DISCRIMINATION LAW

This textbook offers comprehensive coverage of the Equality Act 2010 and also deals with the equality aspects of the common law, the Human Rights Act 1998 and the European Convention on Human Rights. It encourages critical analysis of equality law to equip the reader with an understanding of the enduring challenges that frame equality law and contemporary responses to those challenges. New content includes a chapter on age discrimination and analysis of the Public Sector Equality Duty.

Structured so as to be accessible to the student approaching discrimination law for the first time, the book is also sufficiently detailed and analytical to appeal to the well-informed reader, and to provide those engaged in research with a solid base for further independent study. For the undergraduate student studying discrimination law as a free-standing subject or as part of a wider course, the book provides a one-stop shop. This book is also a key core text for any postgraduate discrimination law course.

Discrimination Law

Text, Cases and Materials

Third Edition

Aileen McColgan KC

•HART•
OXFORD • LONDON • NEW YORK • NEW DELHI • SYDNEY

HART PUBLISHING
Bloomsbury Publishing Plc
Kemp House, Chawley Park, Cumnor Hill, Oxford, OX2 9PH, UK
1385 Broadway, New York, NY 10018, USA
29 Earlsfort Terrace, Dublin 2, Ireland

First published in Great Britain 2023

A catalogue record for this book is available from the British Library.

Library of Congress Cataloging-in-Publication data

Names: McColgan, Aileen, author.

Title: Discrimination law : text, cases and materials / Aileen McColgan KC.

Description: Third edition. | Oxford ; New York : Hart, 2023. | Includes bibliographical references and index. | Summary: "This textbook offers comprehensive coverage of the Equality Act 2010 and deals also with the equality aspects of the Human Rights Act 1998 and European Convention on Human Rights. It encourages critical analysis of equality law to equip the reader with an understanding of the enduring challenges that frame equality law and contemporary responses to those challenges. New content includes a chapter on age discrimination and analysis of the Public Sector Equality Duty. Structured so as to be accessible to the student approaching discrimination law for the first time, the book is also sufficiently detailed and analytical to appeal to the well-informed reader, and to provide those engaged in research with a solid base for further independent study. For the undergraduate student studying discrimination law as a free-standing subject or as part of a wider course, the book provides a one-stop shop. This book is also a key core text for any postgraduate discrimination law course"—Provided by publisher.

Identifiers: LCCN 2023000028 (print) | LCCN 2023000029 (ebook) | ISBN 9781849462464 (paperback) | ISBN 9781509966592 (hardback) | ISBN 9781509928439 (pdf) | ISBN 9781509928446 (Epub)

Subjects: LCSH: Discrimination in employment—Law and legislation—Great Britain. | Great Britain. Equality Act 2010. | LCGFT: Casebooks (Law)

Classification: LCC KD3102 .M338 2023 (print) | LCC KD3102 (ebook) | DDC 344.4101/133—dc23/eng/20230206

LC record available at https://lccn.loc.gov/2023000028

LC ebook record available at https://lccn.loc.gov/2023000029

ISBN: PB: 978-1-84946-246-4
HB: 978-1-50996-659-2
ePDF: 978-1-50992-843-9
ePub: 978-1-50992-844-6

Typeset by Compuscript Ltd, Shannon

In memory of my beloved parents Sam and Eithne and of Sarah Bailey,
late of Arts Council England and Tate and much missed.

Contents

List of Abbreviations

2020 Regs	The Equality Act 2010 (Disability) Regulations 2010
A1P1	Article 1 of the First Protocol to the ECHR
ACAS/Acas	Advicory, Conciliation and Arbitration Service
AC	Appeal Cases
ADA	Americans with Disabilities Act (1990)
Age regulations	Employment Equality (Age Discrimination) Regulations 2006
All ER	All England Reports
AP	approved premises
BAME	Black and Minority Ethnic
BAPIO	British Association of Physicians of Indian Origin
BBC	British Broadcasting Corporation
BC	Borough Council
BHRC	Butterworths Human Rights Cases
BMA	British Medical Association
BME	Black and Minority Ethnic
BMLR	Butterworths Medico-Legal Reports
BNP	British National Party
CA	Court of Appeal
CAC	Convention on the Rights of the Child
CAMHS	Child and Adolescent Mental Health Services
CC	Chief Constable, alternatively (depending on context) City Council, County Council
CCR	Concessions Contracts Regulations 2016
CCT	Compulsory Competitive Tendering
CEDAW	Convention on the Elimination of all Forms of Discrimination against Women
CERD	Convention on the Elimination of all Forms of Racial Discrimination

Ch	Chancery (law reports)
CICS	Criminal Injuries Compensation Scheme
CIPD	Chartered Institute of Personnel and Development
CIPD	Chartered Institute of Personnel and Development
CJ	Chief Justice
CJEU	Court of Justice of the EU (see also ECJ)
CMLR	Common Market Law Reports
CPS	Crown Prosecution Service
CQC	Care Quality Commission
CRE	Commission for Racial Equality (Predecessor to the EHRC with responsibility for race discrimination)
CRPD	Convention on the Rights of Persons with Disabilities
CSIH	Court of Session Inner House (Scotland)
CSO	close supervision centre
DC	District Council
DDA	Disability Discrimination Act 1995 (predecessor to the EqA concerned with disability)
DPP	Director of Public Prosecutions
DEFRA	Department for Environment, Food and Rural Affairs
DRC	Disability Rights Commission (Predecessor to the EHRC with responsibility for disability discrimination)
DSO	direct service organisation
DSPCR	Defence and Security Public Contracts Regulations
DWP	Department for Work and Pensions
EAT	Employment Appeal Tribunal
EC	European Community
ECHR	European Convention on Human Rights
ECJ	European Court of Justice (see also CJEU)
ECNI	Equality Commission of Northern Ireland
ECR	European Case Reports
ECtHR	European Court of Human Rights
EEA	European Economic Area
EHRC	Equality and Human Rights Commission (formally the Commission for Equality and Human Rights)

EHRR	European Human Rights Reports
ELR	Education Law Reports
EOC	Equal Opportunity Commission (Predecessor to the EHRC with responsibility for sex and related discrimination)
EPM	Extra Parochial Ministry Licence
EqA	Equality Act 2010
EqA 2006	Equality Act 2006 (concerned with non-employment-related religion and belief discrimination and created the EHRC)
ERA	Employment Rights Act 1996
ET	Employment Tribunal
EU	European Union
EWCA	England and Wales Court of Appeal (neutral case citation)
EWHC	England and Wales High Court (neutral case citation)
Fam	law report
FCR	Family Court Reports
FEC	Fair Employment Commission (now absorbed into the ECNI)
FEA	Fair Employment Act
FETO	Fair Employment and Treatment (Northern Ireland) Order 1998
FI	Formal Investigation
FRA	Fundamental Rights Agency (EU body)
FTS	Find a Tender service (https://www.findatenderservice.co.uk)
GB	Great Britain
GC	Grand Chamber (ECtHR)
GCHQ	Government Communications Headquarters
GLC	Greater London Council
GMC	General Medical Council
GMB	General and Municipal Boilermakers union
GOR	genuine occupational requirement
GOQ	genuine occupational qualification
GP	General Practitioner
GPA	WTO's plurilateral Agreement on Government Procurement
GRA	Gender Recognition Act 2004
GRC	Gender Recognition Certificate

HA	Health Authority
HC	High Court/House of Commons
HE&FEIs	higher education and further education institutions
HL	House of Lords
HLR	Housing Law Reports
HHJ	His/Her Honour Judge (Circuit Judge)
HM	Her [now His] Majesty's
HMRC	Her [now His] Majesty's Revenue & Customs
HMSO	Her [His] Majesty's Stationery Office
HMP	Her [His] Majesty's Prison
HRA	Human Rights Act 1998
ICCPR	International Covenant on Civil and Political Rights (UN instrument)
ICESCR	International Convention on Economic, Social and Cultural Rights (UN instrument)
ICR	Industrial Case Reports
ILEA	Inner London Education Authority
Imm AR	Immigration Appeal Reports
IOC	International Olympic Committee
IR	Immigration Reports
IRLR	Industrial Relations Law Reports
ISSP	information society service provider
ITV	Independent Television
J	Mr/Mrs Justice
JCHR	Joint Committee on Human Rights
JES	job evaluation scheme
JFS	Jewish Free School
KB	King's Bench Division (also law reports of same name)
LB	London Borough
LBC	London Borough Council
LGA 1988	Local Government Act 1998
LGB	Lesbian, Gay and Bisexual
LGBT	Lesbian, Gay, Bisexual and Trans

LGBTI	Lesbian, Gay, Bisexual, Trans and Intersex
LGHA	Local Government and Housing Act 1989
LGR	Local Government Reports
LJ	Lord Justice of Appeal
LJJ	Lords Justice of Appeal
LLP	Limited Liability Partnership
MBC	Metropolitan Borough Council
MENA	Nigerian, Middle Eastern and north African
MFD	material factor defence
MOD	Ministry of Defence
MOJ	Ministry of Justice
MR	Master of the Rolls
MWRF	manifestly without reasonable foundation
NDN	non-discrimination notice
NGO	Non governmental organisation
NHS	National Health Service
NI	Northern Ireland (also law report of same name)
NICE	National Institute for Care Excellence
NIQB	Norther Ireland Queen's Bench (also law report of same name)
NLDP	Notice of Letting to a Disqualified Person
NMW	National Minimum Wage
OIA;	Office of the Independent Adjudicator for Higher Education
ONS	Office for National Statistics
OECD	Organisation for Economic Cooperation and Development
P	President (of the EAT)
PAFT	Policy Appraisal and Fair Treatment (Northern Irish predecessor of the PSED)
PCP	provision, criterion or practice
PCR	Public Contracts Regulations 2015
PHE	Public Health England
POW	prisoner of war
PSED	public sector equality duty (imposed by s149 EqA)

PSNI	Police Service for Northern Ireland
PTO	Permission to Officiate
QALY	Quality-adjusted life years
QB	Queen's Bench Division (also law reports of same name)
QC	Queen's Counsel
RB Regs	Employment Equality (Religion and Belief) Regulations 2003 (predecessor to the EqA concerned with employment-related religion and belief discrimination)
RC	Regional Council
RMT	National Union of Rail, Maritime and Transport Workers
RRA	Race Relations Act 1976 (predecessor to the EqA concerned with race)
RTE	Raidió Teilifís Éireann (Irish equivalent of the BBC)
RUC	Royal Ulster Constabulary (replaced by PSNI)
SC	Supreme Court
SCA	Senior Courts Act 1981
SDA	Sex Discrimination Act 1975 (predecessor to the EqA concerned with sex)
SD Order	Sex Discrimination (Northern Ireland) Order 1976 (the equivalent of the SDA in NI, still in force)
SJNC	Scottish Joint Negotiating Committee
SO Regs 2007	Equality Act 2006 (Sexual Orientation) Regulations 2007 (predecessor to the EqA concerned with non-employment-related sexual orientation discrimination)
SO Regs	Employment Equality (Sexual Orientation) Regulations 2003 (predecessor to the EqA concerned with employment-related sexual orientation discrimination)
SQV	Special Quota Voucher
SSHD	Secretary of State for the Home Department (Home Secretary)
SSCLG	Secretary of State for Communities and Local Government
SS	Secretary of State
SSHSC	Secretary of State for Health and Social Care
SSJ	Secretary of State for Justice
SSSS	Secretary of State for Social Services
SSWP	Secretary of State for Work and Pensions

TFEU/TEU	Treaty on the Functioning of the EU
TUPE	Transfer of Undertakings (Protection of Employment) Regulations
TUC	Trades Union Congress
UCR	Utilities Contracts Regulations 2016
UK	United Kingdom
UKSC	United Kingdom Supreme Court (neutral case citation)
UKUT	United Kingdom Upper Tribunal (neutral citation)
UN	United Nations
UNHCR	United Nations Human Rights Commission
UNRWA	United Nations Relief and Works Agency
US	United States
VPRS	Vulnerable Persons Resettlement Scheme
WEC	Women and Equalities Committee
WLR	Weekly Law Reports
WTO	World Trade Organisation

Table of Cases

Table of Legislation

National

Australia

Canada

France

Gibraltar

Greece

India

Netherlands

South Africa

United Kingdom

Table of Statutory Instruments and Codes of Practice

Statutory Instruments

Codes of Practice

Table of European Legislation

Primary legislation

Secondary legislation

Table of International Conventions

Publisher's Note

The author and publisher gratefully acknowledge the authors and publishers of extracted material which appears in this book, and in particular the following for permission to reprint from the sources indicated.

Academy of European Law: Colm O'Cinneide, 'Positive Action' (2014) http://www.era-comm.eu/oldoku/SNLLaw/04_Positive_action/2014_April_Cinneide_Paper_EN.pdf

BMJ Publishing Group Ltd: J Harris, 'QALYfying the value of life', (1987) 13 Journal of Medical Ethics, 118–123

Equality and Human Rights Commission – EHRC: England's most disadvantaged groups: Gypsies, Travellers and Roma; Public Sector Equality Duty assessment of hostile environment policies; Being disabled in Britain: a journey less equal (2017) https://www.equalityhumanrights.com/sites/default/files/being-disabled-in-britain.pdf

LSE Business Review: Joan Costa-Font, 'The Covid-19 crisis reveals how much we value old age' https://blogs.lse.ac.uk/usappblog/2020/04/25/the-covid-19-crisis-reveals-how-much-we-value-old-age/

Mind Publications: Mind, 'Lesbians, gay men, bisexuals and mental health' (1996)

National Institute of Economic and Social Research: Nathan Hudson-Sharp and Hilary Metcalf, 'Inequality among lesbian, gay bisexual and transgender groups in the UK: a review of evidence' (2016)

Northern Ireland Assembly: R Russell, 'Fair Employment in Northern Ireland: the decades of change (1990–2010)' (2012) Northern Ireland Assembly Research Paper NIAR 352–12 http://www.niassembly.gov.uk/globalassets/documents/raise/publications/2012/general/12112.pdf

Runnymede Trust: Farah Elahi and Omar Khan, 'Introduction: What is Islamophobia?' in Islamophobia; Still a challenge for us all (2017)

SAGE Publications: For extracts from *International Journal of Discrimination and the Law*: C Davies and M Robison, 'Bridging the gap: An exploration of the use and impact of positive action in the UK' (2016); *Work, Employment and Society*: M Noon, 'the shackled runner: time to rethink positive discrimination?'(2010) 24(4) 728–739

The Independent: Maya Oppenheim, 'There are hundreds more like me, says woman sacked for being pregnant,' 10 January 2020

The University of Chicago Press: E. Anderson, 'What is the Point of Equality' (1999) 109 Ethics 287–337

Wiley: O. Fiss, 'Groups and the Equal Protection Clause' (1976) 109 Philosophy and Public Affairs 107–177

While every care has been taken to establish and acknowledge copyright, and to contact the copyright owners, the publishers apologise for any accidental infringement and would be pleased to come to a suitable agreement with the rightful copyright owners in each case.

1

Introduction

Introduction

This is the third edition of a book first published in 2000, whose second edition was in 2005. Much has changed in the intervening years (not least with the passage of the Equality Act 2010 (EqA), which replaced a morass of primary and secondary legislation with a single, if very complex and substantial, statute[1]). The Act's various predecessors had applied beyond employment to private and, increasingly, public services[2] as well as premises, associations and education, but the large bulk of discrimination challenges started life in the employment tribunals. This was significantly the result of different costs regimes; whereas it is relatively unusual for employment tribunals to award costs, unsuccessful parties routinely bear the successful parties' costs in the civil courts. As discussed in Chapter 5, this has had the effect of making it more or less impossible for most people who regard themselves as having been victims to discrimination in access to goods and services or by associations to sue.

The implementation of the Human Rights Act 1998 (HRA) and the introduction of the public sector equality duties from 2001 shifted this because such claims are generally pursued by way of judicial review where costs may be lower (because disputes concern law rather than facts) and in respect of which legal aid or cost-capping measures may be available. Discrimination challenges began to be brought under the HRA from its early days and from 2005 there was a cascade of public sector equality duty (PSED) challenges which significantly shifted the focus of equality litigation from the employment tribunals into the High Court.[3] The combination of the HRA and the PSED did much to extend the practical reach of equality law beyond the employment sphere and, in particular, into public law.[4]

[1] The EqA does not apply in Northern Ireland, whose legislation is dealt with only in passing in this book.
[2] See further Ch 4.
[3] The PSED is discussed in Ch 3. *R (Elias) v Secretary of State for Defence* [2005] EWHC 1435 (Admin), [2005] IRLR 788 (HC), [2006] EWCA Civ 1293, [2006] 1 WLR 3213 (CA), other aspects of which are discussed in Chs 2 and 7, was the first significant PSED decision.
[4] Though clearly the implementation of the prohibition on discrimination in the exercise of public functions also played a significant part.

The focus of this book remains domestic, but the HRA cannot be understood in isolation from the European Convention on Human Rights (ECHR) and, to a lesser extent, from international legal provisions including the Convention on the Elimination of all Forms of Discrimination against Women and the Convention on the Rights of Persons with Disabilities (CEDAW and CRPD respectively).[5] The EqA must also be interpreted so far as possible to give effect to the ECHR rights, understood where relevant in the context of international legal provisions. Further, and importantly, the EqA cannot be understood in isolation from EU law, which has helped to shape it and which remains relevant to its understanding despite the UK's withdrawal from the EU.

A very short introduction to some of the international legal provisions relating to discrimination is included at pp 21–22 below. The ECHR itself is discussed in some detail in Chapter 2 and the threat to the continued existence of the HRA is referred to at pp 12–13. EU law (including the question of its continued relevance in the UK post-Brexit) is considered at p 22 below. Before turning to these matters, however, it is useful to outline the basic approach of the EqA itself, then to consider the regulation of discrimination by the common law which may well (in view of Brexit and uncertainty over the future of the HRA) assume additional importance in future years.

The Equality Act 2010

Protected Characteristics

The EqA regulates discrimination across a range of 'protected characteristics': age, disability, gender reassignment, marriage and civil partnership, race, religion and belief, sex, and sexual orientation. Race comprises four sub-categories: colour, ethnic origins, nationality and national origins.[6] These characteristics are not treated identically: broadly speaking, colour, ethnic and national origins attract the highest level of protection followed by sex, pregnancy, nationality, disability and gender reassignment; then religion and belief and sexual orientation; then age; and finally marriage and civil partnership. The differences in protection do not necessarily indicate a hierarchy of value, but may instead reflect a need to balance rights (for example between the Article 9 rights of different individuals,[7] or the Article 9 rights of some individuals with the rights of others not to be offended[8]) or a recognition of the unique nature of age as a protected characteristic (being entirely temporal and therefore shared over time). Protection against discrimination on grounds of marriage and civil partnership is an historic anomaly which has been preserved over time and extended with the introduction of civil partnership, but is difficult to justify,[9] while the express regulation of pregnancy discrimination other than as an inevitable aspect of sex discrimination is

[5] Further discussed below.
[6] See s 9 EqA.
[7] This underpins the absence of any express regulation of religion and belief harassment in Parts 3, 4, 6 or 7 (see discussion in Chs 4 and 9).
[8] See the absence of any express regulation of sexual orientation harassment in Parts 3, 4, 6 or 7 (discussed in Chs 4 and 10).
[9] See Ch 6.

the result of a narrow, comparator-driven approach to pregnancy and a failure of imagination on the part of a generation of judges.[10]

The EqA's 'protected characteristics' have not been plucked out of the air but have been selected for protection, albeit at different times and to varying degrees, following the recognition of disadvantage suffered by groups of people defined by reference to those characteristics. This disadvantage has frequently been experienced across multiple axes (access to work, for example, vulnerability to personal violence, housing and criminal justice). They may in some cases have their roots in previous legislative measures (such as criminal prohibitions on sexual contact between men, or entrenched discrimination against women). They may reflect decades or centuries of prejudice (against particular racially minoritised communities, for example) and/or stereotypical views about competence or commitment (such as in the case of disabled people or mothers).

Types of Discrimination

The EqA defines and regulates various forms of discrimination and associated statutory torts which are discussed in Chapter 2 insofar as they are of general application. These consist of direct and indirect discrimination, harassment and victimisation. Harassment and victimisation do not fit the general mould of 'discrimination' adopted by the EqA because neither requires proof of less favourable treatment. The same is true of the two forms of discrimination which are unique to disability (and which are discussed in Chapter 8). These consist of a failure to make reasonable adjustments to disability-related needs and of unfavourable treatment because of something arising in consequence of a person's disability.

'Discrimination' and Disadvantage

No detailed discussion of the various types of discrimination regulated by the EqA will be undertaken here, but it is worth making a general observation about the basic approach of the EqA to discrimination. The protected characteristics referred to above are associated with disadvantage for some (for example women, racially minoritised people, LGB people, disabled people) and with relative advantage for others (men, white people, straight people, non-disabled people).[11]

This is not to say that *all* women, racially minoritised people, LGB people or disabled people are disadvantaged, or that *all* men, white people, straight people or non-disabled people are advantaged. They cannot be, as a single person can simultaneously be relatively disadvantaged in terms (for example) of sex and sexual orientation, while being relatively disadvantaged by race and disability. But at a general level it is true that women are more likely to be disadvantaged *by reason of sex* than are men; racially minoritised people are more likely to be disadvantaged *by reason of race* than are white people; LGB people are more likely to be disadvantaged *by reason of sexual orientation* than are straight people, and disabled people are more likely to be disadvantaged *by reason of disability* than are non-disabled people.

[10] This is now of largely historic interest but was discussed at length in previous editions; see second edition (2005), 487–501. Ch 6 makes clear that pregnancy discrimination remains a huge problem.

[11] The relative disadvantages associated with the various protected characteristics are discussed in Chs 6–11.

Nor is this to say that *all* women are disadvantaged, or *all* men advantaged, by sex (and so on). There will be exceptions, and among groups of people disadvantaged by reference to one protected characteristic will be those whose other characteristics render them relatively (even exceptionally) advantaged in general terms. But none of this is inconsistent with the fact that certain characteristics typically operate to the benefit of some and the detriment of others. Notwithstanding this, the EqA (like its predecessors) adopts a *formal* or *symmetrical* approach to equality, rather than seeking to prohibit discrimination associated with *disadvantage*. In other words, the EqA prohibits discrimination on grounds of sex rather than discrimination against women;[12] prohibits discrimination on grounds of race rather than discrimination against racially minoritised people; and prohibits discrimination on grounds of sexual orientation and religion rather than discrimination against LGB people and those whose actual or assumed religious beliefs render them vulnerable to discrimination.

The only exceptions to the symmetrical approach are in relation to the protected characteristics of disability and married/civilly partnered status (and, to a limited extent only, gender reassignment[13]). The significance of the *asymmetric* approach is that it permits all forms of positive steps to be taken to ameliorate the disadvantage suffered by people with the relevant protected characteristic, whereas ameliorative action may only be taken in connection with other protected characteristics where it consists of lawful positive action (see Chapter 3). While there have not been a great number of challenges brought against attempts to reduce the disadvantage experienced in particular spheres by women, people from racially minoritised communities or other disadvantaged groups, the symmetrical approach to most of the characteristics protected by the EqA imposes a chilling effect on efforts which might otherwise have been made to achieve increased substantive equality.

Areas of Application

The EqA does not prohibit all discrimination which is associated with protected characteristics. Instead, it prohibits such discrimination in a variety of contexts which are dealt with in Parts 3–7 of the EqA.[14] These consist, respectively, of:

- access to goods, facilities and services, and the exercise of public functions (Part 3);
- premises (part 4);
- work (Part 5);
- education (Part 6), and
- associations (Part 7).[15]

Discrimination which falls outside the scope of the EqA (because it relates to characteristics which are not protected, consists in treatment which is not recognised as 'discrimination' or otherwise prohibited by the Act, or takes place in a context which falls outwith Parts 3–7 of EqA) may be regulated by the ECHR, and therefore by the HRA, and/or may be challengeable under the common law. These will now be considered briefly in turn.

[12] Except in the case of pregnancy-related benefits, discussed in Ch 6.

[13] Discussed in Ch 6 as is the asymmetrical protection of married and civilly partnered status.

[14] Part 1 EqA having defined the protected characteristics and Part 2 the conduct prohibited by the Act.

[15] Part 12 EqA contains detailed technical provisions relating to disabled persons transport which are beyond the scope of this book as is Part 15 'Family Property' which, inter alia, abolished the common law rule that 'a husband must maintain his wife'.

Intersectional Discrimination

As is set out above, the EqA regulates discrimination by reference to various separate and distinct protected characteristics there set out. Reference has been made above to the fact that a single person can simultaneously be relatively disadvantaged in terms (for example) of sex and sexual orientation, while being relatively disadvantaged by race and disability. It is of course equally the case that a person may be at the intersection of multiple vectors of disadvantage related to protected (and unprotected) characteristics. Such disadvantage may be the cumulative effect of, for example, racism, sexism and ageism. But it may also relate to the specificity of the individual's identity (young African-Caribbean male). And because people are human, and do not experience themselves as packages of distinct and separable characteristics ('female', 'gay', 'Muslim heritage', 'Black'), it can be difficult to conceptualise, or to challenge, discrimination experienced by people who are relatively disadvantaged by reference to multiple protected characteristics.

The term 'intersectionality' was coined by US academic Kimberlé Crenshaw in the late 1980s.[16] Crenshaw discussed how what she referred to as the 'single-axis framework' of anti-discrimination law in the US:

> **Kimberlé Crenshaw, 'Demarginalizing the Intersection of Race and Sex: A Black Feminist Critique of Antidiscrimination Doctrine, Feminist Theory and Antiracist Politics' (1989) 1 *University of Chicago Legal Forum* 139, 139**
>
> erases Black women in the conceptualization, identification and remediation of race and sex discrimination by limiting inquiry to the experiences of otherwise-privileged members of the group. In other words, in race discrimination cases, discrimination tends to be viewed in terms of sex- or class-privileged Blacks; in sex discrimination cases, the focus is on race- and class-privileged women.
>
> This focus on the most privileged group members marginalizes those who are multiply-burdened and obscures claims that cannot be understood as resulting from discrete sources of discrimination … this focus on otherwise-privileged group members creates a distorted analysis of racism and sexism because the operative conceptions of race and sex become grounded in experiences that actually represent only a subset of a much more complex phenomenon.

Much of Crenshaw's focus was on the 'marginalization of Black women in feminist theory and in antiracist politics' which in her view were 'predicated on a discrete set of experiences that often does not accurately reflect the interaction of race and gender' and 'cannot be solved simply by including Black women within an already established analytical structure'.[17] But Crenshaw framed her work against a critique of cases (*DeGraffenreid v General Motors* (1976),[18] *Moore v Hughes Helicopter* (1983)[19] and *Payne v Travenol* (1982)[20]) in which US courts refused to acknowledge the discrimination experienced by Black women *as Black women*. In *DeGraffenreid*, in which the evidence demonstrated specific discrimination against Black women as a class, the court insisted that the claimants frame their case as involving sex discrimination *or* race discrimination. To do otherwise, the court suggested,

[16] 'Demarginalizing the Intersection of Race and Sex: A Black Feminist Critique of Antidiscrimination Doctrine, Feminist Theory and Antiracist Politics' (1989) 1 *University of Chicago Legal Forum* 139.

[17] *Ibid*, 140.

[18] 413 F Supp 142 (E D Mo 1976).

[19] 708 F2d 475 (9th Cir 1983).

[20] 673 F2d 798 (5th Cir 1982).

would be to 'create a new classification of "black women" who would have greater standing than, for example, a black male', and would threaten to open a 'Pandora's box' of 'new classes of protected minorities, governed only by the mathematical principles of permutation and combination'.

In *Moore*, conversely, the court refused to certify the claimant (a Black woman) as a suitable representative in a sex discrimination action because she 'never claimed … that she was discriminated against as a female, but only as a Black female', which 'raised serious doubts as to [her] ability to adequately represent white female employees'. As Crenshaw pointed out, this

> curious logic … reveals not only the narrow scope of antidiscrimination doctrine and its failure to embrace intersectionality, but also the centrality of white female experiences in the conceptualization of gender discrimination. One inference that could be drawn from the court's statement that Moore's complaint did not entail a claim of discrimination 'against females' is that discrimination against Black females is something less than discrimination against females.

And even if, as Crenshaw acknowledged was more likely,

> the court meant to imply that Moore did not claim that all females were discriminated against but only Black females' and saw Moore's 'attempt to specify her race … as being at odds with the standard allegation that the employer simply discriminated 'against females',

this ignored the fact that any claimant would have a racial identity whether or not it was specified (though the racial identity of a white woman would have been seen as neutral). Finally, in *Payne v Travenol*, the court refused to allow Black women claimants to represent Black men in a class action alleging race discrimination.

The legal difficulties which may confront claimants who are vulnerable to multiple forms of discrimination/disadvantage in the domestic courts were illustrated in the following decision, also discussed in Chapter 5.

***The Law Society v Bahl* [2003] UKEAT 1056_01_3107, [2003] IRLR 640**

The claimant brought a discrimination claim after being accused of bullying staff in her position as Vice President of the Law Society. A tribunal found that she had had been discriminated against *as a black woman*, declaring that:

> We do not distinguish between the race or sex of the applicant in reaching this conclusion … The claim was advanced on the basis that Kamlesh Bahl was treated in the way she was because she is a black woman. Kamlesh Bahl was the first office holder that the Law Society had ever had who was not both white and male … We do not know what was in the minds of [the alleged discriminators] at any particular point. It is sufficient for our purposes to find, where appropriate, that in each case they would not have treated a white person or a man less favourably.[21]

The EAT overturned the tribunal's decision, accepting the argument put for the Law Society that it was 'incumbent on the tribunal to distinguish between the allegation of race discrimination and that of sex discrimination, and to make plain the evidential basis for drawing the inference of unlawful discrimination in respect of each ground'.

[21] Cited by the EAT [2003] IRLR 640 §140.

Elias J (for the EAT):

157. The reason for the tribunal not approaching the matter in that way appears to be because of the tribunal's observations that 'there was no basis in the evidence for comparing her treatment with that of a white female or black male office holder.' We confess to having some difficulty in understanding what this sentence means. It may be that the tribunal was intending to indicate that there was no actual comparator with whom any comparison could be made. That is plainly correct, although in those circumstances the tribunal was entitled to consider how the hypothetical comparator would have been treated in that situation. In the case of sex discrimination that would have involved considering how a male (white or black) would have been treated in otherwise like circumstances, and in the case of race discrimination how a white person (male or female) would have been treated in such circumstances. Alternatively, the tribunal may have meant simply that it could not disentangle the two elements and reach a clear conclusion on either.

158. Plainly it is possible for a tribunal to infer that there may be discrimination both on grounds of race and sex after considering the evidence in respect of each. But if the evidence does not satisfy the tribunal that there is discrimination on grounds of race or on grounds of sex, considered independently, then it is not open to a tribunal to find either claim satisfied on the basis that there is nonetheless discrimination on grounds of race and sex when both are taken together. That would fail to give effect to the fact that the burden of proof is on the applicant. Nor can the tribunal properly conclude, if it is uncertain about whether it is race or sex, that it will find both.

159. Mr de Mello submits [for the claimant] that the tribunal was entitled to adopt this approach. It was not obliged to separate out the two strands of race and sex from the mix. The applicant had put her case before the tribunal on the basis that she was a black woman, and it was entitled to treat the two elements together. It was a unique case and the tribunal was justified in treating the evidence in the round without identifying those aspects which it considered justified the inference of race discrimination and those which justified a finding of sex discrimination.

160. We do not accept that submission. In our view the tribunal did err in law in failing to distinguish between the elements of alleged race and sex discrimination. The result was that it failed to reach properly reasoned findings on the question whether Dr Bahl had satisfied the tribunal – the burden being on her – that discrimination had occurred in respect of either ground. This would, in our view, be a sufficient basis for upholding these appeals even in the absence of any other error of law.

Dr Bahl's appeal against this aspect of the EAT's decision failed, the CA characterising the passage of the tribunal's judgment set out above as 'puzzling' and stating that the tribunal had been obliged 'to find the primary facts in relation to each type of discrimination against each alleged discriminator and then to explain why it was making the inference which it did in favour of Dr Bahl on whom lay the burden of proving her case'.

The references to the burden of proof need to be taken with care in view of the fact that the burden now shifts to the defendant once the claimant has established a prima facie case of discrimination (see discussion in Chapter 5), but it is not clear that the change in the burden of proof would have made a material change to the *Bahl* decision. On the one hand the EAT must have been right to insist that a claimant satisfy whatever burden of proof applies. But the EAT's approach, approved by the Court of Appeal (CA), involves treating race and sex as separate and distinct, such that a claimant (in that case Dr Bahl) ought to be able to prove the operation of race discrimination against her as a non-sexed person (ie, a person whose treatment is not influenced by sex), and/or the operation of sex discrimination against her as a 'raceless' woman (a woman whose treatment is not influenced by race). Because white men have been, and continue to be, treated as the default and as 'neutral', a person whose treatment is not influenced by sex is likely to be (and to be conceived of, whether consciously or unconsciously) as a man, and a woman whose treatment is not influenced by sex is likely to be (and to be conceived of as being) white.

Intersectional discrimination was recognised by the EAT in the following case.

***Ministry of Defence v DeBique* [2009] UKEAT 0048_09_1210, [2010] IRLR 471**

In this case the EAT ruled that the claimant, a single mother and British Army soldier from St Vincent and the Grenadines, was subject to unlawful indirect discrimination on the grounds of her race and sex when she was disciplined for her inability to comply with a requirement to be available to be deployed 24 hours a day, seven days a week.[22] The claimant had put in place childcare arrangements which allowed her to be on duty from 8am until 4.30pm, Monday to Friday, and had been told by her commanding officer that her arrangements were acceptable, but was disciplined for failure to carry out overnight duties. After being issued with warnings about her continued service she sought to have one of her sisters come to live with her from St Vincent and the Grenadine to care for her child. Her application was refused because, in order to comply with UK immigration rules, army policy prohibited 'Foreign and Commonwealth soldiers' from bringing adult relatives to live with them for childcare purposes, whether in a paid or unpaid capacity. The claimant's grievance was dismissed and she was told that inability to comply with 24/7 duties would be regarded as gross misconduct. She issued proceedings for race and sex discrimination. A tribunal upheld her claim, ruling that while the 24/7 requirement was justified notwithstanding its disparate impact on women, its impact, taken in combination with the government's immigration rules, on women whose potential child-carers were foreign nationals was not. The MOD appealed.

Cox J:

> 162. … Mr Morton [for the MOD] contends that the tribunal erred in conflating the two separate PCPs[23] which they found had been applied to the claimant in this case. He submits that it was wrong to consider the combined effect of two PCPs alleged to discriminate indirectly on the separate and distinct grounds of sex and race. Either one or the other, or both independently, are indirectly discriminatory or they are not.
>
> 163. In any event, once this tribunal had found that the 24/7 PCP was justified and, therefore, not unlawful under the provisions of the SDA, it was not open to the tribunal to consider it further in combination with the immigration PCP, which fell to be considered under the RRA. Mr Morton submits that the tribunal's approach leads to the 'absurd conclusion' that a female single parent soldier of Vincentian national origin has been discriminated against on the ground of her sex, whereas a female single parent soldier of British national origin, in identical circumstances, would not have been discriminated against on the ground of her sex. In this case, therefore, the question whether there had been indirect sex discrimination turned on the national origin of the claimant.

[22] Indirect discrimination, which is discussed in Ch 2, is concerned with disparately impacting treatment related to protected characteristics.

[23] Provisions, criteria or practices; see discussion of indirect discrimination in Ch 2.

164. … In our view, however, this submission fails to recognise the cause of the particular disadvantage to which women in this claimant's position and the claimant herself were found to be subject. The female single parent soldier of British national origin could never have been placed in the 'identical circumstances' to which Mr Morton refers. His submission is based, in our view, on an incorrect analysis of this tribunal's reasoning.

165. In general, the nature of discrimination is such that it cannot always be sensibly compartmentalised into discrete categories. Whilst some complainants will raise issues relating to only one or other of the prohibited grounds, attempts to view others as raising only one form of discrimination for consideration will result in an inadequate understanding and assessment of the complainant's true disadvantage. Discrimination is often a multi-faceted experience. The claimant in this case considered that the particular disadvantage to which she was subject arose both because she was a 24/7 female soldier with a child and because she was a woman of Vincentian national origin, for whom childcare assistance from a live-in Vincentian relative was not permitted. The tribunal recognised that this double disadvantage reflected the factual reality of her situation.

166. As the tribunal correctly observed … a comparison of the cases of persons of different sex … must be such that the relevant circumstances in the one case are the same or not materially different in the other.

167. In this case, therefore, when considering the 24/7 PCP in the context of the claimant's allegations, the relevant circumstances of the women and the men in the pool, for the purposes of this 'like for like' comparison, were that they were men and women soldiers in the British Army whose potential childcarers were foreign nationals …. In this pool the women soldiers were at a particular disadvantage because they were more likely than the men to be single parents requiring assistance with childcare ….

168. This is what we understand this tribunal to mean, in referring to the combined effect of the 24/7 and the immigration PCPs, when considering the claim of indirect sex discrimination.

169. Applying the same reasoning, the mirror requirement … that a comparison of the case of a person of a particular racial group with that of a person not of that group … must be such that the relevant circumstances in the one case are the same, or not materially different in the other, led the tribunal to identify the pool as they did at paragraph 177: namely, those of Vincentian national origin and of British national origin in the Army who are or may become single parents. Within that pool the Vincentian soldiers, (who the tribunal found would also be predominantly women), were put at a particular disadvantage, because their extended families and, therefore, their potential childcarers, were more likely to be foreign nationals, unable to stay in the UK for more than six months.

170. This conclusion accurately reflected, in our judgment, the particular disadvantage caused to women of Vincentian origin in the British Army who were single parents. There is no challenge to the tribunal's conclusion that what the tribunal have described as the combined effect of these PCPs put this claimant to that disadvantage.

Shortly after *de Bique* was decided the EqA came into force. Section 14 EqA provides as follows:

Section 14 EqA, Combined discrimination: dual characteristics

(1) A person (A) discriminates against another (B) if, because of a combination of two relevant protected characteristics, A treats B less favourably than A treats or would treat a person who does not share either of those characteristics.

(2) The relevant protected characteristics are—

(a) age;
(b) disability;
(c) gender reassignment;
(d) race
(e) religion or belief;
(f) sex;
(g) sexual orientation.

(3) For the purposes of establishing a contravention of this Act by virtue of subsection (1), B need not show that A's treatment of B is direct discrimination because of each of the characteristics in the combination (taken separately).

(4) But B cannot establish a contravention of this Act by virtue of subsection (1) if, in reliance on another provision of this Act or any other enactment, A shows that A's treatment of B is not direct discrimination because of either or both of the characteristics in the combination …

This provision is far from radical, limited as it is to two protected characteristics and direct discrimination. Notwithstanding its modesty, the provision has not been implemented, and the Coalition Government announced in 2013 that it had 'decided not to take [the provision] forward'.[24] The *DeBique* judgment has not resulted in a rush of reported decisions on multiple/intersectional discrimination, though it is obvious from the discussion of compensation in Chapter 5 that such cases have been successfully brought notwithstanding the failure to implement s 14 EqA.

Discrimination and the ECHR/HRA

At present, the main application of the HRA to discrimination is through its incorporation of Article 14 ECHR which provides that:

Article 14 ECHR

The enjoyment of the rights and freedoms set forth in this Convention shall be secured without discrimination on any ground such as sex, race, colour, language, religion, political or other opinion, national or social origin, association with a national minority, property, birth or other status.

As is evident from the text of Article 14, Article 14 is 'parasitic' in as much as it does not amount to a free-standing prohibition on discrimination, being concerned only with discrimination *in the exercise of other Convention rights.* Protocol 12, Article 1 ECHR provides a free-standing prohibition on discrimination, but it has not been signed or ratified by the UK. In order to succeed in an Article 14 claim a person will have to show discrimination on a protected ground 'within the ambit' of another Convention right.

[24] https://www.gov.uk/guidance/equality-act-2010-guidance. Such a decision is of questionable legality: *R v Secretary of State for the Home Department, ex p Fire Brigades Union* [1995] 2 AC 513, but does not appear to have been challenged.

Convention Rights

The rights provided by the ECHR and given partial effect in domestic law by the HRA are broad and various. In short summary, they cover the following subject areas:

- Article 2: right to life, broadly interpreted to cover core aspects of health;
- Article 3: prohibition of inhuman and degrading treatment and torture;
- Article 4: prohibition of slavery and forced labour;
- Article 5: right to liberty and security;
- Article 6: right to a fair trial in civil and criminal matters;
- Article 7: prohibition on punishment without law;
- Article 8: right to private and family life;
- Article 9: right to freedom of thought, conscience and religion;
- Article 10: right to freedom of expression;
- Article 11: right to freedom of association and assembly;
- Article 12: right to marry;
- Article 1 Protocol 1: right to property;
- Article 1 Protocol 2: right to education;
- Article 1 Protocol 3: right to free elections.

The HRA

The ECHR and, in particular, Article 14 thereof is discussed in Chapter 2 and features across this book. At present it finds much of its force in the UK by reason of the HRA which, in short summary:

- requires public authorities to act consistently with ECHR rights except where required by primary legislation to do otherwise;
- imposes a very strong obligation upon the courts to interpret domestic legislation consistent with ECHR rights;
- requires the courts to strike down secondary legislation which is inconsistent with ECHR rights, except where the inconsistency is required by primary legislation (interpreted so far as possible, to be consistent with ECHR rights); and
- provides for 'declarations of incompatibility' in relation to legislation which cannot be struck down or interpreted compatibly with ECHR rights.

Discrimination which falls outside the EqA may be capable of challenge under the HRA. Examples might include discrimination permitted by statute or by ministerial authorisation, or which occurs outside the geographical scope of the EqA.[25] As discussed in Chapter 2, the

[25] See Ch 4. The extra-territorial application of the HRA as established in *R (Al-Skeini) v Secretary of State for Defence* [2007] UKHL 26, [2008] 1 AC 153 and *Al Skeini v UK* (2011) 53 EHRR 18 is one of the major reasons for current Government hostility to the Act.

approach taken by the European Court of Human Rights (ECtHR) and domestic courts to the question whether discrimination concerns the exercise of these Convention rights is relatively generous. This has had the effect of opening a wide range of public decision-making, including in the form of legislation, to judicial scrutiny. As set out in Chapter 2, this scrutiny has extended to state benefits, criminal injury compensation, prisoner release, compulsory jury service and immigration, rules concerning the allocation of social housing; the upkeep of churches; state pensionable age; birth registration; adoption and fostering agencies; prison sentences and deportation and internment without trial; access to civil partnerships, abortion and marriage; the implantation of embryos; the recording of sex on passports; planning and succession to tenancies.

The Conservative Party has maintained a position of general hostility towards the HRA, which culminated in the introduction into Parliament in June 2022 of the Bill of Rights Bill 2022 whose intended purpose was to 'strike the proper balance of rights and responsibilities, individual liberty and the public interest, rigorous judicial interpretation, and respect for the authority of elected law' by repealing the HRA and replacing it with a 'British Bill of Rights'. The 'flagship policy' of then Secretary of State for Justice Dominic Raab,[26] the Bill itself, like the Consultation Paper which accompanied it, bore no intelligible relationship to the 'Independent Human Rights Act Review' which preceded it in October 2021,[27] or to the overwhelming majority of consultation responses received by the government to its March 2022 consultation paper.[28]

The Bill of Rights Bill will, if adopted, place devolved arrangements under pressure and impose yet further challenges to the constitutional arrangements in Northern Ireland, already under significant threat as a result of the UK's withdrawal from the EU and its proposed unilateral 'fix[ing]' of the Northern Ireland Protocol.[29] The short-lived Truss administration wasted no time in indicating that the Bill would not proceed in its then form. The day after Liz Truss's appointment as Prime Minister, it was reported that she had 'pulled plans to enact a new bill of rights in one of her first acts as prime minister':

Jessica Elgot, Liz Truss halts Dominic Raab's bill of rights plan', *The Guardian*, 7 September 2022

Critics had argued [that the Bill] would not materially affect the UK's relationship to the European court and was unlikely to lead to a resolution to the current impasse. Ministers are understood to be deeply concerned about the overall drafting of the bill, which was due to have its second reading on Monday. There were also advanced plans for amendments to the bill by opposition MPs, including one on expanding abortion rights from the Labour MP Stella Creasy that would have necessitated a free vote on a conscience issue.

A Whitehall source said the bill was now 'unlikely to progress in its current form' and that there was a widespread review on the most 'effective means to deliver objectives through legislative agenda'. Another said there were issues with the drafting, describing it as a 'complete mess'.

[26] J Elgot, Liz Truss halts Dominic Raab's bill of rights plan', *The Guardian*, 7 September 2022.

[27] https://www.gov.uk/guidance/independent-human-rights-act-review.

[28] See 'Human Rights Act Reform: A Modern Bill of Rights', available at https://www.gov.uk/government/consultations/human-rights-act-reform-a-modern-bill-of-rights. This was despite the fact that the consultation itself was, according to the Review's Chair, former appeal Judge Lord Gross, 'not a response to my report': M Fouzder, *Law Society Gazette*, 1 February 2022, available at https://www.lawgazette.co.uk/news/human-rights-act-consultation-not-a-response-to-my-report-gross/5111359.article.

[29] Northern Ireland Protocol Bill, introduced 13 June 2022, available at https://bills.parliament.uk/bills/3182.

In the period between writing this chapter and editing it, Liz Truss was replaced as Prime Minister by Rishi Sunak; and Dominic Raab returned to his former role as Justice Secretary and signaled the revival of the Bill of Rights, which had been declared 'dead in the water' just two months before.[30]

Discrimination and the Common Law

The third potential source of discrimination challenges is the common law. The historical approach of the common law to discrimination left much to be desired. Taking sex discrimination by way of example, the judiciary itself was responsible for doctrines such as coverture by which 'the very being or legal existence of the wife is suspended during the marriage or at least incorporated and consolidated into that of the husband under whose wing, protection and cover she performs everything'. It was not until 1991 that domestic law accepted that the rape of a woman by her husband was a legal possibility.[31] And gains for women in terms of enfranchisement and child custody on divorce were won very slowly by legislative reform in the teeth of determined judicial resistance. Public employers' attempts to pay men and women equally were struck down in *Roberts v Hopwood* [1925] AC 578 as the pursuit of 'some eccentric principles of socialistic philanthropy'.

Nor were the common law's inadequacies in the context of discrimination restricted to the field of sex: in *In re Lysaght* the High Court upheld the validity of a legacy to fund training of British-born non-Jews and non-Roman Catholics.[32] According to that Court the stipulation, though 'undesirable ... [was] not ... contrary to the public policy'. Nor, according to the House of Lords (HL) in *Blathwayt v Baron Cawley*, was a testamentary condition excluding those who were or became Roman Catholic.[33]

Conor Gearty cites *In re Lysaght*, together with *Schlegel v Corcoran* (1942) IR 19 and *Scala Ballroom (Wolverhampton) Ltd v Ratcliffe* [1958] 1 WLR 1057, as illustrative of 'a system of laws which prioritized ... interests in property and contract to the exclusion of other public interests'.[34] In *Schlegel*, an Irish court upheld the reasonableness of a refusal to transfer rooms to a Jewish dentist on the grounds that the practice 'may, under Mr Gross, develop a Jewish complexion ... such an anticipation is not groundless in a locality with a number of Jewish residents.' And in *Scala* the English CA upheld the legality of a bar on 'coloured' entrants to the ballroom as 'a course which [the company was] entitled to adopt in [its] own business interests'.

[30] See, respectively, *The Guardian* article extracted above and the ITV News, 6 November 2022, 'Dominic Raab to bring back British Bill of Rights in bid to curb migrant crossings': https://www.itv.com/news/2022-11-06/raab-to-bring-back-british-bill-of-rights-in-bid-to-curb-migrant-crossings.

[31] *R v R* [1992] 1 AC 599.

[32] [1966] 1 Ch 191. See also *Scala Ballroom v Ratcliffe* [1958] 3 All ER 220.

[33] [1976] AC 397. See also *Horne v Poland* [1922] 2 KB 364, in which the High Court accepted that race discrimination in the provision of insurance was potentially reasonable, and *Cumings v Birkenhead Corporation* [1972] Ch 12 in which the CA upheld the *vires* of an education authority rule that children who had attended Roman Catholic primary school would be considered only for Roman Catholic secondary schools. In *Cumings* Lord Denning insisted that a rule allocating places in according to hair 'or, for that matter,' skin colour 'would be so unreasonable, so capricious, so irrelevant to any proper system of education that it would be *ultra vires* altogether, and this court would strike it down at once.'

[34] 'The Internal and External "Other" in the Union Legal Order: Racism, Religious Intolerance and Xenophobia in Europe in P Alston, M Bustelo and J Heenan (eds), *The EU and Human Rights* (Oxford, OUP, 1999) 327, 341.

In *Nagle v Feilden* [1966] 2 QB 633 the CA reinstated a claim struck out by the lower courts that the discriminatory refusal by the Jockey Club to grant a woman a training licence was 'unlawful and in restraint of trade and contrary to public policy'. Lord Denning remarked that the refusal of training licences to women 'may well be said to be arbitrary and capricious,' women being perfectly capable of training horses, although he did suggest that a different approach might be appropriate in relation to 'an unsuitable occupation for a woman, like that of a jockey or speedway-rider.' The case did not mark a turning point in the judicial approach to questions of discrimination. In *Amin v Entry Clearance Officer, Bombay* [1983] 2 AC 818 the HL ruled, by a majority, that sex discrimination in the context of immigration fell outwith the Sex Discrimination Act 1975 (SDA). Their Lordships further ruled that, this being the case, the discrimination was not open to challenge. According to Lord Fraser, with whom all of their Lordships agreed on this point: 'not all sex discrimination is unlawful … Discrimination is only unlawful if it occurs in one of the fields in which it is prohibited by [the SDA].'[35]

Even as late as 1996, notably liberal senior judges felt powerless to regulate egregious discrimination by common law tools (in particular the prohibition on '*Wednesbury* irrationality').[36]

***R v Admiralty Board ex p Lustig-Prean, R v Ministry of Defence ex p Smith* [1996] QB 517**

The CA upheld a ban on gays in the military against *Wednesbury* challenge. Simon Brown J (as he then was), in the Divisional Court [1995] 4 All ER 427, had remarked on the lack of evidence put before him to justify the '"blanket, non-discretionary, specific," "status based" ban' but had 'albeit with hesitation and regret' decided that the ban was not so irrational as to fail the *Wednesbury* test which requires the court to be satisfied that the administrative action at issue 'is beyond the range of responses open to a reasonable decision-maker.' The CA upheld his decision.

The Court accepted the submission of David Pannick QC, for the claimants, that:

> The court may not interfere with the exercise of an administrative discretion on substantive grounds save where the court is satisfied that the decision is unreasonable in the sense that it is beyond the range of responses open to a reasonable decision-maker. But in judging whether the decision-maker has exceeded this margin of appreciation the human rights context is important. The more substantial the interference with human rights, the more the court will require by way of justification before it is satisfied that the decision is reasonable in the sense outlined above.

But it went on to decide that the policy, which was justified by the MOD on the grounds of 'morale and unit effectiveness, the … role of the services as guardian of recruits under the age of 18, and … the requirement of communal living in many service situations,' was not irrational. Pannick argued that the first reason was rooted in irrational prejudice, the second also in the assumption 'that homosexuals were less able to control their sexual impulses than heterosexuals,' and that, while '[t]he lack of privacy in service life was … a reason for imposing strict rules and discipline [it was] not a reason for banning

[35] And see also *Bernstein v Immigration Appeal Tribunal & Department of Employment* [1988] Imm AR 449.
[36] *Associated Provincial Picture Houses Ltd v Wednesbury Corp* [1948] 1 KB 223, one of the main grounds (with illegality and procedural impropriety) for challenge by way of judicial review.

the membership of any homosexual … each of the appellants had worked in the armed forces for a number of years without any concern being expressed or complaints made about inappropriate behaviour':

> Above all, Mr Pannick criticised the blanket nature of the existing rule. He placed great emphasis on the practice of other nations whose rules were framed so as to counter the particular mischiefs to which homosexual orientation or activity might give rise. He pointed out that other personal problems such as addiction to alcohol, or compulsive gambling, or marital infidelity were dealt with by the service authorities on a case by case basis and not on the basis of a rule which permitted no account to be taken of the peculiar features of the case under consideration.

Sir Thomas Bingham MR, with whose judgment the rest of the CA concurred, ruled that 'The threshold of irrationality is a high one. It was not crossed in this case.'

In *Smith & Grady v UK* the ECtHR ruled that the ban breached Article 8 ECHR.[37]

***Smith & Grady v UK* (2000) 29 EHRR 493**

Judgment:

> … each State is competent to organise its own system of military discipline and enjoys a certain margin of appreciation in this respect … it is open to the State to impose restrictions on an individual's right to respect for his private life where there is a real threat to the armed forces' operational effectiveness, as the proper functioning of an army is hardly imaginable without legal rules designed to prevent service personnel from undermining it. However, the national authorities cannot rely on such rules to frustrate the exercise by individual members of the armed forces of their right to respect for their private lives, which right applies to service personnel as it does to others within the jurisdiction of the State. Moreover, assertions as to a risk to operational effectiveness must be 'substantiated by specific examples.'…
>
> The core argument of the Government in support of the policy is that the presence of open or suspected homosexuals in the armed forces would have a substantial and negative effect on morale and, consequently, on the fighting power and operational effectiveness of the armed forces …
>
> The Court notes the lack of concrete evidence to substantiate the alleged damage to morale and fighting power that any change in the policy would entail … Given the number of homosexuals dismissed between 1991 and 1996 … the number of homosexuals who were in the armed forces at the relevant time cannot be said to be insignificant. Even if the absence of such evidence can be explained by the consistent application of the policy, as submitted by the Government, this is insufficient to demonstrate to the Court's satisfaction that operational effectiveness problems of the nature and level alleged can be anticipated in the absence of the policy …
>
> … The Government … underlined that it is 'the knowledge or suspicion of homosexuality' which would cause the morale problems and not conduct, so that a conduct code would not solve the anticipated difficulties. However, in so far as negative attitudes to homosexuality are insufficient, of themselves, to justify the policy … they are equally insufficient to justify the rejection of a proposed alternative …

[37] *Lustig-Prean & Beckett v UK* (2000) 29 EHRR 548 was in similar terms.

> The Government maintained that homosexuality raised problems of a type and intensity that race and gender did not. However, even if it can be assumed that the integration of homosexuals would give rise to problems not encountered with the integration of women or racial minorities, the Court is not satisfied that the codes and rules which have been found to be effective in the latter case would not equally prove effective in the former. The 'robust indifference'... of the large number of British armed forces' personnel serving abroad with allied forces to homosexuals serving in those foreign forces, serves to confirm that the perceived problems of integration are not insuperable ...
>
> The Court ... notes the evidence before the domestic courts to the effect that the European countries operating a blanket legal ban on homosexuals in their armed forces are now in a small minority. It considers that, even if relatively recent, the Court cannot overlook the widespread and consistently developing views and associated legal changes to the domestic laws of Contracting States on this issue.

In 1994 Constitutional expert Jeffrey Jowell suggested that equality is a 'constitutional principle' in English common law.[38] Scepticism was expressed about this claim in the first edition of this book, which pointed out that many of the cases relied upon by Jowell resulted in decisions striking down attempts to take ameliorative action in favour of disadvantaged groups.[39] It was suggested at that time, however, that the decision of the Privy Council in the following case might mark a significant change in the common law's approach to discrimination.

***Matadeen v Pointu & Ors* [1999] 1 AC 98**

The case concerned a challenge to a change of education rules which had the effect of disadvantaging students who were not studying an oriental language. The claimants argued that, Mauritius being a signatory to the ICCPR, its constitutional prohibitions on discrimination must be read so as to give effect to Article 26 of the Covenant, which provides (as we saw above) that 'the law shall prohibit any discrimination and guarantee to all persons equal and effective protection against discrimination on any ground such as race, colour, sex, language, religion, political or other opinion, national or social origin, property, birth or other status.'

Lord Hoffmann stated, for the HL, that:

> treating like cases alike and unlike cases differently is a general axiom of rational behaviour. It is, for example, frequently invoked by the courts in proceedings for judicial review as a ground for holding some administrative act to have been irrational.

He went on to declare that the protection of the rights guaranteed by Article 26 did not require the incorporation of that provision as such into domestic law, this on the basis that:

> the power to quash the Minister's decision as unreasonable, under the principles in *Associated Provincial Picture Houses v Wednesbury* [[1948] 1KB 223], would have been entirely adequate to secure compliance with the equal treatment provisions of Article 26.

[38] 'Is Equality a Constitutional Principle?' (1994) *Current Legal Problems* 1.

[39] These included *Prescott v Birmingham Corporation* [1955] Ch 210 and *Roberts v Hopwood* [1925] AC 578.

Matadeen raised as many questions as it answered. Immediately after making the statement extracted above Lord Hoffmann went on to declare that:

> the very banality of the principle [of equality] must suggest a doubt as to whether merely to state it can provide an answer to the kind of problem which arises in this case. Of course persons should be uniformly treated, unless there is some valid reason to treat them differently. But what counts as a valid reason for treating them differently? And, perhaps more important, who is to decide whether the reason is valid or not? Must it always be the courts? The reasons for not treating people uniformly often involve ... questions of social policy on which views may differ. These are questions which the elected representatives of the people have some claim to decide for themselves. The fact that equality of treatment is a general principle of rational behaviour does not entail that it should necessarily be a justiciable principle – that it should always be the judges who have the last word on whether the principle has been observed. In this, as in other areas of constitutional law, sonorous judicial statements of uncontroversial principle often conceal the real problem, which is to mark out the boundary between the powers of the judiciary, the legislature and the executive in deciding how that principle is to be applied.
>
> A self-confident democracy may feel that it can give the last word, even in respect of the most fundamental rights, to the popularly elected organs of its constitution. The United Kingdom has traditionally done so; perhaps not always to universal satisfaction, but certainly without forfeiting its title to be a democracy. A generous power of judicial review of legislative action is not therefore of the essence of a democracy. Different societies may reach different solutions.

In the following case the High Court considered a discrimination claim from Nepalese former Gurkhas who had been Japanese POWs while serving for the Indian Army during the Second World War, during which time India was a British Colony and the 'Indian' army was under British command. The claim was brought under common law as well as the HRA because at the time the discrimination complained of would not have been regarded as falling within the scope of A1P1.[40]

***Gurung v Ministry of Defence* [2002] EWHC 2463 (Admin)**

The claimants had been excluded from the terms of a scheme adopted in 2000 to compensate former Japanese POWs. The defendant sought to rely on a distinction which it had used to determine eligibility under a compensation scheme adopted in the 1950s, which relied upon whether POWs had been subject to British military law. The Gurkhas had been subject to Indian, rather than British, military law because they were classified as 'native' as distinct from 'European'. According to what McCombe J referred to in his judgment as an 'embarrassed letter' written at the time, the 1950s compensation scheme had been based on the premise that:

> There is no analogy of any sort between the status of European members of the former Indian Army and that of Nepalese members of the Indian Army. The 'native' personnel of the Indian Army was recruited from Ahirs, Dogras, Garhwalis, Gurkhas, etc. and the fact that the Gurkhas, coming from the independent Kingdom of Nepal, were recruited under special

[40] The scheme being non-contributory. The inclusion of non-contributory benefits from the scope of A1P1 was confirmed in *Stec v UK* (2006) 43 EHRR 47.

treaty arrangements made no difference whatever to their status when mustered into the Indian Army. They were paid like any other Indian sepoy [an Indian soldier serving under British or other European orders], and were subject to the same code of discipline (the Indian Army Act).

There was evidence that the term 'European' was at the material time 'applied to Her Majesty's subjects born or naturalised or domiciled in the United Kingdom or any of the European, American or Australian Colonies or possessions of Her Majesty, or in the Colony of New Zealand, or in the Colony of the Cape of Good Hope or Natal.' McCombe J accepted that the distinction between 'native' and 'European' was 'based upon race'. The question was whether this sufficed to render the 2000 scheme irrational.

McCombe J:

35. … The challenge is founded simply on the basis that the exclusion of the Gurkhas from the scheme was 'irrational' in terms of the Court of Appeal's decision in *Associated Provincial Picture Houses v Wednesbury Corporation* [1948] 1KB 223. Mr Blake [for the claimants] relied upon the following passage in de Smith, Woolf and Jowell, *Judicial Review of Administrative Action* (1995) paragraph 13–040:

'… equality of treatment has shown itself to be a principle of lawful administration in English law … in the nineteenth century Lord Russell considered that by-laws could be held to be unreasonable because of: "partial and unequal treatment as between different classes" (*Kruse v Johnson* [1898] 2 QB 91). Although subsequent cases did not articulate the principle with equal clarity, unequal treatment has justified a number of instances in which the courts have stood down a decision or provision which infringes equality ….'

I was referred to various other materials, both in academic discourse and in the Courts, in which this principle has been examined. I confine myself here to reference to two examples. The first is *Short v Poole Corporation* [1926] Ch 66. It will be recalled that in that case the Defendant had given a woman teacher notice to terminate her engagement 'after satisfying themselves that her husband was able to maintain her'. The decision so to act had been reached by the following reasoning: (1) the duty of the married woman was primarily to look after her domestic concerns and the Defendant regarded it as impossible for her to do so and to act effectively and satisfactorily as a teacher at the same time; and (2) that it was unfair to the large number of unmarried teachers who were then seeking employment that such positions be occupied by married women whose husbands could maintain them. The teacher sought a declaration of illegality and an injunction against the Council restraining it from acting upon the notice. Reversing Romer J, the Court of Appeal refused the plaintiff the relief sought, finding that she had failed to establish that the Defendant had failed to take into account matters other than those which belonged to their educational sphere. The judgment of Warrington LJ, included the following passage (at p. 91)

'… It may be also possible to prove that an act of the public body, though performed in good faith and without the taint of corruption, was so clearly founded on alien and irrelevant grounds as to be outside the authority conferred upon the body, and therefore inoperative. It is difficult to suggest any act which would be held *ultra vires* under this head, though performed bona fide. To look for one example germane to the present case, I suppose that if the defendants were to dismiss a teacher because she had red hair, or for some equally frivolous and foolish reason, the Court would declare the attempted dismissal to be void …'

I quote that passage and refer to the decision in that case for the proposition that the facts there may well provide an example of a danger of decision makers today adopting a 'rationality' based upon the criteria of yesterday. Would an authority reaching such a decision as the Corporation did in 1924 be considered to have acted rationally? The answer must be, 'Surely not.'

36. My second example is a passage from a lecture given by Lord Steyn on 18 September 2002 in honour of Lord Cooke of Thorndon. At page 18 of the printed copy of the lecture, Lord Steyn says:

> 'The importance of the development of constitutional rights has not come to an end with the advent of the Human Rights Act. One illustration is sufficient. The anti-discrimination provision contained in Article 14 of the European Convention is parasitic in as much as it serves only to protect other Convention rights. There is no general or free-standing prohibition of discrimination. This is a relatively weak provision. On the other hand, the constitutional principle of equality developed domestically by English courts is wider. The law and the government must accord every individual equal concern and respect for their welfare and dignity. Everyone is entitled to equal protection of the law, which must be applied without fear or favour. Except where compellingly justified distinctions must never be made on the grounds of race, colour, belief, gender or other irrational ground. Individuals are therefore comprehensively protected from discrimination by the principle of equality. This constitutional right has a continuing role to play. The organic development of constitutional rights is therefore a complementary and parallel process to the application of human rights legislation.'

I cite that passage in demonstration of the continued force of the common law principle of equality and generality of its application. I emphasise the passage where Lord Steyn says that, 'Except where compellingly justified distinctions must never be made on the grounds of race [or] colour'.

37. Mr Sales submitted [for the MOD], however, that the Courts must tread warily in this field and he submitted, in reliance upon the decision of the Privy Council in *Matadeen v Pointer* … that questions of equal treatment are not always justiciable ones …

38. The question in that case was whether the Constitution of Mauritius rendered unconstitutional laws giving rise to inequalities outside the grounds set out in the constitution itself. The Privy Council decided that this was not the effect of the Constitution and that, outside its express terms, questions of legitimate justification for other forms of discrimination or classification was a matter for Parliament or, subject to judicial review, to the relevant minister or other decision maker: see pp.110 and 118.

39. This decision obviously leaves intact the common law principle of equality of which Lord Steyn spoke in his lecture. Moreover, given the terms of the Constitution of Mauritius which proscribed discrimination on racial grounds, it can hardly have been thought that concepts of racial discrimination might not be properly justiciable …

54. … The Gurkhas were excluded on the basis of a Constitutional distinction which was in fact founded upon race.

55. The embarrassment to government in that exclusion is palpable in the 1955 correspondence. The adherence to the same distinction in 2000, particularly if the racial nature of the disciplinary distinction originally made in the 19th century was not appreciated (as seems clear it was not), appears to me (with genuine respect for the aims of the scheme) to be irrational and inconsistent with the principle of equality that is the cornerstone of our law. The 'floodgates' argument, based upon the perceived parallels with Dominion citizens, is difficult to follow in the light of the facts before the court.

56. In these circumstances there seems to me to be little reason for fossilising rationality in its 1951 form and applying it rigidly 50 years later. The decision making process has been helpfully laid bare before the Court. The failure to appreciate what to me is a clear distinction drawn on 'de facto' racial grounds (disguised by 'de jure' Constitutional ones) and to apply that same distinction to the new scheme undermines the rationality of the exclusion of the Claimants. This conclusion is compounded by the new analogy between these Claimants and Dominion citizens, drawn for the first time by the Defendant in reaching its decision in 2000 … For those reasons, it seems to me that the Defendant must be required to think again.

In reaching his conclusion in *Gurung* McCombe J distinguished the decision in *R (ABCIFER) v Secretary of State for Defence* [2002] EWHC 2119 (Admin), in which the High Court had rejected a challenge to the exclusion from a civilian Japanese POW scheme of British civilians who had not (and whose parents and grandparents had not) been born in the UK. The common law aspect of that challenge had been based on legitimate expectations. On appeal to the CA, however, the claimants sought to rely on the claim that the distinction drawn between categories of British citizens on the basis of their place of birth contravened the 'common law principle of equality'.

***R (Association of British Civilian Internees: Far East Region) v Secretary of State for Defence* [2003] QB 1397**

Dyson LJ, for the Court:

> We do not find it necessary to determine whether there is a free-standing principle of equality in English domestic law, since we did not hear argument on the point. We do not, however, think that the Privy Council in *Matadeen's* case was propounding such a principle. It seems to us that what Lord Hoffmann was discussing was how the Wednesbury test should be accommodated in cases of alleged unjustified discrimination …
>
> … whether the question is considered in *Wednesbury* terms, or on an application of a free-standing principle that like cases should be treated alike unless there is a valid reason for treating them differently, the complaint in the present case must be rejected. We have already given our reasons for concluding that the decision to exclude those who did not satisfy the birth criteria was not unreasonable in the *Wednesbury* sense. If a free-standing principle of equality were to be applied, it would have to be on the basis that the court would give the minister a margin of appreciation to determine what was a valid reason for treating internees differently. In our view, the minister's decision to exclude those British subjects who did not satisfy the birth criteria fell comfortably within the margin of appreciation that should be accorded to him by the court. Our reasons are essentially the same as those which led us to conclude that the challenge to the birth criteria fails on an application of the *Wednesbury* test.

The introduction of the PSED and the availability of direct challenges to statutory provisions under the HRA, coupled with the removal of previous limitations on the application of A1P1 to state benefits has reduced the immediate incentive for claimants to bring common law discrimination claims. It remains to be seen what the impact on such claims may be of any changes to the domestic protection of human rights through the HRA. Certainly, there are indications that senior domestic judges, whether or not in response to perceived threats to the HRA, have demonstrated some enthusiasm for the development of common law human rights protection notwithstanding the current applicability, through the HRA, of ECHR rights.[41]

[41] See eg *Rabone v Pennine Care NHS Foundation Trust* [2012] UKSC 2, [2012] 2 AC 72 §113 *per* Lord Brown; *Osborn v Parole Board* [2013] UKSC 61, [2014] AC 1115 § 57 *per* Lord Reed; *Kennedy v Charity Commission* [2014] UKSC 20, [2015] AC 455 §46 *per* Lord Mance.

Discrimination and International Human Rights Obligations

Prohibitions on discrimination figure strongly in international law. The first recital to the Universal Declaration of Human Rights, for example, recognises 'the equal and inalienable rights of all' and the first two articles of the declaration provide that 'All human beings are born free and equal in dignity and rights' and that 'Everyone is entitled to all the rights and freedoms set forth in this Declaration, without distinction of any kind, such as race, colour, sex, language, religion, political or other opinion, national or social origin, property, birth or other status.' The International Covenant on Civil and Political Rights (ICCPR) and the International Covenant on Economic, Social and Cultural Rights (ICESCR), through which the Universal Declaration is given effect, both regulate discrimination. Article 26 of the ICCPR, for example, provides that:

> All persons are equal before the law and are entitled without any discrimination to the equal protection of the law. In this respect, the law shall prohibit any discrimination and guarantee to all persons equal and effective protection against discrimination on any ground such as race, colour, sex, language, religion, political or other opinion, national or social origin, property, birth or other status.

The ICESCR requires contracting parties (Article 2.2) to 'guarantee that the rights enunciated in the present Covenant will be exercised without discrimination of any kind as to race, colour, sex, language, religion, political or other opinion, national or social origin, property, birth or other status'. The European Social Charter of 1961 and the Social Charter of 1996 proscribe discrimination while International Convention on the Elimination of all Forms of Racial Discrimination (CERD), CEDAW and CRPD and the Convention on the Rights of the Child (CRC) all contain detailed provisions by which discrimination is to be eliminated and equality furthered.[42]

These international provisions are mentioned here only to give a flavour of the context in which domestic discrimination law operates. Between them they include a rich variety of approaches varying from blunt prohibitions on differential treatment on listed (and, in some cases, unlisted) grounds to richly detailed substantive requirements (such as, for example, Article 10 ICESCR, which requires a reasonable period of 'paid leave or leave with adequate social security benefits' for maternity and Article 7 of the Convention on the Rights of the Child, which provides that children shall be registered immediately after birth and 'shall have the right from birth to a name, the right to acquire a nationality and, as far as possible, the right to know and be cared for by [their] parents').

The ECHR is unique in the UK in that its provisions have been transposed, albeit partially and at present uncertainly, into domestic law.[43] Other international standards

[42] For general (albeit rather dated) discussion of these and other international provisions see A McColgan, 'Principles of Equality and Protection from Discrimination in International Human Rights Law' [2003] *European Human Rights Law Review* 157–75.

[43] 'Partially' in the sense that they are subject to override by clearly contrary primary legislation.

have legal effect only to the extent that they are reflected in legislation (the UK operating a dualist, rather than monist, approach to international obligations). A seven-judge Supreme Court took the opportunity in *R (SC) v Secretary of State for Work and Pensions* [2021] UKSC 26, [2022] AC 223 to put paid to recent suggestions by a number of its justices that the courts might take into account unincorporated international obligations (such as those imposed by the Convention on the Rights of the Child, or the Convention on the Rights of Persons with Disabilities) in considering the question of justification under Article 14 ECHR.[44] The suggestion had been made with more or less conviction by Lord Carnwath, Lady Hale and Lord Kerr in *R (SG) v SSWP* [2015] UKSC 16, [2015] 1 WLR 1449, Lady Hale (for the majority) in *In re McLaughlin* [2018] UKSC 48, [2018] 1 WLR 4250 and Lord Wilson (for the majority) in *Mathieson v SSWP* [2015] UKSC 47, [2015] 1 WLR 3250 and in *DA* [2019] 1 WLR 3289. There remains some scope for international obligations to find their way into domestic law by becoming part of the context in which ECHR rights are interpreted/developed by the ECtHR, with implications for the domestic courts (at least for the moment) in their application of the HRA.

Discrimination and EU Law

EU law provides a significant backdrop to domestic equality law notwithstanding the UK's withdrawal from the EU, not least in view of the fact that the European Union (Withdrawal) Act 2018 retained the principle that EU law was supreme in relation to legislation (including the EqA) which predated Brexit. There was a time when any proper analysis of domestic law would have required detailed engagement with the EU Treaty and Directive provisions against which domestic law fell to be interpreted. Since the implementation of the EqA and the significant reduction in the pace of EU legislative change, it can be said that current domestic law is more or less compliant with the underpinning EU provisions, which will not be discussed in this book except where directly relevant to a particular case or statutory provision.[45] Further, and to the extent that there may be disparities between the EqA (in its current or future amended form) and EU law as it is interpreted over time, the publication (the day before this text is being written) of the Retained EU Law (Revocation and Reform) Bill makes clear the Government's intention to remove the principle of the supremacy of EU law from domestic law 'after the end of 2023, in relation to any enactment or rule of law (whenever passed or made)'. Assuming that the Bill becomes law in more or less its current form, it is unlikely that domestic judges will swiftly or radically alter the interpretation of large parts of the EqA. It is possible, however, that interpretations adopted by the CJEU and the domestic courts of transposed EU provisions (to the extent that these survive the planned 'bonfire of EU law') will diverge over time. It is also, and regrettably, likely that legislative amendments will be made to aspects of the EqA which are regarded by free market idealogues within the Conservative Party as 'burdensome' on business, perhaps irrespective of whether consultation exercises support this view.[46] At the risk of tempting fate, such changes might involve the imposition of additional hurdles to the enforcement of rights.

[44] See further discussion of this case in Ch 2.

[45] See, for example, *Jessemey v Rowstock Ltd* [2014] EWCA Civ 185, [2014] ICR 550 and *Blackwood v Birmingham & Solihull Mental Health NHS Trust* [2016] EWCA Civ 607, [2016] ICR 903, both discussed in Ch 4.

[46] See discussion in Ch 5 of the repeal of the questionnaire procedure for discrimination claims and the broader powers of tribunals to make recommendations.

The Structure of this Book

This book falls into two parts. The first (Chapters 2–5 inclusive) deals with questions of general application and the second (Chapters 6–11 inclusive) with matters unique, or of particular relevance to, individual protected characteristics.[47] As explained above, Chapter 2 deals with the definitions of discrimination and various associated torts regulated by the EqA.[48] It also discusses the discrimination under Article 14 ECHR and its application in domestic law. Chapter 3 discusses the scope for positive action in domestic law and under the ECHR, and the public sector equality duty (PSED) now found in s149 EqA.[49] Chapter 4 considers the material scope of the EqA (that is, the areas to which it applies[50]) and, to an extent, of the HRA. Chapter 5 discusses enforcement[51] which is of central importance to the effectiveness or otherwise of anti-discrimination/equality law.

Chapter 6 considers matters arising in connection with sex, gender reassignment and married and civilly partnered status; Chapter 7 with race; Chapter 8 disability; Chapter 9 religion and belief; Chapter 10 sexual orientation; and Chapter 11 age. The approach taken in these chapters is not uniform. All of them discuss the nature of disadvantage and discrimination associated with the relevant protected characteristic and those aspects of the EqA which apply uniquely or predominantly in relation to the protected characteristic, but the nature of the materials considered varies significantly as does the extent to which Convention rights or EU law are discussed. The purpose of these Chapters is to introduce readers to the social realities associated with the various protected characteristics, and to seek to demonstrate the law (both the EqA and the HRA/ECHR) in operation. A reader who is interested in only one or a few protected characteristics could gain an adequate grasp of the law by reading Chapters 2–5 in combination with the relevant chapters from Chapters 6–11, though engagement with the book in its entirety will provided a firmer grounding in the subject.

[47] Part 1 EqA and (Ch 8) Part 13 which concerns adjustments to let premises.
[48] This broadly corresponds to Part 2 EqA.
[49] This Chapter broadly corresponds to Part 11 EqA 'Advancement of Equality'.
[50] Parts 3–7, Part 8 ('Prohibited Conduct: Ancillary') EqA and Part 14 ('General Exceptions'). This chapter also makes reference to provisions in Part 10 EqA, 'Contracts etc'.
[51] Including, but not limited to, Part 9 EqA 'Enforcement'.

2

'Discrimination' and Related Conduct

'Discrimination' is the subject matter of this book, and it is the concept which ties together all the legislation and case law here considered. Of central significance is the Equality Act 2010 (EqA), which employs a variety of discrete concepts of discrimination all defined in the EqA. Also of great significance is discrimination as regulated by Article 14 of the European Convention on Human Rights (ECHR), given partial effect in the UK by the Human Rights Act 1998 (HRA; see further Chapter 1). Article 14 discrimination is more fluid than that recognised by the EqA though it overlaps and concepts of direct and indirect discrimination can usefully be employed within Article 14.

The EqA regulates direct and indirect discrimination as well as victimisation and harassment (both of which are considered in this chapter for convenience, though they are not actually defined as forms of discrimination). In addition, in the case of disability, the EqA defines as discrimination a failure to make reasonable adjustments and prohibits discrimination 'because of something arising in consequence of' a person's disability. This last is similar to, but broader than, direct discrimination and, unlike most direct discrimination, is capable of justification under the EqA. The concepts of discrimination and related conduct employed generally by the EqA are considered in this chapter (those specific to disability and to age in Chapters 8 and 11 respectively). Also considered in this chapter is 'discrimination' as it is regulated by Article 14 ECHR.

The Equality Act 2010

Direct Discrimination

Section 13 EqA, Direct Discrimination

Section 13 EqA provides that:

(1) A person (A) discriminates against another (B) if, because of a protected characteristic, A treats B less favourably than A treats or would treat others.

(2) If the protected characteristic is age, A does not discriminate against B if A can show A's treatment of B to be a proportionate means of achieving a legitimate aim.

(3) If the protected characteristic is disability, and B is not a disabled person, A does not discriminate against B only because A treats or would treat disabled persons more favourably than A treats B.
(4) If the protected characteristic is marriage and civil partnership, this section applies to a contravention of Part 5 (work) only if the treatment is because it is B who is married or a civil partner.
(5) If the protected characteristic is race, less favourable treatment includes segregating B from others.
(6) If the protected characteristic is sex—
 (a) less favourable treatment of a woman includes less favourable treatment of her because she is breast-feeding;
 (b) in a case where B is a man, no account is to be taken of special treatment afforded to a woman in connection with pregnancy or childbirth.
(7) Subsection (6)(a) does not apply for the purposes of Part 5 (work).
(8) This section is subject to sections 17(6) and 18(7).

The Basics

As is clear from the foregoing, a justification defence is available in the case of direct age discrimination, but not otherwise (s13(2) EqA). Disability is unusual among the protected characteristics in that the prohibition on direct discrimination operates asymmetrically: in other words, whereas s13 prohibits the *less* favourable treatment of disabled people, s13(3) EqA makes it clear that *more* favourable treatment of disabled than of non-disabled people does not amount to direct discrimination. The protection from discrimination on grounds of marriage/civil partnership, which applies only in relation to work, also applies asymmetrically, and the prohibition on indirect (but not direct) gender reassignment discrimination is asymmetrical.[1] In addition, the language of s13(4) EqA appears to exclude associative discrimination claims (see further pp 38–42 below) in relation to this ground. Section 13(5) EqA specifies that in the case of race, segregation amounts to discrimination. This might be taken to suggest that the same is not true in relation to other grounds, though we shall see at pp 35–38 below that sex segregation has also been recognised as amounting to discrimination.

Discrimination because of breast-feeding amounts to direct sex discrimination other than in the context of work (s13(6)(a) and (7) EqA) and the prohibition on sex discrimination is asymmetrical to the extent (only) that special treatment afforded to a woman in connection with pregnancy or childbirth does not amount to sex discrimination against men (s13(6)(b) EqA). Section 13(6) needs to be read with ss17(6) and 18(7). Section 17(6) provides that, in a non-work context, unfavourable treatment of a woman because of her pregnancy, or because she has given birth within the previous six months, does not amount to direct sex discrimination (this because it is prohibited instead as pregnancy and maternity discrimination). Section 18(7) makes similar provision in the context of work (see further Chapter 6).

Intention, Motivation and Stereotypes

The definition of direct discrimination appears relatively straightforward. But, particularly in the early application of the Sex Discrimination Act 1975 (SDA), the courts at times appeared reluctant to apply it in its full force. The first case to reach the Court of Appeal (CA) under that Act was *Peake v Automotive Products.*

[1] See discussion in Ch 6, pp 329–330.

***Peake v Automotive Products Ltd* [1977] EWCA Civ J0705-1, [1978] QB 233**

The claimant challenged his employer's practice of allowing women to leave the factory five minutes before men. Men and women finished work at the same time, but women were permitted to leave first, according to Lord Denning, 'in the interests of safety so that the women should not be jostled or hurt in the rush through the gates when the men leave work.'

Lord Denning MR:

> Although the [SDA] applies equally to men as to women, I must say it would be very wrong to my mind if this Act were thought to obliterate the differences between men and women or to do away with the chivalry and courtesy which we expect mankind to give womankind. The natural differences of sex must be regarded even in the interpretation of an Act of Parliament. Applied to this case it seems to me that, when a working rule is made differentiating between men and women in the interests of safety, there is no [direct] discrimination. Instances were put before us in the course of argument, such as a cruise liner which employs both men and women. Would it be wrong to have a regulation: 'Woman and children first?' Or in the case of a factory in case of fire? As soon as such instances are considered, the answer is clear. It is not discrimination for mankind to treat womankind with the courtesy and chivalry which we have been taught to believe is right conduct in our society.

Goff and Shaw LJJ agreed with the Master of the Rolls, the latter on the basis that 'The [SDA] was not, in my judgment, designed to provide a basis for capricious and empty complaints of differentiation between the sexes' and that 'discrimination' against men or women 'involves an element of something which is inherently adverse or hostile to the interests of the persons of the sex which is said to be discriminated against.'

Not long after the decision in *Peake* the CA modified its approach.

***Ministry of Defence v Jeremiah* [1980] QB 87**

Mr Jeremiah complained that, whereas men who volunteered for overtime were required to work in the 'colour-bursting shop' (an unpleasant environment in respect of which work attracted an additional premium), women who worked overtime were not so required.

Lord Denning MR:

> A woman's hair is her crowning glory, so it is said. She does not like it disturbed: especially when she has just had a 'hair-do'. The women at an ordnance factory in Wales are no exception. They do not want to work in a part of the factory … which ruins their 'hair-do'…
>
> Mr Jeremiah has little regard for chivalry or for the women's hair-dos. He is a modern man. He says that there should be equality between the sexes. Either the women should be required to do their stint (in the colour-bursting shop), just like the men. Or the men should not be required to do it any more than the women … it is plain that Ministry of Defence here discriminated against Mr Jeremiah. They required him to work in the dirty shop. They treated him less favourably than they treated a woman; and they did it on the ground of his sex, because he was a man … the Ministry relies on *Peake v Automotive Products Ltd* … There were two grounds for the decision. Now on reconsideration, I think the only sound ground was that the discrimination was *de minimis*. Counsel for Mr Jeremiah told us that on a petition to the House of Lords, they refused leave to appeal for that very reason. They thought that the decision was correct on the *de minimis* ground.
>
> In these circumstances, the other ground (about chivalry and administrative practice) should no longer be relied on …

The categorisation of the discrimination in *Peake* as de minimis is questionable, Peter Wallington pointing out that the difference in time worked by men and women amounted to two days per annum.[2] The existence of a *de minimis* defence to a discrimination claim was doubted by the CA in *Gill v El Vino Co Ltd* [1983] QB 425, which ruled that a refusal to serve women at the bar of a wine bar was unlawful, Eveleigh LJ stating in terms that he found it 'very difficult to invoke the maxim *de minimis non curat lex* in a situation where that which has been denied to the plaintiff is the very thing that Parliament seeks to provide, namely facilities and services on an equal basis.' The Court did not, however, overrule its earlier decision and in *R (Dowsett) v SSJ* [2013] EWHC 687 (Admin) the High Court relied on *Peake* in rejecting a challenge to a policy permitting rub-down searches of male prisoners by women prison guards while prohibiting rub-down searches of women prisoners by male prison guards.

Direct discrimination may consist of treating people differently *simply* because of a difference in sex, race, etc.[3] But it will more commonly consist of treating them differently on the basis of attributes stereotypically associated with persons of either sex or a particular racial group. In *R (European Roma Rights Centre) v Immigration Officer at Prague Airport* [2004] UKHL 55, [2005] 2 AC 1, the House of Lords (HL) overturned a decision by the CA ([2004] QB 811) which permitted the application of stereotypical assumptions that Roma travelling to the UK were more likely than others to be prospective asylum-seekers. More recently, an employment tribunal ruled that a worker had been discriminated against when a colleague assumed that, as a mixed-race person, she would have been subject to racial oppression.

'Diversity officer guilty of racism after telling colleague "you must have been oppressed", ***The Telegraph*****, 2 August 2022**

A Sky diversity officer racially discriminated against a mixed race colleague by telling her she must have been 'oppressed' because of her Latina heritage, an employment tribunal has ruled. Jane Bradbury was left 'distressed' after Rosemary Cook made the remark as she prepared to deliver a presentation about racism in the wake of the murder of George Floyd and emergence of the Black Lives Matter movement …

Following the conversation, Mrs Bradbury, 50, became 'very upset' and self-conscious about her skin colour, causing her to take several days off work as she was worried about being treated differently because of her race, the tribunal heard. Now, the field engineer has successfully sued Sky In-Home Services for race discrimination and has been awarded £14,000 in compensation. The tribunal ruled that though Ms Cook had not meant to cause offence, the remark was 'blunt' and an assumption that amounted to stereotyping …

… Mrs Bradbury … was left upset when Ms Cook rang her to discuss her views on the presentation she was preparing to give on issues of inclusion and diversity. 'It was not specifically about race discrimination but that featured as it was taking place against the relatively recent murder of George Floyd in the US, and the emergence of the Black Lives Matter movement …. Ms Cook said to Mrs Bradbury words to the effect that she would have suffered oppression because of her race, and the colour of her skin. Mrs Bradbury expressed her views to the contrary, forcefully,' the panel was told.

After raising the issue with bosses, Mrs Bradbury was told she was being removed from her role as an Inclusion Advocate to protect her 'emotional well-being'…

[2] P Wallington 'Ladies First – How Mr Peake was piqued' [1978] *Cambridge Law Journal* 37.

[3] In such a case an employer, if replying honestly, would affirm that the reason for the differential treatment was the difference in sex, race, etc.

> In its ruling, the panel said Ms Cook's remark did amount to discrimination although it added she did not deliberately use offensive language nor attempt to cause harm. 'Ms Cook appears to have assumed that, as Mrs Bradbury's skin colour is not white, she must have suffered oppression, which is a form of stereotyping. We considered that the remark and the manner in which it was handled by Sky In-Home Services did amount to less favourable treatment. It caused Mrs Bradbury understandable distress.'

The cases thus far considered suggest (*Jeremiah*'s disapproval of *Peake* being taken into account) that a respondent's motive for treating the claimant less favourably will not preclude a finding of discrimination as long as that discrimination was '*because of*' sex or race, etc. The prohibited ground does not have to be the sole ground for the less favourable treatment (*Owen & Brigg v James* [1982] ICR 618), but it must be 'the principal or at least an important or significant cause of the less favourable treatment.'[4]

The lack of any requirement that the discriminator be motivated by the prohibited ground was confirmed by the HL in *R v Birmingham CC ex parte EOC*.[5] The same decision also established that 'less favourable treatment' occurred when a plaintiff was deprived of a choice which was valued by her and by others on reasonable grounds.

***R v Birmingham CC ex parte EOC* [1989] UKHL 8, [1989] 1 AC 1155**

The case was brought by the EOC because, the Council having fewer grammar school places available for girls than for boys, it set the pass mark higher for the former in the '11 plus' examination by which children in the area were selected for secondary education. The HL ruled that, in order to establish that the girls had been discriminated against, it did not have to be shown that grammar school education was better than the alternative. Lord Goff went on to consider the meaning of 'on the grounds of sex'.

Lord Goff (with whom the other Lords agreed):

> There is discrimination under the statute if there is less favourable treatment on the ground of sex[6], in other words if the relevant girl or girls would have received the same treatment as the boys but for their sex. The intention or motive of the defendant to discriminate, though it may be relevant so far as remedies are concerned ... is not a necessary condition to liability ... if [it were] it would be a good defence for an employer to show that he discriminated against women not because he intended to do so but (for example) because of customer preference, or to save money, or even to avoid controversy.[7]

This statement of the law seems clear but it did not settle what was meant by 'on the grounds of', which was then the test for direct discrimination. (The current test for direct discrimination requires that the less favourable treatment be 'because of' rather than 'on the ground of' the protected characteristic, but the change is in wording only and the test itself has not altered.[8]) The HL considered the matter once again in *James v Eastleigh BC*.

[4] In *Neill v Governors of St Thomas More School* [1997] ICR 33 and in *O'Donoghue v Redcar and Cleveland BC* [2001] EWCA Civ 701, [2001] IRLR 615 the EAT and CA respectively asked whether the protected characteristic was an 'effective cause'. The same approach applies in victimisation claims: *Nagarajan v Agnew* [1994] IRLR 61.

[5] Prior to this see *R v CRE, ex p Westminster* [1985] ICR 827.

[6] Note that s13 EqA now refers to 'because of' rather than 'on the ground of'.

[7] Citing *Jenkins v Kingsgate Ltd* [1981] ICR 715 *per* Browne-Wilkinson J and *R v SS Education and Science, ex p Keating* (1985) 84 LGR 469 at 475 *per* Taylor J. See also Lord Denning MR in *MOD v Jeremiah* discussed above.

[8] See §61 of the explanatory notes to the EqA (https://www.legislation.gov.uk/ukpga/2010/15/notes/division/3/2/2/1). See also the discussion at p 39 below.

***James v Eastleigh BC* [1990] UKHL 6, [1990] 2 AC 751**

The applicant had been charged entrance to the local swimming pool on the grounds that, both he and his wife being aged between 60 and 65, she but not he had reached state pensionable age upon which free entrance depended. A county court and the CA had rejected the claimant's complaint of direct sex discrimination, the latter on the ground that direct discrimination required that either the covert or the overt reason for the treatment complained of was sex.

Lord Bridge:

> … the statutory pensionable age, being fixed at 60 for women and 65 for men, is itself a criterion which directly discriminates between men and women in that it treats women more favourably than men 'on the ground of their sex'… It follows inevitably that any other differential treatment of men and women which adopts the same criterion must equally involve discrimination 'on the ground of sex'….
>
> The Court of Appeal's attempt to escape from these conclusions lies in construing the phrase 'on the ground of her sex' in [the prohibition on direct discrimination] as referring subjectively to the alleged discriminator's 'reason' for doing the act complained of. As already noted, the judgment had earlier identified the council's reason as 'to give benefits to those whose resources would be likely to have been reduced by retirement' and 'to aid the needy, whether male or female.' But to construe the phrase, 'on the ground of her sex' as referring to the alleged discriminator's reason in this sense is directly contrary to a long line of authority confirmed by your Lordships' House in [*ex parte EOC* above].

Lord Goff's test, it will be observed, is not subjective, but objective. Adopting it here the question becomes: would the plaintiff, a man of 61, have received the same treatment as his wife *but* for his sex? (emphasis added) An affirmative answer is inescapable.

Lord Goff:

> … As a matter of impression, it seems to me that … it can properly be said that, by applying to the plaintiff a gender-based criterion, unfavourable to men, which [the Council has] adopted as the basis for a concession of free entry to its swimming pool, they [sic] did on the ground of sex treat him less favourably than it treated women of the same age, and in particular his wife. In other words, I do not read the words 'on the ground of sex' as necessarily referring only to the reason why the defendant acted as he did, but as embracing cases in which a gender-based criterion is the basis on which the complainant has been selected for the relevant treatment. Of course, there may be cases where the defendant's reason for his action may bring the case within the subsection, as when the defendant is motivated by an animus against persons of the complainant's sex, or otherwise selects the complainant for the relevant treatment because of his or her sex. But it does not follow that the words 'on the ground of sex' refer only to cases where the defendant's reason for his action is the sex of the complainant and, in my opinion, the application by the defendant to the complainant of a gender-based criterion which favours the opposite sex is just as much a case of unfavourable treatment on the ground of sex …
>
> … as I see it, cases of direct discrimination … can be considered by asking the simple question: would the complainant have received the same treatment from the defendant but for his or her sex? This simple test possesses the double virtue that, on the one hand, it embraces both the case where the treatment derives from the application of a gender-based criterion, and the case where it derives from the selection of the complainant because of his or her sex and on the other hand it avoids, in most cases at least, complicated questions relating to concepts such as intention, motive, reason or purpose, and the danger of confusion arising from the misuse of those elusive terms.

Lord Ackner concurred with Lords Bridge and Goff, Lords Griffiths and Lowry dissenting. The benefit of the 'but-for' test is that it avoids analysis of the motivation for discrimination, though it does not permit a distinction to be drawn between negative and positive discrimination – that is, between discrimination which perpetuates existing disadvantage and that which is designed to ameliorate it (see further Chapter 3). Although subject to repeated challenge before the highest courts the 'but-for' test has stood the test of time. In *R (E) v Governing Body of JFS* [2009] UKSC 15, [2010] 2 AC 728 the Supreme Court (SC) applied the test in deciding that a school which admitted only children recognised as Jewish under Orthodox rules had discriminated directly on racial grounds because the criteria for recognition required descent from an Orthodox Jewish mother or ancestress in the matrilineal line (see further Chapter 7). And in *Essop v Home Office* [2017] UKSC 27, [2017] ICR 640 (see further p 45 below) the SC cited *James v Eastleigh* in declaring that 'even if the protected characteristic is not the overt criterion, there will still be direct discrimination if the criterion used … exactly corresponds with a protected characteristic … and is thus a proxy for it'.

In *Bull v Hall* [2012] EWCA Civ 83, [2012] 1 WLR 2514, discussed in Chapter 10, the CA appeared to extend the bounds of direct discrimination in ruling that discrimination between same-sex partners and married couples amounted to direct discrimination because of sexual orientation because at the time same-sex couples were unable to get married. There is, of course, no exact correspondence between unmarried couples and same-sex couples, though the CA thought that the case was directly analogous with *James v Eastleigh*.[9] The SC ([2013] UKSC 73, [2013] 1 WLR 3741) based its finding of direct discrimination on the difference in treatment between (same sex) civil partners and (heterosexual) married couples in a move which appeared to reinstate the orthodox position (that is, that direct discrimination will result from less favourable treatment of a criterion other than a protected characteristic only where there is an exact fit between that criterion and the protected characteristic for which it is a proxy).[10]

The Comparator Question

The essence of direct discrimination is comparison because a finding of direct discrimination requires *less* favourable treatment, which is by definition relative. This may be contrasted with discrimination arising from disability, and with discrimination because of pregnancy or maternity, each of which is defined (s15, s17 and s18 EqA) as *unfavourable* rather than *less favourable*, treatment.

The EqA now provides that:

Section 23 EqA, Comparison by reference to circumstances

(1) On a comparison of cases for the purposes of section 13, 14, or 19 there must be no material difference between the circumstances relating to each case.

[9] A view with which Lord Dyson MR disagreed in *Black v Wilkinson* [2013] EWCA Civ 820, [2013] 1 WLR 2490, though he regarded himself nonetheless as bound to follow the earlier decision of the CA.

[10] Similarly, in *Taiwo v Olaigbe, Onu v Akwiwu* [2016] UKSC 31, [2016] ICR 756, discussed in Ch 7, the SC ruled that discrimination on grounds of immigrant status did not amount to direct discrimination because of nationality.

(2) The circumstances relating to a case include a person's abilities if—

(a) on a comparison for the purposes of section 13, the protected characteristic is disability;

(b) on a comparison for the purposes of section 14, one of the protected characteristics in the combination is disability.[11]

(3) If the protected characteristic is sexual orientation, the fact that one person (whether or not the person referred to as B) is a civil partner while another is married … is not a material difference between the circumstances relating to each case.

(4) If the protected characteristic is sexual orientation, the fact that one person (whether or not the person referred to as B) is married to, or the civil partner of, a person of the same sex while another is married to, or the civil partner of, a person of the opposite sex is not a material difference between the circumstances relating to each case.

The requirement for less favourable treatment has given rise to difficulties associated with the identification of the comparator against whose treatment that of the claimant falls to be assessed. Prior to the specific regulation of pregnancy discrimination such claims had to be challenged under the prohibition on sex discrimination; the domestic courts proved singularly reluctant to accept that pregnancy (perhaps the greatest cause of women's work-related disadvantage) amounted to or involved sex discrimination. The greatest stumbling block appeared to be the requirement in s5(3) SDA (the predecessor provision of s23 EqA) for comparison between people whose relevant circumstances were 'the same, or not materially different'.[12] The domestic courts were eventually required by EU law to recognise pregnancy discrimination as sex discrimination and in *Shamoon v CC RUC* the HL signalled a less formalistic approach to comparators.

***Shamoon v CC Royal Ulster Constabulary (Northern Ireland)* [2003] UKHL 11, [2003] ICR 337**

The case involved a sex discrimination complaint from a chief inspector whose appraisal duties were removed from her after a number of complaints about her conduct of appraisals. Her sex discrimination claim was upheld by a tribunal but dismissed by Northern Ireland's CA (to which claims from tribunals go directly) on the basis that her chosen comparators – two male chief inspectors – were not similarly situated (this because no complaints had been made against them in connection with their performance of appraisals). The HL agreed that the actual comparators relied upon by the claimant were inappropriate and that the tribunal had given no reasons to justify the finding of sex discrimination. Lord Hope pointed out, however, that:

> the choice of comparator requires that a judgment must be made as to which of the differences between any two individuals are relevant and which are irrelevant. The choice of characteristics may itself be determinative of the outcome … This suggests that care must be taken not to approach this issue in a way that will defeat the purpose of the legislation, which is to eliminate discrimination against women on the ground of their sex in all the areas with which it deals.[13]

Lord Nicholls, with whom Lord Rodger agreed on this point, noted that the general practice of tribunals was to ask, first, 'whether the claimant received less favourable treatment than the appropriate comparator (the "less favourable treatment" issue)' and to treat this

[11] See further Ch 8.

[12] Discussed in previous editions of this book.

[13] Having noted Sandra Fredman's critique of the comparator approach (see *Discrimination Law* (OUP, 2001) 96–99).

question effectively as a 'threshold which the claimant must cross before the tribunal is called upon to decide' the second question – 'whether the less favourable treatment was on the relevant proscribed ground (the "reason why" issue).' This practice could be 'convenient and helpful' but there was 'essentially a single question: did the claimant, on the proscribed ground, receive less favourable treatment than others [received or would have received]?' The 'sequential analysis' could 'give rise to needless problems', 'especially where the identity of the relevant comparator is a matter of dispute. Sometimes the less favourable treatment issue cannot be resolved without, at the same time, deciding the reason why issue. The two issues are intertwined.'

In the instant case it was not possible to answer whether the claimant's chosen comparators were appropriate without addressing the question why she had been relieved of her appraisal duties: if the reason was connected with the complaints against her the comparators were not appropriate. But the action taken against her may have had nothing to do with the complaints, in which case the comparison she advocated would have entailed 'comparing like with like, because in that event the difference between her and her two male colleagues would be an immaterial difference'. Equally, the question whether the claimant was less favourably treated than a hypothetical comparator:

> is incapable of being answered without … identifying the ground on which she was treated as she was. Was it grounds of sex? If yes, then she was treated less favourably than a male chief inspector in her position would have been treated. If not, not. Thus, on this footing also, the less favourable treatment issue is incapable of being decided without deciding the reason why issue. And the decision on the reason why issue will also provide the answer to the less favourable treatment issue.

Lord Nicholls concluded that tribunals:

> may sometimes be able to avoid arid and confusing disputes about the identification of the appropriate comparator by concentrating primarily on why the claimant was treated as she was. Was it on the proscribed ground which is the foundation of the application? That will call for an examination of all the facts of the case. Or was it for some other reason? If the latter, the application fails. If the former, there will be usually be no difficulty in deciding whether the treatment, afforded to the claimant on the proscribed ground, was less favourable than was or would have been afforded to others'

Lord Nicholls' approach fits well with the model of direct discrimination which permits claimants to establish discrimination in relation to a *hypothetical* comparator. Once it has been established that the treatment complained of was *by reason of* a protected ground, the comparator question is largely a formality. But this approach does not solve all the problems to which the analysis of discrimination gives rise. Indeed, it is perhaps precisely because of the difficulties associated with determining the reasons for differential treatment that a comparator-driven approach can appear attractive. The HL's embracing of the 'but-for' test in *James v Eastleigh* was intended to avoid unnecessary confusion as to intention, motive, etc. It operates in practice by emphasising what Lord Nicholls referred to in *Shamoon* as the 'less favourable treatment' question over the 'reason why' question. In order to determine whether a claimant would have been treated more favourably 'but for' her sex, the question required by the comparator-driven approach is whether a similarly situated man was or would have been treated more favourably than she was. But, as their Lordships generally recognised in *Shamoon*, the answer to this may depend on the characteristics assigned to the 'similarly situated' man or other relevant comparator.

The question of comparators was considered by the SC in the *Coll* case, which concerned the differential provision for men and women former prisoners of approved premises to which they might be released on licence.

***R (Coll) v Secretary of State for Justice* [2017] UKSC 40, [2017] 1 WLR 2093**

The claimant had been sentenced to life imprisonment for murder. This being the case it was likely that on her release she would initially be required to live in approved premises (APs). There were 94 such premises for men across England and Wales but only six for women, and the 112 places they provided were inadequate to meet the demand. The claimant feared that she would be required to live far away from her family, which was in London, on her release. She brought judicial review proceedings seeking declarations that the lack of any APs for women in London amounted to unlawful direct and indirect sex discrimination and that the defendant had breached the Public Sector Equality Duty (PSED, discussed in Chapter 3) by failing to have due regard, in relation to the provision of APs in London, to the need to eliminate discrimination against women, and advance equality of opportunity for them.

A judge dismissed the claimant's case except insofar as he made a declaration that the defendant had failed to discharge the PSED. The CA refused the claimant's appeal but the SC ruled that she had been subject to direct sex discrimination and that the defendant could not rely on Schedule 3 para 26 EqA (see further Chapter 6).

Lady Hale (for the Court):

> 26. The appellant's case on direct discrimination is a simple one. Being required to live in an AP a long way away from home is a detriment. A woman is much more likely to suffer this detriment than is a man, because of the geographical distribution of the small number of APs available for women. This is treating her less favourably than a man because of her sex …
>
> 29. [Referring to the argument raised for the Secretary of State that, because not all women suffered the detriment complained of there could not be direct discrimination, which required exact correspondence between the disadvantaged class and the protected characteristic.[14] However, as Ms Rose correctly points out, the 'exact correspondence' test is only relevant where the actual criterion used by the alleged discriminator is not a protected characteristic but something else. In *Patmalniece* it was not having the right to reside in the United Kingdom; in *Bull v Hall*, it was not being married. The question is whether some other criterion is in reality a proxy for the protected characteristic. The best-known example is *James v Eastleigh* …. The differential state retirement ages for men and women meant that a 61-year-old woman got in free whereas her 61-year-old husband did not. This was held to be direct discrimination on grounds of sex. In this case, there is no doubt what the criterion is. It is sex, which is itself a protected characteristic.
>
> 30. Furthermore, it cannot be a requirement of direct discrimination that all the people who share a particular protected characteristic must suffer the less favourable treatment complained of. It is not necessary to show, for example, that an employer always discriminates against women: it is enough to show that he did so in this case. In [*R v Birmingham CC ex parte EOC* [2989 1 AC 1055], some of the girls achieved a high enough pass mark to gain a place at a selective school. What all the girls suffered from was the risk that if they did not get a high enough mark, they would not get a place … In the *Birmingham* case, some of the girls did of course

[14] Citing *Patmalniece v SSWP* [2011] UKSC 11, [2011] 1 WLR 783, discussed in *Bull v Hall* [2013] UKSC 73, [2013] 1 WLR 374, which is extracted in Ch 10.

achieve a high enough mark to get a place. But there were some who achieved a mark which would have been high enough had they been boys but was not high enough because they were girls. That is direct discrimination on grounds of sex.

31. I can see no valid distinction between the *Birmingham* case and this one. In this case, all the women who would be required to live in an AP when released on licence suffered the much greater risk than the men that they would be sent to an AP far from their homes and families. The fact that some of them would not suffer this detriment does not mean that those who do suffer it have not been discriminated against.

32. It was argued in the courts below that there was a material difference between the circumstances of the male and female offenders so that their cases were not comparable for the purpose of s 23 … Cranston J accepted [at first instance] that comparing the women prisoners with the men prisoners was not comparing like with like … The women had different characteristics from the men, fewer being of high or very high risk, and the criteria for admitting them to APs were different. However, in the CA, Elias LJ rejected this argument. Those differences were not material to the present issue, which was accommodating them close to home … I agree. The question of comparing like with like must always be treated with great care – men and women are different from one another in many ways, but that does not mean that the relevant circumstances cannot be the same for the purpose of deciding whether one has been treated less favourably than the other. Usually, those circumstances will be something other than the personal characteristics of the men and women concerned, something extrinsic rather than intrinsic to them. In this case, the material circumstances are that they are offenders being released on licence on condition that they live in an AP. Those circumstances are the same for men and women. But the risk of being placed far from home is much greater for the women than for the men.

The approach adopted by the HL in *James v Eastleigh* was liberal and purposive in defining direct discrimination widely without requiring malign motivation on the part of the discriminator. It does not do away with the need to ask questions about reasons for discrimination and whether they are properly categorised as coming within the protected grounds or not. One example might relate to unfavourable treatment accorded to a pregnant trans man in connection with that pregnancy. We saw above that pregnancy itself is a protected characteristic for the purposes of the ss17 and 18 EqA, defining unlawful discrimination in this context as unfavourable treatment of 'a woman' because of 'a pregnancy of hers' or (in the context of work) 'because of illness suffered by her as a result of' the pregnancy. 'Woman' is defined by s212 EqA as 'a female of any age'. Unless a pregnant trans man is recognised as 'female' despite having a GRC[15] the treatment complained of will not, on its face, fall within ss17 or 18 EqA, though the interpretive obligation imposed by s3 HRA might assist (see further Chapter 1).

If ss17 and 18 EqA do not assist, the trans man would have to fall back on s13 EqA and argue that the treatment amounted to or involved *less* favourable treatment of him than of a suitable relevant comparator for the purposes of s23 EqA. Whether this would assist will depend on the nature of and reasons for the treatment complained of (ie, whether it involves treating the individual less favourably than a woman would have been treated (sex discrimination) or than a person who had not undergone gender reassignment would have been treated (gender reassignment discrimination). If the former is in issue the claimant will

[15] *cf* discussion in Ch 6.

have to establish that there is 'no material difference' between his circumstances and those of a pregnant woman. If the latter is in issue he will have to show that there is 'no material difference' between his circumstances and those of a man who has not undergone gender reassignment. Each of these requirements may impose real difficulties if, for example, the complaint is that the trans man is being denied access to the full range of facilities offered to pregnant women undergoing maternity care.[16]

It is no defence to a claim of discrimination that the alleged discriminator has the same relevant characteristics as the person(s) against whom he or she is alleged to have discriminated. This is made clear by s24 EqA:

> **Section 24 EqA, Irrelevance of alleged discriminator's characteristics**
>
> For the purpose of establishing a contravention of this Act by virtue of section 13(1), it does not matter whether A has the protected characteristic …

Segregation and Discrimination

We saw above that s13(5) EqA provides that 'If the protected characteristic is race, less favourable treatment includes segregating B from others'. No similar provision is made by the EqA in relation to any other protected characteristics. Notwithstanding this, the CA ruled in the *Al-Hijrah* case that the segregation of children by sex in a mixed-sex school involved sex discrimination against both girls and boys.

***HM Chief Inspector of Education, Children's Services and Skill v Interim Executive Board of Al-Hijrah School* [2017] EWCA Civ 1426, [2018] 1 WLR 1471**

The school was a mixed-sex Islamic faith school for children aged between four and 16 which, for religious reasons, separated girls and boys completely after their ninth birthdays (from year 5). This policy was deemed to discriminate on grounds of sex by the Chief Inspector, who was responsible for Ofsted, a conclusion challenged by the school. The High Court ruled that Ofsted had been wrong to draw this conclusion where it had found that the quality of education received by girls and boys in the school was the same, and had not found that the impact of segregation was to reinforce social and cultural stereotypes about female inferiority. Boys and girls were both being denied the opportunity to interact/socialise/learn with or from the opposite sex with the effect that there was no differential treatment of the sexes. The CA disagreed.

Sir Terence Etherton MR and Beatson LJ:

> 45. Ms Helen Mountfield QC, for Ofsted, … submitted that a girl pupil who wishes to mix or socialise with a boy pupil is precluded from doing so because of her sex, a protected characteristic; whereas, if she did not have that characteristic, and was a boy pupil, she would be able to mix or socialise with all the other boys. Equally, if a boy pupil wishes to mix or socialise with a girl pupil, he is precluded from doing so because of his sex; and if he did not have that characteristic, and was a girl pupil, he would be able to mix or socialise with all the other

[16] See eg J Fertray, 'Ensuring pregnant trans men get equal quality care', Public Health England Blog, 13 March 2020, available at https://phescreening.blog.gov.uk/2020/03/13/pregnant-men-best-care; F White, *Trans Pregnancy*, available at https://transpregnancy.leeds.ac.uk/wp-content/uploads/sites/70/2018/05/Trans-Pregnancy-policy-review-UK.pdf.

girls. Ofsted's view was that this restriction on the freedom of a girl pupil to mix or socialise with boy pupils and on a boy pupil to mix or socialise with girl pupils was detrimental to their education …

46. It was submitted that the point can be put on the basis of a comparator, namely (in the case of discrimination against a girl pupil) a boy pupil who can mix with other boy pupils, and (in the case of discrimination against a boy pupil) a girl pupil who can mix with other girl pupils, or it can be advanced without any comparator by simply asking what would have been the position if the girl pupil or the boy pupil did not have the protected characteristic of their sex. It is said that, either way, there is discrimination … Viewed from the perspective of an individual pupil, in that way, both the girl pupil and the boy pupil are treated less favourably than the other.

47. We agree with those submissions of Ofsted.

48. There is no doubt that the restriction on a girl pupil socialising with boy pupils, and on a boy pupil socialising with girl pupils, is by reason of their respective sex. There is no doubt that Ofsted could reasonably take the view, which it did, that the differential treatment, as Ofsted portrays it, was detrimental to both the girl pupil and the boy pupil. As it happens, there was direct evidence from some, albeit a small number, of the pupils in the present case that they regarded the complete separation of the sexes as detrimental to their social awareness and development, and there is equally no doubt that that view was a reasonable one to hold, reasonableness of perception of adverse detriment being the touchstone of detriment in this context …

49. The judge … regarded the key question as whether the denial of the opportunity to mix socially and interact with pupils of the opposite sex amounts to 'less favourable treatment' for the purposes of EA 2010, s 13(1) read in conjunction with EA 2010, s 23(1) … he approached the question of 'less favourable treatment' on the footing that 'each sex must be viewed as a group – there is no material difference (inter se) between any of the boys and the girls – and the comparison must be made between the two groups [and the two groups] … can be considered simultaneously, because that is the effect of segregating them down the middle'.

50. We agree with Ofsted that the judge was wrong to approach the matter in that way. The starting point is that EA 2010, s 13 specifies what is direct discrimination by reference to a 'person'. There is no reference to "group" discrimination or comparison. Each girl pupil and each boy pupil is entitled to freedom from direct discrimination looking at the matter from her or his individual perspective[17] …

51. Viewed in that way, Ofsted's analysis of 'less favourable treatment' is correct. An individual girl pupil cannot socialise and intermix with a boy pupil because, and only because, of her sex; and an individual boy pupil cannot socialise and intermix with a girl pupil because, and only because, of his sex. Each is, therefore, treated less favourably than would be the case if their sex was different.'[18]

The majority judges did not accept that girls were subject to greater psychological harm by the segregation because of the disadvantaged position of women in society and the fact that the segregation resulted from deep-seated cultural and historical perspectives as to the inferiority of the female sex. Gloster LJ, the sole woman on the Court, disagreed.

[17] Citing *R (E) v JFS* [2009] UKSC 15, [2010] 2 AC 728 §90.

[18] The majority also relied on the decisions in *Smyth v Croft Inns Ltd* [1995] NI 292, [1996] IRLR 84 and *R (Coll) v SSJ* [2017] UKSC 40, [2017] 1 WLR 2093 and distinguished *Smith v Safeway plc* [1996] ICR 868 and *G v Head Teacher and Governors of St Gregory's Catholic Science College* [2011] EWHC 1452 (Admin), which dealt with sex-specific appearance codes.

Having set out her conclusions that girls were in practical terms treated less favourably than boys at the school by reason of being exposed to literature which regarded women as inferior and always being made to have their break time after boys, she went on to consider the less practical aspects of sex segregation in this context.

Gloster LJ:

143. … I would also accept Ofsted's more conceptual argument … that, because, as the judge (and indeed the majority) recognized, in general in today's society women have been and remain 'the group with minority power in society' in terms of the distribution of wealth and influence, that means that strict segregation in a mixed sex school, where both girls and boys are educated on the same site, has a greater practical adverse impact on the girls than the boys.

144. Ms Mountfield's argument, in summary, is that, at an impressionable age, those with the minority of power are socialised to be regarded, by themselves and by those with the majority of power, as relevantly different in contexts where gender should be treated as irrelevant; and that creates a particular detriment for females as neither male nor female pupils are socialised to regard women as normal working and social companions for men, or 'like them', in a society in which men still hold the significant majority of power. If men and women find it more natural and comfortable to form exclusive and different social networks around working life only with those of their own sex, women lose out more than men, because women are disproportionately excluded from networks of power and influence in later life.

145. I accept these arguments, nebulous as they might appear to be at first sight. In my judgment, once the principle is accepted, as it was by the judge (and the majority in this court), that, as a generality, men exercise more influence and power in society than women, and that persistent gender inequalities remain in the employment market, evidence is not required to establish that an educational system, which promotes segregation in a situation where girls are not allowed to mix with boys or to be educated alongside them, notwithstanding they are studying the same curriculum and spending their days on the same single school site, is bound to endorse traditional gender stereotypes that preserve male power, influence and economic dominance. And the impact of that is inevitably greater on women than on men. One does not need to have been educated at a women's college at a co-educational university, at a time when women were still prohibited from being members of all-male colleges, to take judicial notice of the career opportunities which women are even today denied, simply because they are prevented from participating in hierarchical male networking groups, whether in the social, educational or employment environment …

147. [Ms Mountfield's argument in relation to *expressive harm*] is that such segregation, viewed in the historical and social context of English perspectives as to the inferiority of the female sex, not only has a practical adverse effect on women, but will also perpetuate and reinforce in the minds of its pupils the notion that females are *inferior* to men in both a social and employment context, despite the fact that they are following the same curriculum or doing the same job. She argues, by analogy with authorities from the United States and other jurisdictions, that, irrespective of the subjective intention of those adopting the policy, segregation based upon gender stigmatises women in an unfavourable way, and sends out the message that women are less worthy or somehow 'different' from men. She also submitted by reference to the comparative jurisprudence that expressive harm falls to be considered even where the message promulgated may be more equivocal; thus '[c]lassifications based upon race carry a *danger* of stigmatic harm' meaning 'unless they are reserved for remedial settings, they *may* in fact promote notions of racial inferiority' (her emphasis added).

148. Ms Mountfield did not seek to argue that faith schools in general, or Islamic schools in particular, segregated the sexes because they regarded females as inferior or took the view that the girls should be separately prepared for a lesser role in society. Thus she did not suggest in

this court (and indeed had not done so below) that the School agrees with, is motivated by, or seeks to perpetuate any message – religious or otherwise – that 'denigrates or deprecates' women, or considers them 'inferior'. Rather, she submitted that treatment which so unequivocally and systematically marks out boys and girls as separate and different will – or is at least liable to – strengthen stereotypical and detrimental perceptions of girls' and women's character, capacity, role or place; the fact that the intention was not malign; or even that it was benign (to satisfy the religious preferences of some parents) was irrelevant for the purposes of s 13 of the Equality Act …

153. I disagree with the judge, and with the majority, that there is a lack of evidence in the present case to support the appellant's arguments in relation to expressive harm. Evidence is not needed to inform the court of the historic, and indeed recent and continuing, struggles of women for equal rights, equal opportunities and equal pay in UK society … As Ms Mountfield cogently submitted, 'protected characteristics are protected because they all have long histories in which one group has been regarded as fundamentally different or inferior in ways which the law today recognises are unjustified and unacceptable but which (the Court can take judicial notice) persist in power imbalances which continue to exist across society at large'. One cannot shut one's eyes to the objective reality that, whatever the good intentions of government and equality legislation, stereotypical attitudes to girls and women, to their role in the family and in society and as to their ability, or entitlement, to command equality of opportunity and pay in the marketplace remain current in certain sections of UK society today. In those circumstances, in my judgment, the segregation by sex on a mixed sex educational campus necessarily endorses and perpetuates, or at the very least risks endorsing and perpetuating, stereotypes about girls and women that are still pervasive in society and which are widely recognised as detrimental and unduly limiting. And that in turn results in expressive harm to girls.

154. The fact that expressive harm caused as a result of segregation on grounds of race in an educational context would be both more obvious and more severe than the expressive harm caused by sex segregation, is not a reason for rejecting the appellant's argument in relation to segregation on grounds of sex, as the judge seemed to have thought …

Association and Perception

The direct discrimination provision of the EqA cover discrimination by association and discrimination on the basis of perceived characteristics. The application of the concept of direct discrimination to discrimination by association was indicated as early as 1984 with the decision of the EAT in *Showboat Entertainment Centre Ltd v Owens* [1984] ICR 65, in which the EAT accepted that a white claimant who was dismissed for refusing to obey an order to discriminate against Black customers had been discriminated against on grounds of race. In *Weathersfield Ltd v Sargent* [1999] ICR 425 the CA agreed with the reasoning in the earlier case and upheld a similar race discrimination claim. More recently, the judgment of the European Court of Justice in *Coleman v Attridge Law* established some of the conceptual parameters of discrimination by association. The claimant claimed that she had been treated less favourably because of the disability of her son, for whom she cared. This would not have fallen within the prohibition on disability discrimination then enshrined in the Disability Discrimination Act 1995 (DDA), which applied only to less favourable treatment 'for a reason which relates to *the disabled person's disability*' (emphasis added). The question for the CJEU was whether Directive 2000/78 (the Equal Treatment Directive) required the regulation of the discrimination complained of by Ms Coleman.

C-303/06 *Coleman v Attridge Law*, EU:C:2008:415, [2008] ECR I-5603, [2008] ICR 1128

47. … the directive seeks to lay down, as regards employment and occupation, a general framework for combating discrimination on one of the grounds referred to in Article 1 – including, in particular, disability – with a view to putting into effect in the Member States the principle of equal treatment. It follows from recital 37 in the preamble to the directive that it also has the objective of creating within the Community a level playing field as regards equality in employment and occupation.

48. … those objectives, and the effectiveness of Directive 2000/78, would be undermined if an employee in the claimant's situation cannot rely on the prohibition of direct discrimination laid down by Article 2(2)(a) of that directive where it has been established that he has been treated less favourably than another employee is, has been or would be treated in a comparable situation, on the grounds of his child's disability, and this is the case even though that employee is not himself disabled …

50. Although, in a situation such as that in the present case, the person who is subject to direct discrimination on grounds of disability is not herself disabled, the fact remains that it is the disability which, according to Ms Coleman, is the ground for the less favourable treatment which she claims to have suffered … Directive 2000/78, which seeks to combat all forms of discrimination on grounds of disability in the field of employment and occupation, applies not to a particular category of person but by reference to the grounds mentioned in Article 1.

51. Where it is established that an employee in a situation such as that in the present case suffers direct discrimination on grounds of disability, an interpretation of Directive 2000/78 limiting its application only to people who are themselves disabled is liable to deprive that directive of an important element of its effectiveness and to reduce the protection which it is intended to guarantee.

Following the *Coleman* decision at the CJEU, and the national case that applied the CJEU decision (*EBR Attridge LLP v Coleman* [2010] ICR 242), the explanatory notes to the EqA state (§59) that the definition of direct discrimination in s13 EqA: 'is broad enough to cover cases where the less favourable treatment is because of the victim's association with someone who has that characteristic (for example, is disabled), or because the victim is wrongly thought to have it (for example, a particular religious belief).'[19] The concept of discrimination by association, also known as associative discrimination, is now well-established law in the UK, as illustrated by the decision below.

***Abrams v EAD Solicitors LLP* [2015] UKEAT 0054_15_0506, [2016] ICR 380**

Mr Abrams, who was a member of the LLP, formed a limited company as a tax avoidance measure, of which he was sole shareholder and director. Mr Abrams' company replaced him as a member of the LLP and employed him to fulfil its partnership obligations to the LLP. The LLP asked Mr Abrams to retire on reaching the agreed retirement age for partners of 62, as a result of which Mr Abrams and his company sued for age discrimination. A tribunal, at a preliminary hearing, accepted that Mr Abrams's company could complain of age discrimination by association with Mr Abrams. On appeal from the

[19] n 8 above.

LLP the EAT ruled that since 'person' could include a body corporate in the absence of a contrary intention, the LLP could be held to have discriminated against 'another' person (whether legal or natural) under s13 EqA where the discrimination was 'because of the protected characteristic' of any person, rather than the person who complained of the discrimination.[20]

In *Lee v Ashers Baking Company Ltd*, also discussed in Chapter 10, the SC made it clear that it did not extend to capture discrimination against a message, rather than a person.

***Lee v Ashers Baking Company Ltd* [2018] UKSC 49, [2020] AC 413**

The claimant was a gay man who volunteered for QueerSpace, an organisation which campaigned for same-sex marriage in Northern Ireland. The respondent was a bakery run by a Christian couple who believed that only heterosexual marriage was consistent with the Bible and acceptable to God. It refused the claimant's request to provide him with a cake iced with the slogan 'Support gay marriage'.

The county court had accepted that the refusal of service amounted to direct discrimination on grounds of sexual orientation and belief and Northern Ireland's CA that it amounted to direct associative discrimination on grounds of sexual orientation.[21] The SC allowed Ashers' appeal, ruling that the CA had erred in finding that Mr Lee had been discriminated against because of his association with the gay and bisexual community in circumstances in which the refusal to supply the cake had related to the cake itself and not the customer.

Lady Hale (with whom Lords Mance, Kerr and Hodge and Lady Black agreed):

> 28. The Court of Appeal held that 'this was a case of association with the gay and bisexual community and the protected personal characteristic was the sexual orientation of that community'. This suggests that the reason for refusing to supply the cake was that Mr Lee was likely to associate with the gay community of which the McArthurs disapproved. But there was no evidence that the bakery had discriminated on that or any other prohibited ground in the past. The evidence was that they both employed and served gay people and treated them in a non-discriminatory way. Nor was there any finding that the reason for refusing to supply the cake was that Mr Lee was thought to associate with gay people. The reason was their religious objection to gay marriage …
>
> 30. In *English v Thomas Sanderson Blinds Ltd* [2008] EWCA Civ 1421, [2009] ICR 543, the applicant complained of harassment at work, because he was repeatedly taunted as if he were gay when in fact he was not. The Court of Appeal held, by a majority, that this was harassment 'on grounds of' sexual orientation. The fact that he was not in fact gay made no difference. As Sedley LJ put it, at para [38]:
>
>> 'If, as is common ground, tormenting a man who is believed to be gay but is not amounts to unlawful harassment, the distance from there to tormenting a man who is being treated as if he were gay when he is not is barely perceptible. In both cases the man's sexual orientation, in both cases imaginary, is the basis – that is to say, the ground – of the harassment.'

[20] Applying *EBR Attridge LLP v Coleman, Showboat Entertainment Centre Ltd v Owens* and *Weathersfield Ltd v Sargent*, all discussed at p 38 above.

[21] In short, the CA accepted that the claimant was discriminated against because he was associated with the gay and bisexual community.

31. There was, however, a powerful dissenting judgment from Laws LJ, who said this at para [21]:

> 'In my judgment, harassment is perpetrated on grounds of sexual orientation only where some person or person's actual, perceived, or assumed sexual orientation gives rise to it, that is, is a substantial cause of it. [Counsel's] case confuses the reason for the conduct complained of with the nature of that conduct. On the facts the reason for the harassment was nothing to do with anyone's actual, perceived, or assumed sexual orientation. It happened to take the form of "homophobic banter" so called, which was thus the vehicle for teasing or tormenting the appellant.'

32. It is of some interest, although not a guide to interpretation, that the Explanatory Notes to the Equality Act (Sexual Orientation) Regulations 2007, which applied in Great Britain, go further than the Memorandum to the Northern Ireland SORs. Paragraph 7.3 states that direct discrimination is 'when a person treats another person less favourably on the grounds of his/her sexual orientation, or what is believed to be his/her sexual orientation, or the sexual orientation/perceived sexual orientation of another person with whom they associate'.

33. That is very far from saying that, because the reason for the less favourable treatment has something to do with the sexual orientation of some people, the less favourable treatment is 'on grounds of' sexual orientation. There must, in my view, be a closer connection than that. Nor would I agree with the Court of Appeal that 'the benefit from the message or slogan on the cake could only accrue to gay or bisexual people'. It could also accrue to the benefit of the children, the parents, the families and friends of gay people who wished to show their commitment to one another in marriage, as well as to the wider community who recognise the social benefits which such commitment can bring.

34. This was a case of associative discrimination or it was nothing. It would be unwise in the context of this particular case to attempt to define the closeness of the association which justifies such a finding. Not only did the District Judge not make such a finding in this case, the association would not have been close enough for her to do so. In a nutshell, the objection was to the message and not to any particular person or persons.[22]

The explanatory notes to the EqA also make clear that the definition of direct discrimination in s13 is broad enough to accommodate discrimination on the basis of *perceived* characteristics, §63 going on to state that 'If an employer rejects a job application form from a white man who he wrongly thinks is black, because the applicant has an African-sounding name, this would constitute direct race discrimination based on the employer's mistaken perception'.[23]

In *J v DLA Piper UK LLP* [2010] ICR 1052 the EAT suggested that discrimination related to perceived disability might not fall within the DDA. The claimant sued in respect of disability discrimination when a job offer previously made to her was withdrawn after she disclosed a history of depression. A tribunal rejected her claim on the basis that she was not disabled. The EAT allowed her appeal on the basis that the tribunal had erred in deciding that she was not disabled,[24] but it rejected her alternative argument (relying on the decision in *Coleman*) that her discrimination claim should have

[22] Subsequent case law has also given rise to the concept of associative victimisation (discussed below).
[23] n 8 above.
[24] It was not in dispute that the claimant had suffered from depression; the tribunal did not accept that the condition was sufficiently severe to amount to a disability for the purposes of the EqA.

succeeded without proof of her disability if she had been discriminated against because the respondent had perceived her to be disabled. Underhill J, as he then was, suggested at §62 that the 'concept of "perceived disability"' presented difficulties in cases in which there is uncertainty as to whether the condition that the alleged discriminator ascribes to the claimant would in fact be likely to last for at 12 months (this being one of the threshold criteria for most disabilities recognised by the EqA). *DLA* was decided under the DDA but the reasoning was equally applicable to the EqA, and in *Peninsula Business Service Ltd v Baker* [2017] ICR 714 the EAT relied on the decision in *DLA* in ruling that a claimant could not succeed in a disability harassment claim under the EqA without proving that he was in fact disabled. In the subsequent case of *CC Norfolk v Coffey* [2020] EWCA Civ 1061, [2020] ICR 145, however, the CA accepted that s13(1) EqA covered a situation in which the discriminator acted because he or she thought that an individual was disabled even if they were not, as long as the 'the putative discriminator believe[d] that all the elements in the statutory definition of disability are present – though it is not necessary that he or she should attach the label "disability" to them'.

Indirect Discrimination

Indirect discrimination is intended to reflect that concept of 'disparate impact' discrimination recognised by the US Supreme Court in its famous decision in *Griggs v Duke Power Co* (1971) 401 US 424. There, Black employees sued under Title VII of the Civil Rights Act 1964 (which, inter alia, prohibits race discrimination), claiming that the employer's practice of requiring a high school diploma or success in an IQ test as a condition of employment in particular jobs discriminated against them on grounds of race, a disproportionate number of Black workers being rendered ineligible by the practice. The lower courts had found that the employer's previous practice of race discrimination had ended, and that there was no evidence that the requirements had been adopted in order to discriminate on racial grounds. The SC found in favour of the plaintiffs.

***Griggs v Duke Power Co* (1971) 401 US 424**

Chief Justice Burger, for the Court:

> … on the record in the present case, 'whites register far better on the Company's alternative requirements' than Negroes … This consequence would appear to be directly traceable to race. Basic intelligence must have the means of articulation to manifest itself fairly in a testing process. Because they are Negroes, petitioners have long received inferior education in segregated schools … Congress did not intend by Title VII, however, to guarantee a job to every person regardless of qualifications. In short, the Act does not command that any person be hired simply because he was formerly the subject of discrimination, or because he is a member of a minority group. Discriminatory preference for any group, minority or majority, is precisely and only what Congress has proscribed. What is required by Congress is the removal of artificial, arbitrary, and unnecessary barriers to employment when the barriers operate invidiously to discriminate on the basis of racial or other impermissible classification.
>
> Congress has now provided that tests or criteria for employment or promotion may not provide equality of opportunity merely in the sense of the fabled offer of milk to the stork and the fox. On the contrary, Congress has now required that the posture and condition of the job-seeker

> be taken into account. It has – to resort again to the fable – provided that the vessel in which the milk is proffered be one all seekers can use. The Act proscribes not only overt discrimination but also practices that are fair in form, but discriminatory in operation. The touchstone is business necessity. If an employment practice which operates to exclude Negroes cannot be shown to be related to job performance, the practice is prohibited.
>
> On the record before us, neither the high school completion requirement nor the general intelligence test is shown to bear a demonstrable relationship to successful performance of the jobs for which it was used. Both were adopted, as the Court of Appeals noted, without meaningful study of their relationship to job-performance ability. Rather, a vice president of the Company testified, the requirements were instituted on the Company's judgment that they generally would improve the overall quality of the work force … good intent or absence of discriminatory intent does not redeem employment procedures or testing mechanisms that operate as 'built-in headwinds' for minority groups and are unrelated to measuring job capability …

Indirect discrimination can go beyond the formalistic approach associated with the regulation of direct discrimination (ie, the requirement to treat like cases alike) and challenge practices which serve to perpetuate the effects of past disadvantage and unequal life chances. In the workplace context such practices include (in the context of sex equality) height/weight/strength requirements;[25] requirements for flexibility as regards hours or place of work;[26] and/or requirements to work full-time,[27] long and/or unsocial hours[28] (this because women tend to bear greater responsibility for childcare than men); age bars or length of service criteria (because women tend to have more periods out of paid work and more fractured work histories).[29] Restrictions on, or preferences for, particular home addresses or universities and requirements for particular qualifications are likely to impact differently on people according to ethnicity[30] as may language requirements while attendance requirements, holiday restrictions and dress codes[31] will impact disparately according to religion, belief and/or ethnicity.[32] Length of service requirements and requirements for particular types of qualification may impact disparately by age[33] while qualification and attendance requirements may impact disproportionately on people with particular types of disability.[34] Whether any such criteria or practices will amount to indirect discrimination in any particular case will turn on their impact on the claimant and upon others in the same relevant group and on the justification put forward by the employer.

[25] Case C-409/1 *Ypourgos Esterkion v Kalliri* EU:C:2017:767, [2018] 2 CMLR 1. Differential physical requirements would be directly discriminatory – see in the case of physical fitness testing *Allcock v CC Hampshire* 36 *EOR Discrimination Case Law Digest* 1. Employers must, accordingly, adopt a single standard whose disparate impact, if any, will be objectively justifiable by reference to the needs of the undertaking.

[26] *London Underground Ltd v Edwards (No 2)* [1999] ICR 494; *Dobson v North Cumbria Integrated Care NHS Foundation Trust* [2021] ICR 1699.

[27] *R v SS Employment ex p EOC* [1995] 1 AC 1; *Allonby v Accrington and Rossendale College* [2001] EWCA Civ 529, [2001] ICR 1189; *Hardy & Hansons plc v Lax* [2005] IRLR 726.

[28] *XC Trains Ltd v CD* [2016] IRLR 748, *Shackletons Garden Centre Ltd v Lowe* UK/EAT/0161/10.

[29] *Meade-Hill v British Council* [1995] ICR 847; *Jones v University of Manchester* [1993] ICR 474.

[30] *Essop v Home Office* [2017] UKSC 27, [2017] ICR 640, discussed below.

[31] *Azmi v Kirklees Metropolitan BC* [2007] ICR 1154; *Eweida & Ors v UK* (2013) 57 EHRR 8.

[32] *Cherfi v G4S Security Services Ltd* UKEAT/0379/10 (24 May 2011, unreported); *MBA v LB Merton* [2013] EWCA Civ 1562, [2014] ICR 357.

[33] *Harrod v CC West Midlands Police* [2017] EWCA Civ 191, [2017] ICR 869; *Heskett v SSJ* [2020] EWCA Civ 1487, [2021] ICR 110.

[34] See respectively *Government Legal Service v Brookes* [2017] IRLR 780; Case C-270/16, *Ruiz Conejero v Ferroser Servicios Auxiliares SA* EU:C:2018:17, [2018] 2 CMLR 27.

The prohibition on indirect (as well as other forms of) discrimination is not confined to the workplace, but applies also (see Chapter 4) to other areas including education, the provision of goods and services, and the performance of public functions. Many of the examples in the case law are from the employment and (increasingly) the public law contexts in which, for reasons discussed in Chapter 5, litigation is more commonplace.

By contrast with direct discrimination, it is of the essence of indirect discrimination that some practices which impact unfavourably upon one or other sex, upon different racial or other groups, may nevertheless be lawful. Indirect discrimination is intended, to reiterate, to capture 'practices that are fair in form, but discriminatory in operation'. The articulation of this concept in domestic law was for a period extraordinarily complex with multiple different definitions between and even within different pieces of legislation, the latter according to whether the subject matter in issue fell within EU law. All of this has been swept away in GB by the EqA[35] which now provides so far as relevant as follows:

Section 19 EqA, Indirect Discrimination

(1) A person (A) discriminates against another (B) if A applies to B a provision, criterion or practice which is discriminatory in relation to a relevant protected characteristic of B's.

(2) For the purposes of subsection (1), a provision, criterion or practice is discriminatory in relation to a relevant protected characteristic of B's if—

(a) A applies, or would apply, it to persons with whom B does not share the characteristic,

(b) it puts, or would put, persons with whom B shares the characteristic at a particular disadvantage when compared with persons with whom B does not share it,

(c) it puts, or would put, B at that disadvantage, and

(d) A cannot show it to be a proportionate means of achieving a legitimate aim.

This definition of indirect discrimination is consistent with that in the various EU directives which refer to the application of apparently neutral provisions, criteria or practices which would put persons having a particular protected characteristics at a particular disadvantage compared with other persons unless the provision, criterion or practice is objectively justified by a legitimate aim and the means of achieving that aim are appropriate and necessary. It does not appear to extend to associative discrimination (that is disadvantage suffered by reason of a person's association with a group of persons identified by reference to a relevant characteristic, even though the individual does not themselves share that characteristic. The CJEU has appeared to include such disadvantage within the concept of indirect discrimination.

Case C-83/12 *CHEZ Razpredelenie Bulgaria AD v Komisia za zashtita ot diskriminatsia*, EU:C:2015:480, [2015] IRLR 746

The claimant had a shop in a predominantly Roma area in which the authorities placed electricity meters on tall pylons with the effect that she could not easily monitor her consumption. This practice was unique to Roma areas whose residents were regarded as more inclined to tampering and fraud. The Court ruled that the claimant, not herself Roma, had been subject to direct associative discrimination, and further that had the practice not amounted to direct discrimination it would have involved indirect discrimination. It did not specifically address the question whether the claimant could have

[35] The EqA does not apply in Northern Ireland.

succeeded in an indirect discrimination claim based on her association with Roma, but at §56 stated that 'the principle of equal treatment ... is intended to benefit also persons who, although not themselves a member of the race or ethnic group concerned, nevertheless suffer less favourable treatment *or a particular disadvantage* on one of those grounds'. The italicised words appear only in the definition of indirect, rather than direct, discrimination, thus suggesting that the concept of associative discrimination applies in that context also.

The constituent elements of indirect discrimination will be considered in turn after discussion of the decisions of the SC in *Essop* and *Naeem*.

***Essop v Home Office, Naeem v Secretary of State for Justice* [2017] UKSC 27, [2017] ICR 640**

Mr Essop was the lead claimant in the *Essop* case which was heard with the *Naeem* case. He was an immigration officer who had been subject to a 'provision, criterion or practice' in the form of a requirement to pass a Core Skills Assessment (CSA) as a pre-requisite to promotion to certain civil service grades. He and the other claimants had failed the CSA, which was not related to the job requirements of the posts in respect of which it was a pre-requisite to promotion. The evidence showed that black and minority ethnic candidates and older candidates had markedly lower pass rates than white and younger candidates, although nobody knew why. A tribunal ruled at a preliminary stage that the claims could proceed only if the claimants were able to establish why black and minority ethnic candidates and older candidates had lower pass rates. The EAT allowed the claimants' appeal and the CA restored the tribunal's decision, ruling that the claimants had to show *both* why the requirement to pass the CSA put the group at a disadvantage and *also* that he or she had failed the test for that same reason. The SC allowed the claimants' appeal.

The *Naeem* case concerned a Muslim prison chaplain who sought to challenge an incremental pay system applicable to chaplains. Prior to 2002 the prison service had employed only Christian chaplains. The claimant, who had been appointed to his role in 2004, did not claim to have been treated differently than a Christian chaplain appointed at the same time, but sought to challenge the fact that that Christians tended to be at the top, and Muslims at the bottom, of the pay scale, and that Muslims had lower average pay than Christians. Part of the case turned on the appropriate pool for comparison (considered at p 58 below). In rejecting Mr Naeem's claim, however, the CA had ruled that it was necessary for him to show that the reason for that disparate impact was something peculiar to the protected characteristic in question. This aspect of the CA's decision was rejected by the SC.

Lady Hale, with whom Lords Clarke, Wilson, Carnwath and Hodge agreed:

23. ... The whole trend of equality legislation since it began in the 1970s has been to reinforce the protection given to the principle of equal treatment. All the iterations share certain salient features relevant to the issues before us.

24. The first salient feature is that, in none of the various definitions of indirect discrimination, is there any express requirement for an explanation of the reasons *why* a particular PCP

puts one group at a disadvantage when compared with others. Thus there was no requirement in the 1975 Act that the claimant had to show why the proportion of women who could comply with the requirement was smaller than the proportion of men. It was enough that it was. There is no requirement in the Equality Act 2010 that the claimant show why the PCP puts one group sharing a particular protected characteristic at a particular disadvantage when compared with others. It is enough that it does. Sometimes, perhaps usually, the reason will be obvious: women are on average shorter than men, so a tall minimum height requirement will disadvantage women whereas a short maximum will disadvantage men. But sometimes it will not be obvious: there is no generally accepted explanation for why women have on average achieved lower grades as chess players than men, but a requirement to hold a high chess grade will put them at a disadvantage.

25. A second salient feature is the contrast between the definitions of direct and indirect discrimination. Direct discrimination expressly requires a causal link between the less favourable treatment and the protected characteristic. Indirect discrimination does not. Instead it requires a causal link between the PCP and the particular disadvantage suffered by the group and the individual. The reason for this is that the prohibition of direct discrimination aims to achieve equality of treatment. Indirect discrimination assumes equality of treatment – the PCP is applied indiscriminately to all – but aims to achieve a level playing field, where people sharing a particular protected characteristic are not subjected to requirements which many of them cannot meet but which cannot be shown to be justified. The prohibition of indirect discrimination thus aims to achieve equality of results in the absence of such justification. It is dealing with hidden barriers which are not easy to anticipate or to spot.

26. A third salient feature is that the reasons why one group may find it harder to comply with the PCP than others are many and various (Mr Sean Jones QC for Mr Naeem called them 'context factors'). They could be genetic, such as strength or height. They could be social, such as the expectation that women will bear the greater responsibility for caring for the home and family than will men. They could be traditional employment practices, such as the division between 'women's jobs' and 'men's jobs' or the practice of starting at the bottom of an incremental pay scale. They could be another PCP, working in combination with the one at issue, as in *Homer v CC West Yorkshire* [[2012] UKSC 15, [2012] ICR 704], where the requirement of a law degree operated in combination with normal retirement age to produce the disadvantage suffered by Mr Homer and others in his age group. These various examples show that the reason for the disadvantage need not be unlawful in itself or be under the control of the employer or provider (although sometimes it will be). They also show that both the PCP and the reason for the disadvantage are 'but for' causes of the disadvantage: removing one or the other would solve the problem.

27. A fourth salient feature is that there is no requirement that the PCP in question put every member of the group sharing the particular protected characteristic at a disadvantage. The later definitions cannot have restricted the original definitions, which referred to the proportion who could, or could not, meet the requirement. Obviously, some women are taller or stronger than some men and can meet a height or strength requirement that many women could not. Some women can work full time without difficulty whereas others cannot. Yet these are paradigm examples of a PCP which may be indirectly discriminatory. The fact that some BME or older candidates could pass the test is neither here nor there. The group was at a disadvantage because the proportion of those who could pass it was smaller than the proportion of white or younger candidates. If they had all failed, it would be closer to a case of direct discrimination (because the test requirement would be a proxy for race or age).

28. A fifth salient feature is that it is commonplace for the disparate impact, or particular disadvantage, to be established on the basis of statistical evidence. That was obvious from the way in which the concept was expressed in the 1975 and 1976 Acts: indeed it might be difficult

to establish that the proportion of women who could comply with the requirement was smaller than the proportion of men unless there was statistical evidence to that effect. Recital (15) to the Race Directive recognised that indirect discrimination might be proved on the basis of statistical evidence, while at the same time introducing the new definition. It cannot have been contemplated that the 'particular disadvantage' might not be capable of being proved by statistical evidence. Statistical evidence is designed to show correlations between particular variables and particular outcomes and to assess the significance of those correlations. But a correlation is not the same as a causal link.

29. A final salient feature is that it is always open to the respondent to show that his PCP is justified – in other words, that there is a good reason for the particular height requirement, or the particular chess grade, or the particular CSA test. Some reluctance to reach this point can be detected in the cases, yet there should not be. There is no finding of unlawful discrimination until all four elements of the definition are met. The requirement to justify a PCP should not be seen as placing an unreasonable burden upon respondents. Nor should it be seen as casting some sort of shadow or stigma upon them. There is no shame in it. There may well be very good reasons for the PCP in question – fitness levels in fire-fighters or policemen spring to mind. But, as Langstaff J pointed out in the EAT in *Essop*, a wise employer will monitor how his policies and practices impact upon various groups and, if he finds that they do have a disparate impact, will try and see what can be modified to remove that impact while achieving the desired result.

Having set out the framework, Baroness Hale made short work of the *Essop* case, stating at §30 that 'All the above salient features of the definition of indirect discrimination support the appellants' case that there is no need to prove the reason why the PCP in question puts or would put the affected group at a particular disadvantage.' She dismissed the employer's arguments that (1) the individual claimant had to show that he or she had been put at 'that disadvantage' (ie, the *same* disadvantage as the relevant group), and that this required the identification of the reasons for the disadvantage; and (2) that it was necessary to prevent 'undeserving' claimants who had failed the CSA for reasons that unrelated to the disparate impact, from 'coat tailing' on the claims of the deserving ones. At §31 Baroness Hale stated that the statutory language required only 'correspondence between the disadvantage suffered by the group and the disadvantage suffered by the individual' and that this would 'largely depend upon how one defines the particular disadvantage in question. If the disadvantage is that more BME or older candidates fail the test than do white or younger candidates, then failure is the disadvantage and a claimant who fails has suffered that disadvantage …' At §32 she stated that the respondent would be free to show that a particular candidate had not been disadvantaged by the requirement (eg because their failure was otherwise explicable), further that a candidate who did not prepare and attend for the test would not be in the same position as one who diligently prepared and would find their claim excluded by s23 EqA (see above), which applies to indirect as to direct discrimination. At §34 Lady Hale emphasised that the 'essential element is a causal connection between the PCP and the disadvantage suffered [here the increased likelihood of failure], not only by the group, but also by the individual. This may be easier to prove if the reason for the group disadvantage is known but that is a matter of fact, not law'. And at §35:

it is a typical feature of indirect discrimination that some members of the disadvantaged group will not in fact suffer the disadvantage. At the level of the group the disadvantage may be no more than likely but that does not make it a different disadvantage from the actual disadvantage

> suffered by those who are affected. The difference is between potential and actual disadvantage but the disadvantage is the same. Thus, in the typical example of a height requirement, women are statistically more likely to fail to meet it, but only some will fail and others will pass. The disadvantage in each case is the same – the failure to meet the height requirement. Any other approach would deprive indirect discrimination of much of its content.

Turning to Mr Naeem:

> 38. The first argument is that the reason why the PCP puts the group at a disadvantage – the 'context factor' – has itself to be related to the protected characteristic. This was the view taken by Underhill LJ in the Court of Appeal in this case .... Thus, at para [22], he held that it cannot:
>
> > 'properly be said that it is the use of the length of service criterion which puts Muslim chaplains at a disadvantage, within the meaning of s 19(2)(b). The concept of 'putting' persons at a disadvantage is causal, and, as in any legal analysis of causation, it is necessary to distinguish the legally relevant cause or causes from other factors in the situation. In my view the only material cause of the disparity in remuneration ... is the (on average) more recent start-dates of the Muslim chaplains. But that does not reflect any characteristic peculiar to them as Muslims: rather, it reflects the fact that there was no need for their services (as employees) at any earlier date.'
>
> 39. But this cannot be right. The same could be said of almost any reason why a PCP puts one group at a disadvantage. There is nothing peculiar to womanhood in taking the larger share of caring responsibilities in a family. Some do and some do not. But (in the context of equal pay) it has been acknowledged that a length of service criterion can have a disparate impact on women because they tend to have shorter service periods as a result of career breaks or later career starts flowing from their childcare responsibilities ... Indeed, it could be said that the lack of need for the Muslim chaplains is more 'peculiar to them as Muslims' than are many of the reasons why women may suffer a particular disadvantage. All that this means is that the employer may have to justify the PCP. In principle, a length of service criterion may be justified as a reward for greater experience and skill, but this gets harder to do the longer the time taken to achieve parity with others.

Provision, Criterion or Practice of General Application

Essop is set out at length above because it provides a clear and authoritative exposition of the nature of indirect discrimination. The first three constituent elements of this form of discrimination can be taken quite quickly, the question of justification requiring more detailed consideration below. The first of these elements is the requirement for a 'provision, criterion or practice' (PCP) of general application. The terms 'provision', 'criterion' and 'practice' are not defined by the EqA. Their introduction into domestic legislation was the result of EU law and they replace the previous formulation of 'requirement or condition' which were interpreted narrowly by the domestic courts and imposed significant threshold barriers for indirect discrimination claims. There is no requirement that a PCP amount to an absolute bar (this by contrast with the previous formulation). Practices may be express or implied, formal or informal, deliberate or not. By way of example, the CA accepted in *United First Partners Research v Carreras* [2018] EWCA Civ 323 that a claimant had been subject to a PCP where he was expected, though not required as such, to work longer hours.

The CA made it clear in *Ishola v TFL* that the terms 'provision', 'criterion' and 'practice' are 'not terms of art, but are ordinary English words' which 'are broad and overlapping, and in light of the object of the legislation, not to be narrowly construed or unjustifiably limited in their application' (§35). Even a single decision or act may constitute a PCP if it signals the likely approach to a future (hypothetical) case. In *British Airways plc v Starmer* [2005] IRLR 862, for example, the EAT accepted that a requirement that a pilot work 75 per cent of full-time hours rather than (as she had requested) 50 per cent involved the imposition of a PCP.

***Ishola v Transport for London* [2020] EWCA Civ 112, [2020] ICR 1204**

Simler LJ, with whom Sir Jack Beatson agreed, categorised at §35 as 'significant' the fact that 'Parliament chose to define claims based on reasonable adjustment and indirect discrimination by reference to these particular words, and did not use the words 'act' or 'decision' in addition or instead'. She went on to state (§37) that 'however widely and purposively the concept of a PCP is to be interpreted, it does not apply to every act of unfair treatment of a particular employee' and that 'provision', 'criterion' and 'practice' each:

> 38. … carry the connotation of a state of affairs (whether framed positively or negatively and however informal) indicating how similar cases are generally treated or how a similar case would be treated if it occurred again. It seems to me that 'practice' here connotes some form of continuum in the sense that it is the way in which things generally are or will be done. That does not mean it is necessary for the PCP or 'practice' to have been applied to anyone else in fact. Something may be a practice or done 'in practice' if it carries with it an indication that it will or would be done again in future if a hypothetical similar case arises … although a one-off decision or act can be a practice, it is not necessarily one.
>
> 39. In that sense, the one-off decision treated as a PCP in *Starmer* is readily understandable as a decision that would have been applied in future to similarly situated employees. However, in the case of a one-off decision in an individual case where there is nothing to indicate that the decision would apply in future, it seems to me the position is different …

A further example of an apparently isolated event indicating an ongoing policy or practice is seen in the *Pendleton* decision discussed below.

Individual Disadvantage

As Lady Hale recognised in *Essop* (p 45 above), a person will not have been subject to indirect discrimination if they were not, as a matter of fact, disadvantaged by comparison with a relevantly similar individual by the PCP applied. By way of example, if one of the claimants in that case had failed the CSA examination because he or she had failed to turn up on the day, or to prepare for the test, the requirement for individual disadvantage would not be met.[36] But the fact that a claimant could comply with a PCP does not mean that they are not disadvantaged by it, as long as compliance involves a detriment.[37]

[36] See by way of example the decision of the EAT in *Ryan v South West Ambulance Services NHS Trust* [2021] ICR 555.

[37] *cf* the earlier statutory provisions in issue in *Clymo v Wandsworth BC* [1989] ICR 250 and *Mandla v Dowell Lee* [1983] 2 AC 548.

Collective Disadvantage

The requirement in s19(2)(c)) that the PCP under challenge 'puts, or would put, persons with whom [the claimant] shares the [protected] characteristic [relied upon] at a particular disadvantage when compared with persons with whom [s/he] does not share' is not a requirement that the disadvantage is severe or significant, rather that it is common to the relevant group.[38] Nor is statistical evidence of disparate impact necessarily required in a case where such impact can be shown without such evidence,[39] or where it is inherent in the nature of the PCP. One example of the latter arose in the CJEU's decision in Case C-237/94 *O'Flynn v Adjudication Officer* ECLI:EU:C:1996:206, [1996] ECR I-2617, [1998] ICR 608, which concerned a challenge to a funeral expenses grant which only covered the expenses of migrant workers if the burial or cremation took place within the territory of the Member State giving the grant. The Court accepted that the rule placed migrant workers at a particular disadvantage because it was 'intrinsically liable to affect migrant workers more than national workers' (§20). A more recent example arose in the case of *Pendleton v Derbyshire CC* in which the EAT accepted that a requirement imposed on a teacher to leave her husband, who had been convicted of making indecent images of children and voyeurism, as a condition of continued employment, disproportionately impacted on her as a Christian who believed that marriage vows were sacrosanct.

***Pendleton v Derbyshire CC* [2016] UKEAT 0238_15_2903, [2016] IRLR 580**

A tribunal had dismissed Ms Pendleton's claim on the basis that the requirement would have impacted on anyone who 'elected to stand by their partner or spouse' and that 'those who share the claimant's religious conviction were at no greater or lesser risk of being dismissed than those who simply exercised their choice to stand by their partner or husband' and that it was 'entirely possible that those who shared the belief and conviction of the claimant could have chosen to leave their spouse (notwithstanding their marriage vows)' (§§6.12–6.13, cited at §§15–16). According to HHJ Eady QC:

> 19. At paragraph 6.12 of its judgment, the ET had failed to answer the two questions it had to determine: (i) did the PCP – the policy of dismissing those who chose not to end a relationship with a person convicted of making indecent images of children and voyeurism … put those sharing the claimant's belief in the sanctity of the marriage vow at a disadvantage; and (ii) did the claimant suffer that disadvantage? The first question was not answered by reflecting on the fact that other groups might also have been put at a disadvantage by operation of the PCP in these circumstances. The ET's earlier finding had clearly recognised the claimant was affected in her faith by the application of the PCP. That, on its face, answered the second question. Further, given that the ET accepted the claimant was thus expressing her religious belief as an Anglican Christian, that was also sufficient to answer the first. As the Equality & Human Rights Commission's Code of Practice made plain, the finding that the claimant was being

[38] *McNeil v Revenue and Customs Commissioners* [2019] EWCA Civ 1112, [2020] ICR 515, in which the CA relied on the decision of the CJEU in Case C-83/12 *CHEZ Razpredelenie Bulgaria AD v Komisia za zashtita ot diskriminatsia*, EU:C:2015:480, [2015] IRLR 746.

[39] The European Commission made it clear in the Explanatory Memorandum to the Racial Equality Directive that the definition of indirect discrimination therein was intentionally chosen to avoid the need for statistical proof and the SC recognised (*per* Lady Hale) in *Homer v CC West Yorkshire Police* [2012] UKSC 15, [2012] ICR 704 that the definition employed in s19 EqA 'was intended to do away with [a previous] need for statistical comparison where no statistics might exist', the though statistics are useful evidence where they are available: *Games v University of Kent* [2015] IRLR 202.

put to the choice of having to elect between her marriage vows and her career was sufficient (see paragraph 4.10 of the Code: 'Sometimes, a provision, criterion or practice is intrinsically liable to disadvantage a group with a particular protected characteristic'). The ET had wrongly focused solely on the disadvantage of dismissal as opposed to the comparative difficulty facing the two groups as a result of the election being forced upon the claimant by the respondents. Disadvantage required only a low threshold, and putting someone to election where they might have to act contrary to their religious beliefs was sufficient to amount to disadvantage for these purposes …

38. Determining the question of comparative collective disadvantage is not simply answered by identifying that the PCP applies to persons both within and without the group sharing the relevant characteristic; that is simply the neutral application of the PCP. In my judgment, it is, moreover, not answered by identifying that others falling outside that group will also consider themselves disadvantaged in some way by the application of the PCP; that again may simply be the product of the neutral application of the PCP. That is, however, what the ET's reasoning at paragraph 6.12 essentially determines; it is not sufficient …

40. … the comparative exercise that the ET had to carry out had to be based upon groups that were – absent the particular protected characteristic – in circumstances that were the same or not materially different (s23 EqA). That meant the comparison of both groups (those sharing the claimant's protected characteristic as compared to those who did not share that characteristic but to whom the PCP would also be applied) would involve persons who were in long-term loving relationships. If facing the very difficult personal circumstances as arose here, both groups would undoubtedly face a very real additional disadvantage if put to the election of choosing between their partner and their career. For some individuals falling into the comparator group (being in a partnership but not married or married but not sharing the same view of their marriage vows as the claimant) that disadvantage might have been the same as that suffered by the claimant. The task for the ET was, however, not to pick out particular individuals who might fall into either group but to consider the potential groups (those sharing the protected characteristic and those who did not) and ask whether – taking, as applicable to both, the difficulty inherent in such circumstances for anyone in a loving and committed relationship – those who also held a religious belief in the particular sanctity of marriage, arising from the sacrosanct nature of vows made before God, face a particular disadvantage?

41. … in answering that question, it was unhelpful for the ET to consider the further hypothetical possibility as to what the claimant, or others sharing her belief, might have done had their spouse not repented. That was not the factual scenario it had to consider and it confused the reasoning. Had it been a relevant factual addition, it would have had to be applied to both groups – not solely that within which the claimant fell – and, again, the question asked whether those with a religious belief in the sanctity of marriage vows faced a particular disadvantage?

42. … the focus on the *general* disadvantage suffered by those falling within each of the comparative groups failed to have proper regard to the statutory requirement, which is to ask whether those falling within the same group as the claimant, sharing the relevant protected characteristic, faced a *particular* disadvantage. A PCP of neutral application may be seen to give rise to a general disadvantage for all concerned (eg the requirement to take a test or to work anti-social hours); that does not mean that it does not give rise to a *particular* disadvantage to those sharing a certain protected characteristic …

44. Having concluded that the ET erred in its approach to this issue, the question arises whether I must remit this matter to the ET for reconsideration? I am satisfied that I need not; there is, in truth, only one answer. Comparing two groups, both comprising individuals in long-term, loving and committed relationships, facing the same difficult circumstances as arose in this case

> and given the choice between remaining with their husband/partner or their career *but* with one group also holding a religious belief in the sanctity of their marriage vows, I conclude the ET was bound to hold that the latter had an additional burden; a particular disadvantage. This was one of those cases (recognised by the ECHR Code of Practice) where the PCP was intrinsically liable to disadvantage a group with a particular protected characteristic.
>
> 45. Specifically, given the findings the ET had made as to the claimant's belief – the tensions that she suffered given the difficulties arising from her belief and the election forced upon her in the circumstances in which she was placed – that would inevitably mean that there would be a particular (collective) disadvantage for others holding the same belief. The finding as to the claimant's belief, and the particular disadvantage to which this gave rise, answered the question of disadvantage on a collective level as well: once the ET had found a sufficiently close nexus with the relevant belief – which it had in its findings in respect of the claimant's own case – it was bound to find that the members of the group sharing that belief inevitably faced an additional dilemma of conscience.
>
> 46. In saying that, I do not suggest that any less respect should be given for those who are in a loving and committed relationship (whether married or not) but who do not share the same view as the claimant as to the sanctity of marriage vows; I am simply recognising that, in these circumstances, those sharing the claimant's belief would suffer a particular disadvantage given the crisis of conscience they would face. Equally, I recognise there may be other forms of belief that could give rise to a particular disadvantage in the same circumstances. That is a hypothetical scenario that was not before the ET and is not before me. It is, however, saying no more than that particular disadvantage might be suffered by different groups as a result of their particular beliefs.

The courts have not always been adept at identifying indirect discrimination:

Homer v CC West Yorkshire Police [2012] UKSC 15, [2012] ICR 704

The claimant was a police legal adviser who challenged, as indirectly discriminatory, a requirement that in order to be eligible for promotion he had to have a law degree. He had become a legal adviser after retiring as a police officer and at 62 did not have time to gain a law degree before reaching the normal retirement age of 65. The EAT overturned a tribunal finding that the claimant had been indirectly discriminated against on grounds of age, it and the CA taking the view that he had been disadvantaged by his impending retirement rather than his age. The SC disagreed. (The case was decided under the Age Discrimination Regulations which predated the EqA (see Chapter 11), but this is not material to the extract below. It was also decided at a time when mandatory retirement was permitted.)

Lady Hale (with whom Lords Brown, Kerr and Hope agreed):

> 12. The EAT and Court of Appeal were however persuaded that what put Mr Homer at a disadvantage was not his age but his impending retirement. Had it not been for that, he would have been able to obtain a degree and reach the third threshold … So Mr Homer must be compared with anyone else who is nearing the end of his employment for whatever reason. Anyone who was contemplating leaving within a similar period – whether for family reasons or some other reason – would face the same difficulty. That is what puts him at a disadvantage and not the age group to which he belongs. Indeed, what Mr Homer is arguing for would put people of his age group at an advantage compared with younger people, because they would be able to get the benefits of the third threshold without having a law degree when others would not.

13. This argument involves taking the particular disadvantage which is suffered by a particular age group for a reason which is related to their age and equating it with a similar disadvantage which is suffered by others but for a completely different reason unrelated to their age. If it were translated into other contexts it would have alarming consequences for the law of discrimination generally. Take, for example, a requirement that employees in a particular job must have a beard. This puts women at a particular disadvantage because very few of them are able to grow a beard. But the argument leaves sex out of account and says that it is the inability to grow a beard which puts women at a particular disadvantage and so they must be compared with other people who for whatever reason, whether it be illness or immaturity, are unable to grow a beard.

14. Ironically, it is perhaps easier to make the argument under the current formulation of the concept of indirect discrimination, which is now also to be found in the Equality Act. Previous formulations relied upon disparate impact – so that if there was a significant disparity in the proportion of men affected by a requirement who could comply with it and the proportion of women who could do so, then that constituted indirect discrimination. But, as Mr Allen QC points out on behalf of Mr Homer, the new formulation was not intended to make it more difficult to establish indirect discrimination: quite the reverse … It was intended to do away with the need for statistical comparisons where no statistics might exist. It was intended to do away with the complexities involved in identifying those who could comply and those who could not and how great the disparity had to be. Now all that is needed is a particular disadvantage when compared with other people who do not share the characteristic in question. It was not intended to lead us to ignore the fact that certain protected characteristics are more likely to be associated with particular disadvantages.

15. In any event, it cannot be right to equate leaving work because of impending retirement with other reasons for doing so. They are materially different. A person who leaves work for family reasons or takes early retirement generally has some choice in the matter. Indeed, she may factor into her decision whether it would be advisable to obtain the law degree and with it the higher grading before doing so. A person who is coming up against the mandatory retirement age does not have the same choice. Any extension depends upon the decision of the employer which cannot be depended upon at the relevant time. At the relevant time for this case, reg 30 of the 2006 Regulations provided that the decision to retire an employee at the age of 65 did not need to be justified. Hence, as Mr Allen puts it, this is a case of running up against the buffers of a mandatory retirement age rather than a matter of choice.

16. Nor is this a question of asking for more favourable treatment for people of their age. It obviously has to be possible to cure the discrimination in a non-discriminatory way. In *London Underground Ltd v Edwards (No 2)* [1999] ICR 494, for example, the new rosters for underground train drivers were held to be indirectly discriminatory because all the men could comply with them but not all the women could do so: it was a 'striking fact' that not a single man was disadvantaged despite the overwhelming preponderance of men in the pool of train drivers affected. The reason, of course, was that the new rosters had a greater impact upon single parents and single parents are predominantly (though not exclusively) female. But the problem could be solved, not by making an exception for the women, but by making arrangements for single parents of whatever sex. This problem could have been solved by making arrangements for people appointed before the new criterion was introduced.

17. Ingenious though the argument put forward by Mr Lewis is, therefore, to my mind it is too ingenious. The law of indirect discrimination is an attempt to level the playing field by subjecting to scrutiny requirements which look neutral on their face but in reality work to the comparative disadvantage of people with a particular protected characteristic. A requirement which works to the comparative disadvantage of a person approaching compulsory retirement age is indirectly discriminatory on grounds of age. There is, as Maurice Kay LJ acknowledged,

'unreality in differentiation between age and retirement' [citing the decision of the Court of Appeal at [2010] ICR 987 §34]. Put simply, the reason for the disadvantage was that people in this age group did not have time to acquire a law degree. And the reason why they did not have time to acquire a law degree was that they were soon to reach the age of retirement. The resulting scrutiny may ultimately lead to the conclusion that the requirement can be justified. But if it cannot, then it can be modified so as to remove the disadvantage.

The mistake made by the EAT and the CA in *Homer* was reflective of earlier case law which rendered the concept of indirect discrimination complex and uncertain, and should have come to an end with the formulation adopted in Council Directive 2000/78 and the implementing legislation.[40] More recently, however, the CJEU itself has misapplied the concept of indirect discrimination in an age-related case.

Case C-154/18 *Horgan v Minister for Education & Skills*, EU:C:2019:113 [2019] IRLR 597

This case involved a challenge to the introduction of salary scales for new teachers which were 10 per cent lower than those applicable to existing teachers. The reductions in salaries (which applied across the public sector) were intended to reduce the cost of the public service at a time of significant budgetary restraints and to correct a significant deficit in the public finances. The reduced salaries applied to teachers regardless of where they were placed on the scale, but affected teachers aged under 25 significantly more than older teachers (who were less likely to be on the newly introduced scale). The CJEU ruled that the application of the reduced salary scales relied exclusively on the date of appointment and was 'manifestly unconnected to any taking into account of the age of the persons recruited' (this because new recruits were predominantly aged under 25 both before and after the change) and that there was no need to consider justification.

The *Horgan* case was remarkable both for the apparent inability of the CJEU to see the obvious point that typically younger, newly qualified, teachers were disadvantaged by being placed on inferior salary scales to their (typically older) peers who had joined teaching before them. The CJEU also took the comparatively rare step of itself rejecting the claim, rather than referring the case back to the national court to determine on the basis of the principles articulated by the CJEU. As the IRLR 'Highlights' pointed out (June 2019), 'this decision appears to fundamentally confuse indirect discrimination with direct discrimination. It is the essence of indirect discrimination that the comparator groups are treated the same. If they are treated differently that is direct discrimination. It is no answer therefore, to an indirect age discrimination claim, to say that the impugned decision did not take age into account.'

A more conventional legal approach to a similar problem was taken by the EAT in *Heskett v SSJ* [2020] EWCA Civ 1487, [2020] ICR 359 in rejecting a challenge to changes made to the incremental payment scale for probation officers the effect of which was to reduce the rate of pay progression for staff, thus disadvantaging those who had not reached

[40] That it did not is clear from the history of the *Essop* and *Naeem* cases.

the top of their scale by comparison with those (predominantly aged over 50) who had. The changes had been introduced in response to a reduction in funding by central government and were intended to be temporary. A tribunal accepted that the change impacted disparately on younger staff and required to be justified, though it found on the facts that it was a proportionate means of achieving the legitimate aims of retaining incentives, rewarding loyalty and experience and avoiding redundancies within the constraints imposed by central government. The EAT rejected the claimant's appeal. By contrast, in the case discussed immediately below, the EAT allowed an appeal from an employment tribunal's ruling that the claimant had not been subject to indirect age discrimination.

***Games v University of Kent* [2014] UKEAT 0524_13_1407, [2015] IRLR 202**

The claimant, an architectural writer and historian born in 1952, lectured part-time at the University. He was excluded from consideration for a full-time position (aged 59) because the School of Architecture had imposed a requirement that candidates have PhDs. The claimant argued that architecture PhDs were unusual when he had been a student and had only subsequently become a requirement for university teaching staff, with the effect that people of his age were discriminated against because they had not anticipated the need for a PhD in order to teach.

The tribunal did not accept that PCP applied by the University disadvantaged people in the same age group as the claimant despite evidence showing that there had been a significant increase in the rate at which doctorates had been awarded since 1970 and that, on a very small sample, a lower proportion of 56+ candidates had PhDs. It took the view that the claimant could have enrolled on a PhD course and that he had not shown statistical evidence of particular disadvantage, further that the requirement was justified by the need to recruit high-calibre candidates to strengthen the school's research credentials and was a proportionate means of achieving that aim.

The EAT ruled that the tribunal had failed to approach the question of indirect discrimination in line with the decision of the SC in *Homer v CC West Yorkshire Police* [2012] UKSC 15, [2012] ICR 704 in which Baroness Hale had declared that the EqA's formulation of indirect discrimination was 'intended to do away with the need for statistical comparisons where no statistics might exist … Now all that is needed is a particular disadvantage when compared with other people who do not share the characteristic in question.' The EAT ruled that statistical evidence was useful but not necessary and that the claimant's own evidence should have been evaluated by the tribunal. The tribunal had also erred in reaching its decision on the basis that the claimant could in the past have acquired a PhD: the time at which the question of disadvantage fell to be determined was the time at which the PCP had been applied; at this time the claimant did not have a PhD.[41] The EAT remitted the case for reconsideration by the tribunal.

Establishing collective disadvantage to the required standard does not impose onerous obligations in the majority of cases but collective disadvantage is of the essence of indirect discrimination, a fact illustrated by the decision of the CA in the case below (one of the Article 14 challenges which was eventually upheld by the ECtHR in *Eweida & Ors v UK* (2013) 57 EHRR 8).

[41] Applying the decision of the Court of Appeal in *Meek v City of Birmingham DC* [1987] IRLR 250.

***Eweida v British Airways* [2010] EWCA Civ 80, [2010] ICR 890**

The claimant was a devout Christian who was employed by British Airways as a member of check-in staff. She regarded the cross as the central image of her faith and wore a plain silver cross. She did not believe this to be a mandatory requirement of her religion, but regarded it as a personal expression of her faith. In 2004 BA's uniform high-necked blouse for women was replaced by an open-neck blouse, the effect of which was that Eweida's cross, previously covered by her clothing, became visible. BA's uniform policy prohibited the wearing of any visible item of adornment around the neck and permitted the visible display of religious items only where wearing the item was a religious requirement, it could not be concealed under the uniform, and management had given its approval. The claimant insisted on wearing her cross and was eventually sent home, where she remained for over four months before BA changed its policy and she was permitted to return to work. Her claim of indirect discrimination on grounds of religion failed before the domestic courts, a tribunal ruling that there was no evidence that the provision put Christians at a particular disadvantage and both the EAT and the CA affirming this decision.

Sedley LJ, with whom Carnwath and Smith LJJ agreed:

10. … Ms Monaghan … concentrated her extremely able submissions on [the argument] that the tribunal had erred in law in looking for evidence of any material group within the BA workforce, and that the EAT had erred in law in upholding them. On a correct reading of the regulation, Ms Monaghan submits, 'persons' in sub-paragraph (i) includes a single individual. Even if on the evidence, therefore, Ms Eweida alone was disadvantaged by the dress code, the test of indirect discrimination is met.

11. This argument faces two major difficulties.

12. The first is that, if it is right, no evidence of group disadvantage is ever necessary: one would simply read 'persons' [in the predecessor provision of s19(2)(b) EqA] as if it were 'any person'. In that event, however, [the predecessor provision of s19(2)(b) EqA] could have been omitted entirely without changing the meaning of the regulation.

13. Moreover, while for my part I would not share the EAT's view (paragraph 59) that 'the whole purpose of indirect discrimination is to deal with the problem of group discrimination' (its overall purpose, as both counsel agree, is to deal with the discriminatory impact of facially neutral requirements), it is entirely right that the way in which equality laws on both sides of the Atlantic have for many years sought to do this is by seeing, first, whether an identifiable group is adversely affected, whether actually or potentially, by some ostensibly neutral requirement and then whether the claimant has in fact been disadvantaged by it …

15. … there is in my judgment no indication that … Directive [2000/78] intended either that solitary disadvantage should be sufficient – the use of the plural ('persons') makes such a reading highly problematical – or that any requirement of plural disadvantage must be dropped. I see no reason, therefore to depart from the natural meaning of [the statutory provision] …

16. The use of the conditional ('would put persons … at a particular disadvantage'), whether in the alternative, as in the domestic legislation, or on its own, as in the Directive, does not in my view have either the purpose or the effect with which Ms Monaghan seeks to invest it. Her contention is that 'would put' requires the tribunal to aggregate the claimant with what may be – and in the present case would be – an entirely hypothetical peer-group to whom the same disadvantage is to be attributed. The effect of the argument is, as before, to permit a finding of indirect discrimination against a solitary employee.

17. The argument loads far too much on to the word 'would'. Its purpose, in my judgment, is the simple one indicated at the end of paragraph 12 above: to include in the disadvantaged

group not only employees to whom the condition has actually been applied but those to whom it potentially applies. Thus, if you take facts like those in the seminal case of *Griggs*, the group of manual workers adversely affected by the unnecessary academic requirement will have included not only those to whom it had been applied but those to whom it stood to be applied.

18. On the narrowest view, its practical application in a case like this would require evidence that other uniformed BA staff would, like the claimant, have wished to wear a cross in a visible place but were deterred by the code from doing so: the fact that, unlike the claimant, they had not chosen to provoke a confrontation would not count against them. On the widest view it would operate wherever evidence showed that there were in society others who shared the material religion or belief and so would suffer a disadvantage were they to be BA employees. On an intermediate view, it would operate by assuming, even if it is not the case, that the workforce includes such others and asking whether they too, or some of them, would be adversely affected by the relevant requirement. All three have difficulties. The narrow view excludes the solitary individual from the protection of the law against indirect discrimination … The wide view places an impossible burden on employers to anticipate and provide for what may be parochial or even factitious beliefs in society at large. The intermediate view, despite its attractions, in practice risks becoming merged with the wide view by inviting proof that in the world outside the workforce are co-religionists or fellow believers, however few, who are to be assumed to have entered the same employment as the claimant and have become subject to the requirement to which the claimant objects.

19. We do not have to resolve this issue because Ms Eweida's evidence failed all three tests[42]. It is also possible that the meaning and effect of the formula differ depending on the form of discrimination alleged: it may be relatively simple, and within the legislative purpose, to aggregate a single female employee with a hypothetical group of other female staff in order to gauge adverse impact, but forensically difficult, even impossible, to do the same for a solitary believer whose fellow-believers elsewhere in society may accord different degrees of importance to the same manifestation of faith …

The decision of the ECtHR in *Eweida* is discussed in Chapter 9. Here it is sufficient to note that, although the Court there ruled that Ms Eweida's Convention rights had been breached by the application to her of the uniform requirement, the CA subsequently confirmed the continuing application of the requirement for collective disadvantage in the *MBA v Mayor and Burgesses of the London Borough of Merton* [2013] EWCA Civ 1562, [2014] ICR 357, also considered in Chapter 9.[43]

In determining whether a PCP places people having the same protected characteristic as the claimant at a particular disadvantage it is necessary to take into account s23 EqA which, as we saw above, provides that 'On a comparison of cases for the purposes of section … 19 there must be no material difference between the circumstances relating to each case'. This is done by defining a 'pool' of people to whom the PCP is or may be applied, which includes people with, and people without, the claimant's protected characteristic. This step was also required under previous approaches to indirect discrimination and generated much case law and significant confusion, not least because there may be more than one possible pool, and disagreement between the claimant and the tribunal as to what the pool is may have the effect that the claimant lacked the necessary evidence to establish particular disadvantage in

[42] On this see the subsequent decision of the EAT in *Chatwal v Wandsworth BC* [2011] All ER (D) 69.

[43] See similarly *Trayhorn v SSJ* [2018] IRLR 502, *Page v NHS Trust Development Authority* UKEAT/0183/18, upheld by the CA at [2021] ICR 941 and considered in Ch 9.

a pool selected by a tribunal. The position is now set out in the decision of the SC in *Naeem v SSJ*. In considering the previous authorities regard should also be had to the fact that many[44] concerned different definitions of indirect discrimination.

***Naeem v Secretary of State for Justice* [2017] UKSC 27, [2017] ICR 640**

The facts of the case are set out at p 45 above. If it was accepted that the relevant pool for comparison included all prison chaplains the claimant would have been able to establish differential impact and accordingly (unless the Home Office succeeded on justification) indirect discrimination because of religion. If, however, the correct pool was determined to contain only those chaplains appointed after 2002 there would have been no disparate impact as between Christian and Muslim chaplains. The tribunal ruled that the pool contained all prison chaplains, EAT allowing the Home Office's appeal and concluding that the relevant pool contained only those appointed after 2002 because the inclusion of the pre-2002 chaplains 'distorted the true comparison'.

Lady Hale, for the SC:

> 40. … In the equal pay case of *Grundy v British Airways plc* [2008] IRLR 74 at para [27], Sedley LJ said that the pool chosen should be that which suitably tests the particular discrimination complained of. In relation to the indirect discrimination claim in *Allonby v Accrington and Rossendale College* [2001] ICR 1189, at para [18], he observed that identifying the pool was not a matter of discretion or of fact-finding but of logic. Giving permission to appeal to the Court of Appeal in this case, he observed that "There is no formula for identifying indirect discrimination pools, but there are some guiding principles. Amongst these is the principle that the pool should not be so drawn as to incorporate the disputed condition."
>
> 41. Consistently with these observations, the [EHRC's] *Statutory Code of Practice* (2011) … at para 4.18, advises that:
>
>> 'In general, the pool should consist of the group which the provision, criterion or practice affects (or would affect) either positively and negatively, while excluding workers who are not affected by it, either positively or negatively.'
>
> In other words, all the workers affected by the PCP in question should be considered. Then the comparison can be made between the impact of the PCP on the group with the relevant protected characteristic and its impact upon the group without it. This makes sense. It also matches the language of s 19(2)(b) which requires that 'it' – ie the PCP in question – puts or would put persons with whom B shares the characteristic at a particular disadvantage compared with persons with whom B does not share it. There is no warrant for including only some of the persons affected by the PCP for comparison purposes. In general, therefore, identifying the PCP will also identify the pool for comparison.
>
> 42. In this case, the PCP identified was the incremental pay structure which affected all the chaplains employed by the Prison Service. This did put the Muslim chaplains at a particular disadvantage compared with the Christians. The appellant suffered this disadvantage and so s 19(2)(b) and (c) were satisfied. The question, therefore, is whether the respondent can justify it as "a proportionate means of achieving a legitimate aim".'

[44] Including the decisions of the HL in *Rutherford v SS Trade and Industry (No 2)* [2006] UKHL 16, [2016] ICR 785 and *Barry v Midland Bank plc* [1999] ICR 859 and that of the CA in *Coker & Osamor v Lord Chancellor* [2001] EWCA Civ 1756, [2002] ICR 321.

It should go without saying that there is no requirement in an indirect discrimination claim that every member of the collective is disadvantaged by the PCP in practice (some women will be able to comply with a requirement to be six feet tall and not all Jewish people keep the Sabbath, or avoid pork). As noted above, it is not necessary to provide statistical evidence of particular disadvantage, though if statistics are available they may be of particular assistance. Absent such evidence, and leaving aside cases in which the disadvantage is intrinsic to the PCP (see discussion of *O'Flynn* at p 50 above), it may be possible to show particular disadvantage by evidence from the claimant and other witnesses about the impact of the disputed PCP on them.[45] A tribunal may also take judicial notice of matters such as the fact that, despite significant progress over recent decades, women continue to bear the disproportionate burden of childcare,[46] but *Eweida*, considered at p 56 above, is a stark reminder that judicial notice may not be taken of matters which might appear obvious to claimants and their advisers.

Justification

This discussion concerns the justification of indirect discrimination. The justification of direct age discrimination is dealt with in Chapter 11 and that of discrimination arising from disability in Chapter 8. The question under s19 EqA is whether the PCP is a 'proportionate means of achieving a legitimate aim'. The same test applies to direct age discrimination and to discrimination arising from disability, though its application differs somewhat between these contexts. It is always for the alleged discriminator to satisfy the tribunal or court on the question of justification.

Prior to the advance of EU legislation and jurisprudence into domestic law the approach to justification was less than rigorous.[47] In *Hampson v Department of Education and Science* [1989] ICR 179, however, the CA took into account the decision of the CJEU in Case C–170/84, *Bilka-Kaufhaus* [1986] ECR 1607, [1987] ICR 110 in which that Court ruled that disparately impacting pay practices were permissible only where they 'correspond to a real need on the part of the undertaking, are appropriate with a view to achieving the objectives pursued and are necessary to that end'. The CJEU's approach in *Bilka* had included an assessment of proportionality. In *Hampson* the CA ruled that the test for justification was an objective one which required a balance to be struck between the needs of the discriminator and the impact of the PCP.

The approach of the CA in *Hampson* was endorsed by the HL in *Rainey v Greater Glasgow Health Board* [1987] AC 224 in which their Lordships ruled that 'necessary' meant 'reasonably necessary', and in *Webb v EMO* [1993] ICR 175.[48] More recently, the SC ruled in *Homer* v *CC West Yorkshire Police* [2012] UKSC 15, [2012] ICR 704 (§22, *per* Lady Hale) that '[t]o be proportionate, a measure has to be *both* an appropriate means of achieving the legitimate aim *and* (reasonably) necessary in order to do so' (original emphasis).

[45] See *Games v University of Kent* n 39 above.

[46] See *London Underground v Edwards (No 2)* [1999] ICR 494, *Dobson v North Cumbria Integrated Care NHS Foundation Trust* [2021] ICR 1699 in which the EAT (Choudhury J) relied, inter alia, on dicta of Lady Hale in *Essop* in running that a tribunal had erred in failing to take judicial notice of this fact. In *Cumming v British Airways Plc* [2021] IRLR 270 the EAT (HHJ Shanks) also relied on the dicta of Lady Hale in *Essop* in concluding that 'I do not think that there was any need for evidence to show that female cabin crew (like any other group of females) bear the bulk of child care responsibilities'.

[47] See eg *Panesar v Nestle Co Ltd* [1980] ICR 14; *Ojutiku & Oburoni v MSC* [1982] ICR 661.

[48] *Rainey* concerned equal pay, *Webb* sex discrimination. The CJEU's approach to proportionality also includes an assessment of the balance between the needs of the alleged discriminator and the impact of the PCP: Case C-83/12 *CHEZ Razpredelenie* Bulgaria, n 38 above.

The express reference to *reasonable* necessity is a domestic rather than an EU inclusion.[49] Subsequent to the decision in *Bilka Kaufhaus* the CJEU made a number of important decisions on justification, many of them in the context of sex discrimination.[50] Although the UK has withdrawn from the EU, EU jurisprudence has become embedded in the domestic approach to justification, as in many other areas, and remains of significance irrespective of the changed constitutional landscape.[51] The classic articulation of the test is now to be found in the dissenting judgment of Lord Reed in the *Bank Mellat* case, which was concerned with the enforcement of sanctions against Iran and not with the EqA or its predecessors.

***Bank Mellat v HM Treasury (No 2)* [2013] UKSC 38–39, [2014] AC 700**

Lord Reed, dissenting, cited the decision of Canada's Supreme Court in *R v Oakes* [1986] 1 SCR 103 as providing 'the clearest and most influential judicial analysis of proportionality within the common law tradition of legal reasoning'. That approach, according to Lord Reed's summary, required the court to determine:

(1) whether the objective of the measure is sufficiently important to justify the limitation of a protected right,
(2) whether the measure is rationally connected to the objective,
(3) whether a less intrusive measure could have been used without unacceptably compromising the achievement of the objective, and
(4) whether, balancing the severity of the measure's effects on the rights of the persons to whom it applies against the importance of the objective, to the extent that the measure will contribute to its achievement, the former outweighs the latter .... In essence, the question at step four is whether the impact of the rights infringement is disproportionate to the likely benefit of the impugned measure.

In considering the question of justification it is necessary to distinguish between: (1) the existence of a legitimate aim; and (2) the (reasonable) necessity and proportionality of the PCP to achieve that aim.[52] There is no definition of 'legitimate aims' in the context of indirect discrimination,[53] though an aim which is itself discriminatory cannot be legitimate and there is case law which limits the extent to which costs savings can amount to such an aim (see discussion in Chapter 11). Among the aims which have been recognised as legitimate in domestic case law are increased efficiency;[54] the avoidance of job losses, privatisation and cuts in hours;[55] the maintenance of trust in a public service;[56] the maintenance of a financial

[49] See also *Barry v Midland Bank*, n 44 above; *Cadman v HSE* [2014] ICR 884.

[50] See eg Case C-171/88 *Rinner-Kühn v FWW Spezial-Gebaudereinigung GmbH* [1989] ECR 2743; Case C-109/88 *Handels-og v Dansk Arbejdsgiverforening (acting for Danfoss)* [1989] ECR 3199; Case C-184/89 *Nimz v Freie* [1991] ECR I–297; Case C-127/92 *Enderby v Frenchay* [1993] ECR I–5535; Case C-226/98 *Jørgensen v Foreningen* [2000] ECR I–02447; Case C-77/02 *Steinicke v Bundesanstalt für Arbeit* [2003] ECR I–0902 and Case C-187/00 *Kutz-Bauer v Freie und Hansestadt Hamburg* [2003] ECR I–02741.

[51] The EU (Withdrawal) Act 2018 s6 now permits the domestic courts to follow or depart from EU law.

[52] See eg *Heskett v SSJ*, n 33 above §17, *per* Underhill LJ.

[53] *cf* the non-exhaustive list of legitimate aims in relation to direct age discrimination in Council Directive 2000/78, Art 6 ('legitimate employment policy, labour market and vocational training objectives').

[54] *Harrod*, n 33 above, discussed in Ch 11.

[55] *Allen v GMB* [2008] EWCA Civ 810, [2008] ICR 1407.

[56] *Page v NHS Trust Development Authority* [2021] ICR 941.

structure which covered the provision of a wide range of public services;[57] the provision of a coherent and efficient system of education;[58] the maintenance of prison security and order;[59] the selection of the best candidate for a job;[60] intergenerational fairness and workforce planning;[61] seeking to provide help as soon as possible to refugees fleeing Syria;[62] and allowing immigration detainees a calm and quiet opportunity to rest and sleep whilst maintaining the safety and security of the detention centre.[63]

The requirement for proportionality has the effect that the more significant the disparate impact of a PCP, the more will be required by way of justification.[64] The proportionality of PCPs of general application must be assessed by reference to their general impact, rather than their impact on the particular claimant.[65] The assessment of proportionality is for the tribunal or court[66] and it is not necessary that the legitimate aim was identified by the alleged discriminator when the PCP was applied,[67] though it may be more difficult to convince a court or tribunal as to proportionality of its application when this was not considered at the time.[68] The court or tribunal must consider proportionality in relation to the legitimate aim identified, rather than asking itself whether a different aim (with a less disparate impact) should have been pursued.[69]

The adoption of a particular PCP in pursuit of a legitimate aim will not be necessary as a matter of logic if a different PCP, with a less discriminatory impact, would have been equally effective. This principle has sometimes been applied in the CJEU case law (which, as pointed out above, tends to refer to necessity rather than reasonable necessity).[70] In other cases that Court has accepted PCPs as being necessary without scrutinising possible alternatives.[71] In so doing it has come closer to the 'reasonable necessity' approach adopted by the domestic courts.[72]

An alleged discriminator will not be able to establish justification by reference to mere generalised assertions[73] or 'subjective impression or stereotyped assumptions',[74] but it will not always be necessary to provide hard evidence, as distinct from 'reasoned and rational

[57] *R (Efthimiou) v City of London* [2022] EWHC 1588 (Admin).
[58] *R (WC) v Somerset CC* [2021] EWHC 2936 (Admin), [2022] ELR 329.
[59] *Trayhorn v SSJ* [2018] IRLR 502.
[60] *Government Legal Service v Brookes* [2017] IRLR 780.
[61] *Seldon v Clarkson Wright and Jakes* [2012] UKSC 16, [2012] ICR 716, discussed in Ch 11; *RMT v Lloyd* [2019] IRLR 897.
[62] *Turani v SSHD* [2021] EWCA Civ 348, [2022] 1 All ER 254.
[63] *R (Soltany) v SSHD* [2020] EWHC 2291 (Admin).
[64] *Hardy & Hansons*, n 27 above.
[65] *Seldon*, n 61 above.
[66] *Hardy & Hansons*, n 27 above. See also *Lockwood v DWP* [2013] EWCA Civ 1195, [2014] ICR 1257: *Harrod*, n 33 above; *Heskett v SSJ*, n 33 above.
[67] *Cadman v HSE*, n 49 above.
[68] *R (Elias) v SSD* [2006] 1 WLR 3213; *Hockenjos v SSSS* [2004] EWCA Civ 1749, [2005] IRLR 471.
[69] *Harrod*, n 33 above.
[70] See eg Case C-546/11 *Dansk Jurist* EU:C:2013:603, [2014] ICR 1; Case C-144/04 *Mangold v Helm* EU:C:2005:709, [2005] ECR I-9981, [2006] IRLR 143. See also Case C-83/12 *CHEZ Razpredelenie Bulgaria*, n 32 above, in which the CJEU stated at §123 that '*assuming that no other measure as effective as the practice at issue can be identified*, the referring court will also have to determine whether the disadvantages caused by the practice at issue are disproportionate to the aims pursued and whether that practice unduly prejudices the legitimate interests of' those affected (emphasis added).
[71] See eg *Danfoss*, n 50 above; Case C-317/93 *Nolte v Landesversich-erungsanatalt Hannover* EU:C:1995:438, [1995] ECR I–4625, [1996] IRLR 225; Case C-17/05 *Cadman v HSE* EU:C:2006:633, [2006] ECR I-9583, [2006] ICR 1623.
[72] See eg *Kapenova v Department of Health* [2014] ICR 884.
[73] *R v SS Employment, ex p EOC* [1995] 1 AC 1; *R v SS Employment, ex p Seymour-Smith* [1995] ICR 995.
[74] *Homer*, n 39 above. See also *Lord Chancellor v McCloud* [2018] EWCA Civ 2844, [2019] ICR 1489 discussed at pp 699–701 below.

judgment'.[75] In *Lumsdon v Legal Services Board* [2015] UKSC 41, [2016] AC 697 the SC stated at §56 that 'much may depend on the nature of the justification and the extent to which it requires evidence to support it. For example, justification based on moral or political considerations may not be capable of being established by evidence. The same may be true of justifications based on intuitive common sense. An economic or social justification on the other hand may well be expected to be supported by evidence'.

At p 104 below we consider the decision of the SC in *R (SC) v SSWP* [2021] UKSC 26, [2022] AC 223, an Article 14 case. That decision shows that a very substantial area of discretion/deference will be given to legislators where matters of economic and/or social decision-making are concerned. In other cases, and with other decision-makers, the margin of discretion will be significantly reduced. This can be illustrated by reference to the decision of the CA in *R (Cornerstone (North East) Fostering & Adoption Services v Ofsted* [2021] EWCA Civ 1390, [2022] 2 All ER 516, also discussed in Chapters 9 and 10. The case was concerned with the lawfulness of an adoption and foster care agency's policy that it would only consider as prospective adoptive parents/carers married couples who adhered to evangelical Christian principles. The High Court had ruled that the policy involved discrimination on grounds of religion for the purposes of the EqA and HRA, but that it fell within EqA exceptions permitting some such discrimination (see discussion Chapter 9) and was justified under Article 9(2). It had also ruled that the policy amounted to direct discrimination because of sexual orientation (or, in the alternative, to unjustified indirect discrimination) and that it was disproportionate to various legitimate aims and therefore unjustified. The exception which would have applied to this form of discrimination (see further Chapter 10) required the discrimination in issue to be proportional so it did not apply.

The CA upheld the decision of the High Court, ruling that the sexual orientation discrimination was direct and that the question of proportionality therefore arose only in relation to the s193 EqA exception.[76] What is significant in this context is that the CA operated on the basis (agreed between the parties) that the same approach applied to proportionality for the purposes of 19(2) EqA, s193 EqA and Articles 8, 9 and 14 ECHR.[77] As to this approach:

***R (Cornerstone (North East) Fostering & Adoption Services) v Ofsted* [2021] EWCA Civ 1390, [2022] 2 All ER 516**

Jackson LJ (with whom Asplin and Davies LJJ agreed):

> 142. … I … accept that some of Cornerstone's arguments deserved to be placed in the balance in its favour on the question of justification. In consequence, I would hold that the real issue arose at stage four of *Bank Mellat* [see above]: whether, balancing the severity of the measure's effects on the rights of the persons to whom it applies against the importance of the objective, the former outweighs the latter. As to that, I have reached the clear conclusion that the Judge was right to find that the different treatment arising under Cornerstone's recruitment policy was not justified, either through the lens of the EA 2010 or of the HRA 1998. My reasons can, after all that has gone before, be shortly stated.

[75] *Homer, ibid.* See also *Seldon v Clarkson Wright and Jakes* [2009] IRLR 267 §73 affirmed by the SC, n 61 above.

[76] This provides, so far as relevant, that the provision of benefits pursuant to charitable instruments may be restricted to persons sharing a protected characteristic (other than colour) if this is a proportionate means of achieving a legitimate aim.

[77] See also the decision of the Supreme Court in *R (Z) v Hackney LBC* [2020] UKSC 40, [2021] 1 WLR 4327, discussed in Ch 3, on s193 justification.

143. The detrimental impact on society and on individuals of discrimination on the ground of sexual orientation has led the law to set a demanding standard of justification. As Baroness Hale said in *Preddy* [above] at [53], we should not underestimate the continuing legacy of centuries of discrimination against homosexuals and, adapting her words to this case, we should be slow to accept that prohibiting fostering agencies from discriminating against homosexuals is a disproportionate limitation on their right to manifest their religion.

144. Further, and critically, the ordinary requirement that such discrimination requires weighty reasons is heavily underscored by statute in the case of a religious organisation that provides services to the public. The Judge was right to accord very considerable significance to this, for the reasons given at paras [39]–[40] and [137] above, and to require nothing less than clear evidence to prove that the discriminatory policy was justified.

145. In the end, although there were matters that the Judge should, I think, have placed on its side of the scales, the simple fact is that this was Cornerstone's claim and its evidence, taken at its highest, fell short of discharging the burden upon it. Ms Birtle's statements set out the organisation's perspective, and there can be no doubting the value of its work or the sincerity of its motives. However, in order to justify a policy of this nature, it needed to provide credible evidence that there would otherwise be a seriously detrimental impact on carers and children. The evidence it actually advanced did not go beyond the level of general assertion. In consequence, the Judge understandably found it impossible to conclude that the ability to discriminate against homosexuals was a matter of such importance to Cornerstone that, without it, the wellbeing of current and future carers and children would be seriously affected. He was entitled to treat assertions of the impact on carers as being at best inconclusive, and no attempt was made to prove any impact on present or future children. In short, while I would not rule out the possibility of an organisation in this position putting up a substantial evidence-based case on justification, Cornerstone simply did not do that, and its claim failed on the facts. In that respect, the outcome mirrors *Catholic Care*[78], but the challenge facing Cornerstone was all the greater because of the implications of Sch 23 EA 2010 for the proportionality assessment.

Before leaving the subject of justification it is useful to consider the decision of the High Court in the following case, also discussed in Chapter 7. The case was decided under the Race Relations Act 1976 (RRA) whose test for justification, like those of the SDA, was whether the matter complained of could be 'show[n] to be justifiable irrespective of the [sex or race] of the person to whom it is applied'.

R (Elias) v Secretary of State for Defence [2005] EWHC 1435 (Admin), [2005] IRLR 788

The claimant, who had been born in Hong Kong as a British subject to Jewish parents originally from Iraq or India, and subsequently interned by the Japanese as a POW. She was excluded from the scheme adopted in 2000 by the British Government to compensate British subjects who had been interned by the Japanese during World War 2 (see further Chapter 1) because neither she, either parent or any of her grandparents had been born in the UK.

The Court did not accept that the scheme directly discriminated on grounds of national origins because someone (like the claimant) whose own national origins were

[78] *Catholic Care (Diocese of Leeds) v Charity Commission for England and Wales* [2010] EWHC 520 (Ch) [2010] 4 All ER 1041, discussed in Ch 4.

non-British could have had a parent or grandparent both in the UK, though it did accept that the scheme discriminated indirectly against those of 'non-British origin'[79] and that this discrimination was not justified.

Elias J:

> 84. In my judgment this is a case where the court should carefully scrutinise the justification claimed. This is not simply because there is some disparate impact on the unlawful grounds. But here it is plain that the extent of the discrimination on grounds of national origin is very marked indeed. I would accept that the court ought in general to give a wide margin of discretion to the executive about how public money should be distributed, but once issues of potentially unlawful discrimination as to the allocation come into play, the scrutiny must become more intense.
>
> 85. It is appropriate to remember that the race relations legislation is designed to prevent the adoption of criteria whose effect is to treat someone less favourably on grounds which are immutable and unrelated to the objective being sought. It is offensive to be singled out in that way. The government can legitimately limit the category of British subjects eligible under the scheme, and to that end can adopt criteria which seek to define more narrowly the necessary connection with the United Kingdom. That is so even although those criteria will involve adverse disparate impact. But the criteria themselves must not themselves be the forbidden grounds. Nor, in my opinion, should they consist of factors which in practice are closely related to them.
>
> 86. In my view the decision of the House of Lords in *Orphanos v Queen Mary College* [1985] AC 761 is particularly relevant when considering the question of justification. In that case different fees were charged for students studying at the College, depending on whether they had been ordinarily resident within the EEC for three years or not. The effect was that in general foreign students were obliged to pay significantly more than British nationals, although the criterion adopted was not strictly nationality. The issue arose as to whether the College could justify imposing different fees by reference to this criterion. Their Lordships held that they could not. The only speech in the House of Lords was given by Lord Fraser (with whose speech Lords Diplock, Keith, Roskill and Bridge concurred). He rejected the justification argument in the following way:
>
>> ... it is necessary to consider ... whether the requirement is 'justifiable irrespective of the colour, race, nationality or ethnic or national origins of the [student] to whom it is applied'. Nationality is the only one of these grounds which is in question in this appeal. 'Justifiable' means, in my opinion, 'capable of being justified'. 'Irrespective of' in that subsection means 'without regard to', as I said in *Mandla (Sewa Singh) v Dowell Lee* [1983] 2 AC 548, and I see no reason to alter that opinion. No doubt the main reason for introducing the residence requirement was, as Mr Scrivener said, to curtail public expenditure on education in the interest of economy. That reason itself did not involve discrimination on racial grounds. But the particular method of curtailment may have done so. Various methods of curtailing the expenditure were possible; grants to all students could have been cut by an equal percentage, and their fees could have been correspondingly increased, or grants could have been restricted by reference to the academic qualifications of applicants. No doubt many other methods were possible. The method chosen was to concentrate grants on home students, and to cease subsidising foreign students. The justification relied on by the college is set out in more detail in the further and better particulars of their defence which includes

[79] The High Court also accepted that the scheme likely discriminated indirectly on grounds of ethnic origins and 'race' (which at the time was, with nationality, colour and national and ethnic origins a sub-category of the protected characteristic of 'race'; of those rejected because of the birth criterion, almost a third were 'non-white' and a similar proportion were Jewish.

> statements … [which] show that the main motive for introducing the residence requirement was economy. But the economy was to be effected at the expense of foreign students. That may have been a perfectly reasonable and justifiable policy for the British Government to adopt but in my opinion the college, on whom the onus lies [to establish justification] has not been able to justify the requirement without having regard to the nationality of the applicants at whose expense the policy was carried into effect …
>
> 88. … the important point for the purposes of this case is that his Lordship considered that the concepts of nationality and residence were so closely interlinked that it could not be said that the criterion was chosen irrespective of nationality. Lord Fraser analysed the case as one of indirect rather than direct discrimination; he did not suggest that the issue of justification did not even arise. But he concluded that where the criterion adopted was so inextricably linked to a forbidden ground of discrimination, the less favourable treatment could not be shown to be irrespective of the unlawful grounds.
>
> 89. In my judgment that is equally the position here. The criteria chosen were very closely linked to national origins. Using these criteria was by no means the only way in which the Minister could achieve his legitimate objective. He could have chosen criteria which narrowed the category of British subjects without linking them so closely with descent and national origins. For example, a simple link to, say, a period of residence in the United Kingdom within a period leading up to internment, or the adoption of criteria based on domicile would have done so. It would, of course, still have involved a disparate impact statistically and the less favourable treatment of those who were not British nationals, but it would in my judgment have been proportionate to the objective being sought.[80]

The test for justification no longer contains the proviso which proved fatal in the *Elias* case. But the test now found in the EqA finds its roots in EU provisions including Council Directives 2000/43 (the Race Directive) and 2000/78 (the Employment Equality Directive), provide that their 'implementation … should not serve to justify any regression in relation to the situation which already prevails in each Member State' (Recitals 25 and 28 respectively). A court confronted with a situation such as that which prevailed in *Elias* may have to adopt a similar approach irrespective of the legislative change.

Harassment

Harassment came to be regulated explicitly by discrimination legislation only relatively late in the day and then as a result of EU law, Council Directives 2000/43 and 2000/78 (the Race and Employment Equality Directives) prohibiting harassment and, further, defining it as a form of discrimination, albeit one which does not require proof of *less favourable* treatment. The 2000 Directives provide that 'discrimination' include 'harassment' which is in turn defined as 'unwanted conduct [which] relates to a protected ground and which takes place with the purpose or effect of violating the dignity of a person and of creating an intimidating, hostile, degrading, humiliating or offensive environment,' going on to provide that 'In this context, the concept of harassment may be defined in accordance with the national laws and practice of the Member States.' Council Directive 2002/73/EC, which

[80] The CA rejected the Secretary of State's appeal that the High Court had misdirected itself on its approach to justification: [2006] EWCA Civ 1293, [2006] 1 WLR 3213.

entered into force in October 2005, made similar provision in relation to sex (not covered by the Employment Equality Directive).[81]

Prior to the statutory regulation of sexual and other forms of harassment domestic protection from such harassment was patchy, and depended on the recognition in any particular case that treatment which demeaned or degraded amounted to less favourable treatment on the relevant ground. Scotland's Court of Session recognised in *Strathclyde v Porcelli* [1986] ICR 564 that the use of 'a particular kind of weapon, based upon the sex of the victim, which ... would not have been used against an equally disliked man' would amount to or entail sex discrimination',[82] but in *Pearce v Governing Body of Mayfield School* [2003] UKHL 34, [2004] ICR 937 the HL cast doubt on this line of authority and ruled that a teacher subject to sustained harassment including the use of taunts such as 'lesbian', 'dyke', 'lesbian shit', 'lemon', 'lezzie' or 'lez' had not been discriminated against on grounds of sex. According to Lord Nicholls, '[t]he fact that harassment is gender-specific in form cannot be regarded as of itself establishing conclusively that the reason for the harassment is gender-based, "on the ground of her sex"' though it would be 'evidence, whose weight will depend on the circumstances, that the reason for the harassment was the sex of the victim ... the observation of Lord Brand in ... *Porcelli* that if a form of unfavourable treatment is meted out to a woman to which a man would not have been vulnerable, she has been discriminated against, and the observation of Lord Grieve in the same case that treatment meted out to a woman on the ground of her sex would fall to be regarded as less favourable treatment simply because it was sexually oriented, could not be approved insofar as they were suggesting that it was not relevant whether the claimant was treated less favourably than a man where the harassment is sexually oriented.'

Section 26 EqA, Harassment

(1) A person (A) harasses another (B) if—

(a) A engages in unwanted conduct related to a relevant protected characteristic, and

(b) the conduct has the purpose or effect of—

(i) violating B's dignity, or

(ii) creating an intimidating, hostile, degrading, humiliating or offensive environment for B.

(2) A also harasses B if—

(a) A engages in unwanted conduct of a sexual nature, and

(b) the conduct has the purpose or effect referred to in subsection (1)(b).

(3) A also harasses B if—

(a) A or another person engages in unwanted conduct of a sexual nature or that is related to gender reassignment or sex,

(b) the conduct has the purpose or effect referred to in subsection (1)(b), and

(c) because of B's rejection of or submission to the conduct, A treats B less favourably than A would treat B if B had not rejected or submitted to the conduct.

(4) In deciding whether conduct has the effect referred to in subsection (1)(b), each of the following must be taken into account—

(a) the perception of B;

(b) the other circumstances of the case;

(c) whether it is reasonable for the conduct to have that effect.

[81] See now Council Directives 2004/113/EC (gender goods and services) and 2006/54/EC of 13 December 2004 (the recast directive, which concerns sex equality in employment and occupation).

[82] See also *Sidhu v Aerospace Composite Technology Ltd* [2001] ICR 167 in relation to racist harassment.

(5) The relevant protected characteristics are—

- age;
- disability;
- gender reassignment;
- race;
- religion or belief;
- sex;
- sexual orientation.'

Note that the EqA does not prohibit discrimination related to pregnancy, marriage or civil partnership, though some such harassment may amount to harassment related to sex or sexual orientation and/or to discrimination because of pregnancy, marriage or civil partnership.

It is clear from ss26(1)(b) and (2)(b) that harassment may be committed intentionally or otherwise. Where the *purpose* of unwanted conduct related to a protected characteristic is to violate a person's dignity or to create an intimidating, hostile, degrading, humiliating or offensive environment for the person, the legislation does not impose any threshold which the unwanted conduct must meet. Particularly where an 'offensive' environment is concerned, this sets the bar for harassment quite low. In the case of inadvertent harassment, by contrast, unwanted conduct related to a protected characteristic will not amount to harassment unless it could reasonably be regarded as violative of dignity or constitutive of an intimidating, hostile, degrading, humiliating or offensive environment for the person whose harassment is alleged.

Section 26 EqA lists the violation of dignity and the creation of an intimidating, hostile, degrading, humiliating or offensive environment as *disjunctive* whereas the definition adopted across the various directives is *conjunctive* ('unwanted conduct related to [a protected characteristic which] takes place with the purpose or effect of violating the dignity of a person *and of* creating an intimidating, hostile, degrading, humiliating or offensive environment' (emphasis added).[83] This definition was the subject of unfavourable comment by the HL and House of Commons Joint Committee on Human Rights when it was adopted in the Equality Act (Sexual Orientation) Regulations (Northern Ireland) 2006, which regulated sexual harassment and discrimination outside the employment context. The harassment-related provisions of those regulations were struck down by Northern Ireland's High Court (see Chapter 10) and legislation in Great Britain has never prohibited harassment related to sexual orientation or religion/belief in access to goods and services or in relation to public functions, education or premises. But in its report on the Northern Irish Regulations the Joint Committee on Human Rights (JCHR), while welcoming the broader regulation of sexual orientation harassment in Northern Ireland, expressed concern that the definition of harassment (identical to that in the EqA):

Joint Committee on Human Rights, *Legislative Scrutiny: Sexual Orientation Regulations*, Sixth Report of Session 2006–07

57. … is drawn too widely and defined too vaguely. Conduct which has the purpose or effect of 'violating dignity' or creating an 'offensive environment' is potentially a very wide category of conduct given the inherent vagueness of the terms 'dignity' and 'offensive'. What constitutes a violation of dignity or an offensive environment will inevitably involve a degree of subjectivity. This is mitigated to some extent by the express requirement that conduct shall be regarded as

[83] eg Directive 2000/78 Art 2(3).

> having these effects only if it should reasonably be considered as doing so, but even then one of the relevant circumstances to which regard must be had 'in particular', is the perception of the person being harassed. The width and vagueness of the definition of harassment … gives rise to a risk of incompatibility with both freedom of speech in Article 10 ECHR and freedom of thought, conscience and religion in Article 9. The potential interference with freedom of speech arises because people may feel inhibited from saying something if they fear that a person may perceive it as a violation of their dignity or as creating an offensive environment. The potential interference with freedom of religion and belief arises because explanations of sincerely held doctrinal beliefs might be perceived as violating a person's dignity or creating an offensive environment … As was explained in the debates on the Northern Ireland Regulations, where a person carrying out an exempt activity seeks to explain why a person has been excluded from that activity, there is a risk that the person being told will regard the explanation as violating their dignity or as offensive, and therefore claim that they have been harassed. We recommend that the new Regulations for Great Britain contain a more precise and narrower definition of harassment, to reduce the risk of incompatibility with the right to freedom of speech and freedom of religion and belief.

This passage was quoted by Mr Justice Weatherup, who struck down the harassment provisions in the Northern Irish Regulations. His Lordship went on there to remark, however, that the general adoption of the broad definition of harassment:

***An application for judicial review by the Christian Institute* [2007] NIQB 66, [2008] IRLR 36**

Mr Justice Weatherup:

> 42. … has not demonstrated any excessive reach of the harassment provisions in relation to gender, race, religious belief or political opinion or sexual orientation in employment. The outlawing of harassment in relation to race, religion and gender involves interference with freedom of speech and a fair balance of rights has been sought to be achieved by permitting interference with such freedom of speech on the ground of the rights of others not to be subject to harassment on the basis of gender or race or religious belief. However in outlawing harassment on the ground of sexual orientation the competing right may not only be the right to freedom of speech but may in addition be the right to manifest a religious belief. Where the exercise of the right to freedom of speech also involves the manifestation of a religious belief there will be an added basis on which to seek to justify the action. This provides an added consideration in the case of sexual orientation that may not apply in relation to harassment on the grounds of gender, race or religious belief …

The Equality Act 2006, which regulated discrimination on grounds of religion or belief outside the context of employment for the first time in Great Britain, did not extend to harassment and the Equality Act (Sexual Orientation) Regulations 2007 adopted the same approach as regards sexual orientation. This was then reflected in the EqA which does not prohibit harassment related to either protected characteristic under Part 3 (services), 4 (premises), 6 (education) or 7 (associations).

In *Richmond Pharmacology Ltd v Dhaliwal* the EAT established guidelines for harassment cases. The case was decided under the RRA, but it remains good law.[84] Its effect is such that harassment is not as broad a concept as the JCHR feared in 2005.

[84] *Chawla v Hewlett Packard Ltd* [2015] IRLR 356.

***Richmond Pharmacology Ltd v Dhaliwal* [2009] UKEAT 0458_08_1202, [2009] ICR 724**

The claimant was British and of Indian ethnic origin. She had a senior role with the respondent. She gave one month's notice to leave her job which was in accordance with her written contract but not with an agreement she had reached some time before to give at least two months' notice. As a result there was some ill feeling with a senior colleague who later told her that her work had deteriorated and advised her that even after she left their paths would probably cross 'unless you are married off in India'. The claimant's claim of racial harassment succeeded before a tribunal but which awarded her £1 000 compensation, and her appeal on remedy was rejected by the EAT as was the employer's appeal on liability.

Underhill J, for the EAT:

> 10. As a matter of formal analysis, it is not difficult to break down the necessary elements of liability under [s26 EqA]. They can be expressed as threefold:
>
> (1) *The unwanted conduct*. Did the respondent engage in unwanted conduct?
> (2) The purpose or effect of that conduct. Did the conduct in question either:
>
> (a) have the purpose *or*
> (b) have the effect
>
> of either (i) violating the claimant's dignity or (ii) creating an adverse environment for her? (We will refer to (i) and (ii) as 'the proscribed consequences'.)
>
> (3) *The grounds for the conduct.* Was that conduct on the grounds of the claimant's [protected characteristic].
>
> 11. ... the question whether the conduct complained of was 'unwanted' will overlap with the question of whether it creates an adverse environment for the claimant. There is also evidently a considerable overlap between the two defined provscribed consequences, notwithstanding that they are expressed as alternatives: many or most acts which are found to create an adverse environment for an employee will also violate her dignity (though it may be less general for the reverse to apply). The tribunal's eventual decision may often depend on what are, in practice, undifferentiated factual issues which cover more than one element in the analysis. Nevertheless, it will be a healthy discipline for a tribunal in any case brought under this section ... specifically to address in its reasons each of the elements which we have identified, in order to establish whether any issue arises in relation to it and to ensure that clear factual findings are made on each element in relation to which an issue arises.
>
> 12. We would make four other points which we hope may be of assistance to tribunals seeking to apply [s26 EqA[85]].
>
> 13. First, such case law as there was in relation to 'harassment' as a variety of discrimination prior to the implementation of the Directive is unlikely to be helpful ... Still less assistance is likely to be gained from the entirely separate provisions of the Protection from Harassment Act 1997 and the associated case law ...
>
> 14. Secondly, it is important to note the formal breakdown of 'element (2)' into two alternative bases of liability – 'purpose' and 'effect'. That means that a respondent may be held liable on the basis that the effect of his conduct has been to produce the proscribed consequences even if that was not his purpose; and, conversely, that he may be liable if he acted for the purposes of producing the proscribed consequences but did not in fact do ...

[85] The fourth point is not reproduced as it was concerned with the requirement that the unwanted conduct be 'on the ground of' the protected characteristic rather than (as now) 'related to' the protected characteristic.

15. Thirdly, although the proviso in [the predecessor provision of s26(4) EqA] is rather clumsily expressed, its broad thrust seems to us to be clear. A respondent should not be held liable merely because his conduct has had the effect of producing a proscribed consequence: it should be *reasonable* that that consequence has occurred … The proscribed consequences are, of their nature, concerned with the feelings of the putative victim: that is, the victim must have felt, or perceived, her dignity to have been violated or an adverse environment to have been created. That can, if you like, be described as introducing a 'subjective' element; but overall the criterion is objective because what the tribunal is required to consider is whether, if the claimant has experienced those feelings or perceptions, it was reasonable for her to do so. Thus if, for example, the tribunal believes that the claimant was unreasonably prone to take offence, then, even if she did genuinely feel her dignity to have been violated, there will have been no harassment within the meaning of the section. Whether it was reasonable for a claimant to have felt her dignity to have been violated is quintessentially a matter for the factual assessment of the tribunal. It will be important for it to have regard to all the relevant circumstances, including the context of the conduct in question. One question that may be material is whether it should reasonably have been apparent whether the conduct was, or was not, intended to cause offence (or, more precisely, to produce the proscribed consequences): the same remark may have a very different weight if it was evidently innocently intended than if it was evidently intended to hurt …

22. … We accept that not every racially slanted adverse comment or conduct may constitute the violation of a person's dignity. Dignity is not necessarily violated by things said or done which are trivial or transitory, particularly if it should have been clear that any offence was unintended. While it is very important that employers, and tribunals, are sensitive to the hurt that can be caused by racially offensive comments or conduct (or indeed comments or conduct on other grounds covered by the cognate legislation to which we have referred), it is also important not to encourage a culture of hypersensitivity or the imposition of legal liability in respect of every unfortunate phrase. We accept that the facts here may have been close to the borderline, as the tribunal indeed indicated by the size of its award. But we are satisfied that the tribunal, which clearly considered the case most conscientiously, was entitled to hold that what it found Dr Lorch to have said did indeed fall on the wrong side of the line. We can see no error of law in its decision and this appeal must be dismissed.

In *English v Thomas Sanderson Blinds Ltd* [2008] EWCA Civ 1421, [2009] ICR 543 the conduct complained of was repeated sexual innuendo suggesting that the claimant was gay (which the harassers did not actually believe him to be). In *Gan Menachem Hendon Ltd v de Groen* [2019] ICR 1023 (also discussed in Chapter 9), in which the claimant was a 23-year-old teacher at an ultra-orthodox Jewish nursey, it consisted of a discussion of her cohabiting status at a meeting during which the claimant was advised that cohabitation and having children outside marriage were wrong, that time was passing for her to have children, and that if she had problems with the idea of marriage she should seek counselling, and at which she was asked to lie about living with her boyfriend. In *Sheffield CC v Norouzi* [2011] IRLR 897 the EAT ruled that mocking the claimant's Iranian accent had amounted to racial harassment. In *Kelly v Covance Laboratories Ltd* [2016] IRLR 338, by contrast, the EAT ruled that a tribunal had not erred in rejecting the claim that an instruction that the (Russian) claimant not speak Russian at work had violated her dignity or created an intimidating, hostile, degrading, humiliating or offensive environment for her.[86] And in *Heafield v*

[86] The instruction had been given because of the employer's concern that the claimant was in fact an animal rights activist who had infiltrated the laboratory.

Times Newspapers Ltd [2013] All ER (D) 265 (Feb) the EAT upheld a tribunal finding that a reference to 'the fucking Pope' shouted across a newsroom (by an editor chasing a delayed article on the Pope's visit to England) had neither the purpose or the effect of violating the Catholic claimant's dignity or creating an adverse environment for him.[87]

***Grant v HM Land Registry* [2011] EWCA Civ 769, [2011] ICR 1390**

The CA ruled that a tribunal had erred in law in ruling that the claimant had been subject to harassment in the form of references to the fact that he was gay when he had previously 'come out' at work (albeit in a previous office). The claimant sought to rely on Article 8 ECtHR to the effect that he was entitled to disclose his sexual orientation at a time and in a manner of his own choosing and that the loss of this ability breached his privacy rights and amounted to a detriment for the purposes of the harassment provisions.

Elias LJ (for the Court):

43. … It is accepted that the fact that the claimant had come out does not mean that remarks or references to his sexuality thereafter cannot constitute discrimination. Clearly they can, an obvious example being where they are vituperative or offensive. Everything depends upon the particular circumstances. So, for example, it will generally be relevant to know to whom the remark was made, in what terms and for what purpose.

44. In my view, it is important to keep separate the privacy issue and the question of discrimination. This is not an Article 8 case. Although initially a claim had been made with respect to that Article, it was not pursued and indeed it was not expressly referred in the analysis of the employment tribunal (although it was raised in argument) or the EAT. The fact that the law must be interpreted consistently with the rights found in the Human Rights Convention does not mean that Convention rights must be actively promoted whenever a statute falls to be construed. Discrimination law cannot be used as a surrogate to enforce rights of privacy. If Article 8 is being relied upon to support the proposition that the disclosure of someone's sexual orientation against his or her wishes may constitute a detriment within the meaning of discrimination law and could in an appropriate case constitute humiliating treatment, then I have no quarrel with it. But one hardly needs to rely on Article 8 to make good the point. Like the courts below, I do not find the Article 8 jurisprudence of any assistance in this appeal.

45. In my judgment, the fact that the claimant had 'come out' in Lytham is a highly significant factor when assessing whether there has been discrimination. This is so whether Sharron Kay [the alleged harasser] knew that this was the case or not. The point can be tested in this way. At any time any one of the 300 or more employees at Lytham could, in conversation with a colleague at Coventry, have revealed perfectly innocently the fact that the claimant was gay. They would have been justified in assuming that the claimant would have no objection to this. It is not suggested that he revealed his sexual orientation in Lytham in circumstances where those in receipt of that information were required or even requested to keep it a secret. If Irene Crothers had been informed by a Lytham employee that the claimant was gay, it would in my view be bizarre if that employee could, by the mere innocent disclosure of that information, be liable for either direct discrimination or harassment. The disclosure would still in fact have been unwanted by the claimant, and no doubt the claimant would have been equally upset by the fact that he was deprived of the opportunity to divulge this information in his own way and in his own time. But it would make a mockery of discrimination law to impose liability in these circumstances. A defendant would be liable for discrimination for doing something which the claimant had reasonably led him or her to believe would not cause the claimant concern.

[87] See also the decision in *Ali v Heathrow Express Operating Company Ltd* [2022] IRLR 558.

> 46. The implications of a finding of discrimination in these circumstances would be far reaching. Similar concepts of direct discrimination and harassment are found in other discrimination legislation, relating to such areas as sex, religion, race and disability. An individual may choose to make generally known in the workplace certain aspects of his or her private life, such as the fact that he or she has contracted some debilitating illness, or is pregnant, or has become a Christian. In my judgment if that information is discussed in the course of conversation, even in idle gossip, provided at least there was no ill intent, that would not make the disclosure of that information an act of disability, sex or religious discrimination, as the case may be. That is so even if the victim is upset at the thought that he or she will be the subject of such idle conversation. By putting these facts into the public domain, the claimant takes the risk that he or she may become the focus of conversation and gossip.
>
> 47. In my judgment, therefore, it would simply not be open to a tribunal to find with respect to the first incident that there is either direct discrimination or harassment. As to the former, in my view there can be no detriment because having made his sexual orientation generally public, any grievance the claimant has about the information being disseminated to others is unreasonable and unjustified. Furthermore, even if in fact the disclosure was unwanted, and the claimant was upset by it, the effect cannot amount to a violation of dignity, nor can it properly be described as creating an intimidating, hostile, degrading, humiliating or offensive environment. Tribunals must not cheapen the significance of these words. They are an important control to prevent trivial acts causing minor upsets being caught by the concept of harassment. The claimant was no doubt upset that he could not release the information in his own way, but that is far from attracting the epithets required to constitute harassment. In my view, to describe this incident as the tribunal did as subjecting the claimant to a 'humiliating environment' when he heard of it some months later is a distortion of language which brings discrimination law into disrepute …
>
> 54. I would add this. Ms Monaghan made powerful submissions to us why it is important that gay persons should be able to reveal their sexual orientation on a confidential basis, and that to break that confidence would be likely to involve a breach of Article 8 and might, depending on the circumstances, also involve sexual orientation discrimination. She referred us in particular to the ACAS guide on sexual orientation in the workplace which states in terms that 'outing' someone might have those consequences. Nothing in this judgment is intended to minimise those concerns or cast doubt on the accuracy of those statements. The circumstances here, however, where someone has chosen widely to reveal his sexual orientation, puts the case into a different category.

In *Reverend Canon Pemberton v Right Reverend Inwood* [2018] EWCA Civ 564, [2018] ICR 1291 the CA ruled that the removal, on his marriage to another man, of the claimant's permission to officiate as an Anglican priest and the refusal to grant him an Extra Parochial Ministry Licence, in each case because his marriage contravened church teaching on same-sex relationships, could not amount to unlawful harassment. A tribunal had accepted that the claimant had been humiliated and degraded but that the respondent's actions had been expressly permitted by the Schedule 9, para 2(3) EqA (see further Chapter 10) as the claimant's marriage had been incompatible with the Church of England's doctrine in relation to marriage. The EAT had rejected the claimant's appeal, pointing out that the claimant had been aware that his marriage would be seen as in conflict with the teachings of the Church and that if the bishop were not to be entitled to make and communicate the decisions which flowed from that fact without committing an act of unlawful harassment there would be a contradiction within the EqA. The CA rejected any suggestion that a defence could properly be read into Schedule 9 in connection with harassment but ruled that, absent any aggravating features, it would not be reasonable for the purposes of s26(4) EqA for unwanted conduct falling within Schedule 9 para 2 to have the effect prohibited in s26(1)(b) EqA.

The change to 'related to' in s26(4) from the 'on grounds of' in the predecessor harassment provisions has extended the scope of harassment since there is no need for any causal relationship between protected characteristic and unwanted conduct.[88] In *Timothy James Consulting Ltd v Wilton* [2015] IRLR 368 the EAT ruled that poor treatment by a director of a senior manager with whom he had previously had a personal relationship, and who he accused of jealously in connection with his subsequent relationship with another member of staff (and his former lover's subordinate) amounted to harassment 'related to' sex.[89] In *Sheffield CC v Norouzi* (see above) the unwanted conduct 'related to' the claimant's ethnicity irrespective of the fact that it was motivated by the desire to upset those in authority. This is not to say, however, that any link between protected characteristic and unwanted conduct will satisfy the 'related to' criteria.

***Bakkali v Greater Manchester Buses (South) Ltd* [2018] UKEAT 0176_17_1005, [2018] IRLR 906**

The claimant, a Muslim bus driver of Moroccan origin, was asked by a colleague whether he was still promoting Islamic State (IS). The question followed an earlier discussion during which the claimant had told his colleague about a journalist's report that IS were very good fighters and had managed to run the country in time, and the colleague subsequently apologised to the claimant because the remark had upset the claimant. An employment tribunal found that the remark was made because of the previous conversation rather than 'because of the claimant's race or religion': 'If the comment had been made without the context, and the speaker knew the claimant was Muslim, it would have appeared that the speaker was linking the claimant's religion to the possibility of him promoting [IS]. However, the context in which [the second driver] made this remark was that it followed a conversation where the claimant had informed [him] about positive sounding comments from a German journalist about [IS].' The tribunal rejected the harassment claim, stating that 'for reasons ... explained in relation to the complaint of direct discrimination, in the context [the remark] was not related to religious belief. There is no evidence it was related to race.'

The EAT rejected the claimant's appeal.

In *Tees Esk and Wear Valleys NHS Foundation Trust v Aslam* [2020] IRLR 495 the EAT rejected a racial harassment claim from an Asian nurse who overheard a psychiatrist stating of a patient with ADHD, 'I've just seen this boy; he should join ISIS that'll sort him.' A tribunal had found that the remark amounted to racial harassment but the EAT ruled that the tribunal had failed to specify what it was about the remark, which had not been directed to the claimant, that was said to be 'related to' race. And in *Bessong v Pennine Care NHS Foundation Trust* [2020] ICR 849 the EAT ruled that a tribunal had not erred in rejecting a claim of harassment arising from an alleged failure by the employer to protect him from racial abuse by a patient. The tribunal accepted that the inaction amounted to unwanted conduct, but did not accept that it was related to race.

[88] See the discussions of this element in *Richmond Pharmacology Ltd v Dhaliwal* [2009] ICR 724 p 69 above, and *Lindsay v LSE* [2014] IRLR 218.

[89] The EAT also ruled that constructive dismissal could not be pleaded as an act of harassment. This aspect of the decision was distinguished in *Urso v DWP* [2017] IRLR 304 in relation to actual dismissal and overruled by the EAT in *Driscoll v V&P Global Ltd* [2021] IRLR 891.

***Forbes v LHR Airport Ltd* [2019] UKEAT 0174_18_2802, [2019] ICR 1558**

The claimant, a security officer, complained about a colleague, Ms Stevens, who shared an image of a golliwog on her Facebook page with the statement 'Let's see how far he can travel before Facebook takes him off.' The image was shared with Ms Stevens' Facebook friends and then shown to the claimant by another colleague. On being challenged she explained that she had shared the picture because it reminded her of a childhood memory about Robertson's Jam[90] and expressed her remorse. The claimant raised a grievance and Ms Stevens was disciplined and received a final written warning. The claimant was subsequently instructed to work alongside Ms Stevens and raised a concern about the situation after which he was moved to work at another location without any explanation. He complained that Ms Stevens' actions amounted to racial harassment. A tribunal dismissed his claim because the image had not been shared by Ms Stevens 'in the course of [her] employment' for the purposes of s109 EqA (see further Chapter 4), also ruling that the act of sharing it did not amount to harassment.

On appeal the claimant argued that the tribunal had not been entitled to take account of the *ex post facto* apology in determining whether Ms Stevens' actions amounted to harassment. The EAT dismissed his appeal.

Choudhury P (for the EAT):

45. Mr Ward submits that in [taking into account Ms Stevens' apology] …, the Tribunal was unduly swayed by the discriminator's motive and whether she intended to cause offence rather than focusing on the 'effect' of the conduct and the fact that it clearly did cause offence.

46. We were referred to an example in the statutory code of practice at para 7.17 thereof, where it was emphasised that the downloading of pornographic images onto office computers could have the effect of creating a hostile and humiliating environment for a female colleague, notwithstanding the fact that those doing the downloading did not do so for the purpose of upsetting the female colleague.

47. In our judgment, the Tribunal did not err in its approach to the s 26 test. It took into account, as it was required to do, the Claimant's perception of the conduct (finding that he was clearly offended by it), the other circumstances of the case and whether it was reasonable for the conduct to have the proscribed effect. The other circumstances identified by the Tribunal included the fact that the images had been shared privately amongst Ms Stevens' friends; that it was not something she did at work; and that the Claimant was not on her friends' list.

48. There was no error in going on also to consider Ms Stevens' apology, as that would fall within the wide rubric of the 'other circumstances' which the Tribunal must take into account in applying s 26 of the EqA. There is no warrant, in our judgment, for treating the reference to the other circumstances under s 26(4)(b) as being confined only to those extant at the time of the alleged act of harassment. Unlike the situation under s109, where the Tribunal, in determining whether an act was in the course of employment, will focus on matters at the time the act took place, under s 26, the Tribunal is required to consider whether conduct has the purpose or effect of creating a hostile and intimidating etc, environment. That may, in appropriate circumstances, include taking account of an apology that is made shortly after the impugned conduct or the immediate cessation of the conduct once it is brought to the employer's attention. Both of those matters could be relevant in assessing whether there was the hostile environment which has been proscribed by the legislation.

[90] Which used to feature a golliwog on its pots.

There has been little reported case law concerning the parameters of 'conduct of a sexual nature' in s26(2) EqA except for the decision in *Raj v Capita Business Services Ltd* [2019] IRLR 1057 in which the EAT ruled that a tribunal had been entitled to hold that brief, unwanted, shoulder massages of the (male) claimant by his (female) team leader amounted neither to conduct of a sexual nature nor to conduct related to sex.[91] There is no reported case law on s26(3) ('*quid pro quo*') harassment though the nature of the conduct targeted by this provision is clear and difficulties more likely to arise from questions of proof (see Chapter 5) than definition.

An issue which arises more often in harassment than in other claims under the EqA concerns vicarious liability. Prior to the decision in *Jones v Tower Boot Co* [1997] ICR 254 it was relatively common for employers to contest liability on the basis that employees were not acting within the course of their employment when they were engaged in harassment. This has become increasingly difficult, as discussed in Chapter 4, but the continuing atomisation of the workforce (which increasingly results in people working side-by-side with workers who are either employed by different employers or who are self-employed or agency workers), has resulted in other difficulties in establishing vicarious liability for harassment.[92] This issue is further considered in Chapter 4.

Victimisation

Section 27 EqA, Victimisation

(1) A person (A) victimises another person (B) if A subjects B to a detriment because—
- (a) B does a protected act, or
- (b) A believes that B has done, or may do, a protected act.

(2) Each of the following is a protected act—
- (a) bringing proceedings under this Act;
- (b) giving evidence or information in connection with proceedings under this Act;
- (c) doing any other thing for the purposes of or in connection with this Act;
- (d) making an allegation (whether or not express) that A or another person has contravened this Act.

(3) Giving false evidence or information, or making a false allegation, is not a protected act if the evidence or information is given, or the allegation is made, in bad faith.

(4) This section applies only where the person subjected to a detriment is an individual.

(5) The reference to contravening this Act includes a reference to committing a breach of an equality clause or rule.

Section 27 suggests that the protected act has to be an act of the victimisation claimant him or herself. EU Directives, by contrast, define victimisation as adverse treatment arising from a complaint or proceedings concerning discrimination. In *Thompson v Central London Bus Company* [2016] IRLR 9 the EAT ruled that a tribunal had erred in striking out an associative victimisation by a claimant who alleged that he had been subject to unfavourable treatment by reason of protected acts carried out by other employees with whom he was associated. The tribunal had interpreted s27 to apply to associative victimisation but struck

[91] See also *R (CC Dyfed Powys Police) v Police Misconduct Tribunal* [2020] EWHC 2032 (Admin), [2020] IRLR 964.

[92] eg *AY & Baker Ltd v Okerago* [2010] IRLR 394; *Forbes v LHR Airport Ltd* [2019] ICR 1558.

out the claim because it regarded as inadequate the evidence of the claimed association between the claimant and the other workers. The EAT allowed the claimant's appeal, stating that the relevant question was 'not whether there is in existence a relationship of some particular kind but whether in the mind of the putative discriminator the protected act of a third party was part of the reason for the treatment of the employee' (§24).

The application of the predecessor provisions of s27 gave rise to a number of difficulties. Some resulted from the requirement (removed by s27 EqA) that the claimant have been treated *less favourably* than another was or would have been in connection with a protected act. Section 27 EqA has dropped the explicit requirement for less favourable treatment though the claimant has to show (1) *detriment* (2) *because of* the protected act.[93]

The concept of detriment is not defined by the EqA other than (s212) so as not to include conduct amounting to harassment. As we shall see in Chapter 4, however, the concept is broad enough to extend to any treatment by which a reasonable worker might regard themselves as having been disadvantaged, but not 'an unjustified sense of grievance'.[94] In *Deer v University of Oxford* [2015] EWCA Civ 52, [2015] IRLR 481 the CA accepted that the conduct of internal procedures could amount to a 'detriment' even if this would not have changed their outcome, though limited damages would be recoverable for such a wrong.

The requirement for causation has given rise to significantly more difficulty as can be seen from the early case law. In *Aziz v Trinity Street Taxis Ltd* [1989] 1 QB 463 the CA rejected a victimisation claim from a taxi driver who had been expelled from his taxi association because it had been discovered that, having become concerned that he was being discriminated against on racial grounds, he had tape-recorded a number of conversations with colleagues. A tribunal had found that he was penalised because of his breach of trust. The CA ruled that the treatment he complained of could not be said to have been 'by reason of'[95] Mr Aziz having done a protected act.[96] The decision was reached under the RRA which did contain an explicit requirement for less favourable treatment, but the CA had rejected as 'absurd' an approach which would have required that the claimant establish that he had been treated less favourably than someone who had performed the same act, but not for a reason connected with the RRA.[97] The Court's approach to causation, however, had the effect that, in order to prove his claim, Mr Aziz would have had to show that he was treated less favourably than another whose perceived breach of trust was not connected with a potential race discrimination claim.

The question which has repeatedly been raised in victimisation claims concerns the relationship between the protected act and the treatment complained of. It is clear from the authorities that a mere causal link between the two is insufficient and that the protected act must play some part on the alleged victimiser's mind.[98] It is equally clear that there is no requirement that the alleged victimiser be consciously motivated by the connection between the claimant's conduct and the discrimination legislation.

[93] See the decision of the EAT in *Woodhouse v West North West Homes* [2013] IRLR 773.

[94] *MOD v Jeremiah* [1980] QB 87; *Shamoon v CC RUC* [2003] UKHL 11, [2003] ICR 337, applied in the context of victimisation by the HL in *St Helens MBC v Derbyshire* [2007] UKHL 16, [2007] ICR 841.

[95] Now 'because'; see s27(1) EqA.

[96] See also the decision of the CA in *Cornelius v University College of Swansea* [1987] IRLR 141.

[97] This having been the approach of the EAT in *Kirby v Manpower Services Commission* [1980] ICR 420.

[98] See eg *Greater Manchester Police v Bailey* [2017] EWCA Civ 425 in which case the detriment complained of would not have happened had the protected act not occurred but was in no way motivated by that act.

***Nagarajan v London Regional Transport* [1999] UKHL 36, [2000] 1 AC 501**

Lord Steyn, with whom Lords Hutton and Hobhouse agreed, ruled that the requirement which had been imposed by the CA in that case for conscious motivation on the part of the alleged victimiser would render victimisation highly unusual as a form of civil liability, further pointed out that motivation was an unusual ingredient even in criminal law. By contrast, the claimant's contention that he was required to prove only that the principal or at least an important or significant cause of the less favourable treatment was the fact that he had done a protected act:

> … postulates that the discriminator's knowledge of the protected act had a subjective impact on his mind [but] … does not require the tribunal to distinguish between conscious and subconscious motivation … Quite sensibly in [direct discrimination] cases the tribunal simply has to pose the question: Why did the defendant treat the employee less favourably? It does not have to consider whether a defendant was consciously motivated in his unequal treatment of an employee. That is a straightforward way of carrying out its task in a [direct discrimination] case. Common sense suggests that the tribunal should also perform its functions in a [victimisation] case by asking the equally straightforward question: Did the defendant treat the employee less favourably because of his knowledge of a protected act? Given that it is unnecessary in [direct discrimination] cases to distinguish between conscious and subconscious motivation, there is no sensible reason for requiring it in [victimisation] cases …[99]

Lord Steyn's ruling that motivation is as irrelevant to a victimisation claim as it is to a claim of direct discrimination was called into question by the subsequent decision of the HL in the *Khan* case.

***CC West Yorkshire Police v Khan* [2001] UKHL 48, [2001] ICR 1065**

The claimant, a police officer, had issued race discrimination proceedings against his employer in connection with his non-promotion (this was because of criticisms of his communication and leadership skills). While the claim was pending he applied for a job in another force whose request for a reference was refused by his employer on the basis that, because of the outstanding claim, the Chief Constable (CC) was 'unable to comment any further for fear of prejudicing his own case before the tribunal.' A tribunal accepted that the claimant had been subject to unlawful victimisation and the CC's appeal was rejected by EAT and the CA ([2000] IRLR 324) but the HL allowed the CC's appeal. Having accepted that the claimant had been treated less favourably than someone who had not made the discrimination claim, their Lordships ruled that the treatment was not 'by reason that' the claimant had brought proceedings against his employer, rather because 'currently and temporarily, [the employer] needs to take steps to preserve his position in the outstanding proceedings'. Employers should, their Lordships ruled, be able 'acting honestly and reasonably, … to take steps to preserve their position in pending discrimination proceedings without laying themselves open to a charge of victimisation'.[100]

[99] The CA confirmed in *Greater Manchester Police v Bailey* (ibid) §12 that the proper approach to causation had not been affected by the change in wording from 'reason' in the predecessor provisions to 'because of' in the EqA.

[100] §31 *per* Lord Nicholls with whom Lords Hoffmann and Hutton agreed. See also *Cornelius v University College of Swansea* (n 96 above), an earlier case whose facts are not entirely dissimilar to those in *Khan*.

This is a difficult distinction to draw, though it is hard to disagree with the view that the employer in this case had no real alternative to refusing to supply Sergeant Khan with a reference while the legal proceedings were outstanding. The reasoning, though not the outcome, in the *Khan* decision was soon revisited by the HL.

***St Helens MBC v Derbyshire* [2007] UKHL 16, [2007] ICR 841**

The Council sent letters to a number of employees who had refused to settle a large equal pay claim brought against the Council (most other employees having agreed the settlement). The letters stated that, if the claimants were to win their claim, the Council would be unable to provide a full school meals service and would be forced to make significant numbers of people redundant. Having won their equal pay claims the claimants sued the Council for victimisation on the basis that the letters had brought them considerable distress and had damaged their relationships with colleagues who had settled. They succeeded before a tribunal which found that the letters 'amounted to an attempt to induce the acquiescence of individuals despite the view of their union ... [were] more than a matter-of-fact reminder of what might happen if they went on with a complaint ... [were] directed against people who were in no position to debate the accuracy of the respondents' pessimistic prognostications' and that they might have resulted in 'surrender induced by fear, fear of public odium or the reproaches of colleagues.' The EAT upheld the tribunal's decision and, after a brief defeat in the CA, the claimants succeeded before the HL.

The CA had regarded the Council's letters as an 'honest and reasonable' to settle the claim (applying *Khan*). Baroness Hale made reference to Directives 2000/43/EC and 2000/78/EC (the Race and Employment Equality directives) which had not been in force at the time of the *Khan* decision whose reasoning 'must now be revisited in the light of the European law' (§35). Having pointed out that the victimisation provisions contained no 'honest and reasonable employer' defence, Baroness Hale identified the relevant questions as whether the employer: (i) had subjected the claimants to 'any other detriment';[101] and (ii) in doing so, treated them less favourably [note that this no longer applies]; (iii) 'by reason' of a protected act (§36). As to (i), she stated that while '[a]n unjustified sense of grievance cannot amount to "detriment"' (citing *Shamoon*), and '[o]rdinary steps in defending the claim and ordinary attempts to settle or compromise the claim do no one any harm and may even do some good ... these were no ordinary attempts to settle the claim' and amounted in her view to the imposition of a detriment. Baroness Hale warned against undue emphasis on (ii) in light of the fact that the Directives did not require it, though she accepted that 'without a difference in treatment, it [might] be difficult to assert that the employer's behaviour was a reaction to the discrimination claim', and noted that differential treatment had been established. Finally, as regards (iii), the employer sent the letters because the claimants were pursuing their claims for equal pay though the others had settled. All this being the case, the victimisation claims succeeded.

Lord Neuberger, with whom Lords Hope and Carswell and Baroness Hale agreed (Lord Bingham delivering a concurring judgment with which Lord Neuberger agreed), suggested that the reasoning in *Khan* was problematic because it appeared to provide a

[101] At the time the requirement for detriment did not feature in the definition of victimisation itself but it was required in order to make the victimisation unlawful

non-statutory defence and assessed detriment, not from the point of view of the claimant, as required by the CA in *MOD v Jeremiah* [1980] QB 87 and the HL in *Shamoon v CC of the RUC* [2003] UKHL 11, [2003] ICR 337, but from that of the employer. Lord Neuberger stated that the court should not ask whether an employer had acted honestly and reasonably but, rather, whether the claimant could properly be regarded as having suffered a detriment, going on to suggest that the application of this test would have led to the same result in *Khan* and 'almost always' as the 'honest and reasonable' test because the distress caused by an 'employer's honest and reasonable conduct in the course of his defence or in the conduct of any settlement negotiations, cannot (save, possibly, in the most unusual circumstances) constitute 'detriment' (§68).[102]

Another issue raised in the House of Lord's decision in *Khan* concerned the nature of the 'protected act' *but for* the performance of which the victimised person would not have suffered less favourable treatment (ie, whether the relationship between the act and the EqA has to operate on the mind of the alleged victimiser. The CA in *Aziz* had demanded a connection between the specific legislation in connection with which the victimised person acted and the treatment relied upon. The respondent in the *Khan* case had argued that the proper comparator for Sergeant Khan was someone who had brought proceedings under different legislation, an argument rejected by EAT, and by the CA in *Brown v TNT Worldwide (UK) Ltd* [2001] ICR 182. Lord Hoffmann, who alone of their Lordships expressly addressed this question, stated that: 'if the fact that the employee had commenced proceedings under the Act was a real reason why he received less favourable treatment, it is no answer that the employer would have behaved in the same way to an employee who had done some non-protected act, such as commencing proceedings otherwise than under the Act' (§60).

Aziz was mentioned above. In that case the CA accepted in essence that the claimant was unprotected by the victimisation proceedings because the alleged victimiser had acted not because he did something (made covert tape recordings) in connection with his prospective race discrimination claim, but rather because of the thing that he did (made covert tape recordings). It might be argued that the making of covert recordings would generally be regarded as unacceptable such that it would be likely to trigger disciplinary proceedings, and that such behaviour ought no more to be protected than the dishonest removal of documents or the use of violence. But too ready an acceptance that it was not 'what the claimant did, but the way that s/he did it', which provoked the treatment complained of risks stripping the victimisation provisions of their protective potential. One particularly stark example of this is seen in an early case, In *Re York Truck Equipment Ltd*, in which the EAT accepted that a woman who complained to her employers of a workplace sexual assault and of the employers' failure properly to investigate it had not been victimised contrary to the (then) SDA 1975, but had been dismissed because of the disruptive manner of her complaints.[103]

That decision is an old one, but its spectre was raised by the decision of the EAT in *Martin v Devonshires Solicitors* [2011] ICR 352 in which the EAT ruled that the dismissal of the claimant for repeatedly pursuing grievances concerning sex discrimination did not

[102] See also, on the application of the victimisation provisions in the context of litigation, the decision of the EAT in *South London & Maudsley NHS Trust v Dathi* [2008] IRLR 350 that correspondence prepared in the context of litigation attracted absolute immunity and so could not form the basis of a victimisation claim, an argument not put in the *St Helen's* claim. See also the decision of the Court of Appeal in *Bird v Sylvester* [2008] ICR 208.

[103] EAT/109/88 (20 October 1989, unreported),

amount to victimisation.[104] This was an extreme case; the claimant suffered from paranoid delusions and her allegations, though genuinely believed by her, were wholly false; she refused to accept that this was the case and was likely to proceed in similar fashion. The EAT stated that 'there would in principle be cases where an employer had dismissed an employee in response to a protected act but could say that the reason for dismissal was not the act but some feature of it which could properly be treated as separable' notwithstanding Underhill P's recognition that this was 'dangerous territory' because false allegations are protected unless brought in bad faith (s27(3) EqA) a claimant ought not to lose protection for bringing a complaint in an unreasonable way. Nevertheless, Underhill P, apparently in defiance of the statutory wording, stated that 'it would be extraordinary if these provisions gave employees absolute immunity in respect of anything said or done in the context of a protected complaint'.

It may be difficult for a tribunal to distinguish between a claimant whose repeated allegations of wrongdoing are the result of delusions and one whose history of ill-treatment has resulted in apparently unreasonable behaviour on their part. The caution displayed by the EAT in *Woodhouse v West North West Homes Leeds* in respect of the *Martin* decision is therefore to be welcomed.

***Woodhouse v West North West Homes Leeds Ltd* [2013] UKEAT 0007_12_0506, [2013] IRLR 773**

The claimant, who was Black, came to believe that he was the victim of race discrimination at work. He issued multiple grievances over a period of years in respect of alleged race discrimination, alleged failures of management support, delay in dealing with his grievances, victimisation and harassment because of his grievances and matters resulting in his redundancy. All but one grievance was dismissed, as eventually was Mr Woodhouse on the basis that he had 'lost all trust and confidence in' his employer and would not regain it unless his allegations of discriminatory conduct were accepted. The claimant issued 9 tribunal claims some of which, including allegations of racial harassment and race discrimination, succeeded, though most were dismissed, a tribunal concluding that all but the first two had repeatedly brought forward empty allegations without any proper evidential basis or grounds.

A tribunal concluded that the claim was 'on all fours' with *Martin v Devonshire's Solicitors* because the reason for dismissal was 'genuinely separable' from the making of the complaints themselves because the claimant's grievances were unfounded and substantially without any significant evidential basis, allegations of racism being 'scattered around in circumstances where, in the majority of cases, there was clearly no basis for suggesting a racial element' and there being 'a repeated pattern of grievances ... which were thoroughly and exhaustively investigated and objectively demonstrated to be false ... the results of those grievances themselves fed what had

[104] See also *HM Prison Service v Ibimidun* [2008] IRLR 940 in which the EAT accepted that the claimant had been dismissed not because he had brought tribunal proceedings complaining of race discrimination but because of the way in which he had pursued them (which included including making unreasonable allegations in order to harass his employer to settlement.

become, by the end, an obsession, a fixation.' The EAT allowed Mr Woodhouse's appeal, pointing out that bad faith had not been relied upon in this case and ruling that there the only proper conclusion had been that he had been victimised for making his complaints.

Judge Hand QC (for the EAT):

> 101. … the real question is can the judgment be supported on the basis of 'genuinely separable features'? Obviously the employment tribunal felt that, as in *Martin*, there was a mixture here of the subjective state of mind of the appellant and the future impact of his behaviour. But we think that a further note of caution ought to be added to the one embedded in the judgment by Underhill J.
>
> 102. In our judgment, *Martin* cannot be regarded as some sort of template into which the facts of cases of alleged victimisation can be fitted. There are no doubt exceptional cases where protected acts have not caused the dismissal or whatever other detriment is at issue. *Martin* is an example of such an exceptional case. But we emphasise the word exceptional; very few cases will have grievances based on paranoid delusions about events that never happened. It seems to us the process of measuring cases against such a yardstick is a dangerous one. One person's conviction that they have been discriminated against is very likely to generate the polar opposite, ie that the complainant is irrational, in the person or organisation complained about. Experience of this type of litigation teaches that grievances multiply and so the fact that here are a series of them is not unusual. It is a slippery slope towards neutering the concept of victimisation if the irrationality and multiplicity of grievances can lead, as a matter of routine, to the case being placed outside the scope of s27 of the EA. All the more so when the origin of the problem is established, as here, to have been a real, as opposed to imaginary, race discrimination.
>
> 103. In our judgment, on any objective basis, this case is not 'on all fours' with *Martin*. This is not only illustrated by the clear factual differences between this case and *Martin* but also by the difficulty, as we perceive it to be, of the employment tribunal being able to articulate what the 'genuinely separable features' are … we think that employment tribunals would do well to start from the proposition that very few cases will be like *Martin*. Moreover, although it is a factor in *Martin* that there was a risk of future repetition … it must not be forgotten that the terms of s27(1) of the EA (see above at paragraph 58 of this judgment) cover future, as well as past, protected acts; in our view the importance of the words 'as a result of that illness' in paragraph 23 of *Martin* should not be underestimated.
>
> 104. Therefore, we conclude that this case is not an analogue of *Martin* and the employment tribunal fell into error when they regarded it as such. But more than that we conclude that the employment tribunal never identified any 'genuinely separable features'. In the end the *Martin* concept is an unchallengeable factual finding of a reason for detrimental action other than the doing of protected act in the past or the potential for such an act in the future. It seems to us all paragraphs 97 and 98 of the judgment of the employment tribunal amount to is that the appellant had raised a number of grievances in the past, which had proved to be unjustified, and his state of mind was such that he was likely to do so in the future. The respondent's position that the appellant was dismissed because he had lost trust and confidence in the organisation when coupled, as the employment tribunal found it to be, with the avoidance of further repetition of grievances by ending the employment relationship, is no more than the appellant being dismissed, if not because of past protected acts, then because of the belief of the likelihood of future protected acts. In our view on the employment tribunal's own factual findings that amounted to victimisation within the scope of s27(1) and the employment tribunal erred by reaching any other conclusion …'

The requirement that the protected act must play a part in the alleged victimiser's decision-making generally means that the decision-maker must have been aware of the protected act.[105] In *Royal Mail v Jhuti* [2019] UKSC 55, [2020] ICR 731 the SC accepted in a whistle-blowing claim (which also requires that the action complained of be causally related to a protected action – there a protected disclosure) that the ultimate decision-maker did not have themselves to be aware of the protected act if a person in the hierarchy of responsibility had hidden behind an invented reason which the decision-maker (innocently) adopted.

***Royal Mail v Jhuti* [2019] UKSC 55, [2020] ICR 731**

The claimant was dismissed after she raised concerns about malpractice within her team, her manager having issued a veiled threat that she would be dismissed if she did not withdraw her concerns. She was subsequently absent by reason of work-related stress and was eventually dismissed by a manager who had no previous involvement with her on the basis of allegedly unsatisfactory performance, which findings depended on evidence invented by the claimant's manager. There was no question that the dismissing manager was motivated by, or even aware of, her disclosures. The SC ruled (overturning the decision of the CA) that the claimant had been dismissed by reason of her protected acts (and therefore that the dismissal was automatically unfair under s103A of the Employment Rights Act 1996).

Lord Wilson (for the Court):

> 60. In searching for the reason for a dismissal for the purposes of [s103A ERA] … courts need generally look no further than at the reasons given by the appointed decision-maker. Unlike Ms Jhuti, most employees will contribute to the decision-maker's inquiry. The employer will advance a reason for the potential dismissal. The employee may well dispute it and may also suggest another reason for the employer's stance. The decision-maker will generally address all rival versions of what has prompted the employer to seek to dismiss the employee and, if reaching a decision to do so, will identify the reason for it. In the present case, however, the reason for the dismissal given in good faith by Ms Vickers turns out to have been bogus. If a person in the hierarchy of responsibility above the employee (here Mr Widmer as Ms Jhuti's line manager) determines that, for reason A (here the making of protected disclosures), the employee should be dismissed but that reason A should be hidden behind an invented reason B which the decision-maker adopts (here inadequate performance), it is the court's duty to penetrate through the invention rather than to allow it also to infect its own determination. If limited to a person placed by the employer in the hierarchy of responsibility above the employee, there is no conceptual difficulty about attributing to the employer that person's state of mind rather than that of the deceived decision-maker.
>
> **Conclusion**
>
> 61. There is no need to remit to the tribunal an issue whether, upon the proper attribution to the company of Mr Widmer's state of mind, the reason for Ms Jhuti's dismissal was that she had made the protected disclosures …

As above, a claimant does not have to establish that the protected act is the only or main reason for the detriment complained of as long as it is 'the principal or at least an

[105] *South London Healthcare NHS Trust v Al-Rubeyi* UKEAT/0269/09 (2 March 2010, unreported); *Thompson v Central London Bus Company* [2016] IRLR 9.

important or significant cause of the less favourable treatment': *Owen & Brigg v James* [1982] ICR 618.[106] Nor does success in a victimisation claim depend on success in the underlying allegations of discrimination. Section 27 EqA does, however, provide a defence where (s27(4)) false evidence or information is provided or a false allegation made in bad faith. In *Saad v Southampton University Hospitals NHS Trust* [2019] ICR 311 the EAT ruled (*per* HHJ Eady QC) that the main question in determining whether there has been bad faith is whether the individual has acted honestly in giving the evidence or information or in making the allegation.

A further limitation in the victimisation provisions became apparent in the following case:

***Waters v Commissioner of Police of the Metropolis* [1997] EWCA Civ J0703-1, [1997] ICR 1073**

The CA rejected a claim brought by a police officer who suffered detriment as a result of her allegation of rape and buggery by a fellow police officer while they were off-duty. Her counsel argued that the victimisation provisions had 'to be construed in such a way as to treat as protected acts any allegations which, objectively considered, are aimed at claiming (ie, provide the basis for development of a claim for) protection under the equality legislation.' The officer's complaint relating to the assault did not amount to a claim that she had been discriminated against contrary to the SDA because her assailants were not regarded as acting within the course of their 'employment' for the purposes of establishing vicarious liability (see further Chapter 4).

Waite LJ (for the CA):

> True it is that the legislation must be construed in a sense favourable to its important public purpose. But there is another principle involved – also essential to that same purpose. Charges of race or sex discrimination are hurtful and damaging and not always easy to refute. In justice, therefore, to those against whom they are brought, it is vital that discrimination (including victimisation) should be defined in language sufficiently precise to enable people to know where they stand before the law. Precision of language is also necessary to prevent the valuable purpose of combating discrimination from becoming frustrated or brought into disrepute through the use of language which encourages unscrupulous or vexatious recourse to the machinery provided by the Discrimination Acts. The interpretation proposed by [counsel for the claimant] would involve an imprecision of language leaving employers in a state of uncertainty as to how they should respond to a particular complaint, and would place the machinery of the Acts at serious risk of abuse. It is better, and safer, to give the words of the subsection their clear and literal meaning. The allegation relied on need not state explicitly that an act of discrimination has occurred ... All that is required is that the allegation relied on should have asserted facts capable of amounting in law to an act of discrimination by an employer .... The facts alleged by the complainant in this case were incapable in law of amounting to an act of discrimination by the Commissioner because they were not done by him, and they cannot (because the alleged perpetrator was not acting in the course of his employment) be treated as done by him ....

This decision is perhaps most generously characterised as unfortunate. From the point of view of the employer, and contrary to Waite LJ's view, it makes no difference whether any allegation made by an employee would, if proven, disclose a breach of the relevant

[106] In *Neill v Governors of St Thomas More School* and in *O'Donoghue v Redcar and Cleveland BC* the EAT and CA respectively asked whether the protected characteristic was an 'effective cause' (see n 4 above). The same approach applies in victimisation claims: *Nagarajan v Agnew* [1994] IRLR 61.

legislation. The claimant had, on her account, been subject to appalling behaviour in the wake of her rape complaint. She had been aggressively treated, transferred between police stations without consultation or the normal periods of notice, her complaint improperly investigated and any semblance of confidentiality related to it breached (this in part resulting in her being ostracised by her colleagues and superior officers). She was transferred from police to civilian duties, denied appropriate time off, her applications for particular placements refused, her personal diary stolen and the theft never investigated. She was given unfair reports, 'harassed and unfairly treated' by her superiors, told 'that she should leave the police force before she was forced to go, given the impression that she, rather than her alleged attacker, was under investigation and told that there would be no disciplinary proceedings against him. She was denied back-up and subjected to pornography by her fellow officers. No attempts were made by senior officers to prevent her harassment (in connection with the rape allegation) by her fellow officers. She was not given notice of court appearances and her complaints about this went unheeded. She was threatened with violence by her Chief Superintendent and 'quite unjustifiably and with a view to intimidating and harassing her', was required to undergo 'psychological analysis' to see if she was 'fit for duty'. Her paperwork started to disappear and she was advised to leave the force by a colleague in his capacity as Police Federation representative. She eventually took sick leave.

The CA's ruling in this case meant that the claimant's allegations were never proven. But, in view of their seriousness, it is difficult to comprehend Waite LJ's assertion that recognising her treatment as victimisation for the purposes of the then legislation would have involved 'an imprecision of language leaving employers in a state of uncertainty as to how they should respond to a particular complaint, and would place the machinery of the Acts at serious risk of abuse.' The facts alleged in *Waters* are certainly at the extreme end of the spectrum. But Waite LJ's approach suggests that, in cases other than those which fall within the victimisation provisions, employers have a right, worthy of legal protection, to respond to complaints by subjecting the complainer to ill-treatment.

Finally, the concept of associative victimisation has been established in the UK in *Thompson v London Central Bus Company Ltd* [2016] IRLR 9, in which the claimant alleged that he was being victimised by his employer for having reported a discrimination claim made by his colleagues, rather than one that he had made on his own behalf. The EAT ruled that, although Mr Thompson had not himself completed a protected act, but rather was associated with those who had made the complaint, his claim of victimisation was nonetheless valid.

The Human Rights Act 1998

Article 14 Discrimination

The approach to Article 14 claims is rather more fluid than that which applies under the EqA. Article 14 provides that:

> **Article 14 ECHR**
>
> The enjoyment of the rights and freedoms set forth in this Convention shall be secured without discrimination on any ground such as sex, race, colour, language, religion, political or other opinion, national or social origin, association with a national minority, property, birth or other status.

***R (SC) v Secretary of State for Work and Pensions* [2021] UKSC 26, [2022] AC 223**

Lord Reed, with whom the rest of the SC agreed, at §37 adopted the approach to Article 14 summarised by the Grand Chamber of the ECtHR in *Carson v UK* (App No 42185/05, judgment of 16 March 2010) (2010) 51 EHRR 13 §61 as follows:

> (1) The court has established in its case law that only differences in treatment based on an identifiable characteristic, or 'status', are capable of amounting to discrimination within the meaning of art 14.
> (2) Moreover, in order for an issue to arise under art 14 there must be a difference in the treatment of persons in analogous, or relevantly similar, situations.
> (3) Such a difference of treatment is discriminatory if it has no objective and reasonable justification; in other words, if it does not pursue a legitimate aim or if there is not a reasonable relationship of proportionality between the means employed and the aim sought to be realised.
> (4) The contracting state enjoys a margin of appreciation in assessing whether and to what extent differences in otherwise similar situations justify a different treatment. The scope of this margin will vary according to the circumstances, the subject matter and the background.

As Lord Reed made clear in *SC*, Article 14 is 'parasitic' in as much as it does not amount to a free-standing prohibition on discrimination, being concerned only with discrimination *in the exercise of other Convention rights*. Protocol 12, Article 1 ECHR provides a free-standing prohibition on discrimination, but it has not been signed or ratified by the UK and so will not be further discussed. In order to succeed in an Article 14 claim a person will have to show discrimination on a protected ground 'within the ambit of another Convention right'. This is further discussed in Chapter 4.

The list of protected grounds in Article 14 is not exhaustive. 'Discrimination' is not defined in Article 14 but may be direct, indirect or '*Thlimmenos*' discrimination, discussed below, and it is possible that new forms of discrimination may be recognised. Direct and indirect discrimination are not subject to the same parameters as imposed by the EqA and all discrimination is capable at least in theory of justification.[107]

The jurisprudence relating to Article 14 has developed significantly in recent years. Not until 2008, with its decision in *DH v Czech Republic* (2008) 47 EHRR 3, did the ECtHR find a breach of Article 14 by way of what it identified as indirect discrimination, though it had indicated as early as 1968 that such a claim might be possible.[108] Meanwhile it had, in *Thlimmenos v Greece* (2001) 31 EHRR 411, accepted that Article 14 might require differential treatment of people in relevantly different situations, as well as similar treatment of those whose situations were relevantly similar. More recently, in *Opuz v Turkey* (2010) 50

[107] Though the justification of direct race discrimination other than positive (ameliorative) discrimination is unlikely to be possible in practice: see *Timishev v Russia* (2007) 44 EHRR 37, §58. The domestic courts initially adopted a formulaic approach to Article 14 cases (see eg *Wandsworth BC v Michalak* [2002] EWCA Civ 271, [2003] 1 WLR 617 §20) but in *R (Carson and Reynolds) v SSWP* [2005] UKHL 37, [2006] 1 AC 173, Lord Nicholls at §3 advocated a 'simple and non-technical' approach which (1) ascertained whether the alleged discrimination is in connection with a Convention right and on a protected ground and (2) determined 'whether the alleged discrimination, that is, the difference in treatment of which complaint is made, can withstand scrutiny': see also *AL (Serbia) v SSHD* [2008] UKHL 42, [2008] WLR 143, §24 and *Ghaidan v Mendoza* [2004] UKHL 30, [2004] 2 AC 557, §§133–134.

[108] *Belgian Linguistic Case (No 2)* (1968) 1 EHRR 252 §4.

EHRR 28 the ECtHR had relied on the jurisprudence developed under the Convention on the Elimination of all forms of Discrimination against Women and other international legal provisions in recognising violence against women as a form of sex discrimination.[109]

The focus of this book is on the domestic case law, but consideration of Article 14 requires consideration of the case law of the ECtHR as well as that of the domestic courts. Having said that, what follows is a very outline sketch of a large body of law.

Positive Obligations

Article 14, like the other provisions of the ECHR, is directed primarily towards *state* actions. The provision may also be breached, however, where the state fails to prevent or to remedy discrimination by others.

ECtHR, *Guide on Article 14 of the European Convention on Human Rights and on Article 1 of Protocol No. 12 to the Convention*[110]

15. The Court [has] pointed out the 'horizontal effect' of Article 14, meaning that the principle of non-discrimination may also apply in purely private situations. Indeed, the Court has held that it could not remain passive where a national court's interpretation of a legal act – be it a testamentary disposition, a private contract, a public document, a statutory provision or an administrative practice – appeared unreasonable, arbitrary or blatantly inconsistent with the prohibition of discrimination enshrined in Article 14 and more broadly with the principles underlying the Convention[111] …

16. In other cases, the Court found that the Contracting States had not taken the necessary measures in order to prevent or punish discrimination between private parties. In *Danilenkov and Others v. Russia* (2014) 58 EHRR 19, 2009, for example, the State failed to afford effective judicial protection against discrimination on the ground of trade-union membership to employees on strike who were fired by their employer.

17. In cases concerning discriminatory violence emanating either from State agents or private individuals, State authorities have been required to conduct an effective and adequate investigation by ascertaining whether there were discriminatory motives and whether feelings of hatred or prejudice based on an individual's personal characteristic played a role in the events.[[112]]

18. Finally, the failure to enforce a judgment acknowledging gender discrimination against a working mother (*García Mateos v Spain*,[[113]] 2013), the refusal to award compensation to a serviceman for discrimination with respect to his right to parental leave (*Hulea v Romania*,[[114]] 2012) and the failure to enforce a judgment of the Court finding a violation of Article 14 (*Sidabras and Others v. Lithuania* [(2006) 42 EHRR 6], 2004) have also resulted in breaches of Article 14.

[109] See also *Unal Tekeli v Turkey* (2006) 42 EHRR 53, §60 in which the ECtHR referred to CEDAW and the ICCPR in determining an Article 14 claim. In *R (SC) v SSWP* [2021] UKSC 26, [2022] AC 223 the Supreme Court emphasised that international law had no independent effect in domestic law but *Opuz* remains illustrative of the fact that such law can find its way into domestic law through the ECHR, at least for as long as the HRA remains in place.

[110] Available at https://www.echr.coe.int/Pages/home.aspx?p=caselaw/analysis/guides&c.

[111] Citing *Pla and Puncernau v Andorra* (2006) 42 EHRR 25 in which the Court ruled that the provision may require a state to take steps in relation to a will which excluded adopted children.

[112] Citing *Abdu v Bulgaria*, App No 38285/09, unreported, judgment of 19 February 2013 §44; *Milanovic v Serbia* (2014) 58 EHRR 33, §90; *Gldani Congregation of Jehovah's Witnesses v Georgia* (2008) 46 EHRR 30; *Identoba v Georgia* (2018) 66 EHRR 17.

[113] App No 38285/09, unreported, judgment of 19 February 2013.

[114] App No 33411/05/09, unreported, judgment of 2 October 2012.

Protected Grounds

Article 14 provides a non-exhaustive list of protected grounds: '*any ground such as* sex, race, colour, language, religion, political or other opinion, national or social origin, association with a national minority, property, birth *or other status*' (emphasis added). It is clear that the grounds protected by Article 14 include age,[115] disability,[116] gender identity[117] and sexual orientation.[118] The fact that these grounds are not enumerated does not mean that they are any less protected than those which are. On the contrary, the ECtHR has recognised a number of 'suspect grounds' which are afforded enhanced protection from discrimination. Disability[119] and sexual orientation[120] are among these grounds as are sex,[121] religion,[122] nationality[123] and, in particular, race.[124] The justification of discrimination on these grounds will generally require 'very weighty reasons', though this may vary according to the context (see further p 101ff below).

Grounds such as disability, sexual orientation, illegitimacy and marital status are well recognised as falling within Article 14, but Article 14 claims may also be brought to challenge differential treatment of different categories of soldier,[125] prisoner[126] or landowner,[127] or associated with place of residence.[128] The boundaries imposed by 'other status' are generous but they are not without limit. In *Kjeldsen, Busk Madsen and Pedersen v Denmark* (1976) 1 EHRR 711 §56 the ECtHR asked whether the ground on which reliance was placed was a 'personal characteristic ("status") by which persons or groups of persons are distinguishable from each other'. Domestic courts became preoccupied at one stage over whether the ground relied upon was created by the rule under challenge, as distinct from existing separately; in *R (Clift & Hindawi) v SSHD* [2006] UKHL 54, [2017] 1 AC 484 the SC ruled that Article 14 did not regulate the differential treatment of prisoners serving long-term determinate sentences from that of prisoners serving life sentences or shorter determinate sentences. One of the reasons for which the Court reached its conclusion was that the status on which the prisoners sought to rely was created by the very legislation they were seeking to challenge and had no independent existence.[129] In *Clift v UK* (App No 7205/07) [2010] ECHR 7205/07, the ECtHR ruled that Article 14 did apply. The Court gave a broad

[115] eg *Schwizgebel v Switzerland* App No 25762/07, unreported, judgment of 15 June 2010.

[116] eg *Glor v Switzerland* App No 13444/04, unreported, judgment of 30 April 2009.

[117] eg *Goodwin v UK* (2002) 35 EHRR 18 (GC).

[118] *Mouta v Portugal* (2001) 31 EHRR 47; *EB v France* (2001) 47 EHRR 21.

[119] *Glor v Switzerland*, n 116 above.

[120] *EB v France*, n 118 above.

[121] *Abdulaziz, Cabales and Balkandali v UK* (1985) 7 EHRR 471.

[122] *Hoffmann v Austria* (1993) 17 EHRR 293, though note the doubt expressed about this by the SC in *R (Cornerstone (North East) Fostering & Adoption Services) v Ofsted* [2021] EWCA Civ 1390, [2022] 2 All ER 516 §129, discussed in Ch 10.

[123] *Gaygusuz v Austria* (1996) 23 EHRR 364. Also illegitimacy: *Marckx v Belgium* (1979) 2 EHRR 330; and marital status: *Sommerfeld v Germany*, (2004) 38 EHRR 35.

[124] In *East African Asians v UK* (1973) 3 EHRR 76, discussed in Ch 7, the European Commission suggested that race discrimination could amount to inhuman and degrading treatment contrary to Art 3 ECHR and in *Timishev v Russia*, n 107 above, the ECtHR stated at §58 that 'no difference in treatment which is based exclusively or to a decisive extent on a person's ethnic origin is capable of being objectively justified in a contemporary democratic society built on the principles of pluralism and respect for different cultures'.

[125] *Engel v Netherlands* (1976) 1 EHRR 647.

[126] *Clift v UK* (App No 7205/07) [2010] ECHR 7205/07.

[127] *James v UK* (1986) 8 EHRR 123, *Chassagnou v France* (2000) 29 EHRR 615.

[128] *R (Carson) v SSWP*, n 107 above.

[129] Lord Bingham §28, Lord Hope §§45–47.

meaning to 'any other status' in Article 14, rejected (at §56) earlier suggestions that it must relate to innate or inherent characteristics, drew attention to the inclusion within Article 14 of 'property' and stated at §60 that 'where a state provides for rights falling within the ambit of the Convention which go beyond the minimum guarantees set out therein, those supplementary rights [must be] applied fairly and consistently to all those within its jurisdiction unless a difference of treatment is objectively justified'. The jurisprudence was considered by the SC in the *Criminal Injuries* case and a broad approach adopted.

***R (A) v Criminal Injuries Compensation Authority* [2021] UKSC 27, [2021] 1 WLR 3746**

Lord Lloyd-Jones (for the Court) (having cited Clift v UK):

43. In *R (Haney) v Secretary of State for Justice* [2014] UKSC 66, [2015] AC 1344 (para [52]), Lord Mance and Lord Hughes observed of [§60 of *Clift v UK*] that, if read literally, it might eliminate any consideration of status. However, in *Mathieson v Secretary of State for Work and Pensions* the Supreme Court accepted this aspect of the judgment in *Clift v UK*. (See further *R (Stott) v Secretary for State for Justice* [2018] UKSC 59, [2020] AC 51 (para [185]) per Lord Hodge.) Lord Wilson observed (at para [22]) that, following *Clift v UK*, it was 'clear that, if the alleged discrimination falls within the scope of a Convention right, the ECtHR is reluctant to conclude that nevertheless the applicant has no relevant status, with the result that the inquiry into discrimination cannot proceed'.

44. Before us Ms Kaufmann submits that the grounds for the difference in treatment in the appellants' case can be characterised in two ways depending upon who are the comparators:

(1) As against other victims of crime who, like them have unspent custodial or community sentences, their status is that they are victims of trafficking.

(2) As against other victims of trafficking, their status is that they have unspent custodial or community sentences …

Victims of trafficking

45. On behalf of the respondents Mr Collins draws attention to the observation of Lord Neuberger (with whom Lords Hope, Rodger, Walker and Mance agreed) in the House of Lords in *R (RJM) v Secretary of State for Work and Pensions* [2008] UKHL 63, [2009] AC 311 (para [45]) that: 'the concept of "personal characteristic" (not surprisingly, like the concept of status) generally requires one to concentrate on what somebody is, rather than what he is doing or what is being done to him. …'

… Mr Collins submits that to seek to define an 'other status' by reference to being a victim of crime can only be a reference to what is being or has been done to the individual concerned. However, this observation by Lord Neuberger needs to be considered in the context of *RJM* where it was held (at paras [45]–[47]) that homelessness is an 'other status' within art 14, even if adopted by choice … Furthermore, *RJM* was decided before the decision of the ECtHR in *Clift v UK* indicated a relaxation of the requirement of status for this purpose which has been reflected in more recent decisions of the Supreme Court.

46. In the light of this more generous approach to status, I have no doubt that being a victim of trafficking does constitute a status for this purpose. Although it is an acquired characteristic resulting from something done as opposed to being inherent or innate, it is plainly a personal identifiable characteristic to which many important legal consequences attach.

Persons with a relevant unspent conviction

48. … The respondents submit that the fact that a person has, in the past, committed an offence and received a particular type of sentence cannot create a personal characteristic which distinguishes that person from others [citing *Clift*] …

51. In *R (Haney) v Secretary of State for Justice* one of the claimants, a serving prisoner, invoked art 14 claiming that he had been discriminated against by the prison authorities in that they prioritised the movement to open prisons of prisoners whose tariff periods had already expired, as opposed to those prisoners whose tariff periods had not. Lord Mance and Lord Hughes, with whom the other members of the Supreme Court agreed, noted the different views taken on the issue of status by the House of Lords in *R (Clift)* and by the ECtHR in *Clift v UK*. They observed (at para [53]) that in light of the ECtHR decision, they saw 'some force in the submission that the difference between pre and post-tariff prisoners should now be taken to represent a relevant difference in status.' However, they did not need to decide the point because the difference in treatment was justified.

52. More recently, in *R (Stott) v Secretary for State for Justice* the Supreme Court considered the rule that an offender serving an extended determinate sentence only became eligible for release on parole after serving two thirds of the appropriate custodial term whereas other prisoners serving determinate sentences became eligible after serving half of their sentence. It held, Lord Carnwath dissenting, that the difference in treatment of prisoners with extended determinate sentences was a difference on the ground of 'other status' within art 14 …

57. The recent jurisprudence in Strasbourg and in the Supreme Court has shown a significant shift towards taking a broad view of status under art 14 and, as a result, the concept of 'other status' must now be generously interpreted. In this context, it seems to me artificial to attempt any longer to distinguish between the gravity of an offence and the characteristics of an individual offender … No doubt, what an offender has done has led to a particular sentence being imposed which reflects the culpability of the offender's conduct, but once imposed the sentence has a significance independent of what the offender has done. This applies with equal force to a custodial sentence and to a community sentence, each of which has its own incidents and consequences. In my view, having an unspent conviction is an identifiable, personal characteristic. Even when the custodial sentence has been served or the community sentence completed, the sentence continues to have significance. As long as a conviction remains unspent it has incidents and consequences, in particular obligations of disclosure, which continue to have far-reaching implications for those who have been convicted.

58. There is, however, a second issue in relation to status which must be addressed in this context. This has been termed 'the individual existence condition'. In the present case the respondents submit [in reliance on *Clift*] that the status founded on unspent convictions for which the appellants contend exists solely by reference to the terms of the legislation which they are challenging. They submit that it has no independent character so as to form any identifiable group of people, as distinct from those who are excluded by the terms of the CICS itself …

60. When the matter came before the ECtHR in *Clift v UK*, that court was dismissive of the point stating at para 60:

> 'Further, the Court is not persuaded that the Government's argument that the treatment of which the applicant complains must exist independently of the "other status" upon which it is based finds any clear support in its case-law. …'…

61. The issue is nevertheless one of importance and since *Clift v UK* it has reappeared frequently in domestic cases. The language of art 14 requires that discrimination should be on the basis of one of a number of identified grounds 'or other status'. If status can be defined solely by the difference in treatment complained of, the words 'on any ground such as …' would add nothing to art 14. (See *R (Clift)*, para [27] per Lord Bingham; *Stott*, para [210] per Lady Hale.) As a result, notwithstanding the judgment of the ECtHR in *Clift v UK*, the position before domestic courts in this jurisdiction remains far from clear.

[Having considered the decisions in *R v Docherty* [2016] UKSC 62, [2017] 1 WLR 181, in which the Supreme Court ruled that, assuming that status as a prisoner subject to a particular regime could in some circumstances amount to sufficient status to bring Art 14 into question (as in *Clift*), it could not do so if the suggested status is defined *entirely* by the alleged discrimination and in Stott] ...

65. In the present appeal the Supreme Court has not been invited to depart from its earlier decision in *Docherty*. In my view, however, it is not necessary to resolve the issue in the present appeal because *Docherty* is distinguishable in this regard. In the present case, to employ the wording of Lord Hope in *R (Clift)* at paras [67]–[68], the distinguishing feature or characteristic which enables persons with an unspent conviction which resulted in a custodial or community sentence to be singled out for separate treatment had been identified as a personal characteristic before it was used for this purpose in the CICS. The distinction drawn by the CICS is between two groups of persons with unspent convictions. That distinction is defined by paras 3 and 4 of Annex D but it does not derive entirely from that provision. There are other consequences of being an offender with an unspent conviction under para 3 which derive from the Rehabilitation of Offenders Act 1974 and other statutes which set out the differing implications of various unspent convictions. As Ms Kaufmann put it in argument, having an unspent conviction within para 3 has significance independent of the CICS. The CICS simply adds a new consequence.

66. I should add, however, that I agree with the observations of Lord Reed on the independent existence issue in his judgment in *R (SC) v Secretary of State for Work and Pensions* [2021] UKSC 26, [2022] AC 223 (paras [69]–[71]) ... Article 14 draws a distinction between relevant status and difference in treatment and the former cannot be defined solely by the latter. There must be a ground for the difference of treatment in terms of a characteristic which is something more than a mere description of the difference in treatment. In the present case the status of the appellants as persons with unspent relevant convictions does, in my view, have a significance independent of the CICS. However, I agree with Lord Reed that there is no requirement that the status should have legal or social significance for other purposes or in contexts other than the difference in treatment of which complaint is made ...

Discrimination

As mentioned above, 'discrimination' under Article 14 is a relatively flexible concept which can accommodate indirect as well as direct discrimination and '*Thlimmenos*' discrimination. These are discussed in turn.

Direct Discrimination

Direct discrimination occurs if there is different treatment (on one or more protected grounds) of individuals who are in comparable situations.

***Carson v UK* (App No 42184/05), judgment of 10 March 2010), (2010) 51 EHRR 13 (Grand Chamber)**

The applicants were former residents of the UK now living abroad who were in receipt of state pensions. Where such individuals were resident in countries with which the UK had reached reciprocal arrangements they would have had their pensions adjusted annually to allow for inflation. The applicants were all resident in countries with which the UK had no such arrangements and so their pensions were frozen at the level paid immediately upon their retirement. They claimed that this breached their Article 14 rights taken with A1P1. Their claims failed in the domestic courts and before the ECtHR.

> 83. … the Court has established in its case law that, in order for an issue to arise under art.14, the first condition is that there must be a difference in the treatment of persons in relevantly similar situations.
>
> 84. The applicants' principal argument in support of their claim to be in a relevantly similar situation to pensioners who receive up-rating is that they also have worked in the United Kingdom and paid compulsory contributions to the National Insurance Fund. However, in common with the national courts and the Chamber, the Grand Chamber considers that the applicants' argument misconceives the relationship between National Insurance contributions and the state pension. Unlike private pension schemes, where premiums are paid into a specific fund and where those premiums are directly linked to the expected benefit returns, National Insurance contributions have no exclusive link to retirement pensions. Instead, they form a source of part of the revenue which pays for a whole range of social security benefits, including incapacity benefits, maternity allowances, widow's benefits, bereavement benefits and the National Health Service. Where necessary, the National Insurance fund can be topped-up with money derived from the ordinary taxation of those resident in the United Kingdom, including pensioners. The variety of funding methods of welfare benefits and the interlocking nature of the benefits and taxation systems have already been recognised by the Court. This complex and interlocking system makes it impossible to isolate the payment of National Insurance contributions as a sufficient ground for equating the position of pensioners who receive up-rating and those, like the applicants, who do not …
>
> 85. The Court does not, therefore, consider that the payment of National Insurance contributions is alone sufficient to place the applicants in a relevantly similar position to all other pensioners, regardless of their country of residence. Moreover, in relation to the comparison with pensioners living in the United Kingdom, it cannot be ignored that social security benefits, including state pensions, are part of a system of social welfare which exist to ensure certain minimum standards of living for residents of the United Kingdom …
>
> 86. Given that the pension system is, therefore, primarily designed to serve the needs of those resident in the United Kingdom, it is hard to draw any genuine comparison with the position of pensioners living elsewhere, because of the range of economic and social variables which apply from country to country. Thus, the value of the pension may be affected by any one or a combination of differences in, for example, rates of inflation, comparative costs of living, interest rates, rates of economic growth, exchange rates between the local currency and sterling (in which the pension is universally paid), social security arrangements and taxation systems. As the CA noted, it is inescapable that the grant of the up-rate to all pensioners, wherever they might have chosen to live, would have random effects. Furthermore, as noted by the domestic courts, as non-residents the applicants do not contribute to the United Kingdom's economy; in particular, they pay no UK tax to offset the cost of any increase in the pension.
>
> 87. Nor does the Court consider that the applicants are in a relevantly similar position to pensioners living in countries with which the United Kingdom has concluded a bilateral agreement providing for up-rating. Those living in reciprocal agreement countries are treated differently from those living elsewhere because an agreement has been entered into; and an agreement has been entered into because the United Kingdom considered it to be in its interests ….
>
> 89. … it would be extraordinary if the fact of entering into bilateral arrangements in the social security sphere had the consequence of creating an obligation to confer the same advantages on all others living in all other countries. Such a conclusion would effectively undermine the right of states to enter into reciprocal agreements and their interest in so doing.

> 90. In summary, therefore, the Court does not consider that the applicants, who live outside the United Kingdom in countries which are not party to reciprocal social security agreements with the United Kingdom providing for pension up-rating, are in a relevantly similar position to residents of the United Kingdom or of countries which are party to such agreements. It follows that there has been no discrimination and, therefore, no violation of art.14 taken in conjunction with [A1P1].

***Burden v UK* (App No 13378/05, judgment of 29 April 2008) (2008) 47 EHRR 38 (Grand Chamber)**

The applicants, unmarried sisters who had lived together all their lives, sought to challenge inheritance tax rules that privileged married and civilly partnered people over others. They claimed that their rights under Article 14 and A1P1 were violated by the fact that they were not entitled to any similar exemption.

> 60. The Court has established in its case law that in order for an issue to arise under Art.14 there must be a difference in the treatment of persons in relevantly similar situations … The contracting state enjoys a margin of appreciation in assessing whether and to what extent differences in otherwise similar situations justify a different treatment, and this margin is usually wide when it comes to general measures of economic or social strategy [citing *Stec v UK* (2006) 43 EHRR 47 §§51–52] …
>
> 62. … the relationship between siblings is qualitatively of a different nature to that between married couples and homosexual civil partners under the United Kingdom's Civil Partnership Act. The very essence of the connection between siblings is consanguinity, whereas one of the defining characteristics of a marriage or Civil Partnership Act union is that it is forbidden to close family members. The fact that the applicants have chosen to live together all their adult lives, as do many married and Civil Partnership Act couples, does not alter this essential difference between the two types of relationship.
>
> 63. Moreover, the Grand Chamber notes that it has already held that marriage confers a special status on those who enter into it. The exercise of the right to marry is protected by Art.12 of the Convention and gives rise to social, personal and legal consequences …
>
> 65. As with marriage, the Grand Chamber considers that the legal consequences of civil partnership under the 2004 Act, which couples expressly and deliberately decide to incur, set these types of relationship apart from other forms of cohabitation. Rather than the length or the supportive nature of the relationship, what is determinative is the existence of a public undertaking, carrying with it a body of rights and obligations of a contractual nature. Just as there can be no analogy between married and Civil Partnership Act couples, on one hand, and heterosexual or homosexual couples who choose to live together but not to become husband and wife or civil partners, on the other hand, the absence of such a legally binding agreement between the applicants renders their relationship of cohabitation, despite its long duration, fundamentally different to that of a married or civil partnership couple. This view is unaffected by the fact that … Member States have adopted a variety of different rules of succession as between survivors of a marriage, civil partnership and those in a close family relationship and have similarly adopted different policies as regards the grant of inheritance tax exemptions to the various categories of survivor; states, in principle, remaining free to devise different rules in the field of taxation policy.
>
> 66. In conclusion, therefore, the Grand Chamber considers that the applicants, as cohabiting sisters, cannot be compared for the purposes of Art.14 with a married or Civil Partnership Act couple. It follows that there has been no discrimination and, therefore, no violation of Art.14 taken in conjunction with Art.1 of Protocol No.1.

'Comparable' does not mean *identical*[130] and, whereas the domestic courts at one stage took a very rigid stance on the question of comparability,[131] they have now adapted to the more flexible approach of the ECtHR, which tends to ask whether any differences in otherwise similar situations justify the differential treatment challenged.[132]

***AL (Serbia) v Secretary of State for the Home Department* [2008] UKHL 42, [2008] 1 WLR 1434**

The claimants had arrived in the UK as unaccompanied minors seeking asylum. They sought to challenge an amnesty granted by the SS by which families who had been in the UK for three or more years were given indefinite leave to remain. The amnesty did not apply to those such as the claimants who had no family in the UK. One of the arguments put for the SS was that the claimants were not comparably situated with those with whom they sought to compare themselves. This attempt was rejected by the HL which accepted, however, that the different treatment was justified.

Baroness Hale, with whom Lord Scott agreed:

> 23. This instantly makes the art 14 right different from our domestic anti-discrimination laws. These focus on less favourable treatment rather than a difference in treatment. They also draw a distinction between direct and indirect discrimination. Direct discrimination, for example treating a woman less favourably than a man, or a black person less favourably than a white, cannot be justified. This means that a great deal of attention has to be paid to whether or not the woman and the man, real or hypothetical, with whom she wishes to compare herself are in truly comparable situations. The law requires that their circumstances be the same or not materially different from one another.
>
> 24. It will be noted, however, that the classic Strasbourg statements of the law do not place any emphasis on the identification of an exact comparator. They ask whether 'differences in otherwise similar situations justify a different treatment'. Lord Nicholls of Birkenhead put it this way in *R (on the application of Carson) v Secretary of State for Work and Pensions* [§3]:
>
>> the essential, question for the court is whether the alleged discrimination, that is, the difference in treatment of which complaint is made, can withstand scrutiny. Sometimes the answer to this question will be plain. There may be such an obvious, relevant difference between the claimant and those with whom he seeks to compare himself that their situations cannot be regarded as analogous. Sometimes, where the position is not so clear, a different approach is called for. Then the court's scrutiny may best be directed at considering whether the differentiation has a legitimate aim and whether the means chosen to achieve the aim is appropriate and not disproportionate in its adverse impact.
>
> 25. Nevertheless, as the very helpful analysis of the Strasbourg case law on art 14, carried out on behalf of Mr AL, shows, in only a handful of cases has the court found that the persons with whom the complainant wishes to compare himself are not in a relevantly similar or analogous position (around 4·435%). This bears out the observation of Professor David Feldman, in *Civil Liberties and Human Rights in England and Wales* (2nd edn, 2002), p 144, quoted by Lord Walker in *Carson*'s case at [65]:
>
>> The way the Court approaches it is not to look for identity of position between different cases, but to ask whether the applicant and the people who are treated differently are in

[130] *Rasmussen v Denmark* (1985) 7 EHRR 371.

[131] See eg *Wandsworth v Michalak*, n 107 above.

[132] *R (Carson) v SSWP*, n 107 above §3, *AL (Serbia) v SSHD*, n 107 above §24.

> 'analogous' situations. This will to some extent depend on whether there is an objective and reasonable justification for the difference in treatment, which overlaps with the questions about the acceptability of the ground and the justifiability of the difference in treatment. This is why, as van Dijk and van Hoof observe ... 'In most instances of the Strasbourg case law ... the comparability test is glossed over, and the emphasis is (almost) completely on the justification test'.
>
> A recent exception, *Burden v UK* ... is instructive. Two sisters, who had lived together for many years, complained that when one of them died, the survivor would be required to pay inheritance tax on their home, whereas a surviving spouse or civil partner would not ... A Grand Chamber found, by fifteen votes to two, that the siblings were not in an analogous situation to spouses or civil partners, first because consanguinity and affinity are different kinds of relationship, and secondly because of the legal consequences which the latter brings. But Judges Bratza and Björgvinsson, who concurred in the result, would have preferred the approach of the Chamber; and the two dissenting judges thought that the two sorts of couple were in an analogous situation. This suggests that, unless there are very obvious relevant differences between the two situations, it is better to concentrate on the reasons for the difference in treatment and whether they amount to an objective and reasonable justification ...
>
> 27. There are, also, as Lord Walker recognised in *Carson*'s case, dangers in regarding differences between two people, which are inherent in a prohibited ground and cannot or should not be changed, as meaning that the situations are not analogous. For example, it would be no answer to a claim of sex discrimination to say that a man and a woman are not in an analogous situation because one can get pregnant and the other cannot. This is something that neither can be expected to change. If it is wrong to discriminate between them as individuals, it is wrong to focus on the personal characteristics which are inherent in their protected status to argue that their situations are not analogous. That is the essential reason why, in *Ghaidan v Godin-Mendoza* [2004] UKHL 30, [2004] 2 AC 557, the argument that same sex couples were not in an analogous position to opposite sex couples, because they could not have children together, did not succeed.'

Indirect Discrimination

As above, the ECtHR was slow to apply the concept of indirect discrimination under Article 14, though it suggested from the first Article 14 decision that this form of discrimination fell within the article. In the *Belgian Linguistics* case the ECtHR had referred to the 'aims and effects' of discriminatory measures[133] and in *Marckx v Belgium* (1979) 2 EHRR 330, §40 to measures whose 'object or result' was discriminatory. In *Abdulaziz, Cabales and Balkandali v UK* (1985) 7 EHRR 471, however, the ECtHR rejected a claim that an immigration rule which required fiancés to have met each other indirectly discriminated against people from the Indian sub-continent, where arranged marriages were commonplace on the basis that the rule's 'main purpose was to prevent evasion of the rules by means of bogus marriages or engagements'. The Court there did not proceed to ask whether the aim was justified notwithstanding the discriminatory impact of the rule, thus suggesting that Article 14 did not in fact extend to indirect discrimination.

In *Jordan v UK* (2003) 37 EHRR 2 the ECtHR did not exclude the possibility that 'a general policy or measure [with] disproportionately prejudicial effects on a particular group

[133] *Belgian Linguistic Case (No 2)*, n 108 above.

… may be considered as discriminatory notwithstanding that it is not specifically aimed or directed at that group' (§154), though it did not accept that statistics showing that the overwhelming majority of people killed by members of the security forces in Northern Ireland were Catholic/nationalist community, and that prosecutions and convictions were rare, could 'in themselves disclose a practice which could be classified as discriminatory within the meaning of Art.14'.[134] In *Hoogendijk v Netherlands* (2005) 40 EHRR SE 22 the ECtHR ruled 'where an applicant is able to show, *on the basis of undisputed official statistics*, the existence of a prima facie indication that a specific rule – although formulated in a neutral manner – in fact affects a clearly higher percentage of women than men, it is for the respondent government to show that this is the result of objective factors unrelated to any discrimination on grounds of sex' (emphasis added). And in *Adami v Malta* (2007) 44 EHRR 3 the ECtHR held on the basis of huge statistical disparities between the number of men and women on jury lists and called for jury service in Malta[135] that there had been differential treatment of men and women in this context. The Court did not set out the criteria for a finding of indirect discrimination, but stated at §76 that 'a discrimination potentially contrary to the Convention may result not only from a legislative measure, but also from a *de facto* situation', referred to the staggering statistical disparities and concluded at §78 that 'the civic obligation of jury service had been placed predominantly on males. Therefore, there had been a difference in treatment between two groups – men and women – which, with respect to this duty, were in a similar situation'. The following year the Court reached its decision in the following important case.

***DH v Czech Republic* (App No 57325/00, judgment of 13 November 2007) (2008) 47 EHRR 3 (Grand Chamber)**

This was a challenge to the massive disproportion in Roma children placed in special schools in the Czech Republic; in one town 2.26 per cent of primary school children, but 56 per cent of those in special schools, were Roma and 50.3 per cent of Roma children, and 1.8 per cent of non-Roma children, were assigned to special schools. The applicants' parents had consented – in some cases requested – their placement in special schools, decisions on placement being taken by headteachers of the schools taking into account the results of psychological tests.

> 178. … According to [the Court's] established case law, proof may follow from the coexistence of sufficiently strong, clear and concordant inferences or of similar unrebutted presumptions of fact. Moreover, the level of persuasion necessary for reaching a particular conclusion and, in this connection, the distribution of the burden of proof are intrinsically linked to the specificity of the facts, the nature of the allegation made and the Convention right at stake.
>
> 179. … In certain circumstances, where the events in issue lie wholly, or in large part, within the exclusive knowledge of the authorities, the burden of proof may be regarded as resting on the authorities to provide a satisfactory and convincing explanation. In the case of *Nachova* [*v Bulgaria* 2004) 39 EHRR 37] the Court did not rule out requiring a respondent Government to disprove an arguable allegation of discrimination in certain cases, even though it considered that it would be difficult to do so in that particular case in which the allegation was that an act

[134] See similarly *McShane v* (2002) 35 EHRR 23; *Hoogendijk v Netherlands* (2005) 40 EHRR SE 22.

[135] There were three times as many men on the lists, only 3% of those placed on the list in the previous years had been women and less than 3% of the previous year's jurors had been women.

of violence had been motivated by racial prejudice. It noted in that connection that in the legal systems of many countries proof of the discriminatory effect of a policy, decision or practice would dispense with the need to prove intent in respect of alleged discrimination in employment or in the provision of services.

180. As to whether statistics can constitute evidence, the Court has in the past stated that statistics could not in themselves disclose a practice which could be classified as discriminatory [citing *Jordan*]. However, in more recent cases on the question of discrimination, in which the applicants alleged a difference in the effect of a general measure or de facto situation [citing *Hoogendilk* and *Adami*], the Court relied extensively on statistics produced by the parties to establish a difference in treatment between two groups (men and women) in similar situations …

181. Lastly, as noted in previous cases, the vulnerable position of Roma/Gypsies means that special consideration should be given to their needs and their different lifestyle both in the relevant regulatory framework and in reaching decisions in particular cases [citing *Chapman v UK* (2001) 33 EHRR 18] …

184. The Court has already accepted in previous cases that a difference in treatment may take the form of disproportionately prejudicial effects of a general policy or measure which, though couched in neutral terms, discriminates against a group [citing *Jordan* and *Hoogendilk*]. In accordance with, for instance, Directives 97/80 and 2000/43, the definition provided by ECRI, such a situation may amount to 'indirect discrimination', which does not necessarily require a discriminatory intent.

185. It was common ground that the impugned difference in treatment did not result from the wording of the statutory provisions on placements in special schools in force at the material time. Accordingly, the issue in the instant case is whether the manner in which the legislation was applied in practice resulted in a disproportionate number of Roma children – including the applicants – being placed in special schools without justification, and whether such children were thereby placed at a significant disadvantage.

186. As mentioned above, the Court has noted in previous cases that applicants may have difficulty in proving discriminatory treatment. In order to guarantee those concerned the effective protection of their rights, less strict evidential rules should apply in cases of alleged indirect discrimination.

187. On this point, the Court observes that Directives 97/80 and 2000/43 stipulate that persons who consider themselves wronged because the principle of equal treatment has not been applied to them may establish, before a domestic authority, by any means, including on the basis of statistical evidence, facts from which it may be presumed that there has been discrimination. The recent case law of the Court of Justice of the European Communities shows that it permits claimants to rely on statistical evidence and the national courts to take such evidence into account where it is valid and significant …

188. In these circumstances, the Court considers that when it comes to assessing the impact of a measure or practice on an individual or group, statistics which appear on critical examination to be reliable and significant will be sufficient to constitute the prima facie evidence the applicant is required to produce. This does not, however, mean that indirect discrimination cannot be proved without statistical evidence …

[The Court went on to discuss the applicants' statistical evidence and evidence provided by third parties which indicated that the disparities complained of were not confined to a single town but were representative of the national picture.]

193. In the Court's view, the latter figures, which do not relate solely to the Ostrava region and therefore provide a more general picture, show that, even if the exact percentage of Roma

children in special schools at the material time remains difficult to establish, their number was disproportionately high. Moreover, Roma pupils formed a majority of the pupils in special schools. Despite being couched in neutral terms, the relevant statutory provisions therefore had considerably more impact in practice on Roma children than on non-Roma children and resulted in statistically disproportionate numbers of placements of the former in special schools.

194. Where it has been shown that legislation produces such a discriminatory effect, the Grand Chamber considers that, as with cases concerning employment or the provision of services, it is not necessary in cases in the educational sphere to prove any discriminatory intent on the part of the relevant authorities.

195. In these circumstances, the evidence submitted by the applicants can be regarded as sufficiently reliable and significant to give rise to a strong presumption of indirect discrimination. The burden of proof must therefore shift to the Government, which must show that the difference in the impact of the legislation was the result of objective factors unrelated to ethnic origin.

Since the decision in *DH v Czech Republic* the ECtHR has found 'a breach' of Article 14 by reason of indirect discrimination in *Biao v Denmark* (2017) 64 EHRR 1, which concerned legislation on family reunion which favoured people who were Danish nationals at birth or had been Dutch nationals for at least 28 years. In *R(SC)* the SC considered an Article 14 challenge to the restriction of the individual element of child tax credit to an amount calculated by reference to two children. Lord Reed, with whom the other members of the SC agreed, referred to the gradual recognition of indirect discrimination by the ECtHR and to the decisions of the ECtHR in *DH* and *Baio*[136] and summarised that Court's approach as being (§53) that once the claimant established 'that a neutrally formulated measure affects a disproportionate number of members of a group of persons sharing a characteristic which is alleged to be the ground of discrimination, so as to give rise to a presumption of indirect discrimination … the burden shifts to the state to show that the indirect difference in treatment is not discriminatory'. The SC in *SC* suggested at §62 that there was some doubt as to whether the concept of indirect discrimination extended beyond 'suspect grounds' but there has been no indication from the ECtHR that the concept is so limited.

R (The Motherhood Plan) v HM Treasury [2021] EWCA Civ 1703, [2022] 3 All ER 727

The CA considered a challenge to the Self-Employment Income Support Scheme (SEISS) introduced by the Government during the first COVID-19 lockdown. The claimants argued that the scheme breached Article 14 ECHR read with A1P1 by discriminating against self-employed women who took a period of leave relating to maternity or pregnancy in any of the three relevant tax years on which SEISS payments were calculated, this because the level of support granted to them under the scheme was not representative of their usual profits. Underhill and Baker LJJ, with whom Davies LJ agreed, cited the dicta of Lord Reed in *R (SC)* as '[t]he most recent authoritative statement of the

[136] Also *Guberina v Croatia* (2018) 66 EHRR 11 and *SAS v France* (2014) 60 EHRR 11.

nature of indirect discrimination in the context of Article 14 of the Convention and continued and recorded as 'common ground before us that Lord Reed's summary is not materially different':

Underhill and Baker LJJ, with whom Davies LJ agreed:

> 54. An important difference between indirect discrimination in the context of Article 14 and indirect discrimination in EU law (which continues to underpin domestic law) is that EU law proscribes only discrimination against persons or groups with specified protected characteristics, whereas under the Convention discrimination may be on the basis not only of the various specified characteristics but 'other status'. But even apart from that, the formulations quoted above are rather more generally expressed than the definition of indirect discrimination adopted in the EU legislation and jurisprudence. The history of that definition is helpfully set out in the judgment of Lady Hale in *Essop v Home Office* [2017] UKSC 27, [2017] ICR 640, at paras 18–22 [see p 45 above]
>
> 55. The EU definition of indirect discrimination is in substance reproduced in English law by section 19 (2) of the Equality Act 2010 … We should also note section 23 (1) of the Act, which provides that '[o]n a comparison of cases for the purposes of section … 19 there must be no material difference between the circumstances relating to each case'.
>
> 56. Notwithstanding those differences in formulation, it is clear that the same principles underlie the concept of indirect discrimination in the Convention, EU and domestic contexts. Broadly speaking, the concept of a 'measure' does the same work as a 'PCP' in EU law, and the requirement that it has 'disproportionately prejudicial effects' (or 'affects a disproportionate number of members') on the relevant group essentially corresponds to the requirement that it puts members of that group at 'a particular disadvantage'. As Lord Reed notes, the Strasbourg case-law is not yet fully developed, and some differences in approach or application may emerge at the margins, but the essential similarities are such that it is in our view legitimate in an Article 14 case at least to have regard to the EU and domestic jurisprudence.
>
> 57. That being so, we think that it is useful to quote from a passage in the judgment of Lady Hale in *Essop* in which she identifies a number of 'salient features' of indirect discrimination, as defined in the EU and domestic legislation. Three of those features are particularly material to the present issue: [his Lordship reproduced §§24–36 of *Essop* p 45 above (the first three 'salient features')] …
>
> 58. A potential ambiguity about terminology should be noted. The status which is characteristic of the disadvantaged group is described in Article 14 as the 'ground' of discrimination, without distinction between direct and indirect discrimination. But the terminology of 'grounds' is sometimes used in a sense specific to direct discrimination, to connote the reason for the treatment complained of, whether in the sense of the criterion employed or the motivation of the relevant decision-taker. In the context of indirect discrimination, the reason why, in that sense, the putative discriminator acted as they did is of course irrelevant …
>
> 59. At para. 40 Whipple J summarised the way that the appellants put their case of indirect discrimination as follows:
>
> > [T]hey argue that the Scheme has a disproportionately prejudicial effect on women who have not worked in the preceding three tax years for maternity reasons; the prejudice is that those women receive smaller payments than they would otherwise be entitled to, and thus the Scheme indirectly discriminates against such women …
>
> 64. It is worth noting that although the appellants chose to include in their definition of the group the fact that the recent mothers in question have 'not worked' in the measurement period, it would have been possible to omit that element and define the group simply as all women eligible for the SEISS who have been pregnant or given birth in the period in question, irrespective

> of whether they stopped work – or indeed as all women eligible for the SEISS, irrespective of maternity. If the appellants' case is otherwise good, the ATP measure would still in principle have a disproportionate impact on the groups so characterised, albeit that it would be diluted by the presence in it of women who had not stopped work (or who were not recent mothers). It would also have been possible to define it as 'recent parents' in recognition of the fact that sometimes, albeit more rarely, self-employed fathers will find their ability to earn adversely impacted by the demands of looking after a young baby …

Whipple J at first instance had relied on a number of cases in which indirect discrimination claims based on past earnings failed,[137] concluding that:

> 64. I am not therefore persuaded that there is any indirect discrimination, approaching the matter on a conventional analysis. The measure imposes no hidden barriers to eligibility. So far as quantum of payment is concerned there is no hidden barrier either: quantum is based on past (average) trading profits, which are a matter of past fact. The same rule applies to all and it is no harder for a woman who has been on maternity leave to qualify or calculate their payment, than someone who has not. The fact that some claimants will receive lower payments than others reflects the fact of lower earnings in past years; I agree with the Defendant that the reasons for lower earnings in past years, in the context of this Scheme with its stated purpose, are not relevant."

Underhill LJ said this:

> 70. The first sentence simply states the conclusion, for which the reasons follow in the rest of the paragraph. We should say that the reference to 'approaching the matter on a conventional analysis' is simply in contradistinction to '*Thlimmenos* discrimination', which we consider separately[138].
>
> 71. The second and third sentences make the point that there are no 'hidden barriers', either as regards eligibility for the SEISS or as regards the quantum of any entitlement … we are not sure what it means in this context. Even if it is in some sense true, it is not an answer to the claim that the adoption of the ATP measure has a disproportionate impact on recent mothers. We say a little more about this at para. 94(2) below.
>
> 72. The fourth sentence begins with the observation that 'the same rule applies to all'. That cannot of course be an answer to the appellants' case: the essence of *prima facie* indirect discrimination is that the same rule applies to everyone *but* that it has a disproportionate impact on the group in question. We are sure the Judge was well aware of that, and we assume she was merely emphasising that this was not a case of directly different treatment; but that in itself does not advance the argument.
>
> 73. The statement in the second part of the fourth sentence that 'it is no harder for a woman who has been on maternity leave to qualify or calculate their payment, than someone who has not' is true, but it does not address the essence of the appellants' case. The complaint is not that recent mothers are disqualified from receiving a SEISS payment, or that calculation of their entitlement is more difficult, but that the adoption of ATP as the measure of their entitlement puts them at a particular disadvantage …
>
> 74. That brings us to the final sentence of para. 64. We should say by way of preliminary that the reference to some claimants receiving 'lower payments than others' is not quite right. We are not in fact sure which 'others' are being referred to; but in any event, as discussed above,

[137] *Barry v Midland Bank*, n 44 above, *Trustees of Uppingham School Retirement Benefits Scheme v Shillcock* [2002] EWHC 64 (Ch), [2002] IRLR 702, and *R (Adiatu) v HM Treasury* [2020] EWHC 1554 (Admin), [2021] 2 All ER 484.

[138] See p 100 below.

the appellants' point is not as such that recent mothers will receive lower SEISS payments than other self-employed people but rather that, compared with such people, they are at disproportionate risk of receiving payments which are unrepresentative of their hypothetical no-Covid earnings. However, that need not undermine the judge's essential point, the essence of which is that the prejudice complained of is immaterial because it 'reflects the fact of lower earnings in past years'...

76. At first sight, the final sentence of para. 64 of Whipple J's judgment is puzzling. Lord Reed's formulation of the circumstances giving rise to *prima facie* indirect discrimination in the Article 14 context requires only that the measure in question has 'disproportionately prejudicial effects on a particular group': see para. 49 of his judgment in *SC*. As noted above, Whipple J appears to have accepted that the ATP measure has a disproportionately prejudicial effect on recent mothers. That being so, it is unclear why it should matter that it 'reflects [i.e. results from] the fact of lower earnings in past years'. As a matter of principle, the fact of the disproportionate effect is enough [citing Lady Hale in *Essop* §24] ... The reasoning is all the more surprising where it is clear that the reason for the 'lower earnings in past years' – that is, lower than would be expected in the hypothetical no-Covid current year – is gender-related.

Having pointed out that the trial judge believed that her approach was required by the decisions in three cases only one of which (*Barry v Midland Bank plc* [1999] UKHL 38, [1999] ICR 859) was binding on the Court, Underhill LJ sought to distil the ratio of that case and distinguished it from the present case.[139] Similarly he did not accept that the other cases relied on had bound the trial judge to decide the case as she had. He accepted that the claimant had succeeded in showing a prima facie case of indirect discrimination, though he went on to rule against her on justification.

Thlimmenos *Discrimination*

This form of discrimination is peculiar to Article 14 and was recognised by the ECtHR in the case of that name: *Thlimmenos v Greece.*

***Thlimmenos v Greece* (App No 34369, judgment of 6 April 2000) (2001) 31 EHRR 15 (Grand Chamber)**

The applicant, a Jehovah's Witness, challenged a law which prevented otherwise qualified individuals with convictions for felonies from registration as chartered accountants. The applicant's conviction related to his refusal, as a Jehovah's Witness (and therefore a pacifist), to undertake military service, which was mandatory at the time in Greece.

41. The Court notes that the applicant was not appointed a chartered accountant as a result of his past conviction for insubordination consisting in his refusal to wear the military uniform. He was thus treated differently from the other persons who had applied for that post on the

[139] The *Barry* case is difficult as Underhill LJ remarked, and has not often featured in the subsequent case law. In it the HL had ruled that calculating the redundancy pay of a woman who had switched from full-time to part-time working for reasons connected with motherhood on the basis of her final (ie part-time) salary only did not raise a prima facie case of indirect sex discrimination. The claimant had argued that the approach disadvantaged her as a woman as women were more likely, on account of maternity, to switch from full-time to part-time work. The House of Lords identified the purpose of the redundancy scheme as replacing lost income and, on that basis, ruled that those in her group were not prejudiced or 'put at a particular disadvantage' by the method of calculation.

> ground of his status as a convicted person. The Court considers that such difference of treatment does not generally come within the scope of Article 14 in so far as it relates to access to a particular profession, the right to freedom of profession not being guaranteed by the Convention.
>
> 42. However, the applicant does not complain of the distinction that the rules governing access to the profession make between convicted persons and others. His complaint rather concerns the fact that in the application of the relevant law no distinction is made between persons convicted of offences committed exclusively because of their religious beliefs and persons convicted of other offences. In this context the Court notes that the applicant is a member of the Jehovah's Witnesses, a religious group committed to pacifism, and that there is nothing in the file to disprove the applicant's claim that he refused to wear the military uniform only because he considered that his religion prevented him from doing so. In essence, the applicant's argument amounts to saying that he is discriminated against in the exercise of his freedom of religion, as guaranteed by Article 9, in that he was treated like any other person convicted of a felony although his own conviction resulted from the very exercise of this freedom. Seen in this perspective, the Court accepts that the 'set of facts' complained of by the applicant – his being treated as a person convicted of a felony for the purposes of an appointment to a chartered accountant's post despite the fact that the offence for which he had been convicted was prompted by his religious beliefs – 'falls within the ambit of a Convention provision', namely Article 9 …
>
> 44. The Court has so far considered that the right under Article 14 not to be discriminated against in the enjoyment of the rights guaranteed under the Convention is violated when States treat differently persons in analogous situations without providing an objective and reasonable justification. However, the Court considers that this is not the only facet of the prohibition of discrimination in Article 14. The right not to be discriminated against in the enjoyment of the rights guaranteed under the Convention is also violated when States without an objective and reasonable justification fail to treat differently persons whose situations are significantly different.
>
> 45. It follows that Article 14 is of relevance to the applicant's complaint and applies in the circumstances of this case in conjunction with Article 9 thereof.

The Court went on to find that the discrimination complained of was not justified because (§47) 'unlike other convictions for serious criminal offences, a conviction for refusing on religious or philosophical grounds to wear the military uniform cannot imply any dishonesty or moral turpitude likely to undermine the offender's ability to exercise this profession'. Further, the applicant had already served a prison sentence for his offence and so the additional punishment was disproportionate. Accordingly, Article 14 had been breached.

In its *Guide on Article 14 of the European Convention on Human Rights and on Article 1 of Protocol No 12 to the Convention* (see above) the court characterises *Thlimmenos* as a form of mandatory positive action.

Justification

In its earliest case on Article 14 the ECtHR ruled that discrimination would breach Article 14 if it had 'no objective and reasonable justification'.[140] The threshold for justification

[140] *Belgian Linguistic Case (No 2)*, n 108 above.

appears low. Appearances are somewhat misleading, however. Even where the basic threshold is in play a discriminator will have to show that the treatment complained of pursues a 'legitimate aim', and that there is a 'reasonable relationship of proportionality between the means employed and the aim sought to be realised'.[141] Further, the ECtHR has imposed a much more demanding approach to justification in cases in which the differential treatment complained of has been on grounds regarded as 'suspect' by the Court, in which case 'very weighty reasons' are required. In the case of race, it is doubtful whether direct discrimination could be justified, except perhaps where the purpose was ameliorative.[142] There is no formal distinction in terms of justification between direct and indirect discrimination though it would perhaps be surprising if it were not easier to justify inadvertent discrimination arising from measures directed towards a non-discriminatory aim than deliberate differential treatment on (at least) a suspect ground.

An example of the approach to be taken in relation to non-suspect grounds is provided by the following case.

Engel v Netherlands (Series A No 22, judgment of 8 June 1976) (1979–80) 1 EHRR 647

The applicants, conscripted soldiers serving in the Dutch armed forces, challenged various penalties imposed upon them for offences against military discipline. They claimed that they were treated less favourably than they would have been had they held higher ranks, or had they been civilians. The ECtHR accepted that military status was an 'other status' for the purposes of Article 14, also that the claim fell within that provision read, inter alia, with Articles 5 and/or 6.

> 72. [The applicants] complain in the first place of distinctions in treatment between servicemen. According to Articles 10 and 44 of the 1903 Act, provisional arrest imposed in the form of strict arrest was served by officers in their dwellings, tent or quarters whereas non-commissioned officers and ordinary servicemen were locked in a cell ... As for committal to a disciplinary unit, privates alone risked this punishment ...
>
> A distinction based on rank may run counter to Article 14 ...
>
> The Court is not unaware that the respective legislation of a number of Contracting States seems to be evolving, albeit in various degrees, towards greater equality in the disciplinary sphere between officers, non-commissioned officers and ordinary servicemen. The Netherlands Act of 12 September 1974 offers a striking example of this tendency. In particular, by abolishing strict arrest and committal to a disciplinary unit, this Act has henceforth put an end to the distinctions criticised by [the applicants]. In order to establish whether the said distinctions constituted discrimination contrary to Articles 5 and 14 taken together, regard must nevertheless be had to the moment when they were in existence. The court will examine the question in the light of its judgment in the *Belgian Linguistic Case*.
>
> The hierarchical structure inherent in armies entails differentiation according to rank. Corresponding to the various ranks are differing responsibilities which in their turn justify certain inequalities of treatment in the disciplinary sphere. Such inequalities are traditionally encountered in the Contracting States and are tolerated by international humanitarian law. In this respect, the European Convention allows the competent national authorities a considerable margin of appreciation.

[141] *Darby v Sweden* (1991) 13 EHRR 774; *Petrovic v Austria* (1998) 33 EHRR 14.
[142] *Timishev v Russia*, n 107 above.

At the time in question, the distinctions attacked by the three applicants had their equivalent in the internal legal system of practically all the Contracting States. Based on an element objective in itself, that is rank, these distinctions could have been dictated by a legitimate aim, namely the preservation of discipline by methods suited to each category of servicemen. While only privates risked committal to a disciplinary unit, they clearly were not subject to a serious penalty threatening the other members of the armed forces, namely reduction in rank. As for confinement in a cell during strict arrest, the Netherlands legislator could have had sufficient reason for not applying this to officers. On the whole, the legislator does not seem in the circumstances to have abused the latitude left to him by the Convention. Furthermore, the court does not consider that the principle of proportionality, as defined in its previously cited judgment in the *Belgian Linguistic Case*, has been offended in the present case.

73. Mr. Engel, Mr. Dona and Mr. Schul in the second place object to inequalities of treatment between servicemen and civilians. In point of fact, even civilians subject by reason of their occupation to a particular disciplinary system cannot in the Netherlands incur penalties analogous to the disputed deprivations of liberty. However, this does not result in any discrimination incompatible with the Convention, the conditions and demands of military life being by nature different from those of civil life.

74. The court thus finds no breach of Articles 5(1) and 14 taken together ...

92. According to the applicants, the disciplinary proceedings of which they complain did not comply with Articles 6 and 14 taken together since they were not attended by as many guarantees as criminal proceedings brought against civilians.

Whilst military disciplinary procedure is not attended by the same guarantees as criminal proceedings brought against civilians, it offers on the other hand substantial advantages to those subject to it (para. 80 above). The distinctions between these two types of proceedings in the legislation of the Contracting States are explicable by the differences between the conditions of military and of civil life. They cannot be taken as entailing a discrimination against members of the armed forces, within the meaning of Articles 6 and 14 taken together.

The approach taken in *Engel* contrasts with that adopted in *EB v France*, which concerned sexual orientation.

***EB v France* (App No 43546/02, judgment of 22 January 2008) (2008) 47 EHRR 21 (Grand Chamber)**

The applicant, who was in a long-term same-sex relationship, challenged the refusal of the French state to allow her to adopt for reasons which were connected with her sexuial orientation. The ECtHR accepted that the discrimination fell within Articles 8 and 14:

91. The Court reiterates that, for the purposes of Art.14, a difference in treatment is discriminatory if it has no objective and reasonable justification, which means that it does not pursue a 'legitimate aim' or that there is no 'reasonable proportionality between the means employed and the aim sought to be realised'. Where sexual orientation is in issue, there is a need for particularly convincing and weighty reasons to justify a difference in treatment regarding rights falling within Art.8.

92. In that connection the Court observes that the Convention is a living instrument, to be interpreted in the light of present-day conditions.

93. In the Court's opinion, if the reasons advanced for such a difference in treatment were based solely on considerations regarding the applicant's sexual orientation this would amount to discrimination under the Convention.

94. The Court points out that French law allows single persons to adopt a child, thereby opening up the possibility of adoption by a single homosexual, which is not disputed. Against the background of the domestic legal provisions, it considers that the reasons put forward by the Government cannot be regarded as particularly convincing and weighty such as to justify refusing to grant the applicant authorisation.

95. The Court notes, lastly, that the relevant provisions of the Civil Code are silent as to the necessity of a referent of the other sex, which would not, in any event, be dependent on the sexual orientation of the adoptive single parent. In this case, moreover, the applicant presented, in the terms of the judgment of the Conseil d'Etat, 'undoubted personal qualities and an aptitude for bringing up children', which were assuredly in the child's best interests, a key notion in the relevant international instruments.

96. Having regard to the foregoing, the Court cannot but observe that, in rejecting the applicant's application for authorisation to adopt, the domestic authorities made a distinction based on considerations regarding her sexual orientation, a distinction which is not acceptable under the Convention.

For some years the domestic courts declined to apply the 'weighty reasons' approach to discrimination on suspect grounds in connection with welfare benefits, relying on *Stec v UK* (2006) 43 EHRR 47 (see Chapter 3) in which the ECtHR adopted a less rigorous approach (the manifestly without reasonable foundation/MWRF test) to sex discrimination, which it regarded as part of a package of measures designed to ameliorate disadvantage. The domestic courts had routinely applied the MWRF test to Convention challenges to economic/social policy irrespective of the protected ground,[143] but in *JD & A v UK* 48 BHRC 36, the ECtHR made it clear that the MWRF test was applicable only to cases involving positive action (see Chapter 3).[144] In *R (SC) v SSWP* the SC revisited the MWRF approach.

***R (SC) v Secretary of State for Work and Pensions* [2021] UKSC 26, [2022] AC 223**

98. According to the settled case law of the European court, the question whether there is an 'objective and reasonable' justification for a difference in treatment is to be judged by whether it pursues a 'legitimate aim' and there is a 'reasonable relationship of proportionality' between the aim and the means employed to achieve it ....[145] It is also well settled that states have 'a margin of appreciation in assessing whether and to what extent differences in otherwise similar situations justify a different treatment': *ibid.* Crucially, in relation to the present issue, '[t]he scope of this margin will vary according to the circumstances, the subject matter and the background.'

99. The court has not itself provided, in its judgments, a systematic analysis of relevant factors or an explanation of how they interact. Its accounts of the general principles it applies are stated at a high level of generality. Nevertheless, patterns emerge, and inferences can be drawn, from a survey of its case law, as I shall explain. It is doubtful whether the nuanced nature of the approach which it follows can be comprehensively described by any general rule. It is more useful to think of there being a range of factors which tend to heighten, or lower, the intensity of review. In any given case, a number of these factors may be present, possibly pulling in

[143] *Humphreys v HMRC* [2012] UKSC 18, [2012] 1 WLR 1545; *R (MA) v SSWP* [2016] UKSC 58, [2016] 1 WLR 4550; *R (DA) v SSWP* [2019] UKSC 21, [2019] 1 WLR 3289.

[144] The case was an appeal from *MA, ibid.* While not a Grand Chamber decision it has been flagged by the ECtHR as a 'key case'.

[145] Citing *Carson v UK* (2010) 51 EHRR 13 §61.

different directions, and the court has to take them all into account in order to make an overall assessment. The case law indicates, however, that some factors have greater weight than others.

100. One particularly important factor is the ground of the difference in treatment. In principle, and all other things being equal, the court usually applies a strict review to the reasons advanced in justification of a difference in treatment based on what it has sometimes called 'suspect' grounds of discrimination. However, these grounds form a somewhat inexact category, which has developed in the case law over time, and is capable of further development by the European court. Furthermore, a much less intense review may be applied even in relation to some so-called suspect grounds where other factors are present which render a strict approach inappropriate, as some of the cases to be discussed will demonstrate.

101. The court originally developed a requirement that 'very weighty reasons' must be shown to justify a difference in treatment based on sex or gender, on the basis that the advancement of gender equality is a major goal in the contracting states …[146]. This approach was soon applied in cases concerning entitlement to welfare benefits ….[147]

102. On the other hand, while continuing to state that 'very weighty reasons' are required for a difference in treatment on grounds of sex to be regarded as compatible with the Convention, the court has found there to be no violation where a state has been acting to correct a historical inequality between the sexes and the pace of change has been reasonable in the context of the contracting states as a whole …[148]

103. These cases illustrate three points of wider significance. The first is that the court's statements that 'very weighty reasons' are required to justify a difference in treatment on a particular ground do not necessarily exclude the possibility that a relatively wide margin of appreciation, and a correspondingly less intense standard of review, may nevertheless be appropriate in particular circumstances, as for example where historical inequalities are being addressed in pace with changes in social attitudes. The second is that the court's case law evolves in the light of the development of common standards among the contracting states. The third is that the court has moved over time towards explaining the need for weighty reasons to justify certain grounds of differences in treatment in terms of the link between those grounds and problems of stereotyping, stigma and social exclusion, which prevent participation in society on an equal footing to others. It is to be noted that this approach differs from that suggested by Lord Walker of Gestingthorpe in *R (RJM) v Secretary of State for Work and Pensions* [2008] UKHL 63, [2009] AC 311, para 5, which focused instead on the relationship between the characteristic in question and the development of an individual's personality …

Lord Reed suggested that the Court had applied the MWRF test to discrimination in the socio-economic context on the suspect grounds of nationality,[149] sexual orientation,[150] ethnicity[151] and religion/ belief before continuing:[152]

112. A relatively strict approach has also been adopted in cases concerned with persons with disabilities, in order to "foster their full participation and integration in society'…[153] In the more recent case of *Guberina* [*v Croatia* (2018) 66 EHRR 11], which concerned a refusal to

[146] Citing *Abdulaziz v UK*, n 121 above, §78.

[147] Citing *Van Raalte v Netherlands* (1997) 24 EHRR 503, §39.

[148] Citing *Petrovic v Austria*, n 141 above; *Markin v Russia* (2012) 56 EHRR 8.

[149] Citing *MS v Germany* (App No 44770/98, unreported, judgment of 20 January 2000); *Ponomaryov* (2011) 59 EHRR 20, §54.

[150] At §107, citing *EB v France*, n 118 above, and *Schalk v Austria* (2010) 53 EHRR 2.

[151] At §108 (citing *Biao v Denmark* (2016) 64 EHRR 1 §§93 and 94).

[152] At §§109–10, citing *Vojnity v Hungary* [2013] 2 FCR 495 and *Eweida*, n 31 above.

[153] Citing *Glor v Switzerland*, n 116 above, §84.

grant a tax exemption for persons with special accommodation needs to the father of a disabled child, the court noted that, on the one hand, a wide margin is usually allowed to the state under the Convention when it comes to general measures of economic or social strategy, including measures in the area of taxation (para 73). On the other hand, it continued:

> ... if a restriction on fundamental rights applies to a particularly vulnerable group in society that has suffered considerable discrimination in the past, then the state's margin of appreciation is substantially narrower and it must have very weighty reasons for the restrictions in question. The reason for this approach, which questions certain classifications per se, is that such groups were historically subject to prejudice with lasting consequences, resulting in their social exclusion. Such prejudice could entail legislative stereotyping which prohibits the individualised evaluation of their capacities and needs.

114. The counterpart of the strict approach taken, other things being equal, to differences in treatment on the grounds discussed above, is less strict scrutiny, other things being equal, of differences in treatment on other grounds, such as age ... immigration status ... prisoner status ... and marital status ... However, as indicated in para 99 above, the case law does not support a straightforwardly binary approach, as a range of factors may be relevant in particular circumstances. For example, although age has not been treated as a "suspect" ground, the best interests of children have been treated by the European court as an important factor in assessing proportionality under art 14 (see, for example, para 86 above), reflecting the fact that individuals in that age group have particular needs and vulnerabilities.

115. In summary, therefore, the court's approach to justification generally is a matter of some complexity, as a number of factors affecting the width of the margin of appreciation can arise from 'the circumstances, the subject matter and its background'. Notwithstanding that complexity, some general points can be identified.

(1) One is that the court distinguishes between differences of treatment on certain grounds ... which for the reasons explained are regarded as especially serious and therefore call, in principle, for a strict test of justification (or, in the case of differences in treatment on the ground of race or ethnic origin, have been said to be incapable of justification), and differences of treatment on other grounds, which are in principle the subject of less intensive review.

(2) Another, repeated in many of the judgments already cited, sometimes alongside a statement that 'very weighty reasons' must be shown, is that a wide margin is usually allowed to the state when it comes to general measures of economic or social strategy ...[154].

(3) A third is that the width of the margin of appreciation can be affected to a considerable extent by the existence, or absence, of common standards among the contracting states ...[155].

(4) A fourth, linked to the third, is that a wide margin of appreciation is in principle available, even where there is differential treatment based on one of the so-called suspect grounds, where the state is taking steps to eliminate a historical inequality over a transitional period. Similarly, in areas of evolving rights, where there is no established consensus, a wide margin has been allowed in the timing of legislative changes ...[156].

(5) Finally, there may be a wide variety of other factors which bear on the width of the margin of appreciation in particular circumstances ...[157]

[154] Citing *Ponomaryov*, n 149 above, §52, (state provision of education); *Schalk*, n 150 above, §97 (legal recognition of same-sex relationships); *Biao v Denmark*, n 151 above, §93 (grant of residence permits); *Guberina*, n 136 above (taxation); *Bah v UK* (2012) 54 EHRR 21, §37 (social housing); *Stummer v Austria* (2012) 54 EHRR 11 §89 (state pension); *Yiðit v Turkey* (2010) 53 EHRR 372 §70 (widow's pension) and noting that the ECtHR had used the MWRF phrase in *Bah*, §37 and *Stummer*, §89.

[155] Citing *Petrovic v Austria*, n 141 above and *Markin v Russia*, n 148 above.

[156] Citing *Inze v Austria* (1988) 10 EHRR 394, *Schalk*, n 150 above, and *Stummer*, n 154 above.

[157] Citing *MS v Germany* (App No 44770/98, unreported, judgment of 20 January 2000); *Ponomaryov*, n 149 above and *Eweida*, n 31 above.

> 116. As the cases demonstrate, more than one of those points may be relevant in the circumstances of a particular case, and, unless one factor is of overriding significance, it is then necessary for the court to make a balanced overall assessment.

Lord Reed went on to point out that the MWRF formulation had first appeared in *Stec v UK* (2006) 43 EHRR 74, which concerned a challenge to a discriminatory rule in a legislative scheme which was designed gradually to equalise pension ages between men and women), stating at §120 that the case 'illustrates how, where a ground of differential treatment is one which could generally be justified only by "very weighty reasons", other factors may nevertheless make it appropriate to allow the state a wide margin of appreciation'. He proceeded to refer to a large number of cases in which the ECtHR had referred to the MWRF test, though in none of these cases had the ECtHR ruled that discrimination on a suspect ground was justified on the basis of that test except where the discrimination was designed to ameliorate past disadvantage (positive discrimination is considered in Chapter 3).

> 129. Up to this point, the cases from *Stec* onwards concerned with welfare benefits and pensions can be seen to have generally followed a consistent approach. Although that approach is far from mechanical, the points noted in para 115 above can readily be discerned.
>
> (1) In relation to the first point, the court has consistently differentiated between cases where 'suspect' and 'non-suspect' grounds of differential treatment have been in issue.
>
> (2) In relation to the second point, the court has almost always recognised the general appropriateness of a wide margin in relation to general measures of economic or social strategy, reflected in the context of welfare benefits, pensions and social housing by the 'manifestly without reasonable foundation' formulation.
>
> (3) In relation to the third point, the relevance of the existence or absence of common standards is evident from such cases as *Stec, Tomás* [*v Spain* (2017) 65 EHRR 24] and *Stummer* [*v Austria* (2012) 54 EHRR 11].
>
> (4) In relation to the fourth point, the relevance of the measure in question forming part of arrangements intended to eliminate an historical inequality over time appears from *Stec, Runkee* [*v UK* [2007] 2 FCR 178], *Andrle* [*v Czech Republic* (2015) 60 EHRR 14] and *British Gurkha* [*Welfare Society v UK* (2017) 64 EHRR 11].
>
> (5) In relation to the fifth point, the potential relevance of other circumstances is illustrated by *Muñoz Díaz v Spain* (2010) 50 EHRR 49, where the court attached importance to the conduct of the domestic authorities in creating a legitimate expectation that the applicant would receive favourable treatment.
>
> 131. The remaining point which can be drawn from the case law up to this point is how the court has balanced different factors when they pull in different directions: notably, where the need for 'very weighty reasons' co-exists with the generally wide margin of appreciation described by the 'manifestly without reasonable foundation' formulation … in cases involving 'suspect' grounds in the field of welfare benefits and pensions, the determinative factor has generally been whether 'very weighty reasons' have been shown, but that the court has taken account of the wide margin generally applicable in that field when making that assessment. Whether a measure has formed part of a scheme intended to address historical inequalities, and the presence or absence of common standards among the contracting states, have also been important factors.

Lord Reed discussed the decision of the ECtHR in *JD & A v UK* 48 BHRC 36 from which he cited at length, including the statement at §88 that 'the court has limited its acceptance to respect the legislature's policy choice as not "manifestly without reasonable foundation" to circumstances where an alleged difference in treatment resulted from a transitional measure forming part of a scheme carried out in order to correct an inequality'.[158] His Lordship suggested at §134–37 that the ECtHR in *JD* had misrepresented its own case law,[159] and that the case did not establish a 'simple rule [that] complaints of discrimination on "suspect" grounds fall outside the scope of the wide margin and "manifestly without reasonable foundation" approach usually accorded in the field of welfare benefits, unless the case concerns "transitional measures"' (§137). He referred to more recent decision of the ECtHR in *Jurčič v Croatia* [2021] 73 EHRR 10 in which the Court had (in a sex discrimination case) had referred to the MWRF test before going on to state that 'outside the context of transitional measures designed to correct historic inequalities[160] very weighty reasons would have to be advanced before a difference in treatment on the grounds of sex could be regarded as being compatible with the Convention and that, in cases of sex discrimination, 'the principle of proportionality does not merely require that the measure chosen should in general be suited to the fulfilment of the aim pursued, but it must also be shown that it was necessary in the circumstances'.[161] Lord Reed observed that the margin of appreciation deployed by the ECtHR has no exact equivalent in the domestic courts, though it tended to be reflected in the width of the 'discretionary area of judgment' provided by the domestic courts:

> 145. In domestic law, as at the Strasbourg level, one would expect closer scrutiny where the case concerns discrimination on a ground such as sex or race, rather than a difference in treatment on less sensitive grounds, especially if it is simply a by-product of a legitimate policy. Distinctions drawn on 'suspect' grounds are inherently appropriate for close judicial scrutiny, notwithstanding the respect due to the judgment of the executive or the legislature.
>
> 146. There is nothing alien or new about an approach which, in general, accords a high level of respect to the judgment of public authorities in the field of economic or social policy, but balances that with the need for close scrutiny where differences of treatment are based on 'suspect' grounds. On the one hand, unjustifiable discrimination by public authorities is likely to be irrational and therefore unlawful at common law: as Lord Hoffmann stated in *Matadeen v Pointu* [1999] 1 AC 98, 109, 'treating like cases alike and unlike cases differently is a general axiom of rational behaviour'. Indeed, the classic example given of unreasonable behaviour in the *Wednesbury* case was of discrimination (*Associated Provincial Picture Houses Ltd v Wednesbury Corpn* [1948] 1 KB 223, 229). At the same time, the general need for judicial restraint in the area of economic policy was made clear by Lord Bridge of Harwich's statement in *R v Secretary of State for the Environment, Ex p Hammersmith and Fulham LBC* [1991] 1 AC 521, 597, that where a 'statute has conferred a power on the Secretary of State which involves the formulation and the implementation of national economic policy and which can only take effect with the approval of the House of Commons, it is not open to challenge on the grounds of irrationality short of the extremes of bad faith, improper motive or manifest

[158] Citing *Stec v UK* (2006) 43 EHRR 47 §§61–66; *Runkee v UK* [2007] 2 FCR 178 §§40–41 and *British Gurkha Welfare Society v UK*, §81.

[159] Though in doing so he did not consider whether the MWRF test had actually been applied in the cases to which he referred (as distinct from having been mentioned under 'general principles' applicable to economic/social cases, and he did not distinguish in referring to non-transitional cases in which it had been referred to between suspect and non-suspect grounds or between cases which had in fact turned on justification or those defeated on other grounds (such as a lack of comparability).

[160] Citing *JD and A v UK* 48 BHRC 36.

[161] Also at §140 to the decision in *Yocheva and Ganeva v Bulgaria* (App Nos 18592/15 and 43863/15, unreported, judgment of 11 May 2021) in which (in a case of illegitimacy discrimination) the Court had referred to the MWRF test before requiring very weighty reasons to justify the difference in treatment, contrasting non-suspect grounds cases in which the ECtHR 'has continued to allow a wide margin, and to repeat the "manifestly without reasonable foundation" formula without qualification', citing *Popovic v Serbia* (2020) 71 EHRR 29.

absurdity'. In other words, the administrative law test of unreasonableness is generally applied in contexts such as economic policy and social policy with considerable care and caution; and the same is true of the Convention test of proportionality. Both tests have to be applied in a way which reconciles the rule of law with the separation of powers.

Having discussed some of the early Article 14 case law[162] Lord Reed acknowledged at §149 that there had been a 'divergence' between the 'reasoning of the European court, as it now appears' and that of the domestic courts from the decision in *Humphreys* [2012] UKSC 18; [2012] 1 WLR 1545, in which the SC interpreted *Stec* as imposing the MWRF test where state benefits were concerned.

151. … it now appears to me that the [Court's] reasoning on justification, following the submissions made, did not reflect the Strasbourg jurisprudence entirely correctly. First, it seems to me that the 'manifestly without reasonable foundation' formulation, as used in the Strasbourg judgments, does not express a test, in the sense of a requirement whose satisfaction or non-satisfaction will in itself necessarily be determinative of the outcome. The phrase indicates the width of the margin of appreciation, and hence the intensity of review, which is in principle appropriate in the field of welfare benefits, other things being equal. As I have explained, however, a number of other factors may also be relevant in the circumstances of particular cases, some of which may call for a stricter standard of review. One might then ask, for example in a case concerned with 'suspect' grounds, whether 'very weighty reasons' have been shown, having regard to the wide margin generally available in that field … However it is put, the question is more complex than a 'test' of whether the policy choice is 'manifestly without reasonable foundation' might appear to be if that were regarded as the entirety of the inquiry.

152. Secondly, the reasoning departed from the Strasbourg approach in its interpretation of *Stec* and *Runkee*, and its consequent rejection of a distinction between 'suspect' and other grounds of differences in treatment in the field of welfare benefits (matters which could only be appreciated in the light of other Strasbourg authorities which were not before the court). As explained … above, differential treatment on a suspect ground, if it is capable of justification at all, generally (but not always) requires to be justified by 'very weighty reasons'. That is so even in the context of measures of social and economic policy which would usually benefit from the 'manifestly without reasonable foundation' approach. The 'manifestly without reasonable foundation' approach does not, therefore, replace or supersede the requirement for 'very weighty reasons' where 'suspect' grounds are in issue. Instead, the degree of deference usually appropriate in relation to social or economic policy choices may have to be taken into account in assessing whether 'very weighty reasons' have been shown.

Lord Reed suggested that, notwithstanding the SC's false move in *Humphreys*, the insistence on the part of Lady Hale (for the Court) that 'careful scrutiny' was required 'was capable of ensuring an appropriate balance between the competing considerations'. He went on to consider a number of subsequent decisions in which the SC had maintained its adherence to the MWRF:[163]

157. In the light of the foregoing discussion, I am not persuaded by the argument, based on *JD*, that the 'manifestly without reasonable foundation' formulation can never have any part to play, even in relation to differences of treatment on 'suspect' grounds, outside the context of transitional measures. I am not convinced that *JD* should be understood as going as far as that, in the light of *Jurčič v Croatia, Yocheva and Ganeva v Bulgaria* and the earlier case law …

[162] *Ghaidan*, n 107 above; *R (RJM) v SSWP*.

[163] *SG* [2015] UKSC 16, [2015] 1 WLR 1449; *MA*, n 143 above (in which 'a wholesale attack was mounted upon the "[MWRF]" but was rejected'); and *DA* [2019] UKSC 21, [2019] 1 WLR 3289 in which 'the court expressed its adherence to "the 'manifestly without reasonable foundation' test" in particularly strict terms'.

158. Nevertheless, it is appropriate that the approach which this court has adopted since *Humphreys* should be modified in order to reflect the nuanced nature of the judgment which is required, following the jurisprudence of the European court. In the light of that jurisprudence as it currently stands, it remains the position that a low intensity of review is generally appropriate, other things being equal, in cases concerned with judgments of social and economic policy in the field of welfare benefits and pensions, so that the judgment of the executive or legislature will generally be respected unless it is manifestly without reasonable foundation. Nevertheless, the intensity of the court's scrutiny can be influenced by a wide range of factors, depending on the circumstances of the particular case, as indeed it would be if the court were applying the domestic test of reasonableness rather than the Convention test of proportionality. In particular, very weighty reasons will usually have to be shown, and the intensity of review will usually be correspondingly high, if a difference in treatment on a 'suspect' ground is to be justified … But other factors can sometimes lower the intensity of review even where a suspect ground is in issue … besides the cases concerned with 'transitional measures'….[164] Equally, even where there is no 'suspect' ground, there may be factors which call for a stricter standard of review than might otherwise be necessary, such as the impact of a measure on the best interests of children.

159. It is therefore important to avoid a mechanical approach to these matters, based simply on the categorisation of the ground of the difference in treatment. A more flexible approach will give appropriate respect to the assessment of democratically accountable institutions, but will also take appropriate account of such other factors as may be relevant. As was recognised in *Ghaidan v Godin-Mendoza* and *R (RJM) v Secretary of State for Work and Pensions*, the courts should generally be very slow to intervene in areas of social and economic policy such as housing and social security; but, as a general rule, differential treatment on grounds such as sex or race nevertheless requires cogent justification.

160. It may also be helpful to observe that the phrase 'manifestly without reasonable foundation', as used by the European court, is merely a way of describing a wide margin of appreciation. A wide margin has also been recognised by the European court in numerous other areas where that phrase has not been used, such as national security, penal policy and matters raising sensitive moral or ethical issues.

161. It follows that in domestic cases, rather than trying to arrive at a precise definition of the ambit of the 'manifestly without reasonable foundation' formulation, it is more fruitful to focus on the question whether a wide margin of judgment is appropriate in the light of the circumstances of the case. The ordinary approach to proportionality gives appropriate weight to the judgment of the primary decision-maker: a degree of weight which will normally be substantial in fields such as economic and social policy, national security, penal policy, and matters raising sensitive moral or ethical issues. It follows … that the ordinary approach to proportionality will accord the same margin to the decision-maker as the 'manifestly without reasonable foundation' formulation in circumstances where a particularly wide margin is appropriate.

162. It is also important to bear in mind that almost any legislation is capable of challenge under art 14. Judges Pejchal and Wojtyczek observed in their partly dissenting opinion in *JD*, para 11:

> Any legislation will differentiate. It differentiates by identifying certain classes of persons, while failing to differentiate within these or other classes of persons. The art of legislation is the art of wise differentiation. Therefore any legislation may be contested from the viewpoint of the principles of equality and non-discrimination and such cases have become more and more frequent in the courts.

[164] Relying on *Schalk*, n 150 above; *Eweida*, n 31 above; and *Tomás v Spain* (2017) 65 EHRR 24.

In practice, challenges to legislation on the ground of discrimination have become increasingly common in the UK. They are usually brought by campaigning organisations which lobbied unsuccessfully against the measure when it was being considered in Parliament, and then act as solicitors for persons affected by the legislation, or otherwise support legal challenges brought in their names, as a means of continuing their campaign. The favoured ground of challenge is usually Article 14, because it is so easy to establish differential treatment of some category of persons, especially if the concept of indirect discrimination is given a wide scope. Since the principle of proportionality confers on the courts a very broad discretionary power, such cases present a risk of undue interference by the courts in the sphere of political choices. That risk can only be avoided if the courts apply the principle in a manner which respects the boundaries between legality and the political process. As Judges Pejchal and Wojtyczek commented (*ibid*):

> Judicial independence is accepted only if the judiciary refrains from interfering with political processes. If the judicial power is to be independent, the judicial and political spheres have to remain separated.

The acceptance by the SC in *SC* that the domestic courts had taken a wrong turning in their approach to justification appears to have been a pyrrhic victory. Lord Reed made it clear at §162 that the decision was not to be seen as providing a green light for discrimination claims. The decision has been heavily relied upon in subsequent Article 14 decisions which have not had high levels of success. Further, the seven-judge SC took the opportunity provided by *SC* to put paid to recent suggestions by a number of its justices that the courts might take into account unincorporated international obligations (such as those imposed by the Convention on the Rights of the Child, or the Convention on the Rights of Persons with Disabilities) in considering the question of justification under Article 14. The suggestion had been made with more or less conviction by Lord Carnwath, Lady Hale and Lord Kerr in *R (SG & Ors) v SSWP* [2015] UKSC 16, [2015] 1 WLR 1449, Lady Hale (for the majority) in *In re McLaughlin* [2018] UKSC 48, [2018] 1 WLR 4250 and Lord Wilson (for the majority) in *Mathieson v SSWP* [2015] UKSC 47, [2015] 1 WLR 3250 and in *DA* [2019] 1 WLR 3289. The decision in *SC* appears indicative of a significantly more conservative court, though it may also demonstrate a pragmatic response to the political threat to the HRA.[165]

Other Discrimination

ECtHR, *Guide on Article 14 of the European Convention on Human Rights and on Article 1 of Protocol No. 12 to the Convention*[166]

30. Harassment and instruction to discriminate can be seen as particular manifestations of direct discrimination. The Court has found violations of Article 14 in cases of harassment and instruction to discriminate ….[167]

[165] Note that the deferential approach to justification is not applicable in cases in which the distribution of resources is not in issue – see for example *R (Steinfeld) v SS International Development* [2018] UKSC 32, (2018) 45 BHRC 169, §32 and the discussion in *Cornerstone*, fn 119 above, §§106 ff, also discussed above.

[166] n 110 above.

[167] Citing *Baczkowski v Poland* (2009) 48 EHRR 19.

37. The Court has confirmed that Article 14 also covers discrimination by association, that is, situations where the protected ground in question relates to another person somehow connected to the applicant.[168]

38. In *Guberina v Croatia*, 2018, the domestic authorities failed to take account of the needs of a child with disabilities when determining his father's eligibility for tax relief on the purchase of suitably adapted property. The Court found that the discriminatory treatment of the father on account of the disability of his child was a form of disability-based discrimination. In *Skorjanec v Croatia*, 2017, the … Court stressed that the obligation on the authorities to seek a possible link between racist attitudes and a given act of violence, which was part of the responsibility incumbent on States under Article 3 taken in conjunction with Article 14, also concerned acts of violence based on a victim's actual or presumed association or affiliation with another person who actually or presumably possessed a particular status or protected characteristic.

39. In *Molla Sali v Greece* [GC], 2018, the first application by the Grand Chamber of the principle of discrimination by association, the Court confirmed that Article 14 of the Convention also covers instances in which an individual is treated less favourably on the basis of another person's status or protected characteristics (§ 134). In that case, in which Sharia law had been applied to an inheritance dispute contrary to the will of the testator, the Court focused on the difference of treatment given the Muslim faith of the testator, and not of the applicant, who was his wife.

[168] Citing *Molla Sali v Greece* (2020) 71 EHRR, SE3; *Guberina*, n 136 above, and *Skorjanec v Croatia* (2018) 66 EHRR 14, discussed immediately below; and *Weller v Hungary* [2009] ECHR 44399/05 which concerned discrimination against children because of the nationality of their parents.

3

Positive Action

Introduction

This chapter discusses the extent to which the Equality Act 2010 (EqA) and the other legal provisions considered in this book allow, and/or require, the taking of positive measures to eradicate discrimination and/or to further equality. The focus is on domestic law, but this requires us to consider EU law and the ECHR, as well as the EqA itself.

Most of the legal tools provided by the EqA are directed towards challenging individual acts of discrimination, whether by employers, service providers, public authorities or other regulated individuals or bodies. Such tools, however, can only have a limited impact, in particular in relation to disadvantage which has resulted from multiple actions and decisions taken over generations by individuals and organisations which, whether because of the passage of time or otherwise, are beyond the reach of the law. It will become clear from Chapters 6–11 that the characteristics protected by the EqA are associated with significant disadvantage experienced by, for example, people with disabilities, those from certain minoritised ethnic and religious communities, and women. Such disadvantages include the economic, educational, social, cultural and political. They are not experienced equally by all those within groups defined by reference to one or more protected characteristics (women, lesbians, Black lesbians, for example), and there may be greater gaps in economic, educational, social and/or political advantage between people in the same 'group' than between individuals in different groups. It is also important to remember that a single individual will occupy many 'groups' defined by reference to protected characteristics (female, Asian, British, over 40, non-disabled, lesbian, agnostic), and may be relatively advantaged in some respects (British, non-disabled) and relatively disadvantaged in others (female, Asian, lesbian). It is important, therefore, not to assume that 'groups' (by which we refer to groups of people defined by reference to one or more protected characteristics) are fixed bodies of homogenous individuals easily distinguishable from others. Nevertheless, reference to groups allows us to recognise the collective nature of some disadvantages, and to consider how they might best be challenged.

The potential of individual challenges to eradicate group disadvantage is limited not only by the difficulties of enforcement outlined in Chapter 5 but also because they can only to a limited extent address the past decisions and actions which have resulted in present disadvantages. It is the case that the regulation of indirect discrimination permits some challenge to, for example, the perpetuation of educational disadvantages stemming from racial segregation (as in *Griggs v Power Duke Co* (1971) 401 US 424). But this applies only to the extent that the imposition of disparately impacting measures (there the requirement for a high school diploma as a condition of access to particular jobs) is not justified by the legitimate aims of the discriminator. Applying the EqA's approach to indirect discrimination, the imposition of a provision, criterion or practice which disparately impacts on persons with particular protected characteristics will be lawful when it is proportional to the legitimate needs of the discriminator. While this is manifestly reasonable in a legal model which is premised on the wrongdoing of the 'discriminator', it clearly falls short of providing a remedy for unjust disadvantage.

Steps taken to redress collective disadvantage, whether in the labour market or elsewhere, may be referred to as 'positive discrimination' or 'reverse discrimination' where they entail the preferential treatment of groups of individuals disadvantaged by sex, race, etc. Neither of these terms has an undisputed meaning, and they are as politically controversial as they are linguistically indeterminate. The terms 'affirmative action' or 'positive action' can encompass not only such preferential forms of treatment but also the taking of steps whose impact will be to ameliorate disadvantage associated with membership of a group defined by race, sex, etc (referred to hereafter as a 'disadvantaged group'), whether or not they are overtly directed at those groups. Permitting employees to work flexibly, for example, will assist women who bear the disproportionate burden of childcare and domestic work, while being open to men; providing adequate Halal, as well as non-Halal, options in a canteen for employees or hospital patients will serve the needs of Muslim as well as other users. 'Affirmative action' or 'positive action' may also include measures which are targeted directly towards members of a disadvantaged group, but which do not involve preferential treatment as regards appointment, promotion etc, as illustrated below.

Paul Burston, 'LGBT equality, diversity and the Metropolitan police', *The Guardian*, 18 May 2012

... LGBT officers first took part in London's annual Pride celebrations in 2003, though it wasn't until 2007 that they marched in uniform. Since September 2004, all new applicants to police forces in England and Wales have been given the option to the declare their sexuality by ticking a box indicating whether they are heterosexual, bisexual, gay or lesbian. And where once people may have been reluctant to come out for fear that it would affect their career prospects, the rise of Brian Paddick to the rank of deputy assistant commissioner proved that this needn't be the case.

A statement from the Met confirms the force's commitment to fair and equal recruitment: 'The Metropolitan police service is an equal opportunities employer and welcomes applications from all communities. We are fully committed to our diversity and equality strategy and we actively engage with LGBT communities to ensure we offer fair opportunities regardless of sexual orientation. We also attend the annual Pride London celebrations to promote the role of special constable, police officer and police community support officer, when we are recruiting externally.'

There are now dedicated LGBT liaison officers in every London borough. And it's not only community liaison officers who know how to deal with members of the LGBT community. In the past few years, I've had dealings with the police on two occasions – once in relation to a homophobic crime and once as a witness to a domestic disturbance involving a neighbour who happened to be transgender. On both occasions, the officers showed a clear understanding of the issues. At my local police station there's a poster which reads – 'Being black or white, lesbian, gay or transgender, having a disability or belonging to a particular faith group is not a crime. Abuse, assault, threats, offensive material or damage towards someone because of their race, faith, disability or sexuality is a crime.' Which is exactly as it should be ...

Of the terms discussed ('positive action', 'positive discrimination', 'reverse discrimination' and 'affirmative action'), 'affirmative action,' though not generally used in the UK, has the longest vintage. It was originally embraced in the US in 1961 when President Kennedy issued Executive Order 10925, which required that those contracting with federal government 'take affirmative action to ensure that applicants are employed, and employees are treated during employment, without regard to their race, creed, color, or national origin.' Previous Executive Orders issued in 1941, 1943 and 1954 had banned race discrimination by federal contractors, but the term 'affirmative action' was first used in Executive Order 10925. The Order was extended to employers who were assisted by federal funds in 1963 and in 1965, following the passage of the Civil Rights Act 1964, it was superseded by President Johnson's Executive Order 11246.

The Civil Rights Act 1964 had prohibited discrimination on grounds of race, colour, national origin, sex and religion. Executive Order 11246 originally referred to race, religion, colour or national origin, but was amended in 1967 to include sex. Importantly, whereas Executive Order 10925 did not demand that contractors do anything other than certify that they would undertake 'affirmative action', regulations issued under Executive Order 11246 required that employers with more than 50 employees, and with federal contracts worth at least $50,000, examine whether their employment practices excluded, disadvantaged or restricted employment opportunities for women or ethnic minorities. If they found that any group was under-represented such employers were required to establish goals and timetables to eliminate the under-representation.

Chris McCrudden has distinguished five different types of 'affirmative action':

Chris McCrudden, 'Rethinking Positive Action' (1986) 15 *Industrial Law Journal* 219, some footnotes omitted

Eradicating discrimination … involves identifying and replacing discriminatory practices …

Facially neutral but purposefully inclusionary policies… seek to increase the proportion of members of the previously excluded or currently underrepresented group … by using criteria which are facially neutral … Thus, for example, the status of being unemployed or of living in a particular geographical area might be stipulated as a relevant condition in order to be eligible for apprenticeship training or entry level employment, with the knowledge that a greater proportion of those who are unemployed or who live in that area are members of the underrepresented group than of the majority group.

Outreach programmes… are designed to attract qualified candidates from the previously underrepresented group … by bringing employment opportunities to the attention of members of the group who might not previously have been aware of them and encouraging them to take up the opportunity to apply … [and] by providing members of the underrepresented group without the necessary skills or qualifications with training …

Preferential treatment in employment… involves a plan to reduce … underrepresentation … more directly … by introducing what has sometimes been called reverse discrimination … at one or more points of the employment relationship such as hiring, promotion and redundancy …

Redefining 'merit' … alters substantially the qualifications which are necessary to do the job by including race, gender, or religion [etc] as a relevant 'qualification' in order to be able to do the job properly. Group membership is a job-related qualification, rather than an exception to it, as it is in the fourth type. Dworkin[1] has argued that there 'is no combination of abilities and skills and traits that constitutes "merit" in the abstract … If a black skin will, as a matter of regrettable

[1] R Dworkin, *A Matter of Principle* (Cambridge MA, Harvard University Press, 1985) 299.

fact, enable another doctor to do a different medical job better, then that black skin is … "merit."' Positive action has been defended, for example, as a means of encouraging the recruitment of more social workers from minority groups on the grounds that '… there are situations when … colour alone can sometimes serve as a source of client-worker identification …'…

McCrudden's first type of 'affirmative action' is unproblematic from a legal perspective in the UK while the third type was expressly permitted under the predecessor provisions to the EqA, discussed below. The second and fifth types of affirmative action are also discussed below. As McCrudden makes clear, the fourth type of affirmative action, which will be referred to below as 'positive discrimination', can be divided into a number of subcategories. At one end are 'quotas' which, in their most extreme form, are used as a caricature by opponents of affirmative action. At the other end of the spectrum, arguably, is a 'tie-break' model whereby, where if candidates are equally qualified, the 'disadvantaged' candidate (female, racially minoritised, etc) will generally be appointed. We shall see below that the EqA permits some tie-break discrimination.

Positive discrimination has traditionally received scant support within the UK where such measures have generally been regarded with suspicion and/or hostility. Although some such treatment is permitted under the EqA, there remains a strong cultural resistance to anything that could be categorised as 'reverse' or 'positive discrimination'. This was evident in the response of large sections of the press to the modest provisions included in the Equality Bill (implemented as the EqA), which generated headlines including 'Now Labour plans law to bar white men from jobs', 'It's not positive, it's just discrimination', 'Harman tells ministers to discriminate in favour of women in latest "equality" drive' and 'Harman's equality law "will hurt white male jobseekers"'.[2] Dominic Raab, variously Deputy Prime Minister, Lord Chancellor, and Secretary of State for Justice, struck a similar note in 2011:

Dominic Raab, 'Perils and injustices in the Equality Act'[3]

Two of the major flaws of the last government – excessive political correctness and ill-thought through legislation – found their perfect form in Harriet Harman's Equality Act. Whilst the aim of bringing together the various disparate strands of anti-discrimination legislation made some sense on grounds of clarity, it was feared that the Bill would become a vehicle for social engineering.

Four hangover provisions of the Act, not brought into force before the 2010 election, left a dilemma for the incoming coalition – the parties have mixed views on them. Ministers acted swiftly to ditch the public sector duty to reduce socio-economic inequality, the notorious 'socialism-in-one clause'. Then, they reined in plans by the previous government to impose mandatory gender pay audits on business – adopting a voluntary approach, working with businesses to increase transparency rather than generating onerous bureaucratic requirements. So far, so good.

However, in April of this year, the government quietly implemented section 159 of the Equality Act – which for the first time licences positive discrimination in recruitment – where several candidates are 'as qualified as each other'. In the Soviet style double-speak of the Equality and Human Rights Commission this is merely 'positive action'. Yet, when it comes to offering a job, the decisive factor may now ultimately be race, gender, sexuality, age, disability, religion, philosophical belief or other social factors – positive discrimination by any other name. It will be voluntary to begin with, but the Commission clearly expects to coax and cajole its increasing use. Such positive discrimination warps the basic value of equality. It smacks of double standards, and has created bitter divisions wherever it has been tried, mainly in countries grappling with historic

[2] Respectively, *Express*, 17 March 2008, *The Telegraph*, 29 June 2008, *Daily Mail*, 18 June 2009 and *Daily Mail*, 3 December 2009.

[3] https://www.conservativehome.com/platform/2011/07/dominic-raab.html.

> injustice or ethnic strife – like Malaysia, South Africa and the United States. Section 159 is a recipe for resentment, stigmatising new recruits and sowing social discord. As Kat Akingbade told the Independent on Sunday when she learnt she had been awarded a new job as a Channel 4 TV presenter on grounds of colour: 'Positive discrimination robs an individual of drive and self-motivation; it completely undermines the achievements and abilities of the hard-working and truly gifted'.

Section 159 EqA is discussed below, as are arguments for and against positive discrimination. It is worth noting, however, that the cultural hostility to positive discrimination (and to positive action more generally), which has been prevalent in the UK, is not typical of other European states. And even in the US, where there have been many successful legal challenges to programmes allowing preferential treatment of minority candidates in, for example, education, employment and contracting situations, there has generally been a significant degree of support across the political spectrum for some forms of preferential treatment.

Over the last 20 years or so there have been important developments across the UK, the effect of which has been to increase the role of positive action in challenging discrimination and promoting equality. Initially these took the form of 'soft' (non-legal) 'goals and timetables' for the advancement of women, racially minoritised and disabled candidates in the public sphere. These were not conspicuously successful but they may have helped to pave the way for the Public Sector Equality Duty (PSED), first introduced into the Race Relations Act 1976 (RRA) in 2001[4] and now found in s149 EqA. The EqA is discussed below, after we consider the approach to positive discrimination under Article 14 ECHR and under EU law. The first is significant both to the application of the Human Rights Act 1998 and the interpretation of the EqA itself. The latter has been important in shaping domestic legislation and continues to be influential even after the UK's withdrawal from the EU.

Positive Discrimination and Article 14 ECHR

> **Article 14 ECHR**
>
> The enjoyment of the rights and freedoms set forth in this Convention shall be secured without discrimination on any ground such as sex, race, colour, language, religion, political or other opinion, national or social origin, association with a national minority, property, birth or other status.

'Discrimination' is undefined in the text of Article 14, but has been interpreted to include direct and indirect discrimination and a failure to treat differently situations which are relevantly dissimilar (see Chapter 2). All discrimination is subject to a defence of justification which varies according to the personal characteristic associated with the discrimination and the context in which the discrimination takes place. The ECtHR has developed a category of characteristics, not all of them among those listed in Article 14, in relation to which 'very weighty reasons' are generally required. These include sex, sexual orientation, nationality and religion, while discrimination on grounds of race is particularly difficult to justify.[5] In *Stec v UK* (2006) 43 EHRR 47 the ECtHR adopted a less rigorous

[4] By the Race Relations 1976 (Amendment) Act 2000, which was implemented in April 2001.

[5] See *Abdulaziz v UK* (1985) 7 EHRR 471 (sex); *EB v France* (2008) 47 EHRR 21 (sexual orientation); *Gaygusuz v Austria* (1996) 23 EHRR 364 (nationality); *Hoffmann v Austria* (1993) 17 EHRR 293 (religion); *DH v Czech Republic* (race).

approach to sex discrimination which it regarded as part of a package of measures designed to ameliorate disadvantage, requiring only that the measure not be 'manifestly without reasonable foundation' (MWRF).[6] The domestic courts interpreted this test as applicable wherever the discrimination in issue occurred in the context of welfare benefits in a number of cases including decisions of the Supreme Court (SC).[7] In *JD v UK*, however, the ECtHR made it clear that it had only applied the MWRF test to cases involving positive action.[8]

***JD v UK* (App nos 32949/17 and 34614/17, judgment of 24 February 2020) (2020) 48 BHRC 36**

The Court:

> 80. The court reiterates that in the enjoyment of the rights and freedoms guaranteed by the Convention, art.14 affords protection against different treatment, without an objective and reasonable justification, of persons in relevantly similar situations [citing *Burden v UK* [2008] 37 EHRR 38].
>
> 81. The court also recalls that the provisions of the Convention do not prevent Contracting States from introducing general policy schemes by way of legislative measures whereby a certain category or group of individuals is treated differently from others, provided that the interference with the rights of the statutory category or group as a whole can be justified under the Convention [citing *Andrejeva v Latvia* (2010) 51 EHRR 28; and *Ždanoka v Latvia* (2007) 45 EHRR 17]. Indeed, measures of economic and social policy often involve the introduction and application of criteria which are based on making distinctions between categories or groups of individuals …
>
> 83. For the purposes of art.14, a difference of treatment based on a prohibited ground is discriminatory if it 'has no objective and reasonable justification', that is, if it does not pursue a 'legitimate aim' or if there is no 'reasonable relationship of proportionality between the means employed and the aim sought to be realised' [citing *Mazurek v France* (2006) 42 EHRR 9] …
>
> 86. … art.14 does not preclude States from treating groups differently even on otherwise prohibited grounds in order to correct 'factual inequalities' between them. Moreover, in certain circumstances a failure to attempt to correct inequality through different treatment may in itself give rise to a breach of the article [citing *Thlimmenos*, *Stec* and *DH v Czech Republic*[9]].
>
> 87. In the context of art.1 of Protocol 1 alone, the court has often held that in matters concerning, for example, general measures of economic or social strategy, the States usually enjoy a wide margin of appreciation under the Convention … Because of their direct knowledge of their society and its needs, the national authorities are in principle better placed than the international judge to appreciate what is in the public interest on social or economic grounds, and the court will generally respect the legislature's policy choice unless it is 'manifestly without reasonable foundation.
>
> 88. However, as the court has stressed in the context of art.14 in conjunction with art.1 Protocol 1, although the margin of appreciation in the context of general measures of economic

[6] See similarly [2007] 2 FCR 178.

[7] *Humphreys v HMRC* [2012] UKSC 18, [2012] 1 WLR 1545; *R (MA) v SSWP* [2016] UKSC 58, [2016] 1 WLR 4550; *R (DA) v SSWP* [2019] UKSC 21, [2019] 1 WLR 3289.

[8] The case was an appeal from *R (MA)*, *ibid.*

[9] *DH v Czech Republic* (2008) 47 EHRR 3.

> or social policy is, in principle, wide, such measures must nevertheless be implemented in a manner that does not violate the prohibition of discrimination as set out in the Convention and complies with the requirement of proportionality ... Thus, even a wide margin in the sphere of economic or social policy does not justify the adoption of laws or practices that would violate the prohibition of discrimination. Hence, in that context the Court has limited its acceptance to respect the legislature's policy choice as not 'manifestly without reasonable foundation' to circumstances where an alleged difference in treatment resulted from a transitional measure forming part of a scheme carried out in order to correct an inequality [citing *Stec* §§61–66; *Runkee v UK* [2007] 2 FCR 178 §§40–41 and *British Gurkha Welfare Society v UK* (2017) 64 EHRR 11].

The MWRF test is easy to satisfy, requiring as it does little more than a rational relationship between means and ends. It is also clear from paragraph 86 of the *JD* decision, and from the decision in *Thlimmenos v Greece* (2000) 31 EHRR 411 discussed in Chapter 2, that Article 14 may *require*, rather than simply *permit*, differential treatment to remedy disadvantage. In *Thlimmenos* the ECtHR ruled that the state was required, in operating a ban on admission to the occupation of chartered accountant on those with criminal convictions, to distinguish between those whose convictions indicated moral turpitude and those whose convictions did not, but were the result of religious belief (there conscientious objection to military service). This aspect of the ECtHR's jurisprudence has yet to be developed, but it is clear that Article 14 ECHR does not impose any significant hurdles to positive discrimination.[10]

Positive Discrimination and EU Law

EU law now regulates discrimination across all characteristics protected by the EqA, though in the case of age, disability, religion and belief, and sexual orientation only in relation to work (broadly defined). The CJEU has typically regarded positive discrimination as an exception to the principle of equality/non-discrimination, which as such falls to be narrowly interpreted. The case law will be dealt with briefly below. It is important to recall, however, that the specific provisions under consideration in the case law have been superseded; Article 2(4) of the original Equal Treatment Directive (Council Directive 76/207/EEC) provided that the prohibition on sex discrimination was 'without prejudice to measures *to promote equal opportunity* for men and women, in particular by removing existing inequalities which affect women's opportunities' in relation to work and, to a more limited extent, social security (emphasis added). That Directive was replaced by Directive 2006/54/EC ('the Recast Directive') which provides, so far as relevant, that:

> **Article 3, Council Directive 2006/54/EC**
>
> **Positive action**
>
> Member States may maintain or adopt measures within the meaning of Article 141(4) of the Treaty with a view to ensuring full equality in practice between men and women in working life.

[10] The ECtHR's *Guide on Article 14 of the European Convention on Human Rights and on Article 1 of Protocol No 12 to the Convention* suggests that *Thlimmenos* is a form of positive discrimination. The guide is available at https://www.echr.coe.int/Pages/home.aspx?p=caselaw/analysis/guides&c.

Article 141(4) has now been superseded by Article 157(4) TFEU which provides that 'With a view to ensuring full equality in practice between men and women in working life, the principle of equal treatment shall not prevent any Member State from maintaining or adopting measures providing for specific advantages in order to make it easier for the underrepresented sex to pursue a vocational activity or to prevent or compensate for disadvantages in professional careers'. That formulation is significantly broader than that in Article 2(4) of the Equal Treatment Directive. A similar rubric is adopted by the Council Directives 2004/113/EC, which regulates sex discrimination in goods and services (Articles 6 and 3 respectively), Article 6 providing that:

Article 6, Council Directive 2004/113/EC

With a view to ensuring full equality in practice between men and women, the principle of equal treatment shall not prevent any Member State from maintaining or adopting specific measures to prevent or compensate for disadvantages linked to sex.

Council Directive 2000/43/EC, which regulates race discrimination in relation to work, education, access to goods and services and premises, and Council Directive 2000/78/EC, which regulates discrimination on grounds of age, disability, religion and belief and sexual orientation in relation to work, make materially identical provision in Articles 5 and 7 respectively, the latter going on to state that:

Article 7, Council Directive 2000/78/EC

With regard to disabled persons, the principle of equal treatment shall be without prejudice to the right of Member States to maintain or adopt provisions on the protection of health and safety at work or to measures aimed at creating or maintaining provisions or facilities for safeguarding or promoting their integration into the working environment.

Leaving aside the provision specific to disabled persons, the same test applies across the protected characteristics: Member States may permit and adopt 'specific measures to prevent or compensate for disadvantages linked to' a protected characteristic.

The original approach of the EU court to positive discrimination was unenthusiastic. In Case C-312/86 *Commission v France* [1988] ECR I-6315 the CJEU took a narrow approach and ruled that the exception provided by Article 2(4) was 'specifically and exclusively designed to allow measures which, although discriminatory in appearance, are in fact intended to eliminate or reduce actual instances of inequality which may exist in the reality of social life.' Subsequently, in Case C-450/93 *Kalanke v Freie Hansestadt Bremen* Case C-450/93 EU:C:1995:322, [1995] ECR I-3051, [1996] ICR 314 the CJEU followed the approach of Advocate General Tesauro, who stated that Article 2(4) permitted only 'measures relating to the organisation of work, in particular working hours, and structures for small children and other measures which will enable family and work commitments to be reconciled with each other ... educational guidance and vocational training' and that it did not permit 'action ... regarded, even less employed, as a means of remedying, through discriminatory measures, a situation of impaired inequality in the past'. The CJEU agreed that Article 2(4) permitted only actions directed towards equality of *opportunity*, rather than *outcome.*

The decision in *Kalanke* was greeted with a great deal of disquiet. The European Commission issued a Communication to the European Parliament and the Council on the interpretation of the judgment to the effect that the decision condemned only the granting of an 'absolute and unconditional right to appointment or promotion', leaving it open to states to take and to permit to be taken 'all other forms of positive action including flexible quotas'.[11] The Commission also unsuccessfully proposed an amendment to the Directive expressly to permit 'the giving of preference, as regards access to employment or promotion, to a member of the under-represented sex, provided that such measures do not preclude the assessment of the particular circumstances of an individual case.'[12]

Within two years, the CJEU adopted the approach advocated by the Commission in its Communication on the *Kalanke* decision in *Marschall v Land Nordrhein-Westfalen*. That case concerned a challenge to legislation (virtually indistinguishable from that at issue in *Kalanke*) providing for preferential treatment of equally qualified and suitable women candidates where there were fewer women than men in a particular career bracket, 'unless reasons specific to an individual [male] candidate tilt the balance in his favour'. Advocate General Jacobs argued that the decision in *Kalanke* was correct and that no distinction could properly be drawn between its facts and those in the present case, although he accepted the argument that legislative reform might well be required. The Court, however, seized upon the 'savings clause' to reach a different conclusion.[13]

Case C-409/95 *Marschall v Land Nordrhein-Westfalen* EU:C:1997:533, [1997] ECR I-6363, [2001] ICR 45

Judgment:

> ... even where male and female candidates are equally qualified, male candidates tend to be promoted in preference to female candidates particularly because of prejudices and stereotypes concerning the role and capacities of women in working life and the fear, for example, that women will interrupt their careers more frequently, that owing to household and family duties they will be less flexible in their working hours, or that they will be absent from work more frequently because of pregnancy, childbirth and breastfeeding. For these reasons, the mere fact that a male candidate and a female candidate are equally qualified does not mean that they have the same chances.
>
> *It follows that* a national rule in terms of which, subject to the application of the saving clause, female candidates for promotion who are equally as qualified as the male candidates are to be treated preferentially in sectors where they are under-represented may fall within the scope of Article 2(4) if such a rule may counteract the prejudicial effects on female candidates of the attitudes and behaviour described above and thus reduce actual instances of inequality which may exist in the real world [emphasis added].

The only qualification imposed by the Court in *Marschall* to its newly permissive approach to positive discrimination was that:

> since Article 2(4) constitutes a derogation from an individual right laid down by the directive, such a national measure specifically favouring female candidates cannot guarantee absolute and unconditional priority for women in the event of a promotion without going beyond the limits of

[11] COM (96) 88 final 3.

[12] (97/C 30/19) OJ C.30/57, 30 January 1997. See further U O' Hare, 'Positive Action Before the European Court of Justice [1996] 2 *Web Journal of Current Legal Issues*; V Sacks, 'What do we think about affirmative action now?' (1996) 2 *International Journal of Discrimination and the Law* 129.

[13] The legislation at issue in *Kalanke* had in fact contained a materially identical clause according to the observations of the Länder reported in the CJEU decision.

> the exception laid down in that provision (see *Kalanke* …) Unlike the rules at issue in *Kalanke*, a national rule which, as in the case in point in the main proceedings, contains a saving clause does not exceed those limits if, in each individual case, it provides for male candidates who are equally as qualified as the female candidates a guarantee that the candidatures will be the subject of an objective assessment which will take account of all criteria specific to the individual candidates and will override the priority accorded to female candidates where one or more of those criteria tilts the balance in favour of the male candidate … It is for the national court to determine whether those conditions are fulfilled on the basis of an examination of the scope of the provision in question as it has been applied.

The CJEU continued to develop a cautious acceptance of positive action in its subsequent caselaw, in Case C-158/97 *Badeck v Hessen* approving German provincial legislation which, inter alia, required that public administrative departments adopt 'women's advancement plans' and take other measures to 'work towards equality of women and men in the public service and the elimination of under-representation of women and to eliminate discrimination on grounds of sex and family status.' Some elements of the action plans were directed towards the elimination of indirect discrimination, but the plans went beyond this to require equality of outcome to a significant degree. Binding targets were required to increase the proportion of women in sectors in which they were under-represented and more than half of all positions arising during the two year duration of each plan were to be designated for women, save where a genuine occupational requirement (GOR)[14] applied or it was 'convincingly demonstrated that not enough women with the necessary qualifications are available'. Promotions of women had, at least, to be in proportion to their relative position in the lower rung of employment and the proportion of women had to be protected in the event of redundancies. Particular measures applied to academic jobs, and quotas were established for training positions in occupations in which women were under-represented. Finally, if the targets were not fulfilled in respect of each two-year plan, every further appointment or promotion of a man in a sector in which women were under-represented was to require the approval of the body which had approved the advancement plan or, in some cases, the provincial government.

Case C-158/97 *Badeck v Hessen* EU:C:2000:163, [2000] ECR I–01875

The CJEU ruled that measures intended to give priority to women in sectors of the public service where they are under-represented were compatible with the Equal Treatment Directive as long as (a) they did not *automatically and unconditionally* give priority to women when women and men were equally qualified, and (b) the candidatures were the subject of an objective assessment which took account of the specific personal situations of all candidates. While it was for the national courts to decide whether these conditions were satisfied, the Court went on to suggest that none of the provisions at issue breached the Directive. It ruled that the Directive does not preclude a national rule which:

Judgment:

— in sectors of the public service where women are under-represented, gives priority, where male and female candidates have equal qualifications, to female candidates where that proves necessary for ensuring compliance with the objectives of the women's advancement plan, if no reasons of greater legal weight are opposed, provided that that rule guarantees

[14] See Ch 4.

> that candidatures are the subject of an objective assessment which takes account of the specific personal situations of all candidates,
> — prescribes that the binding targets of the women's advancement plan for temporary posts in the academic service and for academic assistants must provide for a minimum percentage of women which is at least equal to the percentage of women among graduates, holders of higher degrees and students in each discipline,
> — in so far as its objective is to eliminate under-representation of women, in trained occupations in which women are under-represented and for which the State does not have a monopoly of training, allocates at least half the training places to women, unless despite appropriate measures for drawing the attention of women to the training places available there are not enough applications from women,
> — where male and female candidates have equal qualifications, guarantees that qualified women who satisfy all the conditions required or laid down are called to interview, in sectors in which they are under-represented,
> — relating to the composition of employees' representative bodies and administrative and supervisory bodies, recommends that the legislative provisions adopted for its implementation take into account the objective that at least half the members of those bodies must be women.

In Case C-366/99 *Griesmar v Ministre de l'Economie*, EU:C:2001:648, [2001] ECR I-9383, [2003] 3 CMLR 95 the CJEU disapproved a scheme for French civil servants which provided mothers with additional pension credits in order to address what the French Government characterised as the 'social reality', ie, that such women were professionally disadvantaged by their unequal responsibility for children even where they continued to work.' The CJEU ruled that the arrangement breached Article 2(4) because the credit was not directly linked to maternity leave or child-related absences from work and 'simply took it for granted that they were brought up at the home of their mother'.[15] In the same year, however, in the *Lommers* case, the Court approved a Dutch scheme which provided workplace nursery places for the children of women employees only, save in 'emergency' cases in which a man bringing up children on his own would be similarly eligible. Having ruled that it was for the national court to determine whether women were significantly under-represented and were particularly likely to be disadvantaged by a shortage of suitable childcare facilities, and whether the 'derogation' from the right to equal treatment was 'proportionate,' the Court continued:

Case C-476/99 *Lommers v Minister van Landbouw, Natuurbeheer en Visserij* EU:C:2002:183, [2002] ECR I–9383

Judgment:

> A measure such as that at issue in the main proceedings, whose purported aim is to abolish a *de facto* inequality, might nevertheless also help to perpetuate a traditional division of roles between men and women.

[15] And see Sandra Fredman's criticism of the decision in *Lommers* in 'Facing the future: Substantive Equality under the Spotlight' in O Dupper and C Garbers, *Equality in the Workplace: Reflections from South Africa and Elsewhere* (South Africa, University of Stellenbosch, 2010).

That fact may, admittedly, appear to lend support to the academic legal opinion to which the national court refers and which argues that, if the aim of promoting equality of opportunity between men and women pursued by the introduction of a measure benefiting working mothers can still be achieved if its scope is extended to include working fathers, the exclusion of men from its scope would not be in conformity with the principle of proportionality.

However, in the case now under consideration, account must be taken of the fact that, given the insufficiency of supply mentioned above, the number of nursery places available under the measure at issue is itself limited and that there are waiting lists for female officials working at the Ministry of Agriculture, so that they themselves have no guarantee of being able to obtain a place.

Moreover, a measure such as that at issue does not have the effect of depriving the male employees concerned, any more than other female staff who have not been able to obtain a nursery place under the nursery places scheme subsidised by the Ministry of Agriculture, of all access to nursery places for their children, since such places still remain accessible mainly on the relevant services market …

Next, it must also be remembered that the measure at issue does not totally exclude male officials from its scope … In this respect, a measure which would exclude male officials who take care of their children by themselves from access to a nursery scheme subsidised by their employer would go beyond the permissible derogation provided for in Article 2(4), by interfering excessively with the individual right to equal treatment which that provision guarantees. Moreover, in relation to those officials, the argument that women are more likely to interrupt their career in order to take care of their young children no longer has the same relevance.

In the circumstances described … it cannot be maintained that the fact that the Circular does not guarantee access to nursery places to officials of both sexes on an equal footing is contrary to the principle of proportionality.

All the cases discussed above concerned the application of Article 2(4) of the Equal Treatment Directive which, as set out above, provides (only) that the Directive was 'without prejudice to measures to promote equal opportunity for men and women, in particular by removing existing inequalities which affect women's opportunities'. We saw above that the formulation in Article 157 TFEU which post-dates the decisions, and in the Directives which are currently in force, refers more broadly to measures to prevent or compensate for disadvantages linked to protected characteristics in order to ensure 'full equality'. The decision of the CJEU in the *Abrahamsson* case suggests the change in terminology did not make a great difference to the approach of the CJEU.

Case C-407/98 *Abrahamsson & Anderson v Fogelqvist* EU:C:2000:367, [2000] ECR I–5539, [2002] ICR 932

The CJEU was asked to rule on the legality of Swedish regulations whereby universities which were recruiting to academic jobs in which women were under-represented were required to grant preference to a candidate from the under-represented sex. The regulations, which provided that the less qualified candidate was not to be appointed 'where the difference between the candidates' qualification is so great that such application would give rise to a breach of the requirement of objectivity in the making of appointments,' had been adopted following the failure of earlier regulations which permitted (but did not require) positive action significantly to affect the under-representation of women in the academic sphere. The CJEU ruled that the scheme breached the Equal Treatment Directive, and that it would have done so even if applied only in relation to a predetermined number of posts or to posts created as part of a specific programme of a particular higher educational institution allowing the application of positive discrimination measures. Having reiterated the *Marschall* holding that the Equal Treatment Directive was consistent with the granting of preference to a candidate of the under-represented sex where qualifications were equal and candidatures were subjected to an objective assessment taking account of their specific personal situations of all the candidates, the Court went on to rule that:

> even though [Article 157 TEU] allows the Member States to maintain or adopt measures providing for special advantages intended to prevent or compensate for disadvantages in professional careers in order to ensure full equality between men and women in professional life, it cannot be inferred from this that it allows a selection method of the kind at issue in the main proceedings which appears, on any view, to be disproportionate to the aim pursued.[16]

D Caruso, 'Limits of the Classic Method: Positive Action in the European Union After the New Equality Directives' (2003) 44 *Harvard International Law Journal* 331, 343–44, footnotes omitted

The Commission welcomed the *Abrahamsson* decision. Interestingly, on its official web site, the Commission advertised the case as one that 'upheld Swedish measures to combat female under-representation in employment.' This is only partly true. The Court did confirm the permissibility of positive discrimination in favour of women, and explained that gender may operate as a tie-breaker once a tie is established, thereby rejecting with unprecedented clarity the logic of *Kalanke*. However, *Abrahamsson* significantly curtailed the scope of the Swedish regulation in question. The administrators of the University interpreted it to mean that, because the principle of objective assessment was not violated – the female candidate was certainly worthy of the academic post – the requirement of par qualifications could be mildly relaxed. Quite the contrary, after *Abrahamsson*, the formalistic threshold of equal qualifications must be unquestionably met. The female candidate must be just as good as her male competitor. It is only at that point that, rather than tossing a coin, the University deans can use gender as a basis for their final decision.

The case reveals a serious clash of attitude between the CJEU and a member state on affirmative action. In the view of the Swedish establishment, the *Marschall* prerequisite of par qualifications is clearly inadequate to address representational deficiencies in the academic community. Yet, it continues to control the supranational legitimacy of positive action policies.

The approach of the EU courts to positive discrimination has been relatively narrow, but it has evolved from unpromising beginnings in *Commission v France* and *Kalanke* to allow proportionate measures designed to redress disadvantage, even where those measures take effect at the point of recruitment or promotion.

C O'Cinneide, 'Positive Action' (2014), Academy of European Law,[17] footnotes omitted

… the ECJ[18] appears to have established that positive action to compensate for past disadvantages is permissible when used to distinguish between more or less equally qualified candidates, provided that an opportunity for individual merit assessment is always available … The new shift

[16] And see Case C-319/03 *Briheche v Ministre de l'Interieur* EU:C:2004:574, [2004] ECR I-8807.

[17] https://kipdf.com/positive-action-1-introduction_5aca94461723dda5743afa6a.html, accessed 16 September 2022.

[18] The European Court of Justice, referred to throughout the book as the CJEU (Court of Justice of the European Union).

towards a greater embrace of the substantive equality approach can be seen in the ECJ decisions in the cases of *Schnorbus*[19] and *Briheche*[20]. In these cases, the Court accepted that wide discretion should be given to states in deciding how to us positive action measures to remedy the disadvantages faced by women. In the case of *Lommers*, the ECJ considered that a child care scheme which gave priority to women was compatible with the principle of gender equality, on the basis that the child care scheme in question was intended to address the under-representation of women. However, in the cases of *Abrahamssohn* and *EFTA Surveillance Authority v Norway*[21], the ECJ confirmed that giving automatic preference to females would remain a violation of the principle of gender equality.

This case-law thus continues to cause some difficulties. The ECJ has not yet clarified what exactly constitutes giving automatic preference to women. This means that the position of the Court on positive action remains ambiguous and uncertain. This lack of clarity may at times discourage the use of certain forms of positive action in member states, as governments can be reluctant to risk a negative decision by the ECJ …

Furthermore, in the recent decision of Case C-104/09 *Pedro Manuel Roca Álvarez v Sesa Start España ETT SA* [EU:C:2010:561, [2010] ECR I-8661, [2011] 1 CMLR 861], the ECJ took the view that not every measure designed to reflect the fact that women bear the bulk of child-caring responsibilities will qualify as positive action. In particular, positive action measures which are 'underinclusive' (i.e. only assist a proportion of the disadvantaged group) may be vulnerable.

O'Cinneide went on to cite §§34–38 of the decision, which are as follows:

34. The aim of Article 2(4) is to achieve substantive, rather than formal, equality by reducing de facto inequalities which may arise in society and, thus, in accordance with Article 157(4) TFEU, to prevent or compensate for disadvantages in the professional career of the relevant persons [citing *Kalanke*, *Abrahamsson* and *Briheche*].

35. As stated in paragraph 21 of this judgment, the leave at issue in the main proceedings takes the form of permission to be absent during the working day or a reduction of its duration. Certainly, such a measure could have the effect of putting women at an advantage by allowing mothers whose status is that of an employed person to keep their job and to devote time to their child. That effect is reinforced by the fact that if the father of the child is himself an employed person, he is entitled to take this leave in the place of the mother, who would not suffer adverse consequences for her job as a result of care and attention devoted to the child.

36. However, to hold, as the Spanish Government submits, that only a mother whose status is that of an employed person is the holder of the right to qualify for the leave at issue in the main proceedings, whereas a father with the same status can only enjoy this right but not be the holder of it, is liable to perpetuate a traditional distribution of the roles of men and women by keeping men in a role subsidiary to that of women in relation to the exercise of their parental duties …

[19] Case 79/99 *Julia Schnorbus v Land Hessen* EU:C:2000:676, [2000] ECR I-10997, [2001] 1 CMLR 1025, in which the CJEU ruled that the provision of limited preferential treatment as regards access to legal training of those who had performed national service did not discriminate against women (who were not required to perform such service) because it was objective in nature and prompted solely by the desire to counterbalance the delay to the career progression of those required to perform by military. The CJEU in *Schnorbus* did not make reference to Art 2(4), instead suggesting (arguably wrongly) that the discrimination was direct rather than indirect and that it was thus capable of justification (and justified).

[20] Case 319/03 *Briheche v Ministre de l'Intérieur* EU:C:2004:574 [2004] ECR I-8807, [2005] 1 CMLR 4 in which the CJEU ruled that a provision exempting widows, but not widowers, from an age limit of 45 applied to applicants for certain posts in the public-sector was not rescued by Art 2(4) because it automatically and unconditionally gave priority to the candidatures of certain categories of women, including widows who had not remarried who were obliged to work, but excluded widowers who had not remarried and who were in the same situation.

[21] Case E-1/02, [2003] EFTA Ct Rep 1.

> 37. … to refuse entitlement to the leave at issue in the main proceedings to fathers whose status is that of an employed person, on the sole ground that the child's mother does not have that status, could have as its effect that a woman … who is self-employed, would have to limit her self-employed activity and bear the burden resulting from the birth of her child alone, without the child's father being able to ease that burden.
>
> 38. Consequently, a measure such as that at issue in the main proceedings cannot be considered to be a measure eliminating or reducing existing inequalities in society within the meaning of Article 2(4) of Directive 76/207, nor as a measure seeking to achieve substantive as opposed to formal equality by reducing the real inequalities that can arise in society and thus, in accordance with Article 157(4) TFEU, to prevent or compensate for disadvantages in the professional careers of the relevant persons.

The decision in the *Álvarez* case illustrates the need to balance the recognition of the fact that women tend to bear the more significant burden of responsibility for children, with the danger of perpetuating that position. This need for balance may make positive action cases involving childcare leave and similar arrangements particularly difficult to adjudicate. A more recent example of a CJEU decision on the positive action provisions, and one which does not involve sex, is that extracted immediately below. It is included as a rare example of such a case, though as will become clear, it was one in which the discrimination complained of could not on any proper analysis be regarded as directed at the amelioration of disadvantage.

Case C-193/17 *Cresco Investigation GmbH v Achatzi*, EU:C:2019:43, [2019] IRLR 380

The case concerned a challenge to Austrian legislation ('the ARG') which provided for preferential treatment for members of certain Christian churches who worked on Good Friday (a bank holiday). The claimant, who was not a member of any of the churches whose members benefitted from this rule, claimed that he had been the victim of religious discrimination. The CJEU ruled that the differential treatment complained of amounted to direct discrimination because of religion and that it was not justified under Article 7(1) of Council Directive 2000/78/EC.[22]

The Court:

> 64. Article 7(1) of Directive 2000/78 is specifically and exclusively designed to authorise measures which, although discriminatory in appearance, are in fact intended to eliminate or reduce actual instances of inequality which may exist in society …
>
> 65. Further, in determining the scope of any derogation from an individual right such as equal treatment, due regard must be had to the principle of proportionality, which requires that derogations remain within the limits of what is appropriate and necessary in order to achieve the aim in view and that the principle of equal treatment be reconciled as far as possible with the requirements of the aim thus pursued [citing *Lommers*] …
>
> 66. In the present case, without it being necessary to determine whether the fact that Good Friday, which appears to be one of the most important days for the religion of the employees who are members of the churches covered by the ARG, does not correspond to any of the

[22] The Court also ruled that the discrimination was not justified under Art 2(5) of the Directive, which provides that 'This Directive shall be without prejudice to measures laid down by national law which, in a democratic society, are necessary … for the protection of the rights and freedoms of others', because adherents to other religions did not receive similar provision.

public holidays listed in Paragraph 7(2) of that law constitutes a practical disadvantage in their working life, as referred to in art 7(1) of Directive 2000/78, it should be noted that the national legislation at issue in the main proceedings cannot be regarded as including specific measures the aim of which is to compensate for such a 'disadvantage' in accordance with the principle of proportionality and, as far as possible, the principle of equal treatment.

67. … the provisions at issue in the main proceedings grant a 24-hour rest period on Good Friday to employees who are members of one of the churches covered by the ARG, while employees belonging to other religions, whose important festivals do not coincide with the public holidays set out in Paragraph 7(2) of the ARG, can, in principle, be absent from work in order to perform the religious rites associated with those festivals only if they are so authorised by their employer in accordance with the duty of care.

68. It follows that the measures at issue in the main proceedings go beyond what is necessary to compensate for that alleged disadvantage and establish a difference in treatment between employees who are subject to comparable religious duties that does not guarantee, as far as is possible, observance of the principle of equal treatment.

Positive Discrimination and the Equality Act 2010

The passage of the EqA also involved significant extension to the scope of lawful positive discrimination (that is, preferential treatment related to a protected characteristic). This is not expressly referred to in the EqA, but is presumptively unlawful in the case of most protected characteristics by reason of the generally 'symmetrical' approach to discrimination adopted by the EqA. Except in the case of disability, gender reassignment and married/civil partnership status, the EqA prescribes discrimination against those advantaged by the protected characteristic (straight white men, for example) in like terms as it prescribes discrimination against their disadvantaged equivalents (Black lesbians). Save where it falls within ss158 or 159 EqA,[23] positive discrimination related to the protected characteristics of sex, race, sexual orientation and religion or belief will breach the EqA.

The question of whether 'positive discrimination' should be permitted, in what form and in what circumstances, is further addressed below. First it is useful to consider the limited extent to which the EqA currently permits any such discrimination. Most of the discussion of positive discrimination tends to deal with preferential treatment which would, unless expressly permitted, amount to unlawful direct discrimination. It is worth noting, however, that indirect positive discrimination (McCrudden's second form of affirmative action) may also be unlawful. An employer would be permitted (even required) to alter practices which served to exclude particular groups (by, for example, opening up jobs to part-time working where the failure to do this unjustifiably disadvantages women, or permitting some flexibility over Friday afternoon working where rigid rules would disproportionately disadvantage Jews and Muslims). But where any disadvantage suffered by a group defined by reference to one or more protected characteristics is societal (or not attributable, at any rate, to the

[23] Or other relevant provision.

particular employer), and where action to tackle it is aimed at that particular group, the prohibition on indirect discrimination may create a problem unless ss158 or 159 applies.[24]

Chris McCrudden, 'Rethinking Positive Action' (1986) 15 *Industrial Law Journal* 219, 230–32, footnotes omitted

> It is arguable that an attempt by an employer to redress underrepresentation by adopting a policy which is neutral but intentionally inclusive is unlawful as a discriminatory arrangement under the SDA, the RRA and the FEA.[25] An employer decides to give preference to those who are unemployed in order to reduce the imbalance between majority and minority groups in his workforce. This would have the effect of disproportionately including, for example, racial minorities (given the considerably greater rate of black unemployment) without explicitly or intentionally excluding whites who, if they are unemployed, would also be able to benefit. There would, however be a disparate impact on whites. That is both the intention and the problem. The decision may amount, first, to direct discrimination under the three Acts. It would, second, be for the courts to decide whether this policy was indirectly discriminatory and whether it would be 'justifiable' under the SDA and RRA.

In Case 170/84 *Bilka-Kaufhaus GmbH v Weber von Hartz* [1986] ECR I-1607, [1986] ICR 110 the CJEU adopted an objective for the justification of indirect discrimination, requiring that disparately impacting practices correspond to a real need on the part of the undertaking, are appropriate with a view to achieving the objectives pursued and are necessary to that end. That test, which requires that the aims pursued by disparately impacting practices are linked to the needs of the alleged discriminator itself, was adopted by the House of Lords (HL) in *Rainey v Greater Glasgow Health Authority Board* [1987] 1 AC 224. Subsequent to this, the EAT ruled that indirect discrimination could not be justified by reference to wider social issues.

***Greater Manchester Police Authority v Lea* [1990] IRLR 372**

The case concerned a police authority's policy of preferring applicants for employment who were not already in receipt of an occupational pension. The reasoning behind the policy was that occupational pension recipients were less in need of an employment-related income than were others. It was, however, demonstrated to the satisfaction of EAT that the policy impacted disadvantageously on men who were in the (un)fortunate position of being more likely than women (4.7 per cent as against 0.6 per cent) to receive such a pension. Dealing with the matter of justification, EAT ruled (applying *Hampson v DES* [1991] 1 AC 171):

Knox J:

> It is therefore now clear if it was not before that the test is, as thus stated by Lord Justice Balcombe in particular, of an objective balance being struck between the discriminatory effect of the requirement or condition and the reasonable needs of the person who applies it.
>
> In our judgment if one applies that test the Police Authority fails to satisfy the requirement because … it was held and properly held by the Industrial Tribunal that there was no relevant

[24] See also L Barmes, 'Equality Law and Experimentation: The Positive Action Challenge' [2009] 68 *Cambridge Law Journal* 623, 631–32. *cf* S Fredman, 'Addressing Disparate Impact; Indirect Discrimination and the Public Sector Equality Duty (2014) 43 *Industrial Law Journal*.

[25] Respectively the Sex Discrimination Act 1975, the Race Relations Act 1976, and the Fair Employment (Northern Ireland) Act 1989, which is further discussed below.

> need of the Police Authority in connection with this condition. It was of course not enough as appears from the judgments in *Hampson* for it to be shown, as no doubt the Police Authority did show, that the condition was imposed in pursuance of an intrinsically entirely laudable and otherwise reasonable policy of helping the unemployed. *There has in our judgment to be a nexus established between the function of the employer in this type of case and the imposition of the condition* otherwise it is impossible to carry out the objective balance that the Court of Appeal has identified as the test of justifiability in relation to the needs of the employer. There was some discussion before us on the question whether or not different tests might properly be applied to public authority employers as compared with private employers. It would not in our judgment be useful or safe to seek any general principles in that field. What is appropriate to a public authority employer will, inevitably, in our view, be conditioned by the status, almost certainly statutory, of the employer in question. Generalisations would be inappropriate in that type of context because the particular framework, usually statutory, would need to be considered in any given case [emphasis added].

Employers will be permitted to alter indirectly discriminatory practices of their own making. But, absent a specific defence, an employer who acts out of altruism would have to show that a recruitment practice which was designed to favour the disadvantaged (the poor, the disaffected) but which had a disparate impact on one or more groups defined by reference to one or more protected characteristics, 'corresponds to a real need on the part of the undertaking, is appropriate with a view to achieving the objectives pursued and is necessary to that end.' It is perhaps reasonable to make this demand in circumstances where the targeting of one disadvantaged group (for example, the unemployed) serves to exclude disproportionate numbers of another disadvantaged group (women, for example, if definition as unemployed turns on receipt of benefits); or where targeting one disadvantaged (predominantly white) housing estate disproportionately excludes one or more racially minoritised communities. But where the group to whose advantage the targeting works is disadvantaged both in the sense (for example) of being unemployed and, further, by reference to a protected characteristic, one has to question whether the severity of the approach adopted in *Lea* is warranted.

The test for the justification of indirect discrimination has changed since 1991 (from a requirement that the discriminator show that the criterion, etc under practice is 'justifiable irrespective of the sex of the person to whom it is applied' to one that the discriminator show that it is 'a proportionate means of achieving a legitimate aim'). This test is modelled on that laid down by the CJEU in *Bilka-Kaufhaus* which the Court of Appeal (CA) sought to embrace in the *Hampson* case on which EAT relied in *Lea*. It is distinctly possible, therefore, that *Lea* would be followed in a challenge brought under the EqA. And even if the concept of a 'legitimate aim' might (contrary to the decision in *Lea*) encompass aims beyond an employer's immediate workplace concerns, at any rate in a situation in which efforts are being made to ameliorate disadvantage, any effort to favour minority groups (for example, in an attempt to ameliorate the effects of past or ongoing discrimination) may amount to direct discrimination. This would be the case even if the attempt was covert (a deliberate intention to favour a disadvantaged group defined by race, sex, sexual orientation, etc being pursued by targeting remedial action at an overlapping or wider group defined other than on those lines), though in such circumstances the intention to discriminate on the prohibited grounds might be difficult to establish.

Disability, Gender Reassignment and Married/Civilly Partnered Status

As mentioned above, the EqA prohibits discrimination related to married/civilly partnered status and disability against those who are married/civilly partnered, and those with disabilities respectively. This is the result of the following provisions:

> **Section 8 EqA, Marriage and civil partnership**
>
> (1) A person has the protected characteristic of marriage and civil partnership if the person is married or is a civil partner.
>
> (2) In relation to the protected characteristic of marriage and civil partnership—
>
> (a) a reference to a person who has a particular protected characteristic is a reference to a person who is married or is a civil partner;
>
> (b) a reference to persons who share a protected characteristic is a reference to persons who are married or are civil partners.
>
> **Section 13 EqA, Direct discrimination**
>
> (1) A person (A) discriminates against another (B) if, because of a protected characteristic, A treats B less favourably than A treats or would treat others …
>
> (3) If the protected characteristic is disability, and B is not a disabled person, *A does not discriminate against B only because A treats or would treat disabled persons more favourably than A treats B.*
>
> (4) If the protected characteristic is marriage and civil partnership, this section applies to a contravention of Part 5 (work) [which is the only part which regulates such discrimination] *only if the treatment is because it is B who is married or a civil partner* [emphasis added].

It is clear from these provisions that the protection afforded in relation to these characteristics is asymmetrical; the EqA would impose no barrier to measures designed to benefit those with the characteristic of marriage and civil partnership or disability.

The same is true of pregnancy and maternity. Section 13(6) EqA, which is discussed in Chapter 6, provides that:

> If the protected characteristic is sex …
>
> (b) in a case where B is a man, no account is to be taken of special treatment afforded to a woman in connection with pregnancy or childbirth.

The position as regards gender reassignment differs somewhat.

> **Section 7 EqA, Gender reassignment**
>
> (1) A person has the protected characteristic of gender reassignment if the person is proposing to undergo, is undergoing or has undergone a process (or part of a process) for the purpose of reassigning the person's sex by changing physiological or other attributes of sex.
>
> (2) A reference to a transsexual person is a reference to a person who has the protected characteristic of gender reassignment.
>
> (3) In relation to the protected characteristic of gender reassignment—
>
> (a) a reference to a person who has a particular protected characteristic is a reference to a transsexual person;
>
> (b) a reference to persons who share a protected characteristic is a reference to transsexual persons.

Unlike the position as regards disability and married/civilly partnered status, s13 EqA does not limit protection from discrimination because of gender reassignment to those who have the protected characteristic of gender reassignment, as defined in s7 EqA. It would appear to follow that a person who does not have that status could nevertheless challenge direct discrimination if treated less favourably because of that status (even if the status is that of the more favourably treated person). The position as regards indirect discrimination differs, however; s19 EqA defines such discrimination as occurring where 'A person (A) discriminates against another (B) if A applies to B a provision, criterion or practice which is discriminatory in relation *to a relevant protected characteristic of B's*' (emphasis added). Section 7 providing that only those someone who 'is proposing to undergo, is undergoing or has undergone a process (or part of a process) for the purpose of reassigning the person's sex by changing physiological or other attributes of sex' has the protected characteristic of gender reassignment, it follows that someone who does not have that characteristic will be unable to complain of indirect discrimination against people without the characteristic.

Section 7 of the Local Government and Housing Act 1989 (LGHA) requires that all local authority workers be appointed on the basis of 'merit'. The Constitutional Reform and Governance Act 2010 imposes similar requirements on recruitment to the Civil Service, the Constitutional Reform Act 2005 on the selection of judges and the Governance Code on Public Appointments on ministerial appointments to public bodies. The HL confirmed, in *Archibald v Fife Council (Scotland)* [2004] UKHL 32, [2004] ICR 954, that the duty to make reasonable adjustments imposed by the Disability Discrimination Act 1995 (DDA), and now contained in the EqA, may require the employer to treat the disabled person more favourably than others (see further Chapter 8). Section 7 of the 1989 Act was amended by the EqA to provide that the duty to appoint on the basis of merit is subject to the duty to make reasonable adjustments as well as (where relevant) to the GOR defence (discussed in Chapter 4). In other cases where there is an obligation to appoint on merit, the reasonableness of any adjustments will fall to be interpreted in light of the obligation to appoint on 'merit'. We shall see below that advocates of positive discrimination contest the usual approach to the assessment of 'merit'. We shall also see below that such an approach does not seem to have persuaded those responsible for appointing senior public figures.

Age

As we shall discuss in Chapter 11, age is unique among the protected characteristics because age discrimination in its direct, as well as its indirect, form is capable of justification. This does not mean, however, that all positive discrimination because of age would in fact be justified; the test for justification requires that the measure in question is a proportionate means to achieve a legitimate aim. Further, we shall see in Chapter 11 that the range of legitimate aims is narrower for direct age discrimination than it is for indirect discrimination related to this and other protected characteristics. This being the case, there may be situations in which the legitimacy of age discrimination will have to be defended under s158 or s159 EqA.

Sections 158 and 159 EqA

Sections 158 and 159 EqA provide that certain discrimination, whether direct or indirect, which would otherwise breach the EqA will nevertheless be lawful. The provisions apply to all protected characteristics (age, disability, gender reassignment, marriage and civil partnership, pregnancy and maternity, race, religion or belief, sex and sexual orientation), though for reasons set out above they do not need to be relied on where positive action is taken to favour those with disabilities, or married/ civilly partnered persons. They provide as follows:

Section 158 EqA, Positive action: general

(1) This section applies if a person (P) reasonably thinks that—
  (a) persons who share a protected characteristic suffer a disadvantage connected to the characteristic,
  (b) persons who share a protected characteristic have needs that are different from the needs of persons who do not share it, or
  (c) participation in an activity by persons who share a protected characteristic is disproportionately low.

(2) This Act does not prohibit P from taking any action which is a proportionate means of achieving the aim of—
  (a) enabling or encouraging persons who share the protected characteristic to overcome or minimise that disadvantage,
  (b) meeting those needs, or
  (c) enabling or encouraging persons who share the protected characteristic to participate in that activity …

(4) This section does not apply to—
  (a) action within section 159(3), or
  (b) anything that is permitted by virtue of section 104.

(5) If section 104(7) is repealed by virtue of section 105, this section will not apply to anything that would have been so permitted but for the repeal.

(6) This section does not enable P to do anything that is prohibited by or under an enactment other than this Act.

Section 159 EqA, Positive action: recruitment and promotion

(1) This section applies if a person (P) reasonably thinks that—
  (a) persons who share a protected characteristic suffer a disadvantage connected to the characteristic, or
  (b) participation in an activity by persons who share a protected characteristic is disproportionately low.

(2) Part 5 (work) does not prohibit P from taking action within subsection (3) with the aim of enabling or encouraging persons who share the protected characteristic to—
  (a) overcome or minimise that disadvantage, or
  (b) participate in that activity.

(3) That action is treating a person (A) more favourably in connection with recruitment or promotion than another person (B) because A has the protected characteristic but B does not.

(4) But subsection (2) applies only if—
  (a) A is as qualified as B to be recruited or promoted,
  (b) P does not have a policy of treating persons who share the protected characteristic more favourably in connection with recruitment or promotion than persons who do not share it, and
  (c) taking the action in question is a proportionate means of achieving the aim referred to in subsection (2).

(5) 'Recruitment' means a process for deciding whether to—
  (a) offer employment to a person,
  (b) make contract work available to a contract worker,
  (c) offer a person a position as a partner in a firm or proposed firm,
  (d) offer a person a position as a member of an LLP or proposed LLP,
  (e) offer a person a pupillage or tenancy in barristers' chambers,
  (f) take a person as an advocate's devil or offer a person membership of an advocate's stable,
  (g) offer a person an appointment to a personal office,
  (h) offer a person an appointment to a public office, recommend a person for such an appointment or approve a person's appointment to a public office, or
  (i) offer a person a service for finding employment.

(6) This section does not enable P to do anything that is prohibited by or under an enactment other than this Act.

Section 104 EqA provides for positive discrimination in selection arrangements for candidates of registered political parties. It is discussed at p 149 below. Sections 158 and 159 EqA replace narrower provisions under the SDA and RRA which permitted targeted training and advertising in cases of under-representation, but did not allow discrimination in terms of access to jobs.[26] In addition, the SDA allowed trade unions to reserve some female seats on elected bodies and political parties to operate single-sex shortlists[27] and the RRA (s35) permitted any act done in affording persons of a particular racial group access to facilities or services to meet the special needs of that group in relation to their education, health, welfare or any other ancillary benefit.[28] The Employment Equality (Sexual Orientation) and Employment Equality (Religion and Belief) Regulations 2003 (respectively the SO and RB Regs) each allowed targeted training and advertising in cases of disadvantage linked to sexual orientation, religion and belief but, like the SDA and RRA, did not permit discrimination in terms of access to jobs.

The positive action provisions of the RRA and the SDA were little-used. A survey of 441 employers in 1987 found that only seven had made any use of s48 SDA, which permitted sex-targeted training.[29] Vera Sacks' subsequent study of the application of ss47 (which permitted targeted advertising) and 48 SDA concluded that their limited use could be ascribed to the SDA's symmetrical approach and to their permissive, rather than mandatory, nature.[30] That these concerns were not without foundation was confirmed by the decision in *ACAS v Taylor* in which the EAT upheld a finding that a man had been discriminated against in relation to promotion in part because of guidance circulated to decision-makers which stated that 'more needs to be done to ensure the reality of the claim that ACAS is an equal opportunity employer. For example women make up only 17 per cent of those at Senior Executive Officer level at present and ethnic minorities staff less than 1 per cent', also that 'All staff should be considered on their merits as individuals'.

[26] Sections 47 and 48 SDA; ss37 and 38 RRA.

[27] Sections 49, 33 and 42A SDA.

[28] See *R (Kaur & Shah) v LB Ealing* [2008] EWHC 2062 (Admin), discussed at p 171 below.

[29] EOC, 'Review of the Training Opportunities Scheme' (1978); EOC, 'Equality Between the Sexes in Industry: How Far Have We Come?' (1978).

[30] V Sacks, 'Tackling Discrimination Positively in Britain' in B Hepple and E Szyszczak (eds), *Discrimination: The Limits of Law* (London, Mansell, 1992) 380–81.

ACAS v Taylor **EAT/788/97, unreported (11 February 1998)**

Morison J:

> The sentence 'Please remember that more needs to be done to ensure the reality of the claim that ACAS is an equal opportunity employer' is readily capable of being misconstrued. Furthermore, it begs the question as to what is to be done and by whom. It seems to us that it would have been more appropriate and quite sufficient for the guidance to have reminded the line managers that ACAS was an equal opportunity employer and to draw attention to the fact that women and ethnic minorities staff at SEO level were poorly represented. Such poor representation was itself suggestive of potentially discriminatory practices in the past and the employers were entitled to draw that to the attention of those who had the responsibility for making decisions about promotions in the future. The way the guidance was composed seems to us to be capable of leading the unwary into positive discrimination.

The RRA's positive action provisions were more used than those of the SDA. Research carried out in the early 1990s, mainly in the public sector, found that 82 per cent of employers had used advertisements to encourage applications from racially minoritised workers and that 33 per cent had provided targeted training for such workers. But these 'targeted' advertisements rarely consisted of more than statements that 'all [were] welcome', or that applicants were 'welcome regardless of race', and the use of the provisions was generally 'patchy' and their 'overall impact ... probably limited'.[31]

Sections 158 and 159 EqA now provide relatively generous scope for positive discrimination (preferential treatment related to a protected characteristic) other than in relation to appointment or promotion, though the Government was insistent throughout the consultation process that the provisions permitted *positive action* (defined as 'targeted measures to prevent or compensate for disadvantage or to meet special needs, so that people from disadvantaged groups can compete on equal terms'[32]) while not permitting '*positive discrimination*') (redefined for these purposes as preferential treatment regardless of merit). The-then Solicitor-General, Vera Baird, explained to the Committee which considered the Equality Bill that the clause which became s158 EqA:

HC Debates 30 June 2009, cols 602–03

> establish[es] a permissive framework under which forms of positive action can be taken. Any use of such provisions will be entirely voluntary. There is no requirement for them to be used by specific individuals or organisations. Although they are voluntary, lots of UK businesses have

[31] C Welsh, J Knox and M Brett, *Acting Positively: Positive Action Under the Race Relations Act 1976* (Sheffield, Employment Department, 1994) Research Series No 36, 37. The research found that 61% of employers were influenced in their decision to take some form of positive action by the CRE.

[32] See eg *The Equality Bill – Government response to the Consultation* (July 2008), para 5.2, Cm 7454; Government Equalities Office Equality Act 2010: Quick start guide to positive action in recruitment and promotion (2011) 9: 'Positive discrimination is recruiting or promoting a person solely because they have a relevant protected characteristic. Setting quotas to recruit or promote a particular number or proportion of people with protected characteristics is also positive discrimination. Positive discrimination is unlawful in Great Britain. However, it is important to note that it is not unlawful for an employer to treat a disabled person more favourably in comparison to a non-disabled person)'. *cf* the definition offered by M Noon, 'The shackled runner: time to rethink positive discrimination?' (2010) 24 *Work, Employment and Society* 728, 729–30: 'Positive *discrimination* is the specific recognition of certain characteristics ... considered to have disadvantaged a group of people through no direct fault of their own. It brings consideration of the disadvantage into the formal decision-making process by making these characteristics legitimate criteria for evaluating candidates' (original emphasis).

recognised the benefits of using positive action to create a more diverse work force, to better understand customers' needs and to attract new business. Therefore, the provisions will be used, but it is important to emphasise that they are totally voluntary.

The second characteristic is that it is not … positive discrimination. Positive discrimination would favour a person from a particular underrepresented or disadvantaged group solely because they come from that particular group irrespective of merit. In the main, positive discrimination is unlawful in the UK.

Therefore this is not positive discrimination. We are not talking about favouring somebody just because they come from a particular group. The provisions are about ensuring that people's needs are met, that they have equal opportunities and that they are not held back because of a particular characteristic.

The clause will have effect in cases in which it is reasonable to consider that those with a protected characteristic suffer a disadvantage that is linked to that characteristic, that those who share the characteristic are under-represented in some way, or that those who share the characteristic have particular needs not shared by those without the characteristic in question. In any such situation, the clause will enable organisations, public authorities, employers and service providers to take a wide range of positive action measures to address the disadvantage, and to increase the participation of people with that characteristic. Moreover, any action must be a proportionate way of accomplishing the intended outcome. I am referring to specific training opportunities, targeted health services to address particular needs and providing lessons exclusively for disadvantaged pupils. We want to ensure the appropriate use – we have just canvassed this – of the positive action measures …

Section 158 EqA only allows such positive action as is 'proportionate'. The explanatory notes to the EqA provide (§512) that proportionality 'will depend, among other things, on the seriousness of the relevant disadvantage, the extremity of need or under-representation and the availability of other means of countering them. This provision will need to be interpreted in accordance with European law which limits the extent to which the kind of action it permits will be allowed'. European law and its application to s158 EqA is considered below. The explanatory notes go on to suggest, by way of example, that:

Equality Act 2010, 2010 Chapter 15 Revision Notes §517[33]

- Having identified that its white male pupils are underperforming at maths, a school could run supplementary maths classes exclusively for them.
- An NHS Primary Care Trust identifies that lesbians are less likely to be aware that they are at risk of cervical cancer and less likely to access health services such as national screening programmes. It is also aware that those who do not have children do not know that they are at an increased risk of breast cancer. Knowing this it could decide to establish local awareness campaigns for lesbians on the importance of cancer screening.

There is evidence that s158 has been relied upon by service providers as well as employers.

Chantal Davies and Muriel Robison, 'Bridging the gap: An exploration of the use and impact of positive action in the UK' (2016) *International Journal of Discrimination and the Law*

There are numerous examples of both private and public sector organisations that have demonstrated a commitment to utilising the positive action measures permitted by section 158. In particular:

- The development by HMRC (HM Revenue and Customs) of their 'embrace' programme, which supports and develops talented BAME (Black Asian and Minority Ethnic) employees in order to provide them with equal opportunity in recruitment and promotion;

[33] https://www.legislation.gov.uk/ukpga/2010/15/notes.

- The measures taken by the Barclays Group to engage with and recruit from the broadest graduate BAME talent pool possible;
- Education charity Teach First's move to embed inclusive processes into its graduate recruitment practices and to attract more diverse talent onto its Leadership Development Programme;
- The Chartered Institute of Library and Information Professionals (CILIP) Encompass scheme which uses positive action to encourage those from BAME communities to develop and choose a career in library and information work;
- The BBC setting up the Journalism Talent Pool to help increase the diversity of its workforce;
- The Metropolitan Police Service introducing a positive action talent development programme to nurture BAME junior officers into senior leadership roles.

The list goes on with numerous examples of good practice and innovative positive action measures being implemented by employers … all of those engaging in such measures would appear to recognise not only the social context within which they act, but also the business case for expanding their talent pool by using positive action.

Section 158 EqA has only been considered in one reported case in England and Wales.[34]

***R (Z) v Hackney LBC* [2020] UKSC 40, [2021] 1 WLR 4327**

The claimants challenged Hackney's allocation of a fraction (less than one per cent) of its social housing via a charitable housing association (Agudas Israel Housing Association/ AIHA) which prioritised applicants from the Orthodox Jewish Community. The reason for the priority was that Orthodox Jewish families were disadvantaged in access to general social housing by reason of their tendency to have large families. The claimants – a mother and child who were not Orthodox Jews – complained that they had been unlawfully discriminated against contrary to s13(1) EqA. The local authority accepted that its approach did involve direct discrimination, but sought to rely on s158 as well as on s193 EqA, which permits charities to restrict the provision of benefits to persons who share a protected characteristic where this is (a) a proportionate means of achieving a legitimate aim, or (b) for the purpose of preventing or compensating for a disadvantage linked to the protected characteristic.[35]

The Divisional Court ([2019] EWHC 139 (Admin)) ruled that the arrangements were a proportionate means of overcoming a disadvantage shared by members of the Orthodox Jewish community, and were permitted by s158, as well as s193 EqA. This being the case, the Court was satisfied that the local authority's allocation policy was lawful. The claimants appealed claiming (as far as s158 EqA was concerned) that the discrimination was not proportionate. The claimants' attempt to rely on the Race

[34] Though it was the subject of passing comment by the Divisional Court in *R (Adath Yisroel Burial Society) v HM Senior Coroner for Inner North London* [2018] EWHC 969 (Admin), [2019] QB 251 (see Ch 4). In addition, it has been the subject of consideration by the Scottish courts in *For Women Scotland Ltd (Petitioner)* [2021] CSOH 31 and (on appeal) *For Women Scotland Ltd v The Lord Advocate and The Scottish Ministers* [2022] CSIH 4 in which the Court of Session ruled that the Scottish Government had acted unlawfully in including transgender women as women for the purpose of positive action measures in the Gender Representation on Public Boards (Scotland) Act 2018.

[35] Section 193 provides, so far as relevant, that '(1) A person does not contravene this Act only by restricting the provision of benefits to persons who share a protected characteristic if (a) the person acts in pursuance of a charitable instrument, and (b) the provision of the benefits is within subsection (2). (2) The provision of benefits is within this subsection if it is (a) a proportionate means of achieving a legitimate aim, or (b) for the purpose of preventing or compensating for a disadvantage linked to the protected characteristic'. See discussion in Ch 4.

Directive (Council Directive 2000/43/EC) was rejected by the CA because they had presented the claim as one of religious discrimination alone in the Divisional Court ([2019] EWCA Civ 1099, [2019] PTSR 2272). The appeal to the SC also failed, the Court ruling that the Race Directive did not apply because the discrimination in this case, unlike that in the *JFS* case[36] concerned religious *observance* rather than (as there) recognition as Jewish according to the Office of the Chief Rabbi (which depended on matrilineal descent). The Court also rejected the claim that EU law would have prohibited the discrimination in issue even had it applied.

The claimants sought to argue that EU law permitted positive discrimination only where the aim of the discrimination was to provide equality of *opportunity* rather than equality of *outcome*, and that a disadvantaged person could be given priority only in a 'tie-break' situation (relying on the CJEU cases discussed at pp 119–128 above). Lord Sales stated at §62, for the majority, that 'There is no general doctrine of positive discrimination in EU law, which is subject to the limitations' suggested for the claimants, pointing out that the cases were concerned with the interpretation of Article 2(4) of the Equal Treatment Directive, which provides that the Directive's general prohibition on sex discrimination 'shall be without prejudice to measures to promote equal opportunity for men and women, in particular by removing existing inequalities which affect women's opportunities'.

Lord Sales, with whom Lords Reed, Kerr and Kitchen agreed, Lady Arden concurring:[37]

> 65. … proportionality analysis requires identification of a legitimate aim and then an assessment whether a measure taken to promote that aim is proportionate in its effects in pursuing it, having regard to other interests at stake. For present purposes, what is significant about the Equal Treatment Directive is that art 2(4) identifies the aim which is to be regarded as a legitimate basis for departing from the general obligation of equal treatment imposed by art 2(1), namely promotion of equality of opportunity in employment rather than equality of outcome. In the judgments referred to, rules of national law were held to be compatible with the Directive if limited to securing equality of opportunity but were held to be incompatible if they went beyond promotion of equality of opportunity and sought to achieve equality of outcome in terms of equal representation of men and women in the workforce. This tells one nothing of any significance about the proper approach to proportionality in the context of s 158 and s 193(2)(a) of the 2010 Act. In fact, separate provision is made in the 2010 Act, in s 159, governing positive action in relation to employment.
>
> 66. In each of s 158 and s 193(2)(a), the range of permissible legitimate aims is wider than the legitimate aim specified in art 2(4) of the Equal Treatment Directive and includes seeking to achieve particular outcomes, ie enabling persons who share the protected characteristic to overcome or minimise disadvantages they suffer which are connected to the characteristic or to meet needs particular to persons with the protected characteristic, in the case of s 158; or any legitimate aim in the case of s 193(2)(a) (which includes aims recognised as legitimate under s 158). Accordingly, the correct question, as the Divisional Court and the Court of Appeal rightly appreciated, is whether AIHA's allocation policy is a measure which is proportionate to promoting such aims in relation to ameliorating the position of members of the Orthodox Jewish community. Those aims relate to improving outcomes for that community, not merely equality of opportunity of the more limited kind discussed in the cases on the Equal Treatment Directive …

[36] *R (E) v JFS* [2009] UKSC 15, [2010] 2 AC 728, discussed in Ch 7.

[37] On the basis that the Divisional Court's evaluation of proportionality was one which it was entitled to make, and which could not be set aside on appeal.

74. [Having stated the view that the decision of the CJEU in *Cresco* was more relevant to the instant case because of the broader positive action provision in the Race Directive than in the Equal Treatment Directive[38]] … Since the Divisional Court gave itself a correct self-direction as to the test to be applied, its conclusion that AIHA's allocation policy is a proportionate means of pursuing the legitimate aims identified can only be set aside if the appeal court comes to the view that its conclusion was wrong in the relevant sense. It is not sufficient that an appellate court might think it would have arrived at a different conclusion had it been considering the matter for the first time …

80. Positive action pursuant to s 158 has to address needs or disadvantages experienced in connection with a protected characteristic, and so contemplates that a group-based approach may be adopted, defined by reference to one of the protected characteristics as shared with others (such as gender, disability or religion). Similarly, in the context of s 193, charities typically focus the benefits they aim to provide on defined groups. Charitable status is a way of recruiting private benevolence for the public good (subject to the public benefit test in the Charities Act), and charities focus on providing for particular groups since that is what motivates private individuals to give money, where they feel a particular link to or concern for the groups in question. It is for the public benefit that private benevolence should be encouraged for projects which supplement welfare and other benefits provided by the state, even though those projects do not confer benefits across the board. Accordingly, Parliament contemplated that the proportionality of measures falling within s 158 and s 193 should be assessed on a group basis, by comparing the advantages for groups covered by the measure in question with the disadvantages for groups falling outside it …

85. In the context of state provision of social welfare benefits, it is well established that it is generally a legitimate approach and in accordance with the principle of proportionality for the state to use bright line criteria to govern their availability [citing *R (RJM) v SSWP* [2008] UKHL 63, [2009] AC 1; *Carson v UK* (2010) 51 EHRR 369 §62 and *R (Tigere) v SS Business, Innovation and Skills* [2015] UKSC 57, [2015] 1 WLR 3820. That is to say, the state is entitled to focus provision of social welfare benefits on a particular group, and hence exclude other groups, even though there may be little or no difference at the margins in terms of need between some particular individual in the first group and another particular individual in the excluded groups. Use of bright line criteria in this way is justified because it minimises the costs of administration of a social welfare scheme; it may be the best way of ensuring that resources are efficiently directed to the group which, overall, needs them most; it can reduce delay in the provision of benefits; and it provides clear and transparent rules which can be applied accurately and consistently, thereby eliminating the need for invidious comparisons of individual cases in all their variety, with the risk of arbitrariness in outcomes which that may involve …

86. These points apply *a fortiori* in relation to a proportionality assessment in respect of a measure taken by a charity, such as AIHA's allocation policy. A charity is a private body which does not have the same responsibility as the state for ensuring equal treatment of citizens, so if the state is entitled to use bright line criteria for distribution of social welfare benefits still more will that be true for a charity. Moreover, charities do not have the same resources as the state, so if the state is entitled to use bright line criteria for distribution of benefits, still more will that be true for a charity. It is in the public interest that charities should be able to minimise their costs of administration. That is in order to ensure that maximum resources are made available to address the problems which charities seek to alleviate and since otherwise charitable giving may be deterred, if donors feel excessive amounts of what they give will be spent on administration rather than actually helping people in need. The aims of minimising wastage of resources on administration and encouraging charitable giving are themselves legitimate objectives to be brought into account in the assessment of proportionality.

[38] See p 127 above.

Section 158 EqA is of general application, applying to education, premises, goods and services, associations and public functions as well as in the context of work. It does not apply, however (s158(4)) to 'action within section 159(3)': that is, to 'treating a person (A) more favourably in connection with recruitment or promotion than another person (B) because A has the protected characteristic but B does not'. This is lawful only to the extent permitted by s159 EqA. Section 159 has not been the subject of any appellate decisions, though there has been one tribunal decision on the provision, which is discussed below. The *Quick Start Guide* published by the Government Equalities Office suggested that it 'allows an employer faced with making a choice between two or more candidates who are of **equal merit** to take into consideration whether one is from a group that is disproportionately under-represented or otherwise disadvantaged within the workforce ... where it is a **proportionate** way of addressing the under-representation or disadvantage' (original emphasis).[39]

Government Equalities Office, Equality Act 2010: *Quick start guide to positive action in recruitment and promotion* (2011) 6–9

What does 'equal merit' mean?

In order to use positive action provisions in a tie-breaker situation, the employer must first establish that the candidates are of equal merit. Employers should establish a set of criteria against which candidates will be assessed when applying for a job. This can take into account a candidate's overall ability, competence and professional experience together with any relevant formal or academic qualifications, as well as any other qualities required to carry out the particular job. However, employers should ensure that any criteria do not indirectly discriminate against people who share a protected characteristic – for example, a requirement that staff must work shift patterns that mean they have to be on-call at certain fixed times might put women, who are more likely to be responsible for childcare issues, at a disproportionate disadvantage. This would be unlawful indirect discrimination unless it could be shown that the need for these work patterns could be objectively justified.

Employers must consider whether candidates are of equal merit in relation to the **specific job or position** they are applying for. While two candidates may be considered to be of equal merit for one particular post, the same two candidates might not be equally suitable for another job.

Example

A health and fitness club is faced with making a choice between two applicants for a job as the manager of a leisure facility. One, a woman, has recently completed a Leisure Management Foundation Degree course but has little practical experience. The other candidate is a man who has no formal qualifications but has several years experience of working in leisure centres. Having interviewed both candidates, the employer decides that both could do the job to the same standard but in different ways as each would bring a different set of skills and experiences to the job. Therefore, because the candidates are of equal merit the manager could voluntarily use the positive action provisions when choosing between the candidates and opt to employ the man because all of the other senior positions at the leisure complex were held by women.

Example

A retailer advertises for a trainee fashion buyer. Among the applicants is a person who has a degree in French. None of the other applicants has a degree in any subject. The fact that one candidate has higher academic qualifications than the others does not automatically make that person better qualified for this particular job. The employer will need to decide if that qualification is a relevant factor in assessing who might do the job as a fashion buyer best.

[39] https://www.gov.uk/government/publications/employers-quick-start-guide-to-positive-action-in-recruitment-and-promotion, 5.

What does 'reasonably thinks' mean?

Positive action in recruitment and promotion can be used where an employer **reasonably thinks** that people with a protected characteristic are under-represented in the workforce, or suffer a disadvantage connected to that protected characteristic. Some information or evidence will be required to indicate to the employer that one of those conditions exists – but it does not need to be sophisticated statistical data or research. It may simply involve an employer looking at the profiles of their workforce and/or making enquiries of other comparable employers in the area or sector as a whole. Additionally, it could involve looking at national data such as labour force surveys for a national or local picture of the work situation for particular groups who share a protected characteristic. A decision could be based on qualitative evidence which may be obtained in various ways, for instance through discussion with workers or their representatives.

What does 'proportionate' mean?

'Proportionate' refers to the balancing of all the relevant factors. In considering using the positive action provisions, an employer will need to balance the seriousness of the disadvantage suffered or the extent to which people with a protected characteristic are under-represented against the impact that the proposed action may have on other people. When thinking about proportionality, an employer may find it helpful to consider if the proposed action is the only way to address the under-representation or disadvantage effectively, or if it would it be possible to achieve the same effect by other actions that are less likely to result in the less favourable treatment of other people.

Routinely favouring people with protected characteristics

The new positive action provisions make it clear that employers must not adopt policies or practices designed to routinely favour candidates with a certain protected characteristic, even where there is evidence of under-representation or disadvantage. All suitably qualified candidates must be considered on their individual merits for the post in question. Where one candidate is clearly superior or better qualified for the job than the others, then an employer should offer the position to that candidate. However, this does not prevent an employer having a routine policy of being prepared to use positive action where it is appropriate for it to do so. An employer may go into an appointment exercise prepared to use the 'tie-breaker' provisions, only to identify a clearly superior candidate – any notion of using the 'tie-breaker' would then become irrelevant.

Artificially low thresholds

Appointments should always be made on merit. If one candidate is superior to another the position should be offered to that candidate. If the pass mark in an assessment is set at 70% and one candidate scores 71% and another score 91%, it would generally be wrong to consider that just because both passed the minimum success threshold the two candidates are of equal merit.

Example

A local authority wishes to diversify its workforce and undertakes a large recruitment exercise. In an attempt to create a large pool of 'qualified' people from which it can cherry-pick those with the relevant protected characteristics to make its workforce more diverse, it sets a very low pass mark for the assessment to make sure that a lot of people pass. Picking someone with a particular protected characteristic from the pool in preference to someone who achieved a higher score and was clearly better qualified for the job but didn't have a targeted protected characteristic would not be allowed by the positive action provisions and would be likely to be unlawful discrimination.

How is what the new positive action provisions allow different from positive discrimination?

Positive discrimination is recruiting or promoting a person solely because they have a relevant protected characteristic. Setting quotas to recruit or promote a particular number or proportion of people with protected characteristics is also positive discrimination. Positive discrimination is

> unlawful in Great Britain. However, it is important to note that it is not unlawful for an employer to treat a disabled person more favourably in comparison to a non-disabled person …
>
> *Example*
>
> A department store employs nine senior managers but only two of them are women. When a vacancy arises it seeks to address this under-representation by only interviewing women applicants, regardless of whether they meet the criteria for the post. This would be positive discrimination so would be unlawful.
>
> *Example*
>
> A supermarket reviews its workforce data and finds that 80% of its employees are under the age of 35. When next recruiting, the supermarket manager sets a quota for 50% of new recruits to be over the age of 35, regardless of whether they are of equal merit to other applicants under the age of 35. This would be positive discrimination so would be unlawful.
>
> *Example*
>
> A call centre wishes to diversify the ethnicity of its workforce as it is aware that it is currently predominantly white despite being based in an area with a large Indian population. After interview the top two candidates are both white – but in a bid to create greater diversity the company appoints the third placed candidate because he is Indian. This would be positive discrimination so would be unlawful [original emphasis throughout].

The repeated reference in the *Quick Start Guide* to 'equal merit' is questionable in view of the fact that s159 EqA does not use that test, requiring instead that tie-break discrimination be restricted to cases in which candidates are 'as qualified as' each other. The insistence in the *Quick Start Guide* that 'If one candidate is superior [whatever that means] to another the position should be offered to that candidate' is also open to challenge, as are the assertions about 'artificially low thresholds'. No two candidates will ever be precisely similar, and the extent to which one candidate may be regarded as 'superior' to another depends on what qualifications are accepted as relevant to the appointment. On the one hand, it could be argued that the holding of a masters qualification or doctorate will render one candidate 'superior' to another regardless of whether or not the qualification is relevant to the job in respect of which appointment is sought. On the other hand, to the extent that appointment on the basis of particular qualifications disadvantages a group definable by reference to one or more protected characteristics, reliance on those qualifications will be lawful only where they impact on the ability of the candidate to perform that particular job. By way of example, in *Griggs v Power Duke Co* 401 U.S. 424 (1971) the US Supreme Court ruled that the imposition of a requirement that, in order to be recruited into all but the poorest paying jobs, potential recruits had to have a high school diploma or pass a mechanical or aptitude test, was unlawful. The background was that the company had previously segregated Black staff into the poorest paying department and had introduced the tests on the day on which race discrimination was prohibited by Title VII of the Civil Rights Act 1964. High school diplomas being held by 34 per cent of white men but only 18 per cent of Black men in the area (North Carolina), and Black people having only a six per cent pass rate in the aptitude tests (by comparison with 58 per cent of white people), it seemed clear that the new approach to recruitment was intended to perpetuate racial segregation. Importantly, however, malign intent is not required as an ingredient of indirect discrimination; it is sufficient for a finding of unlawfulness that a disparately impacting practice etc is not reasonably necessary. Such was the case in *Griggs*, which was concerned with qualifications.[40]

[40] And see *Essop v Home Office* [2017] UKSC 27, [2017] ICR 640, discussed in Ch 2.

This being the case, the specification of that which will be regarded as going to qualification for appointment should, arguably, be as narrow as reasonably possible and, when candidates are being compared, the extent of their qualifications should be measured only on the basis of the factors related to the particular job. One result of this would be to multiply the cases in which candidates can be regarded as 'as qualified as' each other. We shall see below, however, that the only decision on s159 EqA to date reflected the approach advocated in the *Quick Start Guide*.

Notwithstanding the narrowness of s159, the provision was subject to trenchant criticism prior to its implementation on the basis that it was inconsistent with equality and likely to result in discrimination against white men.[41] Arguments for and against positive discrimination are discussed from p 155 below, after we consider the operation of s159 EqA. Predictions from the *Daily Mail* and *The Telegraph* that the provision would result in routine discrimination against white men proved to be unfounded. Although there has been very limited empirical research in this area, such as there has been suggests that the provision is seldom used:

Chantal Davies and Muriel Robison, 'Bridging the gap: An exploration of the use and impact of positive action in the UK' (2016) *International Journal of Discrimination and the Law*

[Sections 158 and 159 EqA] ... have the capacity, at least, to address underrepresentation and tackle disadvantage of any protected group. Nonetheless, a feature of the positive action provisions at European, and therefore at domestic, level is of course that such initiatives are voluntary, not mandatory. So, despite the Equality Act allowing employers to take positive action in general and in relation to recruitment and promotion in particular, and Government guidance encouraging its use, anecdotal evidence would suggest that there are relatively few employers who are prepared to embrace positive action initiatives, and even fewer who are prepared to use the tie-break provisions. Indications are then that the broadening of the positive action provisions has had little, if any, impact on the extent to which these initiatives are utilised, and therefore far less to have served the purpose of moving closer to achieving 'full equality in practice' as envisaged by the European provisions ...

[Having referred to the 'numerous examples of good practice and innovative positive action measures being implemented by employers' under s158 EqA] ... Yet, when looking for evidence of employers crossing the rubicon between 'outreach' and 'preferential treatment', the narrative dries up. Whilst there are some notable public sector exceptions (such as the Judicial Appointments Commission in the UK) where there was willingness to utilize 'preferential treatment' as advocated by section 159, most employers are silent on this matter. This has largely been borne out by the initial findings in the authors' study) ...

Meaningful debate on the utility and development of positive action within the UK and beyond can only be achieved by assessing how the current legislative provisions are utilised in practice ... We can make vague assumptions as to why employers are not utilising the permissive positive action provisions. Is it a lack of awareness and/or understanding or is it something less tangible such as a wariness of the new paradigm of equality in the UK suggested by the application of section 159? Anecdote would suggest that it is the permissive nature of legislative positive action that discourages employers. Equally, the potential risks of introducing a viable positive action initiative, in light of possible legal challenge for 'reverse discrimination' from an unsuccessful candidate (for example in a tie-break situation), may be considered overly burdensome ...

Inclination and alacrity

When asked whether they would be willing to use the positive action provisions in the future, respondents returned a diverse range of responses. Whilst the majority (50 percent) of respondents

[41] See eg J McCartney, 'It's not positive, it's just discrimination' *The Telegraph*, 29 June 2008; 'Harman's equality law "will hurt white male jobseekers"' *Daily Mail* 3 December 2009.

were seemingly undecided in this regard, 30 percent were definite in responding that they could envisage utilizing the positive action provisions in the near future. Once again a reticence in relation to section 159 was evident. Concern was apparent regarding the potential legal consequences of applying a 'reverse discrimination' approach to recruitment and promotion. The following comments from two separate respondents provide clear evidence of this:

> Some aspects of the provision are liable for legal challenge.
>
> If we identified areas of particular under representation and were 100% sure that in doing so we wouldn't actually be breaching equality legislation.

Equally, concern was expressed regarding the potential difficulties for employers around use of the 'tie-break' provision and perceptions of difficulty around determining what may amount to an 'equally qualified comparator':

> There is less hunger, amongst some organisations in private and public sector, for more concerted and direct activity through the use of the equally qualified comparator. This may be due to the vague nature of the current CoP [Code of Practice] that requires a test case before the remits of some of the more flexible provisions are clear.

This concern regarding the boundaries and legal consequences of using section 159 was evident even in those respondents who were clearly well informed regarding the detail and coverage of the legal positive action provisions. This would support some of the anecdotal evidence that has become prevalent in this area.

Whilst a clear majority (75 percent) had been reticent about or could not envisage utilising the positive action provisions in their organisations in the near future, in contrast a significant majority (67 percent) expressed a personal view that the positive action provisions were necessary to alleviate disadvantage in the UK. This may suggest a discrepancy between personal subjective opinion, which may well be based on individual mores, and organisational perspectives which may necessarily involve a more objective risk-based approach towards positive action. Some of the qualitative subjective responses to this question appeared to have an in-depth understanding of the theoretical dialogue in this area and indeed were in support of preferential treatment under section 159:

> 'I'd be in favour of a stronger provision such as "threshold selection"'[42]
>
> 'I think it is crucial to get recruiters to think outside the box and to think of new ways of doing things'.

Others appeared to transfer their professional reticence (which was more couched in concern regarding legal liability) into their personal theoretical philosophy:

> 'I believe it's about the right person with the right skills for the right role, and in a fast paced commercial private sector environment that takes priority over diversity and inclusion'.

One organisation linked use of positive action to increased diversity with improved productivity and, as such, focused on the business case argument:

> 'A more proportionate representation in health and social care of various protected groups could result in better service provision'.

Nevertheless, for many respondents, concerns were expressed regarding the business case for utilizing positive action within the workplace. In particular, a number of respondents appeared unconvinced regarding the impact on the productivity and efficacy of the organization:

> 'We have identified areas of under-representation and could use positive action to address this. The benefits would show in our statistics but whether they would show in terms of actually being a more effective organisation, I don't know'.

[42] Citing Noon, n 32 above.

> Others expressed concern that disadvantaged groups may perceive that any measures taken would impact on their credibility and position in the workplace:
>
> > 'Any action taken to tackle disadvantage is a positive one, but just because it is backed up by legislation, doesn't mean it will work. PLUS There is the worry that some may feel segregated.'
>
> Being able to use positive action would have benefits in terms of addressing disproportionality within the workforce, however, there is widespread concern (including from those who groups that are under-represented) that using positive action could undermine their credibility within the workforce.

That the scope for legal positive discrimination remains very limited indeed, and that it does not permit the 'threshold' approach supported by Noon, is indicated by the first tribunal decision on s159 EqA.

***Furlong v CC Cheshire Police* Case No 2405577/18, 13 February 2019**[43]

The claimant was a graduate who had applied for a job as a PC with Cheshire Police. He performed well in tests and at interview but was not appointed. Cheshire had applied a three-stage approach under which applicants were (1) asked to respond to questionnaires, (2) provided with tests and an initial interview at a Search Assessment Centre and (3) if successful in the earlier stages, subjected to a final interview. All those who passed the final interview were deemed to be equal and the final selection was made according to:

1. Whether the candidate identified as having one of the protected characteristics of race, sex sexual orientation or disability
2. Whether the candidate spoke English as a second language
3. Whether the candidate was [had been] employed by Cheshire Police in one of a number of capacities, and
4. The candidates' results from the second stage of the recruitment process.

Cheshire Police had been identified by then Home Secretary Theresa May in 2015 as one of four police forces in the country with no Black officers. At that time *The Guardian* had reported that Simon Byrne, then Cheshire's Chief Constable, had stated that the force 'has tried "every legitimate trick in the book" to diversify recruitment' and had called on the government to 'consider changing the law to allow positive discrimination':

> **'Police chief with no black officers open to positive discrimination', *The Guardian*, 22 October 2015**
>
> Byrne said he regretted not having any African-Caribbean officers, adding that the force had 13 officers who are Asian or mixed race … demographics meant there were only around 3,000 black people in his area from which he could recruit, and that most would be in education or employment already …
>
> Byrne said Cheshire were trying various initiatives, visiting 11 colleges recently and even trying to get ethnic minority officers to leave their forces to join his. 'We are trying very hard to recruit locally and in the region.'…
>
> In her speech on Thursday, the home secretary rejected calls made previously by the police to change the law: 'I am clear that the case for positive discrimination is deeply flawed, and we need to pursue other options if we are to improve diversity in the police. Moreover, convincing

[43] Available at https://www.gov.uk/employment-tribunal-decisions/mr-m-furlong-v-the-chief-constable-of-cheshire-police-2405577-2018.

support for such action does not exist. When the College [of Policing] surveyed every BME officer in the country on the introduction of positive discrimination, while just over a third supported it, just over a third did not, and just under a third were undecided. Forces should instead take the steps that are available to them using existing positive action provisions in the Equality Act.'...

None of the 43 police forces in England and Wales comes close to accurately reflecting the ethnic makeup of its local population, analysis of official figures by the *Guardian* has shown. The analysis showed that in three of the biggest forces – Greater Manchester, West Midlands and West Yorkshire – the percentage of non-white officers was less than a third of the proportion of non-white people in the overall population. A similar picture emerged in the country's biggest police force, the Metropolitan police, where 11.7% of officers came from BME communities, according to figures from March this year, while the 2011 census found an overall minority-ethnic population in London of 40.2% ...

By 2017 the measures adopted by Cheshire had had only limited effect and more radical steps were adopted in relation to the recruitment exercise, as set out above. Mr Furlong was one of 56 candidates who were interviewed but not selected. The Chief Constable sought to rely on s159 EqA. The tribunal referred to the EHRC's Statutory Code of Practice on Employment[44] and the 2014 supplement thereto[45] as well as to the *Quick Start Guide* extracted above, emphasising the warning in the guidance against 'artificially low thresholds' and the examples given in relation thereto. The tribunal also drew attention to the widely differing scores awarded to candidates who had passed the final interview test, in some cases barely, and to concerns expressed by interviewers about the suitability of a number of successful candidates.

105. In essence, the Tribunal find the respondents in using a pass/fail mechanism to assess interview performance at the third stage of the recruitment exercise put forward an artificially low threshold for the recruitment exercise such that substantial numbers were then 'deemed equal' when plainly common sense dictates that they could not be so. They did this in order to put in place their action plan of positive action in the recruitment round for PCs.

106. Having 'deemed' candidates equal at that stage after the 'positive action' candidates were recruited they then reverted to a prioritisation of the quality of candidates by reverting to the Search Assessment scores and appointing in a hierarchy. This shows and undermines any argument of equal suitability ...

109. The nub of the Tribunal's view is that there was clear qualitative data collected by the respondent, albeit not reduced to numerical scoring which gave clear indications of which candidates had demonstrated which qualities, by showing evidential examples to the interview panel of the competencies and values for the role required by the College of Policing.

110. The Tribunal struggles with the concept in itself that 127 people could be viewed 'as of equal merit' for appointment to the role. The Tribunal rejects the contention that the 127 were of 'equal merit' or could be 'deemed to be' of equal merit.

111. Given that the claimant's interview was relatively strong although not the strongest interview on an analysis of the extensive number of forms that the Tribunal has been referred to the Tribunal considers he would have been in the quota of individuals who were nearer the top of the qualitative interview process rather than the bottom.

112. In relation to the question whether the respondent can show that it reasonably thought that persons who share a protected characteristic suffer a disadvantage connected to the

[44] https://www.equalityhumanrights.com/en/publication-download/employment-statutory-code-practice.
[45] https://www.equalityhumanrights.com/sites/default/files/supplementtotheemploymentcofp.pdf.

characteristic, the Tribunal was taken through a plethora of evidence regarding different protected characteristics but particularly gender, BME and sexual orientation. This was not necessarily specific to 'disadvantage' but rather to lack of representation. Although disadvantage was not made out the Tribunal did consider the respondent made out its case in relation to the alternative limb of Section 159(1) in respect of participation …

116. The respondent relies on section 159(4) of the Equality Act 2010. Firstly, the Tribunal has to determine whether the candidates with one or more protected characteristics who were given preferential treatment in being appointed ahead of candidates who did not have that or those protected characteristics were as qualified as the claimant to be recruited. This is the 'equal merit' point. The Tribunal has made findings in the paragraphs above regarding its view of the assessment of the interview as a pass/fail with over 120 applicants with no further qualitative interpretation of data, which was available to the respondent in this process. The Tribunal did not consider that 127 people were as qualified as each other to be recruited at that stage, and further the respondent in using principle 4 (i.e. reverting to the assessment search centre scores) themselves cannot have believed that qualitatively all candidates were equal, given that that is what they did in that second part of the procedure. This undermines the assertion they were of 'equal merit'. 'Deeming' it such does not make it so but makes a fallacy of assessment.

117. The Tribunal refers back to the early part of its considerations in respect of the guidance as quoted in the early paragraphs of this decision, and the Tribunal having been referred to cases by the claimant's counsel regarding the European jurisprudence on 'equal merit or qualifications' [citing *Abrahamsson* and *Badeck*, discussed above, to the effect that] … The specific personal qualification of all the candidates must be considered [and automatic and unconditional prioritisation of people from underrepresented groups is unacceptable] …

118. It is relevant that *Abrahmsson* allowed special positive treatment when there was an express limit on the difference in the level of qualification of the candidates. In the circumstances of the guidance which is referred to in the earlier paragraphs and in reliance on the authorities previously decided in the European cases, the respondent has not shown that there was equal qualification under section 159(4)(a) when applying positive action to those candidates to deemed to have passed the interview process.

119. The next question the Tribunal determined was whether the respondent could show that it did not have a policy of treating persons who shared the protected characteristic more favourably in connection with recruitment to the role of Police Constable than persons who do not share it. The Tribunal accepts the submission that the respondent's actions in giving preferential access to candidates with one or more protected characteristics did amount to a policy. Whilst in the earlier stages of the recruitment process the candidates were selected on merit, at the interview stage the candidates who demonstrated and evidenced their criteria were not prioritised in respect of qualities; they were all 'deemed equal' thereby allowing positive action to in effect, if qualities were visible, pre-select those with the protected characteristics to be appointed. Whilst the respondent sought to argue it did not have a policy it seemed to the Tribunal, the policy was in place post the interview stage of the selection process …

121. … the final question which the Tribunal had to consider was whether the respondent could show that its action in appointing to the role of Police Constable candidates with one or more protected characteristics ahead of candidates who did not share them was a proportionate means of achieving a legitimate aim.

122. The respondent relies on the legitimate aim of increasing diversity in its workforce which falls within subsection (2), the claimant does not dispute that this is a legitimate aim but disputes that the action taken was proportionate. …

127. Plainly the aim of the recruitment exercise in using positive action was to recruit a diverse population of new Police Constables who came from a wider background and were more representative of the community which it was intended they would serve, so that the hope was more

black ethnic minority officers would be recruited, more female officers and more gay/lesbian/bisexual officers and transgender officers would be recruited. This is a laudable aim …

129. The Tribunal accepts and has set out in earlier paragraphs the extensive steps, which the respondent had taken to improve diversity but had not recorded the measurable effects, other than through statistics to March 2018, which were having a desirous impact albeit small on the statistical recruitment of those with protected characteristics. The Insight programme was bearing fruit, albeit in a relatively small way …

132. Taking into account the guidance … 'proportionate' refers to the balancing of all the relevant factors in considering using the positive action provisions an employer will need to balance the seriousness of the disadvantage suffered or the extent to which people with a protected characteristic are underrepresented against the impact that the proposed action may have on other people, the impact on the claimant and on the 34 white male non-disabled candidates.

133. In the Tribunal's view they were rejected where evidence existed in the claimant's case that he was a relatively strong candidate following on from the competency based interview. He had felt he had passed all areas and should have had a green light to appointment. Others of those 34 on analysis may also feel that they were significantly more meritorious candidates than some of those with protected characteristics who were appointed.

134. The knock on effect of discontentment and disillusionment may lead to a lack of confidence in the ability of appointees to the role of police officer and the organisation in general. This would be counter productive and not in the public interest if public confidence in the respondent were undermined.

135. Whilst the Tribunal applauds the respondent's attempts to improve diversity and its attempts to recruit from a wider pool to have more police officers with the protected characteristics, applying positive action to the large volume exercise in this way does not seem to us to be reasonably necessary. Certainly at the juncture of this exercise.

136. Previous measures were bearing fruit, applications from those in protected characteristic groups were increasing, the reputational damage of the Force having had no black officers in 2015 were improving on the basis of the recruitment since that time and the improvement in the statistics as shown in the March 2018 documentation. The impact of the Force being chosen to host the National Black Police Association Conference in 2017 whilst symbolic would raise BME profile and policing in a positive light. The method and manner of recruitment has to be considered in this backdrop.

137. This was a radical and substantial change in the recruitment process. Whilst the Tribunal accept there is a need for change this blanket approach was not a proportionate means of achieving a legitimate aim … the percentage of LGBT and women and BME candidates successful at interview was going up.

138. The application of this selection procedure at the time was in the Tribunal's view premature without a full analysis of the impact of the measures that were already in place. Further there appeared at times a scattergun approach to the individuals with different protected characteristics. The Tribunal considers that the manner of the selection imposed what the Government Equalities Office had counselled against in that it was an artificially low threshold, imposing an artificially low threshold would not be a proportionate response to recruiting to address the issue of a lack of diversity balance.

139. In the circumstances the respondents have not demonstrated the justification for the discriminatory effect of the positive action they applied in this case. The respondents were required to consider first the bedding down of their previous positive action measures, secondly, to measurably assess the impact of those to potentially apply positive action to a smaller exercise in the first place, and to not impose artificially low thresholds in terms of a recruitment procedure, nor to completely ignore a qualitative assessment of candidates and then to re-introduce a merit based analysis in a later part of the recruitment.

140. In the circumstances the Tribunal concludes that the claimant would have succeeded in his application and been appointed as a Police Constable, had the respondent not applied positive action at the interview stage having obtained and ignored qualitative data and where he was a relatively strong candidate and likely on our assessment to have been positioned on the right side of the number needed to fill the vacancies.

Other Domestic Provisions

The first of these provisions is now to be found in s104 EqA, which had its predecessor provisions in the Sex Discrimination (Election Candidates) Act 2002, passed after a tribunal had ruled that the Labour Party's adoption of all-women shortlists in the 1997 general election campaign had breached the SDA.[46] The provision initially applied only to women and was to expire in 2015 but was extended until December 2030 by the EqA when it will expire unless extended by Order:

Section 104 EqA, Selection of candidates

(1) This section applies to an association which is a registered political party.
(2) A person does not contravene this Part only by acting in accordance with selection arrangements.
(3) Selection arrangements are arrangements—
  (a) which the party makes for regulating the selection of its candidates in a relevant election,
  (b) the purpose of which is to reduce inequality in the party's representation in the body concerned, and
  (c) which, subject to subsection (7), are a proportionate means of achieving that purpose.
(4) The reference in subsection (3)(b) to inequality in a party's representation in a body is a reference to inequality between—
  (a) the number of the party's candidates elected to be members of the body who share a protected characteristic, and
  (b) the number of the party's candidates so elected who do not share that characteristic.
(5) For the purposes of subsection (4), persons share the protected characteristic of disability if they are disabled persons (and section 6(3)(b) [which provides that 'a reference to persons who share a protected characteristic is a reference to persons who have the same disability'] is accordingly to be ignored).
(6) Selection arrangements do not include short-listing only such persons as have a particular protected characteristic.
(7) But subsection (6) does not apply to the protected characteristic of sex; and subsection (3)(c) does not apply to short-listing in reliance on this subsection …

Comparison of s104(6) and 104(7) illustrates that women-only shortlists are permissible, but shortlists limited by reference to other protected characteristics are not, and that there is no requirement to establish proportionality in the use of women-only shortlists.

The justification for all-women shortlists can be found in the following statistics, referred to by Baroness Gale, in the House of Lords, on 30 October 2008:

Since 1918, when women were first able to stand as Members of Parliament, only 291 women have been elected, but during the same period 4,363 men were elected. If it was possible to put all the women who have been elected into the House of Commons today, they would still be in the minority.[47]

[46] *Jepson & Dyas-Elliott v Labour Party* [1996] IRLR 166. See R Kelly and I White, *All-women shortlists* (House of Commons Library, Briefing paper 5057, 2016).
[47] Cited in Kelly and White *ibid*, 3.

Between 2008 and 2016, following the 2010 and 2015 elections, an additional 159 women were elected to the House of Commons, a grand total of 450 in the first 98 years. The total number of constituencies is 650. Women comprised 0.1 per cent of MPs in 1918, 3.8 per cent in 1945, 4.1 per cent in 1966, three per cent in 1979, 18.2 per cent in 1997 (101 of the total 120 women were Labour, 35 of whom had been elected from all-women shortlists), 17.9 per cent in 2001, 19.8 per cent in 2005, 22 per cent in 2010 and 29.4 per cent in 2015 (when 91 of the 191 women were Labour, of whom 31 had been elected from all-women shortlists).[48]

The provision permitting women-only shortlists recognises the imperatives of representative democracy. The second major departure from the UK's normal approach to positive discrimination recognised the danger posed to the Peace Process in Northern Ireland of an almost exclusively Protestant police force (the Royal Ulster Constabulary), which was regarded by many Catholics as serving the interests of Protestant people alone. The Police (Northern Ireland) Act 2000 dealt with recruitment to the Police Service for Northern Ireland, which replaced the RUC. Chris (now Lord) Patten chaired a commission on policing in Northern Ireland whose report stated that 'Merit must remain a critical criterion for selection for the police service,' and that 'religious or cultural identity, gender or ethnicity should [not] be regarded as a makeweight for merit', but went on to recommend that all candidates reaching a specified standard of merit 'should then enter a pool from which the required number of recruits can be drawn … an equal number of Protestants and Catholics should then be drawn from the pool.'[49] The 2000 Act made provision accordingly and Council Directive 2000/78/EC expressly provided for this to continue notwithstanding its prohibition of religious discrimination.[50]

The proportion of Catholics in Northern Ireland's police service increased from eight per cent to 30 per cent before the positive action mechanism came to an end in 2011. Since then, concerns have grown that the proportion of Catholics in the PSNI (32 per cent in 2020[51]) remained significantly less than the proportion of Catholics in the population (45 per cent), and that the rate of recruitment of Catholics had fallen significantly (to 31% per cent in 2015[52]). This fall does not appear to have been the result of differential selection by PSNI, as distinct from differential application levels; the 31 per cent recruitment rate in 2015 precisely matched the proportion of Catholics among PSNI applicants in 2020.[53]

Fair Employment and Treatment (Northern Ireland) Order 1998

The question of diversity in the police and other UK institutions is returned to below, after we have considered the third example of more radical domestic provisions: Northern Ireland's FETO which, uniquely in the UK, expressly provides for 'affirmative action'.

[48] Kelly and White (n 46) 5 citing source: Rallings and Thrasher, *British Electoral Facts 1832–2006*; House of Commons Library Research Papers 10/36 *General Election 2010 and CBP-7186 General Election 2015.*

[49] *Report of the Independent Commission on Policing*, paras 15.9–15.10.

[50] Article 15(1) provides that 'In order to tackle the under-representation of one of the major religious communities in the police service of Northern Ireland, differences in treatment regarding recruitment into that service, including its support staff, shall not constitute discrimination insofar as those differences in treatment are expressly authorized by national legislation'.

[51] 'PSNI recruitment campaign: Attracting Catholics still an issue for police' BBC News, 2 February 2020.

[52] 'Why are there still so few Catholics in the PSNI?' *Irish Times*, 4 October 2018.

[53] 'Increase in number of Catholics applying to join PSNI' RTE, 26 February 2020.

Notwithstanding the terminology employed, we shall see that FETO does not permit positive discrimination in the form of preferential treatment. It does, however, impose positive obligations on employers which have proved effective in reducing the religious/ sectarian segregation which characterised employment in Northern Ireland since its creation. FETO like its predecessors, the Fair Employment (Northern Ireland) Act 1976 and the Fair Employment (Northern Ireland) Act 1989, prohibited discrimination on grounds of religion or political belief in Northern Ireland long before the introduction of the RB Regs in Britain. The fair employment legislation is a legacy of the 'Troubles', the conflict in Northern Ireland which spilled into violence in the late 1960s, and a response to the segregation along religious and political lines (Protestant 'Unionist': Catholic 'Nationalist') which marked the jurisdiction.

Raymond Russell, 'Fair Employment in Northern Ireland: the decades of change (1990–2010)' (2012) Northern Ireland Assembly Research Paper NIAR 352-12, footnotes omitted

On 5 October 1968 a Civil Rights march in Derry/Londonderry, which had previously been banned by the then Minister of Home Affairs, was stopped by the police. The ensuing violence and public disorder was filmed by a television camera crew and created headlines in Europe and the United States. The violence grew in scale and intensity throughout the autumn and winter of 1968–1969.

The Governor of Northern Ireland, acting on the advice of the Government of Northern Ireland, appointed a Commission on 3 March 1969 to hold an enquiry into the immediate causes and nature of the disorder. The Cameron Report, as it become known, concluded that a sense of injustice and grievance among large sections of the Catholic community had been a general contributory factor behind the outbreaks of violence …

One of the earliest attempts to examine religion and the labour market was made by Aunger[54], a Canadian academic, who analysed data from the 1971 Census. Aunger found that 41 per cent of economically active Protestants were in professional, managerial, and 'white collar' jobs, compared with 31 per cent of Catholics. By contrast, Catholics were substantially over-represented in the categories of semi-skilled, unskilled and unemployed (52%), compared with their Protestant counterparts (40%). According to Aunger, Catholics predominated in lower status occupations, such as clothing manufacturing, bricklaying, plastering and labouring in the construction industry, and pubs and betting shops. Members of the Catholic middle-class were to be found primarily servicing their own community as doctors, lawyers, teachers, bookmakers and publicans. In contrast, members of the Protestant middle class serviced their own community, but in addition provided province-wide services in sectors such as banking, insurance and public administration.

Hepburn[55] showed that the pattern of disadvantage described above existed in 1901 and did not significantly alter in the ensuing fifty years …

The Northern Ireland Parliament was suspended in March 1972. In August 1972, the new Direct Rule Administration established a Working Party to consider what steps should be taken to counter religious discrimination where it may exist in the private sector in Northern Ireland.

[54] Citing E Aunger (1975) 'Religion and Class: an Analysis of 1971 Census Data' in R Cormack and R Osborne (eds), *Religion, Education and Employment: aspects of Equal Opportunity in Northern Ireland* (Belfast, Appletree, 1987). K McEvoy and C White report, in 'Security Vetting in Northern Ireland: Loyalty, Redress and Citizenship' (1998) 61 *Modern Law Review* 341, that McEvoy and White go on to report that in 1969, by which stage Catholics accounted for one-third of the population, they occupied 6%, 7% and 14% respectively of technical and professional civil service posts, higher administrative civil service positions and government nominated public body appointments.

[55] Citing A Hepburn (1987) 'Employment and Religion in Belfast, 1901–1951' in R Cormack and R Osborne (eds) *Religion, Education and Employment: aspects of Equal Opportunity in Northern Ireland* (Belfast, Appletree, 1987).

> The Working Party was first chaired by Paul Channon MP and then by William Van Straubenzee MP, both Ministers in the Northern Ireland Office.
>
> The Working Party, whose Report was published in May 1973, developed a series of best-practice proposals for combating discrimination in employment based on a review of other jurisdictions, notably Great Britain, the United States, Ontario and New Zealand. The Van Straubenzee Report was to play a central role in the development of fair employment in Northern Ireland.
>
> The Report defined religious and political discrimination; introduced the concepts of equality of opportunity and affirmative action; advocated specific legislation to tackle discrimination (a fair employment Act); and proposed a new body, the Fair Employment Agency (FEA), to oversee the implementation of the legislation. The FEA would have general responsibility for countering religious discrimination in employment, and have specific functions of investigation, conciliation and enforcement.

The FEA 1976 was eventually replaced by FETO, which is still in place. FETO makes provision for 'affirmative action' by employers, defined as follows:

> **Article 4 FETO**
>
> … action designed to secure fair participation in employment by members of the Protestant, or members of the Roman Catholic, community in Northern Ireland by means including—
>
> (a) the adoption of practices encouraging such participation; and
> (b) the modification or abandonment of practices that have or may have the effect of restricting or discouraging such participation.[56]

The fact that the affirmative action obligations apply 'symmetrically; that is, … to concerns where Protestants are under-represented and to concerns where Catholics are under-represented' has been described as a 'crucial feature of the legislation, which sets it apart from all the other well-known examples of affirmative action'.[57] Article 5 defines 'equality of opportunity' under FETO as 'ha[ving] the same opportunity [in terms of employment or occupation] … as [an]other person has or would have … due allowance being made for any material difference in their suitability' and goes on to provide that:

> **Article 5 FETO**
>
> (3) … a person is not to be treated as not having the same opportunity as another person has or would have by reason only of anything lawfully done in pursuance of affirmative action.
> (5) Any reference in this Order to the promotion of equality of opportunity includes a reference to the promotion of affirmative action and, accordingly, any reference to action for promoting equality of opportunity includes a reference to affirmative action.

Northern Irish employers may engage in 'affirmative action' at will, and are not constrained by the under-representation requirements imposed by the EqA. Employers having more than 10 employees are obliged to monitor their workforces by religion and to submit records to the Equality Commission for Northern Ireland (ECNI). In addition, all public sector employers and those in the private sector having at least 250 employees must monitor the

[56] Whereas the direct and indirect discrimination and the victimisation provisions of FETO extend protection beyond Catholic and Protestant to anyone discriminated against on grounds of 'religious belief or political opinion', those provisions dealing with 'fair participation' and 'affirmative action' concern themselves only with the 'two communities'. Such has been the overriding significance of the Protestant/Catholic divide in Northern Ireland that an old joke concerns a Jewish person quizzed as to whether s/he is a 'Protestant Jew' or a 'Catholic Jew'.

[57] R Muttarak, H Hamill, A Heath and C McCrudden, 'Does Affirmative Action Work? Evidence from the Operation of Fair Employment Legislation in Northern Ireland' (2010) 47 *Sociology* 560, 565.

religion of their promotees and of those ceasing to be employed. Failure to supply the ECNI with monitoring returns is a criminal offence.

Article 55 FETO requires that employers 'review the composition of those employed ... and the employment practices of the concern for the purposes of determining whether members of each community [Protestant and Catholic] are enjoying, and are likely to continue to enjoy, fair participation in employment in the concern.' These reviews must take place at least once every three years and must include review of practices relating to recruitment, training and promotion. Where it appears to an employer, as a result of such a review, that 'members of a particular community are not enjoying, or are not likely to continue to enjoy' 'fair participation', Article 55 FETO provides that the employer must 'determine the affirmative action (if any) which would be reasonable and appropriate.' Such action may include the establishment of goals and timetables to set out the 'progress towards fair participation in employment in the concern that can reasonably be expected to be made by members of a particular community' (Article 55(3)). Employers are under no general obligation to submit reviews to the ECNI but (Article 56(4)) the Commission may require information from employers regarding such reviews and is required:

Article 56(5) FETO

> where a review discloses that members of a particular community are not enjoying, or are not likely to continue to enjoy, fair participation in employment in the concern, [to] make such recommendations as it thinks fit as to the affirmative action to be taken and, assuming the action is taken, as to the progress towards fair participation in employment in the concern, by reference to any period or periods, that can reasonably be expected to be made by members of the community.

Where the ECNI has recommended affirmative action, it is empowered to require follow-up information (not more than once every six months) as to the progress being made. And where it is of the view that an employer's monitoring or review processes are not adequate, the ECNI may seek written undertakings from the employer as to changes to those processes and may, in the absence or breach of such undertaking, issue mandatory directions to the employer (Article 58). These may, in the final analysis, be enforced by Northern Ireland's Fair Employment Tribunal.

Neither FETO nor its predecessors define 'fair participation' in pursuit of which affirmative action ought to be undertaken'.[58] A Code of Practice issued by the Fair Employment Commission (merged in 1999 into the ECNI) suggested (para. 3.1) that affirmative action 'should certainly be considered' if, for example, either Protestants or Catholics:

> are applying in fewer numbers than might be expected for either employment, training or promotion,
>
> are being recruited, trained or promoted in numbers proportionately lower than their rate of application,
>
> hold jobs carrying higher pay, status and authority in numbers proportionately lower than their rate of application or availability,
>
> are, in larger undertakings, concentrated in certain branches, shifts, sections or departments,
>
> enjoy less attractive terms, hours or working conditions than others, are likely to be adversely affected by possible redundancies and agreed or traditional schemes such as 'last in first out'.

[58] The Government did not act on the FEC's 1997 proposal (FEC's *Review of Fair Employment Acts*, para 3.34) that the legislation ought to 'clarify that fair participation will not be present where there is an under-representation of one community defined as "fewer members of that community than might be expected".'

FETO appears to provide a much more significant role for positive discrimination than exists under the EqA, because of the obligation it imposes on employers to consider action such as the adoption of goals and timetables. But Christine Bell pointed out in 1996 that only three (now four) forms of 'affirmative action' were explicitly permitted by FETO (then the FEA 1989):

Christine Bell, 'The Employment Equality Review in Northern Ireland' (1996) 2 *International Journal of Discrimination and the Law* 53, 60, footnotes omitted

- special training to enhance limited or non-existent skills among members of the under-represented group …
- adoption of alternative redundancy procedures designed to ensure that attempts to recruit members of the under-represented community into the workforce are not dissipated, for example by disapplying last in first out policies in redundancy situations (not to be defined with specific reference to religion or politics)
- targeted advertising to attract applicants from an under-represented group …

There are several problems with affirmative action as defined by the legislation. Firstly, the fact that only three forms of affirmative action enjoy explicit protection from charges of unlawful discrimination, suggests that other forms of affirmative action are not favoured and are vulnerable to charges of discrimination. This can act to inhibit employers from taking other affirmative action measures because of fear of discrimination suits ….

Since Bell's article was written the scope of lawful affirmative action under the fair employment regime has been widened. Prior to the implementation of FETO, and despite first impressions, the scope for positive action within the fair employment legislation was, despite the talk of 'affirmative action' and 'fair participation', in some respects narrower even than the predecessor provisions to the EqA. Although the express exception covering redundancy selection was unique to the fair employment legislation,[59] the FEA did not permit any religion-specific training regardless of the degree of under-representation of one or other community in the workplace, employers being restricted in these circumstances to training which, being based in a particular geographic area or confined to a class of persons *defined other than on grounds of religious belief or political opinion*, was more accessible to the under-represented group. FETO widened the scope of the training provision, Article 76 permitting employers and other training bodies to provide single-religion training if at any time within the immediately preceding 12 months:

Article 76 FETO

(2)(a) … it appear[ed] to the [ECNI] that—

(i) there are no persons of the religious belief in question among those engaged in that employment at the establishment; or

(ii) that the proportion of persons of that belief among those engaged in that employment at that establishment is small in comparison with the proportion of persons of that belief among all those employed by the employer there or among the population of the area from which that employer might reasonably be expected to recruit persons for employment at that establishment …

[59] See *Brook v LB Haringey* [1992] IRLR 478.

The potential difficulty posed for positive action by the prohibition on indirect discrimination was mentioned above. Recognition of this lay behind the following provision:

Article 75 FETO

(1) The application of any requirement or condition to any person applying to fill a vacancy for employment where the requirement or condition is one that the person applying to fill the vacancy has not been in employment for a specified period of time is not … by virtue of Article 3(2) unlawful …

This provision was inserted to deal with the fact that, because Catholic unemployment rates in Northern Ireland had remained fairly stable at around twice the Protestant level for decades, any attempt to target the unemployed would amount, prima facie, to indirect discrimination the lawfulness of which would have turned on the issue of justification (see discussion in Chapter 2).

The scope for positive action in the provision of training remains considerably narrower under FETO than under even the predecessor provisions to the EqA in that the ECNI must give prior approval of any such training and the training may not be provided 'by an employer, or a person providing training services on behalf of an employer, in relation to any person who is employed by the employer at the time when the act is done.' Returning to the point made by Christine Bell, and despite the apparently generous scope of Articles 5, 55 and 56, the scope afforded for positive action under FETO remains almost as narrow (and in some respects is narrower) than that provided under the EqA. FETO permits such action in relation to the under-represented only to the extent that it encourages them to apply for jobs and, if necessary, provides them with training.[60] It does not permit discrimination in favour of the disadvantaged at the point of hiring.[61] FETO, however, has proven successful in helping to desegregate employment in Northern Ireland.

R Muttarak, H Hamill, A Heath and C McCrudden, 'Does Affirmative Action Work? Evidence from the Operation of Fair Employment Legislation in Northern Ireland' (2010) 47 *Sociology* 560–79, references omitted

… At the beginning of the political conflict, or 'Troubles' in Northern Ireland … Catholics were two and a half times as likely as Protestants to be unemployed. Catholics in employment were over-represented in the semi-skilled and unskilled categories and in lower-status industries such as clothing manufacture and textiles. In contrast, Protestants dominated the relatively higher paid areas of shipbuilding and engineering. Zoning policies and tax incentives that influenced the location of new industries reinforced these differences in employment patterns. These were often in areas where Catholics found it difficult or dangerous to travel. Trade unions acted to maintain the Protestant monopoly in the heavy manufacturing industries. Historically, therefore, workforces were seen as either Catholic or Protestant …

A major tool was made available to the FEC [ECNI] under the legislation … where the Commission considered it was necessary, it could seek to establish agreements to improve the representation of the under-represented group … While the majority of concluded agreements have attempted to remedy Catholic under-representation, a substantial number have also been designed to remedy Protestant under-representation in specific concerns … These affirmative action agreements usually required concerns to introduce changes in the way in which they con ducted their personnel functions, particularly by formalizing advertising, hiring, promotion and dismissal. Additional

[60] Also, in the case of FETO, with *indirect* discrimination in redundancy selection.
[61] See, eg, *Jones v CC Northamptonshire Police* 41 *EOR Discrimination Case Law Digest* 6.

> specified measures deemed most appropriate for that concern were also required, such as the use of advertising specifically targeted to the under-represented group, the use of statements in advertisements particularly welcoming applications from the under-represented group, and (frequently) the adoption of specified numerical goals that concerns committed themselves to achieving in order to reduce under-representation, together with timetables …

The authors reported that between 1990 and 2005 the workforce in Northern Ireland had become more integrated and that the FEC had been able to extend its involvement from large and public sector organisations to medium and small private sector employers. They found that 'affirmative action agreements were successful in increasing the employment share of the under-represented group within concerns that had signed an agreement' in some (but not all) industrial sectors and that such agreements 'directly tackled a fundamental cause of the conflict and contributed to the Peace Process'. They also found that, over the 12 years to 2010, the proportion of Catholics and Protestants nine to four per cent and from 14 to three per cent respectively.

> … key ingredients of the Northern Ireland success may be the regular monitoring of firms' composition, the willingness of the Commission to use its powers … in cases where monitoring reveals serious under-representation, and the extent of external political pressure … negotiated agreements to remedy under-representation can be a successful part of a strategy of bringing about change. It is particularly striking that these changes in composition of workplaces and attitudes to workplace integration have been achieved without the primary use of sanctions such as threatening to withhold government contracts (as in the USA), and without imposing quotas (as in India) …

'Goals and Timetables'

The contested politics of positive discrimination (even positive action) was referred to above, as has the insistence of the UK Government on referring to anything permitted by the EqA as 'positive action', while defining positive discrimination narrowly and classifying it as unlawful. Notwithstanding this, 'goals and timetables' have been adopted in the UK to increase diversity in public sector jobs. As we saw above, 'goals and timetables' are available to (and sometimes required of) Northern Irish employers under FETO, as under its predecessor (the FEA 1989). The Labour Government of 1997–2000 was an enthusiastic adopter of goals and timetables, and these became more prevalent as a result of the adoption of the Public Sector Equality Duty (PSED), discussed from p 165 below.

Outside the Northern Irish context, goals and timetables have not met with marked success in the UK. In late 1998, fewer than one-third of public appointments were held by women, and only 3.6 per cent by members of racially minoritised communities.[62] In July of that year the Government had established a target of 50:50 male:female appointment ratio for men and women in public life[63] and, in the *Modernising Government* White Paper (March 1999),[64] it committed itself to '*pro rata* representation of ethnic minority groups' among the 100,000 public appointments (those serving on NHS Trusts and advisory and

[62] 81 *EOR* News, 8.

[63] Speech by Joan Ruddock, then Minister for Women, to a regional TUC conference on women's work 9 July 1999, press release. A publication from the Women's Unit ('Delivering for Women: the Progress so Far') reports that 1998 appointments were 39% female, up from 32% in 1997.

[64] (CM 4310), the forerunner to the Local Government Act 1999, further discussed in Ch 5.

executive bodies, school governors, magistrates etc). *Modernising Government* also stated the need to 'accelerate progress on diversity' in the public sector, expressing concern at the 'serious underrepresent[ation]' of women, racially minoritised and disabled people 'in the more senior parts of the public service'. The Government committed itself to targets of 35 per cent women in the top 3000, and 25 per cent women in the top 600 Civil Service posts by 2004/05 and 3.2 per cent racially minoritised incumbents in the top 3,000 Civil Service posts,[65] and in summer 2000 it set itself the task of doubling the proportion of disabled persons in top Civil Service jobs to three per cent by 2005.[66]

By 2010 women comprised 35.2 per cent of Senior Civil Servants (these the top 4,000 or so civil servants) and by 2019 this had risen to 45 per cent. The figures for disabled staff were 3.4 and 5.2 per cent respectively and those for racially minoritised staff 4.2 and six per cent[67] in each case well below the representation of women, disabled and racially minoritised staff in the civil service as a whole which in 2010 and 2019 were 53.3, 7.6 and 9.3 per cent, and 53.9, 12.7 and 11.7 per cent respectively.

The impact of 'goals and timetables' on racial diversity in the public sector is further considered in Chapter 7. In 2011 Lizzie Barmes and Kate Malleson suggested that the failure of 'Many years of institutional and regulatory activity designed to promote diversity in the composition of the judiciary in England and Wales ... to bring about significant substantive change' was in part due to the legal restrictions on positive discrimination.[68] The authors referred to a 'regulatory bind' imposed on public authorities, in particular the Judicial Appointments Commission, which was on the one hand obliged to pursue diversity outcomes and on the other bound by an 'extensive web of individual, symmetrical anti-discrimination rights':

Lizzie Barmes and Kate Malleson, 'The Legal Profession as Gatekeeper to the Judiciary: Design Faults in Measures to Enhance Diversity' (2011) 74 *Modern Law Review* 245–71, footnotes omitted

... These cause legal complexity, difficulty and, at worst, risk, for organisations wishing to take targeted action in pursuit of equality ...

... the accretion over the years of individual, symmetrical anti-discrimination rights has left UK equality law with an internal logic that, in spite of many innovations in recent years, calls only for 'tempered passivity' from organisations in relation to group identity. The legally mandated call for organisational passivity is undoubtedly more 'tempered' than it has ever been. It is important that organisations, public and private, are now at times required to adjust what they do in pursuit of equality, particularly in relation to people affected by disability and to women who are either pregnant or who have recently had a child. Equally, the positive race, disability and gender duties require mainly public authorities in several ways to be active in their pursuit of equality.[69] ... Finally it matters that there are new possibilities for lawful positive action in the Equality Act 2010 ... But critically, these do not require, but only permit, such initiatives. Beyond the instances in

[65] 17.8% and 12.7% respectively in 1998.

[66] A headline in the 87 *EOR* (September/October 1999) read 'Middle class white men still rule Civil Service', and reported that ethnic minorities comprise 1.6%, women 16% and disabled people 1.5% of the senior Civil Service: 'the current culture is perceived as encouraging those who are different to comply with the "norms" in order to get on' and that 'being prepared to work long and additional hours was the highest ranked enabler to career progression by two-thirds of [the 1701] respondents'. Networking and patronage were also seen as too influential in assisting career development.

[67] https://www.gov.uk/government/publications/civil-service-diversity-inclusion-dashboard/civil-service-diversity-and-inclusion-dashboard#representation-ensuring-the-civil-service-reflects-the-diversity-of-the-uk.

[68] The authors' other concern is about the relatively non-diverse pool (largely barristers) from which judges are selected.

[69] The PSED obligations were extended to the other protected characteristics with the implementation of the EqA.

> which an active stance is required, moreover, the default setting that UK equality law continues to ask from organisations is that group identity be ignored …
>
> The second element of the regulatory bind in which public authorities, including the JAC, are caught, concerns the direct effect on them of UK equality law's extensive web of individual, symmetrical anti-discrimination rights … the complex of such rights both constrains dynamism in pursuit of equality goals and, in subtle ways, inhibits bodies like the JAC from decisively using even such power as they have to challenge exclusionary practices and hierarchies, especially in the private sector …
>
> … the Equality Act 2010 has made changes to increase the room for manoeuvre that organisations have voluntarily to implement such measures. The bind on the JAC and other public authorities in this respect has therefore been loosened to some extent. But it is very unfortunate that it is not clear that the new positive action provisions comply with relevant EU law on this topic, and that the relevant EU law is somewhat unpredictable. It is likely therefore that this aspect of equality law will continue to be a source of complexity, difficulty and, ultimately, legal risk for organisations …

The Rights and Wrongs of Positive Discrimination

The degree of suspicion with which positive discrimination has historically been viewed in the UK is far from universal. We saw above that the ECtHR takes a liberal approach to action intended to remedy disadvantage and that Article 14 ECHR sometimes requires it. Most of the international legal instruments concerned with equality allow the adoption of 'temporary special measures' to accelerate de facto equality.[70] South Africa's Constitution and Canada's Charter of Rights explicitly permit positive discrimination, the first providing (section 9(2)) that 'To promote the achievement of equality, legislative and other measures designed to protect or advance persons, or categories of persons, disadvantaged by unfair discrimination may be taken' and the second (section 15(2)) that the prohibition on discrimination does not apply to 'any law, program or activity that has as its object the amelioration of conditions of disadvantaged individuals or groups including those that are disadvantaged because of race, national or ethnic origin, colour, religion, sex, age or mental or physical disability'.

Some of the objections were set out by Justice Stewart in his dissenting opinion in *Fullilove v Klutznick*, in which the US Supreme Court upheld the constitutionality of a 10 per cent 'minority business enterprise' set-aside in a federal public works programme.

***Fullilove v Klutznick* 448 US 448 (1980)**

Justice Stewart:

> Our Constitution is color-blind, and neither knows nor tolerates classes among citizens … The law regards man as man, and takes no account of his surroundings or of his color …
>
> Those words were written by a Member of this Court 84 years ago [citing Harlan J, dissenting, in *Plessy v Ferguson*, 163 US 537]. His colleagues disagreed with him, and held that a statute

[70] See, for example, Article 4 of the UN's Convention on the Elimination of all forms of Discrimination against Women (CEDAW); General Comment No 18 of the UN Human Rights Committee (responsible for the implementation of the International Convention on Civil and Political Rights: ICCPR).

that required the separation of people on the basis of their race was constitutionally valid because it was a 'reasonable' exercise of legislative power and had been 'enacted in good faith for the promotion [of] the public good'…

From the perspective of a person detrimentally affected by a racially discriminatory law, the arbitrariness and unfairness is entirely the same, whatever his skin color and whatever the law's purpose, be it purportedly 'for the promotion of the public good' or otherwise … since the guarantee of equal protection immunizes from capricious governmental treatment 'persons' – not 'races' – it can never countenance laws that seek racial balance as a goal in and of itself … Second, there are indications that the [minority business set aside] … may have been enacted to compensate for the effects of social, educational, and economic 'disadvantage.' No race, however, has a monopoly on social, educational, or economic disadvantage, and any law that indulges in such a presumption clearly violates the constitutional guarantee of equal protection …

Laws that operate on the basis of race require definitions of race. Because of the Court's decision today, our statute books will once again have to contain laws that reflect the odious practice of delineating the qualities that make one person a Negro and make another white. Moreover, racial discrimination, even 'good faith' racial discrimination, is inevitably a two-edged sword … Most importantly, by making race a relevant criterion once again in its own affairs the Government implicitly teaches the public that the apportionment of rewards and penalties can legitimately be made according to race – rather than according to merit or ability – and that people can, and perhaps should, view themselves and others in terms of their racial characteristics. Notions of 'racial entitlement' will be fostered, and private discrimination will necessarily be encouraged …

Justice Stewart was in the dissent in *Fullilove*. Fifteen years later, in *Adarand Constructors v Pena*, Justice Thomas concurred with a majority decision finding a similar set-aside programme unconstitutional in delivering the following judgment:

***Adarand Constructors v Pena* 515 US 2000 (1995)**

Justice Thomas:

I believe that there is a 'moral [and] constitutional equivalence,' between laws designed to subjugate a race and those that distribute benefits on the basis of race in order to foster some current notion of equality. Government cannot make us equal; it can only recognize, respect, and protect us as equal before the law …

As far as the Constitution is concerned, it is irrelevant whether a government's racial classifications are drawn by those who wish to oppress a race or by those who have a sincere desire to help those thought to be disadvantaged. There can be no doubt that the paternalism that appears to lie at the heart of this program is at war with the principle of inherent equality that underlies and infuses our Constitution. (See the Declaration of Independence 'We hold these truths to be self-evident, that all men are created equal, that they are endowed by their Creator with certain unalienable Rights, that among these are Life, Liberty, and the pursuit of Happiness') …

Purchased at the price of immeasurable human suffering, the equal protection principle reflects our Nation's understanding that [racial] classifications ultimately have a destructive impact on the individual and our society. Unquestionably, '[i]nvidious [racial] discrimination is an engine of oppression.' It is also true that '[r]emedial' racial preferences may reflect a desire to foster equality in society.' But there can be no doubt that racial paternalism and its unintended consequences can be as poisonous and pernicious as any other form of discrimination. So-called 'benign' discrimination teaches many that because of chronic and apparently immutable handicaps, minorities cannot compete with them without their patronizing indulgence. Inevitably, such programs engender attitudes of superiority or, alternatively, provoke resentment among those who believe that they have been wronged by the government's use of race. These programs stamp minorities with a badge of inferiority and may cause them to develop dependencies or to adopt an attitude that they are 'entitled' to preferences …

In my mind, government-sponsored racial discrimination based on benign prejudice is just as noxious as discrimination inspired by malicious prejudice. In each instance, it is racial discrimination, plain and simple.

It is the case that some of those who might fall to benefit from positive discrimination regard such measures as undermining of them, indicative that they have achieved other than because of 'merit' (see further Chapter 7).[71] More generally, attitudes to positive discrimination vary according to whether the individual concerned favours formal or substantive equality.

Sandra Fredman, 'Substantive equality revisited' (2016) 14 *International Journal of Constitutional Law* 712–38, footnotes omitted

… the meaning of the right to equality is deeply contested. Westen for one argues that 'equality is an idea that should be banished from moral and legal discourse as an explanatory norm.'[72] For others, the right to equality does not go far enough. Even if equality before the law has been established, disadvantage persists, and this disadvantage tends to be concentrated in groups with a particular status, such as women, people with disabilities, ethnic minorities and others.

These concerns have led to the quest for more sophisticated conceptions, moving from a formal understanding focused on like treatment, to more substantive conceptions. Both the SC of Canada and the South African Constitutional Court have embraced the principle of substantive equality in interpreting the right to equality, a trend reflected at international level. Nevertheless, the meaning of the right to substantive equality remains elusive …

It is argued in this article that, whereas it is clear that the right to equality should move beyond a formal conception that likes should be treated alike, a substantive conception resists capture by a single principle. Instead, drawing on the strengths of the familiar principles in the substantive equality discourse, a four dimensional principle is proposed: to redress disadvantage; to address stigma, stereotyping, prejudice and violence; to enhance voice and participation; and to accommodate difference and achieve structural change. Behind this is the basic principle that the right to equality should be located in the social context, responsive to those who are disadvantaged, demeaned, excluded, or ignored …

The recognition of disadvantage and stigma is core to substantive equality, as the following extract shows. In it, the writer is concerned with philosophical conceptions of egalitarianism,

[71] See for example 'Employed because I was black: Positive discrimination robs people of their drive to succeed says TV presenter' *Daily Mail* 3 April 2011.

[72] Citing P Westen, *The Empty Idea of Equality* (1983) 95 *Harvard Law Review* 537.

rather than legal concepts of equality/non-discrimination, but the relevance to the current discussion should be obvious.

Elizabeth Anderson, 'What is the Point of Equality' (1999) 109 *Ethics* 287–337

... Inegalitarian asserted the justice or necessity of basing social order on a hierarchy of human beings, ranked according to intrinsic worth. Inequality referred not so much to distributions of goods as to relations between superior and inferior persons. Those of superior rank were thought entitled to inflict violence oninferiors, to exclude or segregate them from social life, to treat them with contempt, to force them to obey, work without reciprocation, and abandon their own cultures. These are what Iris Young has identified as the faces of oppression: marginalization, status hierarchy, domination, exploitation, and cultural imperialism.[73] Such unequal social relations generate, and were thought to justify, inequalities in the distribution of freedoms, resources, and welfare. This is the core of inegalitarian ideologies of racism, sexism, nationalism, caste, class, and eugenics.

Egalitarian political movements oppose such hierarchies. They assert the equal moral worth of persons. This assertion does not mean that all have equal virtue or talent. Negatively, the claim repudiates distinctions of moral worth based on birth or social identity – on family membership, inherited social status, race, ethnicity, gender, or genes. There are no natural slaves, plebeians, or aristocrats. Positively, the claim asserts that all competent adults are equally moral agents: everyone equally has the power to develop and exercise moral responsibility, to cooperate with others according to principles of justice, to shape and fulfill a conception of their good.

... Egalitarian political movements have never lost sight of the whole range of targets of egalitarian assessment. For example, feminists work to overcome the internal obstacles to choice – self-abnegation, lack of confidence, and low self-esteem – that women often face from internalizing norms of femininity. Gays and lesbians seek the ability to publicly reveal their identities without shame or fear, which requires significant changes in social relations of contempt and hostility, and changes in norms of gender and sexuality. The disabled aim to reconfigure public spaces to make them accessible and adapt work situations to their needs, so that they can participate in productive activity. No mere redistribution of divisible resources can secure the freedoms these groups seek.

Egalitarians base claims to social and political equality on the fact of universal moral equality. These claims also have a negative and a positive aspect. Negatively, egalitarians seek to abolish oppression – that is, forms of social relationship by which some people dominate, exploit, marginalize, demean, and inflict violence upon others. Diversities in socially ascribed identities, distinct roles in the division of labor, or differences in personal traits, whether these be neutral biological and psychological differences, valuable talents and virtues, or unfortunate disabilities and infirmities, never justify the unequal social relations listed above. Nothing can justify treating people in these ways, except just punishment for crimes and defence against violence. Positively, egalitarians seek a social order in which persons stand in relations of equality. They seek to live together in a democratic community, as opposed to a hierarchical one. Democracy is here understood as collective self-determination by means of open discussion among equals, in accordance with rules acceptable to all. To stand as an equal before others in discussion means that one is entitled to participate, that others recognize an obligation to listen respectfully and respond to one's arguments, that no one need bow and scrape before others or represent themselves as inferior to others as a condition of having their claim heard.

Contrast this democratic conception of equality with equality of fortune. First, democratic equality aims to abolish socially created oppression. Equality of fortune aims to correct what it takes to be injustices generated by the natural order. Second, democratic equality is what I shall call a

[73] Citing *Justice and the Politics of Difference* (Princeton, Princeton University Press, 1990).

relational theory of equality: it views equality as a social relationship. Equality of fortune is a distributive theory of equality: it conceives of equality as a pattern of distribution. Thus, equality of fortune regards two people as equal so long as they enjoy equal amounts of some distributable good – income, resources, opportunities for welfare, and so forth. Social relationships are largely seen as instrumental to generating such patterns of distribution. By contrast, democratic equality regards two people as equal when each accepts the obligation to justify their actions by principles acceptable to the other, and in which they take mutual consultation, reciprocation, and recognition for granted. Certain patterns in the distribution of goods may be instrumental to securing such relationships, follow from them, or even be constitutive of them. But democratic egalitarians are fundamentally concerned with the relationships within which goods are distributed, not only with the distribution of goods themselves. This implies, third, that democratic equality is sensitive to the need to integrate the demands of equal recognition with those of equal distribution. Goods must be dis-tributed according to principles and processes that express respect for all. People must not be required to grovel or demean themselves before others as a condition of laying claim to their share of goods. The basis for people's claims to distributed goods is that they are equals, not inferiors, to others. This gives us a rough conception of equality.

Also helpful to the understanding of a more substantive approach to equality is Owen Fiss's influential article on the US Constitution's Equal Protection Clause, which regulates state action. Fiss's reference to the 'antidiscrimination principle' is to the formalistic approach to equality which had been adopted by the US SC in relation to that provision.

Owen Fiss, 'Groups and the Equal Protection Clause' (1976) 109 *Philosophy and Public Affairs* 107–77

The tie between individualism and the antidiscrimination principle may … stem from the fact that it yields a highly individualized conception of rights. Under the antidiscrimination principle, the constitutional flaw inheres in the structure of the statute or the conduct of the administrator, not in its impact on any group or class. Any individual who happens to be burdened by a statute or practice, or any individual excluded from the benefits, can complain of the wrong …

… under the antidiscrimination principle, equal protection rights are not only individualized, but also universalized and this is another source of its appeal. Everyone is protected. There may be a limitation on the laws brought within its sweep-they must contain a discrimination or classification. But once a distinction among persons is made by a state statute or practice, that measure can be tested by anyone who happens to be burdened by it …

The universalizing tendency of the antidiscrimination principle no doubt accounts for its popular appeal-no person seems to be given more protection than another. This universalizing tendency also appeals to a court. It relieves the judiciary of the burden of deciding, who will receive the protection (in the jurisdictional sense) of a constitutional provision and then explaining why some are left out …

One shortcoming of the antidiscrimination principle relates to the problem of preferential treatment for blacks. This is a difficult issue, but the antidiscrimination principle makes it more difficult than it is: the permissibility of preferential treatment is tied to the permissibility of hostile treatment against blacks. The antidiscrimination principle does not formally acknowledge social groups, such as blacks; nor does it offer any special dispensation for conduct that benefits a disadvantaged group. It only knows criteria or classifications; and the color black is as much a racial criterion as the color white. The regime it introduces is a symmetrical one of 'color blindness,' making the criterion of color, any color, presumptively impermissible. Reverse discrimination, so the argument is made, is a form of discrimination and is equally arbitrary since it is based on race …

In my judgment, the preferential and exclusionary policies should be viewed quite differently under the Equal Protection Clause. Indeed, it would be one of the strangest and cruelest ironies to interpret that Clause in such a way that linked-in some tight, inextricable fashion- the judgments

> about the preferential and exclusionary policies. This dilemma can only be avoided if the applicable mediating principle of the Clause is clearly and explicitly asymmetrical, one that talks about substantive ends, and not fit, and one that recognizes the existence and importance of groups, not just individuals. Only then will it be possible to believe that when we reject the claim against preferential treatment for blacks we are not at the same time under- mining the constitutional basis for protecting them. Of course, even if the antidiscrimination principle were not the predominant interpretation of the Clause, it might still be possible to formulate a claim against preferential treatment. The element of individual unfairness to the rejected applicants inherent in preferential treatment could be considered a cost in evaluating the state action in the same way as a loss of liberty or a dignitary harm might be. The failure of the state to include other disadvantaged groups, such as the Chicanos, might also become significant. But the impenetrable barrier posed by the seemingly symmetrical antidiscrimination principle would be gone. The stakes would not be so high …
>
> Equality is a relativistic idea. The concern should be with those laws or practices that particularly hurt a disadvantaged group. Such laws might enhance the welfare of society (or the better-off classes), or leave it the same; what is critical, however, is that the state law or practice aggravates (or perpetuates?) the subordinate position of a specially disadvantaged group. This is what the Equal Protection Clause prohibits.
>
> Implicit in this formulation of the prohibition of the Equal Protection Clause is a view that certain state practices may be harmful to the members of a specially disadvantaged group, and yet not impair or threaten or aggravate the status or position of the group. For example, it is conceivable that a sales tax is harmful to blacks, and yet, due to several factors-such as the diffuseness of the impact and the nature of the deprivation-it need not be viewed as a practice that aggravates the subordinate status of blacks as a group. What is needed in order to bring a state practice within the equal protection ban is a theory of status-harm, one that shows how the challenged practice has this effect on the status of the group.
>
> It is from this perspective – one of a proscription against status-harm – that discriminatory state action should be viewed. Such action is one form of state conduct that impairs the status of a specially disadvantaged group. The Equal Protection Clause prohibits the state, for example, from using race as the criterion of admission to a swimming pool or a public housing project because that practice tends to aggravate the subordinate position of blacks by excluding them from a state facility. The same is true for the dual school system-the practice of assigning students to schools (or other public facilities) on the basis of race in order to segregate them. Once again, this state action is prohibited by the Equal Protection Clause because it aggravates the subordinate position of blacks …
>
> The white applicant who is rejected because of the preference for blacks may have been treated unfairly-may claim that he is being treated unfairly because he is being judged on the basis of an inappropriate criterion (not being black) and because the costs of a social policy are being localized on him. The individual unfairness to the rejected nondisadvantaged applicant is relevant in assessing the justification of the state's refusal to institute the practice of preferential treatment; it might be relevant in fashioning a remedy, or it might even give rise to the violation of another constitutional provision … But I do wish to deny that unfair treatment-such as being judged on the basis of an inappropriate criterion – is the domain of the Equal Protection Clause – even though such unfair treatment may be viewed from the individual perspective as a form of unequal treatment. As a protection for specially disadvantaged groups, the Equal Protection Clause should be viewed as a prohibition against group-disadvantaging practices, not unfair treatment.

It is quite clear that the EqA has not generally adopted an approach such as that advocated by Fiss, which would have entailed a non-symmetrical prohibition on discrimination against those disadvantaged by reference to protected characteristics such as sex, race, etc. Such an approach has been adopted in relation to disability, the prohibition against discrimination on the basis of which protects only those categorised as disabled for the purposes of the EqA. The importance of Fiss's article, however, is that it indicates that the symmetrical approach is not inevitable, and the practice of positive discrimination (preferential treatment designed to ameliorate disadvantage and/or to redress discrimination) is not necessarily to be viewed as inconsistent with a commitment to equality.

Mike Noon, extracted below, quoted US President Lyndon Johnson who said, as he introduced Executive Order 11246 in 1965:

> Imagine a hundred yard dash in which one of the two runners has his legs shackled together. He has progressed 10 yards, while the unshackled runner has gone 50 yards. At that point the judges decide that the race is unfair. How do they rectify the situation? Do they merely remove the shackles and allow the race to proceed? Then they could say that equal opportunity now prevailed. But one of the runners would still be forty yards ahead of the other. Would it not be the better part of justice to allow the previously shackled runner to make up the forty yard gap; or to start the race all over again?[74] …

Noon contrasted 'tie-break' positive discrimination such as that found in s159 EqA with 'threshold' positive discrimination, which 'requires candidates to achieve minimum qualification standards, but then allows managers to make choices in favour of candidates from disadvantaged groups':

> **Michael Noon, 'The shackled runner: time to rethink positive discrimination?' (2010) 24 *Work, Employment and Society* 728–39, references omitted**
>
> To require a 'tie-break' before taking into account social group characteristics would mean that candidates from the disadvantaged social groups have already proved themselves to be more able; they have jumped a higher hurdle to get to the tie-break position. In contrast, the threshold system means taking into account social group characteristics from the point where a candidate has attained the minimum standards required to do the job. The approach candidate from a disadvantaged group does not need to be compared with the highest achiever (a moveable target as it depends on the other candidates) but with the required standard to undertake the job (a fixed target or benchmark). This also has the advantage of encouraging the organisation's managers to consider what really constitutes the job requirements – so it fits with the meritocratic principle … that candidates need to be assessed on their suitability for the job (based on their skills and abilities to perform well in the role), rather than on acceptability (based on dubious assessments of whether they fit with the social norms or workplace 'culture', for example).

Noon challenged the suggestion that positive discrimination prevents the selection of the 'best candidate', suggesting that selection processes are characterised by 'pseudo-scientific rationalism' and high levels of subjectivity. Having pointed out that '[t]he "best" candidate is not necessarily the only appointable candidate', Noon suggested that diversity ought to be one of the criteria which could be 'used to determine what constitutes "best" beyond the appointable standard'. He went on to point out that the merit-based objection to positive discrimination assumes, contrary to the evidence, that appointments are made on this basis if positive discrimination measures are not adopted, also that the notion of merit itself is not value neutral ('Should it be focused on talent and ability, or should it also reflect effort and achievement?'), and that it 'can of course be used to disguise prejudicial views about certain groups being unable or unsuitable to perform certain work':

> laudable, white, able-bodied, heterosexual men have historically benefited from a system that privileges them. It is of little surprise that they react negatively towards changes that seek to remove

[74] n 32 above, extracted immediately below, citing D Bell *The Coming of Post-Industrial Society* (New York, Basic Books, 1973) 429.

those privileges. The enlisting of the social justice argument – that discrimination is morally wrong – rings hollow when issues of fairness have not been a primary concern for those accepting the privileges of their dominance. There is hypocrisy in claiming a concern for social justice only when one becomes a potential victim of injustice.

As commentators such as Young point out, the 'problem' arises because of a belief in the primacy of the principle of non-discrimination[75]. If it is acknowledged that injustice occurs through other means, such as oppression, the moral primacy of non-discrimination disappears. Not discriminating is therefore less important than not taking action that oppresses, subordinates or marginalises a social group. The point being made is that drawing distinctions between people based on social group characteristics and treating them differently (discriminating between people) is not wrong in itself, but if it is done to reduce opportunities or exploit groups then it becomes an oppressive act and is morally questionable. Conversely, drawing such distinctions in order to provide preferential treatment and therefore to redress an existing disadvantage can be construed as morally laudable. At issue is not the treatment, but the purpose and impact of the treatment. This long-standing tension between same (equal) treatment and different treatment is a central antagonism in policy making yet remains a false dichotomy obscuring the core purpose of equality policy if the latter is aimed at providing social justice.

The Public Sector Equality Duty

The first PSED was introduced in Britain by the Race Relations (Amendment) Act 2000, which amended the RRA, similar duties being added to the SDA and DDA in 2006 and 2007 respectively. It had its roots in s75 of the Northern Ireland Act 1998 (NIA) which imposes upon 'public authorities' scheduled to the Act an obligation 'in carrying out [their] functions relating to Northern Ireland' to have 'due regard to the need to promote equality of opportunity … between persons of different religious belief, political opinion, racial group, age, marital status or sexual orientation … men and women generally … persons with a disability and persons without [and] between persons with dependents and persons without.' Section 75(2) of the Act provides that, without prejudice to the obligations imposed by s75(1), public authorities shall also have regard to the desirability of promoting good relations between persons of different religious belief, political opinion or racial group.

Section 75 NIA in turn had its roots in the Policy Appraisal and Fair Treatment (PAFT) guidelines, first issued in Northern Ireland in December 1993, which in turn drew upon British guidelines launched in the 1980s by the Ministerial Group on Women's Issues. The PAFT initiative was intended 'to ensure that, in practice, issues of equality and equity condition policy-making and action in all spheres and at all levels of Government activity, whether in regulatory and administrative functions or in the delivery of services to the public.'[76] The operation of the PAFT guidelines in Northern Ireland was heavily criticised, Christine Bell pointing out in 1996 that they were not made public and, in many cases, did not even reach public authorities responsible for their implementation.[77] The regime established by the NIA (s75 and Schedule 9) took into account the lessons learned from PAFT. Central to it were the 'equality schemes' which all public authorities covered by the Act are required to submit to the ECNI for approval. Schemes may be approved by the Commission or referred to the Secretary of State who may approve them, request the relevant public

[75] Citing IM Young, *Justice and the Politics of Difference* (Chichester, Princeton University Press, 1990).
[76] Central Community Relations Unit's First Annual Report on PAFT (1995).
[77] See C Bell, 'Employment Equality Review' (1996) 2 *International Journal of Discrimination and the Law* 53.

authority to draw up a revised scheme, or impose a scheme on the authority. Public authorities must review their schemes every five years and notify the Commission of the outcome of any such review. The ECNI can receive complaints about any failure on the part of a public authority to comply with its own equality scheme, where such complaints are brought by a person 'who claims to have been directly affected by the failure'. It can also investigate, in the absence of complaint, authorities' compliance with their equality schemes.

The Race Relations (Amendment) Act 2000 was passed in response to the Macpherson Report into the death of Stephen Lawrence and its exposition of 'institutional racism' among the police (see further below). The Act prohibited race discrimination by public authorities, including the police, in the exercise of their functions (see Chapter 4) and replaced what had been a very weak positive obligation with s71 RRA, which was broadly modelled on s75 NIA.[78] The RRA, in its amended form, included a requirement for detailed race equality schemes which are of much less importance today. The RRA model was in turn applied across the EqA's other predecessor provisions. The PSED now contained in s149 EqA[79] differs from its predecessor 'general duty' provisions in several respects but the general judicial approach to the provisions has not significantly changed.

Section 149 EqA, Public sector equality duty

(1) A public authority must, in the exercise of its functions, have due regard to the need to—
   (a) eliminate discrimination, harassment, victimisation and any other conduct that is prohibited by or under this Act;
   (b) advance equality of opportunity between persons who share a relevant protected characteristic and persons who do not share it;
   (c) foster good relations between persons who share a relevant protected characteristic and persons who do not share it.

(2) A person who is not a public authority but who exercises public functions must, in the exercise of those functions, have due regard to the matters mentioned in subsection (1).

(3) Having due regard to the need to advance equality of opportunity between persons who share a relevant protected characteristic and persons who do not share it involves having due regard, in particular, to the need to—
   (a) remove or minimise disadvantages suffered by persons who share a relevant protected characteristic that are connected to that characteristic;
   (b) take steps to meet the needs of persons who share a relevant protected characteristic that are different from the needs of persons who do not share it;
   (c) encourage persons who share a relevant protected characteristic to participate in public life or in any other activity in which participation by such persons is disproportionately low.

(4) The steps involved in meeting the needs of disabled persons that are different from the needs of persons who are not disabled include, in particular, steps to take account of disabled persons' disabilities.

(5) Having due regard to the need to foster good relations between persons who share a relevant protected characteristic and persons who do not share it involves having due regard, in particular, to the need to—
   (a) tackle prejudice, and
   (b) promote understanding.

[78] Originally imposed in England and Wales by the Race Relations Act 1976 (Statutory Duties) Order 2001 (SI 2001/3458).

[79] Which, with various associated provisions (ss 150–57) and ss158 and 159 EqA (positive action) form Part 11 EqA ('Advancement of Equality').

(6) Compliance with the duties in this section may involve treating some persons more favourably than others; but that is not to be taken as permitting conduct that would otherwise be prohibited by or under this Act.

(7) The relevant protected characteristics are—

age;
disability;
gender reassignment;
pregnancy and maternity;
race;
religion or belief;
sex;
sexual orientation …

Geographical Reach of the PSED

The question of territorial application of the EqA is considered in Chapter 4. It should be noted here, however, that the obligations imposed by the PSED do not apply outside Britain.

***Turani v Secretary of State for the Home Department* [2021] EWCA Civ 348, [2022] 1 All ER 254**

The claimants were Palestinians who had fled Syria as refugees to the Lebanon and wished to be considered for resettlement in the UK under the Vulnerable Persons Resettlement Scheme (VPRS). They were excluded from the scheme for reasons discussed in Chapter 4 and claimed both indirect race discrimination and a breach of the PSED. The CA accepted that they were entitled to bring the discrimination claim under Part 3 EqA, but ruled that the PSED did not apply.

Simler LJ, with whom Warby and Underhill LJJ agreed:

101. The starting point, as before, must be the presumption that Parliament legislated for territorial effect only, unless Parliament can reasonably be taken to have intended to legislate for extraterritorial effect. There is nothing in the express words of section 149(1)(b) EqA 2010 to suggest that Parliament intended to extend the territorial reach of subsection 1(b) to persons or matters outside the United Kingdom. The points made earlier which suggest that Parliament did not intend Part 3 to have extraterritorial effect save in limited circumstances apply with equal force to this provision.

102. The duty in subsection (1)(b) is explained by section 149(3) and (5) EqA 2010 as including the need to remove or minimise disadvantages suffered by people who share a protected characteristic that are connected to that characteristic; the need to take steps to meet the needs of people who share a protected characteristic that are different from the needs of people who do not; and the need to encourage people who share a relevant protected characteristic to 'participate in public life or in any other activity in which participation by such persons is disproportionately low'. The latter involves tackling prejudice and promoting understanding. I find it difficult to see why or how Parliament could have expected public authorities to take these steps in relation to people outside the United Kingdom in a place where the authority is unlikely to have any real sphere of operation, or in a place or country where different views may be taken on questions of equality and non-discrimination as reflected in local laws, customs and traditions. Certain characteristics that are protected characteristics in Great Britain are far from protected elsewhere and there may be great sensitivity in this regard. It cannot be for

a public authority in this country to determine how best to advance equality of opportunity between people subject to foreign law, traditions and customs. These points reinforce the force of the normal presumption in this case.

103. Although, as Mr Jaffey submitted [for the claimants], the duty is a procedural one, it seems to me that the purpose of this legislation can properly and effectively be achieved without implying extraterritorial effect. To require a public authority to have regard to the equality needs of people who are outside the jurisdiction and whose equality of opportunity and good relations with others it will necessarily have limited if any scope to influence is not implicit in the statutory scheme and as Elisabeth Laing J noted, would make it '*incoherent*'. It would mean that section 149(1)(b) requires a public authority to have due regard to the need to advance equality for anyone anywhere in the world, regardless of the public authority's actual capacity to advance that person's equality of opportunity. That seems to me to be a meaningless duty. There is nothing to suggest that was Parliament's intention.

104. For a claimant who is not a British citizen, does not live or work here, and has no other link at all with the United Kingdom other than a wish to benefit from a policy of the Secretary of State, the exceptional connection with the United Kingdom which would otherwise be required to establish a territorial extension to the EA 2010 is absent. The fact that government practice may extend to conducting equality impact assessments where the effects are felt outside the United Kingdom is not a guide to the interpretation of this provision, and does not lead me to a different conclusion …

Exceptions to the PSED

Schedule 18 provides that the PSED does not apply:

- in connection with age, to the exercise of a function relating to the provision of education, benefits, facilities or services to pupils in schools or the provision of accommodation, benefits, facilities or services to children in children's homes
- in connection with age, nationality, ethnic or national origins or religion or belief in the exercise of immigration and nationality functions
- to the exercise of a judicial function or a function exercised on behalf of, or on the instructions of, a person exercising a judicial function;
- to the House of Commons, the HL; the Scottish Parliament, the National Assembly for Wales, the General Synod of the Church of England, the Security Service, Secret Intelligence Service or Government Communications Headquarters (GCHQ), or to part of the armed forces which is, in accordance with a requirement of the Secretary of State, assisting GCHQ, when they are exercising public functions other than as public authorities
- to anyone exercising a function in connection with proceedings in the House of Commons or the HL, in the Scottish Parliament (other than a function of the Scottish Parliamentary Corporate Body) or in the National Assembly for Wales (other than a function of the Assembly Commission).

Operation of the PSED

Early indications for the PSED (then 'general duty') were not promising, s71 RRA as amended by the 2000 Act generating no litigation for the first 4 years and scant evidence of compliance by public authorities.[80] In *R (Elias) v SSD* [2005] EWHC 1435 (Admin), [2005] IRLR 788, however, the High Court ruled that the defendant had breached the PSED by failing to have due regard to the need to eliminate unlawful racial discrimination in adopting a compensation scheme for former Japanese prisoners of war, the CA subsequently declaring ([2006] EWCA Civ 1293, [2006] IRLR 934) that the 'clear purpose' of the PSED was 'to require public bodies to whom that provision applies to give advance consideration to issues of … discrimination *before* making any policy decision that may be affected by them. The compensation scheme challenged in *Elias* excluded from entitlement to payment British subjects who had not been born (and whose parents and grandparents had not been born) in the UK. The High Court ruled that, given the 'obvious discriminatory effect of this scheme', the PSED required the Secretary of State to consider in advance of its adoption whether its disparate racial impact was justifiable.

In *R (BAPIO Action Ltd) v SSD* [2007] EWHC 199 (QB) the High Court ruled that changes to the regime for training international medical students in the UK had been made in breach of the PSED. The CA upheld the decision ([2007] EWCA Civ 1139), Sedley LJ stating that the PSED had to be complied with 'not as rearguard action following a concluded decision but as an essential preliminary to any such decision. Inattention to it is both unlawful and bad government'.[81] And in *R(C) v Secretary of State for Justice* the CA quashed amendments to the legislation concerning training for young people in detention which had been made without any analysis of their likely racial impact, stating that that the failure of analysis was '[a]lthough here characterised as a procedural defect … is of very great substantial, and not merely technical, importance'.

Considerations of space precludes a detailed discussion of the extensive case law which has developed under the PSED.[82] The significance of the provision is that it should facilitate proper engagement, on the basis of adequate information,[83] with the equality implication of decisions *before they are made*, the effect of which may well be that those decisions are made differently. It is important to understand that the obligation imposed by the PSED is not one of *results* but of *procedure*; the public authority is required to take equality-related needs into account in reaching decisions, but the weight to be afforded to those needs are a matter for the public authority itself, subject to the normal public law requirements of rationality, legality and procedural propriety.[84]

Much of the benefit of the PSED may be in the avoidance of inadvertent indirect discrimination as a result of the disparate impact of proposed measures being recognised and avoided in advance, though the extent to which the courts are prepared to *require* such action remains limited. *R (BAPIO) v Royal College of General Practitioners* was an unsuccessful PSED challenge to a membership examination imposed by the defendant which had for years had very significant disparate impacts between white applicants, on the one hand, Black and South Asian, on the other. A review carried out in 2013 had made various recommendations, including training a more representative profile of examiners, after which the claimant (the British Association of Physicians of Indian Origin) sought to challenge the defendants' continued use of the membership examination, complaining inter alia of

[80] CRE, *Common Ground* (CRE, 2006).
[81] See also the decision in *R (Kaur) v LB Ealing*, n 28 above.
[82] See instead, for example, A McColgan, extracted below.
[83] See for example *R (Lunt) v Liverpool CC* [2008] EWCA Civ 141, [2008] LGR 239 but see also *CPAG v SSWP* [2011] EWHC 2616 (Admin).
[84] See for example *R (Baker) v SSCLG* [2008] EWCA Civ 141, [2008] LGR 239.

the defendant's failure to undertake an equality impact assessment of the requirements for membership. The Court ruled that the defendant had been under a continuing duty to pay due regard to the need to eliminate discrimination and advance equality of opportunity and had done so by commissioning the review and identifying the respects in which it needed to act to eliminate discrimination and some of the means by which it might do so.

***R (Bapio) v Royal College of General Practitioners* [2014] EWHC 1416 (Admin)**

Mitting J:

31. … Section 149 does not permit a person exercising public functions to identify the need to eliminate discrimination in one of the public functions it exercises and then do nothing about it. If it acted thus it would not be 'having regard' to the need to eliminate discrimination in the exercise of its public function, it would be *disregarding* a specific need which it had itself identified. In many, but I think not in all cases, it might also be infringing s 19 if it acted thus.

32. On the facts of this case, the Royal College has now identified the respect in which, in the discharge of its public functions, it needs to act to eliminate discrimination and has identified some of the means by which that need might be addressed and fulfilled. The time at which it should act upon the information which it has gathered and analysed has either arrived or will do so very soon. If it does not act and its failure to act is the subject of a further challenge, it may well be held to be in breach of its duty under s 149 for that reason alone. As of now, I am not satisfied that it is in breach of its duties under s 149 or was at the time when this claim form was issued.

Sandra Fredman argued at the time that, once it had been established that a proposed policy or practice would or might produce a disparate impact, the relevant decision maker ought to be required to take steps to avert that impact. She described as 'somewhat anomalous' the fact that the PSED required only that 'due regard' be paid to the need to eliminate unlawful discrimination, suggesting that the identification of such discrimination 'triggers the need to take action, even if no complaint has been brought'. Mitting J, she suggested, ought to have found in the *BAPIO* case that the defendant was already in breach of the PSED by reason of its failure already to have taken ameliorative action.

Sandra Fredman, 'Addressing Disparate Impact: Indirect Discrimination and the Public Sector Equality Duty' (2014) 43 *Industrial Law Journal* 349–63, footnotes omitted

Perhaps [Mitting] J thought that, given the strong indications he had given, the Royal College would now act voluntarily to bring about change. He concluded his judgment by stating the claimant had 'achieved, if not a legal victory, then a moral success'. However, it is hard to see why the public body should be left to its own devices, having dragged their heels for so long that the claimant had no other option than to bring judicial proceedings. Indeed, [Mitting] J acknowledged that the claim was only brought because the claimant felt no other course was open to it to rectify what he characterised as an 'anomaly acknowledged by all to exist'. If it was correct that the time the public body should act had arrived or shortly would arrive, it is difficult to see why the Court did not hold in favour of the claimant. Litigation is expensive and time consuming; it is not realistic to require that further litigation be mounted if the Royal College failed to act …

Even apart from the PSED, there is a duty to eliminate unlawful discrimination, which arises regardless of whether a complaint has actually been brought. Thus, section 29 EA states that a service provider 'must not discriminate' (directly or indirectly) against recipients of a public service; and section 39 likewise states that an employer 'must not discriminate' against employees and applicants. This is not dependent on whether a complaint has been brought. In the context of indirect discrimination, as we have seen, the duty requires the institution of alternative, less discriminatory means, which arises pre-emptively in order to establish a justification defence. The PSED's admonition to 'have due regard' to the need to eliminate unlawful discrimination would add nothing to the existing duties under sections 29 and 39, if it did not require alternative means to be explored as soon as there were grounds to suspect, as the court did, that there was a disparate impact, rather than waiting for it to be established …

Mitting J's suggestion that the PSED could be breached by a decision maker which recognised, and then failed to address, the discriminatory impact of a decision has not been followed.

The PSED applies to decision-making by public authorities about their employment as well as other functions and ought to have implications for decision-making which impacts on the gender pay gap and other indicators of workplace inequality. There have been few indications to date, however, that this has occurred.

The PSED requires that due regard be paid not only to the need to eliminate discrimination, but also to the need to advance equality (the term 'promote' had been used in the RRA). Section 149(3) and (4) EqA then make it clear that the 'Having due regard to the need to advance equality of opportunity' requires consideration of positive action measures, and of reasonable adjustments for disabled people.

Aileen McColgan 'Litigating the Public Sector Equality Duty: The Story So Far' (2015) 35 *Oxford Journal of Legal Studies* 453–85, footnotes omitted

… the PSED case law appears to have helped to shift the judicial conceptualisation of equality or non-discrimination as being concerned with the avoidance of treatment which differentiates in form or substance, to something with a more radical edge. In *Kaur & Shah* [*v LB Ealing* [2008] EWHC 2062 (Admin)] the defendant sought to argue that its continued funding of the Southall Black Sisters would have entailed unlawful race discrimination. Moses LJ, in rejecting this submission, relied on section 35 RRA which permitted the provision of access to facilities or services to persons of a particular racial group where the facilities or services 'meet the special needs of persons of that group in regard to their education, training or welfare, or any ancillary benefits'. Refusing to read that provision strictly as an exception to the principle of equality, as was urged upon him by the defendant, his Lordship declared that section 35 was:

> not an exception to the [RRA]. It does not derogate from it in any way. It is a manifestation of the important principle of anti discrimination and equality measures that not only must like cases be treated alike but that unlike cases but must be treated differently.

He went on to rule that there was 'no dichotomy between the promotion of equality and cohesion and the provision of specialist services to an ethnic minority' and that 'in certain circumstances the purposes of [the PSED] and the relevant statutory code may only be met by specialist services from a specialist source'.

Kaur, although reached over 30 years after the enactment of the RRA, was one of very few examples of cases in which that provision fell to be judicially considered, much less determined the outcome. It is unlikely to have been a coincidence that the non-formalistic approach to equality was taken in a case in which the relevant duty was to 'have due regard to the need (a) to eliminate unlawful racial discrimination and (b) *to promote equality of opportunity* and good relations between persons of different racial groups' (emphasis added[85]). With the implementation of the Equality Act 2010 the PSED's reference to the *promotion* of equality was replaced with a requirement to have due regard to the need to *advance* equality of opportunity … any assumption that the reference to equality *of opportunity* as distinct from 'equality of results', 'equality of outcome'

[85] This being the test imposed by the RRA.

or simply 'equality' is meant to indicate a symmetrical approach to concept is contradicted by section 149(3) …

… the application of the PSED to austerity decision-making is not the most promising context for the advancement of equality as distinct from the avoidance of discrimination. Having said this, in [*R (Chavda) v Harrow LBC* [2007] EWHC 3064 (Admin), [2008] LGR 657] … Judge Mackie QC made specific reference to 'the need to promote equality of opportunity *and to take account of disabilities even where that involves treating the disabled more favourably than others*' (emphasis added) and ruled that the failure to draw attention to this obligation rendered the decision unlawful. And in *R (South West Care Homes Ltd) v Devon CC* [[2011] EWHC 2676 (Admin), [2012] PTSR D13], a decision on care home fees was struck down in part because of the defendant's failure to take into account the potential impact on the rights of residents under the [UN Convention on the Rights of Persons with Disabilities]'to choose where they live and to have support so as to prevent isolation or segregation from the community'. In the latter case the judge relied on the decision in *Burnip v SSWP* [[2012] EWCA Civ 629, [2012] LGR 954] in which the CA had ruled, on the strength of the ECtHR's decision in *Thlimmenos v Greece* (2001) 31 EHRR 411, that the defendant's failure to make allowances for the fact that the claimants needed larger properties by reason of their or their children's disabilities, and were therefore placed at a particular disadvantage by the bedroom tax, breached Article 14.

Chavda, *South West Care Homes* and *Burnip* all concerned people with disabilities, and might be seen as no more than applications of the relatively uncontroversial principle that the avoidance of disability discrimination may well require special treatment (this being the underpinning presumption of the duty to make reasonable adjustments). But more recently, in *R (Knowles) v SSWP* [[2013] EWHC 19 (Admin)], Hickinbottom J applied the *Burnip* approach to a challenge to the fact that housing benefit payments in respect of the costs of accommodation at caravan sites are calculated by reference to ordinary sites, and did not allow for the additional costs associated with gypsy sites (additional site management, maintenance, clearance costs, fencing and security, education facilities for children, resolution of disputes, and personal support, which together were estimated to account for about a third of the total costs). The judge accepted that 'the state may have a positive obligation to allocate a greater share of public resources to a particular person or group to ameliorate' what might be termed a *Thlimmenos* difference; that '[a]lthough very different on its facts, conceptually, this case appears to me indistinguishable from *Burnip*, in which the analysis was made in *Thlimmenos* terms'; and that:

> [f]ollowing *Burnip*, there is of course no conceptual or jurisdictional difficulty in finding a *prima facie* positive obligation on the state to allocate resources to remedy such a difference; and then proceeding to consider the reasons for the difference and whether they amount to an objective and reasonable justification.

The claim failed, the bulk of the additional costs being ineligible to be met within the housing benefit scheme, but the case may suggest increased judicial confidence with a non-symmetrical approach to equality. *Knowles* was not a PSED case and it would be wrong to suggest that all of the work in the area of equality law is being done by the PSED. It is however noteworthy that a duty which began with relatively limited apparent potential has proved so significant in practice …

Socio-Economic Inequalities

Finally, mention should be made of s1 EqA which provides that:

Section 1 EqA, Public sector equality duty regarding socio-economic inequalities

(1) An authority to which this section applies must, when making decisions of a strategic nature about how to exercise its functions, have due regard to the desirability of exercising them in a way that is designed to reduce the inequalities of outcome which result from socio-economic disadvantage …

The provision is a less onerous version of s149, but would extend the reach of positive obligations beyond the EqA's protected characteristics to socio-economic disadvantage. It has not been implemented in GB, the EqA having been passed in the final days of the last Labour administration. Section 1 EqA has, however, been implemented in Scotland as the 'Fairer Scotland Duty' in April 2018 and in Wales in March 2021. Research by the EHRC published in March 2021 reported that:

Elaine Wilson Smith, Diego Garcia Rodriguez and June Brawner, *Evaluating the socio-economic duty in Scotland and Wales* (EHRC, 2021) 8

- Some Scottish public bodies reported that the duty had begun to influence and change the outcomes of decisions. Several, however, felt that the duty had not, as yet, made any significant changes to the outcome of decisions that had been made, and had not been used to set or tackle specific priorities to date …

Public bodies in both nations identified a number of elements that are needed to ensure future success and the effective implementation of the duty:

- clear success criteria and measures so that the impact of the duty on inequalities of outcomes can be monitored
- further guidance and support from governments on data use and consultation with those experiencing socio-economic disadvantage
- mechanisms that hold public bodies accountable to the duty
- collective responsibility for the duty among all staff members within public bodies, and
- greater focus on changes to outcomes rather than decision-making processes.

4

Coverage

The Human Rights Act 1998

The main focus of this chapter is on the coverage of the Equality Act 2010 (EqA). Before coming to this, however, it is useful to discuss the other significant statute considered in this book: the Human Rights Act 1998 (HRA). At the time of writing the HRA is threatened (as discussed in Chapter 1), but whatever the future of the HRA, the European Convention on Human Rights (ECHR) rights here discussed are likely to remain of significance in the UK, although the mechanism for their enforcement may alter.

At present, the main application of the HRA to discrimination is through its incorporation of Article 14 ECHR, which provides that:

> **Article 14 ECHR**
>
> The enjoyment of the rights and freedoms set forth in this Convention shall be secured without discrimination on any ground such as sex, race, colour, language, religion, political or other opinion, national or social origin, association with a national minority, property, birth or other status.

As discussed in Chapter 1, Article 14 does not amount to a free-standing prohibition on discrimination, being concerned only with discrimination *in the exercise of other Convention rights*, listed there and immediately below.

Convention Rights

The rights provided by the ECHR and given partial effect in domestic law by the HRA are broad and various. In short summary, they cover the following subject areas:

- Article 2: right to life, broadly interpreted to cover core aspects of health;
- Article 3: prohibition of inhuman and degrading treatment and torture;
- Article 4: prohibition of slavery and forced labour;
- Article 5: right to liberty and security;
- Article 6: right to a fair trial in civil and criminal matters;
- Article 7: prohibition on punishment without law;

- Article 8: right to private and family life;
- Article 9: right to freedom of thought, conscience and religion;
- Article 10: right to freedom of expression;
- Article 11: right to freedom of association and assembly;
- Article 12: right to marry;
- Article 1 Protocol 1: right to property;
- Article 1 Protocol 2: right to education;
- Article 1 Protocol 3: right to free elections.

'Within the Ambit'

As above, Article 14 applies only to discrimination 'in the exercise of' these other Convention rights. The approach of the European Court of Human Rights (ECtHR) and domestic courts is relatively generous, permitting claims about discrimination which falls within the 'ambit' or scope of a Convention right.[1]

> **ECtHR, *Guide on Article 14 of the European Convention on Human Rights and on Article 1 of Protocol No. 12 to the Convention***[2]
>
> 10. For Article 14 to be applicable it is necessary, but also sufficient, for the facts of the case to fall within the wider ambit of one or more of the Convention Articles.[3] As such, the material scope of application of Article 14 – read in conjunction with a substantive provision – cannot be reduced solely to the material scope of application of the substantive provision.
>
> 11. As a consequence, the Court has established that the prohibition of discrimination applies to those additional rights, falling within the general scope of any Article of the Convention, for which the State has voluntarily decided to provide protection.[4]
>
> 12. The Court itself has provided a number of examples of this concept of 'additional rights', explaining that, for instance, Article 6 of the Convention does not compel States to institute a system of appeal courts. A State which does set up such courts consequently goes beyond its obligations under Article 6. However, it would violate that Article, read in conjunction with Article 14, were it to debar certain persons from these remedies without a legitimate reason, while making them available to others in respect of the same type of actions.[5]
>
> 13. To this end, it is necessary that the legal interest to which the non-discrimination requirement applies falls within the ambit of the substantive Article,[6] is linked to the exercise of a right guaranteed by the substantive Article,[7] or does not fall completely outside the ambit of the substantive Article.[8]

[1] *Abdulaziz, Cabales and Balkandali v UK* (1985) 7 EHRR 471 §71; *Inze v Austria* (1988) 10 EHRR 394, §36.

[2] https://www.echr.coe.int/Documents/Guide_Art_14_Art_1_Protocol_12_ENG.pdf.

[3] Citing *Carson v UK* (2010) 51 EHRR 13, §63; *EB v France* (2008) 47 EHRR 21, §47; *Markin v Russia* (2012) 56 EHRR 8, §124; *Sidabras and Dziautas v Lithuania* (2006) 42 EHRR 6, §38.

[4] Citing, inter alia, *Fabian v Hungary* (2018) 66 EHRR 26 §112; *Biao v Denmark* (2017) 64 EHRR 1 §88; *Dogan v Turkey* (2017) 64 EHRR 5 §158; *Carson v UK, ibid* §63; *EB v France, ibid*, §48; *Genovese v Malta* (2014) 58 EHRR 25 §32.

[5] Citing the *Belgian Linguistic Case (No 2)* (1968) 1 EHRR 252 §9.

[6] Citing *Zarb Adami v Malta* (2006) 44 EHRR 49 §49.

[7] Citing *Markin v Russia*, n 3 above §129, or does not fall completely outside the ambit of the substantive Article.

[8] Citing *Van der Mussele v Belgium* (1984) 6 EHRR 163, §43.

> 14. The Court has thus found Article 14, read in conjunction with a substantive right, applicable to a number of circumstances. For example, it recognised that rights such as the right for a single homosexual parent to adopt a child,[9] parental leave and parental allowances[10] and denial of citizenship[11] come within the scope of Article 8 in conjunction with Article 14. By the same token, the Court has found Article 14 in conjunction with Article 1 of Protocol No. 1 applicable to a variety of welfare benefits.[12]

In *M v SSWP* [2006] UKHL 11, [2006] 2 AC 91 Lord Walker, with whom Lords Bingham and Mance agreed, said at §60 that 'no simple bright-line test, general guidance [could] be derived from the Strasbourg case law' but that the guidance 'does not in my opinion lead to the conclusion that even a tenuous link is sufficient' between substantive Convention right and the treatment complained of in an Article 14 claim. At §61 he stated that the necessary connection would vary depending on which substantive right was at issue. The House of Lords (HL) ruled in *M* that child support payments did not fall within the ambit of Article 8 or Article 1 Protocol 1 (A1P1) and, accordingly, that discrimination against non-resident parents in same-sex couples could not be challenged under Article 14. In *R (Clift) v SSHD* [2004] UKHL 54, [2007] 1 AC 484, a case involving the release of prisoners on licence, the HL ruled (*per* Lord Bingham MR) that (§13) 'expressions such as "ambit", "scope" and "linked" used in the Strasbourg cases ... denote a situation in which a substantive convention right is not violated, but in which a personal interest close to the core of such a right is infringed. This calls, as Lord Nicholls said in *M v SSWP* (at §14), for a value judgment. The court is required to consider, in respect of the convention right relied on, what value that substantive right exists to protect.'

The ECtHR in *JM v UK* (2011) 53 EHRR 6 disagreed with the decision of the HL in *M*, ruling that child-support payments did fall within the ambit of A1P1 and that the discrimination complained of breached Article 14. The approach of the HL in *M* and *Clift* remained influential until *In re McLaughlin* [2018] UKSC 48, [2018] 1 WLR 4250 in which Lady Hale, for the majority, suggested that the domestic courts had 'made rather heavy weather of the ambit point' and that the requirement for more than a tenuous connection between the matter complained of and the 'core values' protected by a Convention right may (§22) be 'too restrictive a test', 'core values' being 'a concept derived from the domestic rather than the Strasbourg jurisprudence'. The current approach of the Supreme Court (SC) is illustrated below.

R (A) v Criminal Injuries Compensation Authority [2021] UKSC 27, [2021] 1 WLR 3746

The claimants had grown up in state care in Lithuania and had convictions there prior to being trafficked from Lithuania to the UK and subjected to labour exploitation and abuse. They were denied payments under the Criminal Injuries Compensation Scheme because they had unspent convictions which had resulted in custodial sentences. They challenged their exclusion from the scheme on the basis, inter alia, that it breached Article 14 read with Article 4 (which prohibits slavery and forced labour).

[9] Citing *EB v France*, n 3 above, §43.
[10] Citing *Markin*, n 3 above, §130.
[11] Citing *Genovese v Malta* (2014) 58 EHRR 25.
[12] Citing *Stummer v Austria* (2012) 54 EHRR 11 §82; *Stec v UK* (2006) 43 EHRR 47 §53; *Carson v UK*, n 4 above, §§64–65; *Andrejeva v Latvia* (2010) 51 EHRR 28 7; *Fabian v Hungary*, n 4 above, §117, and contrasting *Dobrowolski v Poland*, App No 45651/11, unreported, judgment of 13 March 2018.

Lord Lloyd-Jones (for the Court):

38. … this is an area where the law has moved on and the attitude of the ECtHR has changed. While 'the English courts have made rather heavy weather of the ambit point' (Re McLaughlin §20, per Lady Hale) the ECtHR has taken a much more relaxed approach to the issue …. This is apparent from Zarb Adami v Malta (2006) 44 EHRR 49. Mr Adami complained of discrimination on grounds of sex in respect of his call for compulsory jury service. He relied, inter alia, on art 4 in conjunction with art 14. The ECtHR held that although art 4(3)(d) excludes 'any work or service which forms part of normal civic obligations' from the prohibition in art 4(2) on 'forced or compulsory labour', the fact that a situation corresponded to a normal civic obligation did not preclude the applicability of art 4 in conjunction with art 14. The concurring judgment of the President, Judge Sir Nicolas Bratza, is particularly illuminating. He observed (at para 7):

> 'The central question which arises is what constitutes 'the ambit' of one of the substantive Articles, in this case art 4. It has been argued that 'even the most tenuous links with another provision in the convention will suffice' for art 14 to be engaged (see Grosz, Beatson and Duffy *The 1998 Act and the European Convention* …, para C14–10). Even if this may be seen as going too far, it is indisputable that a wide interpretation has consistently been given by the court to the term 'within the ambit'. Thus, according to the constant case law of the court, the application of art 14 not only does not presuppose the violation of one of the substantive convention rights or a direct interference with the exercise of such right, but it does not even require that the discriminatory treatment of which complaint is made falls within the four corners of the individual rights guaranteed by the article. This is best illustrated by the fact that art 14 has been held to cover not only the enjoyment of the rights that states are obliged to safeguard under the convention but also those rights and freedoms that a state has chosen to guarantee, even if in doing so it goes beyond the requirements of the convention (see eg *Case Relating to Certain Aspects of the Laws on the Use of Languages in Education in Belgium* (1968) 1 EHRR 252 at para 9; *Abdulaziz v UK* [(1985) 7 EHRR 471] … at para 71). This would indicate in my view that the 'ambit' of an article for this purpose must be given a significantly wider meaning than the 'scope' of the particular rights defined in the article itself. Thus, in the specific context of art 4 of the convention, the fact that work or service falling within the definition of 'normal civic obligations' in para 3 are expressly excluded from the scope of the right guaranteed by para 2 of that article, in no sense means that they are also excluded from the ambit of the article seen as a whole.'

39. In the present case, while the CICS is not limited to victims of trafficking, it extends its benefits to them. In the preparation of the scheme specific attention was paid to its application to victims of trafficking and provisions included in order to accommodate them … The United Kingdom, in applying the scheme to victims of trafficking, has chosen to confer a degree of protection to promote their interests. I consider that in doing so it is applying a measure which has a more than tenuous connection with the core value of the protection of victims of trafficking under art 4. The rights voluntarily conferred in this way under the scheme on victims of trafficking fall within the general scope of art 4 and must, therefore, be made available without discrimination.

It is important to emphasise that the discriminatory treatment complained of need not breach the other Convention right.

***Abdulaziz, Cabales and Balkandali v UK* (1985) 7 EHRR 471**

The applicants were non-citizens entitled to live in the UK. As women, they had no right to have their husbands and fiancés enter the UK to live with them. Men in the same position as the women did have that right. The applicants challenged the immigration rule relying, inter alia, on Article 14 and Article 8 ECHR (the latter of which protects the right to family life). The Article 8 claims failed because Article 8 did not at the time provide a right to family life *in the UK*[13] and the applicants could have joined their husbands and fiancés in the Indian sub-continent. Their Article 14 claims succeeded, however, because the sex discrimination complained of related to their ability to enjoy their family lives (by enjoying it in the UK) and the justification put forward by the UK government was inadequate.

Some sense of the width of discrimination challenges possible under the HRA should have been provided by the cases discussed above (which concerned state benefits, criminal injury compensation, prisoner release, compulsory jury service and immigration). Other discrimination-related claims brought under the HRA have included challenges to rules concerning: the allocation of social housing;[14] the upkeep of churches;[15] state pensionable age;[16] birth registration;[17] adoption and fostering agencies;[18] prison sentences;[19] deportation;[20] access to civil partnerships, to abortion and to marriage;[21] the recording of sex on passports;[22] planning;[23] the implantation of embryos;[24] succession to tenancies;[25] and internment without trial.[26] Some of these cases are discussed elsewhere in the book.

The Equality Act 2010

Returning to the main theme of this chapter, the EqA does not impose a blanket prohibition on discrimination on the basis of the protected characteristics. Instead, the legislation details a number of areas – goods and services, public functions, employment, premises, associations etc – in respect of which discrimination is regulated. These are found in Part 3

[13] Now *cf R (Quila) v SSHD* [2011] UKSC 45, [2012] 1 AC 621.

[14] *R (Z) v Hackney LBC* [2020] UKSC 40 [2021] 1 WLR 4327, discussed in Ch 3; *R (Morris) v Westminster CC* [2005] EWCA Civ 1184, [2006] 1 WLR 505.

[15] *Aston Cantlow v Wallbank* [2003] UKHL 37, [2004] 1 AC 546.

[16] *R (Delve) v SSWP* [2020] EWCA Civ 1199, [2021] 3 All ER 115.

[17] *R (McConnell) v Registrar General for England and Wales* [2020] EWCA Civ 559, [2021] Fam 77.

[18] *R (Cornerstone (North East) Fostering & Adoption Services v Ofsted)* [2021] EWCA Civ 1390, [2022] 2 All ER 516.

[19] *R (Khan) v SSJ* [2020] EWHC 2084 (Admin), [2021] 2 All ER 1033; *R (Stott) v SSJ* [2018] UKSC 59, [2020] AC 51; *R (Clift) v SSHD* [2006] UKHL 54, [2007] 1 AC 484.

[20] *R (Johnson) v SSHD* [2016] UKSC 56, [2017] AC 365.

[21] Respectively *R (Steinfeld) v SS International Development* [2018] UKSC 32, [2018] 4 All ER 1, *R (A) v SS Health* [2017] UKSC 41, [2017] 4 All ER 353 and *R (Baiai) v SSHD* [2007] EWCA Civ 478, [2008] QB 143.

[22] *R (Elan-Cane) v SSHD* [2021] UKSC 56, [2022] 2 All ER 1.

[23] *R (Wilson) v Wychavon DC* [2007] EWCA Civ 52, [2007] QB 801.

[24] *Evans v Amicus Healthcare Ltd* [2004] EWCA (Civ) 727, [2004] 3 All ER 1025.

[25] *Wandsworth BC v Michalak* [2002] EWCA Civ 271, [2003] 1 WLR 617; *Ghaidan v Mendoza* [2004] UKHL, [2004] 2 AC 557.

[26] *A v SSHD* [2004] UKHL 56, [2005] 2 AC 68.

of the Act (goods, facilities, services and public functions), Part 4 (premises), Part 5 (work), Part 6 (education) and Part 7 (associations).[27] It also provides (Part 10) that:

> **Section 142 EqA, Unenforceable terms**
>
> A term of a contract is unenforceable against a person in so far as it constitutes, promotes or provides for treatment of that or another person that is of a description prohibited by this Act.[28]

The scope in respect of which discrimination related to the protected characteristics varies somewhat, as detailed below. Some discrimination which falls outside the scope of the EqA is regulated by the common law or by the HRA, discussed above.

Geographical Reach

The explanatory notes to the EqA provide that the Act applies to England and Wales and (with the exception of s190 and Part 15, which concern improvements to let dwelling houses and family property respectively) to Scotland. The territorial application of the provisions relating to work (Part 5) is left to tribunals to determine (see further p 204 below), and the Act is silent as to the territorial application of its other provisions other than in a few cases in which express provision is made for its application outside Great Britain (GB). These are mentioned where relevant below and in the following chapter. Otherwise, it will be up to the relevant court or tribunal to determine whether the Act applies to matters occurring outside GB.[29]

Part 3: Discrimination in the Provision of Goods, Facilities, Services and in the Exercise of Public Functions

Material Scope of Part 3

> **Section 29 EqA, Provision of services, etc**
>
> (1) A person (a 'service-provider') concerned with the provision of a service to the public or a section of the public (for payment or not) must not discriminate against a person requiring the service[30] by not providing the person with the service.[31]
>
> (2) A service-provider (A) must not, in providing the service, discriminate against a person (B)—
>
> (a) as to the terms on which A provides the service to B;
>
> (b) by terminating the provision of the service to B;
>
> (c) by subjecting B to any other detriment …
>
> (9) In the application of this section, so far as relating to race or religion or belief, to the granting of entry clearance (within the meaning of the Immigration Act 1971), it does not matter whether an act is done within or outside the United Kingdom.

[27] And see Part 8 (Prohibited Conduct: Ancillary') discussed under 'Establishing liability for discrimination' below.

[28] This provision has given rise to no reported case law. Nor has s142(2), which makes similar provision for some non-contractual terms relating to disability.

[29] The extra-territorial application of the HRA is somewhat broader. In *R (Al-Skeini) v Secretary of State for Defence* [2007] UKHL 26, [2008] 1 AC 153 the HL ruled that the territorial application of the HRA should reflect that of the ECHR which (*Al Skeini v UK* (2011) 53 EHRR 18) protects those under the control of UK public authorities, even when those public authorities are operating overseas.

[30] By s31(6) EqA this includes reference to persons who are seeking to obtain or use the service.

[31] Section 31(7) EqA provides that references to the non-provision of service include the failure to provide services of the quality, or on the terms on which, the service provider usually provides to the public (or the relevant section of it).

(10) Subsection (9) does not affect the application of any other provision of this Act to conduct outside England and Wales or Scotland.

Section 29(3)–(5) EqA make similar provision to s29(1)–(2) in relation to harassment and victimisation (see Chapter 2), though the prohibitions on harassment do not apply in relation to religion or belief or to sexual orientation.[32] Section 29(6) EqA then provides that 'A person must not, in the exercise of a public function that is not the provision of a service to the public or a section of the public, do anything that constitutes discrimination, harassment or victimisation', and s29(7) that a duty to make reasonable adjustments(see further Chapter 8) applies to service providers and persons who exercise public functions that do not consist of 'the provision of a service to the public or a section of the public'.[33]

Section 31(2) EqA provides that references to the provision of services include references to the provision of goods or facilities and s31(3) that services include services provided in the exercise of a public function, defined in turn by reference to the HRA. Section 31(7) EqA then provides that s31(1) applies to a failure to provide a service of the quality that the service provider usually provides to the public (or the section of it), or in the manner in which, or on the terms on which, the service is usually provided by the service provider.

By contrast with the predecessor provisions, the EqA does not list any examples of goods, facilities and/or services. By way of example, s29(2) of the Sex Discrimination Act 1975 (SDA) had listed, as examples of the same, 'access to and use of any place which members of the public or a section of the public are permitted to enter'; 'accommodation in a hotel, boarding house or other similar establishment'; 'facilities by way of banking or insurance or for grants, loans, credit or finance'; 'facilities for education'; 'facilities for entertainment, recreation or refreshment'; 'facilities for transport or travel'; and 'services of any profession or trade, or any local or other public authority'. Notwithstanding the omission of such a list, it is reasonable to suppose that all these matters would fall within s29 except to the extent that they are expressly excluded.

The predecessors of s29 EqA were applied to a wine bar's refusal to serve women unless they were seated;[34] a shop's refusal to extend credit facilities to a woman unless her husband stood as a guarantor;[35] *The Lady* magazine's refusal to accept an advertisement for a housekeeper/cook from a man; and a pub's refusal to admit men wearing earrings;[36] to discriminatory charges for access to a public swimming pool;[37] to race discrimination by estate agents, in access to prison work, the provision of tax relief and the issue of marriage licences;[38] and to the failure of both Ryanair and Stansted Airport to provide a disabled passenger with a wheelchair free of charge where he needed the facility to access a flight.[39] More recently, in *Paulley v Firstgroup plc* [2017] UKSC 4, [2017] 1 WLR 423,

[32] Section 29(8) EqA, discussed in Chs 9 and 10. Section 28(1) EqA provides that Part 3 does not apply to discrimination on grounds of marriage or civil partnership or to age discrimination against those aged under 18.

[33] This neutralises the effect of the HL's decision in *Amin v Entry Clearance Officer, Bombay* [1983] 2 AC 818, discussed below.

[34] *Gill v El Vino Co Ltd* [1983] QB 425 (CA).

[35] *Quinn v Williams Furniture Ltd* [1981] ICR 328.

[36] Respectively *Bain v Bowles* [1991] IRLR 356 and *McConomy v Croft Inns Ltd* [1992] IRLR 561. The latter is an unusual case – see Ch 6 for a full discussion of clothing and appearance rules.

[37] *James v Eastleigh* [1990] 2 AC 751.

[38] Respectively *R v CRE ex parte Cottrell* [1980] 1 WLR 1580; *Alexander v Home Office* [1988] ICR 685; *Savjani v IRC* [1981] QB 458 (CA); and *Tejani v The Superintendent Registrar for the District of Peterborough* [1986] IRLR 502.

[39] *Ross v Ryanair Ltd* [2004] EWCA Civ 1751, [2005] 1 WLR 2447. See also *Roads v Central Trains Ltd* [2004] EWCA Civ 1541, 104 ConLR 62, which concerned access to a station platform.

the SC ruled that the rail company had discriminated against the claimant contrary to s29 EqA by failing to take sufficient steps to ensure his access as a wheelchair user to its buses. And in *Plummer v Royal Herbert Freehold Ltd* the county court applied s29 EqA to a failure by the management company of the block of apartments in which the claimant lived to make reasonable adjustments in connection with his access to a leisure club on the premises.[40] There was a dispute between the parties as to whether the club, which was open only to members and their guests, provided a service to 'the public or a section of the public'. Had it not, the discrimination complained of would have fallen to be considered under Part 7 ('Associations', discussed below). Having remarked that Part 7 would apply '[i]n an ideal world' but that it could not, because membership was automatically granted to residents and owners of apartments the judge proceeded to consider whether members (not all of whom were residents and owners) and their guests constituted a 'section of the public' for the purposes of s29 EqA:

***Plummer v Royal Herbert Freehold Ltd*, 25 May 2018, Case No: B01CL659**

District Judge Avent:

334. … if a non-resident applicant is able to satisfy some subjective test applied by [Royal Herbert employee] Mr Onyali, and subject to the overall limit of a maximum of 20 non-resident members, membership of the Club would be granted. In other words, any member of the public who can persuade Mr Onyali that they should be a member will undoubtedly become one. There is no process prescribed by the Rules for a proposer or seconder and no scrutiny, as such, of their suitability …

335 … the Club has been open to members of the public in the past for aerobic, swimming and yoga classes. They may have ended some time ago now but they clearly gave rise to a tension between the residents and the public side of the Club. There may well have been a tightening up of the position over the years but the fact is that the residents do not, and appear never to have had, the exclusivity which … would be essential.

336. Once the Club opened its doors to external members, given the lack of any proper vetting or formality to become a member, it was, in fact, open to 'a section of the public'…

337 … The Club is … the equivalent of a local health club but within the confines of the Estate. If there is no vetting or screening of residents or non-residents members then there is certainly no evidence that there is any assessment in relation to the admittance of guests although members are limited two guests at a time. The reality again, in my view, is that (save for children under a certain age) members of the public who visit residents as guests or who know a non-resident member would be able to gain access to the club without let or hindrance.

338. The position might be best summed up by the availability of, and access given to, the Club's facilities to short let tenants at the time of the 2012 Olympics [who] effectively became honorary residents for the duration of their stay. That, in effect, was an artifice because all of them must have been members of the public, quite possibly from several different countries.

341. I am satisfied that the Club is offering a service to the public or a section of the public …

[40] Central London county court, 27 May 2018, [2018] Lexis Citation 48.

An important exclusion from s29's predecessor provisions related to services provided by public authorities which were not materially similar to those provided by private persons or bodies.[41] The function at issue in *Amin v Entry Clearance Officer*, as in subsequent similar cases, was immigration, in which public authorities generally exercise the coercive power of the state, rather than acting in a manner akin to a private sector provider of 'services'. Another very important function which this line of judicial authority excluded from the scope of the anti-discrimination legislation was police powers, and the aftermath of Stephen Lawrence's murder highlighted the inadequacies of the legislative framework in this area.[42] The critical Macpherson Report on Stephen Lawrence's death and the police reaction thereto resulted in the Race Relations (Amendment) Act 2000 which, inter alia, prohibited race discrimination by public authorities in the exercise of their functions, and this initiative was gradually implemented across the protected characteristics. Section 31(2) EqA now provides that references to the provision of services include the provision of services in the exercise of a public function, while (as we saw above) s29(6) provides that 'A person must not, in the exercise of a public function that is not the provision of a service to the public or a section of the public, do anything that constitutes discrimination, harassment or victimisation'. The CA has ruled that the prohibition on discrimination in the exercise of public functions applies only to the exercise of those functions within GB.[43]

Section 31(4) EqA provides that a 'public function is a function that is a function of a public nature for the purposes of the HRA. The EHRC's Code of Practice suggests (§11.14) that 'public functions' would include the management of a prison or the discharge of child protection responsibilities, whether or not these are provided by private sector bodies. Nothing material turns on the question which sub-section applies, but it is commonplace therefore for both s29(1) or (2) and s29(6) EqA to be pleaded in the alternative when a services claim is brought against a public authority, or a private body exercising what might arguably be a public function.[44] It is important to be aware that, where discrimination by a public authority is alleged, an alternative or additional method of challenge may be via the HRA.

Many of the important cases decided under s29 EqA concern discrimination by public authorities. Among these, in *R (ZK) v Redbridge LBC* [2019] EWHC 1450 (Admin), [2019] ELR 482 the High Court appeared to accept that a challenge to the Council's model of funding special educational needs provision fell within s29, though the claim failed on the facts. And in *R (Diocese of Menevia) v Swansea* the High Court accepted that a transport policy which denied children free transport to attend faith schools, where there was a non-faith school within three miles of their homes involved indirect discrimination in breach of s29 EqA.[45] In *R (Adrath Yisroel Burial Society) v Inner North London Senior Coroner* [2018]

[41] See *Amin v Entry Clearance Officer*, n 33 above.

[42] Note that the police, like the Inland Revenue (see *Savjani*, n 38 above) were accepted as *sometimes* providing services: see *Farah v Commissioner of the Police of the Metropolis* [1998] QB 65.

[43] *R (Hottak) v SS Foreign & Commonwealth* [2016] EWCA Civ 438, [2016] 3 All ER 935.

[44] https://www.equalityhumanrights.com/en/publication-download/services-public-functions-and-associations-statutory-code-practice.

[45] [2015] EWHC 1436 (Admin), [2015] ELR 389. Note that Sch 3 para 11(e) EqA excludes from s29 claims or discrimination on the ground of religion or belief in connection with transport to or from school. In *Menevia* the policy was found to discriminate indirectly against BME students. *cf R (P) v East Sussex CC* [2014] EWHC 4634 (Admin) [2015] ELR 178 in which the High Court rejected a challenge to a council's refusal to make flexible arrangements for the transport to school of a severely disabled child who was prevented from accessing the provision made by the council by reason of multiple hospital appointments.

EWHC 969 (Admin), [2019] QB 251 the Divisional Court ruled that the adoption by the senior coroner of a policy which prevented religion being taken into account by coroners breached s29 EqA as well as Article 14 ECHR read with Article 9. The Court recognised that it was an important element of Orthodox Judaism that the dead should be buried as soon as possible, preferably on the day of death, and the coroner's policy indirectly discriminated against Jewish people. Finally, in *DM v Fife Council* [2016] CSIH 17, [2016] ELR 237, the Scottish Court of Session rejected an appeal against a finding that the council had breached s29 EqA by failing to adjust its normal practice of ceasing to make educational provision for students after the year in which they turned 18 in the case of the claimant, who was disabled.

Part 4 EqA, which regulates discrimination in relation to premises, is considered at p 196ff below. But most of the housing-related case law has concerned access to social housing, which falls within s29 EqA. The CRE, one of the EHRC's predecessor bodies, issued codes of practice on housing in 1991 and 1992 in which lengthy residence qualifications for social housing featured as an example of potentially unlawful race discrimination. More recently, such barriers to social housing have been encouraged by national guidance issued by the Secretary of State under the Housing Act 1996 as amended by the Localism Act 2011. The 1996 Act requires local authorities to have a scheme for determining priorities in allocating housing. The 2011 amendments enabled local authorities to decide, subject to exceptions, what classes of person were qualifying persons, and the guidance encouraged them to prioritise applicants with a local connection, although it also stated that consideration had to be given to the implications of excluding members of groups of non-qualifying persons and to the EqA.

In *Ealing LBC v H*, the CA considered a challenge brought under s29 EqA to a policy governing access to social housing which prioritised 'working households' and 'model tenants', and which was alleged to discriminate against women, the elderly and the disabled.[46] That claim failed on the facts, but the High Court had previously upheld a different challenge against the same Council by a woman fleeing domestic violence who challenged the Council's five-year residence requirement for access to social housing as discriminatory on grounds of sex: *R (HA) v Ealing LBC* [2015] EWHC 2375 (Admin), [2015] LGR 954. The High Court ruled in favour of the claimant under s29 EqA, and also suggested that the discrimination breached Article 14 ECHR read with Article 8. The latter suggestion was subsequently doubted by the CA in the *H* case, but that Court did not question the decision in *HA* on s29 EqA. And in *R (Ward) v Hillingdon LBC, R (Gullu) v Hillingdon LBC* [2019] EWCA Civ 692, [2019] PTSR 1738 the CA accepted that a policy which imposed a 10-year residential qualification other than in exceptional cases discriminated on racial grounds against the claimants, Irish Travellers and a Kurdish refugee.[47]

The decision in *HA* was mentioned just above. Article 14, generally read with Article 8 ECHR, is a significant tool for challenge to discrimination by public authorities which might also fall within s29 EqA, or which might also so fall but for the fact that an exception applies. By way of example, in *JT v First-Tier Tribunal* [2018] EWCA Civ 1735,

[46] [2017] EWCA Civ 1127, [2018] HLR 10.

[47] A more unusual allegation of discrimination in access to social housing arose in *R (Z) v Hackney*, n 14 above, in which the claimant challenged Hackney's allocation of a fraction (less than 1%) of its social housing via a charitable housing association which prioritized applicants from the Orthodox Jewish Community. The reason for the priority was that Orthodox Jewish families were disadvantaged in access to general social housing by reason of their tendency to have large families. The decision is considered in Ch 3.

[2019] 1 WLR 1313 the CA ruled that the claimant's exclusion from the criminal injuries scheme because her sexually abusive step-father had lived in the same home during the period of abuse amounted to unlawful discrimination under Article 14 ECHR and, accordingly, under the HRA.[48] A claim under the EqA would have been blocked by the exception relating to statutory authority, discussed below. And in *R (Joint Council for the Welfare of Immigrants) v SSHD* [2019] EWHC 452 (Admin) [2019] 4 All ER 527 the High Court accepted that a scheme requiring private landlords to satisfy themselves that prospective tenants were entitled to be in the UK fell within the ambit of Article 8, and breached Article 14. That scheme would not have been open to challenge under the EqA because it had statutory authority under the Immigration Act 2014 (see further p 187ff, p 194 below and Chapter 7).

EHRC, 'Services, public functions and associations', Statutory Code of Practice[49]

The Code provides (para 11.3) that 'services' include 'permitting access to and use of any place which members of the public are permitted to enter', as well as services provided:

> by local authorities, such as toilet facilities; government departments and their agencies; some charities; voluntary organisations; hotels; restaurants; pubs; post offices; banks; building societies; solicitors; accountants; telecommunications organisations; public utilities (such as gas, electricity and water suppliers); services provided by bus and train operators, railway stations, airports; public parks; sports stadia; leisure centres; advice agencies; theatres; cinemas; hairdressers; shops; market stalls; petrol stations; telesales businesses; hospitals, and clinics ....

One of the more unusual decisions under s29 EqA is that of Southwark's Consistory Court in *In re All Saints', Sanderstead* [2012] Fam 51, which concerned a complaint by a disabled parishioner of the Church that the proposed removal of communion rails and kneelers would breach her s29 rights by reason of her inability to stand while taking communion. The Court remarked that the concept of 'services' under s29 EqA included 'access to and use of any place which members of the public are permitted to enter'[50] and, accordingly, that it applied to access to churches, though it did not accept that the provision of the communion rail and kneelers amounted to a service, or that a priest celebrating Holy Communion or a church facilitating that celebration was a 'service provider' or a public authority for the purposes of s29.[51]

Schedule 2 EqA makes specific provisions in relation to reasonable adjustments in connection with services and public functions. It will be considered further in Chapter 8, though it should be noted here that, in this context, the duty to make reasonable accommodation is *anticipatory*;[52] that a service provider or public authority may adopt a reasonable alternative method of providing the service or exercising the function; and that a service provider is not required to take any step which would fundamentally alter the nature of the service, or of the provider's trade or profession, or a public authority to take any step it has no power to take. Schedule 2 para 3 provides that a transport provider will never be required by the duty to alter a vehicle', for example by installing hand controls or facilities to stow a wheelchair, though see below and Chapter 8 for specific requirements imposed on transport providers.

[48] As explained above, Art 14 does not contain a free-standing prohibition on discrimination but requires to be read with another ECHR right. The discrimination at issue in *JT* fell within A1P1 (the right to property).

[49] n 44 above.

[50] This because s19(3) of the DDA had listed this as an example of services within the relevant provision of that Act.

[51] See further Ch 9.

[52] This by reason of para 2(2), discussed in Ch 8.

EHRC, 'Services, public functions and associations', Statutory Code of Practice[53]

The Code makes it clear that the duty to make reasonable adjustments in the context of Part 3 EqA is anticipatory and:

> 7.20 … requires consideration of, and action in relation to, barriers that impede people with one or more kinds of disability prior to an individual disabled person seeking to use the service, avail themselves of a function …
>
> 7.21 Service providers should therefore not wait until a disabled person wants to use a service that they provide before they give consideration to their duty to make reasonable adjustments. They should anticipate the requirements of disabled people and the adjustments that may have to be made for them. Failure to anticipate the need for an adjustment may create additional expense, or render it too late to comply with the duty to make the adjustment. Furthermore, it may not in itself provide a defence to a claim of a failure to make a reasonable adjustment.

It follows from the fact that the duty to make reasonable adjustments is owed in this context at large (rather than as in the case of employment, to the individual job applicant or employee), that it applies 'regardless of whether the service provider knows that a particular person is disabled or whether it currently has disabled customers' (§7.22).

Geographical Reach of Part 3

Turani v SSHD **[2021] EWCA Civ 348, [2022] 1 All ER 254**

The claimants were Palestinians who had fled Syria as refugees to the Lebanon and wished to be considered for resettlement in the UK under the Vulnerable Persons Resettlement Scheme (VPRS). This was an *ex gratia* scheme which facilitated resettlement in the UK of refugees who had fled the conflict in Syria and who were referred by the United Nations High Commissioner for Refugees (UNHCR).[54] The resettlement initiative had initially been targeted at Syrian nationals only, but had been opened to non-nationals who had fled Syria from 2017. The claimants could not be referred by the UNHCR because they were under the exclusive mandate of the United Nations Relief and Works Agency (UNRWA) which assists Palestinian refugees in Lebanon, Jordan, Syria the West Bank and Gaza and which did not have a resettlement mandate.

The appellants sought to challenge the Secretary of State's decision to rely exclusively on UNHCR for referrals to the Scheme, and his failure to put in place any alternative mechanism to enable Palestinian Refugees from Syria (PRS) like them to be referred, thereby excluding them from resettlement in the UK under the Scheme. They claimed that the Scheme and New Scheme (the schemes) unlawfully discriminated against them as Palestinians and that the respondent had breached the PSED (see Chapter 3) in implementing it.

The claim failed before the High Court which ruled that the matters complained of fell outside the territorial scope of the EqA, further that the indirect discrimination against non-Syrians was justified and therefore lawful. The CA ruled that the discrimination in

[53] n 44 above.

[54] The VPRS was subsequently replaced by new UK Resettlement Scheme, which was on identical terms.

issue fell within the geographical scope of the EqA, though it agreed with Laing J on justification.[55] Simler LJ, with whom Warby and Underhill LJJ agreed, 'approach[ed] the question of territorial reach from first principles' (§54), ruling at §58 that 'a natural reading of section 29(1) and (6) is that they do not ordinarily extend to things done outside the UK because otherwise section 29(9) would not be necessary'. Simler LJ accepted, however, that s29(9) EqA carried the implication that s26(6) applied to functions exercisable under the Immigration Acts and, accordingly, 'to decisions to grant entry clearance in individual cases' (§60). She further accepted that it was artificial to separate out the various stages of the decision-making process in this case (ie initial policy from final entry clearance acceptance or refusal in the individual case). That being the case, the exception in s29(9) applied to the bring the policies under challenge back within the jurisdiction of the EqA (§§65–71) (emphasis added).[56]

Exceptions to the Prohibitions on Discrimination

General Exceptions

The EqA provides a number of general exceptions to its prohibitions on discrimination. These are set out in ss 191–197 and Schedules 22–23 EqA. They cover:

- in relation to the protected characteristics of age, disability, religion or belief and sexual orientation, acts done under statutory authority (broadly, enactments including Measures of the Church of England's General Synod, and whether pre-dating or post-dating the EqA), or requirements or conditions imposed by ministers of the Crown or Welsh or Scottish equivalents, under such enactments;[57]
- anything proportionate which is done 'for the purpose of safeguarding national security';[58]
- in relation to sex, gender reassignment and age, by doing anything in relation to the participation of another as a competitor in competitive activities which are gender or age affected (that is, where a participant's gender or age respectively will place them at a disadvantage relative to others).[59] Where the protected characteristic is gender reassignment there is an additional requirement that the thing done must be necessary to secure in relation to the activity fair competition, or the safety of competitors, and where the protected characteristic is age the thing done must be necessary to secure in relation to the activity fair competition or the safety of competitors, to comply with the rules of a national or international competition, or to increase participation in that activity;
- in relation to race, by imposing restrictions on nationality or place of birth or length of residence in a particular area or place in selecting one or more persons to represent a

[55] The CA accepted that PRS were extraordinarily disadvantaged and vulnerable and '[a]lthough not assessed by UNHCR for obvious reasons, on the face of it [met] … the criteria for resettlement under the Scheme' and that the Government did not appear to have recognised the impact of using UNHCR as the exclusive gatekeeper for the Scheme had on those, like PRS, who fell outside its mandate.

[56] The CA reached a different conclusion on the claimant's PSED claim, ruling that s149 EqA did not have extra-territorial effect (see Ch 3).

[57] Section 191 and Sch 22 para 1 EqA. This latter does not apply to age (presumably because of the general justification defence applicable to direct discrimination).

[58] Section 192 EqA.

[59] Section 195 EqA. See further Chs 6 and 11.

country, place or area or a related association, in a sport or game or other activity of a competitive nature, or doing anything in pursuance of the rules of a competition so far as relating to eligibility to compete in a sport or game or other such activity;[60]

- the provision of charitable benefits to persons defined by reference to a protected characteristic other than colour where the discrimination is a proportionate means of achieving a legitimate aim, or is for the purpose of preventing or compensating for a disadvantage linked to the protected characteristic.[61] Participation in fund-raising activities may also be restricted on grounds of sex.[62]

Statutory Authority

The exceptions concerning sports and single-sex services are considered further in Chapter 6 and those specific to race in Chapter 7. As to the others, Schedule 22 para 1 provides broad exceptions from the prohibitions on discrimination as follows:

Schedule 22 para 1 EqA, Statutory authority

(1) A person (P) does not contravene a provision specified in the first column of the table, so far as relating to the protected characteristic specified in the second column in respect of that provision, if P does anything P must do pursuant to a requirement specified in the third column.

Specified provision	Protected characteristic	Requirement
Parts 3–7	Age	A requirement of an enactment
Parts 3–7 and 12	Disability	A requirement of an enactment
		A relevant requirement or condition imposed by virtue of an enactment
Parts 3–7	Religion or belief	A requirement of an enactment
		A relevant requirement or condition imposed by virtue of an enactment
Section 29(6) and Parts 6 and 7	Sex	A requirement of an enactment
Parts 3, 4, 6 and 7	Sexual orientation	A requirement of an enactment
		A relevant requirement or condition imposed by virtue of an enactment

(2) A reference in the table to Part 6 does not include a reference to that Part so far as relating to vocational training.

(3) In this paragraph a reference to an enactment includes a reference to—

(a) a Measure of the General Synod of the Church of England;

(b) an enactment passed or made on or after the date on which this Act is passed.

[60] See further Ch 7.

[61] Section 193 EqA, discussed below and in Ch 10. The provision was also considered in *R (Z) v Hackney*, n 14 above, discussed in Ch 3. It is sufficient to say here that in that case the SC confirmed that, where charitable benefits are provided for the purpose of preventing or compensating for a disadvantage linked to the protected characteristic, there is no requirement for proportionality.

[62] Section 194 EqA.

(4) In the table, a relevant requirement or condition is a requirement or condition imposed (whether before or after the passing of this Act) by—

(a) a Minister of the Crown;
(b) a member of the Scottish Executive;
(c) the National Assembly for Wales (constituted by the Government of Wales Act 1998);
(d) the Welsh Ministers, the First Minister for Wales or the Counsel General to the Welsh Assembly Government.

Paragraph 2 of Schedule 22 permits discrimination in work or vocational training which is required to comply with a pre-1975 Act concerned with the protection of women in relation to protecting women in relation to pregnancy or maternity or any other risks specifically affecting them,[63] or with health and safety law, or with provisions concerned with protection of women at work in relation to pregnancy or maternity or any other risks specifically affecting them.

No general exceptions apply in relation to race discrimination done under statutory authority, Schedule 22 para 5 providing only for 'rules restricting to persons of particular birth, nationality, descent or residence' in relation to employment by certain public bodies and to the holding of certain public offices. But para 17 of Schedule 3 to the EqA permits discrimination on grounds of nationality of ethnic or national origins in relation to Part 3 EqA (goods, facilities and services and public functions) 'in the exercise [by a relevant person] of functions exercisable by virtue of a relevant enactment' where a 'relevant person' is a Minister of the Crown acting personally or a person given authorisation by a Minister of the Crown acting personally or by 'a relevant enactment or by an instrument made under or by virtue of a relevant enactment'. The listed 'relevant enactments' in para 17 are concerned with immigration and asylum. In addition, schedule 23 para 1 provides that nationality discrimination is not unlawful where it is '[i]n pursuance of an enactment' or 'an instrument made by a member of the executive under an enactment'. Neither is such discrimination unlawful where it is or 'to comply with a requirement imposed … by a member of the executive by virtue of an enactment' or 'in pursuance of arrangements made … by or with the approval of, or for the time being approved by' or 'to comply with a condition imposed … by a Minister of the Crown', in each case irrespective of when the requirement or condition was imposed or the arrangements made.

Schedule 3 para 17, Schedule 22 para 1 and Schedule 23 para 1 are broadly modelled on s41 Race Relations Act (RRA) which, so far as relevant, permitted certain discrimination 'in pursuance of any enactment or order in Council; or … any instrument made under any enactment by a Minister of the Crown; or in order to comply with any condition or requirement imposed by a Minister of the Crown'. The section was significantly amended to comply with the Race Directive (Council Directive 2000/78/EC). Prior to its amendment, s41 RRA was considered in *Hampson v Department of Education and Science* [1991] 1 AC 171, in which the HL dealt with a challenge by a Hong Kong Chinese woman to her exclusion from UK teaching positions by reason of a requirement in regulations made by Secretary of State that, in order to qualify for such posts, overseas-trained teachers had to have undertaken a teaching course over three consecutive years. The regulations were made under s27 of the Education Act 1980, which allowed the Secretary of State to 'by regulations make provision … for requiring teachers at schools … to possess such qualification

[63] Or any enactment made under such Act, at whatever time.

as may be determined by or under the regulations ....' The claimant's third year of training was completed eight years after the initial two-year course normal in Hong Kong. She had taught during the intervening years. The question for the HL was whether the regulations had been made 'pursuant to' s27. Lord Lowry, who delivered the sole speech, referred to the judgment of Balcombe LJ (dissenting) in the CA in which he framed the question for the Court as being whether the words 'in pursuance of any instrument' applied only to those acts which were 'done in necessary performance of an express obligation contained in the instrument (the narrow construction)', or whether they encompassed also 'acts done in exercise of a power or discretion conferred by the instrument (the wide construction).' Having noted that 'the wide construction is the more natural meaning of the words used', Lord Lowry concluded that the very broad scope of the s41 exception which would result from the wide construction was an indication that the narrow approach was to be preferred and that race discrimination would not be saved by s41 unless it had been 'sanctioned by Parliament'. In the instant case the Secretary of State himself had 'set up and appl[ied] a non-statutory criterion, the setting up and application of which involved the exercise of his administrative discretion and led to the discriminatory act complained'. The scheme, accordingly, fell outside s41 RRA.

The *Hampson* principle has been the subject of more recent judicial consideration. *Amnesty International v Ahmed* is considered immediately below, *R (Goloshvili) v SSHD* [2019] EWHC 614 (Admin), [2019] HLR 37 in Chapter 7 at pp 467–468.

***Amnesty International v Ahmed* [2009] UKEAT 0447_08_1308, [2009] ICR 1450**

The EAT rejected the argument that s41 RRA permitted the employer to decline to promote the claimant, who was of northern Sudanese ethnic origin, to the post of researcher for Sudan on the grounds that, being from the north and having an 'Arab' appearance, she and her colleagues would be exposed to an increased safety risk if she were sent to East Chad. The EAT accepted that Amnesty could have relied on s41 RRA had it been required to discriminate in order to comply with its duty under s2(1) of the Health and Safety at Work Act 1974 'to ensure, so far as is reasonably practicable, the health, safety and welfare at work of all his employees'. On the facts, however, the tribunal had been entitled to reject the defence on the basis that Amnesty could have avoided the risk by appointing the claimant to the position but not sending her to East Chad.

National Security

Section 192 EqA, National security

A person does not contravene this Act only by doing, for the purpose of safeguarding national security, anything it is proportionate to do for that purpose.

The exception in section 192 EqA is materially similar to that previously found as s42 RRA as amended in 2001. Prior to its amendment the RRA had provided a blanket exception which made a Ministerial certificate conclusive evidence of the application of the national security exception, but which was incompatible with the Race Directive once that came into effect.[64] Section 192 EqA and its predecessors are of immensely wide reach, but the only national security provision which has been much relied upon has been that in Northern Ireland's fair employment legislation.

Charitable Benefits

Section 193 EqA, Charities

(1) A person does not contravene this Act only by restricting the provision of benefits to persons who share a protected characteristic if—

(a) the person acts in pursuance of a charitable instrument, and
(b) the provision of the benefits is within subsection (2).

(2) The provision of benefits is within this subsection if it is—

(a) a proportionate means of achieving a legitimate aim, or
(b) for the purpose of preventing or compensating for a disadvantage linked to the protected characteristic ...

(4) If a charitable instrument enables the provision of benefits to persons of a class defined by reference to colour, it has effect for all purposes as if it enabled the provision of such benefits—

(a) to persons of the class which results if the reference to colour is ignored, or
(b) if the original class is defined by reference only to colour, to persons generally ...

Section 193(9) EqA provides that the exception does not apply in relation to work-related discrimination.

The application of one of the predecessor provisions of s193 EqA fell to be considered by the High Court (Chancery Division) in *Catholic Care (Diocese of Leeds) v Charity Commission for England and Wales*.

***Catholic Care (Diocese of Leeds) v Charity Commission for England and Wales* [2010] EWHC 520 (Ch) [2010] 4 All ER 1041**

The charity, which was funded partly by payments from local authorities and partly from charitable donations, wished to continue to provide its services to heterosexual couples only following the prohibition of discrimination because of sexual orientation in access to services. It sought to rely on the predecessor provision of s193 EqA (reg 18 of the Equality Act (Sexual Orientation) Regulations 2007 (SO Regs 2007)). In order to do so, it needed to change its memorandum of association to state that it would 'only provide adoption services to heterosexuals and such services to heterosexuals [would] only be provided in accordance with the tenets of the [Roman Catholic] Church'. The claimant needed the permission of the Charity Commission to make this change, which permission was withheld because the Commission interpreted the word 'benefits' as meaning only benefits of a charitable nature provided to the charity's beneficiaries

[64] A similar provision had been removed from the SDA in the wake of the CJEU decision in Case C-224/84 *Johnston v CC RUC* [1986] ECR 651 in which that Court ruled that the unavailability of judicial review to challenge a similar exemption in the SD Order breached the obligation regarding justiciability in the Equal Treatment Directive. See also *Tinnelly & Sons Ltd and McElduff v UK* (1999) 27 EHRR 249 in which the ECtHR ruled that a materially identical provision in Northern Ireland's Fair Employment Act 1989 (FEA) breached the right to a fair trial protected by Art 6 ECHR.

(the adoptive children), and so concluded that there would be no benefit to the proposed change. The Charity Tribunal disagreed with the Commission, ruling that the provision of benefits to one class of persons (adoptive parents) as a means of achieving an ultimate charitable purpose (assisting adoptive children) would constitute acting in pursuance of a charitable instrument, within the meaning of reg 18 (now s193 EqA). The tribunal also ruled that the provision contemplated only 'a discrete area of pure charitable activity' distinct from matters dealt with elsewhere in the SO Regs 2007, and dismissed the charity's appeal on the grounds that it would not be able to show that there it was involved in a discrete area of adoption-related activity within s193 EqA, which was simultaneously sufficient to permit the charity to continue to be authorised as an adoption agency by the relevant government agency. The High Court allowed the charity's appeal and remitted the matter to the commission for reconsideration.

Briggs J:

> 78. In my judgment the purpose of reg 18 is to afford to charities an exception from the prohibition of differential treatment on grounds of sexual orientation, wherever the public purpose being (or to be) achieved by the charity in question constitutes an art 14 [ECHR] justification for that differential treatment.
>
> 86. The first question of interpretation is whether reg 18(1) applies only to differential treatment in the provision of benefits to the ultimate beneficial class of the charity in question. In my judgment it is not so limited. While such a limitation would have the purely adventitious advantage that it would exclude faith-based publicly-funded adoption charities from making use of reg 18, it is otherwise neither logical, rational, purposive nor responsive to any reasonable linguistic interpretation of the language used.
>
> 87. Charities do not, strictly, exist to serve a beneficial class, they serve publicly beneficial purposes. None the less, even if certain familiar types of charity may loosely be described as serving a beneficial class, it is by no means uncommon for them to achieve that purpose by conferring benefits on persons outside that class. For example, a charity for the relief of sickness may serve that purpose by providing benefits to nurses or to the hospital employing those nurses … A charity for the relief of the disabled may serve its purpose by providing respite care (for example holidays) for the relatives of the disabled who care for them at home. Similarly, Catholic Care and similar charitable adoption agencies serve needy children by making benefits available to prospective adoptive parents. It is a feature of the dependency caused by youth, sickness, disability and old age that relief can often best be achieved by conferring benefits on the carers rather than directly upon the cared.
>
> 88. I can envisage no logical or rational reason why reg 18 should provide a means for enabling justified differential treatment by reference to the sexual orientation of the ultimate beneficial class, while excluding any justified differential treatment of the carers of the beneficial class by reference to their sexual orientation, where the charity's purpose is achieved precisely by affording benefits to those carers.
>
> 89. I have already referred to the irrationality of permitting justified differential treatment by a charity set up to provide counselling for gay teenagers, while denying it to a charity set up to provide counselling for the teenaged children of gay parents, regardless of the children's sexual orientation. It is equally irrational to permit justified differential treatment of such children by a charity set up to provide them with counselling, while denying it to a charity set up to provide their gay parents with the advice and support sufficient to enable them to assist their children …
>
> 92. The second question is whether the tribunal's interpretation, limiting reg 18 to an elusive field of pure private charitable activity which is neither forbidden by, nor within the contemplation

of, any other regulation, is any better than the commission's interpretation. In my judgment it is not. Its first and most serious difficulty is that it seeks to set on its head the opening phrase in reg 18(1) 'Nothing in these Regulations shall make it unlawful …', by limiting reg 18 to activity which is not prohibited by any other regulation …

94. … the notion, lying at the heart of the tribunal's analysis, that reg 18 is in some way confined to purely private activity seems to me to lie uneasily with the essential requirement of a charity, namely that it should confer a public benefit. Returning to my examples of the charities for the provision of counselling to gay teenagers or the children of same-sex parents, it is not obvious why their clear justification (in art 14 terms) should depend under reg 18 on them being privately funded …

96. The third and remaining question is how none the less reg 18 is to be confined by way of interpretation so as to avoid it transgressing the real restrictions imposed by the requirement to construe it compatibly with convention rights, and in particular with the jurisprudence about art 14. In my judgment the answer is to be found in three elements of reg 18. The first is the restriction (unique to reg 18 among these regulations), that it applies only to charities. The second lies in the fact that, as expressly contemplated by reg 18(2), the practical effect of reg 18 is controlled by a public authority, namely the commission, as regulator. The third is that even without an express reference to the need for the proportionate pursuit of a legitimate aim, a convention-right compatible interpretation of reg 18 requires that limitation to be implied. I will take each of those elements in turn.

97. An organisation which proposes to fulfil a purpose for the public benefit will only qualify as a charity if, taking into account any dis-benefit arising from its modus operandi, its activities none the less yield a net public benefit: see above. Thus, a charity which proposed to apply differential treatment on grounds of sexual orientation otherwise than as a proportionate means of achieving a legitimate aim might thereby fail to achieve charitable status (or lose it, if it sought to pursue such activities by amendment of its objects) …

Briggs J noted that the justification on which the charity sought to rely was that it had for many years successfully placed some of the most hard-to-place children with families, acting as the adoption agency of last resort for the local authority. The charity had no option but to seek to rely on reg 18 or to discontinue its adoption services as it was significantly funded by the Roman Catholic Church for these and the other services which accounted for 90 per cent of its activities. Under these circumstances, it argued that the discrimination was proportionate to the aims the charities pursued as same-sex couples could use alternative adoption agencies, and that any competition between the interests of the children and the interests (including the human rights) of prospective adoptive parents could only be properly resolved in favour of the children. He concluded that there was insufficient evidence upon which he could determine the question of justification and remitted the case to the Commission to determine whether to allow the amendment to the charity's objects on the basis of his judgment.

The case returned to the courts three years later after the Charity Commission again refused permission to the charity to amend its objects. The charity appealed to the First-tier Tribunal (Tax and Chancery), which had by this stage absorbed the functions of the Charity Tribunal. It found on the evidence that, were the claimant to be deprived of its ability to function as an adoption agency, the position of hard to place children would not be materially affected. The charity's appeal to the Upper Tribunal failed.[65]

[65] *Catholic Care (Diocese of Leeds) v Charity Commission for England and Wales* [2012] UKUT 395 (TCC), [2013] 2 All ER 1114.

Section 193 EqA was considered again by the High Court and CA in *R (Cornerstone (North East) Fostering & Adoption Services v Ofsted)* [2021] EWCA Civ 1390, [2022] 2 All ER 516, also discussed in Chapters 2, 9 and 10. So far as relevant here, the claimant (an evangelical Christian charitable adoption and fostering service which operated for and on behalf of a number of local authorities) sought to challenge a decision by a regulator that its requirement that prospective adoptive parents and foster carers be married evangelical Christians breached the prohibitions imposed by the EqA and HRA (Articles 8 and 14) on sexual orientation and religious discrimination. The High Court accepted ([2020] EWHC 1679 (Admin), [2020] IRLR 774) that the religious discrimination was lawful by reason of Schedule 23 para 2 (see discussion in Chapter 9), though that provision did not apply in relation to sexual orientation because para 2(10) provided that it did 'not permit anything which is prohibited by section 29, so far as relating to sexual orientation, if it is done (a) on behalf of a public authority, and (b) under the terms of a contract between the organisation and the public authority'). The High Court ruled that Cornerstone's discriminatory policy discriminated directly on grounds of sexual orientation, and alternatively that it was indirectly discriminatory and unjustified because disproportionate. It went on to reject the argument that the discrimination was saved by s193 EqA given the requirement in s193(2) that such discrimination be 'a proportionate means of achieving a legitimate aim'. The CA rejected Cornerstone's appeal, agreeing with the parties that the same approach to proportionality applied to s193 EqA and to s19(2) EqA and Articles 8, 9 and 14 ECHR, and with the judge below that Cornerstone's policy had been disproportionate to any legitimate aims.[66]

Specific Exceptions Applicable to Part 3 EqA

Additional exceptions applicable to s29 EqA are found in Schedule 3 EqA, which provides that the prohibition on discrimination in the exercise of public functions does not apply to legislative, judicial and Parliamentary functions and the security services (paras 1–3 and 5). Nor do the prohibitions on discrimination on grounds of age, disability, gender reassignment or sex in the exercise of public functions 'apply to anything done for the purpose of ensuring the combat effectiveness of the armed forces' (para 4). Further exceptions are provided in relation to discrimination in the exercise of public functions which relate to education (paras 6–12), health and care (paras 13–15), immigration (paras 15A–19), insurance (paras 20–23), marriage (paras 24–25C), separate and single sex services (paras 26–30D) television, radio and online broadcasting and distribution (para 31) and transport (paras 32–34A).

The Schedule 3 exceptions which apply in relation to education are not directed at discrimination by schools, which is regulated by Part 6 of the EqA. They are, rather, concerned with the education functions of local authorities, and they permit discrimination on grounds of:

- age in relation to the provision of schools, school curricula, admission, transport and establishment, alteration or closure of schools;
- religion or belief in relation to the provision of schools, school curricula, admission to schools with a religious ethos, acts of worship or other religious observance organised by or on behalf of a school, transport and establishment, alteration or closure of schools;
- disability insofar as it consists of physical features of premises.

[66] See also the discussion of *R (Z) v Hackney*, n 14 above, in Ch 3.

Paragraphs 13–15 of Schedule 3 allow reasonable refusals of blood donations on the basis of risk assessments based on clinical, epidemiological or other data obtained from a source on which it is reasonable to rely,[67] also the refusal of services to pregnant women[68] based on the reasonable belief that the service would, because of the pregnancy, create a risk to the women's health or safety, where the service provider also refuses the service to persons with other physical conditions because of reasonable concern for their health or safety; and participation in arrangements to treat as a member of a person's family, whether for reward or not, of persons requiring particular care and attention. The exception relating to pregnancy is discussed in Chapter 6.

Paragraphs 15A–19 of Schedule 3 allow discrimination on grounds of age, nationality and national or ethnic origins in the context of immigration where the discrimination is done in the exercise of Ministerial authorisations, also discrimination on grounds of disability and religion or belief in decisions taken on the ground of necessity for the public good in accordance with the immigration rules and concerning entry clearance or leave to remain or (in the case of religion or belief) on the basis that it is undesirable to permit the person to remain in the UK, and decisions (whether or not taken in accordance with immigration rules) concerning entry clearance or leave to remain, taken because a person holds an religious office or post or provides a religious service, or that a religion or belief is not to be treated in the same way as certain other religions or beliefs, or that the exclusion from the UK of a person holding that religious office or post or providing that religious service is conducive to the public good. Para 15A EqA also makes exceptions to the prohibition on age discrimination in respect of acts done in connection with immigration under statutory authority.[69] These provisions are further discussed in Chapters 7 and 9.

Paragraphs 20–23 of Schedule 3 exempt from the scope of s29 EqA discrimination in employment-related financial services (which fall within the scope of Part 5 of the Act) and discrimination in connection with financial services on grounds of age, where the discrimination is based on risk assessment carried out by reference to relevant information from a source on which it is reasonable to rely, or disability on satisfaction of the same condition and the additional condition that the discrimination is reasonable.[70] These provisions are further discussed in Chapters 8 and 11.

Paragraphs 24–25C of Schedule 3 exempt from s29 EqA much discrimination on grounds of gender reassignment and sexual orientation in connection with the religious solemnisation of marriage. These exceptions and others applicable to gender reassignment are considered in Chapter 6 as are the exceptions set out in para 26–28, which permit sex-segregated services. Insofar as they relate to sexual orientation, they are discussed in Chapter 10.

The general silence of the EqA as to its geographical reach was mentioned above. Exceptions relevant here are services provided by an information society service provider (ISSP),[71]

[67] It was reported on 14 June 2021 that the NHS blood service had ceased to question blood donors about their sexual orientation: https://www.blood.co.uk/news-and-campaigns/news-and-statements/landmark-change-to-blood-donation-eligibility-rules-on-today-s-world-blood-donor-day.

[68] Or the imposition of conditions on the provision of service in equivalent circumstances.

[69] Section 29(9) EqA provides that the prohibitions on race discrimination in relation to service provision and the exercise of public functions apply to the granting of entry clearance wherever the act takes place.

[70] Para 23(3), which permits discrimination on grounds of any protected characteristic in an insurance policy of insurance entered into before 1 October 2012, unless such policy was renewed, or its terms reviewed, on or after that date, is likely to be of very limited application in 2020. Para 20 EqA, discussed in Ch 6, permits some sex, pregnancy, marriage/civil partnership and gender reassignment discrimination in relation to insurance.

[71] ISSPs are defined by Sch 25 EqA in line with Art 2(a) of the Council Directive 98/34/ EC (the E-Commerce Directive) to cover services normally provided for remuneration from a distance by means of electronic equipment to consumers, such as online shopping, direct marketing and advertising.

part 3 regulating the provision by ISSPs established in GB of information society services (services normally provided for remuneration from a distance by means of electronic equipment to consumers, eg online shopping, direct marketing and advertising), whether those services are accessed in GB or any EEA Member State other than the UK.[72] If the ISSP is established in an EEA state other than the UK, the EqA does not apply to anything done in providing the information society services. To use examples in the EHRC's Code of Practice, s29 would apply to a refusal by a GB-based online holiday company to accept bookings from same-sex couples for shared accommodation 'regardless of whether the service user was in the Great Britain or another EEA member state' but sex discrimination by an online retailer based in Germany in providing group discounts for the football World Cup 'would have to be brought in the German courts regardless of whether the service user was in Great Britain or another EEA member state'.[73]

Paragraph 29 allows some sex-segregation by religious institutions (see further Chapters 6 and 9), while para 30 permits the provision of services exclusively to persons sharing a protected characteristic, where this has been the way in which the service has generally been provided and the service provider 'reasonably thinks it is impracticable to provide the service to persons who do not share that characteristic'. Specific exceptions are also provided by paras 30A–30D in relation to age discrimination in the form of age-related concessions; age-specific holiday services designed to 'bring[] together … persons of that age group with a view to facilitating their enjoyment of facilities or services designed with particular regard to persons of that age group; age restrictions required by statute and minimum age requirements for residential mobile homes'. These are discussed in Chapter 11.

Paragraph 31 of Schedule 3 provides that s29 EqA does not apply to the 'provision of a content service', as distinct from the provision of an 'electronic communications network, electronic communications service or associated facility'.[74] The EHRC's Code of Practice suggests that a refusal by a broadcasting company to send a signal to a person's home would be challengeable under s29 EqA whereas a decision concerning who should appear in a particular programme or on which day that programme should be transmitted would not.[75]

Paragraphs 32–34A of Schedule 3 provide exceptions for disability discrimination in transport by air, road or rail, with exceptions to the exceptions provided in the case of train coaches and many road vehicles, including taxis. The reason for the exceptions from s29 of these matters is because disability discrimination in these contexts is regulated by EC Regulations which are directly effective in domestic law,[76] the details of which are outside the scope of this work.[77] It is important to be aware that Part 12 EqA applies specifically in relation to transport, making provision for regulations setting access standards for taxis, public service vehicles, and light rail vehicles, and imposing specific duties on the drivers of taxis and private hire vehicles (see further Chapter 8). Section 30 EqA

[72] ie the provision does not apply in N Ireland.

[73] n 41 above, §11.11. Note that the references to GB as 'an EEA state' are no longer correct.

[74] See EHRC Code, n 44 above, §§13.105–13.106.

[75] *ibid*, §13.106.

[76] Regulation (EC) No 1107/2006 of the European Parliament and of the Council of 5 July 2006 concerning the rights of disabled persons and persons with reduced mobility when travelling by air; Regulation (EU) No 181/2011 of the European Parliament and of the Council of 16 February 2011 concerning the rights of passengers in bus and coach transport and amending Regulation (EC) No 2006/2004 and Regulation (EC) No 1371/2007 of the European Parliament and of the Council of 23 October 2007 on rail passengers' rights and obligations.

[77] See *Campbell v Thomas Cook Tour Operators Ltd* [2014] EWCA Civ 1668, [2015] 1 WLR 2007.

limits the application of s29 to the transport of people by, and services provided on, ships and hovercrafts to circumstances in which this has been prescribed, or where the transport or services constitute the exercise of a public function.[78] No secondary legislation is yet in existence. The infrastructure related to the means of transport which does not itself involve the use of the mode of transport itself falls within s29 EqA. Examples of this would include station cafés, airports, train stations and bus stops as well as ticketing arrangements.

Part 4: Housing/Premises

Material Scope of Part 4

Section 33 EqA, Disposals, etc

(1) A person (A) who has the right to dispose of premises must not discriminate against another (B)—
   (a) as to the terms on which A offers to dispose of the premises to B;
   (b) by not disposing of the premises to B;
   (c) in A's treatment of B with respect to things done in relation to persons seeking premises.

(2) Where an interest in a commonhold unit cannot be disposed of unless a particular person is a party to the disposal, that person must not discriminate against a person by not being a party to the disposal.

(3) A person who has the right to dispose of premises must not, in connection with anything done in relation to their occupation or disposal, harass—
   (a) a person who occupies them;
   (b) a person who applies for them.

Section 33(4)–(5) EqA prohibit victimisation in materially identical terms to ss33(1)–(2) and (3) EqA prohibits harassment in connection with the occupation or disposal of premises by a person with the right to dispose of the premises of the occupier of the premises, or of someone who seeks to occupy them. Section 32 EqA provides that the prohibition on discrimination in relation to premises does not apply in relation to the protected characteristics of age, marriage or civil partnership and s33(6) excludes the protected characteristics of sexual orientation and religion or belief from the prohibition on harassment in this context.[79] Section 36 EqA imposes duties of reasonable adjustment on the controllers of premises which are or are to be let, and upon commonhold associations and the person responsible for common parts.[80]

Section 34 EqA applies the same prohibitions on discrimination, harassment and victimisation as are found in s33 to persons whose permission is required for the disposal of

[78] Even then, s30(2) EqA provides that the duty to make reasonable adjustments applies only to the extent prescribed.

[79] Section 33 also does not apply (s33(2)) to discrimination which is (or would other than because of an express exception be) covered by parts 5 or 6 (work or education) or (s33(3) EqA) to the provision of accommodation which is generally intended for short stays by persons resident elsewhere and which is provided only for the purposes of providing a service or exercising a public function (parties in pubs, for example, or hotel stays).

[80] The terms are defined by s36(2)–(7) EqA.

premises, other than persons exercising judicial functions. Section 35 EqA then provides as follows:

Section 35 EqA, Management

(1) A person (A) who manages premises must not discriminate against a person (B) who occupies the premises—

(a) in the way in which A allows B, or by not allowing B, to make use of a benefit or facility;
(b) by evicting B (or taking steps for the purpose of securing B's eviction);
(c) by subjecting B to any other detriment.

Section 35(3) prohibits victimisation in materially identical terms to s35(1), and s35(2) provides that:

(2) A person who manages premises must not, in relation to their management, harass—

(a) a person who occupies them;
(b) a person who applies for them.

As is the case with the disposal of premises, s35 EqA does not apply in relation to the protected characteristics of age, marriage or civil partnership and the prohibition on harassment does not apply to sexual orientation and religion or belief.[81]

A number of cases brought under s35 EqA have concerned challenges to the eviction of disabled tenants. One notable example is discussed immediately below.

***Aster Communities Ltd v Akerman-Livingstone* [2015] UKSC 15, [2015] AC 1399**

The claimant, who had severe prolonged duress stress disorder and was homeless, was provided with temporary accommodation by a local authority. The housing was managed by Aster Communities. The claimant having refused to accept any offer of permanent accommodation, the local authority decided that its main housing duty had ended and required Aster Communities to bring proceedings to evict him so that the property could be made available to another homeless person. The claimant sought to defend the proceedings by arguing that they amounted to discrimination contrary to ss15 and 35(1)(b) EqA. The county court judge held that, in relation to social housing, a court should approach a defence based on alleged disability discrimination as it would approach a defence based on Article 8 ECHR, with the effect that the possession order should be granted as a proportionate means of achieving the twin aims of vindicating the local authority's property rights and enabling the authority to comply with its statutory duties in the allocation and management of its housing stock. The High Court, CA and SC all rejected the claimant's appeal but the SC did so having ruled that, where the possibility of disability discrimination was established, the burden passed to the landlord to show that there was no unfavourable treatment for a reason arising in consequence of the claimant's disability or that, if there was, the possession order was a proportionate means of achieving a legitimate aim. By contrast with the position where Article 8 was relied upon, this could not be assumed. In the instant case, however, the Court was satisfied that a full hearing of the claim would have resulted in its dismissal.

[81] Sections 32, 35(4) EqA.

Exceptions

In addition to the general exceptions from the EqA's prohibitions on discrimination. Schedule 5 provides specific exceptions applicable to owner-occupiers and those concerned with the management or disposal of small premises. Paragraph 1 provides that owner-occupiers are subject only to the prohibition on race discrimination as regards the disposal of their premises as long as they do not use an estate agent or advertise the disposal, though they are subject to the prohibitions on harassment and victimisation. In addition, such owner-occupiers are not subject to the prohibition on discrimination connected with sexual orientation, religion or belief as regards the grant or withholding of permission to dispose of premises (though they are subject to the prohibition on victimisation). Paragraph 3 makes similar provision in relation to the disposal, occupation or management of part of small premises by an individual who lives, or whose relative lives, and intends to continue to live, in another part of the premises, which premises include common parts other than storage or access. 'Small premises' are defined as those not normally sufficient to accommodate more than three other households, or more than six persons other than those in the same household as the discriminator or his or her relative. Such individuals under no duty to make reasonable adjustments. Nor are individuals who let premises which are or have been their only or main home unless they have used a manager in relation to the letting.

These provisions had their predecessors in the RRA but relatively few cases were litigated under the provisions. The CRE carried out a number of Formal Investigations (see further Chapter 5) into race discrimination by local authorities in the provision of housing and in 1984 found that Hackney Council had been guilty of 'direct discrimination against black applicants and tenants who had been allocated housing from the waiting list … in that whites had received better-quality allocations of housing than blacks' and that white applicants were disproportionately likely to be allocated houses, maisonettes, ground- or first-floor and new properties, whilst Black applicants were more likely to be allocated flats.[82] More recently, much of the litigation concerning housing-related discrimination has concerned the allocation of social housing, which falls within s29 (see p 183 above).

Part 5: Work

The core relevant provision of Part 5 EqA is s39.

Section 39 EqA, Employees and applicants

(1) An employer (A) must not discriminate against a person (B)—
   (a) in the arrangements A makes for deciding to whom to offer employment;
   (b) as to the terms on which A offers B employment;
   (c) by not offering B employment.

[82] See M Bryan, 'Discrimination in the Public Provision of Housing: the Commission for Racial Equality Report on Housing in Hackney' [1984] *Public Law* 194, 196.

(2) An employer (A) must not discriminate against an employee of A's (B)—
  (a) as to B's terms of employment;
  (b) in the way A affords B access, or by not affording B access, to opportunities for promotion, transfer or training or for receiving any other benefit, facility or service;[83]
  (c) by dismissing B;[84]
  (d) by subjecting B to any other detriment.

Section 39(3)–(4) EqA make materially identical provision in respect of victimisation, and s39(5) imposes a duty to make reasonable adjustments in the employment context, while s39(6) excludes from the reach of s39 pay-related complaints, other than of direct discrimination, in relation to sex, or pregnancy and maternity.[85] Section 40 EqA provides that an employer may not harass employees or job applicants. Section 40(2) EqA, which imposed liability on employers in some cases for harassment by third parties over whom they had some control, was repealed in 2013. The repeal has proved controversial, in particular in light of increasing public concern about sexual harassment. Liability for harassment and discrimination is considered further below.

Specific provision is made by Part 5 EqA in respect of discrimination against contract workers (s41 EqA), police constables (s42 EqA), partners (ss44–45 EqA), barristers and advocates (ss47–48 EqA) and the holders of personal and public offices (ss49–51 EqA) (see further pp 215–216 below). Broadly speaking, the protection given to these categories of workers is materially similar to that given to those falling within ss39 and 40 EqA, albeit tweaked to take account of the particular issues arising in each case. Thus, by way of example, s41 EqA protects contract workers against discrimination by 'principals' (that is, persons to whom contract workers employed by other parties are supplied under contract), while s51 EqA prohibits discrimination by a person with power to recommend or approve appointment to a public office in like terms as s50 prohibits discrimination by a person with the power to make such an appointment.

Part 5 EqA also regulates discrimination in the broader sphere of employment including discrimination by qualifications bodies (s53 EqA), employment service providers (s55 EqA)[86] and trade organisations including trade unions (section 57), and discrimination against local authority members in the carrying out of their official business (section 58). These provisions, and ss41–51 EqA, are considered below, after a discussion of the scope of 'employment' within s39 EqA.

Scope of 'Employment'

Returning to s39 EqA, 'employment' is defined broadly under the EqA to include 'employment under a contract of employment, a contract of apprenticeship or a contract personally to do work' as well as Crown employment and employment 'as a relevant member'

[83] Section 31(5) EqA provides that, where an employer arranges for another person to provide a service only to the employer's employees, the employer is not to be regarded as the service-provider, but the employees are to be regarded as a section of the public. This has the effect that the employees could challenge discrimination by the employer under s39 and/or discrimination by the service provider under s29.

[84] Including, by virtue of s39(7) EqA constructively or on notice except, in the latter case, where employment is immediately renewed on the same terms.

[85] These have to be brought under the equal pay provisions, discussed in Ch 6.

[86] Note that the claimant in *Chet v Capita Translation and Interpreting Ltd* did not seek to rely on s55 EqA until the EAT appeal, by which stage it was too late to introduce this new head of claim.

of House of Commons or House of Lords staff.[87] This definition applies the protection of the relevant anti-discrimination provisions to a wider category of workers than those entitled to claim unfair dismissal, redundancy payments, etc, under the Employment Rights Act 1996, which applies only to workers employed under contracts *of service*, as distinct from contracts *for services*.

The boundaries of 'employment' under the EqA's predecessor legislation are illustrated by the decision of the CA in the *Gunning* case.

***Mirror Group Newspapers Ltd v Gunning* [1986] ICR 145**

Ms Gunning sought to sue MGN under the SDA when the group refused to permit her to take over her father's area distributorship on his retirement. She, like her father, was an independent newspaper wholesaler who bought papers from newspaper publishers and sold them on to newsagents. A tribunal ruled that the distributorship came within the SDA's definition of 'employment', the contract between MGN and Ms Gunning's father requiring that he exercised day-to-day supervision over the distribution tasks, although he was not obliged to carry them out himself. The CA allowed MGN's appeal on the basis that the contract at issue was not one 'personally to execute any work or labour', this being the test which applied at the material time. Ms Gunning's counsel had argued that 'any' should be read as applying to the *extent* as well as to the *nature* of the work or labour contracted for, so as to afford the protection of the SDA to any contract a 'material' term of which required the personal execution of work or labour by a contracting party. The CA, however, ruled that 'the phrase in its context contemplates a contract whose *dominant* purpose is that the party contracting to provide services under the contract performs personally the work or labour which forms the subject matter of the contract' (emphasis added).

The *Gunning* case was applied to exclude sub-postmasters from the protection of the EqA's predecessor legislation.[88] Also excluded by reason of the SC's decision in *X v Mid Sussex Citizens Advice Bureau* [2012] UKSC 59, [2013] ICR 249 are volunteers. And in *Jivraj v Hashwani*, extracted below, the SC ruled that the extended concept of employment a predecessor provision of s83(2) EqA did not apply to an arbitrator. The Court ruled that, while the arbitrator's services were to be performed pursuant to the contract between the parties, that contract was not one for 'employment under … a contract personally to do any work'. In doing so the Court relied on the decision of the CJEU in the *Allonby* case.

Case C-256/01 *Allonby v Accrington & Rossendale College* EU:C:2004:18, [2004] ECR I-873, [2004] ICR 1328

The claimants in that case were part-time teachers who provided their services through an agency to the college. The CJEU ruled that the term 'worker' for the purposes of EU law included 'a person who, for a certain period of time, performs services for and under

[87] Section 83(2) EqA.

[88] Respectively, *Chambers v Post Office Counters Ltd* 21 February 1995, unreported and *Sheehan v Post Office Counters* EAT/417/98, 16 November 1998, unreported. See also *Commissioners of Inland Revenue v Post Office Ltd* [2003] ICR 546.

the direction of another person in return for which he receives remuneration', though 'the authors of the Treaty did not intend that the term ... should include independent providers of services who are not in a relationship of subordination with the person who receives the services'. The Court ruled that the EU concept of 'worker', which has been transposed for domestic law purposes into the kind of 'employment' contemplated by the EqA, 'cannot be defined by reference to the legislation of the Member States but has a Community meaning [and] ... cannot be interpreted restrictively'. It concluded that the claimants were 'workers' for the purposes of Article 141 [now Article 157 TFEU[89]], and ruled that '[p]rovided that a person is a worker within the meaning of Article 141(1) EC, the nature of his legal relationship with the other party to the employment relationship is of no consequence in regard to the application of that article' and that '[t]he formal classification of a self-employed person under national law does not exclude the possibility that a person must be classified as a worker within the meaning of Article 141(1) EC if his independence is merely notional, thereby disguising an employment relationship within the meaning of that article'.

***Jivraj v Hashwani* [2011] UKSC 40, [2011] ICR 1004**

In this case the SC applied the dicta in *Allonby* to find that an arbitrator was an independent provider of services and was to be regarded as genuinely self-employed, and therefore outside the scope of the employment provisions. The fact that he or she would receive fees for their work, might be providing services for the purposes of VAT, and would render non-delegable personal services was insufficient to establish employment where the services were not provided for, and under the direction of, the parties.

The outcome in *Jivraj* was perhaps unsurprising but, whereas the decision of the CJEU in *Allonby* had been expansive as regards the protection of EU law, its impact through the decision in *Jivraj* was to be felt by relatively humble claimants such as the Romanian interpreter in *Chet v Capita Translation and Interpreting Ltd*[90] and the beauty consultant in *Halawi v WDFG UK Ltd (t/a World Duty Free)* [2014] EWCA Civ 1387, [2015] IRLR 50. The reference to subordination in *Allonby* had started running the hare which resulted in the decision in *Jivraj* and its progeny in *Chet* and *Hilawi*. In the *O'Brien* case, by contrast, the CJEU ruled that the holding of judicial office was insufficient to exclude the claimant, a part-time judge, from the status of 'worker' for the purposes of EU law, though it was for the national courts to examine to what extent the relationship between judges and the Ministry of Justice was, by its nature, substantially different from an employment relationship between an employer and a worker.

[89] Discussed in Ch 6.

[90] (2015) UKEAT/0086/15 24 July 2015, unreported. *cf Capita Translation and Interpreting Ltd v Siacunas* [2017] ICR 887.

Case C-393/10 *O'Brien v Ministry of Justice* EU:C:2012:110, [2012] ICR 955

The CJEU suggested that the factors to be taken into account in determining worker status included the rules for appointing and removing judges, the way in which their working was organised, and their entitlement to sick pay, maternity or paternity pay and other similar benefits. The SC, which had referred the case to the CJEU, referred to the CJEU's distinction between a 'worker' and a 'self-employed person', the latter having 'the comparative luxury of independence' and being able to 'make his own choices as to the work he does and when and where he does it. He works for himself. He is not subject to the direction or control of others. Of course, he must adhere to the standards of his trade or profession. He must face the reality that, if he is to succeed, he must satisfy the needs and requirements of those who engage his services. They may be quite demanding, and the room for manoeuvre may be small. But the choices that must be made are for him, and him alone, to take.'[91] Without making reference to the concept of subordination (or its apparent absence from the relationship between judges and the state, the CJEU ruled that recorders such as the claimant were entitled to be regarded as 'workers' for the purpose of the Part-time Workers Regulations 2000 (which included an individual working under 'any other contract … whereby the individual undertakes to do or perform personally any work or services for another party to the contract whose status is not by virtue of the contract that of a client or customer of any profession or business undertaking carried on by the individual').

In *Bates van Winkelhof* [2014] UKSC 32, [2014] ICR 730 the SC held that subordination was not a 'freestanding and universal' element in employment, ruling that an equity partner in a law firm could be a 'worker' for the purposes of the ERA 1996. The decision of the SC in *Pimlico Plumbers Ltd* is indicative of a more general relaxation on the part of the courts to employment status.

***Pimlico Plumbers Ltd v Smith* [2018] UKSC 29, [2018] ICR 1511**

The SC refused an appeal against a decision that the claimant, a plumber, was a 'worker' for the purposes of the ERA. The particular question in issue concerned whether he had undertaken to 'perform personally' his work or services for Pimlico Plumbers, so the case is of relevance under the EqA as well as the ERA. The SC considered whether the claimant's right to substitute another Pimlico operative for himself was inconsistent with an obligation of personal performance, that is, whether the dominant feature of the contract remained personal performance on his part. The Court pointed out that the right to substitute had not even been expressly referred to in the contract, that the terms of the contract focused on personal performance (referring to 'your skills' and 'your appearance') and that it was unusual for an operative to estimate for a job and then to substitute another operative to effect performance. It found that the Tribunal had 'clearly' been entitled to hold that the dominant feature of the claimant's contracts with Pimlico was an obligation of personal performance and that the restricted nature of the right to substitute was the converse of a situation in which the other party was uninterested in the identity of the substitute, provided only that the work got done. Nor could

[91] [2013] UKSC 6, [2013] ICR 499 §39.

Pimlico be regarded as a client or customer of the claimant's despite the latter's freedom to reject any particular offer of work; his freedom (subject to being available to work for 40 hours over five days) to take outside work, albeit not that offered by Pimlico's clients; the fact that Pimlico had no right to supervise or otherwise interfere with the manner in which Mr Smith did his work; or the fact that there were financial risks, as well as advantages, consequent upon Mr Smith's work for Pimlico. The Court paid regard, in reaching this conclusion, to the tight control exercised by Pimlico over the claimant including in requiring him to wear the Pimlico uniform, drive its branded van (to which Pimlico applied a tracker), carry its identity card, and closely follow the administrative instructions of its control room. Finally, the severe terms as to when and how much it was obliged to pay him, on which it relied, were inconsistent with his being a truly independent contractor.

One question which has arisen from time to time is whether a firm or collective, as distinct from an individual, can complain of discrimination. 'Person' is defined by the Interpretation Act 1978 to include bodies corporate as well as unincorporated.[92] In *Abrams v EAD Solicitors LLP*, a tribunal ruled that a company could bring a claim for associative discrimination under the EqA. This concept is considered further in Chapter 2. It suggests that corporate claimants may be able to proceed under the EqA by framing discrimination claims as claims in respect of *associative* discrimination (that is, discrimination against the association because of the ethnicity, sexual orientation, sex, sexual orientation etc of its staff, customers, clients, etc).

***Abrams v EAD Solicitors LLP* [2015] UKEAT 0054_15_0506, [2016] ICR 380**

Langstaff P:

7. The Interpretation Act 1978 provides in s.5 under the heading 'Definitions':

'In any Act, unless the contrary intention appears, words and expressions listed in Schedule 1 to this Act are to be construed according to that Schedule'.

8. In Schedule 1 the word 'person' is said to include 'a body of persons corporate or unincorporate'. Thus on the face of s.13 the LLP (as person A) may be held to discriminate against another, B, and if the word 'another' means, as it seems to me plain it does, 'another person', B may be a natural or a legal person in accordance with the Interpretation Act unless the contrary intention appears. If, therefore, s.13 is capable in the Equality Act of holding the way in which a corporate body has been treated by an alleged discriminator as being unlawful discrimination, then under s.45 a breach of the Act would be made out once it was shown that, because of a protected characteristic, the limited company had been treated less favourably than A treated or would have treated others. This assumes that s.45 is to be read as including a legal person as well as a natural person as a member.

9. The argument for the claimant before me as it was before the judge is simplicity itself: a person may include a corporation. Within s.13, the opening words 'A person (A)' must include a corporate body, for it is familiar to any employment lawyer that many corporations are alleged to be discriminators and no one has so far considered that is inappropriate. If, then, the word 'person' is to be used at the outset of s.31 as including a corporation, there is no proper basis for reading the same word, albeit introduced by 'another', in any different sense where it appears later in the same section. There is no contrary intention appearing in the statute …

[92] See *Kelly & Loughran v Northern Ireland Housing Executive* [1999] AC 428, and *Patterson v Legal Services Commission* [2004] ICR 312.

11. The argument of Mr Sendall, who appears for the LLP, begins by pointing out that only an individual can have a protected characteristic. Of the nine protected characteristics in s.4 of the Equality Act, only an individual can sensibly be said to have age; disability; be subject to gender reassignment; be entitled to marriage and civil partnership; enjoy pregnancy and maternity; have race; religion or belief; sex; or sexual orientation. That is obvious. Accordingly, he submits that the whole thrust of the anti-discrimination provisions that are contained in the Equality Act is directed towards individuals; it is concerned with their protection. In my view, this argument misses the point that the Equality Act does not deal with individuals on the basis of their protected characteristics but identifies discrimination as being detrimental treatment caused by the protected characteristic or related to it. Detrimental treatment can be given to any person, whether that person is natural or legal. There is no reason to restrict the class of those who can suffer a detriment if what is being complained of, and that which the statute seeks to avoid, is a detriment being suffered because of an individual's protected characteristic.[93]

There has been a great deal of litigation on the employment status of ministers of religion. This is considered in Chapter 9.

Geographical Reach of Part 5

The question of territorial jurisdiction has also loomed large in recent years with many decisions of the SC and lower cases as to whether various individuals working wholly or mainly outside GB have been protected by domestic employment and/or discrimination law. As explained above, the territorial application of the employment-related provisions of the EqA is left to tribunals to determine, save that ss81–82 and regulations made thereunder make specific provision in relation to work on ships and hovercraft, and to seafarers and persons in offshore work.[94]

Walker v Wallem Ship Management Ltd [2020] UKEAT 0236_18_1601, [2020] ICR 1103

The EAT ruled that the claimant, who had, in the UK, been refused employment on a non-UK flagged vessel because she was a woman, could not challenge the discrimination under the EqA. The claimant, a qualified deck officer, had been told by the respondent that it could not 'offer the appropriate on-board environment' for 'girls [who] have a place and a chance to succeed' but who would be better placed in the cruise industry. Section 81 EqA provides that Part 5 EqA applies in relation to work on ships, hovercraft and by seafarers 'only in such circumstances as are prescribed', irrespective of 'whether employment arises or work is carried out within or outside the UK'. The Equality Act 2010 (Work on Ships and Hovercraft) Regulations 2011 set out the circumstances in which Part 5 of the 2010 Act applies in relation to work on ships, hovercraft and by seafarers. They did not apply to work, such as that the claimant sought, on board foreign registered ships sailing in foreign waters. The EAT rejected the argument put for the claimant that, the exclusionary language in s81 being in the present tense ('aris*es*', '*is* carried out'), the provision applied only in cases in which there was an actual employment relationship.

[93] Citing *Showboat Entertainment Centre Ltd v Owens* [1984] ICR 65 and *Weathersfield Ltd v Sargent* [1999] ICR 425, discussed in Ch 2.

[94] See the EqA 2010 (Work on Ships and Hovercraft) Regulations 2011 and *Wittenberg v Sunset Personnel Services Ltd* (2013) UKEATS/0019/13, [2017] ICR 1012; and EqA 2010 (Offshore Work) Order 2010, SI 2010/1835.

Kerr J:

24. … We start, as usual, with the words of the statute, s 81 of the 2010 Act. It is true that the drafter has used the present tense and participle … Similarly, in reg 4 of the 2011 Regulations the present tense is used in the phrase 'a seafarer who works wholly outside Great Britain.' The language used does connote current employment.

25. On the other hand, regs 3 and 4 of the 2011 Regulations apply or disapply the whole of Pt 5, not only parts of it. They do not carve up Pt 5 into applied parts and disapplied parts. Part 5 is entitled *Work*, while Ch 1 (headed Employment, Etc) includes provisions that plainly apply to the pre-employment recruitment process and not just the employment (or worker) relationship …

27. Regulation 5 creates a limited exception in the case of payment, or offered payment, of nationality-based differential rates. The part of reg 5 dealing with offers to pay would be redundant if discrimination in relation to pre-employment offers of work, or offers of work on particular terms, were already excluded (other than in prescribed cases) from the general disapplication of Pt 5 by s 81 …

29. We therefore consider whether there are reasons of policy or justice which impel us to prefer the claimant's construction and, if so, whether we can apply the *Marleasing* principle[95] and adopt a construction that confines the injustice as narrowly as possible by applying the exclusion of Pt 5 only to cases of actual employment, not recruitment. The claimant says that Wallem's construction is unjust on several counts: it infringes the principle that where a wrong is done, there should be a remedy; it denies the claimant rights not to suffer discrimination, conferred by the Equal Treatment Directive and the Charter of Fundamental Rights; and it undermines the common law 'right to work' articulated in *Nagle v Fielden* [1966] 2 QB 633 …

36. Parliament chose, in s 81, to empower the Secretary of State to decide whether and to what extent Pt 5 should apply in relation to work on ships, work on hovercraft and seafarers. In our judgment, the Secretary of State then decided to apply or disapply the whole of Pt 5 of the 2010 Act as provided for in regs 3 and 4 of the 2011 Regulations and to disapply part, but not all, of Pt 5, in the circumstances provided for in reg 5.

37. We consider that we cannot escape from that conclusion by invocation of a beneficent policy-driven construction, whether by applying the *Marleasing* principle or by invoking other general principles of interpretation such as the need for there to be a remedy where a wrong needs righting, or preservation of a right to work. It would strain the language of s 81, read with the 2011 Regulations, too far to do so.

38 …. We must therefore dismiss the claimant's appeal. We do so with some misgivings. The respondent's conduct has been reprehensible, but the tribunal below and this appeal tribunal are powerless to right the injustice done to the claimant.

39. It is, in our judgment, an uncomfortable but inescapable proposition that the 2011 Regulations permit an offshore employment service provider to discriminate, on United Kingdom soil, on the ground of any of the protected characteristics in the 2010 Act, when recruiting in this country personnel to serve on its clients' foreign flagged ships sailing outside United Kingdom waters.

40. No international law obligation of the United Kingdom requires UK domestic law to permit such discrimination. It is, at least, doubtful whether the 2011 Regulations conform to

[95] A reference to the decision of the CJEU in Case C-106/89 *Marleasing SA v La Comercial Internacional de Alimentacion SA* [1990] ECR I-4135, [1992] 1 CMLR 305 which imposes a strong interpretive obligation on national courts to interpret domestic legislation in conformity with EU directives.

the provisions of Directive 2006/54/EC (the Equal Treatment Directive). The claimant has no remedy against the respondent because the latter is not an emanation of the state. The claimant's remedy, if any, lies against the United Kingdom itself.

41. The three members of this appeal tribunal consider that the Secretary of State would be wise to revisit the scope of the 2011 Regulations. We note that he or she is obliged by reg 6 of the 2011 Regulations to review the impact of regs 3–5 every five years. The next quinquennial review must be done by 31 July 2021. The conclusions must be published in a report. The scope of the review includes reference to three directives on equal treatment, including Directive 2006/54/EC. We would not be surprised if the present case and the injustice suffered by the claimant were to feature in that review.

***R (Hottak) v SS Foreign and Commonwealth Affairs* [2016] EWCA Civ 438, [2016] IRLR 534**

The CA rejected an appeal against the decision of the Divisional Court that s39(2) EqA did not apply to locally employed staff working as interpreters for the British forces in Afghanistan. Such interpreters had been targeted by the Taliban as collaborators, intimidated, attacked and killed. They complained that less favourable benefits were available to them than had been provided to interpreters working with the British military in Iraq and sought to challenge this as nationality discrimination contrary to ss29 and s39 EqA. The Divisional Court adopted the approach applied in the context of unfair dismissal to Part 3 EqA[96] and rejected the claims because the claimants did not have stronger connections with GB and with British employment law than with Afghanistan and Afghan employment law. The CA rejected the claimants' appeal, ruling that it was a question of fact and degree whether a connection with GB and British employment law was sufficiently strong to overcome the general rule that the place of employment is decisive, and that (legal misdirection aside) this had been a matter for determination by the Court below.

Employment-Related Protections

Having considered some of the broader questions which arise in relation to employment claims, we will now consider in some more detail the conduct which s39 EqA seeks to regulate. This can be grouped, broadly, into selection (ss39(1)(a) and (c) EqA), terms (s39(1)(b) and (2)(a) EqA); benefits, promotion etc (s39(2)(b) EqA), dismissal (s39(2)(c) EqA) and other detriment (s39(2)(d) EqA). These are considered very briefly in turn below.

Selection

The main distinction between s39(1)(a) and (c) EqA is that, whereas the latter requires that the claimant has applied for and been rejected from the job in question, the former is apt

[96] See *Lawson v Serco Ltd* [2006] UKHL 3, [2006] ICR 250; *Bates van Winkelhof v Clyde & Co LLP* [2012] EWCA Civ 1207, [2013] ICR 883; *Duncombe v SS Children, Schools and Families (No 2)* [2011] UKSC 36, [2011] ICR 1312; *Ravat v Halliburton Manufacturing and Services Ltd* [2012] UKSC 1, [2012] ICR 389; *CreditSights Ltd v Dhunna* [2014] EWCA Civ 1238, [2015] ICR 105.

to cover complaints from those who have been rendered unable to apply (or, presumably, discouraged from so doing).[97] The 'arrangements' to which s39(1)(a) applies might include advertising (including questions of how any advertisements are drafted and where they are placed);[98] the use of recruitment sources such as schools, careers offices, job centres, etc (including the selection of these sources and any instructions issued to them); selection and training of short-listers and interviewers, and the manner in which short-listing, interviewing, and final selection is conducted.[99] Specific provision is made by s60 EqA in relation to enquiries related to health or disability in the recruitment process, which are discussed in Chapter 8.

The EqA (s20 and Schedule 8) places an obligation on employers to make adjustments where (a) a provision, criterion or practice applied by them or on their behalf, (b) any physical feature of premises occupied by them, or (c) any failure to provide an auxiliary aid places an applicant or potential applicant, at a substantial disadvantage by comparison with persons who are not disabled. The duty is to take such steps as it is reasonable to prevent the disadvantage. Employers are not placed under any obligation in cases in which they did not know, and could not reasonably have been expected to know that the disabled person was or might be an applicant.

It is unlawful for employers to indicate that they will discriminate directly against applicants on grounds of race, sex, etc (and, except where objectively justified, age). It is also important to avoid indirect discrimination.

EHRC, 'Employment', Statutory Code of Practice[100]

16.4 The inclusion of requirements in a job description or person specification which are unnecessary or seldom used is likely to lead to indirect discrimination. Employers who use job descriptions and person specifications should therefore review them each time they decide to fill a post. Reliance on an existing person specification or job description, may lead to discrimination if they contain discriminatory criteria.

Example:

An employer uses a person specification for an accountant's post that states 'employees must be confident in dealing with external clients' when in fact the job in question does not involve liaising directly with external clients. This requirement is unnecessary and could lead to discrimination against disabled people who have difficulty interacting with others, such as some people with autism ...

16.8 Where there are different ways of performing a task, job descriptions should not specify how the task should be done. Instead, the job description should state what outcome needs to be achieved.

Example:

A job description includes the task: 'Using MagicReport software to produce reports about customer complaints'. This particular software is not accessible to some disabled people

[97] Although it does require—*LB Croydon v Kuttapan* [1999] IRLR 349 – that an actual vacancy existed.

[98] Though see the decision of the EAT in *Cardiff Women's Aid v Hartup* [1994] IRLR 390 and the IRLR commentary thereto in the August 1994 IRLR 'highlights'. *cf Tanna v The Woods Group Ltd* reported in 130 EOR 'Case Digest'.

[99] See *In re Ballymena BC* NIQB 18 June 1993 (unreported), where selection took place by secret ballot by counsellors divided along sectarian lines. The applicant, who was rejected, succeeded in a complaint under the predecessor provision of s39(1)(c). Had, for some reason, a decision been reached after the ballot to abandon the new position and not appoint, an application could still have been made under s s39(1)(a).

[100] https://www.equalityhumanrights.com/en/publication-download/employment-statutory-code-practice.

> who use voice-activated software. Discrimination could be avoided by describing the task as 'Producing reports about customer complaints'.
>
> 16.9 Job descriptions should not specify working hours or working patterns that are not necessary to the job in question. If a job could be done either part-time, full-time, or through job share arrangements, this should be stated in the job description. As well as avoiding discrimination, this approach can also widen the group of people who may choose to make an application …
>
> 16.13 The person specification should not include criteria that are wholly irrelevant.
>
> Example:
>
> A requirement that the applicant must be 'active and energetic' when the job is a sedentary one is an irrelevant criterion. This requirement could be discriminatory against some disabled people who may be less mobile …
>
> Requiring a UK-based qualification, when equivalent qualifications obtained abroad would also meet the requirement for that particular level of knowledge or skill, may lead to indirect discrimination because of race, if the requirement cannot be objectively justified …
>
> 16.16 The inclusion of health requirements can amount to direct discrimination against disabled people, where such requirements lead to a blanket exclusion of people with particular impairments and do not allow individual circumstances to be considered. Employers should also be aware that, except in specified circumstances, it is unlawful to ask questions about health or disability before the offer of a job is made or a person is placed in a pool of people to be offered a job …

The Code also points out that employers may be required to provide information about jobs in alternative formats by way of a reasonable adjustment to disabled candidates, and to enable such candidates to indicate any relevant effects of a disability and to suggest adjustments, for example, to interview arrangements. Much of the case law which rose under the predecessor provisions of s39(1)(a) concerned discriminatory questioning at interviews.[101] The attitude of the judiciary to such questioning was not always robust.

***R (European Roma Rights Centre) v Immigration Officer at Prague Airport* [2004] UKHL 55, [2005] 2 AC 1**

The CA ([2003] EWCA Civ 666, [2004] QB 811) had rejected the argument that differential question of Roma and other travellers coming to the UK amounted to direct discrimination. Simon Browne LJ had stated for the majority that an employer 'in place of the wholesale rejection of women with children as an unreliable class of employees was entitled to question them more intrusively than others', and indeed that such questioning was 'logically likely'. He had continued:

> Consider similarly an employer interviewing for a job involving heavy lifting. He may not be entitled to refuse to interview women at all, but is he not permitted to question a female applicant for the job more sceptically and rigorously than her male counterpart? … If a terrorist outrage were committed on our streets today, would the police not be entitled to question more suspiciously those in the vicinity appearing to come from an Islamic background? Similarly in the case of sectarian violence in Northern Ireland. These seem to me the relevant analogies here,

[101] See for example *Brennan v J H Dewhurst Ltd* [1984] ICR 52. *cf Saunders v Richmond upon Thames BC* [1978] ICR 75.

not the now defunct practice[102] of repeatedly stopping and searching black youths, clearly an unjustifiable interference with their liberty unless reasonable grounds exist for suspecting those actually stopped.

The HL allowed an appeal. The position of job applicants was not discussed but their Lordships made it clear that treating Roma 'with more suspicion' and subjecting them to 'more intense and intrusive questioning' than non-Roma amounted to direct race discrimination.

Failure to Appoint

Section 39(1)(a) EqA, which we have already considered, concerns discrimination in the *arrangements* made to appoint, s39(1)(c), discrimination consisting of a refusal or deliberate failure to offer an appointment. It requires that the aggrieved individual actually applied for the position and was rejected.

Among the cases which arose under the predecessor provisions of s39(1)(c) EqA were *Martin v Marks & Spencer* (a refusal to appoint by an allegedly racially biased panel), *Price v Civil Service Commission* (application of an age bar which discriminated against women) and *Meer v Tower Hamlets* (application of selection criteria which were alleged to discriminate indirectly on racial grounds).[103] Other examples include the refusal of a job as a community service supervisor to an applicant who suffered from chronic depression, on the grounds that an alternative job as a handyman was deemed less stressful by the employer's occupational health adviser (*Paul v National Probation Service*); the refusal to appoint to the police a woman who had undergone gender reassignment on the basis that she would not be capable of performing intimate searches (*A v CC West Yorkshire Police* [2004] UKHL 21, [2005] AC 51, discussed in Chapter 6[104]); and a refusal to renew an English journalist's fixed-term presenting job on BBC Scotland's 'Rugby Special' (*BBC Scotland v Souster*).[105]

Terms of Appointment

Section 39(1)(b) EqA is concerned with the terms upon which employment is offered, s39(2)(a) with the actual terms of employment.[106] There have been relatively few appellate decisions on these subsections or their predecessors with the exception of *Barclays Bank plc v Kapur* [1991] 2 AC 355, which concerned alleged race discrimination in contractual terms and *Wakeman v Quick Corporation* [1999] IRLR 424, a claim made by locally recruited staff of a Japanese firm who compared their conditions to those applied to staff seconded from Japan. In *Spicer v Government of Spain* [2004] EWCA Civ 046, [2005] ICR

[102] The suggestion that this was a thing of the past was premature: in October 2018 M Shiner, Z Carre, R Delsol and N Eastwood reported massive racial disparities in the use of stop and search: The Colour of Injustice: 'Race', drugs and law enforcement in England and Wales (Stopwatch, LSE and Release), available at http://www.stopwatch.org/uploads/documents/The_Colour_of_Injustice.pdf.

[103] Respectively [1998] ICR 1005, [1977] 1 WLR 943 and [1988] IRLR 399.

[104] The decision pre-dated the introduction of specific GORs applicable in relation to gender reassignment.

[105] Respectively [2004] IRLR 190, [2005] 1 AC 51 and [2001] IRLR 150.

[106] Section 39(6) EqA restricts the application of s39(1)(b) to sex or pregnancy and maternity, claims in relation to which are generally dealt with as equal pay claims and discussed in Ch 6.

213 the CA considered a challenge under the RRA to the payment of expatriate allowances to Spanish civil servants but not to locally recruited UK staff. More recently, in *Air Products plc Cockram* [2018] EWCA Civ 346, [2018] IRLR 755, the CA considered an age discrimination claim brought under s39(2)(a) EqA to a contractual provision which created an exception to a general rule that various incentive awards were forfeited on termination of employment. The exception related to employees who left employment on or after the relevant customary retirement age. In 2010, after UK pension law imposed a minimum pensionable age of 55 on most people, the company interpreted the customary retirement age as being 55. The claimant resigned at 50, by which stage he was entitled to a pension, and sought the benefit of the exception to the forfeiture rule. His claim was ultimately unsuccessful because the employer was seeking to achieve fairness between the generations and treat employees consistently, and even direct age discrimination is capable of justification (see Chapter 11), but the case illustrates the potential application of s39(2)(a) EqA. And in *Naeem v SSJ* [2017] UKSC 27, [2017] ICR 640 (discussed in Chapter 2) s39(2)(a) was relied upon in an indirect discrimination claim brought by a Muslim imam employed by the Prison Service. He complained that, Muslim imams, having been eligible to serve as prison chaplains only from 2002, were (and he was) relatively poorly paid by comparison with longer serving Christian chaplains, this as a result of the fact that employees progressed up pay bands partly according to length of service. The claim failed because the courts, including the SC, accepted that the discrimination was justifiable as a proportionate means of achieving a legitimate aim.

A particular complication exists in relation to alleged sex discrimination concerning contractual terms, which are subject to a specific regime originally found in the Equal Pay Act 1970 (EqPA), rather than the SDA. The equal pay provisions, somewhat modified, are now found at ss64–76 EqA and are considered in Chapter 6. Section 70(1) EqA provides that s39(2), so far as it relates to sex, has no effect in relation to a contractual term which is modified by a sex equality clause (see Chapter 6) or would be so modified but for a defence available to the employer. Section 70(2) EqA provides that: 'Neither of the following is sex discrimination for the purposes of the relevant sex discrimination provision – (a) the inclusion in A's terms of a term that is less favourable as referred to in section 66(2)(a); (b) the failure to include in A's terms a corresponding term as referred to in section 66(2)(b)'. Section 71 then provides that s39(2) has no effect in relation to 'a term of a person's work – (a) that relates to pay, but (b)in relation to which a sex equality clause or rule has no effect … except in so far as treatment of the person amounts to a contravention of the provision by virtue of section 13 or 14' (direct discrimination). In *BMC Software Ltd v Shaikh*, the EAT considered whether a claim under s39(2) EqA was blocked by ss70 and/or 71. HHJ Hand said this:

***BMC Software Ltd v Shaikh* [2017] UKEAT 0092_16_0908, [2017] IRLR 1074**

Judge Hand:

70. … a claim under the SDA was essentially a claim made in (statutory) tort (with s.66(4) expressly providing power to award compensation for injury to feelings), whereas a claim under the E[q]PA was essentially a claim in contract with no similar power to award compensation in relation to injury to feelings …

71. Put very broadly those provisions can be described as having had the effect of making the two statutes mutually exclusive. It seems to me that is also the object of s.70 EqA and that

separation of remedies is preserved by ss.124 (breach of discrimination provisions) and 132 (breach of an equality clause).

72. I can find no precursor to s.71 EqA in either the EPA or the SDA. At first sight, it might seem that ss.70 and 71 are in some way complementary, an impression fostered by the appearance of the phrase 'no effect' in subsection (1) of both sections. On reflection, however, I think this is not the case; in my view, although both are dealing with contractual terms they have the opposite effect; s.70 EqA precludes discrimination provisions from applying to breach of a sex equality clause; s.71 EqA includes direct discrimination in respect of terms as to pay in respect of which a sex equality clause is not effective.

73. Section 70(3) EqA identifies the 'relevant discrimination provision' as being, in an employment case, s.39(2) EqA, which is the provision rendering discrimination during employment unlawful. By s.39(2)(a) an employer must not discriminate against an employee as to his or her terms of employment. The other paragraphs of sub-s 39(2) (ie (b) to (d)) do not refer explicitly to 'terms' but in some circumstances their subject-matter may well involve the terms of employment … By s.70(1) EqA the whole of s.39(2) EqA has 'no effect in relation to' either a term modified by a sex equality clause (section 70(1)(a)) or a term that would be modified were it not for the fact that a material factor defence had been established (section 70(1)(b)). To my mind because the provision has 'no effect', it prevents successful reliance on the employment discrimination provision in s.39(2) EqA in circumstances where s.66 EqA applies. But not only does the 'relevant discrimination provision' have no effect, by s.70(2) a less favourable term (section 70(2)(a)) or no term at all (section 70(2)(b)) cannot amount to sex discrimination.

74. I need go no further in the instant appeal than to say that in my judgment the meaning of s.70 EqA is that although a breach of an equality clause in the form of a failure to pay a woman the same as a man for like work is plainly a form of sex discrimination, a complainant cannot succeed in both an equal pay claim and the sex discrimination claim respect of that breach. Moreover, although these exclusionary concepts may be rather intricate I think that is the clear meaning of s.70 EqA …

76. Unlike s.70, the lack of 'effect' in s.71 does not arise as a result of the operation of the section but it is a precondition to the operation of the section. Thus s.71 deals with situations where the circumstances set out in s.65 EqA are not present and that has the result that s.66 EqA does not have any effect. Put another way, the equality clause has no effect as there is no 'corresponding term' because there is no actual comparator. There is little academic commentary that I can find relating to s.71 EqA although it is addressed in the Explanatory Notes. I accept Explanatory Notes to a statute are not necessarily an accurate or a reliable guide to statutory interpretation. But where there is little else I think they may be consulted. The Explanatory Note to s.71 EqA, gives this example:

> 'An employer tells a female employee "I would pay you more if you were a man" … In the absence of any male comparator the woman cannot bring a claim for breach of an equality clause but she can bring a claim of direct sex discrimination …'

This seems to me to illustrate the territory covered by s.71 EqA. Therefore the section is not an exception to s.70 EqA although it does identify circumstances where a sex discrimination claim can arise out of a term of the contract relating to pay. To my mind far from providing a general exception this reinforces the division made by s.70 EqA between a remedy under the equal pay provisions and sex discrimination. It only applies where s.70 EqA does not and it allows for a sex discrimination claim limited to direct discrimination and based on the 'treatment of the person.'

Discrimination in Access to Promotion, Employment-Related Benefits, etc

Section 39(2)(b) EqA applies to discrimination in access (or the refusal of access) to 'opportunities for promotion, transfer or training, or … any other benefits, facilities or services', Schedule 9 para 19 providing that the 'benefits, facilities or services' to which the section applies do not include those which the employer provides to the public or a section of the public unless the provision to staff is materially different, or is regulated by the contract of employment, or is concerned with training.

In *LB Southwark v Afolabi* [2003] EWCA Civ 15, [2003] ICR 800 the CA upheld tribunal findings that the claimant had been discriminated against contrary to a predecessor provision of s39(2)(b) when he was appointed on a lower grade than that of the post in respect of which he applied, and when he was treated less favourably than white colleagues in a regrading exercise. Other examples of the application of the predecessor provisions include *Greenwood v British Airways* [1999] IRLR 600, in which a senior cargo assistant who had had considerable periods of sick leave associated with a psychiatric problem challenged a refusal to promote him based in part on his sickness record and *O'Donoghue v Redcar & Cleveland BC* [2001] EWCA Civ 701, [2001] IRLR 615, in which a woman whose application for a newly created post in her department was rejected challenged a decision which had been based in part on her 'strong feminist views which she had freely expressed over a period of years.' In *Essop v Home Office* [2017] UKSC 27, [2017] ICR 640, heard by the SC with *Naeem v SSJ* and also discussed in Chapter 2, s39(2)(b) EqA was relied upon by civil servants who challenged the operation of a threshold test for promotion which disadvantaged older and BAME workers.

Section s39(2)(b) EqA also applies in relation to the provision of non-contractual benefits such as discretionary loyalty bonuses (*GUS Home Shopping Ltd v Green*), mortgage subsidy schemes (*Calder v James Finlay Corporation Ltd*), and references (*Cornelius v University College of Swansea*).[107] Discrimination by employers in relation to pensions, health or other forms of insurance, etc would fall within ss39(1)(b) and 39(2)(a) and/or (b), or under s66 EqA, where the benefit was contractual and the discrimination was on grounds of sex. Discrimination by trustees of pension schemes is regulated by ss61 and 67 EqA, discussed in Chapter 6.

Dismissal

Section 39(7) EqA provides that s39(2)(c) EqA applies to the expiry of a fixed-term contract and to constructive dismissal, other than (in the former case) where the employment is renewed on the same terms immediately after termination.[108] The question arose in *BMC Software Ltd v Shaikh*, discussed above, whether the claimant could rely on breaches of her right to equal pay to found a constructive dismissal claim under the EqA. The tribunal had allowed the constructive dismissal claim under both the EqA and the ERA 1996, ruling that 'the equality clause lies at the heart of the relationship of trust and confidence between employer and employee' and is 'fundamental to the relationship' such that 'breach of it is objectively likely to destroy or seriously damage the relationship. Error or misunderstanding by the employer do not amount to proper cause for the breach'. The question for the EAT was whether the claim was blocked by ss70 and/or

[107] Respectively, [2001] IRLR 75, [1989] IRLR 55 and [1988] ICR 735.
[108] The same is true in relation to termination of partnerships and office holdings by reason of ss44–45, 49–51 EqA.

71 EqA (see pp 210–211 above). Having set out his understanding of the relationship between s39 and the equal pay provisions of the EqA, HHJ Hand concluded at §80 that the Tribunal had been 'wrong in law to reach the conclusion that the "constructive dismissal" gave rise to a breach of s.39(2)(c) EqA'.

Post-Termination Discrimination

Post-termination discrimination is now covered by s108 EqA which regulates discrimination which (a) 'arises out of and is closely connected to a relationship which used to exist between' the parties, and which (b) 'would, if it occurred during the relationship, contravene this Act'. In *Jessemey v Rowstock Ltd* [2014] EWCA Civ 185, [2014] ICR 550 the CA confirmed that this section applied to victimisation as well as discrimination by reason of the interpretive obligations imposed on the domestic courts by EU law, this despite the fact that s108(7) EqA appeared to exclude it.[109]

Examples of the application of the post-employment provisions are provided in the Explanatory Notes to the EqA (§354):

- A school or employer refuses to give a reference to an ex-pupil or ex-employee because of his or her religion or belief. This would be direct discrimination …
- A disabled former employee's benefits include life-time use of the company's in-house gym facilities. The employer or owner of the premises must make reasonable adjustments to enable the former employee to continue using the facilities even after she has retired.[110]

***Ford Motor Co Ltd v Elliott* [2015] UKEAT 0327_14_2409, [2016] ICR 711**

The EAT rejected a s108 claim, brought by retired pensioner members of Ford's pension scheme when Ford made compensatory lump sum payments to current employees in connection with changes made to the indexing of staff pensions, but did not make such payments to retired members. The purpose of the payments was to avoid threatened industrial action.

The claimants had complained that the differential treatment amounted to discrimination on grounds of age, and relied on s108 to bring their claim. This succeeded before a tribunal, which accepted that there was a sufficiently close nexus and connection between the claimants' relationship with Ford as former employees and as current pensioners, but Ford successfully appealed. The EAT ruled that the relevant question which the tribunal had been obliged to address, and which it had not, was (a) whether the alleged discrimination arose out of and was closely connected to the employment relationship which had previously existed between the claimants and Ford, and (b) whether the alleged discrimination would have contravened the EqA. The EAT ruled that s108(b) required the Tribunal to determine whether the claimants and their comparators were in the same material circumstances under s23 EqA (see Chapter 2), and that the failure to do this meant that the question of jurisdiction had to be revisited.

[109] The CA ruled that the apparent exclusion of a victimisation claim by s108(7) EqA was a drafting error. In *Butterworth v Police and Crime Commissioner's Office for Greater Manchester* [2016] IRLR 280 the EAT rejected the argument that s108 could impose liability on a third party.

[110] https://www.legislation.gov.uk/ukpga/2010/15/notes.

Detriment

Turning to the 'any other detriment' element of s39(2)(c) EqA, this serves as a 'catch-all' category capable of covering most types of discrimination which might arise during employment and not otherwise covered by s39. The predecessor provisions of s39 EqA gave rise to a considerable number of appellate decisions. The difficulty associated with it is that, whereas discrimination in respect of the other matters covered by s39 EqA is actionable per se, the claimant who alleges discrimination under the second head of s39(2)(b) must convince the tribunal not only that less favourable treatment was accorded her, but also that the treatment was sufficiently disadvantageous to be regarded as an actionable 'detriment.'

The difficulties to which the 'detriment' requirement have given rise were indicated as early as 1977 in the CA's decision in *Peake v Automotive Products Ltd* [1978] QB 233, discussed in Chapter 2, that the employer's policy of allowing women to leave work five minutes before men was not 'discrimination' against men. This aspect of the decision was disapproved of by the same court in the subsequent decision in *MOD v Jeremiah* [1980] QB 87. But the alternative basis for the *Peake* ruling, which was upheld in the latter decision, was that the additional five minutes which the men were required to work was, if it amounted to a 'detriment' at all, *de minimis* and therefore outside the scope of the Act.

The *de minimis* approach has not subsequently been expressly applied to exclude discrimination, having been called into question by the subsequent decision of the CA in *Gill & Coote v El Vino Ltd* [1983] QB 425, also discussed in Chapter 2.[111] But a similar outcome was achieved by the categorisation of particular forms of discrimination (in the sense of differential or differently impacting treatment) as 'not detrimental' to their challengers. This approach has been particularly evident in the context of clothing and appearance rules, discussed in Chapter 6.[112]

Wider Work-Related Protection from Discrimination

Section 39 EqA regulates employment discrimination. The definition of 'employment' for the purposes of the anti-discrimination provisions has been considered above. But the broadly employment-related provisions of the EqA includes not only s39 but also those sections which deal with contract workers, officers, partners, barristers and advocates, office holders, and local authority members.[113] Contract workers will be discussed in some detail below after the other categories of worker (very broadly defined) are dealt with in brief.

[111] [1983] QB 425, in which the CA refused to apply the de minimis maxim where, in a case where women were refused service in a bar unless seated at a table, men being allowed to stand at the bar. Eveleigh LJ found it: 'very difficult to invoke the *maxim de minimis non curat lex* in a situation where that which has been denied to the plaintiff is the very thing that Parliament seeks to provide, namely facilities and services on an equal basis'. *cf*, however, the decision in *Schmidt v Austicks Bookshops* [1978] ICR 85, discussed in Ch 6.

[112] See *Staffordshire CC v Black* [1995] IRLR 234; *Clymo v Wandsworth* [1989] ICR 250. In *MOD v Jeremiah* [1980] QB 87 Brightman LJ stated at 440 that 'a detriment exists if a reasonable worker would or might take the view that the [treatment] was in all the circumstances to his detriment'. In *Shamoon v CC RUC* [2003] UKHL 11, [2003] ICR 337 the HL ruled that there could be a 'detriment' in the employment context where a reasonable worker would or might take the view that he had thereby been disadvantaged in the circumstances in which he had thereafter to work and that, although an unjustified sense of grievance could not amount to a 'detriment, it was not necessary to demonstrate any physical or economic consequence.' And in *Jiad v Byford* [2003] IRLR 232 the CA ruled that a tribunal had erred in striking out a race discrimination claim on the basis that the claimant had suffered no actionable detriment where he experienced psychological stress and humiliation as result of an incident with the director of BBC World Service.

[113] Section 41–59 EqA. Schedule 6 para 4 provides that bishops are not the holders of public offices for these purposes.

'Workers'

The first thing to note is that contract workers, police, barristers and advocates, office holders and local authority members are protected by the EqA even though they do not fit within the broad definition of 'employment' discussed at p 199ff above. Police officers, for example, are office holders rather than employees, but s42 EqA provides that they are to be treated, for the purpose of protection under the Act, as if they were employed.[114] Partners, who would often fall outside the definition of employment (though see the discussion of *Bates van Winkelhof v Clyde & Co LLP* above) are protected by ss44 and 45 EqA as if they were employees. The same is true of barristers and (in Scotland) advocates, who are protected by ss47 and 48 EqA from discrimination, harassment and victimisation in connection with pupillage (devilling in Scotland), tenancy (membership of a stable) and access to work, whether the discrimination is perpetrated by other barristers, clerks or instructing solicitors. Holders (and prospective holders) of personal and public offices are protected by ss49–51 EqA as if they were employed, s51 expressly regulating discrimination by persons with power to make recommendations or give approval to appointments to public offices. Holders of public office include judges, a significant number of whom have recently brought discrimination challenges to changes in judicial pension arrangements.[115] And s58 EqA protects elected members of local authorities from discrimination by the authority as if they were employees of the authority.

Contract Workers

Section 41(1) and (3) EqA provide that a 'principal'[116] must not discriminate against or victimise a contract worker 'as to the terms on which the principal allows the worker to do the work; by not allowing the worker to do, or to continue to do, the work; in the way the principal affords the worker access, or by not affording the worker access, to opportunities for receiving a benefit, facility or service'; or 'by subjecting the worker to any other detriment'. Section 41(2) prohibits the harassment of contract workers by principals while s41(4) imposes a duty to make reasonable adjustments on the principal as well as the employer of a disabled contract worker. In *Harrods Ltd v Remmick* [1997] IRLR 583 the CA applied a predecessor provision of s41 EqA to protect staff employed by concessionaires within Harrods from discrimination by Harrods (which required that employees of concessionaires be approved by Harrods and which had withdrawn approval from the claimants on racial grounds).

***Allonby v Accrington & Rossendale College* [2001] EWCA Civ 529, [2001] ICR 1189**

In this case, also considered above, the CA considered whether a woman retained as a contract worker by the college via an agency could rely on a predecessor provision of s41 EqA to challenge discrimination in terms and conditions between her and a man who was directly employed by the college. The tribunal rejected the claim on the basis that

[114] Other than for equal pay purposes where s79(8) provides that police officers are to be treated as holders of personal offices.

[115] See for example *Lord Chancellor v McCloud* [2018] EWCA Civ 2844, [2019] ICR 1489 discussed at pp 699–701 below.

[116] Defined by s41(5) EqA as 'a person who makes work available for an individual who is (a) employed by another person, and (b) supplied by that other person in furtherance of a contract to which the principal is a party (whether or not that other person is a party to it) while a contract worker is defined by s41(7) as 'an individual supplied to a principal in furtherance of a contract such as is mentioned in subsection (5)(b)'.

the provision only regulated discrimination *between* male and female contract workers. The EAT dismissed her appeal but the CA, after referring some questions to the CJEU, allowed Allonby's appeal and remitted to the employment tribunal the question whether she had been discriminated against contrary to the predecessor provision of s41. Sedley LJ, who delivered the judgment of the Court, stated that there was 'no reason' why the provision should be limited to allowing claims only between contract workers, pointing out that it would be 'remarkable if it … permitted an employer, by bringing in black or female workers on subcontract to work alongside a predominantly white or male employed workforce, to give them inferior conditions so long as they were all treated equally badly or (if differentially treated) were all of the same race or sex and so unable to complain'.

In *MHC Consulting Services v Tansell* [2000] ICR 798 the CA ruled that a predecessor provision of s41 applied to protect a worker who provided services via a personal services company which contracted with an agency which then contracted with the principal. In reaching this conclusion the Court (*per* Mummery LJ) reiterated the 'the importance of giving the wide ranging provisions of the discrimination legislation a generous interpretation'.[117] As is evident from the discussion of *Kemeh v MOD* [2014] EWCA Civ 91, [2014] ICR 625 below, however, the increasing fragmentation of the workforce may leave workers without a remedy when they are subject to harassment or discrimination by people with whom they work, but who are not employed by the same employer.

Trade Unions, etc

Discrimination by trade unions, employers' and trade organisations, and persons concerned with vocational training and guidance is prohibited by ss55 and 57 EqA. Section 55 provides that employment service providers, defined to include those who provide or arrange the provision of vocational training or guidance, must not discriminate in relation to those matters. Section 57 EqA then provides that trade organisations, which are defined to include trade unions, employers' organisations and other organisations 'whose members carry on a particular trade or profession for the purposes of which the organisation exists' must not discriminate or victimise individuals in relation to access to or the terms of membership; access to benefits, facilities or services; deprivation of membership or subjection to any other detriment, and must not harass members or applicants for membership.

The application of the predecessor provisions of s57 EqA has been considered in a number of cases, among them *FTATU v Modgill* [1980] IRLR 142 and *Fire Brigades Union v Fraser* [1998] IRLR 697.[118] The *Modgill* case concerned allegations that the union had discriminated against the claimants by refusing them their own shop steward and failing – on racial grounds – to support their struggles for improved wages, a better pay structure, and the same working hours as others within the same plant. The EAT overturned a tribunal decision in favour of the claimants on the basis that race discrimination had not been proven. But the case gives some indication of the potential breadth of s57 EqA. The same is true of the *Fraser* case in which a man accused of sexual harassment sued his union because it refused him representation in the ensuing disciplinary proceedings. The Court of Session overturned a tribunal decision in his favour because no discrimination was proven – the

[117] Citing, inter alia, *Jones v Tower Boot Co Ltd* [1997] ICR 254.
[118] See also the discussion of *Unite the Union v Nailard* [2018] EWCA Civ 1203, [2019] ICR 28 below.

union had chosen not to represent him because he was accused of harassment and they were representing the accuser, not because he was a man.[119]

More recently, in *RMT v Lloyd* [2019] IRLR 897, the EAT upheld a tribunal decision that the union had discriminated contrary to s57(2) EqA against the claimant, who had been barred from participating in an election to the union's National Executive Committee (NEC) because he would have reached 65 before completing the three-year term; the union's rules provided that members seeking nomination in an election must be able to complete the full period of office prior to reaching the normal retirement age of 65 years. The union accepted that it had (subject to justification) discriminated against the claimant by subjecting him to detriment within the meaning of s57(2)(d) EqA, though it argued unsuccessfully that the discrimination was justified.[120]

Qualifications Bodies

Section 53 EqA prohibits discrimination, victimisation or harassment by a 'qualifying body', defined as 'an authority or body which can confer … an authorisation, qualification, recognition, registration, enrolment, approval or certification which is needed for, or facilitates engagement in, a particular trade or profession', but excluding bodies whose activities are covered by the education-related provisions of the EqA.[121] The discrimination and victimisation which is prohibited relates to 'the arrangements A makes for deciding upon whom to confer a relevant qualification'; 'the terms on which it is prepared to confer a relevant qualification', by failing to confer, or withdrawing, a relevant qualification, by varying the terms on which a person holds such a qualification and by subjecting a person on whom it has conferred a relevant qualification to any other detriment.

Section 53(6) EqA having imposed a duty to make reasonable adjustments on qualifications bodies, s53(7) provides that 'The application by a qualifications body of a competence standard to a disabled person is not disability discrimination unless it is discrimination by virtue of section 19'. Competence standards are further discussed in Chapter 8.

Section 53 EqA's predecessor provisions gave rise to decisions including that in *Tattari v PPP* [1998] ICR 106, in which the CA ruled that a refusal by a health insurance company to add an already qualified doctor to its list of approved plastic surgeons did not fall within the equivalent provision of the RRA. Beldam LJ, for the Court, ruled that the provision did 'not refer to a body which is not authorised to or empowered to confer [a] qualification or permission but which stipulates that for the purpose of its commercial agreements a particular qualification is required'. A similar decision was reached in *Kelly & Loughran v Northern Ireland Housing Executive* [1999] AC 428 in which the HL accepted that Northern Ireland's Housing Executive did not act as a qualifying body in appointing to its panel of solicitors.

In *Patterson v Legal Services Commission*, by contrast [2004] ICR 312, the CA accepted that the award of a franchise by the Legal Services Commission fell within the predecessor provision of s53 EqA, the award of such a franchise amounting to the

[119] In *GMC v Cox* (2002) 70 BMLR 31 the EAT ruled that the General Medical Council was not a trade organisation for the purposes of s57's predecessor provision in the DDA, its primary function being the protection of the public rather than of the interests of doctors. As we shall see below, however, the GMC is covered by s53 EqA (qualifications bodies)

[120] Direct age discrimination, uniquely, being capable of justification under the EqA; see further Ch 11.

[121] Section 212 EqA provides that 'profession' includes 'vocation or occupation'.

conferment of an 'authorisation' to perform publicly funded legal work and 'facilitat[ing]' engagement in the solicitors' profession by making it easier or less difficult to carry on the profession. But in *Triesman v Ali* [2002] EWCA Civ 93, [2002] ICR 1062 the CA took a different approach, ruling that selection as a party candidate for local government elections had 'nothing to do with employment' and that 'the obvious application of … [the provision] is to cases where a body has among its functions that of granting some qualification to, or authorising, a person who has satisfied appropriate standards of competence, to practise a profession, calling or trade … being a local government councillor is … certainly not being engaged in a profession and, while being a councillor occupies some of the time of the councillor who is entitled to receive allowances, it is not an activity from which the councillor will earn his living or receive a salary, and we question whether it is within the intendment of the section'. According to Peter Gibson LJ, for the Court, the Labour Party was 'not the type of qualifying body to which the section is intended to apply, its activities being for its own political purposes … In the present case, we cannot accept that there is any conferment of approval by the Labour Party when a member who has nominated himself or been nominated as a local government candidate has his name go forward to the pool available for selection. No status in any meaningful sense is thereby conferred'.

The decision of the CA in *Triesmann* was approved in *Ahsan v Watt*, in which the HL ruled that, in selecting candidates for local elections, the Labour Party was not a body which conferred an authorisation or qualification needed for engagement in a profession or trade.

***Ahsan v Watt* [2007] UKHL 51, [2008] 1 AC 696**

Lord Hoffmann (with whom the other Law Lords agreed):

> The notion of an 'authorisation or qualification' suggests some kind of objective standard which the qualifying body applies, an even-handed, not to say 'transparent', test which people may pass or fail. The qualifying body vouches to the public for the qualifications of the candidate and the public rely upon the qualification in offering him employment or professional engagements … that is far removed from the basis upon which a political party chooses its candidates. The main criterion is likely to be the popularity of the candidate with the voters, which is unlikely to be based on the most objective criteria. That will certainly be true of selection by vote of the branch and I doubt whether greater objectivity can be expected of a selection committee. The members or selection panel want to choose the candidate who, for whatever reason, seems to them most likely to win or at least put up a respectable showing in the election.

Discrimination by political parties will be returned to at p 230 below. In *Reverend Canon Pemberton v Right Reverend Inwood*, also discussed in Chapter 10, the CA ruled that the appellant, a bishop, was a qualifications body under s53 EqA in relation to the licensing of priests. The claimant, a Church of England priest, married his same-sex partner. As a result, the bishop revoked his Permission to Officiate (PTO) at services, with the effect that he could not conduct services within the diocese. The bishop also refused to grant the claimant an Extra Parochial Ministry Licence (EPM) which would have permitted him to be appointed chaplaincy and bereavement manager in a faith centre at a hospital. The CA accepted that EPML was a 'relevant qualification' though PTO was not, and that the bishop had acted as a qualifications body in refusing EPML, though not in revoking the PTO.

It went on to find that the bishop had been entitled to discriminate against the claimant in pursuit of a GOR (see further Chapter 10):

***Reverend Canon Pemberton v Right Reverend Inwood* [2018] EWCA Civ 564, [2018] ICR 1291, [2018] IRLR 542**

Asplin LJ with whom Underhill and Gloster LJJ agreed:

27. Mr Jones QC on behalf of the Canon submits that both the PTO and the EPML are 'relevant qualifications' and that accordingly, the Bishop is a 'qualifications body'. He drew attention to the breadth of s 54(3) and in particular, to the fact that a 'relevant qualification' may be one which 'facilitates engagement' in a vocation.

28. It is accepted that an EPML would have allowed the Canon to perform 'such offices and services' as were specified in the licence at the hospitals specified and that the offer of work as a Chaplaincy and Bereavement Manager was conditional upon the Canon holding such a licence …

40. … PTO does not in itself lead to remuneration and that it is accepted for the purposes of this appeal that remuneration is necessary for the activity to amount to a trade, profession or vocation. I make no comment upon whether this assumption is correct …

41. Further, as Her Honour Judge Eady QC found on the basis of the findings of fact made by the ET, the PTO and the EPML were not interdependent and did not facilitate each other …

43. I can also find no error of law in the EAT's treatment of the issue of whether the EPML is a 'relevant qualification.' It is clear that the EPML was a condition of the employment on offer. It was needed for, or, at the very least, would have facilitated the appointment and it is common ground that the position of Chaplaincy and Bereavement Manager amounted to a 'vocation' for the purposes of s 212 of the 2010 Act. I am unable to accept Mr Linden's submission [for the Bishop] that the EPML was equivalent to a character reference and could not amount to a 'relevant qualification'. I agree with Mr Jones [for the claimant] that it is quite clear from the job description that the person taking up the post was required to hold the appropriate licence and be 'accredited' by his or her faith body. It was for that reason that they were to be employed …

44. I come to this conclusion despite the fact that the decision to grant an EPML is one for the individual bishop concerned based upon that individual's assessment of the particular applicant. That is an inevitable consequence of the structure of the Church of England and the authority of individual bishops. It is not suggested that a decision of this kind is made upon a whim. In fact, we were referred to the undisputed evidence of the Bishop in relation to the grant of licences to priests from different diocese. It entails obtaining a 'Clergy Current Status Letter' from the 'sending bishop' which contains specific paragraphs about prescribed matters. Those matters are also the subject of detailed Guidance Notes. It seems to me, therefore, that the decision in relation to the grant of a licence is subject to objective criteria even if different bishops may reach different conclusions.

45. The circumstances are not the same as those of the would-be political candidates in the *Triesmann* and *Ahsan* cases. Their selection would not have denoted any particular status at all and it is not clear that any objective criteria would be applied in the selection process. By contrast, the EPML amounts to an authorisation and a vouching to the public that the person in question is qualified and has a particular status within the Church of England which can be relied upon and which was arrived at by the application of particular criteria … the Bishop on behalf of the Church of England was not simply applying a standard for his and its own purposes. Granting an EPML signifies to the NHS Trust in this case and through the Trust to the public that the individual meets a particular standard and has an appropriate status. The circumstances are analogous with those in the *Patterson v Legal Services Commission* case see p 217 above. In granting an EPML a bishop is vouching that a priest has the requisite status within the Church of England for the purpose of the outward facing role which the employment in question entails.

Many of the cases brought under the predecessor provisions of s53 related to proceedings of the General Medical Council which licenses doctors in the UK.[122] In *Rovenska v GMC* [1998] ICR 85, for example, a Czechoslovakian-qualified doctor challenged the GMC's language-related qualifying criteria for full registration in the UK. Such claims were frequently complicated by the predecessor provision of s120(7) EqA which provides that employment tribunals do not have jurisdiction in respect of s53 EqA claims 'in so far as the act complained of may, by virtue of an enactment, be subject to an appeal or proceedings in the nature of an appeal'.

The impact of one of the predecessor provisions of s120(7) EqA was felt in *Khan v GMC* [1993] ICR 627 in which the claimant, who had twice been refused full registration as an overseas qualified practitioner, complained that the GMC's requirements for such registration were indirectly discriminatory. His application, pursuant to the relevant legislation, for review of the Council's decision had been unsuccessful. The CA ruled that the review was 'in the nature of an appeal' despite the fact that the review board had no power to reverse the decision of the Council, its role being restricted to providing an opinion to the President of the Council.[123] More recently, the SC ruled in *Michalak v General Medical Council* [2017] UKSC 71, [2018] ICR 49 that the availability of judicial review against a decision of a GMC fitness to practice panel did not satisfy s120(7) EqA. The Court ruled that judicial review was not in the nature of an appeal, and did not arise 'by virtue of' any statutory source; its origins lay in the common law. The Court also ruled, while employment tribunals should be robust in striking out proceedings commenced in place of those for which specific statutory provision had been made for appeals, the rationale for this would only apply where the alternative route of appeal or review was capable of providing an equivalent means of redress.

Employment Service Providers

Section 55 EqA provides that providers of employment services may not discriminate in the arrangements they make for selecting persons to whom to offer or provide their services, the terms on which they offer or provide those services or by not providing or offering to provide their services, by terminating their provision of services or by subjecting service users to any other detriment. Similar provision is made by s55(3)–(4) EqA as regards harassment and victimisation, and s55(6) provides that a duty of reasonable adjustment applies to service providers 'except in relation to the provision of a vocational service'. Section 56 then defines 'employment services' to include, inter alia, the provision of, or making of arrangements for the provision of, vocational training (including work experience) and guidance;[124] the provision of services for finding employment for persons or for supplying employers with persons to do work; and the provision of careers services and assessments relating to the conferment of relevant qualifications by qualifications bodies[125]). *Walker v Wallem Ship Management Ltd* [2020] ICR 1103, discussed at pp 204–206 above, was brought under s55, Wallem being a company which recruited on behalf of ultimate employers, rather than an employer itself.

[122] See also *Trivedi v GMC* App No EAT/544/96 (unreported, 1 July 1996); *Jeffrey-Shaw v Shropshire County Premier Football League & Shropshire County Football Association* App No EAT/0320/04/TM, 16 September 2004; and, on a related issue, *Chaudhary v BMA* [2003] ICR 1510.

[123] *cf Zaidi v FIMBRA* [1995] ICR 876.

[124] Except (s56(3)–(5) EqA) insofar as it is covered elsewhere in the EqA, including in Part 6 (education).

[125] Except where the assessment is carried out by the qualifications body itself.

The interplay between the work and educational provisions of the EqA (Parts 5 and 6) can give rise to significant difficulties, as illustrated in the following case.

***Blackwood v Birmingham & Solihull Mental Health NHS Trust* [2016] EWCA Civ 607, [2016] ICR 903, [2016] IRLR 878**

The claimant, a nursing student at Birmingham City University, was required to undertake work placements as part of her course. The university arranged a clinical placement for her at a unit operated by the NHS Trust which, when she explained that she would have difficulty working nightshifts and weekends because of her childcare responsibilities, withdrew the placement. She issued proceedings in the employment tribunal against the Trust, which had her claim struck out for lack of jurisdiction. The NHS Trust argued, and tribunal and the EAT accepted, that the claimant was required to proceed in the county court under Part 6 EqA because her work placement had been arranged by her university. Although s56 defines 'employment services' to include 'the provision of vocational training', s56(5) states that this 'does not apply in relation to training or guidance for students of an institution to which section 91 applies in so far as it is training or guidance to which the governing body of the institution has power to afford access'. The claimant appealed to the CA, arguing that if s56(5) EqA disapplied s55, students who were discriminated against on university-arranged work placements would have no effective remedy unless the discriminator was acting as the agent of the university. She further argued that this would place the UK in breach of the Equal Treatment Directive 2006/54. The CA allowed her appeal:

Underhill LJ (with whom Lewison and Patten LJJ agreed):

9. It was common ground before us that the intended consequence of disapplying s.56 is also to disapply the substantive provisions of s.55. Although the drafting is clumsy, I accept that that must be the correct reading.

10. The circumstances which trigger the operation of subsections (3)–(5) are all circumstances in which a remedy against discrimination is afforded by other provisions of the Act. In the case of subsection (3) the only 'other provisions' of Part 5 which apply to 'training' (none refer to 'guidance') are those proscribing discrimination by the various people or institutions who provide work, such as employers (s.39), partnerships (s.44) or persons making appointments to public offices (s.50) … In the case of subsections (4) and (5) the two sections to which they refer, ss.85 and 91, are likewise sections which proscribe discrimination by the institutions in question – that is, schools and universities. That being so, it seems reasonably evident that the purpose of all three subsections is to prevent overlap – that is, to prevent claims in relation to the same 'training or guidance' being brought under more than one provision. The effect of subsections (4) and (5) is that any claims arising out of discrimination in relation to training and guidance to which access is afforded by schools or universities would have to be brought under a different Part of the Act, which in turn means that they would have to be brought in the county court rather than the employment tribunal. However, that is not so in the case of subsection (3), which is designed to prevent overlap with other provisions in the same Part, in respect of which the employment tribunal is equally the allocated forum. Accordingly it does not appear that the draftsman was concerned, or in any event concerned only, with forum allocation …

24. … although the [SDA], like the 2010 Act, included an 'educational exclusion' in the provisions relating to vocational training, it was differently expressed. The liability of the provider under s.14 was excluded only where and to the extent that the discrimination in question

constituted discrimination which was rendered unlawful under the educational provisions: to spell it out, the exclusion depended on whether the acts complained of under s.14(1) could have given rise to a valid claim under s.22. The criterion was not, as under the 2010 Act, expressed as being whether the university had 'power to afford access' to the training in question. The most obvious example of a case where the same acts would be caught by both s.14(1) (subject to subsection (2)) and s.22 would be where the university arranged for the provision of vocational training, though there might also be cases where it provided training itself.

25. The 2010 Act represents in the relevant respects the UK's implementation of its obligations under EU anti-discrimination legislation …

26. I take … [Directive 2006/54] first, since the appeal before us is concerned with sex discrimination … Article 14.1 … reads:

> 'There shall be no direct or indirect discrimination on grounds of sex in the public or private sectors, including public bodies, in relation to:
>
> (a) conditions for access to employment, to self-employment or to occupation, including selection criteria and recruitment conditions, whatever the branch of activity and at all levels of the professional hierarchy, including promotion;
>
> (b) access to all types and to all levels of vocational guidance, vocational training, advanced vocational training and retraining, including practical work experience …'

43. … It is no doubt correct that students have a remedy against their university under s.91 if it discriminates against them by not affording them access to work placements, or in the way in which it does so: see subsection (2). But it seems to me clear that the concept of 'affording access' is concerned only with what the university itself does or does not do in enabling the student to enjoy the benefit in question – that is, in the present context, in making and, so far as necessary, maintaining the arrangements under which the student receives vocational training from the third party. The phrase does not in its natural meaning extend to responsibility for acts done by the work placement provider in the course of the placement. To take Cox J's example of the female trainee plumber on a work placement who is consistently assigned the least attractive tasks, that has nothing to do with the way that her college affords her access to training; likewise where a student nurse is subjected to sexual or racial harassment by a manager. Those are the acts of the work provider, and there is no basis – subject to any indirect liability that might be available on the facts of a particular case – on which they can be caught by the terms of s.91. The relevant provision is plainly that which proscribes discrimination by providers, ie s.55; but if s.56(5) has the meaning found by the EAT a student can have no remedy under that section ….

Having decided that, on ordinary principles of construction, it was not possible to interpret s56 to avoid the lacuna in protection identified in the judgment the Court decided that the obligation imposed on domestic courts by the decision of the CJEU in Marleasing (see fn 95 above) required the provision to be re-written as follows:

> This section does not apply to discrimination in relation to training or guidance for students of an institution to which section 91 applies to the extent that the student is entitled under that section to make a claim as regards that discrimination.

This approach would avoid overlap between ss55 and 91 EqA and reproduced the position as it had been under the SDA. Underhill LJ concluded by summarising the effect of the Court's decision in the following terms:

> 61. …. The starting point in any case is to identify the nature of the student's complaint – that is, whether it is about discriminatory access to a work placement or about discrimination occurring during the placement.

(1) If the claim is about access – either that the university has failed to provide a placement at all or that it has done so in a discriminatory way – it can only be brought under s.91, and thus in the county court. The primary claim will inevitably be against the university, because it is the university that has the responsibility for the provision of access, and it is hard therefore to see any role for ss.109 and 110; but if the provider has induced or aided that contravention it will be secondarily liable under s.111 or 112 and the student can proceed against it (in the county court) as well as, or instead of, the university.

(2) If the claim is about discrimination by the provider in the course of the work placement, the provider will typically discrimination done the act complained of as a principal and will thus be primarily liable for that discrimination under s.55, with the forum for any proceedings being the employment tribunal. There may be untypical cases where the act was done by the provider as the agent of the university. In those cases both the university and the provider will be liable, by virtue of ss.109(2) and 110(1) respectively, but the liability will still arise under s.55, so that the ET will still be the correct forum whether the claimant chooses to proceed against only one of them or against both. The university may of course also in a particular case be liable, depending on the facts, under ss.111 or 112 as having induced or assisted the discrimination. Any such claim will, again, have to be brought in

62. I recognise that on this analysis there may occasionally be cases in which a student wishes to complain both about discrimination in his or her access to a work placement and about discrimination in the course of that placement and that the need to pursue those claims in different forums will involve expense and inconvenience. That is regrettable, but it could only be avoided by denying students the right to bring claims arising out of work placement discrimination at all or by rewriting the Act so as to allow such claims to be brought under Part 6. For the reasons given above neither course is in my view acceptable.

Exceptions to the Prohibitions on Employment-Related Discrimination

General exceptions to the prohibitions on discrimination are considered above at pp 186–193. Others are considered in some detail in the chapters dealing with the various heads of discrimination. All of the defences apply not only in relation to 'employment' itself but also to discrimination by principals against contract workers, to discrimination by partnerships and employment service providers, and to discrimination against office holders, etc. Insofar as it is of general application, the GOR defence is as follows.

Schedule 9, para 1 EqA

(1) A person (A) does not contravene a provision mentioned in sub-paragraph (2) by applying in relation to work a requirement to have a particular protected characteristic, if A shows that, having regard to the nature or context of the work—

(a) it is an occupational requirement,

(b) the application of the requirement is a proportionate means of achieving a legitimate aim, and

(c) the person to whom A applies the requirement does not meet it (or A has reasonable grounds for not being satisfied that the person meets it).

Paragraph 1(2) lists the provisions which regulate discrimination against workers, contract workers, partners and holders of personal or private offices. Specific provision is made as regards the application of para 1 where the protected characteristic is gender reassignment, marriage or civil partnership and sex (see Chapter 6) and provision is made in relation to employment for the purposes of organised religion or similar (paras 2 and 3). This is discussed in Chapter 9. Paragraph 4, further discussed in Chapter 6, provides an exemption for discrimination on grounds of sex and gender reassignment in relation to service in the armed forces and provides that the prohibitions on age and disability discrimination do not apply to such service. Paragraph 5 provides that the same exceptions as are provided by paras 1–4 in relation to work apply to those providing employment services in connection with the offer of such work.

EHRC, 'Employment', Statutory Code of Practice[126]

13.8 Examples of how the occupational requirement exception may be used include some jobs which require someone of a particular sex for reasons of privacy and decency or where personal services are being provided. For example, a unisex gym could rely on an occupational requirement to employ a changing room attendant of the same sex as the users of that room. Similarly, a women's refuge which lawfully provides services to women only can apply a requirement for all members of its staff to be women.

13.9 Example: A local council decides to set up a health project which would encourage older people from the Somali community to make more use of health services. The council wants to recruit a person of Somali origin for the post because it involves visiting elderly people in their homes and it is necessary for the post-holder to have a good knowledge of the culture and language of the potential clients. The council does not have a Somali worker already in post who could take on the new duties. They could rely on the occupational requirement exception to recruit a health worker of Somali origin.[127]

Part 6: Education

Material Scope of Part 6

Part 6 of the EqA regulates discrimination in education at all levels. Insofar as it applies to disability discrimination in schools and further education institutions (though not higher education institutions) the EqA forms an interlocking system with the Special Educational Needs regime, which is outside the scope of this book. The core relevant provisions of the EqA are ss85 and 91 which apply, respectively, to schools and to higher education and further education institutions (HE&FEIs). They are found in chapters 1 and 2 of Part 6, neither of which applies to the protected characteristics of marriage and civil partnership. Chapter 1 (schools) also does not apply to the protected characteristic of age.

Section 85 EqA: Pupils, admission and treatment, etc

(1) The responsible body of a school to which this section applies must not discriminate against a person—

(a) in the arrangements it makes for deciding who is offered admission as a pupil;
(b) as to the terms on which it offers to admit the person as a pupil;
(c) by not admitting the person as a pupil.

(2) **The responsible body of such a school must not discriminate against a pupil—**

(a) in the way it provides education for the pupil;
(b) in the way it affords the pupil access to a benefit, facility or service;
(c) by not providing education for the pupil;

[126] n 100 above.
[127] The EqA also permits positive action, discussed in Ch 3, which is better characterised as an aspect of, rather than an exception to, the prohibitions on discrimination.

(d) by not affording the pupil access to a benefit, facility or service;
(e) by excluding the pupil from the school;
(f) by subjecting the pupil to any other detriment.

Section 85 EqA applies to all schools whether state or independent. Section 85(3) provides that schools must not harass pupils and applicants to the school, and s85(4)–(5) make materially identical provision with respect to victimisation as is made by s85(1)–(2) EqA in respect of discrimination.[128] Section 85(6) EqA imposes a duty of reasonable adjustment on school's 'responsible bodies'.[129] Section 85(10) provides that s85(3)'s prohibition on harassment does not apply in relation to gender reassignment, religion or belief, or sexual orientation. Section 86 EqA provides that pupils may not be subject to victimisation because of the protected acts of their parents or siblings.[130]

Section 91 is materially similar to s85 EqA but applies to the responsible bodies of HEIs and FEIs and to students, as distinct from pupils. One material difference is the inclusion of s91(3) EqA which provides as follows:

Section 91(3) EqA: Students: admission and treatment, etc

(3) The responsible body of such an institution must not discriminate against a disabled person—

(a) in the arrangements it makes for deciding upon whom to confer a qualification;
(b) as to the terms on which it is prepared to confer a qualification on the person;
(c) by not conferring a qualification on the person;
(d) by withdrawing a qualification from the person or varying the terms on which the person holds it.

Section 91(3) EqA applies only to discrimination connected with disability. Section 91(5) EqA provides that the prohibition on harassment, which applies more generally, extends to disabled persons who hold or have applied for a qualification conferred by the institution,[131] and s91(8) makes materially identical provision with respect to the victimisation of disabled people as is made by 91(3) in respect of disability discrimination. A further difference between s81 and s91 EqA is that the latter's prohibition on harassment applies in relation to gender reassignment, religion or belief and sexual orientation as well as to the other protected characteristics.

A number of important discrimination cases have arisen in the education context, among them the decision of the HL in *Birmingham v EOC* and in *Mandla v Lee* (discussed respectively in Chapters 2 and 7);[132] those of the SC in *R (E) v JFS*, *R (Begum) v Denbigh High School* (discussed in Chapters 7 and 9) and *R (Tigere) v SS Business, Innovation and Skills*;[133] and those of the CA in *HM Chief Inspector of Education, Children's Services and*

[128] Harassment and victimisation are discussed in Ch 2.

[129] See s81(9) EqA for the definition of responsible bodies. See also s88 and Schedule 10, which require that local authorities and schools adopt accessibility strategies and plans to increase access to the curriculum and education generally to disabled students.

[130] And note that the protection applies even where the allegation etc of the parent or sibling was not made in good faith as long as the child has acted in good faith.

[131] This is not limited to disability-related harassment.

[132] [1989] AC 1155 and [1983] 2 AC 548 respectively.

[133] [2009] UKSC 15, [2010] 2 AC 728; [2006] UKHL 15, [2007] 1 AC 100; and [2015] UKSC 57, [2015] 1 WLR 3820 respectively.

Skills v Al-Hijrah School (discussed in Chapter 2).[134] While some of these have concerned the application of Article 14 ECHR[135] or other statutory provisions,[136] many have been decided under ss85 or 91 or their predecessor provisions.

In *Mandla v Lee*, for example, the HL upheld a ruling that the refusal of admission of a Sikh pupil to a school because his turban breached the school's uniform policy breached the predecessor provision of s85(1)(b) EqA. In the *JFS* case the SC made a similar ruling in relation to the school's imposition of admission criteria which restricted admission to children who were recognised as Jewish through maternal descent or Orthodox conversion. In *Al-Hijrah* the CA ruled that Ofsted had been entitled to find that a school had discriminated contrary to s85(2) EqA by imposing rigid sex segregation between male and female pupils. In *R (Watkins-Singh) v Aberdare Girls' High School* [2008] EWHC 1865 (Admin) [2008] ELR 561 the High Court ruled that the school had breached the predecessor provision of s85 EqA by punishing the claimant for wearing a Sikh *kara* in defiance of the school's uniform policy. And in *G v St Gregory's Catholic Science College* [2011] EWHC 1452 (Admin) the High Court found that a school's prohibition on cornrows for male pupils amounted to unlawful race discrimination contrary to s85(1)(b) and 2(f) EqA. The school's policy prohibited hair below the collar (for boys), '"Skinhead' or shorn hairstyles', 'razor cuts so as to create lines or designs across the hair or eyebrow', 'outlandish' hair 'in colouring and so on', the wearing of wax, gel or extensions, and required that hair be 'cut uniformly all over without creating a crop or layered effect'.

There have also been a significant number of challenges to school exclusions, many of them alleging disability discrimination. A number of such cases have involved exclusions for behaviour which is connected with a pupil's disability, particularly where that disability is autism-related. Until recently these cases were regularly defeated by a provision in the EqA (Disability) Regulations 2010 which exclude from the definition of 'disability' 'a tendency to physical abuse'. This provision is one of a number of tendencies excluded by the 2010 Regulations including fire-setting, sexual abuse and stealing, as well as exhibitionism and voyeurism. In *X Endowed Primary School v Special Educational Needs and Disability Tribunal* [2009] EWHC 1842 (Admin), [2009] IRLR 1007, also discussed in Chapter 8, the High Court ruled that the exclusion applied to physical violence connected with a condition (such as autism) which would otherwise be protected. It was far from obvious that this had been the intention of the legislation, since its impact was that a school which had been partly responsible for a pupil's violent outbursts (because it had failed to make reasonable adjustments in relation to her disability) would be able to resist a discrimination challenge to any exclusion resulting from the outburst. In *C & C v Governing Body of a School* [2018] UKUT 269, [2019] PTSR 857, also discussed in Chapter 8, the Upper Tribunal ruled that the 'tendency to physical abuse' exclusion was contrary to the HRA insofar as it applied to children whose tendency to such abuse resulted from a condition such as autism, and that it should be disapplied.

[134] [2017] EWCA Civ 1426, [2018] 1 WLR 1471.

[135] See *Tigere*, n 130 above, in which the SC ruled that the non-availability of student loans to the claimant, who had spent most of her life in the UK but who had temporary rather than indefinite leave to remain through no fault of her own, breached Art 14 read with Art 2 of the First Protocol to the ECHR. See also *Menevia*, n 45 above, and *R (ZK) v Redbridge LBC* [2019] EWHC 1450 (Admin), [2019] ELR 482, discussed at p 182 above, which fell within s29 EqA; and *Begum*, which concerned the application of a school uniform policy.

[136] See *Birmingham v EOC* [1989] AC 1155, discussed in Ch 2, in which the HL ruled that the setting of a higher 11 Plus exam pass mark for girls than boys breached s23 SDA, which was concerned with discrimination by local authorities in relation to education.

The EHRC has not produced any Code of Practice applicable to education though it has issued non-statutory 'technical guidance' relating to schools, and separate guidance relating to FEIs and HEIs.[137] The technical guidance for schools suggests that a school might discriminate unlawfully against pupils by:

- imposing different disciplinary sanctions on pupils of different ethnic groups who have been guilty of similar misbehaviour;
- denying a facially disfigured pupil a place on a school team to avoid his being bulled by other pupils because of his disfigurement;
- racially segregating pupils;
- refusing a pupil a place at a Catholic school because his parents are a same-sex couple;
- refusing to allow an effeminate pupil to play rugby because he is assumed to be gay;
- limiting the number of GCSEs which can be taken by a pregnant pupil, or refusing to allow her to undertake work experience in a garage because she is pregnant;
- indicating on its website that it will not accept applications from the Gypsy and Traveller community;
- repeatedly telling a 'transsexual' pupil that 'he' should not dress like a girl and that 'he' looks silly;[138]
- referring to homosexuality as 'unnatural' in class;
- insisting that a Muslim or Jewish pupil handle pork gelatine;
- planning career discussions on a Friday evening where to do so will exclude Jewish students.[139]

Exceptions

In addition to the general exceptions set out at pp 186–193 above, Schedules 11 and 12 EqA provide specific exceptions to the prohibitions on discrimination by schools and HE&FEIs respectively, as follows:

- The prohibitions on sex discrimination in relation to admissions (ss85(1)) and 91(1) EqA) are disapplied in the case of single-sex schools and FE&HEIs, both of which are defined to include bodies which admit pupils or students 'of the opposite sex' either exceptionally or in 'comparatively small numbers' to 'particular courses or classes'.[140] They are also disapplied in relation to single-sex boarding schools (again defined to include schools which permit boarding by 'small' numbers of 'opposite sex' pupils).[141]
- The prohibitions on discrimination on grounds of religion or belief in ss85(1) and (2)(a)–(d) EqA are disapplied in the case of state and independent schools having a religious character,[142] while certain designated HE&FEIs are permitted to give preference

[137] Available at https://www.equalityhumanrights.com/en/publication-download/technical-guidance-schools-england.

[138] See Ch 6 for discussion of the position concerning gender questioning pupils.

[139] §§5.5–5.8, 5.11–5.27.

[140] Schedule 11 para 1 and Sch 12 para 1 EqA respectively.

[141] Schedule 11 para 2. Schedule 11 paras 3–4 and Sch 12 paras 2–3 provide for permissible discrimination in the case of schools and HE&FEIs transitioning from single-sex.

[142] As listed by Sch 11 para 5 EqA.

to persons of a particular religion or belief as regards access to certain non-vocational courses, where this is necessary to preserve the institution's religious ethos.[143]

- The prohibitions on discrimination on grounds of religion or belief in ss85(2)(a)–(d) EqA are disapplied in relation to 'anything done in connection with acts of worship or other religious observance organised by or on behalf of a school (whether or not forming part of the curriculum)'.[144]
- The prohibition on discrimination on grounds of religion or belief in ss85(1)(a) EqA is disapplied in relation to selection on the basis of ability or aptitude insofar as this is otherwise legally permitted.[145]
- The prohibitions on discrimination in s91(a) and (2) EqA do not apply in relation to training for work in respect of which a genuine occupational requirement (GOR) would apply (see further pp 223–224 above and discussions in Chapters 6, 9 and 10).[146]

Importantly, ss89(2) and 92(2) EqA provide that the prohibitions on discrimination by schools and further and higher education establishments do not apply 'to anything done in connection with the content of the curriculum'. This was relied upon by the High Court in *Birmingham CC v Afsar* to dismiss an argument that the teaching of relationships education to young British Pakistani Muslim children discriminated against them on religious grounds.

***Birmingham CC v Afsar* [2019] EWHC 3217 (QB)**

The discrimination argument had been put by way of a defence to a claim for injunctive relief against individuals, including some parents, who had been involved in picketing a primary school in protest at the fact that it taught children about the existence of LGBT people and same-sex families. The protestors claimed, entirely wrongly, that the school had pursued 'a paedophile agenda', taught children how to masturbate, provided 'LGBT sexual education', including teaching on anal sex, and that it had given convicted paedophiles access to the school.

It was argued for the protestors that the school had indirectly discriminated against British Pakistani Muslim children at the school, and those with parental responsibility for them by 'Weaving into lessons through years one to six, without informing parents in advance, that (a) it is ok for a child to have two mummies and two daddies (b) it is ok for two ladies to get married (c) it is ok to be gay (d) it is ok for a boy to dress as a girl and (e) it is up to the parents to teach their child(ren) what they believe at home, without the opportunity for the parents to opt the child out.' This, it was said, amounted to a breach of s85(2)(a) read with s19 EqA. This argument was rejected on the basis that s89(2) EqA excluded the content of the curriculum from the scope of s85(2)(a), the argument put for

[143] Schedule 12 para 5 EqA.

[144] Schedule 11 para 6 EqA.

[145] Schedule 11 para 8 EqA. The scope of state schools, other than grammar schools, to select pupils on the basis of ability or aptitude is set out in s99 of the School Standards and Framework Act 1998; that of grammar schools in s104 of the 1998 Act. Independent schools are free to select 'by reference to general or special ability or aptitude, with a view to admitting only pupils of high ability or aptitude'.

[146] Schedule 12 para 4 EqA. The exception in para 6 concerning benefits for married and civilly partnered persons is of limited application in view of the availability of both statuses to both same-sex and different-sex couples. Para 7 also permits HE&FEIs to provide or facilitate access to childcare for children of particular ages.

the protestors that 'curriculum' in s89(2) EqA extended only to the national curriculum, which did not at that stage require the material in issue to be taught to primary school children being rejected by Warby J. The judge referred to the EqA's explanatory notes which stated (§§302–303) that s89(2) EqA:

> makes it clear that the prohibitions in the Chapter do not apply to anything done in relation to the content of the school curriculum. This ensures that the Act does not inhibit the ability of schools to include a full range of issues, ideas and materials in their syllabus and to expose pupils to thoughts and ideas of all kinds. The way in which the curriculum is taught is, however, covered by the reference to education in section 85(2)(a), so as to ensure issues are taught in a way which does not subject pupils to discrimination …
>
> **Examples**
>
> A school curriculum includes teaching of evolution in science lessons. This would not be religious discrimination against a pupil whose religious beliefs include creationism.
>
> A school curriculum includes The Taming of the Shrew on the syllabus. This would not be discrimination against a girl.

Warby J remarked that the second of these examples was 'very much in point, given the defendants' reliance on specific books … It indicates, rightly in my judgment, that a decision to use a particular text as part of a programme of instruction is likely to be something done in relation to "curriculum content"' and continued:

Warby J:

> 50 I cannot accept [the protestors'] invitation to give the wording of s 89(2) the narrow interpretation for which he contends, on the grounds that giving the words their natural meaning would militate against the purpose of the Act. This seems to me to be circular reasoning, as it presumes a legislative intention to do something other than that which the statutory wording indicates. To adopt this approach would deprive the sub-section of all or most of the effect it is evidently intended to have. It is easy to understand the rationale for the exemption. The purpose of s 89(2) is to enable a school to teach controversial material without being accused of contravening the [EqA] …
>
> 51 The exemption is cast in broad terms; it does not just apply to decisions about the curriculum content, but to 'anything done in connection with' that content. This is consistent with an intention to protect against collateral attack. In my judgment, the PCP alleged by the defendants is entirely concerned with the 'content of the curriculum' within the meaning of s 89(2). None of it is about the 'way education is delivered' so as to fall with s 85(2)(a), and outside the scope of that sub-section.[147]

Part 7: Associations

Material Scope of Part 7

Difficulties arose under s29 EqA's predecessor provisions as to the meaning of 'a section of the public', the effect of which is to exclude private associations. In two cases in the 1970s, the HL ruled that the RRA's equivalent of s29 did not apply to discrimination in access

[147] The protestors' attempt to rely on s29 EqA also failed on the grounds that the school was not engaged in the provision of education to the protestors, including those who were parents of children at the school.

to Conservative and working men's clubs.[148] These decisions resulted in the incorporation into the RRA of a provision regulating discrimination by private members' associations. That provision formed the basis of s101 EqA, which now provides that 'associations' (defined by s107(2) as 'an association of persons' having at least 25 members, admission to whose membership depends upon selection under the group's rules) must not harass members, persons seeking membership or associates[149] and must not discriminate against or victimise:

- individuals as regards the arrangements made 'for deciding who to admit to membership'; the terms of admission or the refusal of admission; or[150]
- members or associate members as regards access to benefits, facilities or services, variation of the terms of or removal of membership or associate membership, or subjection to any other detriment;[151]

Section 102 EqA provides similar protection from discrimination to guests of members. The prohibitions do not apply in relation to the protected characteristic of marriage or civil partnership and the prohibition on harassment does not apply as regards religion, belief or sexual orientation.

The exceptions applicable to Part 7 are somewhat broader than those which apply to Part 4. It remains important therefore to determine which Part discriminatory conduct falls within. We saw in the discussion of *Plummer v Royal Herbert Freehold Ltd* above that the key to the concept of an association is exclusivity.

There was a degree of uncertainty as to whether the predecessor provisions of s101 EqA applied to political parties.[152] This appears to have been put to rest by s104 EqA, which applies to 'an association which is a registered political party' and which permits positive action, including single-sex shortlisting, in relation to the selection of candidates for election. That provision is further discussed in Chapter 3. Similarly, political parties are expressly referred to as 'member associations' in Schedule 16 EqA, which provides exceptions from the prohibition on discrimination by associations.

Exceptions

In addition to the exceptions of general application, Schedule 16 EqA provides (para 1) as follows:

Schedule 16, para 1 EqA

(1) An association does not contravene section 101(1) by restricting membership to persons who share a protected characteristic.

[148] *Race Relations Board v Charter* [1973] AC 868; *Dockers' Labour Club and Institute Ltd v Race Relations Board* [1976] AC 285. The EOC's annual report for 1999–2000 reported (at 8) a county court ruling that the Professional Football Players' Annual Awards Dinner was not 'private' and that, therefore, the exclusion from it in 1997 and 1998 of a woman agent on the ground of her sex was actionable as a breach of the SDA.

[149] Section 100 provides that s101 will apply only where Parts 3–6 (which cover services and public functions, premises, work and education) do not or where they provide an express exception to their prohibitions.

[150] Section 101(1), (5) EqA.

[151] Section 101(2), (3), (6)–(7) EqA.

[152] See *Triesman v Ali* [2002] EWCA Civ 93, [2002] ICR 1026 which concerned alleged discrimination by the Labour Party in the selection of candidates for election to positions as Labour councillors.

(2) An association that restricts membership to persons who share a protected characteristic does not breach section 101(3) by restricting the access by associates to a benefit, facility or service to such persons as share the characteristic.
(3) An association that restricts membership to persons who share a protected characteristic does not breach section 102(1) by inviting as guests, or by permitting to be invited as guests, only such persons as share the characteristic.
(4) Sub-paragraphs (1) to (3), so far as relating to race, do not apply in relation to colour.
(5) This paragraph does not apply to an association that is a registered political party.

Paragraph 1A provides that the exceptions on discrimination by associations do not apply to age-related concessions while para 2 provides a number of pregnancy-related exceptions similar to those which apply in relation to s29 EqA. These are discussed in Chapter 6. Section 193(5) EqA also provides that charities may require 'members, or persons wishing to become members, to make a statement which asserts or implies membership or acceptance of a religion or belief'. This is discussed in Chapter 9.

Associations which are protected by para 1 of Schedule 16 may provide extremely useful support to disadvantaged and/or discriminated groups. To the extent that it permits the maintenance of men-only establishment clubs, however, the provision is controversial. By way of example, an article in *The Guardian* in 2018 linked the continued existence of such clubs to the behaviour of men at the Presidents Club dinner in January 2018, which was exposed by the *Financial Times* and formed part of the #MeToo discussion in the UK.

Amelia Gentleman, 'Men-only clubs and menace: how the establishment maintains male power', *The Guardian*, 25 January 2018

… many senior establishment men cling firmly to their right to spend time in men-only environments outside of the world of finance. Anyone shocked by the idea of 360 men from business, politics and finance gathering at the all-male Presidents Club annual dinner should note that men-only clubs continue to flourish throughout London. Mostly, the atmosphere is tamer, and has none of the sexual harassment present at the Presidents Club, but these remain establishments where powerful men can spend time together without women.

Environment secretary Michael Gove and former attorney general Dominic Grieve belong to the private members, men-only Garrick Club in London, as do actors Hugh Bonneville, Damian Lewis and Stephen Fry, along with broadcasters John Simpson, Jeremy Paxman and Melvyn Bragg and a handful of supreme court judges. Baroness Hale, president of the supreme court, has expressed her despair at judges' membership of men-only institutions, but to no effect. 'I regard it as quite shocking that so many of my colleagues belong to the Garrick Club, but they don't see what all the fuss is about', she has said.

If asked, Garrick members protest that the club is not a networking environment and that discussing work inside the building is frowned upon. But it's a nonsense to pretend that important invisible connections are not forged in these clubs.

The Travellers Club in central London, which has historically been a crucial meeting place for diplomats, continues to refuse female membership. In 2012, members expressed embarrassment that female ambassadors from around the world were unable to join, and issued a proposal to allow 'lady heads of some diplomatic missions in London to be accorded honorary membership for the duration of their tenure'. The motion was rejected. A leaked consultation on the possibility of female membership in 2014 revealed male concerns that the arrival of women would jeopardise the club's reputation as a place where men can enjoy 'male banter, without having to bother with the etiquette that one inevitably must adhere to in female company (whether it be offering her drinks, waiting for her to eat, or standing when she arrives or leaves)'…

Establishing Liability for Discrimination

A breach of the EqA requires that a nexus be established between the claimant and the respondent/defendant.[153] This is the case whether the discrimination at issue is in the field of employment or not (a school, for example, may be liable for discrimination against pupils by its staff, a shop for harassment of customers and a public authority for victimisation of service users).

Part 8 EqA sets out three ways in which employers can be pinned with responsibility for the actions of others. In the first place, s109 EqA imposes vicarious liability upon employers. They may also be liable for the actions of their agents, and may incur direct or personal liability if they assist in discrimination, harassment etc by another.

Vicarious liability

Section 109 EqA, Liability of employers and principals

(1) Anything done by a person (A) in the course of A's employment must be treated as also done by the employer …

(4) In proceedings against A's employer (B) in respect of anything alleged to have been done by A in the course of A's employment it is a defence for B to show that B took all reasonable steps to prevent A—

(a) from doing that thing, or
(b) from doing anything of that description.

(5) This section does not apply to offences under this Act (other than offences under Part 12 (disabled persons: transport)).

Establishing vicarious liability for discrimination, victimisation, etc has rarely given rise to difficulties where the conduct complained of takes the form of arrangements made for recruitment, decisions about recruitment and terms of employment, etc, and dismissals, as in these cases it will generally be easy to attribute the acts of the individual discriminator to the employer. Cases of harassment by colleagues historically created more difficulties because the common law held employers liable only for those actions of their employees which were in some sense 'authorised'.[154] In *Tower Boot Co Ltd v Jones* [1997] ICR 254 the CA ruled that the common law test for vicarious liability did not apply, and that the statutory test established under the RRA was intended to make employers liable for all discriminatory treatment in their workplaces, subject to the reasonable steps defence (see below).[155] In *CC Lincolnshire Police v Stubbs* [1999] ICR 547 the EAT accepted that sexual harassment which took place at a social gathering which could be regarded as 'an extension of the employment' of those involved could be 'within the course of' the harasser's employment as understood post-*Tower Boot*. In the following case the EAT ruled that the sharing of a racist image on a private Facebook page was not an act 'in the course of … employment', though the employee concerned was given a final written warning after the claimant, who had been shown the image by a colleague, raised a grievance in respect of it.

[153] The former term is used in the employment tribunal, the latter in the civil courts. 'Respondent' is also used on appeal to signify the party who is not the appellant.

[154] See for example *Irving v Post Office* [1987] IRLR 289.

[155] The common law test has widened as a result of the HL decision in *Lister v Helsey Hall Ltd* [2001] UKHL 22, [2002] 1 AC 215 and the decisions of the SC in *Catholic Child Welfare Society* [2012] UKSC 56, [2013] 2 AC 1; *Mohamud v WM Morrison Supermarkets plc* [2016] UKSC 11, [2016] AC 677; and *Cox v Ministry of Justice* [2016] UKSC 10, [2016] AC 660.

***Forbes v LHR Airport Ltd* [2019] UKEAT 0174_18_2802, [2019] ICR 1558**

This case, also considered in Chapter 2, concerned a harassment claim arising from a Facebook post of a gollywog, for which the claimant's colleague had apologised and been issued with a final written warning. The claimant appealed against a tribunal's ruling that the post had not been within the colleague's course of employment.

Choudhury J (President):

> 25. … the main principle to be gleaned [from the authorities] is that the question of whether conduct is or is not in the course of employment within the meaning of section 109 of the Equality Act 2010 is very much one of fact to be determined by the tribunal having regard to all the relevant circumstances. It can also be said that the words 'in the course of employment' are to be construed in the sense in which the lay person would understand them and that there is no clear dividing line between conduct that is in the course of employment and that which is not. Each case will depend on its own particular facts.
>
> 26. It is also apparent from these authorities that the relevant factors to be taken into account might include whether the impugned act was done at work or outside of work, and, if done outside of work, whether there is nevertheless a sufficient nexus or connection with work such as to render it in the course of employment. Those kinds of factors are readily understood when one is dealing with the physical environment of the workplace. It is much more difficult to apply them to the virtual landscape in which many people these days spend their time. Thus, it may not be very easy to say whether a person is doing something whilst at work where some of that person's work activity is conducted online at home. Equally, it may be very difficult to ascertain whether there is a sufficient nexus between an activity carried out on a personal social media account and their employment. If that account is used for purposes relating to work then it might well be open to the tribunal to consider that there is a sufficient connection with work to render an act done on that social media account as being done in the course of employment; whereas if the link with work is tangential or more tenuous then it might well be open to the tribunal to conclude otherwise.
>
> 27. We do not consider that it is possible or even desirable to lay down any hard and fast guidance in respect of these matters, especially as the extent to which social media platforms are used continues to increase. Just as is the case with the physical work environment, whether something is done in the course of employment when done in the virtual landscape will be a question of fact for the tribunal in each case having regard to all the circumstances. No clear boundary as to when such conduct will be in the course of employment can be defined …
>
> 31. … The lay person would not consider that the sharing of an image on a private non-work-related Facebook page, with a list of friends that largely did not include work colleagues, was an act done in the course of employment. The factors taken into account by the tribunal also included the fact that Ms Stevens was not at work when the image was posted; that the image had not made reference to the employer or any of the employer's employees; and that she did not use the employer's equipment in sharing the image.
>
> 32. … There was no finding that the image was shared amongst colleagues as such. The only evidence of the image being shared in the workplace was that BW had shown the image to the claimant …
>
> 36. There may of course be many circumstances where the sharing of an image on a Facebook page could be found to be an act done in the course of employment. This could include situations where the Facebook page is solely or principally maintained for the purposes of communicating with work colleagues or is routinely used for raising work-related matters.

> In those circumstances, one can see that an ostensibly private act could be regarded as being sufficiently closely connected to the workplace to render it an act done in the course of employment. Whether or not such an act is seen as such will depend on the facts of the individual case.
>
> 37. The fact that the employer treated the matter as a disciplinary one as far as Ms Stevens was concerned is not determinative. In the first place, the employer's actions were after the event, and, as with BW's sharing of the image with the claimant, was not necessarily probative of the prior question of whether Ms Stevens's sharing of the image was done in the course of her employment. Furthermore, the employer may, depending on its policy, be entitled to take disciplinary action in respect of a Facebook post which it considered to be potentially damaging of its reputation.
>
> 38. However, the fact that the employer considers it appropriate to take such action does not mean that the conduct in question is necessarily done in the course of employment. The employer can, for example, take action, again depending on policies, against an employee where it transpires that he or she has committed criminal acts outside employment, or acts which are otherwise considered offensive or unacceptable. An employee found to be chanting racist slogans at a football match, for example, might be regarded by an employer as engaging in conduct worthy of censure. However, no reasonable person would regard such conduct as being done in the course of employment, unless there was shown to be some connection between attendance at the football match and employment that suggested otherwise. There is, in other words, no necessary correlation in this context between conduct outside of work, which is considered by the employer to be unacceptable, and the statutory test of an act being done in the course of employment …

Particular difficulties arose in establishing vicarious liability on the part of a Chief Constable for the actions of police officers, but s42 EqA provides that, for the purposes of Part 5 EqA, 'holding the office of constable is to be treated as employment' by the Chief Constable or other 'responsible authority'. In *P v Metropolitan Police Commissioner* [2017] UKSC 65, [2018] ICR 560 the SC confirmed that s42 established vicarious liability in Chief Constables or other responsible authorities for the actions of police officers.

One matter which continues to create significant and increasing difficulties (in view of the increasing atomisation of the workforce) concerns the liability of employers for harassment by third parties (client, customers, contract workers and other workers with whom an employee may come into contact in the course of their employment). In *Bessong v Pennine Care NHS Foundation Trust* [2020] ICR 849, for example, a racial harassment claim failed because the harasser was the patient of the Trust and not (for example) a fellow employee for whom the employer would have been vicariously liable.[156] While failure to prevent or deter such harassment could still be actionable under the EqA this would only be the case where any failure of action on the employer's part was itself tainted by race (or other protected characteristic as the case may be).[157]

[156] The EqA as initially enacted imposed liability on an employer for third party harassment which the employer had failed to take reasonable steps to prevent where the employer knew that the employee had been harassed by a third party on at least two previous occasions (s40(2)–(4)).

[157] In reaching this decision the EAT took account of the Race Directive as well as the EqA, distinguishing the decision in *Sheffield CC v Norouzi* [2011] IRLR 897 in which the EAT accepted that the Directive applied to third-party harassment because it had been based on a concession by the council.

The Employer's Defence

Even where an act of harassment or other discrimination is found to be within s109(1) EqA, an employer can escape liability by proving (s109(4)) that they 'took such steps as were reasonably practicable to prevent the employee from doing that act, or from doing in the course of his employment acts of that description.' Whether such steps have been taken will be a matter of fact in any case in which the defence is argued. In most cases in which employers plead the 'due diligence' defence, the issue is one of harassment.[158]

***Canniffe v East Riding of Yorkshire Council* [2000] UKEAT 1035_98_1704, [2000] IRLR 555**

The EAT allowed an appeal against a tribunal decision that an employer had made out the reasonable steps defence in a sexual harassment claim. The claimant had been repeatedly harassed by a work colleague who, on one particular occasion, was alleged to have committed a very serious sexual assault on her. The tribunal ruled that the employers had taken such steps as were reasonably practicable to prevent the harassment, this on the basis that:

> While the applicant has levelled complaints about the culture within which she worked and about the steps taken by the respondent to draw its employees' attention to matters such as the personal harassment policy and equal opportunities, we fail to see that those sorts of steps would have made any difference in the type of acts about which complaint is made. We failed to see that any better implementation of such policies would have any effect in relation to the very serious criminal behaviour perpetrated upon the applicant. It is almost superfluous to have a Code of Conduct and to train employees not to indecently expose themselves or to carry out indecent assaults upon their colleagues, any more than it may be necessary to advise them not to steal from their colleagues or to assault their colleagues in any other way.

The EAT ruled, on appeal, that the tribunal should not have focused entirely on whether anything that the employers did or could have done would have made any difference. The questions it should have asked were: (1) whether the respondents took steps to prevent the employee from doing the act or acts complained of in the course of his employment; and (2) whether there were any further steps the employers could have taken which were reasonably practicable.

Burton J:

> The question as to whether the doing of any such acts would in fact have been successful in preventing the acts of discrimination in question may be worth addressing, and may be interesting to address, but are not determinative either way. On the one hand, the employer, if he takes steps which are reasonably practicable, will not be inculpated if those steps are not successful; indeed, the matter would not be before the court if the steps had been successful, and so the whole availability of the defence suggests the necessity that someone will have committed the act of discrimination, notwithstanding the taking of reasonable steps; but on the other hand, the employer will not be exculpated if it has not taken reasonable steps simply because if he had taken those reasonable steps they would not have led anywhere or achieved anything or in fact prevented anything from occurring ...
>
> It appears to us that the tribunal has found that the respondent took some steps and was satisfied that those steps that the respondent had taken were reasonable. The tribunal has

[158] Though *cf Martin v Marks & Spencer* [1998] ICR 1005.

not however asked itself the missing question, which is: were there any other steps which could reasonably have been taken which the respondent did not take? It appears to us that there is or could be a very substantial difference between the two different scenarios at the workplace. One is where there is no knowledge on the part of employers or managers of risk of any harassment or inappropriate sexual behaviour by an employee, or indeed in particular by one employee towards another particular employee or employees. In those circumstances it may well be sufficient for there to be adequately promulgated a sexual harassment policy, particularly where it can be said that when a one-off incident occurs of a seriousness of the kind that occurred in this case, it must in any event have been known to any employee, never mind a reasonable or honest employee, that the conduct could not possibly be condoned or encouraged by employers. In those circumstances, it may be sufficient for the question simply to be addressed as to whether there was a policy and whether it was promulgated without more. There may, however, be an entirely different situation in which there was knowledge or suspicion in relation to a particular employee of his own predilections or temperament, and certainly of a risk that he might commit inappropriate acts towards a particular employee or particular employees. In this case, there was such a possibility, but the tribunal did not, in our view, adequately address that possibility or ask itself the right questions. It may well be that on a proper consideration of the position of [employees who had been made aware of the harassment], it could be concluded that there was nothing more that those gentlemen could or should have done that was reasonably practicable to do. On the other hand it may well be that on a proper consideration it would be concluded that, because of the failure of those gentlemen to take any further steps, the respondent, who is vicariously liable for them, should be held not to have taken such steps that were reasonably practicable to prevent the kind of conduct which eventually occurred.

Forbes v LHR Airport Ltd [2019] UKEAT 0174_18_2802, [2019] ICR 1558

In this case, also considered at p 233 above, the claimant challenged the tribunal's finding that the employer had been entitled to rely on the s109(4) defence, because there was no evidence that the company took steps to publicise, audit or monitor its policies. He sought to rely on the EHRC's Statutory Code of Practice on employment which stated that reasonable steps which an employer might take under s109 EqA might include, for example, ensuring workers were aware of an equality policy and providing training. The EAT dismissed his appeal.

Choudhury J (President):

50 … Mr Ward [for the claimant] relies upon para 10.51 and 10.52 of the Code of Practice[159] where it is stated that:

10.51 An employer would be considered to have taken all reasonable steps if there were no further steps that they could have been expected to take. In deciding whether a step is reasonable, an employer should consider its likely effect and whether an alternative step could be more effective. However, a step does not have to be effective to be reasonable.

10.52 Reasonable steps might include:

- implementing an equality policy;
- ensuring workers are aware of the policy;

[159] n 100 above.

- providing equal opportunities training;
- reviewing the equality policy as appropriate; and
- dealing effectively with employee complaints.

51 Mr Ward also drew our attention to Ch 18 of the Code of Practice, which contains further information in relation to equalities policies and practice in the workplace. The introduction to that chapter states as follows:

> 18.1. There is no formal statutory requirement in the act for an employer to put in place an equality policy. However, a systematic approach to developing and maintaining good practice is the best way of showing that an organisation is taking its legal responsibility seriously …'

There then follows a series of recommendations, including monitoring and auditing such policies. In our judgment, it is important to bear in mind that the Code of Practice is not to be considered in this regard as comprising a list of statutory requirements, each of which must be met in order for an employer to be regarded as having taken all reasonable steps. The steps that would be reasonable in a particular case would depend on the facts. Moreover, the Code of Practice suggests that the reasonable steps 'might' include those set out; it does not suggest that the failure to take any one of those steps in relation to any policy will necessarily mean that the reasonable steps defence under s 109(4) of the EqA cannot succeed.

52 In the present case, the Tribunal regarded as significant that the employer treated Ms Stevens' conduct seriously and gave her a final written warning. The Tribunal was, in our judgement, entitled in those circumstances to conclude that, notwithstanding the absence of any evidence as to the publication, auditing or monitoring of the policy, the Respondent did take reasonable steps to prevent its employees from doing the discriminatory act in question …[160]

Liability for Agents

Section 109 EqA, Liability of employers and principals

(2) Anything done by an agent for a principal, with the authority of the principal, must be treated as also done by the principal.

(3) It does not matter whether that thing is done with the employer's or principal's knowledge or approval.

In *Lana v Positive Training in Housing (London) Ltd* [2001] IRLR 501 the EAT applied a predecessor provision of s109(2) and (3) in holding a training body liable for discrimination on the part of the organisation with which it had placed a trainee. The decision in *Kemeh v MOD*, however, illustrates the limits of the provision.

***Kemeh v MOD* [2014] EWCA Civ 91, [2014] ICR 625**

The claimant was a British Army cook of Ghanian national origin, stationed in the Falklands, who complained of harassment by Ms Ausher, a contract worker employed in the catering facility in which he worked. She was employed by Sodexo, which was a subcontractor of Serco, which in turn had a contract with the MoD. A tribunal had accepted that Ms Ausher had acted as the MOD's agent and that the MOD was, accordingly, liable

[160] See also *Allay (UK) Ltd v Gehlen* [2021] ICR 645.

under the predecessor provision of s109(2), finding that the MOD 'had delegated to [Serco and Sodexo] the responsibility for carrying out duties which would otherwise have been performed by service personnel', and that 'civilian workers, including Ms Ausher, were subject to day-to-day control by the military'. The EAT allowed the MOD's appeal and the CA rejected Mr Kemeh's appeal, rejecting the argument put for Mr Kemeh that Ms Ausher was acting as the agent of the MOD. The relevant provision was s32 RRA, which is materially similar to s109 EqA.

Elias LJ (with whom Lewison and Kitchin LJJ agreed):

> 11. … In my judgment, Parliament must have intended that the principal will be liable wherever the agent discriminates in the course of carrying out the functions he is authorised to do. It is a moot point whether the common law would in any event impose liability in these circumstances. The scope of the principal's liability for an agent at common law is not entirely clear … but s.32(2) removes the uncertainty which might otherwise exist …
>
> 35. We are concerned with the construction of a statute. The aim must be to give effect to Parliament's intentions as evidenced by the language of the provision having regard to the statutory and social context. I do not find it helpful to talk in the abstract about the need to adopt a purposive construction. It is not permissible to expand the meaning of a statutory concept beyond its legitimate reach because it is thought that the broad objective of the statute would be better effected thereby …
>
> 36. … I readily accept that a broader rather than a narrower meaning should be adopted where two constructions are equally plausible and the broader meaning better achieves the statutory purpose … that was the approach of the court in the *Tower Boot* case. But I do not consider that *Tower Boot* provides any further assistance in seeking to determine the proper meaning of s.32(2). The particular features which enabled the court to adopt a non-technical approach in that case are not present here. Moreover, *Tower Boot* was concerned with the question for what acts the employer should be liable, whereas here the issue is for whose acts the employer should be liable.
>
> 40. … Whatever the precise scope of the legal concept of agency, and whatever difficulties there may be of applying it in marginal cases, I am satisfied that no question of agency arises in this case. In my view, it cannot be appropriate to describe as an agent someone who is employed by a contractor simply on the grounds that he or she performs work for the benefit of a third party employer. She is no more acting on behalf of the employer than his own employees are, and they would not typically be treated as agents. (That is not, of course, to say that employees can never be agents; they might well be, depending upon the obligations cast upon them, such as where a senior manager is authorised to contract with third parties. He will be an employee but will also act as an agent when exercising the authority to deal with third parties.)
>
> 41. In my judgment, Ms Ausher's contract with Sodexo is the source of any authority she has to make decisions relating to the butcher's department in the Mess. It may be, as Ms Romney asserts [for the claimant], that ultimately the MoD would have the right to veto her presence, at least for good reason. But that limited degree of control comes nowhere near constituting an authorisation by the MoD to allow Ms Ausher to act on its behalf with respect to third parties.
>
> 43. … the fact that someone is employed by A would not automatically prevent him from being an agent of B, and I would not discount the possibility that the two relationships can co-exist even in relation to the same transaction. But in my judgment there would, particularly in the latter case, need to be very cogent evidence to show that the duties which an employee was obliged to do as the employee of A were also being performed as an agent of B. It is in general difficult to see why B would either want or need to enter into the agency relationship. That is so whichever concept of agency is employed. There is a complete lack of such cogent evidence here.

46. For these reasons, therefore, this appeal must fail. Whatever the precise scope of the agency concept in s.32 – and in my view it must at least reflect the essence of the legal concept – Ms Ausher does not fall within it. Accordingly, the MoD cannot be liable for her act of discrimination.

47. In reaching this conclusion I fully recognise the force of what, in policy terms at least, was Ms Romney's most powerful argument. If the appellant cannot bring a claim against the MoD, there is a real risk that he has no remedy at all for Ms Ausher's discriminatory act. Sodexo is not liable because although they would in principle be responsible under s.32(1) for her acts, the appellant could only bring proceedings if he were in their employment, and he does not fall even within the wide definition of that term adopted for the purposes of the Act. So he can bring no proceedings against them.

48. The result is that because of the different sets of rules relating to contract workers and employees, the appellant falls in a gap in the statutory protection. Section 7 confers rights upon contract workers like Ms Ausher to bring a claim against the employer for whose ultimate benefit they provide services (the MoD here) but the Act does not impose liabilities on that person for the acts of the to contract worker. Parliament may wish to consider this lacuna, although if it provides a remedy, it will have to decide whether it is the immediate employer rather than the end user of the services who should bear the legal responsibility.

Blackwood v Birmingham & Solihull Mental Health NHS Trust [2016] EWCA Civ 607, [2016] ICR 903

In this case, also discussed at p 221 above, the CA had rejected the argument put for the Trust that the proper route for a student in the claimant's position was to proceed under s91 against the university, and for the courts to take a '"benign" approach to the operation of ss.109 and 110' by 'treat[ing] the relationship of a university and a work placement provider in every case as one of principal and agent, and to regard every act of the provider in the course of that relationship as being done with the authority of the university'. According to Underhill LJ, with whom the rest of the Court agreed:

Underhill LJ (with whom Lewison and Patten LJJ agreed):

57. … It is settled law that references to agency concepts in this legislation are to be given their ordinary common law meaning: see *Kemeh v MOD* … Although I do not rule out the possibility that there may be some kinds of arrangement between a university and a provider of work placements under which the provider acts as the agent of the university, it is inconceivable that this will be universally the case, still less that every act of the provider can be done with the authority of the university. On the contrary, in the case of a typical student work placement, say with a school or hospital, while the university will no doubt have agreed certain parameters with the provider about what work will be provided, it will in the nature of things have no involvement in, or control over, the student's day-to-day working environment. It is hard to see any basis for characterising such a relationship as one of principal and agent as opposed to an arm's length relationship between two principals, and harder still as one where every act of the provider is to be treated as done with the authority of the university. To insist on such a characterisation in every case, as a means of achieving compliance with the requirements of the EU Directives, would be unacceptably artificial. It would also produce unfair results, since it would mean that the university was treated as automatically liable for acts on the part of the provider for which it could not fairly be regarded as having any responsibility. In my view the scheme under ss.109 and 110 of the 2010 Act depends on the concept of agency being applied

> in accordance with the ordinary understanding, and a departure from that approach would be inconsistent with a fundamental feature of the legislation …

Underhill LJ referred to the decision in *Lana* above, stating at §59 that 'The fact that the relationship between the training company and the training provider in that case was one of principal and agent does not mean that such a relationship can be found in every case where a work placement is arranged for a student by a university'.

The case below provides a further illustration of the application of s109 EqA.

Unite the Union v Nailard **[2018] EWCA Civ 1203, [2019] ICR 28**

The CA considered the application of s109(2) EqA in a case in which the trade union had been held liable, in principle, in respect of allegations of sexual harassment and sex discrimination made by an employee of the union against two locally elected lay officials. The claimant was employed as a regional officer at an airport at which the union officials, who were employed by the airport, carried out full-time union duties on behalf of Unite. The claimant's grievance was upheld by the union, which concluded that she had been bullied and sexually harassed, but offered her a transfer to an alternative site. A tribunal found that the union was liable under ss26 (harassment), 39 (employment) and 109 EqA and that the union's employed officers were themselves guilty of sexual harassment and sex discrimination by reason of their failure to investigate and take appropriate action (in particular, because of their decision to transfer the claimant). The EAT agreed that the union was liable for the conduct of its elected officials as its agents within s109(2), although it found that the tribunal had erred in concluding that the paid officers' actions amounted to harassment or sex discrimination without consideration of the conduct and motives of the individual decision-makers.

The CA rejected the union's appeal in respect of the first of these findings. Underhill LJ, with whom Moylan LJ agreed,[161] made reference to s109(3) EqA, which provides that an act may be done with the principal's 'authority' for the purpose of s109(2) even though he or she has no prior knowledge of it, and noted that the 'reasonable steps' defence in s109(4) was available only to employers and not to principals, which he found 'on the face of it rather surprising'.[162] He considered the decision in *Kemeh* (above) and that in *Heatons Transport (St Helens) Ltd v Transport and General Workers' Union* [1973] AC 15, in which the HL held the union liable for the actions of its shop stewards in an industrial action context, which actions were within the union rules. He then made reference to the argument put for the union that it would be liable for the conduct of its lay officials as agents only towards third parties, and not towards those such as the claimant who was also a representative of the union in the meetings in which the harassment occurred.

[161] It being a two-person panel.

[162] This was the case under the EqA's predecessor provisions: see *Lana v Positive Training in Housing (London) Ltd* [2001] IRLR 501, which featured in the reasoning of Elias LJ in *Kemeh*.

Underhill LJ (for the Court):

42. The starting-point is the statement of Elias LJ at para [11] of his judgment in *Kemeh* that the effect of what is now s 109(2) is that 'the principal will be liable wherever the agent discriminates in the course of carrying out the functions he is authorised to do'... That formulation effectively equates the circumstances in which a principal may be liable for the acts of an agent with the 'course of employment' test governing the liability of employers for the acts of their employees. It may well extend the scope of the liability beyond what would apply at common law; but there is no reason why Parliament should not have chosen to effect such an extension in discrimination cases ...

43. If, therefore, the effect of the language of s 109(2) is to render a principal liable for the acts of his or her agents done in the course of the performance of their authorised functions, I can see no justification for limiting that liability in the way proposed by Mr Segal [for the union]. An agent may stand in the shoes of the principal in dealing with A, but if while wearing them he treads on B's toes I see no good reason why he should not be liable to B just as much as if it had been A's toes that were crushed: in both cases the wrong is done in the course of performing the authorised functions.

44. I agree with Mr Carr [for the claimant] that that result makes sense in policy terms. The distinction on which Mr Segal relies would plainly have no application in the case of an employee: indeed in very many, if not most, cases where an employer is liable for an employee's discriminatory acts by virtue of s 109(1) the claimant is a fellow-employee rather than a 'third party'. It would be surprising and unsatisfactory if the position were different where the discriminator was acting on behalf of the organisation in question but under some different arrangement: the conduct complained of would still be being done by the agent in the course of the principal's business. The anomalies which would result are particularly obvious in the case of an organisation where persons who are not employees (even in the extended sense) perform important functions, as in the case of trade unions ...

45. ... I acknowledge that it is an apparent anomaly that the reasonable steps defence is not available to principals as regards the acts of their agents when it is available to employers as regards the acts of their employees. But that anomaly would be present whichever construction of s 109(2) is preferred; and I accept Mr Carr's submission that it cannot be right in principle to adopt what would otherwise be the wrong construction simply so that the anomaly would arise in fewer cases.[163]

The Employee/Agent's Personal Liability

Section 110 EqA, Liability of employees and agents

(1) A person (A) contravenes this section if—

(a) A is an employee or agent,

(b) A does something which, by virtue of section 109(1) or (2), is treated as having been done by A's employer or principal (as the case may be), and

(c) the doing of that thing by A amounts to a contravention of this Act by the employer or principal (as the case may be).

[163] In *Victor-Davis v LB Hackney* UKEAT/1269/01, [2003] All ER (D) 318 (Feb) HHJ McMullen, in the EAT, suggested that it would be 'contrary to the scheme and purpose' of the anti-discrimination legislation for a principal to incur greater liability for the acts of an agent than an employer would incur for acts of an employee and that, accordingly, 'a discriminatory act, done by a person without the knowledge or approval of a principal' could not be 'deemed to have been done by that person as the principal's agent and with this authority where the principal has taken such steps as are practicable to prevent the person from doing that act'.

(2) It does not matter whether, in any proceedings, the employer is found not to have contravened this Act by virtue of section 109(4).
(3) A does not contravene this section if—
   (a) A relies on a statement by the employer or principal that doing that thing is not a contravention of this Act, and
   (b) it is reasonable for A to do so.
(4) A person (B) commits an offence if B knowingly or recklessly makes a statement mentioned in subsection (3)(a) which is false or misleading in a material respect.
(5) A person guilty of an offence under subsection (4) is liable on summary conviction to a fine not exceeding level 5 on the standard scale …

In this circular way, the perpetrators of harassment or other forms of discrimination can personally be held accountable for their actions, and damages awarded against them. Remedies for discrimination are considered in detail in Chapter 5. Here it is sufficient to note *LB Hackney v Sivanandan* [2011] ICR 1374, in which the EAT ruled that, where more than one person has participated in the same act of unlawful discrimination, each person would generally be jointly and severally liable for any award. That case, the reasoning in which was subsequently approved by the CA,[164] concerned sex and race discrimination against an applicant for appointment to a body called Hackney Action for Racial Equality (HARE) by a panel comprising members of HARE's executive committee and an employee of the council. The claim was upheld against the interviewers, the executive committee of HARE, HARE (the company), and the council. And in *Bungay v Saini* UKEAT/0331/10 the same principle was applied to the award of damages against both employees and employers, or agents and their principals.[165]

Other Liability for Assisting Discrimination

Section 111 EqA, Instructing, causing or inducing contraventions

(1) A person (A) must not instruct another (B) to do in relation to a third person (C) anything which contravenes Part 3, 4, 5, 6 or 7 or section 108(1) or (2) or 112(1) (a basic contravention).
(2) A person (A) must not cause another (B) to do in relation to a third person (C) anything which is a basic contravention.
(3) A person (A) must not induce another (B) to do in relation to a third person (C) anything which is a basic contravention.
(4) For the purposes of subsection (3), inducement may be direct or indirect.
(5) Proceedings for a contravention of this section may be brought—
   (a) by B, if B is subjected to a detriment as a result of A's conduct;
   (b) by C, if C is subjected to a detriment as a result of A's conduct;
   (c) by the Commission.
(6) For the purposes of subsection (5), it does not matter whether—
   (a) the basic contravention occurs;
   (b) any other proceedings are, or may be, brought in relation to A's conduct.
(7) This section does not apply unless the relationship between A and B is such that A is in a position to commit a basic contravention in relation to B.

[164] [2013] EWCA Civ 22, [2013] EqLR 249.
[165] The CA refused permission to appeal: [2012] EWCA Civ 574.

(8) A reference in this section to causing or inducing a person to do something includes a reference to attempting to cause or induce the person to do it.
(9) For the purposes of Part 9 (enforcement), a contravention of this section is to be treated as relating—
 (a) in a case within subsection (5)(a), to the Part of this Act which, because of the relationship between A and B, A is in a position to contravene in relation to B;
 (b) in a case within subsection (5)(b), to the Part of this Act which, because of the relationship between B and C, B is in a position to contravene in relation to C.

Section 112 EqA, Aiding contraventions

A person (A) must not knowingly help another (B) to do anything which contravenes Part 3, 4, 5, 6 or 7 or section 108(1) or (2) or 111 (a basic contravention).

Section 111 EqA renders unlawful instructing, causing or inducing discrimination, harassment or victimisation in any of the substantive areas covered by the EqA. In addition, such actions may amount to discrimination contrary to s13 EqA against the person to whom the instruction is issued: see *Showboat Entertainment Centre Ltd v Owens* [1982] ICR 618, discussed in Chapter 2. Section EqA 112 prohibits the provision of knowing assistance to discriminate.

The application of one of the predecessor provisions of s111 EqA was considered in *CRE v The Imperial Society of Teachers of Dancing* [1983] ICR 473, in which the EAT overruled a tribunal decision that 'induce' within s31 did not cover a mere request to discriminate. There the society had suggested that the school which it had invited to send potential filing clerks for consideration did not send anyone 'coloured' as the office was exclusively white. A tribunal ruled that there was no attempted 'inducement' in a mere request. The EAT overturned the tribunal's decision on the basis that 'induce' meant simply 'to persuade or to prevail upon or to bring about' and was sufficiently wide to cover the subject matter of this complaint.

The application of s111 was (briefly) considered by the CA in *Blackwood*, discussed at pp 221 and 239 above, in which the CA ruled at §19 that 'A [the aider or assister] is only liable if B's act is itself a contravention of one of the primary provisions of the Act.' The Court there suggested that the 'effect of ss.111 and 112 is reasonably self-explanatory', drawing attention to the fact that 'A is only liable if B's act is itself a contravention of one of the primary provisions of the Act' and that 'Claims under them must be brought in the forum appropriate to the 'basic contravention'.

In *Anyanwu v South Bank University* [2001] UKHL 14, [2001] ICR 391 the HL ruled that liability under the predecessor provision of s112 did not turn on whether B was the 'prime mover' in an act of discrimination or harassment; in that case the university had expelled and excluded from its premises the claimants, who had been salaried officers of the student union. The result of the university's actions was that the student union had treated the claimants' employment contracts was at an end. The claimants sued the union and the university, but initially met with the response that the university was the prime mover in the alleged discrimination and so could not be regarded as having 'aided' the union. The HL disagreed.

5

Enforcement and Remedies

Introduction

Until relatively recently, the enforcement of equality/discrimination law across the UK was a very individualistic affair. The primary model of enforcement for domestic discrimination legislation consisted in discrimination claims brought by individuals, generally in the employment tribunals.[1] Consideration of 'group' characteristics (such as women's disproportionate responsibility for childcare, or dress codes associated with particular religions) could be taken into consideration in indirect discrimination claims brought by individuals. But prior to the implementation of the Human Rights Act 1998 (HRA) and of the positive duties[2] in domestic discrimination law, most legal challenges to discrimination took the form of legal cases brought by individuals, whose outcomes applied only to those individuals. Trade unions and the equality commissions (now the Equality and Human Rights Commission (EHRC)) supported 'test cases' whose outcome might, in practical terms, reach beyond the individual. And employment tribunals could select 'sample cases' where many litigants were involved in similar claims.[3] But the focus of domestic law prior to the turn of the century was almost exclusively on the individual, and legal success turned on the demonstration of detriment suffered by the individual as a result of discrimination.

The implementation of the HRA, whose repeal is threatened at the time of writing, opened the way to significant changes by facilitating direct challenges to legislation and to well as to government policies and practices. The impact of such challenges can be wide-ranging and rapid change. While the HRA does not permit strike-down of primary legislation which is incompatible with (for example) Article 14, it does require courts to seek to interpret potentially incompatible legislation so as to be consistent with Convention rights.[4] In addition, courts may strike down much secondary legislation as well as ruling many

[1] The reasons for this are discussed below.

[2] Now the public sector equality duty (PSED) discussed in Ch 3.

[3] See, eg, *Ashmore v British Coal* [1990] 2 QB 338, in which the Court of Appeal stayed as abusive cases brought after the dismissal of 12 sample cases of 1,500.

[4] This is one of the aspects of the HRA most disliked by the current Government whose proposed British Bill of Rights would remove this power. The change of leadership in September 2022 appeared to have triggered a rethink but the removal of Liz Truss as PM initiated the return of Dominic Raab, who had championed the 'Bill of Rights' as Secretary of State for Justice, so the future of the HRA cannot be considered secure: see further Ch 1.

actions of public authorities (including central government) unlawful. The Equality Act 2010 (EqA) and its predecessor provisions are more limited in that much government action is exempted from their provisions (see further Chapter 4). Having said this, the implementation of the Public Sector Equality Duty (PSED) and its predecessors (see further Chapter 3) resulted in a huge increase in discrimination challenges directed at state action which have implications for large numbers of people.

Notwithstanding the expansion of collective means of enforcement, it is worth noting that the scope for state action to facilitate or require advancements in equality/non-discrimination is very limited in England and Wales by comparison with, for example, the historical position in the US and Canada.

Structural Challenges to Discrimination

Contract Compliance

Introduction

Contract compliance, also considered in Chapter 3, has had a long history in the US as a major means for the enforcement of anti-discrimination legislation. It consists of conditioning access to government contracts, grants, etc, on compliance with particular criteria. It was used as early as 1914 when President Roosevelt issued an Executive Order to prohibit discrimination by defence contractors.[5] The US federal government has used contract compliance since 1968 in order to require government contractors to adhere to workplace equality standards.[6]

The scope of this book does not permit detailed analysis of the history or operation of contract compliance in the US, which is referred to only to draw attention to one of the mechanisms by which employers could be encouraged or required to comply with the EqA, including (if necessary) by adopting positive measures to increase the diversity of workplaces and to reduce the disadvantages associated with sex, race, disability and other protected characteristics.

Contract Compliance in the UK

Prior to the implementation of the Local Government Act 1988 (LGA 1998, discussed below), a number of local authorities (in particular, the subsequently disbanded Greater London Council (GLC) and Inner London Education Authority (ILEA)) had adopted policies of contract compliance. Chris McCrudden wrote of that period:

Chris McCrudden, 'Codes in a Cold Climate' (1988) 51 *Modern Law Review* 409, 429, footnotes omitted

> Local authorities have basically the same powers to contract as others, including the power to seek to have firms with which they contract accept conditions on how the contract is to be carried out. In all cases, however, these powers are subject to public law requirements, including the

[5] In the same year the Philadelphia Plan, adopted by President Nixon, required all those bidding for federal contracts to establish numerical goals for integration. As Attorney General, the later Chief Justice Rehnquist assured the President that the plan was in conformity with the Civil Rights Act – see R McKeever, *Raw Judicial Power? The Supreme Court and American Society*, 2nd edn (Manchester, Manchester University Press, 1995) 125–26.

[6] Paras 99–100 Fourth Report of the Select Committee on N Ireland, 1998–99, HC 95–I.

> duties to act reasonably, not *ultra vires*, and in compliance with the fiduciary duty to the ratepayers. The … GLC in drawing up its contract compliance policy in 1983, sought counsel's opinion on how best to satisfy these public law duties. As a result of that advice, the GLC relied on section 71 of the Race Relations Act, which imposes on councils a duty to seek to eliminate racial discrimination and promote equality of opportunity, as a primary legal support for its contract compliance policy.[7] Though there was no specific legal obligation for other areas of discrimination, it was considered justifiable on moral grounds for public bodies to seek positively to promote the laws against sex discrimination in equivalent ways. Furthermore, it decided that the detail of any compliance sought 'should relate as closely as possible to officially recognised standards … using the Codes of Practice of the CRE and the EOC' Indeed, one of the architects of the policy has written that, '[b]ecause of the clear legal advice the GLC received, the operational core of the policy turned on the Codes of Practice.' An equivalent policy was also adopted by the Inner London Education Authority. Most importantly, ethnic monitoring and the submission of statistics became standard elements in contract compliance policy.
>
> Although it was open for those subject to local authority contract compliance policies to challenge them by way of judicial review, the Government eventually acceded to requests from the CBI and the construction and civil engineering employers to introduce legislation restricting local authority powers to impose contract compliance policies on those with whom they contracted.

Section 17 LGA 1988 prohibited local and other public authorities from taking into account, in their contracting functions: 'non-commercial matters', these matters being defined to include 'the terms and conditions of employment by contractors of their workers or the composition of, the arrangements for the promotion, transfer or training of or the other opportunities afforded to, their workforces.' The only exception to this prohibition was provided by s18 (2) LGA 1988, which permitted only that local authorities 'ask … approved questions seeking information or undertakings relating to workforce matters and consider … the responses to them' and/or 'include[e] in a draft contract or draft tender for a contract terms or provisions relating to workforce matters and consider … the responses to them … if, as the case may be, consideration of the information, the giving of the undertaking or the inclusion of the term is reasonably necessary to secure compliance with [the Race Relations Act 1976 (RRA), s 71].'[8]

Section 71 RRA at the time imposed upon local authorities an obligation to 'to make appropriate arrangements with a view to securing that their various functions are carried out with due regard to the need (a) to eliminate unlawful racial discrimination; and (b) to promote equality of opportunity and good relations, between persons of different racial groups.' The LGA permitted local authorities to ask six 'approved questions' of prospective contractors concerning, inter alia, their arrangements for complying with the RRA and the existence of any findings of unlawful race discrimination against them in the previous three years. But according to the CRE's second (1992) report on the RRA (41–42):

> … we were disappointed by Government action in relation to the local government legislation of 1988. If it had not been for the existence of [s71 RRA], the probability is that Government would

[7] Section 71 RRA was the predecessor of the PSED: see Ch 3.

[8] Northern Ireland's Fair Employment and Treatment Order (FETO), also discussed in Ch 3, embraces an extremely limited form of contract compliance; Art 64 provides that public authorities shall not enter into goods and services contracts with and 'shall take all such steps as are reasonable to secure that no work is executed or goods or services supplied for the purposes of' such contracts with persons who have been declared unqualified by the NI Equality Commission because of failures to comply with the commission's monitoring regime. C Bell reported in 1996 ('The Employment Equality Review and Fair Employment in Northern Ireland' (1996) 2 *International Journal of Discrimination and Law* 53) that since the legislation had been introduced in 1989 the disqualification provisions had only been applied once, and then only for a short period.

> have banned local authorities altogether from considering equal opportunities in their contracting processes … The [Sex Discrimination Act 1975 (SDA)] contains no similar provision and Government did ban local authorities from considering equal opportunities between men and women in their contracting processes.
>
> Because of Section 71 the Government felt it had to permit some local government action in the area of race, but restricted it. By use of the Approved Questions under the legislation, Government has stopped local authorities obtaining ethnic monitoring data from those they might wish to contract for the supply of goods and services. Yet, in *West Midlands Passenger Transport Executive v Singh* [1988] ICR 614 … and in the Commission's *Code of Practice in Employment*, the value of that data in determining whether equal opportunities is being provided is recognised.

Section 71 RRA was replaced by s71A RRA in 2001, similar provisions gradually being introduced to the other anti-discrimination legislation and resulting in what is now the PSED (s149 EqA), discussed in Chapter 3. This is returned to below. Meanwhile it is important to note that the LGA's prohibition on contract compliance became particularly problematic with the widespread contracting-out of services previously provided by the public sector from 1980 onwards as a result of compulsory competitive tendering which had a devastating impact on the terms and conditions of former public sector jobs.

Linda Dickens, 'Gender, race and employment equality in Britain: inadequate strategies and the role of industrial relations actors' (1997) 28 *Industrial Relations Journal* 282, footnotes omitted

> There has been a disproportionate adverse effect on women and ethnic minorities (in particular black women) who tend to be over-represented in those sectors and jobs which have been effected. Some predominantly male areas, such as refuse collection have been affected, although the stronger union and bargaining position of male workers helped reduce some of the adverse consequences of CCT for them. The major impact has been on women who have lost jobs, had hours reduced and work intensified, experienced pay reductions and loss of benefits … The government policy shift in the public sector towards sub-contracting could have been harnessed for equality through a strategy of contract compliance … [which] had been used to some effect by local authorities in the past. Instead a contrary path was taken with contract compliance being curtailed by [the LGA]
>
> … Nor was there any equality-proofing of the CCT process. Rather than disseminating good practice out from the public sector (which traditionally provides the model of a 'good employer'), increased commercialism within a deregulated framework has weakened the good practice itself.

Dickens states that 'some protection of existing terms and conditions was provided by the need for the UK to conform to European requirements relating to transfers of undertakings.' But, as she points out, this protection was 'belated', the Transfer of Undertakings Regulations 1981 only being amended in 1993 clearly to apply to public sector contracting-out. In any event, their imperfect protection applies only to existing workers, rather than to jobs, so they have little long-term impact on terms and conditions in contracted-out sectors. Research in 1995 by Escott and Whitfield for the EOC further demonstrated that women in particular had suffered as a result of CCT.[9]

Section 17 LGA was amended to accommodate the EqA and the Public Services (Social Value) Act 2012, which requires public authorities to have regard to economic, social and

[9] K Escott and D Whitfield, *The impact of CCT in Local Government* (Manchester, EOC, 1995).

environmental well-being in connection with public services contracts. It now provides as follows:

Section 17 LGA 1988, Local and other public authority contracts: exclusion of non-commercial considerations

(1) It is the duty of every public authority to which this section applies,[10] in exercising, in relation to its public supply or works contracts, any proposed or any subsisting such contract, as the case may be, any function regulated by this section to exercise that function without reference to matters which are non-commercial matters for the purposes of this section …

(3) The contracts which are public supply or works contracts for the purposes of this section are contracts for the supply of goods or materials, for the supply of services or for the execution of works ….

(4) The functions regulated by this section are—

(a) the inclusion of persons in or the exclusion of persons from—

(i) any list of persons approved for the purposes of public supply or works contracts with the authority, or

(ii) any list of persons from whom tenders for such contracts may be invited;

(b) in relation to a proposed public supply or works contract with the authority—

(i) the inclusion of persons in or the exclusion of persons from the group of persons from whom tenders are invited,

(ii) the accepting or not accepting the submission of tenders for the contract,

(iii) the selecting the person with whom to enter into the contract, or

(iv) the giving or withholding approval for, or the selecting or nominating, persons to be sub-contractors for the purposes of the contract; and

(c) in relation to a subsisting public supply or works contract with the authority—

(i) the giving or withholding approval for, or the selecting or nominating, persons to be sub-contractors for the purposes of the contract, or

(ii) the termination of the contract.

(5) The following matters are non-commercial matters as regards the public supply or works contracts of a public authority, any proposed or any subsisting such contract, as the case may be, that is to say—

(a) the terms and conditions of employment by contractors of their workers or the composition of, the arrangements for the promotion, transfer or training of or the other opportunities afforded to, their workforces;

(b) whether the terms on which contractors contract with their sub-contractors constitute, in the case of contracts with individuals, contracts for the provision by them as self-employed persons of their services only …

(10) This section does not prevent a public authority to which it applies from exercising any function regulated by this section with reference to a non-commercial matter to the extent that the authority considers it necessary or expedient to do so to enable or facilitate compliance with—

(a) the duty imposed on it by section 149 of the Equality Act 2010 (public sector equality duty), or

(b) any duty imposed on it by regulations under section 153 or 154 of that Act [powers to impose specific duties).]

(11) This section does not prevent a public authority to which it applies from exercising any function regulated by this section with reference to a non-commercial matter to the extent that the authority considers it necessary or expedient to do so to enable or facilitate compliance with a duty imposed on it by section 1 of the Public Services (Social Value) Act 2012.

[10] These are set out in Sch 2 EqA.

As originally enacted, s17 LGA 1988 was (as mentioned above) subject to s18, which qualified its application where necessary to comply with s71 RRA (the predecessor of the PSED). This provision was repealed by the EqA, which amended s17 LGA to include s17(10). Prior to this, the LGA 1999 had replaced CCT with the Best Value regime, which required public bodies to engage in a rolling programme of review to demonstrate that they are making arrangements that are economic, efficient and effective, and that they have regard to the need to secure continuous improvement in how they provide all their services, whether in-house or contracted-out.[11] The Local Government Best Value (Exclusion of Non-commercial Considerations) Order 2001 and Local Government Best Value (Exclusion of Non-commercial Considerations) (Wales) Order 2002[12] excluded from the category of (forbidden) non-commercial considerations those falling within s17(5)(a) and (d) LGA:

(a) to the extent that a best value authority considers it necessary or expedient, in order to permit or facilitate compliance with the requirements of Part I of the 1999 Act (Best Value), to exercise the functions regulated by that section in relation to its public supply or works contracts with reference to those matters; or
(b) for the purposes of any functions regulated by that section in relation to a public supply or works contract which involves a transfer of staff to which the provisions of the Transfer of Undertakings (Protection of Employment) Regulations 1981 may apply.

These provisions marked a move away from exclusively (ideologically and) commercially driven CCT to Best Value contracting by local authorities which permitted consideration of workers' terms and conditions. Best Value, coupled with the amendments made to the LGA 1988, provided a climate less hostile to contract compliance than did CCT though Higgins and Roper argued at the time that the application of Best Value across the range of local authority activities (by contrast with CCT which only ever applied to specific local authority functions), coupled with the requirement that authorities subject 'all of their services to a fundamental [Best Value] review process over five years and in so doing … address … challenge, consultation, comparison and competition', was likely to result in more, rather than less, outsourcing than took place under CCT.[13] The figures for spend on local authority outsourcing before and after the LGA 1999 are not readily available, but the trend over time for government spending in general suggests that the move to Best Value did not significantly reduce outsourcing.[14]

Contract Compliance and EU Law

The legal position concerning contract compliance is a complicated one, regulated by EU-derived law on public procurement and, more recently, by the PSED. Extensive discussion of public procurement law and its intersection with the PSED is beyond the scope

[11] Prior to 2012 local authorities had to report to the Audit Commission on a range of 'best value' indicators which allowed the Commission to judge whether 'best value' was being achieved (authorities also had to report against 'Best Value Performance Plans' for a numb er of years. Reporting requirements ended with the abolition in 2012 of the Commission.

[12] Adopted under s19 LGA 1999.

[13] P Higgins and I Roper, *Does Best Value Offer a Better Deal for Local Government Workers than Compulsory Competitive Tendering?* (2002, Discussion paper, Middlesex University).

[14] See Figure 1 in T Sasse et al, *Government outsourcing When and how to bring public services back into government hands* (Institute for Government, 2020), available at https://www.instituteforgovernment.org.uk/sites/default/files/publications/government-outsourcing-public-services-government-hands.pdf.

of this chapter, but a short summary will be provided with a focus on the potential of the relevant law to limit equality-related contract compliance initiatives.

The Public Procurement Directives (Council Directives 93/37, 93/36, 92/50 and 93/38) first regulated the contracting process in relation, respectively, to works, supplies, services and utilities. They applied to contracts which exceed specified financial thresholds and require that the tendering process be transparent and that the selection of candidates in the award of tenders be based on objective criteria.[15] They were replaced from January 2006 by Directives 2004/17 and 2004/18, which imposed regulated, respectively, the water, energy, transport and postal services sectors, and public works contracts, public supply contracts and public service contracts. Directive 2004/18 was implemented in the UK by the UK Public Contract Regulations 2006.

The EU Directives have been implemented by the Public Contracts Regulations 2015 (PCR), Utilities Contracts Regulations 2016 (UCR), Concessions Contracts Regulations 2016 (CCR) and Defence and Security Public Contracts Regulations 2011 (DSPCR), which apply respectively to procurement by public sector organisations, by certain utility companies, of works and services concession contracts,[16] and of certain defence and security contracts.[17] The legislation, recently amended, remains in place despite the UK's withdrawal from the EU though contracting authorities have been released from the obligation to comply with 'general EU treaty principles' in relation to contracts below the procurement directives' thresholds.

In short summary, the various regulations apply only to contracts whose commercial value exceeds certain thresholds,[18] requiring that contracting authorities[19] contract on the basis of an advertised competitive contract award process based on objective, relevant and proportionate criteria. Contract award procedures must be open to economic operators from the UK; EU Member States (for procurements covered by the EU–UK Trade and Cooperation Agreement); non-EU GPA states (for procurements covered by the WTO's plurilateral Agreement on Government Procurement (GPA)); and other countries with which the UK has relevant bilateral procurement agreements. Contracting authorities must act transparently and proportionately and must treat bidders equally and without discrimination.

As a general rule contracting authorities must:

- advertise contracts on 'Find a Tender' (FTS)[20] and on the relevant the national online portal for public contracts, providing prescribed details including award criteria and any legal, economic and financial, technical and professional requirements and inviting expressions of interest within given timescales;

[15] Transposed into UK law, respectively, by The Public Works Contracts Regulations 1991; The Public Supply Contracts Regulations 1995; The Public Service Contracts Regulations 1993; and The Utility Supply and Works Contracts Regulations 1992.

[16] Defined as contracts in which consideration consists wholly or partly in the right to exploit the works or services that are the subject of the contract with operating risk transferring to the concessionaire.

[17] The PCR, UCR and CCR apply to England, Wales and Northern Ireland (Scotland having its own similar legislation) and the DSPCR applying to the UK.

[18] Ranging for the two years from 1 January 2022 from £138,760 incl of VAT in the case of supplies and most services contracts entered into by central government bodies works contracts under the PCR to £5,336,937 incl of VAT for works contracts under the PCR, UCR and DSPCR and concession contracts under the CCR.

[19] Defined for present purposes to include non-public authorities contracting under the CCR or DSPCR.

[20] https://www.findatenderservice.co.uk.

- determine whether an economic operator which has expressed an interest has the necessary legal and financial standing and the relevant technical and professional ability to perform the contract;
- invite a shortlist of qualified economic operators, selected on the basis of objective and non-discriminatory rules and criteria, to submit tenders or carry out negotiations before submitting tenders;
- evaluate tenders on the basis of pre-disclosed objective award criteria linked to the subject matter of the contract, so as to determine the most economically advantageous tender;
- notify decisions to all economic operators which have submitted tenders;
- observe a minimum 10-day standstill period;
- conclude contracts after this period only if no legal challenge has been made to the contract award;
- advertise contract awards on FTS.

Focusing in this context on the matters most relevant to the furtherance of equality, contracting authorities may (in determining whether an interested person is eligible to participate in a procurement process) take into account only the applicant's suitability to pursue a professional activity, its economic and financial standing, and its technical and professional ability, as well as whether it has committed certain offences which would normally require or permit its exclusion from the competition.[21] Contracting authorities are obliged to award contracts to the bidder which in its view has the most economically advantageous tender, assessed by reference to price or cost alone, or the best price:quality ratio assessed on the basis of criteria that are linked to the subject matter of the contract. These criteria may include qualitative, environmental or social aspects but may not confer unrestricted freedom of choice on the contracting authority, such as would be the case if the criteria were not clearly defined. The criteria must permit effective competition by allowing an objective comparison of the relative merits of the tenders; and must be accompanied by specifications permitting the information provided by the tenderers to be effectively verified.

The EHRC has provided guidance on how the PSED may intersect with the public procurement framework. It should be noted that the furtherance of equality through contracting is not limited to ensuring that contractors comply with the EqA in relation to their staff, but extends to the contracted-out tasks themselves.[22] Recent local authority trends appear to be towards insourcing,[23] but contract compliance remains a powerful tool for promoting equality where public authorities engage in contractual arrangements.

Returning to the more conventional mechanisms for enforcement of equality-related legislation, the enforcement of the individual-related provisions of the EqA is dealt with at pp 278 and following, of the PSED at pp 272–277 and of HRA at pp 277–278 below. Before turning to these issues, it is worth considering the powers of the Equality and Human Rights Commission (EHRC) to investigate and challenge discrimination.

[21] Exclusion is mandatory for a period of five years for certain offences relating to bribery, corruption, conspiracy, fraud affecting the EU's financial interests, money laundering, as well as certain offences related to terrorism, proceeds of crime, drug trafficking, human trafficking and modern slavery. See below for discretionary exclusion.

[22] EHRC, *Buying better outcomes: Mainstreaming equality considerations in procurement, A guide for public authorities in England* (2022), available at https://www.equalityhumanrights.com/en/publication-download/buying-better-outcomes-mainstreaming-equality-considerations-procurement-guide.

[23] See eg T Sasse, n 14 above.

The EHRC

The EHRC was created in 2006, absorbing the functions of the previous Commission for Racial Equality (CRE), Equal Opportunities Commission (EOC) and Disability Rights Commission (DRC) which had responsibilities for, respectively, race, sex and disability. On its creation, the EHRC was also given responsibilities in respect of sexual orientation, religion and belief and age, as well as human rights. The EHRC had a budget of £70m and the capacity to employ 525 full-time equivalent (FTE) staff when it was established in 2007.[24] This budget had been reduced to £55m in 2010 and to £17.1m in 2020/21, during which year the EHRC employed 183 FTE permanent staff and an additional 16 short-term/agency/seconded staff.[25]

The Equality Act 2006 (EqA 2006), which established the EHRC (formally entitled the Commission for Equality and Human Rights) provides that:

Section 8 EqA 2006, Equality and diversity

(1) The Commission shall, by exercising the powers conferred by this Part—
   (a) promote understanding of the importance of equality and diversity,
   (b) encourage good practice in relation to equality and diversity,
   (c) promote equality of opportunity,
   (d) promote awareness and understanding of rights under the Equality Act 2010,
   (e) enforce that Act,
   (f) work towards the elimination of unlawful discrimination, and
   (g) work towards the elimination of unlawful harassment …

Section 9 EqA 2006, Human rights

(1) The Commission shall, by exercising the powers conferred by this Part—
   (a) promote understanding of the importance of human rights,
   (b) encourage good practice in relation to human rights,
   (c) promote awareness, understanding and protection of human rights, and
   (d) encourage public authorities to comply with section 6 of the Human Rights Act 1998 (c 42) (compliance with Convention rights).

(2) In this Part 'human rights' means—
   (a) the Convention rights within the meaning given by section 1 of the Human Rights Act 1998, and
   (b) other human rights …

Sections 11 and 12 EqA 2006 provide that the EHRC shall 'monitor the effectiveness of the equality and human rights enactments' and also monitor societal progress in relation to ss8 and 9 of the Act. Sections 13 and 17 EqA 2006 provide the EHRC with 'general powers' to disseminate ideas or information, undertake research, provide education and training and provide general advice pursuant to its duties under ss8 and 9 EqA 2006, and to provide grants to other bodies.[26] Sections 14 and 15 EqA 2006 impose powers and duties to

[24] Annual Report 2008–2009, available at https://www.equalityhumanrights.com/sites/default/files/ehrc_ar_2008-09.pdf; Comprehensive Budget Review of the Equality and Human Rights Commission, available at https://assets.publishing.service.gov.uk/government/uploads/system/uploads/attachment_data/file/86430/Comprehensive_Budget_Review_of_the_EHRC_.pdf.

[25] Annual Report 2020–21, available at https://www.equalityhumanrights.com/sites/default/files/annual-report-and-accounts-2020-21.pdf.

[26] Section 13(2) providing that the reference to advice in s13(1) 'does not include a reference to preparing, or assisting in the preparation of, a document to be used for the purpose of legal proceedings'.

issue codes of practice which courts and tribunals are required to take into account where relevant to matters under consideration.[27] Section 16 EqA 2006 provides the EHRC with the power to undertake inquiries into matters relating to equality/ human rights.

EHRC Inquiries and Investigations

Sections 16 and 20 EqA 2006 are set out below. Before turning to consider them, it is useful to place them in historical context. The provisions are the successor to the powers of formal investigation (FI) granted to the CRE and EOC respectively by the RRA and SDA. As we shall see, these powers were subject to marked judicial hostility which rendered them all but unusable. The FI powers were intended to play a very significant role in the enforcement of the early anti-discrimination legislation, having been 'identified in two Government White Papers which preceded the [SDA] and [RRA] as strategic in identifying and eliminating discriminatory practices'.[28] As Vera Sacks and Judith Maxwell pointed out in 1984, the RRA White Paper had stated that: 'The Commission's *main tasks* will be ... to identify and deal with discriminatory practices by industries, firms or institutions' and this could be 'on its own initiative' and 'whether or not there had been individual complaints about the organisation investigated' (emphasis added).[29] Sacks and Maxwell went on to report that 'Extensive investigatory powers were conferred on the [CRE] for this purpose for it was recognised that the individual would usually lack the resources to finance and compile proof, and that what was needed was an independent body acting in the public interest who could undertake a thorough appraisal of practices, policies and procedures which, although apparently neutral, might have a discriminatory impact.'

The CRE made full use of its FI powers in the early years, launching no less than 17 such investigations in its first 18 months of operation (June 1977–January 1979), and a total of 63 to the end of 1999.[30] The CRE displayed considerably more relish for its investigative powers than did the EOC, though, as Ellis and Appleby pointed out, it did have the benefit of years of experience on the part of the Race Relations Board (whose remit, albeit considerably expanded, it inherited).[31] Having said this, the pace of FI slowed considerably after 1984 in the wake of the *Hillingdon* and *Prestige* cases (discussed below), half of the FIs being concluded in the 7.5 years to the end of 1984, the other 50 per cent taking an additional 15 years. The early approach of the CRE to FIs is discussed by Mary Coussey:

Mary Coussey, 'The Effectiveness of Strategic Enforcement of the Race Relations Act 1976', in B Hepple and E Szyszczak (eds), *Discrimination: The Limits of Law*, footnotes omitted

> The strategic investigations carried out by the CRE before the *Prestige* decision in 1984 were chosen with reference to the broad labour market position. It was decided to carry out a rolling programme of general enquiries into the extent of inequality in a number of representative industries located in areas of significant ethnic minority population. In this way, it would be possible to build up a range of models, demonstrating in practical terms how discrimination operates. Over a dozen such enquiries were started. By selecting large companies in industrial sectors in which ethnic minorities were concentrated, it was anticipated that the findings of the investigations would be relevant to other employers in the same industry.

[27] See s15(4) EqA 2006 and discussion in Ch 8 n 23.
[28] V Sacks and J Maxwell, 'Unnatural Justice for Discriminators' (1984) 47 *Modern Law Review* 334, 334–35.
[29] *Ibid.*
[30] C McCrudden, D Smith and C Brown, *Racial Justice at Work* (London, Policy Studies Institute, 1991) 452.
[31] E Ellis and G Appleby, 'Formal Investigations: the CRE and the EOC as Law Enforcement Agencies' (1984) *Public Law* 236. The Race Relations Board had been established under the RRA 1965.

These enquiries combined a strategic and inspectorial approach. However, their aims were not fulfilled because many of the early strategic investigations had to be abandoned after the *Prestige* decision. But the experience gained was the basis for many of the recommendations in the Code of Practice, as these enquiries identified most of the potentially discriminatory practices and other barriers caused by disadvantage in the labour market.

For example, there were five reports published of general investigations, started before the *Prestige* decision, into named organizations. The enquiries covered a wide range of personnel decision-making and practices at different job levels. Many potentially discriminatory practices were identified. These included informal word-of-mouth recruitment, which effectively excluded ethnic minority applicants from access to jobs, and the application of geographical preferences, which in some circumstances disproportionately excluded ethnic minorities (e.g. applicants should not live in Liverpool 8). Discriminatory selection criteria were also found, such as informal oral or written English tests which had little relation to the standards needed for the work, and which screened out a large majority of Asian candidates. Subjective criteria, acceptability criteria and stereotypical judgments were widespread. The use of sponsorship as a qualification for a hackney cab licence was found to be a discriminatory practice. One enquiry was restarted as a 'belief' investigation, and focused more narrowly on promotion procedures, identifying the interview as a discriminatory practice because it rejected ethnic minority candidates for lack of communication skills. This was found to be unjustifiable because the interview did not test the more direct work-related communication require for the job.

Other early investigations published before 1984 (and therefore unaffected by *Prestige*) uncovered a similar array of discriminatory practices. These included direct discrimination and pressure to discriminate by shop stewards, and indirect discrimination by Massey Ferguson in the use of unsolicited letters for recruitment. The latter practice favoured applicants with links with the workforce. As the workforce was overwhelmingly white, the letters of application also came mainly from white people. Inside knowledge also meant that applicants wrote to apply for a specific vacancy as it arose. Ethnic minority applicants had no such networks at the plant, and tended to call at the factory gates. When this occurred, they may have been advised to 'write in,' but few did so. Many had no confidence that their letters would be successful. The company argued that this recruitment practice was not a 'requirement' (which is one of the criteria in the statutory definition of indirect discrimination [see further Chapter 2]) because applicants who applied in other ways were sometimes considered. Had this early case come to the courts, it would have been an interesting test of the meaning of 'requirement or condition' in Section 1(1)(b) of the Race Relations Act, demonstrating as it does the ease with which employers can point to one or two exceptions to challenge the existence of a practice or 'requirement.'

This investigation also showed the powerful effect of a poor company image: the chill factor. It was known among the ethnic minority communities in Coventry, the site of the plant, that it was a 'waste of time' applying to Massey Ferguson for a job if you were black or Asian, because 'no one like me' was employed there. The 'chill factor' is still an important deterrent to ethnic minority candidates, as several recent surveys by employers have shown. See, for example, the recent survey 'Ethnic Minority Recruitment to the Armed Services,' published by the Ministry of Defence in January 1990. According to this research, one-third of Asians and half of Afro-Caribbeans in the survey expected to find racial discrimination when applying to the armed services.

None of the companies involved in these pre-1984 investigations had taken steps to implement equal opportunities policies. The discriminatory practices could flourish unchecked, as there were no records of the ethnic origin of applicants or employees. Ironically; in the absence of such data, it was difficult for the commission to find sufficient evidence of discriminatory practices. The alternative was to rely on employers' records of reasons for rejection or their accounts of selection practices. Not surprisingly, the evidence gleaned from this was often too weak to justify the use of the enforcement powers.

The CRE faced significant resistance from the courts. The disapproval with which elements of the judiciary regarded the investigative powers of the commissions was evident from the start. Lord Hailsham likened the CRE's powers to those of the Star Chamber in the House of Lords debate on the Bill.[32] And in *Science Research Council v Nassé* [1979] QB 144, Lord Denning declared that the CRE's investigative powers enabled it to 'interrogate employers ... up to the hilt and compel disclosure of documents on a massive scale ... You might think that we were back in the days of the inquisition.'

Vera Sacks and Judith Maxwell, 'Unnatural Justice for Discriminators' (1984) 47 *Modern Law Review* 334, 338, footnotes omitted

Lord Oliver in *Mandla v Dowell Lee* [1983] 2 AC 548 has accused the CRE of using the Race Relations Act as an 'engine of oppression,' Lord Denning has likened an investigation to a criminal charge, while Lord Diplock voiced an implied criticism against the CRE for wasting public money – when the waste was in fact occasioned by the courts' interpretation of their powers ... The courts have found in favour of respondents and their multiplicity of challenges to the CRE on procedural grounds.

The *Hillingdon* and *Prestige* cases were mentioned above. In *Hillingdon LBC v CRE* [1982] AC 779 the House of Lords (HL) took its first substantial step towards curbing what it evidently saw as the excessive powers of the Commission by requiring that the CRE, before it began an investigation into a named individual or organisation, had formed a belief that the subject of the investigation might be or have been engaged in unlawful discrimination *of the type* (narrowly defined) which was to be investigated. This involved a strained interpretation of the relevant statutory provision.[33] Their Lordships also required that the subject(s) of any proposed such investigation be provided the opportunity to argue against its launch. The House of Lords reached a similar decision in *R v CRE ex parte Prestige Group plc* [1984] ICR 473, the effect of which was, as Vera Sacks later pointed out, to confine the remit of formal investigations to the 'narrow factual issue' whose report to the Commission triggered the investigation.[34] Sacks attributed the low number of FIs conducted by the EOC in part both to the technicality of the legal provisions, and to their judicial interpretation. The power granted to the EHRC by s16 EqA 2006 to conduct inquiries goes some way to alleviating the problem highlighted by Sacks.

Section 16 EqA 2006, Inquiries

(1) The Commission may conduct an inquiry into a matter relating to any of the Commission's duties under sections 8 and 9.

(2) If in the course of an inquiry the Commission begins to suspect that a person may have committed an unlawful act—

  (a) in continuing the inquiry the Commission shall, so far as possible, avoid further consideration of whether or not the person has committed an unlawful act,

  (b) the Commission may commence an investigation into that question under section 20,

  (c) the Commission may use information or evidence acquired in the course of the inquiry for the purpose of the investigation, and

  (d) the Commission shall so far as possible ensure (whether by aborting or suspending the inquiry or otherwise) that any aspects of the inquiry which concern the person investigated, or may require his involvement, are not pursued while the investigation is in progress.

[32] 373 HL Debs 20 July 1976, col 745.

[33] See Ellis and Appleby, n 31 above, 244.

[34] V Sacks, 'The Equal Opportunities Commission – Ten Years On' (1986) 49 *Modern Law Review* 560.

(3) The report of an inquiry—

(a) may not state (whether expressly or by necessary implication) that a specified or identifiable person has committed an unlawful act, and

(b) shall not otherwise refer to the activities of a specified or identifiable person unless the Commission thinks that the reference—

(i) will not harm the person, or

(ii) is necessary in order for the report adequately to reflect the results of the inquiry.

(4) Subsections (2) and (3) shall not prevent an inquiry from considering or reporting a matter relating to human rights (whether or not a necessary implication arises in relation to the Equality Act 2010).

(5) Before settling a report of an inquiry which records findings which in the Commission's opinion are of an adverse nature and relate (whether expressly or by necessary implication) to a specified or identifiable person the Commission shall—

(a) send a draft of the report to the person,

(b) specify a period of at least 28 days during which he may make written representations about the draft, and

(c) consider any representations made.

Additional provision for inquiries is made in Schedule 2 EqA 2006. The primary point is that the EHRC may not, under s16 EqA 2006, investigate suspicions that any person involved in the inquiry is guilty of unlawful activity. The provision was intended to avoid some of the difficulties associated with formal investigations (now replaced by s20 investigations), discussed below. By April 2022, 15 years after its creation,[35] the EHRC had initiated inquiries into:

- how older and disabled adults and unpaid carers can challenge local council decisions about social care and support in England and Wales;
- the treatment and experience of ethnic minority workers in lower paid roles in the health and social care sectors;
- the experiences of disabled defendants or accused in the criminal justice system;
- how schools are monitoring and recording their use of restraint;
- racial harassment in universities and higher education colleges;
- whether legal aid enables people who raise a discrimination complaint in England and Wales to get justice;
- the availability of accessible and adaptable housing, and the support services around it, in England, Scotland and Wales;
- non-natural deaths of adults with mental health conditions in detention in prisons, police custody and psychiatric hospitals in England and Wales;
- board level appointment practices of the top 350 listed companies;
- disability-related harassment;
- the effectiveness of the English care and support system in protecting and promoting the human rights of older people requiring or receiving home-based care and support;
- trafficking for the purposes of commercial sexual exploitation in Scotland.

[35] See https://www.equalityhumanrights.com/en/our-legal-action/inquiries-and-investigations.

Taking, by way of example, the EHRC's two-year investigation into the harassment of disabled people, in 2011 the commission published *Hidden in Plain Sight*,[36] which reported that many disabled people routinely suffered harassment in respect of which there was a 'culture of disbelief'. Such harassment was under-reported and, whether or not reported, was inadequately responded to by public authorities. The EHRC made a number of initial recommendations in 2011, on publication of its report, and carried out a six-month consultation in which it asked a number of organisations formally to respond to the inquiry and to advise the EHRC of what they planned to do differently as a result of the inquiry. These responses from organisations including HM Government, the CPS, GMC and CQC, Her Majesty's Inspectorates of Constabulary and Probation, and Ofsted were published by the EHRC[37] which 'encourage[d] individuals, disabled people's organisations and others to use these to hold each organisation to account'.[38] Whether or not adequate progress has been made by these and other agencies, the example illustrates the potential of s16 inquiries to result in systemic change.

Suspicions of unlawful activity may only be investigated under s20 EqA 2006 Act which provides procedural protections for those under investigation.

Section 20 EqA 2006, Investigations

(1) The Commission may investigate whether or not a person—
   (a) has committed an unlawful act,
   (b) has complied with a requirement imposed by an unlawful act notice under section 21, or
   (c) has complied with an undertaking given under section 23.

(2) The Commission may conduct an investigation under subsection (1)(a) only if it suspects that the person concerned may have committed an unlawful act.

(3) A suspicion for the purposes of subsection (2) may (but need not) be based on the results of, or a matter arising during the course of, an inquiry under section 16.

(4) Before settling a report of an investigation recording a finding that a person has committed an unlawful act or has failed to comply with a requirement or undertaking the Commission shall—
   (a) send a draft of the report to the person,
   (b) specify a period of at least 28 days during which he may make written representations about the draft, and
   (c) consider any representations made.

(5) Schedule 2 makes supplemental provision about investigations.[39]

The EHRC has carried out only five s20 investigations in the 15 years since its creation.[40] The very low number may be a reflection of the difficulties inherent in such investigations or (or, likely, and) the constraints on the EHRC's budget (see p 252 above).

[36] Available at https://www.equalityhumanrights.com/en/inquiries-and-investigations/inquiry-disability-related-harassment/download-disability-related.

[37] https://www.equalityhumanrights.com/en/inquiries-and-investigations/inquiry-disability-related-harassment/progress-inquiry.

[38] *Out in the open. Tackling disability-related harassment: A manifesto for change*, available at https://www.equalityhumanrights.com/en/publication-download/out-open-tackling-disability-related-harassment-manifesto-change.

[39] Schedule 2 contains detailed provisions relating to, eg, terms of reference, notice to persons under investigation and the opportunity for such persons to make representations, and the collection of evidence by the EHRC.

[40] See https://www.equalityhumanrights.com/en/our-legal-action/inquiries-and-investigations. Note (Ch 7) the formal investigation into Pontins launched in May 2022.

Except in a case where (as in the care agency investigation) an unlawful act is evident on the basis of documentary evidence, a finding of illegality may require consideration of witness evidence which may itself require the possibility of cross-examination, which would in turn indicate quasi-judicial hearings, all carried out under the potential threat of judicial review challenges by bodies under investigation. Seeking to establish unlawful actions on the basis of documentary evidence may require the collection and analysis of huge amounts of material by suitably skilled individuals who are very unlikely (given budgetary constraints on the EHRC) to be directly employed by it. The EHRC has a panel of counsel it instructs to undertake work, including on s20 investigations. The rates paid by the EHRC are likely to be lower than many such barristers would generally command, but even at discounted rates it is unlikely that the EHRC's budget would stretch very far.

Perhaps the highest profile of the EHRC's s20 investigations has been into anti-Semitism within the Labour Party (discussed below). In addition, the EHRC carried out s20 investigations into suspected unlawful pay practices by the BBC; suspected unlawful race, sex and sexual orientation discrimination, harassment and victimisation of employees by the Metropolitan Police Service and suspected disability discrimination by an agency which supplies care staff. Neither the BBC nor the Met Police investigation resulted in findings of unlawful action though the former resulted in the identification of 'some areas where the BBC can make improvements to rebuild trust with women at the organisation and increase transparency around decision-making and communications' and the latter in recommendations for improvement to the Met's complaints procedures. The care agency investigation found that Elite Careplus Limited had 'asked pre-employment health questions on its job application form, between 21 November 2018 and 20 June 2019' and 'failed to show that there was a lawful reason for asking the questions. It therefore committed an unlawful act that breached section 60 of the Equality Act 2010'. The EHRC reported that the agency 'has now removed the questions from its job application form'.

Preventing Further Discrimination

The EHRC may, during the course of and after the completion of s20 investigations, issue unlawful act notices.

Section 21 EqA, Unlawful act notice

(1) The Commission may give a person a notice under this section (an 'unlawful act notice') if—
  (a) he is or has been the subject of an investigation under section 20(1)(a), and
  (b) the Commission is satisfied that he has committed an unlawful act.

(2) A notice must specify—
  (a) the unlawful act, and
  (b) the provision of the Equality Act 2010 by virtue of which the act is unlawful.

(3) A notice must inform the recipient of the effect of—
  (a) subsections (5) to (7),
  (b) section 20(1)(b), and
  (c) section 24(1).

(4) A notice may—
  (a) require the person to whom the notice is given to prepare an action plan for the purpose of avoiding repetition or continuation of the unlawful act;
  (b) recommend action to be taken by the person for that purpose.

(5) A person who is given a notice may, within the period of six weeks beginning with the day on which the notice is given, appeal to the appropriate court or tribunal on the grounds—

 (a) that he has not committed the unlawful act specified in the notice, or
 (b) that a requirement for the preparation of an action plan imposed under subsection (4)(a) is unreasonable.

(6) On an appeal under subsection (5) the court or tribunal may—

 (a) affirm a notice;
 (b) annul a notice;
 (c) vary a notice;
 (d) affirm a requirement;
 (e) annul a requirement;
 (f) vary a requirement;
 (g) make an order for costs or expenses.

(7) In subsection (5) 'the appropriate court or tribunal' means—

 (a) an employment tribunal, if a claim in respect of the alleged unlawful act could be made to it, or
 (b) the county court (in England and Wales) or the sheriff (in Scotland), if a claim in respect of the alleged unlawful act could be made to it or to him.

The EHRC has issued only one unlawful act notice, this in 2020 following its investigation into alleged anti-Semitism in the Labour Party in which it concluded that the Labour Party had breached the EqA by (1) interfering politically in antisemitism complaints and (2) failing to provide adequate training to those handling anti-Semitism complaints, both of which the EHRC found amounted to unlawful indirect discrimination, and (3) engaging in anti-Semitic harassment through Ken Livingstone, former Mayor of London and a former member of the Labour Party's National Executive Committee, and Pam Bromley, a Labour Party local authority councillor in Rossendale, who used anti-Semitic tropes and suggested that complaints of anti-Semitism were fake or smears. The EHRC required that the Labour Party draft an action plan to implement its recommendations that the Party:[41]

- Commission an independent process to handle and determine anti-Semitism complaints, as soon as rule changes allow to last until trust and confidence in the process is fully restored;
- Acknowledge the effect that political interference has had on the handling of anti-Semitism complaints;
- Implement clear rules and guidance that prohibit and sanction any inappropriate interference in the complaints process;
- Put in place long-term arrangements for independent oversight of the complaint handling process, to make sure that standards are monitored and enforced, and adequate resources are in place;
- Audit its complaint handling process to address any ongoing issues;
- Measure staff and stakeholder confidence in the complaint-handling process;
- Publish a comprehensive policy and procedure, setting out how anti-Semitism complaints will be handled and how decisions will be made. This should include published criteria

[41] https://www.equalityhumanrights.com/en/publication-download/investigation-antisemitism-labour-party.

on what conduct will be subject to investigation and suspension, and what will be considered an appropriate sanction for different types of proven anti-Semitic conduct;

- Review and update its 'Code of Conduct: Social Media Policy' to make it clear that members may be investigated and subject to disciplinary action if they share or like any anti-Semitic social media content;
- Commission and provide education and practical training for all individuals involved in the anti-Semitism complaints process. This should be implemented fully within six months of publication of this report and, from that date, should be mandatory before any individual is allowed to be involved in any stage of the anti-Semitism complaints process;
- Make sure that all members found to have engaged in antisemitic conduct undertake an educational course on identifying and tackling anti-Semitism, regardless of the level of sanction applied;
- Engage with Jewish stakeholders to develop and embed clear, accessible and robust principles and practices to tackle anti-Semitism and to instil confidence for the future.

Section 22 EqA 2006 provides that failure to provide an action plan required by a s21 EqA 2006 notice by the specified date may result in an application by the EHRC for a court order to the requiring the preparation of a plan; further, that the EHRC may seek a court order requiring compliance with an agreed action plan for a period of five years from its start date. Failure to comply with a court order is an offence punishable by a fine (s22(9) EqA).

Unlawful act notices may be issued only when the EHRC is satisfied that the recipient has breached the EqA 2010. By contrast, s23 permits the commission to reach agreements with persons (legal or actual) by which the other party to the agreement agrees not to commit 'an unlawful act of a specified kind, and to take, or refrain from taking, other specified action (which may include the preparation of a plan for the purpose of avoiding an unlawful act)', and the commission agrees not to undertake a s20 investigation or issue a s21 unlawful act notice.[42] Such agreements may be made only where the EHRC thinks that the person has committed an unlawful act, but s22(3) provides that by entering into a s22 agreement the other party 'shall not be taken to admit to the commission of an unlawful act by reason only of entering into an agreement under this section'. Both action plans and s23 agreements may be varied, and s23 agreements terminated, by agreement.

Under the predecessor equality legislation, the commissions (EOC, CRE and DRC) had powers to conduct formal investigations and to issue non-discrimination notices (NDNs). The RRA and SDA provided rights of appeal against an NDN to an employment tribunal in employment-related cases, to the county or (in Scotland) sheriff court in other cases, and further provided that the tribunal or court should quash a requirement in an NDN where it 'considers a requirement in respect of which an appeal is brought … to be unreasonable because it is based on an incorrect finding of fact or for any other reason'.[43] This provision was interpreted by the Court of Appeal (CA) in *R v CRE ex parte Amari*

[42] The CRE and EOC had in fact routinely entered into voluntary agreements during the course of, or after the completion of, formal investigations, by which the party under investigation entered binding commitments to the achievement of specified outcomes by particular dates. Details of recent such agreements can be found in the CRE's [and EOC's] *Annual Reports* and included voluntary agreements reached between the CRE and the CPS in September 2001 and between the CRE and the MOD/Household Cavalry which came to an end in 2003, and between the EOC and the Post Office which resulted in the suspension of an FI into sexual harassment in the post office.

[43] Section 59 RRA and s68 SDA.

Plastics [1982] QB 1194, to require a reopening of all the findings of fact, rather than simply the NDN requirements themselves, an approach defended by Browne-Wilkinson J on the basis that 'a requirement "to stop beating your wife" is unreasonable if you have never beaten your wife'.[44] The impact was to impose further procedural hurdles on an enforcement mechanism which had been intended to be an alternative to judicial enforcement. NDNs were also flawed in that, as the CRE pointed out in 1983, the legislation did not permit it 'to postulate what changes, in the Commission's view, are necessary to avoid a repetition of the discriminatory act', as distinct from making recommendations.[45]

The CRE's 1983 recommendation that it be 'given power to state in a non-discrimination notice what changes in the respondents practice are the minimum necessary' fell on deaf ears at the time, but has been answered by s21 EqA 2006,[46] which requires the drawing-up and implementation of action plans agreed with the EHRC. Further, the EqA 2006 does not provide an appeal route to the courts, though judicial review would be available in respect of irrational or procedurally unfair or otherwise unlawful action by the EHRC in connection with investigations.

PSED Assessments

The EqA 2006 also makes provision for the EHRC to carry out assessments of public authorities' compliance with their PSED obligations.

> **Section 31 EqA 2006, Applications to court**
>
> The Commission may assess the extent to which or the manner in which a person has complied with a duty under or by virtue of section 149, 153 or 154 of the Equality Act 2010 (public sector equality duty).
>
> Schedule 2 makes supplemental provision about assessments.
>
> This section is without prejudice to the generality of sections 16 and 20.

Schedule 2 provides, so far as relevant, that the EHRC will provide a person subject to a s31 assessment with the proposed terms of reference and an opportunity to make representations about them, which representations it is required to consider prior to publication of the final terms of reference. The EHRC is also required to take into account representations made by the person under investigation in relation to the substantive matter under assessment and otherwise to act in a similar manner as in s20 investigations.

The power provided to the EHRC by s31 EqA 2006 is in addition to the standard method of enforcement for the PSED, which consists of applications for judicial review by individuals or organisations with an interest in the matter. In April 2022 the EHRC's website recorded two assessments undertaken into compliance with the PSED. These consisted in assessments (1) of the Home Office's 'hostile environment policies' affecting the Windrush generation and (2) of the extent to which the Treasury met its legal obligations to consider the impact of the Government's 2010 Spending Review on people with protected characteristics.[47] The EHRC's assessment of the Home Office, discussed in Chapter 7, was damning.

[44] [1982] 1 QB 265, 272.

[45] CRE, *The Race relations Act – Time for a Change?* (CRE, 1983).

[46] It had also been answered by the Disability Rights Commission Act 1999 which created the DRC, subsequently merged into the EHRC (see s4 of the now repealed DRCA).

[47] https://www.equalityhumanrights.com/en/our-legal-action/inquiries-and-investigations.

Gender Pay Gap Reporting

The EHRC also has powers in relation to the enforcement of obligations in respect of gender pay gap reporting. The Equality Act 2010 (Gender Pay Gap Information) Regulations 2017 and Equality Act 2010 (Specific Duties and Public Authorities) Regulations 2017 impose upon private and voluntary sector employers with 250 or more employees and specified public sector employers in England (and a limited number of non-devolved bodies) obligations to publish, and to submit to the EHRC, information about the gender pay gaps within their organisations. The Regulations could reasonably be characterised as crude in as much as they require reporting on overall hourly pay gaps at the level of the institution, rather than more granular information. They appear to have had some impact, however, in drawing attention to the very significant gaps between male and female wages in number of organisations.

Even before the Regulations came into force the BBC had been required in July 2017, under its new Royal Charter, to publish a list of all employees earning more than £150,000. The list of 96 employees contained 62 men and 34 women, all seven of the highest earners being men. This publication resulted in external and internal criticism of the BBC, the resignation of Carrie Gracie as BBC China Editor, reports that a number of high-profile men at the BBC had agreed to take pay cuts and, eventually, in the EHRC's s20 investigation into the BBC. In 2020 *The Guardian* reported that the BBC had been 'rushing to settle' equal pay claims to give incoming director general Tim Davies 'a clean slate':

'BBC has given rises to 700 female staff since start of pay scandal', *The Guardian*, 14 September 2020[48]

In total at least 84 women were given pay increases through formal processes between July 2017 and March 2020, according to a freedom of information request made by Caroline Barlow, a former BBC employee who received £130,000 in an equal pay dispute. During the same time period 608 women received a pay revision or increase through an informal pay enquiry process started in the wake of the equal pay scandal. The BBC said not all of these cases related to women being paid less than men and an unknown number of men had also seen their pay increase through the same procedure.

In the most high profile case, Newswatch presenter Samira Ahmed successfully took the BBC to an employment tribunal to seek more than £700,000 in back pay after she was paid substantially less than Jeremy Vine for presenting an equivalent programme. The hearings were deeply embarrassing for the BBC, as internal emails about pay negotiations were made public.

New deals over the summer have now pushed the combined number of equal pay settlements and pay revisions for women to over 700, according to sources at the corporation. Following these recent settlements there are now fewer than 10 equal pay cases outstanding but there is still concern among staff that in some cases women are still earning less than the men they are managing …

The BBC has been keen to promote its progress on equalising pay for on-air stars who take home more than £150,000 a year from the corporation. When these figures were first made public in 2017, at the behest of the Conservative government, they revealed that just a third of top-earning presenters were women.

The fall-out resulted in many high-earning men such as Chris Evans and Jeremy Vine either departing the corporation or taking substantial pay cuts. BBC sources say the new annual report will show that 45% of top-earning presenters are now women, including the likes of 6Music presenter Lauren Laverne.

[48] https://www.theguardian.com/media/2020/sep/14/bbc-has-settled-at-least-700-female-employees-equal-pay-claims.

However, these figures have been aided by the removal of high-earning male actors who make shows for the BBC's drama department as they are now classed as working for a commercial organisation. Match of the Day's Gary Lineker is expected to top the list yet again …

The gender pay gap reporting obligations have also had a significant impact in the legal profession, drawing attention as they did to the very large gaps between typical male and female pay in solicitors firms. In 2020 the Law Society reported 'key findings' from an analysis of data from over 40 large law firms.

Law Society, Gender pay gap reporting: what can we learn from the 2020 snapshot?[49]

… Across all organisations reporting … the average gap in men and women's mean hourly pay was 14% and in median pay it was 12.6% … 42 [of the 52 largest law firms] had submitted a gender pay gap report for April 2020 … Among these 42 firms, the average gap in mean hourly pay was 20.3%, and for median hourly pay it was 32.4%. For most firms, this does not include partner pay[50] …

Of the 41 law firms reporting for 2017 and 2020, 28 saw a decrease in their mean gender pay gap based on hourly pay, 12 experienced an increase and one firm saw no change.

Based on the median, 20 firms experienced a decrease and 21 firms saw an increase.

Minimum and maximum pay gaps reported

The range of pay gaps reported by the firms in this report has shifted downwards slightly. The highest reported mean and median pay gaps in 2020 are lower than those reported in 2017. In 2017, the highest mean gender pay gap was 39.1%, and in 2020 it was 38.8%. The highest median gap in 2017 was 68.2%, while in the 2020 snapshot, the highest median was 67.5%.

Gender bonus gaps

On average, the largest law firms reported that a similar proportion of men (58.3%) and women (59.6%) received bonuses in the pay period covering the April 2020 snapshot date. However, on average, men received bonuses that were of higher value. The average gap between the value of men's and women's bonuses in 2020 was 39.4%.

The EHRC is responsible for the enforcement of the Gender Pay Gap Regulations. It reported in March 2022 that its policy is to send warning notices to organisations which fail to report in compliance with the statutory timetable before (possibly) investigating whether organisations are breaching the regulations:

Gender pay gap: our enforcement action[51]

If you are [breaching the Regulations] we will send you a 'statutory unlawful act notice', which is a letter telling you to comply with your reporting obligations. If you are a public body we may carry out a public sector assessment or send you a 'statutory compliance notice', as required. If any organisation fails to comply with a statutory compliance notice, we may seek a court order against you. Failing to comply with the court order is an offence, punishable with an unlimited fine if you are convicted.'

We will make details of any employers that we investigate available on our website.

Action we took in 2021

We took action against 1,400 employers who had registered but failed to report by the extended October 2021 deadline. This included issuing warning notices to over 200 public sector employers

[49] 9 December 2021, available at https://www.lawsociety.org.uk/topics/research/gender-pay-gap-reporting-firms-2020-snapshot.

[50] This because partners are not employees. Where partners' statistics are included the gaps tend to widen significantly.

[51] https://www.equalityhumanrights.com/en/pay-gaps/gender-pay-gap-our-enforcement-action.

and over 1,100 private sector employers across England, Scotland and Wales. By 25 March 2022 99% of the 1,400 employers had taken the steps they needed to comply with the gender pay gap regulations. For those organisations who failed to report their gender pay gap information for the October 2021 deadline, we will consider taking formal enforcement action against repeating non-reporters once the 2022 reporting deadlines have passed.

We consider this approach proportionate in view of the shorter period for enforcement between the extended 5 October 2021 deadline and the 2022 deadlines.

The EHRC as Litigant

The EqA 2006 provides the EHRC with the power to litigate under a number of provisions, as follows:

Section 24 EqA 2006, Applications to court

(1) If the Commission thinks that a person is likely to commit an unlawful act, it may apply—
  (a) in England and Wales, to the county court for an injunction restraining the person from committing the act, or
  (b) in Scotland, to the sheriff for an interdict prohibiting the person from committing the act.

(2) Subsection (3) applies if the Commission thinks that a party to an agreement under section 23 has failed to comply, or is likely not to comply, with an undertaking under the agreement.

(3) The Commission may apply to the county court (in England and Wales) or to the sheriff (in Scotland) for an order requiring the person—
  (a) to comply with his undertaking, and
  (b) to take such other action as the court or the sheriff may specify.

Section 24(2)–(3) EqA 2006 provide the EHRC with power to enforce s23 agreements, but s24(1) is of broader application.

Section 24A EqA 2006, Enforcement powers: supplemental

(1) This section has effect in relation to—
  (a) an act which is unlawful because, by virtue of any of sections 13 to 18 of the Equality Act 2010, it amounts to a contravention of any of Parts 3, 4, 5, 6 or 7 of that Act,
  (b) an act which is unlawful because it amounts to a contravention of section 60(1) of that Act (or to a contravention of section 111 or 112 of that Act that relates to a contravention of section 60(1) of that Act) (enquiries about disability and health),
  (c) an act which is unlawful because it amounts to a contravention of section 106 of that Act (information about diversity in range of election candidates etc),
  (d) an act which is unlawful because, by virtue of section 108(1) of that Act, it amounts to a contravention of any of Parts 3, 4, 5, 6 or 7 of that Act, or
  (e) the application of a provision, criterion or practice which, by virtue of section 19 of that Act, amounts to a contravention of that Act.

(2) For the purposes of sections 20 to 24 of this Act, it is immaterial whether the Commission knows or suspects that a person has been or may be affected by the unlawful act or application.

(3) For those purposes, an unlawful act includes making arrangements to act in a particular way which would, if applied to an individual, amount to a contravention mentioned in subsection (1)(a).

(4) Nothing in this Act affects the entitlement of a person to bring proceedings under the Equality Act 2010 in respect of a contravention mentioned in subsection (1).

There is only one reported example of s24 having been relied upon by the EHRC.

***EHRC v Griffin* [2010] EWHC 3343 (Admin)**

The EHRC sought an injunction under s24 EqA 2006 in respect of the defendants' alleged failure to comply with a county court order issued in 2010 which (broadly speaking) prohibited the party from requiring members to adhere to racially discriminatory principles, and required that the terms of the order be widely publicised by the BNP. The defendants were at the time of the order respectively chairman and National Nominating Officer of the BNP. The EHRC, having made various investigations and enquiries, concluded that the BNP had failed to comply with the judge's order in a number of respects and applied to the county court for an order that the defendants be committed for contempt as well as for other relief, including the sequestration of the BNP's assets. The matter was transferred to the High Court as the county court judge was concerned whether he had jurisdiction to make a sequestration order. The Divisional Court (Lord Justice Moore-Bick and Ramsey J) refused to grant the injunction because it appeared that many alleged breaches by the BNP had been rectified and because the terms of the order were insufficiently clear to permit findings of contempt to be made.

The provision featured more recently in a case which was concerned with the range of remedies available in the First-tier Tribunal.

***Proprietor of Ashdown House School v JKL* [2019] UKUT 259 (AAC), [2019] Lexis Citation 92**

The question arose in a disability discrimination claim against a school whether the First-tier Tribunal had had the power to order that an independent school to reinstate a pupil and, if so, how such an order might be enforced. Having noted that the EqA provided (ss113, 116, Sch 3 and Sch 17) that disability discrimination cases concerning schools must be brought to the First-tier Tribunal which (Sch 3 para 5) could 'make such order as it thinks fit', other than an order for compensation, the Upper Tribunal accepted the argument put on behalf of the claimant that the First-tier Tribunal could order reinstatement. The school sought to argue that, because the tribunal had no power to enforce orders,[52] it was therefore limited to making declarations and recommendations. One of the matters upon which the Upper Tribunal relied in dismissing the school's arguments was that the EHRC could take action under s24 EqA 2006 if a Tribunal order was not complied with.

Judge West:

171. Miss Gannon submitted [for the school] that, whilst the power to seek an injunction was in theory available to the EHRC, it was in practice rarely exercised. Ms Darwin [for the claimant] confirmed that it may be rarely exercised, although in her professional experience sometimes threatened, frequently with efficacious results …

173. Ss. 20 to 24 of the 2006 Act empower the EHRC to conduct investigations into whether or not a person has committed an 'unlawful act', complied with an 'unlawful act notice' under s.21 and complied with an undertaking given under s.23. Under s.24 if the Commission thinks that a person is 'likely' to commit 'an unlawful act' it may apply for an injunction restraining the person from committing the act …

[52] This because the Tribunals, Courts and Enforcement Act 2007 granted First-tier Tribunals enforcement powers only in relation to compensation.

174. An 'unlawful act' is defined in s.24A of the Equality Act 2006. This definition does not in terms state that an unlawful act is a failure to comply with an order of the First-tier Tribunal …

175. In this case, therefore, the unlawful act was a contravention of the terms of s.15 in that, as found by the decision of the Tribunal, the exclusion from the School amounted to an unlawful act of disability discrimination contrary to s.15 of the 2010 Act. That would trigger the EHRC's powers under s.24. They form an exception to the requirements of s.113(1) of the 2010 Act, that proceedings relating to a contravention of the 2010 Act must be brought in accordance with that Part of the 2010 Act, since s.113(2) provides that 'Subsection (1) does not apply to proceedings under Part 1 of the Equality Act 2006' (which includes ss.20 to 24).

176. In that event it seems to me that the EHRC could potentially have intervened and brought proceedings based on the original expulsion even before the Tribunal hearing had taken place (or before the assistance of the Tribunal had been sought by the issue of proceedings) because that expulsion would itself have been an unlawful act under s.15. It did not in fact do so, but the grounds to do so appear nevertheless to have existed. In addition, the EHRC could apply for injunctive relief once the Tribunal order had been made and not complied with, since that too would have been an unlawful act, a breach of s.15 which was not going to be remedied and which was ongoing unless nipped in the bud.

In addition to the powers granted by s24 EqA 2006, s30 of the Act provides specific power for the EHRC to issue judicial review proceedings on its own account and to intervene in proceedings brought by others.

Section 30 EqA 2006, Judicial review and other legal proceedings

(1) The Commission shall have capacity to institute or intervene in legal proceedings, whether for judicial review or otherwise, if it appears to the Commission that the proceedings are relevant to a matter in connection with which the Commission has a function.

(2) The Commission shall be taken to have title and interest in relation to the subject matter of any legal proceedings in Scotland which it has capacity to institute, or in which it has capacity to intervene, by virtue of subsection (1).

(3) The Commission may, in the course of legal proceedings for judicial review which it institutes (or in which it intervenes), rely on section 7(1)(b) of the Human Rights Act 1998 (c 42) (breach of Convention rights); and for that purpose—

(a) the Commission need not be a victim or potential victim of the unlawful act to which the proceedings relate,

(b) the Commission may act only if there is or would be one or more victims of the unlawful act,

(c) section 7(3) and (4) of that Act shall not apply, and

(d) no award of damages may be made to the Commission (whether or not the exception in section 8(3) of that Act applies);

and an expression used in this subsection and in section 7 of the Human Rights Act 1998 has the same meaning in this subsection as in that section.

(4) Subsections (1) and (2)—

(a) do not create a cause of action, and

(b) are, except as provided by subsection (3), subject to any limitation or restriction imposed by virtue of an enactment (including an enactment in or under an Act of the Scottish Parliament) or in accordance with the practice of a court.

Section 30(3) exempts the EHRC from the normal requirement that, in order to pursue a claim under the HRA 1998, the claimant be a *victim* of the alleged breach, but makes it clear that there *must be such a victim*.[53] (As its name suggests, the EHRC has powers related to the HRA as well as the EqA.) The EHRC's website suggests that examples of cases in which it, rather than the victim of a HRA violation, might bring a claim include:

- If the government announces that it is going to introduce a change in the law which the Commission believes will lead to violations of people's human rights, the Commission can threaten judicial review before the legislation is passed or within 3 months of enactment. For example, when the government proposed extending the time for the detention of terrorist suspects to 42 days without charge, the Commission threatened judicial review and the proposal was dropped;
- where the subject matter of the case is one where the Commission is best placed to bring the claim because of its history, statutory duties or particular expertise;
- where there are multiple victims whose experience can be used to illustrate a problem but where a claim brought by any one of them would not tell the whole story; and
- where the actual or potential victims do not have access to lawyers, or cannot fund a claim themselves.[54]

One early example of an equality commission's application for judicial review was *EOC v Birmingham City Council* [1989] AC 1155, discussed in Chapter 2, in which the EOC challenged the council's discriminatory provision of grammar school places. The SDA provided no express power to the EOC to commence judicial review proceedings, but its ability to do so was not challenged in the *Birmingham* case. In *EOC v Secretary of State for Employment* the HL rejected the respondent's argument that the EOC had no right to challenge its imposition of differential qualifying periods for employment protection on full-time and part-time workers and issued a declaration that the discriminatory periods were contrary to EU law.

***EOC v Secretary of State for Employment* [1995] 1 AC 1**

Lord Keith (for the majority):

> [The rules regulating judicial review] provide[] that the court shall not grant leave to apply for judicial review 'unless it considers that the applicant has a sufficient interest in the matter to which the application relates'... Has the EOC a sufficient interest in that matter? Under s.53(1) of the [SDA] the duties of the EOC include: '(a) to work towards the elimination of discrimination; (b) to promote equality of opportunity between men and women generally ...' If the admittedly discriminatory [qualifying periods] ... are not objectively justified,

[53] See *Northern Ireland Human Rights Commission's Application for Judicial Review* [2018] UKSC 27, [2018] HRLR 14 for a case in which that commission's application for judicial review failed because it had not identified a victim of the human rights violations there alleged. (The case challenged the unavailability of abortion in Northern Ireland and the Supreme Court, while formally rejecting the challenge, made abundantly clear its view that the situation was incompatible with the Art 8 rights of women affected by it.) Note however *R (Cornerstone (North East) Fostering & Adoption Services v Ofsted)* [2021] EWCA Civ 1390, [2022] 2 All ER 516 in which the Court of Appeal confirmed that Ofsted could lawfully conclude that a policy of a regulated body was discriminatory without identifying an actual victim (see §137), remarking that the *NIHRC* case 'was a decision about the statutory remit of that body and does not assist Cornerstone'. See also Case C-81/12 *Associata ACCEPT v Consilul National pentru Combaterea Discriminarii* EU:C:2013:275, [2013] ICR 938 in which the CJEU ruled that a claim of direct discrimination contrary to Council Directive 2000/78 did not require an identifiable victim. See similarly Case C-507/18 *NH v Associazione Avvocatura per i diritti LGBTI – Rete Lenford* EU:C:2020:289, EU:C:2019:922, [2020] ICR 1124.

[54] https://www.equalityhumanrights.com/en/court-action.

> then steps taken by the EOC towards securing that these provisions are changed may very reasonably be regarded as taken in the course of working towards the elimination of discrimination. The present proceedings are clearly such a step. In a number of cases the EOC has been the initiating party to proceedings designed to secure the elimination of discrimination. The prime example is *EOC v Birmingham* … in which it was not suggested at any stage that the EOC lacked *locus standi*.[55] In my opinion it would be a very retrograde step now to hold that the EOC has no *locus standi* to agitate in judicial review proceedings questions related to sex discrimination which are of public importance and affect a large section of the population. The determination of this issue turns essentially upon a consideration of the statutory duties and public law role of the EOC as regards which no helpful guidance is to be gathered from decided cases. I would hold that the EOC has sufficient interest to bring these proceedings and hence the necessary *locus standi*.[56]

The potential impact of proceedings such as those in the *EOC* case is difficult to overestimate. Whereas an individual challenge to the qualifying periods would have to be brought by a claimant against her employer under the relevant legislation and would result, if successful, only in the non-application of the period to her alone, action by the EOC resulted in the removal at the national level of the discriminatory provisions.

Section 30(1) EqA 2006 also grants specific power for the EHRC to intervene in cases brought by other parties. The predecessor legislation made no specific reference to intervention and Northern Ireland's Human Rights Commission had to litigate as far as the HL to establish that it had such a power. Northern Ireland's CA had ruled that the Commission had no power to intervene in litigation commenced by individuals concerning an inquest into the deaths of victims of the Omagh bomb in 1998. The Commission wished to make a formal submission on human rights issues, but was refused by the coroner on the basis that it had no statutory power so to do. The Commission's application for judicial review failed as did its appeal to Northern Ireland's CA,[57] but the HL in *In re Northern Ireland Human Rights Commission* [2002] UKHL 25, [2002] HRLR 35 allowed its further appeal (Lord Hobhouse dissenting), ruling that the power to intervene was 'reasonably incidental' to express duties such as, in particular, duties to 'keep under review the adequacy and effectiveness of law and practice relating to the protection of human rights' and to 'promote [understanding] and [awareness of the importance] of human rights in Northern Ireland'.

Importantly, s30 EqA 2006 provides *powers* to the EHRC but does not create any *entitlement* (vis-à-vis the courts) to litigate or to intervene. In other words, the EHRC may apply for permission to bring judicial review proceedings or to intervene, but it is a matter for the court whether not permission should be granted. While it is unlikely that the EHRC would be refused permission in a judicial review claim or an application to intervene in an equality or HRA case because it lacked standing (see further below[58]), permission could be refused

[55] His Lordship also relied on *R v SSD, ex p EOC* (20 December 1991, unreported) in which it was common ground that the EOC had *locus standi*. Another instance is *R v SS Social Security, ex p EOC* Case C-9/91 [1992] ECR I-04297, which went to the ECJ.

[56] Lord Jauncey dissented on the basis that: 'the fact that the commission may properly initiate judicial review proceedings in pursuance of their duties against local authorities or other ministers is not, in my view, conclusive of its ability so to do in relation to the Secretary of State.'

[57] [2001] NI 271.

[58] Assuming that in a HRA case there existed a victim: see s30(3) EqA 2006. *cf* the ruling in *R (Good Law Project & Runnymede Trust) v Prime Minister & SSHSC* [2022] EWHC 298 (Admin), discussed at p 273 below.

in an application for judicial review on the basis of delay or substantive weakness of the claim and in an application to intervene because such intervention might result in unnecessary delay or prejudice to a party, or is not likely to be helpful to the court.

Examples of ECHR Litigation and Interventions

Among the cases in which the EHRC has intervened are:

- a number relating to Article 14 challenges to matters including the 'bedroom tax';[59] the two-child limit for child benefit and tax credit;[60] housing benefit rules;[61] the level of financial support available to asylum seekers;[62] the treatment of foreign prisoners;[63] the application of planning laws to travellers;[64] housing allocation by local authorities[65] and restrictions on Criminal Injuries Compensation;[66]
- EqA/HRA challenges to a refusal of approval to potential foster parents because of concerns about their views on homosexuality and religious views other than their own;[67] the discontinuance of a prosecution because of disability-related concerns about the credibility of a witness[68] and the detention of a vulnerable former prisoner pending his deportation.[69]
- HRA cases concerning the solitary confinement of a child in a young offenders' institution and the deprivation of liberty of incapacitated individuals; the failure to award compensation for a breach of the HRA and the imposition of a smoking ban in a secure mental hospital;[70]
- EU law challenges to mandatory retirement ages;[71] the burden of proof in victimisation claims;[72] the imposition of tribunal fees[73] and the non-application of the EqA to volunteers;[74]

[59] *RR v SSWP* [2019] UKSC 52, 171 BMLR 37.

[60] *SC v SSWP* [2019] EWCA Civ 615, [2019] 1 WLR 5687, which ended in the SC [2021] UKSC 26, [2021] 3 WLR 428 (and see, similarly, *R (DA) v SSWP* [2018] EWCA Civ 504, [2018] PTSR 1606 and *R (TP) v SSWP* [2020] EWCA Civ 37, [2020] PTSR 1785.

[61] *Obrey v SSWP* [2013] EWCA Civ 1584, [2014] HLR 133.

[62] *R (Ghulam) v SSHD* [2016] EWHC 2639 (Admin).

[63] *R (EG) v Parole Board* [2020] EWHC 1457 (Admin), (2021) 52 BHRC 8 (see also *R (EHRC) v SSJ* [2010] EWHC 147 (Admin)).

[64] *R (Moore) v SSCLG* [2015] EWHC 44 (Admin), [2015] LGR 405 See also *Mulvenna v SSCLG* [2017] EWCA Civ 1850, [2017] All ER (D) 34 (Dec).

[65] *R (H) v Ealing LBC* [2017] EWCA Civ 1127, [2018] PTSR 541; *R (Ward) v LB Hillingdon, R (Gullu) v LB Hillingdon* [2019] EWCA Civ 692, [2019] PTSR 1738.

[66] *JT v First-Tier Tribunal* [2018] EWCA Civ 1735.

[67] *R (Johns) v Derby CC* [2011] EWHC 375 (Admin), [2011] 1 FLR 2094.

[68] *R (B) v DPP* [2009] EWHC 106 (Admin), [2009] 1 WLR 2072. This case was brought under the DDA.

[69] *R (MDA) v SSHD* [2017] EWHC 2132 (Admin).

[70] Respectively *R (AB) v SSJ* [2021] UKSC 28, [2021] 4 All ER 777; *Re A & C* [2010] EWHC 978 (Fam) [2010] 2 FLR 1363; *R (SXC) v SSWP* [2019] EWHC 2774 (Admin); and *R (E) v Nottinghamshire Healthcare NHS Trust* [2009] EWCA Civ 795, [2010] PTSR 674.

[71] *R (Age UK) v SS Business, Innovation and Skills* [2009] EWHC 2336 (Admin), [2009] IRLR 1017 and *Seldon v Clarkson Wright & Jakes* [2009] IRLR 267 (which ended in the SC [2012] SC 16, [2012] ICR 579 (see Ch 11)).

[72] *Oyarce v Cheshire CC* [2008] EWCA Civ 434, [2008] ICR 1179; *Pothecary Witham Weld v Bullimore* [2010] IRLR 572; and *Rowstock v Jessemey* [2010] ICR 807.

[73] *R (UNISON) v Lord Chancellor* [2014] EWHC 218 (Admin); *R (UNISON (No 2)) v Lord Chancellor* [2014] EWHC 4198 (Admin), [2015] ICR 390; and *R (UNISON) v Lord Chancellor (No 3)* [2015] EWCA Civ 935, [2016] ICR 1 (which ended in the SC [2017] UKSC 51, [2020] AC 869 (see pp 282–283)).

[74] *X v Citizens Advice Bureau* [2011] EWCA Civ 28, [2011] ICR 460. The case ended in the SC [2012] UKSC 59, [2013] ICR 249.

- EqA/predecessor legislation challenges to the definition of disability and disability discrimination;[75] the approach of local authorities to homelessness;[76] equal pay (comparators and time limits);[77] the justification of indirect discrimination;[78] the treatment by tribunals of disabled claimants[79] and the approach to sexual orientation harassment/discrimination;[80]
- PSED challenges to local authority charges for adult social care;[81] planning decisions;[82] rules determining capability to work;[83] NHS charges to non-UK residents[84] and immigration detention.[85]

The EHRC has also litigated on its own behalf in relation to the definition of torture in guidance issued to Intelligence Officers and Service Personnel on the Detention and Interviewing of Detainees Overseas, and on the Passing and Receipt of Intelligence Relating to Detainees.[86]

EqA: 'Collective' Provisions

The Equal Pay Act 1970 (EqPA), as it was originally enacted, provided (s3) that discriminatory collective agreements or pay structures could be referred to the Central Arbitration Committee (CAC) which had the power to amend the offending terms.[87] This provision was to prove very significant, early commentators on the Act attributing much of the initial hike in women's relative wages to s3 EqPA. One Australian study attributed the success of the UK legislation, relative to that in the US, precisely to this factor 'in terms of institutional mechanisms a comparatively centralised wage-fixing system is a more efficient vehicle for implementing equal pay initiatives … across the board … initiatives such as those seen in Great Britain … are the most effective in reducing sex-based differentials'.[88]

Section 3 EqPA was capable of providing the benefits of 'equal pay' even to women in exclusively female workplaces, in cases where those workplaces were covered by multi-employer collective agreements. And even where women were not covered by collective agreements, 'female rates' within workplaces had to be raised to the level of the lowest 'male rate' regardless, again, of the content of the jobs performed by the men and women respectively. But the powers of the Committee were narrowly defined – in particular, they could revise only those provisions which explicitly applied 'to men only or to women only'.

[75] *Boyle v SCA Packaging Ltd* [2009] UKHL 37, [2009] ICR 1056; *Lewisham LBC v Malcolm* [2008] UKHL 43, [2008] 1 AC 1399; and *Hainsworth v MOD* [2014] EWCA Civ 763, [2014] IRLR 728.

[76] *Lomax v Gosport BC* [2018] EWCA Civ 1846, [2019] PTSR 167.

[77] *Bainbridge v Redcar and Cleveland BC* [2008] EWCA Civ 885, [2009] ICR 1336 and *Slack v Cumbria CC* [2009] EWCA Civ 293, [2009] ICR 1217.

[78] *Wilson v HSE* [2009] EWCA Civ 1074, [2010] ICR 302.

[79] *Anderson v Eespro* [2019] EWCA Civ 815, [2019] ICR 1362.

[80] *Grant v HM Land Registry* [2011] EWCA Civ 769, [2011] ICR 1390.

[81] *R (Domb) v Hammersmith and Fulham LBC* [2009] EWCA Civ 941, [2009] LGR 843.

[82] *R (Harris) v Haringey LBC* [2010] EWCA Civ 703, [2010] LGR 713.

[83] *R (Turner) v SSWP* [2021] EWHC 465 (Admin), [2021] PTSR 1312.

[84] *R (MP) v SSHSC* [2018] EWHC 3392 (Admin), 167 BMLR 102.

[85] *Medical Justice v SSHD* [2017] EWHC 2461 (Admin), [2018] 1 All ER 400; *R (VC) v SSHD* [2018] EWCA Civ 57, [2018] 1 WLR 4781; and *R (ASK) v SSHD* [2019] EWCA Civ 1239.

[86] *EHRC v The Prime Minister* [2011] EWHC 2401 (Admin).

[87] The provisions of the EqPA extend beyond pay to cover all contractual terms.

[88] K MacDermott, *Pay Equity: A Survey of 7 OECD Countries* (Canberra, Australian Government Publishing Service, 1987) Women's Bureau, Information Paper No 5, 77.

And the CAC's liberal approach to these powers – it was prepared to amend agreements and pay structures in which, in the committee's view, insufficient steps had been taken fully to eradicate the effects of past discrimination[89] – was blocked by the Divisional Court in *R v CAC ex parte Hy-Mac Ltd* [1979] IRLR 461, in which it ruled that the Committee had exceeded its jurisdiction in interfering with a collective agreement which did not contain overtly discriminatory 'male' and 'female' payscales.

The *Hy-Mac* decision rendered s3 useless. The SDA 1986 stripped the CAC of its powers under the EqPA, s3 of that Act being replaced by s6 SDA 1986, which provided that discriminatory terms in collective agreements and pay structures were void, but contained no enforcement mechanism.[90] The Trade Union Reform and Employment Rights Act 1993 amended s6 to provide individuals the right of complaint to a tribunal in respect of discriminatory terms of collective agreements and 'rules of undertakings.' These provisions are now to be found in ss145–146 EqA (2010), which provide as follows:

Section 145 EqA, Void and unenforceable terms

(1) A term of a collective agreement is void in so far as it constitutes, promotes or provides for treatment of a description prohibited by this Act.
(2) A rule of an undertaking is unenforceable against a person in so far as it constitutes, promotes or provides for treatment of the person that is of a description prohibited by this Act.

Section 146 EqA, Declaration in respect of void term, etc

(1) A qualifying person (P) may make a complaint to an employment tribunal that a term is void, or that a rule is unenforceable, as a result of section 145.
(2) But subsection (1) applies only if—
   (a) the term or rule may in the future have effect in relation to P, and
   (b) where the complaint alleges that the term or rule provides for treatment of a description prohibited by this Act, P may in the future be subjected to treatment that would (if P were subjected to it in present circumstances) be of that description.
(3) If the tribunal finds that the complaint is well-founded, it must make an order declaring that the term is void or the rule is unenforceable.
(4) An order under this section may include provision in respect of a period before the making of the order.
(5) In the case of a complaint about a term of a collective agreement, where the term is one made by or on behalf of a person of a description specified in the first column of the table, a qualifying person is a person of a description specified in the second column.

The table goes on to provide collective agreements reached by employers can be challenged by their employees (actual or prospective) while those reached by organisations of employers can be challenged by actual or prospective employees of member organisations. Section 146(6) makes similar provision for challenges to 'undertakings', providing that rules made by employers can be challenged by actual or prospective employees, those made by trade organisations of qualifications bodies can be challenged by actual or prospective members of the organisation or body and by persons upon whom the qualifications body has conferred a relevant qualification, or who is seeking the conferment of such a qualification. The provision has not been relied upon in any reported decision.

[89] *See, eg, Prestcold & APECCS* (1978) CAC 78/830, reported in EOC *Annual Report* 1978, 50.

[90] This despite the suggestion by the AG in Case C-165/82 *Commission v United Kingdom* [1983] ECR I-03431, [1983] ICR 192 that the CAC was the most appropriate body to deal with collective cases – B Fitzpatrick 'The Sex Discrimination Act 1986' (1987) 50 *Modern Law Review* 934, 945. Fitzpatrick also points out that, s77 permitting only parties to collective agreements or contractual terms to challenge them, someone covered by discriminatory

The power of individuals to challenge discrimination, other than exclusively as it impacts on them, is very limited.[91] We saw above that the EHRC may in some cases litigate on its own behalf, as well as in support of individuals, as may also exercise investigatory powers. The PSED imposed by s149 EqA also provides the opportunity for broader challenges to discriminatory policies, practices and/or decisions.

Enforcement of the PSED

The PSED imposed by s149 EqA is discussed in Chapter 3. Section 156 EqA provides that 'A failure in respect of a performance of a duty imposed by or under this Chapter does not confer a cause of action at private law'. This being the case, a claim for breach of the PSED is properly brought as a public law claim by way of an application to the High Court for judicial review in which the claimant will argue that the public authority in question has acted unlawfully by failing to comply with the PSED. Claims for judicial review may be brought by anyone with sufficient interest in the matter being litigated to be recognised as having standing (see immediately below). The procedure involves applying for permission to bring a claim, which permission will be granted only if a judge (considering the matter on the papers only) finds that the claim is 'arguable' and has 'a realistic prospect of success'. Applications for judicial review must be brought (Civil Procedure Rules, r54.5(1)) '(a) promptly; and (b) in any event not later than three months after the grounds to make the claim first arose' unless a shorter time limit applies (as in planning cases).

If the judge does not give permission the claimant may, unless the judge has declared the application as being 'wholly without merit', 'renew' the application at a short oral hearing at which the judge may not determine the claim in the claimant's favour (this being a preliminary stage) but may grant or refuse permission to proceed to a full hearing.[92]

Standing

The rule on standing is found in the Senior Courts Act 1981, which provides as follows.

> **Section 31(3) Senior Courts Act 1981, Application for judicial review**
>
> No application for judicial review shall be made unless the leave of the High Court has been obtained in accordance with rules of court; and the court shall not grant leave to make such an application unless –
>
> (a) it considers that the applicant has a sufficient interest in the matter to which the application relates …

Such an interest can be shown by an individual or by an organisation, and an interest may or may not be personal. Questions of standing have not given rise to much difficulty in PSED claims which have been brought by trade unions;[93] charities and other organisations with

collectively agreed term had no power to challenge them. Section 77 SDA and s72 RRA provided for declarations that unlawful terms be unenforceable against the complainant.

[91] The inclusion of a detriment requirement in indirect discrimination is discussed in Ch 2. In cases of direct discrimination the claimant must have been less favourably treated.

[92] The Senior Courts Act 1981 imposes rules about transparency of funding in applications for judicial review (s31(3A)).

[93] *R (Adiatu) v Her Majesty's Treasury* [2020] EWHC 1554 (Admin), [2021] 2 All ER 484.

particular interests in the matters in issue;[94] individual service users affected by public body decisions affecting their service providers;[95] students challenging increases in student fees;[96] organisations incorporated to challenge anti-Semitism in the UK;[97] individuals challenging public authorities' decision-making in relation to them as individuals[98] or members of affected groups;[99] and an association of Indian-origin doctors.[100] In *R (Good Law Project and Runnymede Trust) v Prime Minister*, however, the High Court ruled that the Good Law Project did not have standing to bring proceedings in respect of alleged breaches of the PSED or alleged breaches of the prohibition against indirect discrimination arising from the informal approach taken by the Government to appointment to high-profile public roles. That aspect of the case is considered below, but it is useful first to set out the Court's general approach to standing which it considered having adopted the distinction drawn by Professors Paul Craig and Peter Cane between 'associational', 'surrogate' and 'public interest' group challenges:[101]

***R (Good Law Project and Runnymede Trust) v Prime Minister & SS Health and Social Care* [2022] EWHC 298 (Admin)**

Singh LJ and Swift J:

> 20. Associational standing is typified by an organisation suing on behalf of its members. Surrogate standing covers the case where a pressure group represents the interests of others, who may not be well placed to bring the action, for example the Child Poverty Action Group in cases concerning social security benefits. Public interest standing is asserted by those claiming to represent the wider public interest, rather than merely that of a group with an identifiable membership. As Professor Craig puts it
>
> > In this type of case the decision may affect the public generally, or a section thereof, but no one particular individual has any more immediate interest than any other, and a group seeks to contest the matter before the courts.
>
> 21. … It is correct that in a number of cases the courts have accepted that claimants had standing even though they were not directly affected by a decision: e.g., pressure groups and even public-spirited individuals have been recognised as having standing in appropriate cases. But what is notable, is that, as the Claimants themselves say in their written submissions, such examples of judicial review challenges have been brought by NGOs 'in their fields of interest'. Numerous examples can be found, some of which are set out by the Claimants: e.g., *R v Secretary of State for Foreign and Commonwealth Affairs, ex p. World Development Movement Ltd* [1995] 1 WLR 386; *R (Refugee Legal Centre) v Secretary of State for the Home Department* [2004] EWCA Civ 148; [2005] 1 WLR 2219; and *R (Motherhood Plan) v HM Treasury* [2021] EWCA Civ 1703, [2022] IRLR 324. The last case is of particular interest because it shows that even a newly established campaigning organisation may be permitted to complain of a breach of the public sector equality duty, or other ground

[94] *R (Motherhood Plan) v Her Majesty's Treasury* [2021] EWHC 309 (Admin), [2022] 3 All ER 727. The HRA aspect of this claim is discussed in Ch 2. See also *R (Adath Yisroel Burial Society) v HM Senior Coroner for Inner North London* [2018] EWHC 969 (Admin), [2019] QB 251.

[95] *R (Kaur & Shah) v LB Ealing* [2008] EWHC 2062 (Admin); *R (Hajrula) v London Councils* [2011] EWHC 448 (Admin).

[96] *R (Hurley) v SS Business, Innovation and Skills* [2012] EWHC 201 (Admin), [2012] ELR 297.

[97] *R (Jewish Rights Watch Ltd) v Leicester CC* [2018] EWCA Civ 1551, [2018] 4 All ER 1040.

[98] *R (Ibrahim) v Westminster CC* [2021] EWHC 2616 (Admin).

[99] *Turani v SSHD* [2021] EWCA Civ 348, [2022] 1 All ER 254

[100] *R (BAPIO Action Ltd) v Royal College of General Practitioners* [2014] EWHC 1416 (Admin).

[101] §20, citing Paul Craig, *Administrative Law*, 9th edn (London, Sweet & Maxwell, 2021) §25-023.

of public law. What is of importance is that in all such cases of which we are aware the NGO concerned did have a particular interest and in a sense was representative of an identifiable group in society which was affected by the decision or policy in question. Even in the case of Lord Rees-Mogg, we note that he was a member of the House of Lords and therefore had a particular interest, as a member of the UK's legislature, in ensuring that the Government acted in accordance with constitutional law: see *R v Secretary of State for Foreign and Commonwealth Affairs, ex p. Rees-Mogg* [1994] QB 552. In that case, there was no dispute as to the applicant's standing: see page 561 (per Lloyd LJ). The Divisional Court accepted 'without question that Lord Rees-Mogg brings the proceedings because of his sincere concerns for constitutional issues': see page 562.

22. Mr Jason Coppel QC, for the Claimants, relied on the decision of the Court of Appeal in *R (Independent Workers Union of Great Britain) v Mayor of London* [2020] EWCA Civ 1046; [2020] 4 WLR 112. In that case the challenge was directed to changes made in the London congestion charge scheme. The claim was brought under sections 19 and 29 [EqA]. Although the claim ultimately failed and the appeal was dismissed, Mr Coppel points out that no-one suggested that the claimant union lacked standing to bring the proceedings, including an argument that the legislation in question gave rise to indirect discrimination. But, in our judgement, that was an example of what Professors Cane and Craig call 'associational' standing: the union was seeking to vindicate the interests of its members, who were individually affected. Furthermore, that was a case of a public law decision, not a decision relating to an individual appointment to a post. In cases of individual employment, it is obvious that an individual could bring proceedings in the Employment Tribunal under the Act. Where no individual has done so, we find it difficult to accept that a claim for judicial review could nevertheless be brought by other individuals or an NGO.

23. We have found helpful the statements of principle as to the correct approach to standing in two decisions of the Supreme Court.

24. In *AXA General Insurance Ltd v HM Advocates* [2011] UKSC 46; [2012] 1 AC 868 the Supreme Court aligned the test for standing in claims for judicial review in Scotland with the position in England and Wales. Although in Scotland the question is whether a person is 'directly affected' by the issue raised, the Supreme Court held that this was in substance the same as the question whether they have a sufficient interest. At paragraph 170, Lord Reed JSC said:

> 'For the reasons I have explained, such an approach cannot be based upon the concept of rights and must instead be based upon the concept of interests. A requirement that the applicant demonstrate an interest in the matter complained of will not however operate satisfactorily if it is applied in the same way in all contexts. In some contexts, it is appropriate to require an applicant for judicial review to demonstrate that he has a particular interest in the matter complained of the type of interest, which is relevant, and therefore required in order to have standing, will depend upon the particular context. In other situations, such as where the excess or misuse of power affects the public generally, insistence upon a particular interest could prevent the matter being brought before the court, and that in turn might disable the court from performing its function to protect the rule of law. I say 'might', because the protection of the rule of law does not require that every allegation of unlawful conduct by a public authority must be examined by a court, any more than it requires that every allegation of criminal conduct must be prosecuted. Even in a context of that kind, there must be considerations which lead the court to treat the applicant as having an interest which is sufficient to justify his bringing the application before the court. What is to be regarded as sufficient interest to justify a particular applicant's bringing a particular application before the court, and thus as conferring standing, depends therefore upon the context, and in particular upon what will best serve the purposes of judicial review in that context.'

At paragraph 172, Lord Reed explained that 'standing should depend upon demonstrating a sufficient interest in the issues raised by the applications.'

> 25. Lord Reed returned to this theme in *Walton v Scottish Ministers* [2012] UKSC 44; 2013 SC 67, at paragraphs 89 and following. At paragraph 92, Lord Reed said:
>
> > As is clear from that passage, a distinction must be drawn between the mere busybody and the person affected by or having a reasonable concern in the matter to which the application relates. The words 'directly affected', upon which the Extra Division focused, were intended to enable the court to draw that distinction. A busybody is someone who interferes in something with which he has no legitimate concern. The circumstances which justify the conclusion that a person is affected by the matter to which an application relates, or has a reasonable concern in it, or is on the other hand interfering in a matter with which he has no legitimate concern, will plainly differ from one case to another, depending upon the particular context and the grounds of the application. As Lord Hope made plain in the final sentence, there are circumstances in which a personal interest need not be shown.
>
> 26. At paragraph 94, he continued:
>
> > In many contexts it will be necessary for a person to demonstrate some particular interest in order to demonstrate that he is not a mere busybody. Not every member of the public can complain of every potential breach of duty by a public body. But there may also be cases in which any individual, simply as a citizen, will have sufficient interest to bring a public authority's violation of the law to the attention of the court, without having to demonstrate any greater impact upon himself than upon other members of the public. The rule of law would not be maintained if, because everyone was equally affected by an unlawful act, no one was able to bring proceedings to challenge it …
>
> 28. We also note that not everyone who has a strong and sincere interest in an issue will necessarily have standing, not even a public official such as the Mayor of London, who had an obvious interest in tackling crime and in the operation of the criminal justice system as it applies to London, including in relation to support provided for victims of crime: see *R (D) v Parole Board* [2018] EWHC 694 (Admin); [2019] QB 285, at paragraphs 105-111. As the Divisional Court (Sir Brian Leveson P, Jay and Garnham JJ) noted in that case, at paragraph 111:
>
> > The test for standing is discretionary and not hard-edged.
> >
> > One consideration which the Court took account of when reaching that conclusion was that there are, or would be, 'obviously better-placed challengers': see paragraph 110 …

The attempt by both the Good Law Project and Runnymede Trust to challenge particular appointments made as being incompatible with the prohibitions on indirect discrimination in the context of employment (see further Chapter 4) failed because the Court ruled that any challenges to these appointments could and should have been brought (in the employment tribunal) by individuals 'directly and personally affected by the decisions under challenge' (§31).[102] The Court did accept, however, that the Trust, 'an organisation which exists specifically to promote the cause of racial equality', but not the Good Law Project, had standing to bring the PSED claim:

> 55. … The Good Law Project Limited (GLP) is a private company limited by guarantee …

[102] The court further considered that the appointment decisions were not amenable to judicial review.

56. … The current set of Articles were drafted during 2021. They were approved by the GLP Board on 30 November 2021 and were formally adopted on 15 December 2021 (coincidentally, that was the final day of the hearing in this court). The Articles were registered at Companies House on 20 December 2021. Those Articles define the objects of the GLP as follows:

2.1 to provide the sound administration of the law and to challenge injustice and inequality;
2.2 to uphold democracy and promote changes to the law and public administration with the aim of improving social justice, equality and inclusion;
2.3 to uphold high standards in public administration in accordance with democratic principles;
2.4 to enable and promote access to justice and the law, particularly for those whose access is curtailed because of poverty, social or economic disadvantage or discrimination;
2.5 to protect and preserve the environment for benefit of mankind now and in the future;
2.6 to advance education and research into good application and development of the law and of administrative practice;
2.7 to promote compliance with the law by public and private actors and to address imbalances of economic power in the application of the law; and
2.8 further any other philanthropic or benevolent purpose ancillary to the above proposes.

57. No individual, even with a sincere interest in public law issues, would be regarded as having standing in all cases. We do not consider that the position differs simply because there is a limited company which brings the claim. It also cannot be right as a matter of principle that an organisation could in effect confer standing upon itself by drafting its objects clause so widely that just about any conceivable public law error by any public authority falls within its remit.

58. In all the circumstances of this case, we are not persuaded that such a general statement of objects as is now set out in the GLP's Articles of Association can confer standing on an organisation. That would be tantamount to saying that the GLP has standing to bring judicial review proceedings in any public law case. This can be contrasted with the approach which was taken by the Divisional Court in the case of *D*, where even a statutory authority (the Mayor of London) was not regarded as having a sufficient interest in the matter in issue in that case. It cannot be supposed that the GLP now has *carte blanche* to bring any claim for judicial review no matter what the issues and no matter what the circumstances …

Remedies

Section 31 Senior Courts Act 1981

(1) An application to the High Court for one or more of the following forms of relief, namely—

(a) a mandatory, prohibiting or quashing order;
(b) a declaration or injunction under subsection (2); or
(c) an injunction under section 30 restraining a person not entitled to do so from acting in an office to which that section applies,

shall be made in accordance with rules of court by a procedure to be known as an application for judicial review.

(2) A declaration may be made or an injunction granted under this subsection in any case where an application for judicial review, seeking that relief, has been made and the High Court considers that, having regard to—

(a) the nature of the matters in respect of which relief may be granted by mandatory, prohibiting or quashing orders;
(b) the nature of the persons and bodies against whom relief may be granted by such orders; and
(c) all the circumstances of the case,

it would be just and convenient for the declaration to be made or of the injunction to be granted, as the case may be.

A mandatory order requires the person to whom it is addressed to do something. A prohibiting order requires the individual or organisation not to do something. A quashing order has the effect of rendering null something that the person has purported to do. Orders in successful judicial review cases will generally include costs and, in suitable cases, may include damages.[103]

Except where there are reasons of 'exceptional public interest' the High Court must refuse a remedy[104] if (s31(2A) Senior Courts Act) 'it appears to the court to be highly likely that the outcome for the applicant would not have been substantially different if the conduct complained of had not occurred'.

Enforcement of the HRA

The HRA can be enforced by application to the High Court or county court, but not by way of application to the employment tribunal whose jurisdiction is limited by statute. Tribunals may, however, deal with HRA arguments made in relation to statutes in respect of which they have jurisdiction, as in *Gilham v Ministry of Justice* [2019] UKSC 44, [2019] ICR 1655, in which a district judge relied on the HRA to extend the scope of 'workers' entitled to protection in respect of whistleblowing. Insofar as challenges are brought to decisions of public authorities or to statutory provisions this will typically occur by way of judicial review and will be subject to the same rules as those discussed immediately above.

Generally only a victim of a Convention breach can establish such a breach (this being a prerequisite for a breach of the HRA). Section 6(1) HRA having stated that 'It is unlawful for a public authority to act in a way which is incompatible with a Convention right', s7 then provides:

Section 7 HRA, Proceedings

(1) A person who claims that a public authority has acted (or proposes to act) in a way which is made unlawful by section 6(1) may—

(a) bring proceedings against the authority under this Act in the appropriate court or tribunal, or

(b) rely on the Convention right or rights concerned in any legal proceedings,

but only if he is (or would be) a victim of the unlawful act …

(3) If the proceedings are brought on an application for judicial review, the applicant is to be taken to have a sufficient interest in relation to the unlawful act only if he is, or would be, a victim of that act …

(5) Proceedings under subsection (1)(a) must be brought before the end of—

(a) the period of one year beginning with the date on which the act complained of took place; or

(b) such longer period as the court or tribunal considers equitable having regard to all the circumstances,

but that is subject to any rule imposing a stricter time limit in relation to the procedure in question [three months if the proceedings are brought by way of judicial review] …

[103] Section 31(4) Senior Courts Act 1981 provides that the High Court may make an award for damages, restitution or the recovery of a sum due in a judicial review claim where such a claim is made and 'the court is satisfied that such an award would have been made if the claim had been made in an action commenced by the applicant at the time of making the application'. No damages are awardable for breach of the PSED but damages may be awarded in HRA claims brought by way of judicial review (see below).

[104] And (s31(3C) SCA 1981) must also refuse permission.

We saw above (s30(3) EqA 2006) that the EHRC may itself bring proceedings for breach of the HRA of which it is not a victim as long as a victim exists. Otherwise the standing rules for HRA claims, whether or not brought by way of judicial review, are considerably tighter than those which apply to non-HRA judicial reviews. The breadth of claims which have been brought under the HRA is discussed in Chapter 4.

Enforcement of the EqA by Individuals

It was mentioned above that the enforcement of discrimination law in the UK relies in the main upon actions taken by individuals. In order to win EqA cases, individuals have to bring their employment-related claims to employment tribunals and non-employment cases to the county court or (in public law challenges brought by way of judicial review) the High Court. Equality-related claims under the HRA must be brought in the civil courts, the jurisdiction of tribunals being limited by statute and not including claims brought directly under the HRA (though the interpretive obligations imposed by that Act can be relied upon in tribunal litigation).

The vast majority of discrimination cases which are litigated in England and Wales are litigated in the employment tribunals. Figures 5.1 and 5.2 below show the numbers of discrimination and equal pay cases disposed of by tribunals in each year between 2007 and 2020 (equal pay claims are separated out because many involve are brought by multiple claimants and their inclusion in the discrimination chart would make it more difficult to see the difference in the number of claims relating to the different protected characteristics).

Figure 5.1 Discrimination claims disposed of by employment tribunals 2007–20[105]

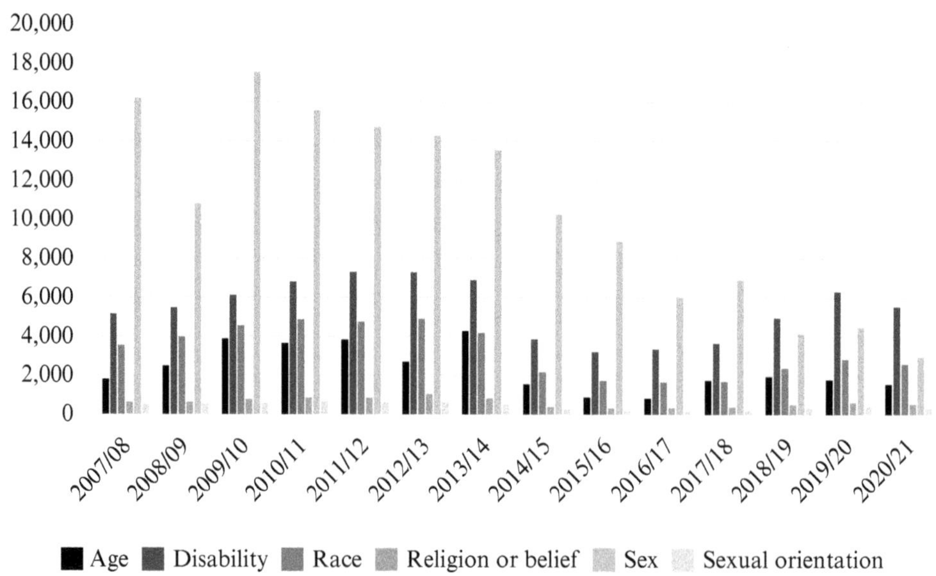

[105] Table ET2, available at https://www.gov.uk/government/statistics/tribunal-statistics-quarterly-july-to-september-2021.

Sex discrimination claims accounted for the majority (often the very significant) majority of cases every year until 2018/19 when they were overtaken by disability discrimination cases. The impact of the tribunal fees regime (see pp 282–283 below) can be seen in the reduction in cases disposed of after 2013/14. The continued depression in the number of cases disposed of may be the result of tribunal backlogs exacerbated by the swingeing cuts made to the number of employment tribunal judges during the period when fees were chargeable.

Figure 5.2 Equal pay claims disposed of by employment tribunals 2007–20[106]

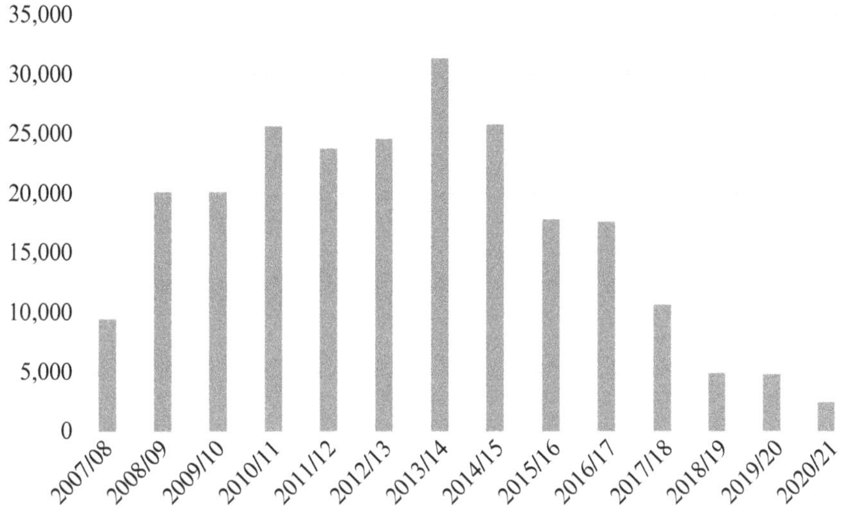

Figures 5.3 and 5.4 below show the proportion of successful claims in employment tribunals by protected characteristic and in equal pay claims in the same period.

Figure 5.3 Claims succeeding at tribunal 2007–21[107]

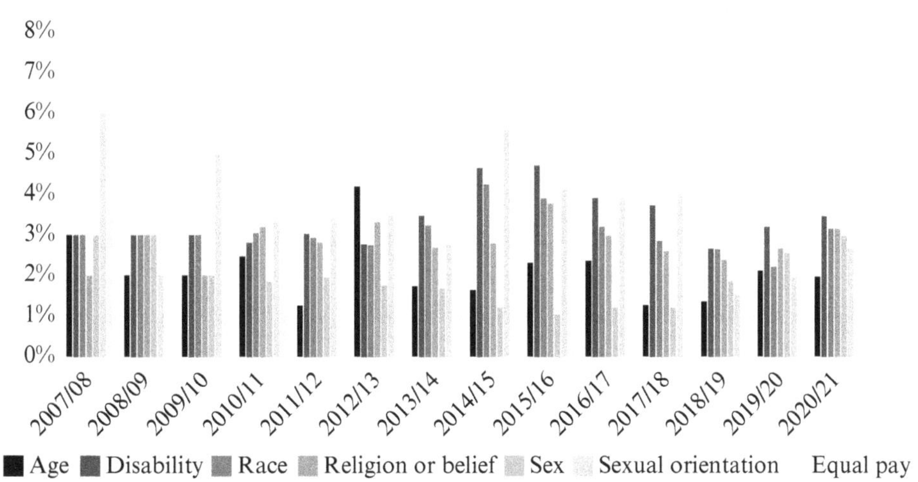

[106] *Ibid.*

[107] Table ET3, available at https://www.gov.uk/government/statistics/tribunal-statistics-quarterly-april-to-june-2022.

Figure 5.4 Claims failing at tribunal or at preliminary hearing 2007–21[108]

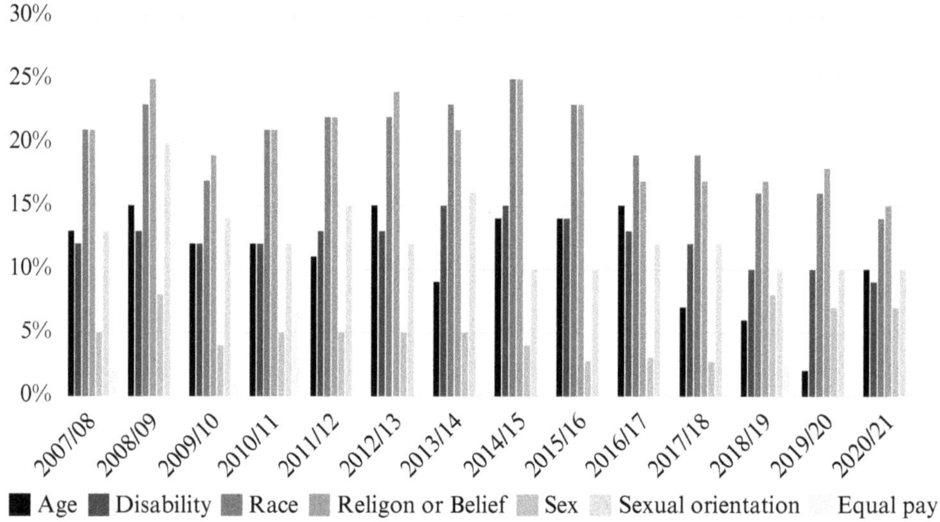

It is clear from the above that the majority of discrimination and equal pay claims, particularly of the latter, do not reach the tribunal. Those which do not are variously settled, withdrawn or struck out without a hearing. Figure 5.5 below shows the number of awards of compensation by employment tribunals in the period 2007–20. It is instructive to compare this chart with Figure 5.1 above to get a sense of the proportion of cases which result in awards of compensation.

Figure 5.5 Number of awards of compensation by employment tribunals 2007–20[109]

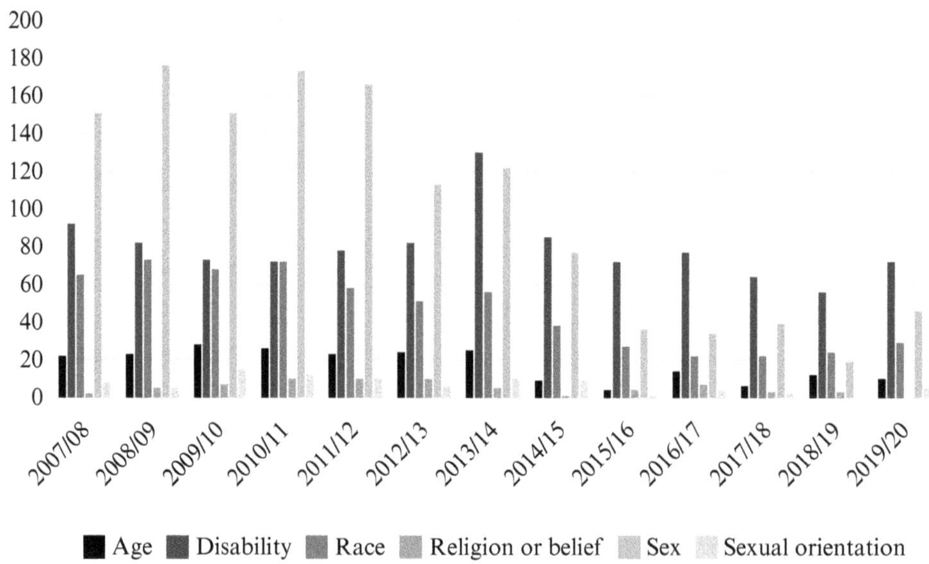

[108] *Ibid.*

[109] Table E2: available at https://www.gov.uk/government/statistics/tribunal-statistics-quarterly-april-to-june-2020/tribunal-statistics-quarterly-april-to-june-2020.

The Costs of Litigation

Discrimination cases are legally and, often, factually complex and generally require expert (and expensive) legal assistance. Even in employment tribunals, which were established with the intention of being accessible to unrepresented individuals, most claimants are represented by lawyers, generally at significant expense.

Figure 5.6 Representation of claimants at employment tribunals 2005–20[110]

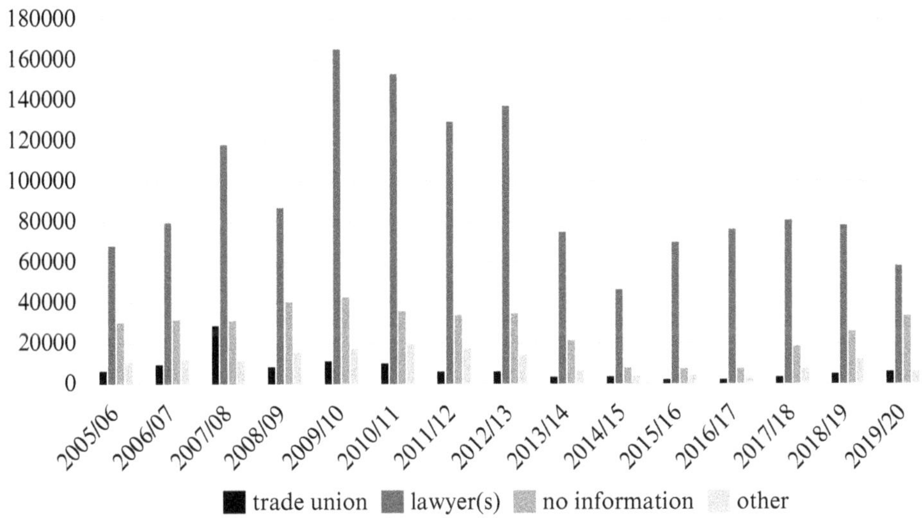

Some employment claims may be covered by household insurance, and legal aid is, in theory, available in discrimination claims including, in exceptional cases, in the employment tribunal. In 2019, however, the EHRC reported that there was 'a real danger of our rights being rights on paper only. The numbers are startling. Between 2013/14 and 2017/18, not a single workplace discrimination case received legal aid funding for representation in the employment tribunal, and only 1 in 200 cases taken on by discrimination specialists received funding for representation in court.'[111] Those who regard themselves as the victims of discrimination can apply to the EHRC itself for financial and other assistance but, as pointed out above, the EHRC's budget in 2021 was about 25 per cent what it was in 2007. The EHRC's 2018–19 Annual Report stated that the EHRC had supported 32 cases under its Legal Support Projects in that year.[112] The Annual Report for 2019–20 stated that the commission had supported 22 cases under its 'legal support project for transport' and a case concerning race discrimination in adoption,[113] and the 2020–21 report referred only to

[110] Table E1: available at https://www.gov.uk/government/statistics/tribunal-statistics-quarterly-april-to-june-2020/tribunal-statistics-quarterly-april-to-june-2020. Representation is recorded at the date of application and is likely to change prior to any hearing. 'No information' cases include those in which the claimant represented him or herself.

[111] EHRC, *Access to Legal Aid for Discrimination Cases* (June 2019), available at https://www.equalityhumanrights.com/en/publication-download/access-legal-aid-discrimination-cases).

[112] At 16. The report referred to 84 cases supported in total, but this included 21 interventions.

[113] https://www.equalityhumanrights.com/en/publication-download/annual-report-and-accounts-1-april-2019-31-march-2020 20, 22.

a single case which the Commission had funded in the relevant period.[114] By contrast, the EOC alone had in 1999–00 granted legal assistance in 101 cases.[115] Additional barriers to litigation are imposed by court fees and the threat of costs (discussed below).

Court Fees

Court fees, which are payable in the county court and High Court, range from £35 for a money claim of up to £300 and £332 in a non-money claim in the county court and £569 in an application for judicial review to £10k in a county court claim for over £200k.[116] Fees were imposed in employment tribunals in 2013[117] but were abolished in 2017 after the Supreme Court (SC) ruled in *R (UNISON) v Lord Chancellor (Respondent)* [2017] UKSC 51, [2020] AC 869 that they had been unlawfully imposed. Band A fees, in simpler cases, were set at £160 for issue and £320 for hearing while Band B fees for more complex cases, including all discrimination cases, were set at £250 for issue and £950 for hearing. Remission of fees was possible in cases of financial hardship, but only the very poorest would have been eligible. During the period in which fees operated the number of single claimant employment tribunal cases issued each quarter fell by 68 per cent from just under 13,500 to around 4,300, while multi-claimant cases fell 75 per cent from around 1,500 per quarter to 400.[118] The SC's decision in the *UNISON* case is discussed in the briefing paper extracted below.

Doug Pyper, Feargal McGuinness and Jennifer Brown, *Employment tribunal fees* (House of Commons briefing paper no 7081[119])

… The [Supreme] Court [declared t]he Fees Order … unlawful *ab initio*, meaning it was from the start unlawful; all fees have been deducted based on an unlawful instrument … Giving the lead judgment, Lord Reed highlighted the importance of access to justice as a component of the rule of law:

> The constitutional right of access to the courts is inherent in the rule of law. The importance of the rule of law is not always understood. Indications of a lack of understanding include the assumption that the administration of justice is merely a public service like any other, that courts and tribunals are providers of services to the 'users' who appear before them, and that the provision of those services is of value only to the users themselves and to those who are remunerated for their participation in the proceedings. The extent to which that viewpoint has gained currency in recent times is apparent from the consultation papers and reports discussed earlier. It is epitomised in the assumption that the consumption of ET and EAT services without full cost recovery results in a loss to society, since 'ET and EAT use does not lead to gains to society that exceed the sum of the gains to consumers and producers of these services'.

[114] *Ibid*, 18 and 28.
[115] The EOC, which had had statutory responsibility for sex alone, was merged into the EHRC in 2007.
[116] Such a claim would be highly unusual in a non-employment discrimination claim where the bulk of compensation is often for injury to feelings (see pp 316–318 below). Figures accurate as of 11 April 2022. Additional fees of between £27 (for a small claims track claim of up to £300) to £1,175 (for a multitrack claim) are also payable in respect of the hearing.
[117] By the Employment Tribunals and the Employment Appeal Tribunal Fees Order 2013. For a history of employment tribunal fees see D Pyper et al, *Employment tribunal fees*, extracted below.
[118] *Ibid*, 13.
[119] https://commonslibrary.parliament.uk/research-briefings/sn07081.

His Lordship went on to emphasise the public interest in maintaining access to justice as a means of underpinning employment law:

> When Parliament passes laws creating employment rights, for example, it does so not merely in order to confer benefits on individual employees, but because it has decided that it is in the public interest that those rights should be given effect. It does not envisage that every case of a breach of those rights will result in a claim before an ET. But the possibility of claims being brought by employees whose rights are infringed must exist, if employment relationships are to be based on respect for those rights. Equally, although it is often desirable that claims arising out of alleged breaches of employment rights should be resolved by negotiation or mediation, those procedures can only work fairly and properly if they are backed up by the knowledge on both sides that a fair and just system of adjudication will be available if they fail. Otherwise, the party in the stronger bargaining position will always prevail. It is thus the claims which are brought before an ET which enable legislation to have the deterrent and other effects which Parliament intended, provide authoritative guidance as to its meaning and application, and underpin alternative methods of dispute resolution.

The Court did, however, recognise that the imposition of some form of fees could be reconciled with the common law right of access to justice if set at a lower level or mitigated in some other way … [though 'I]n order for the fees to be lawful, they have to be set at a level that everyone can afford, taking into account the availability of full or partial remission[']. After surveying the evidence, Lord Reed concluded that fees were set at an unaffordable level, and that neither the remission system, nor the Lord Chancellor's rarely used power to remit fees in exceptional circumstances, were sufficient to mitigate this. This conclusion was based on a combination of factors. First, statistical evidence:

> The fall in the number of claims has in any event been so sharp, so substantial, and so sustained as to warrant the conclusion that a significant number of people who would otherwise have brought claims have found the fees to be unaffordable.

Second, the Government's own review of fees estimated that between 3,000 and 8,000 people per year, who were unable to resolve their disputes through Acas conciliation, did not issue a claim because they were unable to pay. This, Lord Reed noted, suggested fees were set at an unaffordable level, a conclusion fortified by consideration of hypothetical examples that indicated the impact of fees on claimants in low to middle income households …

Third, the Court was swayed by argument that fees restricted access to justice when set at levels that, compared to the amounts at stake, made it irrational to bring claims …

The Court thus concluded that 'the Fees Order effectively prevents access to justice and is therefore unlawful'. While it was ultimately this new ground of argument – the common law right of access to justice – that proved decisive, the Government lost its case on all other fronts, namely: that the Fees Order contravened the rule that specific statutory rights are not to be cut down by subordinate legislation passed under the authority of a different Act; that the Fees Order imposed disproportionate limitations on the exercise of EU rights and so was unlawful under EU law; and that the higher Type B fees constituted unjustified indirect discrimination.

The last of these claims was based on the fact that the fees imposed a disparate impact on women who brought the majority of Band B cases.

Costs

Turning to costs, the normal rule in civil litigation is that the losing side pays the winning side's legal costs. This makes litigation a high-risk activity; even if a claimant can minimise or gain assistance with his or her own legal costs, defeat will mean having to pay the costs of the winning party, which may be significantly higher than the claimant's own.

Respondent costs will routinely run into five figures and in long cases in the employment tribunal will often exceed £100k. Employment tribunals do not generally award costs to successful parties, which means that the risk of litigating in such tribunals is considerably less than in the county court. (The downside, of course, is that a claimant who wins in the employment tribunal may have spent a great deal of money on legal fees, which money will in effect come out of any compensation awarded.)

The general rule in employment, as in other, tribunals is 'no costs'. This rule is subject to exceptions, however.

Employment Tribunals Rules of Procedure, Schedule 1, Rule 76

(1) A Tribunal may make a costs order or a preparation time order, and shall consider whether to do so, where it considers that—

(a) a party (or that party's representative) has acted vexatiously, abusively, disruptively or otherwise unreasonably in either the bringing of the proceedings (or part) or the way that the proceedings (or part) have been conducted; or

(b) any claim or response had no reasonable prospect of success or

(c) a hearing has been postponed or adjourned on the application of a party made less than 7 days before the date on which the relevant hearing begins.

A costs order is obtainable only where the party claiming it has been legally represented but a preparation time order allows an unrepresented party or one represented or assisted by a non-lawyer to claim payment at £41 per hour[120] in respect of reasonable time spent preparing for (though not attending) tribunal.[121]

A claimant will act 'vexatiously' by issuing or pursuing a claim which 'has little or no basis in law (or at least no discernible basis)', the effect of which 'whatever the intention of the proceedings may be … to subject the defendant to inconvenience, harassment and expense out of all proportion to any gain likely to accrue to the claimant; and [which] involves an abuse of the process of the court, meaning by that a use of the court process for a purpose or in a way which is significantly different from the ordinary and proper use of the court process'.[122] Rule 76(1)(a) also allows costs to be awarded for 'disruptive' or 'abusive' conduct by a party or his or her representative, as well as for conduct that is 'otherwise unreasonable'. Costs may be awarded under Rule 76(1)(a) in cases, for example, in which parties have deliberately lie about a matter central to the claim, waste time or make outrageous and unevidenced claims. Late and inadequately justified withdrawal of claims may result in an award of costs, though it is not routine for withdrawal to do so. Costs may be awarded under Rule 76(1)(a) against a *successful* party, though this would be unusual.

Tribunals may at any stage strike out claims or responses with no real prospects of success and may at the preliminary stage require the payment of a deposit of up to £1,000 by a party if it considers that any specific allegation or argument made by the party in a claim or response has little reasonable prospect of success (Rule 39(1)). Before making such an order it must make reasonable enquiries into the ability of the party to pay the deposit, and must take this into account in setting the amount of any deposit (Rule 39(2)). Failure to pay any required deposit will result in strike-out of the claim or response. Rule 84 of the Tribunal Rules also provide that ability to pay may (not *must*) be taken into account in making any costs order.

Table 5.1 below shows the number and amount of costs awards made against claimants ('C') and respondents ('R') in alternate years up to 2019–20 (the latest statistics available).

[120] Set at £33/hr by rule 79(2) from July 2013 and increasing by £1 each 6 April thereafter.

[121] A party cannot claim both preparation time and costs.

[122] *A-G v Barker* [2000] 1 FLR 759, [2000] 2 FCR 1 §19, *per* Lord Bingham CJ.

Table 5.1 Costs awards by employment tribunals 2007–20[123]

	2007–08		2009–10		2011–12		2013–14		2015–16		2017–18		2019–20	
	C	R	*C*	R	*C*	R	*C*	R	*C*	R	*C*	R	*C*	R
<£200	*22*	33	*4*	30	*9*	829	*47*	124	*99*	20	*41*	7	*5*	2
£201–£400	*6*	34	*15*	36	*6*	40	*36*	40	*129*	12	*45*	12	*5*	7
£401–£600	*14*	47	*14*	52	*8*	77	*16*	58	*29*	15	*7*	21	*4*	12
£601–£800	*11*	24	*8*	12	*8*	21	*7*	28	*5*	10	*9*	9	*3*	4
£801–£1,000	*15*	35	*10*	37	*10*	39	*14*	62	*1*	19	*4*	19	*1*	14
£1,001–£2,000	*26*	60	*18*	52	*24*	72	*37*	109	*72*	36	*34*	21	*6*	21
£2,001–£4,000	*18*	47	*15*	40	*22*	98	*28*	88	*26*	36	*10*	28	*6*	25
£4,001–£6,000	*10*	19	*1*	26	*10*	54	*19*	36	*10*	38	*9*	14	*3*	9
£6,001–£8,000	*3*	9	–	9	*6*	23	*3*	30	*7*	18	*5*	7	*4*	8
£8,001–£10,000	*6*	17	*2*	29	*3*	3	*11*	29	*1*	4	*4*	141	*3*	7
£10,000+	*3*	2	*1*	–	*10*	38	*24*	43	*14*	57	*1*	31	*7*	21
Total	*134*	327	*88*	323	*116*	1294	*242*	647	*393*	265	*169*	310	*47*	130

It is evident that costs awards have fallen over this period from 134 in favour of and 327 against claimants from 47 in favour of and 130 against claimants in 2019–20. The largest number of costs awards in favour of and against claimants were in 2015–2016 and 2022–12 respectively. In 2016–17 the figures were 297 for and 182 against 51 and 158 for and against claimants respectively. There was a huge spike in 2011–12 in costs awarded against claimants, this as a result of a costs award in a multiple claim involving 800 claimants who were all made liable (at the rate of £5 each) for a costs award of £4,000 to the respondent. The overall trend for awarding costs appears to be downwards since about 2013–15, as illustrated by Figure 5.7 below.

Figure 5.7 Number of costs awards made by employment tribunals 2007–20[124]

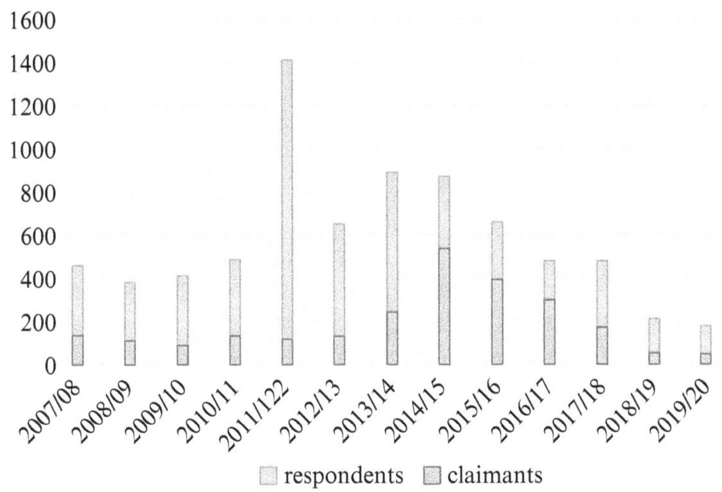

[123] Table E10: available at https://www.gov.uk/government/statistics/tribunal-statistics-quarterly-april-to-june-2020/tribunal-statistics-quarterly-april-to-june-2020.

[124] Table E10: available at https://www.gov.uk/government/statistics/tribunal-statistics-quarterly-april-to-june-2020/tribunal-statistics-quarterly-april-to-june-2020.

Costs are significantly more likely to be awarded against rather than in favour of claimants, but the likelihood of costs awards should be kept in perspective: Figure 5.8 shows the number of cases disposed of by the employment tribunals in the period 2008–20:

Figure 5.8 Number of cases disposed of by employment tribunals 2007–20[125]

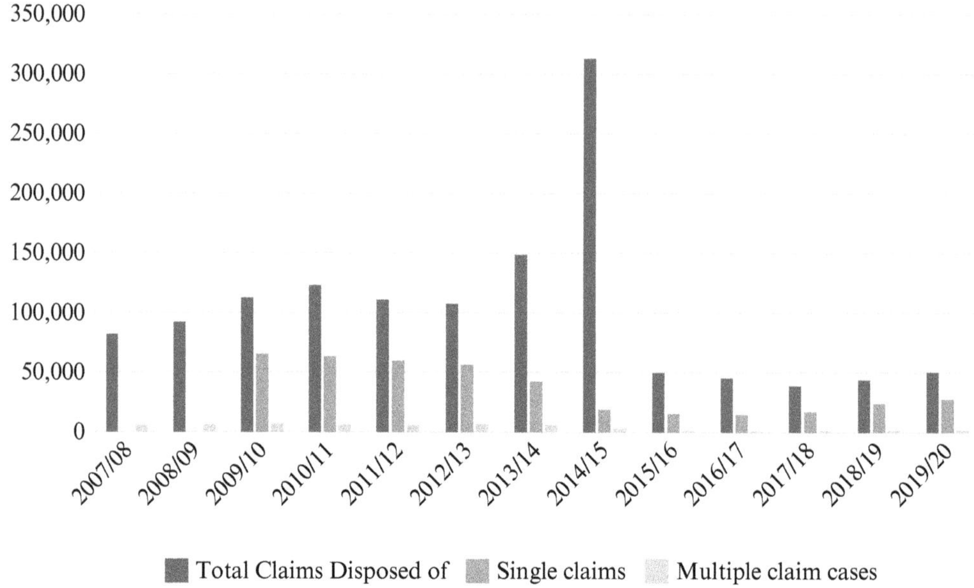

These numbers are high by comparison with costs awards, though the majority of cases which are received by tribunals do not proceed to a hearing.

Department for Business, Energy and Industrial Strategy, Survey of Employment Tribunal Applications: *Findings from the 2018 Survey*[126]

Executive Summary …

A settlement was reached in 58 per cent of all cases surveyed. In 17 per cent of cases surveyed, an offer for settlement was made but no settlement was reached between the parties. In cases where an offer of settlement was made, the combined samples of claimants and employers indicate it was mostly the employer (44 per cent) or an employer representative (12 per cent) who proposed the first offer. In line with 2012, financial reasons (46 per cent) and saving time (26 per cent) were the main reasons cited by employers who either settled or offered a settlement. Among those employers who did not propose an offer, reasons for not doing so focused around the employer believing that they had a strong case.

Claimants were most likely to settle because they thought it was less stressful than proceeding with the claim (40 per cent). If claimants withdrew their case, it was most likely to be because of cost (33 per cent) or stress (23 per cent) …

[125] Table S1: available at https://www.gov.uk/government/statistics/tribunal-statistics-quarterly-july-to-september-2021.

[126] BEIS Research Paper Number 2020/007, available at https://www.gov.uk/government/publications/survey-of-employment-tribunal-applications-2018.

Outcomes

The outcomes of ET claims in 2017 broadly reflect those in 2012. The analysis of the combined samples of claimants and employers shows that more than half of cases (58 per cent) were settled in 2017 (54 per cent in 2012): 40 per cent through Acas (the same as in 2012) and 18 per cent privately (13 per cent in 2012). Multivariate analysis indicates that the following variables had a significant effect on the outcome of the case; specifically, whether the case went to a tribunal hearing rather than being withdrawn/dismissed or settled:

- In general, compared with other jurisdictions, discrimination cases were more likely to be withdrawn/dismissed or settled than to go to a hearing. In particular, breach of contract (fast track) and unauthorised deductions from wages cases were more likely than discrimination cases to go to a hearing …

In the claimant data, 17 per cent of all claims went to a full tribunal hearing. Overall, claimants at a full tribunal hearing were more likely to be unsuccessful than successful.

Multivariate analysis of the claimant data showed that:

- The claimant was more likely to be successful in breach of contract (fast track) and unauthorised deductions from wages cases, compared with other jurisdictions. This applied to the analysis of both the claimant and employer data.
- Both claimants and employers were more likely to have a successful outcome if they were represented at the hearing:
  - According to the claimant data, the claimant was more likely to be successful if they had a representative at the hearing;
  - In the employer data, the claimant was much less likely to be successful if the employer had a representative at the hearing.
- According to the employer data, the claimant was more likely to be successful if a settlement offer had previously been made.
- Claimants were considerably more likely to be successful in cases involving small or medium-sized employers (up to 250 employees) than large employers (with 250 or more employees) …

It is worth noting here that only a very small fraction of discrimination claims which reach tribunals are upheld.

The table extracted on the following page shows that claimants were successful at hearing in only three per cent of discrimination claims in both 2012 and 2017 (this by comparison with success rates of five and eight per cent respectively in unfair dismissal cases, 12 and nine per cent in breach of contract cases and 12 and 12 per cent of unauthorised deduction cases). Claims failed at tribunal in eight and 10 per cent of discrimination claims in 2012 and 2017 respectively, the figures for unfair dismissal cases, breach of contract cases and unauthorised deduction cases being 12 per cent and 16 per cent, seven per cent and seven per cent, and six and five per cent in 2012 and 2017 respectively. Discrimination cases were also relatively likely to be withdrawn (as distinct from being settled), the proportion of such cases running at 20 and 15 per cent in 2012 and 2017 respectively by comparison with 11 and nine per cent in breach of contract and 11 and 10 per cent in unauthorised deduction cases, though this outcome was also relatively likely for unfair dismissal claims (18 per cent and 17 per cent in 2012 and 2017 respectively).

Department for Business, Energy and Industrial Strategy, Survey of Employment Tribunal Applications: *Findings from the 2018 Survey*[127]

Table 5.2 Claimants' and employers' survey combined: SETA outcome by primary jurisdiction, summary jurisdiction and year

													Per cent, bases are counts	
	Primary Jurisdiction [CJURM]													
	Unfair Dismissal		**Breach of Contract**		**Unauthorised Deductions**		**Redundancy Payments**		**Discrimination**		**Other**		**All**	
	2012	**2017**	**2012**	**2017**	**2012**	**2017**	**2012**	**2017**	**2012**	**2017**	**2012**	**2017**	**2012**	**2017**
SETA Outcome [CSVOUT2]														
Claimant successful at hearing	5	8	12	9	14	12	8	[5]	3	3	5	5	8	7
Claimant unsuccessful at hearing	12	16	7	7	4	6	5	[8]	8	10	10	12	8	10
Acas settled	42	37	43	43	32	31	33	[48]	43	43	45	37	41	40
Privately settled	10	13	11	20	19	13	11	[10]	15	20	14	19	13	18
Withdrawn	18	17	11	9	11	10	15	[10]	20	16	15	12	15	13
Dismissed/disposed	11	9	7	5	5	9	6	[8]	10	7	8	8	9	7
Default judgment in favour of claimant	1	*	10	8	15	20	22	[11]	1	*	3	6	6	5
Any settled	52	51	54	62	51	44	44	[57]	58	63	59	57	54	58
unweighted base	1136	501	1158	850	333	192	122	[49]	827	781	423	290	3999	2663

Table source: SETA 2018 and SETA 2013: All claimants/employers.
Table weight: SETA 2018 and SETA 2013: Case weight.
Table notes: Table 5.2 in SETA 2013.
Due to the changes to the Employment Tribunal system since the last SETA and the introduction of the mandatory early conciliation process, sample profile of 2013 and 2018 surveys are not directly comparable. Comparison, if made, should be indicative only

[127] *Ibid.*

Figure 5.9 below shows the median and mean awards of costs in 2007–20 (awards for and against claimants being considered together and the 800 awards of £5 being ignored for these purposes)) while Figure 5.10 shows the maximum costs award in each year.

Figure 5.9 Median and mean costs awards by employment tribunals 2007–20[128]

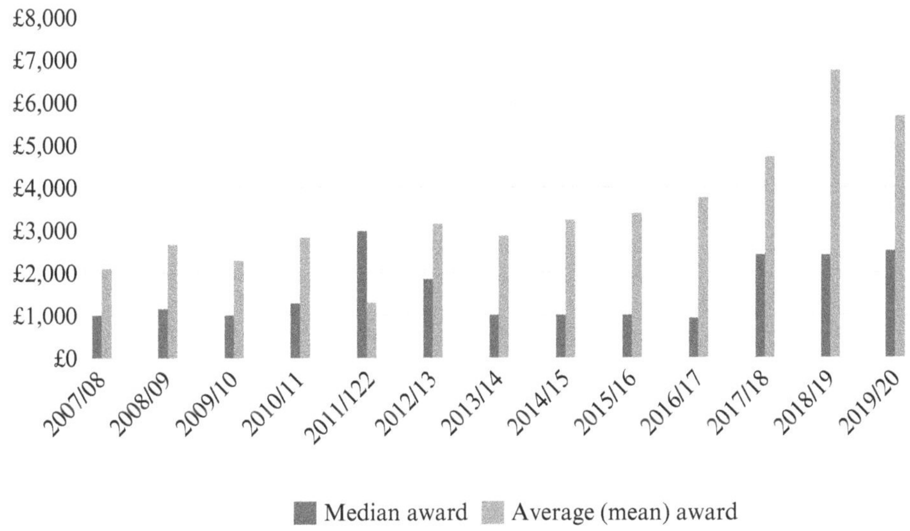

Figure 5.10 Maximum costs awarded by employment tribunals 2007–20[129]

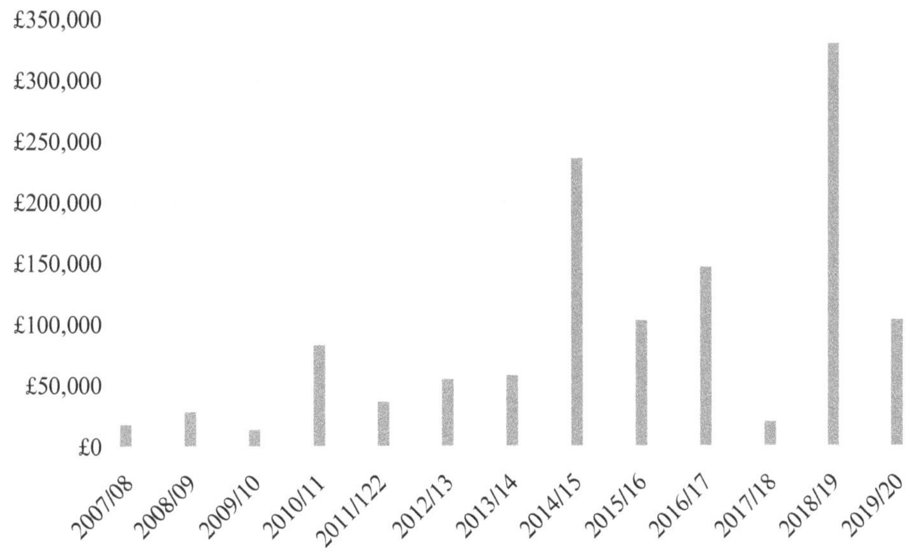

[128] Table E10: available at https://www.gov.uk/government/statistics/tribunal-statistics-quarterly-april-to-june-2020/tribunal-statistics-quarterly-april-to-june-2020.
[129] *Ibid.*

The maximum award of costs in 2018–19 was an eye-watering £330k. At the time this was without precedent, but in November 2020 a tribunal awarded £432k, believed to be the largest award of costs in an employment tribunal to date. The award was made against an individual claimant who had sued his employer for unfair dismissal, discrimination because of race and sexual orientation, victimisation, harassment, whistleblowing detriment and unlawful deductions from wages. More recently still, in April 2021 a costs award of £300k was made against the claimant in a religious discrimination claim.[130]

DAC Beachcroft, 'Tribunal costs awards: Employer recoups record £432,000 in legal costs'[131]

Mr Tan was employed by Copthorne Hotels Limited. Copthorne Hotels dismissed him in 2017, giving redundancy as the reason for his dismissal … The employment tribunal found that redundancy was the genuine reason for the termination of Mr Tan's employment, and that a fair procedure had been followed. It dismissed all his other claims too.

During his employment, Mr Tan had made covert recordings of conversations with other employees. By his own admission, there were tens of thousands of hours of recordings. These included recordings of peers, senior and junior employees, and of the company's OH doctor. The employment tribunal described his behaviour as 'duplicitous' and 'underhand', and held that the covert recordings (had Copthorne Hotels known about them) would have completely eroded any trust and confidence, so that Mr Tan would have been dismissed in any event had Copthorne found out about the recordings.

Mr Tan's witness statement was 61 pages long, and the employment tribunal bundles ran to over 3,000 pages. Mr Tan introduced 17 comparators for his claim of discriminatory pay, which the employment tribunal described as a 'fishing expedition'. The employment tribunal also held that he had a 'scattergun approach', introducing multiple causes of action that he believed to be behind the redundancy. Elements of his claim were described as 'speculative'.

Proving Claims

The Burden of Proof

The burden of proof in discrimination cases is on the claimant, though the EqA provides for a shift in the burden once a prima facie case has been established. It is not necessary to prove that the protected characteristic is the sole cause of the less favourable treatment, but it must be shown to have been 'the principal or at least an important or significant cause of the less favourable treatment.'[132]

Section 136 EqA, Burden of proof

(1) This section applies to any proceedings relating to a contravention of this Act.
(2) If there are facts from which the court could decide, in the absence of any other explanation, that a person (A) contravened the provision concerned, the court must hold that the contravention occurred.
(3) But subsection (2) does not apply if A shows that A did not contravene the provision.

[130] See Harrison Clark Rickerbys, '£300,000 costs awarded against claimant at employment tribunal', 12 April 2021, available at https://www.hcrlaw.com/blog/300000-costs-awarded-against-claimant-at-employment-tribunal/.

[131] Published 5 November 2020 at https://www.dacbeachcroft.com/en/gb/articles/2020/november/tribunal-costs-awards-employer-recoups-record-432-000-in-legal-costs.

[132] See eg *Neill v Governors of St Thomas More Roman Catholic Voluntary Aided Upper School* [1997] ICR 33; *O'Donoghue v Redcar and Cleveland BC* [2001] EWCA Civ 701, [2001] IRLR 615; *Igen Ltd v Wong* [2005] EWCA Civ 142, [2005] ICR 931 and (in victimisation claims) *Nagarajan v LRT* [2000] 1 AC 501.

(4) The reference to a contravention of this Act includes a reference to a breach of an equality clause or rule[133]
(5) This section does not apply to proceedings for an offence under this Act.
(6) A reference to the court includes a reference to—
 (a) an employment tribunal;
 (b) the Asylum and Immigration Tribunal;
 (c) the Special Immigration Appeals Commission;
 (d) the First-tier Tribunal;
 (e) the Education Tribunal for Wales;
 (f) the First-tier Tribunal for Scotland Health and Education Chamber.

Section 136 EqA has its roots in EU law, Council Directive 97/80 on the burden of proof providing (Article 4) that the burden of disproving sex discrimination must shift to the defendant/respondent once the claimant had established 'facts from which it may be presumed that there has been direct or indirect discrimination'.[134] This approach was reflected in each of the subsequent discrimination directives. Its implementation in domestic law displaced a series of decisions to the effect that a court or tribunal *might*, but was *not obliged to*, make a finding of discrimination where a defendant/respondent failed to provide an adequate explanation of differential treatment and a protected characteristic.[135] The impact of the revised burden of proof was confirmed by the CA in *Igen Ltd v Wong*, which concerned the SDA's predecessor provision to s136 EqA. Peter Gibson LJ, for the Court, ruled that s63A SDA, which had been introduced to implement Article 4 of the burden of proof directive, altered rather than consolidated the previous position,[136] and that a respondent's failure to provide an adequate explanation for a prima facie case *required*, rather than *permitted*, a tribunal to make a finding of discrimination. The CA approved the guidance set out by the EAT in *Barton v Investec Henderson Crosthwaite Securities Ltd* [2003] ICR 1205 as follows:

***Igen Ltd v Wong* [2005] EWCA Civ 142, [2005] ICR 931**

Peter Gibson LJ (for the Court):

14. … (1) Pursuant to s.63A [SDA], it is for the [claimant] who complains of sex discrimination to prove on the balance of probabilities facts from which the tribunal could conclude, in the absence of an adequate explanation, that the employer has committed an act of discrimination against the [claimant] which is unlawful by virtue of Part II or which by virtue of s.41 or 42 [SDA] is to be treated as having been committed against the claimant. These are referred to below as 'such facts.'

(2) If the [claimant] does not prove such facts he or she will fail.

(3) It is important to bear in mind in deciding whether the [claimant] has proved such facts that it is unusual to find direct evidence of sex discrimination. Few employers would be prepared to admit such discrimination, even to themselves. In some cases the discrimination will not be an intention but merely based on the assumption that 'he or she would not have fitted in'.

[133] See Ch 6 for discussion of equal pay and equal pension cases.
[134] The Directive was extended to the UK by Council Directive 98/52 of 13 July 1998. The term 'defendant' is routinely used in the civil courts at first instance, 'respondent' in the tribunals and, on appeal, to indicate the party who is not the appellant.
[135] *North West Thames RHA v Noone (No 2)* [1988] ICR 813; *King v The Great Britain-China Centre* [1992] ICR 516; *Glasgow CC v Zafar* [1998] ICR 120.
[136] Dismissing as *obiter* comments to the contrary by Simon Brown LJ, as he then was, in *Nelson v Carillion Services Ltd* [2003] ICR 1256.

> (4) In deciding whether the [claimant] has proved such facts, it is important to remember that the outcome at this stage of the analysis by the tribunal will therefore usually depend on what inferences it is proper to draw from the primary facts found by the tribunal.
>
> (5) It is important to note the word is 'could'. At this stage the tribunal does not have to reach a definitive determination that such facts would lead it to the conclusion that there was an act of unlawful discrimination. At this stage a tribunal is looking at the primary facts proved by the [claimant] to see what inferences of secondary fact could be drawn from them.
>
> (6)These inferences can include, in appropriate cases, any inferences that it is just and equitable to draw in accordance with s 74(2)(b) [SDA] from an evasive or equivocal reply to a questionnaire or any other questions that fall within s 74(2) … [The questionnaire procedure has since been repealed: see fn 143.]
>
> (7) Likewise, the tribunal must decide whether any provision of any relevant code of practice is relevant and if so, take it into account in determining such facts … This means that inferences may also be drawn from any failure to comply with any relevant code of practice.
>
> (8) Where the [claimant] has proved facts from which inferences could be drawn that the employer has treated the claimant less favourably on the grounds of sex, then the burden of proof moves to the employer.
>
> (9) It is then for the employer to prove that he did not commit, or as the case may be, is not to be treated as having committed that act.
>
> (10) To discharge that burden it is necessary for the employer to prove, on the balance of probabilities, that the treatment was in no sense whatsoever on the grounds of sex, since 'no discrimination whatsoever' is compatible with the Burden of Proof Directive.
>
> (11) That requires a tribunal to assess not merely whether the employer has proved an explanation for the facts from which such inferences can be drawn, but further that it is adequate to discharge the burden of proof on the balance of probabilities that sex was not any part of the reasons for the treatment in question.
>
> (12) Since the facts necessary to prove an explanation would normally be in the possession of the employer, a tribunal would normally expect cogent evidence to discharge that burden of proof. In particular, the tribunal will need to examine carefully explanations for failure to deal with the questionnaire procedure and/or code of practice.[137]

The CA in *Igen v Wong* at §23 accepted the claimant's argument that 'it may be helpful for the *Barton* guidance to include a paragraph stating that the ET must assume no adequate explanation at the first stage'. The core of the *Igen v Wong* approach is to impose a two-stage approach to the burden of proof by which (1) the claimant establishes facts from which an inference of discrimination *could* be drawn and then (2) the respondent is able to avoid the drawing of any such inference by providing an adequate alternative explanation. In *Madarassy v Nomura International plc* [2007] EWCA Civ 33, [2007] ICR 867 the CA ruled that it was not necessary for tribunals to divide evidence and argument into two distinct stages, the stages instead referring to the analysis to be undertaken in light of all the evidence, further that evidence from the employer could be taken into account at the stage of determining whether a prima facie case of less favourable treatment had been established, though not (at that stage) in considering the reason for any such treatment. The SC has recently confirmed that the *Igen v Wong* approach, as subsequently elaborated and clarified in *Madarassay* and a number of other cases, applies equally to s136 EqA.

[137] The references in the CA's judgment are to tribunals and employers but the same approach applies to courts and other respondents. Again it is important to note that the statutory questionnaire procedure referred to in the judgment no longer exists.

Efobi v Royal Mail Group Ltd [2021] UKSC 33, [2021] ICR 1263

Lord Leggatt (for the Court):

17. The guidance given by the Court of Appeal in *Wong v Igen Ltd* and *Madarassy* was in turn approved by the Supreme Court in *Hewage v Grampian Health Board* [2012] UKSC 37; [2012] ICR 1054.

18. Two points established by this guidance are significant for present purposes.

19. First, although the old provisions required the tribunal to adopt a two-stage process of analysis, they did not require the tribunal to divide hearings into two parts to correspond to those analytical stages and tribunals were discouraged from doing so …

20. Second, although the language of the old provisions referred to the complainant having to prove facts, and there was no mention of evidence from the respondent, the courts held that the tribunal was not prevented from taking account at the first stage of evidence adduced by the respondent in so far as it was relevant in deciding whether the burden of proof had moved to the respondent …

Has the law changed?

24. As Singh LJ observed in *Ayodele* [*v Citylink Ltd* [2018] ICR 748 §100], for seven years after the enactment of the 2010 Act the legal community proceeded on the assumption that no change of substance was made by s 136. That was evidently the government's view when the 2010 Act was enacted, as is clear from the Explanatory Notes which accompanied the Bill during its passage through Parliament …

25. The claimant submits that this understanding fails to take account of how the relevant wording has changed. Section 136(2) no longer uses the words '[w]here … the complainant proves facts'. Instead, it adopts a neutral formulation: '[i]f there are facts …'. The meaning of this provision must be discerned from the language used, and not from the language of the old provisions which were repealed by the 2010 Act. The claimant argues that the appeal tribunal was right to hold that the language used in s 136(2) has brought about a substantive change in the law. As it was put by the appeal tribunal (at para 78):

> Section 136(2) does not put any burden on a claimant. It requires the ET, instead, to consider all the evidence, from all sources, at the end of the hearing, so as to decide whether or not "there are facts etc" … Its effect is that if there are such facts, and no explanation from A, the ET must find the contravention proved. If, on the other hand, there are such facts, but A shows he did not contravene the provision, the ET cannot find the contravention proved …

26. The central point made in this passage is that s 136(2) requires the employment tribunal to consider all the evidence from all sources, not just the claimant's evidence, so as to decide whether or not 'there are facts etc'. I agree that this is what s 136(2) requires. I do not, however, accept that this has made a substantive change in the law. The reason is that this was already what the old provisions required as they had been interpreted by the courts. As discussed at paras 20–23 above, it had been authoritatively decided that, although the language of the old provisions referred to the complainant having to prove facts and did not mention evidence from the respondent, the tribunal was not limited at the first stage to considering evidence adduced by the claimant; nor indeed was the tribunal limited when considering the respondent's evidence to taking account of matters which assisted the claimant. The tribunal was also entitled to take into account evidence adduced by the respondent which went to rebut or undermine the claimant's case.

27. The desirability of making this clear explains why the relevant wording has been changed. I would adopt what Singh LJ said in *Ayodele* at para [103]:

> What then is to be made of the fact that the wording of s 136 is different from the predecessor provisions? It seems to me that the answer lies in the fact that the previous wording was not entirely clear that what should be considered at the first stage was *all* the evidence, from whatever source it had come, and not only the evidence adduced by the *claimant*. Its express wording was apt to mislead in that regard, as it referred only to the complainant. This had been clarified in the case law on the predecessor provisions, in particular by the EAT in *Laing* [v *Laing v Manchester City Council* [2006] ICR 1519], which was approved by this court in *Madarassy*. Parliament can be taken to have known of that case law when it enacted s 136. The provision can sensibly be read as making that point clear on the face of the legislation. [Emphasis in *Ayodele*]

28. The aspect of s 136(2) which is the focus of this appeal is not the only respect in which the opportunity was taken to alter the wording of the old provisions so as more clearly to reflect the way in which they had been interpreted by the courts. The old provisions referred to 'an adequate explanation' (or 'a reasonable alternative explanation'). Those phrases were also apt to mislead in that they could have given the impression that the explanation had to be one which showed that the employer had acted for a reason which satisfied some objective standard of reasonableness or acceptability. It was, however, established that it did not matter if the employer had acted for an unfair or discreditable reason provided that the reason had nothing to do with the protected characteristic: see eg *Glasgow City Council v Zafar* [1998] ICR 120; *Bahl v The Law Society* [2004] EWCA Civ 1070, [2004] IRLR 799; *Laing v Manchester City Council*, para 51. It seems likely that the change of wording to refer to 'any other explanation' was intended to make this clearer.

29. Unfortunately, as this case has shown, replacing '[w]here … the complainant proves facts' by '[i]f there are facts' created the possibility for a different misunderstanding that there is no longer any burden of proof on a claimant. There is nothing in the background to the 2010 Act which provides any support for a suggestion that this was or might have been a goal of the legislation: see *Ayodele*, paras [96]–[100]. Indeed, the Explanatory Notes [to the Equality Bill] … positively suggest otherwise. Furthermore, there was no need to state in s 136(2) that the burden of proving facts from which the requisite inference can be drawn lies on the claimant because that is the effect of the general law. Any court or tribunal which is required to make findings of fact may face a situation in which it is unclear from the evidence whether something is a fact or not. To enable a court or tribunal to know how to proceed in such a situation, the law has developed rules about the burden and standard of proof. In civil cases (including employment disputes) the general rule is that a court or tribunal must find that something asserted by a party is a fact if, and only if, its truth is shown by sufficient evidence to be more probable than not.

30. As counsel for the claimant properly accepted when questioned on this point, it follows from the application of this basic rule of evidence that an employment tribunal may only find that 'there are facts' for the purpose of s 136(2) of the 2010 Act if the tribunal concludes that it is more likely than not that the relevant assertions are true. This means that the claimant has the burden of proving, on the balance of probabilities, those matters which he or she wishes the tribunal to find as facts from which the inference could properly be drawn (in the absence of any other explanation) that an unlawful act was committed. This is not the whole picture since, as discussed, along with those facts which the claimant proves, the tribunal must also take account of any facts proved by the respondent which would prevent the necessary inference

> from being drawn. But that does not alter the position that, under s 136(2) of the 2010 Act just as under the old provisions, the initial burden of proof is on the claimant to prove facts which are sufficient to shift the burden of proof to the respondent …
>
> 34. Accordingly, in agreement with the Court of Appeal in *Ayodele*, I conclude that the change in the language used in s 136(2) of the 2010 Act has not made any substantive change in the law.

The decisions of the HL and CA respectively in *Glasgow City Council v Zafar* [1998] ICR 120 and in *Bahl v The Law Society* were referred to with approval by the SC in *Efobi.* These cases risk encouraging alleged discriminators to run the so-called 'bastard' defence: 'yes I treated the claimant badly/unfairly/unreasonably/appallingly. But I would have treated someone of a different sex/race/etc equally badly …'. In *Anya v University of Oxford* [2001] ICR 847 the CA ruled that, where an alleged discriminator seeks to argue that *unfavourable* treatment of a claimant was not *less favourable treatment* (because s/he would treat everyone equally badly) the onus is on the alleged discriminator to provide evidence of this and that it did not fall to the claimant to prove that s/he had been singled out. In *Bahl v The Law Society*, however, the CA made clear that this did not place any burden of proof on the respondent.

***Bahl v The Law Society* [2004] EWCA Civ 1070, [2004] IRLR 799**

The claimant, a former Chair of the EOC, brought her discrimination claim after being accused of bullying staff in her position as Vice President of the Law Society. A tribunal found that she had been the victim of race and sex discrimination, a finding which was successfully appealed by the Law Society and the EAT's decision upheld by the CA. Mr Justice Elias, for the EAT, had stated that a tribunal could only infer discrimination from a finding of less favourable treatment which was explained by an alleged discriminator if the 'explanation … was inadequate or unsatisfactory in the sense that the tribunal did not accept it as genuine, not in the sense that it was a genuine, non-racial explanation, albeit that it was unreasonable because it resulted in unreasonable treatment.' He went on to say that 'it is the human condition that we all at times act foolishly, inconsiderately, unsympathetically and selfishly and in other ways which we regret with hindsight. It is, however, a wholly unacceptable leap to conclude that whenever the victim of such conduct is black or a woman then it is legitimate to infer that our unreasonable treatment was because the person was black or a woman. All unlawful discriminatory treatment is unreasonable, but not all unreasonable treatment is discriminatory, and it is not shown to be so merely because the victim is either a woman or of a minority race or colour. In order to establish unlawful discrimination, it is necessary to show that the particular employer's reason for acting was one of the proscribed grounds. Simply to say that the conduct was unreasonable tells us nothing about the grounds for acting in that way'. The claimant appealed.

Peter Gibson LJ (delivering the judgment of the Court):

> 100. … it is appropriate to refer to *Anya*, a decision of this Court. Its ratio takes matters no further than *King v The Great Britain-China Centre* [1992] ICR 516 and *Zafar*, both of

which are cited in the judgment of the Court [in *Anya*] given by Sedley LJ However, the judgment contains an obiter passage which has attracted debate in a number of cases including the present appeal. It reads ...

> As Neill LJ pointed out in *King* ... such hostility [ie unreasonableness] *may* justify an inference of racial bias if there is nothing else to explain it: whether there is such an explanation ... will depend not on a theoretical possibility that the employer behaves equally badly to employees of all races but on evidence that he does.

It has been suggested, not least by Mr de Mello in the present case, that Sedley LJ was there placing an important gloss on *Zafar* to the effect that it is open to a tribunal to infer discrimination from unreasonable treatment, at least if the alleged discriminator does not show by evidence that equally unreasonable treatment would have been applied to a white person or a man.

101. In our judgment, the answer to this submission is that contained in the judgment of Elias J in the present case. It is correct, as Sedley LJ said, that racial or sex discrimination may be inferred if there is no explanation for unreasonable treatment. This is not an inference from unreasonable treatment itself but from the absence of any explanation for it. However, the final words in the passage which we have quoted from *Anya* are not to be construed in the manner that Mr de Mello submits. That would be inconsistent with *Zafar*. It is not the case that an alleged discriminator can only avoid an adverse inference by proving that he behaves equally unreasonably to everybody. As Elias J observed (paragraph 97):

> Were it so, the employer could never do so where the situation he was dealing with was a novel one, as in this case.

Accordingly, proof of equally unreasonable treatment of all is merely one way of avoiding an inference of unlawful discrimination. It is not the only way. He added (*ibid*):

> The inference may also be rebutted – and indeed this will, we suspect, be far more common – by the employer leading evidence of a genuine reason which is not discriminatory and which was the ground of his conduct. Employers will often have unjustified albeit genuine reasons for acting as they have. If these are accepted and show no discrimination, there is generally no basis for the inference of unlawful discrimination to be made. Even if they are not accepted, the tribunal's own findings of fact may identify an obvious reason for the treatment in issue, other than a discriminatory reason.

We entirely agree with that impressive analysis. As we shall see, it resonates in this appeal.

Statistical and Other Evidence

Among the most powerful evidence from which discrimination may be inferred is statistical evidence relating to an employer's past or current practice. It was not until 1987 that EAT accepted the relevance of statistical evidence in *West Midlands Passenger Transport Executive v Singh*, a decision upheld by the CA. The case involved a race discrimination claimant who applied for disclosure of the ethnic origins of all applicants for senior inspector posts with the employer over a particular period, which post he had unsuccessfully applied for. This information was collected by the employer in pursuit of its equal opportunities policy. The Transport Executive resisted the application and appealed against an industrial tribunal order which was subsequently upheld by EAT. EAT ruled that the statistics sought were logically probative as evidence from which an inference might be drawn that the employers had adopted a racially discriminatory policy. The CA also rejected the employer's appeal. Having remarked on the special difficulties of proving discrimination, and the need for inferences to be drawn from primary facts, Balcombe LJ continued:

***West Midlands Passenger Transport Executive v Singh* [1988] ICR 614**

Balcombe LJ (for the Court):

Statistical evidence may establish a discernible pattern in the treatment of a particular group: if that pattern demonstrates a regular failure of members of the group to obtain promotion to particular jobs and to under-representation in such jobs, it may give rise to an inference of discrimination against the group. That is the reason why the Race Relations Code of Practice … recommends ethnic monitoring of the workforce and of applications for promotion and recruitment, a practice adopted by the appellants in their own organisation. Statistics obtained through monitoring are not conclusive in themselves, but if they show racial or ethnic imbalance or disparities, then they may indicate areas of racial discrimination …

If a practice is being operated against a group then, in the absence of a satisfactory explanation in a particular case, it is reasonable to infer that the complainant, as a member of the group, has himself been treated less favourably on grounds of race. Indeed, evidence of discriminatory treatment against the group in relation to promotion may be more persuasive of discrimination in the particular case than previous treatment of the applicant, which may be indicative of personal factors peculiar to the applicant and not necessarily racially motivated …[138]

The suitability of candidates can rarely be measured objectively; often subjective judgments will be made. If there is evidence of a high percentage rate of failure to achieve promotion at particular levels by members of a particular racial group, this may indicate that the real reason for refusal is a conscious or unconscious racial attitude which involves stereotyped assumptions about members of that group …

Balcombe LJ pointed out that an order for disclosure (then discovery) did not follow automatically upon a finding of relevance, the question being whether such an order was necessary for the fair disposal of the proceedings[139] and, in particular, whether the party seeking the request was 'fishing' or the request 'oppressive' in the sense that: '(1) It may require the provision of material not readily to hand, which can only be made available with difficulty and at great expense [or] … (2) It … may … require the party ordered to make discovery to embark on a course which will add unreasonably to the length and cost of the hearing.' It was for the tribunal to decide, as it had done here, whether the discovery order ought to be granted.

The limits of the *Singh* decision became apparent in the following case:

***Carrington v Helix Lighting Ltd* [1990] ICR 125**

Ms Carrington, who had applied for a light assembly job, was interviewed for only a couple of minutes and was rejected without notification, advertisements for the jobs in question continuing to appear in the local press. She sought disclosure of statistical material relating to the ethnic composition of the respondents' workforce. The employer did not conform to the CRE's Code of Practice in respect of ethnic monitoring, and so did not have this information to hand. The claimant's application was refused by the tribunal on the grounds that, the documents sought not already being in existence, their disclosure could not be ordered. EAT rejected her appeal.

[138] If evidence of a non-discriminatory attitude on the part of an employer is accepted as having probative force, as being likely to have governed his behaviour in the particular case [as was the case in *Owen and Briggs v James* [1982] ICR 618, then evidence of a discriminatory attitude on his part may also have probative effect …'

[139] Citing *Science Research Council v Nassé* [1979] QB 144.

The rules of disclosure, which differ somewhat between employment tribunals and the county court, are outside the scope of this book. It is sufficient to note here that, even where statistical information does exist, it may not be possible for the claimant to obtain it from the alleged discriminator. Reference was made in the *Singh* case to 'fishing expeditions' and tribunals will not order disclosure of information in which (*per* Choudhury P in *Tesco Stores v Element*) 'a party is trying to see if they can find a case, either of complaint or defence, of which they know nothing or which is not yet pleaded.'[140] But disclosure may be ordered 'to narrow and particularise existing' claims,[141] and Choudhury P there rejected the argument put for the respondent that disclosure should not be granted in an equal pay case unless a prima facie case had established. Particular arguments arise in discrimination cases because the information sought by claimants may be highly confidential. Confidentiality is not a barrier to disclosure which will be ordered where necessary for the fair disposal of the proceedings but, as the HL recognised in *Science Research Council v Nassé* [1979] QB 144, it is a factor which may be taken into account by a tribunal in the exercise of its discretion.[142] In addition, the disclosure of extensive information such as that which a discrimination claimant may seek to access may be regarded as oppressive to the respondent even where relevant to the claimant.[143]

Jurisdiction

The EqA provides (s113) that, except as specified, claims must be brought in the court or tribunal specified in Part 9 of the Act.[144] Section 113(2)–(3) EqA provide that this does not apply to applications made by the EHRC under s24 EqA 2006, to claims for judicial review (see above), or to claims brought under the Immigration Acts or Special Immigration Appeals Commission Act 1997 (see Chapter 7). Section 113(5) EqA provides that the jurisdictional restriction applies to claims in respect of breach of an equality clause or rule, though we shall see at p 302 below that this does not prevent claimants from bringing equal pay claims in the civil courts.

[140] UKEAT/0228/20 (13 January 2021, unreported, §32) citing the *White Book* §18.1.13.

[141] *Ibid* §73.

[142] Where disclosure is ordered, the employment judge must consider whether and what steps may be taken to avoid unnecessary sharing of confidential elements of information (eg names and addresses of comparators whose information may be provided).

[143] See eg *Perera v Civil Service Commission* [1980] ICR 699. Note that the EqA, like the predecessor anti-discrimination provisions, originally provided for a questionnaire procedure which was intended to ameliorate some of the difficulties of proving discrimination by allowing questions to be put to the respondent prior to or after issue of a discrimination claim and for adverse inferences to be drawn, where a tribunal thought appropriate, from absent, evasive or equivocal responses. The procedure was widely regarded, including by many employers, as sensible, not least because it allowed for the narrowing-down of issues between the parties, and the responses to the consultation paper which proposed abolition were overwhelmingly negative. Section 138 EqA was, however, repealed by the Enterprise and Regulatory Reform Act 2013 from 6 April 2014. There is nothing to prevent a claimant (or prospective claimant) from putting questions to a suspected discriminator and from putting the answers (or the failure to answer) before a tribunal. Absent statutory underpinning, however, this has become much less common.

[144] Section 113(2) EqA provides that this does not apply in relation to claims brought under part 1 (socio-economic inequalities) which has not been brought into effect.

Claims in respect of Part 3 (services and public functions), Part 4 (premises), Part 6 (education), Part 7 (associations) must be brought in the county court (in Scotland, the sheriff court),[145] save that:

- Challenges to decisions of immigration authorities relating to the entitlement of a person to enter or remain in the United Kingdom which would otherwise fall within Part 3 must be brought in immigration appeal proceedings where possible, and may not be brought where an immigration appeal authority has decided that the act complained of has not breached Part 3 EqA;[146]
- Challenges relating to disability discrimination in education must be brought before the First-tier Tribunal (in England and Scotland), the Education Tribunal in Wales (ss114(1)(c) & 116 EqA)];[147]
- Proceedings in respect of EqA offences or penalties imposed by Part 12 in relation to transport for disabled persons.[148]

Section 120 provides that employment tribunals have jurisdiction in relation to Part 5 (work),[149] including in relation to pension equality (see Chapters 4 and 6),[150] save where the complaint relates to enquiries made about the health of the applicant[151] or is made about alleged discrimination by a qualifications body is subject to a statutory appeal. Claims relating to pension schemes may be brought not only by members but also by trustees or managers of the scheme; employer whose employees are, or may be, members of the scheme and any person exercising an appointing function in relation to an office the holder of which is, or may be, a member of the scheme.

Section 121 provides that Part 5 claims brought in connection with service in the armed forces must first be brought as service complaints, the time limit for applications to the employment tribunal (see below) being extended to accommodate such complaints. Section 122 allows any court dealing with an equality challenge relating to a pension scheme to strike out the claim if it is of the view that the claim could more conveniently be dealt with by a tribunal (see p 302 below), or to refer or require the referral of a question to the employment tribunal and to stay proceedings meanwhile.

Jurisdiction and EU Law

Some of the detail of the EU equality law is considered throughout the book. It is sufficient here to make clear that employment tribunals do not have jurisdiction to consider free-standing claims brought under EU law provisions, irrespective of their direct enforceability. Employment tribunals are created by statute and only have only the powers provided to them by statute (eg by the EqA and various employment statutes). A claim which arises

[145] Section 114, as must claims brought under ss108, 111 or 112 EqA relating to Parts 3, 4, 6 or 7 (see further Ch 4).

[146] Sections 114(2) and 115 EqA.

[147] Section 114(6) and 116 EqA.

[148] Penalties are established by the EqA in respect of non-compliance with gender gap reporting (s78), false statements about the application of the EqA (s110), the provision of assistance to discriminators.

[149] And claims brought under s108, 111 or 112 EqA relating to Part 5.

[150] Note (see pp 302–304 below) that this jurisdiction is not exclusive insofar as claims are contractual.

[151] See s60 EqA, discussed in Ch 8; the only remedy for breach of this provision is an action by the EHRC or the drawing of inferences in a discrimination claim brought under Part 5 EqA.

under EU law alone must be brought in the county court or High Court whose jurisdiction is not limited. More often, however, it is possible to rely on EU law in the interpretation of domestic statutes,[152] even where this 'interpretation' involves a degree of vandalism to the domestic statute.[153]

Time Limits

A further significant difficulty which discrimination complainants frequently encounter relates to the time limits imposed by legislation. The EqA provides, broadly speaking, for time limits of six months in county court claims and three months in employment tribunal claims, with the exception of equal pay cases where the time limit is (broadly) six months. Section 123, which applies to discrimination claims in the employment tribunal, is simpler than s118 (which applies to county court claims) and is set out below, followed by an explanation of how county court time limits work and a discussion broadly applicable to both jurisdictions.

Section 123 EqA, Time limits

(1) Subject to section 140B, proceedings on a complaint within section 120 [employment tribunal claims] may not be brought after the end of—

(a) the period of 3 months starting with the date of the act to which the complaint relates, or
(b) such other period as the employment tribunal thinks just and equitable.

(2) Proceedings may not be brought in reliance on section 121(1) after the end of—

(a) the period of 6 months starting with the date of the act to which the proceedings relate, or
(b) such other period as the employment tribunal thinks just and equitable.

(3) For the purposes of this section—

(a) conduct extending over a period is to be treated as done at the end of the period;
(b) failure to do something is to be treated as occurring when the person in question decided on it.

(4) In the absence of evidence to the contrary, a person (P) is to be taken to decide on failure to do something—

(a) when P does an act inconsistent with doing it, or
(b) if P does no inconsistent act, on the expiry of the period in which P might reasonably have been expected to do it.

Section 140B EqA provides for an extension of time when the dispute has been subject to Acas conciliation. Claimants must register proposed claims with Acas prior to the normal limitation date at which point time ceases to run until Acas issues a conciliation certificate which confirms that early conciliation has not resulted in a settlement of the proposed claim. Conciliation is not mandatory and will be attempted by Acas only with the claimant's agreement. Claimants have a minimum one month after the date of when any such certificate is received within which to bring a claim irrespective of when limitation would otherwise apply.

[152] See the decision of the CJEU in Case C-106/89, *Marleasing SA v Comercial Internacional de Alimentacion SA* EU:C:1990:395, [1991] I-ECR 4135, [1992] 1 CMLR 305.

[153] See eg discussions of *EBR Attridge Law v Coleman* (No 2) [2010] ICR 242 and *Rowstock Ltd v Jessemmy* [2014] EWCA Civ 185, [2014] ICR 550 in Ch 2 and *Blackwood v Birmingham & Solihull Mental Health NHS Trust* [2016] EWCA Civ 607, [2016] ICR 903 in Ch 4.

Section 118 EqA is in materially similar terms to s123 EqA in that it provides for the extension of the time limit by reference to s140AA EqA (to accommodate alternative dispute resolution in certain cross border or domestic contractual disputes), allows the time limit (there of six rather than three months) to be extended where the county court or sheriff thinks just and equitable; provides for 'continuing acts' (see s123(3) EqA) and makes specific provision for discrimination by omission (s123(3)–(4) EqA).[154] Section 118(3) EqA, in addition, extends the time limit from six to nine months where a higher education claim has been referred within six months of the Office of the Independent Adjudicator for Higher Education (the OIA) which operates a complaint scheme for students. Section 123(5) EqA provides for an extension of time in immigration cases in which complaints of discrimination under Part 3 EqA (services and public functions) are required first to be raised in an immigration appeal (s115 EqA).

It is important to note that under both s118 and 123 EqA time begins to run from the date on which the alleged act of discrimination occurred, and not the date on which the claimant became aware of it, or became aware that it was or may have been discriminatory.[155] This can obviously work against the interests of claimants, but it may also work in their favour: where, for example the alleged act of discrimination consists of a dismissal time begins to run at the date of the dismissal rather than when the claimant was given notice.[156]

Equal Pay/Pension Cases

Time limits in equal pay/pension claims are set out in s129 EqA which provides for a non-extendable (except where Acas has been involved) six-month limitation period.[157] Time will generally begin to run from 'the last day of the employment or appointment' (s129(3)), though in a 'stable work case' ('where the proceedings relate to a period during which there was a stable working relationship between the worker and the responsible person (including any time after the terms of work had expired[158] time runs from the day on which the stable working relationship ended. In addition, where the responsible person (employer or the trustees or managers of the occupational pension scheme) has deliberately concealed a core factual element of the claim from the worker) or where the worker had an incapacity, time will not begin to run until, respectively, 'the day on which the worker discovered (or could with reasonable diligence have discovered)' the core factual element and 'the day on which the worker ceased to have the incapacity'.[159]

Section 129(4) also makes provision for cases involving armed services personnel who may bring their claims within nine months of 'the last day of the period of service during which the complaint arose', subject to the same extensions in cases of concealment or incapacity. In each case the time periods, generally not capable of extension, are also subject to a carve-out to facilitate Acas conciliation.

[154] S118(1), (6) & (7) EqA.

[155] See *Virdi v Commissioner of Police of the Metropolis* [2007] IRLR 24 (EAT) *per* Elias P at §25. The same rule applies to discriminatory policies: *Murali v BMA* UKEAT/0850/02, [2003] All ER (D) 152 (Dec) at §19, *per* HH Judge Wakefield.

[156] See eg *Lupetti v Wrens Old House Ltd* [1984] ICR 348.

[157] Nine months in cases involving military personnel: s129(4) EqA.

[158] Section 130(3) EqA.

[159] Where there is concealment and incapacity the later of the two relevant dates.

The equal pay provisions have always imposed different time limits from the anti-discrimination provisions. In addition, the equal provisions, uniquely, impose a back-stop on the period in respect of which damages (in the form of back-pay) are recoverable (see further pp 327–328 below).[160] As originally enacted, the six-month limitation period and two-year backstops were absolute, but provisions permitting the extension of the limitation period in concealment and incapacity cases, extending the two-year backstop to six and disapplying it in concealment and incapacity cases were implemented as a result of a number of CJEU decisions challenging the effectiveness and equivalence of remedies in equal pay claims.[161]

Claimants may escape the short limitations periods applicable in the employment tribunals by issuing equal pay claims in the civil courts. This step is not available in respect of discrimination claims in respect of which the EqA provides exclusive jurisdiction to employment or other tribunal or to the civil courts depending on the context in which the discrimination is alleged to have occurred. Equal pay claims are different because ss ss64–76 EqA operate by inserting an 'equality clause' into the successful claimant's contract of employment. The SC confirmed in *Abdulla v Birmingham City Council* that this clause can then be enforced in the ordinary way, though claimants who issue equal pay claims in the civil courts will be at greater risk of costs if their claims do not succeed (see pp 283–286 above).

***Abdulla v Birmingham CC* [2012] UKSC 47, [2012] ICR 1419**

The claimants brought equal pay claims in the High Court at a time when they would have been out of time to bring their claims in the employment tribunal but were within the normal six-year limitation period for contract claims in the civil courts. The council applied to the court for a direction that the claims be struck out pursuant to s2(3) of the 1970 Act, which provided that 'Where it appears to the court in which any proceedings are pending that a claim or counter-claim in respect of the operation of an equal pay clause could more conveniently be disposed of separately by an employment tribunal, the court may direct that the claim or counterclaim shall be struck out.'[162] The High Court rejected the Council's application on the ground that 'it cannot be more convenient for a claim to be disposed of separately by an employment tribunal in circumstances where the … tribunal could not determine the claim on its merits but would be bound to refuse jurisdiction to deal with the claim because it was time barred.' The Council appealed unsuccessfully to the CA and then to the SC which, by a majority, dismissed the appeal.

[160] The short time limits imposed by the discrimination provisions will in most cases prevent recovery in respect of long-past wrongs, but it remains a possibility in cases of continuing discrimination or where (at least in theory) a tribunal extends time.

[161] See eg Case C-326/96 *Levez v Jennings*, EU:C:1998:577 [1999] ECR I–07835, [1999] ICR 521 and in C-78/98 *Preston v Wolverhampton Healthcare NHS Trust* EU:C:2000:247, [2000] ECR I-03201; Case C-246/96 *Magorrian and Cunningham v Eastern HSSB and DHSS* EU:C:1997:605, [1997] ECR I–7153, [1998] ICR 979; and see *Levez v Jennings (Harlow Pools) Ltd, Hicking v Basford Group Ltd (No 2)* [2000] ICR 58.

[162] The same provision is found in s128 EqA.

Lord Wilson (with whom Lady Hale and Lord Reed agreed, Lords Sumption and Carnwath dissenting):

6. Were it not for one feature, the claims could have been presented by way of complaint to an employment tribunal .... Such claims are usually brought in the tribunal, which offers to litigants many advantages not on offer in a court, including greater expertise in their determination (even, in a specified situation, provision to them free of charge of an expert report ..., less cost and, in principle, faster resolution. Indeed, in the course of giving the only substantive judgment in the Court of Appeal, Mummery LJ, whose experience of this area of the law is unrivalled, observed that he had never previously encountered a claim under the Act which had been presented to a court rather than the tribunal.

7. The feature which precludes the claimants from presenting their claims to the tribunal is that they would be out of time for doing so ...

12. In his judgment Mummery LJ held that the 'basic assumption' behind the first part of s.2(3) was that both the court and the tribunal would have jurisdiction to decide the claim on its merits; that the purpose behind the provision was, in that context, to identify the forum more fitted for its resolution; that, in that Birmingham was not alleging that the claims represented an abuse of the process of the court, the reasons why the claims had not been made to the tribunal were irrelevant; and that the deputy judge's decision had been correct. Nevertheless Mummery LJ expressed himself in terms more qualified than those used by the deputy judge: he said that, in the exercise of the discretion under the first part of the subsection, the fact that a complaint to the tribunal would be time-barred would be no more than 'a circumstance of considerable weight in most cases'. He added that it would be exceptional for the reasons for not presenting a complaint in time to the tribunal to be relevant to the exercise of the discretion but that, for example, they would be relevant where they were such as to render the claim made to the court an abuse of its process. As an aside, Mummery LJ addressed the word 'separately' in the first part of the subsection, upon which nothing in the appeal turned; and he observed, helpfully, that Parliament may in particular have had in mind the presentation to the court of a mixed claim, of which one component was of breach of an equality clause and of which others were such as the tribunal had no jurisdiction to entertain. In the light of his conclusion Mummery LJ explained that he had no need to address the principle of equivalence ...

[Having considered the historical development of the EqPA which had involved providing to tribunals for the first time a limited jurisdiction over contractual claims, so as to permit them to deal with equal pay claims]

17. Although it thus conferred on the tribunal jurisdiction to determine a claim of breach of contract in this regard, Parliament did not oust the jurisdiction of the court to determine such a claim. That there was concurrent jurisdiction in the tribunal and the court is plain from (among others) the subsection, namely s.2(3), which is central to this appeal; and, over the four subsequent decades, such has been frequently acknowledged and never doubted ...

20. A striking feature of the limitation period of six months set by s.2(4) of the [Equal Pay] Act was that Parliament never made it extendable. For almost all of the many other claims which, by 2010, could be made to the tribunal, Parliament prescribed limitation periods which it permitted the tribunal to extend; in some cases to extend them in so far as it was just and equitable to do so and, in other cases in which it had not been reasonably practicable for the complaint to be presented in time, to extend them for such further period as the tribunal might consider reasonable ... It is strongly arguable that Parliament tolerated an unusually absolute time limit for the presentation to the tribunal of a claim under the Act only because it recognised that, were she to fall foul of that time limit, the claimant would nevertheless be likely to remain in time for making her claim in court ...

26. … No doubt in most cases it will be more convenient for the tribunal to dispose of a claim in respect of the operation of an equality clause, provided that it can still be brought there, rather than for the court to do so. If the claim can no longer be brought there, the effect of Birmingham's submissions in this appeal … would be to convert the reasons why the claimant had failed to present her claim in time to the tribunal into the factor determinative of whether it be struck out by the court. But I do not regard the reasons for her failure as relevant in any way to the notion of convenience. In my view Birmingham aspires in effect to re-write s.2(3); and to introduce into the law a principle which would in some cases in effect serve to shorten the period of limitation allowed by Parliament for the bringing of claims in court …

29. I would hold that the present claims cannot more conveniently be disposed of by the tribunal … I prefer the categorical terms favoured by the deputy judge to the qualified terms favoured by Mummery LJ. The latter referred to cases of abuse of process. Nothing can detract from the inherent jurisdiction of the court to strike out a claim in respect of the operation of an equality clause if it were to represent an abuse of its process; one example might be that of a claimant who had been invited to present a complaint in time to the tribunal but who had spurned the invitation in order to secure what the court considered to be an illegitimate advantage by bringing the claim before itself. But the subject of s.2(3) was not abuse of process; and I would hold, for the purpose both of the first part of the subsection and of its successor, namely s.128 of the Equality Act 2010, that a claim in respect of the operation of an equality clause can never more conveniently be disposed of by the tribunal if it would there be time-barred.

30. No doubt one aspect of Birmingham's concern about the prospect that claims in respect of the operation of an equality clause may be brought against employers in court, rather than in the tribunal, relates to the court's general rule, which does not apply in the tribunal, to make an order for costs against the unsuccessful party. But the court may make a different order and, in deciding what order (if any) to make in respect of costs, it must have regard to all the circumstances, including the conduct of the parties: CPR rule 44.3(4)(a). It is to this latter inquiry that the factor incorrectly urged as relevant to this appeal might well become relevant. The court's conclusion that, instead of bringing it in court, a claimant should, in all the circumstances, reasonably have presented her claim, in time, to the tribunal might well be relevant to its survey in relation to costs under the subrule: in so far as, had she done so, she would not have obtained an order for costs, such might well be relevant to the court's decision as to the appropriate order.

31. Even in circumstances in which the presentation of a claim to the tribunal would be time-barred, the power of the court under both the second part of s.2(3) of the Act and its successor, namely s.128(2) of the 2010 Act, to refer to the tribunal a question as to the operation of an equality clause still remains; and should not be forgotten. Nevertheless Parliament might well wish to consider introducing a relaxation of the usual limitation period for the presentation of a claim to the tribunal in cases in which a claim in respect of the operation of an equality clause has been brought, in time, before the court and, were it not for the effect of the usual limitation period, would more conveniently be disposed of by the tribunal.

Continuing Acts

Whether discrimination is alleged to have taken place over a period of time, whether in the sphere of employment or elsewhere, the EqA provides that time will not begin to run until the end of that period (s118(6); s123(3)). The case law distinguishes 'continuing acts' from 'continuing consequences'[163] (the consequences of a discriminatory failure to appoint or promote, for example, will persist over time but the three-month period will run from the

[163] See eg *Sougrin v Haringey HA* [1992] ICR 650, for example, and *Owusu v London Fire & Civil Defence Authority* [1995] IRLR 574.

date of the non-appointment or promotion). That the distinction can be difficult to draw can be seen in *Okoro v Taylor Woodrow Construction Ltd* [2012] EWCA Civ 1590, [2013] ICR 580 in which a prohibition on the claimant working on the respondent's building sites was found by the CA to be to be a one-off act with continuing consequences.

The cases below were decided under the EqA's predecessor provisions but the statutory formula has not changed and the cases remain good law.

The EAT ruled in *Owusu v London Fire & Civil Defence Authority* [1995] ICR 650 (*per* Mummery J as he then was) that a 'continuing act' refers to 'some policy, rule or practice, in accordance with which decisions are taken from time to time'. In that case, a fire safety case worker complained of a persistent failure on the part of his employers to promote, regrade, or shortlist him for promotion. The effect of EAT's acceptance that the 'continuing act' complained of was the practice of discriminatorily excluding the claimant from regrading was that a race discrimination complaint which specified a number of failures on the part of the employer to regrade the claimant was within the three-month time limit, despite the fact that more than three months had elapsed since the last act alleged.

A similar approach was taken by the CA in the following case.

***Cast v Croydon College* [1998] EWCA Civ 498, [1998] ICR 500**

The claimant had been denied permission to transfer from full-time to part-time work after her return from maternity leave. The employer's written policy was one of 'receptiveness to proposals for jobsharing at all levels', but Ms Cast was informed that it was essential for the holder of her post (information centre manager) to work full-time in order properly to coordinate the work of the centre's part-time employees. She resigned a month after her return to work and made her sex discrimination claim two months later. The claim was rejected by a tribunal and the EAT on the grounds that the act of discrimination (if it was such an act) took place prior to the claimant's return from maternity leave (the date of her first request).[164] The complaint, accordingly, was long out of time. Further, both the tribunal and the EAT denied that the employer's refusal (despite repeated requests on Ms Cast's part) amounted to a policy, Judge Hargrove declaring that '[t]he mere repetition of a request ... cannot convert a single managerial decision into a policy, practice or rule. The CA allowed Ms Cast's appeal.

Auld LJ (for the Court):

> 25. The fact that a specific act out of time may have continuing consequences within time does not make it an act extending over a period ...[165]

[164] See also *Commissioner of the Police for the Metropolis v Harley* [2001] ICR 927 in which EAT ruled that the time limit in a constructive dismissal case under the DDA ran from the repudiatory act rather than its acceptance.

[165] Citing *Amies v Inner London Education Authority* [1977] ICR 308: failure to appoint to a position; and *Sougrin v Haringey HA* n 163 above: refusal to upgrade an employee. For a decision on this issue under the FEA (as it then was) see *Kearney v Northern Irish Civil Service Commission* [1996] NI 415.
Citing *Owusu*, n 163 above, and Lord Griffiths in *Barclays Bank v Kapur* [1991] 2 AC 355 who, in turn, cited with approval a passage from the judgment of Bristow J in *Amies, ibid*: 'So, if the employers operated a rule that the position of head of department was open to men only, for as long as the rule was in operation there would be a continuing discrimination and anyone considering herself to have been discriminated against because of the rule would have three months from the time when the rule was abrogated within which to bring the complaint.'

> 26. As to an act extending over a period, the authorities make clear … that it is the existence of a policy or regime, not a specific act of an employer triggering its application to the complainant, that matters. A moment's consideration of the [statutory formula] 'any act extending over a period shall be treated as done at the end of that period' (my emphasis) – shows that that must be so. If the 'act extending over a period' required a specific act by an employer to give it effect there would be no need or room to 'treat … it as done at the end of the period'…
>
> 27. There may be a policy or regime for this purpose even though it is not of a formal nature or expressed in writing; and it may be confined to a particular post or role …
>
> 40. The passage from … Judge Hargrove's judgment [above] confuses the question whether the repetition of requests, and it would seem corresponding refusals, can convert a single decision into a policy with the question whether there was a single decision or several decisions. His conclusions that the industrial tribunal had been 'forced to the view that this was a single act' and, implicitly, that it had so found are not, in my judgment, justified on the material before the tribunal or evident from the way it expressed its findings …
>
> 43. To acknowledge that there may be successive acts of discrimination in this way does not negate the time bar provided by s.76, provided that decision-makers make clear in responding to further requests whether they have reconsidered the matter. If they have, time begins to run again; if they have not, and merely refer the complainant to their previous decision, no new period of limitation arises. However, where the successive acts are such as to indicate and/or are pursuant to a policy or regime, different considerations arise …

The decision of the CA in *Hendricks* is the leading case on continuing discrimination. It marked a judicial softening of approach, Mummery J (now LJ) resiling from his requirement in *Owusu* for a 'policy, rule or practice, in accordance with which decisions are taken from time to time'.[166]

***Hendricks v Commissioner of Police for the Metropolis* [2002] EWCA Civ 1686, [2003] ICR 530**

The claimant complained of more than 100 acts of race and sex discrimination over the course of her 11 years' service in the Met police. Most had taken place in the first five years of her service but she alleged that discrimination had continued up to the date of her claim notwithstanding that in the year immediately prior to it she had been on long-term stress-related sick leave. A tribunal ruled as a preliminary matter that complaints related to a 'continuing act' and were therefore to be treated as done at the end of the period over which the act extended: 'In our view, on the basis of the applicant's as yet untested allegations, a policy, rule or practice could be detected as result of which female officers and officers from ethnic minorities were treated less favourably than white male officers.' The EAT overturned on the basis that the claimant's allegations could not support findings of a generalised discriminatory policy so as to amount to a 'continuing act' – this on the basis that she did not allege a 'policy' as such or claim that others had been the victims of it. The CA reinstated her claim.

[166] See also *Kells v Pilkington plc* [2002] IRLR 693.

Mummery LJ:

27. On the 'continuing act' point it was made clear by the counsel then appearing for Miss Hendricks that, although the acts complained of appeared on their face to be separate incidents, they in fact constituted a 'seamless whole of continual and continuing less favourable treatment by the respondent's officers.'...

47. On the crucial issue whether this is a case of 'an act extending over a period' ... I am satisfied that there was no error of law on the part of the employment tribunal.

48. On the evidential material before it, the tribunal was entitled to make a preliminary decision that it has jurisdiction to consider the allegations of discrimination made by Miss Hendricks. The fact that she was off sick from March 1999 and was absent from the working environment does not necessarily rule out the possibility of continuing discrimination against her, for which the Commissioner may be held legally responsible ... She is, in my view, entitled to pursue her claim beyond this preliminary stage on the basis that the burden is on her to prove, either by direct evidence or by inference from primary facts, that the numerous alleged incidents of discrimination are linked to one another and that they are evidence of a continuing discriminatory state of affairs covered by the concept of 'an act extending over a period.' I regard this as a legally more precise way of characterising her case than the use of expressions such as 'institutionalised racism,' 'a prevailing way of life,' a 'generalised policy of discrimination,' or 'climate' or 'culture' of unlawful discrimination.

49. At the end of the day Miss Hendricks may not succeed in proving that the alleged incidents actually occurred or that, if they did, they add up to more than isolated and unconnected acts of less favourable treatment by different people in different places over a long period and that there was no 'act extending over a period' for which the Commissioner can be held legally responsible as a result of what he has done, or omitted to do, in the direction and control of the Service in matters of race and sex discrimination. It is, however, too soon to say that the complaints have been brought too late.

50. I appreciate the concern expressed about the practical difficulties that may well arise in having to deal with so many incidents alleged to have occurred so long ago; but this problem often occurs in discrimination cases, even where the only acts complained of are very recent. Evidence can still be brought of long-past incidents of less favourable treatment in order to raise or reinforce an inference that the ground of the less favourable treatment is race or sex.

51. In my judgment, the approach of both the employment tribunal and the Appeal Tribunal to the language of the authorities on 'continuing acts' was too literal. They concentrated on whether the concepts of a policy, rule, scheme, regime or practice, in accordance with which decisions affecting the treatment of workers are taken, fitted the facts of this case ... The concepts of policy, rule, practice, scheme or regime in the authorities were given as examples of when an act extends over a period. They should not be treated as a complete and constricting statement of the indicia of 'an act extending over a period.' I agree with the observation made by Sedley LJ, in his decision on the paper application for permission to appeal, that the Appeal Tribunal allowed itself to be sidetracked by focusing on whether a 'policy' could be discerned. Instead, the focus should be on the substance of the complaints that the Commissioner was responsible for an ongoing situation or a continuing state of affairs in which female ethnic minority officers in the Service were treated less favourably. The question is whether that is 'an act extending over a period' as distinct from a succession of unconnected or isolated specific acts, for which time would begin to run from the date when each specific act was committed.[167]

[167] See also *Spender v HM Prison Service* [2004] All ER (D) 94 (Mar) in which EAT ruled that absence from work (there on maternity and parental leave) did not prevent discrimination continuing for the purpose of extending time.

Just and Equitable Extension

We saw above that ss111(2)(b) and 123(1)(b) EqA allow tribunals and courts to determine discrimination claims which are brought outside the normal time limit but within 'such other period as the [court or] tribunal thinks just and equitable'. The discretion thus provided to disapply time limits is much wider than that afforded to tribunals in unfair dismissal and other employment claims, ss11(4), 23(4), 34(2), 48(3) and 111(2) of the Employment Rights Act 1996 providing that a tribunal 'shall not consider' a claim made out-of-time unless made 'within such further period as the tribunal considers reasonable in a case where it is satisfied that it was not reasonably practicable' for the complaint to be presented in time.[168] The EAT should not readily overturn the exercise of such discretion.

***LB Southwark v Afolabi* [2003] EWCA Civ 15, [2003] ICR 800**

The CA ruled that a tribunal had not erred in hearing a race discrimination complaint which concerned the terms of his appointment to a position some nine years before. It was not until shortly prior to the issue of the complaint that the claimant had seen his personnel file which revealed that the employer's refusal to appoint him to the position he had originally sought (as distinct from the more junior one in which he was taken on) was made notwithstanding very high ratings he had received at his interview. The tribunal ruled that it was just and equitable to consider his complaint, there having been no reason for him to inspect his personal file before he did, and Mr Afolabi having brought his claim within three months of seeing the file. The tribunal took the view that the lapse in time would be no more prejudicial to the respondent than it was to the claimant himself. EAT and the CA upheld the tribunal's exercise of discretion, although Peter Gibson LJ (with whom Rix LJ expressly agreed on this point) suggested that:

> 35. ... it can only be in a wholly exceptional case that the [tribunal] could properly conclude that despite a delay of a magnitude anywhere approaching nine years it was just and equitable to extend time. The policy of the Act is made clear by the brevity of the limitation period; that period of three months is in marked contrast to the limitation periods in ordinary litigation. Parliament having envisaged that complaints within the jurisdiction of the [tribunal] will be determined within a short space of time after the events complained of, it will be an extremely rare case where the [tribunal] can properly decide that there can be a fair trial so long after those events. Had Southwark duly applied itself to what it needed to prove and submitted appropriate evidence, the result may well have been different. As it is, I am compelled to conclude that, on the findings which it was open for the [tribunal] to make, the decision to extend time cannot be impugned.

Section 33 of the Limitation Act 1980, which applies to claims before the civil courts, sets out a number of factors which the court must consider in determining whether to extend time. These include the prejudice to each party resulting from the grant or refusal of an extension and all the other circumstances, in particular: (a) the length of and reasons for the delay; (b) the extent to which the cogency of the evidence is likely to be affected by the delay; (c) the extent to which the party sued had co-operated with any requests for information;

[168] These provisions relate, respectively, to claims in respect of employment particulars, unauthorised deduction from pay, guarantee payments, unlawful detriment and unfair dismissal.

(d) the promptness with which the claimant acted once he or she knew of the facts giving rise to the cause of action; and (e) the steps taken by the claimant to obtain appropriate professional advice once he or she knew of the possibility of taking action.

The EAT suggested in *British Coal Corpn v Keeble* [1997] IRLR 336 that tribunals might consider the list of factors in s33 in considering whether to extend time in discrimination cases. In *Abertawe Bro Morgannwg University Local Health Board v Morgan* [2018] EWCA Civ 640, [2018] ICR 1194, however, the CA disapproved of this approach. Leggatt LJ (with whom Bean LJ agreed) stated at §18 that Parliament had chosen to give tribunals 'the widest possible discretion' under the EqA, by contrast with the position under the Limitation Act 1980, and had not included any list of mandatory considerations. Under these circumstances, he stated, it would be 'wrong … to put a gloss on the words of the provision or to interpret it as if it contains such a list'. His Lordship referred to the earlier decision in *Alofabi* §33 as authority that 'the tribunal is not required to go through such a list, the only requirement being that it does not leave a significant factor out of account: That said, factors which are almost always relevant to consider when exercising any discretion whether to extend time were, his lordship stated (§19): (a) the length of, and reasons for, the delay and (b) whether the delay has prejudiced the respondent (for example, by preventing or inhibiting it from investigating the claim while matters were fresh).'

More recently, in *Adedeji v University Hospitals Birmingham NHS Foundation Trust* [2021] EWCA Civ 23, [2021] ICR D5 the CA expressed concern that tribunals continued to rely on s33 of the 1980 Act despite the guidance of the CA in *Abertawe*.

***Harvey on Industrial Relations* Division L: Equal Opportunities**

[832] The following is a non-exhaustive list of factors which may prove helpful in assessing individual cases:

- the presence or absence of any prejudice to the respondent if the claim is allowed to proceed (other than the prejudice involved in having to defend proceedings);
- the presence or absence of any other remedy for the claimant if the claim is not allowed to proceed;
- the conduct of the respondent subsequent to the act of which complaint is made, up to the date of the application;
- the conduct of the claimant over the same period;
- the length of time by which the application is out of time;
- the medical condition of the claimant, taking into account, in particular, any reason why this should have prevented or inhibited the making of a claim;
- the extent to which professional advice on making a claim was sought and, if it was sought, the content of any advice given.

… Whichever factor is relevant to be taken into account, it must be responsible for causing the time limit to be missed …

Individual Remedies

The primary remedies available for discrimination claims are set out in ss119 and 124 EqA, which provide, so far as relevant, as follows:

Section 119 EqA, Remedies

(1) This section applies if the county court or the sheriff finds that there has been a contravention of a provision referred to in section 114(1).

(2) The county court has power to grant any remedy which could be granted by the High Court—

(a) in proceedings in tort;
(b) on a claim for judicial review …

(4) An award of damages may include compensation for injured feelings (whether or not it includes compensation on any other basis).
(5) Subsection (6) applies if the county court or sheriff—

(a) finds that a contravention of a provision referred to in section 114(1) is established by virtue of section 19, but
(b) is satisfied that the provision, criterion or practice was not applied with the intention of discriminating against the claimant or pursuer.

(6) The county court or sheriff must not make an award of damages unless it first considers whether to make any other disposal.
(7) The county court or sheriff must not grant a remedy other than an award of damages or the making of a declaration unless satisfied that no criminal matter would be prejudiced by doing so.

Section 119(2)(b) EqA provides county courts with the power to issue injunctions and declarations, where appropriate, as well as to order compensation. Section 124 EqA, which governs remedies in the employment tribunal, provides that:

Section 124 EqA, Remedies: general

(1) This section applies if an employment tribunal finds that there has been a contravention of a provision referred to in section 120(1).
(2) The tribunal may—

(a) make a declaration as to the rights of the complainant and the respondent in relation to the matters to which the proceedings relate;
(b) order the respondent to pay compensation to the complainant;
(c) make an appropriate recommendation.

(3) An appropriate recommendation is a recommendation that within a specified period the respondent takes specified steps for the purpose of obviating or reducing the adverse effect on the complainant of any matter to which the proceedings relate …

Section 124(4) EqA is in similar terms to s119(5), providing that in cases of unintentional indirect discrimination a tribunal must not award compensation without first considering whether to make a declaration or recommendation under s124(2). Section 124 EqA then goes on to provide that:

(6) The amount of compensation which may be awarded under subsection (2)(b) corresponds to the amount which could be awarded by the county court or the sheriff under section 119.
(7) If a respondent fails, without reasonable excuse, to comply with an appropriate recommendation, the tribunal may—

(a) if an order was made under subsection (2)(b), increase the amount of compensation to be paid;
(b) if no such order was made, make one.

Section 126 makes specific provision for remedies where discrimination in occupational pension schemes is challenged, giving tribunals power to make declarations admitting claimants to schemes from which they have been excluded, or for their inclusion on non-discriminatory terms, in addition to any remedy which the tribunal could grant under s124 EqA, and restricting the damages payable under s124 to compensation for injury to feelings.

Declarations

Section 124(a) EqA provides that a tribunal may make a declaration by way of remedy in a successful discrimination claim. This is likely to provide cold comfort to the theoretically successful claimant who is unlikely to recover the costs of their claim, and may themselves be vulnerable to an application for costs from a respondent who has made a settlement offer.

Recommendations

Tribunals have no power to issue injunctions in discrimination claims but may make recommendations and declarations. As originally enacted, s124(3) EqA empowered tribunals to make recommendations 'that within a specified period the respondent takes specified steps for the purpose of obviating or reducing the adverse effect of any matter to which the proceedings relate (a) on the complainant; (b) on any other person'. The inclusion within the EqA of a provision allowing recommendations whose impact could extend beyond the claimant was a response to decades of campaigning by the CRE and EOC. The impact was to permit recommendations to be made to remedy discriminatory practices by a respondent whether or not it continued to employ the claimant. The wider power was removed in 2015 together with the EqA's provision for questionnaires in discrimination and equal pay cases in pursuit of a government drive to reduce 'red tape' and notwithstanding the overwhelming disagreement of those who responded to the consultation paper.

Appellate decisions relating to recommendations are relatively rare. In *Noone v North West Thames Regional Health Authority (No 2)* [1988] ICR 813 the CA ruled that the RRA's equivalent of s124 EqA did not empower a tribunal to recommend that the claimant be appointed to the next suitable job because it did not permit 'positive' discrimination (see further Chapter 3). In *British Gas plc v Sharma* [1991] ICR 19 the EAT reached a similar conclusion in relation to a recommendation that the claimant be promoted to the next suitable vacancy.

Neither s124(3) EqA or its various predecessors provide(d) any express power to order reinstatement or re-engagement (*cf* ss 112–115 ERA 1996 on an unfair dismissal claim). In *CC West Yorkshire Police v Vento (No 2)* [2003] ICR 318, however, Wall J characterised the discretion given to tribunals the SDA as 'extremely wide', and there seems to be no reason in principle why a tribunal could not recommend reinstatement or re-engagement. In *Smith v Ingram Motoring Group Ltd* (2004, reported in 'Case Digest' 126 *Equal Opportunities Review*) a tribunal recommended that the claimant, who had won a claim relating to a refusal to permit her to return part-time after maternity leave, be permitted to return on that basis. The decision of the CA below provides an example of the potential width of the power to make recommendations, albeit now limited (again) to those which may impact on the claimant him or herself.

***Hill v Lloyds Bank plc* Appeal No UKEAT/0173/19/LA, [2020] IRLR 652**

The EAT considered the appropriateness of a recommendation, made in a reasonable adjustments disability case, that the respondent provide an undertaking that it would not require the claimant to work with either of two managers and that, if there was no alternative to her so doing, that it would offer her a severance package equivalent to that provided on redundancy. Having made this recommendation, the employment tribunal reconsidered it at the respondent's invitation and concluded that it was not properly made because it included matters relating to remuneration (severance pay) which was inappropriate for a recommendation, and because it was not possible to specify a period of time for compliance with the recommendation or to specify the period during which it would apply in the future (s124(3) EqA providing that an appropriate recommendation was one that that *within a specified period* the respondent take specified steps for the purpose of obviating or reducing the adverse effect on the complainant of any matter to which the proceedings relate).

The EAT dealt first with the employer's objection to the substantive finding that the failure to give the claimant that she would not be required to work with either of the named managers and that, if this proved unsustainable, she would be given a severance package. Having ruled that the tribunal was entitled to find that the undertaking sought by the claimant was a reasonable adjustment and that the refusal to agree it amounted to disability discrimination, the EAT went on to consider the appropriateness of the recommendation initially made by the tribunal.

Judge Shanks (for the EAT):

> 20. … The form of recommendation made by the ET originally was as follows:
>
> 'The Tribunal makes the following recommendation:
>
> The Respondent undertakes to ensure that the Claimant does not work or interact in any capacity with Mr B or Ms M and that in the event that this is not possible that the Respondent and the Claimant explore suitable alternative employment with the Respondent and if this fails that the Respondent uses its best endeavours to ensure that the Claimant can leave the Respondent with a severance package equivalent to its redundancy payment scheme applicable at the time of her departure.'
>
> That recommendation was, as we have said, set aside by the ET on reconsideration, so that as matters stand there is no recommendation in place. We observe there were plainly problems with the recommendation as made originally and, indeed, we are puzzled as to why the ET did not just make a recommendation in the terms Mrs Hill had asked, which reflected precisely the terms of the reasonable adjustments she was suggesting should have been made. To identify the problems with the recommendation made by the ET very briefly: first, there was no time limit on the requirement to give an undertaking; second, there was no requirement that it should be in writing; third, the undertaking to see that the Claimant did not interact in any capacity with Mr B or Ms M seems to us a rather wide undertaking to require; fourth, the undertaking would have required things to be done by the Claimant exploring suitable alternative employment, which is not really a suitable form of undertaking to be given by the Bank; fifth, there was provision for 'best endeavours' to be used which was perhaps rather vague.
>
> 21. On those grounds, we would agree that the recommendation as originally made should be set aside and consideration given to a fresh form of recommendation. However, the real issue that arises in this Tribunal is whether a recommendation along the general lines proposed can be upheld in principle. The Bank say that it cannot and in effect they persuaded the ET of that on the Reconsideration Hearing …
>
> 25. We can see no objection of principle to a requirement by undertaking that a particular employee should be treated as redundant in certain circumstances. The whole point of the

reasonable adjustments regime is that it is designed to benefit disabled employees and many recommendations can have financial implications. My colleagues in discussion mentioned provisions about carrying on with sick pay on at a full rate in certain circumstances or provisions that a particular employee is moved from A to B which may have financial implications for both employer and employer. Therefore, we cannot see any objection in principle to a recommendation (or indeed an undertaking) that will have potential financial implications. Also, we have already referred to the fact that the purpose of this particular part of the undertaking was in fact to reinforce the basic undertaking that the Claimant would not be required to work with B or M. Therefore, we do not consider that this objection to the recommendation in principle is valid.[169]

26. The second reason that the ET relied on in para 6 of their Reconsideration Judgment was that it was not possible to specify a period of time for compliance with the recommendation or to specify the period during which it would apply in the future. The first answer to this point again is that the time limit to be applied would have been a time limit on the giving of the written undertaking which could not involve any problem. However, in any event, we can see no problem with a requirement that 'steps' once taken must remain in place indefinitely. That is likely to be case in relation to very many straightforward recommendations. For example, a recommendation that a Claimant's place of work is moved to another place carries with it the inevitable implication that that is a state of affairs which should continue to apply indefinitely, so the fact that a recommendation or an undertaking may go on for an indefinite period does not seem to us to be a valid objection at all …

29. In general, we can see no objection in principle to a recommendation that an employer give an undertaking in suitable (perhaps rare) cases. Here, the ET had found that the very step that was required to alleviate the disadvantage being suffered by Mrs Hill was an undertaking that she could rely on to give her comfort. The failure to give that very undertaking was the basis for her success on the disability discrimination claim. In those circumstances, we see no reason why the ET should not have made a recommendation along the lines proposed. We shall therefore allow the appeal in relation to the Reconsideration Decision and remit the question of what recommendation should be made to be considered again by the ET …

32. Therefore, drawing it all together, we allow the appeals in relation to the recommendation made originally and the reconsideration Decision and in relation to anonymity. Those matters should all be remitted for decision by the ET.

Compensation

By far the most common remedy under the EqA is compensation which, by contrast with that available in unfair dismissal claims, is uncapped (this as a result of the CJEU's decision in *Marshall v Southampton and South-West Hampshire Area Health Authority (No 2)*, Case C-271/91 [1993] ECR I–04367, [1993] IRLR 445). The awards made by tribunals in discrimination cases are considered at pp 324–327 below (no comparable figures being collated by the civil courts). The heads under which discrimination may be

[169] Note, however, the decision of the CA in *Irvine v Prestcold Ltd* [1981] ICR 777 that a tribunal had erred in recommending that the claimant, who had been discriminated against by being refused promotion, should receive a higher salary until promotion; monetary compensation should be awarded as compensation rather than in the form of a recommendation. The decision in *Hill* is not inconsistent with that in *Irvine* but *Irvine* indicates the boundaries of recommendations relating to financial matters

awarded in a discrimination claim (whether by a tribunal or a court) were set out by the CA in the following case:

***Alexander v Home Office* [1988] ICR 685**

May LJ (for the Court):

14. … damages for this relatively new tort of unlawful racial discrimination are at large, that is to say that they are not limited to the pecuniary loss that can be specifically proved … compensatory damages may and in some instances should include an element of aggravated damages where, for example, the defendant may have behaved in a high-handed, malicious, insulting or oppressive manner in committing the act of discrimination.[170] … The material passage from Lord Diplock's speech in *Cassell & Co Ltd v Broome* [[1972] 1 AC 1027] is in these terms:

> The three heads under which damages are recoverable for those torts for which damages are 'at large' are classified under the following heads. (1) Compensation for the harm caused to the plaintiff by the wrongful physical act of the defendant in respect of which the action is brought. In addition to any pecuniary loss specifically proved the assessment of this compensation may itself involve putting a money value upon physical hurt, as in assault on curtailment of liberty, as in false imprisonment or malicious prosecution on injury to reputation, as in defamation, false imprisonment and malicious prosecution on inconvenience or disturbance of the even tenor of life, as in many torts, including intimidation. (2) Additional compensation for the injured feelings of the plaintiff where his sense of injury resulting from the wrongful physical act is justifiably heightened by the manner in which or motive for which the defendant did it. This Lord Devlin calls 'aggravated damages.' (3) Punishment of the defendant for his anti-social behaviour to the plaintiff. This Lord Devlin calls 'exemplary damages.'

Claimants, then, can recover compensation for pecuniary losses flowing from the discrimination, and for non-pecuniary losses. Claimants may recover in respect of future as well as part pecuniary losses (in particular, in employment tribunal claims, for loss of future earnings). The aim of compensation is to put claimants in the position in which they would have been had the discrimination established had not taken place.[171] The CA ruled, by a majority, in *Essa v Laing Ltd* [2004] EWCA Civ 02, [2004] ICR 746 that the discriminator's liability is not limited by the doctrine of reasonable foreseeability, finding that a tribunal had erred in refusing the claimant losses connected with a dramatic personality change resulting from racial harassment. The tribunal had refused to compensate in respect of these losses which, it had ruled, were not reasonably foreseeable. The CA ruled that the only question was whether there was a direct causal link between the discrimination and the losses.[172]

[170] Citing *Rookes v Barnard* [1964] AC 1129 *per* Lord Devlin, *Cassell & Co Ltd v Broome* [1972] AC 1027.
[171] *Hurley v Mustoe (No 2)* [1083] ICR 422; *MOD v Cannock* [1994] ICR 918.
[172] The Court reached this decision in respect of direct discrimination and harassment and left open the question whether the same would apply in other types of discrimination and associated conduct.

Compensation for Pecuniary Losses

Compensation for pecuniary losses is subject to a duty to mitigate.[173] The calculation of recoverable pecuniary losses is a matter for the tribunal, taking into account the evidence before it, including expert evidence if necessary (eg as to the claimant's medical condition or the state of the relevant job market, or the extent to which the discrimination complained of contributed to the loss,[174] and with reference (as regards future losses) to the Government Actuary-produced Ogden tables with due regard being given to all relevant contingencies.[175] Compensation is available not only in respect of losses already incurred at the date of the tribunal hearing but also in respect of future losses, which may be a significant element in dismissal cases in particular.

In *Vento v CC West Yorkshire Police (No 2)* [2002] EWCA Civ 1871, [2003] ICR 318 the CA ruled that a tribunal had been entitled to calculate the compensation due to the claimant, a probationary police constable discriminatorily dismissed, on the basis that she would likely have served with the police for 21 years before retiring at 55. The evidence before the tribunal had been that only nine per cent of women who had left the respondent force had served for more than 18 years, but most women left to have children; the claimant could not have any more children; and the respondent had introduced 'family-friendly' employment policies since the statistics had been collected. The EAT ruled that the tribunal had been entitled to calculate the claimant's compensation on the basis that there was a 75 per cent chance that she would have remained with the respondent until age 55.

In most cases future losses will not be calculated on a 'whole career' basis, the CA ruling in *Wardle v Credit Agricole Corporate and Investment Bank* [2011] EWCA Civ 545, [2011] IRLR 604 that tribunals should generally assess future losses by reference to date by which the claimant is likely, rather than certain, to have secured an equivalently remunerated job. The Court went on to rule in *Wardle* that, where it is appropriate to assess future losses on a 'whole career' basis, such losses should be increasingly discounted for increasingly distant time periods because the chances of claimants securing equivalent work would increase over time, and should also be subject to reduction to reflect the vicissitudes of life.[176] The CA in *Chagger v Abbey National and Hopkins* [2009] EWCA Civ 1202, [2010] IRLR 47 accepted that the calculation of future losses could take account of 'stigma damage': the fact that having complained of discrimination may make it more difficult for a claimant to obtain future work.

Compensation for Non-Pecuniary Damages

Non-pecuniary damages in discrimination cases may include compensation for personal injury, pain, suffering and loss of amenity ('general damages') as well as compensation for injury to feelings, aggravated damages and exemplary damages. The availability of personal injury damages under the RRA (and, by implication, the other discrimination legislation) was confirmed by the CA in *Sheriff v Klyne Tugs (Lowestoft)* [1999] ICR 1170,

[173] Note however that it is for the respondent to evidence to demonstrate that the loss could have been mitigated. By contrast with the position in unfair dismissal cases (to which recoupment provisions apply) social security payments received by the claimant will be deducted from any award as will invalidity benefits received as a result of the discriminatory act: *Chan v Hackney LBC* [1997] ICR 1014.

[174] *BAE Systems (Operations) Ltd v Konczak* [2017] EWCA Civ 1188, [2018] ICR 893.

[175] *Abbey National and Hopkins v Chagger* [2009] ICR 624.

[176] eg the possibility of dismissal for a non-discriminatory reason.

in which it ruled that the county court was correct to strike out a claim in negligence seeking damages for personal injury arising out alleged racial harassment. The Court ruled that the claimant, who had brought and compromised an employment tribunal claim arising from the same incident, could have made his personal injury claim in the tribunal and so was estopped from bringing his action in the county court. In *Essa v Laing Ltd* [2004] ICR 746, considered above, the CA confirmed that damages were recoverable under the RRA for financial losses resulting from psychiatric injury arising from racial harassment.

Injury to Feelings

A very significant element of compensation in many discrimination cases is compensation for injury to feelings. In *Alexander v Home Office* May LJ had suggested that such awards were not automatic, but in *Ministry of Defence v Sullivan* [1994] ICR 193 Tucker J suggested that it would be surprising if such an award was not made in a discrimination claim.[177] As is the case with every other element of compensation for discrimination with the sole exception of aggravated damages, awards for injury to feelings are compensatory, not punitive.[178]

The leading case on this category of compensation is *Vento v CC West Yorkshire Police (No 2)* which established guidelines which remain in place, albeit the indicative figures for compensation in each category have been updated on several occasions since the decision.

***Vento v CC West Yorkshire Police (No 2)* [2002] EWCA Civ 1871, [2003] ICR 318**

The claim was brought by a police officer who was sexually harassed and eventually dismissed. A tribunal awarded her £257,844 including £65,000 for injury to feelings including £15,000 by way of aggravated damages and £9,000 for personal injury. The award for injury to feelings reflected the tribunal's finding that the claimant had been bullied by her superiors following the breakdown of her marriage, that this had contributed to her suffering clinical depression, that she had then suffered shock and disappointment and lost a 'satisfying and genial career' because of her dismissal, and that she had been subject to a tribunal hearing at which her private life had been subjected to minute scrutiny. The additional award for aggravated damages reflected the tribunal's finding that the employers had 'throughout acted in a high-handed manner' and that their attitude was one of 'institutional denial.'

The EAT reduced the award for injury to feelings, including aggravated damages, from £65,000 to £30,000 on the basis that the tribunal's award was well outside the range which any tribunal properly directing itself to the cited authorities would have made. The CA allowed the respondent's appeal against EAT's failure to substitute a lower figure than £30,000 as compensation for injury to feelings, taking into account the award of an additional £9,000 by the tribunal for psychiatric injury. The Court reduced to £18,000 and £5000 the awards for injury to feelings and aggravated damages, leaving the award for psychiatric injury at £9,000.

[177] See also *Murray v Powertech (Scotland) Ltd* [1992] IRLR 257, This is subject to the specific provision made in relation to unintentional indirect discrimination (see pp 318–320 below).
[178] See eg *ICTS (UK) Ltd v Tchoula* [2000] ICR 1191.

Mummery LJ (for the Court):

> 46. This is the first time for many years that the Court of Appeal has had the opportunity to consider the appropriate level of compensation for injury to feelings in discrimination cases. Some decisions in the employment tribunal and in the Appeal Tribunal have resulted in awards of substantial sums for injury to feelings, sometimes supplemented by compensation for psychiatric damage and aggravated damages …
>
> 47. Compensation of the magnitude of £125,000 for non-pecuniary damage creates concern as to whether some recent tribunal awards in discrimination cases are in line with general levels of compensation recovered in other cases of non-pecuniary loss, such as general damages for personal injuries, malicious prosecution and defamation. In the interests of justice (social and individual), and of predictability of outcome and consistency of treatment of like cases (an important ingredient of justice) this court should indicate to employment tribunals and practitioners general guidance on the proper level of award for injury to feelings and other forms of non-pecuniary damage.
>
> 50. It is self-evident that the assessment of compensation for an injury or loss, which is neither physical nor financial, presents special problems for the judicial process, which aims to produce results objectively justified by evidence, reason and precedent. Subjective feelings of upset, frustration, worry, anxiety, mental distress, fear, grief, anguish, humiliation, unhappiness, stress, depression and so on and the degree of their intensity are incapable of objective proof or of measurement in monetary terms. Translating hurt feelings into hard currency is bound to be an artificial exercise.

Having concluded that the compensation awarded in the claim was manifestly excessive the CA went on to set out guidelines for tribunals to take into account in determining awards for injury to feelings 'as distinct from compensation for psychiatric or similar personal injury':

> 65. (i) The top band should normally be between £15,000 and £25,000. Sums in this range should be awarded in the most serious cases, such as where there has been a lengthy campaign of discriminatory harassment on the ground of sex or race. This case falls within that band. Only in the most exceptional case should an award of compensation for injury to feelings exceed £25,000.
>
> (ii) The middle band of between £5,000 and £15,000 should be used for serious cases, which do not merit an award in the highest band.
>
> (iii) Awards of between £500 and £5,000 are appropriate for less serious cases, such as where the act of discrimination is an isolated or one-off occurrence. In general, awards of less than £500 are to be avoided altogether, as they risk being regarded as so low as not to be a proper recognition of injury to feelings.[179]
>
> 66. There is, of course, within each band considerable flexibility, allowing tribunals to fix what is considered to be fair, reasonable and just compensation in the particular circumstances of the case.
>
> 67. The decision whether or not to award aggravated damages and, if so, in what amount must depend on the particular circumstances of the discrimination and on the way in which the complaint of discrimination has been handled.
>
> 68. Common sense requires that regard should also be had to the overall magnitude of the sum total of the awards of compensation for non-pecuniary loss made under the various headings of injury to feelings, psychiatric damage and aggravated damage. In particular, double recovery should be avoided by taking appropriate account of the overlap between the individual heads of damage. The extent of overlap will depend on the facts of each particular case.

[179] In *Base Childrenswear Ltd v Otshudi* UKEAT/0267/18 (28 February 2019, unreported), the EAT ruled that one-off acts of discrimination would not always fall into band 1 of *Vento*.

Annual guidance issued by the Presidents of the Employment Tribunals now uprates the *Vento* bands for inflation.[180] The latest guidance indicates that, in the case of claims presented on or after 6 April 2023, the *Vento* bands should be £33,700 to £56,200 for the most serious cases, £11,200 to £33,700 for the middle band and £1,100 to £11,200 for the lowest band, with awards in excess of £56,200 being reserved for exceptionally serious cases. The guidance is not formally binding, but a tribunal which wished to depart from it would have to provide reasons for so doing.

Refusal of Damages in Unintentional Indirect Discrimination Claims

We saw above that ss119(5)–(6) and 124(4)–(5) EqA provide that a court or tribunal may not make an award of compensation in a case of unintentional indirect discrimination without first considering whether to make any other disposal (in the case of the county court) or a declaration and/or recommendation (in the case of the employment tribunal). Section 124 (4)–(5) EqA were challenged in the CA in the case below.

Wisbey v Commissioner of the City of London Police **[2021] EWCA Civ 650, [2021] ICR 1485**

The claimant, a police officer, brought a successful claim for indirect sex discrimination after he was removed from advanced driving duties when he failed a colour vision defect tests in his annual medical examinations in 2017, not being reinstated until 2018 when he passed additional tests. His indirect sex discrimination claim succeeded. About eight per cent of men and only 0.25 per cent of women had colour vision defects, and the tribunal found no evidence that it was necessary to bar an officer with any but the most severe colour vision defects from driving duties. The tribunal declared that the claimant had been subjected to indirect sex discrimination but refused to award any compensation because it found that the indirect discrimination had been unintentional (ie, that the respondent had been unaware that men were more likely than women to have defective colour vision[181]). The claimant appealed unsuccessfully to the EAT and then to the CA, arguing that s 124(4)–(5) were not compliant with EU law, the EU Charter or the ECHR because they imposed an additional threshold or hurdle to be met by a tribunal before any consideration could be given to awarding compensation in a case of unintentional indirect discrimination, with the result that the remedies available for that form of discrimination were neither effective nor dissuasive.

Simler LJ (with whom Lewis and Jackson LJJ agreed):

27. Article 2 of the Recast Directive … provides as follows:

> '18. Member States shall introduce into their national legal systems such measures as are necessary to ensure real and effective compensation or reparation as the Member States so determine for the loss and damage sustained by a person injured as a result of discrimination on grounds of sex, in a way which is dissuasive and proportionate to the damage

[180] See most recently https://www.judiciary.uk/wp-content/uploads/2013/08/Vento-bands-presidential-guidance-April-2022-addendum.pdf.

[181] In *London Underground v Edwards* [1995] ICR 574 the EAT ruled that an intention to apply the disputed requirement or condition, coupled with the knowledge of its impact on the claimant as a member of the group upon which it impacted disadvantageously, amounted to intentionality in the context of indirect discrimination. See also *JH Walker Ltd v Hussain* [1996] ICR 291.

suffered. Such compensation or reparation may not be restricted by the fixing of a prior upper limit, except in cases where the employer can prove that the only damage suffered by an applicant as a result of discrimination within the meaning of this Directive is the refusal to take his/her job application into consideration.'

28. So far as the Charter is concerned, it is given legal effect by art 6 of the Treaty on European Union which provides that the EU recognises the rights, freedoms and principles set out in the Charter (and also that the EU shall accede to the Convention) and that these rights shall constitute general principles of EU law. Article 21 of the Charter prohibits discrimination based on any ground such as sex, race, colour, ethnic or social origin (amongst others). Ms Monaghan [for the Claimant] placed particular reliance on art 47 which provides, among other things, for the rights to an effective remedy as follows:

'47. Everyone whose rights and freedoms guaranteed by the law of the Union are violated has the right to an effective remedy before a tribunal in compliance with the conditions laid down in this Article. …'

29. Finally, arts 8, 13 and 14 of the Convention are relied on by Ms Monaghan. It is unnecessary to set them all out, but art 13 provides:

'13. Everyone whose rights and freedoms as set forth in [the] Convention are violated shall have an effective remedy before a national authority notwithstanding that the violation has been committed by persons acting in an official capacity.'…

30. In developing her submission that s 124(4) and (5) EA 2010 are not compliant with EU law, Ms Monaghan emphasised the particular importance placed on the principle of non-discrimination and the task of combating 'social exclusion and discrimination' and the promotion of 'social justice and protection'… Where financial compensation is the measure adopted to achieve the objective of equality, the CJEU has consistently held that it must be adequate to enable the damage actually sustained as a result of discriminatory treatment to be made good in full: see *Von Colson and Kamann v Land Nordrhein-Westfalen* 14/83 [1984] ECR 1891, C-14/83; and *Marshall* [*v South West Area Health Authority* C-271/91, EU:C:1993:335, [1994] QB 126]. A provision allowing for the award of *no* compensation in the face of a finding of unlawful discrimination self-evidently cannot meet the requirement to be 'effective' and 'dissuasive and proportionate' (especially where compensation is the chosen remedy).

31. Similar arguments by reference to both the Charter and the Convention were advanced ….

33. Although Ms Monaghan advanced these submissions with conspicuous clarity and erudition, I do not accept them … First, I do not accept that as a matter of statutory construction s 124(4) and (5) EA 2010 restrict the right to adequate and proportionate compensation for a breach of the prohibition on indirect sex discrimination; nor that they do not have appropriate dissuasive effect …

40. Having first considered the remedies of a declaration and a recommendation, there is no restriction or prohibition in s 124(5) on a tribunal's power to make a compensation order where loss is sustained as a consequence of established unlawful but unintentional indirect discrimination. If, after consideration, a tribunal decides that a declaration and a recommendation are appropriate, nothing in the terms of the statute precludes a tribunal from also awarding compensation, still less requiring a tribunal to reach a conclusion that loss sustained by reason of the unintentional indirect discrimination should nevertheless be uncompensated for that reason. The prohibition on awarding damages for unintentional indirect discrimination was repealed by Parliament and has not been reintroduced in any way by the EA 2010. The 'consideration' requirement is not and is not to be read as an obstacle to an award of compensation where compensation is due. There can be no doubt that employment tribunals have discretion under s 124(5) to award compensation once the other remedies have been considered

> and, importantly, if loss and damage have been sustained as a consequence of the indirect discrimination suffered, it is to be expected that compensation will be awarded. Moreover, such compensation should be both adequate to compensate for the loss and damage suffered and proportionate to it.
>
> 41. It is common ground that the provisions of the Recast Directive and the Charter referred to above, allow Member States to determine what measures to implement in order to ensure that the Recast Directive is effective in domestic law in accordance with its stated purpose and objective. That is subject to the requirement that the measures adopted provide for real and effective compensation or reparation for loss and damage sustained by a person as a consequence of discrimination, in a way which is both dissuasive and proportionate. These principles of EU law continue to apply in this case. Although the United Kingdom ceased to be a member of the EU on 31 January 2020, Parliament has provided that those provisions of EU law continue to apply to cases that had been started, but not concluded, before the United Kingdom left the European Union: see para 39 of Sch 8 to the European Union (Withdrawal) Act 2018.
>
> 42. However, for the reasons set out above, there is nothing in the terms of s 124(4) and (5) that operates as a restriction on or an obstacle to the right to compensation for loss and damage consequent on a breach of the prohibition on unlawful sex discrimination. For the same reason I do not consider this provision to be in breach of the principle of effectiveness. Requiring a tribunal to first consider whether to make a declaration or a recommendation before compensation can be awarded does not inhibit or make it more difficult for a complainant to vindicate their domestic or EU rights. Accordingly, I do not believe there is a difference in treatment as between discrimination claims and other employment-related claims which could form the basis of an indirect sex discrimination claim. The discretion to make a compensation order in either case is ultimately the same, subject only to the order in which potential remedies must be considered in unintentional indirect discrimination cases, and this is by no means a hurdle or barrier to awarding compensation. It is unnecessary to address the remaining arguments based on EU law, the Charter and the Convention in these circumstances. They add nothing and fail for the same reasons as set out above ...[182]

One of the difficulties with the approach of the CA is that it operates as a profound disincentive for legal challenge to indirectly discriminatory policies etc of general application; claimants who succeed in legal challenges may find themselves with nothing to show for their efforts except a theoretical victory and very significant legal costs.

Aggravated Damages

The EAT ruled in *Armitage, Marsden and HM Prison Service v Johnson* [1997] ICR 275 that aggravated damages are available for an act of discrimination.[183] Such damages, which must be compensatory and not punitive in nature, are available where a claimant is caused distress by, eg, the 'high-handed, malicious, insulting or oppressive' way in which a tort was committed;[184] the fact that a respondent has been motivated by prejudice, animosity, spite

[182] For another example of an unsuccessful attempt to rely on EU law and the ECHR, there to challenge the unavailability of interim relief in discrimination/victimisation claims, see the decision of the EAT in *Steer v Stormsure Ltd* [2021] IRLR 172.

[183] This is not the case in Scotland where aggravated damages are not available in any claim.

[184] *Broome v Cassell* [1972] AC 1027, HL, *per* Lord Reid.

or vindictiveness[185] or by subsequent conduct, for example in the conduct of the case, or the treatment of the claimant or the discriminator, or a failure to apologise.[186]

In the following case the EAT upheld a tribunal award of aggravated damages.

ICTS (UK) Ltd v Tchoula [2000] ICR 1191

Judge Peter Clark:

> Mr Martin [for the employers] submits that the tribunal failed to apply the correct principles in making an extra award of aggravated damages to the applicant over and above that for injury to feelings. There was no finding by the tribunal that the respondent had acted maliciously towards the applicant ...
>
> ... The first question must always be, do the facts disclose the essential requirements for an award of aggravated damages?
>
> In this present case we are satisfied that on their findings of fact this tribunal was entitled to answer that case in the affirmative. In the liability decision the tribunal found that Mr Dewane was 'going after' the applicant in the hope of finding him in dereliction of his duty, consciously motivated by the applicant's claims of racial discrimination made against him (complaints which, although dismissed, we infer the tribunal found were made in good faith ... Mr Lewis carried out a disciplinary procedure which was seriously flawed, again consciously motivated by the applicant's original complaint of unlawful discrimination, culminating in his dismissal. Further, the tribunal conducted these proceedings over 22 days. They are the best judges of whether the proceedings were improperly conducted to any extent as they found at paragraph 20 of the remedies reasons. Without spelling it out, it is clear to us that the tribunal regarded that combination of factors as amounting to high-handed, malicious, insulting or oppressive behaviour directed towards the applicant, to borrow the words of May LJ in *Alexander*. In these circumstances we are satisfied that the tribunal was entitled to make an award of aggravated damages.

There is potential for double recovery if a claimant claims an uplift for failure to comply with the Acas Code of Practice where, for example, a grievance about discrimination has been inadequately dealt with, and also claims aggravated damages in respect of the same matter.[187] The potential for double recovery also arises where awards are made in respect of injury to feelings and aggravated damages. The EAT recognised this in *Commissioner of Police of the Metropolis v Shaw* [2012] IRLR 291 in which it ruled (*per* Underhill P) that

[185] Though this will not cause a claimant distress unless the claimant is or becomes aware of it.

[186] See eg *Baker v Lennox Thompson*, reported in 'Compensation Awards 2002' 124 *EOR*, in which the respondents not only replied to a race discrimination questionnaire to the effect that the allegations were 'a creative fabrication to which we are unable to offer any kind of clarification', but cross-examined the claimant in a grossly offensive manner at tribunal. The tribunal awarded £10,000 injury to feelings plus £8,500 aggravated damages. The award of aggravated damages in respect of the conduct of the hearing was approved by EAT in *Zaiwalla v Walia* [2002] IRLR 697. See also *BT plc v Reid* [2004] IRLR 327 in which the Court of Appeal approved an award of aggravated damages in respect of the promotion of the claimant's harasser when her complaints against him were outstanding. In *Franklin v Pectel Ltd* (discussed in 'Compensation Awards 2003' 133 *EOR*) a tribunal awarded £5,000 on top of £17,000 compensation for injury to feelings to a woman subject to sexual harassment, 'malicious and insulting behaviour' and tribunal proceedings during which her harasser had sought 'to belittle ... the hurt and anguish caused to her' by stating, for example, that she had been denied a pay rise due to her incompetence (rather than, as the tribunal found as a fact, because she was pregnant), and had questioned her truthfulness. The quantum of damages in these cases has to be treated with caution in light of the subsequent caselaw but they remain illustrative of where aggravated damages might be appropriate.

[187] See eg *Base Childrenswear Ltd v Otshudi* [2020] IRLR 118 (CA).

tribunals should have regard to the total award made in respect of injury to feelings and aggravated damages (where both are made) to ensure that the sum is not excessive, and should formulate any award of aggravated damages as a sub-category of injury to feelings. A similar approach was taken by Langstaff J, who succeeded Underhill P as President of the EAT, in *HM Land Registry v McGlue* UKEAT/0435/11. Langstaff P there warned against allowing double recovery and ruled that in any case in which there was conduct which would permit an award of aggravated damages (in order to compensate the claimant rather than to punish the discriminator) the tribunal should consider whether, from an objective perspective, the conduct complained of was capable of having aggravated the claimant's sense of injustice and injured his or her feelings yet further.

Exemplary Damages

The CA in *Alexander v Home Office* made reference to exemplary damages. In *Gibbons v South West Water Services Ltd* [1993] 2 WLR 507 the CA ruled that exemplary damages were available in respect only of those torts, whether statutory or common law, which existed prior to the decision of the HL in *Rookes v Barnard* [1964] AC 1129. On this view, such damages were not available in respect of sex or race discrimination.[188] In *Kuddus v CC Leicester Constabulary* [2001] UKHL 29, [2002] 2 AC 122, however, the HL held that the availability of exemplary damages depended on the conduct of the public authority rather than the cause of action sued upon, and that such damages were available in that case on a complaint of misfeasance in public office notwithstanding the fact that the tort had not been accepted as a cause of action before 1964. Liability for such damages will only arise where compensation is insufficient to punish the discriminator and if (a) there has been oppressive, arbitrary or unconstitutional action by the state agents, or (b) the discriminator's conduct has been calculated to make a profit which may exceed the compensation payable to the claimant. Awards of exemplary damages are available only in the most egregious cases;[189] *Michalak v Mid Yorkshire NHS Trust*, also discussed below by reason of the size of the overall award made (£4.5m), is a rare example of such a case.[190]

***Michalak v Mid Yorkshire NHS Trust*, Case No 1810815/2008**[191]

The claimant, a consultant physician, had been subject to a campaign of sex and race-related harassment and false allegations after she went on maternity leave (the first consultant physician at her workplace ever to have done so). She was eventually dismissed and suffered depression as a result. Having won her claims for unfair dismissal and harassment/discrimination she was awarded £4.5m (see below) including £4,000 in exemplary damages. The tribunal rejected the argument put for the respondent that exemplary damages were not, on principle, available against the respondent, a hospital trust, relying on *Bradford City Metropolitan Council v Arora* [1990] ICR 226 in which the CA had accepted that interviewing the claimant 'for a senior position in a college for

[188] See also *Deane v Ealing LBC* [1993] ICR 329.

[189] See *Ministry of Defence v Fletcher* [2010] IRLR 25.

[190] *cf MOD v Fletcher* [2010] IRLR 25 in which the EAT ruled that the tribunal had erred in awarding exemplary damages.

[191] Case No 1810815/2008, available at http://www.ajustnhs.com/wp-content/uploads/2012/05/michalak-ET-judgment-2011.pdf.

which the Council had authority was properly to be regarded as an exercise of a public function by a public authority capable of attracting an award of exemplary damages for its abuse'.

Employment Judge Burton (for the ET):

> 50. We conclude that in one narrow respect it is appropriate to award exemplary damages in this case. When the Respondents decided to suspend the Claimant they did so within the provisions of the MHPS which, we understand to be, a policy document prescribed by Government as to the way in which disciplinary action against medical staff should be pursued. The exercise of the power to suspend derives from that policy document and, to that extent, in exercising that power, we believe that that is analogous to an NHS Trust exercising Governmental functions. The whole purpose of the provisions relating to suspension is to ensure that taxpayers' money is not improperly wasted by paying doctors significant salaries for significant periods of time when they are not providing valuable work. That is why the safeguards exist requiring regular review of suspension, requiring consultation with NCAS and imposing a maximum period of six months except for cases involving criminal investigations …
>
> 51. These Respondents abused that power by failing to carry out proper reviews, by failing to allow the Claimant to return to work when, as a matter of fact, the suspension had lapsed, by not telling the truth to NCAS in order to obtain their endorsement of the Claimant's continuing suspension and by unlawfully continuing the extension beyond six months despite the fact that no criminal activity was suspected. The protection of appointing a designated Board Member … was taken away when Mr Grasby retired and his successor wholly failed in her responsibilities. Finally when the Claimant sought to challenge that suspension in the High Court the Respondents opposed that application and relied upon the wholly untruthful evidence of Mrs Diane Nicholls. Those circumstances, it seems to us, properly amount to oppressive arbitrary or unconstitutional action by the Servants of the Government and justify, we find, an award of exemplary damages. We do think it appropriate within this decision to impose a level of punishment for the Respondents' conduct in that regard but would restrict that, in the light of the remaining award that we are making, to the sum of £4,000.

Interest

Interest is also available in respect of pecuniary losses prior to the date on which damages are awarded, and in respect of compensation for injury to feelings. The Employment Tribunal (Interest on Awards in Discrimination Cases) Regulations 1996 provide (Reg 2(1)) that tribunals must consider whether to award interest irrespective of whether it has been asked it to do so. Tribunals are not required to award interest if they take the view that a 'serious injustice' would be caused if interest were awarded. The Regulations provide that interest will generally be calculated as simple interest which accrues daily (Reg 3(1)) at a rate fixed in England and Wales by s17 of the Judgment Acts 1838 (currently eight per cent). Interest for past pecuniary losses will generally be calculated on the basis of the midpoint between discrimination and the date of calculation with interest in respect of injury to feelings compensation being calculated in respect of the entire period from discrimination to calculation (Reg 6(1)). If a tribunal decides not to award interest or to do so on a basis other than that set out in the Regulations it should provide its reasons for not doing so, and its decision may be subject to appeal.[192]

[192] See eg *Derby Specialist Fabrication Ltd v Burton* [2001] ICR 833.

Quantum of Awards in Discrimination Claims

Notwithstanding the fact that compensation in discrimination claims is not subject to any statutory cap the level of awards is typically modest. Figures 5.11 and 5.12 below show the median and average awards made by tribunals in successful claims by protected characteristic between 2007 and 2020.

Figure 5.11 Median awards in employment tribunal discrimination cases 2007–20[193]

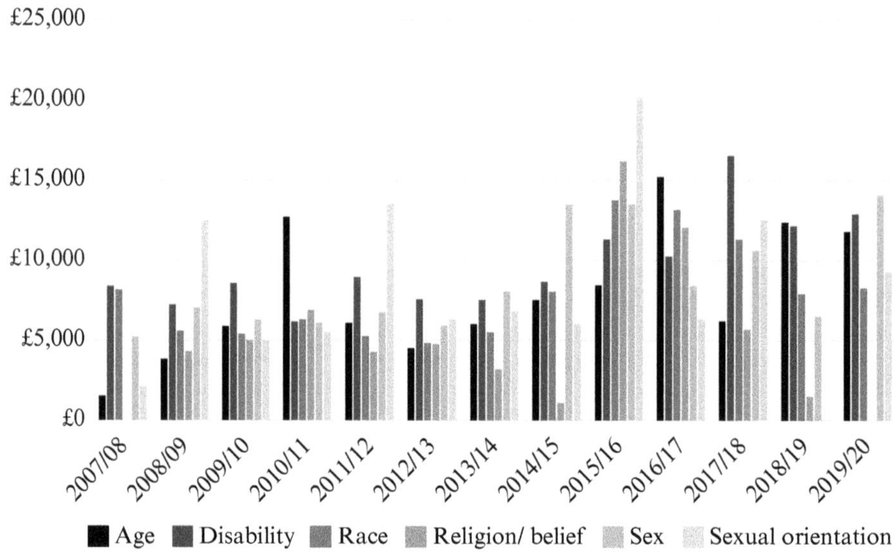

Figure 5.12 Average awards in employment tribunal discrimination cases 2007–20[194]

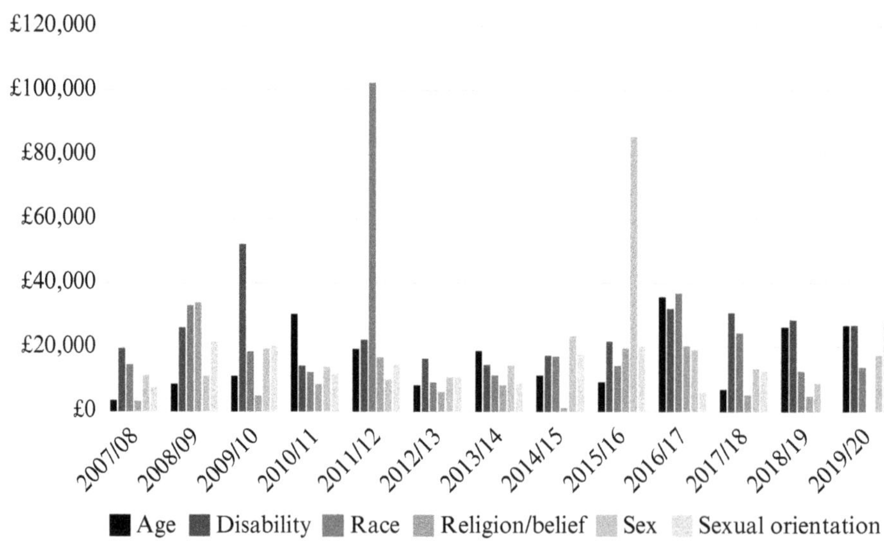

[193] Table E2: available at https://www.gov.uk/government/statistics/tribunal-statistics-quarterly-april-to-june-2020/tribunal-statistics-quarterly-april-to-june-2020.

[194] *Ibid.*

The significant spikes in average awards in race claims in 2011/12 and in sex claims in 2015/16 are explained by a number of exceptionally high awards in those years (see further Figure 5.13 below). For this reason, the median awards give a more representative picture of the trend over time which is generally upwards with no clear relationship between protected characteristic and quantum.

Figure 5.13 Maximum awards in employment tribunal discrimination cases 2007–20[195]

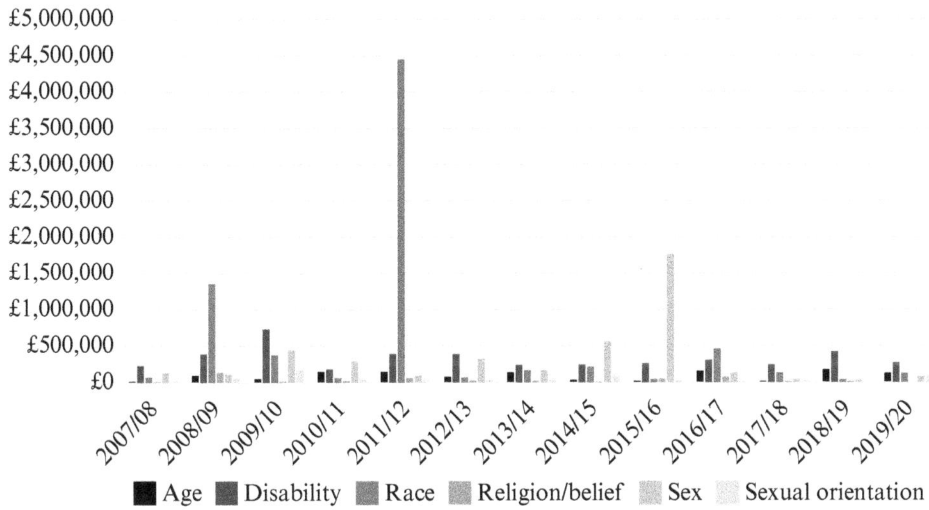

Figure 5.13 illustrates that discrimination claims occasionally result in large awards, notably awards of over £1m and £4m in race claims in 2008/09 and 2011/12 respectively, and in a sex discrimination claim of over £1.5m in 2015/16.

Awards in excess of £500 000 are exceptional, and they are excluded from Figure 5.14 below in order better to show the maximum awards typically made by tribunals by protected characteristic over time. Once the exceptional outlying awards are excluded it can be seen that in most years and for most protected characteristics the maximum awards are below £200 000 (54 of 78), and often below £100 000 (36 of 78). It is also clear that the trend is, if anything, down rather than up over time. More often than not the biggest awards are made in disability claims in which future losses are likely to be exacerbated by the claimant's disabilities.

Returning to the 2012 case in which £4.5m was awarded, *Michalak v Mid Yorkshire NHS Trust*[196] is listed in the Ministry of Justice's statistics as a race claim, but also involved a successful sex discrimination claim.[197] Of the £4.5m awarded more than £1.5m related

[195] Tables E4–E9: available at https://www.gov.uk/government/statistics/tribunal-statistics-quarterly-april-to-june-2020/tribunal-statistics-quarterly-april-to-june-2020.

[196] See n 191 above.

[197] Dr Michalak also sued the GMC which had begun fitness to practise proceedings against her following a referral from the Trust. (The Trust had made the referral prior to the determination of her tribunal claim against it and later accepted that there had been no proper grounds for the referral.) In *Michalak v General Medical Council* [2017] UKSC 71, [2018] ICR 49, the SC ruled that Dr Michalak was entitled to pursue a discrimination claim

Figure 5.14 Maximum awards in employment tribunal discrimination cases 2007–20 excluding large outliers[198]

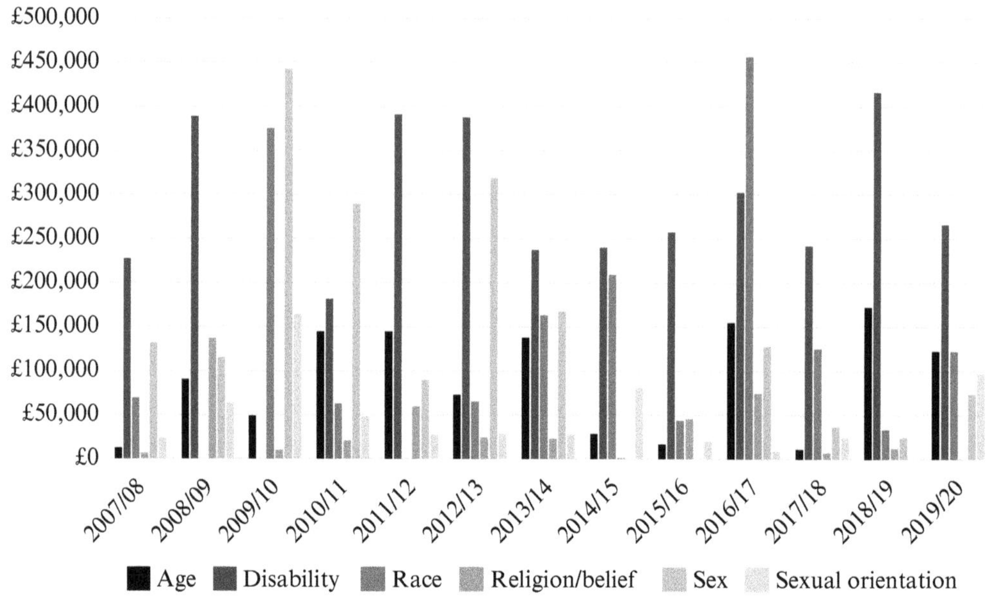

to future earnings and pension losses (£992k and £666k respectively), £168k related to past losses of earnings, £124k to past and future care and medical costs and £15k to life insurance. The sum also included £30k for injury to feelings, £56k for psychiatric injury, £4k in exemplary damages and £20k in interest. These figures were all then subject to a 15 per cent uplift for the respondent's failure to comply with the Acas procedures and the resulting total was more than doubled to account for the tax that the claimant would have to pay on it.[199]

Not included in the statistics above are awards made in March 2018 and April 2021 of £4.7m and £2.6m in disability discrimination claims against Lloyds Bank and Kellog Brown and Root (UK) respectively. In *AB v Royal Bank of Scotland*, an appeal from which was refused by the EAT in February 2020,[200] a bank worker who had been run over by a car established that she had been subjected to six years of harassment and bullying by colleagues at Nat West (owned by RBS) and that her employers had demoted her, failed to provide her with OT or reasonable adjustments, refused her a transfer and constructively dismissed her. AB was left severely depressed with anxiety and conversion disorders and was unlikely to work again.

relating to the manner in which it has pursued the FtP proceedings against the GMC as a qualifying body in the employment tribunal (see further Ch 4).

[198] *Ibid.*

[199] The 'grossing up' of awards to take into account claimants' liability to pay tax on them is required in order to place them in the same position as they would have been in had the discrimination not occurred.

[200] UKEAT/0266/18/DA, 27 February 2020. The Court of Appeal rejected the bank's further appeal: [2021] EWCA Civ 345.

***Barrow v Kellog Brown and Root (UK) Ltd,* Case No 2303683/18V**[201]

The claimant had started work with the respondent as a graduate trainee and had spent all but two of his 38 working years with it prior to being dismissed in 2018. He began to be treated for skin problems in 2017 and was eventually diagnosed with a form of skin cancer. Prior to this, steroid treatment had affected his mental health. During the course of his treatment the claimant, whose work performance had always been good, was told by his line manager that the respondent 'could not employ him anymore' and he was escorted from the office, his colleagues being informed that he had been dismissed for poor performance. Following the claimant's cancer diagnosis he was subject to another process which concluded with his dismissal in May 2018 on the grounds of an alleged breakdown in the implied term of trust and confidence. He succeeded in claims of unfair dismissal, disability discrimination, harassment, victimisation and failure to make reasonable adjustments, the tribunal concluding that the process which resulted in his 2018 dismissal was a sham whose process had been predetermined by his line manager. The claimant, who was 60 at the time of his dismissal, was awarded damages on a 'career-long' basis as he was unlikely to work again, together with £7 500 aggravated damages and £25,000 in respect of pain, suffering and loss of amenity. The overall figure included an eight per cent uplift for failure to comply with the Acas Code.

Harvey on Industrial Relations reports (Division L) awards of compensation by employment tribunals in respect of (separate and distinct) findings of race discrimination and of sex and religion discrimination in the form of enforced hijab in *Rai v Mr and Mrs Al Mutari*;[202] of sex and age discrimination in *Kent v (1) Krazy Kidz (2) Sykes* Reading;[203] of sexual and racial harassment in *Mahmoud v Islamic Cultural Centre and the London Central Mosque*;[204] of race and religious discrimination in the case of *Munir v Shaw & Lisle Catering Ltd*;[205] of race and sex discrimination connected with allegations of sexual assault in *Lobo v London Underground Ltd*,[206] and relating to assumptions made about Sikh women in *Vohra v Kader*.[207]

Equal Pay/Pension Cases

The primary remedy on an equal pay complaint is the equalisation of the claimant's relevant contractual provision(s) to that or those of her comparator(s), which provides (at least in theory) for equality going forward. In addition, s132 EqA provides that, in non-pension claims, a court or tribunal which has found a breach of an equality clause (in other words, the fact that the claimant's contractual term(s) were less favourable than those of her comparator(s)) may 'make a declaration as to the rights of the parties in relation to the matters to which the proceedings relate' and 'order an award by way of arrears of pay or

[201] The liability and remedies judgments are at https://www.gov.uk/employment-tribunal-decisions/mr-d-barrow-v-kellog-brown-and-root-uk-ltd-2303683-slash-2018.
[202] Case No 2704089/2011 [2013] EqLR 188, discussed at Harvey Division L [1129.01].
[203] Case No 2701208/07 (12 May 2008) discussed at Harvey Division L [1130].
[204] Case No 2202694/05 [2007] All ER (D) 204 (Jul) discussed at Harvey Division [L 1131].
[205] Case No 1800364/17 discussed at Harvey Division L [1131.1].
[206] Case No 3300654/05 discussed at Harvey Division L [1132].
[207] Case No 1804053/2009 discussed at Harvey Division L [1132.01].

damages in relation to the complainant'. Such a payment may not relate to a period of time more than six years prior to the date of issue of the equal pay claim except in a concealment or incapacity case (see p 302 above) in which case it may be backdated to the point at which the claimant first became entitled to equal pay.[208]

In cases in which the EqA is relied on to challenge pension inequality the Act provides as follows.

Section 133 EqA, Remedies in pensions cases

(1) This section applies to proceedings before a court or employment tribunal on a complaint relating to—
   (a) a breach of an equality rule, or
   (b) a breach of an equality clause with respect to membership of, or rights under, an occupational pension scheme.[209]

(2) If the court or tribunal finds that there has been a breach as referred to in subsection (1)—
   (a) it may make a declaration as to the rights of the parties in relation to the matters to which the proceedings relate;
   (b) it must not order arrears of benefits or damages or any other amount to be paid to the complainant.

(3) Subsection (2)(b) does not apply if the proceedings are proceedings to which section 134 applies.
(4) If the breach relates to a term on which persons become members of the scheme, the court or tribunal may declare that the complainant is entitled to be admitted to the scheme with effect from a specified date.
(5) A date specified for the purposes of subsection (4) must not be before 8 April 1976.
(6) If the breach relates to a term on which members of the scheme are treated, the court or tribunal may declare that the complainant is, in respect of a specified period, entitled to secure the rights that would have accrued if the breach had not occurred.
(7) A period specified for the purposes of subsection (6) must not begin before 17 May 1990.
(8) If the court or tribunal makes a declaration under subsection (6), the employer must provide such resources to the scheme as are necessary to secure for the complainant (without contribution or further contribution by the complainant or other members) the rights referred to in that subsection.

The dates set out in s133(5) and (7) are those on which EU law first prohibited sex discrimination in access to occupational pension schemes and as regards the terms of such schemes respectively.

Section 134 EqA, which applies to claims made by pensioner members of occupational pension schemes, is in similar terms to s133(1) and (2) but imposes the same backstop on pension-related claims as applies to equal pay claims (see p 302 above). There is no backstop to s133 claims which are made by workers who have not yet become pensioner members of schemes. Section 134 also requires employers to make additional payments to pension schemes where such is required to accommodate claims made under s133 EqA.

[208] Note that 'pay' here refers to all contractual terms not merely to pay, however broadly defined.

[209] Contractual discrimination against existing employees as regards access to pension schemes will fall to be challenged under the equal pay provisions which cover all contractual terms, but the remedy is provided by s133 EqA.

6

Sex, Gender Reassignment and Relationship Status

Introduction and Scope of this Chapter

This chapter considers the prohibition of discrimination on grounds of sex and the other protected characteristics discrimination on the basis of which was originally regulated by the Sex Discrimination Act 1975 (SDA) as amended over time. These other protected characteristics consist of:

- gender reassignment (s7 Equality Act 2010 (EqA))
- marriage and civil partnership (s8 EqA).

The protected characteristics considered in this chapter are set out below.

> **Section 11 EqA, Sex**
>
> In relation to the protected characteristic of sex—
>
> (a) a reference to a person who has a particular protected characteristic is a reference to a man or to a woman;
>
> (b) a reference to persons who share a protected characteristic is a reference to persons of the same sex.

Section 212(1) EqA defines 'man' as 'a male of any age' and 'woman' as 'a female of any age'.

The prohibition on sex discrimination applies equally to men as to women except that special treatment afforded to a woman in connection with pregnancy or childbirth does not amount to sex discrimination against men (s13(6)(b) EqA). By contrast, the prohibition on discrimination relating to marriage and civil partnership is asymmetric and that relating to gender reassignment is partly asymmetric.

> **Section 7 EqA, Gender Reassignment**
>
> (1) A person has the protected characteristic of gender reassignment if the person is proposing to undergo, is undergoing or has undergone a process (or part of a process) for the purpose of reassigning the person's sex by changing physiological or other attributes of sex.

(2) A reference to a transsexual person is a reference to a person who has the protected characteristic of gender reassignment.
(3) In relation to the protected characteristic of gender reassignment—
  (a) a reference to a person who has a particular protected characteristic is a reference to a transsexual person;
  (b) a reference to persons who share a protected characteristic is a reference to transsexual persons.[1]

Section 8 EqA, Marriage and Civil Partnership

(1) A person has the protected characteristic of marriage and civil partnership if the person is married or is a civil partner.
(2) In relation to the protected characteristic of marriage and civil partnership—
  (a) a reference to a person who has a particular protected characteristic is a reference to a person who is married or is a civil partner;
  (b) a reference to persons who share a protected characteristic is a reference to persons who are married or are civil partners.

The EqA does not regulate discrimination against those who are single or divorced, s13(4) EqA providing that 'If the protected characteristic is marriage and civil partnership, this section applies to a contravention of Part 5 (work)[2] only if the treatment is because it is [the person discriminated against] who is married or a civil partner.'

The EqA does regulate discrimination *in favour of* persons who are proposing to undergo, are undergoing or have undergone a process (or part of a process) of gender reassignment because s13 EqA does not limit protection from discrimination because of gender reassignment to those who have the protected characteristic of gender reassignment, as defined in s7 EqA. It would, therefore, appear that a person who does not have protected characteristic of gender reassignment could nevertheless challenge direct discrimination if treated less favourably because of that protected characteristic (even if the person with the protected characteristic is the person who has been more favourably treated person). The position as regards indirect discrimination differs, however; s19 EqA defines such discrimination as occurring where 'A person (A) discriminates against another (B) if A applies to B a provision, criterion or practice which is discriminatory in relation *to a relevant protected characteristic of B's*' (emphasis added). Section 7 providing that only those someone who 'is proposing to undergo, is undergoing or has undergone a process (or part of a process) for the purpose of reassigning the person's sex by changing physiological or other attributes of sex' has the protected characteristic of gender reassignment, it follows that someone who does not have that characteristic will be unable to complain of indirect discrimination against people without the characteristic.[3]

Sex and gender reassignment are considered in some detail below after brief consideration of the protected characteristic of marriage and civil partnership. Its inclusion is largely an accident of history. Marriage bars, by which married women were ineligible for appointment or continued employment, operated until the mid-1900s in many professions in Britain, and until 1973 in the foreign and diplomatic service. Even where such formal barriers did not exist, married women continued to experience particular disadvantages in

[1] The term 'transsexual' is not generally used now but remains the statutory language.
[2] Which is the only Part of the Act in which such discrimination is regulated.
[3] Indirect discrimination in relation to marriage and civil partnership is asymmetrical for the same reason (see definition of the protected characteristic in s7 above).

the workplace and so the SDA prohibited discrimination on grounds of married status in the context of employment (but not more generally). When civil partnerships were recognised by law in 2004, the SDA was amended to protect from discrimination because of civil partnership as well as that of marriage, and the provisions survived into the EqA. The prohibition of such discrimination has given rise to relatively little case law. It applies only to discrimination which is related specifically to the fact of marriage or civil partnership, and does not extend to discrimination because, for example, of concerns about the potential for conflict of interest arising from an intimate relationship.[4]

***Gould v St John's Downshire Hill* [2020] IRLR 863**

The claimant, vicar of a conservative and evangelical church, was dismissed after a period during which his marriage encountered difficulties and ultimately failed. During this period he had shared very personal details about the difficulties, suggested that his wife might not be a Christian and that she had a personality disorder, and appeared to try to isolate her from the fellowship which was central to the church. He had also chosen to preach a series of sermons on marriage. The church's leadership team was concerned that the claimant's marital problems were harming the church and had concerns with a number of aspects of his performance. After requiring the claimant to take a six-month period of sabbatical during which he persisted, in the face of instructions, in contacting members of the congregation, and after undertaking mediation, the church's trustees unanimously decided that the relationship of trust and confidence had broken down and that he should be dismissed. The claimant claimed that he had been dismissed because of a belief that 'broken marriage equals broken ministry', but the tribunal was satisfied on the evidence that the relationship between the claimant and the trustees, leadership team, certain members of staff and other members of the congregation had broken down. It considered that the claimant's marriage breakdown was the background to some of the reasons why trust and confidence in the relationship had irretrievably broken but that neither it nor his marriage was the reason for the dismissal.

The EAT refused his appeal, ruling that the task for the tribunal had been to determine whether the church leadership was consciously or subconsciously influenced by its views or assumptions about, or attitudes to, marriage or civil partnership as distinct types of human relationship. The EAT suggested that it would generally be helpful to ask whether, had the claimant and their partner been unmarried, or not in a civil partnership, but the circumstances had otherwise been the same, they would have been treated more favourably. Examples of situations in which a claim might succeed would include those in which the church acted because of views about the importance of sexual fidelity in marriage, about separation or about the taking steps to divorce (though not about the fact of divorce given that the asymmetric nature of the protection provided by s8 EqA). The question was whether the alleged discriminator would have treated an unmarried unfaithful or separating partner (in such cases) in the same way as the claimant.

The claimant's case failed because there was no evidence that the church had dismissed him because of the fact that he was married.

[4] See for example *Hawkins v Atex Group Ltd* [2012] ICR 1315. *cf Dunn v Institute of Cemetery and Crematorium Management* [2012] ICR 941.

The *Gould* decision illustrates the very limited protection afforded by s8 EqA. The question might sensibly be asked whether the continued prohibition of such discrimination plays any function in a context in which child-bearing has been significantly decoupled from married status (only 52 per cent of children born in the UK in 2016 being born to married or civilly partnered couples);[5] there is scant evidence that being in a formally coupled state is associated with disadvantage and the opening of marriage to same-sex couples (and of civil partnership to heterosexual couples) demonstrates that marriage, as an institution, has moved a long way from its patriarchal roots and purposes.

'Gender'/'Gender Identity' and 'Sex'

As is clear from s7 EqA, the Act does not expressly regulate discrimination on grounds of 'gender' or 'gender identity'. Further, as can be seen above, it defines 'transsexual', which is the term it employs, narrowly by reference to a process of (actual or anticipated) gender reassignment. The term 'gender reassignment' is also used in EU law. Neither Council Directive 2006/54 (which regulates work-related sex discrimination) nor Council Directive 2004/113 (which regulates sex discrimination in access to goods and services, etc) expressly prohibits such discrimination, and Directive 2004/113 is completely silent on the matter. But Recital 3 to Directive 2006/54 states that 'The Court of Justice has held that the scope of the principle of equal treatment for men and women cannot be confined to the prohibition of discrimination based on the fact that a person is of one or other sex. In view of its purpose and the nature of the rights which it seeks to safeguard, it also applies to discrimination arising from the gender reassignment of a person'.[6] The approach taken by the CJEU in the context of work-related discrimination can be assumed to apply equally to discrimination in the context of goods and services.

The terms 'sex' and 'gender' terms have until relatively recently tended to be used interchangeably, and are so used by the EqA (see in particular s7(1), above) and the Gender Recognition Act 2004 (GRA). They are, however, conventionally understood to refer respectively to biology (sex) and social construction/stereotypes (gender). Thus, for example, in 2019 the UK Office of National Statistics said this.

UK Office of National Statistics, What is the difference between sex and gender?[7]

The UK government defines sex as:

- referring to the biological aspects of an individual as determined by their anatomy, which is produced by their chromosomes, hormones and their interactions
- generally male or female
- something that is assigned at birth[8]

[5] https://www.ons.gov.uk/peoplepopulationandcommunity/birthsdeathsandmarriages/livebirths/bulletins/birthsbyparentscharacteristicsinenglandandwales/2016.

[6] See Case C-13/94, *P v S & Cornwall* EU:C:1996:170, [1996] ECR I-2143, [1996] ICR 795; Case C-117/01, *KB v NHS Pensions Agency* EU:C:2004:7, [2004] ECR I-541, [2004] ICR 781 (both discussed below); Case C-423/04, *Richards v SSWP*, EU:C:2006:256, [2006] ECR I-3585, [2006] ICR 1181 and, more recently, Case C-451/16, *MB v SSWP* EU:C:2018:492, [2019] ICR 115.

[7] https://www.ons.gov.uk/economy/environmentalaccounts/articles/whatisthedifferencebetweensexandgender/2019-02-21#:~:text=8.-,Summary,woman%2C%20or%20another%20gender%20identity.

[8] The use of this phrase is itself controversial, as noted at p 333 below.

The UK government defines gender as:

- a social construction relating to behaviours and attributes based on labels of masculinity and femininity; gender identity is a personal, internal perception of oneself and so the gender category someone identifies with may not match the sex they were assigned at birth
- where an individual may see themselves as a man, a woman, as having no gender, or as having a non-binary gender – where people identify as somewhere on a spectrum between man and woman …

… gender identity … refers to an individual's personal concept about their gender and how they feel inside. It is a deeply held internal sense of self and is typically self-identified. Gender identity differs from sexual identity and is not related to an individual's sexual orientation …

The EqA defines 'sex' as a protected characteristic by reference to 'men' and 'women' (see s11 above) and defines these concepts in turn by reference to 'male' and 'female' (see s212(1) EqA, referred to above), which are biologically determined categories.

'Gender reassignment' is defined by the EqA by reference to a transition between sexes (that is, from 'male' to 'female' or vice versa). This being the case, the EqA would not appear to prohibit discrimination against someone because they are non-binary or otherwise gender non-conforming, though some examples of such discrimination may amount to or involve discrimination because of sex or sexual orientation (real or perceived).[9] The 'category of 'trans' people, as it is often now conceptualised, is significantly broader than the protected characteristic of 'gender reassignment'.

Mark Walters, Jenny Paterson, Rupert Brown and Liz McDonnell, 'Hate Crimes Against Trans People: Assessing Emotions, Behaviors, and Attitudes Toward Criminal Justice Agencies' (2017) 35 *Journal of Interpersonal Violence* 4583, citations omitted

'Trans' identity refers to gender identities and expressions that go beyond biological sex as is assigned at birth. It is an inclusive term that embraces a broad range of identity categories and includes individuals who consider themselves transgender (those whose lifestyles appear to be in conflict with gender norms – for example, by dressing or presenting themselves in their preferred gender role); those who consider themselves not cisgender in any other way, rejecting binary categories – for example, genderfluid, nonbinary, genderfuck, genderless, agender, nongendered, third gender, two spirit, bigender, and trans man and trans woman; and transsexuals (those who experience a disjuncture between their gender identity and physical bodies, many of whom will wish to undergo surgery or hormone therapy to realign their bodies with their gender identity).

The reference to sex being 'assigned at birth' is itself controversial, many scientists and others taking the view that sex is a biological reality which precedes birth and is *recorded* (correctly or, very occasionally, incorrectly) at birth. The extract above nevertheless indicates the chasm between the protected characteristic of 'gender reassignment' and the social category of 'trans' people.

Discrimination relating to gender identity and/or gender reassignment is considered further below.

Sex-Based Disadvantage

It is important to understand why SDA and its sister legislation, the Equal Pay Act 1970 (EqPA), were enacted, and how the position of women in the UK has changed in the

[9] To the extent that the employment tribunal decision in *Taylor v Jaguar Land Rover Ltd* ET Case 1304471/2018 (available at https://www.gov.uk/employment-tribunal-decisions/ms-r-taylor-v-jaguar-land-rover-ltd-1304471-2018) suggests the contrary, it is not consistent with the text of the EqA.

intervening period. The seeds of the prohibition on sex discrimination were sewn in the late 1960s and early 1970s with the design and implementation of the EqPA and the SDA in December 1975. The EqPA was required by reason of the UK's impending accession to the EEC, as it then was, Article 119 of the founding Treaty of Rome prohibiting unequal pay for equal work as between men and women. In 1970 it was commonplace for UK employers to have different pay structures for men and women, women invariably being entitled to less pay than men regardless of the nature and/or value of their work, and including in cases in which men and women did precisely the same jobs. The SDA was the product of a domestic recognition that women were significantly disadvantaged by comparison with men. The White Paper which preceded the Act captured what were regarded as the main disadvantages experienced by women at the time.

Equality for Women **Cmnd 5724 (1974)**

Employment and Related Matters

6 … In the generations before the second world war, women used to work for several years between leaving school and getting married, whereupon they withdrew from the labour market. The typical woman worker was therefore young and single … Today, nearly half of all married women are in paid employment … Women's working lives have been transformed. Instead of work being an interlude between school and motherhood, work now increasingly tends to follow motherhood.

7. Paradoxically, the very improvements in the position of women have, in some ways, made their lives harder than before. To the physical and emotional strain of bearing children and caring for them on their early infancy have been added the demands of work in offices, shops and factories.

8. But, while more is being demanded of women, generally their treatment at work continues to be unequal and unjust. Most women do low-grade jobs in a narrow range of industries and services at much lower rates of pay that unskilled men. Most of them are segregated into 'women's work'. Women do not have the same chances as men of training for skilled work or promotion. Proportionately five times as many boys as girls take up apprenticeships, and most of the girls are apprentices in hairdressing and manicure. Five times as many men attend further education establishments on day release by their employers. The restricted nature of the opportunities open to young women to train for skilled work reinforces the tendency for women to fill the lowest paid, lease satisfying jobs. They are less likely to be promoted than men and are generally treated as unsuitable to be in authority over men …

9 … Women employees lag well behind men in relation to fringe benefits, particularly occupational benefits. And the absence of adequate provision for the special needs of married women employees makes it impossible for many fully-qualified married women to do responsible well-paid and fulfilling work …

11 … in the professions, women are even less well presented than in the ranks of senior and middle management. There has been little improvement in the proportion of women in the professions since the removal of sex disqualifications by Parliament in 1919. Less than one-seventh of all medical practitioners are women, and some medical schools have limited the number of women they accept. Women are in a majority in the teaching profession, but there are relatively few women in top teaching jobs. In primary school over three quarters of all teachers, but only two-fifths of head teachers, are women. In higher education, only 46 of more than 3,000 university professors in 1969 were women.

Education

12. There is a similar pattern of inequality in the educational system. Many children are brought up from their earliest years in the belief that the social and economic roles of men and women are radically different. This is reflected in the differences which are common in the curricula for boys and girls. For example, in England and Wales, at 'A' level, there is a marked difference in the

proportionate distribution between boys and girls taking arts and sciences, and at all examination levels from C.S.E. upwards there are fewer subject entries from girls than from boys … more girls than boys leave school at the minimum school-leaving age …

13. … In 1971–72, 4.2 per cent of girl school leavers and 7.3 per cent of boy school leavers were destined for the universities, whereas 1.4 per cent of boy school leavers and 5.0 per cent of girl school leavers went to colleges of education [teacher training colleges]. Male students at the universities outnumbered female students by a ratio of over two to one.

14. … The gap between the sexes has tended to narrow … [but] in the 25–34 age group … only two and a half per cent of women as against seven and a half per cent of men have university degrees or equivalent qualifications and 59 per cent of women compared with 48 per cent of men have no formal qualifications of any kind … In 1971 three-quarters of all women with qualifications at 'A' level or above were in the health and education fields while similarly qualified men were in a much wider range of occupations … in science and social science men outnumbered women by about five to one …

Facilities and services

15 …. Women … may be denied facilities for banking, insurance, mortgages, grants, loans, credit and finance on equal terms with men [or] … simply because they are women, or because they are married, or because they cannot provide a suitable male to guarantee their obligations … women may be refused tenancies, both by local authorities and property companies, solely on the ground of sex or marriage …

Much has changed since 1974, not least the proportion of pupils going on to university and the relative educational attainment of men and women. Women's participation rate in higher education caught up with that of men in 1992 and has exceeded it since that date.[10] In 2016/17, 177,525 men and 236,710 women graduated with a first degree.[11]

Table 6.1 First degree by sex, 2016/17

	2016/2017			Female % of total
	Female	**Male**	**Total[12]**	
Medicine and dentistry	11,645	7,490	19,205	60.6
Subjects allied to medicine	67,640	17,640	85,360	79.2
Biological and sports sciences	16,745	17,440	34,210	48.9
Psychology	26,040	5,700	31,825	81.8
Veterinary science	1,870	415	2,290	81.7
Agriculture, food & related subjects	3,620	1,795	5,415	66.9
Physical sciences	8,275	12,165	20,465	40.4
Mathematical sciences	5,640	8,625	14,295	39.5
Engineering & technology	11,085	41,260	52,375	21.2

(continued)

[10] S. Broecke and J. Hamed, *Higher Education Participation*, Department for Innovation, Universities and Skills, DIUS Research Report 08 14, 2, available at https://dera.ioe.ac.uk/8717/1/DIUS-RR-08-14.pdf.

[11] Taken from HESA, Higher Education Student Statistics: UK, 2019/20 – Qualifications achieved, available at https://www.hesa.ac.uk/news/27-01-2021/sb258-higher-education-student-statistics/qualifications.

[12] Includes 'other' who accounted for 1,000 of the total 800,335.

Table 6.1 ***(Continued)***

	2016/2017			Female % of total
	Female	**Male**	**Total**[12]	
Computing	7,165	26,380	33,600	21.3
Geographical & environmental studies (natural sciences)	4,220	3,490	7,715	54.7
Architecture, building & planning	8,325	11,815	20,150	41.3
Total science subject areas	172,850	154,725	327,940	52.7
Geographical & environmental studies (social sciences)	2,595	1,810	4,410	58.8
Humanities & liberal arts (non-specific)	1,190	605	1,795	66.3
Social studies	52,465	28,640	81,220	64.6
Law	25,450	14,305	39,800	63.9
Business & management	74,570	67,975	142,605	52.3
Communication & media	12,375	6,365	18,770	65.9
Languages & area studies	22,415	8,710	31,200	71.8
Historical, philosophical & religious studies	14,285	11,755	26,110	54.7
Creative arts & design	40,045	21,775	61,990	64.6
Education & teaching	46,635	14,695	61,370	76.0
Combined & general studies	1,765	1,350	3,115	56.7
Total non-science subject areas	293,785	177,980	472,395	62.2
Total	466,635	322,705	800,335	58.3

The proportion of all women graduating in 2019/20 was 57.1 per cent. It is clear from the table above, however, that women and men are concentrated in different areas of study, with very large numbers of women (25,000+) graduating in subjects allied to medicine, psychology, social studies, law, business & management studies and creative arts & design. Men were concentrated in business & management (67,975), engineering & technology (41,260), computing (26,380) and social sciences (28,640). Psychology and veterinary science were over 80 per cent and subjects allied to medicine and education almost 80 per cent female while computer science and engineering & technology were almost 80 per cent male.

The participation of women in paid work has also increased enormously over the last 50 years. Whereas in 1971 only 53 per cent of women in the UK were involved in paid work, the female employment rate reached 72.7 per cent in late 2019, declining to 72.2 per cent two years later.[13] 15.66 million women in the UK aged 16 and over were in employment in January 2020, 47.5 per cent of the total workforce.[14]

Women remain more likely than men to work part-time (part-time working accounting for 38 per cent of female employment, but only 13 per cent of male employment, in 2019[15]).

[13] ONS, *Women in the labour market* (2013), available at https://www.ons.gov.uk/employmentandlabourmarket/peopleinwork/employmentandemployeetypes/articles/womeninthelabourmarket/2013-09-25); S Irvine, H Clark, M Ward and B Francis-Devine, *Women and the Economy*, House of Commons Library Paper, SNO6838, March 2022, 3.

[14] B Francis-Devine and N Foley, *Women and the Economy*, House of Commons Library Paper, SNO6838, March 2020, 6.

[15] *Women and the Economy* (2022) n 13 above, 7.

The proportion of women working full-time rather than part-time has, however, increased markedly over time. Whereas in 1985, about 32 per cent of working aged women worked part-time and about 29 per cent worked full-time, by 2018 the first of these figures had remained about the same but the proportion of working aged women working full-time had increased to almost 45 per cent.[16]

Men and women work in different sectors of the economy, with women being concentrated in health and social work (over 3.5 million women's jobs in September 2021); wholesale and retail and education (over two million each).[17] Men and women also work in different jobs, as Figure 6.1 shows.

Figure 6.1 Employment by sex and occupation in the UK 2018–19[18]

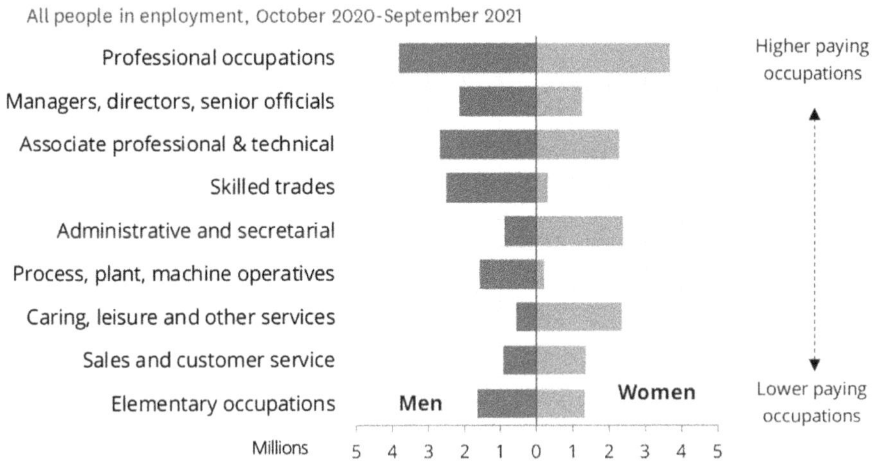

Note: Occupations ranked based on median hourly pay (excluding overtime) for employees as of April 2021.
Source: ONS, Employment by status and occupation, via Nomis and Annual Survey of Hours and Earnings via NOMIS.

In 2019, 79 per cent of jobs in the health and social work sector and 70 per cent of jobs in education were held by women, but only 15 per cent of construction jobs, 16 per cent of mining and quarrying jobs and 23 per cent of transportation and storage jobs.[19]

Much has changed, but women remain at a significant disadvantage by comparison with men. The median hourly pay gap (excluding overtime) between full-time women workers and full-time male workers stood at 7.9 per cent in 2021, while women part-time workers earned 2.7 per cent more per hour than their male counterparts. But because the rate of pay for part-time workers generally is lower than that for full-time, the median hourly pay gap between all male and female workers stood at 15.4 per cent in 2021.[20]

At the bottom of the hierarchy the pay gap between men and women is minimal because most staff are paid minimum wage (the pay gap was 0.5 per cent among bar staff in 2019,

[16] B Roantree and K Vira, *The rise and rise of women's employment in the UK*, Institute for Fiscal Studies, IFS Briefing Note BN234 (2020), Fig 2.

[17] *Women and the Economy* (2022), n 13 above, 10.

[18] Chart taken from Women and the Economy (2022), n 13 above, 11, chart 5.

[19] *Women in the Economy* (2020), n 13 above.

[20] *Women and the Economy* (2022) n 12 above, 15.

for example, and –2.6 per cent among kitchen and catering assistants).[21] Elsewhere, women are paid less than men in most occupational categories. Among the most highly paid full-time workers the hourly pay gap between men and women in 2019 was 39 per cent for dental practitioners, 36 per cent for aircraft pilots and flight engineers, 33 per cent for financial institution directors and managers, and 20 per cent for legal professionals and medical practitioners. There have been changes over time. Women who work as nurses, teachers, police and fire service officers earned within five per cent of their male colleagues in 2019, while women were paid marginally (three–six per cent) more than men when they worked in a variety of occupations including secretarial and related occupations, as youth and community workers, clergy and probation officers. The pay gap in favour of women was highest, at 33 per cent, for archivists and curators, and in excess of 20 per cent for counsellors, PAs and other secretaries, and other drivers and transport operatives.[22] It remains the case, however, that in the majority of jobs women are paid less than their male colleagues.

'GP gender pay gap "far higher" than average at 33%, finds Government review', *Pulse*, 29 March 2019

Male GPs earn 33% more than their female counterparts, according to a major review of the gender pay gap in the NHS. Interim results from the Department of Health and Social Care-commissioned review, published today, found the gender pay gap in general practice is 'far higher than the average in medicine'. The results also showed a lack of women represented in senior medical grades across the NHS, with women over-represented in lower-paid specialties … The report also showed:

- Male doctors earning £1.17 for every £1 earned by female doctors in the NHS, with two in three consultants being men
- There is a lack of women represented in senior medical grades, with nearly 32,000 male consultants to just 18,000 female
- Although two-thirds of doctors in training grades are women the number drops to less than half in consultant grades
- Women are over represented in lower paid specialties, such as public health and occupational health, while being under represented in the highest paying specialties including urology and surgery
- There is variation across medical specialities, with male-dominated specialties such as urology showing a higher gender pay gap …

Classroom pay: 'My male colleague was paid £7,000 more than me', *The Guardian*, 8 March 2018

the gender pay gap is as live an issue in schools as it is elsewhere. Government figures show that although young female teachers earn slightly more than male colleagues, they slip back as their careers progress. A woman under 25 in a local authority secondary school, for instance, might on average expect to earn £24,500 – £500 more than a male colleague. But by age 55–59 she would find herself on £44,700, while a man would earn £47,900.

Although two-thirds of secondary teachers are women, fewer than four out of 10 secondary heads are female. In primaries, one classroom teacher in seven is male, but more than a quarter of heads are men. The reasons for this are complex – women are more likely to take career breaks; they are more likely to go into part-time roles where promotion is less likely. But those aren't the only reasons why women earn less in schools … women are often held back by a culture in which jobs are offered through personal connections and in which if you don't ask, you don't get …

[21] https://www.ons.gov.uk/employmentandlabourmarket/peopleinwork/earningsandworkinghours/datasets/annualsurveyofhoursandearningsashegenderpaygaptables and https://www.ons.gov.uk/employmentandlabourmarket/peopleinwork/earningsandworkinghours/bulletins/genderpaygapintheuk/2019.

[22] *Ibid.*

> When schools compete with each other for staff, and when posts are often filled without advertisement, then those who are less forceful in their demands can lose out. There's a belief, too, that academisation has played its part in deepening this gender divide. And there are figures that back up this view. Government statistics show female teachers in local authority primary schools earn on average £1,800 a year less than male colleagues, while those in primary academies earn £2,800 less. In local authority secondaries the gender gap is £2,600; in secondary academies it is £3,000 …

Orthodox economists sometimes attempt to explain the wage gap in terms of 'human capital' – the skills, training and education, etc, in which workers invest. It is often argued that women have lower human capital than men – that they are less well educated, trained, motivated and/or skilled than men. But these arguments have been countered by research (much of it conducted in Britain) which has shown that women are paid less not *because* they were concentrated in jobs requiring less skill, but *despite* their working in jobs very similar to those performed by men in different organisations;[23] and that women's jobs were traditionally ungraded:

C Craig, Jill Rubery, Roger Tarling and Frank Wilkinson, *Labour Market Structure, Industrial Organisation and Low Pay* (Cambridge, CUP, 1982) 84

> firms would often recognise differences in skill between the women workers … but nevertheless pay all of them at the same rate, justifying the practice on the basis that any differentiation would cause resentment amongst the other women workers. The fact of women's pay being less than men's cannot therefore simply be explained on the grounds that women's work is less skilled, for even within women's work there is little or no differentiation of reward by skill … the predominant influence on the shape and structure of the pay and employment system was the sex of the workers.

Jan Waldfogel, 'Women Working for Less' (London, LSE, 1993) 47

> only a small proportion of the gender gap … is due to differences in characteristics between young men and women … if women had the same characteristics they do now but received the same returns as men in the labour market, the gender gap at age 23 would fall 84 per cent (from 19 per cent to 3 per cent) and at age 33 would fall 70 per cent (from 30 per cent to 7 per cent). This means that the much greater part (84 per cent at age 23 and 70 per cent at age 33) of the gender gap is due to differential treatment.[24]

In 2010 a major report commissioned by the Government Equalities Office concluded that, even after a 'series of key covariates' was controlled for, 'gender itself was still found to be the biggest cause of the gender pay gap. It accounted for 71 per cent of the gender pay gap in 2007 … The second largest factor causing the pay gap in both time periods was occupational segregation, and that factor had more impact in 2007 than it did in 1997.'[25] And in 2018 the Office for National Statistics reported that men's average lifetime earnings were £643,000 while those of women were £380,000.[26]

[23] S Horrell, J Ruberry and B Burchell, 'Unequal Jobs or Unequal Pay?' (1990) 20 *Industrial Relations Journal* 176. Job skills were compared using index allocating points for responsibility, degree of supervision, autonomy, training and education.

[24] 'Women Working for Less: A Longitudinal Analysis of the Family Gap' (London, LSE, 1993) 47. P Sloane, 'The Gender Wage Differential' in A Scott (ed), *Gender Segregation and Social Change: Men and Women in Changing Labour Markets* (Oxford, OUP, 1994) 191, found that discrimination accounted for approximately one-third of the wage gap between single men and women, one-quarter of that between married men and women. It should be noted, however, that Sloane included as factors distinct from 'sex' (the latter being the measure of discrimination) some, such as marriage and experience, which might be considered themselves to be discriminatory.

[25] W Olsen, V Gash, L Vandecasteele, P Walthery and H Heuvelman, *The Gender Pay Gap in the UK 1995–2007: Part 1 – Research report* (University of Manchester, 2010) 65.

[26] https://www.ons.gov.uk/peoplepopulationandcommunity/wellbeing/articles/humancapitalestimates/2004to2018.

For many women, the point at which work-related disadvantage bites hardest is after childbirth. Many jobs at the top of the economic hierarchy are still structured on the assumption not only that the holder has no caring obligations, but also that he does not even have to look after himself. Women face a very difficult task in attempting to reconcile such jobs with motherhood no matter how comprehensive and high-quality their childcare arrangements. Further down the scale, relatively few jobs pay sufficient to buy good-quality childcare so women are dependent on informal arrangements which require a significant degree of flexibility on their part. Many women 'choose' part-time work as part of this balancing act, only to find themselves denied promotion, downgraded or having to accept work for which they are over-qualified.

The problems faced by racially minoritised women are particularly acute. Racially minoritised and white women have different working patterns. As Kathleen Henehan and Helena Rose pointed out in 2018, in 2016–17 the employment rate for women aged 22–64 varied in 2016–17 between 75 per cent for white women through 70 per cent and 69 per cent respectively for Black and Indian women to only 39 per cent for Pakistani/Bangladeshi women. Conversely, the economic inactivity for women from these groups stood at 22 per cent, 23 per cent, 27 per cent and 56 per cent respectively.[27]

These figures are not static; the researchers report that the employment rate of white women grew by 13 per cent in the 20 years to 2006–07 but that that for Pakistani/Bangladeshi women it increased by almost 115 per cent. Pay growth for the various groups was not even; whereas Indian men and women had fared very well (relatively speaking), and white men and women and Pakistani/Bangladeshi men reasonably well (though in all these cases except white and Indian men from a low base), Pakistani/Bangladeshi women had seen their pay increase by less than these other groups, Black women by less still and Black men by least of all.

Henehan and Rose reported raw pay gaps relative to white men of between 24 per cent for Black men, four per cent for Indian men and 27 per cent for Pakistani/Bangladeshi men (for graduates) and 15 per cent for Black men, 12 per cent for Indian men and 31 per cent for Pakistani/Bangladeshi (non-graduates). There was a raw pay gap of 18 per cent between white women and white men graduates and of 19 per cent between non graduates. The raw figures for Black, Indian and Pakistani/Bangladeshi graduates relative to white women graduates were nine per cent, five per cent and 15 per cent, while that for non-graduate Pakistani/Bangladeshi non-graduates 12 per cent (those for Black and Indian non-graduate women being statistically meaningless).[28]

The researchers did not directly compare the pay of white men and of Black, Indian or Pakistani/Bangladeshi women, but it is clear from the comparative figures for white men and women, and those for white and Black, Indian and Pakistani/Bangladeshi women, that the gaps between white men and racially minoritised women are very large (though smaller than those between white and minoritised men). Having adjusted the raw statistics to take into account differences in educational attainment the researchers found that:

- White women had made little progress over the past 20 years by comparison with white men;
- The pay penalty experienced by Black women by comparison with white women had not reduced;

[27] 'Opportunities Knocked? Exploring pay penalties among the UK's ethnic minorities' (Resolution Foundation, 2018) Fig 1.

[28] Tables 6.1 and 6.2 respectively.

- Pakistani/Bangladeshi women faced large pay gaps compared with white women but these gaps reduced by more than 50 per cent when the statistics were adjusted, though they remained at 8 per cent for both graduates and non-graduates.

In 2017 the Living Wage Foundation reported that:

- 'Women make up nearly two thirds (62%) of workers currently struggling to make ends meet on less than the real Living Wage';
- 'This amounts to 3.4 million women compared to 2.1 million men';
- 'Nearly 1/3 of all UK working women (26%) are still earning less than the Living Wage, compared to just 16% of all working men'.[29]

The disadvantage that women face is not limited to unequal pay.

EHRC, *Is Britain Fairer? The state of equality and human rights 2018* (2019)[30]

Executive Summary

In some ways women's equality has progressed significantly. The employment gap and pay gap with men has narrowed, and the number of women in higher pay occupations and represented on company boards has increased. However, full gender equality has not been achieved and there are still many factors holding women back at work – some of which stem from gender stereotypes and emerge from school or earlier. For example, gender differences in career aspirations can be seen at an early age. This trickles through to higher education, where women are under-represented in most science, technology, engineering and maths courses, despite girls performing better than boys in education. Gender segregation is also prominent in apprenticeships. All of these factors contribute to women still being more likely to be in low-pay occupations.

Bullying and sexual harassment are widespread in the workplace and in education, and three-quarters of new mothers have had a negative or potentially discriminatory experience at work as a result of pregnancy or maternity. Sexual and domestic violence is a persistent and growing concern, and affects women and girls disproportionately. These negative experiences and the inequalities we continue to observe relate closely to stereotypes and perceptions of women and girls, and limit women's choices and opportunities …

There is an urgent need to improve the experiences of women across Britain. Schools should record and monitor prejudice-based bullying and sexual harassment in order to tackle these effectively …

Among the EHRC's more detailed findings in 2018 were that:

- although '[o]n average, boys continue to do worse than girls at school' and '[b]oys are more likely than girls to be excluded from school', '[g]ender differences in career aspirations emerge at an early age. Boys aged 7–11 are 20 times more likely than girls to aspire to be an engineer or architect';
- 'Girls are more likely than boys to be bullied; more than a third of young women experience sexist comments online';
- although '[w]omen are more likely than men to pursue higher education" and "perform better than men in higher education, on average', they 'continue to be under-represented in most science, technology, engineering and maths (STEM) courses';

[29] https://www.livingwage.org.uk/news/news-women-continue-be-hit-hardest-low-wages-uk.
[30] https://www.equalityhumanrights.com/en/publication-download/britain-fairer-2018.

- 'Apprenticeships remain strongly segregated by sex and women are still under-represented in the construction and engineering sectors';
- only one in ten FTSE 100 executive directors was a woman in 2017;
- 'Women are much more likely to be in low-pay occupations than men' though the proportion of women in high-pay occupations had risen.

The disproportionate impact of poverty on women is also evident from the following.

The Women's Budget Group, *The Female Face of Poverty* (2018)[31]

1.2. Poverty with a female face

Poverty is gendered. Women in the UK are slightly more likely to live in poverty than men when this is measured on the usual household basis (21% of adult women, compared to 19% of adult men in 2016-17) and female- headed households are poorer than comparable male-headed households. For example, almost half (48%) of single-parent households are living in poverty, compared to a quarter (24%) of couple households. In the vast majority (86%) of such households, the single parent is the mother. In older age-groups, 23% of single female pensioners are living in poverty compared to 18% of single male pensioners …

1.3. Why are women more likely to be poor than men?

… **Family and Care**

Women's looser attachment to the labour market is a consequence of gendered roles and expectations about who should shoulder caring responsibilities. The design of the benefits system and lack of investment in transport, child care and social care also hinder women's ability to combine care commitments with paid employment.

Social security provision

Women tend to rely more on means-tested benefits and men more on national insurance benefits which are not means tested. It can be harder for women to qualify for national insurance benefits because of periods out of paid work. With the new Universal Credit system, cuts in work allowances, taper rates and the single monthly payment particularly hit women by reducing work incentives for some second earners and potentially increasing women's vulnerability to poverty and financial abuse. Cuts in benefits and public spending since 2010 have disproportionately affected women, and BME women in particular.

Benefit sanctions have been increasing in severity and conditionality is now applied to previously exempt groups (e.g. more lone parents and disabled people). These sanctions are having a particular toll on vulnerable groups such as the victims of sexual and domestic violence and are pushing many people into destitution and ill health.

1.4. The consequences of poverty for women

Housing

Restricted access to good quality housing is a consequence of poverty.

Financial vulnerability limits the choice of living location and therefore the availability of family support, good jobs for low-income women and schools for children. It also limits women's ability to flee violent and abusive relationships. Homelessness is particularly prevalent among single parents, with nearly half (47%) of all homeless households being single-mother households.

[31] The Women's Budget Group, *The Female Face of Poverty* (2018), http://wbg.org.uk/wp-content/uploads/2018/08/FINAL-Female-Face-of-Poverty.pdf, citing DWP, Households Below Average Income – Percentage of individuals in low-income groups by various family and household characteristics (AHC) (2018) 1994/95–2016/17.

Health

The burden of managing poverty has an impact on women's health. Women are often responsible for budgeting in low-income families with children and this is associated with poor health and low morale. Mothers will often shield their families from poverty by going without food, clothing or warmth themselves. Cuts to public services are leaving many people with unmet care needs, particularly older women, who tend to live longer and more often on their own, and so tend to have greater caring needs than older men.

Debt

Women represented roughly two-thirds of those with severe debt problems in the UK in 2013. Rising housing costs, cuts to housing benefit and caps to Local Housing Allowance (to meet private rents) are forcing many people into rent arrears and/or to turn to foodbanks to feed their families. People struggling financially may be forced to accept credit at high interest rates or doorstep loans to avoid rent arrears.

Domestic violence and abuse

Poverty may exacerbate domestic abuse and violence by increasing or prolonging women's exposure to it and by reducing their ability to flee. The relationship between poverty and domestic violence is a complex one but we know they are correlated. For half of domestic violence victims living with their abuser, financial abuse prevents them from leaving the relationship.

Men take on a more significant share of unpaid domestic work than they did 30 years ago, but women continue to bear the disproportionate burden of childcare and housework, and are much more likely to take leave from paid work in order to look after children. According to the latest OECD statistics, women in the UK spend an average 248.6 minutes per day (over four hours) in unpaid work and 216.2 minutes in paid work, whereas men spend an average 140.1 minutes per day in unpaid work and 308.6 minutes in paid work.[32] The TUC reported in 2019 that only one per cent of new parents took shared parental leave in 2018,[33] and less than a third of men take the paternity leave to which they are entitled.[34]

One of the major markers and causes of gender inequality is sexual violence against women. Recent years have seen a particular concentration on sexual harassment as a result of the global #MeToo movement. The House of Commons Women and Equalities Committee has conducted no fewer than three inquiries into sexual harassment covering, respectively, schools, public places and the workplace. Some of the Committee's findings are reproduced below. It is important to emphasise that, whereas much harassment in schools and in public places falls outside legal regulation (unless and until it reaches the threshold for criminality), sexual harassment in workplaces has been prohibited for decades. That it remains so prevalent may be attributable in part to shortcomings in the law (in particular, the fact that the EqA generally imposes liability on employers only for the actions of their staff, rather than those of third parties, including customers and co-workers employed by other employers. More significant, however, as regards the continued flourishing of sexual harassment in the workplace, are the difficulties of enforcement which are discussed in Chapter 5.

[32] https://stats.oecd.org/index.aspx?queryid=54757.

[33] 'Shared parental leave' is the term given to leave previously only open to mothers which may now be shared with the other parent.

[34] https://www.tuc.org.uk/news/tuc-calls-overhaul-shared-parental-leave; http://hrnews.co.uk/less-than-a-third-of-eligible-men-now-take-any-paternity-leave-percentage-declines-for-fourth-year-in-a-row.

House of Commons Women and Equalities Committee, *Sexual harassment and sexual violence in schools*, Third Report of Session 2016–17, HC 91, footnotes omitted

Introduction

13. Despite the lack of centralised data on incidents of sexual harassment and sexual violence in schools, we are able to gain a deeper understanding of the extent of this problem through the extensive quantitative and qualitative data submitted to this inquiry. A number of large scale surveys find girls and young women consistently reporting high levels of sexual harassment and sexual violence in school:

- 59% of girls and young women aged 13–21 said in 2014 that they had faced some form of sexual harassment at school or college in the past year.
- Almost a third (29%) of 16–18-year-old girls say they have experienced unwanted sexual touching at school.
- 41% of UK girls aged 14 to 17 who reported an intimate relationship experienced some form of sexual violence from their partner.
- 22% of young girls aged 7–12 have experienced jokes of a sexual nature from boys.
- Nearly three-quarters (71%) of all 16–18-year-olds (boys and girls) say they hear sexual name-calling with terms such as "slut" or "slag" used towards girls at schools on a daily basis or a few times a week.
- 28% of 16–18-year-olds say they have seen sexual pictures on mobile phones at school a few times a month or more …

19. Young people who gave evidence to us noted the ubiquity of sexual harassment in school:

> I guess the thing that people would say they see the most, and we see as well, is slapping of bums and flicking [lifting up] of skirts. That is a common thing that people see in schools. There is also derogative term calling – calling women bitches and stuff like that – which is also a common thing that you see in school, on a daily basis really.

You see it every day in my school. I wouldn't say it was appropriate, but it still happens …

23. The Addressing Sexual Bullying Across Europe (ASBAE) Project, which interviewed young people across five EU countries between 2013–2015 found sexual harassment was often taken for granted:

> It became apparent that, whilst sexual bullying was widespread, the young people had previously accepted most sexual bullying behaviours as just a 'normal' part of their everyday lives. … The findings from the professionals further supported this … viewing sexual bullying as a widespread problem that had become normalised by young people, and suggesting that the ubiquity made it difficult for young people to identify problematic behaviours as sexual bullying.

The researchers also noted that this normalisation of sexual harassment and abuse makes it less likely that victims will identify behaviour as abusive and are therefore unlikely to report it.

24. There is strong evidence that young women are more likely to be targets of sexual harassment and sexual violence than young men …

34. Members of the ATL teaching union reported some of the consequences of sexual harassment that they had observed. These included:

- girls being 'even more unwilling to take risks even in academic areas'
- girls being less likely to participate in activities and 'do anything that will make them stand out and attract attention'
- girls being more self-conscious about appearance 'and not appearing too geeky'
- sexual harassment 'taking up a lot of teacher time.'…

36. Other impacts of sexual harassment at school have been identified as: post-traumatic stress disorder; self-harm; isolation and withdrawal; substance use; sexually transmitted diseases; depression and anxiety; and lack of attendance at school …

House of Commons Women and Equalities Committee, *Sexual harassment and sexual violence in schools*, Third Report of Session 2016–17, HC 91, footnotes omitted

Introduction …

12 … Women and girls experience a wide range of behaviours as sexual harassment, including behaviour that is unwanted but not necessarily unlawful as well as sexual assault and other criminal offences …

13. We heard about a wide range of behaviours including unwanted sexual comments in the street, rape threats on public transport, sexual assault in bars and clubs, racial abuse when sexual propositions were rejected, men exposing themselves in public, being masturbated at, sexual rubbing on a crowded train, and we heard from a group of women who had experienced sexual harassment in prison and elsewhere in the criminal justice system …

14. Sexual harassment in public places is overwhelmingly experienced by women and girls. Surveys show that sexual harassment is, in fact, the most common form of violence against women and girls and that young women are particularly targeted:

A survey published by the EU Fundamental Rights Agency in 2014 found that sexual harassment was the most common form of violence against women across the EU, with 68 per cent of women respondents in the UK saying they had experienced sexual harassment since the age of 15 and 25 per cent having been sexually harassed in the past 12 months;

- 85 per cent of women aged 18–24 and 64 per cent of women of all ages reported that they had experienced unwanted sexual attention in public places and 35 per cent had experienced unwanted sexual touching, in a survey carried out by the End Violence Against Women coalition in 2016;
- A survey of 14–21 year olds by Plan UK in 2018 found that 38 per cent of girls experience verbal harassment including sexual comments in public places at least once a month, while 15 per cent are being touched, groped or grabbed at least once a month;
- 63 per cent of girls and young women aged 13–21 experience (or know someone who has experienced) not feeling safe walking home alone, according to the Girls Attitudes Survey 2018. A range of other findings from this survey indicates that girls feel less safe online than they did five years ago – 25 per cent said they had had threatening things said about them on social media compared with 21 per cent in 2013, and 24 per cent had been sent photos or content by people they knew that they found upsetting, compared with 17 per cent in 2013 …

15. Girls often first experience sexual harassment below the age of 18; we were particularly disturbed to hear from a number of women about the sexual harassment they experienced as a girl from men and boys …

16. Even more disturbingly, for some girls their first experience happens below the age of 10. One woman told us: 'I have experienced sexual harassment in public since I was a young child. I remember the first time I was [under 12]. […] I continued to be sexually harassed almost daily throughout my childhood.' Many girls in Plan UK's 2016 research described witnessing or experiencing the harassment of girls aged eight and upwards, among whom girls in uniform appeared to be 'a particular target, with girls describing feeling fetishised by "older men targeting school girls".' This experience then becomes 'normalised' for girls and young women; it helps to shape the messages boys and girls receive about what is acceptable behaviour between men and women, and teaches girls to minimise experiences of harassment and abuse.

17. Sexual harassment can intersect with other forms of abuse such as disability-related harassment and racialised sexual harassment. Marai Larasi, Director of Imkaan, told us 'we hear that a lot of black and minority ethnic women and girls are being victimised in ways that include racialised abuse – being called a black bitch, for example, might be one of the things that happens.' …

18. Sexual harassment has significant and widespread impacts, both on individuals as well as on society. Sexual harassment in public reduces women and girls' freedom to enjoy public life, and can

negatively affect feelings of safety, bodily autonomy and mental health. Being sexually harassed can be a degrading, humiliating, and harmful experience in itself, but the effects are damaging more widely. It helps to keep women and girls unequal by perpetuating a culture in which they are sexualised; it is the backdrop to a society in which sexual violence can be normalised or excused.

19. Women and girls often fear and experience retaliation from men and boys perpetrating sexual harassment. Plan UK told us that girls talked about the backlash they could receive if they 'rejected' unwanted approaches, with harassment often turning into verbal aggression …

20. While some men and boys experience sexual harassment in public, harassment directed from unknown men to women and girls has a particular meaning given both the prevalence of sexual violence and the routine ways in which responsibility is put on women and girls themselves for preventing it … A 2014 survey found that 87 per cent of women reported changing their route as a result of harassment and nearly 80 per cent chose different forms of transport, for example calling a cab instead of walking or taking a bus …

21. Women also told us that they doubted themselves, questioning whether anything had happened, or blamed themselves …'Unwritten rules' for women and girls to keep themselves safe become accepted as 'common sense', meaning that society places the onus on them to avoid putting themselves in 'risky' situations. When sexual harassment is trivialised or treated as no big deal, it can reinforce the problem. Victims do not want to speak out in case they are told that what they experienced is trivial, a joke, or a compliment.

22. One of the effects of sexual harassment can be that girls feel that they do not control their bodies in public spaces and that they are seen as sexual objects, whether or not the experience is explicit …

24. In the UK, as elsewhere in the world, men and boys are overwhelmingly the perpetrators of sexual harassment in public places … Nearly one in three of the young men surveyed in the UK had made sexually harassing comments to a woman or girl they didn't know in a public place – such as the street, their workplace, their school or university, or an online space – in the previous month …

As mentioned above, much of the harassment described above is not subject to legal regulation other than, at the extreme, by the criminal law. Sexual harassment in the workplace, by contrast, has been the subject of regulation for many years. This being the case, the Women and Equalities Committee's inquiry into sexual harassment at work makes sobering reading.

House of Commons Women and Equalities Committee, *Sexual harassment in the workplace*, Fifth Report of Session 2017–19, HC 725, footnotes omitted

Introduction

1. In October 2017, allegations about sexual harassment in the entertainment industry began to appear in the media in the US and the UK. Many of these allegations concerned celebrities and other high-profile figures, but the stories sparked a mass movement of women from all walks of life and in many different fields of work sharing their own experiences of being sexually harassed in the workplace or elsewhere …

2. In the wake of #MeToo, a wide range of employers found themselves scrambling to respond to allegations of sexual harassment in their organisations or sectors …

8. Surveys commissioned by media and other organisations, of which there was a spate following the emergence of #MeToo, therefore provide valuable insights into prevalence. The impression such surveys give of a widespread problem across many sectors is borne out by evidence we have received about, for example, the entertainment industry, teaching, journalism, hospitality, retail, healthcare, the music industry and the international charity sector. Throughout the world of work, in spite of the law, sexual harassment is an everyday, common occurrence.

9. Research by ComRes for the BBC in November 2017 (surveying 6,206 adults in Great Britain) found that 40 per cent of women and 18 per cent of men (29 per cent overall) had experienced some form of unwanted sexual behaviour in the workplace, including nine per cent in the preceding year.

This ranged from displays of pornographic material and unwelcome jokes or comments of a sexual nature to serious sexual assaults. A ComRes poll for BBC Radio 5 Live in October 2017 (surveying 2,031 adults) found that 53 per cent of women and 20 per cent of men (37 per cent overall) said they had experienced sexual harassment at work or a place of study, and one in 10 of the women who had been harassed said they had been sexually assaulted. Surveys that ask about experience of 'sexual harassment', as opposed to specific unwanted behaviours, tend to show lower rates of incidence, perhaps because respondents may not categorise all those behaviours as harassment.

10. Men can also be victims of sexual harassment (perpetrated by both women and men), and women can be perpetrators (against both men and women). We acknowledge a risk that portraying it as an issue that only affects women could discourage male victims from reporting complaints. However, women are significantly more likely to experience sexual harassment than men. Perpetrators are disproportionately men. Sexual harassment can be considered both a cause and consequence of sex inequality, and some of the evidence we received drew links between sexual harassment and other manifestations of gender inequality in the workplace such as the gender pay gap and the underrepresentation of women in leadership roles.

11. Specific groups are disproportionately affected or susceptible to sexual harassment at work, such as young women between the ages of 18 and 24, employees with a disability or long-term illness, and members of sexual minority groups. Workers with irregular, flexible or precarious employment contracts, common in the services sector, and freelancers are more likely to experience sexual harassment. Specific factors may affect different racial groups, and experience of sexual harassment can be bound up with racial harassment. TUC research found that no BME women who had reported an incident to their employer felt it had been dealt with satisfactorily, compared to seven per cent of white women.

12. Sexual harassment can have a devastating impact on those who are subjected to it. Mental and physical health often suffer, leading to anxiety, poor sleep, depression, loss of appetite, headaches, exhaustion or nausea. Victims feel humiliation, mistrust, anger, fear and sadness. Women who have experienced harassment often take it on themselves to alter their own behaviour and habits or curtail their activities to avoid their harasser or similar situations, while observing that perpetrators suffer no negative consequences …[35]

Pregnancy-Related Discrimination

Women are particularly vulnerable to workplace discrimination during pregnancy. In 2005 the EOC published the final report into its formal investigation into pregnancy discrimination which it had commenced in 2003:

***Greater expectations,* Final report of the EOC's investigation into discrimination against new and expectant mothers in the workplace (2005)**

EXECUTIVE SUMMARY

The EOC has undertaken a two-year investigation into pregnancy related discrimination at work. What we found was far worse than even we expected.

[35] Note the recent coverage of sexual harassment of women nurses and doctors, teachers, women barristers, school children: https://www.nursingtimes.net/news/workforce/exclusive-survey-reveals-majority-of-nurses-have-experienced-sexual-harassment-03-06-2021, https://www.independent.co.uk/news/health/sanction-doctors-sexual-misconduct-b2015338.html; https://www.theguardian.com/education/2021/apr/06/very-intimidating-teachers-on-sexual-harassment-by-pupils; https://www.counselmagazine.co.uk/articles/interview-behind-the-gown; https://www.theguardian.com/society/2021/mar/27/how-schoolgirls-finally-found-voice-to-tell-of-sexual-abuse; https://www.theguardian.com/education/2021/jun/10/sexual-harassment-is-a-routine-part-of-life-schoolchildren-tell-ofsted.

The extent and impact of pregnancy discrimination

A million pregnant women are likely to experience discrimination at work over the next 5 years, if current trends continue. Our research has established that:

- Each year almost half of the 440,000 pregnant women in Great Britain experience some form of disadvantage at work, simply for being pregnant or taking maternity leave. 30,000 are forced out of their jobs.
- Women who lose their jobs miss out on £12m a year in Statutory Maternity Pay each year and, on average, return to hourly earnings 5% lower than they could have expected, 14% less for those on lower incomes.
- Yet the majority of women take little or no action to assert their rights. Around 3% of those who lose their job will attempt to seek financial compensation for their dismissal at an Employment Tribunal. Less than one in 20 will seek advice.
- This discrimination has serious, far-reaching implications for Government and employers, too. Women are nearly half the workforce and increasingly highly qualified. Unfair treatment at work during pregnancy makes it much less likely that they will return to their old jobs after maternity leave. And six times more likely that they will consider never going back to work at all. Employers not only lose out on their skills and experience, they also face extra recruitment and training costs.
- All women of childbearing age are potentially affected. Employer concerns about managing pregnancy may be having a wider impact on women's access to work. More research is needed but anecdotal evidence is shocking: 80% of HR professionals replying to one on-line survey said that they think twice before employing women of childbearing age. This needs to be tackled if the UK economy is to continue to grow.

In 2018 the EOC's successor, the EHRC, published the results of research it had commissioned with the Department for Business, Innovation and Skills into the prevalence and nature of pregnancy discrimination and disadvantage in the workplace. Interviews were carried out with 3,034 employers and 3,254 mothers. The main findings were as follows:

EHRC, *Pregnancy and maternity discrimination research findings* (2018)[36]

The majority of employers reported that it was in their interests to support pregnant women and those on maternity leave and they agreed that statutory rights relating to pregnancy and maternity are reasonable and easy to implement. However, the research found that:

- Around one in nine mothers (11%) reported that they were either dismissed; made compulsorily redundant, where others in their workplace were not; or treated so poorly they felt they had to leave their job; if scaled up to the general population this could mean as many as 54,000 mothers a year.
- One in five mothers said they had experienced harassment or negative comments related to pregnancy or flexible working from their employer and /or colleagues; if scaled up to the general population this could mean as many as 100,000 mothers a year.
- 10% of mothers said their employer discouraged them from attending antenatal appointments; if scaled up to the general population this could mean up to 53,000 mothers a year …
- A third (36%) of private sector employers agree that it is reasonable to ask women about their plans to have children in the future during recruitment.
- Six in 10 employers (59%) agree that a woman should have to disclose whether she is pregnant during the recruitment process.
- Almost half (46%) of employers agree it is reasonable to ask women if they have young children during the recruitment process.

[36] https://www.equalityhumanrights.com/en/managing-pregnancy-and-maternity-workplace/pregnancy-and-maternity-discrimination-research-findings.

- 44% of employers agree that women should work for an organisation for at least a year before deciding to have children.
- 40% of employers claim to have seen at least one pregnant woman in their workplace 'take advantage' of their pregnancy.
- A third believe that women who become pregnant and new mothers in work are 'generally less interested in career progression' when compared to other employees in their company.
- Four in 10 (41%) employers agreed that pregnancy in the workplace puts 'an unnecessary cost burden' on the workplace.
- Half (51%) of employers agree that there is sometimes resentment amongst employees towards women who are pregnant or on maternity leave.
- Around a third (36%) of employers disagree that it is easy to protect expectant or new mothers from discrimination in the workplace.

The Women and Equalities Committee was so concerned about the research findings which resulted in the 2018 EHRC report that it conducted an inquiry into pregnancy and maternity discrimination in 2016.

House of Commons Women and Equalities Committee, *Pregnancy and maternity discrimination*, First Report of Session 2016–17[37]

Shockingly, pregnant women and mothers report more discrimination and poor treatment at work now than they did a decade ago. With record numbers of women in work in 2016, the situation is likely to decline further unless it is tackled effectively now. Urgent action and leadership is needed, but the approach that the Government is taking forward lacks urgency and bite. There is a lack of detail about the Government's objectives, how and when it expects to achieve them, and how the effectiveness of its approach will be assessed. We welcome the awareness-raising work that the Government is doing with the EHRC and businesses, but it needs to set out a detailed plan outlining the specific actions it will take to tackle this unacceptable level of discrimination. This work must be underpinned by concrete actions to increase significantly compliance by employers and so improve women's lives.

The Government must make changes in laws and protections to ensure a safe working environment for new and expectant mothers, to prevent discriminatory redundancies and to increase protection for casual, agency and zero-hours workers. It must also provide incentives and ensure better enforcement to encourage better employer practice. Currently, the burden of enforcement rests with the individual experiencing discrimination, but the number of women taking enforcement action is low. The Government must take urgent action to remove barriers to justice and should seek ways of reducing the burden on women and making it easier for them to take action. It must also set out how it will monitor whether outcomes are improving for women.

A summary of our key recommendations is outlined here …

2. Employers should be required to undertake an individual risk assessment when they are informed that a woman who works for them is pregnant, has given birth in the past six months or is breastfeeding. …
3. The right to paid time off for antenatal appointments should be extended to workers. The Government should review the pregnancy and maternity-related rights available to workers and legislate to give greater parity between workers and employees …
4. The Government should increase protection from redundancy so that new and expectant mothers can be made redundant only in specified circumstances …
5. The Government should review the three-month time limit for bringing a tribunal claim in maternity and pregnancy discrimination cases …

[37] https://publications.parliament.uk/pa/cm201617/cmselect/cmwomeq/90/90.pdf.

6. The Government should monitor access to free, good-quality, one-to-one advice on pregnancy and maternity discrimination issues and assess whether additional resources are required …

The Government did not commit to action on any of these recommendations.[38] In June 2019 it was reported that pregnancy discrimination claims has risen by over 50 per cent in a year.

'Experts "surprised" by rise in pregnancy discrimination claims', ***People Management*****, 10 June 2019**[39]

In 2017/18, the number of pregnancy-related ET claims reached 1,357 – an increase of 56 per cent on 2016/17, according to official figures.

This rate of growth was over twice as fast as the overall increase in the number of tribunal cases, which rose almost 20 per cent over the same period, from 143,950 in 2016/17 to 172,730 in 2017/18.

Claire McCartney, senior policy adviser at the CIPD, said that while the removal of tribunal fees may have accounted for some of the increase, there has also been a greater awareness of maternity and paternity rights, and an increased willingness to make claims …

> The legislation is really helpful, but it's about creating culture change,' she said. 'Prevention is better than cure, so it's about organisations talking about the fact they're not going to discriminate in this area, what their policies are, what their values are, making sure they are modelling these in general. …

Any assumption that pregnancy discrimination is becoming a thing of the past should be dispelled by a report on the *Independent* in January 2020. The newspaper reports on a successful claim against the Liz Earle Beauty Company by Helen Larkin, who was sacked when she was eight months pregnant. According to the paper Larkin, who was given two weeks' notice of a purported redundancy dismissal after working for the company for five years, had been contacted by 'hundreds' of women who reported similar experiences:

'There are hundreds more like me, says woman sacked for being pregnant', ***The Independent*****, 10 January 2020**[40]

A woman who was sacked by a leading beauty brand because she was eight months pregnant has been contacted by hundreds of others who say they have also faced discrimination at work while expecting a baby.

Helen Larkin was awarded £17,303 by an employment tribunal on Thursday over her unfair dismissal from the Liz Earle Beauty Company. The 38-year-old, from Portsmouth, told *The Independent* a new senior employee saw her pregnancy as 'standing in the way' of a company restructure, and her applications for two other positions were rejected without interview because she would soon be taking maternity leave. She said the 'sexist treatment' the company subjected her to is part of a wider problem in which women across the UK face unfair discrimination because of their pregnancy …

> 'I have had hundreds of women reach out to me from different companies, across all sectors, saying they have also experienced similar treatment. So many have been silenced or did not know what to do. Hopefully my case will raise awareness of the scope and breadth of

[38] *Government response to the House of Commons Women and Equalities Committee report on pregnancy and maternity discrimination*, January 2017, available at https://www.parliament.uk/globalassets/documents/commons-committees/women-and-equalities/Government-response/Pregnancy-and-maternity-discrimination.pdf.

[39] https://www.peoplemanagement.co.uk/news/articles/experts-surprised-rise-pregnancy-discrimination-claims.

[40] © M Oppenheim, available at https://www.independent.co.uk/news/uk/home-news/pregnant-woman-sacked-discrimination-work-baby-tribunal-employment-a9278736.html.

> the problem of pregnancy discrimination and make businesses look at their processes and procedures, as well as encouraging other women to speak up and realise they can take these companies on by themselves.'

Ms Larkin, who had been working at the beauty firm for five years and has 14 years of digital marketing experience, said she was only given two weeks' notice of her redundancy in June 2018. The mother-of-two said the ordeal has had a 'huge impact' on her mental health and that she was very stressed about the case while pregnant.

> 'I was worried about finances because I was the main earner … I was also worried about the stress it was putting on my own health and my unborn. Being stressed while pregnant can be dangerous and have long-term health implications for the baby. The day before my C-section I had to do forms for the employment tribunal. I feel shocked and angry that they took something which should have been a special time with my new-born baby away from me and I'll never get that time back.'…

Joeli Brearley, founder of campaign group Pregnant Then Screwed, said: 'This is a monumental win not only for Helen but for women everywhere. Hundreds of thousands of women across the UK are cheering Helen on: women who have faced their own version of pregnancy or maternity discrimination but, due to cost, time limits, stress, mental-health issues or the sheer complexity of managing a tribunal claim and a new baby, were unable to challenge their employer. Taking a case of pregnancy or maternity discrimination to tribunal isn't easy. You have three months less one day to raise the claim; the costs can be horrifically expensive with a straightforward case costing between £5,000 and £10,000, and more complex cases costing upwards of £30,000; and the stress and strain on new mums can be totally overwhelming. Companies often have finances and legal representation that far outweigh that of the victim, making it feel like David vs Goliath.'

These factors lead to only one per cent of those who experience pregnancy or maternity discrimination raising a tribunal claim, the campaigner said.

> 'Even fewer make it to tribunal, as once the company realises their previous employee is serious about legal action, they will offer a financial settlement tied to a non-disclosure agreement which prevents them speaking publicly,' she added. Ms Brearley said the public rarely hears about cases such as Ms Larkin's due to firms using 'powerful and legal tools' to 'gag and silence' their victims.

The Liz Earle Beauty Company, which denied discrimination at the employment tribunal, told the hearing: 'The wellbeing of our people is of the highest importance to us and we always aim to ensure they are treated fairly. Over the course of the tribunal hearing … it seemed that we fell short of our standards in some areas, which we sincerely regret.'

Disadvantages Experienced by Trans People

In 2019 the EU's Fundamental Rights Agency conducted a survey of 140,000 people across the EU, North Macedonia and Serbia.[41] It was said by the FRA to be the largest survey of its kind.[42] It reported that 36 per cent of trans people in the UK always or often avoided certain locations for fear of being assaulted, threatened or harassed because of sexual orientation/gender identity. Some of the findings of the survey are included in Table 6.2 below.

[41] https://fra.europa.eu/en/data-and-maps/2020/lgbti-survey-data-explorer#contentSection.

[42] FRA, *A Long Way to go for LGBTI Equality*, 3, available at https://fra.europa.eu/en/publication/2020/eu-lgbti-survey-results.

Table 6.2 Experiences of trans people in the UK

	Trans people[43]	**Trans women**	**Trans men**
Percentage of trans people who report avoiding certain places 'often' or 'always' avoid certain places or locations for fear of being assaulted, threatened or harassed because of sexual orientation/ gender identity	40%	57%	47%
Locations/situations in which openness about sexual orientation/gender identity is avoided for fear of being assaulted, threatened or harassed			
– At home	16%	10%	20%
– Around family	23%	33%	35%
– At school	20%	11%	30%
– In the workplace	33%	25%	28%
– In healthcare settings	28%	19%	25%
– In cafés, restaurants and pubs and clubs	46%	54%	52%
– On public transport	56%	56%	58%
– In the street, squares, parks or car parks and other public places	57%	61%	56%
– In public premises or buildings	44%	45%	47%

Forty-five per cent of trans men, 30 per cent of trans women and 55 per cent of trans people generally are never or rarely open about being trans, while 32 per cent of trans men and trans people and 24 per cent of trans women hide it at work.

Table 6.3 Discrimination against trans people in the UK

	Trans people[44]	**Trans women**	**Trans men**
Percentage of trans people discriminated against in the previous 12 months because of their sexual orientation/gender identity			
In one of more of the listed contexts	56%	66%	73%
In a work-related context	36%	46%	48%
– While looking for work	31%	48%	45%
– At work	31%	38%	40%
In a non-work-related context	51%	61%	71%
– While looking for housing	17%	27%	17%[45]
– In healthcare/social services	35%	44%	50%
– In education (as parent or student)	30%	27%	50%
– In a café, restaurant, pubs or nightclub	28%	41%	32%
– In a shop	28%	41%	34%
– When showing ID/ an official document	24%	39%	45%

[43] Defined to include non-binary, cross-dressing, gender queer and gender fluid, agender and polygender people.
[44] Defined as above.
[45] Very small sample size.

Twenty-seven per cent of UK respondents reported that the discrimination they had most recently experienced also related to their sexual orientation, and five per cent, two per cent and three per cent respectively reported that it also related to their ethnicity or immigration background, their skin colour, or their religion or belief and 17 per cent to their sex. Only 14 per cent of trans people had reported the last incident of discrimination they had experienced. The survey also asked about violence and harassment were also reported by UK respondents.

Table 6.4 Violence and harassment against trans people in the UK

	Trans people[46]	Trans women	Trans men
Experience of physical or sexual attacks or harassment because of sexual orientation/gender identity			
Percentage of the population which had experienced such physical or sexual attacks in the past five years	16%	26%	19%
Of those, the number who had experienced			
– One such attack	47%	42%	49%
– Three or more such attacks	27%	30%[47]	37%[48]
Percentage of the population which had experienced such physical or sexual attacks in the past 12 months	8%	13%	11%
Percentage of the population which had experienced such harassment in the past 12 months	49%	66%	68%
– Verbal, in-person harassment	36%	51%	51%
– Non-verbal/ in-person harassment	35%	50%	42%

Fifty per cent of those who had experienced trans harassment attributed it also to their sexual orientation, seven per cent to their ethnicity or immigrant background and three per cent to their skin colour. Four per cent thought that their religion or belief had played a part and 20 per cent thought that their sex was also involved. Forty-nine per cent of trans respondents in the UK, but 60 per cent of those aged 15–17, reported having experienced having been ridiculed, teased, insulted or threatened at school because of their sexual orientation or gender identity. Such reports were higher for trans men (63 per cent) than for trans women (50 per cent).[49]

The Legal Regulation of Sex Discrimination

In this chapter we consider the EqA's prohibitions on discrimination as they apply to sex, as well as the provisions which are directed at gender unequal pay. The dual approach to sex discrimination (non-contractual and contractual) is the result of legislative history

[46] Defined as above.
[47] Small sample size.
[48] Small sample size.
[49] See also discussion in Ch 10 of evidence aggregating disadvantages reported by LGBT people.

and the origins of the EqPA 1970 in EU law. As is the case in respect of much discrimination law, the domestic provisions cannot be considered in isolation from the relevant European provisions which in their most recent form consist of Article 157 of the Treaty on the Functioning of the European Union (TFEU, formerly Article 141 of the Treaty of the European Communities, and before that Article 119 of the Treaty of Rome), and Council Directive 2006/54 (previously Council Directives 75/117 and 76/207).

Prior to the implementation of the Human Rights Act 1998 (HRA) and the application of anti-discrimination law to public functions, there were limited tools available to challenge much of the discrimination from which women suffer ('domestic' violence, sexual assault, the dual burden of paid and unpaid work). Much has changed in the last 20 years, however. The HRA has allowed women to challenge cuts to housing benefit which indirectly discriminated against women as victims of domestic violence; the non-availability to unmarried partners of widowed parents' allowance, and the non-availability to family members of criminal injuries compensation because they lived in the same home as their sexual abusers.[50] As discussed in Chapter 1, the HRA is under threat at the time of writing though the UK is likely to remain subject to the European Convention on Human Rights (ECHR). The Public Sector Equality Duty (PSED, discussed in Chapter 3) has allowed a challenge to be brought to the 2010 'emergency budget' on the basis that it had been prepared without due regard to its impact on women.[51] The application for judicial review which was brought by the Fawcett Society did not succeed, but the litigation focused public attention on the unequal impact of austerity cuts and it has been suggested that it contributed to the EHRC's formal assessment of the Treasury's compliance with the PSED.[52] The PSED also resulted in a successful challenge to funding cuts imposed by Ealing Council on domestic violence services for racially minoritised women (see further Chapter 3).[53]

The PSED and the HRA have been discussed in the preceding chapters. Here we turn to those issues which are unique to the regulation of sex discrimination. Two of the main subjects of the chapter are the equal pay provisions of the EqA, which apply only to gender unequal pay, and the exceptions to the prohibitions on sex and gender reassignment discrimination. Dress codes will also be considered, as will pregnancy and the degree to which 'gender identity' is protected by the EqA and/or the HRA.

Equal Pay

Sections 64–76 EqA apply only to pay differences related to sex and pregnancy/maternity. Like much else in the EqA the provisions adopt a symmetrical approach insofar as they deal with sex, and permit claims by men as well as women. The similarities between these provisions of the EqA, on the one hand, and the Act's other provisions, on the other, do not extend far beyond their shared symmetry of approach. Parts 3, 4, 6 and 7, and Chapters 1 and 2 of Part 5 EqA, prohibit 'discrimination,' direct or indirect, in a number of situations, and impose duties of reasonable adjustment. Hypothetical comparators may be used to

[50] See, respectively, *A v UK* 48 BHRC 36; *In re McLaughlin* [2018] UKSC 48, [2018] 1 WLR 4250 and *JT v First-Tier Tribunal* [2018] EWCA Civ 1735, [2019] 1 WLR 1313.

[51] *R (Fawcett Society) v Chancellor of the Exchequer* [2010] EWHC 3522 (Admin).

[52] TUC (2011), *The Gender Impact of the Cuts – a year on*, available at https://www.tuc.org.uk/sites/default/files/tucfiles/genderimpactofcutsrevisited.pdf.

[53] *R (Kaur) v LB Ealing* [2008] EWHC 2062 (Admin).

establish discrimination. Sections 64–76 EqA, on the other hand, do not actually use the term 'discrimination', much less distinguish its direct and indirect varieties. Instead, they set out three situations in which there is a de facto right to the same contractual terms (including pay) as another, or to equivalent pension provision. Pension claims are dealt with briefly at pp 383–384 below, the focus of this section being on equal pay claims.

In order to succeed in an equal pay claim the claimant must prove that she (or he) falls within one of three situations – ie, that she does the same work, work which has been rated by the employer as equivalent (in value) or work which a tribunal has determined to be of equal value, to that done by someone of the opposite sex in the 'same employment' as her. Where the claimant does this she is entitled, subject to the material factor defence (MFD, discussed further below), to have an 'equality clause' inserted into her contract which gives her the same contractual term(s) as that (those) enjoyed by her comparator and sought by her.

Before we turn to the detail of 64–76 EqA it is necessary to mention Article 157 TFEU which provides a right as between men and women to equal pay for work of equal value. In Case C-43/75 *Defrenne v Sabena (No 2)* [1976] ECR 455, [1976] ICR 547 the CJEU accepted that the predecessor provision of Article 157 TFEU was directly effective. Since that date individuals within the various Member States have been able to rely on Article 157 to claim equal pay in their national courts.

Article 157 TFEU

(1) Each Member State shall ensure that the principle of equal pay for male and female workers for equal work or work of equal value is applied.

(2) For the purposes of this Article, 'pay' means the ordinary basic or minimum wage or salary and any other consideration, whether in cash or in kind, which the worker receives, directly or indirectly, in respect of his employment from his employer.
Equal pay without discrimination based on sex means:

- (a) that pay for the same work at piece rates shall be calculated on the basis of the same unit of measurement;
- (b) that pay for work at time rates shall be the same for the same job …

This provision is, for the most part, given effect in domestic law. The starting point in domestic law is s66 EqA.

Section 66 EqA, Sex equality clause

(1) If the terms of A's work do not (by whatever means) include a sex equality clause, they are to be treated as including one.

(2) A sex equality clause is a provision that has the following effect—

(a) if a term of A's is less favourable to A than a corresponding term of B's is to B, A's term is modified so as not to be less favourable;

(b) if A does not have a term which corresponds to a term of B's that benefits B, A's terms are modified so as to include such a term …

(4) In the case of work within section 65(1)(b), a reference in subsection (2) above to a term includes a reference to such terms (if any) as have not been determined by the rating of the work (as well as those that have).

The majority of claims brought under ss64–66 EqA concern pay, but it is clear from s66 that the EqA's scope is wider than this. Section 64 EqA provides that ss66–70 EqA[54] apply

[54] That is, equal pay and pension provisions including the MFD.

where 'a person (A) is employed on' or holds a personal or public office and does 'work that is equal to the work that a comparator of the opposite sex (B) does', whether or not contemporaneously. And s65(1) provides that work is 'equal' in one of three situations, namely, where it is like work, work rated as equivalent, or work of equal value. Section 65(2)–(6) EqA then provide that:

- 'A's work is like B's work if A's work and B's work are the same or broadly similar, and such differences as there are between their work are not of practical importance in relation to the terms of their work', further that 'on a comparison of one person's work with another's for the purposes' of determining whether the work is 'like', 'it is necessary to have regard to – (a) the frequency with which differences between their work occur in practice, and (b) the nature and extent of the differences';
- 'A's work is rated as equivalent to B's work if a job evaluation study gives an equal value to A's job and B's job in terms of the demands made on a worker, or would give an equal value to A's job and B's job in those terms were the evaluation not made on a sex-specific system', a system being 'sex-specific if, for the purposes of one or more of the demands made on a worker, it sets values for men different from those it sets for women'; and
- 'A's work is of equal value to B's work if it is neither like B's work nor rated as equivalent to B's work, but nevertheless equal to B's work in terms of the demands made on A by reference to factors such as effort, skill and decision-making'.

Sections 72–75 EqA make materially similar provision to ss64–66 EqA in the case of women on maternity leave, such women being entitled to the benefit of a 'maternity equality clause' to bring their contractual entitlement to the same level as it would have been had they not taken maternity leave. This does not have the effect of requiring that the woman be paid while on maternity leave as she would have been had she been at work, rather to ensure (broadly) that she benefits from any pay increases on her return to work that she would have received had she not taken leave, and that she is entitled to receive bonus payments which are attributable to the period before or after her maternity leave see pp 395–396 below.

An equal pay claimant does not have to prove that she has been discriminated against, simply that she has been less favourably treated in some contractual term than a suitable comparator.[55] In these circumstances, it might be said that a presumption of discrimination arises. The employer can displace that presumption, and escape the imposition of an equality clause, by proving that the difference in pay (or other contractual term) is due to a 'material factor' which is 'not the difference of sex'. The MFD is considered further below. A 'material factor' which is 'not the difference of sex' does not discriminate directly between men and women and, if it is indirectly discriminatory (in the sense that reliance upon it disfavours women as a matter of fact), reliance upon it must be justified in line with the test established under Article 157 TFEU.[56]

[55] ie, like work, work rated as equivalent or work of equal value. Sections 67–68 EqA make provision as regards the terms of A's occupational pension (if any), separate provision being required because pension payments are the responsibility of occupational pension scheme trustees, rather than by employers.

[56] Article 157 TFEU may (at the time of writing) be relied upon in the UK courts, generally by way of having the EqA interpreted (however contrary to its express terms) so as to give effect to the European provision. Article 157 does not (*Biggs v Somerset CC* [1996] ICR 364) give rise to any 'free-standing' cause of action but must be applied through the domestic provisions (see further Ch 1); see also *Preston v Wolverhampton Healthcare NHS Trust (No 3)* [2004] ICR 993. This used to be a matter of great significance given inadequacies in the domestic legislation but many of the shortcomings in the law have been addressed over time.

The particular 'equalising' mechanism employed by ss64–66 EqA, ie, the insertion of an 'equality clause' to modify any term of A's which 'is less favourable to [her] than a corresponding term of' her comparator's is to him, would appear to allow 'leap-frogging', ie, attempting to 'cherry pick' any particularly favourable terms of a comparator's contract which may, in theory or practice, be balanced by terms which are more favourable to the claimant than her comparator's equivalent are to him. It was argued by the employers in the early equal pay case of *Hayward v Cammell Laird*, that the EqPA 1970 did not permit such an approach.

***Hayward v Cammell Laird Shipbuilders Ltd (No 2)* [1988] 1 AC 894**

The case was brought by a canteen worker who named, as her comparators, a painter, a joiner and an insulation engineer. By way of defence her employers claimed that, although her basic and overtime rates of pay were lower than those of her comparators, her sickness benefits and meal breaks were better than theirs with the effect that, taken as a whole, her contractual terms were no less favourable to her than theirs were to them. A tribunal, the EAT and the CA all agreed that the claimant was not entitled to relief if, as the employer argued, her contract, taken as a whole, was no less favourable than those of her comparators.[57] The House of Lords (HL) allowed her appeal, unanimously deciding that s1(2) EqPA (which was materially similar to 66 EqA) meant what it said.

Lord Goff (with whom Lords Griffiths, Bridge and Brandon agreed, Lord Mackay delivering a concurring judgment):

> 34 .... If I look at the words used ['where the woman's contract does not include a term corresponding to a term benefitting the male comparator included in his contract'], and give them their natural and ordinary meaning, they mean quite simply that one looks at the man's contract and at the woman's contract, and if one finds in the man's contract a term benefiting him which is not included in the woman's contract, then that term is treated as included in hers. On this simple and literal approach, the words 'benefiting that man' mean precisely what they say, that the term must be one which is beneficial to him, as opposed to being burdensome. So if, for example, the man's contract contains a term that he is to be provided with the use of a car, and the woman's contract does not include such a term, then her contract is to be treated as including such a term.

The employers in *Hayward*, and the lower courts, had made much of the 'absurd and unreal consequences' which would follow a literal interpretation of s1(2) EqPA, the former using an example of a woman with a salary of £7,500 and a car worth £3,500 pa who sought to compare her wages with those of a man paid £11,000 but without a company car. Lord Mackay accepted that 'one can envisage difficult examples' but 'in the ordinary case such as the present ... it would be wrong to depart from the natural meaning of the words Parliament has used because of the difficulty in their application to particular examples especially when those examples do not arise in actual cases.' Neither Lord Mackay nor Lord Goff found it necessary to examine the European legislation in view of their conclusion on the clarity of the UK provisions. Nevertheless, both took the view that it supported their

[57] [1988] QB 12 (CA) and [1987] 1 All ER 503 (EAT).

approach. In the event, the CJEU decisions in Case C-381/99 *Brunnhofer v Bank der österreichischen Postsparkasse AG* EU:C:2001:358, [2001] ECR I-4961, [2001] IRLR 571 and in Case C-236/98 *Jämställdhetsombudsmannen v Örebro Läns Landsting* EU:C:2000:173, [2000] ECR I–02189, [2001] ICR 249 confirm that the approach under Article 157 TFEU is the same, the principle of transparency requiring equivalence in each aspect of pay in the absence of objective justification. Dealing with the concern of the lower courts as to the potential of their interpretation to lead to 'mutual enhancement or leap-frogging, as terms of the woman's contract and the man's contract are both, so to speak, upgraded to bring them into line with each other,' Lord Goff suggested that the MFD might apply in relation to 'compensating' terms such as those upon which the employer in the present case sought to rely. Lord Mackay was not convinced of this, suggesting 'at the very least' that MFD required the establishment of a causal link between the woman's unfavourable term and that which claimed to balance it, but Lord Goff's provisional view was supported by Lord Bridge in *Leverton v Clwyd CC* [1989] 1 AC 706. The decision is considered further at p 264 below. On the question, however, whether a woman's unfavourable pay could be balanced against her shorter hours, Lord Bridge concluded, perhaps not surprisingly, that:

> 19 .... Where a woman's and a man's regular annual working hours, unaffected by any significant additional hours of work, can be translated into a notional hourly rate which yields no significant difference, it is surely a legitimate, if not a necessary, inference that the difference in their annual salaries is both due to and justified by the difference in the hours they work in the course of a year and has nothing to do with the difference in sex.

The decision of the HL in *Hayward* denied employers *carte blanche* to decide on their workers' behalf the manner in which they should be paid, to the extent that this differed between men and women.[58]

'Like Work'

Turning to consider the various equal pay claims in more detail, the concept of 'like work' now found in s65 EqA (see p 356 above) was regarded by the framers of the EqPA 1970 as quite a broad and generous provision. The courts initially adopted a very narrow approach to the provision, the EAT in *Eaton Ltd v Nuttall* [1977] ICR 272 ruling that a woman production scheduler who was responsible for ordering 2,400 units per week of a value up to £2.50 did not do like work with a male production scheduler who was responsible for ordering 1,200 units per week of a value ranging between £5 and £1,000. In reaching this conclusion the EAT overlooked the fact that the only other female production scheduler in employment, who was paid the same rate as the claimant, had replaced a man who had been paid on the same (higher) rate as that paid to the only male production scheduler whose rate of pay was known.

Shortly thereafter, the EAT ruled in *Capper Pass Ltd v Lawton* [1977] QB 852 that no account should be taken, in determining the question of 'like work', of 'trivial differences or differences not likely in the real world to be reflected in the terms and conditions of

[58] See also *Matthews v Kent & Medway Towns Fire Authority* [2004] ICR 257 in which EAT declared, *obiter*, that an employment tribunal had correctly insisted on comparing each individual term enjoyed by part-time and full-time firefighters for the purposes of a claim under the Part-time Workers Regulations, see below). The CA ([2005] ICR 84) did not comment on this appropriate method of comparison.

employment.' In *Shields v Coomes* the CA approved of this approach. The claimant, who worked in a betting shop, was paid less than her male colleague who, in addition to those duties he shared with her, was required to work longer hours, to open the shop, and to carry cash to and from it. The employers, who usually staffed their shop with women, had a policy of employing one man in each of their shops which they considered to be in 'rough' areas. The employers took the view that these men, who were all paid at the higher rate, functioned 'as a cover or precaution against illegal entry'.

A tribunal took the view that the man's security and cash-carrying duties constituted a difference 'of practical importance in relation to terms and conditions of employment' so as to defeat a like work claim. The EAT disagreed, a ruling upheld by the CA. Lord Denning MR cited the decision in *Capper Pass Ltd v Lawton* with approval and ruled that the tribunal should consider the 'nature and extent' of the differences between the tasks performed by the woman and her comparator(s) and well as their frequency, focusing on the jobs and not the workers.

***Shields v E Coomes (Holdings) Ltd* [1978] ICR 1159**

Lord Denning MR:

> 31 .... The employer should not be able to avoid the principle by introducing comparatively small differences in 'job content' between men and women; nor by giving the work a different 'job description'...
>
> 32. Nor should the employer be able to avoid the principle of 'equal value' by having the work (at the same job) done by night or for longer hours. The only legitimate way of dealing with night work or for longer hours is by paying a night shift premium or overtime rate assessed at a reasonable figure ...
>
> 37. In this case the woman and the man were employed on work of a broadly similar nature. They were both counterhands. There were several differences between the things she did and the things which he did. For instance, he started at opening time and worked longer hours; but this did not, by itself, warrant a difference in the 'rate for the job.' He carried cash from shop to shop or to head office. But this difference was, by itself, 'not of practical importance.' The one difference of any significance between them was that the man filled a protective role. He was a watchdog ready to bark and scare off intruders. This difference, when taken with the others, amounted to differences which the majority of the industrial tribunal found were 'real and existing and of practical importance.' Accepting this finding, I do not think these differences could or did affect the 'rate for the job.' Both the woman and the man worked alongside one another hour after hour, doing precisely the same work. She should, therefore, receive the same hourly rate as he. It is rather like the difference between a barman and a barmaid. They do the same work as one another in serving drinks. Each has his or her own way of dealing with awkward customers. Each is subject to the same risk of abuse or unpleasantness. But, whichever way each adopts in dealing with awkward customers, the job of each, as a job, is of equivalent rating. Each should, therefore, receive the same 'rate for the job.' It [amounts to] 'like work.'

Work Rated as Equivalent

The 'work rated as equivalent' provision of the EqPA 1970, which was materially identical to that now found in s65 EqA (see p 358 above), In *Eaton Ltd v Nuttall* the EAT declared that, in order to found a 'work rated as equivalent' claim, the job evaluation scheme (JES) must be (§13):

> thorough in analysis and capable of impartial application. It should be possible by applying the study to arrive at the position of a particular employee at a particular point in a particular salary grade without taking other matters into account except those unconnected with the nature of the work. It will be in order to take into account such matters as merit or seniority etc, but any matters concerning the work (eg responsibility) one would expect to find taken care of in the evaluation study.

In *Springboard Sunderland Trust v Robson* [1992] ICR 554 a question arose as to whether the claimant's job and that of her comparator had, as a matter of fact, been rated as equivalent under the scheme in question. The claimant's job had been awarded 410 points and that of her comparator 429 points on a scheme which placed jobs rated between 360 and 409 points on grade 3, and those rated 410 to 449 points on grade 4. The employers did not pay the claimant a grade 4 salary and argued that a 'work rated as equivalent' claim was only available to those claimants whose jobs had been awarded precisely equal point scores on a JES, rather than those whose point scores placed them within the same grade as that of their comparators. Both the tribunal and EAT ruled in the claimant's favour.

Work of Equal Value

We saw above that the gender-pay gap is associated with occupational sex segregation. If a woman has to prove that she is doing the same job as a man in order to be entitled to receive the same pay, that part of the gender-pay gap which results from this type of segregation goes unchallenged. The establishment in 1984 of the 'equal pay for work of equal value claim' opened the possibility of real challenge to this part of the pay gap.

> **David Pannick, *Sex Discrimination Law* (Oxford, OUP, 1985) 102**
>
> Equal pay for work of equal value is an essential element of anti-discrimination law in a society in which occupational segregation of men and women persists. The anthropologist Margaret Mead explained that all societies tend to undervalue work done by women:
>
> > Men may cook or weave or dress dolls or hunt humming-birds, but if such activities are appropriate occupations of men, then the whole society, men and women alike, votes them as important. When the same occupations are performed by women, they are regarded as less important.

In equal value claims a tribunal has to consider the relative value of the woman's job and that of her male comparator in terms of (s65(6) EqA) 'the demands made … reference to factors such as effort, skill and decision-making'. The EqPA provided for the appointment of 'independent experts' to advise tribunals on the issue of value, and tribunals were not initially permitted to determine an equal value claim in favour of a claimant until it had received the report of the independent expert. Since 2004, however, tribunals have been able to choose whether or not to appoint an expert or to determine an equal value claim without one. Section 131 EqA now provides that a tribunal may appoint an expert from a panel maintained by Acas and, if it does so, that it may not determine the question of value unless it has received the expert's report or withdrawn the request. Section 131 EqA then provides that, where a question has arisen about whether A's job is of equal value to B's, and the jobs have been given different values by a job evaluation study:

Section 131 EqA, Assessment of whether work is of equal value

(6) The tribunal must determine that A's work is not of equal value to B's work unless it has reasonable grounds for suspecting that the evaluation contained in the study—

(a) was based on a system that discriminates because of sex, or
(b) is otherwise unreliable.

(7) For the purposes of subsection (6)(a), a system discriminates because of sex if a difference (or coincidence) between values that the system sets on different demands is not justifiable regardless of the sex of the person on whom the demands are made.

In *Eaton v Nutall*, mentioned above, the EAT ruled that a 'work rated as equivalent' claim could not succeed unless the JES on the basis of which it was made was 'analytical, in the sense of being 'thorough in analysis and capable of impartial application'. In *Bromley v Quick* [1988] ICR 623 the CA imposed a similar requirement on a JES on which an employer sought to rely to block a work rated as equivalent claim. The provisions under consideration were of the EqPA but the principle remains the same.

In order to bring an equal pay claim a woman must first discover what potential comparators earn. This is likely to prove difficult, particularly in non-unionised workplaces. Between 2003 and 2014 the legislation provided a questionnaire procedure which permitted actual or prospective claimants to ask questions of their employers about matters including whether the employer accepts that the questioner is employed on equal work with that of her (potential) comparator(s), whether she is receiving less pay than their (potential) comparator (s) and, if so, why. Failure or refusal to answer appropriate questions in a timely and satisfactory manner would allow a tribunal to draw adverse inferences against the employer. With the abolition of the questionnaire procedure the hurdles facing potential equal pay claimants have become more intense.[59]

In *Pickstone v Freemans plc* [1988] 1 AC 66 the HL confirmed that equal value claims could be brought notwithstanding the presence of a man in the same job as the claimant (or one which has been rated as equivalent). According to Lord Keith, the alternative: 'would leave a large gap in the equal pay provision, enabling an employer to evade it by employing one token man on the same work as a group of potential women claimants who were deliberately paid less than a group of men employed on work of equal value with that of the women. This would mean that the United Kingdom had failed yet again fully to implement its obligations under art [157 TFEU] ....'

One interesting result of the decision in *Pickstone* was seen in *Milligan v South Ayrshire Council* [2003] IRLR 153. In *South Ayrshire Council v Morton* [2002] IRLR 256, the Court of Session had held that a female primary school headteacher employed by South Ayrshire Council could claim equal pay with a male secondary school headteacher working for Highland Council. This decision is considered further below. The applicant in *Milligan* was a male primary school teacher who wished to use as his comparator a female primary school headteacher whose wages would, as a result of the *Morton* litigation, be increased to match those of a male secondary school teacher (all such teachers were male so the applicant in *Milligan* could not use this direct method of comparison for the purposes of an equal pay claim). The Court of Session permitted Mr Milligan to make a 'contingent'

[59] Section 77 EqA, discussed at p 362 below, protects pay-related discussions but does not require the disclosure of pay-related information.

('piggy back') claim and, further, to have this claim stayed until the resolution of his comparator's equal pay claim. The Court took the view that the applicant would suffer 'real prejudice in relation to back pay' if he was required to await the outcome of his comparator's pay claim prior to launching his claim (see further Chapter 5 for the limits on back-dating in equal pay claims). The *Milligan* decision was followed by the EAT in *Hartlepool BC v Llewellyn* [2009] IRLR 796, a case involving mass litigation against three local authorities including Hartlepool. Among the claimants were a small number of men who had sought to make piggy back claims. The questions for the EAT were (1) whether the men could bring claims before the women's succeeded; (2) whether, the women's claims having succeeded, the men's claims would too; and (3) if so, whether the men would be entitled to up to six years' back pay (as the women had been) or to back pay only to the date the women's claims succeeded. The EAT ruled that the men had been entitled to bring claims contingent on the outcome of the women's claims, that the claims succeeded, and that the men had the same entitlement to back pay as the women had had. The EAT also ruled that a tribunal had been correct to rule that in the case of one employer who had settled the women's claims, the refusal to settle the men's claims had amounted to unlawful sex discrimination.[60]

Since 2010, employers have been prohibited from penalising employees for seeking or making disclosures about pay to colleagues in connection with possible EqA claims. Section 77 EqA, which had no equivalent under the previous legislation, provides that:

Section 77 EqA, Discussions about pay

(1) A term of a person's work that purports to prevent or restrict the person (P) from disclosing or seeking to disclose information about the terms of P's work is unenforceable against P in so far as P makes or seeks to make a relevant pay disclosure.

(2) A term of a person's work that purports to prevent or restrict the person (P) from seeking disclosure of information from a colleague about the terms of the colleague's work is unenforceable against P in so far as P seeks a relevant pay disclosure from the colleague; and "colleague" includes a former colleague in relation to the work in question.

(3) A disclosure is a relevant pay disclosure if made for the purpose of enabling the person who makes it, or the person to whom it is made, to find out whether or to what extent there is, in relation to the work in question, a connection between pay and having (or not having) a particular protected characteristic.

(4) The following are to be treated as protected acts for the purposes of the relevant victimisation provision[61]—

(a) seeking a disclosure that would be a relevant pay disclosure;
(b) making or seeking to make a relevant pay disclosure;
(c) receiving information disclosed in a relevant pay disclosure …

The prohibition on victimisation is considered in Chapter 2. Welcome as s77 EqA is, it does not impose any requirement on potential comparators to discuss pay and many are very reluctant so to do. Meanwhile, the removal of the questionnaire procedure has served to strengthen the ability of employers to rely on the provisions of data protection legislation.[62]

[60] For an alternative approach to 'piggy back' claims see M Malone, 'The Concept of Indirect Discrimination by Association: Too Late for the UK? (2017) 46 *Industrial Law Journal* 144, section 11.

[61] Defined as the relevant prohibition on victimisation against employees or holders of public or private office, as the case may be.

[62] Originally the Data Protection Act 1998, more recently the Data Protection Act 2018 and the General Data Protection Regulation.

EHRC, *Equal pay for equal work: what the law says*[63]

Confidentiality and the principle of transparency

The principle of transparency doesn't mean that someone has the automatic right to know what someone else earns. It means that employees have the right to know how the calculations are made …

There needs to be a balance between the ideal of transparency and the rights of individual privacy. A woman cannot require an employer to disclose confidential information, unless she asks for an order from the employment tribunal and the tribunal orders the employer to do so.

A woman can write to her employer to request key information. In many cases an employer will be able to answer detailed questions in general terms, while still preserving the anonymity and confidentiality of other employees.

The Data Protection Act 1998 and the General Data Protection Regulations 2018

Although much of the information a woman may request won't be confidential, some of it might be. For example, the exact details of a comparator's pay package.

Pay records will usually include personal data covered by the Data Protection Act and General Data Protection Regulations, which can only be disclosed in accordance with data protection principles. Other personal information, such as ethnic origin and medical details, are also subject to particular safeguards.

The disclosure of confidential information in the employment context is also protected by the implied duty of trust and confidence owed by an employer to an employee …

The EqA also imposes duties on larger employers to publish information on the gender pay gaps within their organisations (s78 EqA). While this obligation has proven useful in raising women's awareness of the general pay gaps within their workplaces, and led to high-profile claims against the BBC, and indirectly into the EHRC's formal investigation into that organisations pay practices,[64] the information whose disclosure is required does not include that relating to identifiable individuals.

All potential equal pay claimants face difficulties in accessing information which would allow them to determine whether their claims might have reasonable prospects of success. But equal value claims pose particular difficulties for prospective claimants. A potential claimant may be able to decide, with a fair degree of certainty, that her job is the same as that done by a man. She may also be able to make an informed decision that her job and that of a man have been rated as equivalent by her employer. But she simply cannot know whether or not her job will be regarded as 'equal' to that done by a male comparator. This being the case, the only reasonable chances of success in equal pay for work of equal value cases lie with women who select as their comparators men who are paid more for jobs which are apparently much less demanding, and with women whose pay claims are organised (as in the *Enderby*, *Ratcliffe*, and *British Coal* cases, all referred to below[65]) by well-informed and well-financed unions committed to improving the wages of their women members.

[63] https://www.equalityhumanrights.com/en/advice-and-guidance/equal-pay-equal-work-what-law-says.

[64] See further Chs 3 and 5.

[65] Respectively Case C-127/92 Case C-127/92 *Enderby v Frenchay Health Authority* EU:C:1993:859, [1993] ECR I-5535, [1994] ICR 112; *Ratcliffe v North Yorkshire CC* [1995] ICR 833; and *British Coal Corp v Smith* [1994] ICR 810.

Cross-Establishment Comparisons

It is clear from the foregoing that the equal value claim is not an easy one to bring. Having said this, ss64–68 EqA are capable – at least in theory – of permitting challenge to that part of the gender-pay gap which results from occupational sex segregation (this through the equal value pay claim). But part of the gender-pay gap is associated with women's industrial and workplace segregation – that is, their concentration in predominantly female workplaces. This, by contrast, is largely outwith the scope of ss64–66 EqA which apply only in relation to differentials between men and women employed essentially by the same employer. Under the EqA, the successful claimant's comparator must (as we saw above) be engaged in 'like work', 'work rated as equivalent' or 'work of equal value' to that done by the equal pay claimant. Section 79 EqA further provides that comparators must be employed 'by A's employer or by an associate of A's employer' where A is employed, and must work at the same establishment as her, or at an establishment at which 'common terms apply … (either generally or as between A and B)'. Section 79(9) provides that 'employers are associated if (a) one is a company of which the other (directly or indirectly) has control, or (b) both are companies of which a third person (directly or indirectly) has control'. In the case of a claimant who holds personal or public office, the comparator must also hold a personal or public office and the same person must be responsible for paying A and B.

The HL and, more recently, the Supreme Court (SC), have adopted a consistently generous approach to the question whether 'common terms' apply between establishments, but the fact that there have been so many decisions of the highest courts on this issue is testament to the numerous difficulties that equal pay litigants face. The first significant case on the question was *Leverton v Clwyd CC*, which involved a nursery nurse whose comparators occupied a variety of posts the terms of which were, like hers, determined by a collective agreement covering local authority administrative, professional, technical and clerical staff. All were employed by the council, but they worked in a variety of establishments. They argued that the claimant was not in the 'same employment' as her comparators (the test established by the EqA was whether 'common terms and conditions of employment [we] re observed either generally or for employees of the relevant classes.' This argument won favour with the CA, which ruled, somewhat bizarrely, that the 'common terms' provision assisted only those claimants who were employed on the same terms and conditions as their comparators (1989] AC 706). (Such women would, of course, have little need of an equal pay claim.) The HL allowed the claimant's appeal, ruling ([1989] 1 AC 706, *per* Lord Bridge) that 'Terms and conditions of employment governed by the same collective agreement … represent the paradigm, though not necessarily the only example, of the common terms and conditions of employment contemplated by the subsection.' His Lordship went on to declare his rejection of a construction of s.1(6) EqPA which 'frustrates rather than serves the manifest purpose of the legislation … it cannot, in my opinion, possibly have been the intention of Parliament to require a woman claiming equality with a man in another establishment to prove an undefined substratum of similarity between the particular terms of her contract and his as the basis of her entitlement to eliminate any discriminatory differences between those terms.'

Notwithstanding the strong terms adopted by the HL in *Leverton* the CA once again adopted a very narrow approach to s1(6) in *British Coal Corp v Smith* [1994] ICR 810, requiring that the woman and her comparator(s) were employed in establishments in which the prevailing terms and conditions were, not merely 'broadly similar' or 'essentially similar' but were (exactly) 'the same'. The HL ([1996] ICR 515) once again overruled, adopting a purposive approach and characterised the CA's demand for identical terms and conditions as 'far too restrictive' (*per* Lord Slynn).

More recently, the SC rejected the argument put for employers that cross-establishment comparisons could not be made under the predecessor provision of s79 EqA unless there was at least a possibility that the male comparator might actually be transferred to the claimants' place of work.

***North v Dumfries and Galloway Council* [2013] UKSC 45 [2013] 4 All ER 413**

The claim was brought by female classroom and other assistants and nursery nurses who were employed by the Council under the Administrative, Professional, Technical and Clerical national collective agreement and the Blue Book supplement to it. They sought to compare themselves with manual workers employed elsewhere by the authority as groundsmen, refuse collectors, refuse drivers and leisure attendants under the Scottish Council for Local Authorities' Services (Manual Workers) Schemes of Pay and Conditions of Service, a collective agreement referred to as the Green Book.[66] One significant difference in pay between the Blue and Green Books concerned bonuses; whereas the male comparators were entitled to substantial bonus payments or supplements in addition to their basic pay, the women were not.

The EAT ruled that the women and their comparators were not employed under common terms so as to permit the women to rely on the men as comparators because it did not accept that there was a real possibility that groundsmen, refuse collectors, refuse drivers or leisure attendants would in practice have been employed at schools or nurseries. The Court of Session refused the women's appeal, but the SC unanimously disagreed and restored the finding of the employment tribunal that the claimants could seek to rely on the men as their comparators.

Lady Hale (for the Court):

> 12. The principles to be derived from [*Leverton* and *British Coal*] are … plain. First, the 'common terms and conditions' referred to … are not those of, on the one hand, the women applicants and, on the other hand, their claimed comparators. They are, on the one hand, the terms and conditions under which the male comparators are employed at different establishments from the women and, on the other hand, the terms and conditions under which those male comparators are or would be employed if they were employed at the same establishment as the women. Second, by 'common terms and conditions' the subsection is not looking for complete correspondence between what those terms are, or would be, in the woman's place of work. It is enough that they are, or would be, broadly similar.
>
> 13. It is also plain from the reasoning of both Lord Bridge in *Leverton*'s case … and Lord Slynn in the *British Coal Corp* case … that it is no answer to say that no such male comparators ever would be employed, on those or any other terms, at the same establishment as the women. Otherwise, it would be far too easy for an employer so to arrange things that only men worked in one place and only women in another. This point is of particular importance, now that women are entitled to claim equality with men who are doing completely different jobs, provided that the women are doing jobs of equal value. Those completely different jobs may well be done in completely different places from the jobs which the women are doing …

[66] See further C McLaughlin, 'Equal Pay, Litigation and Reflexive Regulation: the Case of the UK Local Authority Sector (2014) 43 *Industrial Law Journal* 1.

30. Not surprisingly, Ms Dinah Rose QC, on behalf of the appellant claimants, argues that the tribunal should not speculate about the adjustments to the comparators' present terms and conditions which might be made in the unlikely event that they were transferred to the claimants' workplace. The hypothesis is that the comparators are transferred *to do their present jobs* in a different location. The question is whether in that event, however unlikely, they would remain employed on the same or broadly similar terms and conditions to those applicable in their current place of work. As Lord Slynn had recognised in *British Coal Corp v Smith* ... the object of the legislation was to allow comparisons to be made between workers who did not and never would work in the same workplace. An example might be a manufacturing company, where the (female) clerical workers worked in an office block, whereas the (male) manufacturers worked in a factory ...

33. I have no hesitation in preferring the arguments presented by Ms Rose. In the first place, it is by no means clear from the facts reported in the *British Coal Corp* case that all the women claimants were based in collieries where there might also be surface mineworkers employed. In the second place, there is no hint of a 'real possibility' or 'feasibility' test in that case and I find it difficult to discern a genuine difference in principle between them. Both add an unwarranted gloss to the wording of the subsection as interpreted in the *British Coal Corp* case.

34. In the third place, to adopt such a test would be to defeat the object of the exercise. This is not just a matter of preventing employers from so organising their workplaces that the women work in one place and the men in another. There may be perfectly good reasons for organising the work into different places. But the object of the legislation is to secure equality of treatment, not only for the same work, but also for work rated as equivalent or assessed by the experts to be of equal value. It stands to reason, therefore, that some very different jobs which are not or cannot be carried out in the same workplaces may nevertheless be rated as equivalent or assessed as having equal value. One example is the (female) office worker who needs office equipment in a clean environment and the (male) factory worker who needs machines which create dirt and dust. But another is the (female) factory worker who puts microscopic circuits on silicon chips in one factory and the (male) factory worker who assembles computer parts in another. The fact that of necessity their work has to be carried on in different places is no barrier to equalising the terms on which it is done. It is well known that those jobs which require physical strength have traditionally been better rewarded than those jobs which require dexterity. It is one of the objects of the equality legislation to iron out those traditional inequalities of reward where the work involved is of genuinely equal value.

35. In the fourth place, it is not the function of the 'same employment' test to establish comparability between the jobs done. That comparability is established by the 'like work', 'work rated as equivalent' and 'work of equal value' tests. Furthermore, the effect of the deemed equality clause is to modify the relevant term of the woman's contract so as not to be less favourable than a term of a similar kind in the contract under which the man is employed or to include a beneficial term in her contract if she has none ... That modification is clearly capable of taking account of differences in the working hours or holiday entitlement in calculating what would be equally favourable treatment for them both. Moreover, the equality clause does not operate if a difference in treatment is genuinely due to a material factor other than sex ... The 'same employment' test should not be used as a proxy for those tests or as a way of avoiding the often difficult and complex issues which they raise (tempting though this may be for large employers faced with multiple claims such as these). Its function is to establish the terms and conditions with which the comparison is to be made. The object is simply to weed out those cases in which geography plays a significant part in determining what those terms and conditions are.

36. In the fifth place, the construction of s 1(6) favoured by the appellants is more consistent with the requirements of European Union law than is the construction favoured by the respondents ...

42. I would therefore allow this appeal and restore the decision of the employment tribunal ...

In *Asda Stores Ltd v Brierley* the CA considered the first collective private sector equal pay claim which was brought by 30,000 claimants working in supermarkets who sought to compare themselves with male employees employed at depots. Both the tribunal and the EAT accepted that such a comparison was possible, whereupon Asda unsuccessfully appealed.

***Asda Stores Ltd v Brierley (No 3)* [2019] EWCA Civ 44, [2019] ICR 1118**

Underhill LJ (for the Court):

> 23. As a matter of domestic law, the claimants acknowledge that they do not work in the same establishments as any of their comparators, because Asda's stores and its depots are entirely separate; but they claim that common terms of employment apply at both, either generally or as between themselves and their comparators, so that they can rely on s 79(4)(c) of the 2010 Act …
>
> 35. Th[e] ratio [in *Leverton*] involves the explicit rejection of the approach taken by the majority in the IT[67] and this Court, which had involved considering the degree of similarity or otherwise between the terms of the applicant and the comparator(s): see, most explicitly Lord Bridge's statement that Parliament did not intend that a woman 'should have to prove an undefined substratum of similarity between the particular terms of her contract and [her comparator's]'. Although this approach should therefore be dead, the history of the present case shows that it is not willing to lie down.
>
> 36. It also follows from the correct approach that it is not necessary that any employees in the comparator's class should actually be employed in the claimant's establishment …
>
> 41. In my view the ratio of *Smith* is, and is only, that in considering whether common terms and conditions are observed as between employees in the comparator's class at two establishments – that is, the claimant's establishment and the comparator's – it is not necessary that all the terms are common: 'broad commonality' is enough· Nothing else was in issue …
>
> 53. In his oral submissions Mr Jeans submitted that '[for Asda that] … Lady Hale [in *North*] only understood comparability to be possible where an employer agrees to collective agreements applying across its workforce' and 'is not operating separate businesses in separate locations'. That was important because Asda's retail and distribution operations were in substance different businesses, with wholly different origins and locations …. I do not believe that Lady Hale meant any such thing … It is in fact clear … that she envisaged cross-establishment comparisons being possible between very different kinds of operation of the same employer …

The Court also rejected Asda's argument that the change in wording between s1(6) EqPA and s79(4)(c) EqA (that is, from 'establishments … at which common terms and conditions of employment are observed either generally or *for employees of the relevant classes*' to 'common terms apply at the establishments (either generally or *as between A and B*)') had the effect of overturning the decision of the HL in *Leverton*. Underhill LJ conceded, for the Court, that this might be the most natural reading of the provision but expressed confidence that this had not been what the legislature intended and that the suggestion that the terms applicable to claimant and comparator had to be similar to allow comparison under s79(4)(c)

[67] Industrial tribunal, the predecessor to the employment tribunal.

EqA was the result of a drafting error which could be overcome by an 'amending construction' even without falling back on a *Marleasing* approach.[68]

Cross-Employer Comparisons

Section 79 EqA clearly allows cross-establishment comparisons, but it requires, as did its predecessor provision, that comparators must be employed by the same employer as the claimant, or by an 'associated employer'. An employer is only 'associated' with another for the purposes of s79 EqA if both are companies one of which controls the other, or both of which are controlled by a third party. The narrowness of this approach became particularly evident in the context of contracting out by which discrete functions of public and private employers are 'hived-off' to contractors. The contracting-out process became increasingly common in the public sector during the 1980s when it was driven by 'compulsory competitive tendering' (CCT), which required local authorities to put cleaning, waste disposal, catering and other functions out to tender at regular intervals, and allowed them to retain these functions only where they were won, in competition, by direct services organisations (DSOs) which had to be financially separate from the local authority and run as commercial enterprises.[69]

CCT brought huge deterioration in the terms and conditions of the workers, in particular the women workers, affected by it. Part of that deterioration resulted from the failure of the Transfer of Undertakings (TUPE) Regulations 1981 adequately to give effect to the Acquired Rights Directive – the Regulations originally excluded 'non-commercial' undertakings, such as most public authority functions, from their protection. The consequence of this was that most contractors competing for public functions did so on the basis of radically reduced labour costs. In many cases low-paid workers were brought into the authority from outside. In others, workers were made redundant and re-employed by the private contractors at reduced wages. The reduced working conditions were felt particularly by women workers whose wages had been protected by collective bargaining in the public sector, and had been pegged considerably higher (often as a result of job evaluation) than the rates prevalent in the private sector.

Even where workers managed to retain their jobs, they did so frequently because DSOs, in preparing 'in house' bids, slashed labour costs in order to compete with the market. One example of this resulted in *Ratcliffe v North Yorkshire CC* [1995] ICR 833 (HL). For current purposes the point of interest is that, prior to the CCT exercise, the claimants' jobs had been rated as equivalent in value to those done by their comparators. But, whereas the 'dinner ladies' DSO had to reduce labour costs by 25 per cent in order to compete with outside tenders, the DSOs employing their comparators did not. According to the tribunal:

> It was clear to [the DSO manager] that he had to have regard to the market forces and, in particular, that because of low pay in the catering industry in general, and particularly in those areas where women were exclusively employed, he could not afford to continue to engage staff on [National Joint Council] terms, conditions and pay …
>
> … [the DSO manager] … perceived that it was necessary to [reduce those terms from the NJC terms] in order to be able to compete in the open market, that is to say due to his perception

[68] In Case C-106/89 *Marleasing MSA v La Comercial Internacional de Alimentacion SA*, EU:C:1990:395, [1990] ECR I-4135 the CJEU imposed onerous duties of interpretation on national courts where required to give effect to relevant EU directives.

[69] CCT is further discussed in Ch 3.

> of market forces in a market which is virtually exclusively female doing work which is convenient to that female workforce and which, but for the particular hours and times of work, that workforce would not be able to do … It was clear to [him] that it was a workforce that would, by and large, continue to do the work, even at a reduced rate of pay, when the alternative was no work or ceasing to have the advantages of remaining a county council employee and becoming an employee of a commercial catering organisation doing the same work for less favourable terms in any event.
>
> It is clear that both the DSO and the employees were over the proverbial 'barrel' due to the fact that competitors only employed women and, because of that, employed them on less favourable terms than the council did previously under the NJC agreement.

In *Ratcliffe v North Yorkshire CC* [1995] ICR 833 the women eventually won their equal pay claim. The issue of the MFD, with which that case was primarily concerned, is discussed below. But the claim succeeded only because the claimants were, in fact, employed by the DSO which, like their comparators' DSO, was still part of the local authority. By contrast, women whose terms and conditions suffered when their jobs were contracted out (as many were), would be able to use, as comparators, only those men employed by the same contractor. This would remain the case even (see *Lawrence v Regent Office Care*, extracted below) where they continued to do precisely the same job in the same workplace as their former colleagues, with whose jobs theirs had (prior to contracting-out) been rated as equivalent.

The TUPE Regulations were amended in 1995 to apply to local authority contracting-out. By this stage a lot of the damage had been done to the wage levels in public-sector-related predominantly female jobs. Even where workers are transferred under TUPE, there is nothing to prevent their terms and conditions from falling behind those which apply in respect of former comparators' jobs which have remained in the public sector. And while CCT came to an end in 1997, local authorities and other public bodies were thereafter obliged to achieve 'Best Value' in all their services.[70] The formal requirement to tender at particular intervals has been replaced with a rolling obligation to assess whether services could be better performed other than by the authority itself. Women have continued to shoulder the burden of cost-cutting imposed on local authorities by decades of under-funding by central government.

It is clear that the EqA does not permit cross-employer comparisons save between 'associated employers', this concept being very narrowly defined. But it was not clear that Article 157 TFEU or its predecessor provisions adopted so narrow an approach. In Case C-43/75 *Defrenne v Sabena (No 2)* [1976] ECR 455, [1976] ICR 547 the CJEU ruled that Article 157 requires equal pay 'for equal work which is carried out in the same establishment or service, whether private or public.' In *Scullard v Knowles*, the EAT accepted that the approach required under EU law (then Art 119 Treaty of Rome now Article 157 TFEU) was wider than that set out under the EqPA.[71] There, a unit manager employed by a Regional Advisory Council sought to name, as her comparators, male unit managers employed by other such bodies, all of which were independent and of the Secretary of State for Employment, but funded by the Department of Employment.

[70] The 2003 Code of Practice on Workforce Matters in Local Authority Service Contracts, which was intended to safeguard the interests of contracted-out workers, was repealed in 2011. See further Ch 5.

[71] See also *Hasley v Fair Employment Agency* [1989] IRLR 106 (NICA).

***Scullard v Knowles & Southern Regional Council for Education & Training* [1996] ICR 399**

Mummery J:

> 10 .... s 1(6) [EqPA] ... excludes, for example, employees of different employers who, though not companies, are all under the direct or indirect control of a third party and have common terms and conditions of employment. The crucial point is that the class of comparators defined in s.1(6) is more restricted than that available on the application of Article [157 TFEU], as interpreted by the European Court of Justice. Article [157] is not, for example, confined to employment in undertakings which have a particular legal form, such as a limited company ...
>
> 13. In *Defrenne* no distinction is drawn between work carried out in the same establishment or service of limited companies and of other employers, whether incorporated or not ...
>
> 18 .... (4) The crucial question for the purposes of Article [157] is, therefore, whether Mrs Scullard and the male unit managers of the other councils were employed 'in the same establishment or service.' The tribunal did not ask or answer that question. To the extent that that is a wider class of comparators than is contained in s 1(6) of the [EqPA], s 1(6), which is confined to 'associated employers,' is displaced and must yield to the paramount force of Article [157] ...

Scullard went some way towards addressing the shortcomings of s1(6) EqPA. But the gaping hole in the protection offered by that Act was exposed in *Lawrence v Regent Office Care.*

Case C-320/00 *Lawrence v Regent Office Care*, EU:C:2002:498, [2002] ECR I-7325, [2013] ICR 1092

The case was brought by 'dinner ladies' who had, like the claimants in *Ratcliffe*, been employed by North Yorkshire CC. During the course of the *Ratcliffe* litigation the council lost some tenders for school meal provision to the private sector. The women in the *Lawrence* case were among those whose jobs were transferred into the private sector. Some were transferred on the understanding that TUPE applied, others on the assumption that it did not. Nevertheless (and this is testament to the ineffective nature of TUPE), all women ended up working on less favourable terms and conditions than had applied during their employment by the council. They sought to rely on Article 157 to compare themselves with men still employed by the council whose jobs had, pre-contracting out, been rated as equivalent to those of the claimants. Their claims were dismissed both by the tribunal and by EAT following which the CA, referred the following question to the CJEU:

> 1. Is Article [157] directly applicable in the circumstances of this case ... [such] that it can be relied upon by the applicants in national proceedings to enable them to compare their pay with that of men in the employment of the North Yorkshire CC who are performing work of equal value to that done by the applicants?

The decision of the CJEU was as follows:

> 17. There is ... nothing in the wording of Article [157 TFEU] to suggest that the applicability of that provision is limited to situations in which men and women work for the same employer. The Court has held that the principle established by that article may be invoked before national courts, in particular in cases of discrimination arising directly from legislative provisions or

collective labour agreements, as well as in cases in which work is carried out in the same establishment or service, whether private or public …

18. However, where, as in the main proceedings here, the differences identified in the pay conditions of workers performing equal work or work of equal value cannot be attributed to a single source, there is no body which is responsible for the inequality and which could restore equal treatment. Such a situation does not come within the scope of Article [157 TFEU]. The work and the pay of those workers cannot therefore be compared on the basis of that provision.

19. In view of all of the foregoing, the answer to the first question must be that a situation such as that in the main proceedings, in which the differences identified in the pay conditions of workers of different sex performing equal work or work of equal value cannot be attributed to a single source, does not come within the scope of Article [157 TFEU].

Shortly before the decision of the CJEU in *Lawrence* the Scottish Court of Session had reached what was described in the IRLR commentary as a 'remarkable decision' in *South Ayrshire Council v Morton* [2002] IRLR 256 (see also p 361 above). The claimant was a female headteacher who was employed by a local education authority in Scotland. The Court of Session ruled that she could choose as her comparator a male headteacher employed by a different Scottish education authority. According to the Court, the use by the CJEU in Case C-43/75 *Defrenne v Sabena (No 2)* [1976] ECR 455, [1976] ICR 547 of the term 'same establishment or service' was merely a description of specific examples of cases which fell within Article 157 TFEU and was not to be taken as requiring, for an Article 157 claim to be made out, that the claimant's comparator be in the same 'service'.[72] In the instant case the Court took the view that pay was determined under statutory authority and overall governmental control, and that this amounted to the type of national collective agreement contemplated by the CJEU in *Defrenne (No 2)* when it ruled that 'among the forms of direct discrimination which may be identified solely by reference to the criteria laid down by Article [157] must be included in particular those which have their origin in legislative provisions or in collective labour agreements and which may be detected on the basis of a purely legal analysis of the situation.'

As noted above, the decision in *Morton* was delivered shortly before that of the CJEU in *Lawrence*. It is not clear that it would have been any different had it followed, rather than preceded, the CJEU's judgment. The salary scales of primary and secondary school teachers in Scotland were set at the relevant time by the Scottish Joint Negotiating Committee, which was a quasi-autonomous body set up by the Education (Scotland) Act under the general control of the Secretary of State. The Act provided that individual education authorities were obliged to implement the SJNC settlement and that its terms were incorporated into every teacher's contract of employment. Each education authority had autonomy over the employment terms of its own employees and the way in which salary scales were implemented in relation to individual employees, but the Court of Session noted the tribunal's finding that 'in reality there is very little scope for individual local authorities to vary, either by increasing or decreasing, an individual teacher's salary. In effect, councils are regulated by what is known as the "Yellow Book" and any attempt to depart from the terms of that scheme of terms and conditions is likely to be subject to judicial review.'

[72] The case concerned Art 119 Treaty of Rome but Art 157 is in materially identical terms.

The emphasis of the CJEU on a 'single source' gave rise to a number of cases in the UK in which employers sought to avoid equal pay claims by arguing that the devolution of decision-making over pay even *within* a single employer had the effect that no 'single source' was responsible for the pay of claimants and their comparators. In *Robertson v DEFRA* [2005] ICR 750, the CA ruled that the claimants, male civil servants in DEFRA, could not compare their pay with that of women civil servants in other government departments whose jobs had been rated as equivalent under a JES. The CA ruled that, responsibility for pay bargaining for civil servants having been delegated from the Treasury to individual government departments, they would not be regarded as being in the 'same employment' by reason of being employed by the Crown unless their pay and conditions could be attributed to a single common source. The Court did not accept that the Treasury, which retained overall budgetary control, had sufficient control over civil servants' pay to be regarded as a single source.

The same approach was indicated by the CA in *Armstrong v Newcastle upon Tyne NHS Hospital Trust* [2005] EWCA Civ 1608, [2006] IRLR 124, in which female domestic ancillary workers sought to compare themselves with male ancillary workers employed by the same NHS Trust. Pay for the two groups had evolved differently as a result of the women's jobs having been subject to CCT when the men's were not, the women's jobs later being taken in-house but at the cost to them of bonus payments which the male comparators had continued to enjoy. There was then a period during which the men and women had been employed by different Trusts that had been created from a single health authority, the Trusts subsequently being merged as the Newcastle upon Tyne NHS Hospital Trust. The EAT had ruled, following *Robertson*, that the hospital Trust had not been responsible for setting the terms of both groups of employees despite having taken some part in the negotiation of terms and conditions at departmental level and despite there being some evidence of the harmonisation of terms and conditions. The CA approved of this though it did not make a formal ruling to this effect, determining the case on the MFD (see p 374 below).

In *North v Dumfries and Galloway Council*, discussed at pp 365–466 above, the SC cast doubt on this line of authority. Lady Hale having pointed out at §40 that 'researches of counsel have discovered no case in the Court of Justice in which the principle of equal pay has not been applied between men and women who work for the same employer', she referred to *Robertson*, and noted the position taken by the EHRC that the decision was wrong 'because it did lie within the power of the Crown to put matters right.' Her Ladyship stated at §41 that 'It is not necessary for us to determine that question now. In this case it is quite clear that the difference in treatment between the claimants and their comparators is attributable to a single source, namely the local authority which employs them and which is in a position to put right the discrepancy if required to do so.'

In *Asda Stores Ltd v Brierley*, also discussed at p 367 above, the CA also considered the 'single source' question.

***Asda Stores Ltd v Brierley (No 3)* [2019] EWCA Civ 44, [2019] ICR 1118**

Underhill LJ (for the Court):

> 59. … *North* is in my view binding authority that the fact that claimant and comparator have the same employer will in the ordinary case mean that the terms have a single source and thus that EU law permits comparison between them for equal pay purposes …

60. It is convenient at this stage to deal with Asda's second ground of appeal before us, which is that 'single source' is not a sufficient basis for comparison. Mr Jeans submitted that the parameters for comparison since *Defrenne* had been that the relevant employees should be 'in the same establishment or service'. He emphasised the centrality of the concept of the establishment across many fields of EU employment law and referred us to authority showing that it typically refers to a particular workplace … He was constrained to acknowledge that the phrase 'or service' might widen the scope of permitted comparison to some extent; but he said that it did not go so far as to cover all employees of the same employer. The issue in *Lawrence* itself was whether the claimants could pursue a comparison with employees of a different employer: what it established was that identity of employer was a necessary criterion, but it was not concerned with whether it was sufficient. He accepted that some domestic authorities had appeared to understand it that way, but he argued that they were wrong and not binding on us. …

61. I do not believe that this ground of appeal can succeed in the light of *North*. The Supreme Court decided, as part of its ratio, that on the facts of the case before it identity of employer was as a matter of EU law a sufficient basis for comparison. Those facts are essentially typical; although Lady Hale left open the possibility that there might be cases where the employer was not the 'source' of all its employees' terms that could only be on the basis of exceptional facts of some kind …

80. … I believe that as a matter of EU law comparison should ordinarily be possible between establishments of the same employer, and a construction of s79(4)(c) which inhibits such comparison should be avoided if possible …

107. I reach th[e] conclusion [about the application of s79 EqA] … without seeking any support from EU law. I am, however, prepared to say that I believe that the claimants' and the comparators' terms did in fact have a single source, within the meaning of *Lawrence*, because they were set by the same employer, which had the power to equalise them. It follows that it would be a breach of EU law if a comparison between them were not permissible; and, like the Supreme Court in *North*, I regard that as an additional reason for upholding the ET's finding that the cross-establishment comparisons on which the claimants rely are permitted by s 79(4)(c) …

108. The case advanced by Asda in the ET was that there were different 'sources' for retail and distribution terms because they were arrived at by wholly different processes within Asda, reflecting the complete managerial separation between its retail and distribution operations. Retail pay was set by a committee of Asda's board, and distribution pay by 'depot management', principally (though, as we have seen, not wholly) through collective bargaining. No doubt formally the ultimate responsibility lay with the Asda board and/or Wal-Mart, who inevitably exercised budgetary oversight; but they were not the effective decision-makers as regards actual terms. As regards Distribution in particular Mr Stansfield gave evidence of the high degree of autonomy he enjoyed. Asda's case was that its effective delegation of responsibility to different internal structures was analogous to the delegation by the Crown of responsibility for pay to the different government departments, which was held in *Robertson* to preclude inter-departmental comparison.

109. That case was rejected by the employment judge, who held, at para 190 of his reasons:

> 'The Executive Board of Asda and the members or subcommittees of that Board had and exercised budgetary control and oversight over both distribution and retail at all material times. The Executive Board was responsible for the differences in pay and could, or could subject to the overarching control of Wal-Mart, have introduced equality.'

He observed (at para 184) that the devolution of responsibility in *Robertson* was wholly different from the delegation of responsibility within a company or corporate structure.

110. Kerr J in the EAT ([2017] IRLR 1058) upheld that reasoning. I quote paras 56–59 of his judgment in full:

'56. For all the intensity of Asda's attack on the judge's reasoning and conclusions, far from considering them perverse I find them unassailable. This was an ordinary case of a large organisation delegating the setting of pay to separate internal organs …

57. In my judgment, [*Robertson*], if as I assume it is correctly decided, was wholly exceptional and turned on the unique position within the civil service, where the setting of pay and most other terms of civil servants on a departmental not national basis, was enshrined in statutory and other instruments that would have to be expressly revoked if the power was to be reclaimed by the Treasury and exercised centrally.

58. Here, by contrast, Asda or Wal-Mart could interfere at the stroke of a pen or, more likely, the click of a mouse. The Industrial Relations Board ("IRB") included senior employees including the Asda's CEO, with an interest in pay across both retail and distribution staff. Moreover, the IRB received regular updates on distribution staff pay negotiations, while retail pay was signed off by the executive board.

59. It would be unjust and little short of absurd if the presence of a single source turned on whether Asda's or Wal-Mart's board happened to have overruled Mr Stansfield, or the CEO or the board happened to have overruled Ms Tatum. It was quite enough to justify the judge's conclusion that the evidence showed that they regularly scrutinised the work done to set pay in, respectively, retail and distribution, and could overrule their decisions at any time.'

111. I agree entirely with that passage, save only that I doubt whether it was necessary even to show that the Asda or Wal-Mart boards 'regularly scrutinised' the relevant pay: it should in my view be enough that the board as a matter of ordinary company law had the power to set or change the terms. I agree that *Robertson* turns on its particular facts (by which I mean what I say – it is not a euphemism for saying that I think it is wrongly decided.) …

The Material Factor Defence

Section 69 EqA, Defence of material factor

(1) The sex equality clause in A's terms has no effect in relation to a difference between A's terms and B's terms if the responsible person shows that the difference is because of a material factor reliance on which—

(a) does not involve treating A less favourably because of A's sex than the responsible person treats B, and

(b) if the factor is within subsection (2), is a proportionate means of achieving a legitimate aim.

(2) A factor is within this subsection if A shows that, as a result of the factor, A and persons of the same sex doing work equal to A's are put at a particular disadvantage when compared with persons of the opposite sex doing work equal to A's.

(3) For the purposes of subsection (1), the long-term objective of reducing inequality between men's and women's terms of work is always to be regarded as a legitimate aim …

(6) For the purposes of this section, a factor is not material unless it is a material difference between A's case and B's.

As Lord Nicholls put it in *Glasgow CC v Marshall* [2000] ICR 196 (albeit discussing the predecessor provision of s69: s1(3) EqPA), 'The scheme of the Act is that a rebuttable presumption of sex discrimination arises once the gender based comparison shows that a woman, doing like work or work rated as equivalent or work of equal value to that of a man, is being paid or treated less favourably than the man.'[73]

As is clear from s69 EqA, the burden is on the employer to establish that the factors upon which it seeks to rely in fact caused the pay differential under challenge. In addition, the employer must establish that the factor is 'material'; that is (*Rainey v Greater Glasgow Health Board* [1987] AC 224) significant and relevant. An illustration of the former is provided by the case below.

***BMC Software Ltd v Shaikh* [2019] EWCA Civ 267, [2019] IRLR 653**

The claimant challenged a pay disparity with two male comparators with whom she was engaged in like work. The employer sought to rely under s69 EqA on the fact that one comparator had been promoted and received a pay rise of £5,000, though there was no record of the process of the promotion or of why the comparator had received the pay increase seven months after it, no evidence that the promotion was the effective cause of the increase, and no evidence to show why the comparator was paid more than the claimant for a job which other evidence suggested was of a lower grade than hers. The employer claimed that it had had to pay the other comparator a higher salary in order to recruit him, but did not provide any evidence of the recruitment process. The employer also sought to rely on 'merit adjustments', but again provided no evidence as to merit it had awarded in any particular case, why the increase was initiated, by whom, when, or how it was considered. The tribunal concluded in relation to each factor that BMC had not discharged the burden under s 69(1) EqA of proving the defence and allowed the claim. The EAT (HHJ Hand) having allowed BMC's appeal on the basis that the tribunal's reasons had been inadequate, the CA upheld the claimant's appeal.

Underhill LJ (for the Court):

> 17. … The common theme is that as regards each of the three factors BMC had not advanced any particularised explanation of the factor relied upon, let alone any evidence specifically supporting such an explanation, and had relied on a general assertion; the Tribunal did not believe that that was good enough. In each case it identifies with specificity the lacunae in the evidence …
>
> 18. Judge Hand's concerns seem to have focused in particular on whether the Tribunal was making a finding that BMC's explanations for the differentials complained of were not 'genuine'. That is a slippery term, but it was certainly not necessary, if this is what he meant, for the Tribunal to make a finding that the explanation was a deliberate sham, or otherwise disingenuous: see my judgment in *Bury Metropolitan Borough Council v Hamilton* … [2011] ICR 655,

[73] A factor relied upon by the employer under s69 EqA must be 'significant and relevant' but there is no requirement for the employer to *justify* reliance upon it (as distinct from *proving*) such reliance, unless the factor is indirectly discriminatory: see *Strathclyde RC v Wallace* [1998] ICR 205; *Glasgow CC v Marshall* [2000] ICR 196. In *Tyldesley v TML Plastics*, the EAT ruled that 'a difference in pay explained by a factor not itself a factor of sex, or tainted by sex discrimination, should, in principle, constitute a valid defence' to an equal pay claim. There, the employer had appointed the claimant's comparator at a higher wage on the mistaken view that he was in possession of a particular qualification. A tribunal had ruled in the claimant's favour on the basis, inter alia, that 'the employer had not established a good and objectively justified ground' for the pay differential. The EAT allowed the employer's appeal, ruling that (per Mummery J) the tribunal had 'erred in law in requiring the employer to satisfy a test of objective justification'.

at para 18. It was sufficient for it to decide, as it did, that BMC had not proved that the differentials complained of were due to any of the three pleaded factors; and of course to explain, as it did, the defects in the explanations and evidence advanced that led to that decision … It is important not to overlook, as Judge Hand arguably comes close to doing, that the burden is on the employer to prove (by sufficiently cogent and particularised evidence) that the factor relied on explains the difference in pay complained of.

19. … If an employer is going to seek to justify a pay disparity based on a factor such as the comparator's promotion or superior 'merit' or 'market forces' it needs to be able to explain with particularity what those factors mean and how they were assessed and how they apply in the circumstances of the case. It is evident from the Tribunal's findings that BMC was simply unable to do that, because of its chaotic and wholly non-transparent 'employment systems'. The equal pay risks in having non-transparent pay systems is a commonplace of equal pay law.

The MFD failed because the employer failed to satisfy the tribunal that the factors upon which it relied were in fact caused the pay differentials.

Section 69 EqA makes it clear that a factor will not found an MFD if it is directly or indirectly discriminatory. Directly discriminatory pay-related factors are relatively unusual now but were not so in the early days of the EqA, separate male and female pay structures having been commonplace before the implementation of the Act. In *Snoxell v Vauxhall Motors Ltd* [1978] QB 11, for example, the EAT ruled that the employer could not rely on the fact that comparators' salaries had been red circled when the previously female and male grades had been assimilated into a new unisex pay structure (women not having been eligible for appointment to the grade in respect of which the men's wages were red-circled): 'To allow such an answer would, we think, be contrary to the spirit and intent of the [EqPA], construed and interpreted in the manner we have already explained. It is true that the original discrimination occurred before 29 December 1975, and accordingly was not then unlawful; nonetheless it cannot have been the intention of the [EqPA] to permit the perpetuation of the effects of earlier discrimination'.[74]

Direct discrimination also defeated the MFD in *Ratcliffe v North Yorkshire CC* [1995] ICR 833, the facts of which have been mentioned above. The tribunal had found that the wages of dinner ladies (including the claimant) had been driven downwards during CCT by the 'general perception in the United Kingdom, and certainly in North Yorkshire, that a woman should stay at home to look after the children and if she wants to work it must fit in with that domestic duty and a lack of facilities to enable her, easily, to do otherwise.' Lord Slynn, who delivered the sole judgment, concluded that the fact that the employers 'paid women less than their male comparators because they were women constitutes direct discrimination and *ex hypothesi* cannot be shown to be justified on grounds "irrespective of the sex of the person" concerned'.[75]

[74] Citing, in support, the US decision in *Corning Glassworks v Brennan* (1974) 417 US 188. See *Bainbridge v Redcar and Cleveland BC* [2008] EWCA Civ 885, [2009] ICR 133 in which CA cited *Snoxell* with approval in ruling that a tribunal may have to look at the underlying reason, and not just the immediate reason, for a difference in pay.

[75] Lord Slynn's suggestion that the MFD 'must be interpreted … without bringing in the distinction between so-called 'direct' and 'indirect' discrimination' did not survive the subsequent decision of the House in *Strathclyde v Wallace*, considered below, but it did not appear to be his intention to preclude justification of an indirectly discriminatory MFD.

'Turning to indirectly discriminatory factors, s69 EqA states in terms that disparately impacting factors will found a defence only if reliance upon them is objectively justifiable. This had not immediately been apparent in relation to s69's predecessor provision, s1(3) EqPA, which provided that the GMF would apply 'if the employer proves that [a] variation is genuinely due to a material factor which is not the difference of sex'. The HL accepted in *Rainey v Greater Glasgow Health Board* [1987] AC 224 that s1(3) EqPA regulated indirect as well as direct discrimination.

The domestic courts were not always astute to recognise disparately impacting pay factors and on occasion imposed procedural hurdles on women seeking to challenge indirect discrimination in pay. One example occurred in the following case.

***Case C-127/92 Enderby v Frenchay Health Authority* EU:C:1993:859, [1993] ECR I-5535, [1994] ICR 112**

The EAT rejected an equal pay claim from a group of women senior speech therapists who sought to compare themselves with male principal grade pharmacists and clinical psychologists who were paid about 60 per cent more than them. The EAT ruled that the difference was due to the separate negotiating structures which determined the pay of the claimants and their comparators. In doing so, it rejected the argument that the employer's pay policies indirectly discriminated against the claimants because the salaries of speech therapists were artificially depressed because of the profession's predominantly female composition, while their comparators benefitted from the fact that their professions contained far greater proportions of men.

The EAT ruled that an employer would only be required to justify a factor relied upon for the GMF defence if it was shown to have imposed a barrier, requirement or condition which caused disparate impact. It did not accept that women were disadvantaged as regards entry to the professions of clinical psychologist or pharmacist and so it did not accept that there was any indirect discrimination which required justification.

The CA referred to the CJEU the question whether the employer's reliance on the separate negotiating structures which governed the pay, respectively, of the claimant and her comparators, was objectively justifiable within Article 157. The employers (and the UK Government) argued that objective justification could only be required in cases which fitted within the SDA's definition of indirect discrimination – where the claimant could point to criteria which a considerably smaller proportion of women than men could comply with and which had discriminatory effects because of the sex of the worker concerned.[76] The CJEU took a different view:

The Court:

> 13. It is normally for the person alleging facts in support of a claim to adduce proof of such facts. Thus, in principle, the burden of proving the existence of sex discrimination as to pay lies with the worker who, believing himself to be the victim of such discrimination, brings legal proceedings against his employer with a view to removing the discrimination.

[76] This, as the CA in *Enderby* pointed out, appears contrary to the dicta of Lord Bridge in *Leverton*: 'the appellant, if she could establish that she was employed on work of equal value to that of "a man in the same employment,"' would prima facie be entitled under s1(2)(c) to have the terms of her contract treated as modified as provided by the section to bring them into line with the terms of his contract.

14. However, it is clear from the case law of the Court that the onus may shift when that is necessary to avoid depriving workers who appear to be the victims of discrimination of any effective means of enforcing the principle of equal pay. Accordingly, when a measure distinguishing between employees on the basis of their hours of work has in practice an adverse impact on substantially more members of one or other sex, that measure must be regarded as contrary to the objective pursued by Article 141 of the Treaty, unless the employer shows that it is based on objectively justified factors unrelated to any discrimination on grounds of sex ... Similarly, where an undertaking applies a system of pay which is wholly lacking in transparency, it is for the employer to prove that his practice in the matter of wages is not discriminatory, if a female worker establishes, in relation to a relatively large number of employees, that the average pay for women is less than that for men [citing *Danfoss*[77]] ...

22. The fact that the rates of pay at issue are decided by collective bargaining processes conducted separately for each of the two professional groups concerned, without any discriminatory effect within each group, does not preclude a finding of prima facie discrimination where the results of those processes show that two groups with the same employer and the same trade union are treated differently. If the employer could rely on the absence of discrimination within each of the collective bargaining processes taken separately as sufficient justification for the difference in pay, he could ... easily circumvent the principle of equal pay by using separate bargaining processes.

23. Accordingly ... the fact that the respective rates of pay of two jobs of equal value, one carried out almost exclusively by women and the other predominantly by men, were arrived at by collective bargaining processes which, although carried out by the same parties, are distinct, and, taken separately, have in themselves no discriminatory effect, is not sufficient objective justification for the difference in pay between those two jobs ...

In *British Road Services Ltd v Loughran* [1997] IRLR 92 Northern Ireland's CA accepted that an *Enderby* approach applied where the claimants belonged to a group which was only 75 per cent, rather than almost exclusively, female. That Court demanded that the employer establish that the MFD[78] relied upon was non-discriminatory. And in the case below the CA accepted that a tribunal had been entitled to apply the *Enderby* approach where the claimant's group (prison service administrative staff) was 50.7 per cent female and the comparator group (prison officers, and industrial and non-industrial support staff) was predominantly male, and 51 per cent of women in the claimants' and comparator groups taken together were disadvantaged, by comparison with nine per cent of men.

***Bailey v Home Office* [2005] EWCA Civ 327, [2005] IRLR 369**

Peter Gibson LJ:

30. I can see no justification for the imposition of a high threshold for satisfying the test of prima facie discrimination. Where, as here, there is one group of employees of an employer which contains a significant number, even though not a clear majority, of female workers

[77] Case C-109/88 *Handels-og v Dansk Arbejdsgiverforening (acting for Danfoss)* [1989] ECR 3199, in which the CJEU also ruled that, where a pay system lacked transparency and resulted in lower wages for women than for men, the burden passed to the employer to disprove discrimination.

[78] At the time referred to as the GMF (genuine material factor) defence.

> whose work is evaluated as equal to that of another group of employees of the employer who are predominantly male and who receive greater pay, it would be very surprising if an ET were to be precluded by the presence in the disadvantaged group of a significant number of men from holding that that disparity in favour of men required justification by the employer. In the present case it may well be that, as the Home Office suggests, there is a genuine material factor which is not the difference of sex and which justifies that disparity. Whether there is such factor is for further determination …
>
> *Waller LJ:*
>
> 34. On the words of the subsection, if a woman can point to a job being performed by a man on a higher rate of pay, which is the same job as she is performing or its equivalent in value, the subsection seems simply to place the onus on the employer of proving that 'genuinely' there is a material factor explaining the difference which has nothing to do with the difference in sex … I have to say that I do not read the subsection at least at first blush, as imposing a two stage process in which the woman having pointed to a higher paid man has some burden of establishing a prima facie case that there is discrimination, which then imposes an evidential burden on the employer to justify the factor.
>
> 39. … s.1(3) cannot demand a high threshold for the establishment of a disparity which prima facie is due to sex. Thus where a difference in pay is established, and statistics seem to indicate a possibility of a disproportionate impact on women when looking at both the advantaged and disadvantaged groups as a whole, those statistics must provide sufficient evidence to get those carrying the burden over the hurdle of placing the onus on the employer to show that there were material factors which were not the difference in sex.[79]

In the *Bailey* case Waller LJ, with whom Sir Martin Nourse agreed, relied on the speech of Lord Nicholls in *Glasgow CC v Marshall* [2000] ICR 196 to suggest that there should be no burden on a claimant to establish that a factor had a disparate impact, s1(3) EqPA imposing the burden of disproving discrimination on the employer once a finding of unequal pay for equal work had been made. He accepted, however, that 'that route is not available', and it is clear from the authorities that, where an employer establishes that the factor upon which it seeks to rely caused the difference in pay, and is significant and relevant (material), it falls to the claimant to establish facts which indicate potential (indirect) discrimination.[80]

Many cases have concerned the point at which the burden of justification passes to the employer. The general approach was summarised by the EAT in *Bury MBC v Hamilton* [2011] ICR 655, in which caterers, cleaners, carers, school support staff and leisure centre attendants, sought to compare themselves with gardeners, road sweepers, drivers and refuse collectors. The comparators had benefited from productivity bonus payments before the introduction of 'single status', which amalgamated previously distinct pay structures, after which time transitional arrangements extended the period during which the comparators continued to receive bonus payments denied to the claimants.

[79] Sir Martin Nourse agreed with both judgments. The HL granted leave to appeal but the appeal was not pursued.

[80] *Nelson v Carillion Services Ltd* [2003] EWCA Civ 544, [2003] ICR 1256; C-427/11, *Kenny v Minister for Justice, Equality and Law Reform* EU:C:2013:122, [2013] IRLR 463.

***Bury MBC v Hamilton* UK/EAT/241/09 & EK/EAT/413/09, [2011] ICR 655**

Underhill P:

14. … (1) It is necessary first to identify the explanation for the differential complained of … The burden of proof is on the employer.

(2) It is then necessary to consider whether that explanation is 'tainted with sex'. What that not altogether happy metaphor means is that the explanation relied on must not itself involve sex discrimination, whether direct or indirect …

(3) In considering whether the explanation involves direct or indirect discrimination, the ordinary principles of the law of discrimination apply. That means that:

(a) if the differential is the result of direct discrimination (in the sense established in *Nagarajan v London Regional Transport* [2000] 1 AC 501) the defence under s.1(3) will fail;
(b) if the differential involves indirect discrimination of either the 'PCP' or '*Enderby*' type – as to this distinction, see paragraph 16 below – the defence will fail unless the employer proves that the differential is objectively justified, applying the classic proportionality test;
(c) if the employer's explanation involves neither direct nor indirect discrimination the defence will succeed, even if the factor relied on cannot be objectively justified – this is most vividly illustrated by the 'mistake' cases such as *Yorkshire Blood Transfusion Service v Plaskitt* [1994] ICR 74 and *Tyldesley v TML Plastics* [1996] ICR 356, approved in [*Strathclyde RC v*] *Wallace* [[1998] ICR 205].

(4) In conducting the exercise under (3), the ordinary principles governing the burden of proof in discrimination claims will apply. Thus if the claimant shows a prima facie case of discrimination … the burden shifts to the employer to prove the absence of discrimination.

15. … The difficulty lies in the fact that the starting point required by the [EqPA] in every case is a one-on-one comparison by a particular woman with a particular man. That comparison may indeed be at the heart of the analysis in a straightforward case of individual (typically direct) discrimination in pay. But in cases like the present, where the differential complained of is evidently the result of pay arrangements applying to groups of workers, the one-on-one comparison tells us nothing: in such cases the need for an individual comparator is a mere matter of form and can indeed be a distraction from the real issue, namely whether those arrangements are discriminatory at the collective level. This peculiarity of the drafting of the 1970 Act can, in 'collective' cases, lead to confusion between the 'rebuttable presumption' established by the initial comparison … which does no more than bring s.1(3) into play, and the rules governing the burden of proof which operate in considering the issues under s.1(3), which will be the real battleground …

16. We refer at paragraph 14(3)(b) above to two distinct types of 'indirect discrimination'. …

1 The first kind of indirect discrimination occurs where the employer 'applies' a 'provision criterion or practice' (or 'PCP' in the jargon) which puts or would put women at a particular disadvantage when compared with men – or, as it is often put, has a 'disparate adverse impact': that is the formulation adopted in the relevant EU legislation and now incorporated also in the UK statutes.

2 The second kind of indirect discrimination was first recognised in the decision of the European Court of Justice in *Enderby*… In cases of the *Enderby* type, indirect discrimination is found where two groups of employees doing work of equal value receive different pay and there is a sufficiently substantial disparity in the gender break-down of the two groups. Mr Cavanagh [for the employer] referred to indirect discrimination of the *Enderby* type as 'tainting by numbers'

> 17. The essential difference between the two kinds of discrimination is that in the first case the employer has demonstrably done something (ie applied a PCP) to produce the disparity complained of, whereas in the second case no act on the part of the employer is identified but the nature and extent of the disparity is such as to justify the inference that it must nevertheless be the result of past discrimination (direct or indirect). It follows that this kind of indirect discrimination is essentially evidential in character … In the case of both types, once the disparity has been established, the differential will – subject to the point which we consider below – be treated as unlawfully discriminatory unless the employer can show that it is 'objectively justified'…
>
> 18. … s.1(3) provides expressly that an employer invoking the defence must show that the differential is 'genuinely' due to the factor on which he seeks to rely. The word 'genuinely' can be used in more than one sense. It is sometimes simply an intensifier, equivalent to something like 'really'. But it can also be used more specifically, to point a contrast with something which is false or dishonest … in *Wallace* Lord Browne-Wilkinson observed, at p.146, that 'the requirement of genuineness would be satisfied if … the reason put forward was not a sham or a pretence'; and Lord Nicholls said the same, using virtually the same language in *Marshall*, at p.274. Neither of them was making any particular point about the significance of the requirement of genuineness: they were simply engaged in the process of analysing the statutory language, and in that context using the phrase 'sham or pretence' as an antonym for 'genuine'. But in at least one reported case in this family … the employment tribunal treated the question of whether the explanation was a sham as if it were the central question for decision … this will not normally be a helpful approach. The terms 'sham or pretence' are, as we have said, essentially concerned with honesty: an explanation which is a sham is one which has been deliberately fabricated in order to present things otherwise than as they are. No doubt there will be cases where employers do dishonestly put forward explanations for pay differentials which they know to be untrue; but these will not be typical. Debates about the correct explanation of allegedly discriminatory pay differentials will generally turn on how properly to characterise or analyse primary facts which are not themselves in issue rather than on the bona fides of individuals. The draftsman's use of the word 'genuinely', though unexceptionable as far as it goes, will be misleading if it sends tribunals off down a track that will not in the typical case lead anywhere relevant. We would counsel tribunals against treating the question 'genuine or sham?' as the normal starting point in the structured analysis of equal pay cases.

On the facts of the cases before it the EAT concluded that the transitional arrangements had a disparate impact on men and women and that they were not objectively justifiable in view of the fact that the bonuses had ceased some time before to bear any relationship to productivity.

A potential pitfall for claimants was established in *Armstrong v Newcastle Upon Tyne NHS Hospital Trust* [2005] EWCA Civ 1608, [2006] IRLR 124 in which the CA ruled that statistics relied upon by the claimants were insufficient to place a burden of justification on the employer. The claimants were female domestic ancillary workers who sought to compare themselves with male ancillary workers who benefited from bonus payments. The evidence established that the bonus payments impacted differently on men and women. Buxton LJ suggested, however, that in such a case an employer could escape a finding of indirect discrimination by showing that the difference between the man's and the woman's contract was 'not discriminatory, in the sense of being attributable to a difference of gender' and that objective justification was required only if the employer failed to do this (§110). The CA has accepted on a number of occasions that *Armstrong* was binding, though it is strongly arguable that the change in wording of the GMF/MFD between s1(3) EqPA and s69 EqA robbed the decision of effect.[81] In any event, the decision of the SC in *Essop v Home Office; Naeem v Ministry of Justice* [2017] UKSC 27, [2017] ICR 640 that prima facie indirect discrimination can arise even if the disadvantage suffered is wholly unconnected with the protected characteristic in issue (see Chapter 2) strongly indicates that the decision in *Armstrong* is wrong in principle.[82]

Explaining Part of the Pay Gap

In *Enderby* the EAT accepted, as an MFD, a factor which explained only ten per cent of the pay differential at issue, ruling that: 'where market forces are genuinely material, it is the whole of the difference which is justified', the alternative being to 'involve the Tribunal in a wage-fixing role [which] would be an unreal approach.' The CA specifically referred to the CJEU the question whether this satisfied Article 141, the response of that Court being to the effect that 'if … the national court has been able to determine precisely what proportion of the [difference] is due to [there,] market forces [and, it must be presumed, free of sex discrimination], it must necessarily accept that the pay differential is objectively justified to the extent of that proportion. When national authorities have to apply Community law, they must apply the principle of proportionality.' If, on the other hand, it is not possible to determine precisely the extent to which the factor relied upon explains the pay differential 'it is for the national court to assess whether the role of the [factor] in determining the rate of pay was sufficiently significant to provide objective justification for part or all of the difference.'

IDS, Employment Law Handbooks, *Equal Pay*

- *MacDougall v Taggarts Motor Group Ltd ET Case No S/5598/94*: M, a female management accountant employed by a motor company at its Glasgow dealership, claimed equal pay on the basis of like work with S, whose pay was £8,000 more than hers. A tribunal found that there was no significant difference between M and S in terms of qualifications, experience or workload. The only difference was that S could drive but M could not. This limited her ability to manage more than one dealership in the employer's group at any one time and so, to some extent, limited her flexibility as a dealership accountant. That factor, according to the tribunal, was not of sufficient practical importance to preclude M being regarded as employed on like work with S. Nor, with regard to the employer's material factor defence, was it sufficient to explain in full the £8,000 pay difference. In the tribunal's view, S's ability to drive explained the salary difference to the extent of around £1,000. The remainder of the difference was not based on any other material factor and was therefore presumed to arise because of the difference of sex.
- *Pollard v Crown Prosecution Service ET Case No 2300481/16*: the employment tribunal found that P was entitled to equal pay with S, a higher-paid man, as from 1 April 2014. S had been employed by the CPS on a higher salary than P since January 2007 but was only transferred to a role that involved equal work at that later date. However, the tribunal accepted that part of S's higher pay was referable to a pay protection measure known as 'old scale maximum'

[81] *Bainbridge v Redcar and Cleveland BC (No 1)* [2008] EWCA Civ 885, [2008] IRLR 776, *Gibson v Sheffield CC* [2010] IRLR 311 (in which a majority of the CA expressed the view that it was also right in principle) and see *Bury MBC v Hamilton* [2011] ICR 655, §17.

[82] This was recognised by the CA in *LC v McCloud* [2019] ICR 1489, §220 pp 700–701 below.

> (OSM), which was paid to those who were in post before May 2007, when a previous pay scale applied. The tribunal found that there was no 'sex taint' in relation to OSM and so the material factor defence was established in relation to this element of the difference in pay. The tribunal considered that Enderby permits partial justification of a pay disparity and so decided that it should disregard the OSM element when calculating the difference between P's and S's salaries for the purpose of remedy.

The Handbook goes on to discuss *Cumbria CC v Dow (No 1)* [2008] IRLR 91 in which Elias P 'seemed to accept the principle behind making a "proportionate award" in respect of partial explanation/justification in a case concerning productivity bonuses paid to (predominantly male) road sweepers but not to the (predominantly female) claimants, who were engaged in work of equal value'. Elias J accepted that the employer might have been able to justify part of the resulting wage disparity by reference to productivity gains made by the road sweepers but stated that 'The problem is that the employer was attempting to justify the whole of the differential on productivity grounds. It may very well be that it would in principle be open to an employer to show that even if the full differential could not be justified on a productivity basis, a certain proportion of it could be, just as with market forces. That might have justified differentiating between the road workers and the other comparators. However, that possible partial justification was not argued in this case, and the question will have to await another day'.

Pension Claims

Sections 67 provides, so far as relevant, as follows:

Section 67 EqA, Sex equality rule

(1) If an occupational pension scheme does not include a sex equality rule, it is to be treated as including one.

(2) A sex equality rule is a provision that has the following effect—

  (a) if a relevant term is less favourable to A than it is to B, the term is modified so as not to be less favourable;

  (b) if a term confers a relevant discretion capable of being exercised in a way that would be less favourable to A than to B, the term is modified so as to prevent the exercise of the discretion in that way.

(3) A term is relevant if it is—

  (a) a term on which persons become members of the scheme, or

  (b) a term on which members of the scheme are treated.

(4) A discretion is relevant if its exercise in relation to the scheme is capable of affecting—

  (a) the way in which persons become members of the scheme, or

  (b) the way in which members of the scheme are treated.

(5) The reference in subsection (3)(b) to a term on which members of a scheme are treated includes a reference to the term as it has effect for the benefit of dependants of members.

(6) The reference in subsection (4)(b) to the way in which members of a scheme are treated includes a reference to the way in which they are treated as the scheme has effect for the benefit of dependants of members.

(7) If the effect of a relevant matter on a person (A) differs according to the effect it has on a person of the same sex as A, according to whether A is married, in a civil partnership, or for some other reason due to A's family status, a comparison for the purposes of this section of

the effect of that matter on persons of the opposite sex must be with a person of the opposite sex to A who is in the same position as A and in particular—

(a) where A is married to, or the civil partner of, someone of the opposite sex, A is to be compared to a person of the opposite sex to A ("B") where B is married to or (as the case may be) the civil partner of someone of the opposite sex to B;

(b) where A is married to, or the civil partner of, someone of the same sex, A is to be compared to B where B is married to or (as the case may be) the civil partner of someone of the same sex as B.

(8) A relevant matter is—

(a) a relevant term;
(b) a term conferring a relevant discretion;
(c) the exercise of a relevant discretion in relation to an occupational pension scheme.

(9) This section, so far as relating to the terms on which persons become members of an occupational pension scheme, does not have effect in relation to pensionable service before 8 April 1976.

(10) This section, so far as relating to the terms on which members of an occupational pension scheme are treated, does not have effect in relation to pensionable service before 17 May 1990a.

An equality rule will apply to a claimant in the same circumstances as an equality clause would (ie, where she can point to a suitable comparator who enjoys more favourable terms, or has been subject to a more favourable exercise of discretion). Section 67 makes it clear that sex equality rules are as applicable to terms of a pension scheme which provide for dependents' benefits as they are to terms directly conferring benefits on members. The backstops in s67(9)–(10) are set at the dates on which EU law first requires sex equality in access to membership of and treatrment by occupational pension schemes.

Section 68 EqA empowers the trustees and managers of occupational pension schemes to make such alterations as are necessary to comply with s67 EqA.

Hypothetical Comparators

It should be clear from the discussion above that ss64–68 EqA do not allow for hypothetical comparators. The SDA did not permit discrimination claims to be brought about the contractual terms of employment, the effect of this being that the only way in which a person could challenge sex discrimination in such terms was via a comparator-based EqA claim. Concerns were raised as to whether this was compatible with EU law. The EqA now allows sex discrimination (as distinct from equal pay) claims to be made about contractual terms, but only so far as allowed by the complex interplay between ss70 and 71 EqA, which provide as follows:

Section 70 EqA, Exclusion of sex discrimination provisions

(1) The relevant sex discrimination provision has no effect in relation to a term of A's that—

(a) is modified by, or included by virtue of, a sex equality clause or rule, or
(b) would be so modified or included but for section 69 or Part 2 of Schedule 7.

(2) Neither of the following is sex discrimination for the purposes of the relevant sex discrimination provision—

(a) the inclusion in A's terms of a term that is less favourable as referred to in section 66(2)(a);
(b) the failure to include in A's terms a corresponding term as referred to in section 66(2)(b).

(3) The relevant sex discrimination provision is, in relation to work of a description given in the first column of the table, the provision referred to in the second column so far as relating to sex.

Description of work	Provision
Employment	Section 39(2)
Appointment to a personal office	Section 49(6)
Appointment to a public office	Section 50(6)

The effect of this is that no sex discrimination claim can be brought in respect of a contractual difference which would breach the equal pay provisions, or to which the employer would have an MFD defence. Section 71 EqA then provides that:

Section 71 EqA, Sex discrimination in relation to contractual pay

(1) This section applies in relation to a term of a person's work—
  (a) that relates to pay, but
  (b) in relation to which a sex equality clause or rule has no effect.

(2) The relevant sex discrimination provision (as defined by section 70) has no effect in relation to the term except in so far as treatment of the person amounts to a contravention of the provision by virtue of section 13 or 14.

These provisions were considered by the EAT in *BMC Software Ltd v Shaikh* [2017] IRLR 1074 (considered above and in Chapter 4). There the EAT ruled that s70 EqA 'precludes discrimination provisions from applying to breach of a sex equality clause' while s71 'includes direct discrimination in respect of terms as to pay in respect of which a sex equality clause is not effective'. The decision in *Shaikh* was largely concerned with whether the claimant could rely on a failure to comply with the equal pay provisions of the EqA to found a constructive dismissal claim (the effect of s70 EqA was that she could not). HHJ Hand also considered s71 EqA, ruling at §76 that 's.71 deals with situations where the circumstances set out in s.65 EqA are not present and that has the result that s.66 EqA does not have any effect. Put another way, the equality clause has no effect as there is no "corresponding term" because there is no actual comparator', drawing on the Explanatory Notes to the EqA which indicate that a claimant could rely on s39 EqA if an employer told a female employee without a male comparator that he would pay her more if she were a man. HHJ Hand's analysis in *Shaikh* suggests that it would not be open to a woman who did have an appropriate male comparator to bring her claim under s39 EqA, though an employer may be reluctant to respond to s s39 claim with the assertion that the claimant is paid less than a man engaged in equal work.

The approach taken by the EqA and its predecessor provisions to gender unequal pay has long been criticised on the basis that it applies an individualistic (risk and expensive) solution to a systemic problem. This has the effect that the individuals who are vulnerable to victimisation by their employers are required to engage in complex and expensive litigation in order to challenge unequal pay. For many, particularly for those who do not belong to unions, this renders the right to equal pay theoretical. As Sandra Fredman has pointed out, even successful claims by individuals do not generally result in systemic changes to pay in their workplaces. Fredman's article, extracted below, discuss developments in the late 1980s and 1990s in local government and the NHS by which unions and employers, working together, sought to rationalise pay by and to improve the pay of those (predominantly women) at the bottom of the pay hierarchy. As she points out, these efforts were hampered by central government's unwillingness to make the necessary funds available which led to 'acute dilemmas for trade unions representing' male as well as female workers.

Sandra Fredman, 'Reforming Equal Pay Laws' (2008) 37 *Industrial Law Journal* 193, 206–10, footnotes omitted

Two major sources of dispute have concerned bonuses paid to predominantly male occupations and the protection of pay for men who stand to lose in the process. Particularly problematic was the exclusion of bonuses and productivity payments from the 1987 manual workers agreement. Given that these payments are attached to predominantly male jobs, it is not surprising that the gender pay gap quickly reasserted itself. This problem remained deliberately unresolved in the 1997 Single Status Agreement, which provided that existing local bonus schemes were not affected by the agreement. Yet in many situations, bonuses no longer represent genuine productivity rewards. Similarly, Agenda for Change did not deal with compensation for historic pay discrimination, and questions remain over the agreed arrangements for protected pay in the transitional period.

These problems demonstrate that collective bargaining could not on its own substitute for the statutory framework under the EqPA. This is partly because, without a firm rights-based framework, the collective process is inevitably based on interest bargaining, reaching pragmatic compromises of the complex conflicting interests at stake. The challenge is to ensure that the collective process operates within a clear rights-based framework. But this does not mean that resort to individual litigation can resolve the issues. Protracted litigation over these contested issues might produce small pockets of real gains for claimants, but the thousands of equal pay cases launched by unions and solicitors in the public sector only expose the weaknesses of the complaints-led system and the opacity of the legislation itself. Meanwhile, attempts at collective resolution are suspended pending the outcome of litigation which could take many years. Above all, none of these cases has been able to produce the much needed funding from central government, exacerbating the perception that equal pay for women can only be achieved at a cost to other important values. Instead, the collective process should be guided by fair and clear principles, and resolution of disputes should take a collective form.

Gender Reassignment

In *P v S & Cornwall* the ECJ ruled that the prohibition on sex discrimination in Council Directive 76/207 had to be interpreted to apply to gender reassignment as to sex. P had been employed as a man and was dismissed after informing her employers that she proposed to undergo surgical gender reassignment. The ECJ ruled that:

Case C-13/94, P v S & Cornwall **EU:C:1996:170, [1996] ECR I-2143, [1996] ICR 795**

17. The principle of equal treatment 'for men and women' to which the Directive refers in its title, preamble and provisions means, as Articles 2(1) and 3(1) in particular indicate, that there should be 'no discrimination whatsoever on grounds of sex'...

18. ... the Directive is simply the expression, in the relevant field, of the principle of equality, which is one of the fundamental principles of Community law. Moreover, as the Court has repeatedly held, the right not to be discriminated against on grounds of sex is one of the fundamental human rights whose observance the Court has a duty to ensure ...

20. Accordingly, the scope of the Directive cannot be confined simply to discrimination based on the fact that a person is one or other sex. In view of its purpose and the nature of the rights

which it seeks to safeguard, the scope of the Directive is also such as to apply to discrimination arising, as in this case, from the gender reassignment of the person concerned.

21. Such discrimination is based, essentially, if not exclusively, on the sex of the person concerned. Where a person is dismissed on the ground that he or she intends to undergo, or has undergone, gender reassignment, he or she is treated unfavourably by comparison with persons of the sex to which he or she was deemed to belong before undergoing gender reassignment.

22. To tolerate such discrimination would be tantamount, as regards such a person, to a failure to respect the dignity and freedom to which he or she is entitled, and which the Court has a duty to safeguard.

In *Chessington World of Adventures Ltd v Reed* [1998] ICR 97 the EAT interpreted the SDA so as to provide the same protection to private sector employees. Shortly thereafter, the Sex Discrimination (Gender Reassignment) Regulations 1999[83] incorporated this approach expressly into the SDA and it found its way in turn into the EqA. And in Case C-117/01, *KB v NHS Pensions Agency* EU:C:2004:7, [2004] ECR I-541, [2004] ICR 781 the ECJ ruled that the restriction of survivors' benefits to married partners amounted to sex discrimination against the claimant who, as a woman, was unable to marry her partner (a transgender man).[84]

The decision in the *P v S & Cornwall* was driven in part by the jurisprudence of the ECtHR which had in *B v France* (1993) 16 EHRR 597 ruled that France had breached Article 8 ECHR by refusing to allow the applicant, a post-operative trans woman, to adopt a woman's name or change her civil status. By the time of the decision in *KB* the ECtHR had decided in *Goodwin v UK* (2002) 35 EHRR 18 that the UK had breached the Article 8 and 12 rights of the applicant, a post-operative transgender woman, by denying her recognition, and the right to marry, as a woman.

The UK's response to the ECtHR's decision in *Goodwin* was to implement the GRA which provides that:

Section 1 GRA, Applications

(1) A person of either gender who is aged at least 18 may make an application for a gender recognition certificate on the basis of—
  (a) living in the other gender, or
  (b) having changed gender under the law of a country or territory outside the United Kingdom …

Section 9 GRA, General

(1) Where a full gender recognition certificate is issued to a person, the person's gender becomes for all purposes the acquired gender (so that, if the acquired gender is the male gender, the person's sex becomes that of a man and, if it is the female gender, the person's sex becomes that of a woman).

(2) Subsection (1) does not affect things done, or events occurring, before the certificate is issued; but it does operate for the interpretation of enactments passed, and instruments and other documents made, before the certificate is issued (as well as those passed or made afterwards).

(3) Subsection (1) is subject to provision made by this Act or any other enactment or any subordinate legislation.

[83] SI 1999 No 1102.

[84] The case preceded the GRA and the recognition of same-sex marriage in GB.

Issue of a GRC certificate requires in England and Wales that the applicant has a diagnosis of gender dysphoria, though it does not require that any medical or hormonal treatment has been undertaken. The general requirements for diagnosis and that an applicant has lived 'in gender' for two years have proved controversial and there has been much lobbying for 'self-identification'.[85] That argument is outside the scope of this book. It is important to be aware of the GRA, however, because it sheds light on the interpretation of the EqA in this area.

Gender Reassignment and Discrimination

Direct discrimination because of gender reassignment will occur when an individual 'X' is treated less favourably 'because of' the protected characteristic of gender reassignment (s13 EqA), that is, because X 'is proposing to undergo, is undergoing or has undergone a process (or part of a process) for the purpose of reassigning the person's sex by changing physiological or other attributes of sex'. If X has a gender recognition certificate then she falls to be regarded as a women for most legal purposes (s9 GRA), and so a refusal to allow X access female services or associations etc will amount to direct discrimination because of gender reassignment. The circumstances under which such discrimination is lawful are considered at pp 397–414 below.

If X does not have a gender recognition certificate then she is not considered to be a woman as a matter of law. This being the case, a refusal to allow X to access female services or associations etc will fall to be considered as direct discrimination because of *sex* rather than direct discrimination because of gender reassignment: in other words, X is being denied access to the service or association etc because she is regarded as a man, rather than because she 'is proposing to undergo, is undergoing or has undergone a process (or part of a process) for the purpose of reassigning the person's sex by changing physiological or other attributes of sex'. The circumstances under which direct sex discrimination is lawful are considered at pp 397–411 below.

Refusing X access to female services or associations etc may well amount to *prima facie* indirect discrimination, because a policy or practice of refusing access to men will is likely to put X, and other men who propose to undergo, are undergoing or have underdone gender reassignment at a disadvantage by comparison with other people who are less likely to be placed at a disadvantage by a refusal to permit men to access female services, associations, etc. Whether this is lawful will depend on whether the policy or practice is justified. In circumstances in which such a policy or practice is lawful despite entailing direct sex discrimination, it is likely to be justifiable despite being indirectly discriminatory on grounds of gender reassignment.

Much of the discussion of this protected characteristic is in the section relating to exceptions below.

Clothing and Appearance Rules

It is common for employers (and, indeed, schools), to impose regulations concerning clothing and appearance. In the employment field these rules are generally regarded as falling within the sphere of managerial discretion. A number of challenges were mounted against the operation of clothing and appearance rules under the SDA, generally in cases where differential rules were imposed on men and women, and under the Race Relations Act 1976. These latter claims tended to be quite different from those considered here, the alleged discrimination consisting in the disparate impact of the rules on persons of different race-related religious groups.

[85] The Gender Recognition Reform (Scotland) Act 2023 would remove the diagnostic requirement and make other changes to the GRA as it applies in Scotland. The Act has been blocked by the Westminster Government and it is unclear at the time of writing whether it will become law, and in what form.

It might be thought that any application of different rules to men and to women should be regarded, in the absence of express provision to the contrary, as breaching the prohibition on sex discrimination. Thus, for example, employers should not be permitted to require that women wear skirts or, indeed, that men wear trousers (unless the same requirement exactly is applied to both sexes). This type of interpretation was rejected by the CA in *Smith v Safeway plc* [1996] ICR 868, in which Phillips LJ declared that:

> 16 … a code which made identical provisions for men and women, but which resulted in one or other having an unconventional appearance, would have an unfavourable impact on that sex being compelled to appear in an unconventional mode. Can there be any doubt that a code which required all employees to have 18-inch hair, earrings and lipstick would treat men unfavourably by requiring them to adopt an appearance at odds with conventional standards?

This statement is difficult to dispute. But what it overlooks is that any code which applied those standards of appearance to women forces them to conform with a particular model of 'appropriate' femininity. It is damaging to women in a different and less obvious way than it is damaging to men. But it is damaging nonetheless. And, whereas Phillips LJ used his argument to support the imposition of what were regarded by the court as 'sex appropriate' sex-specific appearance codes, it is equally consistent with a different approach.

The judicial approach which prevails to this day was established by EAT in *Schmidt v Austicks Bookshops*. The claimant complained that she was prohibited from wearing trousers to work and, in addition, required to wear overalls while serving customers. Men, by contrast, were subject to the sole restriction that they were not permitted to wear t-shirts at work. Her claim failed before the tribunal and the EAT. Phillips J, for the Court, disregarded the matter of the overalls (which, presumably, gave female staff a subordinate appearance by comparison with men) as too trivial to amount to a 'detriment' (see further Chapter 5) before going on to establish the general approach to clothing rules:

***Schmdt v Austicks Bookshops* [1978] ICR 85**

Phillips J:

> 8 …. although there was less scope for positive rules [ie, 'no skirts'] in the case of the men, in that the choice of wearing apparel was more limited, there were restrictions in their case, too. For example, they were not allowed to wear [tee] shirts; and it is quite certain, on a reasonable examination of the evidence, that they would not have been allowed to wear, had they sought to do so, any out-of-the-way clothing. And so they were subjected to restrictions, too, albeit different ones – because, as we have already said, the restrictions to which the women were subjected were not appropriate to the men. Experience shows that under the [SDA] a lot depends on how one phrases or formulates the matter of which complaint is made. Here it has been formulated in the terms of skirts and overalls. As has been pointed out, in another case it might be in terms of ear-rings for men, long hair, all sorts of possibilities. But it seems to us that the realistic and better way of formulating it is to say that there were in force rules restricting wearing apparel and governing appearance which applied to men and also applied to women, although obviously, women and men being different, the rules in the two cases were not the same. We should be prepared to accept … an alternative contention … 'that in any event, in so far as a comparison is possible, the employers treated both female and male staff alike in that both sexes were restricted in the choice of clothing for wear whilst at work and were both informed that a certain garment should not be worn during working hours.' It seems to us, if there are to be other cases on these lines, that an approach of that sort is a better approach and more likely to lead to a sensible result, than an approach which examines the situation point by point and garment by garment …

The *Schmidt* approach operates, within the structure of the EqA, by accepting that a 'sex appropriate dress code' can be a 'relevant circumstance' within s23 EqA (see further Chapter 2), and by finding discrimination only if the terms of the code, as they apply to one sex, are significantly less favourable than those which apply to the other.

Such less favourable treatment has, on occasion, been found by tribunals. In January 2000 Judy Owen won a claim under the SDA against the Professional Golfers' Association, which had required her to wear trousers at work. Such decisions are, however, rare. In *Schmidt*, as we saw above, a dress code forbidding women from wearing trousers and requiring them to wear overalls was regarded as not significantly less favourable than that forbidding men from wearing T-shirts. In *Burrett v West Birmingham Health Authority* [1994] IRLR 7, a uniform which required women nurses to wear a linen cap was not regarded as imposing upon them significantly less favourable treatment than in the case of men, who had no obligation in respect of headgear. And in *Smith v Safeway plc* [1996] ICR 868 the CA ruled that the prohibition, in the case of male employees, of long hair (female employees were permitted to wear their hair long and tied back) was not discriminatory. In doing so, the Court overruled the EAT which had ([1995] ICR 472) distinguished the code, bearing as it did on the employee's appearance outside employment, from those upheld in *Schmidt* and in *Burrett*.[86]

Schmidt permits employers to reinforce, through dress codes, the very stereotypes of 'male' (serious, responsible, mature) and 'female' (decorative handmaidens) which disadvantage women at work. Because they are in line with stereotyped notions of what is appropriate to men and women respectively, these dress codes are not seen 'objectively' to 'demean' women even where they serve to mark them out as 'second class'.

The approach of the British courts to appearance codes has been widely criticised. In 1995, Leo Flynn suggested that 'the starting point produced by the EAT in *Schmidt* was ill-founded and is not convincing. The boundaries of acceptable male and female dress can, and have, shifted significantly over the centuries and have altered with dramatic speed in the past few decades. Efforts to fix this process through an ascription of natural limits to 'female' and 'male' apparel cannot be reconciled with the basic philosophy of anti-discrimination legislation'.[87] And Paul Skidmore characterised the approach of Phillips LJ in *Smith* (and of Phillips J, as he had been, in *Schmidt*) an 'unacceptable gloss on "less favourable treatment"', choosing 'firstly to look at the dress code as a whole, rather than item by item, and assum[ing] secondly that any overall package which reinforces conventional gender stereotypes (or as he put it 'a conventional standard of appearance') does not give rise to less favourable treatment'.[88]

A number of cases decided post *Smith v Safeway* suggested that the tide might have turned; Judy Owen's success in *Owen v Professional Golf Association* (2000) was mentioned above. Female Eurostar guards persuaded their employer to allow them to wear trousers at work after a dispute. And the EOC (predecessor to the EHRC) won a settlement in a well-publicised case involving a challenge brought by a schoolgirl to a uniform requirement that girls wore skirts rather than trousers. But the orthodox approach was restated in *Department for Work and Pensions v Thompson* [2004] IRLR 348, in which the EAT overturned a tribunal

[86] See also *Cootes v John Lewis plc* EAT/1414/00, which concerned an unsuccessful challenge to a uniform policy on the grounds that it made women appear junior to their male peers.

[87] L Flynn, 'Gender Equality Law and Employer's Dress Codes' (1995) 25 *Industrial Law Journal* 255.

[88] P Skidmore, 'Sex, Gender and Comparators in Employment Discrimination Law' (1997) 26 *Industrial Law Journal* 51.

finding that a requirement that male employees wear a shirt and tie, while women had to 'dress appropriately and to a similar standard', amounted to sex discrimination.

Smith v Safeways was applied by the EAT in *Dansie v Commissioner of the Metropolitan Police* UKEAT/0234/09 in rejecting a sex discrimination claim from a trainee PC threatened with disciplinary action for refusing to have his hair cut. It was also relied upon by the High Court in *G v Head Teacher and Governors of St Gregory's Catholic Science College* [2011] EWHC 1452 (Admin) to defeat a sex discrimination challenge against a prohibition on boys, but not girls, wearing their hair in cornrows. The Court having ruled that the prohibition amounted to unlawful indirect race discrimination, Collins J went on to declare at §§59–60 that:

> although cornrows for boys are by no means unusual, I am not persuaded that the defendants are wrong to regard them as not being conventional ... The claimant is protected by the indirect race discrimination. I see no good reason why a choice of cornrows should be permitted on grounds of sex discrimination. A rigid appearance policy at a school is clearly entirely reasonable provided it complies with equality law. Permitting long hair for girls and not for boys may be regarded as discriminatory since boys nowadays not unusually wear their hair longer. But I have no doubt that 'not unusual' does not equate to conventional and an appearance policy such as the one operated by the defendants is not discriminatory albeit it applies different rules to girls than for boys.

The difficulties created by the law in this area were highlighted by the House of Commons Petitions Committee and Women and Equalities Committee in their 2017 report, 'High heels and workplace dress codes'. The report was the product of an inquiry commenced in response to a petition initiated by Nicola Thorp, who commenced work in 2015 as a temporary receptionist at PwC's offices, employed by Portico (a 'specialist provider of high quality, tailored front and back of house guest services'). On arrival, she was told that Portico's dress code required her to wear heels of between two and four inches. (The code also prohibited opaque tights and required that make-up be 'worn at all times [by women] and regularly reapplied, with a minimum of light blusher, lipstick or tinted gloss, mascara, eye shadow, light foundation/powder'. Permissible nail colours were specified and visible roots prohibited.[89]) Ms Thorp was given the option to buy a pair of high heels and, when she refused, was sent home without pay.

Nicola Thorp's petition, which called for a ban on any requirement for women staff to wear high heels at work, was signed by over 150,000 people. The Government response was that 'Employers are entitled to set dress codes for their workforce but the law is clear that these dress codes must be reasonable'. The Petitions Committee was unimpressed with this response and it and the WEC conducted a joint inquiry.

House of Commons Women and Equalities Committee, *High heels and workplace dress codes*, First Joint Report of Session 2016–17, HC 291

32. Many women used our web forum to describe how mandatory high heel dress codes made them feel in the workplace. The picture these contributions paint is a stark one. Workers find dress codes which require them to wear high heels to be 'humiliating and degrading', and 'demeaning'. Some commenters felt 'sexualised' by their employer's insistence on high heels ...

34. We heard from [one witness] how she found her dress code as an air hostess made her feel 'extremely uncomfortable, particularly because it was being done for the business.' She explained:

> For me personally, it was a bit dehumanising and humiliating to be made specifically to wear items of uniform that sexualised my appearance or enhanced my sexuality – no aspect of the

[89] Box 1 in the Joint report.

> men's uniform was designed to enhance their male sexuality. They looked very smart – they all looked immaculate – but none of them was enhancing their sexuality to somehow improve the image of the airline or the service we were providing.

[Another witness] told us:

> I felt offended, in retail, by the request to get better sales by flaunting myself, whereas I was a very good salesperson and I could use my skills and my product knowledge to do that. I felt offended that [the employer] would think less of my skills and more of the clothes that I was wearing.

She explained that her employer had encouraged her and her colleagues to wear shorter skirts and unbutton their blouses more at Christmas time, when a higher proportion of male shoppers was anticipated.

36. Gender-based dress codes also seem, on the evidence we heard, to go hand in hand with a work environment in which women – especially young women – are objectified and left vulnerable to sexual harassment and unwanted sexual attention …

37. [One witness] told us about the harassment which young female flight attendants can suffer:

> The harassment suffered by some of these colleagues was absolutely unbelievable, particularly online. People would take the name off their name badges and send a lot of Facebook messages and stuff like that, to try to find them … They would get a lot of messages on social media from passengers who had flown with them and perhaps got the wrong idea about how friendly they were. People would try to find out which hotel we were staying in all the time. There would be a fair amount of grooming towards girls half or a third of their age about taking them out and stuff like that, which was highly inappropriate.

38. Sexual harassment is not the only type of workplace harassment which might be linked to gender-based dress codes. One in four trans people, and one in five LGB people, have reported being discriminated against at work. Gender-based dress codes may exacerbate this …

In response to the Committees' call for action by government, the Government Equalities Office issued guidance in May 2018. This suggested that it might be unlawful to require female employees to wear high heels and states that while '[d]ress policies for men and women do not have to be identical … the standards imposed should be equivalent'.[90] It provides that 'Transgender employees should be allowed to follow the organisation's dress code in a way which they feel matches their gender identity', that 'Employers should be flexible and not set dress codes which prohibit religious symbols that do not interfere with an employee's work' and that requiring staff 'to dress in a provocative or revealing fashion' might, even if applicable to both men and women, 'contribute to an environment in which employees may be vulnerable to unwanted sexual attention and harassment'.

Pregnancy

We saw above that women are particularly likely to face discrimination, especially in relation to work, in connection with child-bearing. Many indirect sex discrimination claims have involved challenges to disadvantage experienced by women who have taken time out of paid work in connection with child-bearing and -rearing, and/or who have sought to work

[90] *Dress codes and sex discrimination – what you need to know*, available at https://www.gov.uk/government/publications/dress-codes-and-sex-discrimination-what-you-need-to-know.

shorter hours to help them reconcile paid and unpaid labour.[91] Notwithstanding 45 years of sex discrimination legislation, women continue to be penalised because they are or may become mothers.

Previous editions of this book detailed the reluctance of the domestic courts to regulate pregnancy and related discrimination as sex discrimination. That is now largely a thing of the past, pregnancy and maternity now being classified as a protected characteristic and the EqA specifically defining such discrimination to exclude the need for a comparator, real or hypothetical; whereas direct discrimination because of sex, race, etc is defined as *less favourable* treatment because of the relevant characteristic, ss17 and 18 EqA define pregnancy-related discrimination as *unfavourable* treatment related to pregnancy. Sections 17 and 18, which apply respectively to non-work and work-related cases, provide as follows:

Section 17 EqA

(2) A person (A) discriminates against a woman if A treats her unfavourably because of a pregnancy of hers.

(3) A person (A) discriminates against a woman[92] if, in the period of 26 weeks beginning with the day on which she gives birth[93], A treats her unfavourably because she has given birth.

(4) The reference in subsection (3) to treating a woman unfavourably because she has given birth includes, in particular, a reference to treating her unfavourably because she is breast-feeding …

Section 18 EqA

(2) A person (A) discriminates against a woman if, in the protected period in relation to a pregnancy of hers, A treats her unfavourably—

(a) because of the pregnancy, or

(b) because of illness suffered by her as a result of it.

(3) A person (A) discriminates against a woman if A treats her unfavourably because she is on compulsory maternity leave.

(4) A person (A) discriminates against a woman if A treats her unfavourably because she is exercising or seeking to exercise, or has exercised or sought to exercise, the right to ordinary or additional maternity leave.

(5) For the purposes of subsection (2), if the treatment of a woman is in implementation of a decision taken in the protected period, the treatment is to be regarded as occurring in that period (even if the implementation is not until after the end of that period).

(6) The protected period, in relation to a woman's pregnancy, begins when the pregnancy begins, and ends—

(a) if she has the right to ordinary and additional maternity leave, at the end of the additional maternity leave period or (if earlier) when she returns to work after the pregnancy;

(b) if she does not have that right, at the end of the period of 2 weeks beginning with the end of the pregnancy.

[91] See for example *Price v Civil Service Commission* [1978] ICR 27; *Jones v University of Manchester* [1992] ICR 52; *Falkirk Council v Whyte* [1997] IRLR 560; or those whose childcare commitments preclude full-time or other particular patterns of work (*Clymo v Wandsworth* [1989] ICR 250; *Cast v Croydon* [1998] ICR 500; *London Underground v Edwards* [1995] ICR 574; *XC Trains Ltd v CD, Aslef* [2016] IRLR 748).

[92] The EqA provides (s212) that 'woman means a female of any age'. This would include trans men without GRCs. It would not appear to extend to trans men with GRCs, though a purposive interpretation of the EqA against the requirements of EU law and the ECHR should have this effect.

[93] Defined by s17(5) to include miscarriage/stillbirth after 24 weeks.

Sections 17(6) and 18(7) EqA exclude pregnancy-related discrimination falling within ss17 and 18 respectively from the prohibition on direct sex discrimination.

Section 13 EqA, which defines direct discrimination, provides (subsection (6)) that (a) 'less favourable treatment of a woman [because of sex] includes less favourable treatment of her because she is breast-feeding', also, (b) that, in determining whether direct sex discrimination has occurred, 'no account is to be taken of special treatment afforded to a woman in connection with pregnancy or childbirth.' Section 13(7) then provides that s13(6)(a) 'does not apply for the purposes of Part 5 (work)'. The result is that, whereas women are protected in respect of breast-feeding outside the context of work both before their child reaches six months (by s174 EqA) and after this time (by s13(6)(a)), discrimination because of breastfeeding in the context of work is not explicitly prohibited by the EqA.[94] Employers are required by health and safety legislation to provide somewhere suitable for a breast-feeding employee to rest, though not to provide somewhere for breastfeeding employees to breastfeed, and Acas advises employers to 'provide a private, hygienic and safe place for employees to breastfeed, and express breast milk and then store it somewhere cool (which doesn't need to be for breast milk only)'.[95] Discrimination associated with breastfeeding may, depending on the facts, amount to direct sex discrimination.[96]

Schedule 7 para 2 EqA provides that 'A sex equality clause does not have effect in relation to terms of work affording special treatment to women in connection with pregnancy or childbirth.' In *Hextall v CC Leicestershire Police* [2019] EWCA Civ 900, [2019] IRLR 695 the CA ruled that a tribunal had erred in considering a complaint by a male police officer that he was paid at a lower rate in respect of 14 weeks' shared parental leave than he would have been had he been a woman on maternity leave under s39(2)(a) EqA. The tribunal had rejected his claim of indirect sex discrimination and the EAT, which agreed that the claim fell within s39(2)(a) EqA, disagreed with the tribunal on the question of indirect discrimination and reverted the case for reconsideration. On the CC's appeal the CA ruled that PC Hextall's claim should have been considered under the equal pay provisions, and that it was defeated by Schedule 7 para 2.

The CJEU ruled in Case C-506/06 *Mayr v Bäckerei und Konditorei Gerhard Flöckner OHG* 06, EU:C:2008:119, [2008] ECR I-1017, [2008] IRLR 387 that a woman who was undergoing fertility treatment would not be regarded as pregnant until the embryo was transferred into her womb. The claimant had been dismissed after fertilisation and three days before implantation occurred. In those circumstances the CJEU ruled that the dismissal, if because of the treatment, would amount to direct sex discrimination. That being the case, while the woman would not be regarded as 'pregnant' for the purposes of the EqA prior to implantation, she ought to be protected by the Act's prohibition on sex discrimination.

Where a surrogate is used the protection provided by ss17 and 18 EqA applies only to the pregnant woman and not to the women who has provided the eggs, if she does not carry the foetus. In Case C-167/12, *CD v ST*, EU:C:2014:169, [2014] IRLR 551 and Case

[94] As in the case of ss17 and 18 EqA, the protection in respect of breast (chest) feeding would not appear to extend to trans men with GRCs, though a purposive interpretation of the EqA against the requirements of EU law and the ECHR should have this effect.

[95] *Pregnancy and maternity discrimination: key points for the workplace*, https://archive.acas.org.uk/media/4945/Pregnancy-and-maternity-discrimination-key-points-for-the-workplace/pdf/Pregnancy___Maternity_Discrimination.pdf.

[96] This question is likely to give rise to the same difficulties as regards appropriate comparators as did pregnancy discrimination (see 2nd edition of this book).

C-363/12, *Z v A Government Department* EU:C:2014:159, [2014] IRLR 563 the CJEU ruled that the 'commissioning mother' is not regarded as pregnant and is not entitled to maternity leave, and that the denial of maternity leave to the commissioning mother is not disability discrimination as infertility is not to be regarded as a disability for the purposes of Council Directive 2000/78. The Law Commission and the Scottish Law Commission undertook a consultation on possible reforms to employment law relating to surrogacy, including the possible extension of maternity leave for commissioning mothers, which closed in October 2019.[97]

Women remain entitled to their contractual and non-contractual benefits during any period of maternity leave *except where these relate to remuneration*.[98]

Schedule 9 para 17 EqA: Non-contractual payments to women on maternity leave

(1) A person does not contravene section 39(1)(b) or (2), so far as relating to pregnancy and maternity, by depriving a woman who is on maternity leave of any benefit from the terms of her employment relating to pay.

(2) The reference in sub-paragraph (1) to benefit from the terms of a woman's employment relating to pay does not include a reference to—

(a) maternity-related pay (including maternity-related pay that is increase-related),

(b) pay (including increase-related pay) in respect of times when she is not on maternity leave, or

(c) pay by way of bonus in respect of times when she is on compulsory maternity leave.

(3) For the purposes of sub-paragraph (2), pay is increase-related in so far as it is to be calculated by reference to increases in pay that the woman would have received had she not been on maternity leave …[99]

EHRC, 'Employment', Statutory Code of Practice[100]

8.38 If a woman receives a pay rise between the start of the calculation period for Statutory Maternity Pay (SMP) and the end of her maternity leave, she is entitled to have her SMP recalculated and receive any extra SMP due. She may also, as a result of recalculation following such a pay rise, become eligible for SMP where previously she was not. Employers are reimbursed all or some of the cost of SMP …

8.39 The Act has a specific exception relating to non-contractual payments to women on maternity leave [Schedule 9 para 17]. There is no obligation on an employer to extend to a woman on maternity leave any non-contractual benefit relating to pay, such as a discretionary bonus. For the purposes of this exception, 'pay' means a payment of money by way of wages or salary.

8.40 However, this exception does not apply to any maternity-related pay (whether statutory or contractual), to which a woman is entitled as a result of being pregnant or on maternity leave. Nor does it apply to any maternity related pay arising from an increase that the woman would have received had she not been on maternity leave.

Example: A woman on maternity leave is receiving contractual maternity pay, which is worked out as a percentage of her salary. The date of her employer's annual review of staff pay falls while she is on maternity leave. All other staff are awarded a 2% pay rise with immediate effect. If the woman on maternity leave does not receive the increase, this would be unlawful

[97] https://s3-eu-west-2.amazonaws.com/lawcom-prod-storage-11jsxou24uy7q/uploads/2019/06/Surrogacy-consultation-paper.pdf.

[98] Unless (as regards remuneration) the contract of employment provides otherwise.

[99] Pay is defined by para 17(5).

[100] https://www.equalityhumanrights.com/sites/default/files/employercode.pdf.

discrimination. Her contractual maternity pay should be recalculated so that it is based on her salary plus the 2% increase given to all her colleagues. Any other benefits linked to salary should also be adjusted to take into account the pay rise. When she returns to work her normal pay must reflect the pay rise.

8.41 Any non-contractual bonus relating to the period of compulsory maternity leave is not covered by the exception, so the employer would have to pay this. Neither does the exception apply to pay relating to times when a woman is not on maternity leave.

In the case extracted below the EAT upheld a tribunal finding that the claimant, a police dog-handler, had been discriminated against contrary to s18 EqA when, one of her two police dogs, having been allocated to another police officer when she became pregnant pursuant to a policy which prohibited pregnant police officers from continuing to operate as dog-handlers in most cases, her request to have her dog reallocated to her on her return to work was refused. The EAT also allowed the claimant's appeal against the rejection by the tribunal of her complaint that her employer's policy of removing and reallocating police dogs where a handler was likely to be non-operational for a while indirectly discriminated on grounds of sex.

***Commissioner of Police of the Metropolis v Keohane* [2014] ICR 1073**

Langstaff P:

36. … The fact that the needs of the Metropolitan Police to keep Nunki Pippin operational may have been a major, or indeed *the* major, reason for the decision does not mean to say that the claimant's pregnancy was not also a cause of it. In any event, here (as we have observed already) the act of removal, and failure to reallocate a dog was not in itself a detriment. They subjected the claimant to one: namely being put at risk that upon her return to work she would both have no second dog and have lost the opportunity of overtime, and that her career prospects would have been damaged. It is not difficult to see that the cause of that detriment was clearly suffered because of her pregnancy. The focus of the risk is upon the conditions she was to face on return to work following pregnancy and maternity leave, and that they should be no worse than they were as a consequence of her taking such leave, but the risk arose immediately upon the apparently permanent removal of Nunki Pippin …

37. The risk might have been obviated if the respondent had promised that the claimant would be allocated a passive dog on her return to work, such that she would not suffer loss of income or career, but the fact the detriment might have been avoided did not prevent it being such in the first place …

45. … The reason why the tribunal concluded that there was no indirect discrimination was that it could not be said for certain that the policy to reallocate dogs where their pregnant handlers became non-operational put or would put women to a particular disadvantage compared with men for, by para 28: "There is merely the risk of that occurring." The concept that "risk" could not be a detriment was repeated in para 30: "the policy only amounts to *potential* discrimination, because it does not uniformly result in reallocation of the dog" (emphasis added) …

47. In our view, the tribunal identified a detriment. Being exposed to a risk that one's police dog might be reallocated is sufficient, providing it is a real risk. It creates a detriment. If the application of a policy has the inevitable result that a woman will suffer that disadvantage, whereas a man will not, it will be directly discriminatory … It is only where the consequence of suffering that disadvantage is neither automatic nor inevitable that indirect discrimination can come into play at all. Sometimes – though not always – such disadvantage will materialise. If where it does, however, it arises disproportionately in respect of one gender, then the basis for a finding of indirect discrimination is laid …

Section 18 EqA is not a panacea, though it has significantly improved the protection of pregnant women and those on maternity leave. Its main limitations concern the duration of the protected period and the non-application of the provision to indirect discrimination.

The first of these limitations is illustrated by the decision in *Lyons v DWP Jobcentre Plus* [2014] ICR 668 in which the EAT ruled that neither s18 nor s13 EqA protected the claimant from dismissal for reasons connected with post-natal depression which extended beyond the protected period. The EAT took into account the jurisprudence of the CJEU in concluding at §31 that 'When a pregnancy-related illness arises during pregnancy or maternity leave and persists after the maternity leave period, an employer is permitted to take into account periods of absence due to that illness, after the end of maternity leave, in computing any period of absence justifying dismissal, in the same way that a man's absences for illness are taken into account'.

Turning to the question of indirect discrimination, in *Interserve FM Ltd v Tuleikyte* [2017] IRLR 615 the EAT allowed the employer's appeal against a tribunal ruling that the claimant had been subject to unlawful discrimination contrary to s18 when she was erased from her employer's employment records. She had earned too little to receive statutory maternity pay, and she was recorded as a leaver in pursuit of the employer's policy that employees who had been absent without pay for three months were erased from the employment records. The tribunal had ruled that the application of the blanket policy to the claimant when she was absent on maternity leave had the automatic consequence of treating her unfavourably because she was on maternity leave, and that unlawful discrimination was therefore inherent in the employer's blanket policy. The EAT ruled that the tribunal had erred in treating the case as one of direct discrimination unless the claimant's absence on maternity leave formed part of the reason or grounds for her treatment in having her name deleted from the employer's records. It remitted the claim to the tribunal for further consideration.

In addition to the protection provided by the EqA, ss77 and 99 of the Employment Rights Act 1996 (ERA) provide some additional protection against redundancy during maternity leave and make dismissals solely or principally because of pregnancy or maternity leave automatically unfair.[101]

Exceptions

The general exceptions provided by the EqA are discussed in Chapter 4. Here we will consider the exceptions which apply in relation to sex and gender reassignment in particular. The most important of these consist of the single-sex services provisions which apply in relation to services and public functions (Part 3) and the genuine occupational requirement (GOR) defences which apply to work (Part 5). In addition, there are exceptions related to participation as a competitor in competitive activities where a participant's sex will place them at a disadvantage relative to others). Positive action is considered in Chapter 3.

[101] See *Sefton BC v Wainwright* [2015] ICR 652 for a decision on the interplay between the EqA and the ERA and associated regulations.

Part 3 EqA: Single-Sex Services

Schedule 3 permits sex-segregated services, including in the exercise of public functions, where 'a joint service for persons of both sexes would be less effective, and the limited provision is a proportionate means of achieving a legitimate aim' (para 26). The segregated service can differ between men and women where, in addition to satisfaction of these conditions, 'the extent to which the service is required by one sex makes it not reasonably practicable to provide the service otherwise than as a separate service provided differently for each sex'. And services and public functions can be provided *exclusively* to members of one sex where the limited provision is a proportionate means of achieving a legitimate aim, and any of the following conditions are satisfied (para 27):

1. only persons of that sex have need of the service;
2. the service is also provided jointly for persons of both sexes, and would be insufficiently effective were it only to be provided jointly;
3. a joint service for persons of both sexes would be less effective, and the extent to which the service is required by persons of each sex makes it not reasonably practicable to provide separate services;
4. the service is provided at a place which is, or is part of a hospital, or another establishment for persons requiring special care, supervision or attention;
5. the service is provided for, or is likely to be used by, two or more persons at the same time, and the circumstances are such that a person of one sex might reasonably object to the presence of a person of the opposite sex;
6. there is likely to be physical contact between a person (A) to whom the service is provided and another person (B), and B might reasonably object if A were not of the same sex as B.

Schedule 3 para 28 provides as follows:

Schedule 3 para 28 EqA, Gender reassignment

(1) A person does not contravene section 29 [EqA], so far as relating to gender reassignment discrimination, only because of anything done in relation to a matter within sub-paragraph (2) if the conduct in question is a proportionate means of achieving a legitimate aim.

(2) The matters are—

(a) the provision of separate services for persons of each sex;
(b) the provision of separate services differently for persons of each sex;
(c) the provision of a service only to persons of one sex.

The para 26 provisions were considered in *R (Coll) v Secretary of State for Justice* in which the SC ruled that the Secretary of State had discriminated against women offenders in relation to approved hostels in which prisoners may be required to live as a condition of release from prison. Whereas there were 94 hostels across the country to which male prisoners could be released on parole, there were only six to which women could be released. The result of this is that the claimant, who had been sentenced to life imprisonment for murder, feared that she would be released to live in approved premises far from her family in London as a condition of her release on licence upon the expiry of her tariff. The SC having ruled that the AP provision was directly discriminatory on grounds of sex (see Chapter 2), it went on to consider the application of Schedule 3 para 26.

R (Coll) v Secretary of State for Justice **[2017] UKSC 40, [2017] 1 WLR 2093**

Lady Hale (for the Court):

37. … Ms Rose argues that the provision of APs is not 'separate but equal' because of the limited number and distribution of APs for women compared with those for men. The applicable exception is in para 26(2), dealing with 'separate but different' services … I agree with her, because the services are different in this important respect. They may very well be different in other respects too, because the needs of women offenders are recognised to be different from the needs of male offenders, but that is by the way.

38. In any event, it does not matter which sub-paragraph is applicable here, because the issue is the same whichever it is. Ms Rose accepts that a joint service for persons of both sexes would be less effective. Expecting women offenders, with their many vulnerabilities, to share premises with male offenders who by definition present a high or very high risk of harm is not likely to be an effective way of helping them with the transition to an independent and law abiding life in the outside world. Ms Rose also accepts that para 26(2)(b) is fulfilled – the much lesser extent to which women require the service makes it 'not reasonably practicable' to provide it otherwise than as a separate service provided differently. It would not be reasonably practicable to provide 94 APs for the 112 places for women required. This must be correct. The minimum staffing costs, for example, are the same no matter how many residents there are.

39. The crucial question, therefore, is whether the limited provision is a proportionate means of achieving a legitimate aim. In discussing justification, Cranston J [at first instance] focused principally on the problem of cost. The cost of building or converting a building into an AP was between £1.5 and £2.2m. No matter how small, the annual running cost of an AP was said to be in the region of £500,000 to £750,000 per annum. There was also likely to be community opposition to establishing new APs. Female APs were under-used, so that women who needed them would readily find a place. The average stay was only 80 days on average. So the current provision was proportionate … Elias LJ did not think that the only objective was saving cost in a time of austerity. It was also to ensure that men and women were in similarly appointed establishments, because there was a real risk of discrimination claims if they were not. Given the limited disadvantage, because of the short average stay, the finding of justification was in principle sustainable …

40. Saving cost is, of course, a legitimate objective of public policy. But, as the Court of Justice of the European Union emphasised in *O'Brien v Ministry of Justice* (Case C-393/10) EU:C:2012:110, [2012] ICR 955, 'budgetary considerations cannot justify discrimination' (para 66). In other words, if a benefit is to be limited in order to save costs, it must be limited in a non-discriminatory way. There was no evidence and no finding that the aim was to ensure that men and women were accommodated in similarly appointed premises. Given that the Act permits different provision to be made if their needs are different, this would not by itself be a sound basis for the discrimination.

41. … Ms Rose accepts that in principle the different provision made for men and women might be justified. Her complaint is that the Ministry of Justice has never properly addressed its collective mind to the problem of providing sufficient and suitable places in APs for women which achieve, so far as practicable, the policy of placing them as close to home as possible. There are other options which could have been considered, including: replacing one or more of the current, relatively large women's APs with a larger number of smaller units, more widely spread; closing one or more of the existing women's APs and replacing them with APs closer to the areas where large numbers of serious women offenders have their homes and families; redesignating one of the men's APs in London for women and one of the women's APs for men to make up the loss of male places; or considering alternative forms of accommodation for women released on licence.

42. Cranston J's finding that the Secretary of State was in breach of the public sector equality duty also means that the Ministry is not in a position to show that the discrimination involved in the different provision made for men and for women is a proportionate means of fulfilling a legitimate aim. It may or may not be. But it is for the respondent to show that the discrimination is justified. Given that the Ministry has not addressed the possible impacts upon women, assessed whether there is a disadvantage, how significant it is and what might be done to mitigate it or to meet the particular circumstances of women offenders, it cannot show that the present distribution of APs for women is a proportionate means of achieving a legitimate aim.

The question of single-sex services has generated extraordinary levels of conflict in recent years. In 2009 the Ministry of Justice lost a judicial review brought against it by a transgender woman with a GRC who had been accommodated in a male prison; in *R (AB) v SSJ* [2009] EWHC 2220 (Admin), [2010] 2 All ER 151 the High Court ruled that the Ministry had breached the prisoner's Article 8 rights. Following this decision, Prison Service Instruction PSI 07/2011 on Care and Management of Transsexual Prisoners in England and Wales indicated that prisoners should normally be located in the prison estate of their sex as recognised by UK law, and that transgender prisoners would not normally be accommodated in accordance with their gender, as distinct from their sex, without a GRC, though exceptions could be made for trans prisoners who were 'sufficiently advanced in the gender reassignment process'.

In October 2015 there was a public outcry after Tara Hudson, a transgender woman who did not have a GRC, was held in a male prison. Shortly thereafter, two transgender prisoners, neither of whom had GRCs, were found dead or dying in their cells in male prisons.[102] The inquest into one of these prisoners, Vikki Thompson, was later to conclude that she was correctly held in a male prison and that she had not intended to kill herself, though she had been 'let down by various departments including the NHS, Leeds Community Healthcare NHS Trust, the Prison Service and also by her family'.[103] The inquest had heard from Thompson's mother that Thompson had not indicated that she had a problem being in a men's prison. Joanne Latham, the other prisoner, had been held in a close supervision centre (CSC), reserved for the most dangerous and vulnerable prisoners, after being sentenced to a third life sentence having attempted to kill three people in separate incidents over 10 years, all while living as a man. She had changed her name from Edward the summer before she killed herself, but had not requested a transfer to a woman's prison. According to a report in *The Guardian*, Latham would have been ineligible for transfer in any event as there are no CSC units in women's prisons.

In 2016 the Women and Equalities Committee published a report, *Transgender Equality*, which stated at §320 that:

> While the safety and welfare of all offenders is paramount, caring for and managing trans offenders appropriately is crucial. There is a clear risk of harm (including violence, sexual assault, self-harming and suicide) where trans prisoners are not located in a prison or other setting appropriate to their acquired / affirmed gender. Neither is it fair or appropriate for them to end up in solitary confinement solely as a result of their trans status.[104]

[102] J Beard, *Transgender Prisoners*, House of Commons Briefing Paper No 07420 (2018).

[103] 'Trans prisoner Vikki Thompson "let down by prison, NHS and family"', BBC News, 19 May 2017, available at https://www.bbc.co.uk/news/uk-england-leeds-39974601.

[104] First Report of Session 2015–16 Report, HC 390, §320 (available at https://publications.parliament.uk/pa/cm201516/cmselect/cmwomeq/390/39002.htm).

Shortly thereafter, the MOJ published its Review on the Care and Management of Transgender Offenders, which declared that 'policy in this area needs to evolve and take as its starting presumption a wish to respect someone in the gender in which they identify, once in the care of the criminal justice system' and that 'People who are living in a gender different to that of their assigned sex[105] at birth should, as a general presumption, be treated by offender management services according to the gender in which they identify, though there would be 'circumstances when a transgender person's location cannot be straightforwardly reconciled with their views. This may be due to a lack of evidence (or the presence of counter-evidence) relating to the gender in which they identify and/or concerns raised via an assessment of all known risks, indicating they cannot be safely managed in a prison that does match their self-identified gender'.[106] Shortly thereafter Prison Service Instruction 17/2016 came into force.

Jacqueline Beard, *Transgender Prisoners*, House of Commons Briefing Paper No 07420, 2018, 3–10

The new policy guidelines, Prison Service Instruction 17/2016 state that 'all transgender prisoners (irrespective of prison location) must be allowed to express the gender with which they identify'. Such prisoners must be asked their view of the part of the prison estate that reflects this; however a decision to locate them in a prison which does not accord with their legal gender can only be made following a Transgender Case Board. Those who wish to be placed in a prison location which is not consistent with their legally recognised gender must provide evidence of living in the gender with which they identify. Assessments will be made on a case by case basis.

Also in November 2016, the Ministry of Justice published the first official statistics on transgender prisoners. A data collection exercise in March/April 2016 showed that there were 70 transgender prisoners in 33 of the 123 public and private prisons in England and Wales.

A Ministry of Justice report published in November 2017 said there were 125 transgender prisoners in England and Wales who had had a local transgender case board when data was collected in March/April 2017. 47 of the prisons in England and Wales said that they had 1 or more transgender prisoners.

In Scotland, policy guidelines state that the social gender in which the prisoner is living should be fully respected, regardless of whether or not they have a GRC …

The key shift in policy [post 2016] is that, in the majority of cases, the prison service will try to accommodate prisoners in the *gender with which they identify* [original emphasis], even if they are not seeking medical interventions or GRCs [then citing the 2016 review]:

> Current instructions and practice place an emphasis on gender at birth, the possible acquisition (or desire to acquire) a gender recognition certificate (GRC), and on a person's decision to undergo surgery or undertake other significant medical intervention. While those people with a GRC must be treated in the acquired gender in every respect, it must also be taken into account that not all these factors are equally important to all transgender people. Many successfully live their lives without such interventions and therefore policy in this area needs to evolve and take as its starting presumption a wish to respect someone in the gender in which they identify, once in the care of the criminal justice system.
>
> Allowing transgender offenders to experience the system in the gender in which they identify will, in the great majority of cases, represent the most humane and safest way to act. We believe it will also assist successful rehabilitation.

[105] The controversial nature of this term has been remarked on above.

[106] https://assets.publishing.service.gov.uk/government/uploads/system/uploads/attachment_data/file/566828/transgender-review-findings-web.pdf.

However, there will be a minority of cases where this will not be possible:

> In the minority of cases where that is not possible, the reasons for departing from this starting presumption must be clear, explicit and made known to the person they affect, especially when it involves assigning someone to a male or female prison. The majority of such cases are likely to concern transgender people convicted of serious offences, where both public protection and the best interests of the person themselves may not be compatible with the general presumption described above. However, this will not be true of all transgender serious offenders and it is important that policy for the majority should not be founded upon the highly complex considerations raised by a minority …

The Women and Equalities Committee's First Report of 2015–16 on *Transgender Equality* was mentioned above. The report also called for GRCs, which have the effect of changing people's legal sex for most purposes, to be available on the basis of self-identification and for the Government to 'work with Sport England to produce guidance which help sporting groups realise that there are likely to be few occasions where exclusions are justified to ensure fair competition or the safety of competitors' (see discussion below). It also recommended that the EqA be amended to protect 'gender identity' rather than gender reassignment, and 'so that the occupational requirements provision and/or the single-sex/separate services provision shall not apply in relation to discrimination against a person whose acquired gender has been recognised under the [GRA]'.

The Government initially responded to the WEC that it 'agree[d] with the principle … that those who … have secured a [GRC] – should be afforded the full legal and social status of their acquired gender', stating that it was 'keen to ensure that that law in this area operates fairly and is not abused, therefore we are keen to receive further representations and evidence on the availability and use of the exceptions in the Equality Act 2010 from all affected parties to take into account for future policy discussions'.[107] It also 'agree[d] that there are likely to be few occasions in sport where exclusions are justified to ensure fair competition or the safety of competitors'. A consultation process was launched in July 2018 about proposed changes to the GRA. Stonewall, in particular, lobbied for the right of those aged 16+ to self-identify gender identity, including non-binary identities,[108] but initial enthusiasm from government for radical changes gave way to concerns about the implications of such reform. By this stage the changes to prison rules had generated their own controversies.

> **'Karen White: how 'manipulative' transgender inmate attacked again', *The Guardian*, 11 October 2018**
>
> Transgender politics – like any politics – can be divisive. Yet in the case of Karen White, who is legally still a man but was put in a female-only prison, both sides of the transgender rights debate are united in the belief mistakes were made. White entered the UK prison system as transgender. However, despite dressing as a woman, the 52-year-old had not undergone any surgery and was still legally a male. She was also a convicted paedophile and on remand for grievous bodily harm, burglary, multiple rapes and other sexual offences against women.
>
> In September last year she was transferred to New Hall prison in West Yorkshire. During a three-month period at the female prison she sexually assaulted two other inmates …

[107] *Government Response to the Women and Equalities Committee Report on Transgender Equality* CM 9103, July 2016, available at https://www.gov.uk/government/publications/transgender-equality-report-government-response, 14.

[108] https://www.stonewall.org.uk/gender-recognition-act.

> It is believed the decision to place White in a women's prison was made only at the first level – by a local case board ... the board should have taken into account all offending history but [it has been suggested that it] failed to do so ...
>
> Born in July 1966 as Stephen Terence Wood, the former Manchester drag artist was convicted in 2001 on two charges of indecent assault and gross indecency with a child of primary school age, and jailed for 18 months ...
>
> Frances Crook, the chief executive of the Howard League for Penal Reform, said grave mistakes were made in the White case and the safety of vulnerable women should be paramount.
>
> Crook has previously said: 'It is a very toxic debate, but I think prisons have probably been influenced by some of the extreme conversations and have been bullied into making some decisions that have harmed women.
>
> > 'In my view, any man who has committed a serious sexual or violent offence against women, who then wants to transfer but has not gone through the whole process, still has a penis and still has male hormones, should not be put into a women's prison. There may be a case for having separate provision; that is a debate to be had.'...
>
> Whatever the case with White, it is clear the prison service is under increasing pressure in this 'rapidly developing area of policy'.

In July 2019 HM Chief Inspector of Prisons for England and Wales reported that two per cent of prisoners categorised themselves as transgender, which would amount to almost 1,650 prisoners. This would suggest a remarkable increase from the figure of 125 in November 2017 (see p 401 above), and a much higher proportion of the prison population than of society more generally.[109] Meanwhile, in March 2019 it had been reported that a separate prison unit had been established in HMP Downview to house transwomen prisoners with GRCs who are regarded as posing an unacceptable risk to women prisoners.[110]

In September 2020 the Government announced that no changes would be made to the EqA or the GRA in England and Wales:

***Bailey v Stonewall Equality Ltd, Garden Court Chambers Ltd,* Case No: 2202172/2020**[111]

Employment Judge Goodman (for the tribunal):

> 50. ... The debate continues. In December 2021 the House of Commons Women and Equalities committee published the results of its own enquiry, recommending changes. In Scotland legislation making changes is proposed.
>
> 51. Opposition to proposed changes has focused on the need to preserve single sex spaces for natal women, and the single sex exemptions in the Equality Act. Some fear that self-identification of gender identity could facilitate abuse of women. Lesbians and gays are concerned that young people exploring their sexual identity may identify in another gender when they are only same-sex attracted, or even that same-sex orientation will be erased.
>
> 52. The debate on reform has been polarised, often uncompromising, and sometimes hostile and abusive. Men and women who oppose gender self identity can be labelled transphobes. Transgender people are in turn accused of homophobia and misogyny. It is probably relevant to the uncompromising tone that the issue is not one of philosophy but of the practical

[109] *Annual Report* 2018–19, HC 2469, 31, 97.
[110] See 'Ministry of Justice opens Britain's first transgender-only prison unit', *The Independent*, 3 March 2019.
[111] https://www.judiciary.uk/wp-content/uploads/2022/07/Bailey-judgment.pdf.

consequences. Many transpeople live in fear of challenge, ridicule and threats. Transwomen are subjected to open abuse and sometimes violence – as gay men sometimes are, possibly by the same people, policing masculinity. They also fear unpleasant challenges from women if they try to use women's toilets and changing rooms. From the other side, the long and continuing history of male violence towards women can make women fearful and mistrustful of admitting people with male bodies to protected spaces where they are vulnerable, such as rape crisis centres, public toilets, changing rooms and refuges. Others fear losing the chance to correct historic disadvantage, for example, in collecting equal pay statistics. People who are same-sex attracted are concerned that younger people may find it hard to recognise they are gay or lesbian when it is suggested to them that their confused feelings mean they are in fact of another gender. Opponents talk of women, or gays or lesbians, being 'erased'.

The appropriate accommodation of trans prisoners is perhaps an extreme example of the difficulties which have arisen in attempting to reconcile the competing interests in this area, but it is not the only one. In 2019, *The Guardian* reported that the City of London Corporation, which is responsible for Hampstead Heath, had formally opened Hampstead Ladies' Pond to transgender women.[112] According to the newspaper, the consultation which had preceded the decision 'was accompanied by an intense debate. In May last year women went into the heath's men-only pond, some dressed in fake beards, claiming that a policy based on how people identify themselves was open to abuse. Meanwhile LGBT charity Stonewall attacked a "toxic" media debate around the issue, stating that the Equality Act 2010 'already said trans people should be allowed to access single-sex spaces that match their gender without discrimination …'.

As should be evident from above, Stonewall's statement, as reported, is inaccurate because:

(1) the EqA permits sex-segregation;
(2) it only protects from gender reassignment discrimination those who are 'proposing to undergo, [are] undergoing or [have] undergone a process (or part of a process) for the purpose of reassigning [their] sex by changing physiological or other attributes of sex', as distinct from (all) trans people;
(3) a person is entitled to be treated as having a sex other than that on their original birth certificate only where they have acquired a GRC; and
(4) even people with GRCs may be denied access to single sex services where this is proportionate.

As discussed at p 388 above, preventing a transgender woman without a GRC from using the Ladies' Pond will amount to *sex* discrimination if admission is refused, Schedule 3 para 27 permitting the discrimination if the admission of women only 'is a proportionate means of achieving a legitimate aim' and it is accepted that woman using the pond might 'reasonably object to the presence of a person of the opposite sex'. Such objection might be raised, in the case of an observant Muslim or orthodox Jewish woman, on the basis that her religious beliefs or community values prohibit her from being undressed in the presence of men. Other women might object to being semi-naked in the presence of men

[112] 'Trans women given formal access to Hampstead Heath pond', *The Guardian*, 23 May 2019.

because of concerns about their appearance, past experience of sexual assault or fear of sexual harassment.[113] In circumstances in which Hampstead also boasts a Men's Pond and a mixed pond for swimming, maintenance of a women's pond might reasonably be regarded as legitimate to encourage access to outside swimming by women who might not otherwise be able to enjoy it.

If a trans woman with a GRC were to be refused access to the pond this would be because of gender reassignment and the question which would then arise is whether Schedule 3 para 28 permitted the discrimination, ie, whether the denial of access is 'a proportionate means of achieving a legitimate aim'. It may be more difficult to prove the proportionality of a 'no trans women' policy but, at least as regards the women users whose concerns are of a religious nature, the admission even of trans women with GRCs would have the same effect of denying their access.

The *Jewish Chronicle* reported that the impact of the change to the rules governing the Ladies' Pond was to prevent Orthodox Jewish women from continuing to use it.

> **'Strictly Orthodox women "to take action" against opening Hampstead Heath Ladies Pond to transgender swimmers', *Jewish Chronicle*, 23 May 2019**
>
> Under halacha, no one can change their gender, and so trans women would not be considered women.
>
> While Jewish law permits Strictly Orthodox Jewish women to be in a state of undress in front of other women, it is forbidden in front of men.
>
> University of Reading Professor Rosa Freedman said on Twitter she had 'explained [the concept of] trans to an ultra orthodox chassidic Jewish Rabbi whose wife and her friends will no longer be able to swim at Hampstead Ladies Pond … perhaps the most difficult conversation I have had on the issue to date.'
>
> The rabbi's wife, Prof Freedman said, 'swims there every day … and she wanted to know 'what can we do? and how do we do it?' She is currently creating a group of religious women to take action …

It is worth bearing in mind that Orthodox Jewish women such as those affected by the decision on the Ladies' Pond cannot mix with men other than their husbands when fully or partially undressed without breaching their religious, family and community values. They cannot, consistent with those values, access mixed-sex services.

Particularly severe difficulties can arise where a trans woman seeks to access intimate services such as massage or waxing. This came to prominence in Canada where trans woman Jessica Yaniv brought multiple claims against beauticians, a number of them migrant women working alone, who refused to wax her (male) genitalia. Yaniv's campaign went on for several years before British Columbia's Human Rights Tribunal dismissed her complaints, ruling that Yaniv 'had sought to target small businesses for financial gain "or to punish certain ethnic groups which she perceives as hostile to the rights of LGBTQ+ people."'[114]

[113] In this context note the *Women and Equalities Committee reports, Sexual harassment of women and girls in public places*, Sixth Report of Session 2017–19, HC 701; *Sexual harassment and sexual violence in schools*, Third Report of Session 2016–17, HC 91 and *Sexual harassment in the workplace*, Fifth Report of Session 2017–19, HC 725, extracted at p 346–347 above.

[114] 'Transgender woman denied waxing of male genitals wasn't discriminated against: Tribunal', *Global News Canada*, 22 October 2019.

In April 2022 the EHRC released its non-statutory guidance, *Separate and single-sex service providers: a guide on the Equality Act sex and gender reassignment provisions.*[115] Having provided examples of cases in which single-sex services might be provided: 'if women of a particular religion or belief will not use the local swimming pool at the same time as men, women-only swimming sessions could be provided as well as mainly-mixed sessions'; 'a women-only support unit for women who have experienced domestic or sexual violence can be set up, even if there is no parallel men-only unit because of insufficient demand'; 'single-sex wards in hospitals and nursing homes'; 'separate male and female changing rooms'; 'sports sessions involving a high degree of physical contact or any service involving intimate personal health or hygiene', it continues:

EHRC, *Separate and single-sex service providers: a guide on the Equality Act sex and gender reassignment provisions*

You must also be able to show that providing the service on a single-sex basis is a proportionate means of achieving a legitimate aim. Again, proportionality requires that you balance the impact on all service users of providing services only to one sex.

If you have met the conditions set out above and have established a separate or single-sex service, you should consider your approach to trans people's use of the service. In considering your approach and when taking decisions you must meet the conditions set out under the gender reassignment provisions.

Under these provisions, your approach must be a proportionate means of achieving a legitimate aim. This will depend upon the nature of the service and may link to the reason the separate or single-sex service is needed. For example, a legitimate aim could be the privacy and dignity of others. You must then show that your action is a proportionate way to achieve that aim. This requires that you balance the impact upon all service users.

Example: A group counselling session is provided for female victims of sexual assault. The organisers do not allow trans women to attend as they judge that the clients who attend the group session are likely to be traumatised by the presence of a person who is biologically male.

Example: A domestic abuse refuge offers emergency accommodation to female survivors. Feedback from survivors indicates that they would feel uncomfortable sharing accommodation with trans women for reasons of trauma and safety. The provider decides to exclude trans women from the refuge. It compiles a list of alternative sources of support in the local area which can be provided to trans women who approach the centre for help.

Example: A leisure centre introduces some female-only fitness classes. It decides to exclude trans women because of the degree of physical contact involved in such classes.

Example: A gym has separate-sex communal changing rooms. There is concern about the safety and dignity of trans men changing in an open plan environment. The gym therefore decides to introduce an additional gender-neutral changing room with self-contained units.

Example: A small cafe with limited space and facilities for public use has separate lockable, self-contained male and female toilets with hand basins in single units. To ensure they are fully inclusive, and to make the most effective use of the available facilities, the cafe decides to make them all gender neutral.

Example: A community centre has separate male and female toilets. It conducts a survey in which some service users say that they would not use the centre if the toilets were open to members of the opposite biological sex, for reasons of privacy and dignity or because of their religious belief. It decides to introduce an additional gender-neutral toilet. It puts up signs telling all users that

[115] https://www.equalityhumanrights.com/en/advice-and-guidance/when-you-can-provide-separate-or-single-sex-service.

> they may use either the toilet for their biological sex or to use the gender-neutral toilet if they feel more comfortable doing so.
>
> If the toilets you provide for service users are also used as staff toilets, you will also need to take account of the Workplace (Health, Safety and Welfare) Regulations 1992 which require employers to provide a certain number of toilets and to provide separate toilet and washing facilities for men and women in some circumstances ...[116]

Part 3 EqA: Religion

In addition to the general provisions permitting sex-segregation discussed above, para 29 of Schedule 3 allows the provision of separate and single-sex services by ministers of religion where such services are provided at a place which is (permanently or for the time being) occupied or used for those purposes, and the limited provision of the service is necessary in order to comply with the doctrines of the religion or is for the purpose of avoiding conflict with the strongly held religious convictions of a significant number of the religion's followers. The provision defines 'minister' so as to exclude those whose office is held within wholly or mainly commercial organisations.

Schedule 3 para 24 EqA excludes from s29 EqA's prohibition on gender reassignment refusals by clergy in the Churches of England and Wales to solemnise marriage, and refusals to permit marriages in buildings registered for the solemnisation of religious marriages. The specific provisions relating to Anglican clergy are necessary because, the Anglican church being established in England and Wales, Anglican clergy have common law duties to marry parishioners.

Part 5 EqA: Genuine Occupational Requirements

The normal GOR defence provided by Schedule 9 para 1 EqA is discussed in Chapter 4 and applies to sex/married and civilly partnered status and gender reassignment as it applies to other protected characteristics.[117] Whereas para 1(3) of Schedule 9 EqA generally provides that the GOR applies if 'the person to whom A applies the requirement does not meet it (or A has reasonable grounds for not being satisfied that the person meets it)', para 1(4) states that the GOR defence applies as regards sex where 'the person to whom A applies the requirement does not meet it'.

The SDA recognised a number of 'genuine occupational qualifications' (GOQs) which disapplied the prohibition on sex discrimination in specific situations, and contained no

[116] The guidance was criticised by many for permitting the exclusion of trans women from single sex services. It is, however, accurate, a statement of the law in its present form. In particular, the decision in of the HL in *A v CC West Yorkshire Police* [2005] AC 51, which tends to be cited in support of the suggestion that trans women must be treated as women, relied on the decisions of the CJEU in *P v S & Cornwall* and *KB v NHS*, discussed above, but predated the implementation of the GRA which provided the protection required by those decisions without (as was necessary in the *West Yorkshire Police* case) requiring robust interpretation of the EqA or its predecessors. The *West Yorkshire Police* case involved a challenge to a refusal to recruit a trans woman into the police because, as a woman police officer, she would have to conduct intimate searches. Lady Hale expressly stated that the 'questions of demarcation and definition' that the HL was required to answer applied '[u]ntil the matter is resolved by legislation'. She also referred to the fact that the claimant in that case had 'done everything that she possibly could do to align her physical identity with her psychological identity. She has lived successfully as a woman for many years. She has taken the appropriate hormone treatment and concluded a programme of surgery. She believes that she presents as a woman in every respect'. Note also that schools are required to maintain separate toilets for girls and boys where they have pupils aged at least eight and that workplaces are required to maintain single sex sanitary facilities unless all facilities are self-contained.

[117] Note that para 9(1)(3)–(4) make technical provision to accommodate the GOR in view of the (non-symmetrical) prohibitions on gender reassignment and married/civil partnership status.

proportionality requirement. These have been displaced by the EqA, but they provide some examples of situations in which sex may be a GOR. These included (s7(2) SDA), situations in which: '(a) the essential nature of the job [or aspects of it] calls for a man [or woman] for reasons of physiology (excluding physical strength or stamina) or, in dramatic performances or other entertainment, for reasons of authenticity, so that the essential nature of the job would be materially different if carried out by a woman [or man]'; (b) a number of situations in which 'the job needs to be held by a man [or woman] to preserve decency or privacy' (eg because aspects of it would be performed where men (women) might be in a state of undress or using sanitary facilities, or involved physical contact and men (women) might reasonably object to it being carried out by a woman (man)); or (ba) because the job would be carried out, or involve the holder living, in a private home and objection might be taken to allowing a woman (or man) doing it 'the degree of physical or social contact with a person living in the home, or the knowledge of intimate details of such a person's life, which is likely, because of the nature or circumstances of the job or of the home, to be allowed to, or available to, the holder of the job' or because '(e) the holder of the job provides individuals with personal services promoting their welfare or education, or similar personal services, and those services can most effectively be provided by a man'.

Discrimination which would have been lawful under s7(2) SDA will be permitted by Schedule 9 para 1 EqA only where it is a proportional means of achieving a legitimate aim. The provision also permits discrimination which would not have come within the closed list provided by s7 SDA, and would accordingly have breached that Act. Examples of this might include the recruitment of drivers for women-only taxi services.

Among the cases which arose under s7 SDA were *Etam v Rowan* [1989] IRLR 150 in which EAT accepted that a job in a women's clothing shop could come within s7(2)(b) where it involved assisting in a changing area. And in *Buckinghamshire CC v Ahmed*, the EAT allowed an appeal against a finding of unlawful discrimination in respect of a man who had been refused work as a Punjabi interpreter, ruling that the tribunal had erred in rejecting as a GOQ the Council's evidence that:

***Buckinghamshire CC v Ahmed* App. No EAT/124/98, 18 June 1998 (unreported)**

Hull J:

> in a number of the ethnic communities with which they dealt and in particular the Punjabi Muslim community, there was great delicacy in dealing with women who were concerned in various social or medical or other problems. It was said that if an interpreter were to go into one of the homes, or to see women collectively at perhaps a 'well woman' session, or women's health session or something of that sort, it would be regarded generally in the community and by the woman concerned as inappropriate that the interpreter should be a man. It was said that although if (say) a white social worker went to a house that might be in order, if a person who was a Punjabi went there it were better, it said, that it should be a woman than a man, out of feelings of delicacy and tact.
>
> It was not said, of course, that it was essential that it should be a woman interpreter but what was said was that the services could be provided more effectively: it would be easier for a Punjabi Muslim woman, on many occasions, to explain in such matters as the case perhaps where her children had been involved in matters which had attracted the attention of the Police, or where she herself had medico-social problems or something like that. It would be easier for her to speak to a woman and would not attract the sort of comment that might happen if a male Punjabi-speaker, particularly a Punjabi himself, were to go to the house.

Another example of where a sex GOR might apply concerns the delivery of services to women victims of gender violence, whether sexual or otherwise. Some rape crisis and similar services are provided exclusively by women, to women, sometimes in premises to which only women are allowed access. There have been no successful challenges in the UK to the application of a GOQ/GOR in these circumstances. The Explanatory Notes to the EqA suggest that 'A counsellor working with victims of rape might have to be a woman and not a transsexual person, even if she has a [GRC], in order to avoid causing them further distress'.[118] The Women and Equalities Committee, whose 2016 report is discussed above, heard evidence from Women's Aid that it had applied the gender reassignment GOR to positions, though this policy was at the time under review. As stated above, the Committee recommended that the GOR cease to apply to individuals with GRCs.[119] A different approach had been taken in 2003 by British Columbia's Supreme Court.

S Jay, 'Court confirms any woman's human right to organize with peers' December 2003[120]

On December 19, 2003, the British Columbia SC set aside the decision of the Human Rights Tribunal which had held, in error, that the Vancouver Rape Relief and Women's Shelter had breached the Human Rights Code when it refused to allow Kimberly Nixon, a person without the life experience of being treated as a woman, to train as a volunteer peer counselor at the women-only rape crisis centre and shelter for battered women. Kimberly Nixon is a post-operative male to female transsexual … The Court also set aside the Tribunal's award of damages, which means that Kimberly Nixon must now return the $7,500 that the non-profit volunteer run organization was ordered to pay. Until it was overruled, it was the highest ever amount awarded to compensate for hurt feelings.

Vancouver Rape Relief argued that their organization did not discriminate and, as well, is protected by the section of the Human Rights Code (sec. 41) which protects charitable groups and their right to freedom of association.

'Vancouver Rape Relief argued that the tribunal's decision failed to recognize the rights of women to organize independently in order to address historic experiences of inequality and oppression. In fact the tribunal's decision opened the way for men to demand entry into women's organizations. In Vancouver Rape Relief's case such a situation would have undermined the peer-based self-help objectives of the organization,' explains Gwendoline Allison, co-counsel for Vancouver Rape Relief and Women's Shelter.

Christine Boyle, Professor of Law at the University of British Columbia, also represented Vancouver Rape Relief. She said, 'This decision reinforces existing case law which rejects a formal equality approach to human rights. Ms Nixon had argued for a "disadvantage neutral" approach to human rights. Vancouver Rape Relief had argued that the analysis of discrimination should be contextual and take into account the needs of equality-seeking groups.

'Other women's groups felt intimidated by the threat of human rights complaints for organizing exactly as we are entitled to organize,' says Suzanne Jay of Vancouver Rape Relief and Women's Shelter, 'Women are an historically disadvantaged group and there is provision in the Charter of Rights and Freedoms and in the Human Rights Code for us to group independently to address these experiences of inequality'.

[118] https://www.legislation.gov.uk/ukpga/2010/15/notes.
[119] n 104 above.
[120] https://sisyphe.org/spip.php?article834.

In March 2019 it was reported that Vancouver's Rape Relief and Women's Shelter, then Canada's oldest rape crisis centre, had been 'stripped of city funding' by Vancouver by reason of its refusal to open its services to trans women.[121]

> **'Canada's oldest rape crisis centre stripped of city funding for refusing to accept trans women', *National Post* 18 March 2019**
>
> After the vote, Vancouver city councillor Christine Boyle[122] posted a tweet to her account accusing the organization of 'supporting transphobia.' 'Trans women are women and sex work is work … I can't support (organizations) who exclude them,' Boyle wrote in an accompanying note.
>
> The defunding is the latest flashpoint in an ongoing struggle between transgender activists and feminist organizations who maintain that female-born and male-born women should remain distinct groups. One of the figures leading the defunding charge against Vancouver Rape Relief was Morgane Oger, a longstanding transgender advocate …
>
> In 2017, the official opening of the Vancouver Women's Library, a space with links to Vancouver Rape Relief, was hijacked by protesters who handed out pamphlets reading 'this library is run by women who hate other women.' When the Licorice Parlour, an East Vancouver candy store, put up a poster in support of a Vancouver Rape Relief fundraiser in May, the shop was hit with online harassment and negative reviews for being 'oppressive' and 'transphobic.'
>
> Vancouver Rape Relief has said that while they believe trans women need support and protection from violence, their 'lived experience' is fundamentally different from a female-born woman. 'We do not have the experience to offer services to people without the same life experience … this is not our work,' Vancouver Rape Relief representative Hilla Kerner told a City a Vancouver committee last week.
>
> In denying service to trans women, Kerner said their group was no different than other city-supported organizations who reserve their services towards a particular demographic group, be it immigrants, Chinese-speakers or native youth. 'Because we are an oppressed group who fights for equality we have a right to decide who are membership is and who we serve,' she said.
>
> Men are strictly banned from spaces operated by Vancouver Rape Relief, and the organization has previously argied that their clients, all of whom are recovering from male violence, do not feel comfortable while in the presence of someone who used to live as a man. 'Even deep voices, male insignia like baseball caps and boots can make women nervous,' wrote Lee Lakeman, a founder of the centre, in 2006.

Part 5 EqA: Religious Organisations

Also of significance here is Schedule 9 para 2, also discussed in Chapter 10, which provides that:

> **Schedule 9 para 2 EqA, Religious requirements relating to sex, marriage etc, sexual orientation**
>
> (1) A person (A) does not contravene a provision mentioned in sub-paragraph (2) by applying in relation to employment a requirement to which sub-paragraph (4) applies if A shows that—
>
> (a) the employment is for the purposes of an organised religion,
>
> (b) the application of the requirement engages the compliance or non-conflict principle, and
>
> (c) the person to whom A applies the requirement does not meet it (or A has reasonable grounds for not being satisfied that the person meets it) …

[121] 'Canada's oldest rape crisis centre stripped of city funding for refusing to accept trans women', *National Post*, 18 March 2019.

[122] Not the same Christine Boyle as that referred to in the previous article.

The provisions in para 2(2) are section 39(1)(a) and (c) and (2)(b) and (c) EqA (which regulate access to jobs, promotion, transfer or training and any other work-related benefits, facilities or services, and dismissal), and the equivalent provisions applicable to public and private offices. Para 2(3) makes similar provision as regards qualifications for posts to which para 2(1) applies. Para 2(4) then provides that the requirements referred to in para 2(1) include:

- to be of a particular sex;
- not to be a transsexual person;
- not to be married or a civil partner;
- not to be married to, or the civil partner of, a person who has a living former spouse or civil partner; or
- related to circumstances in which a marriage or civil partnership came to an end.

Paras 2(5)–(6) provide that the application of a requirement engages the compliance principle if it is applied so as to comply with the doctrines of the religion, and the non-conflict principle if, 'because of the nature or context of the employment, the requirement is applied so as to avoid conflicting with the strongly held religious convictions of a significant number of the religion's followers'. The significance of para 2 is that, unlike para 1, it does not impose any requirement of proportionality. It is further discussed in Chapter 9.

Part 5 EqA: The Military

Schedule 9 para 4 permits the application of a requirement to be a man or not to be a 'transsexual' person 'in relation to service in the armed forces' if it is shown that 'the application is a proportionate means of ensuring the combat effectiveness of the armed forces'. The provision is modelled on the following:

> **Article 14(2), Council Directive 2006/54**
>
> Member States may provide, as regards access to employment including the training leading thereto, that a difference of treatment which is based on a characteristic related to sex shall not constitute discrimination where, by reason of the nature of the particular occupational activities concerned or of the context in which they are carried out, such a characteristic constitutes a genuine and determining occupational requirement, provided that its objective is legitimate and the requirement is proportionate.

In *Sirdar v Secretary of State for Defence* Case C-273/97 [1999] ECR I–7403, [2000] ICR 130 the CJEU rejected a challenge to the prohibition which then applied to the admission of women into the marines by reason of that unit's principle of 'interoperability' – that is, the rule that all marines must be capable of operating in a commando unit. Women were at that time prohibited from active combat service.[123] Shortly afterwards, in Case C-285/98 *Kreil v Germany* EU:C:2000:2, [2000] ECR I–69, the CJEU ruled that a complete prohibition on women in the armed services was disproportionate.[124] Since that time women have

[123] This rule was maintained after an MOD review: 'Women in the Armed Forces', May 2002.

[124] In Case C-186/01 *Dory v Germany* EU:C:2003:146, [2003] ECR I-2479 the CJEU ruled that the German requirement for men (but not women) to perform national service did not fall within the scope of the Equal Treatment Directive. The CJEU categorised the exclusively male obligation as a 'choice[] of military organisation for the defence of their territory or of their essential interests.'

increasingly been deployed in the armed services across the EU, and since October 2018 all roles in the British armed forces have been open to women.

Part 5 EqA: Insurance

Schedule 9 para 20 EqA, Insurance contracts, etc

(1) It is not a contravention of this Part of this Act, so far as relating to relevant discrimination, to do anything in relation to an annuity, life insurance policy, accident insurance policy or similar matter involving the assessment of risk if—

(a) that thing is done by reference to actuarial or other data from a source on which it is reasonable to rely, and
(b) it is reasonable to do it.

(2) 'Relevant discrimination' is—

(a) gender reassignment discrimination;
(b) marriage and civil partnership discrimination;
(c) pregnancy and maternity discrimination;
(d) sex discrimination.

The Explanatory Notes to the EqA state that this provision is designed to replace a similar exception in the SDA, but does not otherwise seek to justify it. The example provided is of an employer which 'makes access to a group insurance policy available as a result of being employed by it. The employer, not the insurer, is responsible for ensuring that the provision of benefits under the policy complies with this Act .... In providing access to these group policies the employer may take advantage of this exception.'[125]

General Exception: Sport

Section 195 EqA, Sport

(1) A person does not contravene this Act, so far as relating to sex, only by doing anything in relation to the participation of another as a competitor in a gender-affected activity.
(2) A person does not contravene section 29, 33, 34 or 35, so far as relating to gender reassignment, only by doing anything in relation to the participation of a transsexual person as a competitor in a gender-affected activity if it is necessary to do so to secure in relation to the activity—

(a) fair competition, or
(b) the safety of competitors.

(3) A gender-affected activity is a sport, game or other activity of a competitive nature in circumstances in which the physical strength, stamina or physique of average persons of one sex would put them at a disadvantage compared to average persons of the other sex as competitors in events involving the activity.
(4) In considering whether a sport, game or other activity is gender-affected in relation to children, it is appropriate to take account of the age and stage of development of children who are likely to be competitors ...

[125] n 118 above.

Controversies over the inclusion of transwomen in sport have been commonplace over recent years. In October 2018 Rachel McKinnon, a transwoman, won the women's UCI Masters Track World Championship. In September 2019 a BBC piece on Kelly Morgan, who had played representative rugby for East Wales as a teenager before transitioning and returning to play for Porth Harlequins Ladies, garnered much critical attention for its light-hearted recounting of one incident in which Kelly had 'folded an opponent "like a deckchair"', and of the team founder's quip that 'She's going to be a good, good player for the next few years, as long as we can stop her injuring players in training'.[126] *The Times* reported shortly afterwards that referees were quitting women's rugby because of concerns about serious injuries to women, having been 'warned not to challenge bearded or heavily muscled players appearing for women's teams' and to 'take it on trust' that trans players have been cleared to play by the Rugby Football Union.[127]

Also in September 2019 the International Olympic Committee, which has since November 2015 allowed transwomen to compete as women if they had maintained levels of testosterone below 10 nanomoles per litre for at least 12 months, failed to reach agreement on stricter guidelines which were to be introduced in advance of the Tokyo Olympics.[128] *The Guardian* reported that the IOC's 'panel of scientists is struggling to reach agreement on such a thorny issue' and that 'the IOC's draft guidelines have been parked, for now, because the whole subject is so politically charged and sensitive'. The article referred to interventions from 'high-profile athletes, including Martina Navratilova, Kelly Holmes and Paula Radcliffe, [who] have … spoken out about the potential damage to women's sports by allowing trans women to compete when they are potentially bigger, stronger and faster having gone through male puberty. The British swimmer Sharron Davies, a silver medallist at the 1980 Olympics, put it earlier this year: "I believe there is a fundamental difference between the binary sex you are born with and the gender you may identify as. To protect women's sport, those with a male sex advantage should not be able to compete in women's sport."' *The Guardian* also quoted Joanna Harper, adviser to the IOC: 'Transgender women after hormone therapy are taller, bigger and stronger on average than cisgender women. But that does not necessarily make it unfair. In high levels of sport transgender women are substantially under-represented. That indicates that, whatever physical advantages transgender women have – and they certainly exist – they are not nearly as large as the sociological disadvantages."'

In February 2020, the families of three female high-school runners issued a legal challenge to the inclusion of trans athletes in female college sports in the US, arguing that its effect had been to deprive them of titles and scholarship opportunities. Sports scholarships are worth a great deal of money in the US and can gain students access to elite universities for which they would not otherwise qualify. The legal claim is that the inclusion of trans athletes violates Title IX, which requires equal opportunities for women in education and athletics.[129] More recently, the victory of Lia Thomas, who had as a man been ranked in the mid-500s among US college swimmers, in the US National Collegiate Athletic Association competition in 2022 generated significant unrest (Thomas was pictured towering above her

[126] Original BBC article at https://www.bbc.co.uk/sport/rugby-union/49298550. For critical commentary see eg https://www.thepostmillennial.com/british-transgender-rugby-star-celebrated-for-injuring-women/ and https://www.thetimes.co.uk/article/injury-fears-over-rugbys-trans-women-drive-referees-off-pitch-877hjsfz0.

[127] 'Too strong trans players in women's rugby are driving referees away', 28 September 2019.

[128] 'OC delays new transgender guidelines after scientists fail to agree', *The Guardian*, 24 September 2019.

[129] 'Teen runners sue to block trans athletes from girls' sports', *The Guardian*, 13 February 2020.

competitors). Later in 2022 trans women who have experienced male puberty were banned from competing against women in elite swimming and bans were also imposed in Britain in triathlon and rugby.

Other

The EqA's exceptions to the prohibition on discrimination in education which are designed to permit single-sex (and predominantly single-sex) schools and further and higher education institutes, were mentioned in Chapter 4.[130] Section 193 EqA, which allows charitable bodies to discriminate in favour of groups defined by reference to protected characteristics other than colour, is discussed in Chapters 4, 9 and 10.

Exceptions to the Prohibition on Pregnancy Discrimination

Schedule 3 para 14 EqA, Health and safety

(1) A service-provider (A) who refuses to provide the service to a pregnant woman does not discriminate against her in contravention of section 29 because she is pregnant if—
   (a) A reasonably believes that providing her with the service would, because she is pregnant, create a risk to her health or safety,
   (b) A refuses to provide the service to persons with other physical conditions, and
   (c) the reason for that refusal is that A reasonably believes that providing the service to such persons would create a risk to their health or safety.

(2) A service-provider (A) who provides, or offers to provide, the service to a pregnant woman on conditions does not discriminate against her in contravention of section 29 because she is pregnant if—
   (a) the conditions are intended to remove or reduce a risk to her health or safety,
   (b) A reasonably believes that the provision of the service without the conditions would create a risk to her health or safety,
   (c) A imposes conditions on the provision of the service to persons with other physical conditions, and
   (d) the reason for the imposition of those conditions is that A reasonably believes that the provision of the service to such persons without those conditions would create a risk to their health or safety.

Similar provision is made by Schedule 16 para 2 in relation to membership associations. There is room for concern about the potential these provisions have to allow individuals to police the behaviour of pregnant women, as in the following examples.

'Pregnant woman "humiliated" by barman's refusal to serve her glass of wine', *The Telegraph*, 27 September 2013

A heavily pregnant bank executive was left 'humiliated' when a barman refused to serve her a small glass of wine, saying he did not want it 'on his conscience'. Jane Hampson, 37, who is expecting her first child and currently past her due date, had been out for a walk with her partner before stopping at a bar for a drink. However, to her astonishment and embarrassment the bartender said he would not sell her a small glass of red wine because of her condition.

[130] Schedule 11 para 2; Sch 11 paras 3–4 and Sch 12 paras 2–3 provide for permissible discrimination in the case of schools and Higher and Further Education Institutions transitioning from single-sex.

Miss Hampson … had done extensive research on the effects of drinking alcohol while pregnant. She said: 'I couldn't believe it – it was so humiliating. There is no way I would endanger my unborn baby yet it was being insinuated that I was doing just that and being irresponsible.

'At the time the bar was packed and all the customers were looking over at us to see what all the commotion was about. We felt we had no choice but to leave because it was so embarrassing …'

Miss Hampson and her partner, Alistair Townend, 37, had gone for a long stroll around Liverpool's Sefton Park on Tuesday night before visiting the nearby Pi bar. She said that the young bartender appeared to take a 'sharp intake of breath' when she ordered a small glass of red wine. 'The barman came up to me and said he wouldn't serve me because he couldn't have serving a pregnant woman alcohol on his conscience. It was outrageous and embarrassing … The barman who refused to serve me was only in his 20s. It's not up to him to decide what I should and shouldn't be putting in my body. I felt like asking whether he refuses to serve fat people pies, or whether the bar checks how much caffeine a woman has consumed that day before they serve her a cup of coffee. There is recent research that suggests baldness is linked to alcohol consumption, are they going to start measuring people's hairlines before they serve them a pint?'…

Ben Reynolds, the area manager of Pi Bar, apologised to Miss Hampson and described the incident as an 'unfortunate misunderstanding'…

'Woman steps in after mum-to-be is "womb shamed" by Starbucks barista over her order', *The Mirror*, 21 May 2019

… A Starbucks barista recently felt this irrepressible urge when a mum-to-be ordered a drink with him. Happily for her, comedian Tiffany Stevenson overheard the exchange and decided to intervene. Tiffany later tweeted about the "womb-shaming" incident and wrote:

"Unbelievable bit of womb bothering in Starbucks at services. A pregnant woman got her Caramel Macchiato and the guy behind the counter said:

'Oh, it's for you. Do you want me to make a decaf?

She said 'No, thanks'.

Him: 'No I should because caffeine is bad for the baby.'

Her: 'It's fine I have one a day.'

Him: 'But … you shouldn't.'

Me *almost spontaneously combusting* 'Are you a man, telling a woman what she should and shouldn't have during a pregnancy?

Then he says: 'Oh just because it's bad for the baby so that's why I'm saying it.'

Me: 'Unbelievable. Stop it.'

Tiffany then added that the barista spent five minutes trying to justify 'policing a stranger'. She finished with, 'He was maybe 30 years old max. Are they also doing Ob/Gyn training at Starbucks these days?'"

7

Race

AILEEN McCOLGAN KC AND EDDIE BRUCE-JONES

Introduction

Legislative prohibitions on race discrimination have been in place in Britain for over 50 years. Despite this, people from racially minoritised communities suffer persistent discrimination and disadvantage. This experience differs between, and even within, minoritised communities according to factors such as sex, educational attainment and economic activity. But for all the heterogeneity of experience of people from these groups, there is for many a shared experience of relative disadvantage.

Recognition of various forms of race discrimination has become more widespread over the past decades, including by way of EU law (in particular Council Directive 2000/43: the Race Directive). But the extension of legal prohibitions on race discrimination has not been accompanied by a commensurate level of conceptual innovation in dealing with broad patterns of racism, legal prohibitions on race discrimination having continued to focus on discrimination by single actors (eg, employers, service providers, public authorities) rather than on interventions at the level of sector, industry or state policy. The Equality Act 2010 (EqA) provides some possibility for structural challenge in the form of the public sector equality duty (PSED), discussed in Chapter 3. Limited as it is to *process* rather than *substance*, its impact has been relatively insignificant.[1] The partial incorporation into domestic law of the European Convention on Human Rights (ECHR), in particular Article 14 thereof, also provides the possibility of legal challenge at the macro, rather than the micro, level. We saw in Chapter 2, however, that the domestic courts have been very reluctant to

[1] Though see *R (Bridges) v Chief Constable of South Wales Police* [2020] EWCA Civ 1058 [2021] 2 All ER 1121 in which the Court of Appeal (CA) ruled that the introduction of facial recognition software was unlawful because the Chief Constable had taken inadequate consideration of its potentially discriminatory effects.

find against the Government in challenges which could be characterised as relating to socio-economic rights.[2]

This chapter considers race discrimination and disadvantage in a number of contexts (criminal justice, health, education and employment) before dealing with those aspects of the EqA which are specific to race.

Conceiving of Racism: Individual, Institutional and Structural Racism

Racism in the UK is multidimensional. It spans various sectors including employment, schooling, housing, policing and health care and affects most, if not all, aspects of social life. It has a structural dimension, affecting the meanings assigned to race and racial difference in society. It has an institutional dimension, being designed and maintained, intentionally and unintentionally, by organisations. And it has an interpersonal dimension, affecting how individuals behave to and with each other. In recent years, patterns of racism have been recognised and examined by government and civil society including in the form of government audits on racism,[3] independent parliamentary review,[4] civil society investigations (eg, by the Runnymede Trust and the Institute for Race Relations) and academic research.[5] Public attention has also been raised in the past decade by events and policies including the 2012 London unrest, the Government's 2012 Hostile Environment Policy (later renamed the Compliant Environment Policy), the Prevent Duty, aspects of the Brexit debate, the Windrush deportation scandal, and the Grenfell Tower fire. Part of the challenge in considering the role of equality law is to discern when and where the EqA and other legal provisions are applicable without losing sight of the larger frame in which race and racism shape thinking, behaviour and institutional postures that may fall beyond the scope of such law.

Whilst racism cuts across various sectors of social life, two influential inquiries have informed the way many in the UK understand the concept of institutional racism. The first was the Scarman Report, written in the 1980s after the Brixton riots of 1981 which followed the deaths of 13 Black teenagers and young adults in a suspicious house fire in New Cross in January 1981, and years of concern about racist policing including the use of stop and search against the Black community. Lord Scarman's report found racial targeting and over-policing of Black residents of Brixton, but attributed this to individual officers acting inappropriately.[6] This 'bad apples' thesis is now regarded by many as an inaccurate representation of a culture of policing practice that supported and maintained such discriminatory over-policing.[7]

[2] See discussion of *R (SC) v SSWP* [2021] UKSC 26, [2022] AC 223 in Ch 2. *See also R (Roberts) v Commissioner of Police of the Metropolis* [2015] UKSC 79, [2016] 2 All ER 1005; *R (Adiatu) v HM Treasury* [2020] EWHC 1554 (Admin), [2021] 2 All ER 484; *R (Joint Council for the Welfare of Immigrants) v SSHD* [2020] EWCA Civ 542, [2020] 4 All ER 1027.

[3] See eg the 2017 race disparity audit: https://www.gov.uk/government/publications/race-disparity-audit.

[4] See eg the Lammy Review: https://www.gov.uk/government/organisations/lammy-review; and the Angiolini Review: https://www.gov.uk/government/publications/deaths-and-serious-incidents-in-police-custody.

[5] See eg Nicola Rollock, Gurminder Bhambra, Paul Gilroy and Nadine El-Enany.

[6] Lord Leslie Scarman, *The Brixton Disorders, 10–12th April (1981)* (HMSO, 1981).

[7] The report was however welcomed at the time, including by the CRE whose chairman David Lane 'called it a historic document which offered "a brilliant analysis of Britain's urban and racial problems and an urgent prescription for action"': 'The home secretary promises to respond to the call to create better relations between the police and the community', *The Guardian*, 26 November 1981.

The second major report was the Macpherson Report, which was published in 1999 and concerned the police mishandling of the racist murder of London teenager Stephen Lawrence. It offered a corrective to the analysis in the Scarman Report in as much as it recognised institutional racism rather than attributing disparate policing outcomes merely to the decisions of individual officers.[8] The report defined institutional discrimination as:

Sir William Macpherson, The Stephen Lawrence Inquiry, London, Home Office, 1999, §6.34

> The collective failure of an organisation to provide an appropriate and professional service to people because of their colour, culture, or ethnic origin. It can be seen or detected in processes, attitudes and behaviour which amount to discrimination through unwitting prejudice, ignorance, thoughtlessness and racist stereotyping which disadvantage minority ethnic people.

The era following the publication of the Macpherson Report was important for several reasons. First, there was a significant reckoning with the reality of racist attitudes and practices within policing institutions in particular; this is not to say that policing institutions accepted this phenomenon, rather that there was a sharpened public debate about the racism endemic within the police. Second, the concept of institutional racism became visible within British policy whereas the term had previously been mainly used by academics and activists. The concept opened new avenues for assessing the principles of equality, even if it did not necessarily expedite effective remedies. The decades since 1999 have been characterised by scholars, activists and policy-makers as a wasted opportunity for meaningful action against institutional racism and, by extension, against institutional forms of discrimination and exclusion more generally. Problems identified by Macpherson persist, including victim-blaming, under-serving and over-policing vulnerable groups, and failures to identify systemic ways in which these practices are mapped onto the structures of social institutions (particularly the police). And diversity and unconscious bias training and hiring diversity schemes have come to be understood as not only involving superficial treatment of a complex problem, but also as a distraction from more fundamental, structural change.[9]

The decade following the Macpherson Inquiry was characterised by changes in political discourse and social understandings of institutional racism. In *Policing and the Legacy of Lawrence*, Nathan Hall et al note changes across a range of areas including culture, governance, politics, law, intelligence and international relations that have influenced policing and policy changes.[10] Despite this, many were disappointed because the recognition of institutional forms of discrimination did not translate into effective remedies against racism. In the political domain and in the wake of the London bombings of 7 July 2005 the focus continued to be on training and internal cohesion among police institutions rather than on more foundational changes in policing practice. This also contributed to delays in carrying out the Macpherson recommendations.[11]

Notwithstanding these concerns, the 2010s did see a shift in public focus from *institutional* to *structural* forms of racism, that is, from patterns of institutional practice to expressions of racism that are embedded in the fabric of social life, within and across institutions and

[8] The Scarman report had declared by contrast that 'Institutional racism does not exist in Britain; but racial disadvantage and its nasty associate, racial discrimination, have not yet been eliminated. The poison minds and attitudes; they are, and so long as they remain, will continue to be a potent factor of unrest'.

[9] See N Rollock, *Report: The Stephen Lawrence Inquiry 10 Years On: An Analysis of the Literature* (The Runnymede Trust, 2009).

[10] N Hall et al, *Policing and the Legacy of Lawrence* (London: Willan Publishing, 2009) 6–21.

[11] *Ibid*, 11.

their discourses, practices and forms of communication. Much of the racism that operates on a structural level remains out of reach of individual discrimination claims levied against employers, service providers or other individuals/organisations. Structural racism involves wider societal ideas and finds its expression in the ways that we think about the world around us, and how those thoughts get translated via media, education, law, policy and work, for example, into action. Recognising such racism impacts on the conception both of equality generally and of the role of law in combating discrimination and promoting equality.

The past decade or so has witnessed broad discussions between civil society organisations, advocates, policy-makers, community organisers and experts about structural racism. Examples include debates about the responses to the London unrest of 2012; the impacts of legal aid cuts on racialised communities and of the Hostile Environment Policy on people without settled migration status; the racial animus caused by the 2015 Prevent Duty; the role and operation of the Home Office in the Windrush scandal (see further below); the racial and class implications of social housing policies and practices in the context of the Grenfell Tower fire; symbols of national heritage and colonialism amidst the international Black Lives Matter protests; and calls to decolonise school and university curricula. Most recently, there have been discussions about the racially disparate effects of the COVID-19 pandemic on Black and South Asian communities in the UK (also discussed further below).[12] These debates, while they cannot always be brought squarely within the remit of the EqA, do involve meaningful questions about the role of law and policy in recognising and responding to racism at the level of institutions and broad social structures.

In 2017, the first ever extensive review of policing related deaths was commissioned by the-then Prime Minister Theresa May. The review, led by Dame Elish Angiolini,[13] examined matters ranging from police testimonial evidence to the financial effects of policing-related deaths on bereaved families. It revealed the profound impact of policing practices on racially minoritised communities, people experiencing mental ill health, and people at the intersection of these groups.[14] The review indicates how disadvantage is structured into policing policies and practices, shedding light on structural racism and other forms of disadvantage.[15]

Race, Discrimination and Disadvantage in Britain

Health

The COVID-19 pandemic shone a light on the relationship between race and disadvantage. Public Health England's (PHE's) *COVID-19: review of disparities in risks and outcomes*, reported in June 2020 that people from racially minoritised communities were dying disproportionately, with those of Bangladeshi origin who contracted COVID-19 being up to twice as likely as, and people from other racially minoritised communities being up to 50 per cent more likely than, white Britons to die, though it did not at that stage suggest the reasons for

[12] R Mathur et al, 'Urgent actions and policies needed to address Covid-19 among UK ethnic minorities', *The Lancet*, 12 December 2020, 1866–68. The article suggests that health disparities resulted from 'intersecting forms of disadvantage', including structural racism and economic class.

[13] n 4 above.

[14] E Bruce-Jones, 'Mental health and death in custody: the Angiolini Review', 62 *Race & Class* (2021) 8–9.

[15] *Ibid.*

the disparity or make any proposals to deal with it.[16] *The Guardian* reported in the same month that the British Medical Association (BMA) had called two months previously for an inquiry into the high death rate among racially minoritised healthcare workers, but to no avail.[17]

The disproportionate racial impact of COVID-19 was not restricted to the UK. An article in US *Medical News Today* reported in June 2020 that the limited available statistics indicated that the death rate for Black Americans was up to three times as high, and that for Latinx people almost twice as high, as that for white Americans. In some states Black and/or Latinx death rates were as much as five or 10 times higher than white death rates.[18] The *Medical News Today* article linked disparate death rates in the US to significant and enduring economic disadvantage. In the UK, too, poverty, unemployment and inadequate housing are unevenly distributed. We discuss the employment disparities below. In 2018, the EHRC reported that Pakistani/Bangladeshi and Black adults were more likely to live in substandard accommodation than white people, with 30.9 per cent of Pakistani/Bangladeshi, 26.8 per cent of Black and 8.3 per cent of white people living in overcrowded accommodation; that 35.7 per cent racially of minoritised and 17.2 per cent of white people lived in poverty and that the mortality rate for Black African women in the UK was four times that for white women.[19]

ITV News reported in May 2020, at a time when seven times as many racially minoritised as white NHS staff had died, that 50 per cent of 2,000 racially minoritised NHS workers surveyed felt that discriminatory behaviour had contributed to this death toll, with 20 per cent claiming to have been the victims of discrimination.[20] According to the report, one respondent had stated that 'All BAME nurses [have been] allocated to red wards and my white colleagues [are] constantly in green wards' and that another said that 'Only BAME doctors from the department have been put forward for deployment'. A British consultant cardiologist of Pakistani origin was quoted as saying that 'Many of the white doctors are in management positions leaving more BAME on the coal face' while a doctor working in A&E told ITV that 'colleagues, "particularly" non-BAME staff, "literally avoid going to covid areas pushing me and my junior colleagues there even when we have patients, we [are] already seeing". Of those surveyed who had been redeployed to meet the needs of the coronavirus outbreak, more than half said they did not feel comfortable raising their concerns about the move'. BMA Council Chair Dr Chaand Nagpaul 'told *ITV News*: "Our own BMA surveys of the past have shown bullying and harassment of doctors and ethnic minority doctors to be much greater than white doctors"'.

When Public Health England's report was published in June 2020 Dr Nagpaul complained that it 'fails to mention the staggering higher proportion of BAME healthcare workers who have tragically died from Covid-19 – with more than 90 per cent of doctors being from BAME backgrounds,' and failed properly to consider the 'occupations of BAME

[16] *COVID-19: review of disparities in risks and outcomes*. An updated version of the report (August 2020) is available at https://www.gov.uk/government/publications/covid-19-review-of-disparities-in-risks-and-outcomes.

[17] 'Calls mount for public inquiry into UK BAME Covid-19 death rate', https://www.theguardian.com/world/2020/jun/02/calls-mount-for-public-inquiry-into-uk-bame-covid-19-death-rate.

[18] 'Racial inequalities in COVID-19 – the impact on black communities' 5 June 2020, available at https://www.medicalnewstoday.com/articles/racial-inequalities-in-covid-19-the-impact-on-black-communities.

[19] 'Race report statistics', available at https://www.equalityhumanrights.com/en/race-report-statistics.

[20] 'Discrimination' on frontline of coronavirus outbreak may be factor in disproportionate BAME deaths among NHS staff', ITV, 13 May 2020, available at https://www.itv.com/news/2020-05-13/discrimination-frontline-coronavirus-covid19-black-minority-ethnic-bame-deaths-nhs-racism.

victims, exposure to the virus and availability of personal protective equipment (PPE) as risk factors'. A report in the *Health Service Journal* stated that '[a]n earlier draft of the [PHE's June report] which was circulated within government last week contained a section which included responses from the 1,000-plus organisations and individuals who supplied evidence to the review. Many of these suggested that discrimination and poorer life chances were playing a part in the increased risk of covid-19 to those with BAME backgrounds … One source with knowledge of the review said the section "did not survive contact with Matt Hancock's office" over the weekend'.[21]

The Times reported that the published version of the PHE report had also excluded recommendations on how to protect racially minoritised people from COVID-19.[22] According to that newspaper: 'a 69-page document … sent to the government at the end of May' included seven PHE recommendations, 'including targeted health advice and risk assessments for BAME staff working in hospitals'. The failure to publish this was, *The Times* reported, 'because of "current global events" including the wave of anti-racism protests'.

Part 2 of the PHE's *Understanding the impact of COVID-19 on BAME groups* was published on 16 June 2020, a fortnight after Part 1.[23] It makes for chilling reading. The report summarised the results of a literature review on the relationship between COVID-19 outcomes and ethnicity and the results of PHE's engagement with 'over 4,000 people with a broad range of interests in BAME issues'. The literature review cited the only study to date of mortality in healthcare workers in the UK by ethnicity[24] which 'used data gathered from social media, news reports, and other publicly available "In memoriam" websites to gather outcome data, meaning it is high risk of bias'. This found that 'Of the deaths in healthcare workers reported, 63 per cent were in BAME groups: 36 per cent were of Asian ethnicity (compared to 10 per cent of NHS workforce) and 27 per cent were of black ethnicity (compared to 6 per cent of the NHS workforce)'.

Some of the factors to which the PHE report attributed the disparate impact of COVID-19 were social, economic and structural. Among these were the fact that overcrowding and inter-generational living were more commonplace among racially minoritised groups and that people from these groups were 'more likely to work in occupations with a higher risk of COVID-19 exposure' including health and social care, cleaning, public transport and retail: 'Often, BAME workers are in lower paid roles within the NHS, which mean that these roles cannot be done remotely this leads to greater exposure with other members of the community. It has also been noted by several research groups that individuals in BAME groups are more likely to use public transportation to travel to their essential work, leading to additional routes of exposure':

PHE, *Beyond the data: Understanding the impact of COVID-19 on BAME groups*, references omitted

Individuals that identify as being part of an BAME group may feel marginalised, have experienced racism, or have had previous experiences with a culturally insensitive health service that

[21] 'Exclusive: Government censored BAME covid-risk review' 2 June 2020, available at https://www.hsj.co.uk/coronavirus/exclusive-government-censored-bame-covid-risk-review/7027761.article.

[22] 'Ministers failed to publish coronavirus advice for ethnic minorities', *The Times*, 12 June 2020, available at https://www.thetimes.co.uk/article/ministers-failed-to-publish-coronavirus-advice-for-ethnic-minorities-m9xzhg8pf.

[23] Beyond the data: Understanding the impact of COVID-19 on BAME groups, available at https://www.gov.uk/government/publications/covid-19-understanding-the-impact-on-bame-communities.

[24] T Cook, E Kursumovic and S Lennane, 'Exclusive: deaths of NHS staff from COVID19 analysed' (2020) *Health Services Journal*, available at https://www.hsj.co.uk/exclusive-deaths-of-nhs-staff-from-covid-19-analysed/7027471.article.

could create barriers to engagement. Research has shown that individuals from BAME backgrounds often have poorer access to healthcare services as well as poor past experiences of care and treatment. This may mean they are less likely to seek care when needed or as NHS staff less likely to speak up when they have concerns about PPE or testing …

Some [stakeholders] reported that they had personally experienced or received reports from colleagues about racism, bullying and harassment at work. This meant that they were reluctant to speak up about issues (such as PPE shortages), which placed them at higher risk.

Others believe that BAME front line workers were sometimes given substandard quality or inadequate PPE given the nature of their roles and the risk of exposure. Numerous examples were given of staff not able to access appropriate PPE to protect themselves adequately in line with national guidance and being afraid to speak up about this.

> 'Requests for risk assessments or additional PPE by BAME workers are more likely to be refused, or whether those requests are less likely to be made because of fear of adverse treatment'

Differential treatment in the workplace

Many feel this is a long-standing issue which existed prior to COVID-19. BAME staff are concerned about raising issues because of past experiences and fear of consequences for speaking up. Others raised issues about fairness in the workplace. Staff want support and an environment for staff to express their concerns and have these met effectively.

> 'Reports we have received since the outbreak of the pandemic suggest that there have been a significant number of instances of direct and indirect discrimination based on ethnicity.
>
> A high number of our BAME members have felt concerned about raising issues because of either previous instances of poor treatment, or a fear that they will face adverse consequences if they speak up.'

Health disparities are not limited to the impact of COVID-19. There is, for example, evidence that the health-related impact of environmental pollution falls disproportionately on people from minoritised communities:

Sam Wong, 'Ethnic minorities and deprived communities hardest hit by air pollution' (Imperial College, 2015)[25]

Air pollution levels are linked to many forms of ill health, including higher risk of respiratory and cardiovascular diseases, especially for more vulnerable groups such as children and the elderly.

Researchers at Imperial College London and the National Institute for Public Health and the Environment in the Netherlands examined data on two types of air pollution: particulate matter (PM_{10}) and nitrogen dioxide (NO_2) …

The EU Ambient Air Quality Directive set limits of 40 micrograms per cubic metre ($\mu g/m^3$) at monitoring stations for both PM_{10} and NO_2 pollution. Concentration averages across all neighbourhoods in England … were within this limit for PM_{10}, but 11 per cent of neighbourhoods in England … exceeded the NO_2 limit, accounting for an affected population of 5.4 million …

In England, the most deprived 20 per cent of neighbourhoods had higher air pollution levels than the least deprived neighbourhoods – 1.5 $\mu g/m^3$ higher PM_{10} and 4.4 $\mu g/m^3$ NO_2 after adjusting for other factors – but this was not the case in the Netherlands. The biggest differences in air pollution levels according to socioeconomic status were in London.

The worst air pollution levels were seen in ethnically diverse neighbourhoods, defined as those where more than 20 per cent of the population are non-white. Even after allowing for the fact that some of these neighbourhoods are more deprived, in England, this difference was 3.0 $\mu g/m^3$ for PM_{10} and 10.1 $\mu g/m^3$ for NO_2. In the Netherlands, differences were lower, with 1.1 $\mu g/m^3$ higher PM_{10} and 4.5 $\mu g/m^3$ NO_2.

[25] https://www.imperial.ac.uk/news/163408/ethnic-minorities-deprived-communities-hardest-pollution.

The following year *The Guardian* reported that Black communities in London were disproportionately exposed by illegal levels of NO_2 pollution by comparison with white and Asian communities.[26] 'Southwark, Lambeth and Hackney were among the boroughs with an overlap of both a higher proportion of black residents and [on 2013 measures] the higher pollution levels'. *The Guardian* reported that the study was 'an update of a report which the former mayor Boris Johnson was accused of burying when Khan took office' and which had shown that '433 primary schools were exposed to NO_2 above the limits in 2010, with that number falling to 360 by 2013 in today's study'. The verdict of the coroner in the 2020 inquest into the death of Ella Adoo-Kissi-Debrah that the nine-year-old had died as a result of air pollution, the first such verdict in the UK, refocused attention on the disproportionate exposure of minoritised communities to air pollution.

Education

People from racially minoritised groups are under-represented and under-served within the UK's education system as school pupils, university students and educators. These dimensions of marginalisation are not unrelated, as the pipeline from school education to academic teaching, research and leadership is populated by those graduates who reach the most elite universities, which is affected by unequal access to resources at the earlier stages of education. While statistics do not tell the complete story of racial disparity, marginalisation and exclusion in education, they do raise questions for policy-makers about how to address what should be presumed to be the cumulative impacts of racism in society's structures.[27]

Exclusion from schools has been noted to affect racialised communities disproportionately. Government statistics from 2020 show that, in each of the 12 years to which the data related (2006–18), the rate of permanent exclusions of Black and mixed pupils was higher than that of white pupils,[28] though the disparity declined over time.[29] The statistics reveal high rates of exclusion for Black and mixed pupils in certain boroughs and cities, and generally higher rates in secondary than in primary school.[30] Research published by a number of London education charities in 2020 showed that Black Caribbean and Gypsy, Roma and Traveller children in London were 'more likely to be excluded than their peers'.[31] The charities reported that tens of thousands of exclusions (fixed-term as well as permanent) are issued in London each year, and that the official statistics on which they relied understated the extent of exclusions because they do not take into account unofficial exclusions including 'off-rolling', by which schools encourage or pressure parents to remove children from schools.

[26] 'London's black communities disproportionately exposed to air pollution – study', *The Guardian*, 10 October 2016, available at https://www.theguardian.com/environment/2016/oct/10/londons-black-communities-disproportionately-exposed-to-air-pollution-study.

[27] E Bruce-Jones, 'The United Kingdom on Race: A Warning for Europe', VerfBlog, 13 April 2021, available at https://verfassungsblog.de/uk-racism, accessed 19 September 2022.

[28] UK Government, 'Pupil Exclusions', 27 January 2020, available at https://www.ethnicity-facts-figures.service.gov.uk/education-skills-and-training/absence-and-exclusions/pupil-exclusions/latest#temporary-exclusions-by-ethnicity-over-time.

[29] *Ibid.*

[30] *Ibid.* See also H Richardson, 'Pupils face trebled exclusion rate in some areas of England,' BBC News, 30 July 2020, available at https://www.bbc.co.uk/news/education-53516009.

[31] Just for Kids Law, 'Race, Poverty and School Exclusions in London' (2020), https://justforkidslaw.org/sites/default/files/fields/download/Race%2C%20poverty%20and%20school%20exclusions%20in%20London.pdf.

Irish Traveller heritage children had an exclusion rate of 450 per cent the general level, and Gypsy and Roma children of almost 400 per cent. Black Caribbean children had exclusion rates of 270 per cent and Mixed White and Caribbean of more than 200 per cent.

Just for Kids Law et al, *Race, Poverty and School Exclusions in London* (2020), footnotes omitted[32]

Only 7% of children who were permanently excluded and 18% of children who received multiple fixed period exclusions went on to achieve good passes in English and maths GCSEs. Being excluded can exacerbate existing mental ill health and trigger long-term psychiatric illness. It affects children's self-esteem and wellbeing …

89% of children in Young Offender Institutions in 2018 had been excluded and 63% of adult prisoners in 2012 reported being temporarily excluded when at school. Children who are outside of mainstream education are more vulnerable to becoming the victim of childhood criminal exploitation, the process of manipulating, threatening or coercing children into engaging in criminal activity, often to transport drugs in so called 'county lines' operations. Conversely, children who have experienced exploitation will then be more vulnerable to exclusion. There is evidence to show that criminals have orchestrated a child's behaviour that leads to exclusion in order to further that child's exploitation.

Exclusions can also affect parents' ability to work, as they need to take time off to attend meetings and be at home during the exclusion period …

Black children can be subject to different treatment, including in response to their behaviour, as a result of racist stereotyping and labelling by teachers [which] … even if unconscious, have been shown to affect teachers' perceptions of children's behaviour and personalities, and their educational expectations for them …

Institutional racism can shape schools' and teachers' views on what is, and is not, acceptable behaviour. The RSA reported that young people had been punished by school for 'actions like "spudding" (or "fist bumping")' and noted other similar cases reported in the media, for example 'kissing teeth' breaching a school's behaviour policy. Schools' uniform policies can also discriminate against Black children on the basis of their hair, for example there have been cases of children being excluded for wearing natural afros or fades …

95 percent of teachers in English schools in 2018 were white, compared with 87 percent of the population. Educational psychologists are predominantly middleclass White women. The ethnic makeup of staff and, in particular, heads and senior management in London schools fails to reflect the students and families they are working with …

On 29 April 2020, in the midst of the first COVID-19 lockdown, the EHRC warned Ofqual that its plan to use predicted grades in place of GCSE and A level examinations in 2020 'could deepen the existing inequality in education and put the future of disadvantaged young people at risk if not correctly implemented'.[33] The EHRC advised that there was research evidence 'of conscious or unconscious race bias' in grade prediction and called on the Department for Education to issue guidance to schools on the approach to grade predictions and student ranking in order to minimise the risk of bias and for Ofqual to 'publish a report evaluating the predicted grades process and outcomes for pupils' and to take action if disparities related to 'protected characteristics'. The EHRC consultation response followed a letter sent on 2 April 2020 from 21 academics, coordinated by the Runnymede Trust, which advised that 'students from lower socio-economic backgrounds (particularly higher

[32] *Ibid.*

[33] https://www.equalityhumanrights.com/en/our-work/news/predicted-grading-during-covid-19-could-limit-young-peoples-futures.

attaining students from lower SES [socioeconomic status] backgrounds) are more likely to have their final grades under-predicted compared to higher attaining students from more advantaged backgrounds'.[34] That letter warned that 'well over a quarter of black and minority ethnic (BAME) GCSE students (including much higher proportions of Gypsy, Roma and Irish Traveller students) are on free school meals', and expressed concern that 'this issue of under-predictions in grades for students from lower socio-economic backgrounds will impact on BAME students disproportionately. We are also aware that "teachers' expectations of black students and their working-class peers tend to be systematically lower than warranted by their performance in class"'.[35]

The 2 April letter referred to research from Dr Gill Wyness for the Sutton Trust which showed a strikingly consistent inverse relationship between socio-economic disadvantage and predicted grades:[36] the poorer the student, the less likely they are to benefit from over-predictions and the more likely they are to have their grades under-predicted. The opposite was true for the wealthiest students.[37]

The disadvantage experienced by racially minoritised pupils is reflected in educational attainment at third level and beyond. AdvanceHE's 2021 *Students statistical report 2021*, which considers only UK domiciled students, found 'pronounced differences in continuation and degree awarding outcomes for white and Black, Asian and minority ethnic students, with lower rates of Black, Asian and minority ethnic students continuing or qualifying and receiving a first/2:1 compared with their white peers'.[38] There were particularly large disparities in continuation rates and degree attainment between white and Black students and BAME students were more likely than white students to be unemployed, and less likely to be in full-time work, 15 months post-qualification.

AdvanceUK reported an 82.3 per cent increase in the number of BAME students between 2003–04 and 2019–20, with increases of 3.6 per cent, 3.2 per cent, 2.8 per cent and 0.9 per cent respectively in the proportion of students who were Black, Asian, Mixed and 'Other', and a 0.1 per cent decrease for Chinese students.[39] BAME students were markedly more represented among first degree undergraduates and taught postgraduates (26.7 per cent and 23.6 per cent, respectively) than research postgraduates (18.6 per cent) and other undergraduates (16.8 per cent).[40] 90 per cent of white students continued or completed their degrees against 82.8 per cent each of Black Caribbean students and of those from another Black background (93.6 per cent of Chinese and 91.1 per cent of Indian students).[41] And 86.0 per cent of white students received a first/2:1 by comparison with 75.2 per cent of BAME students (an attainment gap of 10.8 per cent). This gap was largest between white and 'other Black' students (23.7 per cent), Black African and Black Caribbean students (20.1 and 17.4 per cent respectively) and reduced to 3.7 per cent,

[34] https://www.runnymedetrust.org/blog/predicted-grades-bme-students-letter-to-ed-sec.

[35] Citing D Gillborn, 'Racism as Policy: A Critical Race Analysis of Education Reforms in the United States and England' (2014) 78 *The Educational Forum* 26.

[36] *Rules of the Game: Disadvantaged students and the University admissions process*, available at https://www.suttontrust.com/wp-content/uploads/2017/12/Rules-of-the-Game.pdf.

[37] See further pp 441–447 below for discussion of discrimination against and disadvantage experienced by people from Gypsy and Traveller communities.

[38] Available at https://www.advance-he.ac.uk/knowledge-hub/equality-higher-education-statistical-report-2021, 126. The reports are based on HESA data covering all students in the UK.

[39] *Ibid*, 127.

[40] *Ibid*.

[41] *Ibid*, 128.

3.3 per cent and 2.2 per cent between white and mixed, Indian and Chinese students respectively.[42] Fifteen months after qualifying, 59.7 per cent of white students and 51.6 per cent of BAME students were in full-time work, 47.2 per cent and 40.2 per cent respectively in professional work and 5.5 per cent and 9.7 per cent respectively were unemployed.

Employment

Racial inequalities persist in employment, income, promotion, and workplace harassment and discrimination. In 2018, for example, according to government statistics, 31.2 per cent of white Gypsy/Roma or Traveller people, and 25.3 per cent, 24.4 per cent and 19.7 per cent of those of Bangladeshi, Pakistani and Arab origin respectively were 'long term unemployed or never worked', by comparison with 4.8 per cent of white people.[43] 15.4 per cent and 12 per cent of people of Indian and white Irish origin respectively were in higher managerial, administrative or professional jobs, compared with 2.5 per cent of White Gypsy/Roma or Traveller people, and 4.2 per cent and 4.9 per cent respectively of those of Bangledeshi and mixed white/Black Caribbean origin.

The 2017 *Racism at Work* survey, carried out by the TUC and analysed by researchers at the University of Manchester, revealed that Black workers are paid 8.3 per cent less than white workers (an average difference of £1.15 an hour). Black workers qualified to A level earn 10 per cent less than their white peers (an average £1.20 per hour) and racially minoritised workers are over a third more likely than white workers to be in temporary or zero-hours work. More than a third (37 per cent) of racially minoritised workers have been bullied, abused or singled out at work and more than half (57 per cent) of racially minoritised women affected by bullying and harassment reported having suffered mental health problems.[44]

Among the key findings of the *Racism at Work* survey were that:

- Over 70 per cent of Asian and Black workers had experienced racial harassment at work in the previous five years;
- Around 60 per cent of Asian and Black, and almost 40 per cent of Mixed heritage workers had been subjected to race discrimination;
- 46 per cent of Black, Asian and Mixed heritage, and 32 per cent of non-White Other, workers had been subjected to 'verbal abuse and racist jokes';
- A third of Black, Asian and Mixed heritage background workers had been bullied and/ or subjected to ignorant or insensitive questioning, with 11 per cent also experiencing racist violence at work;
- Minoritised workers reported having been to 'excessive surveillance and scrutiny by colleagues, supervisors and managers, as well as being denied promotion and development/ 'acting up' opportunities'. 'given unfair performance assessments' and 'treated as being intellectually inferior to their White counterparts';

[42] *Ibid*, 128.

[43] 'Socioeconomic status', available at https://www.ethnicity-facts-figures.service.gov.uk/uk-population-by-ethnicity/demographics/socioeconomic-status/latest#ethnic-groups-by-socio-economic-status.

[44] TUC, 'BME People Still Facing Racism and Discrimination at Work, TUC Says' March 2018, available at https://www.tuc.org.uk/news/bme-people-still-facing-racism-and-discrimination-work-says-tuc.

- Workers on non-permanent contracts were more likely to experience race discrimination and harassment and part-time workers more likely to experience racial harassment than full time workers,
- 56 per cent of Asian, Black and Mixed heritage workers who experienced racism at work had reported impacts on their mental health and 28 per cent reported impacts on their physical health. 28 per cent had taken sick leave in connection with such racism.[45]

The survey suggested that employers did not take race discrimination seriously and that workers who experienced such discrimination found it 'extremely difficult' to challenge. Over 40 per cent of workers who did report found themselves ignored and/or treated as troublemakers and more than 10 per cent were subjected to disciplinary action or dismissed for so doing.

The researchers who analysed the TUC's survey findings highlighted the need to understand workplace race discrimination in the UK in historical context, in intersectional terms, and in light of structural and institutional forms of racism.

Stephen Ashe, Magda Borkowska and James Nazroo, *Racism Ruins Lives: An Analysis of the 2016–17 Trade Union Congress Racism at Work Survey* (TUC, University of Manchester, April 2019)[46]

> Key findings
>
> … a considerable number of women identifying as Black reported that they had been pressurised, if not explicitly forced, to 'straighten' their hair, as well as being objectified in hypersexualised ways. What is more, almost 15% of ethnic minority women and 8% of ethnic minority men stated that racial discrimination had caused them to leave their job. In light of this, future discussions on how to address workplace racism must also recognise that racism occurs alongside sexism, homophobia, transphobia and disablism, thus making some people vulnerable to multiple forms of discrimination and domination …
>
> The personal statements provided by survey participants also draw attention to the ways in which contemporary workplace racism is rooted in forms of racial thinking that once underpinned imperialism, colonialism, slavery and scientific racism. For example, people racialised as non-White continue to be thought of as 'intellectually inferior' to White people, 'child-like', 'degenerate' and 'subhuman'. What is more people racialised as non-White were also framed as belonging to places characterised as 'dirty', 'wild', 'uncivilised' and 'backwards'. Indeed, this was also evident in terms of the gendered ways in which many survey participants experienced racism at work.
>
> … xenophobia remains a significant problem. Indeed, the survey demonstrates that the prevalence and deepening of anti- immigrant sentiment before, during and after the EU Referendum has had a profound impact of the working lives of participants who self-identified as White European. In doing so, the survey sheds further light on the exclusionary, if not probationary, nature of Whiteness.

The researchers expressed concern that workers who identified themselves as White British had 'suggested that globalisation, deindustrialisation, neoliberalism and austerity have had a disproportionate, detrimental impact on the "White working class"… [and] used the survey to downplay the nature and extent of workplace racism, express various forms of White resentment and/or allege the pervasiveness of "reverse racism"'. They drew attention

[45] S Ash, M Borkowska and J Nazroo, *Racism Ruins Lives*, available at http://hummedia.manchester.ac.uk/institutes/code/research/projects/racism-at-work/tuc-full-report.pdf.

[46] *Ibid.*

to 'the role played by historically coded forms of racial thinking, as well as the structural and institutional dimensions of racism in the workplace and 'the hegemonic nature of Whiteness', suggesting that the survey 'provides a number of critical insights in terms of the anti-racist educational work that must now be carried out' and that 'racism remains an integral feature of workplace culture and everyday working life for a substantial number of people in this country'.

The TUC survey is not the only evidence of continuing racial disadvantage at work. The Centre for Social Investigation at Nuffield College at the University of Oxford found that people from racially minoritised communities had to make 60 per cent more job applications to receive a positive response than white people of British origin, with Pakistani and Nigerian applicants having to make 70 per cent and 80 per cent more applications respectively than their white counterparts, and Nigerian graduates with relevant work experience having to make twice as many applications as white candidates to secure a call back in software engineering and marketing assistant applications.[47]

'Minority ethnic Britons face "shocking" job discrimination', *The Guardian*, 17 January 2019[48]

Black Britons and those of south Asian origin face 'shocking' discrimination in the labour market at levels unchanged since the late 1960s, research has found. A study by experts based at the Centre for Social Investigation at Nuffield College, University of Oxford, found applicants from minority ethnic backgrounds had to send 80% more applications to get a positive response from an employer than a white person of British origin. A linked study by the same researchers, comparing their results with similar field experiments dating back to 1969, found discrimination against black Britons and those of south Asian origin – particularly Pakistanis – unchanged over almost 50 years.

The research, part of a larger cross-national project funded by the European Union … prompted concerns that race relations legislation had failed … The researchers sent almost 3,200 applications to both manual and non-manual jobs – including software engineers, marketing, chefs and shop assistants – advertised on a popular recruitment platform between November 2016 and December 2017 … On average, 24% of applicants of white British origin received a positive response from employers, compared with 15% of minority ethnic applicants applying with identical CVs and cover letters. All of the minority applications clearly stated that they were either British-born or had arrived in the country by the age of six and had obtained all their education and training in Britain.

Minority ethnic applicants, including white minorities, had to send 60% more applications to get a positive response from an employer than a white person of British origin. While applicants originating from western Europe and the US were treated almost as well as the majority group, people of Pakistani origin had to make 70% more applications. The figures were even higher for those of Nigerian, Middle Eastern and north African (MENA) origin, at 80% and 90% respectively. The researchers said the high levels of discrimination from countries with a sizeable Muslim population echoed 'strong anti-Muslim attitudes recorded in recent surveys'.

Valentina Di Stasio and Anthony Heath, *Are employers in Britain discriminating against ethnic minorities?* (European Research Centre on Migration and Ethnic Relations, Utrecht University) 5–7[49]

… To put these findings in perspective, in a meta-analysis summarizing results from several field experiments conducted in Britain, we found that there has been virtually no change over

[47] See discussion in *The Guardian* article immediately below.

[48] https://www.theguardian.com/world/2019/jan/17/minority-ethnic-britons-face-shocking-job-discrimination.

[49] Available at http://csi.nuff.ox.ac.uk/wp-content/uploads/2019/01/Are-employers-in-Britain-discriminating-against-ethnic-minorities_final.pdf.

time in the level of discrimination faced by Pakistanis: the studies from the 1970s and from the 21st century show almost identical patterns of discrimination despite being almost forty years apart …

Two theories have been proposed in the economics literature to explain why employers may be prone to discriminate. Statistical discrimination theory attributes discrimination to a lack of information during the hiring process, which leads profit-maximizing employers to use ethnic group membership as a signal to infer the productivity of potential employees. Taste-based theory of discrimination, on the other hand, argues that some employers have a distaste for members of (specific) minority groups and would even prefer to incur economic costs rather than hire applicants from the outgroup …

in our study adding information to the resume and cover letter did not reduce discrimination. Applicants from Pakistan, Bangladesh, Africa or the MENA countries who stressed their competence and past achievements in the job application still received significantly lower callbacks from employers than white British applicants who did not include information on performance in their application. These result speak against statistical discrimination theory, although it is possible that employers regard the individual signals of productivity for minority group members as totally uninformative. Overall, our findings show that culturally more distant, non-Western minorities experience severe discrimination, regardless of the occupation considered and the information included in the application. These patterns are consistent with a model of 'lexicographic search' by employers, who simply reed no further when they see a Middle East-sounding or African-sounding name …

The finding of shockingly high levels of discrimination towards applicants from countries that have a sizeable Muslim population (Pakistan, Bangladesh, the MENA region) also echoes the strong anti-Muslim attitudes recorded in recent surveys …

British employers treat minorities of European background relatively fairly. It is non-European, and mostly non Western/non-white minorities that are very strongly discriminated in the British context.

Even the *Daily Mail*, not generally known for its concerns about discrimination, used the word 'shocking' in a headline and quoted the researchers' statement that 'It's not just covert racism or unconscious bias that we need to worry about; it's overt and conscious racism, where applicants are getting shortlisted on the basis of their ethnicity and/or name'.[50]

A House of Commons briefing paper reported in July 2022 that unemployment rates for minoritised communities, already higher than those of white people before COVID-19, had disproportionately increased.[51] Whereas 3.6 per cent of white people had been unemployed in January to March 2020 (pre-pandemic) and 3.1 per cent in January to March 2022, the figures for Chinese people were 4.7 per cent and 7.2 per cent, for mixed/multiple ethnic groups 5.2 per cent and 7.4 per cent, and for Pakistani people 5.9 per cent and 7.6 per cent. Other ethnic groups had also seen rises in unemployment rates from 5.8 per cent to 6.9 per cent, Indian people from 3.7 per cent to 4.1 per cent, and Black/African/Caribbean/Black British people from 8.9 per cent to 9.0 per cent. The unemployment rate for Bangladeshi people had remained stable at 9.3 per cent.

[50] 'Revealed: British workers from minority backgrounds face "shocking" discrimination when job hunting and have to submit 80 per cent more applications than a white person to get a positive response', 18 January 2019, discussing the Di Stasio and Heath research extracted above.

[51] B Francis-Devine and H Clark, Unemployment by ethnic background (House of Commons Library, Research Briefing 6385, July 2022), available at https://commonslibrary.parliament.uk/research-briefings/sn06385.

Brigid Francis-Devine and Harriet Clark, *Unemployment by ethnic background* (House of Commons Library, Research Briefing 6385, July 2022) 5–6

All ethnic groups experienced an increase in unemployment at the beginning of the coronavirus pandemic, but the unemployment rate for people from a minority ethnic background increased much more sharply, and has been slower to recover …

Among people aged 16-24, unemployment rates were highest for people from a Black (31%) ethnic background in January-December 2021. This compared to a rate of 10% for people from an Indian ethnic background and 11% for people from a White ethnic background …

The unemployment rate was highest for women from a Pakistani or Bangladeshi (11.7%) and Black (10.6%) ethnic background, compared to an overall female unemployment rate of 4.2%.

On 28 October 2020 the Resolution Foundation had reported that racially minoritised workers, like young workers, were disproportionately likely to have been adversely affected by the pandemic. Among the report's key findings were that minoritised workers and those aged 18–24 were disproportionately represented among the nine per cent of furloughed workers who had lost their jobs (22 per cent and 19 per cent respectively).[52]

Government statistics from January 2021 show that employment rates for white people between the ages of 16 and 64 are higher than people of other backgrounds, in some cases by a large margin.

Table 7.1 Percentage of 16- to 64-year-olds who were employed, by ethnicity and gender[53]

	All	Men	Women
All	76%	80%	72%
Asian	65%	77%	54%
Indian	76%	82%	69%
Pakistani/ Bangladeshi	56%	73%	39%
Asian Other	65%	74%	58%
Black	69%	71%	67%
Mixed	69%	71%	67%
White	78%	81%	74%
White British	77%	80%	74%
White Other	83%	89%	78%
Other	63%	73%	54%

Women are employed at a lower rate than men across all ethnicity categories, but the employment gap within the Pakistani/Bangladeshi community is particularly high and the employment rate of Pakistani/Bangladeshi women 15 points lower than that of the nearest group ('other' women). In 2012 the All-Party Parliamentary Group on Race and Community reported that, while there were various reasons underlying the low employment rates for Pakistani and Bangladeshi women, discrimination permeated every level of their employment experience.[54]

[52] *Jobs, Jobs, Jobs*, available at https://www.resolutionfoundation.org/publications/jobs-jobs-jobs.

[53] Ethnicity Facts and Figures, 'Employment', available at https://www.ethnicity-facts-figures.service.gov.uk/work-pay-and-benefits/employment/employment/.

[54] V Butler, Ethnic minority female unemployment: Black, Pakistani and Bangladeshi heritage women, available at https://www.bl.uk/collection-items/ethnic-minority-female-unemployment-black-pakistani-and-bangladeshi-heritage-women.

In 2022 the Runnymede Trust and Fawcett Society published a significant report on racially minoritised women at work. Among the report's key findings were that:

Michelle Gymiah et al, *Broken Ladders: The myth of meritocracy for women of colour in the workplace*[55]

- **75% of women of colour reported having experienced one or more forms of** racism at work – from 'banter' about ethnicity or culture, surprise at their ability to speak English, micro-aggressions such as repeated mispronunciation of their name or outright racial slurs.
- **61% of women of colour (compared to 44% of white women) had performed the 'mental gymnastics' of changing something about themselves** – they had changed their language, topics of conversation, hairstyle, their name or what they eat at work a great deal' or 'quite a bit' – to 'fit in' within the workplace.
- **Women of colour are more likely than white women to report a manager having blocked their progression at work (28% compared with 19%)** – as well as experiencing 'sticky floors' and 'concrete ceilings'. And self-employed women of colour are often expected to lower their fees or work for free … [original emphasis]

The authors reported that racially minoritised women were often advised to 'lower their ambitions' while at school and that their career choices are also disproportionately hobbled by limited financial resources. Racially minoritised women reported a '"constant guessing game" involving code switching and changing aspects of themselves to "fit in" with wider expectations about class, background and ethnicity' and the 'mental gymnastics' required to negotiate discriminatory hiring processes. They also reported a lack of access to training that is rationed by employers and 'over reliance on informal networks for progression' which excluded them. They were 'significantly more likely than white women to report being passed over for promotion, despite frequent good feedback (42% versus 27%)' and were more likely (particularly if of Pakistani, Bangladeshi or Indian heritage) than white women 'to report a manager having blocked their progression at work (28%, compared with 19%)'. And racially minoritised women report being 'told how calm, professional or well-spoken they are in comparison to others within their ethnicity'.

> The message most women of colour receive throughout is one of exclusion and othering – the idea that they do not belong in these spaces. This is reinforced through overt means such as direct racism and discrimination, and through subtle cues that force women of colour to change who they are to assimilate …
>
> These everyday adaptations that women of colour make directly challenge the notion of 'bring your whole self to work' that many employers claim they want …
>
> The illusion of meritocracy in the workplace and the narrative of 'merit' obscures the power and influence of invisible and informal networks at work, of which women of colour are often excluded.
>
> - **A less acceptable leader:** Being a woman of colour was significantly associated with being seen as a less acceptable leader; with women of Pakistani and Bangladeshi heritage most likely to report being told they do not have the right leadership qualities (36%).
> - **A mistaken leader:** Women of colour in senior roles reported attending conferences and being mistaken as hospitality service staff or taking part in meetings and being addressed as the secretary.
> - **Restricted expertise:** An additional problem is the issue of 'leadership fit' where women of colours' expertise and skills are restricted to what is seen as in line with their racialised and gendered identity, rather than a broader recognition of their leadership qualities … [original emphasis]

[55] Available at https://www.runnymedetrust.org/partnership-projects/broken-ladders.

Race Discrimination and EU Law

While race discrimination has been prohibited in the UK for decades prior to any such prohibitions at EU level, EU law has nevertheless contributed significantly to the current domestic law. As with other protected characteristics, the evolution to date of domestic law (including by reason of EU case law) and the withdrawal of the UK from the EU means that EU legislation and case law will become less important over time in the development of domestic law. It is important, however, to have some understanding of the relevant EU provisions, if only to understand the context within which domestic law has developed.

Prior to July 2003, when the Race Directive (Council Directive 2000/78/EC) was transposed, the only EU provision which impacted directly on domestic race discrimination law was Article 19 of the Treaty on the Functioning of the European Union (TFEU),[56] which provides:

> **Article 19 TFEU**
>
> Without prejudice to the other provisions of the Treaties and within the limits of the powers conferred by them upon the Union, the Council, acting unanimously in accordance with a special legislative procedure and after obtaining the consent of the European Parliament, may take appropriate action to combat discrimination based on sex, racial or ethnic origin, religion or belief, disability, age or sexual orientation.

Article 19's predecessor generated scant litigation in the UK context, its protections being considerably weaker for most purposes than those provided at the time by the Race Relations Act 1976 (RRA).[57] The adoption of the Racial Directive altered the position to some extent, though EU protections against race discrimination remain far from satisfactory. Many of the criticisms raised in Bob Hepple's article, written a year after the transposition of the Race Directive into domestic law and extracted below, remain true today.

> **Bob Hepple, 'Race and Law in Fortress Europe' (2004) 67 *Modern Law Review* 1, 3–13, footnotes omitted**
>
> two features of these important legal instruments [the Racial Directive and the European Convention on Human Rights] … in my view, prevent them from being as effective as they might be in promoting a pluralistic culture of human rights in Europe. The first is that the universality of human rights is undermined by being restricted to those who are nationals of the EU states. The second is that these instruments are incapable of redressing collective racial disadvantage because they do not provide for the enforcement of positive social, economic and cultural obligations … discrimination on grounds of nationality is altogether excluded from [the] scope [of the Racial Directive]. The member states were worried that their immigration controls might be susceptible to challenge. So they secured changes to the draft in order to limit its application.

Hepple's criticism of the individualistic focus of the Race Directive has been echoed by the European Commission, which recently published the EU Anti-racism Action Plan 2020–2025. This plan calls for a more integrated, intersectional and structural approach to understanding racism in Europe.[58]

[56] Previously Art 13 of the Treaty Establishing the European Community (TEC), under which the Race Directive and the Employment Equality Directive were adopted.

[57] See E Szyszczak, 'Race Discrimination: The Limits of Market Equality' in B Hepple and E Szyszczak (eds), *Discrimination: The Limits of Law* (London, Mansell, 1992) 125.

[58] For a brief assessment of the structural dimension of the Action Plan, see European Network Against Racism, 'EU Anti-Racism Action Plan Explained: A Blog Series', 13 October 2020, available at https://www.enar-eu.org/eu-anti-racism-action-plan-explained-a-blog-series.

European Commission, *A Union of equality: EU Anti-Racism Action Plan 2020–2025*, (2020) 1–2, footnotes omitted[59]

There is now a moment of reckoning. Over half of Europeans believe that such discrimination is widespread in their country. The conflict between our values of equality and the reality of ingrained racism cannot be ignored: the global Black Lives Matter movement has acted as a stark reminder. It is time to acknowledge and act against the prevalence of racism and racial discrimination, to consider what we can do, engaging at local, national, EU and international levels. The EU is built on diversity and on fostering a society of pluralism, tolerance and non-discrimination: we need to act not only out of responsibility, but also to be true to our values. Upholding values starts at home, in our own institution. The Commission will take measures to significantly improve the diversity of its staff and ensure that all can equally thrive and contribute in the working environment.

Racism comes in different forms. Overt expressions of individual racism and racial discrimination are the most obvious. All too often, racial or ethnic origin is used as a ground to discriminate – the COVID-19 pandemic and the aftermath of terrorist attacks are just the most recent cases where blame has been unjustly directed at people with a minority racial or ethnic background. People of Asian and African descent, Muslims, Jewish and Roma people have all suffered from intolerance. But other, less explicit forms of racism and racial discrimination, such as those based on unconscious bias, can be equally damaging. Racist and discriminatory behaviours can be embedded in social, financial and political institutions, impacting on the levers of power and on policy-making. This structural racism perpetuates the barriers placed in the way of citizens solely due to their racial or ethnic origin. Every day, people affected by racism can feel its impact on their access to jobs, healthcare, housing, financing or education, as well as cases of violence.

There are different forms of racism, for example anti-black racism, antigypsyism, antisemitism and anti-Asian racism, that link to religion or belief in cases such anti-Muslim hatred. All share the reality that the value of a person is undermined by stereotypes based on prejudice. In addition to religion or belief, racism can also be combined with discrimination and hatred on other grounds, including gender, sexual orientation, age, and disability or against migrants. This needs to be taken into account through an intersectional approach.

Any improvement to the EU's approach comes too late for the UK.

The Equality Act 2010

Race as a Protected Characteristic

The EqA provides that:

Section 9 EqA, Race

(1) Race includes—

(a) colour;
(b) nationality;
(c) ethnic or national origins.

[59] https://ec.europa.eu/info/policies/justice-and-fundamental-rights/combatting-discrimination/racism-and-xenophobia/eu-anti-racism-action-plan-2020–2025_en.

(2) In relation to the protected characteristic of race—

(a) a reference to a person who has a particular protected characteristic is a reference to a person of a particular racial group;

(b) a reference to persons who share a protected characteristic is a reference to persons of the same racial group.

(3) A racial group is a group of persons defined by reference to race; and a reference to a person's racial group is a reference to a racial group into which the person falls.

(4) The fact that a racial group comprises two or more distinct racial groups does not prevent it from constituting a particular racial group.

(5) A Minister of the Crown … —

(a) must by order amend this section so as to provide for caste to be an aspect of race …

Notwithstanding the mandatory terms of s9(5) EqA, which was introduced in 2013, no legislation has been implemented to give it effect.[60] Caste discrimination may, however, fall within the EqA where it also amounts to indirect discrimination on grounds of colour, ethnic origin or national origin, or otherwise entails discrimination because of one or more of these factors (see further pp 453–454 below).

Section 9 EqA classifies as race discrimination less favourable treatment because of skin colour, as well as discrimination against Albanians or Australians (nationality), or against those of African or Welsh descent (national origins). The concept of ethnic origins is more expansive than the other categories of race discrimination and is discussed at pp 437–440 below.

Colour

There is little case law on 'colour' discrimination. It is worth noting however that this form of discrimination attracts the highest possible discrimination under the EqA. Section 193 EqA, which permits charities to be created to benefit groups of people classified according to protected characteristics, provides (s193(4)) that 'If a charitable instrument enables the provision of benefits to persons of a class defined by reference to colour, it has effect for all purposes as if it enabled the provision of such benefits – (a) to persons of the class which results if the reference to colour is ignored, or (b) if the original class is defined by reference only to colour, to persons generally.' And Schedule 16 para 1 EqA, which permits associations to restrict membership to people sharing particular characteristics, does not apply to colour.

Nationality

The prohibition on nationality discrimination is subject to more exceptions than other forms of race discrimination (see pp 466–474 below). Much of the disadvantage which is associated with nationality arises in connection with immigration status which determines people's entitlement to live and work in the UK and, accordingly, their ability to access education and services, and to seek the assistance and protection of the state. The prohibition of nationality discrimination has, failed to protect those rendered vulnerable by their (nationality-related) immigration status to exploitation and abuse.

[60] In its original form s9 *permitted* rather than *required* the inclusion of caste within the EqA.

***Taiwo v Olaigbe; Onu v Akwiwu* [2016] UKSC 31, [2016] ICR 756**

The first claimant was a Nigerian national who had entered the UK lawfully with a migrant domestic worker's visa obtained for her by the first respondents, her employers, who subjected her to physical and mental abuse. The second claimant, who was also Nigerian, had entered the UK on a domestic worker's visa obtained by deceit for her by the second respondents, her employers, who had removed her passport and threatened and abused her. Neither claimant would have been so treated had they not been vulnerable migrant workers whose lawful presence in the UK depended on their continued relationship with their abusive employers.

The claimants claimed direct and indirect race discrimination. The first claimant's claims were dismissed by a tribunal, which found that she had been treated as she was because she was a vulnerable migrant worker who was reliant on her employers for her continued employment and residence in the UK, not because she was Nigerian. The second claimant's claims were upheld by a tribunal, which ruled that her status as a migrant worker was 'clearly linked' to her race, and also found that she had been harassed by reason of race. The EAT rejected the first claimant's appeal and upheld the second respondent's appeal, ruling that the treatment of the second claimant was bound up not with her race but with her subordinate position and the relative economic benefits of her work in the UK compared with the poverty of her situation in Nigeria. The EAT further rejected the claim that the mistreatment of migrant workers amounted to indirect race discrimination because such mistreatment was not a neutral criterion which disadvantaged some of those to whom it applied disproportionately when compared with others to whom it applied. The CA upheld the EAT's findings and the Supreme Court (SC) rejected the claimants' appeals.

Lady Hale (for the Court:

> 14. … These employees were treated disgracefully, in a way which employees who did not share their vulnerable immigration status would not have been treated. As the employment tribunals found, this was because of the vulnerability associated with their immigration status. The issue for us is a simple one: does discrimination on grounds of immigration status amount to discrimination on grounds of nationality … On the face of it, the two are different. What basis is there for saying that they are the same? […]
>
> 26. … there are many non-British nationals living and working here who do not share this vulnerability. No doubt, if these employers had employed British nationals to work for them in their homes, they would not have treated them so badly. They would probably not have been given the opportunity to do so. But equally, if they had employed non-British nationals who had the right to live and work here, they would not have treated them so badly. The reason why these employees were treated so badly was their particular vulnerability arising, at least in part, from their particular immigration status. As Mr Rahman pointed out, on behalf of Mr and Mrs Akwiwu, it had nothing to do with the fact that they were Nigerians. The employers too were non-nationals, but they were not vulnerable in the same way.
>
> 27. That, in my view, is enough to dispose of the direct discrimination claim. But it is consistent with the approach of this court in the cases of *Patmalniece v Secretary of State for Work and Pensions* [20111] UKSC 11, [2011] 1 WLR 783, which in turn applied the approach of the European Court of Justice in the cases of *Schnorbus v Land Hessen* (Case C-79/99) [2000] ECR I-10997 and *Bressol v Gouvernement de la Communauteì Française, Chaverot v Gouvernement de la Communauteì Française* (Case C-73/08) [2010] ECR I-2735, and *Bull v Hall* [[2013] UKSC 73, [2013] 1 WLR 374].

28. *Patmalniece* was about whether a residence requirement, which all British nationals, but not all non-British nationals, could meet was directly discriminatory on grounds of nationality. In *Schnorbus*, Advocate General Jacobs had said this (at para 33):

> 'The discrimination is direct where the difference in treatment is based on a criterion which is either explicitly that of sex or necessarily linked to a characteristic indissociable from sex. It is indirect where some other criterion is applied but a substantially higher proportion of one sex than of the other is in fact affected.

This concept of indissociability was taken up by Advocate General Sharpston in *Bressol*, where the facts were very similar to those in *Patmalniece*, and formulated thus (at para 56):

> 'I take there to be direct discrimination when the category of those receiving a certain advantage and the category of those suffering a correlative disadvantage coincide exactly with the respective categories of persons distinguished only by applying a prohibited classification.'

In all three cases, the discrimination was held to be indirect rather than direct (the Court of Justice disagreeing with the Advocate General in *Bressol*). There was not an exact correspondence between the advantaged and disadvantaged groups and the protected characteristic, as some of those distinguished by their nationality were not disadvantaged, although others were.

29. The same approach was adopted in *Bull v Hall*, where Christian hotel keepers would deny a double bedded room to all unmarried couples, whether of opposite sexes or the same sex. That would undoubtedly have been indirect discrimination, as same sex couples were not then able to marry and thus fulfil the criterion, whereas opposite sex couples could do so if they chose. But the majority held that it was direct discrimination, because the hotel keepers expressly discriminated between heterosexual and non-heterosexual married couples. The couple in question were in a civil partnership, which for all legal purposes is the same as marriage.

30. Mr Allen argues [for the claimants] that these cases can be distinguished, because they were cases in which an express criterion was being applied, be it nationality or heterosexuality, whereas these appeals are not concerned with such a criterion or test, but with the mental processes of the employers. But that makes no difference. In 'mental processes' cases, it is still necessary to determine what criterion was in fact being adopted by the alleged discriminator – whether sex, race, ethnicity or whatever – and it has to be one which falls within the prohibited characteristics. The point about this case is that the criterion in fact being adopted by these employers was not nationality but, as Mr Allen freely acknowledges, being 'a particular kind of migrant worker, her particular status making her vulnerable to abuse'.[61]

31. Mr Allen accepts that this is not a case of indirect discrimination. It is direct discrimination or nothing. In my view he is wise to do so, but the fact that these cases cannot be fitted into the concept of indirect discrimination is further support for the view that the mistreatment here was not because of the employees' race but for other reasons …

32. [Indirect discrimination occurs when an] … employer or supplier has a rule or practice which he applies to all employees or customers, actual or would-be, but which favours one group over another and cannot objectively be justified. Requiring all employees to sport a moustache is obviously indirectly discriminatory against women. The problem in this case is that no-one can think of a 'provision, criterion or practice' which these employers would have applied to all their employees, whether or not they had the particular immigration status of these employees. The only PCP which anyone can think of is the mistreatment and exploitation of workers who are vulnerable because of their immigration status. By definition, this would not be applied to workers who are not so vulnerable. Applying it to these workers cannot therefore be indirect discrimination within the meaning of section 19 [EqA].

[61] See also discussion in Ch 9 (direct and indirect discrimination in context of religion).

Ethnic Origins

The leading decision on the scope of 'ethnic origins' remains the decision in *Mandla v Dowell Lee*, in which the HL considered whether Sikhs were properly considered a racial group. Prior to this decision EAT had accepted, in *Seide v Gillette* [1980] IRLR 427, that Jews were properly regarded as a racial group, with the result that anti-Jewish discrimination was caught by the provisions of the RRA. The drafters of the RRA had intended that Sikhs be treated as a racial group[62] and the early case law had treated them as such,[63] but doubt was cast on this by the CA in the unreported case of *CRE v Genture Restaurants Ltd*. The county court judge in the *Mandla* case had ruled that Sikhs were not a racial group and the CA agreed ([1983] QB 1), interpreting 'ethnic origins' to refer (as a subcategory of 'race') to 'characteristics or attributes which are, by their nature, unalterable.' The HL restored the previous orthodoxy.

***Mandla v Dowell Lee* [1983] 2 AC 548**

The *Mandla* case was brought on behalf of a schoolboy who was refused access to a private school on the grounds that he, consistent with the requirements of his Sikh religion, wore a turban. The school's argument was that the turban would draw attention to the boy's origins and 'accentuate religious and social distinctions in the school which, being a multiracial school based on the Christian faith, the headmaster desired to minimise' (by assimilating all pupils to the (white Christian) 'norm'.

The HL decided unanimously that Sikhs comprised a 'racial group' for the purposes of the RRA. The effect of this was that the application of a 'no turban' rule amounted, subject to its justifiability, to indirect discrimination against the boy. Lord Fraser who, with Lord Templeman, delivered the leading speeches, accepted that Sikhs were indistinguishable from other groups, especially those in the Punjab, 'by reference to colour, race, nationality or national origins', but ruled that a group defined by reference to 'ethnic origins' was one which regarded itself, and was regarded by others:

Lord Fraser, with whom Lords Edmund-Davies, Roskill and Brandon agreed:

> 11. … as a distinct community by virtue of certain characteristics. Some of these characteristics are essential others are not essential but one or more of them will commonly be found and will help to distinguish the group from the surrounding community. The conditions which appear to me to be essential are these: (1) a long shared history, of which the group is conscious as distinguishing it from other groups, and the memory of which it keeps alive (2) a cultural tradition of its own, including family and social customs and manners, often but not necessarily associated with religious observance. In addition to those two essential characteristics the following characteristics are, in my opinion, relevant: (3) either a common geographical origin, or descent from a small number of common ancestors (4) a common language, not necessarily peculiar to the group (5) a common literature peculiar to the group (6) a common religion different from that of neighbouring groups or from the general community surrounding it (7) being a minority or being an oppressed or a dominant group within a larger community, for example a conquered people (say, the inhabitants of England shortly after the Norman conquest) and their conquerors might both be ethnic groups.

[62] See I McKenna, 'Racial Discrimination' (1983) 46 *Modern Law Review* 759, 759–60. Convention at the time (pre-*Pepper v Hart* [1993] AC 593) prevented judges from looking officially at statements made in Parliament in interpreting the meaning of legislation.

[63] See eg *Singh v Rowntree Mackintosh Ltd* [1979] ICR 504 and *Panesar v Nestlé Co Ltd* [1980] ICR 144.

Lord Fraser stated that a group which satisfied the test set out above would not cease to do so because some of its members were converts and/or because it excluded 'apostates', and that converts would be treated as sharing the ethnic origins of the group for the purposes of the RRA if they regarded themselves and members, and were accepted as such by other members.[64] Lord Fraser pointed out that the Sikh community, although originally founded at about the end of the fifteenth century by Guru Nanak as a religious community, was now (quoting the county court judge) 'a distinctive and self-conscious community [with] a history going back to the fifteenth century [and] a written language which a small proportion of Sikhs can read but which can be read by a much higher proportion of Sikhs than of Hindus [which was] at one time politically supreme in the Punjab'. He concluded on the basis of this that Sikhs were 'a group defined by a reference to ethnic origins ... although they are not biologically distinguishable from the other peoples living in the Punjab'.

Lord Templeman, who delivered the other main speech, and with whom Lords Edmund-Davies, Roskill and Brandon also agreed, declared that 'a group of persons defined by reference to ethnic origins must possess some of the characteristics of a race, namely group descent, a group of geographical origin and a group history'. He concluded that Sikhs satisfied this test and that, although physically indistinguishable from 'other inhabitants of the Punjab', 'they constitute a separate and distinct community derived from the racial characteristics I have mentioned', as well (he pointed out) as Lord Fraser's conditions.

The approach taken by the HL in *Mandla* has not gone uncriticised:

G Tony Pagone, 'The Lawyer's Hunt for Snarks, Religion and Races' [1984] *Cambridge Law Journal* 218, 218–22, footnotes omitted

To the social scientist … the lawyer's attempt at definition must seem like the famous hunt for Snarks described by Lewis Carroll and the object of the hunt as dangerous as the Boojum, for if you ever catch sight of a Boojum you 'will softly and suddenly vanish away.' So too with 'race,' 'ethnicity' and 'religion,' since the closer the definition approaches the concept the less it appears as a definition at all …

> Lord Fraser. considered the competing senses in which 'ethnic' is used and attempted to strike a balance between (a) the need of lower courts and public officials for guidance and certainty in the administration of the law and (b) an awareness that a rigid legal definition of such concepts would be inappropriate … in deciding that Sikhs were an 'ethnic' group and hence a 'racial group' for the purposes of the Act, the House of Lords has adopted a definition which seeks to contain the elusiveness of the concept under discussion by allowing for future changes and variation in the nature of the concept …
>
> It could be argued that there is no compelling reason why the House of Lords … needed to provide any definition at all. The court[] could, for example, have taken the view that what is a 'race' is a question of fact to be determined by the trier of fact …
>
> In the final analysis, however, [the] court[] provide[d a] solution[] which g[a]ve recognition to the impossibility of fixed and certain meanings. Ultimately, whether any group of people can be called an 'ethnic group' or 'race'… requires a judgment for which no amount of legal training can assist. The lawyer is neither equipped nor entitled to give fixed legal definitions for such important social phenomena and at best the law can do little more than point to the general direction of what seems an elusive concept. It is thus not surprising that in the end the

[64] Note that such people, as well as apostates, will in any event be protected from discrimination because of their *perceived* membership of the group: see Ch 2.

> approach[] of … the House of Lords should be to list what appear to be some relevant factors and leave additions, weightings and orderings of importance in each case as, and when, it arises.

Pagone takes issue with the very attempt to define 'ethnic group'. Benyon and Lore, whose article is extracted below, comment on the disparities between Lord Fraser's judgment and that of Lord Templeman who, while setting out a substantially different test, appeared also to agree with Lord Fraser. The writers point out that both Law Lords regarded a historical element as an 'essential characteristic' but that 'there the similarity ends' with Lord Fraser's 'cultural tradition', 'language,' 'literature,' 'religion' and 'oppressed or dominant group' not featuring at all in Lord Templeman's list, and Lord Templeman's required characteristics of 'group descent' and 'group of geographical origin' being regarded by Lord Fraser as 'non-essential' though 'relevant characteristics'. Having drawn attention to the disparities between the approaches of Lord Fraser and Lord Templeman, they suggest, in light of the latter's apparent agreement with the former, that actual consensus cannot be found because:

Helen Benyon and Nigel Love, 'Mandla and the Meaning of "Racial Group"' (1984) 100 *Law Quarterly Review* 120, 121–23, footnotes omitted

> conditions which Lord Templeman states 'must' exist ('group descent' and 'geographical origin') Lord Fraser merely regards as 'relevant'… There is surely a crucial difference between 'must' and 'may,' of between a necessary condition and a contingent characteristic, even if, as will shortly be shown, other aspects of Lord Fraser's speech suggest that in other respects he attached little importance to the distinction he was here at pains to draw. So, at the very least, even if (a dubious point) Lord Fraser and Lord Templeman concurred in requiring a 'cultural tradition' as well as a 'group history' (lengthy or otherwise), they did not concur as to whether or not 'group descent' and 'geographical origin' were essential (Lord Templeman) or merely relevant (Lord Fraser) …
>
> Lord Fraser's interpretation of 'racial group' might well embrace gipsies as nomads and itinerants, even though Lord Templeman's clearly would not, since nomads and itinerant as such would fall foul of Lord Templeman's second requirement of 'geographical origin.' In fact, Lord Fraser's definition would seem to embrace many groups quite outside the intended scope of the [RRA], such as the British Royal Family, or the working class. Do they not each possess, in their different ways, 'long shared histories' and 'cultural traditions, including family and social customs and manners …'? One response to this might be that although both the Royal Family and the working class possess Lord Fraser's characteristics, they are not 'defined by reference to' them. They are instead probably 'defined by reference to' consanguinity or affinity with a reigning monarch, and occupation, respectively. A perfectly sensible response, indeed, but not one open to anyone supporting Lord Fraser's interpretation of the Act, since he himself, as will be shown, did not use 'defined by reference to' in this limiting sense. So, another possible response might be that, however distinctive the family and social customs of the Royal Family and the working classes, they do not amount to a 'cultural tradition,' but only to a 'sub-cultural' tradition. But if so, the infinite regress towards which that tends is another argument against Lord Fraser's interpretation …

Gypsies (but not 'travellers') were accepted as a 'racial group' by the CA in the following case.

***Commission for Racial Equality v Dutton* [1988] EWCA Civ 17, [1989] QB 783**

The CRE challenged a 'No Travellers' sign displayed in the Cat and Mutton pub in Hackney's Broadway Market. In his evidence the pub's landlord defined 'Traveller' as a 'person who travels around in a caravan and parks on illegal sites and gives him "hassle".' The CRE's view that 'Travellers' in fact referred to 'Gypsies' was rejected by the county court and, on appeal, by the CA. Having pointed out that the word 'Gypsy' or 'Gipsy' was used both to refer to Romanies and also to people with nomadic lifestyles, Nicholls LJ continued:

Nicholls LJ:

> 9. … if the word 'gipsy' is used in this second, colloquial sense it is not definitive of a racial group within the Act. To discriminate against such a group would not be on racial grounds, namely, on the ground of ethnic origins. As the judge observed, there are many people who travel around the country in caravans, vans converted buses, trailers, lorries and motor vehicles, leading a peripatetic or nomadic way of life. They include didicois, mumpers, peace people, new age travellers, hippies, tinkers, hawkers, self-styled 'anarchists,' and others, as well as (Romany) gipsies. They may all be loosely referred to as 'gipsies,' but as a group they do not have the characteristics requisite of a racial group within the Act …

Having clarified that he would use the word 'Gipsy' in the first of these senses, Nicholls LJ observed that the 'Travellers' prohibited from entering the pub would include those (Romany) Gipsies who had preserved a nomadic way of life[65] and went on to consider whether Gipsies were a 'racial group' for the purposes of deciding whether the notice amounted to unlawful indirect discrimination against them.

> 21. On the evidence it is clear that such gipsies are a minority, with a long-shared history and a common geographical origin. They are a people who originated in northern India. They migrated thence to Europe through Persia in medieval times. They have certain, albeit limited, customs of their own, regarding cooking and the manner of washing. They have a distinctive, traditional style of dressing, with heavy jewellery worn by the women, although this dress is not worn all the time. They also furnish their caravans in a distinctive manner. They have a language or dialect, known as 'pogadi chib,' spoken by English gipsies (Romany chals) and Welsh gipsies (Kale) which consists of up to one-fifth of Romany words in pace of English words. They do not have a common religion, nor a peculiar, common literature of their own, but they have a repertoire of folktales and music passed on from one generation to the next. No doubt, after all the centuries which have passed since the first gipsies left the Punjab, gipsies are no longer derived from what, in biological terms, is a common racial stock, but that of itself does not prevent them from being a racial group as widely defined in the Act.

Nicholls LJ rejected the county court judge's conclusion that, because (he found) Gypsies preferred to be referred to as 'Travellers' and more than half were settled, Gypsies had lost their separate, group identify and were no longer a community recognisable by ethnic origins. He went on to rule that the 'No Travellers' rule amounted to indirect discrimination against Gypsies, subject to the question of justification which he referred back to the county court for decision. Taylor and Stocker LJJ concurred, though the latter expressed reservations about the qualification as an 'ethnic group' of Gypsies given what he saw as the degree of their absorption into the wider population.[66]

[65] Though not, he thought, settled Gypsies.

[66] A decade or so after this case was decided the Cat and Mutton displayed a sign stating that the management 'reserve[d] the right to refuse admission'. The pub has subsequently changed hands several times: see 'Cat and Mutton pub closes', *Hackney Citizen*, 17 December 2013, available at https://www.hackneycitizen.co.uk/2013/12/17/cat-and-mutton-pub-closes.

Gypsies, Travellers and Roma

The Irish Traveller Community is expressly recognised as a racial group by the Race Relations (Northern Ireland) Order 1997. In *O'Leary v Allied Domecq* (unreported, 2000), the Central London county court accepted that Irish Travellers were an ethnic group for the purposes of the RRA despite their lack of express inclusion in the statute. According to Judge Goldstein, who ruled in favour of a number of Irish Travellers denied access to a pub: 'Modern Irish Travellers are guided by culture and traditions which have been handed down by generations.' In March 2005 the Joint Committee on Human Rights raised concerns about the discrimination faced by Gypsies and Travellers in the UK, referring to their:

Joint Committee on Human. Rights, *The Convention on the Elimination of Racial Discrimination*, Fourteenth Report of 2004–2005[67]

95. … higher child mortality rate, exclusion from schools, shorter life expectancy, poor housing conditions, lack of available camping sites, high unemployment rate and limited access to health services'…

96. … evidence presented to us, attests to the multiple discrimination faced by Gypsies and their exceptional level of social exclusion. Poor levels of health, even compared with other marginalised groups, high rates of infant mortality, and difficulties in accessing healthcare were cited in the evidence. Poor school attendance, low educational attainment and high levels of illiteracy were also referred to as particularly acute problems for Gypsy and Traveller children …

100. It is unequal access to adequate and culturally appropriate accommodation, however, which lies at the root of many of the inequalities that face Gypsies and Travellers. In their evidence to us, the Gypsy and Traveller Law Reform Coalition (G&TLRC) emphasised the consequences of insecurity of tenure for the health and education of Travellers, and the Children's Society testified to the detrimental impact which eviction and the lack of secure sites had on the welfare of Traveller children …

102. The House of Commons Select Committee on the Office of the Deputy Prime Minister, in a Report on Gypsy and Traveller Sites published in November 2004, estimated that over 3,500 Gypsies and Travellers, 20% of the Travelling community, have no legal place where they can stop their caravans. These caravans are therefore on unauthorised encampments and their occupants are defined as homeless under the Housing Act 1996. In addition, these encampments are often a source of tension between Gypsies/Travellers and the settled community. The G&TLRC state in their evidence that in England there is a shortage of 4,500 transit and residential pitches.

The JCHR drew attention to the multiple legal difficulties faced by Gypsies and Travellers in connection with sites which in the Committee's view risked breaches of the Convention on the Elimination of Racial Discrimination and of Article 14 ECHR read with A1P1 (the right to property). In 2009 the EHRC published a 360-page review entitled *Inequalities experienced by Gypsy and Traveller communities*, which catalogued the various disadvantages experiences by these groups.[68] The authors found that 'The lack of suitable, secure accommodation underpins many of the inequalities that Gypsy and Traveller communities experience', planning policy having 'shifted away from publicly owned sites, which local housing authorities administer, to self-provision by the communities themselves' which were often denied planning permission. The 'considerable shortfall in the quantity of residential

[67] https://publications.parliament.uk/pa/jt200405/jtselect/jtrights/88/8804.htm.

[68] https://www.equalityhumanrights.com/sites/default/files/research_report_12inequalities_experienced_by_gypsy_and_traveller_communities_a_review.pdf.

and transit accommodation available to Gypsies and Travellers who do not wish to reside in conventional housing' resulted in people living 'under motorways or next to sewage works' and experiencing 'health hazards (such as contamination by vermin), decayed sewage and water fittings, poor-quality utility rooms, and failings in fire safety' and 'a cycle of evictions, typically linked to violent and threatening behaviour from private bailiff companies'.[69] Insecure living arrangements and associated 'instability and trauma' impacted on the health of Gypsies and Travellers 'while severe disruptions occur to access to education for children, healthcare services and employment opportunities'.

The 2009 report also found that the general social unacceptability of overt racism did not apply to its deployment against Gypsies and Travellers who were subject to racism in the press and by local and national politicians as well as by employers and others:

Sarah Cemlyn et al, *Inequalities experienced by Gypsy and Traveller communities* (EHRC) v–vi[70]

While Gypsies and Travellers have experienced such hostility for centuries, what is remarkable – and shameful – is that this continues in the present day, despite a wealth of legislation to promote equality and human rights and protect against discrimination …

The following points highlight a few key areas of concern from among the severe, wide-ranging and mutually reinforcing inequalities and problems faced by members of the communities that are the focus of this report. It is by no means an exhaustive list.

- Gypsies and Travellers die earlier than the rest of the population.
- They experience worse health, yet are less likely to receive effective, continuous healthcare.
- Children's educational achievements are worse, and declining still further (contrary to the national trend).
- Participation in secondary education is extremely low …
- There is a lack of access to pre-school, out-of-school and leisure services for children and young people.
- There is an unquantified but substantial negative psychological impact on children who experience repeated brutal evictions, family tensions associated with insecure lifestyles, and an unending stream of overt and extreme hostility from the wider population.
- Employment rates are low, and poverty high.
- There is an increasing problem of substance abuse among unemployed and disaffected young people.
- There are high suicide rates among the communities.
- Within the criminal justice system – because of a combination of unfair treatment at different stages and other inequalities affecting the communities – there is a process of accelerated criminalisation at a young age, leading rapidly to custody …
- Policy initiatives and political systems that are designed to promote inclusion and equality frequently exclude Gypsies and Travellers. This includes political structures and community development and community cohesion programmes.
- There is a lack of access to culturally appropriate support services for people in the most vulnerable situations, such as women experiencing domestic violence.
- Gypsies' and Travellers' culture and identity receive little or no recognition, with consequent and considerable damage to their self-esteem.

In 2016 the EHRC declared Gypsies, Travellers and Roma among the four most disadvantaged groups in Britain (the others were homeless people, people with learning disabilities and migrants, refugees and asylum-seekers).

[69] *Ibid*, iv.
[70] *Ibid*.

EHRC, *England's most disadvantaged groups: Gypsies, Travellers and Roma*, references omitted[71]

Education

Although the educational attainment of Gypsy, Roma and Traveller children in England improved between 2008/09 and 2012/13, the attainment gap between Gypsy and Roma children, and White pupils appears to have widened, while the gap between Travellers of Irish heritage and White pupils has not changed. Gypsy, Roma and Traveller children were less likely to achieve 'a good level of development' in their early years (EYFS) in 2013/14 (19.1% for Gypsy and Roma children, and 30.9% for Traveller children, compared with 61.8% other White children). Similarly, a lower percentage of Gypsy and Roma children (13.8%) and Traveller children (17.5%) achieved the GCSE threshold in 2012/13 compared with other White children (60.3%) and the attainment gap widened between 2008/09 and 2012/13.

Gypsy, Roma and Traveller children were also among those most likely to be excluded from school. Their exclusion rates were four to five times higher than the national average in 2012/13: Gypsy and Roma (136.3 per 1,000) and Traveller (169.4 per 1,000) children compared with other White children (41.8 per 1,000) in 2012/13. Gypsy, Roma and Traveller children are particularly vulnerable in a school setting and subjected to bullying). Because of the transience of these pupils, head teachers report difficulties in quickly accessing funding, for example, the pupil premium, for new pupils. There was also a shortage of expertise to provide effective support to Roma pupils.

Work and standard of living

In 2011, Gypsy or Irish Travellers had the lowest recorded economic activity in England and Wales (47% compared with 63%) … Roma were often in low-paid waged employment, faced discrimination in employment agency work, and worked informally for 'cash in hand' work … There is a twice-yearly count of Traveller caravans, which takes place in January and July. Since 2010, the number of Traveller caravans on unauthorised sites has decreased. The number on authorised private sites has increased and on socially rented sites has remained relatively stable. In January 2015, 20,123 Traveller caravans were counted in England: 6,867 (34%) on socially rented sites and 10,585 (53%) on privately rented sites, with the remainder on unauthorised sites …

Health

Compared with the general population, Gypsies and Travellers are more likely to suffer bad health. This includes lower life expectancy, high infant mortality rates, high maternal mortality rates, low child immunisation levels, higher prevalence of anxiety and depression, chronic cough or bronchitis (even after smoking is taken into account), asthma, chest pain and diabetes … and higher rates of smoking (Aspinall and Mitton, 2014). This is exacerbated by the fact that many Gypsies and Travellers remain unregistered with GPs (RCGP, 2013). In 2011, 14.1% of Gypsies and Irish Travellers in England and Wales rated their health as bad or very bad, compared with 5.9% of White British and 9.2% of White Irish people (ONS, 2013). While the variability in general health among different ethnic groups can sometimes be explained by an older age profile, this is not the case for Gypsies and Irish Travellers, of whom only 6% were aged 65 and above in 2011 and who had a low median age of 26 … Improved life expectancy of Gypsy and Traveller communities appears to be associated with the availability of established site provision and access to medical

[71] EHRC, *England's most disadvantaged groups: Gypsies, Travellers and Roma* (one of four 'spotlight reports following the EHRC's 2016 *Is England Fairer?* Report) (2016); www.equalityhumanrights.com/sites/default/files/is-england-fairer-2016-most-disadvantaged-groups-migrants-refugees-asylum-seekers.pdf#:~:text=The%20Equality%20and%20Human%20Rights%20Commission%E2%80%99s%20first-ever%20report,disadvantaged%20groups%3A%20Homeless%20people%20Gypsies%2C%20Travellers%20and%20Roma.

care … There is emerging evidence that health inequalities of Roma people are similar to those identified among Gypsies and Travellers, including a high prevalence of diabetes, cardiovascular disease, premature myocardial infarction, obesity, asthma and mental health issues such as stress, anxiety and depression … Poor familiarity with healthcare provisions and language barriers may make it difficult for them to access health services … Cultural norms may prevent some Roma people from accessing services for support with mental health, sexual health, and drug and alcohol misuse … Infrequent contact with health providers may also be exacerbating the health problems of some Roma patients …

Prisons

Gypsies, Roma or Travellers are considerably over-represented in prison. In 2013–14, 4% of the prison population identified as Gypsy, Roma or Traveller in the HMIP prisoner survey, whereas only 0.1% of the population identified as such in the 2011 census … The exact size of the population in prison is not known because levels of self reporting were low and the option to record a prisoners' ethnicity as 'Gypsy or Irish Traveller' was only added to the Prison National Offender Management Information System monitoring system for the first time in 2011 … Gypsies, Roma and Travellers were more likely to report feeling unsafe in prison (46%) compared with other prisoners (33%), and more likely to say they had been victimised by other prisoners (36% compared with 23%) and by staff (40% compared with 27%). They were also more likely to report that they been physically restrained or had been in segregation in the previous six months (14% compared with 6%) (HMIP, 2014). Their vulnerability in prison may further be heighted by separation from their families, high levels of mental illness, lack of adequate mental health support and not being able to read or write ….

Stigmatising treatment

Negative attitudes towards Gypsy, Roma and Traveller communities were still widely held.

- According to the Spring 2014 Global Attitudes survey, 50% of people in Britain reported having an unfavourable view of Roma …
- Discrimination and harassment of Gypsies, Roma and Travellers was common across Britain, not only on the part of the general public but also by the police and other authorities …
- Evidence from a study carried out in Devon found that some people from Gypsy, Roma and Traveller communities had hidden their ethnic identity in order toaccess employment and services, and others said their children were bullied at school and that they had been refused entry to pubs and cinemas …
- Britain has failed to make progress on all of the measures aimed at fighting discrimination that are part of the European Commission's Framework for National Roma Integration …

Hostility towards individuals and groups on the basis of ethnicity is often channelled through political rhetoric and the media, which has been criticised by human rights monitoring bodies and highlighted by the Leveson Inquiry:

- The Irish Traveller Movement in Britain provided numerous examples of bias, racism and stereotyping in the media in relation to the reporting of Gypsy, Roma and Traveller issues and claimed that it was making the integration of these communities more difficult …
- There were many examples of 'prejudicial or pejorative references' to particular races or ethnicities in the press. For example, in 2013 an opinion piece in *The Spectator* described Gypsy, Roma and Traveller people as lazy, criminal and unintelligent. The author Rod Liddle claimed that usage of the terms 'gyppo' and 'pikey' were a 'useful means of lumping them all together' …
- Channel 4's series 'Big Fat Gypsy Weddings' has also been found to have perpetuated negative stereotypes. In 2012, the broadcaster was criticised by the Advertising Standards Agency for an advertising campaign which featured posters with the words 'Bigger. Fatter. Gypsier'. The decision that the complaints did not warrant investigation was challenged by the Irish

Traveller Movement and eight other complainants, and an independent review of the agency's decision led to the case being re-opened. The Advertising Standards Agency took advice from the EHRC and upheld that the adverts were offensive because they were racist, denigrating and portrayed Gypsies and Travellers in a negatively stereotypical way. It also stated that the adverts were irresponsible because they depicted negative stereotypes of Gypsies and Travellers, and endorsed prejudice against them …

In 2019 the House of Commons Women and Equalities Committee painted a similarly bleak picture and was sharply critical of Government policy-making in this area.

House of Commons Women and Equalities Committee, *Tackling inequalities faced by Gypsy, Roma and Traveller communities*, Seventh Report of Session 2017–19[72]

Summary

… Given that three in four Gypsies and Travellers live in non-caravan accommodation, we are deeply concerned that Government policy-making is overwhelmingly focused on planning and accommodation issues. Other important areas of public policy and service provision seem to consist of small-scale projects that are funded for a short time and then not taken forward strategically. Specialist support in education and health that has been put in place has not been sustained and is increasingly reliant on small, voluntary agencies. We have found that trust is low between Gypsy, Roma and Traveller communities and public services, due to historic and ongoing discrimination. Gypsy, Roma and Traveller people feel that they are, at best, ignored and, at worst, actively discriminated against in public services and policy making. While pockets of good practice exist, these tend to be driven by committed individuals developing creative solutions to overcome barriers. When individuals move on, the trust that has been built up dissipates, along with any progress that has been made. Gypsy, Roma and Traveller communities have every right to live their lives according to their values and beliefs within the law that that applies to every UK resident. But we have concluded that actions that fall outside the law are not as effectively tackled by local authorities, law enforcement agencies and other public bodies as they are for settled communities. This creates unnecessary tensions and prejudiced attitudes. This also lets down vulnerable members of the Gypsy, Roma and Traveller communities, especially those suffering domestic abuse and children who are not receiving their legal right to education. This is completely unacceptable and must be addressed through both sensitive work by public bodies and through the Communities being willing to work with them in good faith.

Among the particular issues raised by the 2019 report were the obligations of the state towards Gypsy and Traveller children and to women subject to domestic violence:

81. We have heard compelling evidence that the education of boys and girls in Gypsy and Traveller communities is heavily gendered, with boys being removed from school to join their fathers in business and girls being removed to look after younger children and to become homemakers. While all young people from Gypsy and Traveller communities may be affected by this, we have spoken to girls and women for whom life chances are particularly limited. However, we have also heard that this situation is changing, with more young women going onto further and higher education. We nonetheless believe that young women from Gypsy and Traveller communities are not able to fulfil their potential and that they are experiencing discrimination by being prevented from accessing education.

82. The Department for Education draft guidance for relationship and sex education in secondary schools makes it clear that the teaching should include an understanding of the religious and cultural context of the children in the school. It also includes the 'right to withdraw' a child from sex education

[72] Available at https://publications.parliament.uk/pa/cm201719/cmselect/cmwomeq/360/360.pdf.

classes, should the parent choose to do so. It does not, however, give parents the right to withdraw their children from education entirely. All children benefit from age-appropriate relationship and sex education, but more needs to be done to ensure that Gypsy, Roma and Traveller parents do not remove their children from school because of an objection to it. Schools must have a plan for how to have constructive conversations with parents to explain to them the benefits of relationship and sex education in a way that is reassuring.

83. Schools have a duty to proactively plan for how they will have conversations with Gypsy, Roma and Traveller parents about what relationship and sex education involves and what parents' options are for their children, short of removing them from school. These plans should be explicit and Ofsted should take them into account during inspections and assess schools accordingly …

163. Gypsy, Roma and Traveller Women who are trying to leave abusive homes face barriers that go beyond those that non-Gypsy, Roma and Traveller women experience. Gypsy and Traveller women often lose their extended community network when a relationship ends. While this can be due to ostracisation, it is also likely that a woman will be living either on a site or very near to her extended family and, if she needs to leave her home, she will need to be housed far away for her own safety. One woman told us:

> As a Traveller woman, you do not have the support of family. [If you leave] you lose your community and you lose who you are because you are leaving everything you have ever known and everyone behind.

164. When informal support networks are absent, women must turn to external agencies for help. Several women we spoke to found support from a particular social worker who they trusted. However, the women expressed a general mistrust of social services, a view we heard repeated throughout the inquiry. This often manifested in the fear that, if a woman were to approach social services for help, she risked having her children taken into care. One of the women we spoke to told us:

> I think social services are one of the biggest barriers in why Traveller women are not asking for help or not trying to break free. You have to stay at home, be a punch bag and cover up your bruises in order to keep your children. That is how Traveller women feel.

165. The police were also seen as untrustworthy by witnesses, although some had had good experiences of support …

167. Support for Gypsy, Roma and Traveller women fleeing violence must provide women with viable and sustainable options to keep them safe. Organisations with strong records of working with and for Gypsy, Roma and Traveller communities are the obvious choice to provide such services, although we note that some women may choose to use non-Traveller services instead. The funding for these services is currently short-term and unsustainable, however, and does not provide Gypsy, Roma and Traveller women with the safety they need.

168. Local authorities should ensure that Gypsy, Roma and Traveller women have access to a single, trusted contact who provides them with the information and support they need. Should this contact be from a charitable organisation, local authorities must ensure that the organisation has sufficient funding to sustain the necessary support… [original emphasis throughout]

In May 2022 the EHRC announced the commencement of a formal investigation into alleged discrimination by Pontins holiday parks against Gypsies and Travellers.[73] Pontins had entered a 12-month agreement with the Commission in 2021 following allegations that it

[73] For discussion of Formal Investigations see Ch 5.

had published a list of 'undesirable' guests which contained common Irish surnames, and had refused or cancelled bookings by people suspected of being Gypsies or Travellers. The EHRC was not satisfied that Pontins was taking the steps required under the agreement and so launched a formal investigation into:

- 'whether Pontins has committed race discrimination against Gypsy and Traveller guests, prospective guests or their associates in how it provides its services';
- 'whether Pontins' booking policies directly or indirectly discriminate on the basis of race, including a requirement that guests, or prospective guests, are on the electoral register';
- 'whether Pontins' intelligence, information and record-keeping systems are operating in a way that discriminates directly or indirectly on the basis of race'.[74]

It is not evident that the Government has absorbed the 2019 message from the Women and Equalities Committee. The Policing, Crime, Sentencing and Courts Act 2022 has been criticised for targeting Roma and travelling communities.[75] Part 4 of the Act ('unauthorised encampments') amends the Criminal Justice and Public Order Act 1994 to criminalise the setting up of certain unauthorised encampments which previously resulted in civil liability alone.[76] The actions which are criminalised by s60C of the 1994 Act, as amended, are (1) failing to comply with a request to (a) leave or (b) to remove his or her property from land, or (2) returning to land with the intention to reside on it, where (A) the adult in question had resided or intended to reside on the land without the consent of the occupier of the land, (B) having or intending to have with them at least one vehicle, and (C) the individual has been asked to leave, or to remove his or her property from, the land by the occupier, a representative of the occupier or a police officer. According to a briefing by the organisation Fair Trials at the second reading stage prior to the (then) Policing, Crime, Sentencing and Courts Act Bill becoming law, Part 4 would result in 'the over-criminalisation, and further over-representation of Gypsy Roma and Traveller … people in the criminal justice system.'[77]

Minority Languages and Ethnicity

In *Gwynedd County Council v Jones*, two non-Welsh-speaking Welsh complainants sought to argue that they had been discriminated against on grounds of their ethnic origin by the application of a Welsh language requirement. A tribunal accepted their claims, ruling that the Welsh could be divided into two ethnic groups: English-speaking-Welsh and Welsh-speaking-Welsh. The EAT allowed the employers' appeal.

[74] https://www.equalityhumanrights.com/en/our-work/news/ehrc-investigate-pontins-over-fears-racial-discrimination-against-gypsies-travellers.

[75] George Monbiot, 'The UK is heading towards authoritarianism: just look at this attack on a minority', *The Guardian*, 12 January 2022, available at https://www.theguardian.com/commentisfree/2022/jan/12/uk-authoritarianism-minority-policing-bill-roma-gypsy-traveller.

[76] The Policing, Crime, Sentencing and Courts Act 2022, Part 4.

[77] Fair Trials, 'Policing, Crime, Sentencing and Courts Bill: Fair Trials' Briefing for a Second Reading', 15 March 2021, available at https://www.fairtrials.org/app/uploads/2022/01/Fair-Trials-Police-Crime-Sentencing-and-Courts-Bill-briefing-for-Second-Reading.pdf.

***Gwynedd County Council v Jones* [1986] ICR 833**

Sir Ralph Kilner Brown:

> ... it was wrong in law to use the language factor alone and in isolation as creating a racial group. Even if ... this approach is said to be a question of fact, the decision is wholly unreasonable ... We cannot believe that, for example, a Mrs Jones from Holyhead who speaks Welsh as well as English is to be regarded as belonging to a different racial group from her dear friend, a Mrs Thomas from Colwyn Bay who speaks only English. This concept seems to us to be as artificial as the proposition that 5,000 or so spectators at Cardiff Arms Park who are fluent in Welsh are a different racial group from the 45,000 or so whose command of the Welsh tongue is limited to the rendering of the Welsh national anthem, or 'Sospan fach.' An Englishman who dared to suggest this would be in danger of his life!

Wilson McLeod, 'Autochthonous language communities and the Race Relations Act' (1998) 1 *Web Journal of Current Legal Issues*, footnotes omitted

> Language cannot properly be considered something that stands alone; in particular, it very often tends to create among its speakers 'a cultural tradition of [their] own' (*Mandla* ...), and it is certainly arguable that such a distinct tradition can be discerned among Welsh speakers ...
>
> Although the principal factor differentiating the Gaels from other Scots is the use of the Gaelic language itself, it can well be argued that the language is actually the medium of a distinct and separate culture, manifested in a variety of ways including deep-rooted traditions of poetry, song and music, and unique forms of religious worship. To some extent at least, this distinctiveness extends to material existence as well, the present-day crofting communities remaining substantially different in their way of life from the highly urbanised Scottish mainstream. The claim of Gaelic speakers to recognition as an ethnic group is also strengthened by the fact that a very high proportion of Gaelic speakers, relative to the UK's other autochthonous language communities, are native speakers born and brought up in Gaelic-speaking communities in the Hebrides and West Highlands. It would be safe to say that at least 90% of Gaelic speakers come from such backgrounds, whereas the Welsh language community contains significant proportions of learners and non-traditional speakers. In the case of Gaelic, then, there is a very significant link between the ability to speak the language and a distinct culture and way of life, and the language is the badge of a community that has long been outside the societal mainstream.
>
> Significantly from a legal standpoint, this 'combination of shared customs, beliefs, traditions and characteristics' is largely 'derived from a common ... past,' distinct from the social institutions and practices of Lowland Britain ... Although Gaelic was once the language of almost all Scotland, language shift and cultural divergence began as early as 1100, and already by 1380 the Gaels were identified as an entirely distinct and separate group. Marginalised by geography and outsiders' hostility, the Gaels have without question emerged from a common history and experience not shared by others ...

One potential gap in the EqA's coverage of race concerns its regulation of discrimination based on the identity (English/Scottish/Welsh/Northern Irish) of people sharing British nationality. In *Boyce v British Airways plc* (App No EAT/385/97, unreported) the EAT ruled that the Scots and the English could not be distinguished on the grounds of *ethnic origins*. We also saw just above the decision in *Gwynned CC v Jones*, and the criticism of it. Section 9 EqA, however, also defines discrimination on the basis of *national origins* as race discrimination.

National Origins

The meaning of 'national origins' was considered by the HL in the following case, which arose under the RRA 1965:

***Ealing London Borough Council v Race Relations Board* [1972] AC 342, 363**

Lord Simon of Glaisdale:

> [The] words ['national origins'] are part of a passage of vague terminology in which the words seem to be used in a popular sense. 'Origin,' in its ordinary sense, signifies a source, someone or something from which someone or something else has descended. 'Nation' and 'national,' in their popular, in contrast to their legal, sense, are also vague terms. They do not necessarily imply statehood. For example, there were many submerged nations in the former Hapsburg Empire. Scotland is not a nation in the eye of international law, but Scotsmen constitute a nation by reason of those most powerful elements in the creation of national spirit – tradition, folk memory, a sentiment of community. The Scots are a nation because of Bannockburn and Flodden, Culloden and the pipes of Lucknow, because of Jenny Geddes and Flora MacDonald, because of frugal living and respect for learning, because of Robert Burns and Walter Scott. So, too, the English are a nation – because Norman, Angevin and Tudor monarchs forged them together, because their land is mostly sea-girt, because of the common law and of gifts for poetry and parliamentary government,[!] because (despite the Wars of the Roses and Old Trafford and Headingley) Yorkshireman and Lancastrian feel more in common than in difference and are even prepared at a pinch to extend their sense of community to southern folk. By the Act of Union English and Scots lost their separate nationalities, but they retained their separate nationhoods, and their descendants have thereby retained their national origins. So, again, the Welsh are a nation – in the popular, though not in the legal, sense – by reason of Offa's Dyke, by recollection of battles long ago and pride in the present valour of their regiments, because of musical gifts and religious dissent, because of fortitude in the face of economic adversity, because of the satisfaction of all Wales that Lloyd George became an architect of the welfare state and prime minister of victory. To discriminate against Englishmen, Scots and Welsh, as such, would, in my opinion, be to discriminate against them on the ground of their national origins ...

In *Northern Joint Police Board v Power* [1997] IRLR 610 the EAT confirmed that a Scots/English distinction could be drawn on grounds of national origin.[78] And while *Gwynned CC v Jones* rejected a challenge by Welsh non-Welsh speakers to a Welsh language requirement, requirements designed to encourage, for example, the continued and expanded use of Welsh or Scots Gallic may involve indirect discrimination on grounds of national origin against, for example, English Irish and Scots (in Wales), Welsh Irish and English (in Scotland).

The following decision is interesting for a number of reasons among them because it was the first decision on the PSED, also because of its approach to justification (see further Chapter 2). It is considered here because it makes very clear the fact that, just as 'national origins' is not synonymous with 'nationality', nor should it be equated with 'birthplace'.

[78] See also *BBC Scotland v Souster* [2001] IRLR 150 in which the Court of Session confirmed that discrimination against an English journalist amounted to discrimination on grounds of national origins, rather than nationality. A subsequent attempt by the claimant in *Boyce* to re-argue his claim as one of discrimination on grounds of *national origins* was dismissed by the Court of Session [2001] IRLR 157 as *res judicata*.

***R (Elias) v Secretary of State for Defence* [2005] EWHC 1435 (Admin), [2005] IRLR 788**

The claimant, who had been born in Hong Kong as a British subject to Jewish parents originally from Iraq or India and subsequently interned by the Japanese as a POW. She was excluded from the scheme adopted in 2000 by the British Government to compensate British subjects who had been interned by the Japanese during World War 2 (see further Chapter 1) because neither she, either parent or any of her grandparents had been born in the UK.

The Court did not accept that the scheme directly discriminated on grounds of national origins because someone (like the claimant) whose own national origins were non-British could have had a parent or grandparent both in the UK, though it did accept that the scheme discriminated indirectly against those of 'non-British origin'[79] and that this discrimination was not justified (see Chapter 2). The Court rejected the claimant's argument that the decision in *Ealing* had been superseded by the RRA (which, unlike the 1965 Act, expressly regulated discrimination in grounds of 'nationality' as well as 'national origins').

Elias J:

> **41 The meanings of national origins**
>
> The leading authority on the meaning of national origins is *Ealing London Borough Council v Race Relations Board* [in which] the House of Lords had to consider whether discrimination on grounds of national origins encompassed discrimination on grounds of nationality … The House of Lords … held by a majority (Lord Donovan, Viscount Dilhorne, Lord Simon of Glaisdale, Lord Cross of Chelsea, Lord Kilbrandon dissenting) that it did not. Their Lordships considered what was meant by the concept of national origins. Viscount Dilhorne referred to a passage from *Oppenheim's International Law* eighth edn (1955) in which the author had distinguished between two meanings of nationality, one in the sense of citizenship of a state and the other membership of a certain nation in the sense of race. He concluded, bearing in mind the racial objects of the race relations legislation, that in the context of this Act the concept 'national origins' meant national in the sense of race and not citizenship.
>
> 42. Lord Simon agreed, expressing the view that given that the concept of 'race' is so elusive, the intention was to ensure that there was no loophole in the application of that concept. Lord Cross expressed a similar view (p.366B). He also sought to define what was meant by national origins in the following way:
>
>> 'To me it suggests a connection subsisting at the time of birth between an individual and one or more groups of people who can be described as a "nation" – whether or not they also constitute a sovereign state. The connection will normally arise because the parents or one of the parents of the individual in question are or is identified by descent with the nation in question, but it may also sometimes arise because the parents have made their home among the people in question. Suppose, for example, that a man of purely French descent marries a woman of purely German descent and that the couple have made their home in England for many years before the birth of the child in question. It could, I think, fairly be said that the child had three "national origins": French through the father, German through the mother and English not because he happened to have been born here but because his parents made their home here. Of course, in most cases a man has only a single "national

[79] The High Court also accepted that the scheme likely discriminated indirectly on grounds of ethnic origins and 'race' (which at the time was, with nationality, colour and national and ethnic origins a sub-category of the protected characteristic of 'race'); of those rejected because of the birth criterion, almost a third were 'non-white' and a similar proportion were Jewish.

origin" which coincides with his nationality at birth in the legal sense and again in most cases his nationality remains unchanged throughout his life. But "national origins" and "nationality" in the legal sense are two quite different conceptions and they may well not coincide or continue to coincide'.

43. It was suggested in argument that *Ealing* no longer represents the law as to the proper scope of the concept of national origin. Their Lordships were concerned with the 1968 Race Relations Act and that is different to the 1976 Act which does now, as a consequence of the Ealing decision, expressly include discrimination on grounds of nationality. In my view, far from casting doubt on the continuing relevance of the Ealing case, it reinforces its significance … Moreover, *Ealing* has been followed in a number of subsequent decisions of the Court of Appeal including *Tejani v The Superintendent Registrar for the District of Peterborough* [1986] IRLR 502 and *Naraine v Hoverspeed Ltd* [1999] All ER (D) 1265.

44. In *Naraine*, Mr Naraine and his wife and two children wished to take a day trip by the Hoverspeed Ferry to France. The company refused to take them because Mr Naraine had only a British Visitor's Passport and it showed that he had been born in Guiana. The French would not admit into their country someone with such a passport who was born outside the United Kingdom … It was alleged that Hoverspeed had infringed his right to freedom of movement under European Union law and also had discriminated on grounds of his national origin under the Race Relations Act. The Court of Appeal rejected both arguments. As to the latter, one of his submissions was that in requiring that someone travelling on the ferry should have been born in the UK, there had been direct discrimination on the grounds of national origins. This argument failed. Lord Bingham, then Lord Chief Justice, observed that in Ealing the House of Lords had distinguished national origins from place of birth. Lord Justice May made observations to the same effect:

> 'A person's place of birth may be entirely fortuitous to say that a person was born a German is different from saying he was born in Germany. There is an intrinsic distinction between narrow national origins and place of birth. The distinction was recognised in the opinions of the House of Lords in *Ealing London Borough Council v Race Relations Board …*'

45. Mr Rabinder Singh for the claimant, and Mr Pannick for the Commission for Racial Equality, accept that to discriminate purely by reference to the place of birth does not constitute discrimination on grounds of national origin. But they contend that in this case there is a combination of features about the criteria adopted which, when taken together, do amount to discrimination on grounds of national origin. They refer to the fact that the birth criteria focus on origins, and origins of a national character; they are analogous to the other grounds of race and ethnic origins in that they are immutable characteristics imposed at birth (even if they can exceptionally be acquired subsequently); they relate not merely to the birth place of the individual whose entitlement to compensation is under consideration but also the birth place of the parents and grandparents; and they must be seen in a context where the express purpose in adopting the criteria was to identify those who could show a concept of 'belonging' to the United Kingdom in a more specific way than simply through being British subjects.

46. They advance a variation of this argument, namely that even if the birth criteria are not identical to national origins, they are nonetheless so closely related to that concept, and in practice would lead to an almost identical differentiation as the adoption of national origins criteria would do, that it should be treated as such discrimination. They recognise that there may be exceptional cases where persons are eligible to receive compensation who are not of British national origin but submit that this does not change the principle. There is discrimination on grounds of colour if, say, a barman serves the odd black man he has got to know but refuses to serve others. Similarly, it is said that in this case Mrs Elias has been discriminated against on grounds of national origin, even if some others of non-British national origin would have qualified for the compensation.

47. There is force in this submission. By linking the place of birth back through three generations it is very unlikely that someone whose origins are British will be excluded, even if he or she were not born in Britain. It must be highly likely that someone with British national origins will have at least one parent or grandparent who was born here, although no doubt there are a few exceptions such as those whose families have lived in the former Empire.

48. At the same time, however, a criterion which involves looking back over three generations also increases the chances that someone who does not have British national origins will nevertheless qualify because some relevant relative happened to be born here. There are no statistics to indicate the proportion of such persons, although I would imagine it is still small although by no means fanciful.

49. Mr Sales [for the defendant] denies that the distinction drawn by the criteria can properly be defined as direct discrimination on grounds of national origin, even if the statistics fall out as I have suggested. He accepts that the authorities establish that the concept of national origins is wide enough to include non-British national origins: see the recent decision of the Court of Criminal Appeal in *Attorney General's Reference (no 4 of 2004); R v D* [2005] EWCA Crim 889; [2005] All ER (D) 332. But he submits that the differentiation being made in this case is different to one which is related to national origin, and that the grounds of discrimination are precisely as the criteria indicate, namely, place of birth. Even accepting – as he does – that it is legitimate to give concepts a broad meaning in this field (see the observations of the Inner House of the Court of Session in *BBC Scotland v Souster* [2001] IRLR 150), nonetheless as a matter of construction it is simply not possible to say that there has been discrimination on the forbidden ground of national origins. He also submitted – and I think there is force in this point – that since direct discrimination can never be justified, the courts ought not to strain unduly to find direct discrimination. If the proportionality test is not satisfied, the criteria will be unlawful in any event. If they can be justified, it would be unfortunate that the merits of the criteria adopted were not considered because of the rigid principle (applicable under domestic legislation but not under the case law of the European Court of Human Rights) that direct discrimination can never be capable of justification (save where the statute specifically allows it).

50. I am persuaded that Mr Sales' submission is correct. I accept that the effect of adopting the criteria used in this scheme is likely in fact to produce a very similar outcome as would have resulted had a national origins criterion been adopted. Nevertheless, it is not an identical form of differentiation. This case is distinguishable from the well-known and controversial case of *James v Eastleigh Borough Council* [1990] 2 AC 751 … In that case the concept used, namely the state pension age was inextricably linked with discrimination on grounds of sex so that the same result was achieved whichever criterion was used. That is not the case here.[80]

Caste

It was noted at p 434 above that the EqA has not yet been amended expressly to include caste as a subcategory of race despite s9(5) requiring this amendment. Section 9(5), in its present form, was included in 2013 at which stage the Coalition Government intended to legislate in summer 2015.

[80] The claimant's appeal on the finding that she had not been subject to direct race discrimination was rejected ([2006] EWCA Civ 1293, [2006] 1 WLR 3213) as was the Secretary of State's appeal on justification).

Douglas Pyper, *The Equality Act 2010: caste discrimination* (House of Commons briefing paper No 06862, 2018)[81]

Summary

The concept of 'caste' is complex, although is generally understood to refer to hereditary, endogamous (marrying within the group) communities differentiated according to different functions of life, such as occupation. The concept is associated with South Asia, particularly India and its diaspora.

Caste discrimination is not expressly prohibited under UK equality legislation, although section 9 of the Equality Act 2010, as amended, currently requires the Government to introduce secondary legislation to make caste an aspect of race, thereby making caste discrimination a form of race discrimination. The Coalition Government initially indicated that this legislation would be introduced to Parliament during summer 2015.

The Conservative Government reviewed its position on the need to introduce legislation, following the Employment Appeal Tribunal's decision in *Chandhok v Tirkey* [2014] UKEAT 0190_14_1912. In that case the Employment Appeal Tribunal noted that caste discrimination is capable of being unlawful under current law, provided that the circumstances of the case fall within the existing prohibition of race discrimination.

On 2 September 2016 the Government announced that it would conduct a public consultation on the issue. The consultation was published on 28 March 2017 and ran until 18 September 2017. The Government published its response on 23 July 2018, concluding against further legislation, preferring to rely on developments in case law. The Government has therefore committed to repealing the duty, under the amended section 9 of the *Equality Act*, to legislate to prohibit caste discrimination.

***Chandhok v Tirkey* [2014] UKEAT 0190_14_1912, [2015] ICR 527**

The claimant (Ms Tirley) and both respondents were of Indian origin. The claimant worked as a domestic worker for the respondents. She claimed that she had been discriminated against because she was regarded as being of. a lower caste than her employers, and that this amounted to race discrimination. A tribunal found that caste was arguably an aspect of ethnic origin and the claimant's claim concerned ethnic and national origins, with which her caste and lower status were bound up. It refused the respondents' application to strike out the claim. The EAT dismissed the appeal. Much of the judgment concerned procedural aspects of the case but the EAT's then-President, having considered the decisions in *Mandla* and *R (E) v Governing Body of JFS* [2009] UKSC 15, [2010] 2 AC 728, see pp 455–457 below, had this to say about caste:

Langstaff P:

> 42. The effect of the principles expressed in *Mandla* and *JFS* is to give a wide and flexible scope to the meaning of 'ethnic origins'. Given the stress to be placed on the word 'origins' in that phrase, descent is, as JFS shows, clearly to be included within it, at least where it is linked to concepts of ethnicity. This is emphasised by the fact that the argument that 'descent' was not part of 'race' as defined by the [RRA] Act was made by counsel for the school, urging that any inclusion of it depended on applying Article 1(1) of [the International Convention on the Elimination of Racial Discrimination]; it should not be, he submitted, since the inspiration for that Article had been caste based discrimination, and it was confined to it. This argument was rejected. However, this demonstrates to me the close link between descent and caste …

[81] https://commonslibrary.parliament.uk/research-briefings/sn06862.

44. … I was referred to the summary by a leading academic writer, Annapurna Waughruay, in 'Capturing Caste in Law: Caste discrimination and the Equality Act 2010' (2012) 14 *Human Rights Law Review* 359–379, in which she said:

> 'There is no agreed sociological or legal definition of caste, but a number of salient features can be identified. Castes are enclosed groups, historically related to social function, membership of which is involuntary, hereditary (that is determined by birth) and permanent … Unlike class, it is not generally possible for individuals or their descendants to move into a different caste. Caste is governed by rules relating to commensality (food and drink must only be shared by others of the same caste) and is maintained by endogamy (marriage must be within the same caste). It entails the idea of innate characteristics and hierarchically graded distinctions based on notions of purity and pollution, with some groups considered to be ritually pure and others ritually impure. A crucial feature of caste in South Asia is the concept of "Untouchability", whereby certain people are considered to be permanently and irredeemably polluted and polluting, hence "untouchable", with whom physical and social contact is to be avoided. Despite the notional nature of caste, Untouchability is conceptualised as an innate physical property separating the Untouchables from the rest of society'.

45. The fact that there is no single definition of caste, as the parties before me were agreed, does not mean that a situation to which that label can, in one of its manifestations, be attached cannot and does not fall within the scope of 'ethnic origins'.

46. … the essential case is … that when applying s.9, as it has been and should be interpreted, an allegation that a claimant was treated disadvantageously because of her having a status which was heavily related to an inherited position in society cannot be ruled out as being established on the evidence. The tribunal hearing such a claim will need to establish what it accepts of the treatment alleged and, in relation to the acts which it accepts, why the respondent did them in respect of the claimant. If the reason or reasons establish factually that the respondents treated the claimant as they did for reasons which more than minimally included their view of her status or origins, and if that status, or that view is bound up with her ethnic origins as understood in domestic case law, the claimant will succeed in a claim for discrimination … It is not necessary in order for her to succeed that the label 'caste', or even 'lower status' should be applied to her: her case must stand or fall by that which the facts establish, not whether all or some of those facts might be adequately and appropriately summarised or grouped under some label (other than the label 'ethnic origins') for which a significance of its own above and apart from those facts is claimed. But that is not to say that facts which establish that a person is seen as belonging to a particular caste are irrelevant to whether a person is within the scope of s.9(1) of the Equality Act 2010.

51. … there may be factual circumstances in which the application of the label 'caste' is appropriate, many of which are capable – depending on their facts – of falling within the scope of s.9(1), particularly coming within 'ethnic origins', as portraying a group with characteristics determined in part by descent, and of a sufficient quality to be described as 'ethnic'. As the judge put it, caste 'is an integral part of the picture' in the present case.

'Race' and 'Religion'

The decision of the HL in *Mandla v Dowell Lee* was considered at pp 437–439 above. Prior to that decision it had been accepted that Jews were a racial group for the purposes of the RRA (*Seide v Gillette* [1980] IRLR 427, EAT). In *Dawkins v Department of the Environment* [1993] ICR 517 the CA ruled that Rastafarians did not comprise a racial group for the purposes of the RRA. The claimant, whose job application had been rejected because he refused to cut his hair, claimed that he had been discriminated against on grounds of race. A tribunal was satisfied that Rastafarians shared a distinct cultural tradition, a common language and geographical origin and that there was a long shared history dating from 1930 of which the group was conscious as distinguishing it from other groups. It concluded that Rastafarians were an ethnic group and upheld the complaint. The EAT, by a majority ([1991] ICR 583), ruled that 60 years did not comprise a 'long shared history' and that there was insufficient basis on which otherwise to distinguish Rastafarians from other African-Caribbeans. The CA agreed. The decision was criticised by one writer who suggested that the Court in *Dawkins* had placed 'undue emphasis' on Lord Fraser's initial observation [in *Mandla*] that 'the word 'ethnic' still retains a racial flavour'.[82]

The SC revisited the *Mandla* decision in 2009:

***R (E) v Governing Body of JFS* [2009] UKSC 15, [2010] 2 AC 728**

E, the father of a Jewish teenager, challenged the admissions policy of a faith school which gave preference to pupils recognised as Jewish by the Office of the Chief Rabbi of the United Hebrew Congregation of the Commonwealth. Such recognition was reserved to those whose mothers were 'automatically and inalienably Jewish', including by conversion to Orthodox Judaism. Such conversion was a longer and more difficult process than conversion to Masorti, Reform or Liberal Judaism. E was Jewish and worshipped at a Masorti synagogue, as did his son M. E's wife, who taught at JFS, was a previously Roman Catholic Italian who had converted to Judaism under the auspices of a non-Orthodox synagogue. M was refused admission to the school, which was over-subscribed, because he was not recognised as Jewish. E brought judicial review proceedings in the High Court, claiming that the policy discriminated directly on grounds of race and had been adopted in breach of the PSED.[83]

The school sought to argue that M was racially Jewish for the purposes of the *Mandla* test and that the discrimination against him was on grounds of religion alone. (The significance was that religious discrimination in admission to the school would have been lawful.) The SC accepted, as had the CA, that the motive for the discrimination against M was religious, but ruled that the policy nevertheless discriminated on grounds of race.

Lord Phillips P:

33. Initially I found Lord Pannick's argument [for the school] persuasive, but on reflection I have concluded that it is fallacious. The fallacy lies in treating current membership of a *Mandla* ethnic group as the exclusive ground of racial discrimination. It ignores the fact that the definition of 'racial grounds' ... includes 'ethnic or national *origins*' (my emphasis). Origins require one to focus on *descent*. Lord Pannick is correct to submit that descent simpliciter is not a ground of racial discrimination. It will only be such a ground if the descent in question is one which traces racial or ethnic origin.

34. This leads me to a further argument advanced on behalf of JFS ... that the matrilineal test is a religious test and that discrimination on the basis of that test is religious, not racial. This argument falls into two parts: (i) the matrilineal test is a test laid down by Jewish religious law;

[82] W McLeod, 'Autochthonous language communities and the Race Relations Act' (1998) 1 *Web Journal of Current Legal Issues*, extracted above.

[83] See Ch 3.

> (ii) the matrilineal test is not a test of ethnic origin or ethnic status but a test of religious origin and religious status.
>
> 35. The first part of this argument focuses … on the reason why the matrilineal test is applied. The reason is that the JFS and the OCR apply the test for determining who is a Jew laid down by Orthodox Jewish religious law. What subjectively motivates them is compliance with religious law, not the ethnicity of the candidates who wish to enter the school. My reaction to this argument will already be clear. It is invalid because it focuses on a matter that is irrelevant – the motive of the discriminator for applying the discriminatory criteria. A person who discriminates on the ground of race … cannot pray in aid the fact that the ground of discrimination is one mandated by his religion …
>
> 45. The question of the 'status' of the matrilineal descendant may thus depend upon whether one is applying the subjective viewpoint of a Jew or the objective *Mandla* test. But one thing is clear about the matrilineal test; it is a test of ethnic origin. By definition, discrimination that is based upon that test is discrimination on racial grounds …
>
> 46. Lord Pannick is correct to say that it is possible to identify two different cohorts, or groups, with an overlapping membership, those who are descended by the maternal line from a Jew, and those who are currently members of the Jewish ethnic group. Discrimination against a person on the grounds that he or she is, or is not, a member of either group is racial discrimination. JFS discriminates in its admission requirements on the sole basis of genetic descent by the maternal line from a woman who is Jewish, in the *Mandla* as well as the religious sense. I can see no escape from the conclusion that this is direct racial discrimination …

Lady Hale and Lords Mance, Kerr and Clarke delivered concurring judgments, each with their own particular reasoning. Lady Hale declared that M had been refused access to the school 'because of his mother's ethnic origins, which were Italian and Roman Catholic' and that the fact that these origins would have been overlooked had she undergone a conversion acceptable to the Chief Rabbi made 'no difference to this fundamental fact [that] M was rejected … because his mother was not descended in the matrilineal line from the original Jewish people … a particular ethnic group'. She pointed out that the school was not concerned with M's own religious beliefs and that it accepted 'pupils who practise all denominations of Judaism, or none at all, or even other religions entirely, as long as they are halachically Jewish, descended from the original Jewish people in the matrilineal line'. Lord Mance agreed that 'the Orthodox Jewish test of descent in the matrilineal line must … be regarded as a test based on ethnic origins' and that the fact that 'the Jewish people was from its outset also defined by its religion does not lead to a different conclusion'. The case could not, he declared, 'be viewed as a mere disagreement between different Jewish denominations, for example about the criteria for conversion. It turns, more fundamentally, on whether it is permissible for any school to treat one child less favourably than another because the child does not have whatever ancestry is required, in the school's view, to make the child Jewish'.

Lord Kerr stated that 'Jews, whether they be Orthodox, Masorti, Liberal or Progressive, constitute an ethnic group' to which M belonged, but that this was 'not comprehensive of his ethnicity'. The fact that he was in the same ethnic or racial group as those admitted to the school did not preclude a finding of discrimination where it was 'because of his lack of the requisite feature of Jewishness that he has received less favourable treatment'. And Lord Clarke, agreeing with Lords Phillips, Mance and Kerr and Lady Hale, declared that 'the discrimination was on both religious and ethnic grounds because the criteria were arrived at on religious grounds but, since those religious grounds involved discrimination on ethnic grounds, it follows that the admissions policy of JFS … discriminated against M and others on racial grounds …'.

Lords Hope and Walker dissented on the basis that the admissions policy was based on Jewish law and not on race.[84] Lord Rodger declared that M's mother 'could have been as Italian in origin as Sophia Loren and as Roman Catholic as the Pope for all that the governors cared: the only thing that mattered was that she had not converted to Judaism under Orthodox auspices' and that the governors would have considered 'a boy whose mother had converted under Orthodox auspices … for admission without pausing for a single second to enquire whether he or his mother came from Rome, Brooklyn, Siberia or Buenos Aires, whether she had once been a Roman Catholic or a Muslim, or whether he or she came from a close-knit Jewish community or had chosen to assimilate and disappear into secular society'. And Lord Brown opined at §239 that:

> M's real complaint here is that in deciding who is a Jew the OCR's approach to conversion is misguided. That, however, is not an issue which is, or ever could be, before the court. No court would ever intervene on such a question or dictate who, as a matter of Orthodox religious law, is to be regarded as Jewish.

Lord Brown went on to characterise as 'quite unrealistic, given that those being treated less favourably and those being treated more favourably by JFS's policy are all (save, of course, for those who have no connection with Judaism whatsoever) in the same ethnic group, to regard the policy as discriminatory on racial rather than religious grounds'.

It is clear from the JFS case that the distinction between race and religion, and the boundaries of 'ethnic origins' are open to disagreement even at the highest level. Discrimination because a person is (or is not) Jewish or Sikh will amount to race discrimination. The same is not true for Christians or Muslims, though there will be some cases in which such discrimination may amount to indirect race discrimination.[85] These religions, by contrast with the Sikh or Jewish faith, are not associated with particular geographical areas. Prior to the prohibition on religious discrimination this left Muslims, very often disadvantaged and discriminated against, largely unprotected by discrimination law.

Sebastian Poulter, 'Muslim Headscarves in School: Contrasting Approaches in England and France' (1997) 17 *Oxford Journal of Legal Studies* 43, 64, footnotes omitted

So far, – in four cases decided by industrial tribunals and the Employment Appeal Tribunal, it has been held that Muslims are not an ethnic group but a religious one. As the South London Industrial Tribunal explained in *Nyazi v Rymans Ltd*:

> 'Muslims include people of many nations and colours, who speak many languages and whose only common denominator is religion and religious culture.'

More importantly, perhaps, Muslims worldwide do not possess a 'shared history' and many perceive themselves not as members of an ethnic group but as part of an essentially religious community or 'ummah.' To some extent, this definitional hurdle can be circumvented through a plaintiff's reliance on membership of a group which does fall clearly within the terms of the Act. A Muslim pupil whose parents came to Britain from Pakistan could plead, for example, that any discrimination against her was based on her Pakistani nationality, her Pakistani 'national origin'

[84] Though they concluded that there was unjustified indirect race discrimination.
[85] Where, for example, there is a high degree of correlation between Muslim or Christian faith and ethnicity within a workplace.

> (if she was a British citizen) or her Asian 'race.' On the other hand, the daughter of one of the growing number of white or black (Afro-Caribbean) British converts to Islam could not take advantage of this approach.

Nyazi v Rymans Ltd concerned a complaint from a Muslim woman who had been denied leave to celebrate Eid. The EAT quoted the tribunal's judgment which was that it was:

Nyazi v Rymans Ltd, App No EAT/6/88 (unreported)

Wood J:

> ... unable to conclude that Muslims ... come within the meaning of 'ethnic group.' All we can say is that Muslims profess a common religion in a belief in the Oneness of God and the prophethood of Muhammed. No doubt there is a profound cultural and historical background and there are traditions of dress, family life and social behaviour. There is a common literature in the sense that the Holy Quaran is a sacred book. Even so, many of the other relevant characteristics would seem to be missing.
>
> The Muslim faith is widespread, covering many nations, indeed many colours and languages, and it seems to us that the common denominator is religion and a religious culture. In other words we believe Muslims are a group defined mainly by reference to religion and that being so we must find that we have no jurisdiction under the Act.

The EAT rejected the claimant's appeal, ruling that the tribunal had not 'erred either in the exercise of its discretion, or in the conclusion it reached on the facts which were before it.'

In *Walker v Hussain* a tribunal accepted that, on the facts of the particular case, discrimination against Muslims amounted to discrimination against Asians and thence to race discrimination.[86] There, Asians were less able to comply with a requirement to work through the summer than were non-Asians in the workplace. Eid fell during the summer months and observant Muslims could not work during that period. Their race discrimination claim succeeded because, most Asians in the workplace being Muslim and the tribunal adopting a workplace pool for comparison, the claimants could demonstrate that Asians were significantly less likely than non-Asian employees to be in a position to comply.

The reasoning adopted by the tribunal in *Walker* would not have applied in a workplace in which the majority of Asian workers were not Muslim, and, if a tribunal were to select the pool from the general population, rather than the workplace, Asians may not be significantly more likely than non-Asians to be devout Muslims so as to be unable to comply, for example, with a requirement to work through Eid. So, for example, in *Safouane v Bouterfas* (1996), the dismissal of two Muslim employees for praying during work breaks did not constitute indirect race discrimination because they were from the same North African ethnic Arab community as the respondents.[87]

Where direct discrimination against Muslims is at issue, the question whether indirect race discrimination has occurred depends upon whether people of the claimant's racial group are put at a particular disadvantage by a requirement not to be Muslim (what the

[86] This aspect of the decision was not appealed to EAT whose decision in the case is at [1996] ICR 291.

[87] EAT/12506/95/LS, 12568/95, 17 July 1996, unreported, discussed in B Hepple and T Choudhury, 'Tackling religious discrimination: practical implications for policy-makers and legislators' (Home Office Research Study 221), para 1.8.

relevant 'racial group' is will differ from case to case).[88] But where the discrimination against Muslims takes the indirect form (as in the discussion of hijab wearing, below), the prohibition on race discrimination will be breached only where the relationship between religion and race is so close that the provision, criterion or practice complained of places people of the claimant's 'racial group' at a particular disadvantage, as well as disadvantaging the claimant herself.

Much of the gap has been filled by the prohibition on religion or belief discrimination (see Chapter 9), though the decision of the SC in *R (E) v JFS* demonstrates why it may still matter whether discrimination against Muslims, Jews or any other group amounts to *racial* as well as *religious* discrimination. Conceptual also questions remain about whether Islamophobic behaviour is best characterised as being concerned with religion, or whether it (like anti-Semitism) is more accurately seen as a form of racism.

Farah Elahi and Omar Khan, 'Introduction: What is Islamophobia?' ***in Islamophobia; Still a challenge for us all*** **(Runnymede Trust, 2017)**[89]

... Islamophobia is any distinction, exclusion or restriction towards, or preference against, Muslims (or those perceived to be Muslims) that has the purpose or effect of nullifying or impairing the recognition, enjoyment or exercise, on an equal footing, of human rights and fundamental freedoms in the political, economic, social, cultural or any other field of public life. We have offered these definitions to forestall further confusion about the nature of Islamophobia, but also to focus policy and social change on what could best tackle Islamophobia and so improve British Muslims' lives. The definition therefore is not simply what Runnymede thinks is the best analytical account of what Islamophobia is, but also points to our various recommendations on how to respond to it.

We recognize that Islamophobia as a form of racial discrimination is not the only challenge facing British Muslims. There are clearly widespread bigoted and false perceptions about Islam as a faith. These feed Islamophobia as a form of discrimination, for example justifying discrimination in the labour market. Justifying discrimination or inequality by referencing the cultural practices of minority groups is a defining characteristic of all forms of prejudice and racism.

As indicated above, our longer-form definition derives from the UN definition of racism. It is perhaps necessary to explain our use of the term 'racism', and why we have chosen it over a possible alternative: 'anti-Muslim hate'.

Among sociologists it is common to talk about different forms of racism, processes of 'racialization', and even 'racism without races'. The notion that 'race' is a social construct is more familiar today and indeed widely affirmed even outside the university and across the political spectrum. Just because something is a social construct, that doesn't mean it doesn't drive or explain individual and group outcomes in the real world. In fact, it is sometimes argued that the relevance of race to social outcomes was first justified by Enlightenment thinkers who deliberately created an essentialized notion of race to deny the otherwise universal proposition of equal moral worth to those human beings who were enslaved and colonized by Europeans.

The UN definition above picks out the ways racism operates: not simply as an attitude or prejudice, but by denying people dignity, rights and liberties across a range of political, economic, social and cultural institutions. Referring only to 'anti-Muslim hate' (or even 'anti-Muslim prejudice

[88] In *Walker*, for example, it was 'Asians' while in *CRE v Precision Manufacturing Services Ltd* COIT 4106/91, 26 July 1991 a tribunal categorised direct discrimination against Muslims as indirect discrimination against 'coloureds', which term is no longer regarded as acceptable.

[89] Runnymede Trust, Farah Elahi and Omar Khan, 'Introduction: What is Islamophobia?' in *Islamophobia; Still a challenge for us all* (Runnymede Trust, 2017), available at https://assets.website-files.com/61488f992b58e687f1108c7c/61bcd30e26cca7688f7a5808_Islamophobia%20Report%202018%20FINAL.pdf.

and discrimination') doesn't fully capture the widespread (or structural) ways racial inequalities persist. It may also get things back to front: prejudicial attitudes about a group develop to justify the economic or political disadvantages experienced by that group.

This helps us understand how all forms of racism have contained a 'cultural' component. It is sometimes argued that current forms of racism are more 'cultural' than previous forms of racism based more on skin colour. It is understandable why far right groups might want to assert such a defence, especially where public understandings of racism still focus on 'colour': they claim only to object to the culturally illiberal or otherwise undesirable practices of certain groups, but assert that they are not otherwise 'racist'. Yet all forms of racism have contained a cultural element, symptomatically by attributing pathological, dangerous or aberrant behaviours to groups ranging from black to Chinese to Jewish people. Nonetheless, the focus on culture as a key component of current forms of racism is useful for understanding why racism and its effects persist even as essentialist biological claims about race have become unfashionable.

Discrimination and Segregation

For the most part the definition of discrimination as it applies to race is the same as that which applies to the other protected characteristics.[90] The exception is that the definition of direct discrimination in s13(2) EqA stipulates (uniquely in the case of race) that segregation is considered less favourable treatment. This provision's predecessor generated only one reported case (*FTATU v Modgill* [1980] IRLR 142) in which the EAT overturned findings that the claimants (16 African Asians who had been represented inadequately by their union and poorly treated by their employers), had been discriminated against on grounds of race. Part of the difficulties experienced by the claimants related to their concentration in one part of the employer's organisation, the paint shop, in which there were the only workers. There was evidence that the company's personnel officer had said that it was good to keep the Asians together because they spoke the same language (not all of the claimants speaking English well) and the claimants argued that Asians were employed in the paint shop because other workers did not wish to be. The EAT ruled that segregation amounted to race discrimination only if it was deliberate, and did not accept that it was so in this case.

FTATU v Modgill [1980] IRLR 142

Slynn J:

34. … [The company's] Mr Barron agreed, so the Tribunal recite in their decision, that he had not had from the personnel department any applicants during the past two years, except in one instance when white persons were sent to him but they were persons who were not interested in the job. And so the facts appear to be that here, for a period of something like two years, the personnel department of the company had not had to select or interview persons for employment in this particular area. Those who worked there had produced candidates for appointment to Mr Barron and he had found men who were able and willing to take on the job. It seems to us that the Tribunal accepted that there arose a situation, really by the acts of those working in the paint shop itself, that all the workers were in fact Asian. This had not always been the position …

[90] Though note that additional types of discrimination are also regulated in the case of disability and direct age discrimination (uniquely) may be justified.

35. … it [appears to have been] the opinion of the Industrial Tribunal, not so much that the company had by its own acts segregated these men in this particular area away from others, but that it had not prevented the men themselves from coming together in this way. What appears to be suggested is that the company ought to have taken steps to ensure that for some of these jobs, white or non-Asian or coloured men were put in, and that Asians were not allowed to take on these jobs on the grounds of their colour, in order to prevent this segregation in fact arising. We repeat that had there been here evidence of a policy to segregate, and of the fact of segregation arising as a result of the company's acts, that might well have constituted a breach of the legislation; but it does not seem to us that there was evidence to support that position. We do not consider that the failure of the company to intervene and to insist on white or non-Asian workers going into the shop, contrary to the wishes of the men to introduce their friends, itself constituted the act of segregating persons on racial grounds … A refusal to appoint other applicants because of their colour, or because they were Asians, might in itself indeed have amounted to discrimination within the meaning of the Act.

In the *Al-Hijrah* case, discussed at some length in Chapter 2, the CA ruled that sex segregation (which was there deliberate) could amount to sex discrimination notwithstanding the lack of any express statement to this effect in the EqA.[91]

Positive Action

The law relating to positive action is the same in relation to race as it is to the other protected characteristics in relation to which protection is symmetrical.[92] In Chapter 3 we considered the possibilities of and legal limitations on positive action in domestic law, and the limited impact of various 'goals and timetables' adopted in the UK to increase diversity in public sector jobs. These 'goals and timetables' have not been limited to questions of racial diversity, but the limited nature of their impact is perhaps best illustrated by reference to race.

Goals and Timetables

In 2014 Michael Drugher, vice-chair of the Labour party, told the IPPR that Labour would set new targets (18 and 24 per cent respectively) for racially minoritised and working class candidates' entry to the civil service fast-stream graduate entry programme. The writer of the following extract pointed out that the proportion of Black and Asian civil servants had increased by only 2.8 per cent between 1997 and 2009 (when the Labour Party was in Government) while the proportion of Black and Asian senior managers had remained stable at 3.5 per cent (as against a target of five per cent).

Clara Arokiasamy, 'How about all-black shortlists for senior civil service jobs?', *The Guardian*, 30 April 2014

More importantly, the same period and subsequent years have seen the gradual departure of the few who did make it to the top. The key reasons cited to me by those affected were invisible and

[91] *HM Chief Inspector of Education, Children's Services and Skill v Interim Executive Board of Al-Hijrah School* [2017] EWCA Civ 1426, [2018] 1 WLR 1471 see pp 35–38 above.

[92] See pp 35–38 above.

> overt racism in the workplace and a lack of support from the champions (chief officers and politicians) who had actively encouraged their recruitment.
>
> I have recently spoken to several BME civil service middle managers who welcome Drugher's announcement. But they also feel that the fast stream is only a small pipeline of people accessing middle management at higher executive officer grade, and there is no guarantee that these would make it to senior management. Instead, they would like to see Labour's commitment to all-women shortlists for parliamentary candidates extended, with the creation of all-black shortlists for the senior civil service. Additionally, they stressed that the piecemeal initiatives to date have squandered the precious resources allocated to improving employment opportunities for BME staff, due to ineffective leadership and a lack of input from those who are supposed to benefit. What is needed is a long-term and comprehensive strategy with the capacity to address the cumulative effects of decades of racial inequality at every level of the civil service.
>
> If Labour is to succeed in its quest to improve diversity in senior management through fast tracking, or any other initiatives for that matter, its first task must be to change the culture in Whitehall to make sure future recruits are not subjected to hostility and differential treatment or racist and discriminatory practices. Mandarins must ensure that they are not recruiting clones of themselves and are supporting freedom in thinking and implementation of ideas.
>
> The recruitment schemes must be supported by a culture of listening, taking advice and accepting dissenting views from a cross-section of the BME civil society, rather than just apparatchiks from Labour's BME political class, advisers and thinktanks – who are just as remote from the wider BME community as their white counterparts. The thinktanks, some of whose own workforces need to better reflect cultural diversity, must shift from regarding black and Asian people as mere evidence material to treating them as equal partners with robust opportunities to put forward challenging and different perspectives in research and policy development …

Targets had been set in summer 2000 for women and racially minoritised staff in top NHS jobs. In 2004 the Department of Health adopted a Race Equality Action Plan and in 2008 the NHS chief executive David Nicholson called for 30 per cent BAME representation at the top tiers of the service.[93] In 2014 it was reported that the proportion of minoritised ethnic NHS Chief Executives and Board Chairs had fallen from 5.4 per cent in 2009 to 2.5 per cent and the proportion of minoritised ethnic members on London NHS Trust Boards had fallen from 9.6 per cent to eight per cent.[94] Forty-one per cent of NHS staff in London and 45 per cent of the population were from minoritised communities, but 40 per cent of London NHS Trust Boards had no racially minoritised members and the proportion of very senior minoritised NHS staff had not increased since 2008, and had fallen slightly in the previous three years: 'little or no progress has been made in meeting those goals' and 'Matters of diversity in the leadership, workforce and service delivery of the NHS appear to receive little attention'. Women represented 40 per cent of NHS Boards, but this was 'well below that of the NHS workforce or the local population' and women were 'especially under-represented at chair and chief executive level'. The position in London was reported to be consistent with that nationally, 'BME executives being entirely absent and women being disproportionately absent, from the Boards of NHS England, Monitor, the NHS Trust Development Authority, Health Education England, and the Professional Standards Authority'.[95]

[93] R Kline, 'The "snowy white peaks" of the NHS: a survey of discrimination in governance and leadership and the potential impact on patient care in London and England', available at https://www.england.nhs.uk/wp-content/uploads/2014/08/edc7-0514.pdf, 6.

[94] *Ibid*, 28.

[95] *Ibid*, 3–4.

Also in 2014, *The Guardian* published a response to the introduction of workplace diversity schemes in the civil service in which the writer, a civil servant, complained that diversity schemes 'are not the right answer for BME people in the civil service' and that they 'breed doubt and resentment' and expressed her disagreement with the proposals made by Michael Dugher, and comments of Clara Arokiasamy (above):

> **'Positive discrimination: am I only here because I'm black and working class?', *The Guardian*, 29 May 2014**[96]
>
> I don't feel I've experienced any discrimination while in post, neither positive nor negative, and I'd like to think that's because I'm capable of doing the jobs I've been given and doing them well. But after reading initiatives such as the ones being proposed (and similar ones that have gone before), I'm forced to stop and reconsider. Am I in the position I'm currently in on merit alone? Or am I just part of a bigger plan to 'boost the numbers'? And the worst thing isn't necessarily my own negative concerns, but rather the possible doubts of future managers and co-workers who might assume I'm the product of more lenient standards because I tick the right boxes: BME, working class – and a successful fast-stream candidate to boot …
>
> I don't support attempts to skew what I feel is already a rigorous and thorough recruitment process … I disagree with any mechanism (be it ethnicity, gender or social background) that precludes other candidates from consideration. Whichever way you spin it, it's an example of positive discrimination and it serves not only to lessen the sense of achievement for those on the right side of the coin, but also to foster resentment for those who aren't part of the chosen minority. To suggest that any and every recruitment process should be a true meritocracy seems naive, even to me. But special measures for particular interest groups, or entirely homogeneous shortlists, won't solve the underlying issue here – that of unconscious bias, something we're all guilty of …

The perspective of those such as the writer is important, though it appears to underestimate the extent of discrimination which permeates recruitment decisions more generally, whether or not in the civil service (see eg the discussion of Di Stasio and Heath's research at pp 428–429 above).

Positive Action and the Police

Perhaps most high profile of all 'goals and timetables' in GB concerned the racial diversification of the police, fire and prison services in the aftermath of the Macpherson Inquiry into the death of Stephen Lawrence and its exposition of 'institutional racism' among the police (see Chapter 3[97]). The general approach has been hostile to positive discrimination and the introduction of 'goals and timetables' has almost invariably been accompanied by protestations that they, unlike 'quotas' do not entail 'unlawful' positive discrimination. In setting targets in 1999 for racial integration of the police service, for example, then Home Secretary Jack Straw declared:

> Let me be clear about what I am not doing. I am not setting quotas and saying that you have to take somebody on because of the colour of their skin. I am setting targets that will enable the police service to more fairly represent the community [the police] serve.[98]

The 1999 *Modernising Government* White Paper, too, was at pains to emphasise that the targets in respect of female and racially minoritised community representation in public

[96] https://www.theguardian.com/public-leaders-network/2014/may/29/positive-discrimination-civil-service-black-working-class.

[97] The steps taken in Northern Ireland to recruit Catholics into the PSNI are also discussed in Ch 3.

[98] Speech to a major police conference in April 1999 reproduced in 87 *EOR*.

sector appointments were to be 'on the basis of merit'. This indicated, perhaps, that the targets were to be achieved by the outreach methods then permitted under the Sex Discrimination Act 1975 (SDA) and RRA, or by conscious efforts to eliminate discrimination in appointment decisions together with networking initiatives directed, in particular, at minoritised staff.

The Commissioner for Public Appointments, whose task is 'to set the standards for recruiting and to regulate the recruitment process for appointments in public bodies,'[99] was established in the wake of the Nolan Committee's investigation into how appointments to public bodies (Quangos) are made. The Commissioner is responsible for monitoring the appointments process to ensure that such appointments are made on merit after fair and open competition. In 2001 the Commissioner published a Code of Practice for ministerial appointments to public bodies which highlighted seven principles including 'merit' and 'equal opportunities'. It was replaced in 2016 with the governance code on public appointments which provides, inter alia, that 'All public appointments should be governed by the principle of appointment on merit' and that 'Public appointments should reflect the diversity of the society in which we live and appointments should be made taking account of the need to appoint boards which include a balance of skills and backgrounds.'[100]

Disapproval of positive discrimination is not universal. On the same day that the *Daily Mail* reported the *Furlong* case (see pp 145–149 above) under the headline 'Too white to be a copper? Graduate, 25, who wanted to follow in his detective father's footsteps was turned down by the police because he isn't disabled, gay or black',[101] one of the UK's most senior police officers told *The Guardian* that legal change was required to allow positive discrimination by the police in favour of racially minoritised candidates in order to avoid a continued lack of ethnic diversity for decades to come.

> **'Police leader calls for laws to allow positive race discrimination', *The Guardian*, 22 February 2019**[102]
>
> In an interview to mark the 20th anniversary of the Macpherson report into the death of Stephen Lawrence, Sara Thornton said police had made huge progress, but 'unconscious bias' still existed and the way they used their powers needed to be seen to be fair …
>
> Thornton said new laws should be passed to 'shock the system'. Since 1999 police have been trying to get the proportion of officers from ethnic minorities to match the proportion in the populations they serve. But not one of the 43 forces in England and Wales has achieved that and it will be 2052 at the earliest before that happens. It is likely to be even decades beyond that if, as expected, the minority ethnic population grows …
>
> While 14% of the population are from an ethnic minority, just 7% of police in England and Wales are – up from 2% when Macpherson reported 20 years ago. Thornton said a quarter or even 30% of new recruits in some big forces were from an ethnic minority. But changing the overall makeup of forces was slow and budget cuts meant few new officers joined between 2010–2015. 'It will take a long time. The turnover of police officers is really quite slow, so it is about 6% a year, it's always going to take you a long time, and it's about whether we can wait,' she said.

[99] See the OCPA website at http://www.ocpa.gov.uk/pages/capa.htm.

[100] Para 2.1, available at https://publicappointmentscommissioner.independent.gov.uk/regulating-appointments/governance-code.

[101] *Daily Mail*, 22 February 2019.

[102] https://www.theguardian.com/uk-news/2019/feb/22/police-leader-calls-for-laws-to-allow-positive-race-discrimination.

> Police chiefs such as the former Metropolitan police commissioner Lord Hogan-Howe have favoured the move, but the government has balked at the idea of introducing positive discrimination on the grounds of race ...
>
> Thornton said: 'I think there's an argument that we could select on merit and put people into a pool [of recruits] and then appoint on representation.'...
>
> Thornton said 'unconscious bias' still existed in policing and there were problems in promotion, and minority ethnic officers being more likely to face disciplinary action ...
>
> She gave the example of one large force, Greater Manchester, holding a promotion board during Ramadan, when Muslim candidates would be fasting and thus possibly physically weaker and at a disadvantage ... Thornton said: 'For marginalised communities, policing can represent the tyranny of state power. 'Let's be candid about this, if within communities there is a sense of being over-policed and under-protected, it's not the sort of occupation parents are going to encourage their youngsters to get involved in.

In 2014 Sir Bernard Hogan-Howe, then Commissioner of the Metropolitan Police, had declared that the Met needed to appoint a racially minoritised officer for each white appointment in order to rid itself of a reputation for 'racism in the ranks' and called for legal change to allow a five-year period of positive discrimination such as that which changed the face of policing in Northern Ireland (see discussion in Chapter 3).[103] At that time only 20 per cent of Met police recruits and 10 per cent of the Met force came from minoritised communities, by comparison with 40 per cent of Londoners. And in February 2020 Labour's Shadow Minister for Policing, Louise Haigh, called for positive discrimination to diversify the police as research showed that the police had become less, rather than more, racially diverse since 2000 despite targets having been adopted to improve diversity.[104]

> **'Labour backs positive discrimination to close racial gap in policing', *The Guardian*, 24 February 2020**[105]
>
> Haigh said: 'The government [plans to recruit 20,000 extra officers within three years] represents a clear opportunity to address the lack of progress on targets set 21 years ago. It is the only opportunity to address the enormous imbalance in the police compared to their communities. Cuts to neighbourhood policing have taken the police even further away from the communities, and it is even more urgent now that it was 10 years ago. What is being lost is the presence in communities and relationship with the communities. It leads to a more reactive style of police service which leads to a more distant relationship and more conflict.'...
>
> The largest gap is in Britain's largest force, the Metropolitan police, which covers London – a region with a 43% ethnic minority population, while its police force has only 14% ethnic minority officers. The Met's own internal estimates say it could be nearly a century away from its goal. Haigh said: 'The pace of change is so glacial the Metropolitan police will still be disproportionately white for another 100 years at this rate of change. We still have not reached those targets 21 years later. Diversity has fallen away among senior police leaders both on race and gender. There's only been one ethnic minority police and crime commissioner and there's only ever been one ethnic minority chief constable ....'
>
> New research commissioned by Labour showed that when the police last continuously grew from 2000 to 2009, the race gap in English and Welsh forces which were using positive action,

[103] 'Met Police should take on one ethnic minority officer for every white recruit, says Hogan-Howe in new 50/50 recruitment drive', *The Daily Mail*, 27 March 2014.

[104] 'Labour backs positive discrimination to close racial gap in policing', *The Guardian*, 24 February 2020, available at https://www.theguardian.com/uk-news/2020/feb/24/labour-backs-positive-discrimination-to-close-racial-gap-in-policing.

[105] https://www.theguardian.com/uk-news/2020/feb/24/labour-backs-positive-discrimination-to-close-racial-gap-in-policing.

grew, from 4.9% to 6.9%. In Northern Ireland, which used a form of positive discrimination, Catholic representation massively increased from 8% in 2001 to 30% in 2011. That gap has also grown since 2000, the year after the Macpherson report was published. In 2000, around 2.3% of officers were from ethnic minorities compared to 7.2% of the population in England and Wales, a gap of 4.9%. In 2019 the percentage of BAME officers was 6.9%, but the BAME population had doubled to 14.5%, a gap of 7.6%. Haigh said: 'If it is the best they can achieve under the current framework then they need to have firm targets written into legislation.'…

Exceptions

The general exceptions provided by the EqA are discussed in Chapter 4. Here we will consider the exceptions which apply in relation to race in particular. The most important of these relates to immigration and is discussed below, after a brief discussion of the exception related to participation as a competitor in competitive activities.

Section 195 EqA, Sport

(5) A person who does anything to which subsection (6) applies does not contravene this Act only because of the nationality or place of birth of another or because of the length of time the other has been resident in a particular area or place.

(6) This subsection applies to—

(a) selecting one or more persons to represent a country, place or area or a related association, in a sport or game or other activity of a competitive nature;

(b) doing anything in pursuance of the rules of a competition so far as relating to eligibility to compete in a sport or game or other such activity.

This provision has given rise to no litigation, and does not appear to relate to the discrimination which is experienced by people from racialised minority groups in accessing sports in the UK.[106] Of more significance is Schedule 3 EqA para 17, which is entitled 'Immigration' and provides, so far as relevant, as follows:

Schedule 3, Para 17, Nationality and ethnic or national origins

(1) This paragraph applies in relation to race discrimination so far as relating to—

(a) nationality, or

(b) ethnic or national origins.

(2) Section 29[107] does not apply to anything done by a relevant person in the exercise of relevant functions.

(3) A relevant person is—

(a) a Minister of the Crown acting personally, or

(b) a person acting in accordance with a relevant authorisation.

[106] See eg K Hylton, J Long, D Parnell, A Rankin, *'Race', racism and participation in sport* (Race Equality Foundation, 2015) available at https://raceequalityfoundation.org.uk/health-care/race-racism-and-participation-in-sport; S Ingle, 'Survey finds 83% of BAME competitors have experienced racism in British sport', *The Guardian*, 3 July 2020, available at https://www.theguardian.com/sport/2020/jul/03/survey-finds-83-of-bame-competitors-have-experienced-racism-in-british-sport.

[107] Which regulates discrimination in the exercise of public functions as well as in relation to goods, services and facilities: see Ch 4.

(4) A relevant authorisation is a requirement imposed or express authorisation given—
  (a) with respect to a particular case or class of case, by a Minister of the Crown acting personally;
  (b) with respect to a particular class of case, by or under anything mentioned in sub-paragraph (5)(a) to (c).

Paragraph 17(5)–(6) provides that the relevant functions relate to immigration and asylum, other than in relation to powers of arrest and entry.

The width of the exception created by Schedule 3 para 17 EqA is illustrated by the decision below.

***R (Goloshvili) v SSHD* [2019] EWHC 614 (Admin), [2019] HLR 37**

Amnesty International v Ahmed [2009] ICR 1450 (see p 189 above) concerned the application of s41 RRA. This more recent decision was concerned with its EqA equivalents (specifically Schedule 3 para 17). The case involved a challenge to a statutory scheme which prohibits landlords from letting residential premises to people who require leave under to enter or remain in the UK but who do not have it ('disqualified persons'). Under the scheme, a landlord who was given notice by the Secretary of State that one or more occupiers of a rented property was not entitled to be in the UK (a 'Notice of Letting to a Disqualified Person'; NLDP) is required to give notice to the tenant(s) to leave the property. The claimant, a Georgian national with leave to remain in the UK, was given notice by her landlord after he received a NLDP which had been issued in error by the Home Secretary. She initiated judicial review proceedings, claiming that the issue of the NLDP amounted to discrimination on grounds of nationality contrary to s29 EqA.

The relevant sections of the Immigration Act 2014 defined disqualified persons and provided (s33D(2)) that landlords were entitled to terminate tenancy agreements where:

> … the Secretary of State has given one or more notices in writing to the landlord which, taken together,—
>
> (a) Identify the occupier of the premises or (if there is more than one occupier) all of them,
> (b) State that the occupier or occupiers are disqualified as a result of their immigration status from occupying premises under a residential tenancy agreement.'

The judge accepted that the issue of the NLDP involved nationality discrimination which would be unlawful unless permitted by the EqA. The claimant argued that the decision in *Hampson v Department of Education and Science* [1991] 1 AC 171 (see pp 188–189 above) had the effect that Schedule 23 para 1 applied to permit the discrimination only if s33(2)(D) expressly required or authorised the service of a NLDP, which it did not. She also argued that, because the defendant had a discretion under s21(3) to grant permission to rent, the issue or service of a NLDP was discretionary and therefore fell outside Schedule 3 para 17. The judge accepted the Secretary of State's argument that the necessary implication of s33D(2) of the Immigration Act 2014 was that the discrimination at issue was permitted by statute.

Martin Spencer J:

> 50 … By reason of para.17(2) of Sch.3, s.29 [EqA], which is the relevant provision for the purposes of this claim, does not apply to anything done by a relevant person in the exercise of functions exercisable by virtue of a relevant enactment. The paragraph is expressly applicable to race discrimination on grounds of nationality.

51. … s.33D(2) of the Immigration Act 2014 … amounts to authorisation of the issue or service of a NLDP under the Act. Where s.33D refers to the condition being that the Secretary of State 'has given one or more notices in writing to the landlord' it thereby confers on the Secretary of State express authorisation to issue such notices. Otherwise … s.33D would be a meaningless provision and the issue of any NLDP would be an act of race discrimination entitling the tenant to sue the Home Office, a result which the legislation certainly cannot have intended. For this reason, to give appropriate respect to primary legislation, it is necessary to interpret s.33D(2) as containing express authorisation whether to issue such notices …

53. I cannot accept [the claimant's] submission that the issuing or service of a NLDP is not covered by the exemption because the defendant has a discretion under s.21(3) of the Immigration Act 2014 to grant permission to rent. In my judgment, the reliance … on the decision of the House of Lords in *Hampson* … is inapposite …

The House of Lords found that the Secretary of State could not rely on s.41 because any wide construction of the expression would be irreconcilable with the purpose of the Act and would allow the imposition of conditions or requirements capable of racial discrimination without any prior opportunity for parliamentary scrutiny. In my judgment, the position is quite different where the act in question is expressly authorised (as I have found) by a provision in the Act itself which has, of course, been subject to parliamentary scrutiny. In relation to acts authorised by Acts of Parliament, there is no such principle that the acts done are restricted to acts done in the 'necessary performance of an expressed obligation' and that this does not extend to acts done in exercise of a power or discretion. Even if the issue of a NLDP can properly be described as a discretionary act by virtue of the provisions of s.21(3) of the Immigration Act 2014, which I doubt, this does not render the issue of a NLDP unlawful given the critical part which it plays in the overall Scheme, a Scheme which is authorised by primary legislation and where the issue of a NLDP is, as I have found, expressly authorised by s.33D(2).'

The judge also rejected the argument put for the claimant that accepted that the references in Schedule 3 para 17 EqA to the Minister acting 'personally' meant that that provision only allowed discrimination which resulted from the decision of ministers, rather than of civil servants acting on their behalf.

Immigration rules also prohibit employers from employing people whose immigration status does not permit them to work, which in turn may permit (indeed require) employers to discriminate. The Home Office has issued a Code of Practice to assist employers to comply with their immigration-related legal obligations without breaching the EqA.

Home Office, 'Code of practice for employers: Avoiding unlawful discrimination while preventing illegal working' (2022)[108]

3: How to avoid discrimination

Employers should:

- be consistent in how they conduct right to work checks on all prospective employees, including British citizens.
- ensure job selections are made on the basis of suitability for the post.
- Ensure that no prospective job applicants are discouraged or excluded, either directly or indirectly, because of known or perceived protected characteristics.

[108] https://www.gov.uk/government/publications/right-to-work-checks-code-of-practice-on-avoiding-discrimination.

Employers should not:

- discriminate when conducting right to work checks.
- only check the status of those who appear to the employer likely to be migrants
- Make assumptions about a person's right to work in the UK or their immigration status on the basis of their colour, nationality, ethnic or national origins, accent, surname or the length of time they have been resident in the UK.

Otherwise, you may be acting in a discriminatory manner and it could be used as evidence against you in proceedings under the [EqA] …

It is inevitable that prohibitions on race discrimination contain some exemptions relating to nationality, since the control of borders is one of the central functions of the state. The exception relating to ethnic or national origins is more controversial, permitting as it would discrimination (for example) against Iraqi Kurds or Uyghur Muslims. It is easy to understand why the state ought to be able to discriminate *in favour of* racially minoritised groups which are facing persecution abroad. The reverse is perhaps less obvious.

East African Asians

The history of the UK in this area is not a happy one. In 1973 the European Commission on Human Rights (ECmHR, which at that time had a triage function in relation to the ECtHR), ruled that the UK had breached Article 3 ECHR (which prohibits torture and unhuman and degrading treatment) in the exercise of its immigration functions. The applicants were UK citizens of Asian origin who sought to enter the UK in order to join their wives, who were already resident in the UK.

The background to the *East African Asians* case is set out in the blog post below.

Asad Ali Khan, 'British nationality claims: The Case of the East African Asians' (2010, Immigration Law Blog)[109]

There is a large population of South Asians in East Africa. Their presence there dates back to the time of the British Empire when large numbers of South Asian workers were brought to East Africa by the British. Today, Kenyan Asians number 100,000. Tanzania and Uganda are reported to have Asian populations of 90,000 each.

At the time of independence of the East African countries, the nationality arrangements were such that most Asians became citizens of the newly independent country in which they were living. However, a significant number of Asians did not, and instead retained citizenship of the UK and colonies.

After the independence of Kenya, the Africanisation programme of the Kenyan authorities resulted in the persecution of the Asian community. Large numbers of Asians with British passports began to migrate to the UK. In 1968, this migration resulted in an Act of Parliament of the UK that still remains a stain on the reputation of the UK. Lord Lester of Herne Hill QC, a celebrated barrister who represented a number of East African Asians in their fight against the UK government before the European Court of Human Rights, describes the events in 1968 as follows:

> After a highly effective populist campaign led by Enoch Powell MP and Duncan Sandys MP to deprive the British Asians of their right to enter the UK, the Wilson Government introduced emergency legislation – the Commonwealth Immigrants Act 1968 – and drove it through all its parliamentary stages in three tumultuous days and nights … Upon its face, the 1968 Act

[109] https://asadakhan.wordpress.com/2010/06/30/british-nationality-claims-the-case-of-the-east-african-asians.

> was merely applying a familiar set of qualifications for the acquisition of UK citizenship to UK immigration law; but, as members of all political parties, the press and the general public recognised at the time, the real purpose of this provision was to deprive the British Asians of their right of entry on racial grounds. A group of British citizens, temporary in public office, successfully used their legislative majority to abridge the basic rights and freedoms of another group of British citizens, because of their colour and ethnic origins. And because the Westminster Parliament was all-powerful under the British constitution with unbridled legislative powers, British courts could not strike down this obnoxious and unsightly measure.

The legal challenge to the Commonwealth Immigrants Act 1968 reached the European Commission in 1973.

East African Asians v UK **(1973) (1981) 3 EHRR 76**

> 196 … The Commission … is not faced with the general question whether racial discrimination in immigration control constitutes degrading treatment as such. The question is rather whether the legislation applied in the applicants' cases … discriminated on the ground of race or colour and, if that be the case, whether its application in the following special circumstances of the present cases constituted 'degrading treatment' in the sense of Article 3 of the Convention:
>
> - the 'pledge' of free entry, which is said to have been given previously to the citizens of the United Kingdom and colonies in East Africa who were affected by the Act;
> - the fact that the persons concerned were not aliens, but were and remained citizens of the United Kingdom and colonies, and that as such, although they had the same duties as other citizens, under the 1968 Act they no longer had the same right of entry;
> - the increasingly difficult situation with which these persons were faced in East Africa: most of them were deprived of their livelihood and rendered destitute; their continued residence in East Africa became illegal; and, being refused entry by the only State of which they were citizens – the United Kingdom – they had nowhere else to go …
>
> 199. The Commission finds it established that the 1968 Act had racial motives and that it covered a racial group. When it was introduced into Parliament as a Bill, it was clear that it was directed against the Asian citizens of the United Kingdom and colonies in East Africa and especially those in Kenya …
>
> It notes in particular that a former Secretary of State for the Colonies had proposed legislation to limit the rights of Asians from Kenya to enter the United Kingdom, and that the main purpose of the Government's Bill was apparently to exclude that 'most of the 200,000 Asians in East Africa would continue to be free to come here at will'.
>
> 200. The Government, while claiming that the Act was based on geography, nevertheless admitted that it had racial motives: the Home Secretary stated in the House of Commons on 27 February 1968 'that the origin of this Bill lies … in a considered judgment of the best way to achieve the idea of a multi-racial society'; and the Government submitted in the present proceedings that the Act was intended to promote 'racial harmony'.

The ECmHR concluded that the 1968 Act discriminated against UK citizens of Asian origin and breached Article 3 ECHR. The UK Government entered into a friendly settlement by virtue of which a Special Quota Voucher Scheme ('SQV Scheme') was introduced to benefit UK citizens whose rights had been restricted by the 1968 Act. Almost 25 years later, a decision of the CA showed that the wrongs identified by the European Commission had not been undone.

***NH (India) v Entry Clearance Officer* [2007] EWCA Civ 1330, [2008] INLR 154**

The claimant appealed against a refusal to allow him to enter the UK. His mother was a UK citizen whose right to reside in the UK had been restricted by the 1968 Act and who subsequently obtained a British overseas citizen passport in 1998 and a British passport in 2003. The claimant's mother was not covered by the SQV Scheme because, as a married woman, she was not the head of a household. Her husband (the claimant's father) and the claimant (who was born in 1985) were refused entry to the UK in 2004. The Immigration and Asylum Tribunal had allowed the claimant's appeal and granted him entry on Article 8 grounds, noting that there was 'historic discrimination' against his mother on grounds of race and sex. The Secretary of State appealed. The CA rejected the appeal, Sedley LJ referring to the 'historic injustice' perpetrated on the claimant's mother which meant that the IAT had been entitled to regard his claim as exceptional and his exclusion disproportionate.

In [2015], in *AP (India) v Secretary of State for the Home Department* [2015] EWCA Civ 89, [2015] INLR 431, Elias LJ referred to the mistreatment of East African Asians as a 'shameful episode in British history'. In that case the Court unanimously granted entry clearance to the claimant who would have been entitled to enter had his father not been disadvantaged by the 1968 Act.

Windrush

The East African Asians scandal has not been the only one to blight the UK's record on immigration. In 2018 public attention was drawn to the plight of people of Caribbean origin who had arrived in the UK as UK citizens prior to 1973, at which point additional restrictions were imposed on such entry. People were misclassified and detained as unlawful immigrants, refused re-entry to the UK and/or wrongly deported. Many lost homes and jobs, access to medical treatment and benefits or medical care to which they were entitled. The scandal was linked to the embrace Theresa May, in her period as Home Secretary, of the Hostile Environment Policy intended to drive out of the UK people without leave to remain in it.

Wendy Williams, *Windrush Lessons Learned Review*, 2020[110]

Executive Summary

Members of the Windrush generation and their children have been poorly served by this country. They had every right to be here and should never have been caught in the immigration net. The many stories of injustice and hardship are heartbreaking, with jobs lost, lives uprooted and untold damage done to so many individuals and families.

However, despite the scandal taking the Home Office by surprise my report sets out that what happened to those affected by the Windrush scandal was foreseeable and avoidable.

The causes of the Windrush scandal can be traced back through successive rounds of policy and legislation about immigration and nationality from the 1960s onwards, the aim of which was to restrict the eligibility of certain groups to live in the UK.

[110] https://assets.publishing.service.gov.uk/government/uploads/system/uploads/attachment_data/file/876336/6.5577_HO_Windrush_Lessons_Learned_Review_LoResFinal.pdf.

The 1971 Immigration Act confirmed that the Windrush generation had, and have, the right of abode in the UK. But they were not given any documents to demonstrate this status. Nor were records kept. They had no reason to doubt their status, or that they belonged in the UK. They could not have been expected to know the complexity of the law as it changed around them.

But over time those in power forgot about them and their circumstances, which meant that when successive governments wanted to demonstrate that they were being tough on immigration by tightening immigration control and passing laws creating, and then expanding the hostile environment, this was done with a complete disregard for the Windrush generation.

A range of warning signs from inside and outside the Home Office were simply not heeded by officials and ministers. Even when stories of members of the Windrush generation being affected by immigration control started to emerge in the media from 2017 onwards, the department was too slow to react.

The report identifies the organisational factors in the Home Office which created the operating environment in which these mistakes could be made, including a culture of disbelief and carelessness when dealing with applications, made worse by the status of the Windrush generation, who were failed when they needed help most …

While I am unable to make a definitive finding of institutional racism within the department, I have serious concerns that these failings demonstrate an institutional ignorance and thoughtlessness towards the issue of race and the history of the Windrush generation within the department, which are consistent with some elements of the definition of institutional racism.

A compensation scheme for Windrush victims was announced in December 2018, but three years later the home affairs select committee reported that only five per cent of those eligible for compensation had received it.[111]

Amelia Gentleman, 'Windrush: Home Office has compensated just 5% of victims in four years', *The Guardian*, 24 November 2021[112]

The report from the home affairs select committee found that the compensation scheme, for which up to 15,000 people were expected to qualify, had compounded injustices faced by the Windrush generation, with some applicants saying the process has become a source of further trauma rather than redress.

Twenty-three eligible applicants have died before getting a payment, the committee found. It recommended transferring the scheme from Priti Patel's department to an independent organisation in order to 'rebuild trust'…

The new report identifies a 'litany of flaws in the design and operation' of the compensation scheme including an excessive burden on claimants to provide documentary evidence of the losses they suffered, long delays in processing applications and making payments, inadequate staffing of the scheme and a failure to provide urgent and exceptional payments to those in desperate need.

It was 'staggering' that the Home Office failed adequately to prepare for, resource and staff the Windrush compensation scheme before its launch, the report notes.

[111] *The Windrush Compensation Scheme*, available at https://committees.parliament.uk/committee/83/home-affairs-committee/news/159118/compensation-scheme-failures-have-compounded-injustices-faced-by-windrush-generation-committee-finds/. See also National Audit Office, *Investigation into the Windrush Compensation Scheme* (2021), available at https://www.nao.org.uk/reports/investigation-into-the-windrush-compensation-scheme; Public Accounts Committee, *Windrush Compensation Scheme* (2021), available at https://publications.parliament.uk/pa/cm5802/cmselect/cmpubacc/174/17402.htm and Justice, Reforming the Windrush Compensation Scheme, available at https://justice.org.uk/our-work/administrative-justice-system/current-work-administrative-justice/reforming-the-windrush-compensation-scheme.

[112] https://www.theguardian.com/uk-news/2021/nov/24/windrush-home-office-has-compensated-just-5-of-victims-in-four-years.

The Home Office's own research has identified lack of trust as a barrier, with 12% of respondents in a survey it carried out saying they believed the Windrush schemes were set up to 'send people who are in the UK illegally back to their country of origin'.

The report says: 'No amount of compensation could ever repay the fear, humiliation, hurt and hardship that was caused to individuals who were affected. That the design and operation of this scheme contained the same bureaucratic insensitivities that led to the Windrush scandal in the first place is a damning indictment of the Home Office, and suggests that the culture change it promised in the wake of the scandal has not yet occurred.'…

EHRC, *Public Sector Equality Duty assessment of hostile environment policies* (2020)[113]

… we found insufficient evidence of the Home Office taking the required steps to show due regard to the need to advance equality of opportunity in relation to colour. This included the documents the Home Office supplied to show compliance. We have therefore concluded that the department did not comply with section 149 of the Equality Act 2010 (the PSED) in understanding the impact on the Windrush generation and their descendants when developing, implementing and monitoring the hostile environment policy agenda. We also agree with the Windrush Lessons Learned Review conclusion that the experiences of the Windrush generation were 'foreseeable and avoidable'. Specifically, we have found:

- When negative equality impacts were identified by the Home Office and stakeholders, they were repeatedly ignored, dismissed, or their severity disregarded at crucial points of policy development. This happened particularly when they were seen as a barrier to implementing hostile environment policies in a highly-politicised environment.
- Limited engagement with stakeholders representing members of the Windrush generation and their descendants, even as the severe effects of hostile environment policies began to emerge. The engagement that did take place was too focused on groups that would help to implement the measures, and not those who could make sure the department fully understood the equality implications of its policies.
- That equality impacts were often considered too late to form a meaningful part of many decision-making processes, with their reputational or legal implications for the Home Office given greater weight than the real-life consequences for the people affected.
- That exceptions to the PSED for immigration functions were often interpreted too broadly, incorrectly and / or inconsistently.
- A lack of organisation-wide commitment, including by senior leadership, to the importance of equality and the Home Office's obligations under the PSED. Any action taken to record and respond to negative equality impacts was perfunctory, and therefore insufficient.

Our recommendations for change

Our recommendations are designed to help the Home Office to comply effectively and meaningfully with its PSED obligations in the future development, implementation and monitoring of immigration policy and practice. In summary, it is our view that the Home Office should:

- Prioritise, act early and use a range of sources and evidence to understand the equality impacts of its policies and practices – particularly through proper engagement with affected groups.
- Fully consider the historical context and cumulative implications of its immigration policies for certain groups.
- Make sure ministers and other decision-makers receive and consider detailed equality information, including options for mitigating any negative impacts, at an appropriately early stage to inform the policymaking process.

[113] https://www.equalityhumanrights.com/sites/default/files/public-sector-equality-duty-assessment-of-hostile-environment-policies.pdf.

- Regularly review equality impacts as policies are implemented, act on this information in a way that is proportionate to the severity of the impacts, and document decisions taken to adopt or not adopt particular mitigation measures.
- Take meaningful action to improve its internal capability to fully understand and comply with the PSED, to fulfil its commitment to equality.
- Be fully transparent and open to scrutiny about the department's commitment and approach to advancing equality.

EHRC, *Home Office signs legal agreement to improve practices following Windrush*[114]

The Home Office has signed a legal agreement with us, setting out the actions it will take to address its failure to comply with equality law when implementing 'hostile environment' measures …

This agreement, under section 23 of the Equality Act 2006, commits the Home Office to a two-year action plan of improvements it will make to demonstrate that it:

- looks for and properly considers evidence and feedback from stakeholders representing affected groups to understand the equality impacts of policies and practices;
- has a clear understanding of equality data and evidence that it uses to inform decisions and policymaking at all levels, including of the potential and actual impact of the department's work on different protected characteristic groups; and
- has taken meaningful action to improve internal knowledge and expertise on how to comply with the PSED.

As part of the action plan Home Office will establish a Community Stakeholder and Engagement Hub and take steps to improve the advice given to Ministers about equality.

[114] 1 April 2021, available at https://www.equalityhumanrights.com/en/our-work/news/home-office-signs-legal-agreement-improve-practices-following-windrush.

8

Disability

Introduction

People with disabilities are far from homogeneous; they include children born with severely debilitating disease whose expected lifespan is short, middle-aged company executives with diabetes or heart disease, and former labourers or GPs with lung cancer caused by exposure to asbestosis as well as those with limitations to mental capacity or mobility and people experiencing mental ill health. The rate of disability increases with age: according to the report below, from eight per cent in children and 19 per cent of working-age adults to 45 per cent of pensioners. It is generally the case, however, that disability is associated with significant disadvantage in terms of education, work, health and care, justice and detention, and participation and identity. People with disabilities are also more likely to experience poverty, which in turn has implications for their access to decent housing and to life chances generally, and (where they are adults) to the life chances of their children.

EHRC, *Being disabled in Britain: a journey less equal* (2017)[1]

Executive Summary

It is a badge of shame on our society that millions of disabled people in Britain are still not being treated as equal citizens and continue to be denied the everyday rights non-disabled people take for granted, such as being able to access transport, appropriate health services and housing, or benefit from education and employment. The disability pay gap is persistent and widening, access to justice has deteriorated, and welfare reforms have significantly affected the already low living standards of disabled people. It is essential that as a society we recognise and address these structural problems urgently and comprehensively …

Education

Disabled pupils in England, Wales and Scotland have much lower attainment rates at school than non-disabled pupils, and are significantly more likely to be permanently or temporarily excluded. Furthermore, there is a need to address bullying experienced by disabled children and the levels of support they are offered.

[1] https://www.equalityhumanrights.com/en/publication-download/being-disabled-britain-journey-less-equal. The EHRC's findings on work are not included as they have been superseded by the information discussed below.

In England and Wales, in 2014/15 the educational attainment of children with Special Educational Needs (SEN) was nearly three times lower than for non-disabled children. Across Britain in 2015/16, disabled young people aged 16–18 were at least twice as likely as their non-disabled peers to not be in education, employment or training (NEET) … the proportion of disabled people with no qualifications was nearly three times that of non-disabled people in 2015/16, and the proportion of disabled people with a degree remained lower than that of non-disabled people …

Standard of living

More disabled people than non-disabled are living in poverty or are materially deprived. Social security reforms have had a particularly disproportionate, cumulative impact on rights to independent living and an adequate standard of living for disabled people.

UK data from 2014/15 shows that 30% of working-age adults in families where at least one member is disabled were living in households with below 60% of contemporary median income after housing costs, compared with 18% for those living in families with no disabled members …

Across the UK, 18.4% of disabled people aged 16–64 were considered to be in food poverty in 2014 compared with just 7.5% of non-disabled people. Disabled people over the age of 65 were twice as likely as non-disabled people in the same age group to be in food poverty: 6.8% compared with 3.3% …

Disabled people face problems in finding adequate housing and this is a major barrier to independent living. There is a shortage of accessible housing across Britain: of councils in England with a housing plan, fewer than 17% have set out strategies to build disabled-friendly homes. In Scotland the amount of wheelchair-adapted local authority housing for physically disabled people has decreased.

As resources become scarcer, and funding for specialist services for disabled people disappears, disabled people are finding it more and more difficult to access support.

Health and care

Disabled people are more likely to experience health inequalities and major health conditions, and are likely to die younger than other people. The extent of these health inequalities is difficult to assess because of limited data on outcomes for disabled people collected by NHS providers and commissioners. Accessibility of services is problematic, and disabled people are less likely to report positive experiences in accessing healthcare services.

Despite a commitment by governments to make improvements to the provision of mental health services, considerable shortcomings remain in all three countries (England, Scotland and Wales), where disabled adults are more likely to report poor mental health and wellbeing than non-disabled adults …

- On average, men with mental health conditions die 20 years earlier than the general population, and women 13 years earlier.
- 'Do not attempt resuscitation' (DNAR) notices are being placed on patients' files without their consent or knowledge.
- Action is needed to reduce the use of physical and chemical restraint for the purposes of behaviour management in hospital and care settings.

Justice and detention

There is an urgent need for prisons to monitor and report on prisoner mental health. Prisoners are more likely to have mental health conditions compared with the general population, and 70% of prisoners that died from self-inflicted means between 2012 and 2014 had an identified mental health need.

Detentions in health and social care settings under the Mental Health Act 1983 are continuing to increase in England and Wales and this is a strong concern, particularly as evidence suggests there are flaws in the way those detained are assessed and treated.

- The use of section 136 of the Mental Health Act 1983 (under which people are brought to hospital as a 'place of safety') increased by 18% to 22,965 in 2016, while the number of detentions in hospitals increased between 2009/10 and 2016 (from 46,600 in 2009/10 to 63,622 in 2016).

The UK continues to be the only country in the European Union with no time limit on immigration detention, and there is a concern that immigration detention facilities are inadequately equipped to deal with detainees who have a mental health condition.

Disabled people in Britain are more likely to have experienced crime than non-disabled people … Disability hate crimes recorded by the police in England and Wales increased by 44% in 2015/16 on the previous year, possibly reflecting improved reporting and recording practices. Despite this improvement, a joint inspection team from HMI Constabulary, HM Crown Prosecution Service Inspectorate and HMI Probation found that criminal justice agencies do not always understand what forms disability hate crime can take, and that more needs to be done to understand how disabled people experience hate crime. This includes the ways in which disabled people are targeted and the difficulties they face in getting public authorities to respond …

Changes to legal aid in England and Wales have negatively affected disabled people's access to justice in family law, housing, employment, debt and welfare benefits cases. Across Great Britain, there has been a 54% drop in employment tribunal claims on grounds of disability discrimination between 2012/13 and 2015/16.

Participation and identity

Disabled people continue to encounter barriers to exercising their right to vote. Disabled people are also under-represented in political office and public appointments, and face continued challenges to achieving equal representation. There is an urgent need for the implementation of section 106 of the Equality Act 2010, so that political parties are required to publish diversity data about their candidates.

Poor access to transport, leisure and other services can affect the community and social life of disabled people, creating a barrier to independence and their enjoyment of day-to-day activities. Across Great Britain, there was an overall increase between 2009–11 and 2012–14 in the percentage of disabled and non-disabled adults who reported having difficulty accessing services in the areas of health, benefits, tax, culture, sport and leisure. In 2012–14 this was 45.3% for disabled people compared with 31.7% for non-disabled people.

The wide gap in internet usage between disabled and non-disabled people has persisted … Disabled people reported difficulties accessing their bank, having a credit history and affording insurance, all of which exacerbate the financial penalty they face and can limit their family life and opportunities to learn, work and participate in society.

Negative attitudes towards disabled people remain prominent in Britain, and people with a mental health condition, learning disability or memory impairment remain particularly likely to be stigmatised …

Joseph Rowntree Foundation, *UK Poverty 2022: The essential guide to understanding poverty in the UK*, 57–58[2]

Disabled people face a higher risk of poverty and have done so for at least the last 20 years. This is driven partly by the additional costs associated with disability and ill-health, and partly by many

[2] https://www.jrf.org.uk/report/uk-poverty-2022.

> disabled people being less able to access work. With potential for work often limited, disabled people and/or families where someone is disabled frequently rely on benefits as a source of income, which at current rates will almost inevitably lead to higher poverty rates …
>
> Overall, around 1 in 5 people are disabled in the UK: looking at this by age, 8% of children, 45% of pensioners and 19% of working-age adults self-report being disabled. Just over one third of all families have at least one person who is disabled.
>
> The poverty measure that has been used in this section is based on after housing costs, excluding disability benefits from household income. These disability benefits are designed to cover the costs associated with being disabled. This means including these disability benefits as income can give a misleadingly lower assessment of the poverty risk.
>
> In the published headline figures where disability benefits are included as income, the poverty rate for disabled people is 27%. Excluding these benefits from income increases the poverty rate for disabled people by 5 percentage points to 32%, some 12 percentage points above those who are not disabled. The difference is particularly stark for working-age adults: those who are disabled are more than twice as likely to live in poverty than those who are not (38% and 17% respectively).

According to the Department for Work and Pension's publication, *The employment of disabled people 2021*:[3]

- one-fifth of the working age population in the UK had a disability in 2021, eight per cent having a severe disability and one in three having a long-term health condition;[4]
- 4.4m disabled people were employed in the UK in 2021, an increase of 300,000 since the previous year, of 390,000 since 2019 and of 1.5m since 2013;
- the employment rate for people with disabilities was 52.7 per cent in 2021 while that for non-disabled people was 81.0 per cent. The figure for disabled people was an increase of 0.3 percentage points since 2020, 0.1 percentage points since 2019 and 9.0 percentage points since 2013, while the gap between the rates of employment for disabled and non-disabled people was 28.4 percentage points in 2021, down by 0.7 percentage points since 2020, by 0.6 percentage points since 2019 and by 4.8 percentage points since 2013;
- the disability employment gap was wider for disabled men, disabled white people, older disabled people (aged 50–64) and those with no qualifications, lower for disabled people with mental health conditions and with five or more health conditions;
- disabled people were more likely than non-disabled people to be working in lower-skilled occupations (but as likely as non-disabled people to be in 'quality work'[5]), to be self-employed, working part-time and in the public sector, and to be working in health, retail or education.

Fifty per cent of the increase in the number of disabled workers in employment between 2013 and 2021 was attributable to increased prevalence of disability (with 6.9m people aged between 16 and 64 self-reporting as disabled in 2013 and 8.3m in 2021).[6] This increase was

[3] https://www.gov.uk/government/statistics/the-employment-of-disabled-people-2021/the-employment-of-disabled-people-2021.

[4] *Ibid.* All statistics relate to the second quarter of the relevant year except where the contrary is stated.

[5] Defined by the ONS as work with good hours (under 48 per week), without low pay and with the contract type (indefinite or otherwise) preferred by the worker.

[6] Figures from the Annual Population Survey.

driven by an increase in people (particularly young women) reporting mental health conditions. Reports of mental health conditions increased by 850,000 (68.6 per cent) of which 340,000 were from women aged 16–34 (for whom this was a rise of 131.5 per cent).

The official figures show that the employment rates, but also the disability employment gap, was lowest for younger workers (16–24) with the disability employment gap increasing with age at each step (25–34, 34–49 and 50–64). Women with disabilities are slightly more likely to be employed than men with disabilities and White disabled workers experience the highest employment gap (by comparison with White non-disabled workers). The relationship between category of disability and employment is shown in Figure 8.1 below.

Figure 8.1 Proportion of disabled people in employment by main or secondary health condition, 2020–21[7]

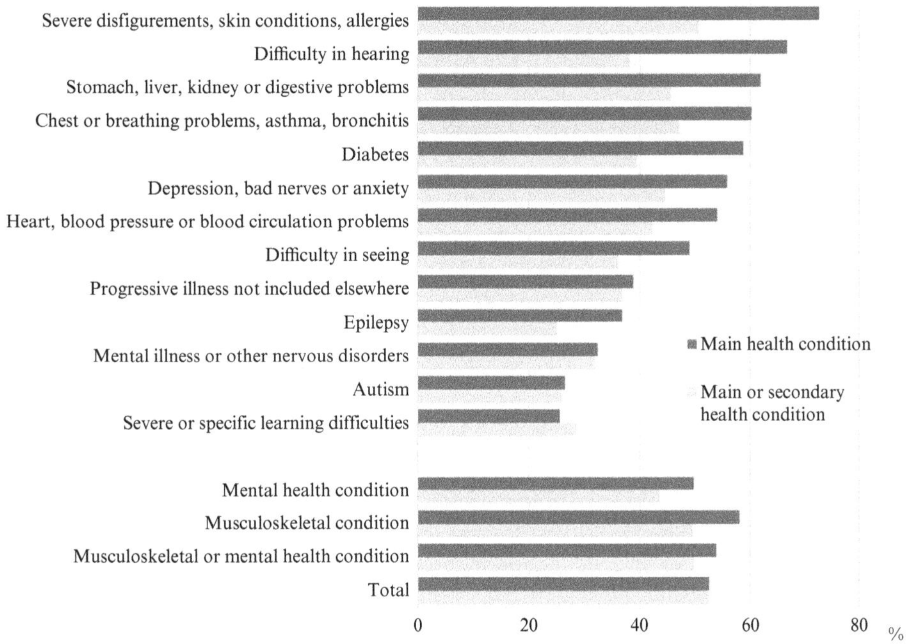

Perhaps unsurprisingly, the disability employment gap increases with the number of health conditions disabled people have. Whereas almost two-thirds of disabled people with one health condition were in employment in 2021, employment rates decline by 10.5 percentage points for each additional condition, with an employment rate of under a third for those with five or more conditions. Education acts as a protective factor, disabled people with A levels being as likely to be employed as non-disabled people without any qualifications and disabled people with higher levels of qualifications having higher employment rates. Figure 8.2 below shows the employment gaps between disabled and non-disabled workers by occupational category.

[7] Department for Work and Pensions, *The employment of disabled people 2021,* n 3 above, Fig 8.

Figure 8.2 Proportion of by occupation and disability status, 2020–21[8]

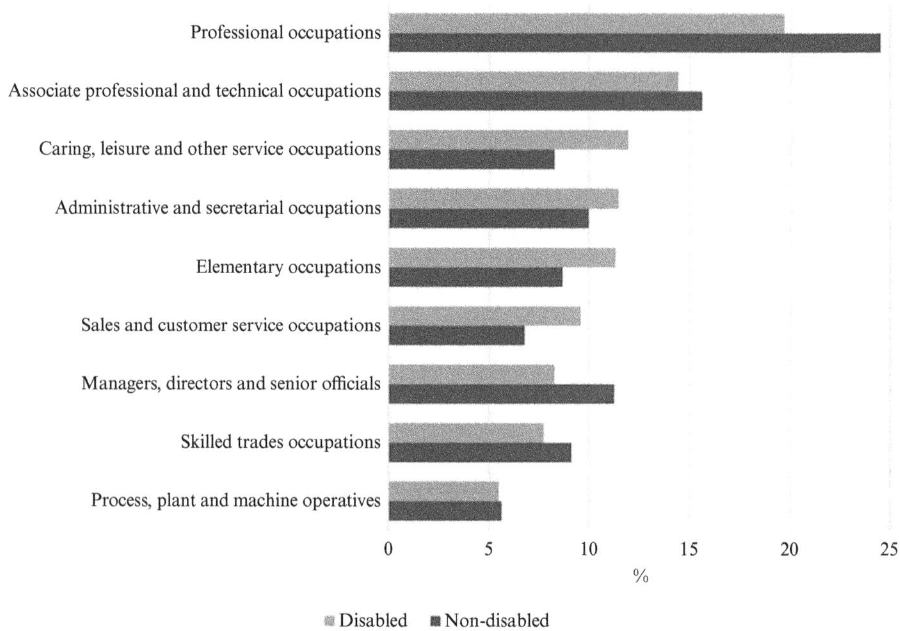

The Equality Act 2010

Disability as a Protected Characteristic

By contrast with its approach to most other protected characteristics (sex, race, sexual orientation, age, religion or belief[9]), the EqA's regulation of disability discrimination is *asymmetric*; generally speaking, only those regarded as disabled for the purposes of the EqA are protected against discrimination related to disability. This rule is not absolute: non-disabled people may be protected from discrimination related to their (mistakenly) *perceived* disability, or their *association with* a disabled person (see generally Chapter 2). Non-disabled people are also protected from victimisation connected with complaints of disability discrimination, and from disability-related harassment (see generally Chapter 2). But protection from direct disability discrimination and s15 discrimination (see below) apply only to people recognised as disabled for the purposes of the EqA. By contrast, those who are generally advantaged, rather than disadvantaged, by their sex, race, age, sexual

[8] Department for Work and Pensions, *The employment of disabled people 2021,* n 3 above, Fig 15.
[9] The position differs for marriage or civil partnership which are also asymmetrically protected and, to some extent, for gender reassignment (see further Ch 2).

orientation and (absence of) religion or belief are entitled to the full protection of the EqA (though not necessarily by the provisions permitting positive action).[10]

Section 6 EqA, Disability

(1) A person (P) has a disability if—

(a) P has a physical or mental impairment, and

(b) the impairment has a substantial and long-term adverse effect on P's ability to carry out normal day-to-day activities.

(2) A reference to a disabled person is a reference to a person who has a disability.

(3) In relation to the protected characteristic of disability—

(a) a reference to a person who has a particular protected characteristic is a reference to a person who has a particular disability;

(b) a reference to persons who share a protected characteristic is a reference to persons who have the same disability.

(4) This Act (except Part 12 and section 190) applies in relation to a person who has had a disability as it applies in relation to a person who has the disability; accordingly (except in that Part and that section)—

(a) a reference (however expressed) to a person who has a disability includes a reference to a person who has had the disability, and

(b) a reference (however expressed) to a person who does not have a disability includes a reference to a person who has not had the disability …

Included and Excluded Conditions

Section 6(6) EqA gives effect to Schedule 1 EqA, which provides that:

- the effect of an impairment is to be regarded as long-term if it has lasted, or is likely to last, for at least 12 months, or is likely to last for the rest of the life of the person affected (para 2);
- an impairment is to be regarded as continuing to have a substantial adverse effect on a person's ability to carry out normal day-to-day activities if it ceases to have such an effect, but is likely to recur (para 2);
- a severe disfigurement is to be treated as having a substantial adverse effect on the ability of the person concerned to carry out normal day-to-day activities (para 3);
- except in the case of eye glasses, an impairment is to be treated as having a substantial adverse effect on the ability of the person concerned to carry out normal day-to-day activities if, but for measures[11] being taken to treat or correct it, it would be likely to have that effect (para 5);
- cancer, HIV infection and multiple sclerosis are regarded as disabilities irrespective of impairment (para 6);
- other progressive conditions will be regarded as having a substantial adverse effect on a person's ability to carry out normal day-to-day activities once they have any adverse effect on this ability if the condition is likely to have a substantial adverse impact (para 8).

[10] See Ch 3.

[11] Including in particular medical treatment and the use of a prosthesis or other aid.

The meaning of the word 'likely' in the predecessor provision to paras 2 and 5 was considered by the House of Lords (HL) in the following case.

***SCA Packaging Ltd v Boyle* [2009] UKHL 37, [2009] ICR 1056**

The claimant, who suffered from hoarseness and vocal nodes, successfully followed a stress-reduction regime involving sipping water, increasing humidity, avoiding certain foods and drinks, throat clearing, singing, humming and raising her voice, limiting phone calls and resting her voice periodically. An industrial tribunal in Northern Ireland ruled that the claimant was disabled because the vocal nodes were 'likely' to recur if she did not follow her regime. Northern Ireland's Court of Appeal (CA) (to which tribunal appeals go direct) rejected the employer's appeal on the basis that 'likely' meant 'could well happen'. The employer further appealed on the basis that 'likely' meant 'more probable than not', as the EAT had held in *Latchman v Reed Business Information Ltd* [2002] ICR 1453. The HL rejected the appeal.

Lady Hale, with whom Lords Hope, Brown, Neuberger and Rodger agreed:

65. Discussion

The Northern Ireland Department of Economic Development has issued Guidance on the matters to be taken into account in determining questions relating to the definition of disability ... The Guidance current at the time was issued in 1996 and is to the same effect as the Guidance issued by the Secretary of State for England and Wales (both have since been replaced). Both state, at para. B7, that 'It is *likely* that an event will happen if it is more probable than not that it will happen'. This curious statement appears to have got 'likely' and 'probable' the wrong way round. It is probable that an event will happen if it is more likely than not that it will do so. Probability denotes a degree of likelihood greater than 50%. Likelihood, on the other hand, is a much more variable concept ...

67. ... The Guidance has, of course, to be taken seriously into account when it deals with the factual matters which are relevant to the application of the legal tests. It is common for statutory Guidance to try to explain, not only how the legislation should be put into effect by the people who have to apply it, but also what the legislation means. But that is simply being helpful to practitioners who are not lawyers and may never read the legal texts. Statutory construction remains a matter for the courts, not for Departmental Guidance. If the court considers that the Guidance is a mis-statement or mis-application of what Parliament has enacted, then it must say so.

68. It is significant that, apart from the EAT decisions cited above, our attention has been drawn to no case in which 'likely' has been held to mean 'more likely than not'. This is scarcely surprising, as Parliament can always use the word 'probable' if that is what it means. In *Cream Holdings Ltd v Banerjee* [2004] UKHL 44, [2005] 1 AC 253, Lord Nicholls of Birkenhead said this, at paragraph 12:

> 'As with most ordinary English words "likely" has several different shades of meaning. Its meaning depends upon the context in which it is being used. Even when read in context its meaning is not always precise. It is capable of encompassing different degrees of likelihood, varying from "more likely than not" to "may well".'...

In that case, the House related the degree of likelihood of success at trial, required by s.12(3) of the Human Rights Act 1998, to the potential adverse effects of disclosure. This is very similar to the position in childcare cases, where the degree of likelihood of harm required by s.31(2) of the Children Act 1989 is related to the seriousness of the consequences if nothing is done.

As Lord Nicholls said in *In re H (Minors) (Sexual Abuse: Standard of Proof)* [1996] AC 563, at p.585:

> 'The context shows that … likely is being used in the sense of a real possibility, a possibility that cannot sensibly be ignored having regard to the nature and gravity of the feared harm in the particular case'.

69. There are very good reasons for concluding that, in this case too, Parliament did not intend that 'likely' should mean 'more likely than not'. We are used, in civil proceedings, to deciding whether or not something has happened in the past 'on the balance of probabilities'. We ask ourselves whether it is more likely than not that something happened. We usually have a good deal of evidence to help us decide what went on. Once we have done so the event is treated as a fact: it was probable, therefore it was certain …

70. But predictions are very different from findings of past fact. It is not a question of weighing the evidence and deciding whom to believe. It is a question of taking a large number of different predictive factors into account. There are cases, as my noble and learned friend Lord Rodger of Earlsferry points out, in which the doctors can predict with all too much confidence what will happen to the patient. But in many others, putting numbers on what may happen in the future is a guessing game. Who can say whether something is more than a 50/50 chance? That is what the doctor in *Latchman* found so difficult. But assessing whether something is a risk against which sensible precautions should be taken is an exercise we carry out all the time. As Girvan LJ put it in the Court of Appeal, at paragraph 19:

> 'The prediction of medical outcomes is something which is frequently difficult. There are many quiescent conditions which are subject to medical treatment or drug regimes and which can give rise to serious consequences if the treatment or the drugs are stopped. These serious consequences may not inevitably happen and in any given case it may be impossible to say whether it is more probable than not that this will occur. This being so, it seems highly likely that in the context of para. 6(1) in the disability legislation the word "likely" is used in the sense of "could well happen".'

It has often been emphasised in the cases that the burden of proving disability rests with the applicant, who must bring medical evidence to establish this. Witnesses from any branch of medicine (including the professions related to medicine such as speech therapy) will be far more comfortable with assessing the reality of the risk rather than putting precise percentages upon it.

71. Furthermore, as Mr Allen points out, the finding of disability is a threshold. In most cases, the question is whether the employer should have made reasonable adjustments to cater for the disability. The real issue in this case is whether it was reasonable to expect the employer to continue to adjust the working environment to take account of Mrs Boyle's problems with her voice or whether it was not. The employer needs to know this in real time, and not to have to wait until a tribunal has heard all the evidence and reached a conclusion about what is more likely than not to happen in the future. As with the childcare cases, the question here should be, are these adverse effects sufficiently likely to require us to consider what, if any, adjustment should be made to take account of them? …

73. Conclusion

I therefore conclude that the Court of Appeal in Northern Ireland applied the right test. *Latchman* should be overruled and dicta to the same effect disapproved. That being so, there is no need for us to go on to consider whether the tribunal's findings of fact were perverse in the light of the evidence before her. But I would have been very reluctant to do so. There was clear evidence of an underlying propensity to develop serious problems with the voice. The person who was closest to the regime which the patient was following was the speech therapist, whose evidence was that failure to follow the regime would lead to deterioration in voice and

> recurrence of the vocal nodules. The ENT surgeons found it more difficult to be so confident but that does not mean that the tribunal should not have reached the conclusion which she did.
>
> 74. However, the fact that the surgeons found it so difficult to put precise numbers on their predictions, when all were agreed on the underlying propensity to voice problems, supports the view that this was not the exercise which Parliament expected of them.

Provision is made by Schedule 1 for regulations prescribing certain matters. The Equality Act 2010 (Disability) Regulations 2010 ('2010 Regs') provide, so far as relevant, that the following are not to be treated as impairments for the purposes of the EqA:

- addictions to alcohol, nicotine or any other substance, unless originally the result of administration of medically prescribed drugs or other medical treatment (Reg 3);
- a tendency to set fires, to steal, to physical or sexual abuse of other persons, exhibitionism or voyeurism (Reg 4);
- seasonal allergic rhinitis (hayfever), save where it aggravates the effect of any other condition (Reg 4);
- tattoos or non-medical piercings or attachments (save where the former has been removed) (Reg 5).

Regulation 6 states that a child under six years of age who has an impairment which does not have a substantial and long-term adverse effect on the child's ability to carry out normal day-to-day activities will nevertheless be regarded as disabled where the impairment would normally have that effect on the ability of a person aged six years or over to carry out normal day-to-day activities. Regulation 7 provides that persons certified as blind, severely sight impaired, sight impaired or partially sighted by a consultant ophthalmologist will be regarded as disabled for the purposes of the EqA.

Obesity is not listed as a disability, but it may result in impairments which do amount to disabilities.[12] While additions themselves are excluded from recognition as disabilities, the impact of additions (lung cancer, cirrhosis, emphysema, hepatitis, depression) is not.[13] This approach is narrower than that adopted in Canada, where human rights legislation recognises addiction as a disability, and the US, in which the Americans with Disabilities Act (ADA), although excluding current illegal drug users and 'current' alcoholics, protects non-using addicts.

In *Murray v Newham Citizens Advice Bureau (No 2)* [2003] ICR 643, the EAT ruled that the claimant, who was discriminated against in connection with a conviction for violence as a result of which he had been diagnosed as a paranoid schizophrenic, was 'disabled' for the purposes of the Disability Discrimination Act 1995 (DDA). A tribunal had rejected his claim on the basis that he had a tendency to violence ('physical abuse' within the 2010 Regs). The EAT overturned on the basis (*per* Judge Serota QC) that the conditions set out in the Regulations are 'freestanding' rather than 'the direct consequence of a physical or mental impairment, within the meaning of s.1(1).' The claimant's physical violence was a consequence of his paranoid schizophrenia and, accordingly, a manifestation of his disability.

[12] This was recognised by the EAT in *Walker v Sita Information Networking Computing Ltd* UKEAT/0097/12, [2013] EqLR 476 and the CJEU in Case C-354/13, *Fag og Arbejde v Kommunernes Landforening* EU:C:2014:2463, [2015] ICR 322.

[13] See eg *Power v Panasonic UK Ltd* [2003] IRLR 151.

The decision of EAT in *Murray* was the subject of negative judicial comments in the subsequent decision in *Edmund Nuttall Ltd v Butterfield* [2006] ICR 77. The claimant was dismissed in connection with offences of indecent exposure. A tribunal found that he had been discriminated against in connection with his disability (depression) which in the tribunal's view had resulted in his offending behaviour. On appeal the employer argued that it was permitted to treat the claimant less favourably by reason of his tendency to exhibitionism notwithstanding its connection to his depression. The EAT allowed the employer's appeal, stated that the concept of 'free-standing conditions' adopted by the EAT in *Murray* was unhelpful and ruled that the tribunal should have considered the critical question, which was one of causation. If the claimant had been dismissed because of his exhibitionism his claim would fail. If, on the other hand, his depression had been an effective cause of the less favourable treatment his claim would succeed, subject to the possibility of justification. The EAT was satisfied that the claimant had been dismissed solely because of his indecent exposure and so it set aside the finding of discrimination. It expressly rejected the proposition that 'a legitimate medical impairment underlying an excluded condition, where that condition is the reason for less favourable treatment, means that disability is a reason for the less favourable treatment'.

The issue of excluded conditions has also given rise to litigation in the education context, in particular where discrimination claims are brought on behalf of children with learning difficulties and/or disabilities who have been excluded from school because of behaviour which may have arisen by reason of the schools' failures to make appropriate adjustments to manage their education related needs. In *Governing Body of X Endowed Primary School v Special Educational Needs and Disability Tribunal* [2009] EWHC 1842 (Admin), [2009] IRLR 1007 the High Court referred with approval to the decision in *Butterfield* in dismissing an appeal relating to a primary school-aged child with Attention Deficit and Hyperactivity Disorder who was excluded from school following a physical assault on a staff member. The only aspect of the child's disability in respect of which the school had failed to make reasonable adjustments was his tendency to physical abuse, which was excluded by Reg 4(1)(c) of the 2010 Regs. The High Court in *X Endowed Primary School* was not invited to consider the application of the Human Rights Act 1998 (HRA) whose provisions require that secondary legislation be disapplied to the extent that it is inconsistent with European Convention on Human Rights (ECHR) rights.[14] In *C & C v The Governing Body of a School*, however, the Upper Tribunal found that Reg 4 was inconsistent with the child's A1P1 and Article 14 rights to an education free from unjustifiable discrimination and so disapplied it.

C & C v The Governing Body of a School [2018] UKUT 269 (AAC), [2019] PTSR 857

C and C were the parents of L, a child with autism, anxiety and Pathological Demand Avoidance. They complained of discrimination on the grounds of L's disability when he was subject to a fixed-term exclusion for aggressive behaviour towards other pupils and a teaching assistant. The First-tier Tribunal dismissed this claim on the basis that L had been excluded because of his 'tendency to physical abuse', and so was not to be treated as disabled under the EqA. The parents appealed, seeking to rely on Article 14 and A1P1 ECHR.

[14] As noted in Ch 1, the continued existence of the HRA is in doubt.

Judge Rowley:

74. … there is nothing before me to suggest that I should have any reassurance that there has been a proper evaluation of the competing interests or that the appropriate scrutiny has been given in other relevant spheres. It is accepted, for example, that there has been no proper consultation, there has been no scrutiny or endorsement by Parliament on the issue relating to the fair balance, there was no impact assessment of the Regulations when they were passed, nor were the Regulations considered and approved by affirmative resolution …

77. … The current application of regulation 4(1)(c) acts as what Mr. Broach [for the claimants] described as a 'knockout blow' to any claim under the 2010 Act, to the extent that the claim relates to a tendency to physical abuse. It effectively allows schools to exclude children like L without necessarily trying to meet their needs so far as that behaviour is concerned and/or provide the support that may enable them to manage their behaviour. Thus, even if the behaviour complained of was brought about by a school's failure to make reasonable adjustments, the school's decision to exclude as a result of it could not amount to discrimination under Equality Act. This means that schools may exclude children like L without having to explain or be held accountable for what, if any, reasonable adjustments they may or may not have made in respect of managing what may loosely be described as the physically aggressive behaviour.

78. As Mr. Broach pointed out, it is crucially important to note that if the regulation were not to apply to cases such as L's, schools would still not be required to tolerate violent behaviour at all costs, nor could it be said that they would be powerless to exclude such children. Rather, they would be able to rely upon a statutory justification defence to any claim brought against them. For example, a school could argue that a claim of discrimination arising from a disability should fail because it could show that the treatment complained of was 'a proportionate means of achieving a legitimate aim' (section 15(1)(b) of the Equality Act). So long as the school could show that the exclusion of a pupil who had been violent as a result of his/her disability was a proportionate response, taking into account the legitimate aim of protecting the needs, well-being and interests of the other pupils and staff, and any reasonable adjustments that have been made, the exclusion would in all likelihood be a lawful one. The emphasis is on 'reasonable' adjustments. There is no need to show that all possible adjustments have been made, irrespective of cost or practicalities. Further, naturally, the more serious the behaviour the easier it would be to justify the exclusion under the terms of the Equality Act.

79. … Mr. Lever (the Chief Executive Officer of NAS [National Autistic Society, which intervened in the case]) cited figures from the Department for Education showing that, nationally, just over four in ten of the reasons given by headteachers for excluding pupils with autism were physical assault against an adult or pupil. As Mr. Broach said, it is very likely that those children would be deemed to have 'a tendency to physical abuse' under the current interpretation of the regulation. Mr. Broach supported this submission by reference to other figures produced by Mr. Lever. Just over 30% of the 260 enquiries made in February and March 2018 to the NAS's dedicated School Exclusions Service involved a tendency to physical abuse. I am under no illusion, therefore, that the numbers involved are particularly significant.

80. Mr. Lever says that NAS believes that it is impossible to separate behaviour caused by a lack of support for an autistic child's needs from the disability itself. Excluding such children often has a massive impact upon them. They may have struggled to find school placements in the first place and if excluded they may struggle to find them again. They may find themselves in pupil referral units with inappropriate peer groups, exposed to significant misbehaviour. They may be out of school for long periods …

81. To my mind, a particularly weighty factor to be put in the balance is that aggressive behaviour is not a choice for autistic children. Mr. Broach forcefully submitted that it is not right that children such as L should lose the protection of the Equality Act through no fault of their own.

> Mr. Lever's evidence (backed-up by academic literature) is that an autism meltdown is not the same as a temper tantrum. It is not 'bad' or 'naughty' behaviour and should not be considered as such. Rather, such challenging behaviour is increasingly being described as 'distressed behaviour.' An autistic child who feels very anxious and stressed – for example, because they are experiencing sensory overload, or are overwhelmed by social demands and interactions – may behave in a way that cannot reasonably be described as a choice. They may not understand the effect of their behaviour and any prospect of punishment is unlikely to have any deterrent effect upon them. Nevertheless, according to the guidance given in the Second X Case, the fact that they are unaware that what they are doing is wrong is an irrelevant consideration in assessing whether they have a tendency to physical abuse …
>
> 89. It is for me to weigh all of the above factors in determining whether a fair balance has been struck between the competing rights and interests. I am firmly of the view that regulation 4(1)(c) comes nowhere near striking a fair balance between the rights of children such as L on the one side and the interests of the community on the other. The profound severity of the consequences of the measure on the status group weigh extremely heavily and the arguments put in favour of the countervailing public interest by no means counterbalance them. Indeed, in my judgment, this is not a case in which the issues are finely poised. Rather, the requirements for the protection of the status group's fundamental rights comprehensively outweigh the arguments put forward for the protection of the interests of others …
>
> 93. For the reasons set out above I conclude that, in the context of education, regulation 4(1)(c) of the 2010 Regulations violates the Convention right of children with a recognised condition that is more likely to result in a 'tendency to physical abuse' not to be discriminated against under Article 14 read in conjunction with A2P1 …
>
> 100. … Identifying the subordinate legislation which has a discriminatory effect (namely regulation 4(1)(c) of the 2010 Regulations) is a perfectly straightforward task in this case. It follows that, under the provisions of section 6(1) of the Human Rights Act, it would be unlawful for me to do anything other than to decide that that regulation should be disapplied in the circumstances of this case.

Social and Medical Models of Disability

The model of disability adopted by s6 EqA is a medical, rather than a social, one. The 'social' model of disability recognises 'the close connection between the limitation experienced by individuals with disabilities, the design and structure of their environments and the attitude of the general population.'[15] It identifies social barriers and the infrastructure of society as the cause of disability; preventing participation on equal terms and denying equality of opportunity. Thus, for example, the interim analytical report of the Prime Minister's Strategy Unit in the Cabinet Office, *Improving the Life Chances of Disabled People* (June 2004) recognised that: '*Disability* is the disadvantage or restriction of activity caused by a society which takes little or no account of people who have impairments and thus excludes them from mainstream activity. *Impairment* is a characteristic, feature of attribute within an individual …' (original emphasis). The 'medical model' by contrast locates the problem of disability in the disabled person, regarding disability as an individual impairment and referring solely to physical conditions or impairments. This approach to disability rights has long been criticised.

[15] See United Nations Standard Rules on the Equalization of Opportunities for Persons with Disabilities, para 5, cited by B Doyle, 'Disabled Workers' Rights, the Disability Discrimination Act and the UN Standard Rules' (1996) 25 *Industrial Law Journal* 1, 11.

K Wells, 'The Impact of the Framework Employment Directive on UK Disability Discrimination Law' (2003) 32 *Industrial Law Journal* 253, 261–62, footnotes omitted

... anti-discrimination legislation based on the social model does not necessarily require a definition of disability with no reference to medical impairment at all. Indeed, some reference to impairment is required for the sake of identifying this issue specifically as one of disability, as opposed to disadvantage through belonging (or a perception of belonging) to a discriminated group. In considering the definition of disability in the European context, Whittle writes that the concept of impairment is a necessary basis for the definition, but goes on to make two points. First, 'it is crucial that the legislative concept of impairment does not (a) incorporate the phraseology that will encourage an assessment as to the extent of an individual's functional limitations and (b) ignore the social dimension to disability.' Second, 'the concept of impairment must be defined in a comprehensive manner to ensure that the question for the judiciary is more to do with whether an individual's past, present future or perceived impairment constitutes an appropriate disability for the purposes of the law.' Essentially, the key focus of an anti-discrimination law should be the occurrence of disability discrimination itself; such a law should not exclude victims of discrimination through its definition of disability.

The current UK system falls down on all these counts, and may be vulnerable to challenge on the basis that these failings frustrate the objectives of the Framework Employment Directive. The DDA's focus is on individual functional impairment, and not on impairments created by society. Even though the DDA contains a duty on employers to make adjustments for disabled people, it nonetheless fails to support a social construction of disability: the basis of the definition of disability on medical factors, and the tendency of tribunals to interpret this definition in a rigid and formal way, seriously undermines the potential of the legislation to address the systemic and social factors that prevent disabled people from enjoying equal employment opportunities. The DDA definition of disability may not be enough to combat discrimination 'on grounds of disability,' and the formal approach taken by tribunals in interpreting the definition may be inconsistent with the purposive approach required by Community law.

Wells' prediction has not yet proven correct (see pp 493–494 below). Even as a medical model of disability, the approach taken by the EqA is very narrow in that it adopts a functional approach which for the most part requires actual, substantial, impairment in relation to normal, day-to-day activities. This echoes the approach taken by the ADA, upon which the DDA was modelled in many respects. The ADA prohibits discrimination against those who are 'disabled' in the sense that they have: (a) a physical or mental impairment that substantially limits one or more of the[ir] major life activities ... or (b) a record of having such an impairment; or (c) [that they are] ... regarded as having such an impairment'. Australia's Disability Discrimination Act 1992, by contrast, defines as 'disability':

(a) total or partial loss of the person's bodily or mental functions; or
(b) total or partial loss of a part of the body; or
(c) the presence in the body of organisms causing ... or
(d) ... capable of causing disease or illness; or
(e) the malfunction, malformation or disfigurement of a part of the person's body; or
(f) a disorder or malfunction that results in the person learning differently from a person without the disorder or malfunction; or
(g) a disorder, illness or disease that affects a person's thought processes, perception of reality, emotions or judgement or that results in disturbed behaviour.

The Australian definition of 'disability' requires no limitation of activities (as in the case of the ADA) or 'effect on' the disabled person's 'ability to carry out ... activities' over and above the medical conditions listed.

Maeve McDonagh, 'Disability Discrimination in Australia' in Gerald Quinn, Maeve McDonagh and Cliona Kimber (eds), *Disability Discrimination Law in the US, Australia & Canada* (Dublin, Oak Tree Press, 1993) 128, footnotes omitted

The definition of disability in the [Australian] DDA follows closely the recommendations of the HREOC's (Human Rights & Equal Opportunities Commissions) Draft Position Paper. It is interesting to note therefore that the HREOC in that document expressly rejected the definition of disability set out in the … ADA.

The HREOC argued that the requirement that a person's impairment substantially limits major life activities is a source of unnecessary legal difficulties or complexities. In particular, it saw such a definition as posing difficulties for people whose condition has disabling effects only intermittently rather than continuously or whose condition is controlled by medication and/or other treatments (for example many people with epilepsy, some forms of mental illness or asthma). In addition there are those people whose disability relates to physical disfigurement, rather than loss of any functional capacity and who are not limited in any major life activities but who are nonetheless discriminated against because of prejudice. Finally, there are people who have overcome any loss of capacity (through their own efforts, with or without any assistance and the use of aids or appliances), for example, many hearing impaired people who would deny that they are limited in their ability to lead a full and active life, other than by prejudice and discrimination. As the HREOC argues 'the need for protection against discrimination does not disappear as a person becomes more able to participate in the community.' Apart from the legal difficulties raised by such definitions, it is also questionable whether a person in seeking the assistance of anti-discrimination law in asserting their ability and entitlement to participate equally may paradoxically find it necessary to argue that their ability to participate fully is in fact limited by their impairment in order to qualify for the protection of the law.

Determining Disability

The general approach to determining whether a claimant is disabled within the meaning of the EqA was set out by EAT in *Goodwin v Patent Office*. That case was decided under the DDA but remains good law.[16] Note that the *Goodwin* test will not apply where a claimant is deemed to be disabled by reason of a condition such as cancer. Nor will it assist a claimant whose 'impairment' consists of or results in an excluded matter such as a tendency to exhibitionism.[17]

***Goodwin v Patent Office* [1998] UKEAT 57_98_2110, [1999] ICR 302**

A tribunal had decided that the claimant, who had been diagnosed with paranoid schizophrenia and who had been dismissed partly because of 'bizarre behaviour' consistent with that diagnosis, was not disabled. The tribunal had concluded that the claimant's normal day-to-day activities were not substantially adversely affected by his condition which resulted in paranoia, 'thought broadcasting' when he imagined that other people could access his thoughts, and auditory hallucinations which, in turn, affected his ability to concentrate on his work and to watch television. According to the majority, the claimant 'must have been able to remember, to organise his thoughts and plan a course of action and execute it, in order to carry out his day-to-day activities of looking after

[16] See eg *Saad v University Hospital Southampton NHS Trust* UKEAT/0184/14, [2014] All ER (D) 77 (Dec), though note the degree of caution expressed by the CA in *Sullivan v Bury Street Capital Ltd* [2022] IRLR 159 §75 about the EAT's approach in *Goodwin* to the EHRC's Code of Practice.

[17] Subject for the moment to the HRA.

himself at home, getting to and from work and carrying out his work.' The EAT ruled that the tribunal had erred in concluding 'from the finding that the claimant was able to cope at home ... that, therefore, he fell outwith the provisions of the Act'. It based its decision partly on the tribunal's failure to refer to the statutory guidance then in force[18], though Morison J warned that 'in many cases the question whether a person is disabled within the meaning of the Act can admit of only one answer. In these cases it would be wrong to search the Guide and use what it says as some kind of extra hurdle over which the applicant must jump.' Rather than remit to a tribunal the question whether or not the claimant was disabled, the EAT concluded that: 'in this case the question whether the applicant was, at the relevant time, disabled within the meaning of the Act admitted only one conclusion: he was.'

Morison J, for the Court, interpreted the guidance then in force as establishing four 'conditions' which had to be satisfied before a complainant could be regarded as 'disabled.'

> *(1) The impairment condition*
>
> The applicant must have either a physical or mental impairment ...[19]
>
> *(2) The adverse effect condition*
>
> In many ways, this may be the most difficult of the four conditions to judge ... The fact that a person can carry out such activities does not mean that his ability to carry them out has not been impaired ... Furthermore, disabled persons are likely, habitually, to 'play down' the effect that their disabilities have on their daily lives. If asked whether they are able to cope at home, the answer may well be 'yes,' even though, on analysis, many of the ordinary day-to-day tasks were done with great difficulty due to the person's impaired ability to carry them out ...'
>
> *(3) The substantial condition*
>
> 'Substantial' might mean 'very large' or it might mean 'more than minor or trivial.' Reference to the Guide shows that the word has been used in the latter sense ... The tribunal will wish to examine how the applicant's abilities had actually been affected at the material time, whilst on medication, and then to address their minds to the difficult question as to the effects which they think there would have been but for the medication: the deduced effects. The question is then whether the actual and deduced effects on the applicant's abilities to carry out normal day-to-day activities is clearly more than trivial.
>
> In many cases, the tribunal will be able to reach a conclusion on these matters without reference to the statutory Guidance (which is there to illuminate what is not reasonably clear ... Although Parliament has linked the effect of medication to the 'substantial condition,' as we have already said, splitting the statutory words into conditions should not divert attention from the definition as a whole, and in determining whether the adverse effect condition is fulfilled the tribunal will take into account deduced effects.
>
> *(4) The long-term condition*
>
> Paragraph 2 of Schedule 1 applies, as does paragraph B of the Guidance, where reference to it is necessary. The provisions appear to be straightforward and we have nothing useful to say about them.

[18] See now The Disability Unit, 'Guidance on matters to be taken into account in determining questions relating to the definition of disability' (https://www.gov.uk/government/publications/equality-act-guidance/disability-equality-act-2010-guidance-on-matters-to-be-taken-into-account-in-determining-questions-relating-to-the-definition-of-disability-html), discussed at pp 491–493 & 499–501 below.

[19] At the time a mental condition had to be 'clinically well recognised'. That is no longer the case. Nor does an 'impairment' does not have to result from a recognised illness: *Millar v ICR* [2006] IRLR 112.

The question is not whether the claimant is disabled at the time of the tribunal hearing but whether he or she was disabled at the time of the alleged discrimination.[20] In determining whether a claimant was so disabled a tribunal should avoid being unduly influenced by how a claimant presents him or herself and should focus on the statutory questions rather than adopting a 'common sense' approach.[21] Medical evidence will often be necessary but the determination of disability for the purposes of the EqA is a legal rather than a medical task and it is for the tribunal to determine whether impairments relied upon were substantial (see further below).[22]

Impairment

The Government has issued guidance 'on matters to be taken into account in determining questions relating to the definition of disability'. The current guidance was issued under the EqA in 2011 but it is very similar to previous guidance issued under the DDA. Schedule 1 para 12 EqA provides that an employment tribunal or court which is determining for any purpose of the Act whether a person's impairment has a substantial and long-term adverse effect on their ability to carry out normal day-to-day activities, is required to take into account any of this guidance which appears to it to be relevant though, as the Guidance itself makes clear, it 'does not impose any legal obligations in itself, nor is it an authoritative statement of the law.' It is clear from a series of cases that failures by tribunals to refer to the relevant sections of the Guidance may well result in a successful appeal.[23]

The Guidance provides (A4) that 'It is not possible to provide an exhaustive list of conditions that qualify as impairments for the purposes of the Act' and that 'Any attempt to do so would inevitably become out of date as medical knowledge advanced'. It goes on to state, however, as follows:

HM Government Office for Disability Issues. *Guidance on matters to be taken into account in determining questions relating to the definition of disability* (2011)[24]

A5. A disability can arise from a wide range of impairments which can be:

- sensory impairments, such as those affecting sight or hearing;
- impairments with fluctuating or recurring effects such as rheumatoid arthritis, myalgic encephalitis (ME), chronic fatigue syndrome (CFS), fibromyalgia, depression and epilepsy;
- progressive, such as motor neurone disease, muscular dystrophy, and forms of dementia;
- auto-immune conditions such as systemic lupus erythematosis (SLE);
- organ specific, including respiratory conditions, such as asthma, and cardiovascular diseases, including thrombosis, stroke and heart disease;

[20] *McDougall v Richmond Adult Community College* [2008] ICR 431.

[21] *Mahon v Accuread Ltd* UKEAT/0081/08, [2008] All ER (D) 217 (Oct); *Vicary v British Telecommunications plc* [1999] IRLR 680.

[22] *Abadeh v British Telecommunications plc* [2001] ICR 156.

[23] *Archibald v Fife Council* [2004] ICR 954 but note the statement in *Goodwin* that the guidance did not need to be referred to where the position was clear. See also *Elliott v Dorset CC* [2021] IRLR 880 in Judge James Tayler stated that the EHRC's Codes and the Guidance were often very helpful but are not to be followed without thought or where inconsistent with statute, or to be construed as if statutes, and that where a statutory provision provides a simple answer additional complexity should not be introduced by consideration of the Code or Guidance. Doubt has been cast upon aspects of the current guidance by the EAT in *Banaszczyk v Booker Ltd* [2016] IRLR 273 (see pp 494–496 below). See also *SCA Packaging v Boyle*, extracted at pp 482–484 above, in which the House of Lords stated that 'statutory construction remains a matter for the courts, not for Departmental Guidance', and *Sullivan v Bury Street Capital*, n 16 above, in which the CA said that failure to mention something in the statutory guidance could not be regarded as an error of law, particularly if the parties had not drawn attention to it.

[24] n 18 above.

- developmental, such as autistic spectrum disorders (ASD), dyslexia and dyspraxia;
- learning disabilities;
- mental health conditions with symptoms such as anxiety, low mood, panic attacks, phobias, or unshared perceptions; eating disorders; bipolar affective disorders; obsessive compulsive disorders; personality disorders; post traumatic stress disorder, and some self-harming behaviour;
- mental illnesses, such as depression and schizophrenia;
- produced by injury to the body, including to the brain.

A6. *It may not always be possible, nor is it necessary, to categorise a condition as either a physical or a mental impairment.* The underlying cause of the impairment may be hard to establish. There may be adverse effects which are both physical and mental in nature. Furthermore, effects of a mainly physical nature may stem from an underlying mental impairment, and vice versa … [original emphasis].

Adverse Effect

It follows from the requirement (except in specified cases) for functional impairment that people are not protected by the EqA from discrimination by reason of a relatively minor medical condition has some real or perceived impact on their ability to perform a particular function, or because of a genetic predisposition to cancer or some other condition.[25] It is important to remember, however, that someone who has had a qualifying impairment in the past but who is no longer functionally impaired continues to be protected as a disabled person by the EqA.[26]

The DDA had provided a list of capabilities including mobility, manual dexterity and the ability to concentrate, learn and understand which were to be considered when assessing impact on normal day-to-day activities. This list was excluded from the EqA in order to make it easier for people to demonstrate disability and so some caution may be required in dealing with pre-EqA caselaw.

The adverse effect has to be on 'normal day to day activities'. The DDA contained a list of qualifying normal day-to-day activities. The EqA does not.

HM Government Office for Disability Issues. *Guidance on matters to be taken into account in determining questions relating to the definition of disability* (2011)

D2. … It is not possible to provide an exhaustive list of day-to-day activities, although guidance on this matter is given here and illustrative examples of when it would, and would not, be reasonable to regard an impairment as having a substantial adverse effect on the ability to carry out normal day-to-day activities are shown in the Appendix.

D3. In general, day-to-day activities are things people do on a regular or daily basis, and examples include shopping, reading and writing, having a conversation or using the telephone, watching television, getting washed and dressed, preparing and eating food, carrying out household tasks, walking and travelling by various forms of transport, and taking part in social activities. Normal day-to-day activities can include general work-related activities, and study and education-related activities, such as interacting with colleagues, following instructions, using a computer, driving, carrying out interviews, preparing written documents, and keeping to a timetable or a shift pattern.

D4. The term 'normal day-to-day activities' is not intended to include activities which are normal only for a particular person, or a small group of people. In deciding whether an activity is a

[25] The GDPR however impacts on the ability of employers to perform or rely on genetic testing.

[26] Other than in relation to in Part 12 (Transport) and s190 EqA (improvements to let dwelling houses).

normal day-to-day activity, account should be taken of how far it is carried out by people on a daily or frequent basis. In this context, 'normal' should be given its ordinary, everyday meaning.

D5. A normal day-to-day activity is not necessarily one that is carried out by a majority of people. For example, it is possible that some activities might be carried out only, or more predominantly, by people of a particular gender, such as breast-feeding or applying make-up, and cannot therefore be said to be normal for most people. They would nevertheless be considered to be normal day-to-day activities …

D8. Where activities are themselves highly specialised or involve highly specialised levels of attainment, they would not be regarded as normal day-to-day activities for most people. In some instances work-related activities are so highly specialised that they would not be regarded as normal day-to-day activities.

[example]

A watch repairer carries out delicate work with highly specialised tools. He develops tenosynovitis. This restricts his ability to carry out delicate work though he is able to carry out activities such as general household repairs using more substantial tools.

Although the delicate work is a normal working activity for a person in his profession, it would not be regarded as a normal day-to-day activity for most people.

D9. The same is true of other specialised activities such as playing a musical instrument to a high standard of achievement; taking part in activities where very specific skills or level of ability are required; or playing a particular sport to a high level of ability, such as would be required for a professional footballer or athlete. Where activities involve highly specialised skills or levels of attainment, they would not be regarded as normal day-to-day activities for most people.

[example]

A woman plays the piano to a high standard, and often takes part in public performances. She has developed carpal tunnel syndrome in her wrists. This does not prevent her from playing the piano, but she cannot achieve such a high standard.

This restriction would not be an adverse effect on a normal day-to-day activity, because playing the piano to such a specialised level would not be normal for most people.

In *Ekpe v Commissioner of Police of the Metropolis* [2001] ICR 1084 the EAT overruled a tribunal decision that the claimant's inability to put rollers in her hair or to use her right hand to apply make-up did not impair her 'normal day-to-day activities,' as these activities were carried on almost exclusively by women and were therefore not to be considered 'normal'(!). The EAT ruled that 'normal' under the DDA is anything not abnormal or unusual, rather than something the majority of people do.

The emphasis on normal day-to-day activities does not mean that the effect of an impairment on work activities is irrelevant, as work might well include normal day-to-day activities.[27] Notwithstanding this, there is a question whether the EqA's approach to disability is consistent with that of the CJEU to Council Directive 2000/78's regulation of disability discrimination. In Case C-13/05, *Chacon Navas v Eurest Colectividades SA* EU:C:2006:456 [2006] ECR I-6467, [2007] ICR 1 the CJEU ruled that 'disability' included a 'limitation which results in particular from physical, mental or psychological impairments and which hinders the participation of the person concerned in professional life'. This raised the possibility that someone ought to be considered disabled under the Directive because of a functional impairment with a work-related activity which might nevertheless not be considered as a 'normal day to day activity'. And in Case C-355/11, *HK Danmark, acting on*

[27] See eg *Law Hospital NHS Trust v Rush* [2001] IRLR 611.

behalf of Ring v Dansk almennyttigt Boligselskab EU:C:2013:222, [2013] ICR 851 ('*Ring*'), the CJEU remarked that the EU was a signatory to the UN Convention on the Rights of Persons with Disabilities which required that the concept of disability be 'understood as referring to a limitation which results in particular from physical, mental or psychological impairments which in interaction with various barriers may hinder the full and effective participation of the persons concerned in professional life on an equal basis with other workers'.[28] The Court also made clear that disability did not require a complete exclusion from work or professional life. It is entirely possible that the CJEU, as it now is, would regard the watch repairer in the example above as disabled by reason of the impact of his tenosynovitis on his ability to carry out delicate work or the pianist as disabled by her carpal tunnel syndrome. This was recognised by the EAT in the following decision.

***Banaszczyk v Booker Ltd* [2016] UKEAT 0132_15_0102, [2016] IRLR 273**

The claimant was employed as a picker by the respondent which operated a chain of wholesale warehouses. His job was to select and load cases of goods. Workers were expected to have a 'pick rate' of pick 210 cases per hour. After suffering a spinal injury the claimant was unable to meet the minimum pick rate and was dismissed on the ground of incapability. His disability discrimination claim was rejected by an employment tribunal which ruled that his admitted long-term impairment did not impact on his ability to carry out normal day-to-day activities. The EAT allowed his appeal.

HHJ Richardson (for the EAT):

21. EU law

It is common ground between the parties that UK employment tribunals must apply European law relating to disability discrimination in employment and occupation …

22. The Equality Directive itself did not lay down any definition of disability. The European Court of Justice has done so most recently in *Ring*, revisiting *Chacón Navas* in the light of the EU's approval of the United Nations Convention on the Rights of Persons with Disabilities …

33. … the definition of disability in the 2010 Act and the Guidance do not apply only in the field of employment and occupation. In that field, however, it is now established law that the definition of 'disability' must be applied in a way which gives effect to EU law.

34. In *Paterson* [*v Metropolitan Police Comr* [2007] ICR 1522] the claimant suffered from dyslexia. This condition had not prevented him from passing a number of examinations and rising to the post of chief inspector. His case was that he required adjustments to the processes for determining whether he might be promoted to superintendent. The employment tribunal held that the taking of promotion examinations or assessments was not a normal day-to-day activity. The Employment Appeal Tribunal allowed the appeal.

[28] See similarly Case C-354/13, *Fag og Arbejde v Kommunernes Landforening* EU:C:2014:2463, [2015] ICR 322; Case C-395/15, *Daouidi v Bootes Plus SL* EU:C:2016:917, [2017] ICR 420. In *Sullivan v Bury Street Capital*, n 16 above, the CA rejected an argument that the EqA's approach to disability was inconsistent with these authorities. Note also that in In Case C-363/12, *Z v A Department* EU:C:2014:159, [2014] IRLR 563 the CJEU interpreted the concept of disability narrowly so as to exclude from protection the claimant, who had been born without a womb and wished to access paid leave in connection with a surrogacy arrangement; the claimant's womb-less state, though an impairment, did not hinder her full and effective participation in professional life on an equal basis with other workers.

35. On the question of day-to-day activity the Employment Appeal Tribunal held that carrying out an assessment or examination is properly to be described as a normal day-to-day activity. The Employment Appeal Tribunal said

> '66. … We would have reached that conclusion simply taking domestic law on its own without any reference to the decision in *Chacón*. In our view carrying out an assessment or examination is properly to be described as a normal day-to-day activity. Moreover, as we have said, in our view the act of reading and comprehension is itself a normal day-to-day activity. In any event, whatever ambiguity there may be about that, in our view the decision of the Court of Justice in *Chacón Navas* is decisive of this case.
>
> 67. We must read s.1 [of the 1995 Act] in a way which gives effect to EU law. We think it can be readily done, simply by giving a meaning to day-to-day activities which encompasses the activities which are relevant to participation in professional life. Appropriate measures must be taken to enable a worker to advance in his or her employment. Since the effect of the disability may adversely affect promotion prospects, then it must be said to hinder participation in professional life.'

36. On the question whether the impairment had a substantial effect on the claimant's ability to carry out the normal day-to-day activity, the Employment Appeal Tribunal said:

> '68. … In our judgment, the only proper basis, as the Guidance makes clear, is to compare the effect on the individual of the disability, and this involves considering how he in fact carries out the activity compared with how he would do if not suffering the impairment. If that difference is more than the kind of difference one might expect taking a cross-section of the population, then the effects are substantial.'

37. The focus is therefore upon the impact of the impairment on the individual. The question is not whether the individual is disadvantaged compared with the population as a whole. The Employment Appeal Tribunal explained why this was so in paragraph 70 of its judgment:

> '70. … The purpose of the legislation, at least in part, is to assist those who are disabled to overcome the disadvantages which stem from a physical or mental impairment … Take the case of someone who has all the skills to be a highly successful accountant, but lacks manual dexterity. This may require that he or she should be given longer to do the relevant examinations. It would surely be no answer and would be wholly inconsistent with the purposes of the legislation, simply to say that that individual was not disadvantaged when compared with the population at large and therefore no obligation to make the adjustment arose …'

38. This approach was applied in [*CC Dumfries & Galloway Constabulary v*] *Adams* [[2009] ICR 1034] (police work on night shifts a normal day-to-day activity) and *Sobhi* [*v Commissioner of Police of the Metropolis* [2013] EqLR 785] (completion of an application to become a police officer, including a security questionnaire, a normal day-to-day activity) …

46. It is plain that the claimant's physical impairment had an adverse effect on his ability to do his work. The first question for the employment judge was whether the activities affected were 'normal day-to-day activities', applying the approach laid down in *Paterson* and *Ring*. The facts about his normal day-to-day activities at work were undisputed. He was a warehouse operative lifting and moving goods in part manually and in part by the use of a pallet truck; and the goods might weigh up to 25kg. This is, in the context of work, a normal day-to-day activity: no-one with any knowledge of modern UK life working life could doubt that large numbers of people are employed to work lifting and moving cases of up to 25kg across a range of occupations, including in particular occupations concerned with warehousing and distribution.

47. Miss Quigley [for the employer] focused her submissions on the pick rate: she argued that this feature of the claimant's work meant that what he did was not a 'normal day-to-day

activity'. I reject that submission. It confuses the activity itself with a particular requirement of an employer as to the speed with which the activity is performed. It is to my mind essential, if disability law is to be applied correctly, to define the relevant activity of working or professional life broadly: care should be taken before including in the definition the very feature which constitutes a barrier to the disabled individual's participation in that activity. In this case the activity was the lifting and movement of goods manually; the employer's 'pick rate' was not the activity, but a particular requirement of the employer as to the manner and speed of performance.

48. Miss Quigley also sought to equate the claimant's case with that of the specialist worker such as the silversmith or watchmaker. I think she may have intended to submit that it was the high 'pick rate' which took the claimant into the class of specialist worker. I have already explained why the day-to-day activity is not to be defined by reference to the 'pick rate'. If she intended to say that the activity of lifting and moving cases itself took the claimant into the class of specialist worker, I disagree. I confess to some doubt whether the 2011 Guidance relating to specialised activities remains entirely correct in the employment context in the light of the *Ring* definition; but I need not address that matter further since it is not remotely arguable that the claimant's activities could be said to fall into that class.'

The broad approach to disability adopted by the EAT in *Banaszczyk v Booker Ltd* [2016] IRLR 273 was also adopted by the CA in the following case.

***CC Norfolk v Coffey* [2019] EWCA Civ 1061, [2020] ICR 145**

The claimant's application for a transfer from her police constable role in Wiltshire Police to one with Norfolk was denied because she had some hearing loss and tinnitus. The claimant claimed to have been discriminated against on the basis of perceived disability. An employment tribunal upheld her claim and the EAT dismissed the appeal after which the Chief Constable appealed again. One question on appeal concerned the parameters of 'normal day-to-day activities':

Underhill LJ (for the Court):

37. … Mr Strelitz [for the Chief Constable] submitted that the requirements of the role of a front-line police officer were exceptional in character and could not sensibly be treated as falling within that description. He referred us to the Guidance … paras D8–D10 ….

38. … The ET appears to have taken it for granted that if the Claimant's hearing loss prevented her from performing a front-line role the statutory definition would be satisfied. In the EAT Judge Richardson did address the issue, but only at a fairly general level. At paras 52–53 of his judgment he said:

'52. It is established law that in the field of employment and occupation the definition of "disability" in the 2010 Act must be applied in a way which gives effect to EU law. The definition of disability has been laid down by the ECJ[29] most recently in [the *Ring* case] …

53. This impacts in particular on the definition of "day-to-day activities"; the phrase must be given an interpretation which encompasses the activities which are relevant to participation in professional life. Thus, in the leading UK case, *Paterson v Commissioner of Police of*

[29] The European Court of Justice, also referred to throughout this book at the CJEU (Court of Justice of the European Union).

> *the Metropolis* [2007] IRLR 763 it was held that the taking of a professional examination for promotion to a high grade was a day-to-day activity.'…

40. Mr Strelitz submitted that Judge Richardson's reliance on *Paterson* and *Ring* was misplaced. He referred to the decision of Lady Smith in the EAT in *Chief Constable of Lothian and Borders Police v Cumming* [2010] IRLR 109. The claimant was a civilian police employee who was also a special constable. She suffered from amblyopia in one eye, resulting in mildly impaired vision, but when she had been appointed a special constable she was given a certificate of fitness and found to have excellent binocular vision. She applied to become a police officer and was rejected because her eyesight did not meet the prescribed standard. She brought proceedings for disability discrimination, but she relied on actual rather than perceived disability. The ET found that her impairment had a substantial adverse effect, on two alternative bases – (a) that her rejection as a police constable recruitment itself constituted a substantial adverse effect, relying on what was said to be the reasoning in *Chacón Navas* and *Paterson*; and (b) that in any event the effect of the amblyopia on her vision was substantial. The EAT allowed the Chief Constable's appeal. Mr Strelitz relied on Lady Smith's reasoning on the first alternative. In summary, she held that it was not legitimate to shortcut the enquiry into the actual physical/mental adverse effects of an impairment and rely simply on the fact that it had led to a refusal of employment. As she put it at para 36 of her judgment (p 113):

> 'The status of disability for the purposes of the [1995 Act] cannot be dependent on the decision of the employer as to how to react to the employee's impairment yet that is, in essence, the argument that the claimant seeks to advance.'

She said that the claimant's approach 'proceeds on a misunderstanding of *Paterson* and *Chacón Navas*'.

41. Mr Strelitz submitted that Lady Smith's reasoning in *Cumming* was authority for the proposition that *Chacón Navas* and *Ring* are only concerned with 'ordinary work activities' and that that excluded the duties of a front-line police officer, which he described as 'unique'. I do not accept that submission. As appears from the previous paragraph, the issue which she was addressing in the passage on which he relies had nothing to do with what constitute 'normal day-to-day activities' in a work context, or, more particularly, in the context of front-line police work: indeed the submission that she was addressing, and rejecting (as it seems to me, rightly), would have meant that that question did not even arise.

42. I return, therefore, to Judge Richardson's approach. The proposition that he was concerned to establish – see para 53 of his judgment – was simply that; '[the phrase "normal day-to-day activities"] should be given an interpretation which encompasses the activities which are relevant to participation in professional life'. That seems to me wholly unexceptionable, save that 'working life' might be more appropriate than 'professional life' (which I think he used only because it appeared in *Paterson*). However, it does not directly address Mr Strelitz's submission before us … that the particular activities required of a front-line police officer are not 'normal' and are more akin to the highly specialised capabilities required of the watchmaker or concert pianist mentioned in the Guidance.

43. As to that, the impairment with which we are here concerned relates to hearing. There was no evidence before the ET, and it seems unlikely, that front-line officers need to have peculiarly acute hearing: they are not piano-tuners or audio engineers. I accept, of course, that there will be occasions in the course of their duties when it is important that they be able to listen carefully or hear particular sounds (even if not a fly's foot-fall), but that is characteristic of many situations both at work and outside it. Although I fully accept that the work of a front-line police officer is in many respects unique and that it is often challenging and sometimes dangerous, the multifarious activities that it involves – or at least those for which good hearing is relevant – are nevertheless for the purpose of the Act 'normal day-to-day activities'…

In *Igweike v TSB Bank plc* [2020] IRLR 267 the EAT ruled that a tribunal had been entitled to rule that a worker was not disabled by the impact on him of his father's death, which had produced in him an adverse grief reaction. Judge Auerbach ruled that there was a distinction between such a reaction and an impairment for the purposes of the EqA. He went on to state, however, that the effect on normal day-to-day activities required for a finding of disability could be established by reference to work activities even if there was no effect on activities outside work or the particular job.

Substantial Effects and Progressive Conditions

A 'substantial' effect is one (s212 EqA) which is 'more than minor or trivial'. This is not a high threshold: in *Aderemi v London and South Eastern Railway Ltd* [2013] ICR 591 Langstaff P stated that 'the Act itself does not create a spectrum running smoothly from those matters which are clearly of substantial effect to those matters which are clearly trivial but provides for a bifurcation: unless a matter can be classified as within the heading "trivial" or "insubstantial", it must be treated as substantial. There is therefore little room for any form of sliding scale between one and the other'.

The Guidance provides (section B) that whether any particular impairment should be considered 'substantial' requires consideration of: the time taken by the person 'to carry out a normal day-to-day activity'; the way in which such an activity is carried out; the 'cumulative effects' where more than a single day-to-day activity is affected; the extent to which the person has or ought to have developed 'coping strategies'; and the effects of the environment on the impairment. Among the examples of substantial impairment provided by the Guidance are those of:

- a 10-year-old child with cerebral palsy who is able to do most things for himself but who because of muscle stiffness, poor balance and uncoordinated movements associated with his condition takes much longer to eat, drink, wash, and get dressed;
- A person with obsessive compulsive disorder (OCD) who 'constantly checks and rechecks that electrical appliances are switched off and that the doors are locked when leaving home';
- Someone with depression who experiences symptoms including 'loss of energy and motivation that makes even the simplest of tasks or decisions seem quite difficult', forgetfulness and inability to plan ahead as a result of which he 'finds it difficult to get up in the morning, get washed and dressed, and prepare breakfast … often run[s] out of food before he thinks of going shopping again' and frequently leaves household tasks undone';
- A person who has mild learning disability and a mild speech impairment which together result in slower than average assimilation of information and an impaired ability to form certain words';
- A woman with rheumatoid arthritis for the last three years whose effects are particularly bad during autumn and winter months but mild during the summer months. The Guidance advises that 'It is necessary to consider the overall impact of the arthritis, and the extent to which it has a substantial adverse effect on her ability to carry out day-to-day activities such as walking, undertaking household tasks, and getting washed and dressed.'

HM Disability Unit, *Guidance on matters to be taken into account in determining questions relating to the definition of disability* (2011)[30]

B7. Account should be taken of how far a person can *reasonably* be expected to modify his or her behaviour, for example by use of a coping or avoidance strategy, to prevent or reduce the effects of an impairment on normal day-to-day activities. In some instances, a coping or avoidance strategy might alter the effects of the impairment to the extent that they are no longer substantial and the person would no longer meet the definition of disability. In other instances, even with the coping or avoidance strategy, there is still an adverse effect on the carrying out of normal day-to-day activities.[31]

For example, a person who needs to avoid certain substances because of allergies may find the day-to-day activity of eating substantially affected. Account should be taken of the degree to which a person can reasonably be expected to behave in such a way that the impairment ceases to have a substantial adverse effect on his or her ability to carry out normal day-to-day activities …

B8. Similarly, it would be reasonable to expect a person with a phobia to avoid extreme activities or situations that would aggravate their condition. It would not be reasonable to expect him or her to give up, or modify, normal activities that might exacerbate the symptoms.

The Guidance states that it might be 'reasonable to expect a person who has chronic back pain to avoid extreme activities such as skiing' or someone with 'acrophobia (extreme fear of heights which can induce panic attacks) … to avoid the top of extremely high buildings, such as the Eiffel Tower' but 'not … to expect the [first] person to give up, or modify, more normal activities that might exacerbate the symptoms; such as shopping, or using public transport' or the second to avoid all multi-storey buildings'. Also, and importantly:

B9. Account should also be taken of where a person avoids doing things which, for example, cause pain, fatigue or substantial social embarrassment, or avoids doing things because of a loss of energy and motivation. It would not be reasonable to conclude that a person who employed an avoidance strategy was not a disabled person. In determining a question as to whether a person meets the definition of disability it is important to consider the things that a person cannot do, or can only do with difficulty.

[example]

In order to manage her mental health condition, a woman who experiences panic attacks finds that she can manage daily tasks, such as going to work, if she can avoid the stress of travelling in the rush hour. In determining whether she meets the definition of disability, consideration should be given to the extent to which it is reasonable to expect her to place such restrictions on her working and personal life.

B10. In some cases, people have coping or avoidance strategies which cease to work in certain circumstances (for example, where someone who has dyslexia is placed under stress). If it is possible that a person's ability to manage the effects of an impairment will break down so that effects will sometimes still occur, this possibility must be taken into account when assessing the effects of the impairment …

The Appendix to the Guidance provides 'an illustrative and non-exhaustive list of factors which, if they are experienced by a person, *it would be reasonable* to regard as having a

[30] n 18 above.

[31] Note that the imposition of significant 'coping' obligations would be inconsistent with the caselaw: see, for example, *Vicary* n 21 above.

substantial adverse effect on normal day-to-day activities' (original emphasis). These include:

- 'Difficulty carrying out activities associated with toileting, or caused by frequent minor incontinence';
- 'Difficulty preparing a meal, for example, because of restricted ability to do things like open cans or packages, or because of an inability to understand and follow a simple recipe';
- 'Difficulty eating; for example, because of an inability to co-ordinate the use of a knife and fork, a need for assistance, or the effect of an eating disorder';
- 'Difficulty going out of doors unaccompanied, for example, because the person has a phobia, a physical restriction, or a learning disability';
- 'Difficulty waiting or queuing, for example, because of a lack of understanding of the concept, or because of pain or fatigue when standing for prolonged periods';
- 'Difficulty using transport; for example, because of physical restrictions, pain or fatigue, a frequent need for a lavatory or as a result of a mental impairment or learning disability';
- 'Difficulty entering or staying in environments that the person perceives as strange or frightening;
- Behaviour which challenges people around the person, making it difficult for the person to be accepted in public places';
- 'Persistent difficulty crossing a road safely, for example, because of physical restrictions or a failure to understand and manage the risk';
- 'Persistent general low motivation or loss of interest in everyday activities';
- 'Inability to converse, or give instructions orally, in the person's native spoken language';
- 'Frequent confused behaviour, intrusive thoughts, feelings of being controlled, or delusions';
- 'Persistently wanting to avoid people or significant difficulty taking part in normal social interaction or forming social relationships, for example because of a mental health condition or disorder';
- 'Compulsive activities or behaviour, or difficulty in adapting after a reasonable period to minor changes in a routine'.

Among the 'factors which, if they are experienced by a person, *it would not be reasonable* to regard as having a substantial adverse effect on normal day-to-day activities' (original emphasis) are:

- 'Inability to move heavy objects without assistance or a mechanical aid, such as moving a large suitcase or heavy piece of furniture without a trolley';
- 'Experiencing some discomfort as a result of travelling, for example by car or plane, for a journey lasting more than two hours';
- 'Experiencing some tiredness or minor discomfort as a result of walking unaided for a distance of about 1.5 kilometres or one mile';
- 'Minor problems with writing or spelling';
- 'Inability to reach typing speeds standardised for secretarial work';

- 'Inability to fill in a long, detailed, technical document, which is in the person's native language, without assistance';
- 'Inability to speak in front of an audience simply as a result of nervousness';
- 'Inability to articulate certain sounds due to a lisp';
- 'Inability to hold a conversation in a very noisy place, such as a factory floor, a pop concert, sporting event or alongside a busy main road';
- 'Inability to concentrate on a task requiring application over several hours';
- 'Simple inability to distinguish between red and green, which is not accompanied by any other effect such as blurring of vision';
- 'Infrequent minor incontinence';
- 'Inability to undertake activities requiring delicate hand movements, such as threading a small needle or picking up a pin'.

In *Leonard v Southern Derbyshire Chamber of Commerce* [2001] IRLR 19 EAT emphasised that tribunals ought not to balance what a claimant could against what she could not do for the purposes of determining whether her condition substantially impaired her ability to carry out normal day-to-day activities. In that case the claimant, who was clinically depressed, was able to eat and drink and catch a ball, but could not negotiate pavement edges safely. EAT ruled that the tribunal had erred in balancing the former abilities against the latter disability as her ability to catch a ball did not assist the claimant in negotiating pavements. The tribunal ought to concentrate on what a claimant cannot do or can do only with difficulty. In *Vicary v British Telecommunications plc* [1999] IRLR 680 the EAT ruled that a tribunal had erred in deciding that the claimant, who could not 'carry a washing basket, bag of shopping, a suitcase, briefcase or hand-held handbag', was not disabled because she could 'rely upon shoulder bags rather than hand-held bags and carry washing in small quantities and unloading shopping in trolleys in small quantities' (§15 *per* Morison J). Similarly in *Aderemi v London and South Eastern Railway Ltd* (p 498 above) Langstaff P emphasised the importance of focusing (§14) 'upon that which a Claimant maintains he cannot do as a result of his physical or mental impairment.'

The Guidance suggests at B1 that 'The requirement that an adverse effect be substantial reflects the general understanding of "disability" as a limitation going beyond the normal differences in ability which may exist among people. A "substantial" effect is more than would be produced by the sort of physical or mental conditions experienced by many people which have only minor effects. A "substantial" effect is one which is more than "minor" or "trivial".' As *Harvey on Industrial Relations* points out (Division L [156]) this 'gloss' was called into question in *Elliott v Dorset County Council* [2021] IRLR 880.

***Harvey on Industrial Relations* Division L, [156]**

In *Elliott*, Judge Tayler identified that there are differences in ability amongst people who are not disabled that are much more than minor or trivial. He recognised the great assistance that the Code and Guidance often provide but said that they are not to be followed without thought, or to be construed as if statutes, and must always give way to the statutory provisions if, on a proper construction, they differ from the Code or Guidance. Where consideration of the statutory provision provides a simple answer, it is erroneous to find additional complexity by considering the Code or Guidance. On the right approach to 'substantial adverse effect', he said:

> 'There is a potential internal inconsistency between an adverse effect being something that is "more than minor or trivial" and looking for a "limitation going beyond the normal differences

> in ability which might exist among people". [...] The starting point is to remember that the statutory definition of the word "substantial" is "more than minor or trivial". If the adverse effect has a more than minor or trivial effect on the ability of a person to carry out day-to-day activities the definition is met; no consideration of the abilities of some group of people, or section of the population, can alter that determination.' (at [38])
>
> 'The ... adverse effect of an impairment on a person is to be compared with the position of the same person, absent the impairment. If the impairment has a more than minor or trivial effect on the abilities of the person compared to those s/he would have absent the impairment, then the substantial condition is made out. (at [43])'

As *Harvey* makes clear, Judge Tayler went on to comment on the decision in *Paterson*, in which Elias J had said both that the question whether an adverse impact is substantial does not require a comparison with 'the population at large ... [but] between the way in which the individual in fact carries out the activity in question and how he would carry it out if not impaired' (§27) and (at §68) that the difference between how the claimant carries out the activity and how he or she would do if not suffering the impairment would indicate a substantial adverse effect if it is 'more than the kind of difference one might expect taking a cross-section of the population':

> Judge Tayler concluded that the opinion of Elias J at [68] in *Paterson* could be reconciled with this because the EAT in the latter case plainly did not make a comparison with a cross-section of the population as a whole but were suggesting a comparison with a broad cross-section of people broadly similar to the claimant, other than that they did not have the alleged disability, which Judge Tayler said one might imagine as a rough and ready cross-section of the population taken at approximately a claimant's level. Judge Tayler stressed that he was not suggesting that there should be some elaborate construction of pools of comparison, or detailed analysis of groups of 'people', because the key question was the effect of the impairment on the claimant as compared with the position of the same person, absent the impairment.

Note that the requirement for any *substantial* adverse effect does not apply to *progressive* conditions which are likely to have such an impact, and which are recognised as disabilities as soon as they have any impact on the individual's ability to carry out normal day-to-day activities (Schedule 1, para 8). 'Likely' here is interpreted as elsewhere in the context of disability (see *SCA Packaging v Boyle* discussed at pp 482–484 above). See also the decision in *Taylor v Ladbrokes Betting and Gaming Ltd* [2017] IRLR 312, discussed at pp 506–507 below.

Long-Term and Recurring Conditions

In order to qualify as 'disabled' under the EqA, the 'substantial ... adverse effect' of the claimant's impairment 'on his or her ability to carry out normal day-to-day activities' has to be 'long-term' (s6 EqA), a 'long-term' effect being defined as one which has lasted or is likely to last for at least 12 months from onset, or which is likely to last for the remainder of the disabled person's life (Schedule 1 para 2 EqA). It is important to emphasise that whether the impact on the claimant's functioning was long-term must be assessed as of the date of the discrimination; the fact that the condition has *in fact* lasted at least 12 months does not, for example, mean that it was likely at the date of the discrimination to do so.[32]

[32] See *Cruickshank v Motorcast* [2002] ICR 729, approved by the CA in *McDougall v Richmond Adult Community College* [2008] ICR 431; *All Answers Ltd v W* [2021] EWCA Civ 606, [2021] IRLR 612.

Paragraph 2 of Schedule 1 EqA provides that an impairment is to be regarded as continuing to have a substantial adverse effect on a person's ability to carry out normal day-to-day activities if it ceases to have such an effect, but is likely to recur. The meaning of 'likely' in this context, as in others relevant to disability, is as set out by the HL in *SCA Packaging v Boyle* (see pp 482–484 above). The point at which the likelihood of recurrence falls to be judged is, in common with other aspects of disability, at the point of the discrimination.

***Sullivan v Bury Street Capital Ltd* [2021] EWCA Civ 1694, [2022] IRLR 159**

The claimant, a senior sales executive who had been employed by the company since 2009, came to believe that he was being followed and subject to surveillance by Russians connected with a Ukrainian woman he had been involved with between March and May 2013. He saw a doctor about this in September 2017 and was advised to take four weeks off work. Later that day he was dismissed. He claimed to have subject to s15 EqA discrimination (see below). An employment tribunal found that he had suffered paranoid throughout the period from May 2013 until his dismissal, but that these delusions had only had a substantial impact on his ability to carry out normal day-to-day activities for four to five months from May 2013 and between April and July 2017. It did not accept that the recurrence of the substantial effect was likely to last at least 12 months because it had occurred at a time when the claimant was under particular stress because of pay-related discussions which would have resolved within a relatively short time. Nor did the tribunal accept that the effect was likely to recur, and so it found that the claimant was not disabled. Further, the tribunal stated that, had it found that the claimant was disabled, it would have concluded that the company did not have actual or constructive knowledge of the disability. The claimant's appeals to the EAT and the CA failed.

Singh LJ, with whom Peter Jackson and Elisabeth Laing LJJ agreed:

> 93. In *McDougall v Richmond Adult Community College* [2008] EWCA Civ 4, [2008] ICR 431 the Court of Appeal had to consider the phrase 'likely to recur' in para 2(2) of Sch 1 to the 1995 Act. In reversing the decision of the EAT, this Court held that the question whether an employer had committed an act of disability discrimination had to be judged on the basis of the evidence available at the time of the act alleged to constitute discrimination and that, therefore, in determining whether the adverse effect of a person's impairment was 'likely to recur', the ET should not have regard to subsequent events. As Pill LJ put it, at para [23], the exercise involves 'a prediction on the available evidence'. In a similar vein, at para [33], Rimer LJ said:
>
> > '… The evidence relating to the relevant time either will, or will not, prove the likelihood of recurrence. If it does prove it, evidence of subsequent events is unnecessary and irrelevant. If it does not prove it, evidence of those events cannot fill the gap. That is because it is fallacious to assume that the occurrence of an event in month six proves that, viewing the matter exclusively as at month one, that occurrence was likely. It does not. It merely proves that the event happened, but by itself leaves unanswered whether, looking at the matter six months earlier, it was *likely* to happen, a question which has to be answered exclusively by reference to the evidence then available …' (Emphasis in original)
>
> 94. In *All Answers Ltd v W* [2021] EWCA Civ 606, [2021] IRLR 612 this Court confirmed the legal position. In that case the ET had fallen into error because it had looked at the position as at the date of the preliminary hearing before it. This Court confirmed that the relevant question is whether, as at the time of the alleged discriminatory act, the effect of an impairment is

likely to last at least 12 months. That must be assessed by reference to the facts and circumstances existing at the date of those alleged acts.

95. The facts of the present case raise a different issue, as the EAT recognised in granting permission to appeal. In this case the substantial adverse effect did in fact recur in 2017. As the EAT rightly said, in the light of *McDougall*, it was irrelevant, for the purposes of determining whether there was a disability in 2013, that the adverse effect did recur in 2017. What *McDougall* did not decide, however, is what is the relevance of the events of 2013 to the likelihood of recurrence when considering the events of 2017. Nevertheless, I agree with the EAT that there is no one answer that must be given to that question as a matter of law. The question remains one of fact. As Choudhury J put it, at para 38, although in many instances the fact that the SAE has recurred episodically might strongly suggest that a further episode is something that 'could well happen', that will not always be the case. Where, as here, the SAE was (in the judgment of the ET) triggered by a particular event that was itself unlikely to continue or to recur, then it is open to the ET to find that it is not likely to recur. The triggering event in this case was, as the ET found, the discussions between the parties in 2017 about remuneration. On those facts, I can see no error of approach by the ET. I agree with the conclusion of the EAT on this point …

97. … Mr Milsom [for the claimant] submits that the ET failed to ask itself the right questions about knowledge. The question for the ET should have been framed around what the employer knew through its employees. He submits that a properly directed ET could 'only' have concluded in this case that BSC had knowledge. Further, he submits that there was a failure on BSC's part to make enquiries about the duration of a known/potential condition, in other words that it had constructive knowledge. Again, it seems to me that these are essentially complaints about the findings of fact made by the ET. They go to the weight it should have ascribed to certain aspects of the evidence rather than to the ET's approach. I do not accept that the ET failed to ask itself the question of constructive knowledge: it expressly referred to what the Respondent could reasonably have been expected to know ….

The Effect of Medical Treatment

Except where visual impairments are corrected by glasses or contact lenses, no account should be taken by a tribunal or court, in assessing the question of disability, of the effects of treatment upon it.[33] 'This … applies even if the measures result in the effects being completely under control or not at all apparent' (Guidance para B13). Thus:

HM Government Office for Disability Issues. *Guidance on matters to be taken into account in determining questions relating to the definition of disability* (2011)

B13. … Where treatment is continuing it may be having the effect of masking or ameliorating a disability so that it does not have a substantial adverse effect. If the final outcome of such treatment cannot be determined, or if it is known that removal of the medical treatment would result in either a relapse or a worsened condition, it would be reasonable to disregard the medical treatment in accordance with paragraph 5 of Schedule 1.

B14. For example, if a person with a hearing impairment wears a hearing aid the question as to whether his or her impairment has a substantial adverse effect is to be decided by reference to what the hearing level would be without the hearing aid. Similarly, the case of someone with diabetes which is being controlled by medication or diet should be decided by reference to what the effects

[33] Schedule 1 para 5 EqA.

of the condition would be if he or she were not taking that medication or following the required diet.

[example]

A person with long-term depression is being treated by counselling. The effect of the treatment is to enable the person to undertake normal day-to-day activities, like shopping and going to work. If the effect of the treatment is disregarded, the person's impairment would have a substantial adverse effect on his ability to carry out normal day-to-day activities …

B16. Account should be taken of where the effect of the continuing medical treatment is to create a permanent improvement rather than a temporary improvement. It is necessary to consider whether, as a consequence of the treatment, the impairment would cease to have a substantial adverse effect. For example, a person who develops pneumonia may be admitted to hospital for treatment including a course of antibiotics. This cures the impairment and no substantial effects remain …

B17. However, if a person receives treatment which cures a condition that would otherwise meet the definition of a disability, the person would be protected by the Act as a person who had a disability in the past …

The theory may be straightforward but tribunals may face a difficult task distinguishing between the effects of a medical impairment and the impact of treatment on those effects. In *Carden v Pickerings Europe Ltd* [2005] IRLR 720, for example, the claimant had had a metal pin and plate inserted in his ankle some 20 years prior to the discrimination of which he complained. The EAT ruled that the question which the tribunal had to determine was whether the pin and plate were in the nature of ongoing 'treatment', in which case it would have had to consider the claimant as he would be without their assistance, or whether they were remnants of previous treatment the result of which was to eliminate the claimant's (past) impairment. It is worth bearing in mind here that even if the latter were the case the claimant would have continued to be protected as someone with a past disability (s 6(4) EqA).

The decision in *SCA Packaging v Boyle* is considered above (pp 482–484). It is clear from that decision that a behavioural regime designed to control a physical problem can amount to 'treatment' for the purposes of Schedule 1 para 5 EqA. The same is true of professional counselling with a qualified professional, though in any case in which a claimant seeks to rely on para 5 it will be advisable to have clear medical evidence as to the likely impact of the impairment absent the treatment (the 'deduced effects').[34] In *Metroline Travel Ltd v Stoute* [2015] IRLR 465 the EAT ruled that merely avoiding sugary drinks in the case of type 2 diabetes did not amount to or involve medical treatment for the purposes of para 5, HHJ Serota QC disclosing that he had the same condition. The judge suggested at §10 that the only impact on the claimant's day-to-day activities was the requirement to abstain from sugary drinks, complaining that the employment tribunal's decision was 'perverse' and would 'also mean that people with other conditions such as nut allergies, intolerance to lactose or what have you would also be regarded as disabled'. He took the view that this act of avoidance (as distinct from the adoption of a more severe regime) was more akin to the type of reasonable strategy envisaged by para B7 of the Guidance (see p 499) which involves altering the effects of an impairment so that they are no longer substantial. He did not, however, refer to para B14 of the Guidance which states in terms that 'the case of someone

[34] *Kapadia v London Borough of Lambeth* [2000] IRLR 699; *Woodrup v LB Southwark* [2002] EWCA Civ 1716, [2003] IRLR 111, discussed at pp 507–508 below.

with diabetes which is being controlled by medication or diet should be decided by reference to what the effects of the condition would be if he or she were not taking that medication or following the required diet.' A similar issue arose in the case immediately below.

***Taylor v Ladbrokes Betting and Gaming Ltd* [2016] UKEAT 0353_15_1612, [2017] IRLR 312**

In this case HHJ Hand QC remitted to a tribunal the question whether the claimant's type 2 diabetes, which was accepted as amounting to a progressive condition, was 'likely to result in [him] having ... an impairment' with a substantial adverse effect at a future date. The medical evidence was that the claimant could easily control his diabetes by means of lifestyle, diet, and exercise, which would likely halt its progression, but had failed to take 'basic steps in this regard which might reasonably have been expected of him'. An employment judge had concluded that the claimant was not disabled, but the EAT allowed the claimant's appeal.

HHJ Hand QC:

> 32. One then comes ... to the issue that seems to me to be the most difficult aspect of this case: how is one to construe para. 8(2) and the words 'if the condition is likely to result in P having such an impairment'? The issue between Mr Hills and Mr Young on this matter of interpretation is as to whether if there is a small possibility that is within the concept of 'likely to result'. To an extent, that depends upon whether one can qualify 'likely' by taking some aspect of the guidance in B7. It seems to me that this must clearly be what Employment Judge Gaskell has done.
>
> 34. Looking at the language of the Schedule and [para 8(2)], it is not immediately apparent to me that one should include the concept of reasonable conduct on the part of the allegedly disabled person within para. 8(2). At first sight, it looks as though it is simply a question of causation. The question is this: is the condition likely to result in his having an impairment? *Boyle*, of course, was concerned with what the word 'likely' means, and Lord Rodger, as he explained in his judgment at paragraph 41, was prepared to accept that there was no error on the part of the Court of Appeal of Northern Ireland by Girvan LJ's use of the phrase 'it could well happen' as analogue for or as being synonymous with the word 'likely'. Mr Hills submits that that still leaves open the question of whether even if this is a small possibility that is something likely to happen. That is an entirely understandable approach to concepts of predicting the future, but I do not regard it as consistent with the judgment of the House of Lords in *Boyle*. What is at issue is not whether something is likely to occur by reference to any definite percentage or proportion of the population in whom the condition may occur, recur or deteriorate. It is, as explained by the House of Lords, an issue of whether a doctor would consider there is a chance of something happening.
>
> 35. Consistent with the approach of Lord Rodger, it does not seem to me that the way in which a doctor would approach a condition that might deteriorate would be on the basis as to there being just a very small chance of it deteriorating or there being a small chance of it deteriorating but on the basis as to whether in terms of medical science in any given population it was a risk to which that population was exposed and that some proportion of that population would suffer a deterioration. In the terms used by Employment Judge Gaskell, it seems to me that even if there is a small possibility of deterioration in a population that is enough to make it likely that it might result in the particular individual having such an impairment.
>
> 36. Moreover, it seems to me that one must be very careful with the concept of the effect of medical treatment. Mr Hills submits that if somebody could take steps that would result in the

risk of future deterioration either being eliminated or very much reduced then if they failed to take steps, what the guidance of para. B7 envisages is that one will take account of their behaviour and if they have failed to use what is called in the guidance a coping or avoidance strategy then that person must be presumed not to be disabled. He says that the way in which Employment Judge Gaskell has interpreted [the medical evidence] is that the chances are that if the appellant modifies his lifestyle, exercises and is careful in terms of diet then his condition is not likely to result in the impairment having a substantial adverse effect in the future and if he does not modify his lifestyle then that is unreasonable conduct on his part. That is how para. 8(2) is intended to work. Plainly, looking at paragraphs 14 and 15, that is how Employment Judge Gaskell approached this matter.

37. Mr Young pointed out the wording of para. B10, which I referred to earlier, and said that meant the possibility of somebody being unable to keep to a particular regime notwithstanding its health-giving benefits is something that ought to also be taken into account and this was clearly so in the case of the appellant …

38. In ground 3, it is said that the judge erred by taking into account wrong lifestyle choices on the part of the appellant and these were not measures under para. 5, as was demonstrated by the *Metroline* case …

39. It seems to me that this case has been tackled by Employment Judge Gaskell on the basis of the material that he had before him. He is not to be criticised for having approached this matter by doing his best to distil from [the medical evidence] what he thought was relevant to the decision that he had to make. It does not seem to me, however, that he has clearly enough had in mind what it was that he actually had to decide. He has extracted from Dr Hurel's material what, in my judgment, is currently not to be found in it. In my view, it is not the case that absent medication the possibility of a deterioration is a small possibility. On the contrary, it is not clear to me exactly what Dr Hurel is saying about the future. On my analysis, he has answered the questions that he has been asked, but he has mixed together the present and the future.

40. What, in my judgment, Employment Judge Gaskell needs to assist him is a clear view as to what is the progression of type 2 diabetes … It is possible to construct the progression, as Mr Young has done, from the medical material provided by Dr Hurel, but whether one is constructing it accurately or not is something that I am concerned about. It seems to me that this is a process, understandably entered into with the best of motives by both the parties and Employment Judge Gaskell but it deprived Employment Judge Gaskell of the clarity that was necessary for him to make a proper and reasoned decision within the parameters set out in s.6 and Schedule 1.

41. I do not propose to decide the extent to which any issue under para. 8(2) can be decided by taking account of the guidance in para. B7, but what, in my judgment, has gone wrong in this case is that Dr Hurel, who is no doubt a busy man, has either not been asked the right questions or the whole process would have benefited from Dr Hurel being present so that he could have answered clearly the questions that might have arisen. Neither of those occurred and I have reached the conclusion that this was an unsound analysis by Employment Judge Gaskell, for which he is blameless but which should be undertaken again by either a much clearer set of questions being addressed in terms of the Schedule to Dr Hurel or by Dr Hurel coming to the tribunal, giving evidence and being cross-examined …

In *Kapadia v LB Lambeth* [2000] IRLR 14, the EAT accepted that counselling being received by a claimant who had suffered from reactive depression was 'treatment' for the purposes of the DDA, despite the fact that it was directed at the alleviation of symptoms of the illness rather than at its cause. Thus the claimant was entitled to have his claim to disability assessed on the basis of what his condition would have been absent the counselling (there being uncontested medical evidence that without the counselling there was a strong likelihood that he would have had a mental breakdown). In *Abadeh v British Telecommunications* [2001] ICR 156 EAT distinguished between continuing and concluded medical treatment ruling that, in the latter case, the 'deduced effect' provisions had no application and the claimant had to be assessed as he or she presented. The EAT further distinguished between continuing medical treatment which has resulted in a permanent improvement, and that which has not. As in the case of concluded medical treatment, continuing treatment whose impact is permanent (or, more precisely, which was permanent at the time of the discrimination) ought not to be disregarded for the purposes of determining whether the claimant is 'disabled'. Tribunals ought, however, to bear in mind that a claimant who is discriminated against on the basis that he or she has been disabled in the past is also protected by the EqA.

The CA in *Woodrup v LB Southwark* [2003] IRLR 52 took a very narrow approach to the 'deduced effects' provisions of the DDA and ruled that, where someone sought to rely on the effects a condition *would have had* in the absence of treatment (but *did not in fact have*, because of the treatment being received), the claimant 'should be required to prove his or her alleged disability with some particularity.' The Court there dismissed an appeal by a claimant who had failed to provide medical evidence in support of her argument that, if her psychotherapy treatment for anxiety neurosis had been discontinued, her impairment would have had a substantial adverse effect on her ability to carry out normal day-to-day activities. According to Simon Brown LJ, who delivered the leading judgment: 'Those seeking to invoke this peculiarly benign doctrine … should not readily expect to be indulged by the tribunal of fact' and an employment tribunal should not have to 'pretend that the applicant is in fact disabled when it knows that he or she is not.'

Knowledge

A finding of disability discrimination may require that the discriminator had actual or constructive/imputed knowledge of the disability (that is, that the discriminator knew or *should in all the circumstances have known* that the claimant was disabled).[35] The CA ruled in *Gallop v Newport CC* [2013] EWCA Civ 1358, [2014] IRLR 211 that the required knowledge is not of the *diagnosis* or of the fact that the claimant falls within the statutory definition of disability. Rather, it relates to the *facts*, namely (1) that the claimant has a physical or mental impairment which (2) has a substantial and long-term adverse effect on (3) his or her ability to carry out normal day-to-day activities. The employer in the *Gallop* case had relied on (incorrect and unreasoned) advice from its Occupational Health advisers that the claimant did not meet the statutory definition of disability. The CA ruled that this advice did not alter the fact that the employer had constructive knowledge of the claimant's disability. The outcome might well have been different had the employer been incorrectly advised as to the *facts* (that is, whether the claimant had a physical or mental impairment, whether it impacted on the claimant's ability to carry out normal day-to-day activities and, if so, whether this impact was substantial and long-term). It might also have been different had the OH advice been reasoned.

[35] *Gallop v Newport CC* (direct discrimination); s15(2) EqA (s15 discrimination, though the burden of proof is on the respondent) and Schedule 8 para 20 EqA (failure to make reasonable adjustments, which relates to Part 5 only).

***Donelien v Liberata UK Ltd* [2018] EWCA Civ 129, [2018] IRLR 535**

The claimant claimed disability after she was dismissed in connection with absenteeism. She had told her employer that she experienced low energy levels and tiredness in the morning related to high blood pressure, subsequently blaming work-related stress. GP's letters referred to high blood pressure, stomach problems and wrist pain, then to high blood pressure and stress and to work-related stress. The employer sought occupational health (OH) advice in relation to which the claimant refused access to her GP. OH advised that she was not disabled and that her problems were 'managerial not medical'. The adviser stated that the claimant's 'issues' were 'linked … to some … dispute with the company rather than any underlying psychiatric condition or indeed primarily to her high blood pressure', that hypertension was 'an extremely unlikely cause of long term certification' and that there was 'no evidence of any underlying psychiatric condition'. A tribunal ruled that the claimant was disabled but that the employer had done everything it could reasonably have been expected to do to determine whether this was the case and that it did not have actual or constructive knowledge of the disability. The EAT and the CA rejected her appeals. Having pointed out that all but one of the GP letters were written at a time when the tribunal concluded that the claimant was not (yet) disabled, that they did 'not give a clear or consistent picture', and that the employers (who were not medical experts) had sought external OH advice which (§29) 'suggested that [the claimant] was not in fact suffering from any mental or physical impairment at all, or in any event one which had a substantial impact on her ability to carry out day-to-day activities', the Court turned to consider the decision in *Gallop*.

Underhill LJ, with whom Lindblom and Singh LJJ agreed:

> 32. It seems that there was some concern following the decision in *Gallop* that it raised a serious question about whether employers in a case of this kind were entitled to attach weight to advice from occupational health consultants about whether an employee was suffering from a disability within the meaning of the 1995 Act. It was explicitly for that reason that Judge Richardson, when permitting the appeal in the EAT to proceed, directed that it be heard by a tribunal that included lay members. In my view it is plain that Rimer LJ did not intend generally to discount the value of such advice. The basis on which the employee's appeal was allowed was that the ET had found that the employer was entitled to rely, and rely exclusively, on the opinion of the occupational health advisers in circumstances where that opinion was worthless because it was unreasoned. That is perhaps most clear from para [42] of Rimer LJ's judgment ('relying *simply* on its *unquestioning* adoption of OH's *unreasoned* opinion') but equally from paras [40] and [43] ('he cannot simply rubber-stamp the adviser's opinion'). That is very far from saying that an employer may not attach great weight to the informed and reasoned opinion of an occupational health consultant. That was the view of the EAT, and in particular of the lay members, in the present case. Having expressed at para [30] of his judgment essentially the same view as me about the ratio of *Gallop*, Langstaff J went on to say, at para [31], that while an ET will 'look for evidence that the employer has taken its own decision … the lay members sitting with me in this case would wish to emphasise that in general great respect must be shown to the views of an Occupational Health doctor', though such views should not be followed uncritically.
>
> 33. Taking that approach to the present case, I do not believe that the ET fell into the same error as the tribunal in *Gallop*. At para [152] of its reasons it did not treat the fact that the respondent had received advice from occupational health consultants as conclusive. It said in terms that Maitland's advice 'chimed with their own experience and impressions, and the two

letters that they had received from the GP', and it emphasised that they not only took occupational health advice but had their own meetings with the appellant and took account of the GP letters. I should also say that it expressly approved the summaries of the relevant information which Ms Prendergast gave to Maitland on each occasion that she sought their advice; and it will be noted that when Dr Bellamy's initial report proved unsatisfactory Ms Prendergast went back to Maitland for clarification. This was clearly not a 'rubber stamp' case …

36. I stand back from all of this and revert to the point which I made earlier. It is not for this court to decide whether it might have found that the respondent could reasonably have been expected to know in September or October 2009 that the appellant was suffering from a disability. The question is whether it was open to the ET, on the evidence that it heard, to find that it could not. It will be apparent from what I have said already that the respondent was presented with a good deal of not very clear information, and getting a good understanding of it was not helped by the appellant's rather uncooperative and confrontational stance. The EAT also endorsed a submission made by Mr Brown that not all of the appellant's absences reflected her being truly unable to work: there was an element of unwillingness too, mixed in with her substantive complaints about pay and working conditions. As it observed, the ET had to disentangle what the appellant could not do from what she would not do. This is not an easy exercise: employers are not doctors, or psychologists.

37. In those circumstances I have no difficulty understanding why the ET came to the conclusion that it did that the respondent 'did all they could reasonably be expected to have done to find out about the nature of the health problem that the claimant was experiencing'. This court should be very slow, absent any explicit misdirection, to depart from the considered assessment of an experienced employment judge and two lay members, endorsed by the President of the EAT and two lay members. Even if – which I am not saying is the case – I would have reached a different conclusion from the ET I am quite sure that it was entitled to reach the decision which it did.

The authorities relating to knowledge of disability were summarised by HHJ Eady QC (as she then was) in *A Ltd v Z* [2020] ICR 199, cited with approval by the CA in *Sullivan v Bury Street Capital Ltd* [2022] IRLR 159 (extracted at pp 503–504 above).

A Ltd v Z [2019] UKEAT 0273_18_2803, [2020] ICR 199

23. In determining whether the employer had requisite knowledge for s 15(2) purposes, the following principles are uncontroversial between the parties in this appeal:

(1) There need only be actual or constructive knowledge as to the disability itself, not the causal link between the disability and its consequent effects which led to the unfavourable treatment, see *City of York Council v Grosset* [2018] ICR 1492 at para 39.

(2) The respondent need not have constructive knowledge of the complainant's diagnosis to satisfy the requirements of s 15(2); it is, however, for the employer to show that it was unreasonable for it to be expected to know that a person (a) suffered an impediment to his physical or mental health, or (b) that that impairment had a substantial and (c) long-term effect, see *Donelien v Liberata UK Ltd* (2014) UKEAT/0297/14 at para 5, per Langstaff P, and also see *Pnaiser v NHS England* [2016] IRLR 170 EAT at para 69 per Simler J.

(3) The question of reasonableness is one of fact and evaluation, see [*Donelien v Liberata UK Ltd*] [2018] IRLR 535 CA at para [27]; nonetheless, such assessments must be adequately and coherently reasoned and must take into account all relevant factors and not take into account those that are irrelevant.

(4) When assessing the question of constructive knowledge, an employee's representations as to the cause of absence or disability related symptoms can be of importance: (i) because, in asking whether the employee has suffered substantial adverse effect, a reaction to life events may fall short of the definition of disability for [Equality Act] purposes (see *Herry v Dudley Metropolitan Borough Council* [2017] ICR 610, per His Honour Judge Richardson, citing *J v DLA Piper UK LLP* [2010] ICR 1052), and (ii) because, without knowing the likely cause of a given impairment, 'it becomes much more difficult to know whether it may well last for more than 12 months, if it has not [already done so]', per Langstaff P in *Donelien* EAT at para 31.

(5) The approach adopted to answering the question thus posed by s 15(2) is to be informed by the code, which (relevantly) provides as follows:

'5.14 It is not enough for the employer to show that they did not know that the disabled person had the disability. They must also show that they could not reasonably have been expected to know about it. Employers should consider whether a worker has a disability even where one has not been formally disclosed, as, for example, not all workers who meet the definition of disability may think of themselves as a "disabled person".

5.15 An employer must do all they can reasonably be expected to do to find out if a worker has a disability. What is reasonable will depend on the circumstances. This is an objective assessment. When making inquiries about disability, employers should consider issues of dignity and privacy and ensure that personal information is dealt with confidentially.'

(6) It is not incumbent upon an employer to make every enquiry where there is little or no basis for doing so (*Ridout v T C Group* [1998] IRLR 628; *Alam v SSDWP* [2010] ICR 665).

(7) Reasonableness, for the purposes of s 15(2), must entail a balance between the strictures of making enquiries, the likelihood of such enquiries yielding results and the dignity and privacy of the employee, as recognised by the Code.'

Disability Discrimination

This chapter will consider only those aspects of discrimination which are unique to the protected characteristic of disability. The more general approach to discrimination is considered in Chapter 2, while Chapter 4 considers those areas in which discrimination is regulated under the DDA and other legislation.[36] It is worth noting here that, in cases of direct disability discrimination, specific provision is made concerning comparators. Section 23(1) EqA having stated that 'On a comparison of cases for the purposes of section 13 … or 19 there must be no material difference between the circumstances relating to each case', s23(2) then provides:

Section 23 EqA, Comparators

(2) The circumstances relating to a case include a person's abilities if—

(a) on a comparison for the purposes of section 13, the protected characteristic is disability …[37]

The effect of this provision is illustrated by the EAT's decision below.

[36] Note that the detailed technical provisions set out in Part 12 Equality Act 2010 (EqA) relating to disabled persons' transport are beyond the scope of this book.

[37] Section 23 EqA also refers to s14 (dual discrimination) which has not been brought into effect.

***Bennett v MiTAC Europe Ltd* EA-2020-000349-LA, [2022] IRLR 25**

The claimant was sales manager of the MiTAC Europe which was the European subsidiary of a company based in Taiwan. He had been recruited by Mr Balaam, UK sales and marketing director, who was shortly thereafter diagnosed with suspected kidney cancer. Both the claimant and Mr Balaam were dismissed shortly thereafter, allegedly because of poor performance. The claimant brought an associative discrimination claim, arguing that he had been dismissed because Mr Balaam had cancer. A tribunal dismissed his claim having found that Mr Balaam had not been dismissed for this reason and that the claimant's dismissal had been by reason of his performance. The claimant appealed. Much of the decision concerned the burden of proof but the EAT also considered the test for direct disability discrimination.

Judge James Tayler:

> 40. Because in the case of disability discrimination the circumstances include a person's abilities, when assessing a claim of direct disability discrimination it is necessary to compare the treatment of the complainant with an actual or hypothetical person with comparable abilities. Thus, if the consequence of a disability is a reduction in a person's ability to do a job and that reduction in ability is the reason for adverse treatment it will not be possible to make out a claim of direct discrimination because the comparator would have the same level of ability as the disabled person. That is why s 15 EqA 2010 is necessary, which provides for discrimination because of something arising in consequence of disability. However, if stereotypical assumptions are made about the ability and/or likely future ability of a disabled person this can amount to direct disability discrimination: *Chief Constable of Norfolk Constabulary v Coffey* [2019] EWCA Civ 1061, [2020] ICR 145 …
>
> 54. The Tribunal held that Mr Chang probably 'did not make allowances for the possible effects of the cancer in contributing to [Mr Balaam's] poor past performance' and that Mr Chang probably 'did consider that the treatment and possible continuing effects would impact on his future performance' but that 'This was not direct discrimination, but would have been unfavourable treatment because of something arising from disability' possibly capable of justification. In respect of the effect that the treatment had on Mr Balaam's past performance that probably is properly analysed as discrimination because of something arising in consequence of disability, whereas if Mr Chang made assumptions, as the tribunal found was probably the case, about Mr Balaam's future performance that could be direct disability discrimination …[38]

Discrimination Arising from Disability

This type of discrimination is the successor to the concept of discrimination related to disability, which was regulated by s3A(1) DDA but through which the HL (Lady Hale dissenting) drove a coach and horses in *Lewisham LBC v Malcolm* [2008] UKHL 43, [2008] 1 AC 1399.

Section 15 EqA, Discrimination arising from disability

(1) A person (A) discriminates against a disabled person (B) if—

- (a) A treats B unfavourably because of something arising in consequence of B's disability, and
- (b) A cannot show that the treatment is a proportionate means of achieving a legitimate aim.

[38] See also Case C-795/19, *XX v Tartu Vangla* EU:C:2020:961, EU:C:2021:606, [2022] IRLR 86.

(2) Subsection (1) does not apply if A shows that A did not know, and could not reasonably have been expected to know, that B had the disability.

Perhaps the most significant element of s15 EqA discrimination is the absence of any requirement for *less* favourable treatment; the claimant only needs to challenge *un*favourable treatment because of something arising in consequence of his or her disability and the burden of justification, or of establishing an absence of knowledge, then falls on the alleged discriminator. Under s15's predecessor provision it had been held that the claimant was required to be disabled, perception being insufficient.[39] It has been suggested that the same restriction applies to s15 EqA.[40]

Unfavourable Treatment

The meaning of 'unfavourable' was dealt with by the Supreme Court (SC) in the following case.

***Williams v Trustees of Swansea University Pension and Assurance Scheme* [2018] UKSC 65, [2019] ICR 230**

The claimant had worked full-time but transitioned to work half-time by reason of disability before seeking early retirement. He received a sum which consisted of (1) a lump sum and annuity, calculated on the basis of his actual salary at the relevant times, payable immediately and without any actuarial reduction for early receipt, and full time or part time (2) an enhancement to both his lump sum and annuity, payable immediately and without any actuarial reduction for early receipt, calculated by reference to his actual salary at date of retirement and as if he had continued to work until his Normal Pension Date. The claimant claimed that the calculation of his enhanced element on the basis of his half-time pensionable salary was unfavourable treatment because his reduced working hours arose as a consequence of his disability. A tribunal found in his favour but the EAT allowed his employer's appeal, and his subsequent appeals were rejected by the CA and the SC which ruled that he had not been subject to any unfavourable treatment by his employer.

Lord Carnwath (with whom Lords Kerr, Hodge and Kitchin and Lady Black agreed):

15. At the beginning of Langstaff J's judgment [in the EAT], he had commented on the effect of the scheme for Mr Williams, which he described as 'immensely favourable':

'Under the rules of the pension scheme applicable to him employees were entitled to a pension on retirement at age 67, but not earlier, unless retiring when their ill-health was such that they were plainly incapable of continuing in work. In the latter case, employees would be entitled not only to the immediate payment of pension – without actuarial reduction – in respect of the work they had already done (accrued pension) but also to an enhanced pension. This was also paid without actuarial reduction for early receipt as if they had continued working until normal retirement age (in the claimant's case 67) continuing to receive the salary they had been receiving when they retired. This was plainly an immensely favourable arrangement for anyone eligible for it. Those eligible for it were

[39] *Aitken v Commissioner of Police of the Metropolis* [2011] EWCA Civ 582, [2012] ICR 78.
[40] See *CC Norfolk v Coffey* [2019] EWCA Civ 1061, [2020] ICR 145, fn 9.

> necessarily disabled (within the meaning of the [EqA]. Any other 38-year-old who left the service of the university at that age would have no prospect of receiving the payment of any accrued pension entitlement until they reached what would have been their normal retirement age, nor any prospect of receiving any enhanced pension' (para 1).

16. In a section under the heading 'Unfavourably', he gave his own view of the meaning of the term (paras 27–29). He did not think the word could be equated with the word 'detriment' used elsewhere in the Act; nor, as was agreed, did it require a comparison with an identifiable comparator, actual or hypothetical. It was to be measured 'against an objective sense of that which is adverse as compared with that which is beneficial'. He noted that the same word was used elsewhere in the Act, in provisions 'which have a longer pedigree', in relation to discrimination on the grounds of pregnancy (s 18(2)). In that context it had the sense of 'placing a hurdle in front of, or creating a particular difficulty for, or disadvantaging a person …' It was likely to be intended to have 'much the same' sense in s 15.

17. It was 'for a tribunal to recognise when an individual has been treated unfavourably', and it was not possible to be prescriptive. However, in his view:

> '… treatment which is advantageous cannot be said to be "unfavourable" merely because it is thought it could have been more advantageous, or, put the other way round, because it is insufficiently advantageous. The determination of that which is unfavourable involves an assessment in which a broad view is to be taken and which is to be judged by broad experience of life. Persons may be said to have been treated unfavourably if they are not in as good a position as others generally would be.'…

19. In the Court of Appeal ([2017] IRLR 882), the leading judgment was given by Bean LJ. He adopted a similar approach to that of Langstaff J, although he also considered the application of the competing interpretations to different hypothetical examples. For the substance of his reasoning it is sufficient to refer to two passages. In the first (paras 42–43) he distinguished decided cases, including *[Lewisham LBC v] Malcolm* [[2008] UKHL 43, [2008] 1 AC 1399], in which there had been an act which in itself caused disadvantage:

> 'In the leading cases cited to us the "treatment" complained of has been an act which itself disadvantages the claimant in some way. In *Clark v Novacold* [[1999] ICR 951] the claimant was dismissed. In the *Lewisham* case Mr Malcolm was evicted. In *Shamoon v Chief Constable of the Royal Ulster Constabulary* [2003] ICR 337 the claimant Chief Inspector had part of her duties as a manager (the appraisal of subordinates) removed. The House of Lords held that it was not necessary for her to show financial loss in order to establish a detriment; it was enough that she might reasonably feel demeaned by this decision in the eyes of those over whom she had authority.

Ms Casserley [counsel for Mr Williams] placed the *Shamoon* case at the forefront of her argument, but I do not consider that it assists her. Mr Williams' case does not turn on a question of reasonable perception. His pension is undoubtedly less advantageous or less favourable than that of a hypothetical comparator suddenly disabled by a heart attack or stroke. But it is far more advantageous or favourable than it would be if he had not become permanently incapacitated from his job. The *Shamoon* case is not authority for saying that a disabled person has been subjected to unfavourable treatment within the meaning of s 15 simply because he thinks he should have been treated better.'

20. In the second (paras [48]–[49]) he rejected what he saw as counsel's implicit comparison with the treatment of different disability:

> 'Ms Casserley's argument begins by treating "unfavourable" as not requiring any comparator but in reality it does depend on a comparator, namely another disabled member of the Scheme with a different medical history.

> No authority was cited to us to support the view that a disabled person who is treated advantageously in consequence of his disability, but not as advantageously as a person with a different disability or different medical history would have been treated, has a valid claim for discrimination under s 15 subject only to the defence that the treatment was a proportionate means of achieving a legitimate aim. If such a claim were valid it would call into question the terms of pension schemes or insurance contracts which confer increased benefits in respect of disability caused by injuries sustained at work, or which make special provision for disability caused by one type of disease (for example cancer). The critical question can be put in this way: whether treatment which confers advantages on a disabled person, but would have conferred greater advantages had his disability arisen more suddenly, amounts to "unfavourable treatment" within s 15. In agreement with the President of the EAT I would hold that it does not.'…

22. The submissions in this court

For Mr Williams, Ms Crasnow's submissions, as I understood them, had a somewhat different emphasis from the case below. … her central submission can be shortly stated. In the words of her speaking note, it was 'unfavourable' to calculate the enhanced element of his pension using his final salary (that is, the lower part-time salary) given that he had been working part-time: '… *only* because of his disabilities. Had he not been disabled he would have continued to work full-time.'…

23. Her supporting submissions took issue with various aspects of the reasoning of the EAT and the Court of Appeal, including the suggestion of Langstaff J that the word 'unfavourably' must be taken to have a different meaning from the word 'detriment' as used elsewhere in the Act. She referred to the guidance given in the Equality and Human Rights Commission's Code of Practice (2011), which she said adopts a more flexible approach. Under the heading 'What is "unfavourable treatment"?', the Code states:

> '5.7 For discrimination arising from disability to occur, a disabled person must have been treated "unfavourably". This means that he or she must have been put at a disadvantage. Often, the disadvantage will be obvious and it will be clear that the treatment has been unfavourable; for example, a person may have been refused a job, denied a work opportunity or dismissed from their employment. But sometimes unfavourable treatment may be less obvious. Even if an employer thinks that they are acting in the best interests of a disabled person, they may still treat that person unfavourably.'

The reference in that passage to 'disadvantage' took her to an earlier passage dealing with the word 'disadvantage' as it appears elsewhere in the statute (s 19):

> '4.9 "Disadvantage" is not defined by the Act. It could include denial of an opportunity or choice, deterrence, rejection or exclusion. The courts have found that "detriment", a similar concept, is something that a reasonable person would complain about – so an unjustified sense of grievance would not qualify. A disadvantage does not have to be quantifiable and the worker does not have to experience actual loss (economic or otherwise). It is enough that the worker can reasonably say that they would have preferred to be treated differently.'

Those passages, Ms Crasnow submitted, show that words such as unfavourably, disadvantage, and detriment are similar in effect. The last sentence also supports a test which is not purely objective; regard may be had to what is reasonably seen as unfavourable by the person affected. In this connection she relied also on the UN Convention on the Rights of Persons with Disabilities, which was said to require a broad interpretation of discrimination, and in particular to support the need to have regard to 'the subjective experience' of the person concerned, 'albeit tempered by a reasonableness test.'…

27. Discussion

Since I am substantially in agreement with the reasoning of the Court of Appeal, I can express my conclusions shortly, without I hope disrespect to Ms Crasnow's carefully developed submissions. I agree with her that in most cases (including the present) little is likely to be gained by seeking to draw narrow distinctions between the word 'unfavourably' in s 15 and analogous concepts such as 'disadvantage' or 'detriment' found in other provisions, nor between an objective and a 'subjective/objective' approach. While the passages in the Code of Practice to which she draws attention cannot replace the statutory words, they do in my view provide helpful advice as to the relatively low threshold of disadvantage which is sufficient to trigger the requirement to justify under this section. It is unnecessary to refer to more remote sources such as the United Nations Conventions. Nor do I find it useful to speculate about the application of the section or the Code in hypothetical cases which are not before the court.

28. On the other hand, I do not think that the passages in the Code do anything to overcome the central objection to Mr Williams' case as now formulated, which can be shortly stated. It is necessary first to identify the relevant 'treatment' to which the section is to be applied. In this case it was the award of a pension. There was nothing intrinsically 'unfavourable' or disadvantageous about that. … Ms Crasnow's formulation, to my mind, depends on an artificial separation between the method of calculation and the award to which it gave rise. The only basis on which Mr Williams was entitled to any award at that time was by reason of his disabilities. As Mr Bryant says, had he been able to work full time, the consequence would have been, not an enhanced entitlement, but no immediate right to a pension at all. It is unnecessary to say whether or not the award of the pension of that amount and in those circumstances was 'immensely favourable' (in Langstaff J's words). It is enough that it was not in any sense 'unfavourable', nor (applying the approach of the Code) could it reasonably have been so regarded.

29. For these reasons I would dismiss the appeal.

'Something Arising in Consequence of Disability'

Section 15 EqA could protect from unfavourable treatment because of disability-related absenteeism (whether in the context of work or education), difficulties with concentration, time-keeping, or the physical or emotional demands imposed by a job or a course of study. In order to fit unfavourable treatment within s15 EqA it must be shown (1) that the treatment was because of 'something',[41] and (2) that the 'something' arose in consequence of the claimant's disability, though in practice these steps are often elided. The following decision shows that the test of causation which applies in s15 discrimination is fairly loose.

Sheikholeslami v University of Edinburgh [2018] UKEAT 0014_17_0510, [2018] IRLR 1090

The claimant was a professor in the university's school of engineering. She raised concerns about sex discrimination and then went on sick leave after being diagnosed with work-related stress and depression. She sought to return to work via a different department of the University. Her request was not met and she was dismissed just under two years' later when her work permit expired. A tribunal rejected her claim of s15 EqA discrimination. The tribunal accepted that she was disabled and that she 'found it difficult to work in the

[41] *Per* Langstaff P in *Basildon & Thurrock NHS Foundation Trust v Weerasinghe* [2016] ICR 305.

school … because she believed that she had been discriminated against or because her colleagues may have been hostile to her on her return' but did not 'consider that [she] was dismissed because she was absent. She was dismissed because she was unwilling or unable to return to work in her existing post and this triggered issues with her work permit …. There is no evidence … that there was a causal link between the claimant's disability and her refusal to return to her post … It appears that she was able to return to work (or at least was asserting that she was) but that she would not return to her previous role'. The EAT allowed the claimant's appeal.

Simler P:

62. On causation, the approach to s15 Equality Act 2010 is now well established and not in dispute on this appeal. In short, this provision requires an investigation of two distinct causative issues: (i) did A treat B unfavourably because of an (identified) something? and (ii) did that something arise in consequence of B's disability? The first issue involves an examination of the putative discriminator's state of mind to determine what consciously or unconsciously was the reason for any unfavourable treatment found. If the 'something' was a more than trivial part of the reason for unfavourable treatment then stage (i) is satisfied. The second issue is a question of objective fact for an employment tribunal to decide in light of the evidence [citing *City of York Council v Grosset* [2018] EWCA Civ 1105, [2018] ICR 1492].

63. Adopting that approach, the first question accordingly was whether the alleged unfavourable treatment (or any of it) occurred and was because of the claimant's ongoing absence from her existing post at the School of Engineering and/or her failure to return to it (the identified 'something' on the claimant's case). That question involved a consideration of the reasons why each relevant decision-maker acted as he or she did in treating the claimant unfavourably. Different treatment might have involved different decision-makers or different reasons, but the tribunal did not descend into this sort of detail.

64. The tribunal, as indicated, focused on the three aspects of unfavourable treatment identified at [203] and implicitly accepted that unfavourable treatment occurred in these respects. In relation to these, the tribunal accepted that *the respondent* believed 'that the claimant was not prepared to return to work in the position for which the work permit had been granted and that, in these circumstances, it believed that there was no possibility of the claimant's work permit being extended' … Leaving aside criticisms made by Mr Gorton [for the claimant] of this finding … and the failure to identify who at the respondent held that belief), the second question for the tribunal was whether the claimant's absence or failure to return to her existing post (which might have been viewed as two sides of the same coin) was as a matter of objective fact 'something arising in consequence of [her mental health] disability'.

65. In concluding … that there was in effect no evidence of any link between the claimant's disability and her absence or refusal to return to her post in the School of Engineering, I consider that the tribunal erred in law … Although the causal connection between the something that causes unfavourable treatment and the disability for s 15 purposes, may involve several links depending on the facts of a particular case, the tribunal appears not to have contemplated this possibility. In other words, more than one relevant consequence of the disability may require consideration, but this does not appear to have been considered: even if the respondent mistreated the claimant on the work permit issue because it believed she was not prepared to return … the tribunal did not consider why the claimant was not prepared to return to her existing post. In fact, on the tribunal's findings, it was the claimant's mental health disability that caused her to be ill and absent from the School of Engineering (as certified by doctor's notes); and this continued until termination of her contract. Further, there was evidence from the claimant that she believed her discriminatory treatment in the School

of Engineering caused her disability, and she perceived hostility from those at the School of Engineering as a result of it. Although the cause of the disability might be irrelevant in many cases, in a case like the present one, where the disability, its cause, and its effects are all so interlinked, it seems to me, in agreement with Mr Gorton, that the broad causation question in s 15 was capable of being satisfied on this basis.

66. Further, it seems to me contrary to the arguments of Mr Reade [for the university], that the incorrect language of causation used by the tribunal … [205] 'because of her disability') fed into the tribunal's error, so that too strict a causation test was imposed by the tribunal in error. The tribunal described the critical question … to be answered as whether the claimant's refusal to return to her previous role was 'because of her disability or because of some other reason, such as she considered she had been badly treated in that department', but this was not a binary question. Both reasons might be in play: her disability caused her to experience anxiety, stress and (on her case) an inability to return to the place where she perceived the mistreatment and hostility to be located, leading to her refusal. The critical question was whether on the objective facts, her refusal to return arose in 'consequence of' (rather than being caused by) her disability. This is a looser connection that might involve more than one link in the chain of consequences. The tribunal did not approach it on that basis. The correct question was not asked in either paragraph; nor was it correctly answered by the tribunal …

Although s15(2) EqA requires actual or constructive knowledge of the disability on the part of the discriminator, there is no requirement that the discriminator know that the 'something' is connected with that disability.[42] Thus, for example, in *City of York Council v Grosset* (referred to by Simler P in the extract immediately above), the CA ruled that a tribunal was entitled to find that a teacher who had been dismissed for showing children an unsuitable film had been discriminated against contrary to s15 where the error in judgment was the result of stress which in turn arose in consequence of the efforts he had to make to manage his cystic fibrosis. It did not matter whether the employer was aware that the claimant's stress was related to his cystic fibrosis. As Arden LJ put it at §67, 's 15(2) is inconsistent with any suggestion that lack of knowledge of the consequences is a defence. I can also well understand that Parliament could have taken the view that if lack of knowledge of the consequences were a defence, that could well in practice undermine the wide protection already given by s 15(1) EqA'.

Examples of s15 discrimination outside the employment context are provided by the EHRC's Code of Practice. The last of these examples also illustrates where a discriminator might be regarded as having constructive (or imputed) knowledge of a disability.

EHRC, 'Services, public functions and associations', Statutory Code of Practice, 84–88[43]

An association – in the form of a private members' club – rejects an applicant for membership because she cannot, as a result of her disability, attend its monthly meetings. Even though the club would reject others who cannot attend their monthly meetings, the woman has been treated unfavourably because of something arising in consequence of her disability. This will be unlawful unless the club can show that the treatment is a proportionate means of achieving a legitimate aim …

[42] *City of York Council v Grosset* [2018] EWCA Civ 1105, [2018] ICR 1492.

[43] https://www.equalityhumanrights.com/en/publication-download/services-public-functions-and-associations-statutory-code-practice.

> A mother seeks admission to a privately run nursery for her son who has Hirschsprung's disease, which means that he does not have full bowel control. The nursery says that they cannot admit her son because he is not toilet trained and all the children at the nursery are. The refusal to admit the boy is not because of his disability itself; but he is being treated unfavourably because of something arising in consequence of his disability …
>
> A disabled person is refused service at a bar because they are slurring their words, as a result of having had a stroke. In these circumstances, the disabled person has been treated unfavourably because of something arising as a consequence of their disability …
>
> A member of staff at Jobcentre Plus refuses to interview a member of the public, who wishes to complete an application for Jobseeker's Allowance, because he is swearing. However, his swearing is a result of his having Tourette syndrome …
>
> A pub employee orders a customer who is lying prone on a bench seat to leave the premises. However, the customer has Chronic Fatigue Syndrome and is lying down because she needs to as a result of her disability. The pub employee refuses to accept her explanation and makes no attempt to talk to the bar staff, who had served her with only one drink. Because relevant information was available about the disabled person, the service provider could reasonably have been expected to know that she was disabled. As a result, the pub is likely to be liable for discrimination arising from disability unless it can show that the treatment is objectively justified.

It is important to note that, as with other forms of discrimination, the 'something' relied upon in s15 discrimination does not have to be the main or sole cause of the unfavourable treatment complained of, as long as it is a 'significant influence' or 'an effective cause'.[44]

***Risby v LB Waltham Forest* UKEAT/0318/15, unreported, 18 March 2016[45]**

Mr Risby was paraplegic and a wheelchair user. He was known to be short-tempered for reasons unrelated to his disability. He lost his temper after being invited to a workshop in a venue which was not wheelchair accessible. He sought out the personal assistant of the event's organiser and shouted at her. She sought assistance from another of the employer's staff to whom the claimant said loudly that 'the Council would not get away with this if they said that no fucking n*****s were allowed to attend.' The PA, who was of mixed race (unknown to the claimant), thought that this was directed at her. Later on the same day the claimant was overheard to state that he was being treated 'like a n****r in the woodpile'. He was summarily dismissed following disciplinary proceedings and claimed s15 discrimination. A tribunal found that the claimant had been dismissed because of conduct which was caused (1) by his disability, which resulted in his indignation and (2) by his bad temper which was unrelated to his disability. Having found no 'direct linkage' between the disability and the conduct the tribunal dismissed the s15 claim. The EAT allowed his appeal, ruling that it was not necessary to have a direct link between the disability and the unfavourable treatment. Further, the tribunal's finding that one of the effective causes of the dismissal had arisen in consequence of the claimant's disability was sufficient to satisfy s15 irrespective of the existence of another effective cause (his bad temper). The EAT remitted the claim to the tribunal to determine whether the s15 discrimination was justified.

[44] *Hall v CC West Yorkshire Police* [2015] IRLR 893.

[45] Discussed in Discrimination Law Association *Briefings* No 59, November 2016, available at https://www.bindmans.com/uploads/files/documents/risby.pdf.

Justification

The test for justification in s15 EqA is the same as that which applies to indirect discrimination ie, the alleged discriminator must 'show that the treatment is a proportionate means of achieving a legitimate aim'. This is an objective test upon which the tribunal must reach its own decision. Its application is discussed in Chapter 2. Here it is important to note that, as Judge Auerbach pointed out in *Stott v Ralli Ltd* [2022] IRLR 148, the matters required to be justified vary between s19 and s15 EqA. Whereas, in an indirect discrimination claim, the alleged discriminator is required to establish that the general application of the disparately impacting provision, criterion or practice is a proportionate means of achieving a legitimate aim, in a s15 claim the justification relates to the unfavourable treatment of the individual disabled person. The significance of this is illustrated by the EAT's decision below.

***Buchanan v Commissioner of Police of the Metropolis* [2016] UKEAT 0112_16_3009, [2017] ICR 184**

The claimant, a police motorcyclist, brought a s15 EqA claim in connection with his treatment after a serious motorbike accident which happened while he was responding to an emergency call. He developed serious post-traumatic stress disorder and was unable to return to work. After an absence of eight months the police force commenced its unsatisfactory performance procedure, which was based on Police Regulations, and gave the claimant a series of dates to return to work with which he was unable to comply. He challenged the police force's use of the procedure. An employment tribunal found that the unfavourable treatment which it accepted was related to something arising in consequence of his disability was justified, having decided that it would look at the 'overall scheme' rather than the individual steps applied to the claimant. The EAT upheld the claimant's appeal.

Judge David Richardson:

42. Discussion and conclusions

The starting-point must be the words of s.15(2)(b) of the Equality Act 2010. This requires the putative discriminator A to show that 'the treatment' of B is a proportionate means of achieving a legitimate aim. The focus is therefore upon 'the treatment'; and the starting point therefore must be that the ET should apply s.15(2)(b) by identifying the act or omission which constitutes unfavourable treatment and asking whether that act or omission is a proportionate means of achieving a legitimate aim.

43. There will be cases where the A's treatment of B is the direct result of applying a general rule or policy to B. In such a case whether B's treatment is justified will usually depend on whether the general rule or policy is justified.

44. *Seldon* was such a case. The claimant, a partner in a solicitors' firm, was required to retire when he reached the age of 65 in accordance with a term in the firm's partnership deed. The Supreme Court accepted that the provision, although amounting to less favourable treatment because of age, was a proportionate means of achieving a legitimate aim. But it was also argued that it had to be justified in the particular case of the claimant at the time. The Supreme Court rejected that argument. Baroness Hale said:

'64. The answer given in the EAT, at [58], with which the Court of Appeal agreed, at [36], was that:

"Typically, legitimate aims can only be achieved by the application of general rules or policies. The adoption of a general rule, as opposed to a series of responses to particular

> individual circumstances, is itself an important element in the justification. It is what gives predictability and consistency, itself an important virtue."
>
> Thus the EAT would not rule out the possibility that there may be cases where the particular application of the rule has to be justified, but they suspected that these would be extremely rare.
>
> 65. I would accept that where it is justified to have a general rule, then the existence of that rule will usually justify the treatment which results from it …'
>
> 45. … If the treatment is the direct result of applying a rule or policy, it will usually be the rule or policy which has to be justified. Suppose for example that A has a strict attendance policy which requires all employees to be dismissed upon reaching a certain level of absence; and the policy admits of no exceptions for disability. B, if dismissed as a direct result of that policy, could bring a claim for discrimination arising from disability or a claim for indirect discrimination; and the issue of justification would in practical terms be the same for each. Thus Elias LJ said in *Griffiths* [*v SSWP* [2015] EWCA Civ, [2017] ICR 160]:
>
> '27. … it is in practice hard to envisage circumstances where an employer who is held to have committed indirect disability discrimination will not also be committing discrimination arising out of disability, at least where the employer has, or ought to have, knowledge that the employee is disabled. Both require essentially the same proportionality analysis. Strictly, in the case of indirect discrimination it is the PCP which needs to be justified whereas in the case of discrimination arising out of disability it is the treatment, but in practice the treatment will flow from the application of the PCP. Accordingly, once the relevant disparate impact is established, both forms of discrimination are likely to stand or fall together …'
>
> 46. In cases of indirect discrimination, the whole basis of claim depends on the application to the claimant and his group of a policy, criterion or practice which causes comparative disadvantage. It is therefore not surprising that in such cases it is the PCP which must be justified …
>
> 47. I therefore accept that there are cases where the question whether B's treatment by A was justified will depend on whether an underlying policy or procedure was itself justified. But … I do not accept that this was such a case.
>
> 48. In my judgment it will be rare in disability cases concerned with attendance management for the approach in *Seldon* to be applicable. This is because generally speaking the policies and procedures applicable to attendance management do allow (adopting the words of Elias LJ quoted by Baroness Hale in *Seldon*) for a series of responses to individual circumstances. And this is in keeping with the purpose underlying disability discrimination law. It is to secure more favourable treatment for disabled people and it requires employers to assess on an individual basis whether allowances or adjustments should be made for them: see *Griffiths* at paragraphs 15–16.
>
> 49. … the respondent's policies allowed for such an individual assessment; and (while they did not deal specifically with disability) so did the Regulations. The various steps which the claimant criticised were not mandated by the Regulations or the respondent's policies. It is therefore impossible to assess whether such a step was a proportionate means of achieving a legitimate aim simply by asking whether the Regulations or the respondent's policies were justified. The ET was required by s.15(2) to look at the treatment itself and ask whether the treatment was proportionate …

We saw above that the regulation of disability discrimination is *asymmetric*, that is, that it is unlawful to discriminate against disabled people for reasons connected with disability, but that the EqA does not prohibit disability discrimination *in favour of* disabled people. This being the case, there is no impediment to making exceptions to generally applicable policies or practices to avoid unfavourable treatment contrary to s15 EqA. Further, the duty to make reasonable adjustments may *require* such exceptions to be made (see further below).

Before leaving the discussion of s15 discrimination it is important to emphasise that, where an alleged discriminator has failed to make a reasonable adjustment the effect of which would have been to avoid the unfavourable treatment complained of, justification is likely to be very difficult. Under the DDA there was a specific provision to the effect that no justification was possible under the forerunner to s15 discrimination unless, had the duty to make reasonable adjustments been complied with, the basis on which the discrimination was claimed to be justified would have still existed. The EqA contains no such express provision but the EHRC's Employment Code of Practice and Technical Guidance for Schools both suggest that a failure to make reasonable adjustments is likely to defeat a justification defence on a related s15 claim.[46]

***City of York Council v Grosset* [2018] EWCA Civ 1105, [2018] ICR 1492**

As discussed above, the Court ruled that a tribunal was entitled to find that a teacher who had been dismissed for showing children an unsuitable film had been discriminated against contrary to s15 where the error in judgment was the result of stress which in turn arose in consequence of the efforts he had to make to manage his cystic fibrosis.

Sales LJ, with whom Peter Jackson LJ agreed (Arden LJ dissenting on their reliance on the Code of Practice):

> 57. A particularly strong factor underlying the ET's conclusion that the dismissal was not proportionate was its unchallenged assessment that, if the respondent had put in place reasonable adjustments as required by ss 20 and 21 EqA, by reducing the work pressure on the claimant, he would not have been subjected to the same level of stress ... Although the ET did not refer to the Code of Practice on this issue, para 5.21 of the Code of Practice, set out above, makes it clear that a link between a failure to put in place reasonable adjustments and the unfavourable treatment in issue under s 15(1)(a) EqA may be an important factor to be taken into account under s 15(1)(b). By virtue of s 15(4) of the Equality Act 2006 the Code of Practice should 'be taken into account by a court or tribunal in any case in which it appears to the court or tribunal to be relevant'. The ET was plainly entitled to give the weight it did to the impact of the respondent's failures to make such reasonable adjustments as it should have put in place.

Failure to Make Reasonable Adjustments

The duty to make reasonable adjustments is core to the prohibition of disability discrimination, and marks this type of discrimination out from most other forms. This was recognised

[46] Respectively §5.21 of the Employment Code, available at https://www.equalityhumanrights.com/en/publication-download/employment-statutory-code-practice and §4.11 of the technical guidance for schools, available at https://www.equalityhumanrights.com/en/publication-download/technical-guidance-schools-england. It is, however, clear from the decision in *Monmouthshire CC v Harris* UKEAT/0010/15 (23 October 2015, unreported) that a past failure to make a reasonable adjustment which duty had ceased to apply by the date on which the alleged s15 discrimination occurred will not necessarily defeat a justification claim.

by Brian Doyle, later to be President of English Employment Tribunals, at the inception of the DDA.

Brian Doyle, 'Enabling legislation or dissembling law? The Disability Discrimination Act 1995' (1997) 60 *Modern Law Review* 64, 74, footnotes omitted

The duty to make reasonable adjustments will assume ... great[ ] importance as a means to prevent (or to require the adjustment of) unjustifiable practices, rules, policies, requirements or conditions which have a harsh or adverse impact upon access by disabled persons and to compensate for the absence of an explicit prohibition on indirect disability discrimination. The concept of a reasonable accommodation or adjustment is at the heart of disability discrimination statutes in other jurisdictions. It is an example of legally mandated positive action rather than a requirement of reverse or positive discrimination.

The imposition upon employers and others of duties to make adjustments to accommodate the needs of disabled people are, in one sense, radical, none of the other discrimination legislation imposing, *in express terms*, any duty of adjustment. It is true that the concept of indirect discrimination can, on occasion, impose an obligation to adjust (by, for example, permitting parents to work part-time). But, whereas the restrictions on positive discrimination limit the extent to which such adjustments can be tied to particular characteristics, this is not the case where the protected characteristic is disability, and the expectation is that the employer or service provider will adjust. In *Archibald v Fife Council (Scotland)* [2004] UKHL 32, [2004] ICR 954, the HL made clear that the duty to make reasonable adjustments may require an employer to treat a disabled person more favourably than a non-disabled person.

The duty to make adjustments (more accurately, the duties to make adjustments) are now set out in ss20 and 21 EqA and in various associated Schedules to the Act. Sections 20 and 21 are set out and discussed immediately below, the Schedules (which deal with the application of the duty in various contexts) after discussion of the general elements of the duty to make reasonable adjustment.

Reasonable Adjustments: General

Section 20 EqA, Duty to make adjustments

(1) Where this Act imposes a duty to make reasonable adjustments on a person, this section, sections 21 and 22 and the applicable Schedule apply; and for those purposes, a person on whom the duty is imposed is referred to as A.
(2) The duty comprises the following three requirements.
(3) The first requirement is a requirement, where a provision, criterion or practice of A's puts a disabled person at a substantial disadvantage in relation to a relevant matter in comparison with persons who are not disabled, to take such steps as it is reasonable to have to take to avoid the disadvantage.
(4) The second requirement is a requirement, where a physical feature puts a disabled person at a substantial disadvantage in relation to a relevant matter in comparison with persons who are not disabled, to take such steps as it is reasonable to have to take to avoid the disadvantage.
(5) The third requirement is a requirement, where a disabled person would, but for the provision of an auxiliary aid, be put at a substantial disadvantage in relation to a relevant matter in comparison with persons who are not disabled, to take such steps as it is reasonable to have to take to provide the auxiliary aid.
(6) Where the first or third requirement relates to the provision of information, the steps which it is reasonable for A to have to take include steps for ensuring that in the circumstances concerned the information is provided in an accessible format.

(7) A person (A) who is subject to a duty to make reasonable adjustments is not (subject to express provision to the contrary) entitled to require a disabled person, in relation to whom A is required to comply with the duty, to pay to any extent A's costs of complying with the duty.

(8) A reference in section 21 or 22 or an applicable Schedule to the first, second or third requirement is to be construed in accordance with this section.

(9) In relation to the second requirement, a reference in this section or an applicable Schedule to avoiding a substantial disadvantage includes a reference to—

(a) removing the physical feature in question,
(b) altering it, or
(c) providing a reasonable means of avoiding it.

(10) A reference in this section, section 21 or 22 or an applicable Schedule (apart from paragraphs 2 to 4 of Schedule 4) to a physical feature is a reference to—

(a) a feature arising from the design or construction of a building,
(b) a feature of an approach to, exit from or access to a building,
(c) a fixture or fitting, or furniture, furnishings, materials, equipment or other chattels, in or on premises, or
(d) any other physical element or quality.

(11) A reference in this section, section 21 or 22 or an applicable Schedule to an auxiliary aid includes a reference to an auxiliary service …[47]

Equality Act 2010, 2010 Chapter 15, revision Notes[48]

82. This section defines what is meant by the duty to make reasonable adjustments for the purposes of the Act and lists the Parts of the Act which impose the duty and the related Schedules which stipulate how the duty will apply in relation to each Part. The duty comprises three requirements which apply where a disabled person is placed at a substantial disadvantage in comparison with non-disabled people. The first requirement covers changing the way things are done (such as changing a practice), the second covers making changes to the built environment (such as providing access to a building), and the third covers providing auxiliary aids and services (such as providing special computer software or providing a different service).

83. The section makes clear that where the first or third requirements involves the way in which information is provided, a reasonable step includes providing that information in an accessible format.

84. It sets out that under the second requirement, taking steps to avoid the disadvantage will include removing, altering or providing a reasonable means of avoiding the physical feature, where it would be reasonable to do so.

85. It also makes clear that, except where the Act states otherwise, it would never be reasonable for a person bound by the duty to pass on the costs of complying with it to an individual disabled person …

Examples

- A utility company knows that significant numbers of its customers have a sight impairment and will have difficulty reading invoices and other customer communications in standard

[47] Section 21(13) then provides that the relevant schedules for Part 3 (services and public functions), Part 4 (premises), Part 5 (work), Part 6 (education) and Part 7 (associations) are Schedules 2, 4, 8, 13 and 15, with Schedule 21 being applicable to all. See further pp 535–541 below.

[48] https://www.legislation.gov.uk/ukpga/2010/15/notes.

print, so must consider how to make its communications more accessible. As a result, it might provide communications in large print to customers who require this.

- A bank is obliged to consider reasonable adjustments for a newly recruited financial adviser who is a wheelchair user and who would have difficulty negotiating her way around the customer area. In consultation with the new adviser, the bank rearranges the layout of furniture in the customer area and installs a new desk. These changes result in the new adviser being able to work alongside her colleagues.
- The organiser of a large public conference knows that hearing-impaired delegates are likely to attend. She must therefore consider how to make the conference accessible to them. Having asked delegates what adjustments they need, she decides to engage BSL/English interpreters, have a palantypist and an induction loop to make sure that the hearing-impaired delegates are not substantially disadvantaged.

The duty is a continuing one.

EHRC, 'Services, public functions and associations', Statutory Code of Practice[49]

7.27 The duty to make reasonable adjustments is a continuing duty. Service providers should keep the duty and the ways they are meeting the duty under regular review in light of their experience with disabled people wishing to access their services. In this respect it is an evolving duty, and not something that needs simply to be considered once only, and then forgotten. What was originally a reasonable step to take might no longer be sufficient, and the provision of further or different adjustments might then have to be considered.

Example: A large sports complex amends its 'no dogs' policy to allow entry to assistance dogs. It offers assistance dog users a tour of the complex to acquaint them with routes. This is likely to be a reasonable step for it to have to take at this stage. However, the complex then starts building work and this encroaches on paths within the complex, making it difficult for assistance dog users to negotiate their way around. Offering an initial tour is therefore no longer an effective adjustment as it does not make the complex accessible to assistance dog users. The service provider therefore decides to offer assistance dog users appropriate additional assistance from staff while the building work is being undertaken. This is likely to be a reasonable step for the service provider to have to take in the circumstances then existing.

Section 21 EqA, Failure to comply with duty

(1) A failure to comply with the first, second or third requirement is a failure to comply with a duty to make reasonable adjustments.

(2) A discriminates against a disabled person if A fails to comply with that duty in relation to that person.

(3) A provision of an applicable Schedule which imposes a duty to comply with the first, second or third requirement applies only for the purpose of establishing whether A has contravened this Act by virtue of subsection (2); a failure to comply is, accordingly, not actionable by virtue of another provision of this Act or otherwise.

The general approach to s20 EqA discrimination was established by the EAT in *Environment Agency v Rowan*. The case was decided under the DDA but it remains applicable under the EqA.[50]

[49] n 43 above.

[50] See *Newham Sixth Form College v Saunders* [2014] EWCA Civ 734 and the EAT in *Muzi-Mabaso v HMRC* UKEAT/0353/14 13 November 2015, both unreported.

Environment Agency v Rowan **[2007] UKEAT 0060_07_0111, [2008] ICR 218**

The claimant, who was employed part-time as a clerk/typist, commenced long-term sickness absence in 2003 following a workplace accident in 1993 and related surgery in 1997. She sought to work from home but was subjected to capability procedures after her employer concluded that she did not wish to return, and resigned. An employment tribunal found that her employer had failed to make reasonable adjustments by refusing to let her work from home. The employer successfully appealed.

HHJ Serota QC:

> 32. … Ms Moore [for the Agency] … submitted that the employment tribunal had made no findings as to the nature and extent of the claimant's substantial disadvantage caused by being required to work in an office and did not give adequate consideration as to how the proposed adjustment would have prevented the claimant being place at a substantial disadvantage. It had also failed to identify the steps that might have been taken by the respondent to prevent office working placing her at a substantial disadvantage …
>
> 33. More crucially, the employment tribunal had made no findings (a) as to the nature of the claimant's disability, (b) as to why this disability placed her at a substantial disadvantage, (c) as to what that substantial disadvantage was, and (d) as to the claimant's duties or roles or the breakdown of the tasks required of her …
>
> **55. Conclusions on issues of disability discrimination**
>
> … we are satisfied that the respondent has made out its principal point; the employment tribunal failed to identify clearly the nature and extent of the substantial disadvantage suffered by the claimant. In the absence of such findings the employment tribunal was unable to determine properly what adjustments were reasonable to prevent the requirement to work in the respondent's office, (the provision, criterion or practice or feature that placed the claimant at a substantial disadvantage having that effect). We accept that there was evidence that might have justified a finding that the claimant was placed at a substantial disadvantage; however, that is not the point. There was a volume of conflicting evidence and powerful points were made by the respondent which the employment tribunal simply has not addressed. We cannot be sure of what facts were found by the employment tribunal.
>
> 56. The employment tribunal, because it has failed to identify clearly the nature and extent of the substantial disadvantage suffered by the claimant has not explained how the proposed adjustment (a trial period of home-working) would alleviate the claimant's substantial disadvantage. The substantial disadvantage not having been clearly identified it is impossible to know how home-working would have overcome this disadvantage and the employment tribunal fails to explain in its decision how home-working would have overcome the adverse effects said to have been suffered by the claimant. As we have said there may have been evidence that would have justified the finding but the evidence was conflicting and we can only guess as to what was accepted and what was not. There must be some explanation as to why home-working would alleviate the substantial disadvantage said to have been suffered by the claimant. The parties when considering the decision should not be expected to have to make assumptions as to facts found by the employment tribunal in a case where there was powerful evidence to suggest that home-working was not a reasonable adjustment and without an explanation having been given by the employment tribunal as to why the respondent's evidence and explanations were rejected …
>
> 59. In the circumstances the appeal must be allowed on this ground …

In *Newham Sixth Form College v Saunders* [2014] EWCA Civ 734, in which the CA approved the approach in *Rowan*, Laws LJ also stated that it was also necessary to consider the alleged discriminator's knowledge of the disadvantage as an alleged discriminator 'cannot … make an objective assessment of the reasonableness of proposed adjustments unless he appreciates the nature and extent of the substantial disadvantage imposed' upon the claimant.

Triggering the Duty to Adjust

Provision, Criterion or Practice

"Provision, criterion or practice' should be interpreted in line with s19 EqA (see Chapter 2) save that, by contrast with the provision, s20(3) does not require that a PCP relied upon in the context of a reasonable adjustments claim has been 'applied' to the claimant. In *Roberts v North West Ambulance Service* [2012] ICR D14 the EAT ruled that an employer who operated a 'hot-desking' space had discriminated against the claimant by failing to ensure that his preferred seat, which the employer had accepted he could have while working, was reserved for his exclusive use during any shift prior to his. The practice was that anyone sitting in the claimant's preferred seat on his arrival would be asked to move to accommodate him, and that the hot-desking policy would not be applied to the claimant. An employment tribunal found that it would have been impracticable for the employer to reserve his seat as requested and that, in any event, the requirement for hot-desking had not been applied to him. The EAT (Judge Richardson) allowed the claimant's appeal, ruling that the tribunal had been required to determine whether the policy placed the claimant at a substantial disadvantage irrespective of not having been applied to him and, if so, whether there were further steps which it was reasonable for the employer to have had to take.

The EHRC's Code of Practice on Employment states at §6.10 that the phrase 'should be construed widely so as to include, for example, any formal or informal policies, rules, practices, arrangements or qualifications including one-off decisions and actions' and provides an example of an employer whose policy is to provide designated car parking spaces to senior managers only: 'A worker who is not a manager, but has a mobility impairment and needs to park very close to the office, is given a designated car parking space. This is likely to be a reasonable adjustment to the employer's car parking policy'.[51]

Harvey on Industrial Relations points out that the non-payment of sick pay or other allowances may amount to a PCP as may being required to walk a particular distance from a car parking space to an office.[52]

***Harvey on Industrial Relations* Division L [389], [396.01], [402.01]**

The application of policies to manage attendance frequently arises for consideration where disabled employees may have more absences. The proper approach to the comparative exercise has been considered in a number of cases at EAT level.[53] In both cases the EAT held that the correct comparator group must consist of persons, who, by reason of illness, were subject to the [attendance management policy] but not disabled. As there was no difference in treatment, the duty to make adjustments was said not to arise. The CA have now held, however, that the correct formulation of the PCP is a requirement for an employee to maintain a certain level of attendance at work in order not to be subject to the risk of disciplinary sanctions[54]. In so formulating the PCP it was clear that a disabled employee whose disability increases the likelihood of absence from work is disadvantaged when compared to non-disabled employees as they are obviously at greater risk

[51] https://www.equalityhumanrights.com/en/publication-download/employment-statutory-code-practice.
[52] *Harvey on Industrial Relations*, Division L [389].
[53] Citing *Rider v Leeds CC* UKEAT/0243/11 and *Bailey v Hillingdon LBC* UKEAT/0421/12.
[54] Citing *Griffiths v SSWP* [2015] EWCA Civ 1265, [2017] ICR 160.

of being absent on grounds of ill health. It may then be a reasonable adjustment to alter trigger points at which disciplinary action will be considered …

The duty to adjust is, as a matter of policy, to enable employees to remain in employment, or to have access to employment. In *Croft Vets Ltd v Butcher [2013] EqLR 1170* it was held this could include the funding of private psychiatric counselling. However, the duty will not extend to matters which would not assist in preserving the employment relationship, such as matters relating to compensation for being unable to work. This was the reasoning of the EAT in *Tameside Hospital NHS Foundation Trust v Mylott UKEAT/0352/09* (11 March 2011, unreported) where the contention that the duty to make adjustments could require an employer to offer ill health retirement was rejected.

In *Kenny v Hampshire Constabulary* [1999] ICR 27, which was decided under the DDA (s6(2) of which referred not to PCPs but to 'any arrangements made by or on behalf of an employer') the EAT ruled that the 'arrangements' had to be job-related and did not extend to the provision of personal assistance to enable a cerebral palsy sufferer to use the toilet.

Physical Features

It is clear from s20(10)) EqA, extracted above, that the definition of 'physical features' is broad. Note the particular provision made in relation to the application of the second requirement in relation to Part 4 (premises) and where consent to changes is necessary (Schedule 21).

Auxiliary Aids

Section 20(11) EqA provides that auxiliary aid includes auxiliary service.

EHRC, 'Services, public functions and associations', Statutory Code of Practice[55]

7.47 An auxiliary aid or service is anything which provides additional support or assistance to a disabled person. Examples include:

- a special piece of equipment;
- the provision of a sign language interpreter, lip-speaker or deaf-blind communicator;
- extra staff assistance to disabled people;
- an electronic or manual note-taking service;
- induction loop or infrared broadcast system;
- videophones;
- audio-visual fire alarms;
- readers for people with visual impairments;
- assistance with guiding; and
- telephone services to supplement other information.

Example:

A person with both learning disabilities and mobility impairments needs to move to a more accessible property. The local authority choice-based letting scheme advertises properties in a weekly paper as available to people with different categories of assessed need. The properties are allocated on a first come, first-served basis. The local authority agrees with the disabled person that it will allocate a staff member to provide the necessary assistance to enable him to have equal access to housing choice. This is likely to be a reasonable step for the local authority to have to take.

Provision of information

7.48 The Act states that where the absence of an auxiliary aid or service places a disabled person at a substantial disadvantage, and this relates to the provision of information, the steps which it is

[55] n 43 above.

reasonable for a service provider to take, include steps to ensure that the information is provided in an accessible format.

Example:

A cinema chain ensures that subtitled performances of films are shown in all its branches, and that the times of these are advertised prominently. It also purchases equipment to provide audio description of films for visually impaired customers. These are likely to be reasonable steps for the cinema chain to have to take.

7.49 Nothing in the Act requires a service provider to provide an auxiliary aid or service to be used for personal purposes unconnected to the services being provided or to be taken away by the disabled person after use …

There is relatively little case law on auxiliary aids. In *Mallon v AECOM Ltd* [2021] IRLR 438, extracted at p 530 below, Judge James Tayler indicated that the case could have been better analysed as an auxiliary aid claim, (the aid being the provision of assistance to the claimant to complete an online application): 'Tribunals should have in mind when determining the issues in reasonable adjustments claims that it may not be a PCP case but may be about physical features (including furniture etc) or auxiliary aids (including services). For example, it is all too common for claims in which an employee contends that s/he needed an ergonomic chair, or voice recognition software, for the claim to be incorrectly analysed in terms of PCPs' (§27).

Substantial Disadvantage

In order to determine whether a PCP, physical feature or the absence of an auxiliary aid has placed the claimant at a 'substantial disadvantage' it will be necessary to determine the nature of the disadvantage (as in *Environment Agency v Rowan*) and to compare this with the impact of the PCP etc on people who are not disabled.

***London Clubs Management Ltd v Hood* [2001] IRLR 719**

In this case, which concerned the application of the-then s6(1) DDA, EAT overruled a tribunal which found that the claimant had been discriminated against contrary to the DDA when he was denied sick pay in respect of disability-related absence. The EAT criticised the tribunal's failure to give due weight to the fact that the employer had exercised its discretion to deny sick pay to all staff (this as a result of concern about the levels of absenteeism). Further:

Elizabeth Slade QC:

21. … it is not apparent … that [the tribunal] considered the question of whether Mr Hood was placed at a substantial disadvantage by the non-payment of sick pay in comparison with persons who were not disabled. If the tribunal is to be taken to have concluded that Mr Hood suffered a substantial disadvantage because of the sick pay arrangements, the reason for that conclusion is not evident from the decision. We consider that if such a conclusion were reached, it was particularly important to give the reasons for doing so in the circumstances of this case where the evidence appears to have indicated that non-disabled employees in common with Mr Hood had significant periods of unpaid sickness absence. Thus in our judgment insufficient reasons were given for the tribunal's conclusion that there had been discrimination.

***Mallon v AECOM Ltd* UKEAT_0175_20_LA (V), [2021] IRLR 438**

The claimant, who had dyspraxia, claimed that the company had breached the duty to make reasonable adjustments to its application process by failing to allow him to make an 'oral application' instead of completing an online application. The claim was struck out because the claimant had been able to make online job applications in the past and had made his ET1 application online. He had also made more than 30 previous ET claims, 29 of which he had withdrawn and three of which had been dismissed on the merits, the claimant having been required to pay costs in one of them. The tribunal, accordingly, did not accept that the PCP imposed by the company had placed the claimant at a significant disadvantage. The EAT allowed the claimant's appeal.

Judge James Tayler:

The Employment Judge analysed the Claimant's case from para 15 of his Judgment:

> '15. The Claimant stated that he requested an oral application instead of the online with the Respondent in this matter but this was not provided. He stated that he was genuine in his desire to work in London as he has had very long commutes to work for significant periods in previous roles.
>
> 16. … The Respondent sent several emails to the Claimant asking the Claimant to provide details of the assistance he required in submitting the form so that his disability could be accommodated. The Claimant did not respond with any details. However, he consistently requested an "oral application". The Claimant's position was that the only way in which he was prepared to progress the application would be by way of oral application.
>
> 17. He stated before me that he cannot engage with online forms, password characters and dropdown menus. This was not conveyed to the Respondent at the time who were, on the face of it reasonably requesting from the Claimant what parts of the online process were said to be problematic. Further, the Respondent in this matter was also aware that the Claimant had in fact completed online forms for them when he worked with them previously.
>
> 18. The Claimant asserted that he could not ask his wife for help in completing the online form as she was not his carer; he was embarrassed to asked friends for help as they did not know that he suffers from dyspraxia; and it would have taken too much time to go to an advice centre for assistance. In respect of the online form that he had previously submitted to the Respondent, he stated he asked his wife for assistance with that because it was a job offer as opposed to an application. I was unable to accept this distinction as likely to be credible.
>
> 19. It is evident that it was the Claimant's choice about who to ask and who to seek assistance from. It is reasonable to infer that if the Claimant was genuinely interested in the role he would have sought assistance in progressing the online application form. In view of the fact that the Claimant was aware of previous Tribunal findings against him on this specific matter it is [likely] to be implausible for the Claimant to continue to maintain that he could not have availed of assistance.
>
> 20. When addressing the submission that the online form was not more involved than the numerous online Employment Tribunal claims he has made, the Claimant stated that he was now experienced at submitted Employment Tribunal claims and was familiar with the process. This did not apply to online processes that he had not encountered before and he would need time to handle them.'…

[Having stressed that claims should only be struck out in the clearest of cases]

22. If an employer, would otherwise be under a duty to make an adjustment, care should be taken before it is assumed that the adjustment is not reasonably required because someone else can make the adjustment. Friends and family may be prepared to help a disabled person, but they should not be expected to step in and make a reasonable adjustment for an employer, or potential employer, to save it from the trouble of having to make the adjustment itself. Similarly, great care should be taken before concluding that a PCP does not place a disabled person at a disadvantage because someone other than the employer, or potential employer, can provide the help that would otherwise have been required as a reasonable adjustment …

35. It does not follow from the fact that there was no time frame in which to complete the online application, that the Claimant was not put at a more than minor or trivial disadvantage, if filling in the online application would take him significantly more time than a person who is not disabled … even if unlimited time is available, a disabled person could still be at a substantial disadvantage if s/he has to spend much longer completing the form than a person who is not disabled …

36. Similarly, the fact that the Claimant could seek assistance in completing the online application, did not necessarily mean that he was not put at a substantial disadvantage by having to do so. If a person who did not have a disability could complete the form without assistance, depending on the facts of the case, the requirement for assistance, itself, could be a disadvantage that is more than minor or trivial. Most people would want to be able to complete a job application themselves, without having to rely on their friends and family. Proper determination of this point is likely to be fact sensitive …

37. Even if it is correct that the Claimant's demand for an oral application, without further elaboration, was unreasonable, this does not go to the question of whether the Claimant was put at a substantial disadvantage by being required to complete an online application, which was the only matter in issue in the strike out application. The claim was not dismissed on the basis that there was no reasonable prospect of establishing that a member of the Respondent's staff speaking to the Claimant by telephone, entering his details into the online form and uploading the CV he had sent by email, could be a reasonable adjustment. The correspondence in the bundle seems to show a degree of intransigence on both sides, that would require consideration on a proper analysis of the evidence. If it was contended that the Claimant requested an oral application because he knew that the Respondent would not provide one, and so he would have a basis for a claim, despite not really wanting the job, and so was at no disadvantage, that is a matter that could not be assumed on a summary consideration at this preliminary hearing, and would have to be put fairly to the Claimant …

38. … I do not consider that it necessarily follows from the fact that a person has previously been able to complete an online form that s/he may not be at a substantial disadvantage in doing so, depending on how long it takes, and what assistance is required. Any difficulties that the Claimant faced in completing claims to the Employment Tribunal would be likely to require fact finding. I also do not consider that the Claimant's argument that he finds it much easier to fill in an online form once he has already completed one of that type, is so obviously without merit that it should be dismissed summarily …

43. I do not consider that on the material that was before this Employment Judge, on the basis of the arguments advanced and his analysis of them, it could properly be said that this claim had no reasonable prospects of success. I consider that the Employment Judge erred in law in striking out the claim …

48. The Claimant told me that he is focused on obtaining work. His chances of obtaining work will increase if he explains to any prospective employers the nature of his disability and the effects it has on his ability to complete online forms; and co-operates with them to find effective means for him to make his applications. The Claimant told me that his applications are for jobs that he genuinely wants. Were that not the case, and were it to be established that multiple applications were being made for jobs that he does not want, with the aim of bringing claims, possibly to achieve settlements, that is a matter that could result in strike out and costs.

The Reasonableness of Adjustments

The adjustments which are required by s20 EqA are those steps which are reasonable, in all the circumstances of the case, for the employer, service provider, etc to have to take in order to avoid the substantial disadvantage otherwise caused by the PCP, etc. This requires that the disabled person be treated more favourably than those others to whom the PCP, etc applies.

EHRC, 'Services, public functions and associations', Statutory Code of Practice[56]

7.29 The duty to make reasonable adjustments places service providers under a responsibility to take such steps as it is reasonable, in all the circumstances of the case, to have to take in order to make adjustments. The Act does not specify that any particular factors should be taken into account. What is a reasonable step for a particular service provider to have to take depends on all the circumstances of the case. It will vary according to:

- the type of service being provided;
- the nature of the service provider and its size and resources; and
- the effect of the disability on the individual disabled person.

7.30 However, without intending to be exhaustive, the following are some of the factors which might be taken into account when considering what is reasonable:

- whether taking any particular steps would be effective in overcoming the substantial disadvantage that disabled people face in accessing the services;
- the extent to which it is practicable for the service provider to take the steps;
- the financial and other costs of making the adjustment;
- the extent of any disruption which taking the steps would cause;
- the extent of the service provider's financial and other resources;
- the amount of any resources already spent on making adjustments; and
- the availability of financial or other assistance.

Example:

Customers in a busy post office are served by staff at a counter after queuing in line. A disabled customer with severe arthritis wishes to purchase a vehicle tax disc. He experiences pain if he has to stand for more than a couple of minutes. Other customers would not expect to have to undergo similar discomfort in order to buy a vehicle tax disc. Thus, the post office's queuing policy places the disabled customer at a substantial disadvantage. Consideration will have to be given as to how the queuing policy could be adjusted so as to accommodate the requirements of such disabled customers. Depending on the size of the post office, staff could ask the customer to take a seat and then serve him in the same way as if he had queued. Alternatively, it might provide a separate service desk with seating for disabled customers.

[56] n 43 above.

7.31 It is more likely to be reasonable for a service provider with substantial financial resources to have to make an adjustment with a significant cost than for a service provider with fewer resources …

EHRC, 'Employment: Statutory Code of Practice'[57]

6.24 There is no onus on the disabled worker to suggest what adjustments should be made (although it is good practice for employers to ask). However, where the disabled person does so, the employer should consider whether such adjustments would help overcome the substantial disadvantage, and whether they are reasonable.

6.25 Effective and practicable adjustments for disabled workers often involve little or no cost or disruption and are therefore very likely to be reasonable for an employer to have to make. Even if an adjustment has a significant cost associated with it, it may still be cost-effective in overall terms – for example, compared with the costs of recruiting and training a new member of staff – and so may still be a reasonable adjustment to have to make.

6.26 Many adjustments do not involve making physical changes to premises. However, where such changes need to be made and an employer occupies premises under a lease or other binding obligation, the employer may have to obtain consent to the making of reasonable adjustments …

6.27 If making a particular adjustment would increase the risk to health and safety of any person (including the disabled worker in question) then this is a relevant factor in deciding whether it is reasonable to make that adjustment. Suitable and sufficient risk assessments should be used to help determine whether such risk is likely to arise.

The Employment Code of Practice suggests the types of adjustment which may be reasonable (though what is reasonable will depend on the particular circumstances of each case). These include (§6.33):

- 'Making adjustments to premises' (eg 'widening a doorway, providing a ramp or moving furniture for a wheelchair user');
- 'Providing information in accessible formats';
- 'Allocating some of the disabled person's duties to another worker' (eg 'the job involves occasionally going onto the open roof of a building but the employer transfers this work away from a worker whose disability involves severe vertigo');
- 'Transferring the disabled worker to fill an existing vacancy'[58] ('Such a post might also involve retraining or other reasonable adjustments such as equipment for the new post or transfer to a position on a higher grade');
- 'Altering the disabled worker's hours of work or training';
- 'Assigning the disabled worker to a different place of work or training or arranging home working';
- 'Allowing the disabled worker to be absent during working or training hours for rehabilitation, assessment or treatment';

[57] n 51 above.

[58] See eg *Archibald v Fife* [2004] UKHL 32, [2004] ICR 95; *Abertawe Bro Morgannwg University Local Health Board v Morgan* [2018] ICR 1194; C-485/20, *XXXX v HR RAIL SA*, EU-C-2022-85, [2022] ICR 881, in which the CJEU ruled that a worker who was incapable, by reason of disability, of performing the essential duties of his or her post should be reassigned to another post for which he or she was competent, capable and available, subject to a disproportionate burden defence.

- 'Giving, or arranging for, training or mentoring (whether for the disabled person or any other worker)';
- 'Acquiring or modifying equipment' ('There is no requirement to provide or modify equipment for personal purposes unconnected with a worker's job, such as providing a wheelchair if a person needs one in any event but does not have one. The disadvantages in such a case do not flow from the employer's arrangements or premises');
- 'Modifying procedures for testing or assessment';
- 'Providing a reader or interpreter';
- 'Providing supervision or other support';
- 'Allowing a disabled worker to take a period of disability leave';
- 'Participating in supported employment schemes, such as Workstep';
- 'Employing a support worker to assist a disabled worker' (eg 'An adviser with a visual impairment is sometimes required to make home visits to clients. The employer employs a support worker to assist her on these visits');
- 'Modifying disciplinary or grievance procedures for a disabled worker' ('A worker with a learning disability is allowed to take a friend (who does not work with her) to act as an advocate at a meeting with her employer about a grievance');
- 'Adjusting redundancy selection criteria for a disabled worker' (eg 'Because of his condition, a man with an autoimmune disease has taken several short periods of absence during the year. When his employer is taking the absences into account as a criterion for selecting people for redundancy, they discount these periods of disability-related absence');
- 'Modifying performance-related pay arrangements for a disabled worker' (eg 'A disabled worker who is paid purely on her output needs frequent short additional breaks during her working day – something her employer agrees to as a reasonable adjustment. It may be a reasonable adjustment for her employer to pay her at an agreed rate (for example, her average hourly rate) for these breaks').

The Code warns that employers may have to take a combination of steps.

Associative Discrimination

The concept of associative discrimination has been discussed in Chapter 2 and featured in *Bennett v MiTAC Europe Ltd* [2022] IRLR 25, discussed above. The CA ruled in *Hainsworth v Ministry of Defence* it does not apply in relation to reasonable adjustments.

Hainsworth v Ministry of Defence **[2014] EWCA Civ 763, [2014] IRLR 728**

The claimant, whose daughter was severely disabled, was a civilian employee of the Ministry of Defence based in Germany. She wished to transfer to the UK because there were no appropriate MOD schools for her daughter in Germany. She argued that Article 5 of Directive 2000/78 required the MOD to make adjustments to a PCP applied to her to enable her daughter, a person 'associated' with her, to undergo training and education. to establish that her employer should have permitted her to move workplace to enable her daughter to undergo training. That provision requires that '… employers shall take appropriate measures … to enable a person with a disability to have access to, participate in, or advance in employment, or to undergo training …'

Laws LJ, with whom Tomlinson and Briggs LJJ agreed:

> 19. … it seems to me that the obvious and entire focus of Article 5 is upon provisions to be made by an employer …
>
> 25. … Article 5 is limited so as to require measures only for the assistance of disabled employees or prospective employees of the employer in question
>
> 33. … neither the UN Convention [on the Rights of Persons with Disabilities', nor the EU Charter of Fundamental Right or the European Social Charter (which is also relied on) begins to be capable of qualifying what to my mind is the plain and inescapable meaning of Article 5 of the Directive'.

The duty to make adjustments being dependent upon disability-related substantial disadvantage, it follows that it does not apply in cases of perceived disability.

Reasonable Adjustments: Particular

Schedules 2, 4, 8, 15 and 13 make specific provision for reasonable adjustments in relation to services and public functions (Part 3 EqA), premises (Part 4), work (Part 5), education (Part 6) and associations (Part 7), with Schedule 21 making provision in relation to reasonable adjustments for cases in which alterations to premises would require the consent of third parties (and see also Part 4 Regulations). The most significant provisions of Schedule 2 are extracted and discussed below, the other Schedules being dealt with more briefly and largely by way of comparison with Schedule 2.

Schedule 2 EqA, Reasonable adjustments: services and public functions

The duty

(1) A must comply with the first, second and third requirements.

(2) For the purposes of this paragraph, the reference in section 20(3), (4) or (5) to a disabled person is to disabled persons generally.

(3) Section 20 has effect as if, in subsection (4), for 'to avoid the disadvantage' there were substituted—

'(a) to avoid the disadvantage, or

(b) to adopt a reasonable alternative method of providing the service or exercising the function.'

(4) In relation to each requirement, the relevant matter is the provision of the service, or the exercise of the function, by A.

(5) Being placed at a substantial disadvantage in relation to the exercise of a function means—

(a) if a benefit is or may be conferred in the exercise of the function, being placed at a substantial disadvantage in relation to the conferment of the benefit, or

(b) if a person is or may be subjected to a detriment in the exercise of the function, suffering an unreasonably adverse experience when being subjected to the detriment.

(6) In relation to the second requirement, a physical feature includes a physical feature brought by or on behalf of A, in the course of providing the service or exercising the function, on to premises other than those that A occupies (as well as including a physical feature in or on premises that A occupies).

(7) If A is a service-provider, nothing in this paragraph requires A to take a step which would fundamentally alter—

(a) the nature of the service, or
(b) the nature of A's trade or profession.

(8) If A exercises a public function, nothing in this paragraph requires A to take a step which A has no power to take.

Specific provision is made in relation to transport by para 3 of Schedule 2 the detail of which is beyond the scope of this book. It is worth noting that the duty of reasonable adjustment is owed (in the context of services and public functions) to disabled people generally. The effect of this is that it is an *anticipatory* duty rather than one which arises only in relation to specific disabled persons. The significance of this cannot be overstated:

EHRC, 'Services, public functions and associations', Statutory Code of Practice[59]

7.20 In relation to all three areas of activity (services, public functions and associations) the duty is anticipatory in the sense that it requires consideration of, and action in relation to, barriers that impede people with one or more kinds of disability prior to an individual disabled person seeking to use the service, avail themselves of a function or participate in the activities of an association.

7.21 Service providers should therefore not wait until a disabled person wants to use a service that they provide before they give consideration to their duty to make reasonable adjustments. They should anticipate the requirements of disabled people and the adjustments that may have to be made for them. Failure to anticipate the need for an adjustment may create additional expense, or render it too late to comply with the duty to make the adjustment. Furthermore, it may not in itself provide a defence to a claim of a failure to make a reasonable adjustment.

Example: A person with a visual impairment regularly receives printed letters regarding his social security benefits, despite the fact that on previous occasions he has indicated his need for Braille and this has been provided. He finds this repeated need to telephone to ask for Braille frustrating and inconvenient, but is told that the software, which generates communications, does not enable a record to be kept of customers' needs for alternative formats. This may constitute a failure to make reasonable adjustments if it is judged to have left the disabled person at a substantial disadvantage and there was a reasonable adjustment that could have been made.

7.22 Because this is a duty to disabled people at large, it applies regardless of whether the service provider knows that a particular person is disabled or whether it currently has disabled customers, members etc.

7.23 When disabled customers request services, the service provider must already have taken all reasonable steps to ensure that they can be served.

7.24 Service providers are not expected to anticipate the needs of every individual who may use their service, but what they are required to think about and take reasonable steps to overcome are barriers that may impede people with different kinds of disability. For example, people with dementia, mental health conditions or mobility impairments may face different types of barriers.

7.25 Disabled people are a diverse group with different requirements – for example, visually impaired people who use guide dogs will be prevented from using services with a 'no dogs' policy, whereas visually impaired people who use white canes will not be affected by this policy. The duty will still be owed to members of both groups.

[59] n 43 above.

7.26 Once a service provider has become aware of the requirements of a particular disabled person who uses or seeks to use its services, it might then be reasonable for the service provider to take a particular step to meet these requirements. This is especially so where a disabled person has pointed out the difficulty that they face in accessing services, or has suggested a reasonable solution to that difficulty.

Example: A disabled person attending the annual general meeting of an association experiences a flare-up of their medical condition, as a result of which they would have experienced severe back pain when sitting on the hard chairs provided for the meeting. Despite the lack of notice, those organising the meeting were able to find a more suitable chair and make this available to the association member.

It is also worth noting the limitation imposed by Schedule 2, para 2(7), which provides that service providers are not required to 'take a step which would fundamentally alter (a) the nature of the service, or (b) the nature of [the service provider's] trade or profession.

EHRC, 'Services, public functions and associations', Statutory Code of Practice[60]

Example: A restaurant that offers a 'dining in the dark' experience is unlikely to have to make the reasonable adjustment of leaving its lights on for a deaf customer who needs to be able to lip read to communicate as this would fundamentally alter the nature of the service being offered.

The reasonable adjustment duty which applies to associations contains a similar qualification, the Code of Practice suggesting (§12.44) that a wine club which 'meets specifically to drink and discuss the merits of different types of wine' would not be required to 'expand its activity to include the tasting of fruit juices' to accommodate the alcohol intolerance of a prospective member.

Premises

Schedule 4 EqA (premises) provides, so far as relevant (para 2), that the controllers of let premises must comply with the first and third requirements (further that 'provision, criterion or practice' includes the terms of letting[61]). In this context, by contrast with services and public functions, the duty of adjustment is owed only to tenants and those otherwise entitled to occupy premises, the requirement to make adjustments applies only on request and there is never a requirement to remove or alter any physical feature of the premises, though 'physical features do not include furniture, furnishings, materials, equipment or other chattels in or on the premises' and that replacing or providing a sign or notice, replacing taps or door handles, replacing, providing or adapting door bells or door entry system and changing the colour of a wall, door or any other surface do not amount to altering physical features. Paragraph 3 makes similar provision in relation to the controllers of premises *to be let*, the duty of adjustment being owed to disabled persons who are considering taking a letting of the premises. Paragraph 4 makes materially similar provision to 'commonhold associations' (associations which manages a commonhold unit, the duty being owed to disabled persons who are unit-holders or are entitled to occupy units of the commonhold. Paragraph 5 requires that those responsible for common parts must comply with the second requirement in relation to physical features of the common parts, this duty being owed to

[60] n 43 above.

[61] Though a term of a letting which prohibits the tenant from making alterations is required to be changed only so far as is necessary to enable a disabled tenant to make alterations to the let premises so as to avoid the relevant disadvantage.

disabled persons who are tenants, unit-holders or are otherwise entitled to occupy the premises *and who use or intend to use the premises as their only or main home*. Paragraph 6 imposes duties of consultation before steps are taken to comply with para 5 and para 7 requires that any steps taken under para 5 must be subject to written agreement between A and B as the 'the rights and responsibilities of each of them in relation to the step', A being entitled to insist that B bears the costs of alteration and subsequent restoration.

Work

Schedule 8, like Schedule 3 EqA, provides that A (here, broadly, employers) must comply with the first, second and third requirements imposed by s20 EqA,[62] para 2(2)(c) stating that 'the reference in section 20(3), (4) or (5) to a disabled person is to an interested disabled person'. An 'interested person' is defined in Schedule 8 Part 2, as 'A person who is, or has notified A that the person may be, an applicant for the employment' (this where the duty of adjustment is said to arise in connection with a decision as to who to offer employment) or, where the duty is said to arise in connection with employment, an applicant to or employee of A. Schedule 8 Part 2 EqA makes materially similar provision in relation to principals in contract work, partnerships, LLPs, barristers, advocates and clerks, persons making appointments to public bodies, qualifications bodies, employment service providers, trade organisations, local authorities and occupational pension providers. In each case the duty to make reasonable adjustments is owed to specific disabled people rather than to disabled people generally. Schedule 8 Part 2 also makes specific provision for the application of the duty of reasonable adjustment to the employers of contract workers.

Schedule 8 Part 1 EqA provides (para 2(5)) that 'If two or more persons are subject to a duty to make reasonable adjustments in relation to the same interested disabled person, each of them must comply with the duty so far as it is reasonable for each of them to do so'. Paragraph 3 makes similar provision in relation to employment services. Schedule 8 Part 3 EqA imposes limitations on the duty to make reasonable adjustments where A 'does not know, and could not reasonably be expected to know … that an interested disabled person is or may be an applicant for the work in question' or 'that an interested disabled person has a disability and is likely to be placed at the disadvantage referred to in the first, second or third requirement', going on to set out what is meant by 'applicant' in relation to employment, partnership etc.

In this context, unlike in the context of service provision, the duty to make adjustments is *reactive* rather than *anticipatory*. It was suggested above that employers ought to discuss with disabled staff/applicants what adjustments might be suitable, though the failure to do so will not itself amount to a breach of the duty. The responsibility for determining what adjustments are reasonable remains firmly on the employer.

***Cosgrove v Caesar & Howie* [2001] UKEAT 1432_00_1705, [2001] IRLR 653**

The claimant was a legal secretary at a firm of solicitors. She was dismissed after being absent for a year with depression and claimed that she had been subject to discrimination including by reason of the employer's failure to make reasonable adjustments. An employment tribunal dismissed her complaint because 'neither the applicant nor her

[62] Except in relation to applicants in respect of whom the second requirement does not apply.

medical witness were able to state what adjustments the respondents could have made to improve her situation and to facilitate an eventual return.'

Lindsay J (P):

> 6. … the duty to make adjustments … is upon the employer. The employer, consistently with its view that there was no disability, had said in its particulars: 'The respondents did not consider any steps or adjustments could be made as in their view the applicant was not suffering from a disability.' And a little later in the same particulars: 'The respondents did not consider any further adjustments as in their view the applicant was not suffering from a disability.' That was confirmed in evidence. The tribunal held:
>
> > 'Mr Borrowman (a partner in the firm) confirmed in evidence that he was aware of the terms of the Act as staff partner, although he did not consider that the Act applied in connection with the applicant's condition. He therefore did not consider what steps he might be able to take to assist her.'
>
> The tribunal jumped from the evidence given at the employment tribunal that Ms Cosgrove's general practitioner and she herself could not think of any useful adjustment to the conclusion that no useful adjustment could be made …
>
> But whether *the employer* could, had it considered … the duty thereby imposed upon it, have thought up any useful adjustment was not a question as to which, as far as one can tell, evidence on the employer's part was adduced. The employer, as Mr Borrowman's evidence made clear, never turned its mind to adjustments or their possibilities.
>
> 7. There will, no doubt, be cases where the evidence given on the applicant's side alone will establish a total unavailability of reasonable and effective adjustments. But it does not seem to us to follow that because a former secretary, long absent from the firm and clinically depressed to the point of disability and her general practitioner also (the latter, at least, being unlikely to know what office or other practicabilities were open to the employer) could postulate no useful adjustment, that the … duty on the employer should, without more, be taken to have been satisfied. Indeed, in the course of argument before us, Mr Millar accepted that the doctor and the applicant were not the most appropriate persons to be asked as to what adjustments could be made. The tribunal said:
>
> > 'Perhaps most importantly both the applicant and Dr Brook stated in evidence that the applicant's condition could not have responded to any adjustments to the workplace. She could not think of anything that the respondents could have done which would have improved the situation.'
>
> That relates only to Ms Cosgrove's ability to discern some adjustment and to the possibility of adjustment to the workplace (and not, be it noted, *at* the workplace). But if the employer had turned its mind to adjustments, might a transfer to another office of the firm have been a possibility? Would it have so reduced the stress which she had suffered at, and could well have suffered on return to, the Bathgate office and upon her working with the partners and staff at that office that a return to work similar to the work she had undertaken earlier or at least a return to some work would become possible … She was under a degree of stress by reason of her having to look after her mother, who was found to have Alzheimer's disease; would an alteration of her working hours … to allow her the better to cope with her mother's needs have so reduced Ms Cosgrove's symptoms that a return to her erstwhile work or to some work would have become possible? Would a very gradual return, building slowly from part-time working in gentle duties to full-time working on her erstwhile duties, have materially facilitated a return? … We do not suggest that there would necessarily have been a positive answer to such questions, but there can be no assurance at all that there would not have been since, unfortunately, such questions were not asked at or around the time of dismissal, or indeed, as it would

seem, even at the tribunal. It cannot, it seems to us, be as *decisive* as the tribunal took it to be on the issue of whether any reasonable adjustments were available that might have prevented Ms Cosgrove's inability to work by reason of her medical condition that neither she, a mentally disabled person, could, at the tribunal itself, suggest any, nor that her doctor, who, as far as we can tell, had no such questions posed to him and could not, presumably, in any event be expected to know what office possibilities the employer could offer, had, at the tribunal, not been able to suggest any either.

Education

Schedule 13 para 2 EqA states, in relation to schools, that 'responsible bodies' must comply with the first and third requirements imposed by s20 EqA. Para 2(3)(b) provides that the duty of adjustment is owed to disabled persons generally where it applies in relation to deciding who is offered admission as a pupil, and that it is owed to disabled pupils generally where it applies in relation to the provision of education or access to a benefit, facility or service.

Paragraph 3 provides that the responsible bodies of higher and further education institutions are subject to all three requirements imposed by s21 EqA. The duty is owed to disabled persons generally where it concerns decisions as to who is offered admission as a student; to disabled students generally where it concerns the provision of education or access to a benefit, facility or service, and to interested disabled persons where it concerns decisions relating to qualifications.[63] Importantly, paragraph 3 goes on to provide as follows:

Schedule 13 para 3 EqA, competence standards

(2) A provision, criterion or practice does not include the application of a competence standard.
(3) A competence standard is an academic, medical or other standard applied for the purpose of determining whether or not a person has a particular level of competence or ability.

Burke v College of Law [2012] EWCA Civ 37, [2012] ELR 195 was brought under the 'qualifying body' provisions of the DDA, and therefore initially heard by an employment tribunal. The CA dismissed an appeal from the claimant, who had multiple sclerosis, and who sought to challenge a requirement that legal professional examinations be conducted within particular time periods (he had been granted 60 per cent additional time as well as a number of other adjustments and had been provided with an amanuensis who could also be required to act as a reader, additional breaks, his own room for taking the exam, an extra desk and a number of attempts at the examination). An employment tribunal had found that the ability to work at speed under time pressure was part of the competence to be assessed in the examination and therefore that the time requirement was a competence standard, and the EAT had agreed. The CA dismissed the appeal on the basis that all reasonable adjustments had been made, though without determining the 'particular and interesting question whether the time requirement is a competence standard' (§39 *per* Kitchin LJ, with whom Laws and Tomlinson LJJ agreed). In *Islam v Bar Standards Board* [2012] All ER (D) 05 (Aug) the claimant, who was registered blind, unsuccessfully sought to challenge minimum entry standards imposed by the Bar Standards Board for entry to

[63] An interested disabled person is defined as a person who is, or has notified A that the person may be, an applicant for the conferment of the qualification, where the decision concerns upon whom to confer a qualification; applicants for the conferment by A of the relevant qualification and persons upon whom A confers the qualification in the case of qualifications conferred by A.

the profession of barrister. The High Court was satisfied that no duty to make adjustments applied to the minimum entry criteria. And in *Koci v University College London* [2014] All ER (D) 232 (Jan) the county court struck out a reasonable adjustments challenge to the threshold criteria for UCL's LLM course, though it allowed the claimant's s15 EqA claim to proceed to a full hearing.[64]

Provision is made by Schedule 13 para 4 EqA in relation to providers of further or higher education courses not falling within paragraph 3 and by para 6 to providers of recreational or training facilities falling within s93 EqA. Paragraph 9 makes provision for qualifications bodies and para 7 provides that 'In deciding whether it is reasonable for A to have to take a step for the purpose of complying with the first, second or third requirement, A must have regard to relevant provisions of a Code of Practice issued under section 14 of the Equality Act 2006'.[65] Paragraph 8 provides that where a person has 'made a confidentiality request of which A is aware', A must take into consideration whether that request is consistent with an adjustment in determining whether such an adjustment is reasonable.[66]

Reasonable Adjustments: Associations

Schedule 15 EqA provides that associations must comply with all three requirements imposed by s20 EqA, the duty of reasonable adjustment being owed to disabled persons who 'are, or are seeking to become or might wish to become, members, are associates, or are, or are likely to become, guests.' It further provides that, where s20(4) EqA makes reference to the avoidance of disadvantage resulting from a physical feature, it should be read to include an option for A to take reasonable steps 'to adopt a reasonable alternative method of affording access to the benefit, facility or service or of admitting persons to membership or inviting persons as guests.' Note also (Schedule 15 para 2(7)) that the duty to make reasonable adjustment does not require an association 'to take a step which would fundamentally alter (a) the nature of the benefit, facility or service concerned, or (b) the nature of the association'. Paragraph 2(8) provides that nothing requires 'a member or associate in whose house meetings of the association take place to make adjustments to a physical feature of the house'.

Exceptions

The exceptions considered here are in addition to the general exceptions from the EqA's prohibitions on discrimination which are discussed in Chapter 4.

Part 3 EqA: Services

Schedule 3 EqA, which contains exceptions applicable to s29 EqA (the prohibition on discrimination in connection with public functions, goods and services) provides that local authorities in England or Wales are not required to remove or alter any physical feature

[64] Permission to appeal has been granted against the decision of the county court in *Abrahart v University of Bristol* (decision of 20 May 2022, [2022] Lexis Citation 81), which adopted a narrow approach to competence standards.

[65] No such Code has been issued, the EHRC instead having issued non-statutory technical guidance for schools.

[66] A confidentiality request is a request that the nature or existence of a disabled person's disability be treated as confidential, such a request having been made by the person's parent or by the person themselves in circumstances in which A 'reasonably believes that the person has sufficient understanding of the nature and effect of the request'.

on premises in performing their functions under the Education Acts.[67] Schedule 3 para 16 EqA provides that the prohibition on disability discrimination does not apply to decisions to refuse entry clearance or leave to enter or remain in the UK, cancel or to vary or refuse to such leave, or to anything done in pursuance of such decisions, or to decisions taken, or guidance given, by the Secretary of State in connection with a decision within sub-paragraph, or to decisions taken in accordance with guidance given by the Secretary of State in connection with such decisions Schedule 3 para 21 EqA provides that anything done in connection with insurance business if will not amount to disability discrimination contrary to s29 EqA if 'that thing is done by reference to information that is both relevant to the assessment of the risk to be insured and from a source on which it is reasonable to rely, and it is reasonable to do that thing'. This is in addition to the general exception related to insurance policies entered into before October 2010 discussed in Chapter 4.

Part 9 of Schedule 3 (paras 32–34A) provide a number of exceptions to the prohibition of disability discrimination relating to transport and falling within s29 EqA. These provisions are meant to exclude from the EqA those matters already covered by various EU laws which are still in force in the UK, though it is unclear at the time of writing for how long. Paragraph 33 exempts transport by air and service on a vehicle for transporting people by air save to the extent that the same is governed by Regulation (EC) No 1107/2006 of the European Parliament and of the Council of 5 July 2006 concerning the rights of disabled persons and persons with reduced mobility when travelling by air. Paragraph 34 provides that s29 EqA will only apply to the transport of people in certain vehicles, though these include passenger transport vehicles, goods transport vehicles weighing no more than 3.5 tonnes, private hire vehicles and taxis, public service vehicles, trams and break-down recovery vehicles designed to transport drivers and passengers. Paragraph 34 states that the no duty of reasonable accommodation applies under s29 to 'anything that is governed by Regulation (EU) No 181/2011 of the European Parliament and of the Council of 16 February 2011 concerning the rights of passengers in bus and coach transport and amending Regulation (EC) No 2006/2004.' And para 34A excludes from the scope of s29 EqA 'anything governed by Regulation (EC) No 1371/2007 of the European Parliament and of the Council of 23 October 2007 on rail passengers' rights and obligations.

Part 5 EqA: Work

Schedule 9 para 4(3) provides that Part 5 EqA 'so far as relating to age or disability, does not apply to service in the armed forces; and section 55 [which applies to employment service providers], so far as relating to disability, does not apply to work experience in the armed forces'. Note that this exclusion applies irrespective of the justifiability of the discrimination. The Explanatory Notes to the EqA states that para 4 'replicates the effects of exemptions for the armed forces in previous legislation, but narrows the scope of the former combat effectiveness exception so that this applies only to direct discrimination in relation to recruitment and access to training, promotion and transfer opportunities' (§799).[68]

Part 6 EqA: Education

Schedule 11 para 8 EqA allows 'permitted forms of selection' in schools including grammar schools, independent schools and other selective schools.

[67] These relate to the organisation of and support for education rather than its direct provision.
[68] n 48 above.

9

Religion and Belief

Introduction

Prior to December 2003, Northern Ireland was unique in the UK in having legislation (the Fair Employment and Treatment Order (FETO) 1998, previously the Fair Employment Act 1989) which explicitly regulated discrimination on grounds of religion. In 2003 the Employment Equality (Religion or Belief) Regulations ('RB Regs') prohibited discrimination and harassment on grounds of religion and belief in the context of work, broadly defined in Great Britain (GB; see further Chapter 4). The Equality Act 2006 extended the regulation of discrimination on grounds of religion or belief to cover goods, facilities and services, public functions, premises and education and the Equality Act 2010 (EqA) extended that regulation to cover associations and added religion or belief to the protected characteristics to which Public Sector Equality Duty (PSED) applies (see Chapter 3). Some differences remain between religion and belief (and sexual orientation), on the one hand, and other protected characteristics. In particular, harassment on the basis of these protected characteristics is not regulated under Part 3 (services), Part 5 (premises), Part 6 (education) or Part 7 (associations). Other notable differences between religion and belief and other characteristic relate to the genuine occupational requirement (GOR) defence and to the extent to which the religious or other ethos of organisations can legitimise discrimination by that organisation on grounds not only of religion or belief, but also of sex, sexual orientation, gender reassignment and marriage or civil partnership status.

The regulation of discrimination on grounds of religion and belief gives rise to difficulties not generated by most other protected characteristics.[1] Whereas one person's right not to be subjected to race discrimination is unlikely to conflict with another person's such right (the same being true in relation to sex, sexual orientation, disability, etc), anti-discrimination rights connected with religion and belief may well clash with each other, and with anti-discrimination rights connected with other grounds such as sex and sexual orientation. This 'clash of rights' arises in part from the fact that religious bodies, as well as individuals, claim protection for freedom of religion and belief. In order to maintain its religious ethos, a body

[1] Though see Ch 6 for a discussion of the tensions between sex and gender reassignment as protected characteristics.

may wish to exclude others who do not share that ethos, or whose behaviour is otherwise considered not to be in conformity with the ethos of the collective. This is relatively uncontroversial where, for example, a church or religious organisation wishes to discriminate, on grounds of religion, in the appointment of a minister. Most would agree that such discrimination is an exercise of the organisation's religious freedom and that any state interference with that decision would be an unwarranted intrusion into the organisation's autonomy, at least other than in the case of established churches. Certainly, interference by the state in the selection of religious ministers is an interference with rights protected by Article 9 of the European Convention on Human Rights (ECHR), and is likely to breach that provision absent very compelling justification (though such justification might be present in the case of established churches). It follows that any prohibition on religious discrimination will almost inevitably contain qualifications relating to the appointment of ministers, etc. The GOR defence has already been mentioned. Similarly, exceptions are provided to the EqA's prohibition on discrimination in the provision of services where those services are of a religious nature (see pp 602–604 below). Even where no explicit exception applies, the courts will be reluctant to intervene in disputes as to the suitability of candidates for religious ministry. In the following case, for example, an application for judicial review of the Chief Rabbi's decision to terminate the claimant's position as a Rabbi because he was 'no longer religiously and morally fit to occupy his position as rabbi' following allegations of adultery with members of his congregation was rejected on the basis (*per* Simon Brown J, as he then was) that:

***R v Chief Rabbi, ex parte Wachman* [1993] 2 All ER 249, 255**

> the court is hardly in a position to regulate what is essentially a religious function – the determination whether someone is morally and religiously fit to carry out the spiritual and pastoral duties of his office. The court must inevitably be wary of entering so self-evidently sensitive an area, straying across the well-recognised divide between church and state.
>
> One cannot, therefore, escape the conclusion that if judicial review lies here, then one way or another this secular court must inevitably be drawn into adjudicating upon matters intimate to a religious community.

A similar approach would be expected where, for example, a Catholic priest was removed from the priesthood on the grounds that he was sexually active (celibacy being required of members of the priesthood).

Judicial reluctance to intervene is evident also in the approach to unfair dismissal claims by ministers of religion which are met, almost invariably, with the response that no contract exists between the minister and the church. Typical of this approach is the dicta below.

***President of the Methodist Conference v Parfitt* [1984] QB 368**

Dillon LJ:

> … I do not think it is right to say that any contract, let alone a contract of service, comes into being between the church and the minister when the minister accepts an invitation from a circuit steward to become a minister on a particular circuit … it seems to me that it follows, from a correct appreciation of the spiritual nature of the minister's position and relationship with the church, that the arrangements between the minister and the church in relation to his

> stationing throughout his ministry and the spiritual discipline which the church is entitled to exercise over the minister in relation to his career remain non-contractual …
>
> … the spiritual nature of the work to be done by a person and the spiritual discipline to which that person is subject may not necessarily, in an appropriate context, exclude a contractual relationship under which work which is of a spiritual nature is to be done for others by a person who is subject to spiritual discipline. On any view the spiritual nature of the work and the spiritual discipline under which it is performed must be very relevant considerations when it has to be decided whether or not there is a contractual relationship.

The courts have declined to find contracts in existence between Presbyterian ministers, Anglican curates, Sikh priests and Muslim khateebs and their churches/congregations.[2] The House of Lords (HL) accepted in *Davies v Presbyterian Church of Wales* [1986] ICR 280 that an intention to create contractual relations could be found in an individual case, though it upheld the decisions of the EAT and the Court of Appeal (CA) that the claimant (a Presbyterian pastor) was not an employee for the purposes of an unfair dismissal claim. For decades, the dicta in *Davies* was honoured wholly in the breach, courts and tribunals being overwhelmingly unlikely to find that no contract existed. The approach appeared to shift with the decision in *Percy v Church of Scotland* [2005] UKHL 73, [2006] 2 AC 28, in which the HL accepted that a Church of Scotland minister was employed under a 'contract personally to execute work' and that she was entitled to bring a sex discrimination case, the House making reference to the importance of ensuring the broad application of the discrimination legislation and the influence of EU law. Lord Nicholls favoured a reversal of the assumption in *Parfitt* against the intention to create contractual relations and ruled that office holding did not exclude a contractual relationship. The HL did not, however, explicitly overrule any of the previous case law and it became clear in *New Testament Church of God v Stewart* [2007] EWCA Civ 1004, [2008] ICR 282 that the careful scrutiny of the evidence required by the HL in *Percy* would not necessarily result in the conclusion that contractual intention existed. In *Stewart* itself and in a number of following cases tribunals (upheld on appeal) ruled that ministers of religion were not 'employed', and in the following case the Supreme Court (SC) itself upheld such a conclusion in relation to a Methodist minister.

***President of the Methodist Conference v Preston* [2013] UKSC 29, [2013] 2 AC 163**

Lord Sumption (for the majority) remarked in Preston (at §§4–5) that the 'recurrent themes' in the case law concerned (1) 'the distinction between an office and an employment' and (2) 'a tendency to regard the spiritual nature of a minister of religion's calling as making it unnecessary and inappropriate to characterise the relationship with the church as giving rise to legal relations at all'. His Lordship remarked that the effect of the decision in Percy was that 'the question whether a minister of religion serves under a contract of employment can no longer be answered simply by classifying the minister's occupation by type: office or employment, spiritual or secular. Nor, in the generality of cases, can it be answered by reference to any presumption against the contractual character of the service of ministers of religion generally'.

[2] Respectively, *Davies v Presbyterian Church of Wales* [1986] ICR 280; *Diocese of Southwark v Coker* [1998] ICR 140; *Santokh Singh v Guru Nanak Gurdwara* [1990] ICR 309; *Birmingham Mosque Trust Ltd v Alavi* [1992] ICR 435.

Lord Sumption (with whom Lords Hope, Wilson and Carnwath agreed, Lady Hale dissenting):

10. … The primary considerations are the manner in which the minister was engaged, and the character of the rules or terms governing his or her service. But, as with all exercises in contractual construction, these documents and any other admissible evidence on the parties' intentions fall to be construed against their factual background. Part of that background is the fundamentally spiritual purpose of the functions of a minister of religion.

Having expressly ruled, contrary to the submissions made by the Methodist Conference, that the test was *not* whether it was *necessary* to imply a contract, Lord Sumption went on to consider the facts of the particular case. He analysed the Deed of Union, the standing orders of the Methodist Conference, and the specific arrangements agreed with the claimant to ascertain whether the relationship between the parties could properly be characterised as contractual, and found that it could not.[3]

20. … First, the manner in which a minister is engaged is incapable of being analysed in terms of contractual formation. Neither the admission of a minister to full connexion nor his or her ordination are themselves contracts. Thereafter, the minister's duties are not consensual. They depend on the unilateral decisions of the Conference. Secondly, the stipend and the manse are due to the minister by virtue only of his or her admission into full connexion and ordination. While he or she remains in full connexion and in the active life, these benefits continue even in the event of sickness or injury, unless he or she is given leave of absence or retires. In addition to the stipend and the manse, the minister has certain procedural rights derived from the disciplinary scheme of the Deed of Union and the standing orders, which determine the manner in which he or she may be suspended or removed from ministerial duties. But the disciplinary scheme is the same for all members of the church whether they are ministers or ordinary lay members. Third, the relationship between the minister and the church is not terminable except by the decision of the Conference or its Stationing Committee or a disciplinary committee. There is no unilateral right to resign, even on notice. I conclude that the ministry described in these instruments is a vocation, by which candidates submit themselves to the discipline of the church for life. Unless some special arrangement is made with a particular minister, the rights and duties of ministers arise, as it seems to me, entirely from their status in the constitution of the church and not from any contract.

The general approach of the domestic courts may have to be reconsidered in light of the decision of the Grand Chamber of the ECtHR in the following case in which that Court rejected a claim by a trade union of Romanian Orthodox priests that the refusal of the state to recognise it breached Article 11 ECHR (which protects freedom of association). The Romanian Orthodox Church had resisted the registration of the union because it claimed that it was incompatible with the principle of religious freedom.

***Sindicatul 'Pastorul Cel Bun' v Romania* (App No 2330/09, judgment of 9 July 2013) (2014) 58 EHRR 10 (Grand Chamber)**

Judgment:

136. The Court reiterates that religious communities traditionally and universally exist in the form of organised structures. Where the organisation of the religious community is at

[3]Though he did accept that, had the relationship been contractual, it would have been a relationship of employment.

issue, Article 9 of the Convention must be interpreted in the light of Article 11, which safeguards associations against unjustified State interference. Seen from this perspective, the right of believers to freedom of religion encompasses the expectation that the community will be allowed to function peacefully, free from arbitrary State intervention. The autonomous existence of religious communities is indispensable for pluralism in a democratic society and is an issue at the very heart of the protection which Article 9 affords. It directly concerns not only the organisation of these communities as such but also the effective enjoyment of the right to freedom of religion by all their active members. Were the organisational life of the community not protected by Article 9, all other aspects of the individual's freedom of religion would become vulnerable ...[4]

140. The question whether the applicant union's members were entitled to form the union raises the issue of whether Article 11 was applicable to them. On this point, the Grand Chamber does not share the Government's view that members of the clergy must be excluded from the protection afforded by Article 11 of the Convention on the ground that they perform their duties under the authority of the bishop, and hence outside the scope of the domestic rules of labour law ...

142. ... the International Labour Organisation considers that the determination of the existence of such a relationship should be guided primarily by the facts relating to the performance of work and the remuneration of the worker, notwithstanding how the relationship is characterised in any contrary arrangement, contractual or otherwise, that may have been agreed between the parties. In addition, the ILO's Convention no. 87 ... which is the principal international legal instrument guaranteeing the right to organise, provides in Article 2 that 'workers and employers, without distinction whatsoever' have the right to establish organisations of their own choosing. Lastly, although Council Directive 78/2000/EC ... accepts the existence of a heightened degree of loyalty on account of the employer's ethos, it specifies that this cannot prejudice freedom of association, in particular the right to establish unions.

143. Having regard to the above considerations, the Court observes that the duties performed by the members of the trade union in question entail many of the characteristic features of an employment relationship. For example, they discharge their activities on the basis of a decision by the bishop appointing them and setting out their rights and obligations. Under the bishop's leadership and supervision, they carry out the tasks assigned to them; besides performing liturgical rites and maintaining contact with parishioners, these include teaching and management of parish assets; members of the clergy are also responsible for the sale of liturgical items ... In addition, domestic law provides for a specific number of posts for members of the clergy and laity which are largely funded from the State and local authority budgets, the post-holders' wages being set with reference to the salaries of Ministry of Education employees ... The Romanian Orthodox Church pays employer's contributions on the wages paid to its clergy, and priests pay income tax, contribute to the national social security scheme and are entitled to all the welfare benefits available to ordinary employees, such as health insurance, a pension on reaching the statutory retirement age, or unemployment insurance.

144. Admittedly, as the Government pointed out, a particular feature of the work of members of the clergy is that it also pursues a spiritual purpose and is carried out within a church enjoying a certain degree of autonomy. Accordingly, members of the clergy assume obligations of a special nature in that they are bound by a heightened duty of loyalty, itself based on a personal, and in principle irrevocable, undertaking by each clergyman. It may therefore be a delicate task to make a precise distinction between the strictly religious activities of members of the clergy and their activities of a more financial nature.

[4] Citing, inter alia, *Hasan & Chaush v Bulgaria* (2002) 34 EHRR 1339.

> 145. However, the question to be determined is rather whether such special features are sufficient to remove the relationship between members of the clergy and their church from the ambit of Article 11. In this connection, the Court reiterates that para. 1 of Article 11 presents trade union freedom as one form or a special aspect of freedom of association and that para. 2 does not exclude any occupational group from the scope of that Article. At most the national authorities are entitled to impose 'lawful restrictions' on certain of their employees in accordance with Article 11 para. 2 ... Moreover, other occupational groups, such as the police or the civil service, are likewise subject to particular constraints and special duties of loyalty without their members' right to organise being called into question ...
>
> 147. The Court further notes that the domestic courts have already explicitly recognised the right of members of the clergy and lay employees of the Romanian Orthodox Church to form a trade union ...
>
> 148. Having regard to all the above factors, the Court considers that, notwithstanding their special circumstances, members of the clergy fulfil their mission in the context of an employment relationship falling within the scope of Article 11 of the Convention. Article 11 is therefore applicable to the facts of the case.

The Court went on to rule that the interference with Article 11 rights was justified taking into account the church's Article 9 rights. The significance of the case for present purposes is that it suggests that the typical exclusion of the clergy from protection against unfair dismissal (this by virtue of the general reluctance of the courts to find that they are employed on contracts of employment) may give rise to incompatibilities with Convention rights (where, for example, this prevented a member of the clergy from protecting his or her rights under Article 8 (private life) or Article 11. It is important to note, however, that the cases discussed above either pre-dated the implementation of the EqA or were brought under the Employment Rights Act 1996, which applies only to those with a contract of employment. Not only does the EqA apply an extended definition of 'employment' (see Chapter 4), it also applies its protections to holders of personal and public offices. Because the EqA defines the former to include 'an office or post – (a) to which a person is appointed to discharge a function personally under the direction of another person, and (b) in respect of which an appointed person is entitled to remuneration', it is likely to cover many ministers of religion.[5] The GOR applicable to such appointments will be discussed below.

The Legal Regulation of Discrimination because of Religion or Belief

Article 9 ECHR

In Chapters 2 and 3 we considered the definitions of discrimination contained in the EqA, the operation of the PSED and the extent to which positive discrimination is permitted by the EqA and the underlying EU provisions. In Chapters 4 and 5 we considered the scope of the regulation of discrimination and the enforcement of the relevant law. Here we consider those aspects of the law which are unique to religion and belief, or which are

[5] Note, however, that Sch 6 para 4 EqA provides that bishops do not hold public offices for the purposes of the EqA.

of particular significance in relation to them. These consist of the meaning of 'religion or belief', the exceptions to its prohibition, the circumstances in which the religion or belief of the discriminator or others permit discrimination which would not otherwise be lawful, and the extent to which the EqA requires the accommodation of religious beliefs and/or practices. Central to much of this discussion will be Article 9 ECHR, which provides that:

Article 9 ECHR

1. Everyone has the right to freedom of thought, conscience and religion; this right includes freedom to change his religion or belief and freedom, either alone or in community with others and in public or private, to manifest his religion or belief, in worship, teaching, practice and observance.
2. Freedom to manifest one's religion or beliefs shall be subject only to such limitations as are prescribed by law and are necessary in a democratic society in the interests of public safety, for the protection of public order, health or morals, or for the protection of the rights and freedoms of others.[6]

Article 9 can be read in isolation or in combination with Article 14 of the Convention (also discussed in Chapter 2) which provides that:

Article 14 ECHR

The enjoyment of the rights and freedoms set forth in this Convention shall be secured without discrimination on any ground such as sex, race, colour, language, religion, political or other opinion, national or social origin, association with a national minority, property, birth or other status.

The protection afforded by Article 9 to 'to freedom of thought, conscience and religion' including the 'right to change religion or belief' is unqualified. The right to *manifest* religion is, however, subject to 'such limitations as are prescribed by law and are necessary in a democratic society in the interests of public safety, for the protection of public order, health or morals, or for the protection of the rights and freedoms of others.'

Where someone is discriminated against solely on grounds of their religious or other beliefs, the question whether Article 9 has been breached will turn on (1) whether the discrimination is classified as 'interference' with the right and, if so, (2) whether the state can be held responsible for any interference either directly (where the state itself has interfered) or indirectly (where its failure to prevent or remedy the interference is sufficiently culpable to make it appropriate for the state to be held liable for the interference). In cases where the discrimination has been in connection with the *manifestation* of religious or other beliefs there is a third question: whether the interference was 'necessary in a democratic society in the interests of public safety, for the protection of public order, health or morals, or for the protection of the rights and freedoms of others'. Where the interference with religious or other beliefs has been discriminatory, Article 14 may also come into play.

The second of the questions outlined above is not unique to Article 9 and has been considered in Chapter 3, in which the extent of the positive obligations imposed by the Convention was discussed.

The European Court's Approach

The first Article 9 case considered by the ECtHR was *Kokkinakis v Greece* which concerned a claim brought by a Jehovah's Witness who had been invited into the home of an Orthodox

[6] Article 10, which protects freedom of expression, also has some relevance, though the ECtHR is reluctant to consider this in cases where Art 9 applies (whether or not it is breached); see *Kokkinakis v Greece* below.

Christian cantor and his wife (Georgia Kyriakaki) and had had a conversation with Ms Kyriakaki about religion after which he was arrested, convicted and fined for proselytism, which was contrary to Greek law. He complained of breaches of Articles 9, 10 and 14 ECHR. The ECtHR found (though only by a 6:3 majority) that the state had breached Article 9, declining to consider Articles 10 or 14.

The Greek Court of Appeal had concluded that the claimant had 'tak[en] advantage of [Ms] Kyriakaki's inexperience, her low intellect and her naïvety', having 'visited [her and told] her he brought good news, pressed her to let him into the house, where he began by telling her about the politician Olof Palme and by expounding pacifist views. He then took out a little book containing professions of faith by adherents of the aforementioned sect and began to read out passages from Holy Scripture, which he skilfully analysed in a manner that the Christian woman, for want of adequate grounding in doctrine, could not challenge, and at the same time offered her various similar books and importunately tried, directly and indirectly, to undermine her religious beliefs'. The characterisation of events had been challenged by one of the national appeal judges, in dissent, who remarked that 'none of the evidence shows that Georgia Kyriakaki … was particularly inexperienced in Orthodox Christian doctrine, being married to a cantor, or of particularly low intellect or particularly naïve'. Ms Kyriakaki's evidence was that her beliefs were unaffected by the visit.

Kokkinakis v Greece **(App No 14307/88, judgment of 25 May 1993), (1994) 17 EHRR 397**

44. … the Court considers that the impugned measure was in pursuit of a legitimate aim under Article 9(2), namely the protection of the rights and freedoms of others, relied on by the Government …

47. The Court has consistently held that a certain margin of appreciation is to be left to the Contracting States in assessing the existence and extent of the necessity of an interference, but this margin is subject to European supervision, embracing both the legislation and the decisions applying it, even those given by an independent court. The Court's task is to determine whether the measures taken at national level were justified in principle and proportionate …

48. First of all, a distinction has to be made between bearing Christian witness and improper proselytism. The former corresponds to true evangelism, which a report drawn up in 1956 under the auspices of the World Council of Churches describes as an essential mission and a responsibility of every Christian and every Church. The latter represents a corruption or deformation of it. It may, according to the same report, take the form of activities offering material or social advantages with a view to gaining new members for a Church or exerting improper pressure on people in distress or in need; it may even entail the use of violence or brainwashing; more generally, it is not compatible with respect for the freedom of thought, conscience and religion of others.

Scrutiny of section 4 of Act 1363/1938 shows that the relevant criteria adopted by the Greek legislature are reconcilable with the foregoing if and in so far as they are designed only to punish improper proselytism, which the Court does not have to define in the abstract in the present case.

49. The Court notes, however, that in their reasoning the Greek courts established the applicant's liability by merely reproducing the wording of section 4 and did not sufficiently specify in what way the accused had attempted to convince his neighbour by improper means. None of the facts they set out warrants that finding.

> That being so, it has not been shown that the applicant's conviction was justified in the circumstances of the case by a pressing social need. The contested measure therefore does not appear to have been proportionate to the legitimate aim pursued or, consequently, 'necessary in a democratic society … for the protection of the rights and freedoms of others.'

The ECtHR's Article 9 jurisprudence was notable, until recently, for the very limited protection it afforded. Some of the cases may have been explained by the fact that they arose in the context of employment, and so the Court was concerned to balance individuals' rights against the contractual obligations they had undertaken. But the limited nature of the protection went beyond a willingness to find justified interferences with Article 9(1) rights to a reluctance even to acknowledge such interferences.

We have noted above that the protection given by Article 9 to the *holding* of beliefs is absolute in the sense that interferences for which the state can be held responsible (or which it culpably fails to remedy) are incapable of justification. Such interferences are by their nature rare, however, at least outside totalitarian states. Far more common is the situation in which an individual is subject to penalty or restriction because of their expression of religious views whether directly (in preaching or otherwise proselytising), or because of their observance of requirements or practices concerning appearance, rest, food and/or worship. Article 9 protects these incidents of religion or belief only in so far as they are recognised as being *manifestations* of religion or belief, and in so far as the actions complained of are recognised as *interferences* with those manifestations. Prior to *Kokkinakis* the European Commission of Human Rights, which at the time had a sifting role in Convention claims, had shown a marked reluctance to do either.

One example of the early jurisprudence is *Ahmad v UK* in which the claimant, a Muslim schoolteacher, claimed a breach of Article 9 after he was refused time off work on a Friday afternoon in order to attend prayers at the mosque. The Commission dismissed the claim as manifestly unfounded.

***Ahmad v UK* (App No 22954/93, decision of 12 September 1995), (1982) 4 EHRR 126 (Commission)**

Judgment:

> With regard to the applicant's claim, that the school authorities should have arranged their time-table so that he could attend Friday prayers, the Commission observes that the object of Article 9 is essentially that of protecting the individual against unjustified interference by the State, but that there may also be positive obligations inherent in an effective 'respect' for the individual's freedom of religion.
>
> *Article 9 of the Convention:*
>
> … The applicant's complaint is confined to the freedom to manifest his religion in worship 'in community with others'…
>
> The applicant states that it is the religious duty of every Muslim to offer prayers on Fridays and, if considerations of distance permit, to attend a mosque for this purpose. A mere contractual obligation cannot excuse absence – a man cannot willingly put himself into a position where he cannot attend. When the applicant commenced his employment with the ILEA in 1968 there was only one mosque in the London area and it was physically impossible for him

to work with the ILEA and to attend Friday prayers. After his transfer, in February 1974, to Division 5 he found himself nearer to mosques. He was then obliged by his religion to attend Friday prayers …

The Commission has already stated that the freedom of religion, as guaranteed by Article 9, is not absolute, but subject to the limitations set out in Article 9(2). Moreover, it may, as regards the modality of a particular religious manifestation, be influenced by the situation of the person claiming that freedom …

The Commission here notes that the applicant did not, when he was first interviewed for his teaching position, nor during the first six years of his employment with the ILEA, disclose the fact that he might require time off during normal school hours for attending prayers at the mosque. The Government state that such a disclosure might have resulted in the applicant being offered only part-time employment. The applicant submits that the United Kingdom should not operate a system in which a job applicant must indicate his religion and thus risk not to be appointed because of his religious obligations. The Commission observes that the present case does not raise the general issue of the confidentiality of information concerning one's religion, but the question whether an employee should inform his employer in advance that he will be absent during a part of the time for which he is engaged. It considers it relevant for the appreciation of the parties' position during the relevant period that the applicant had at no time before and during the first six years of his employment brought to the attention of the ILEA his wish to have time off during normal school hours for attending prayers at the mosque.

The Commission further observes that, throughout his employment with the ILEA between 1968 and 1975, the applicant remained free to resign if and when he found that his teaching obligations conflicted with his religious duties. It notes that, in 1975, the applicant did in fact resign from his five-day employment and that he subsequently accepted a four-and-a-half day employment enabling him to comply with his duties as a Muslim on Fridays. The applicant points out that his present employment means less not only as regards his pay but also concerning his pension rights, chances of promotion and security of employment. He submits that his case could have been better solved by a re-arrangement of the school time-table permitting his absence for about 45 minutes at the beginning of the afternoon sessions on Fridays. The Government contest this possibility …

The Commission accepts that the school authorities, in their treatment of the applicant's case on the basis of his contract with the ILEA, had to have regard not only to his religious position, but also to the requirements of the education system as a whole; it notes that the complex education system of the United Kingdom was during the relevant time faced with the task of gradual adaptation to new developments in its society. The Commission is not called upon to substitute for the assessment by the national authorities of what might be the best policy in this field but only to examine whether the school authorities, in relying on the applicant's contract, arbitrarily disregarded his freedom of religion …

The Commission concludes that there has been no interference with the applicant's freedom of religion under Article 9(1) of the Convention.

The Commission reached a similar decision in the case of *Stedman v UK* (1997) 23 EHRR CD, in which a woman was dismissed for refusing to accept a contractual variation requiring her to work on Sundays. She, like Mr Ahmad, relied on her right to freedom of religion under Article 9. Unlike him, she was employed in the private sector, the alleged obligation on the part of the state being to protect her rights from interference by others, rather than to abstain itself from interference with them (see further Chapter 1). Also unlike

Mr Ahmad, she had not 'voluntarily' accepted employment inconsistent with her religious obligations.

Just as the Commission, in cases such as *Ahmad* and *Stedman*, had been reluctant to recognise that work-related obligations could amount to interferences with Article 9 rights, so it was also reluctant to accept that a variety of practices associated with religious or other beliefs amounted to *manifestations* of such beliefs. Requirements relating directly to religion, such as in *Ahmad* and *Stedman*, were likely to be accepted as such a manifestation. But the limitations of the concept of 'manifestation' were made clear in *Arrowsmith v UK* (1978) 3 EHRR 110 in which the Commission dismissed as manifestly unfounded a claim by a pacifist that her prosecution for handing out leaflets to soldiers urging them not to serve in Northern Ireland breached her Article 9 rights. According to the Commission, her action in handing out these leaflets was not a 'manifestation' of her pacifist beliefs: 'where actions of individuals do not actually express the belief concerned they cannot be considered to be as such protected by Article 9(1), even when they are motivated by it.'

The Commission and Court proved particularly unsympathetic to challenges brought by Muslim women to restrictions on the wearing of *hijab* and other indicia of Muslim identity. In *Karaduman v Turkey* (1993) 74 DR 93 the Commission rejected a challenge to a Turkish rule prohibiting the claimant from graduating from university unless she was photographed without a scarf. A similar decision was reached in *Dahlab v Switzerland* [2001] ECHR 42393/98. Not until 2004, with the decision in *Şahin v Turkey* (2005) 41 EHRR 8, did the ECtHR recognise a restriction on clothing or appearance as an interference with the manifestation of religious belief.

Şahin v Turkey (App No 44774/98, judgment of 10 November 2005), (2007) 44 EHRR 5 (Grand Chamber)

The case concerned a challenge to a university rule prohibiting the wearing of headscarves on campus. The Court restated the proposition that 'Article 9 does not protect every act motivated or inspired by a religion or belief and does not in all cases guarantee the right to behave in the public sphere in a way which is dictated by a belief' but accepted that, in this particular case, taking into account the fact that Şahin regarded herself as bound to cover her head, it would 'proceed on the assumption' that there was an interference with her rights. It went on to find, however, that the interference was necessary and proportionate to the legitimate aims of protecting public order and the rights and freedoms of others. The Grand Chamber rejected Şahin's appeal, endorsing the Chamber's findings that her Article 9 rights had been interfered with but also that the interference was justified

Judgment:

> 106. In democratic societies, in which several religions co-exist within one and the same population, it may be necessary to place restrictions on freedom to manifest one's religion or belief in order to reconcile the interests of the various groups and ensure that everyone's beliefs are respected …
>
> 107. The Court has frequently emphasised the State's role as the neutral and impartial organiser of the exercise of various religions, faiths and beliefs, and stated that this role is conducive to public order, religious harmony and tolerance in a democratic society. It also considers that the State's duty of neutrality and impartiality is incompatible with any power on the State's part to assess the legitimacy of religious beliefs or the ways in which those beliefs are expressed and

that it requires the State to ensure mutual tolerance between opposing groups. Accordingly, the role of the authorities in such circumstances is not to remove the cause of tension by eliminating pluralism, but to ensure that the competing groups tolerate each other.

108. Pluralism, tolerance and broadmindedness are hallmarks of a 'democratic society'. Although individual interests must on occasion be subordinated to those of a group, democracy does not simply mean that the views of a majority must always prevail: a balance must be achieved which ensures the fair and proper treatment of people from minorities and avoids any abuse of a dominant position. Pluralism and democracy must also be based on dialogue and a spirit of compromise necessarily entailing various concessions on the part of individuals or groups of individuals which are justified in order to maintain and promote the ideals and values of a democratic society. Where these 'rights and freedoms' are themselves among those guaranteed by the Convention or its Protocols, it must be accepted that the need to protect them may lead states to restrict other rights or freedoms likewise set forth in the Convention. It is precisely this constant search for a balance between the fundamental rights of each individual which constitutes the foundation of a 'democratic society'.

109. Where questions concerning the relationship between state and religions are at stake, on which opinion in a democratic society may reasonably differ widely, the role of the national decision-making body must be given special importance. This will notably be the case when it comes to regulating the wearing of religious symbols in educational institutions, especially in view of the diversity of the approaches taken by national authorities on the issue. It is not possible to discern throughout Europe a uniform conception of the significance of religion in society and the meaning or impact of the public expression of a religious belief will differ according to time and context. Rules in this sphere will consequently vary from one country to another according to national traditions and the requirements imposed by the need to protect the rights and freedoms of others and to maintain public order. Accordingly, the choice of the extent and form such regulations should take must inevitably be left up to a point to the state concerned, as it will depend on the domestic context concerned.

110. This margin of appreciation goes hand in hand with a European supervision embracing both the law and the decisions applying it. The Court's task is to determine whether the measures taken at national level were justified in principle and proportionate. In delimiting the extent of the margin of appreciation in the present case the Court must have regard to what is at stake, namely the need to protect the rights and freedoms of others, to preserve public order and to secure civil peace and true religious pluralism, which is vital to the survival of a democratic society …

112. The interference in issue caused by the circular of February 23, 1998 imposing restrictions as to place and manner on the rights of students such as Ms Şahin to wear the Islamic headscarf on university premises was, according to the Turkish courts, based in particular on the two principles of secularism and equality …

114. As the Chamber rightly stated, the Court considers this notion of secularism to be consistent with the values underpinning the Convention. It finds that upholding that principle, which is undoubtedly one of the fundamental principles of the Turkish State which are in harmony with the rule of law and respect for human rights, may be considered necessary to protect the democratic system in Turkey. An attitude which fails to respect that principle will not necessarily be accepted as being covered by the freedom to manifest one's religion and will not enjoy the protection of Art.9 of the Convention …

116. … it is the principle of secularism, as elucidated by the Constitutional Court, which is the paramount consideration underlying the ban on the wearing of religious symbols in universities. In such a context, where the values of pluralism, respect for the rights of others and, in particular, equality before the law of men and women are being taught and applied in practice,

> it is understandable that the relevant authorities should wish to preserve the secular nature of the institution concerned and so consider it contrary to such values to allow religious attire, including, as in the present case, the Islamic headscarf, to be worn …
>
> 120. Furthermore, the process whereby the regulations that led to the decision of July 9, 1998 were implemented took several years and was accompanied by a wide debate within Turkish society and the teaching profession. The two highest courts, the Supreme Administrative Court and the Constitutional Court, have managed to establish settled case law on this issue. It is quite clear that throughout that decision-making process the university authorities sought to adapt to the evolving situation in a way that would not bar access to the university to students wearing the veil, through continued dialogue with those concerned, while at the same time ensuring that order was maintained and in particular that the requirements imposed by the nature of the course in question were complied with …
>
> 122. In the light of the foregoing and having regard to the contracting states' margin of appreciation in this sphere, the Court finds that the interference in issue was justified in principle and proportionate to the aim pursued.

Judge Tulkens dissented, disagreeing with the wide margin of appreciation granted Turkey in light of the fact that it was the only Council of Europe member to impose such a ban on university students, and characterising the approach of the majority as amounting to a failure to exercise any supervision on the state. She declared that the principles of secularism, equality and liberty should be harmonised rather than weighed against each other, and that religious freedom was 'a founding principle of democratic societies' and protested that the majority had failed to show any 'pressing social need' for the ban, relying on 'mere worries or fears' rather than 'indisputable facts and reasons whose legitimacy is beyond doubt'.

Judge Tulkens took issue with the view of the majority (§114) that 'wearing the headscarf contravenes the principle of secularism', pointing out that the applicant's evidence was that she agreed with the principle of secularism and that there was 'no evidence to show that the applicant, through her attitude, conduct or acts, contravened that principle'. She also distinguished between the present case and those such as *Dahlab*, stating that the 'principle of secularism requires education to be provided without any manifestation of religion and while it has to be compulsory for teachers and all public servants, as they have voluntarily taken up posts in a neutral environment' but that the position of pupils and students was different. There was, she pointed out, no suggestion that Şahin's headscarf 'had been ostentatious or aggressive or was used to exert pressure, to provoke a reaction, to proselytise or to spread propaganda and undermined – or was liable to undermine – the convictions of others'. Nor had there been 'any disruption in teaching or in everyday life at the university, or any disorderly conduct, as a result of the applicant's wearing the headscarf'.

Judge Tulkens denied, contrary to the view of the majority, that the effect of the headscarf on non-wearers could amount to a 'pressing social need', contrasting the outcome in the instant case with that in *Gündüz v Turkey* (2003) 41 EHRR 5 in which the Court had found a breach of Article 10 in a case in which the applicant, 'a Muslim religious leader had been convicted for violently criticising the secular regime in Turkey, calling for the introduction of the sharia and referring to children born of marriages celebrated solely before the secular authorities as "bastards". Thus, manifesting one's religion by peacefully wearing a headscarf may be prohibited whereas, in the same context, remarks which could be construed as incitement to religious hatred are covered by freedom of expression'. She protested that the Court had taken into account 'the threat posed by "extremist political movements" seeking to "impose on society as a whole their religious symbols and conception of a society founded on religious precepts" in its response to '[m]erely wearing the headscarf [which] cannot be associated with fundamentalism ... Not all women who wear the headscarf are fundamentalists and there is nothing to suggest that the applicant held fundamentalist views. She is a young adult woman and a university student and might reasonably be expected to have a heightened capacity to resist pressure, it being noted in this connection that the judgment fails to provide any concrete example of the type of pressure concerned. The applicant's personal interest in exercising the right to freedom of religion and to manifest her religion by an external symbol cannot be wholly absorbed by the public interest in fighting extremism'.

Judge Tulkens was equally unimpressed with the Court's reliance on arguments about equality:

> O-II11. ... the majority focus on the protection of women's rights and the principle of sexual equality. By converse implication, wearing the headscarf is considered synonymous with the alienation of women. The ban on wearing the headscarf is therefore seen as promoting equality between men and women. However, what, in fact, is the connection between the ban and sexual equality? The judgment does not say. Indeed, what is the signification of wearing the headscarf? ... wearing the headscarf has no single meaning; it is a practice that is engaged in for a variety of reasons. It does not necessarily symbolise the submission of women to men and there are those who maintain that, in certain cases, it can even be a means of emancipating women. What is lacking in this debate is the opinion of women, both those who wear the headscarf and those who choose not to.
>
> O-II12. On this issue, the Grand Chamber refers in its judgment to the *Dahlab v Switzerland*, citing what to my mind is the most questionable part of the reasoning in that decision, namely that wearing the headscarf represents a 'powerful external symbol', which 'appeared to be imposed on women by a religious precept that was hard to reconcile with the principle of gender equality' and that the practice could not easily be 'reconciled with the message of tolerance, respect for others and, above all, equality and non-discrimination that all teachers in a democratic society should convey to their pupils'.
>
> O-II12. It is not the Court's role to make an appraisal of this type – in this instance a unilateral and negative one – of a religion or religious practice, just as it is not its role to determine in a general and abstract way the signification of wearing the headscarf or to impose its viewpoint on the applicant. The applicant, a young adult university student, said – and there is nothing to suggest that she was not telling the truth – that she wore the headscarf of her own free will. In this connection, I fail to see how the principle of sexual equality can justify prohibiting a woman from following a practice which, in the absence of proof to the contrary, she must be taken to have freely adopted. Equality and non-discrimination are subjective rights which must remain under the control of those who are entitled to benefit from them. 'Paternalism' of this sort runs counter to the case law of the Court, which has developed a real right to personal autonomy on the basis of Art.8. Finally, if wearing the headscarf really was contrary to the principle of the equality of men and women in any event, the State would have a positive obligation to prohibit it in all places, whether public or private.

Notwithstanding these criticisms, the decision in *Şahin* did suggest progress in the ECtHR jurisprudence in that the court at least addressed itself to the question of justification rather than determining the case on threshold considerations or manifestation or interference.

The subsequent decision of the majority of the HL in *R (Begum) v Headteacher and Governors of Denbigh High School* is reflective of the ECtHR's pre-, rather than post-*Şahin* approach. The claimant, a Muslim pupil, sought to rely on Article 9 to challenge her exclusion from school by reason of her insistence on wearing a *jilbab* (full-length draped garment) in place of the uniform option of *shalwar kameeze*, which had been adopted as part of the school's uniform after an extensive consultation involving local faith leaders. The HL considered the case on the school's appeal from the CA which had upheld Begum's claim. A majority of the Court (Lords Bingham, Hoffmann and Scott) ruled that there had been no interference with the claimant's right to manifest her religious beliefs because (1) the right to manifest belief was qualified and that what constituted interference would depend on all the circumstances of the case; (2) the claimant's parents had chosen the school with knowledge of its uniform requirements and (3) the claimant could have changed schools. Lord Nicholls and Baroness Hale, in the minority, took the view that there had been an interference with the manifestation of Begum's religious beliefs, though that interference was justifiable in the circumstances of the case. Baroness Hale drew heavily on the dissenting judgment in *Şahin*.

R (Begum) v Headteacher and Governors of Denbigh High School **[2006] UKHL 15, [2007] 1 AC 100**

Baroness Hale:

94 .... If a Sikh man wears a turban or a Jewish man a yarmulka, we can readily assume that it was his free choice to adopt the dress dictated by the teachings of his religion. I would make the same assumption about an adult Muslim woman who chooses to wear the Islamic headscarf ...

95. But it must be the woman's choice, not something imposed upon her by others. It is quite clear from the evidence in this case that there are different views in different communities about what is required of a Muslim woman who leaves the privacy of her home and family and goes out into the public world. There is also a view that the more extreme requirements are imposed as much for political and social as for religious reasons. If this is so, it is not a uniquely Muslim phenomenon. The Parekh Report on *The Future of Multi-Ethnic Britain* (Runnymede Trust (2000) pp 236–237 (para 17.3)), for example, points out that:

> 'In all traditions, religious claims and rituals may be used to legitimise power structures rather than to promote ethical principles, and may foster bigotry, sectarianism and fundamentalism. Notoriously, religion often accepts and gives its blessing to gender inequalities.'

Gita Saghal and Nira Yuval-Davis, discussing 'Fundamentalism, Multiculturalism and Women in Britain' (in *Refusing Holy Orders, Women and Fundamentalism in Britain* (2000) p 14) argue that the effect of and on women is—

> 'central to the project of fundamentalism, which attempts to impose its own unitary religious definition on the grouping and its symbolic order. The "proper" behaviour of women is used to signify the difference between those who belong and those who do not; women are also seen as the "cultural carriers" of the grouping, who transmit group culture to the future generation; and proper control in terms of marriage and divorce ensures that children who are born to those women are within the boundaries of the collectivity, not only biologically but also symbolically.'

According to this view, strict dress codes may be imposed upon women, not for their own sake but to serve the ends of others. Hence they may be denied equal freedom to choose for themselves. They may also be denied equal treatment. A dress code which requires women to conceal all but their face and hands, while leaving men much freer to decide what they will wear, does not treat them equally. Although a different issue from seclusion, the assumption may be that women will play their part in the private domestic sphere while men will play theirs in the public world. Of course, from a woman's point of view, this may be a safer and more comfortable place to be. Gita Saghal and Nira Yuval Davis go on to point out (p 15) that:

> 'One of the paradoxes … is the fact that women collude, seek comfort, and even at times gain a sense of empowerment within the spaces allocated to them by fundamentalist movements.'

96. If a woman freely chooses to adopt a way of life for herself, it is not for others, including other women who have chosen differently, to criticise or prevent her. Judge Tulkens [dissenting], in *Şahin v Turkey* … draws the analogy with freedom of speech. The European Court of Human Rights has never accepted that interference with the right of freedom of expression is justified by the fact that the ideas expressed may offend someone. Likewise, the sight of a woman in full purdah may offend some people, and especially those western feminists who believe that it is a symbol of her oppression, but that could not be a good reason for prohibiting her from wearing it.

97. But schools are different. Their task is to educate the young from all the many and diverse families and communities in this country in accordance with the national curriculum. Their task is to help all of their pupils achieve their full potential. This includes growing up to play whatever part they choose in the society in which they are living. The school's task is also to promote the ability of people of diverse races, religions and cultures to live together in harmony. Fostering a sense of community and cohesion within the school is an important part of that. A uniform dress code can play its role in smoothing over ethnic, religious and social divisions. But it does more than that. Like it or not, this is a society committed, in principle and in law, to equal freedom for men and women to choose how they will lead their lives within the law. Young girls from ethnic, cultural or religious minorities growing up here face particularly difficult choices: how far to adopt or to distance themselves from the dominant culture. A good school will enable and support them. This particular school is a good school: that, it appears, is one reason why Shabina Begum wanted to stay there. It is also a mixed school. That was what led to the difficulty. It would not have arisen in a girls' school with an all-female staff.

98. In deciding how far to go in accommodating religious requirements within its dress code, such a school has to accommodate some complex considerations. These are helpfully explained by Professor Frances Radnay in 'Culture, Religion and Gender' [2003] 1 *Int J of Constitutional Law* 663:

> 'genuine individual consent to a discriminatory practice or dissent from it may not be feasible where these girls are not yet adult. The question is whether patriarchal family control should be allowed to result in girls being socialised according to the implications of veiling while still attending public educational institutions … A mandatory policy that rejects veiling in state educational institutions may provide a crucial opportunity for girls to choose the feminist freedom of state education over the patriarchal dominance of their families. Also, for the families, such a policy may send a clear message that the benefits of state education are tied to the obligation to respect women's and girls' rights to equality and freedom … On the other hand, a prohibition of veiling risks violating the liberal principle of respect for individual autonomy and cultural diversity for parents as well as students. It may also result in traditionalist families not sending their children to the state educational institutions. In this educational context, implementation of the right to equality is a complex matter, and the determination of the way it should be achieved depends upon the balance between these two conflicting policy priorities in a specific social environment.'

It seems to me that that was exactly what this school was trying to do when it devised the school uniform policy to suit the social conditions in that school, in that town, and at that time … Social cohesion is promoted by the uniform elements of shirt, tie and jumper, and the requirement that all outer garments be in the school colour. But cultural and religious diversity is respected by allowing girls to wear either a skirt, trousers, or the shalwar kameez, and by allowing those who wished to do so to wear the hijab. This was indeed a thoughtful and proportionate response to reconciling the complexities of the situation. This is demonstrated by the fact that girls have subsequently expressed their concern that if the jilbab were to be allowed they would face pressure to adopt it even though they do not wish to do so. Here is the evidence to support the justification which Judge Tulkens found lacking in *Şahin v Turkey*.

The readiness of the ECtHR in *Şahin* to accept that the interference there at issue was justified seemed rooted in an anxiety about Islam, though subsequent decisions have not differentiated between Muslims and Sikhs in this regard. In 2008 the ECtHR rejected a challenge by a French Muslim pupil who was expelled from school because of her insistence on wearing a headscarf during physical education classes.[7] The following year it rejected claims by a number of Muslim girls and Sikh boys expelled for refusals to comply with prohibitions on covering their heads in school.[8] The Court also rejected a complaint by a French Sikh that he had been required to remove his turban for a security check, and by another that he had been required to appear bare-headed on photographs for identity documents.[9]

In 2013 the ECtHR found in favour of one of the applicants in *Eweida v UK*, a claim brought by four individuals two of whom had been subjected to dress codes which they regarded as inconsistent with their Article 9 rights. Eweida was a devout Christian who was employed by British Airways as a member of check-in staff. She regarded the cross as the central image of her faith and wore a plain silver cross. She did not believe this to be a mandatory requirement of her religion, but regarded it as a personal expression of her faith. In 2004 BA's uniform high-necked blouse for women was replaced by an open-neck blouse, the effect of which was that Eweida's cross, previously covered by her clothing, became visible. BA's uniform policy prohibited the wearing of any visible item of adornment around the neck and permitted the visible display of religious items only where wearing the item was a religious requirement, it could not be concealed under the uniform, and management had given its approval. The claimant insisted on wearing her cross and was eventually sent home, where she remained for over four months before BA changed its policy and she was permitted to return to work. Shirley Chaplain was a Christian nurse who wished to wear a cross in a visible fashion. Her employers prohibited the wearing of necklaces on health and safety grounds. After a change in uniform which rendered Chaplain's cross visible she was asked to remove it and was moved to non-nursing duties when she refused. The other claims, which are considered further below, did not concern dress codes. The ECtHR upheld Eweida's claim and dismissed Chaplain's. It accepted in both cases that the dress codes had interfered with the women's Article 9 rights, though it accepted in Chaplain's case that the interference was justified.

[7] *Dogru v France* (2008) 49 EHRR 179.

[8] *Aktas v France* (App No 43563/08); *Bayrak v France* (App No 14308/08); *Gamaleddyn v France* (App No 18527/08); *Ghazal v France* (App No 29134/08); *Singh v France* (App No 25463/08); and *Singh v France* (App No 27561/08).

[9] *Phull v France* (App No 35753/03) (admissibility decision, 11 January 2005); *Singh v France* (App No 24479/07) (admissibility decision, 11 June 2007).

***Eweida v UK* (App Nos 48420/10, 59842/10, 51671/10 and 36516/10, judgment of 15 January 2012) (2013) 57 EHRR 8 (4th Section)**

Judgment:

81. The right to freedom of thought, conscience and religion denotes views that attain a certain level of cogency, seriousness, cohesion and importance … Provided this is satisfied, the State's duty of neutrality and impartiality is incompatible with any power on the State's part to assess the legitimacy of religious beliefs or the ways in which those beliefs are expressed …

82. Even where the belief in question attains the required level of cogency and importance, it cannot be said that every act which is in some way inspired, motivated or influenced by it constitutes a 'manifestation' of the belief. Thus, for example, acts or omissions which do not directly express the belief concerned or which are only remotely connected to a precept of faith fall outside the protection of Article 9(1) … In order to count as a 'manifestation' within the meaning of Article 9, the act in question must be intimately linked to the religion or belief. An example would be an act of worship or devotion which forms part of the practice of a religion or belief in a generally recognised form. However, the manifestation of religion or belief is not limited to such acts; the existence of a sufficiently close and direct nexus between the act and the underlying belief must be determined on the facts of each case. In particular, there is no requirement on the applicant to establish that he or she acted in fulfilment of a duty mandated by the religion in question …

83. It is true … that there is case law of the Court and Commission which indicates that, if a person is able to take steps to circumvent a limitation placed on his or her freedom to manifest religion or belief, there is no interference with the right under Article 9(1) and the limitation does not therefore require to be justified under Article 9(2). For example, in … *Cha'are Shalom Ve Tsedek* case, the court held that 'there would be interference with the freedom to manifest one's religion only if the illegality of performing ritual slaughter made it impossible for ultra-orthodox Jews to eat meat from animals slaughtered in accordance with the religious prescriptions they considered applicable'. However, this conclusion can be explained by the Court's finding that the religious practice and observance at issue in that case was the consumption of meat only from animals that had been ritually slaughtered and certified to comply with religious dietary laws, rather than any personal involvement in the ritual slaughter and certification process itself … More relevantly, in cases involving restrictions placed by employers on an employee's ability to observe religious practice, the Commission held in several decisions that the possibility of resigning from the job and changing employment meant that there was no interference with the employee's religious freedom … However, the court has not applied a similar approach in respect of employment sanctions imposed on individuals as a result of the exercise by them of other rights protected by the Convention, for example the right to respect for private life under Article 8; the right to freedom of expression under Article 10; or the negative right, not to join a trade union, under Article 11 … Given the importance in a democratic society of freedom of religion, the Court considers that, where an individual complains of a restriction on freedom of religion in the workplace, rather than holding that the possibility of changing job would negate any interference with the right, the better approach would be to weigh that possibility in the overall balance when considering whether or not the restriction was proportionate.

89. … It was not disputed in the proceedings before the domestic tribunals and this court that Ms Eweida's insistence on wearing a cross visibly at work was motivated by her desire to bear witness to her Christian faith. Applying the principles set out above, the court considers that Ms Eweida's behaviour was a manifestation of her religious belief, in the form of worship, practice and observance, and as such attracted the protection of Article 9 …

91. The Court considers that the refusal by British Airways between September 2006 and February 2007 to allow the applicant to remain in her post while visibly wearing a cross amounted to an interference with her right to manifest her religion. Since the interference was not directly attributable to the State, the Court must examine whether in all the circumstances the State authorities complied with their positive obligation under Article 9; in other words, whether Ms Eweida's right freely to manifest her religion was sufficiently secured within the domestic legal order and whether a fair balance was struck between her rights and those of others ...

93. When considering the proportionality of the steps taken by British Airways to enforce its uniform code, the national judges at each level agreed that the aim of the code was legitimate, namely to communicate a certain image of the company and to promote recognition of its brand and staff. The employment tribunal considered that the requirement to comply with the code was disproportionate, since it failed to distinguish an item worn as a religious symbol from a piece of jewellery worn purely for decorative reasons. This finding was reversed on appeal to the Court of Appeal, which found that British Airways had acted proportionately. In reaching this conclusion, the Court of Appeal referred to the facts of the case as established by the employment tribunal and, in particular, that the dress code had been in force for some years and had caused no known problem to the applicant or any other member of staff; that Ms Eweida lodged a formal grievance complaint but then decided to arrive at work displaying her cross, without waiting for the results of the grievance procedure; that the issue was conscientiously addressed by British Airways once the complaint had been lodged, involving a consultation process and resulting in a relaxation of the dress code to permit the wearing of visible religious symbols; and that Ms Eweida was offered an administrative post on identical pay during this process and was in February 2007 reinstated in her old job.

94. It is clear, in the view of the Court, that these factors combined to mitigate the extent of the interference suffered by the applicant and must be taken into account. Moreover, in weighing the proportionality of the measures taken by a private company in respect of its employee, the national authorities, in particular the courts, operate within a margin of appreciation. Nonetheless, the Court has reached the conclusion in the present case that a fair balance was not struck. On one side of the scales was Ms Eweida's desire to manifest her religious belief. As previously noted, this is a fundamental right: because a healthy democratic society needs to tolerate and sustain pluralism and diversity; but also because of the value to an individual who has made religion a central tenet of his or her life to be able to communicate that belief to others. On the other side of the scales was the employer's wish to project a certain corporate image. The Court considers that, while this aim was undoubtedly legitimate, the domestic courts accorded it too much weight. Ms Eweida's cross was discreet and cannot have detracted from her professional appearance. There was no evidence that the wearing of other, previously authorised, items of religious clothing, such as turbans and hijabs, by other employees, had any negative impact on British Airways' brand or image. Moreover, the fact that the company was able to amend the uniform code to allow for the visible wearing of religious symbolic jewellery demonstrates that the earlier prohibition was not of crucial importance.

95. The court therefore concludes that, in these circumstances where there is no evidence of any real encroachment on the interests of others, the domestic authorities failed sufficiently to protect the first applicant's right to manifest her religion, in breach of the positive obligation under Article 9 ...

98. The second applicant's employer was a public authority, and the Court must determine whether the interference was necessary in a democratic society in pursuit of one of the aims set out in art 9(2). In this case, there does not appear to be any dispute that the reason for the restriction on jewellery, including religious symbols, was to protect the health and safety of

nurses and patients. The evidence before the Employment Tribunal was that the applicant's managers considered there was a risk that a disturbed patient might seize and pull the chain, thereby injuring herself or the applicant, or that the cross might swing forward and could, for example, come into contact with an open wound. There was also evidence that another Christian nurse had been requested to remove a cross and chain; two Sikh nurses had been told they could not wear a bangle or kirpan; and that flowing hijabs were prohibited. The applicant was offered the possibility of wearing a cross in the form of a brooch attached to her uniform, or tucked under a high-necked top worn under her tunic, but she did not consider that this would be sufficient to comply with her religious conviction.

99. The Court considers that, as in Ms Eweida's case, the importance for the second applicant of being permitted to manifest her religion by wearing her cross visibly must weigh heavily in the balance. However, the reason for asking her to remove the cross, namely the protection of health and safety on a hospital ward, was inherently of a greater magnitude than that which applied in respect of Ms Eweida. Moreover, this is a field where the domestic authorities must be allowed a wide margin of appreciation. The hospital managers were better placed to make decisions about clinical safety than a court, particularly an international court which has heard no direct evidence.[10]

100. It follows that the Court is unable to conclude that the measures of which Ms Chaplin complains were disproportionate. It follows that the interference with her freedom to manifest her religion was necessary in a democratic society and that there was no violation of art 9 in respect of the second applicant.

A number of European states initiated bans on the wearing of full-face veils in public spaces from around 2010 (a ban was imposed by France in 2010, a similar ban by Belgium in 2011 with Latvia, Bulgaria, Italy, Austria, Spain, Switzerland and Denmark subsequently imposing partial or complete bans on the wearing of full-face veils in public spaces).

Ronan McCrea, 'The Ban on the Veil and European Law' (2013) 13 *Human Rights Law Review*, 57–97, footnotes omitted

… As Laborde notes, the [French] legislation defines public space 'in the most extensive way possible, as referring to any space outside the home'. As the long list of exemptions, coupled with the absence of a general religious exemption shows, this legislation is quite clearly motivated by a desire to restrict the wearing of the full face veil by Muslim women. It and similar laws in other European states are, without doubt, influenced by xenophobia and other discriminatory motives. However, such familiar and unworthy impulses are only part of the story of such laws. Legislation of this kind is also representative of something more complex and is also supported by many who are sincere in their egalitarianism and their commitment to tolerance and liberalism. Conflict on the issue of public veiling represents an important instance of a broader struggle to define and apply boundaries to religion's role and influence in European societies at a time when established boundaries are being challenged by greater religious diversity. The more muscular religiosity of many members of communities of immigrant origin, particularly those communities with roots in mainly Muslim societies, is raising complex and difficult issues for European states. As Roy notes, many Europeans feel 'threatened by the emergence of communities not bound by old compromises painstakingly worked out between cathos and laicques.' They are reacting by seeking to define more strictly the boundaries of the settlement between law, society and faith, boundaries

[10] See also more recently *Grimmark v Sweden* [2020] IRLR 554 in which the Court rejected a claim that the refusal of a job as a midwife to the applicant on the grounds that she would not, for religious reasons, assist in carrying out abortions, breached her rights under Arts 9 and 14.

> which have to date been a matter of cultural convention rather than legal rule in many European states. Thus, as cultural consensus breaks down, the law moves in to replace cultural norms with legal rules. Matters are complicated by the fact that this is happening against a background of widespread hostility to migration and severe discrimination against some minority populations. These developments, particularly attempts to change a cultural reticence to publicly express faith into a legal obligation, have brought major challenges for European human rights law, most notably in relation to the wearing of religious dress

In 2014 the Grand Chamber rejected a challenge to the French law. The applicant, a Muslim woman who wore the *burqa* and *niqab*, was prepared to remove her facial coverings for security checks at banks, airports, etc but challenged the wider ban as contrary to Articles 8, 9, 10 and 14 (the last of these because she claimed that it discriminated on grounds of sex, religion and ethnic origin). The Grand Chamber accepted that the ban fell within the scope of Articles 8 and 9 and that the applicant's rights had been interfered with. It accepted that the interference was justified, but it did not follow precisely the same approach as it had in *Şahin*. The Grand Chamber scrutinised the aims on which the French Government sought to rely ('public safety' and 'respect for the minimum set of values of an open and democratic society') with some care. It accepted that the first amounted to a legitimate aim but did not accept this of two of the three 'values of an open and democratic society' relied upon ('respect for equality between men and women, respect for human dignity and respect for the minimum requirements of life in society'):

SAS v France (App No 43835/11, judgment of 1 July 2014), (2015) 60 EHRR 11 (Grand Chamber)

Judgment:

> 119. [The Court] does not doubt that gender equality might rightly justify an interference with the exercise of certain rights and freedoms enshrined in the convention … It reiterates in this connection that advancement of gender equality is today a major goal in the member states of the Council of Europe … Thus a state party which, in the name of gender equality, prohibits anyone from forcing women to conceal their face pursues an aim which corresponds to the 'protection of the rights and freedoms of others' within the meaning of the second paragraphs of arts 8 and 9 of the convention (see *Şahin v Turkey* §111). The court takes the view, however, that a state party cannot invoke gender equality in order to ban a practice that is defended by women – such as the applicant – in the context of the exercise of the rights enshrined in those provisions, unless it were to be understood that individuals could be protected on that basis from the exercise of their own fundamental rights and freedoms …
>
> 120. Secondly, the court takes the view that, however essential it may be, respect for human dignity cannot legitimately justify a blanket ban on the wearing of the full-face veil in public places. The court is aware that the clothing in question is perceived as strange by many of those who observe it. It would point out, however, that it is the expression of a cultural identity which contributes to the pluralism that is inherent in democracy. It notes in this connection the variability of the notions of virtuousness and decency that are applied to the uncovering of the human body. Moreover, it does not have any evidence capable of leading it to consider that women who wear the full-face veil seek to express a form of contempt against those they encounter or otherwise to offend against the dignity of others.
>
> 122. The court takes into account the respondent state's point that the face plays an important role in social interaction. It can understand the view that individuals who are present in places open to all may not wish to see practices or attitudes developing there which would

fundamentally call into question the possibility of open interpersonal relationships, which, by virtue of an established consensus, forms an indispensable element of community life within the society in question. The court is therefore able to accept that the barrier raised against others by a veil concealing the face is perceived by the respondent state as breaching the right of others to live in a space of socialisation which makes living together easier. That being said, in view of the flexibility of the notion of 'living together' and the resulting risk of abuse, the court must engage in a careful examination of the necessity of the impugned limitation …

128. Pluralism, tolerance and broadmindedness are hallmarks of a 'democratic society'. Although individual interests must on occasion be subordinated to those of a group, democracy does not simply mean that the views of a majority must always prevail: a balance must be achieved which ensures the fair treatment of people from minorities and avoids any abuse of a dominant position … Pluralism and democracy must also be based on dialogue and a spirit of compromise necessarily entailing various concessions on the part of individuals or groups of individuals which are justified in order to maintain and promote the ideals and values of a democratic society … Where these 'rights and freedoms of others' are themselves among those guaranteed by the convention or the Protocols thereto, it must be accepted that the need to protect them may lead states to restrict other rights or freedoms likewise set forth in the convention. It is precisely this constant search for a balance between the fundamental rights of each individual which constitutes the foundation of a 'democratic society'…

129. It is also important to emphasise the fundamentally subsidiary role of the convention mechanism. The national authorities have direct democratic legitimation and are, as the court has held on many occasions, in principle better placed than an international court to evaluate local needs and conditions. In matters of general policy, on which opinions within a democratic society may reasonably differ widely, the role of the domestic policy-maker should be given special … As regards art 9 of the convention, the state should thus, in principle, be afforded a wide margin of appreciation in deciding whether and to what extent a limitation of the right to manifest one's religion or beliefs is 'necessary' …

139. … the court understands that a state may find it essential to be able to identify individuals in order to prevent danger for the safety of persons and property and to combat identity fraud. It has thus found no violation of art 9 of the convention in cases concerning the obligation to remove clothing with a religious connotation in the context of security checks and the obligation to appear bareheaded on identity photos for use on official documents … However, in view of its impact on the rights of women who wish to wear the full-face veil for religious reasons, a blanket ban on the wearing in public places of clothing designed to conceal the face can be regarded as proportionate only in a context where there is a general threat to public safety. The government have not shown that the ban introduced by the law of 11 October 2010 falls into such a context. As to the women concerned, they are thus obliged to give up completely an element of their identity that they consider important, together with their chosen manner of manifesting their religion or beliefs, whereas the objective alluded to by the government could be attained by a mere obligation to show their face and to identify themselves where a risk for the safety of persons and property has been established, or where particular circumstances entail a suspicion of identity fraud. It cannot therefore be found that the blanket ban imposed by the law of 11 October 2010 is necessary, in a democratic society, for public safety, within the meaning of arts 8 and 9 of the convention.

140. The court will now examine the questions raised by the other aim that it has found legitimate: to ensure the observance of the minimum requirements of life in society as part of the 'protection of the rights and freedoms of others'…

141. The court observes that this is an aim to which the authorities have given much weight. … It indeed falls within the powers of the state to secure the conditions whereby individuals can live together in their diversity. Moreover, the court is able to accept that a state may find it

essential to give particular weight in this connection to the interaction between individuals and may consider this to be adversely affected by the fact that some conceal their faces in public places …

143. It remains to be ascertained whether the ban is proportionate to that aim …

145. First, it is true that only a small number of women are concerned … about 1,900 women wore the Islamic full-face veil in France at the end of 2009, of whom about 270 were living in French overseas administrative areas … This is a small proportion in relation to the French population of about 65m and to the number of Muslims living in France. It may thus seem excessive to respond to such a situation by imposing a blanket ban.

146. In addition, there is no doubt that the ban has a significant negative impact on the situation of women who, like the applicant, have chosen to wear the full-face veil for reasons related to their beliefs. As stated previously, they are thus confronted with a complex dilemma, and the ban may have the effect of isolating them and restricting their autonomy, as well as impairing the exercise of their freedom to manifest their beliefs and their right to respect for their private life. It is also understandable that the women concerned may perceive the ban as a threat to their identity.

147. It should furthermore be observed that a large number of actors, both international and national, in the field of fundamental rights protection have found a blanket ban to be disproportionate. This is the case, for example, of the French National Advisory Commission on Human Rights … non-governmental organisations such as the third-party interveners, the Parliamentary Assembly of the Council of Europe … and the Commissioner for Human Rights of the Council of Europe … The court is also aware that the law of 11 October 2010, together with certain debates surrounding its drafting, may have upset part of the Muslim community, including some members who are not in favour of the full-face veil being worn.

149. In this connection, the court is very concerned by the indications of some of the third-party interveners to the effect that certain Islamophobic remarks marked the debate which preceded the adoption of the law of 11 October 2010 … It is admittedly not for the court to rule on whether legislation is desirable in such matters. It would, however, emphasise that a state which enters into a legislative process of this kind takes the risk of contributing to the consolidation of the stereotypes which affect certain categories of the population and of encouraging the expression of intolerance, when it has a duty, on the contrary, to promote tolerance … The court reiterates that remarks which constitute a general, vehement attack on a religious or ethnic group are incompatible with the values of tolerance, social peace and non-discrimination which underlie the convention and do not fall within the right to freedom of expression that it protects …

151. … while it is true that the scope of the ban is broad, because all places accessible to the public are concerned (except for places of worship), the law of 11 October 2010 does not affect the freedom to wear in public any garment or item of clothing – with or without a religious connotation – which does not have the effect of concealing the face. The court is aware of the fact that the impugned ban mainly affects Muslim women who wish to wear the full-face veil. It nevertheless finds it to be of some significance that the ban is not expressly based on the religious connotation of the clothing in question but solely on the fact that it conceals the face …

152. As to the fact that criminal sanctions are attached to the ban, this no doubt increases the impact of the measure on those concerned. It is certainly understandable that the idea of being prosecuted for concealing one's face in a public place is traumatising for women who have chosen to wear the full-face veil for reasons related to their beliefs. It should nevertheless be taken into account that the sanctions provided for by the law's drafters are among the lightest that could be envisaged, because they consist of a fine at the rate applying to second-class petty

> offences (currently 150 euros maximum), with the possibility for the court to impose, in addition to or instead of the fine, an obligation to follow a citizenship course.
>
> 153. Furthermore, admittedly, as the applicant pointed out, by prohibiting everyone from wearing clothing designed to conceal the face in public places, the respondent state has to a certain extent restricted the reach of pluralism, since the ban prevents certain women from expressing their personality and their beliefs by wearing the full-face veil in public. However, for their part, the government indicated that it was a question of responding to a practice that the state deemed incompatible, in French society, with the ground rules of social communication and more broadly the requirements of 'living together'. From that perspective, the respondent state is seeking to protect a principle of interaction between individuals, which in its view is essential for the expression not only of pluralism, but also of tolerance and broadmindedness without which there is no democratic society … It can thus be said that the question whether or not it should be permitted to wear the full-face veil in public places constitutes a choice of society.
>
> 154. In such circumstances, the court has a duty to exercise a degree of restraint in its review of convention compliance, since such review will lead it to assess a balance that has been struck by means of a democratic process within the society in question. The court has, moreover, already had occasion to observe that in matters of general policy, on which opinions within a democratic society may reasonably differ widely, the role of the domestic policy-maker should be given special weight …
>
> 155. In other words, France had a wide margin of appreciation in the present case.
>
> 156. This is particularly true as there is little common ground among the member states of the Council of Europe … as to the question of the wearing of the full-face veil in public … there is no European consensus against a ban. Admittedly, from a strictly normative standpoint, France is very much in a minority position in Europe: except for Belgium, no other member state of the Council of Europe has, to date, opted for such a measure. It must be observed, however, that the question of the wearing of the full-face veil in public is or has been a subject of debate in a number of European states. In some it has been decided not to opt for a blanket ban. In others, such a ban is still being considered …
>
> 157. Consequently, having regard in particular to the breadth of the margin of appreciation afforded to the respondent state in the present case, the court finds that the ban imposed by the law of 11 October 2010 can be regarded as proportionate to the aim pursued, namely the preservation of the conditions of 'living together' as an element of the 'protection of the rights and freedoms of others'.

The following year, in *Ebrahimian v France* [2015] ECHR 1041, the ECtHR rejected an Article 9 claim from a hospital social worker whose contract was not renewed because she wore hijab. The Court ruled that the French authorities regarded the *hijab* as an 'ostentatious manifestation of religion that was incompatible with the requirement of neutrality incumbent on public officials in discharging their functions' and that its prohibition was necessary to uphold the secular character of the State and to protect hospital patients from any risk of influence or partiality in the name of their right to their own freedom of conscience.

EU Law

It had been assumed by some that Council Directive 2000/78 would provide more protection to those, particularly Muslim women, whose religious beliefs or identity are often manifest in their appearance. It became apparent in 2017, with the decision of the CJEU in Case C-157/15 *Achbita v G4S Secure Solutions NV*, EU:C:2017:203, [2018] ICR 102, that this was not the case. The claimant, a receptionist, complained of discrimination when she was dismissed because she began to wear *hijab* and continued to do so despite her employer's insistence on a 'rule', which was initially unwritten, that the workplace was neutral and that workers would not be permitted to display any sign of political, philosophical or religious belief. The Belgian Court of Cassation referred to the CJEU the question whether the prohibition on direct religious discrimination in Council Directive 2000/78 would be breached by a general rule of this sort. The CJEU concluded that it would not, and went on to declare that, if such a rule had a disparate impact such that justification was required, the desire to display a policy of political, philosophical or religious neutrality in relations with customers would be legitimate, particularly where it impacted only on customer-facing workers, and such a rule would be appropriate provided that it was genuinely pursued in a consistent and systematic manner. It further stated that the prohibition imposed by such a general rule would have to be limited to what was strictly necessary, and it was for the referring court to ascertain whether, without the employer being required to take on an additional burden, it could have offered the claimant a post which was not customer-facing instead of dismissing her.

The CJEU reached a different decision on justification in Case C-188/15 *Bougnaoui v Micropole SA* EU:C:2017:204, [2018] ICR 139 in which the claimant, a design engineer, was dismissed after she wore *hijab*, against instruction, while working at a customer site, and the customer complained. The French court referred to the CJEU the question whether the GOR in Article 4(1) of Council Directive 2000/78 had to be interpreted to cover an employer's desire to take account of customer wishes. The CJEU ruled that the GOR applied only to requirements that are objectively dictated by the nature of the occupational activities concerned or of the context in which they are carried out, and could not cover subjective considerations, such as this.

The decision in *Achbita*, in particular, was the subject of considerable criticism. Lucy Vickers, extracted below, discusses the contrasting opinions of AG Kokott, in *Achbita*, and AG Sharpston, in *Bougnaoui*. AG Kokott appeared to adopt a 'margin of appreciation' approach which marks the jurisprudence of the CJEU but which, as Vickers points out, does not appear to have a role in EU equality law which 'has traditionally set common standards to eradicate inequality across the EU', while AG Sharpston 'was clear that different standards of protection should not be applied to different equality grounds' and 'warned strongly against businesses relying on customer prejudice to justify discrimination, suggesting that arguments based on established practice should not be accepted as justifying a refusal to accommodate religious manifestations at work'.

Lucy Vickers, '*Achbita* and *Bougnaoui*: One Step Forward and Two Steps Back for Religious Diversity in the Workplace' (2017) 8 *European Labour Law Journal* 232–57, footnotes omitted

The failure of the Court to reflect on the insights that come from equality thinking is seen particularly in its approach to limiting visible symbols in public facing roles. This has the potential to create very significant limits on the protection of religious dress at work, given just how many roles can be public-facing … Confining protection for religious expression to non-visible or back room roles can thus be seen as a backwards step in terms of promoting equality for minority groups. The effect is to restrict not only employment opportunities, but also broader inclusion of groups such as Muslim women and Sikh men at work, thereby creating invisibility for religious minorities. In contrast to the usual approach in equality law, which has been to encourage participation of protected groups by addressing their needs (for example, the introduction of maternity leave), the

> courts seems to revert to an approach where the minority group has to take responsibility to solve any difficulties by removing themselves from parts of the workforce. In effect, the onus seems to be on religious minorities to 'fix' themselves, rather than changing the discriminatory practices …
>
> The reason for the backwards step in terms of equality can best be understood in the context of a deeper reluctance on the part of the CJEU to address issues of state sovereignty which arise when considering the highly contentious question of the proper scope of protection for religion or belief in Europe. Its failure to address this deeper matter of the integration of standards across the EU can be seen as second backwards step on the part of the CJEU …
>
> The EU's move from an economic union to a social and political union has involved an agenda to promote integration. The EU Equality Directives can be seen to form part of this process … Although integration policy involves integration of minority groups within and between Member States, integration policy also operates at the level of the EU as a whole, including in the constitutional sphere. Within this broader constitutional context, matters of religion or belief have proved intractable … different national approaches to religion appear unamenable to such levels of EU integration, with very different approaches to religious dress codes remaining accepted …

As Vickers indicates, the decisions of the ECtHR and the CJEU should not be taken to be reflective of the position in domestic law, the courts in the UK having generally taken a much more robust approach to restrictions on dress than either European court.[11] And in its subsequent decision in the *IX and MH Muller Handels* case the CJEU ruled added that the mere desire of an employer to pursue a policy of neutrality, while a legitimate aim, was not sufficient to justify objectively a difference of treatment indirectly based on religion or belief.

Cases C-804/18 and C-341/19 *IX and MH Muller Handels GmbH v WABE eV and MJ* EU:C:2021:594, [2022] ICR 190

IX was employed as a special needs carer by WABE, which ran child daycare centres in Germany, MJ as a sales assistant and cashier in a store operated by MH. Both wore headscarves as an expression of their Muslim identities. In 2018, following its adoption of a policy of political, philosophical and religious neutrality which prohibited the wearing of headscarves, *kippahs* and crucifixes IX was suspended for wearing her scarf. In 2016 MJ was asked to remove the headscarf and was sent home when she refused. MH claimed that it had from that date applied a policy prohibiting the use of conspicuous, large-sized political, philosophical or religious signs in all its stores in order to maintain neutrality and to prevent conflicts between employees such as had occurred in the past. German courts referred to the CJEU questions relating to whether the policies constituted direct or indirect discrimination on the grounds of religion or belief contrary to Directive 2000/78.

The Court:

> 52. As regards … the question whether an internal rule of a private undertaking prohibiting the wearing of any visible sign of political, philosophical or religious beliefs in the workplace

[11] Note, more recently, the decision of the CJEU in Case C-193/17 *Cresco Investigation GmbH v Achatzi* [2019] IRLR 380 that the provision of additional paid public holidays to members of certain Christian churches which were not provided to non-members of these churches breached the prohibition in Council Directive 2000/78 on direct religious discrimination, rejecting the argument put for the Austrian government that the discrimination was justified by Art 2(5) of the Directive, which provided that the directive 'shall be without prejudice to measures laid down by national law which, in a democratic society, are necessary … for the protection of the rights and freedoms of others'.

constitutes direct discrimination on the grounds of religion or belief, within the meaning of art 2(2)(a) of Directive 2000/78, the Court has already held that such a rule does not constitute discrimination of that sort provided that it covers any manifestation of such beliefs without distinction and treats all workers of the undertaking in the same way by requiring them, in a general and undifferentiated way, inter alia, to dress neutrally, which precludes the wearing of such signs [citing *Achbita*]. Since every person may have a religion or belief, such a rule, provided that it is applied in a general and undifferentiated way, does not establish a difference of treatment based on a criterion that is inextricably linked to religion or belief …

53. That finding is not called into question … by the fact that some workers observe religious precepts requiring certain clothing to be worn. Although the application of an internal rule such as that referred to in para 52 above is indeed capable of causing particular inconvenience for such workers, that has no bearing on the finding, set out in that paragraph, that that rule, reflecting a policy of political, philosophical and religious neutrality on the part of the employer, does not, in principle, establish a difference of treatment between workers based on a criterion that is inextricably linked to religion or belief, within the meaning of art 1 of Directive 2000/78 …

59. As regards the question of a difference of treatment indirectly based on religion or belief … it should be recalled that such a difference exists where it is established that the apparently neutral obligation which a rule encompasses results, in fact, in persons adhering to a particular religion or belief being put at a particular disadvantage [citing *Achbita*]. Although it is for the referring court to verify that point, it should be noted that, according to the findings of that court, the rule at issue in Case C-804/18 concerns, statistically, almost exclusively female workers who wear a headscarf because of their Muslim faith, and the Court therefore starts from the premiss that that rule constitutes a difference of treatment indirectly based on religion.

60. … a difference of treatment … does not amount to indirect discrimination, within the meaning of art 2(2)(b) of Directive 2000/78, if it is objectively justified by a legitimate aim and if the means of achieving that aim are appropriate and necessary [citing *Bougnaoui*] …

61. In that respect, the concept of a legitimate aim and the appropriate and necessary nature of the means taken to achieve it must be interpreted …

63. … an employer's desire to display, in relations with both public- and private-sector customers, a policy of political, philosophical or religious neutrality may be regarded as legitimate. An employer's wish to project an image of neutrality towards customers relates to the freedom to conduct a business that is recognised in art 16 of the Charter and is, in principle, legitimate, in particular where the employer involves in its pursuit of that aim only those workers who are required to come into contact with the employer's customers [citing *Achbita*] …

64. That being said, the mere desire of an employer to pursue a policy of neutrality – while in itself a legitimate aim – is not sufficient, as such, to justify objectively a difference of treatment indirectly based on religion or belief, since such a justification can be regarded as being objective only where there is a genuine need on the part of that employer, which it is for that employer to demonstrate.

65. In those circumstances, in order to establish the existence of objective justification and, therefore, of a genuine need on the part of the employer, account may be taken, in the first place, of the rights and legitimate wishes of customers or users. That is the case, for example, of parents' right to ensure the education and teaching of their children in accordance with their religious, philosophical and teaching beliefs recognised in art 14 of the Charter or their wish to have their children supervised by persons who do not manifest their religion or belief when they are in contact with the children with the aim, inter alia, of 'guaranteeing the free and personal development of children as regards religion, belief and policy', as mentioned in the staff instructions adopted by WABE …

70. In the light of the foregoing … art 2(2)(b) of Directive 2000/78 must be interpreted as meaning that a difference of treatment indirectly based on religion or belief, arising from an internal rule of an undertaking prohibiting workers from wearing any visible sign of political, philosophical or religious beliefs in the workplace, may be justified by the employer's desire to pursue a policy of political, philosophical and religious neutrality with regard to its customers or users, provided, first, that that policy meets a genuine need on the part of that employer, which it is for that employer to demonstrate, taking into consideration, inter alia, the legitimate wishes of those customers or users and the adverse consequences that that employer would suffer in the absence of that policy, given the nature of its activities and the context in which they are carried out; secondly, that that difference of treatment is appropriate for the purpose of ensuring that the employer's policy of neutrality is properly applied, which entails that that policy is pursued in a consistent and systematic manner; and, thirdly, that the prohibition in question is limited to what is strictly necessary having regard to the actual scale and severity of the adverse consequences that the employer is seeking to avoid by adopting that prohibition …

[turning to the second case]

77. … a policy of neutrality within an undertaking, such as that referred to by the first question in Case C-341/19, can be effectively pursued only if no visible manifestation of political, philosophical or religious beliefs is allowed when workers are in contact with customers or with other workers, since the wearing of any sign, even a small-sized one, undermines the ability of that measure to achieve the aim allegedly pursued and therefore calls into question the consistency of that policy of neutrality.

78. … art 2(2)(b)(i) of Directive 2000/78 must be interpreted as meaning that indirect discrimination on the grounds of religion or belief resulting from an internal rule of an undertaking prohibiting, at the workplace, the wearing of visible signs of political, philosophical or religious beliefs with the aim of ensuring a policy of neutrality within that undertaking can be justified only if that prohibition covers all visible forms of expression of political, philosophical or religious beliefs. A prohibition which is limited to the wearing of conspicuous, large-sized signs of political, philosophical or religious beliefs is liable to constitute direct discrimination on the grounds of religion or belief, which cannot in any event be justified on the basis of that provision.

Ronan McCrea, 'Hijab ruling presents the thorny problem of legislating for all EU member states', *The Conversation*, 22 July 2021[12]

… *Religion and the workplace*

There are two contrasting approaches for people of different religious identities and viewpoints to share a workplace. One is to protect the right of everyone to be fully themselves at work and to wear symbols of religion or belief if they so choose. The second way sees coexistence as best achieved by requiring everyone to refrain from expressing their beliefs at work by adhering to a policy of visible religious neutrality.

Restricting religious symbols at work curtails the religious freedom of employees. Furthermore, what is considered to be 'neutral' in any society will bear the imprint of that society's history and culture. Complying with a 'neutral' standard is likely to be more difficult for minority groups. Still, encouraging religious expression at work is controversial. Most mainstream religions have teachings on matters such as gender and sexuality that people can legitimately find offensive.

[12] https://theconversation.com/hijab-ruling-presents-the-thorny-problem-of-legislating-for-all-eu-member-states-164722.

Commentators have expressed disappointment in the EU court's ruling, accusing the court of failing to take religious discrimination seriously – and even pandering to prejudice. Regulating religion brings particular difficulties. Religion is both a matter of what you believe and who you are. It is hard to protect religious identity without appearing to privilege religious over other forms of belief. If a religious employee can wear a crucifix or a hijab at work, can an atheist employee wear a 'There is no God' t-shirt? Can a vegan employee wear a sticker saying 'Meat is murder?'

Ruling for the whole EU

In cases like these, the EU court faces the delicate task of interpreting legislation that applies to 27 member states, all with different values and approaches to religious freedom. As EU anti-discrimination legislation can only be amended with the agreement of every member state, if the court gets it wrong, the EU is likely to be stuck with its interpretation indefinitely.

In France, the approach has often been to pursue coexistence by pushing people to hold back on expressing religious identity in shared contexts. In the UK, by contrast, the approach has been to facilitate religious expression. Each approach has its detractors on both the right and the left. Many in France see the French way of doing things as oppressive and as exclusionary towards minorities, and tainted with elements of colonialist thinking. On the other hand, some in the UK feel that cohesion has been poorly served by approaches that emphasise religious differences. Statistics on which approach is better at producing mutual respect, friendship across religious lines and religious beliefs compatible with liberal democratic values are mixed. With such different views among nations and no historical precedent, it would have been wrong for a multinational court to decide it had identified the ideal approach and impose it on all 27 member states.

The EU court was right to allow states to continue to experiment with different ways of managing this situation. States that want to encourage religious reticence in shared contexts can do so. Those that wish to provide greater protection for religious expression at work may also do. It was also right to impose some limits by ensuring bans cannot target one faith. Too often in Europe, secularist principles have been cynically embraced by those with exclusionary agendas. Marine Le Pen's National Rally, for example, appeared to only discover a love for secularist principles after realising they could be used as a stick with which to beat French Muslims. For a multinational court, dealing with virtually unamendable legislation and a rapidly changing and unpredictable situation, that is about as much as it was prudent to do.

The Equality Act 2010

'Religion or Belief'

Section 10 EqA, Religion or Belief

(1) Religion means any religion and a reference to religion includes a reference to a lack of religion.
(2) Belief means any religious or philosophical belief and a reference to belief includes a reference to a lack of belief.
(3) In relation to the protected characteristic of religion or belief—
  (a) a reference to a person who has a particular protected characteristic is a reference to a person of a particular religion or belief;
  (b) a reference to persons who share a protected characteristic is a reference to persons who are of the same religion or belief.

The initial prohibition in GB of discrimination related to religion or belief was designed to implement Council Directive 2000/78 which regulated such discrimination in the context of work. That provision was also influenced by Article 9 ECHR. Neither the Act nor Council

Directive 2000/78 further defines 'religion or belief', though recital 13 of the preamble to the original proposal for the Directive referred to the EU's Declaration on the status of churches and non-confessional organisations, attached to the Amsterdam Treaty, which 'has explicitly recognised that it respects and does not prejudice the status which churches and religious associations or communities enjoy in the Member States under national law *and that it equally respects the status of philosophical and non-confessional organisations*' (emphasis added).

In *R (Williamson) v Secretary of State for Education and Employment*, an Article 9 case, the HL held that a court could enquire into whether a claimant actually held beliefs that he or she claimed to hold, but could not investigate whether the belief was 'valid', as distinct from 'not an artifice'. The case involved a claim by Christian parents that their religious beliefs required that their children be subject to corporal punishment, where appropriate, by their schoolteachers. The Secretary of State had argued that the infliction of corporal punishment could not be regarded as part of the claimants' religious convictions.

***R (Williamson) v Secretary of State for Education and Employment* [2005] UKHL 15, [2005] 2 AC 246**

Lord Nicholl, with whom Lords Walker, Brown and Bingham and Lady Hale agreed):

> 22. ... When the genuineness of a claimant's professed belief is an issue in the proceedings the court will inquire into and decide this issue as a question of fact. This is a limited inquiry. The court is concerned to ensure an assertion of religious belief is made in good faith, 'neither fictitious, nor capricious, and that it is not an artifice', to adopt the felicitous phrase of Iacobucci J in the decision of the Supreme Court of Canada in *Syndicat Northcrest v Amselem* (2004) 241 DLR (4th) 1 at §52. But, emphatically, it is not for the court to embark on an inquiry into the asserted belief and judge its 'validity' by some objective standard such as the source material upon which the claimant founds his belief or the orthodox teaching of the religion in question or the extent to which the claimant's belief conforms to or differs from the views of others professing the same religion. Freedom of religion protects the subjective belief of an individual. As Iaccobucci J also noted (§54)) religious belief is intensely personal and can easily vary from one individual to another. Each individual is at liberty to hold his own religious beliefs, however irrational or inconsistent they may seem to some, however surprising ... The relevance of objective factors such as source material is, at most, that they may throw light on whether the professed belief is genuinely held.[13]

The SC had cause to consider the definition of religion in *R (Hodkin) v Registrar General of Births, Deaths and Marriages* [2013] UKSC 77, [2014] AC 610. The case concerned the Church of Scientology which had in 1970 been found by the CA in *Ex p Segerdal* [1970] 2 QB 697 (*per* Lord Denning) not to be involved in 'religious worship' because its ceremonies did not involve reverence or veneration of God or a Supreme Being. The claimant sought in 2011 to have one of the Church's chapels registered as a 'place of meeting for religious worship' under s2 of the Places of Worship Registration Act 1855 and as a building for the solemnisation of marriages under the Marriage Act 1949, so that she could marry in it. The application was refused by the Registrar General of Births, Deaths and Marriages

[13] And see *Gareddu v London Underground Ltd* [2017] IRLR 404 in which the EAT upheld the rejection by a tribunal that the claimant's religious belief required him to so attend five weeks of festivals in Sardinia with his family every summer.

who regarded himself as bound by the CA's decision in *Ex p Segerdal.* The claimant's challenge reached the SC which ruled both that Scientology was a religion and that its services included 'religious worship'.

R (Hodkin) v Registrar General of Births, Deaths and Marriages [2013] UKSC 77, [2014] AC 610

Lord Toulson (with whom Lords Neuberger, Clarke and Reed agreed):

51. Unless there is some compelling contextual reason for holding otherwise, religion should not be confined to religions which recognise a supreme deity. First and foremost, to do so would be a form of religious discrimination unacceptable in today's society. It would exclude Buddhism, along with other faiths such as Jainism, Taoism, Theosophy and part of Hinduism. The evidence in the present case shows that, among others, Jains, Theosophists and Buddhists have registered places of worship in England. Lord Denning in *Ex p Segerdal* … acknowledged that Buddhist temples were 'properly described as places of meeting for religious worship' but he referred to them as 'exceptional cases' without offering any further explanation. The need to make an exception for Buddhism (which has also been applied to Jainism and Theosophy), and the absence of a satisfactory explanation for it, are powerful indications that there is something unsound in the supposed general rule.

52. Further, to confine religion to a religion which involves belief in a 'supreme deity' leads into difficult theological territory. On the evidence of Mrs Wilks, Scientologists do believe in a supreme deity of a kind, but of an abstract and impersonal nature. Ideas about the nature of God are the stuff of theological debate …

54. For the purposes of charity law, s 3(2)(a) of the 2011 Act now states that: '"religion" includes – (i) a religion which involves belief in more than one god, and (ii) a religion which does not involve belief in a god.'

55. That definition … has no direct application to s 2 of the 1855 Act, but it is a further indication that the understanding of religion in today's society is broad.

57. … For the purposes of the 1855 Act, I would describe religion in summary as a spiritual or non-secular belief system, held by a group of adherents, which claims to explain mankind's place in the universe and relationship with the infinite, and to teach its adherents how they are to live their lives in conformity with the spiritual understanding associated with the belief system. By spiritual or non-secular I mean a belief system which goes beyond that which can be perceived by the senses or ascertained by the application of science. I prefer not to use the word 'supernatural' to express this element, because it is a loaded word which can carry a variety of connotations. Such a belief system may or may not involve belief in a supreme being, but it does involve a belief that there is more to be understood about mankind's nature and relationship to the universe than can be gained from the senses or from science. I emphasise that this is intended to be a description and not a definitive formula.

59. The legislation … makes separate provision for religious wedding ceremonies on registered premises and secular wedding services on approved premises.

62. I interpret the expression 'religious worship' as wide enough to include religious services, whether or not the form of service falls within the narrower definition adopted in *Ex p Segerdal.* This broader interpretation accords with standard dictionary definitions …

63. The broader interpretation accords with the purpose of the statute in permitting members of a religious congregation, who have a meeting place where they perform their religious rites, to carry out religious ceremonies of marriage there. Their authorisation to do so should not depend on fine theological or liturgical niceties as to how precisely they see and express their

relationship with the infinite (referred to by Scientologists as 'God' in their creed and universal prayer). Those matters, which have been gone into in close detail in the evidence in this case, are more fitting for theologians than for the Registrar General or the courts.

64. There is a further significant point. If, as I have held, Scientology comes within the meaning of a religion, but its chapel cannot be registered under the 1855 Act because its services do not involve the kind of veneration which the CA in *Ex p Segerdal* considered essential, the result would be to prevent Scientologists from being married anywhere in a form which involved use of their marriage service. They could have a service in their chapel, but it would not be a legal marriage, and they could have a civil marriage on other 'approved premises' under s 26(1)(bb) of the 1949 Act, but they could not incorporate any form of religious service because of the prohibition in s 46B(4). They would therefore be under a double disability, not shared by atheists, agnostics or most religious groups. This would be illogical, discriminatory and unjust. When Parliament prohibited the use of any 'religious service' on approved premises in s 46B(4), it can only have been on the assumption that any religious service of marriage could lawfully be held at a meeting place for religious services by registration under the 1855 Act.

There has been very little discussion in the domestic or EU case law about the parameters of 'religion' in the context of the EqA, its predecessor legislation or Council Directive 2000/78. By contrast, there have been a large number of cases in the domestic courts which have concerned the scope of protected *beliefs*. The original consultation document on the implementation of the Employment Equality Directive stated that, because of 'the wide variety of different faiths and beliefs in this country, we have reached the view that we should not attempt to define "religion or belief," and that it would be better to leave it to the Courts to resolve definitional issues as they arise [nevertheless] we do intend to make it clear that the term "belief" does not apply to political belief – which is not covered by the Directive. In our view, "belief" extends only to religious beliefs and profound philosophical convictions similar to religious belief which deserve society's respect.'[14] By the second round of consultation (*Equality and Diversity: The Way Ahead*) the Government had decided 'not … to give any further definition of these terms except to say that "belief" should be taken to refer to a religious or similar belief, but not a political belief more generally.' The word 'similar' was originally included in the RB Regs but was removed by the Equality Act 2006. It had been suggested that '[t]o be defined as "similar" to religion was viewed as offensive to some humanists and atheists',[15] though the Attorney General Baroness Scotland indicated in the Parliamentary debates that the word was being removed because it:

HL Debates 13 July 2005, cols 1109–10

added nothing and was, therefore, redundant. This is because the term 'philosophical belief' will take its meaning form the context in which it appears; that is, as part of the legislation relating to discrimination on the grounds of religion or belief. Given that context, philosophical beliefs must therefore always be of a similar nature to religious beliefs. It will be for the courts to decide what constitutes a belief … but case law suggests that any philosophical belief must attain a certain level of cogency, seriousness, cohesion and importance, must be worthy of respect in a democratic society and must not be incompatible with human dignity. Therefore an example of a belief that might meet this description is humanism, and examples of something that might not … would be support of a political party or a belief in the supreme nature of the Jedi Knights.[16]

[14] *Towards Equality and Diversity*.
[15] Lucy Vickers, *Religious Freedom, Religious Discrimination, and the Workplace* (London, Bloomsbury, 2008) 23.
[16] Equality Bill *Hansard* (HL Debates) 13 July 2005, cols 1109–10.

The approach of the courts has not been exactly as Baroness Scotland anticipated. The starting point is the decision of the EAT in *Grainger v Nicholson* in which the claimant alleged that he had been dismissed because of his strong belief that mankind was heading towards catastrophic climate change and that there was a moral duty to live in a manner which mitigated or avoided that catastrophe for the benefit of future generations and to persuade others to do the same. He claimed that this belief affected his choice of home, his travel, his purchases, his consumption of food and drink, how he disposed of his waste, and his hopes and fears. The EAT ruled that the claimant's belief could constitute a 'philosophical belief'.

Grainger v Nicholson **[2009] UKEAT 0219_09_0311, [2010] ICR 360**

Burton J:

20. … Allowance must be made for the fact that the article 9 *belief* need not be a philosophical belief, though an article 2 of the First Protocol *conviction* must be *philosophical*. Prior to *Campbell [v UK]* 4 EHRR 293, the only matters said to be of any potential relevance are two decisions of the European Commission on Human Rights. The first [was] *Arrowsmith v United Kingdom* (1978) 3 EHRR 218, in which the Commission was of the opinion, at para 69, that pacifism is a philosophy. In a subsequent decision of the Commission, *CW v United Kingdom* (1993) 16 EHRR CD 44, the Commission noted that the United Kingdom Government did not contest that veganism was capable of concerning belief within the meaning of article 9 of the Convention. Though neither of those decisions, and certainly not the latter, which was based upon a concession, could be in any way binding, it is significant that, clearly by reference to them, Lord Walker of Gestingthorpe was able to state in his speech in *R (Williamson) v Secretary of State for Education and Employment*, §55:

> "pacifism, vegetarianism and total abstinence from alcohol are uncontroversial examples of beliefs which would fall within article 9 (of course pacifism or any comparable belief may be based on religious convictions, but equally it may be based on ethical convictions which are not religious but humanist …)"

And *Arrowsmith v United Kingdom* is expressly approved by Lord Nicholls in §24 …

24. … I shall endeavour to set out the limitations, or criteria, which are to be implied or introduced by reference to the jurisprudence set out above. (i) The belief must be genuinely held. (ii) It must be a belief and not, as in *McClintock v Department of Constitutional Affairs* [2008] IRLR 29, an opinion or viewpoint based on the present state of information available. (iii) It must be a belief as to a weighty and substantial aspect of human life and behaviour. (iv) It must attain a certain level of cogency, seriousness, cohesion and importance. (v) It must be worthy of respect in a democratic society, be not incompatible with human dignity and not conflict with the fundamental rights of others (§36 of *Campbell* and §23 of *Williamson's* case) …

27. I conclude that it is not a bar to a *philosophical belief* being protected … if it is a one-off belief and not shared by others, a fortiori where it is likely that others do share the belief. Pacifism and vegetarianism can both be described as one-off beliefs in the sense in which I understand it to be being used by Mr Bowers, namely a belief that does not govern the entirety of a person's life. Hence, provided that there are the limitations referred to above, which I accept as being appropriately applied to the Regulations, I would subscribe, even were the jurisprudence of the Convention not otherwise, as I conclude it to be, persuasive, if not binding upon me, to the proposition that, as concluded by the court in *Campbell v United Kingdom* §36, the philosophical belief in question does not need to constitute or "allude to a fully-fledged system of thought", *provided that* it otherwise satisfies the limitations set out in §24 above. As it was put in argument, such philosophical belief does not need to amount to an "-ism".

> 28. … There is nothing to my mind in the make-up of a philosophical belief – particularly against the background of article 14 of the Convention referred to above – which would disqualify a belief based on a political philosophy. The belief asserted by the claimant in this case, by reference to his alleged philosophical belief in anthropogenic climate change, if established, is likely to be characterised as a political belief … But I do not see that as a ground for excluding it, if it be otherwise qualified as a genuinely held philosophical belief. It seemed to me that the real concern that Mr Bowers had, and one which the court would naturally share, would be the fear that reliance could be placed upon an alleged philosophical belief based on a political philosophy which could be characterised as objectionable: a racist or homophobic political philosophy for example. In my judgment, the way to deal with that would be to conclude that it offended against the requirement set out in §36 of *Campbell*, that the belief relied on must be "worthy of respect in a democratic society and not incompatible with human dignity" or, in accordance with §23 of *Williamson*, a belief "consistent with basic standards of human dignity or integrity". Paragraph 36 in *Campbell* expressly refers, as the source of this requirement/caveat, to article 17 of the Convention, which deals with 'Prohibition of abuse of rights'…
>
> 30. In my judgment, if a person can establish that he holds a philosophical belief which is based on science, as opposed, for example, to religion, then there is no reason to disqualify it from protection by the Regulations. The employment judge drew attention to the existence of empiricist philosophers, no doubt such as Hume and Locke. The best example, as it seems to me, which was canvassed during the course of the hearing, is by reference to the clash of two such philosophies, exemplified in the play *Inherit the Wind*, ie one not simply between those who supported Creationism and those who did not, but between those who positively supported, and wished to teach, only Creationism and those who positively supported, and wished to teach, only Darwinism. Darwinism must plainly be capable of being a philosophical belief, albeit that it may be based entirely on scientific conclusions (not all of which may be uncontroversial).

Among the beliefs which have been accepted as falling (at least arguably) within the *Grainger* test, and hence within the EqA or its predecessor have been the following:

- A belief that lying is always wrong, this in a case brought by a Christian telesales agent who alleged that he was dismissed for his belief that potential customers should not be lied to: *Hawkins v Universal Utilities Ltd t/a Unicom* ET/2501234/2012;
- A police officer's belief in the need for the efficient use of money in the public sector: *Harron v CC Dorset Police* [2016] IRLR 481;
- A commitment to public service, this in the case of a full-time school social exclusion officer who also worked full-time as the mayor of Liverpool: *Anderson v Chesterfield High School*;[17]
- A belief in democratic socialism/left-wing democratic socialism: *Olivier v Department for Work and Pensions* ET/1701407/2013;
- A belief in humanism: *Streatfeild v London Philharmonic Orchestra Ltd* ET/2390772/2011;
- A belief in Scottish independence extended beyond the merely political to a 'fundamental belief in the right of Scotland to national sovereignty'; *McEleny v Ministry of Defence* S/4105347/2017;[18]

[17] The EAT decision (which did not concern the scope of 'belief'), is at UKEAT/0206/14/MC.
[18] https://www.gov.uk/employment-tribunal-decisions/mr-c-mceleny-v-ministry-of-defence-4105347-2017.

- A belief in the sanctity of life which resulted in opposition to fox hunting and hare coursing: *Hashman v Milton Park (Dorset) Ltd t/a Orchard Park* ET/3105555/2009;
- A belief in spiritualism, life after death and the ability of mediums to contact the dead: *Greater Manchester Police Authority v Power* UKEAT/0087/10/JOJ;
- A belief in the 'higher purpose' of public service broadcasting: *Maistry v BBC* ET/1313142/10;
- Anti-monarchy or republican belief: *Gibbins v British Council* ET/2200088/2017;[19]
- 'Ethical veganism: *Casamitjana Costa v The League of Cruel Sports*: ET/3331129/2018.[20]

By contrast, the following have been found to fall outside the *Grainger* parameters:

- *Vegetarianism: Conisbee v Crossley Farms Limited* ET/3335357/2018;[21]
- A belief in the claimant's statutory human or moral right to own copyright and moral rights of her own creative works and output': *Gray v Mulberry Company (Design) Ltd* [2019] EWCA Civ 1720, [2020] IRLR 29;
- A belief that poppies should be worn in early November: *Lisk v Shield Guardian Co Ltd* ET/3300873/11;
- A belief that the London bombings of 7 July 2005 and the 11 September 2001 attack on the World Trade Center in New York were carried out by the US and UK governments as part of a 'gigantic' and 'evil' conspiracy: *Farrell v South Yorkshire Police Authority* ET/2803805/10;
- The beliefs that 'homosexuality is contrary to God's law and nature' and that 'no Jewish people were killed by the use of poison gas in concentration camps during the Second World War': *Ellis v Parmagan Ltd* ET/1603027/2013;
- 'Extreme' Marxist/Trotskyist beliefs: *Kelly and others v UNISON* ET/2204854/08; and
- A fanatical devotion to a football club (*McClung v Doosan Babcock Ltd* ET/4110538/2019).[22]

Employment tribunals found in *Mackereth v Department of Work and Pensions* ET/1304602/2018 and *Forstater v CGD Europe* ET/2200909/2019 that beliefs which might be described as 'gender critical' were not protected. The claimant in *Forstater* believed that there were only two sexes, male and female, and that a Gender Recognition Certificate did not have the effect of changing actual (as distinct from legal) sex. The claimant in *Mackereth* was a Christian doctor who believed that a person could not change his or her sex or gender at will and that attempting to do so was pointless, self-destructive and sinful, that society should not accommodate or encourage what he saw as '*impersonation*' in this context, and that it would be irresponsible and dishonest for a health professional to accommodate or encourage such 'impersonation' by a patient. Both lost their cases at first instance on the basis that their beliefs were not protected but Ms Forstater successfully appealed against the

[19] https://assets.publishing.service.gov.uk/media/59fc55a140f0b63683389ef3/Ms_A_Gibbins_v_British_Council_2200088-2017_-_Final_and_Reasons.pdf.

[20] https://www.gov.uk/employment-tribunal-decisions/mr-j-casamitjana-costa-v-the-league-against-cruel-sports-3331129-2018.

[21] https://www.gov.uk/employment-tribunal-decisions/mr-g-conisbee-v-crossley-farms-ltd-and-others-3335357-2018.

[22] https://www.gov.uk/employment-tribunal-decisions/mr-e-mcclung-v-doosan-babcock-ltd-and-others-4110538-slash-2019.

tribunal decision (see below) and subsequently won her case. On his appeal Dr Mackereth established that his belief was protected by s10 EqA but his appeal failed because the tribunal had proceeded, despite its findings on the *Grainger* criteria, to consider his claims on the merits and found on the facts that he had not suffered the acts of less favourable treatment/harassment complained of, and that his beliefs (as distinct from the manner of their manifestation) were not the reason for the respondents' conduct. The tribunal had also been entitled to find that any indirect discrimination against the claimant was justified by the needs of potentially vulnerable service users and the risks the claimant posed to those individuals and, in consequence, to the respondents.[23]

***Forstater v CGD Europe* [2021] UKEAT 0105_20_1006, [2022] ICR 1**

The claimant, a researcher and visiting fellow of a think tank, was subject to detriment after she expressed concerns about proposed amendments to the Gender Recognition Act 2004 to allow 'self-identification' by transgender people in their preferred gender. Her views were regarded by certain colleagues as transphobic. She brought proceedings alleging direct discrimination because of her 'gender-critical' beliefs but her claim was struck out at a preliminary hearing on the basis that her core beliefs – that sex was biologically immutable, that that there were only two sexes, male and female, and that sex was determined by biology – were 'absolutist' and unworthy of respect in a democratic society, and were therefore not protected by the EqA. The claimant successfully appealed.

Choudhury P:

> 57 .... It is clear from the passage in *Grainger* cited at para 21 above, that Burton P derived *Grainger* V from certain passages in two earlier decisions: the first is para 36 of the decision of the ECtHR in *Campbell and Cosans v UK* (App 7511/76) (1983) 4 EHRR 293 …
>
> 58. In accepting that the applicants' views on corporal punishment did amount to philosophical convictions, the ECtHR said as follows at para 36 of its judgment:
>
> > '… Having regard to the Convention as a whole, *including Article 17*, the expression "philosophical convictions" in the present context denotes, in the Court's opinion, such convictions as are worthy of respect in a "democratic society" and are not incompatible with human dignity; in addition, they must not conflict with the fundamental right of the child to education, the whole of Article 2 being dominated by its first sentence. The applicants' views relate to a weighty and substantial aspect of human life and behaviour, namely the integrity of the person, the propriety or otherwise of the infliction of corporal punishment and the exclusion of the distress which the risk of such punishment entails. They are views which satisfy each of the various criteria listed above; it is this that distinguishes them from opinions that might be held on other methods of discipline or on discipline in general.' [Choudhury J's emphasis]
>
> 59. The ECtHR.s reference to art 17, ECHR, is instructive. Article 17, ECHR, prohibits the use of the ECHR to destroy the rights of others. It becomes relevant where a State, group or person seeks to rely on Convention rights in a way that blatantly violates the rights and values protected by the Convention. One cannot, for example, rely on the right to freedom of expression to espouse hatred, violence or a totalitarian ideology that is wholly incompatible with the principles of democracy … The level at which art 17 becomes relevant is

[23] [2022] EAT 99, [2022] IRLR 721.

> clearly (and necessarily) a high one. The fundamental freedoms and rights conferred by the Convention would be seriously diminished if art 17, and the effective denial of a Convention right, could be too readily invoked … Thus, when the ECtHR refers to art 17 (as it did in *Campbell and Cosans v UK*) in considering whether a philosophical conviction is worthy of respect in a democratic society and not in conflict with the fundamental rights of others, it would have had in mind that it is only a conviction that eg challenges the very notion of democracy that would not command such respect. To maintain the plurality that is the hallmark of a functioning democracy, the range of beliefs and convictions that must be tolerated is very broad. It is not enough that a belief or a statement has the potential to 'offend, shock or disturb' [citing *Vajnai v Hungary* (2010) 50 EHRR 44 §46] a section (or even most) of society that it should be deprived of protection under arts 9 (freedom of thought conscience and belief) or art 10 (freedom of expression). The stipulation that the conviction or belief must not be in conflict with the fundamental rights of others must also be viewed with regard to art 17. The conflict between rights in this context of satisfying threshold requirements is not merely that which would arise in any case where the exercise of one right might have an impact on the ECHR rights of another; in order for a conviction or belief to satisfy threshold requirements to qualify for protection, it need only be established that it does not have the effect of destroying the rights of others.

Choudhury P then referred to the decision in *Williamson* which he said at §61 was 'consistent with the principle that only the gravest violations of Convention principles should be denied protection. Such violations go far beyond what might be regarded as potentially justifiable interference with a right: they seek to destroy such rights'. He went on to consider the ECHR decisions in *Ibragimov v Russia* (App nos 1413/08 and 28621/11) [2018] ECHR 1413/08 and *Lilliendahl v Iceland* (App no 29297/18):

> 66. It is clear from these judgments that, in assessing whether a person's rights under art 9 or art 10 have been infringed, there is a preliminary question as to whether the person qualifies for protection at all, or, to use the ECtHR's terminology, as to whether the person 'fall[s] outside the scope of protection of art 10 of the Convention by virtue of art 17': *Lilliendahl* at para 39. Where the expression amounts to the 'gravest form of hate speech' then the protection would not apply, as art 17 would operate to deprive the person of the protection that they seek to invoke. However, if the expression does not fall into that first category, then the question is whether the steps taken by the State to restrict such expression are justified within the meaning of art 10(2). Thus even comments which are 'serious, severely hurtful and prejudicial', or which promote intolerance and detestation of homosexuals would not fall outside the scope of art 10 altogether. However, that does not mean that the individual making such comments has free rein to make them in any circumstance at all. The individual's freedom to express their views is limited to the extent provided for by art 10(2) and it will then be for the Court to assess whether any limitation imposed by the State is justified.
>
> 67. In many art 9 cases, that two-stage analysis will not arise because it will be obvious that the religion or belief is one which falls within scope of the protection afforded by that Article, and the analysis will move swiftly to whether there was an interference with the right and, if so, whether that was justified. However, where it does arise, it is important to bear in mind the extremely limited circumstances in which a belief would be considered so beyond the pale that it does not qualify for protection at all.
>
> 68. … In relation to *Grainger* V, that means that only those beliefs whose characteristics are such that they would fall outside the scope of art 9, ECHR by virtue of art 17 would fail to satisfy that criterion.
>
> 79. In our judgment, it is important that in applying *Grainger* V, Tribunals bear in mind that it is only those beliefs that would be an affront to Convention principles in a manner akin to

> that of pursuing totalitarianism, or advocating Nazism, or espousing violence and hatred in the gravest of forms, that should be capable of being not worthy of respect in a democratic society. Beliefs that are offensive, shocking or even disturbing to others, and which fall into the less grave forms of hate speech would not be excluded from the protection. However, the manifestation of such beliefs may, depending on circumstances, justifiably be restricted under art 9(2) or art 10(2) as the case may be ...
>
> 111. ... the Claimant's belief does not get anywhere near to approaching the kind of belief akin to Nazism or totalitarianism that would warrant the application of art 17. That is reason enough on its own to find that *Grainger* V is satisfied. The Claimant's belief might well be considered offensive and abhorrent to some, but the accepted evidence before the Tribunal was that she believed that it is not 'incompatible to recognise that human beings cannot change sex whilst also protecting the human rights of people who identify as transgender': see para 39.2 of the Judgment. That is not, on any view, a statement of a belief that seeks to destroy the rights of trans persons. It is a belief that might in some circumstances cause offence to trans persons, but the potential for offence cannot be a reason to exclude a belief from protection altogether.
>
> 112. In the present case, there are two further factors which, upon analysis, are wholly at odds with the view that the belief is not one worthy of respect in a democratic society.
>
> 113. First, there is the evidence that the gender-critical belief is not unique to the Claimant, but is widely shared, including amongst respected academics. The popularity of a belief does not necessarily insulate it from being one that gravely undermines the rights of others; history is replete with instances where large swathes of society have succumbed to philosophies that seek to destroy the rights of others. However, a widely shared belief demands particular care before it can be condemned as being not worthy of respect in a democratic society.
>
> 114. Second, the Claimant's belief that sex is immutable and binary is, as the Tribunal itself correctly concluded, consistent with the law .... The leading case is still *Corbett v Corbett* [1970] 2 All ER 33 (at 47, 48 and 49) per Ormrod J ...
>
> 115. Where a belief or a major tenet of it appears to be in accordance with the law of the land, then it is all the more jarring that it should be declared as one not worthy of respect in a democratic society ...
>
> 116. Just as the legal recognition of Civil Partnerships does not negate the right of a person to believe that marriage should only apply to heterosexual couples, becoming the acquired gender 'for all purposes' within the meaning of GRA does not negate a person's right to believe, like the Claimant, that as a matter of biology a trans person is still their natal sex. Both beliefs may well be profoundly offensive and even distressing to many others, but they are beliefs that are and must be tolerated in a pluralist society.

It is difficult to argue with Choudhury P's conclusion at §115. It is perhaps more questionable whether similar protection should be afforded by the EqA to a belief in the need for efficiency in the public sector, or in the 'higher purpose' of public service broadcasting, as is given to ethnicity or sexual orientation. It is the case that the protection of the EqA is generally symmetrical, that is, it applies to men as well as to women, to white as well as racially minoritised people and to heterosexual as well as LGB people. But, whereas gender, ethnicity and sexual orientation are significantly and broadly related to life chances, this is clearly not the case for many of the beliefs which have been protected under the EqA.

Direct Discrimination

In *Lee v Ashers Baking Company Ltd*, also discussed in Chapters 2 and 10, the SC considered whether a refusal, based on the bakers' religious beliefs, to provide the claimant with a cake iced with the slogan 'Support gay marriage', amounted to or entailed discrimination on grounds of the claimant's belief.

***Lee v Ashers Baking Company Ltd* [2018] UKSC 49, [2020] AC 413**

The claimant was a gay man who volunteered for QueerSpace, an organisation which campaigned for same-sex marriage in Northern Ireland. Ashers was a bakery run by a Christian couple who believed that only heterosexual marriage was consistent with the Bible and acceptable to God. It refused the claimant's request to provide him with a cake iced with the slogan 'Support gay marriage'.

The county court had accepted that the refusal of service amounted to direct discrimination on grounds of the claimant's beliefs (the Northern Irish Fair Employment and Treatment Order applying unambiguously to political as well as other beliefs). The CA did not consider this aspect of the claim. The SC ruled that the claimant had not been discriminated against on grounds of his belief contrary to FETO[24] or (see Chapter 10) his sexual orientation.

Lady Hale (with whom Lords Mance, Kerr and Hodge and Lady Black agreed):

41. … The District Judge held that support for gay marriage was a political opinion for this purpose. There was a political debate going on in Northern Ireland at the time about whether same sex couples should be allowed to marry in Northern Ireland as they are in the rest of the United Kingdom. The Assembly had debated a motion calling for same sex marriage three times over a period of 18 months and had rejected it for a third time only the week before. Political opinion is not defined in the legislation, but in *McKay v Northern Ireland Public Service Alliance* [1995] IRLR 146, it was defined as 'an opinion relating to the policy of government and matters touching the government of the state' and in *Ryder v Northern Ireland Policing Board* [2007] NICA 43, it was said that 'the type of political opinion must be one relating to the conduct of the government of the state or matters of public policy'. There is no need for an association with a particular political party or ideology, although no doubt that would also count. I see no reason to doubt that support for gay marriage is indeed a political opinion for this purpose.

42. However, it is not entirely clear on what basis the District Judge upheld this aspect of the claim. She clearly held, in two places, that the reason why the order had not been fulfilled was the McArthurs' religious belief. Among the arguments presented to her on behalf of Mr Lee was that it was immaterial whether the bakery knew of Mr Lee's religious belief or political opinion, because 'under the 1998 Order, discrimination can take place on the grounds of the discriminator's religious belief and political opinion'.

43. Not surprisingly, Mr Scoffield, for the bakery, argues that this cannot be right. The purpose of discrimination law is to protect a person (or a person or persons with whom he is associated) who has a protected characteristic from being treated less favourably because of that characteristic. The purpose is not to protect people without such a characteristic from being treated less favourably because of the protected characteristic of the alleged discriminator. This was reflected, for example, in s 45(1) of the Equality Act 2006 which made it clear that the discrimination has to be on the ground of the religion or belief of someone other than the alleged discriminator. It is also a well-established principle of equality law that the motive of the alleged discriminator is irrelevant: see, *R (E) v Governing Body of JFS* [2009] UKSC 15,

[24] See p 543 above.

[2010] 2 AC 728, eg at paras [13]–[20], citing *R v Birmingham City Council ex parte EOC* [1989] AC 1155 and *James v Eastleigh Borough Council* [1990] 2 AC 751.

44. In *In re Northern Ireland Electricity Service's Application* [1987] NI 271, Nicholson J did observe *obiter* that the words of s 16(2) of the Fair Employment (Northern Ireland) Act 1976, which are essentially the same as those in art 3(2)(a) of FETO, were capable of being read widely enough to encompass acts done based on the religious belief or political opinion of the person doing the act. There are similar dicta in *In re O'Neill's Application* [1995] NI 274, at 279–280, and in *Ryder v Northern Ireland Policing Board* [2007] NICA 43, para [11]. However, such a reading would be inconsistent with [the definition of direct discrimination] which requires a comparison between the person receiving the less favourable treatment and 'other persons': this would not be possible if the treatment were on the grounds of the discriminator's beliefs because everyone would be treated alike. It would also be inconsistent with the definition of indirect discrimination, which requires, in art 3(2)(b)(ii), that the discriminator cannot show that the requirement or condition with which the person to whom it is applied cannot comply is 'justifiable irrespective of the religious belief or political opinion of the person to whom it is applied'. Another pointer are the exemptions in art 31(3)(a) and (4)(a) for goods, facilities and services provided by a religious denomination or political party, the essential nature of which requires them to be provided only to persons holding or not holding a particular belief or opinion.

45. For all those reasons, of policy, principle and language, in my view the less favourable treatment prohibited by FETO must be on the grounds of religious belief or political opinion of someone other than the person meting out that treatment. To the extent that the District Judge held that the bakery had discriminated unlawfully because of its owners' religious beliefs she was wrong to do so.

46. However, that may not be an entirely fair reading of her judgment. She rejected the submission that the bakery had no reason to know about Mr Lee's political opinions. They clearly did know that he supported gay marriage, because of the message he wanted on the cake … there appears to have been no evidence of Mr Lee's religious beliefs. Once a claim based on the McArthurs' religious beliefs is dismissed, the claim must be made, if at all, on the basis of his political opinion …

47. It may well be that the answer to this question is the same as the answer to the claim based on sexual orientation. There was no less favourable treatment on this ground because anyone else would have been treated in the same way. The objection was not to Mr Lee because he, or anyone with whom he associated, held a political opinion supporting gay marriage. The objection was to being required to promote the message on the cake. The less favourable treatment was afforded to the message not to the man. It was not as if he were being refused a job, or accommodation, or baked goods in general, because of his political opinion, as for example, was alleged to have happened in *Ryder v Northern Ireland Policing Board*. The evidence was that they were quite prepared to serve him in other ways. The situation is not comparable to people being refused jobs, accommodation or business simply because of their religious faith. It is more akin to a Christian printing business being required to print leaflets promoting an atheist message.

48. However, there is here a much closer association between the political opinions of the man and the message that he wishes to promote, such that it could be argued that they are 'indissociable' for the purpose of direct discrimination on the ground of political opinion. This would not always be the case, because the person ordering a particular message may in fact be indifferent to it. But in this case Mr Lee was perceived as holding the opinion in question. It becomes appropriate, therefore, to consider the impact of the McArthurs' Convention rights upon the meaning and effect of FETO.

49. IV The Convention Rights

The Convention rights to freedom of thought, conscience and religion and freedom of expression are clearly engaged by this case … In its first case dealing with art 9, *Kokkinakis v Greece* (1993) 17 EHRR 397, para [31], the European Court of Human Rights expressed the importance of the right in a passage which has been much-cited since:

> 'As enshrined in article 9, freedom of thought, conscience and religion is one of the foundations of a "democratic society" within the meaning of the Convention. It is, in its religious dimension, one of the most vital elements that go to make up the identity of believers and their conception of life, but it is also a precious asset for atheists, agnostics, sceptics and the unconcerned. The pluralism indissociable from a democratic society, which has been dearly won over the centuries, depends on it.'

One is free both to believe and not to believe.

50. Furthermore, obliging a person to manifest a belief which he does not hold has been held to be a limitation on his art 9(1) rights. In *Buscarini v San Marino* (1999) 30 EHRR 208, the Grand Chamber held that it was a violation of art 9 to oblige non-believers to swear a Christian oath as a condition of remaining members of Parliament. The court reiterated that freedom of thought, conscience and religion 'entails, inter alia, freedom to hold or not to hold religious beliefs and to practise or not to practise a religion'.

51. The Judicial Committee of the Privy Council took the same view in *Commodore of the Royal Bahamas Defence Force v Laramore* [2017] UKPC 13, [2017] 1 WLR 2752 …

52. The freedom not to be obliged to hold or to manifest beliefs that one does not hold is also protected by art 10 of the Convention. A recent example in this jurisdiction is *RT (Zimbabwe) v Secretary of State for the Home Department* [2012] UKSC 38, [2012] 4 All ER 843. The issue was whether asylum seekers should be sent back to Zimbabwe where they would face a real risk of persecution if they refused to demonstrate positive support for the then regime in that country. Citing, among other cases, both *Kokkinakis* and *Buscarini*, Lord Dyson held that the principle applied as much to political opinions as it did to religious belief: 'Nobody should be forced to have or express a political opinion in which he does not believe' (para [42]).

53. The respondent suggests that the jurisprudence in relation to 'compelled speech' has been developed principally in the United States as a result of the First Amendment. There is indeed longstanding Supreme Court authority for the proposition that 'the right to freedom of thought protected by the First Amendment against state action includes both the right to speak freely and the right to refrain from speaking at all': see *Wooley v Maynard* (1977) 430 US 705, 714, per Burger CJ, citing *West Virginia State Board of Education v Barnette* (1943) 319 US 624, 633–634. But in the light of *Laramore* and *RT (Zimbabwe)*, and the Strasbourg case law on which they are based, it cannot seriously be suggested that the same principles do not apply in the context of arts 9 and 10 of the Convention.

54. The District Judge did not accept that the defendants were being required to promote and support a campaign for a change in the law to enable same sex marriage. The Court of Appeal, while not deciding the point, appears to have agreed with this: 'the fact that a baker provides a cake for a particular team or portrays witches on a Halloween cake does not indicate any support for either'. These are, in fact, two separate matters: being required to promote a campaign and being associated with it. As to the first, the bakery was required, on pain of liability in damages, to supply a product which actively promoted the cause, a cause in which many believe, but a cause in which the owners most definitely and sincerely did not. As to the second, there is no requirement that the person who is compelled to speak can only complain if he is thought by others to support the message. Mrs McArthur may have been worried that others would see the Ashers logo on the cake box and think that they supported the campaign.

But that is by the way: what matters is that by being required to produce the cake they were being required to express a message with which they deeply disagreed.

55. Articles 9 and 10 are, of course, qualified rights which may be limited or restricted in accordance with the law and insofar as this is necessary in a democratic society in pursuit of a legitimate aim. It is, of course, the case that businesses offering services to the public are not entitled to discriminate on certain grounds. The bakery could not refuse to provide a cake – or any other of their products – to Mr Lee because he was a gay man or because he supported gay marriage. But that important fact does not amount to a justification for something completely different – obliging them to supply a cake iced with a message with which they profoundly disagreed. In my view they would be entitled to refuse to do that whatever the message conveyed by the icing on the cake – support for living in sin, support for a particular political party, support for a particular religious denomination. The fact that this particular message had to do with sexual orientation is irrelevant to the FETO claim.

56. Under s 3(1) of the Human Rights Act 1998, all legislation is, so far as it is possible to do so, to be read and given effect in a way which is compatible with the Convention rights. I have already indicated my doubts about whether this was discrimination against Mr Lee on the grounds of his political opinions, but have acknowledged the possibility that it might be. But in my view, FETO should not be read or given effect in such a way as to compel providers of goods, facilities and services to express a message with which they disagree, unless justification is shown for doing so.

57. As the courts below reached a different conclusion on this issue, they did not have to consider the position of the company separately from that of Mr and Mrs McArthur. It is the case that in *Company X v Switzerland* (App No 7865/77) (1981) 16 DR 85, and in *Kustannus Oy Vapaa Ajattelija AB v Finland* (App no 20471/92) (1996) 85 DR 29, the European Commission of Human Rights held that limited companies could not rely upon art 9(1) to resist paying church taxes. In this case, however, to hold the company liable when the McArthurs are not would effectively negate their convention rights. In holding that the company is not liable, this court is not holding that the company has rights under art 9; rather, it is upholding the rights of the McArthurs under that article ...[25]

Gan Menachem Hendon Ltd v de Groen [2019] UKEAT 0059_18_1202, [2019] ICR 1023

This case concerned an appeal against a tribunal's finding that a Jewish nursery teacher who had been dismissed by an ultra-orthodox Jewish nursery because she co-habited with her boyfriend, and was not prepared to lie about this state of affairs, had been subject to unlawful direct and indirect discrimination on grounds of religious belief, and to direct sex discrimination. The reasons given for her dismissal were that she had presented herself 'in contravention of the nursery's culture, ethos and religious beliefs' and that she had damaged the nursery's reputation through parental complaints leading to potential financial detriment. The employment tribunal upheld her claims but the EAT allowed the nursery's appeal against the tribunal's finding of direct discrimination on grounds of

[25] Lady Hale added a postscript distinguishing the decision of the US SC in *Masterpiece Cakeshop Ltd v Colorado Civil Rights Commission* 138 S Ct 1719; 201 L Ed 2d 35 which was published during the SC's deliberations. Although that case also dealt with a 'gay cake', the discrimination there involved the refusal of service to customers (who wished to order a cake for their same-sex wedding) *because of the baker's opposition to same-sex marriage*, rather than (as here) objection to the message on a cake which could have been ordered by anyone.

religion or belief, the tribunal having based this finding on its conclusion that the nursery had discriminated against the claimant because of its (the nursery's) religious beliefs.

Swift J:

> 20. The conclusion that s 10(1) of the 2010 Act prohibits less favourable treatment by an employer on the basis of its own religion or belief is wrong. It is a conclusion that cannot survive the reasoning of Baroness Hale in her judgment in *Lee v Ashers Baking Co Ltd* ...
>
> 21. ... The purpose of discrimination law, she said, was the protection of a person who had a protected characteristic from less favourable treatment because of that characteristic, not the protection of persons without that protected characteristic from less favourable treatment because of a protected characteristic of the discriminator. Any conclusion to the contrary would run against the principle that a discriminator's motive for the less favourable is immaterial. More importantly any direct discrimination claim that rested on the discriminator's protected characteristic would be doomed to fail because any comparison between the person receiving the less favourable treatment and 'other persons' would always produce the result that there had been no difference in treatment since it could safely be assumed that a discriminator acting on the grounds of his own political (or religious) belief would act in the same way regardless of who was affected.
>
> 24. ... Based on the tribunal's own findings, I do not consider that it was either correct or sustainable as a conclusion reasonably available, for the tribunal to characterise the less favourable treatment as treatment afforded to Ms de Groen because of her lack of religious belief ...
>
> 30. This is a case about differing religious belief within a religion. Ms de Groen is Jewish; she considers herself a practising Jew. It is not her case that her belief is either novel or outside the scope of Judaism. For the purposes of this part of my judgment I must assume (contrary to what I have said above at §§24–25) that the root cause of the events that resulted in her dismissal was the disagreement about whether adherence to Judaism excluded cohabitation outside marriage. The tribunal recorded that some Jews consider cohabitation outside marriage to be impermissible, but others do not. In the course of this appeal, neither party sought to persuade me otherwise. Disagreements on such matters are not exclusive to Judaism. It is entirely possible in any organised religion that disagreements exist as to whether some or other practice or value is an important part of the religion, or to the extent of its importance. It is in the nature of many organised religions that there will be differences of opinion. Members of the religion may disagree but, absent schism, they remain members of the same religion ...

Swift J dismissed the appeal against the Tribunal's finding that the GOR defence did not apply, this because the claimant had not been subject to any requirement not to co-habit; it was clear from the tribunal's findings of fact that the requirement which the nursery sought to impose related to her informing parents about her situation, which was not a requirement that she have 'a particular protected characteristic' for the purposes of Schedule 9 para 3 EqA (see further below).

Accommodating Difference

Members of minoritised religious groups are regularly placed at a disadvantage by the lack of fit between the requirements imposed upon them by their religious practice, and the demands of the 'secular' world.

Sandra Fredman, 'The Future of Equality in Britain' (EOC Working Series No 5, 2002) 19, footnotes omitted

> ... The Church of England enjoys a privileged position in many walks of life, from schools to the House of Lords. Even more fundamentally, many apparently secular practices are in fact Christian, whether it is the working week, the day of rest, the mode of dressing or the dietary laws. Thus, an approach which purports to be neutral and ignores the imbalances of power between minority religions and the majority will fail to address the real issues. This is seen clearly in the approach of the ECHR [in *Ahmad v UK*, discussed at pp 551–552] which rejected a discrimination claim by a Muslim teacher who asked for time off for Friday prayers on the grounds that all minorities had to conform to the dominant Christian working week.
>
> Instead, an important function of equality laws is to make sure that all religious groups are equally capable of expressing their religious identity. This receives legal expression through a duty to accommodate, and applies to differences in dress, religious holidays, days of rest and times of prayer, diet and so on. At the same time, equality extends to the interaction between different minority religions, as well as to those who choose to have no religion.

Acas has published guidance on religion and belief in the workplace which provides extensive information on the various obligations imposed by Baha'i, Buddhism, Hinduism, Islam, Jainism, Orthodox Judaism, Rastafarianism, Sikhism and Zoroastrianism concerning prayer, fasting, diet, clothing and appearance, purification, holy days, pilgrimage and contact between the sexes.[26] It is clear that any meaningful attempt to render 'equal' in the workplace those who adhere to minoritised religions requires not merely the prohibition of direct discrimination on grounds of religion and belief, but also the imposition of requirements to accommodate difference. The concept of indirect discrimination has been discussed in Chapter 2, and many examples given of its application in the case law there and in Chapter 4. For reasons which included the complexities of the original definition of indirect discrimination and the extent to which true equality requires the accommodation of difference in this context, Hepple and Choudhury floated, in 2001, the idea that transposition of the religion and belief provisions of the Council Directive 2000/78 might include the imposition of explicit duties to accommodate.

Bob Hepple and Tufail Choudhury, *Tackling religious discrimination: practical implications for policy-makers and legislators* (Home Office Research Study 221) 37–40, footnotes omitted

> ... In the context of religious discrimination in Britain it is argued that there is a need to accommodate diversity because our society is already structured around basic Christian assumptions and therefore already accommodates the needs of Christians, for example Christmas and Easter are recognised as public holidays, and shop workers and betting workers have the right to object to Sunday working.[27] In a multi-faith multi-cultural society, the needs of individuals with different religious faiths should be met. This was something understood by Lord Scarman in 1978 when, in [*Ahmad*,] a case involving a dispute between a Muslim teacher who requested time to attend Friday prayers and the local education authority, he argued that 'room has to be found for teachers and pupils of the new religions in the educational system, if discrimination is to be avoided. This calls not for a policy of the blind eye but for one of understanding. The system must be made flexible to accommodate their beliefs and their observances. Otherwise they will suffer discrimination.' Justice McIntyre in the Canadian Supreme Court also recognised that 'the accommodation of differences ... is the essence of true equality.'[28] Others have pointed towards the dangers of

[26] Acas, 'Religion or Belief and the Workplace', Appendix 2, available at www.staffs.ac.uk/students/docs/pdf/student-support/edi/acas-religion-or-belief-and-the-workplace.pdf.

[27] Under the Employment Rights Act 1996 ss36–39, though this applies only to those continually employed in a protected job since 1994.

[28] Citing *Andrews v Law Society of British Columbia* 10 CHRR D/5719.

reasonable accommodation. Lord Denning in *Ahmad* took the view that it would do a minority group 'no good, if they were to be given preferential treatment over the great majority of people. If it should happen that, in the name of religious freedom, they were given special privileges or advantages, it would provoke discontent, and even resentment among those with whom they work ... and so the cause of racial integration would suffer. So, whilst upholding religious freedom to the full, I would suggest that it should be applied with caution, especially having regard to the setting in which it is sought.' Lord Justice Orr also objected to pursuing a policy of reasonable accommodation. He argued that this would lead to 'resentment among non-Moslem staff at having to assume additional burdens and possibly to a situation in which education authorities would have been reluctant to employ more Moslem teachers.' ...

The reasonable adjustment approach [applicable to disability] places the onus on the individual to disclose a disability and explain that the arrangements place him or her at a substantial disadvantage. If he or she succeeds in doing this the result will be an individualised solution. The next disabled person will have to go though the same process of disclosure and negotiating reasonableness. The indirect discrimination approach, on the other hand, requires 'equality proofing'. The onus is on the employer or service provider to consider in advance whether or not a provision or practice indirectly discriminates and, if so, whether it is objectively justifiable. The indirect discrimination approach is easier for the individual and can have a much more significant impact in terms of promoting participation and access by the disadvantaged group ....

The *Ontario Human Rights Code* has ... attempted to combine the concept of reasonable adjustment within the concept of indirect discrimination. It goes further than ... directive [2000/78] by applying this to religious discrimination. The Code introduces the concept of 'constructive discrimination' which is similar to indirect discrimination. Section 11 of the Code provides a defence to claims of constructive discrimination where 'the requirement, qualification or factor is reasonable and bona fide in the circumstances.' The provision goes on to state that 'a court shall not find that a requirement, qualification or factor is reasonable and *bona fide* in the circumstances unless it is satisfied that the needs of the group of which the person is a member *cannot be accommodated without undue hardship* on the person responsible for accommodating those needs, considering the cost, outside sources of funding, if any, and health and safety requirements, if any.' This formulation has the advantage of clarifying the relationship between indirect discrimination and the duty to make reasonable adjustments.

The EqA does not impose a duty to make reasonable accommodation as such. The prohibition of indirect discrimination does require that a degree of accommodation be made to practices which have a disparate impact on people with adherences to different beliefs. The Acas guidance suggests that policies such as 'no headwear' rules may be indirectly discriminatory against Sikh staff as will a prohibition on pony tails for men. Acas recommends that companies avoid arranging inflexible interviews for Friday afternoons but suggests that a requirement imposed by a small financial company to work on Friday afternoons may be justified irrespective of its impact on Jewish staff if it is necessary to analyse stock prices in the American finance market which arrive late on Friday because of global time differences. It warns against holding recruitment events in venues where alcohol is served and counsels employers to make appropriate provision for Halal or Kosher requirements (eg by providing at least vegetarian options) and suggests that employers should take account of staff requirements for religious observance, including during working hours, of significant religious festivals, of fasting and clothing requirements and of particular sensitivities as regards eg physical contact or nakedness associated with some religions.

It is clear from the Acas guidance that the prohibition on indirect discrimination goes a significant way towards accommodating religious beliefs. The limitations on this type of discrimination became evident in the *Eweida* case, the facts of which are set out at p 559 above. The employment tribunal dismissed Ms Eweida's claim because it did not accept that Christians were put at a particular disadvantage by BA's uniform policy, as was required for a finding of indirect discrimination. The EAT dismissed her appeal, ruling that the whole purpose of the prohibition on indirect discrimination was to deal with group disadvantage and that the claimant had failed to establish that the uniform policy disadvantaged Christians disproportionately. The CA also dismissed her appeal.

***Eweida v British Airways Plc* [2010] EWCA Civ 80, [2010] ICR 890**

Sedley LJ (with whom Smith LJJ and Carnwath agreed):

> 13. ... while for my part I would not share the Employment Appeal Tribunal's view ... that 'the whole purpose of indirect discrimination is to deal with the problem of group discrimination' (its overall purpose, as both counsel agree, is to deal with the discriminatory impact of facially neutral requirements), it is entirely right that the way in which equality laws on both sides of the Atlantic have for many years sought to do this is by seeing, first, whether an identifiable group is adversely affected, whether actually or potentially, by some ostensibly neutral requirement and then whether the claimant has in fact been disadvantaged by it.
>
> 14. This familiar model, originating in the United States Supreme Court's landmark decision in *Griggs v Duke Power Co* (1970) 401 US 424, brought in its train considerable problems of implementation. In particular, the schematisation of it in the Sex Discrimination Act 1975 and the Race Relations Act 1976 required the isolation of 'pools' within which the proportion of disadvantage could be gauged, a task which defeated three decades' judicial attempts to find a workable formula. Council Directive 2000/78/EC (OJ 2000 L303 p 16) avoided this snare by defining indirect discrimination as occurring:
>
> > 'where an apparently neutral provision, criterion or practice would put persons having a particular religion or belief, a particular disability, a particular age, or a particular sexual orientation at a particular disadvantage compared with other persons' article 2(2)(b) ...
>
> 15. ... there is in my judgment no indication that Directive 2000/78 intended either that solitary disadvantage should be sufficient – the use of the plural ('persons') makes such a reading highly problematical – or that any requirement of plural disadvantage must be dropped. I see no reason, therefore to depart from the natural meaning of regulation 3. That meaning, as Ms Simler submits [for BA], is that some identifiable section of a workforce, quite possibly a small one, must be shown to suffer a particular disadvantage which the claimant shares ...
>
> 22. ... the jurisprudence on article 9 does nothing to advance the claimant's case. The European Court of Human Rights in *Kalaç v Turkey* (1999) 27 EHRR 552, para 27, said:
>
> > "Article 9 does not protect every act motivated or inspired by a religion or belief. Moreover, in exercising his freedom to manifest his religion, an individual may need to take his specific situation into account."
>
> 23. In *R (SB) v Governors of Denbigh High School* [2007] 1 AC 100, para 23, Lord Bingham of Cornhill commented on this and other Strasbourg decisions:
>
> > "The Strasbourg institutions have not been at all ready to find an interference with the right to manifest religious belief in practice or observance where a person has voluntarily accepted an employment or role which does not accommodate that practice or observance and there are other means open to the person to practise or observe his or her religion without undue hardship or inconvenience."

> 24. … While my reasoning … follows a slightly different course [from that of the EAT], and at one point differs from it, my conclusion is the same as theirs. In particular I would respectfully endorse what they held at para 60:
>
> > 'In our judgment, in order for indirect discrimination to be established, it must be possible to make some general statements which would be true about a religious group such that an employer ought reasonably to be able to appreciate that any particular provision may have a disparate adverse impact on the group.'

A majority of the CA went on to declare that, even had the claimant been able to establish a prima facie case of indirect discrimination, it would (contrary to the tribunal's decision) have been inclined to regard the discrimination as justified in view of the claimant's intransigence (she had refused to be redeployed to non-customer-facing duties but had instead chosen 'to stay away from work and claim her pay as compensation'; the fact that (per Sedley LJ) the cross did not (contrary to the tribunal's formulation) 'represent … the core of [the claimant's] being', but 'a personal preference on her part'; the fact that the uniform policy had 'for some seven years … apparently caused Ms Eweida, along with the rest of BA's staff, no known problem'; and that 'When the issue was raised by her, it was conscientiously addressed – not perhaps as speedily as it might have been, but then it had been raised by a single employee and had no apparent urgency'. As we saw above, the ECtHR found that Eweida's Article 9 rights had been breached.

The ECtHR's decision in Eweida made clear that the EqA's prohibition on indirect discrimination on grounds of religion will not always be sufficient to guarantee the rights protected by Article 9. The relevance of collective and disadvantage to indirect discrimination arose again in *Mba v Merton.*

***Mba v Mayor and Burgesses of the London Borough of Merton* [2013] EWCA Civ 1562, [2014] ICR 357**

The claimant, a Christian care assistant, complained of unlawful indirect discrimination when her employer, which had previously sought to accommodate her concern not to work on Sundays, sought to require her to comply with her contractual duty to work a rota system which included some Sundays. A tribunal accepted that she had been subject to a PCP requiring Sunday working and that this was a proportionate means of achieving the Council's legitimate aim of running its business effectively, further stating that Mrs Mba's belief that Sunday should be a day of rest and worship, whilst deeply held, was 'not a core component of the Christian faith'.

Maurice Kay LJ:

> 14. The primary issue for us is whether, in carrying out the proportionality exercise, the ET was entitled to give weight to its finding that Mrs Mba's belief that Sunday should be a day of rest and worship 'is not a core component of the Christian faith'. This raises the complex difficulty

identified by Lord Justice Rix in the Court of Appeal in *R (Williamson) v Secretary of State for Education* and *Employment* [2003] QB 1300, at §123:

> 'The question, of course, is not what the status of a belief in angels is: but the argument proceeds by distinguishing between the belief in issue, which is accorded a distinct and subsidiary status, and on the other hand an "article of faith" or belief which embodies or defines religious faith ... which is accorded a higher status. I am concerned that a secular court is ill equipped for such distinctions. I am concerned that it is not only ill-equipped, but that it lacks in this case the conventional means by which it would normally proceed to make such distinctions, which is evidence. I am in any event uneasy about the efficacy of such evidence: one of the problems of religion is the diversity of belief even within the umbrella of a single faith.'

This sensitivity to the diversity of beliefs between and *within* religions is something which flows from the respect that is accorded to the range of sincerely held religious beliefs ...

17. ... it is not necessary to establish that all or most Christians, or all or most non-conformist Christians, are or would be put at a particular disadvantage. It is permissible to define a claimant's religion or belief more narrowly than that. In my judgment, this is where the ET went wrong. It described Mrs Mba's Sabbatarian belief as 'not a core component of the Christian faith'. By so doing it opened the door to a quantitative test on far too wide a basis.

18. It is clear ... that, for some Christians, working on Sundays is unacceptable. It is also clear that Mrs Mba's religious belief genuinely embraces that injunction ....

Maurice Kay LJ went on to consider whether the extent to which a view was commonly held by adherents to a religion could be taken into account other than in determining whether the test for collective disadvantage had been met in the context of an indirect discrimination claim. He was inclined to think that it should not, suggesting at §19 that, if it were to be relevant to justification, the fact that only a small number of people were disadvantaged by a requirement could either work in the interest of the employee (because it could more easily be accommodated) or the employer. Elias LJ agreed that the tribunal should not have taken into account whether a refusal to work on Sunday was 'a core component of the Christian faith' 'in the balance in support of the justification defence, but for a different reason than' that given by Maurice Kay LJ (§30).[29]

Elias LJ:

31. If one considers this case purely as a domestic law indirect discrimination case, independently of Article 9 considerations, then in my view it would at least indirectly be a legitimate factor for the employment tribunal to consider. This is because if the belief which results in the disadvantage is a core principle or belief of a particular religion, a policy, criterion or practice which interferes with the manifestation of that belief will impinge upon a greater number of potential adherents than would otherwise be the case; and in general the greater the impact, the harder it is to justify the provision. As Baroness Hale pointed out in *Homer v Chief Constable of West Yorkshire* [2012] UKSC 15; [2012] ICR 704, §24 [discussed in Chapter 2], what has to be justified is the particular policy, criterion or practice, but

> 'Part of the assessment of whether the criterion can be justified entails a comparison of the impact of that criterion upon the affected group as against the importance of the aim to the employer'.

32. In my judgment, an evaluation of the impact must include its extent ...

[29] Vos LJ delivered a speech which was largely in agreement with that of Elias LJ.

> 34. … The protection of freedom of religion conferred by that Article does not require a claimant to establish any group disadvantage; the question is whether the interference of that individual right by the employer is proportionate given the legitimate aims of the employer [citing *Eweida v United Kingdom*] …
>
> 35. … the claimant's Article 9 right is incapable of direct enforcement in the employment tribunal. However, domestic law must be read so as to be consistent with Convention rights where possible, in accordance with s.3 of the Human Rights Act. In my judgment, it is simply not possible to read down the concept of indirect discrimination to ignore the need to establish group disadvantage. But I see no reason why the concept of justification should not be read compatibly with Article 9 where that provision is in play. In that context it does not matter whether the claimant is disadvantaged along with others or not, and it cannot in any way weaken her case with respect to justification that her beliefs are not more widely shared or do not constitute a core belief of any particular religion. It is for this reason that in my view the employment tribunal was wrong to make reference to this factor as one assisting the employer.
>
> 36. This is not to say that the number of employees sharing a particular belief will necessarily be irrelevant to a justification challenge where Article 9 is engaged. Assuming that the employer's criterion is designed to achieve a legitimate end, the greater the number of employees affected, the more difficult it is likely to be for an employer to accommodate those beliefs in a way which is compatible with his business objectives. So paradoxically, if a belief is not widely shared, which is more likely to be the case where it is not a core belief of a particular religion, that is a factor which under Article 9 is likely to work in favour of the employee rather than against.
>
> 37. It follows that, in my view, it is the Article 9 dimension of this case which made it inappropriate for the employment tribunal, when assessing justification, to weigh in the employer's favour the fact that the appellant's religious belief was not a core belief of her religion so that any group impact was limited. However, I am wholly satisfied that this was a peripheral part of the proportionality analysis of the employment tribunal and did not materially affect its conclusion …

In *Trayhorn v Secretary of State for Justice* [2018] IRLR 502 the question of collective disadvantage was squarely in issue. The EAT confirmed that the concept of indirect discrimination requires collective disadvantage, dismissing an appeal from a Christian prison gardener/horticulturalist who had been invited to a disciplinary meeting after he volunteered to help at services in the prison chapel (he was also a Pentecostal minister) and had there been reported to have stated that god 'hat[ed] prostitutes and gays'. An employment tribunal decided that PCPs of requiring employees to adhere to disciplinary and to equality policies did not put those of a Christian faith or Pentecostals at a disadvantage as a group (further, that they did not disadvantage the claimant as an individual) and, if they had, that they would have been proportionate means of achieving the wholly legitimate aims of maintaining the security and order of the prison. The EAT rejected the claimant's appeal, relying on the decision in *Mba* on the requirement for group disadvantage and agreeing with the tribunal's findings on justification.

Accommodating Intolerance

The accommodation of religious requirements concerning working time or dress codes may cause inconvenience or expense, but it does not give rise to any significant issues of principle. The decision in *Mba* illustrates that considerations of cost or the impact on other staff may justify PCPs which disadvantage those with particular beliefs. Other examples include *Azmi v Kirklees MBC* [2007] ICR 1154 in which the EAT dismissed an appeal from a teaching assistant employed to provide support for children for whom English was a second language, who had sought to wear a full-face veil in class despite evidence that her function was more effectively performed when her face was visible.

Different considerations arise in relation to beliefs which are, or may be, in tension with core rights of others. Examples of such beliefs arose in the *Eweida* case, discussed above,[30] in which two of the applicants sought the accommodation of their beliefs concerning homosexuality. One of these, Lillian Ladele, was a registrar of births, marriages, civil partnerships and deaths. She had strong Christian beliefs, including that marriage was a life-long union of one man and one woman. In December 2005, the Civil Partnership Act 2004 came into force, allowing same-sex couples to enter civil partnerships (subsequently marriage was opened to same-sex couples and civil partnerships to other couples). Ms Ladele, who had previously been a registrar of births, marriages and deaths, was a registrar of births, marriages, civil partnerships and deaths in line with her employer's policy of taking this step in relation to all registrars. This resulted, in due course, in disciplinary action being taken against Ms Ladele, who claimed that she had been discriminated against on grounds of her religious beliefs. An employment tribunal ruled in her favour. In so far as relevant here, it ruled that the Council's policy served the legitimate aim of providing effective civil partnership arrangements, but was a disproportionate means of achieving that aim, since the accommodation of Ms Ladele's views would not have impaired the quality of its registry services. The EAT allowed the Council's appeal, ruling that the aim of the Council's policy was to provide the registrar service on a non-discriminatory basis, and that it had been entitled to require that all registrars to perform the full range of services. The claimant appealed to the CA. (Note that the case refers to the RB Regs, which prohibited discrimination against Ms Ladele, and the Equality Act (Sexual Orientation) Regulations ('the SO Regs 2007') which prohibited discrimination against LGB service users.

***Ladele v LB Islington* [2009] EWCA Civ 1357, [2010] ICR 532**

Lord Neuberger MR (with whom Dyson and Smith LJJ agreed):

45. The problem with the ET's analysis is, as the EAT pointed out, that it wrongly identifies Islington's aim, as it overlooks the point that the service which Islington stated that they aimed to provide was not merely one which was effective in terms of practicality and efficiency, but was also one which complied with their overarching policy of being 'an employer and a public authority wholly committed to the promotion of equal opportunities and to requiring all its employees to act in a way which does not discriminate against others'...

46. Islington wished to ensure that all their registrars were designated to conduct, and did conduct, civil partnerships as they regarded this as consistent with their strong commitment to fighting discrimination, both externally, for the benefit of the residents of the borough, and internally in the sense of relations with and between their employees ...

49. The EAT was therefore entitled, indeed effectively obliged, to address the issue of whether Islington's designation and requirement of Ms Ladele in relation to civil partnerships, and their treatment of Ms Ladele in the light of her refusal to officiate at such partnerships, was a proportionate means of achieving their legitimate aim which the EAT had correctly identified. On that issue, as the EAT said in §111 of Elias J's judgment, '[o]nce it is accepted that that the aim of providing the service on a non-discriminatory basis was legitimate – and in truth it was

[30] See pp 559–562 and 588–589 above.

bound to be – then … it must follow that [Islington] were entitled to require all registrars to perform the full range of services.' As the EAT went on to point out, permitting Ms Ladele to refuse to perform civil partnerships 'would necessarily undermine the council's clear commitment to' what the EAT described as 'their non-discriminatory objectives which [they] thought it important to espouse both to their staff and to the wider community'…

52. … Ms Ladele was employed in a public job and was working for a public authority; she was being required to perform a purely secular task, which was being treated as part of her job; Ms Ladele's refusal to perform that task involved discriminating against gay people in the course of that job; she was being asked to perform the task because of Islington's Dignity for All policy, whose laudable aim was to avoid, or at least minimise, discrimination both among Islington's employees, and as between Islington (and its employees) and those in the community they served; Ms Ladele's refusal was causing offence to at least two of her gay colleagues; Ms Ladele's objection was based on her view of marriage, which was not a core part of her religion; and Islington's requirement in no way prevented her from worshipping as she wished.

53. So, in agreement with the EAT, I consider that there were no grounds to support the ET's conclusion that Islington was guilty of indirect discrimination under the 2003 Regulations against Ms Ladele …

62. I now turn to what might be characterised as a potentially overriding argument, pressed by Ms Monaghan QC, on behalf of Liberty, and now supported by Ms Mountfield for Islington, namely that … Islington had no alternative but to require Ms Ladele to perform civil partnership duties along with all the other registrars. The EAT declined to deal with the argument, on the grounds that it was unnecessary to do so. I fully understand that view, but, the point has been fully argued, as a result of which court time and costs have been devoted to it, and it may be an issue of some importance, so I consider that it is right to address it.

68. Liberty's argument is simple, and is based purely on the natural meaning of the [SORs 2007], and it has three stages. The first stage is an assertion that a refusal to perform civil partnerships, on the part of someone who is quite prepared to perform marriages, amounts to discrimination … The second stage involves the contention that officiating at marriages and civil partnerships involves 'the provision to the public or a section of the public of … services' ….

69. I find it hard to see any logical flaw in those two stages of the argument, at least once Ms Ladele had been designated a civil partnership registrar. The third, and final, stage in Liberty's argument is that, even if Ms Ladele had succeeded in establishing that Islington would not otherwise have been entitled to require her to perform civil partnerships, the effect of this analysis of the impact of the [SO Regs] means that, at least once Ms Ladele was designated a civil partnership registrar, Islington were not merely entitled, but obliged, to require her to do so. This argument effectively involves saying that the prohibition of discrimination by the [SORs 2007] takes precedence over any right which a person would otherwise have by virtue of his or her religious belief or faith, to practice discrimination on the ground of sexual orientation.

70. Such an argument, in my view, accords with the natural meaning of the [SORs 2007], and is supported by the provisions of reg. 14, which identifies the relatively limited circumstances in which it is permissible to discriminate against anyone on grounds of sexual orientation because of one's religious belief: those circumstances are essentially limited to the membership and operation of 'organisations relating to religion or belief', which plainly does not cover performing civil partnership unions, which is self-evidently a secular activity carried out in a public sphere under the auspices of a public, secular body.

71. Once it is decided that there is nothing in the [RB Regs] which entitles Ms Ladele, having been designated a civil partnership registrar, to insist on her right not to have civil partnership duties assigned to her because of her religious beliefs in relation to marriage, it means that there is no inconsistency, so far as other legislation is concerned, in giving the subsequent

[SORs 2007] their natural meaning, namely that it is simply unlawful for Ms Ladele to refuse to perform civil partnerships. It is also hard to resist the conclusion that this means that Islington had no alternative but to insist on her performing such duties together with their other registrars.

72. It would also appear to follow that it would be difficult for Islington, having designated her a civil partnership registrar, to justify the offer they made Ms Ladele, namely that she officiate only at civil partnerships which involve no ceremonies …

73. I see the force of that point. Nonetheless, it appears to me that, however much sympathy one may have with someone such as Ms Ladele, who is faced with choosing between giving up a post she plainly appreciates or officiating at events which she considers to be contrary to her religious beliefs, the legislature has decided that the requirements of a modern liberal democracy, such as the United Kingdom, include outlawing discrimination in the provision of goods, facilities and services on grounds of sexual orientation, subject only to very limited exceptions.

74. It is right to add that this conclusion may well not have applied if Islington had not designated Ms Ladele (along with all the other registrars) a civil partnership registrar. If they had not so designated her, it seems to me that there would have been a powerful case for saying that she would then have had no cause to refuse to officiate at civil partnerships, and accordingly no problem of discrimination under the [O Regs] could arise. Accordingly, I doubt whether a decision by Islington that she would not be designated a civil partnership registrar, at her request because of her religious problems with officiating at civil partnerships, would fall foul of the [O Regs].

75. However, the fact that some registration authorities have (as I understand to be the case) decided not to designate registrars who shared Ms Ladele's beliefs as civil partnership registrars, and the fact that such decisions may well be lawful certainly do not undermine the conclusions reached by the EAT …

Ms Ladele's appeal to the ECtHR also failed.

***Eweida v UK* (App Nos 48420/10, 59842/10, 51671/10 and 36516/10, judgment of 15 January 2012), (2013) 57 EHRR 8 (4th Section)**

Judgment:

105. The Court of Appeal held in this case that the aim pursued by the local authority was to provide a service which was not merely effective in terms of practicality and efficiency, but also one which complied with the overarching policy of being 'an employer and a public authority wholly committed to the promotion of equal opportunities and to requiring all its employees to act in a way which does not discriminate against others'. The Court recalls that in its case law under Article 14 it has held that differences in treatment based on sexual orientation require particularly serious reasons by way of justification … It has also held that same-sex couples are in a relevantly similar situation to different-sex couples as regards their need for legal recognition and protection of their relationship, although since practice in this regard is still evolving across Europe, the Contracting States enjoy a wide margin of appreciation as to the way in which this is achieved within the domestic legal order … Against this background, it is evident that the aim pursued by the local authority was legitimate.

106. It remains to be determined whether the means used to pursue this aim were proportionate. The court takes into account that the consequences for the applicant were serious: given the strength of her religious conviction, she considered that she had no choice but to face disciplinary action rather than be designated a civil partnership registrar and, ultimately, she

lost her job. Furthermore, it cannot be said that, when she entered into her contract of employment, the applicant specifically waived her right to manifest her religious belief by objecting to participating in the creation of civil partnerships, since this requirement was introduced by her employer at a later date. On the other hand, however, the local authority's policy aimed to secure the rights of others which are also protected under the Convention. The Court generally allows the national authorities a wide margin of appreciation when it comes to striking a balance between competing Convention rights … In all the circumstances, the Court does not consider that the national authorities, that is the local authority employer which brought the disciplinary proceedings and also the domestic courts which rejected the applicant's discrimination claim, exceeded the margin of appreciation available to them. It cannot, therefore, be said that there has been a violation of Article 14 taken in conjunction with Article 9 in respect of the third applicant.

The same conclusion was reached in relation to Gary McFarlane, a Christian who worked as a relationship counsellor for Relate, and who was dismissed in connection with his refusal to provide psychosexual therapy for same-sex couples. The Court accepted that McFarlane's objection was a manifestation of his religion and belief, but declared at §109 that 'the most important factor to be taken into account is that the employer's action was intended to secure the implementation of its policy of providing a service without discrimination' and that '[t]he state authorities therefore benefitted from a wide margin of appreciation in deciding where to strike the balance between Mr McFarlane's right to manifest his religious belief and the employer's interest in securing the rights of others'.[31]

The protection of religion and belief by the EqA is also limited insofar as it applies to proselytism. Many evangelical Christians regard proselytism as a mandatory Christian duty. Such behaviour, however, has the capacity to interfere with the rights and interests of others and may be regarded as incompatible with professional obligations. By way of example:

Wasteney v East London NHS Foundation Trust **[2016] UKEAT 0157_15_0704, [2016] ICR 643**

The claimant, an evangelical Christian, was head of forensic occupational therapy at a mental health services facility who had been counselled and informally warned about the need for boundaries between her spiritual and professional lives. Subsequently EN, a Muslim woman of Pakistani heritage, complained that the claimant had tried to impose her religious views on her during EN's first 12-month post-training placement as an occupational therapist: inviting her to services at the church, praying with her, and laying hands on her. EN spoke of feeling 'groomed' by the claimant, and of the claimant's attention having begun to make her feel ill and having 'completely ruined her first year of practice'. The claimant complained of unlawful discrimination and harassment and a breach of Article 9 after she was given a written warning with a recommendation of training. A tribunal rejected her complaint and the EAT refused her appeal, ruling that the disciplinary action against the claimant did not relate to any legitimate manifestation of her religious beliefs.

[31] *cf* the decision of the CA in *R (Ngole) v University of Sheffield* [2019] EWCA Civ 1127, [2019] ELR 443 that the university had breached the claimant's Art 9 and 10 rights when it removed him from his social work course as a result of homophobic religious views which he had expressed online.

***Kuteh v Dartford and Gravesham NHS Trust* [2019] EWCA Civ 818, [2019] IRLR 716**

Here the CA dismissed an appeal by a Christian nurse who had been dismissed because of repeated infractions of an instruction not to discuss her Christian views with patients unless they asked her to. One of her tasks was to ascertain whether patients had any religious adherence. A number of complaints had been made by patients about her proselytisim before the instruction was issued. She was eventually dismissed for gross misconduct including breach of the Nursing and Midwifery Council Code by the inappropriate expression of personal beliefs. The CA accepted that Article 9 could protect proselytism but ruled that its protection did not extend to improper proselytism, such as was at issue here. The respondent had not imposed a blanket ban on religious speech at the workplace and the claimant's conduct had generated complaints from patients. The respondent's decision to dismiss her had clearly been within the range of reasonable responses.

***Page v NHS Trust Development Authority* [2021] EWCA Civ 255, [2021] ICR 941**

The claimant, who was also a magistrate, had been removed from the judiciary as a result of repeated media interviews following a reprimand for his refusal to authorise the adoption of a child by a same-sex couple, and in breach of a requirement to notify the Trust about such interviews. He had told the press that same-sex adoption was not in the best interests of any child and was 'not normal', that 'homosexual activity' was wrong and that he did not agree with same-sex marriage. He brought proceedings under the EqA, also relying on Articles 9 and 10 ECHR. These were rejected by an employment tribunal and by the EAT, the claimant then appealing to the CA. The Court ruled that the action taken against him been based on the public expression of his Christian beliefs rather than on the beliefs themselves, and that this expression was not intimately linked to his religion or his beliefs.[32] Even if it had been (such that Article 9 would have been engaged) the tribunal had not erred in ruling that any interference with his rights under Article 9 (and Article 10) was justified by the Trust's genuine and reasonable concern that the claimant's statements to the national media risked impairing the willingness of gay people with mental health difficulties to engage with NHS service.

Underhill LJ, with whom Jackson and Simler LJJ agreed:

> 59. The extent to which it is legitimate to expect a person holding a senior role in a public body to refrain from expressing views which may upset a section of the public is a delicate question which can only be decided by reference to the facts of each particular case. It is right to acknowledge that the Appellant had a particular interest in expressing publicly his views about same-sex adoption in the context of his removal as a magistrate, which was a legitimate matter of public debate: his media appearances were not in that sense gratuitous. It is also right to acknowledge that he expressed his views in temperate terms. This is not therefore a case in which it is obvious from the start that the proportionality balance comes down in

[32] The CA was more prepared to accept that the claimant's media comments did manifest what was characterised on appeal as the claimant's beliefs in 'traditional family values', but ruled that interference with the manifestation of this belief was justified in any event.

> the Authority's favour. However, there are three reasons in particular why I believe that the Tribunal was entitled to reach the conclusion that it did.
>
> 60. First, the Appellant's expressed views about homosexuality went beyond what Mr Diamond somewhat blandly characterises … as 'a sceptical opinion on same-sex adoptions' [which] … and were accordingly the more likely to cause offence or invite misinterpretation … Secondly, this was not … a case where the justification advanced is merely that some or many members of the public, or members of the Trust's staff, both gay and straight, might find the Appellant's views about homosexuality offensive or disturbing; nor is it based on some generalised perceived reputational damage to the Trust. On the contrary, it is based specifically on the risk that the fact that a member of its board held the views that the Appellant did about homosexuality might deter mentally ill gay people in the Trust's catchment area from engaging with its services. That risk relates directly to the ability of the Trust to perform its core healthcare functions …
>
> 62. Third, the Appellant's conduct made it in practice impossible to try to find a way forward that might have respected both parties' interests …

The Court went on to decide that the claimant had not been subject to either direct or indirect discrimination under the EqA because of his beliefs.

> 68. … In the context of the protected characteristic of religion or belief the EAT case-law has recognised a distinction between (1) the case where the reason is the fact that the claimant holds and/or manifests the protected belief, and (2) the case where the reason is that the claimant had manifested that belief in some particular way to which objection could justifiably be taken. In the latter case it is the objectionable manifestation of the belief, and not the belief itself, which is treated as the reason for the act complained of. Of course, if the consequences are not such as to justify the act complained of, they cannot sensibly be treated as separate from an objection to the belief itself[33] …
>
> 72 …. The Authority took disciplinary action against the Appellant not because he was a Christian or because he held the traditional family belief but because he expressed the latter belief (and his other views about homosexuality) in the national media in circumstances which, on the Tribunal's findings, justified the action taken …

As to the indirect discrimination claim, it was hard to see how the tribunal's conclusion on justification in relation to Article 9 would not have read over to defeat it.

Harassment

It was noted above that harassment related to religion or belief (or sexual orientation) is not regulated under Part 3 (services), Part 5 (premises), Part 6 (education) or Part 7 (associations) of the EqA. The Bill, which became the Equality Act 2006, which first regulated discrimination on grounds of religion outside the work context in GB, had initially provided for the regulation of harassment as well as discrimination but it was amended following a HL defeat for the Government. Lord Lester, a prominent discrimination lawyer and Liberal Democrat peer, convinced his colleagues that the harassment provisions were unsatisfactory as drafted and that question whether religion/belief harassment should be

[33] Citing *Chondol v Liverpool CC* (2009) UKEAT 0298/08, [2009] All ER (D) 155 (Feb); *Grace v Places for Children* (2013) UKEAT 0217/13; and *Wasteney v East London NHS Foundation Trust* [2016] ICR 643.

regulated outside the workplace context required further consideration and the provisions were removed from the Bill.[34]

HL Debs 19 November 2005, Cols 650–52[35]

To meet the criticism of extreme vagueness of religious harassment, the Home Office relies on the fact that similar language has been used in regulations to give effect to EU directives. That is true and it is regrettable that the Government have not exercised the option under the directives to define harassment more precisely to accord with the British legal tradition. In any event, the provisions of Part 2 of the Bill are not required by EU law; we have a free hand …

… the religious harassment provisions would … catch proselytising by way of religious displays and materials such as posters, Bibles, crucifixes and so on because they involve deliberate attempts to persuade people of a different faith or no faith to join the church and they may be interpreted as harming human dignity – whatever that means – or creating an offensive environment. The display of a 'Jews for Jesus' poster to persuade me to see the light would violate the dignity of observant Jews and create an offensive environment with the necessary mental element to constitute the tort. That is why the amendment tabled by the noble Baroness, Lady Miller, is not good enough. It would be a deliberate act causing offence to many Jews. Yet why should it be forbidden by law? It was because of concern for free speech that the Home Office did not apply religious harassment to booksellers. But the same considerations apply to what remains of religious harassment in the Bill.

… the tort … suffers from the twin vices of vagueness and over-breadth …

I will give a few examples before I conclude. Suppose the Christian evangelical owner of a block of flats illuminates his property with Christmas lights around a model depicting Jesus in the crib in the manger, and he does so intentionally to spread the good news of the birth of Christ to his tenants so that they may abandon their Jewish or Muslim faith – or no faith at all. Or suppose that a secular Muslim property owner wishes to display in the entrance hall a copy of the artistic work that unfortunately had to be removed under pressure from Tate Modern showing the Koran in a broken condition and in need of repair. Suppose she does so with the intention of persuading fundamentalist Muslims to modernise their religious practices and utterances, like the editor of the women's magazine in Afghanistan who was recently given two years' imprisonment for challenging a belief that Muslims who convert to other religions should be stoned to death.

Such action in those two examples would constitute deliberate religious harassment and could give rise to legal proceedings for damages or a declaration or an injunction. That would seriously threaten free speech – the very reason which prompted the Home Office to exclude religious harassment from the provision of goods, services and facilities. The exemption for religious objects would be no defence.

Given the undefined nature of what constitutes 'religion or belief', of 'violating human dignity', or of 'an offensive environment' … the inclusion of this tort would, we believe, encourage divisions within the community and litigation that was against the public interest.

Exceptions to the Prohibitions on Discrimination

The tension which may arise between religious and other rights was mentioned above. Churches, religious organisations and individuals are entitled to freedom of religion and belief (which includes a qualified entitlement to *manifest* religion and belief, as well as an

[34] See HL Debs 13 July 2005 cols 1116–21; HL Debs 19 November 2005 cols 648–67. Lord Lester's amendment to remove harassment was withdrawn, but the Government did not legislate in respect of harassment as well as discrimination in the Equality Act 2006 which prohibited religious discrimination, or in the SO Regs 2007, which were made under the 2006 Act.

[35] *Ibid.*

absolute right to hold it. The question will, from time to time, arise: where are the boundaries to be drawn between one person or organisation's entitlement to manifest religion or belief and another person's entitlement not to be disadvantaged, whether on grounds of religion or belief or otherwise, by that manifestation? Here we consider the cases in which discrimination because of religion or belief is permitted by the EqA. These are in addition to the exceptions of a general nature which are discussed in Chapter 4. These exceptions are helpfully considered bearing in mind that some are intended to permit discrimination (on grounds not limited to religion) by reason of the religion or belief of *the discriminator*, others are intended to permit discrimination by reason of *the other's* religion or belief. The first category of cases is considered here and in Chapter 10 since they typically involve discrimination on grounds of sexual orientation. The second is considered below.

Protection of the right not to be discriminated against because of religion, or because of personal characteristics such as sex or sexual orientation, requires that religious organisations be subject where appropriate to the normal rules applicable to those who provide work, services, etc. But religious organisations are also protected by Article 9, as illustrated by the decision of the Grand Chamber of the ECtHR in *Sindicatul 'Pastorul Cel Bun' v Romania*. The case was considered above in connection with the Article 11 rights of clergy. Here we are interested in its discussion of the Article 9 rights of the Romanian Orthodox Church.

***Sindicatul 'Pastorul Cel Bun' v Romania* (App No 2330/09, judgment of 9 July 2013) (2014) 58 EHRR 10 (Grand Chamber)**

Judgment:

137. In accordance with the principle of autonomy, the State is prohibited from obliging a religious community to admit new members or to exclude existing ones. Similarly, Article 9 of the Convention does not guarantee any right to dissent within a religious body; in the event of a disagreement over matters of doctrine or organisation between a religious community and one of its members, the individual's freedom of religion is exercised through his freedom to leave the community …

138. Lastly, where questions concerning the relationship between the State and religions are at stake, on which opinion in a democratic society may reasonably differ widely, the role of the national decision-making body must be given special importance … This will be the case in particular where practice in European States is characterised by a wide variety of constitutional models governing relations between the State and religious denominations.

161 …. In the proceedings before the courts with jurisdiction to examine the union's application for registration, the Archdiocese, which was opposed to its recognition, maintained that the aims set out in the union's constitution were incompatible with the duties accepted by priests by virtue of their ministry and their undertaking towards the archbishop. It asserted that the emergence within the structure of the Church of a new body of this kind would seriously imperil the freedom of religious denominations to organise themselves in accordance with their own traditions, and that the establishment of the trade union would therefore be likely to undermine the Church's traditional hierarchical structure; for these reasons, it argued that it was necessary to limit the trade union freedom claimed by the applicant union.

163. In this connection, the Court observes that in Romania, all religious denominations are entitled to adopt their own internal regulations and are thus free to make their own decisions concerning their operations, recruitment of staff and relations with their clergy … The principle of the autonomy of religious communities is the cornerstone of relations between

the Romanian State and the religious communities recognised within its territory, including the Romanian Orthodox Church. As the Government indicated, members of the Romanian Orthodox clergy, and hence the priests belonging to the applicant union, perform their duties by virtue of their ministry, their undertaking towards the bishop and the decision issued by the latter; the Romanian Orthodox Church has chosen not to incorporate into its Statute the labour law provisions which are relevant in this regard, a choice that has been approved by a Government ordinance in accordance with the principle of the autonomy of religious communities ...

166. Having regard to all the information in its possession, the Court shares the respondent Government's view that in refusing to register the applicant union, the State was simply declining to become involved in the organisation and operation of the Romanian Orthodox Church, thereby observing its duty of neutrality under Article 9 of the Convention. It remains to be determined whether the examination carried out by the county court in refusing the union's application satisfied the conditions for ensuring that the refusal of its registration was necessary in a democratic society (see paragraph 159 above).

167. The majority of the Chamber answered this question in the negative. They held that the county court had not taken sufficient account of all the relevant arguments, having justified its refusal to register the trade union on purely religious grounds based on the provisions of the Church's Statute ...

168. The Grand Chamber does not agree with that conclusion. It observes that the county court refused to register the applicant union after noting that its application did not satisfy the requirements of the Church's Statute because its members had not complied with the special procedure in place for setting up an association. It considers that by taking this approach, the county court was simply applying the principle of the autonomy of religious communities; its refusal of the applicant union's registration for failure to comply with the requirement of obtaining the archbishop's permission was a direct consequence of the right of the religious community concerned to make its own organisational arrangements and to operate in accordance with the provisions of its Statute.

169. Furthermore, the applicant union did not put forward any reasons to justify its failure to request permission formally from the archbishop. Nevertheless, the national courts compensated for this omission by obtaining the opinion of the Archdiocese of Craiova and examining the reasons it gave. The county court concluded, endorsing the reasons put forward by the Archdiocese of Craiova, that if it were to authorise the establishment of the trade union, the consultative and deliberative bodies provided for by the Church's Statute would be replaced by or obliged to work together with a new body – the trade union – not bound by the traditions of the Church and the rules of canon law governing consultation and decision-making. The review undertaken by the court thus confirmed that the risk alleged by the Church authorities was plausible and substantial, that the reasons they put forward did not serve any other purpose unrelated to the exercise of the autonomy of the religious community in question, and that the refusal to register the applicant union did not go beyond what was necessary to eliminate that risk.

170. More generally, the Court observes that the Statute of the Romanian Orthodox Church does not provide for an absolute ban on members of its clergy forming trade unions to protect their legitimate rights and interests. Accordingly, there is nothing to stop the applicant union's members from availing themselves of their right under Article 11 of the Convention by forming an association of this kind that pursues aims compatible with the Church's Statute and does not call into question the Church's traditional hierarchical structure and decision-making procedures. The Court notes that the applicant union's members are also free to join any of

> the associations currently existing within the Romanian Orthodox Church which have been authorised by the national courts and operate in accordance with the requirements of the Church's Statute …
>
> 171. Lastly, the Court takes note of the wide variety of constitutional models governing relations between States and religious denominations in Europe. Having regard to the lack of a European consensus on this matter … it considers that the State enjoys a wider margin of appreciation in this sphere, encompassing the right to decide whether or not to recognise trade unions that operate within religious communities and pursue aims that might hinder the exercise of such communities' autonomy.
>
> 172. In conclusion, regard being had to the reasons set out in its judgment, the county court's refusal to register the applicant union did not overstep the margin of appreciation afforded to the national authorities in this sphere, and accordingly was not disproportionate.

It is tempting to consider the approach adopted in *Sindicatul 'Pastorul Cel Bun'* as permitting religious organisations more freedom to discriminate than other bodies. This is true to some extent, though part of what is at stake is rather an exercise of differentiating the areas in which secular law may properly apply and those in which it has no role. The point is perhaps best made by reference to the decision in *R v Chief Rabbi, ex p Wachman* [1993] 2 All ER 249, mentioned at p 544 above; no religious body could claim to be free from state interference if a court could police decisions made in accordance with the internal rules or practices of that body about matters properly characterised as spiritual, or pertaining to questions of doctrine or religious practice. Where, on the other hand, a religious body enters into the commercial domain, it may be held to the same legal rules as non-religious bodies. To the extent that the EqA or other legislative regimes provide exemptions to religious organisations from rules of general application, those exemptions are generally intended to strike a balance between the Article 9 or similar rights of the body, and the legal rights (including non-discrimination rights) of those with whom its relationship is not exclusively internal (in the sense of being solely concerned with religious or spiritual matters). Different jurisdictions may strike different balances as regards, for example, the entitlement of ministers to maternity or parental leave or minimum process rights, or the freedom of religious bodies engaged in operating schools or hospitals to restrict access to certain positions within those organisations on religious or related grounds, but the principle of permitting some exemptions from the generally applicable rules is consistent with human rights norms. This point will be returned to in the discussion below.

Religious Organisations

Schedule 23 EqA provides that an organisation which falls within para 2(1) 'does not contravene Part 3, 4 or 7 [which prohibit discrimination in access to services, goods or facilities, in public functions, in relation to premises and by associations], so far as relating to religion or belief or sexual orientation, only by restricting:

Schedule 23, para 2(3) EqA

(a) membership of the organisation;
(b) participation in activities undertaken by the organisation or on its behalf or under its auspices;

(c) the provision of goods, facilities or services in the course of activities undertaken by the organisation or on its behalf or under its auspices;
(d) the use or disposal of premises owned or controlled by the organisation.[36]

Organisations which fall within para 2(1) are those whose sole or main purpose is not commercial, and whose purpose is:

(a) to practise a religion or belief,
(b) to advance a religion or belief,
(c) to teach the practice or principles of a religion or belief,
(d) to enable persons of a religion or belief to receive any benefit, or to engage in any activity, within the framework of that religion or belief, or
(e) to foster or maintain good relations between persons of different religions or beliefs.

The application of Schedule 23 para 2 was considered by the High Court in *R (Cornerstone (North East) Fostering & Adoption Services v Ofsted)* [2020] EWHC 1679 (Admin), [2020] IRLR 774, also considered in Chapters 2, 4 and 10. So far as relevant here, the claimant (an evangelical Christian charitable adoption and fostering service) sought to challenge a decision by a regulator that its requirement that prospective adoptive parents and foster carers be married evangelical Christians breached the prohibitions imposed by the EqA and ECHR (Articles 8 and 14) on sexual orientation and religious discrimination. The Charity Commission, which regulates charities, had accepted in 2011 that Cornerstone's discrimination was lawful by reason of Schedule 23 para 2 EqA. Cornerstone failed on its sexual orientation challenge (see Chapter 10) but succeeded in overturning Ofsted's conclusion that it had discriminated unlawfully on grounds of religion or belief. The High Court accepted that the discrimination fell within Schedule 23 para 2, and was not prohibited by the EqA.[37] Further, this provision representing 'Parliament's considered response to the question of whether, and if so how far, religious organisations should be allowed to discriminate on grounds of religion', 'it would be fundamentally incompatible with Parliament's intention to hold under Article 14 that a religiously based fostering agency cannot restrict its services to applicants holding the same faith, when Parliament in para of Sch 23 has clearly and unambiguously permitted it to do so.'[38]

Schedule 23 para 2(5) provides that:

Schedule 23, para 2(5) EqA, Organisations relating to religion or belief

'A minister does not contravene Part 3, 4 or 7, so far as relating to religion or belief or sexual orientation, only by restricting—

(a) participation in activities carried on in the performance of the minister's functions in connection with or in respect of the organisation;
(b) the provision of goods, facilities or services in the course of activities carried on in the performance of the minister's functions in connection with or in respect of the organisation.[39]

[36] Paragraph 2(4) provides similarly that 'A person does not contravene Part 3, 4 or 7, so far as relating to religion or belief or sexual orientation, only by doing anything mentioned in sub-para (3) on behalf of or under the auspices of the organisation'

[37] Note that para 2(1) does not permit (Sch 23 para 2(10)) 'anything which is prohibited by s 29, so far as relating to sexual orientation, if it is done (a) on behalf of a public authority, and (b) under the terms of a contract between the organisation and the public authority.' It was this provision which prevented Cornerstone relying on para 2(1) in relation to sexual orientation discrimination.

[38] This ruling was not appealed.

[39] This exception is discussed in Ch 10 in so far as it relates to sexual orientation, to which its application is narrower than it is to religion.

Schedule 23 para 2(6) then provides that paras 2(3)–(5) only permit a restriction relating to religion or belief which are 'imposed (a) because of the purpose of the organisation, or (b) to avoid causing offence, on grounds of the religion or belief to which the organisation relates, to persons of that religion or belief'. The Explanatory Notes to the EqA state that para 2 would permit a Catholic seminary to restrict places for students to Catholics.[40]

The exceptions set out above apply to discrimination which would otherwise fall within Part 3, 4 or 7 of the EqA. In addition, Schedule 3 para 29 allows the provision by a minister of religion of separate and single-sex services where the services are for the purposes of an organised religion, are provided at a place which is (permanently or for the time being) occupied or used for those purposes, and where the limited provision of the service is necessary in order to comply with the doctrines of the religion or is for the purpose of avoiding conflict with the strongly held religious convictions of a significant number of the religion's followers. The exception does not apply to organisations whose sole or main purposes are commercial. The Explanatory Notes to the EqA state that this would permit a synagogue to have separate seating for men and women at a reception following a religious service.[41]

In order to fall within the exceptions provided by Schedule 23 para 2(5) and Schedule 3 para 29, 'ministers' must be 'accredited, approved or recognised for purposes of, a relevant organisation in relation to the religion', a 'relevant organisation being defined as one whose sole or main purpose is not commercial and is to practise or advance the religion, to teach its practice or principles, to enable persons of the religion to receive benefits, or to engage in activities, within the framework of that religion, or to foster or maintain good relations between persons of different religions'.

The significance of the reference to segregation at the *reception* as distinct from the *service* in the Explanatory Notes to Schedule 3 para 29 is that the latter would fall outwith Part 3 of the EqA in any event. The decision of Southwark's Consistory Court in *In re All Saints', Sanderstead* was discussed in Chapter 4. There the Consistory Court, which has jurisdiction over a variety of matters internal to the Church of England, considered a complaint by a disabled parishioner that the proposed removal of communion rails and kneelers would breach her rights under s29 EqA by reason of her inability to stand while taking communion. The Court ruled that no duty to make reasonable adjustments arose in connection with the 'celebration of Holy Communion' because characterising 'the administration of the sacrament in the context of divine worship as provision of a service is not appropriate' (§63). Nor did the administration of the sacrament involve the exercise of a public function:

***In re All Saints', Sanderstead* [2012] Fam 51**

Petchey Ch:

> 66. Absent authority, I would incline to the view that a priest is fulfilling a function of a public nature in respect of the celebration of Holy Communion … However, in *Aston Cantlow and Wilmcote with Billesley Parochial Church Council v Wallbank* [2004] 1 AC 546 the House of Lords emphasised that in order for the European Convention for the Protection of Human Rights and Fundamental Freedoms to apply the function needs to be of a *governmental* nature

[40] https://www.legislation.gov.uk/ukpga/2010/15/notes.
[41] *Ibid.*

> [citing Lord Rodger of Earlsferry, at §§164–170]. Lord Rodger specifically seemed to exclude the generality of Church of England services. He said, at para 170:
>
> > 'For the most part, in performing his duties and conducting the prescribed services, the minister is simply carrying out part of the mission of the Church, not any governmental junction of the state. On the other hand, when in the course of his pastoral duties the minister marries a couple in the parish church, he may be carrying out a governmental function in a broad sense and so may be regarded as a public authority for purposes of the 1998 Act.'
>
> 67. The contrast Lord Rodger was drawing was between the purely 'religious' services (which would include Holy Communion) and the celebration of marriage. One may readily see that the latter involves a governmental function in the way that other services do not. Lord Hobhouse of Woodborough drew a similar distinction, at para 86:
>
> > 'Thus the priest ministering in the parish may have responsibilities that are certainly not public, such as the supervision of the liturgies used or advising about doctrine, but may have other responsibilities which are of a public nature, such as a responsibility for marriages and burials and the keeping of registers.'...
>
> The point that is being made is that in its religious functions the Church of England is in relation to the Convention in no different position to that of say, the Roman Catholic Church or the Methodist Church: the fact of the establishment makes no difference in this regard.

Some complications arise in the case of the Church of England by reason of its status as the established Church which means, for example, that individuals who have no connection with the Church are entitled by virtue of residence to marry according to its rites. Further, as mentioned in the *All Saints* decision, some ministers of religion perform public functions in that marriage ceremonies have legally binding effect. Religious services themselves, however, fall outside the EqA. So, it is suggested, would restrictions on membership of religious organisations even where those restrictions did not fall within the exceptions provided by Schedule 23 para 2 (ie, sexual orientation or religion and belief). By way of example, we considered in Chapter 7 the *JFS* case[42] in which the SC decided that the restriction of admission to the school along Orthodox Jewish lines (that is, by reference to maternal lineage rather than religious practice) amounted to race discrimination. The same, by definition, is true of access to membership of the Orthodox Jewish community itself. Restrictions on such access would not fall within the exceptions provided by Schedule 23 para 2 because they would entail discrimination on grounds of ethnicity. It is inconceivable, however, that they would be regarded as breaching the EqA since this would constitute a direct interference by secular law with religious doctrine, and would certainly breach Article 9 ECHR. This being the case, it follows that the exceptions provided by Schedule 23, para 2 EqA must apply to a wider spectrum of organisations/conduct than would fall outside the scope of the EqA in any event. This might include scouting associations organised along religious lines, or outreach work by religious organisation.

Work

We considered the GOR provided by Schedule 9 para 1 EqA in Chapter 4. This would apply to permit, for example, that an NHS trust require that applicants for a position as an Anglican or Muslim chaplain be Anglican or Muslim respectively (this on the assumption

[42] *R (E) v Governing Body of JFS* [2009] UKSC 15, [2010] 2 AC 728: see pp 455–457.

that the trust took a proportional approach to the overall body of chaplains). Schedule 9 para 3, and Article 4(2) on which it is based, are capable of permitting wider discrimination, though only by 'churches and other public or private organisations the ethos of which is based on religion or belief'. The requirement that someone be of a certain religion or belief must be legitimate and proportionate 'having regard to [the organisation's] ethos,' but there is no need to justify that ethos.

Schedule 9 para 3 provides as follows:

Schedule 9 para 3 EqA, Other requirements relating to religion or belief

A person (A) with an ethos based on religion or belief does not contravene a provision mentioned in paragraph 1(2) by applying in relation to work a requirement to be of a particular religion or belief if A shows that, having regard to that ethos and to the nature or context of the work—

(a) it is an occupational requirement,
(b) the application of the requirement is a proportionate means of achieving a legitimate aim, and
(c) the person to whom A applies the requirement does not meet it (or A has reasonable grounds for not being satisfied that the person meets it).

Schedule 9 para 1(2) extends to employees, public and private office-holders, contract workers and partners. Schedule 9 para 3 is very similar to para 1 (the general GOR defence), which was considered in Chapter 4, the only difference being that it allows the ethos of the discriminator as well as the nature or context of the work to be taken into account in assessing proportionality.[43]

Schedule 9 para 1 is based on Article 4(1) of Council Directive 2000/78. Schedule 1 paras 2 and para 3 are based on Article 4(2) of the Directive which provides, so far as relevant, as follows:

Article 4, Council Directive 2000/78

1. Notwithstanding Article 2(1) and (2) [which prohibit discrimination on grounds including religion or belief], Member States may provide that a difference of treatment which is based on a characteristic related to any of the grounds referred to in Article 1 shall not constitute discrimination where, by reason of the nature of the particular occupational activities concerned or of the context in which they are carried out, such a characteristic constitutes a genuine and determining occupational requirement, provided that the objective is legitimate and the requirement is proportionate.
2. Member States may maintain national legislation in force at the date of adoption of this Directive or provide for future legislation incorporating national practices existing at the date of adoption of this Directive pursuant to which, in the case of occupational activities within churches and other public or private organisations the ethos of which is based on religion or belief, a difference of treatment based on a person's religion or belief shall not constitute discrimination where, by reason of the nature of these activities or of the context in which they are carried out, a person's religion or belief constitute a genuine, legitimate and justified occupational requirement, having regard to the organisation's ethos. This difference of treatment shall be implemented taking account of Member States' constitutional provisions

[43] The predecessor provision differed from the general GOR in that the latter required that the GOR was a genuine and determining occupational requirement, whereas the predecessor provision of para 3 required only that it was a genuine occupational requirement. The terms 'genuine' and 'determining' are no longer included in Sch 9 paras 1, 2 or 3. The Government made it clear in the debates on the Equality Bill that this change was not intended to have any substantive effect and had been made because the words added nothing to 'requirement' (*Hansard*, 2 March 2010 pm, col 1387). The Explanatory Notes to the EqA, n 39 above, state at §787 that an occupational requirement must be 'crucial to the post, and not merely one of several important factors' (see also IDS Handbook Vol 4, *Discrimination at Work*, §31.10).

> and principles, as well as the general principles of Community law, and should not justify discrimination on another ground.
>
> Provided that its provisions are otherwise complied with, this Directive shall thus not prejudice the right of churches and other public or private organisations, the ethos of which is based on religion or belief, acting in conformity with national constitutions and laws, to require individuals working for them to act in good faith and with loyalty to the organisation's ethos.

In Case C-414/16, *Egenberger v Evangelisches Werk für Diakonie und Entwicklung eV* EU:C:2018:257, [2018] IRLR 762 the Grand Chamber of the CJEU considered whether an auxiliary organisation of the Protestant Church which pursued charitable, benevolent and religious purposes was entitled to restrict access to a research job relating to Germany's compliance with international race discrimination law to membership of a Protestant church. The CJEU ruled that Germany could not, consistent with the Directive, allow religious organisations to determine the application of the GOR provided for by Article 4(2) without recourse to the courts. It also ruled that, in applying Article 4(2), the national courts must, other than in very exceptional cases, refrain from assessing whether the actual ethos of the church or organisation concerned was legitimate, but that they must nonetheless ensure that workers were not discriminated against contrary to the Directive. The lawfulness of a difference of treatment on grounds of religion or belief turned on whether there was an objectively verifiable direct link between the occupational requirement imposed by the employer and the activity concerned, whether because of the nature of the activity (as where a worker would determine the ethos of the church or organisation in question or contribute to its mission of proclamation), or the circumstances in which the activity is to be carried out (such as where the worker was responsible for presenting the organisation to the outside world). National courts would be required to determine (1) whether the requirement relating to religion or belief appeared to be necessary because of the importance of the occupational activity in question for the manifestation of that ethos or the exercise by the church or organisation of its right of autonomy; (2) that the requirement was not used to pursue an aim unrelated to that ethos or the exercise; (3) that the supposed risk of causing harm to the organisation's ethos or right of autonomy had been shown to be probable and substantial, such that the imposition of the requirement was necessary; and (4) that the imposition of the requirement was proportionate.

In Case C-68/17, *IR v JQ* EU:C:2018:696, [2019] ICR 417, the CJEU indicated that Article 4(2) would not permit the dismissal by IR, a company set up to carry out the work of Catholic charitable organisations including through the operation of hospitals, of the head of department at such a hospital, when he remarried after divorce. JQ, who was Catholic, had a contract of employment based on canon law and IR argued that by entering a marriage which was invalid under canon law, JQ had breached his contractual obligations. The Grand Chamber of the CJEU ruled that Article 4(2) permitted discrimination only in relation to occupational activities for which religion or belief was a genuine, legitimate and justified occupational requirement in the light of the organisation's ethos. While the matter was one for the national court to decide, the CJEU suggested that adherence to that part of the Catholic ethos which regarded religious marriage as sacred and indissoluble was not necessary for the promotion of IR's ethos in view of the fact that JQ's role was to manage a department concerned with the provision of medical advice and care in a hospital setting.

Article 4(2) of Council Directive 2000/78 expressly applies only to discrimination on grounds of religion though much of the concern expressed in relation to it has been concerned with the scope it may permit for religious organisations to discriminate against, for example, gay men and lesbian women on the grounds that active homosexuality is inconsistent with 'good faith and ... loyalty to [their] ethos.' This aspect of the Directive is considered further in Chapter 10. Here we concentrate primarily on the transposition of Article 4(1) and (2) Council Directive 2000/78 by Schedule 9 para 2 EqA.

In *Glasgow CC v McNab* [2007] IRLR 476 the EAT ruled that a local authority could not rely on the equivalent of Schedule 9 para 3 in connection with its refusal to interview an atheist teacher for a role involving pastoral care at a Catholic school. An employment tribunal having ruled that a local authority could not possess a religious ethos, the EAT emphasised that the authority had no business seeking to follow or further any such ethos. And in *Sheridan v Prospects for People With Learning Disabilities* ET Case 2901366/06, 22 May 2008, unreported, an employment tribunal ruled that a Christian charity which provided support services to people with learning disabilities could not rely on the exemption in connection with its 'Christians-only' employment policy.

IDS, *Discrimination at Work* (Employment Law Handbooks Volume 4), §§32.26–32.27

The tribunal approached the issue in three stages. First, it considered the charity's ethos, the nature of the employment and the context in which it was carried out. Then it asked whether a particular religion or belief was a GOR for the support worker posts in question. Finally, it asked whether the GOR was proportionate in the circumstances.

On the first point, the tribunal accepted that the charity had a Christian ethos but rejected the assertion that it primarily existed to serve Christ and therefore required Christian staff to fulfil this 'mission': the charity's primary objective was to provide support services to people with learning difficulties. The tribunal found that the overwhelming support given was secular in nature, that the majority of people supported were not Christians and that a significant number of the charity's support workers were not practising Christians. As to whether being a practising Christian was essential to performing the functions of a support worker, the tribunal found that the fact that the charity had, for some years, run its services with a significant number of non-practising Christians in these roles, coupled with its decision not to dismiss them after reasserting its 'Christians-only' employment policy in 2005, pointed away from there being a GOR for these roles. On the question of proportionality, the tribunal found that a few functions of the support worker posts had a Christian element but the concept of proportionality required the charity to consider whether these functions could be carried out by other members of staff or whether it was sufficient to apply a lesser requirement than being a practising Christian – such as requiring staff to be ethos sympathetic. The charity had not done so.

Charities

Section 193(5) EqA, which permits some discrimination in the context of charitable giving (see further Chapter 4), also expressly provides that charities may 'require members, or persons wishing to become members, to make a statement which asserts or implies membership or acceptance of a religion or belief; and for this purpose restricting the access by members to a benefit, facility or service to those who make such a statement is to be treated as imposing such a requirement'. This is perhaps less extensive an exception than it might appear to be because charities are only recognised as such if they operate overall for the public benefit, taking into account any dis-benefit arising from factors such as the restrictions they impose on beneficiaries.[44]

[44] See the discussion of the *Catholic Care* case in Ch 4 (*Catholic Care (Diocese of Leeds) v Charity Commission for England and Wales* [2010] EWHC 520 (Ch), [2010] 4 All ER 1041 and [2012] UKUT 395 (TCC), [2013] 2 All ER 1114 and see generally the discussion in Ch 2.

Education

The prohibitions on discrimination in education are found in Part 6 in so far as they apply to schools and institutions of higher and further education. Some of the important exceptions to the prohibitions on religious discrimination in education, however, relate to Part 3 which prohibits discrimination (including as regards their education functions) by local authorities. For that reason, the exceptions relating to both schools and the education functions of local education authorities are considered together here.

Schedule 3 EqA provides that Part 3's prohibitions on discrimination because of religion or belief do not apply to local authorities as regards the provision of schools, or to:

Schedule 3 para 9 EqA, Education

'anything done in connection with—

(a) the curriculum of a school;[45]
(b) admission to a school which has a religious ethos;
(c) acts of worship or other religious observance organised by or on behalf of a school (whether or not forming part of the curriculum);
(d) the responsible body of a school which has a religious ethos;
(e) transport to or from a school;
(f) the establishment, alteration or closure of schools.

Schedule 11 EqA then provides (para 5) that the prohibition on discrimination because of religion or belief as regards access to schools, and the provision of education and related benefits, facilities and services by schools, does not apply to schools having a religious character, such schools being designated as such under s69(3) School Standards and Framework Act 1998 or (in the case of independent schools) listed as such in the register of independent schools for England or for Wales.[46] In addition, para 6 provides that the prohibition on religion or belief discrimination in the provision of education and related benefits, facilities and services by schools does not apply as regards 'anything done in connection with acts of worship or other religious observance organised by or on behalf of a school (whether or not forming part of the curriculum)'. None of these provisions permit discriminatory exclusion of pupils or their subjection to other detriments.

The effect of the exceptions in Schedules 3, as they apply to education, and 11, is to safeguard the position of schools with a religious ethos, and to avoid religion/belief discrimination challenges based on the content of teaching in schools. As to the first, we saw above that the restrictions of admission to the *JFS* school breached the RRA because they were found to entail discrimination on grounds of *race* as well as *religion*. As a result of the decision of the SC in that case many Jewish schools have revised their entrance criteria. Examples of criteria applied in 2019 by a variety of UK Jewish schools include the following:

- documentary evidence of attendance by a parent/carer or child at a minimum of four synagogue services in the six months prior to the application;
- documentary evidence of a child's engagement in formal Jewish education (either provided, where relevant, at a school having a Jewish religious character, a Cheder/Hebrew school, or equivalent, or by a tutor) on at least three occasions in the six months prior to application *and* documentary evidence of a parent/carer or child's involvement

[45] See discussion in Ch 4 including of the decision in *Birmingham CC v Afsar* [2019] EWHC 3217 (QB), [2020] 4 WLR 168.

[46] Different criteria apply in Scotland.

in any Jewish communal, charitable or welfare activity on at least three occasions in the six months prior to application in a volunteer capacity;

- a Certificate of Religious Practice (CRP) based on criteria such as the family's synagogue attendance, prior commitment to Jewish education and voluntary work within the community.
- membership of a Jewish prayer group *or* enrolment in any formal Jewish education for at least six months in the previous 12 *or* attendance by a parent / carer or child at a minimum of four synagogue or other organised Jewish prayer group services in the previous 12 months *or* parent's/carer's regular (at least monthly) involvement as a volunteer in any Jewish communal, charitable or welfare activity of at least a year's duration in previous two years *or* parent's /carer's regular (at least 6 individual occurrences) involvement in any combination of the following in the year before the application closing date: private or family celebration of Shabbat or Jewish festivals; organised Jewish learning (eg London Jewish Cultural Centre courses, Limmud sessions, Jewish Museum courses; Jewish youth movement activities; organised Jewish community activities (eg Mitzvah Day, Jewish Community Centre events, Jewish Book Week events);
- Parental ability to demonstrate commitment to Orthodox Jewish observances and practices including by certifying their observance of Jewish dietary laws and Shabbat and involvement in Jewish religious education, as well as verified regular attendance at Orthodox Synagogue.

The provisions discussed above are relevant to primary and secondary schools. Schedule 12, which is concerned with further and higher education institutions, provides that:

Schedule 12 para 5 EqA, Institutions with a religious ethos

(1) The responsible body of an institution which is designated for the purposes of this paragraph does not contravene section 91(1), so far as relating to religion or belief, if, in the admission of students to a course at the institution—

(a) it gives preference to persons of a particular religion or belief,
(b) it does so to preserve the institution's religious ethos, and
(c) the course is not a course of vocational training.

(2) A Minister of the Crown may by order designate an institution if satisfied that the institution has a religious ethos.

The Equality Act 2010 (Designation of Institutions with a Religious Ethos) (England and Wales) Order 2010 lists 16 institutions which are designated for the purposes of Schedule 12, all of them Catholic sixth-form colleges.

Schools having a religious ethos are also able to discriminate on grounds of religion as regards employment.

Schedule 22 para 4 EqA, Educational appointments, etc: religious belief

A person does not contravene this Act only by doing anything which is permitted for the purposes of—

(a) section 58(6) or (7) of the School Standards and Framework Act 1998 (dismissal of teachers because of failure to give religious education efficiently);
(b) section 60(4) and (5) of that Act (religious considerations relating to certain appointments);
(c) section 124A of that Act (preference for certain teachers at independent schools of a religious character);
(d) section 124AA(5) to (7) of that Act (religious considerations relating to certain teachers at Academies with religious character).

Section 58 of the 1998 Act requires that foundation or voluntary controlled schools which have a religious character have teachers 'selected for their fitness and competence to give religious education' and specifically appointed so to do. These teachers, who are referred to as 'reserved teachers', may comprise up to 20 per cent of the total staff of the school and may be dismissed if the school considers that they have 'failed to give such religious education efficiently and suitably'.[47] Section 60 provides that foundation or voluntary schools having a religious character may have regard to the ability of a prospective headteacher's ability and fitness to preserve and develop the religious character of the school in making his or her appointment. It also permits voluntary-aided schools to give preference to persons whose religious opinions are in accordance with the tenets of the school's religion or religious denomination, who attend religious worship in accordance with those tenets, or who give, or are willing to give, religious education at the school in accordance with those tenets, in connection with their appointment, remuneration or promotion, and that they may have regard to any conduct by a teacher which is incompatible with the precepts, or with the upholding of the tenets, of the religion or religious denomination of the school in connection with his or her dismissal. Section 124A makes the same provision for teachers at independent schools having a religious character (other than Academies) as s60 does for foundation and voluntary schools. And s124AA makes similar provision to ss58 and 60 in respect of academies with a religious character.

The effect of these exceptions is very significant. In 2014, 37 per cent of state-funded primary schools and 19 per cent of state-funded secondary schools had a religious character. About three-quarters of the seven per cent of schools which were independent had. Areligious character and most of the remainder had a religious ethos.[48]

Richy Thompson, 'Religion, Belief, Education and Discrimination' (2015) 14 *Equal Rights Review* 71–105, footnotes omitted

Schools that teach faith-based religious education would certainly be able to claim a GOR for the head of their RE department, and might also be able to claim a GOR for the headteacher and other senior teaching posts. Some schools might argue that they require a certain proportion of teachers to be of a certain faith, in order to ensure the religious ethos of the school. But surely it goes beyond GOR to permit every voluntary aided school to require every single teacher to share the faith of the school. The evidence clearly shows that schools go beyond what is permitted by GOR. For instance, the clear policy of the Catholic Education Service for England and Wales (CES), the agency of the Catholic Bishops' Conference of England and Wales that is responsible for education, is that 'the posts of Headteacher, Deputy Headteacher and Head or Coordinator of Religious Education are to be filled by baptised and practising Catholics'; for other 'Teacher posts – Applicants are advised that schools/colleges are entitled to give priority to practising Catholic applicants.' For non-teaching posts, discrimination is explicitly limited to where a GOR can be demonstrated:

> Applicants are advised that schools/colleges (in England only) are entitled to give priority to practising Catholic applicants where it can be demonstrated that it is a proportionate means of achieving a legitimate aim (commonly known as a 'genuine occupational requirement').

Similarly, the CES's policy is that:

> The Bishops require that the Headteacher or Principal, Deputy Headteacher or Vice-Principal, and Head of RE/RE Co-ordinator must be practising Catholics. Preferential consideration

[47] More than 20% in cases where the teaching staff is not a multiple of five, in which case the numbers of staff are to be rounded to the next five to determine the maximum number of 'reserved teachers'.

[48] R Thompson, 'Religion, Belief, Education and Discrimination' (2015) 14 *Equal Rights Review* 71.

> should also be given to practising Catholics for all teaching posts and for non-teaching posts where there is a specific religious occupational requirement, i.e., chaplaincy post. In England and Wales statutory provision allows for such preferences to be made.
>
> The meaning is clear: the CES believes that every teacher in every Catholic school can be required to be a practising Catholic, and furthermore that preferential consideration should be given to practising Catholics for every teaching post. The fact that it is not required that Catholics fill every teaching post, and that only preferential consideration is given to practising Catholics for these posts, shows that it cannot be said to be a GOR that the posts are filled by Catholics …

The ability of schools to discriminate in the recruitment of staff is not limited to those having a Catholic ethos, as Thompson points out in the extract above.

Services and Public Functions

Schedule 3 EqA also provides that the prohibition on discrimination because of religion or belief does not apply as regards (para 18) anything done for the purposes of or in pursuance of a decision taken in accordance with immigration rules to refuse a person entry to the UK or the ability to remain in the UK where the decision to refuse entry is taken on the grounds that a person's exclusion from the UK is conducive to the public good, or the decision to prevent a person from remaining in the UK is taken on the grounds that it is undesirable to permit the person to remain in the UK. Para 18 further provides that the prohibition on discrimination because of religion or belief does not to a decision (whether or not taken in accordance with immigration rules) in connection with an application for entry clearance or for leave to enter or remain in the UK which is taken on the ground (a) that a person holds an office or post in connection with a religion or belief or provides a service in connection with a religion or belief, (b) that a religion or belief is not to be treated in the same way as certain other religions or beliefs, or (c) that the exclusion from the UK of a person to whom paragraph (a) applies is conducive to the public good.

Equality Act 2010, 2010 Chapter 15 Revision Notes §711[49]

- The immigration services may differentiate between certain religious groups in order to allow a person such as a minister of religion to enter the UK to provide essential pastoral services, without being challenged by groups which could operate against the public interest, but which might also claim to represent a religion.
- A decision to prevent a person who holds extreme religious views from entering or remaining in the country if his or her presence is not conducive to the public good, for example, preachers who use the pulpit to incite violence, would not constitute unlawful discrimination because of religion or belief.

[49] https://www.legislation.gov.uk/ukpga/2010/15/notes.

10

Sexual Orientation

Sexual Orientation Discrimination: Past and Present

In this chapter we consider the Equality Act 2010's (EqA) prohibitions on discrimination as they apply to sexual orientation. The EqA has replaced the previous legislative provisions: the Employment Equality (Sexual Orientation) Regulations 2003 ('SO Regs') and the Equality Act (Sexual Orientation) Regulations 2007 ('SO Regs 2007'). The SO Regs, which prohibited sexual orientation discrimination at work, were adopted to implement the requirements of Council Directive 2000/78 (the Employment Equality Directive), whose relevant provisions are discussed below. The SO Regs 2007, which prohibited discrimination on grounds of sexual orientation in the provision of goods, facilities and services, education, disposal and management of premises and exercise of public functions, were not the result of any EU initiatives and, this being the case, EU law has limited impact on the interpretation of the Equality Act 2010 (EqA) as it applies to sexual orientation outside the context of work.

The Past

The extract immediately below was included in the previous edition of this book and helps to illustrate how much change has been made in this area in a relatively short time.

MIND, 'Lesbians, gay men, bisexuals and mental health' (1996)

In 1885 all male homosexual relationships were declared illegal. Many gay men were given prison sentences simply because they had homosexual relationships. This often resulted in blackmail and suicides. The first change in the law followed from the recommendations of the 1957 Wolfenden Report. In 1967 the Sexual Offences Act came into force. The Act did not incorporate all the recommendations made in the report. It decriminalised a small number of 'offences' and extended tolerance of homosexuality only slightly.

The Wolfenden Report and the resulting Sexual Offences Act did not refer to lesbianism. In fact, lesbians have never been directly legislated against and relationships between women have never been officially illegal. Lesbianism was last discussed in Parliament as a distinct issue in 1921 when

The Criminal Law Amendment Act attempted to legislate with regard to the age of consent. However, the absence of legislation does not mean that lesbian relationships have been more acceptable. Lesbians have been discriminated against indirectly simply because of their invisibility in any legislation. Their relationships have remained largely unrecognised and the law offers scant protection in many areas of their lives. Throughout history the social climate has made it extremely difficult for women to live together independently of men. Lesbians have been seen as a threat to the traditional notions of the nuclear family and to the assigned gender roles men and women in modern western society are supposed to adopt. Society has suppressed lesbianism by making these roles very difficult to break, and women who have not conformed to society's expectations have found themselves considerably disadvantaged, socially, personally and economically.

Following the 1967 Act, men over the age of 21 were permitted to have sexual relationships with each other. The law only applied to England, although Scotland and Northern Ireland passed similar legislation some time after this. In 1992 the Isle of Man finally brought its law into line with the rest of the UK after its autonomy was threatened because of its consistent refusal to implement even the 1967 Sexual Offences Act.

The 1967 Act does not address many of the legal issues facing lesbians and gay men in Britain today. There is no legal framework for lesbian and gay partnerships and no law against the unequal treatment in society of lesbians and gay men.

Legal discrimination still remains in the 1956 Sexual Offences Act and the 1967 Sexual Offences Act. Other legislation, whilst it does not directly discriminate against gay men and lesbians, does not afford the same privileges to gay partnerships as it does to heterosexual ones. This reflects a general lack of civil rights throughout the legislative framework …

The introduction of the 1983 Mental Health Act did not take into account lesbian and gay relationships. This Act grants the 'nearest relative' specific rights: for example, the right to make an application for the patient to be admitted to hospital against their will under Section 2 of the Act, or to be discharged or to be given certain important information. The Act identifies the nearest relative according to a hierarchy: first choice is husband or wife (which can include common law heterosexual spouse of six months standing), then son or daughter, then other family members ending with nephew or niece. This order can only be altered if the 'patient' has lived with someone else for at least 5 years … this means that if a lesbian or gay man has lived with a partner for 4 years, the 'nearest relative' could be a nephew whom they hardly know. Meanwhile a heterosexual partner would gain nearest relative status after only six months and a married heterosexual partner immediately.

This discrimination was deliberate. In 1982 Parliament debated an amendment to the Act which would have given gay and lesbian partners equal rights with heterosexuals. David Ennals MP argued that gay men and lesbians often do not have very good relationships with their families because of their sexuality, and therefore family members should not automatically be given nearest relative status over a partner. Others argued against the amendment along the lines of strengthening family relationships and ties, some expressed outright moral censure, and others were worried that affording gay partners equal rights within the Mental Health Act would mean that other areas of law would be challenged, thus 'opening up the floodgates.' Despite these weak arguments and unsubstantiated claims the 1982 amendment was defeated.

Section 28 of the Local Government Act, introduced in 1987, was largely seen as an attempt by the Government to curtail the growing inclusion of lesbians and gay men in equal opportunities policies. The Act prevented 'a local authority from giving financial or other assistance to any person for the purpose of publishing or promoting homosexuality as an acceptable family relationship, or for the purpose of teaching acceptability in any maintained school.' Despite the mass efforts of lesbians and gay men, Section 28 passed into law and remains there today.

In fact, Section 28 works mainly as a deterrent to local authorities. Many have drastically cut funding for projects set up specifically for gay men and lesbians, and local authorities who wish to review their equal opportunities policies to include discrimination on the basis of sexuality are put off by the clause. Even though the legislation applies only to local government and grant maintained schools, many local authorities have applied it to other areas and some voluntary organisations have been discouraged from expanding their equal opportunities policies to include sexual orientation.

No legal proceedings have ever taken place on the interpretation of the concepts enshrined in Section 28. Many lawyers believe that 'promoting homosexuality' would mean local authorities directly persuading their populations to become homosexual – something that is very difficult, and arguably impossible, to do.

Until 1994 the age of consent for sexual relations between homosexuals remained at 21. The House of Commons voted to equalise this with heterosexual relationships by bringing the age of consent down to 16. The outcome of this vote was to lower the age from 21 to 18, still not granting gay people the same rights as heterosexuals. A bill to lower the age of consent to 16 was defeated by the House of Lords in the summer of 1998 [but see immediately below].

There have been profound changes across the UK in the status of LGB (lesbian, gay and bisexual) people. Section 28 Local Government Act 1988 was repealed in Scotland in 2000 and in the rest of the UK in 2003 in which year the SO Regs prohibited sexual orientation discrimination at work. In 2001 the UK Government lifted the previous ban on LGB people serving in the armed forces and equalised the age of consent for sex between men was equalised, at 16, with that applicable to sex between women and between men and women. Same-sex couples gained equal adoption rights in 2002,[1] the right to enter civil partnerships in 2004 and the right to be recognised as the legal parents of children conceived through the use of donated sperm, eggs or embryos in 2008.[2] The SO Regs 2007 prohibited discrimination on grounds of sexual orientation in the provision of goods, facilities and services, education, disposal and management of premises and exercise of public functions and in 2014 same-sex couples gained the right to marry.[3] By this stage the SO Regs and SO Regs 2007 had been consolidated into the EqA.

The attitude then prevalent among many was captured by discussion in the House of Lords (HL) about the Equality Act (Sexual Orientation) Regulations (Northern Ireland) 2006 (the Northern Irish equivalent of the SO Regs 2007), which the Democratic Unionist Party's Lord Morrow sought to have annulled on the basis that they attacked 'fundamental religious freedoms'.[4] Lord Morrow protested that while:

HL Debs 9 January 2007, Col 181

Homosexual people are entitled to be able to buy their groceries and have their bins emptied, just like everyone else', the regulations would 'make it possible for homosexual activists to sue people who disagree with a homosexual lifestyle because of their religious beliefs. Bed and breakfast owners and Christian old people's homes will be sued for not giving a double bed to homosexual civil partners. Wedding photographers will be made to pay compensation for not taking bookings for civil partnership ceremonies. Christians in business could even be sued for sharing their faith with customers. Worst of all, they require religious organisations to choose between obedience to God and obedience to the state.

[1] The Adoption and Children Act 2002.
[2] Human Fertilisation and Embryology Act.
[3] The Marriage (Same-Sex Couples) Act 2013 came into effect in 2014.
[4] HL Debs 9 January 2007, Col 180.

Having referred to judicial review proceedings which had been issued against the Northern Irish regulations (see pp 623–627 below), Lord Morrow continued:

HL Debs 9 January 2007, Cols 182–83

One might have hoped for some humility from Government in the face of these allegations, some willingness to reconsider. Instead, Ministers have been engaged in knocking down straw men. I have here a letter dated 13 December from Mr David Hanson, the Minister of State for Northern Ireland, which says that bed and breakfast places can still refuse to give a double bed to a homosexual couple so long as they also refuse double beds to unmarried heterosexual couples, but what about the issue of civil partnerships? The consultation paper repeatedly declared the Government's intention to ensure that civil partners receive the same treatment as married couples. So, if a Christian bed and breakfast establishment refused a double room to a homosexual couple living in a civil partnership, they could be sued and so in effect closed down purely because of their religious beliefs.

Education will also be affected. The Minister says that the regulations apply only to access to benefits and not the curriculum. I believe that he is mistaken. There is absolutely nothing in the wording that excludes the curriculum from the scope of litigation …

There is another glaring hole in the exceptions for religious groups. Regulation 16(8) states that the exception does not apply where an organisation contracts with the state to provide a particular service. This means that religious bodies providing a service on behalf of the state must fully comply with the new laws. So a Christian old people's home receiving state funding for some places which refused a double room to two civil partners would be unlawfully discriminating. The home is faced with a choice: defend legal actions or turn down state funding. Either way, the costs would mean that the home will close …

Government have failed to provide robust evidence to support the claim that homosexual individuals are denied access to essential healthcare. As that claim seems to be one of the main bases for introducing [the Regulations], the burden of responsibility rests with the Minister to produce robust and convincing evidence that homosexual individuals are denied access to essential healthcare. It is most important that the Government ensure that the proposed SORs will not be abused by malicious claims as has happened in other countries. I give the example of Canada.

I am firmly convinced that the freedom to manifest one's religion is seriously undermined. The regulations threaten to override the consciences and free speech of Christians and others who object to homosexual practice. This contravenes Articles 9 and 10 of the European Convention on Human Rights. However, the Government have achieved one thing: they have united Protestant, Catholic and Dissenter in opposition to these SORs. I am not aware of any – I underline the word 'any' – church denomination, large or small, in Northern Ireland that supports the regulations. As a matter of fact, I confidently stand here tonight and tell noble Lords that there is none. Not a single denomination, small or large, in Northern Ireland supports these regulations.

Former Lord Chancellor Lord Mackay of Clashfern suggested that the regulations 'differ considerably from any of the legislation outlawing discrimination on other grounds'.

HL Debs 9 January 2007, Col 185

The sexual orientation regulations are not confined in their effect to the tendency of a person – orientation means, I think, tendency. These regulations are not about outlawing a particular tendency. They do more than that. They state that people who give services, supply goods or provide facilities must not discriminate on the ground of sexual orientation. The regulations imply that if those people interact with people of that orientation, they must also be prepared to allow them, if appropriate, to use the facilities that they provide for the purpose of homosexual practice. That is quite different from the other types of discrimination. It is the practice of homosexual acts that some Christians – but not the noble Lord who has just spoken – and considerable numbers

> of people of other major religions believe is wrong and sinful, and they do not think that they can conscientiously do anything to promote or further it.
>
> I shall take one illustration, that of a person who provides bed and breakfast for people in his house. In that situation, if he receives a same-sex couple in a double room in his house, he is liable to be convinced of the fact that he is allowing a sinful practice of which he disapproves. That is the difference between this type of regulation and the discrimination regulations with which we are familiar and which most, if not all, Christians and other religious people support wholeheartedly …
>
> … these regulations … would make it unlawful for a person to refuse to accept a same-sex couple into their boarding house. I am much too old to offer any such facilities and the regulations are unlikely to affect me in any way whatever; I am thinking of a person who has a religious conviction of the kind that I have just mentioned and who does not believe that it is right in conscience to accept people into their house who would use it to practise a way of life that they considered sinful. That is the essence of the problem. The regulations seek to override their conscientious objection to that behaviour in their home.
>
> The adoption agencies are another area of difficulty. There may be a regulation that helps to exempt adoption agencies that are charities – at least it does so on one construction of it – but there is a difficulty if an adoption agency declines to place children with same-sex couples on the ground of religious conviction. Again, that might be outlawed by the regulations. The regulations are not particularly easy to construe and I am not going to attempt to do so, because they are quite complicated, but this is the essence of the matter as I see it – differentiating these regulations and the kind with which we are familiar …

Cross-bench peer Lord Moran demanded to know 'why this Government are apparently so obsessed with extending the rights and privileges of gays. People may begin to wonder if they are planning to make homosexuality compulsory. This never-ending stream of measures for a particular lobby is surely likely to produce a backlash and make life for gays worse rather than better.'[5] And former Cabinet Minister Lord Tebbit declared that 'We would not wish to discriminate against people for being black or on grounds of their sexual orientation' but that 'The concerns being expressed this evening are primarily about sodomy rather than about sexual orientation – that is, doing not being', going on to ask whether 'a woman patient in a hospital who declined to be treated or examined by an openly lesbian doctor [would] be guilty of harassment?'.

The Northern Irish Regulations, unlike the SO Regs 2007, regulated sexual orientation harassment as well as sexual orientation discrimination outside the employment sphere. Lord Moran expressed concern that the regulations 'while seeking quite reasonably to meet the concerns of lesbians, gay men and bisexuals, may have damaging effects on Christians and Christian churches of all denominations, Christian schools, Christian adoption agencies, Christian printers and Christian conference centres' and 'will certainly have an adverse effect on freedom of speech. A Christian teacher would, it appears, risk prosecution if he or she were to teach the importance of marriage and add that sexual partnerships outside marriage should be avoided.'[6] And referring to the removal of religious harassment from the Bill which became the Equality Act 2006 (see p 623 below), Lord Morrow complained that the regulation of sexual orientation harassment had 'major implications for religious liberty and freedom of speech. For example, if church membership were denied to a homosexual and the minister explained in orthodox, theological terms the religious belief that justified

[5] HL Debs 9 January 2007, Cols 189–90.
[6] *Ibid.*

the denial, it would be open to the person to bring a claim for harassment'. He pointed out that the Regulations exempted the restriction of participation by a minister in activities carried on in the performance of his functions but not 'any subsequent explanations. If he quotes from the Bible, he could be in trouble. What could be more fundamental than the right to decide who is a member of your church? Yet that is jeopardised by the regulations'.

HL Debs 9 January 2007, Col 182

The Minister also says that the harassment provisions will not stop a Christian bookshop promoting marriage. That is very good. But what he does not say is what happens when members of staff in a Christian bookshop share the Gospel with a homosexual customer. If they urge the customer to repent and turn to Christ – as in Northern Ireland they might often do – they could easily find themselves on the wrong end of a legal action for harassment. The bookshop would not want to discriminate in any way – it would happily sell the person, sell anyone, a book – but it can still be sued for harassment.

The protestations of Lord Morrow and others did not succeed and the motion to annul the Northern Irish Regulations was defeated though the application for judicial review succeeded in striking down the harassment provisions of the Regulations (see pp 623–627 below). We shall consider below the extent to which the concerns raised about religious freedom have been vindicated.

The Present

Law is not a panacea and discrimination and disadvantage experienced by LGB people has not disappeared. A research review commissioned by the Government Equalities Office and published in 2016 provides an overview though (as it points out) the research which it reviews tends to treat trans people (considered in Chapter 2) and LGB people as a single group, which makes it difficult to determine the extent to which some of the matters discussed are related to sexual orientation, on the one hand, or gender identity, on the other.

Nathan Hudson-Sharp and Hilary Metcalf, *Inequality among lesbian, gay bisexual and transgender groups in the UK: a review of evidence* (National Institute of Economic and Social Research, 2016)

Executive summary

… the evidence base for an effective assessment of inequality and relative disadvantage by sexual orientation and gender identity is deficient and has major gaps. To a large extent this stems from a shortage of robust, representative data, as well as a failure of research to disaggregate disadvantage into single LGB&T groups. In particular, the report identifies a dearth of evidence on inequality by gender identity, and finds evidence on inequality between LGB&T groups to be lacking. The report shows across policy areas how a lack of representative quantitative research data precludes a comprehensive and reliable assessment of the extent of disadvantage for LGB&T people in the UK.

Education

Homophobic, biphobic and transphobic (HBT) bullying remains a major problem in schools and, to an extent, in further and higher education. A number of measures, such as directly addressing incidents of HBT bullying, are thought by teachers to be effective but there is evidence that these measures fail to be universally implemented. Heterosexism and heteronormativity are prevalent in educational institutions reinforcing feelings of alienation among LGB&T students and leaving their specific support needs largely unaddressed. The evidence also finds teachers in need of leadership and support, including training.

The evidence in relation to discrimination in education is weak, based on non-robust studies and with little comparison between groups. There is no reliable evidence on the extent of perceived or expected discrimination, and little reliable evidence on inequalities between groups. However, there is evidence that expectations of discrimination are higher amongst transgender people than LGB people.

Safety

Evidence finds LGB&T people at greater risk of being victim to hate crime compared to heterosexual people, with recorded incidences increasing over time. Certain LGB&T groups are found to be at particular risk of hate crime – notably gay men, young people and those from black and ethnic minority groups. Some survey-based research suggests significant under-reporting of incidences of hate crime and that this may be explained by unsatisfactory treatment from services.

The prevalence of domestic violence among LGB&T people is unclear, as well as which groups are most at risk. Some limited evidence suggests LGB&T people are discouraged from using generic domestic violence services. This has been explained by fear of potential homophobic, biphobic, and/or transphobic treatment from service providers and other service users, as well as expectations of inadequate staff diversity, knowledge and skills.

Health

More research has been conducted into LGB people's health than other policy areas. Much of the research, however, does not adjust for standard mediating factors such as age and class and may therefore misidentify health inequalities. There is evidence that LGB people's general health worse than that of heterosexual people. It was unclear whether this results from a higher incidence of mental health problems amongst LGB people, evidenced in the review, or also of physical health problems, for which there was no evidence.

More LGB&T people than heterosexual people are dissatisfied with health services. Experiences of discrimination, heteronormativity, and a lack of information and/or staff knowledge on LGB&T people's health needs are identified as main sources of dissatisfaction. Mental health services are the most often perceived to be discriminatory. Research evidence in the area of health is lacking for transgender people. In respect of mental health, there is some evidence of 'pathologisation' (i.e. attributing mental health problems to their transgender status). There is evidence of a lack of mental health inpatient provision for transgender people, restricting access to mental health care. There is also evidence of long waiting times in first referral to a gender identity clinic, with consequences for mental health. The evidence points to some possible improvements to service provision by gender identity clinics.

Access to and experience of services

Heteronormative assumptions as well as experiences and/or fears of discrimination prevent LGB&T people from accessing mainstream services. For this reason, LGB&T people have a preference for and are more engaged with specialist LGB&T organisations. There is some evidence that LGB&T people may be disproportionately negatively affected by spending cuts on voluntary and community sector (VCS) services, which are poorly funded. Evidence suggests services do not routinely monitor the sexual orientation and/or gender identity of their staff and/or service users, nor are LGB&T people routinely involved in consultative processes.

Employment

There is, at best, weak, inconsistent evidence of inequality of employment outcomes by sexual orientation. Much of this evidence points towards higher employment rates, occupational levels and earnings for LGB people than for heterosexual people. However, some of these differences disappear when other characteristics are taken into account. Lack of data prevents a view on the relative performance of transgender people in the labour market.

There is evidence of discrimination in recruitment, in promotion, deployment and access to social networks within particular occupations. The workplace remains LGB&T-unfriendly for many LGB and even more so for transgender people, with many experiencing harassment and bullying, impacting on job choice, reduced progression and inability to openly identify at work.

LGB&T families, adoption and fostering

There is evidence of familial rejection of LGB&T children and young adults, impacting on mental health and resulting in homelessness. There is no evidence of either detrimental effects or, beneficial effects on mental health and gender adjustment among children raised by same-sex parents. While children of same-sex couples do not view having same-sex parents as problematic, they experience negative responses by others, including through homophobic bullying at school. LGB people expect to encounter barriers to adoption and fostering because of their sexual orientation.

Homelessness and access to housing provision

Despite claims in the research evidence that LGB&T people are at increased risk of homelessness, supporting evidence is weak and non-comparative. HBT abuse has been identified as the most prolific cause of homelessness, with young people in the process of coming out thought to be at particular risk. Consistent evidence finds LGB&T people experience and expect discriminatory practice from housing services. There is also some evidence that the needs of LGB people may not be being adequately addressed within housing services.

Civic society

Fear of HBT abuse, as well as expectations of discrimination, have been identified as barriers to engagement in public and political life. For transgender people, there is evidence of an additional barrier in lack of recognition of transgender issues in the formation of government policy and amongst LGB&T groups themselves. Overall, evidence points to an improvement in general public attitudes on the acceptability of LGB people in public positions.

Public attitudes

Evidence suggests that the UK has become more accepting of LGB people in recent years and the public increasingly supports legal equality. This support varies by issue, with adoption by same-sex couples, for example, being viewed less positively than same-sex marriage.

Asylum

No evidence is available on the experiences of transgender or bisexual people seeking asylum. Qualitative research has found lesbian and gay asylum seekers subjected to inappropriate questioning by staff from the UK Border Agency (now known as UK Visas and Immigration). Evidence of the impact of this on approval of refugee status based on sexual orientation is mixed. There is evidence that lesbian and gay asylum seekers face additional barriers to securing suitable housing, employment and financial stability as a direct result of their sexual orientation.

Young people

Evidence from across all the policy areas covered by the review shows young LGB&T people face a hostile environment – in education, at home and in wider society – at a stage in their lives when they are particularly in need of support and approbation. Young people are subject to extensive homophobia, biphobia, transphobia, greater mental ill health and unwanted and risky sex. Experiences at this age have life-long implications for mental health and resilience. There is little evidence on the inequalities experienced by young transgender people, and no evidence was found on young LGB&T young people who were not in education, education or training (NEET).

> ***Older people***
>
> Evidence from across all the policy areas covered by the review shows older LGB people, compared with older heterosexual people, are more concerned about the implications of ageing in relation to care needs, independence and mobility, health, housing and mental health. Research suggests that LGB people are more likely than heterosexual people to be concerned about having to move into residential accommodation as they age, because of fears of homophobia and heteronormativity. Evidence is, however absent on the actual experiences of older LGB&T people in residential homes …

A survey conducted in 2019 by the EU's Fundamental Rights Agency provided disaggregated information on the experiences of LGBT people across the EU, North Macedonia and Serbia.[7] The survey involved 140,000 people and was said by the FRA to be the largest survey of its kind.[8] It reported that 64 per cent of LGB people in the UK always or often avoided holding hands in public with a same-sex partner for fear of being assaulted, threatened or harassed.[9] The disaggregated statistics for lesbians, gay men and bisexual men and women are set out in Table 10.1 below, which also shows other reported forms of disadvantage and discrimination reported by LGB people in the UK.

Table 10.1 Experiences of LGB people in the UK

	LGB people	**Lesbians**	**Gay men**	**Bisexual women**	**Bisexual men**
Percentage of the relevant population which reports the relevant behaviour/experience as happening 'often' or 'always' for fear of being assaulted, threatened or harassed because of sexual orientation/ gender identity					
Avoid holding hands in public with a same-sex partner	64%	51%	73%	49%	71%
Avoid certain places or locations	32%	37%	41%	21%	28%
Locations/situations in which openness about sexual orientation/gender identity is avoided for fear of being assaulted, threatened or harassed					
At home	13%	8%	7%	18%	18%
With/around family	28%	19%	16%	39%	37%
At school	18%	14%	11%	24%	24%
In the workplace	27%	18%	19%	30%	39%
In healthcare settings	19%	17%	16%	19%	18%
In cafés, restaurants and pubs and clubs	41%	40%	42%	36%	48%
On public transport	62%	61%	66%	59%	61%
In the street, squares, parks or car parks and other public places	62%	63%	70%	54%	62%
In public premises or buildings	41%	36%	45%	37%	48%

The FRA also reported that 39 per cent of lesbians, gay men and bisexuals in the UK reported having experienced discrimination in the previous 12 months in one or more of the context set out in Table 10.2 below.

[7] https://fra.europa.eu/en/data-and-maps/2020/lgbti-survey-data-explorer#contentSection.

[8] FRA, *A Long Way to go for LGBTI Equality* (14 May 2020) 3, available at https://fra.europa.eu/en/publication/2020/eu-lgbti-survey-results. The survey's results relating to trans people are discussed in Ch 2.

[9] n 7 above.

Table 10.2 UK LGB experience of discrimination within the last 12 months because of their sexual orientation/gender identity

	LGB people	Lesbians	Gay men	Bisexual women	Bisexual men
In one of more of the listed contexts	39%	47%	39%	39%	31%
In a work-related context	19%	24%	22%	16%	16%
While looking for work	6%	8%	9%	3%	5%
At work	18%	22%	20%	16%	15%
In a non-work-related context	34%	42%	37%	35%	26%
While looking for housing	7%	10%	8%	4%	4%
In healthcare/social services	13%	19%	11%	13%	8%
In education (as parent or student)	17%	23%	12%	20%	11%
In a café, restaurant, pubs or nightclub	20%	24%	22%	19%	15%
In a shop	11%	16%	12%	8%	9%

Nine per cent of UK respondents reported that the discrimination they had most recently experienced also related to their gender identity or expression, and eight per cent, four per cent and four per cent respectively reported that it also related to their ethnicity or immigration background, their skin colour, or their religion or belief. Twenty-five per cent of women and six per cent of men reported that their sex had also played a role. Only 11 per cent of LGB people had reported the last incident of discrimination they had experienced.

The survey also asked about violence and harassment were also reported by UK respondents. The figure for harassment (42 per cent) was higher than the EU average of 38 per cent.

Table 10.3 UK LGB experience of physical or sexual attacks or harassment because of sexual orientation/ gender identity

	LGB people	Lesbians	Gay men	Bisexual women	Bisexual men
Experience of physical/sexual attacks or harassment because of sexual orientation/gender identity					
Percentage of the population which had experienced such physical or sexual attacks in the past five years	10%	9%	14%	8%	9%
One such attack	66%	54%	63%	63%	59%
Three or more such attacks	20%	11%	19%	20%[10]	19%[11]
Percentage of the population which had experienced such physical or sexual attacks in the past 12 months	4%	4%	5%	3%	4%
Percentage of the population which had experienced such harassment in the past 12 months	42%	51%	48%	40%	32%
Verbal, in-person harassment	32%	39%	37%	29%	25%
Non-verbal/ in-person harassment	28%	24%	27%	23%	16%

[10] Small sample size.
[11] Small sample size.

Fifty per cent of those who had experienced LGB harassment attributed it also to their gender identity or expression, seven per cent to their ethnicity or immigrant background and four per cent to their skin colour. Five per cent thought that their religion or belief had played a part and 20 per cent (25 per cent of women) thought that their sex was also involved.

Fifty-five per cent of LGB respondents in the UK reported having experienced having been ridiculed, teased, insulted or threatened at school because of their sexual orientation or gender identity. This was more widely reported among younger people.

Table 10.4 School bullying of LGB people in the UK

	LGB people	**Lesbians**	**Gay men**	**Bisexual women**	**Bisexual men**
Percentage of the relevant population ridiculed, teased, insulted or threatened at school because of their sexual orientation or gender identity					
All age groups	55%	55%	72%	45%	48%
15–17	61%	60%	74%	48%	64%

There was a low rate of satisfaction with government action in the UK though respondents reported a significantly better than average satisfaction with life relative to that of the general population.[12]

Sexual Orientation Discrimination and the Law

The Equality Act 2010

We have considered the definitions of discrimination contained in the EqA in Chapter 2 (direct and indirect discrimination, victimisation, harassment, the issue of instructions and the provision of assistance to discriminate). In Chapter 3 we considered the extent to which the EqA permits or requires positive action while the scope of the EqA was dealt with in Chapter 4, and enforcement issues in Chapter 5. Here we consider those aspects of the EqA which are unique to sexual orientation discrimination. The impact of the European Convention on Human Rights (ECHR) is evident in the case law discussed below, but the Convention, and its implementation in the UK, is also considered at the end of the chapter.

In considering this area of law it is important to recognise the tension which may exist between rights or interests in freedom of religion, on the one hand, and non-discrimination on grounds of sexual orientation on the other. This tension is not unique to these protected characteristics and also exists within the protected characteristic of religion, in particular, where one person's right to express their religious beliefs is another person's blasphemy (see further Chapter 9). It surfaced in the parliamentary debates on the Equality Act 2006 which set out to regulate discrimination on grounds of religion or belief for the first time in Great Britain. As explained in Chapter 9, prominent discrimination lawyer and Liberal Democrat

[12] n 7 above, 17 and 29.

peer Lord Lester passed an amendment removing the harassment provisions from the Bill having expressed grave concern about the fact that they would 'catch proselytising by way of religious displays and materials such as posters, Bibles, crucifixes and so on because they involve deliberate attempts to persuade people of a different faith or no faith to join the church and they may be interpreted as harming human dignity – whatever that means – or creating an offensive environment. The display of a "Jews for Jesus" poster to persuade me to see the light would violate the dignity of observant Jews'.

Lord Lester's influence on the development of the EqA 2006 was referred to in the parliamentary discussions of the Northern Irish 2006 Regulations extracted above. Recognition of the potential impact of rights against discrimination also resulted in the partial success of the judicial review challenge to those Regulations which resulted in the annulment of their harassment provisions, though the bulk of the Regulations survived unscathed.

***An application for judicial review by the Christian Institute* [2007] NIQB 66, [2008] IRLR 36**

The applicants were named individuals representing a large range of Irish Protestant churches and organisations. The claim also featured interveners representing a number of archbishops as well as the Northern Ireland Human Rights Commission, the Equality Commission for Northern Ireland and the Coalition on Sexual Orientation. The applicants argued, inter alia, that there had been inadequate consultation on the Regulations which, further, disproportionately interfered with ECHR rights to freedom of religion and expression and non-discrimination. They also argued that the Regulations had been adopted in the mistaken belief that they provided the same treatment to sexual orientation as to religion or belief whereas there was no protection in Northern Ireland against harassment related to religion or belief other than in the context of work.

The High Court ruled in favour of the applicants and set aside the harassment provisions of the Regulations. In so doing the judge discussed the application of the ECHR and the balance which fell to be struck between freedom of religion and expression, on the one hand, and the right to be free from discrimination, on the other. He accepted (relying on the decision of the HL in *R (Williamson) v Secretary of State for Education and Employment* [2005] UKHL 15, [2005] 2 AC 246 (see p 572) that the applicants' beliefs in the sinfulness of same-sex relationships was protected for the purposes of Article 9 (this was an 'orthodox Christian belief … a long established part of the belief system of the world's major religions') but declined to strike down the regulations in their entirety as an unwarranted interference with their Article 9 rights.

Mr Justice Weatherup:

> 9. Callum Webster, the Northern Ireland officer of the first applicant, Christian Institute, gave examples of the areas where he considers the Regulations will have an unwarranted effect. As illustrations of the consequences of the Regulations Archbishop Brady set out a number of examples as follows:
>
> > 'A. Under the harassment provisions, Catholic teachers, volunteers, staff, or priests in schools, youth clubs, parishes, St Mary's University College or university chaplaincies who seek to present the Catholic Church's teaching on sexual orientation, marriage and the family could be subject to claims of harassment on the basis of "violating the dignity" of persons with a homosexual orientation who are present or "creating an intimating, hostile, degrading, humiliating or offensive environment". This scenario becomes particularly problematic when, as is often the case, the person making the presentation of Catholic doctrine is doing so by

invitation and outside of a Catholic institution, or during a church organised course or event which is open to the general public and held in a non-church building.

B. The likelihood of such claims is heightened when in the context of maintaining an environment consistent with the ethos of a Catholic institution, the management or staff of that institution take preventative or proactive action in support of that ethos which may be regarded by a person with a homosexual orientation as either harassment or indirect discrimination. For example, if the management of St Mary's University College, in the interests of maintaining the Catholic ethos of the institution and thereby upholding the teaching of the church, were to issue a Directive forbidding the students' union, of say an affiliate of the Union of Students of Ireland (USI) from inviting a gay and lesbian lobby group supported by the USI to make a presentation to students of the college, the management may be subject to an action under the Regulations. The same might apply if the management of the college removed posters within the college grounds promoting such an event. Parallel scenarios could easily be multiplied for Catholic schools, youth clubs and parishes. The Regulations have the potential to become particularly problematic in terms of actions taken by the management of a Catholic school, youth club or chaplaincy in the interests of the ethos of the institution, in response to displays of physical affection and intimacy by a homosexual couple over the age of consent, even if such actions would also have been taken in response to similar behaviour by a heterosexual couple. The scale of the services provided by the church to young people in second and third level education as well as youth organisations is such that this could become a significant source of such actions, especially if pursued in organising a coordinated fashion by a lobby group. This opens up the real possibility of Catholic staff being harassed because of their religious belief.

C. … it is not clear whether in giving an explanation, based on the magisterial teaching of the Catholic church, for a lawful action taken under the exemptions provided for the ministers of religion, the explanation itself could become the source of a claim for harassment.

D. A potential problem arises in respect of access sought by same sex couples, whether civilly registered or not, to marriage and relationship counselling courses offered by Accord or Diocese and Family Ministry Services. Acceptance of same sex couples for relationship counselling on the same terms as married couples would be in contravention of the doctrinal principles by granting public and *de facto* equivalence to a same sex union. Yet, if the Catholic agency, in compliance with its doctrinal position, was to decline such services to a same sex couple they may become subject to an action on the basis of the current regulations, either on the basis of the refusal to provide the service and/or on the basis of the explanation given for such action.

E. A similar problem arises in relation to adoption placement and access to parenting courses run by the Catholic church related institutions. If a Catholic adoption agency was to consider a same sex couple as a potential adoptive couple, on the same terms as a married couple, this would be in contravention of the doctrinal principles. As the court will be aware, the political debate around the parallel legislation to be introduced in Britain has already conceded that the consequence of the legislation is the likely closure of Catholic adoption agencies. A similar principle applies in regard to the increasingly likely situation whereupon a same sex couple will seek to be accepted on a parenting course run by a church based agency, or even as trainee volunteers to work in support of a family ministry programme. Again, in each of these cases, both the refusal to allow participation, on the basis of implying equivalence, as well as the explanation for the action, could give rise to court action under the Regulations.

F. Given the high number of youths and other groups using church owned halls and facilities to host their events, situations may arise where such groups will organise activities or permit behaviour which, in terms of the doctrinal position of the church, the church management of such facilities, in the interests of protecting the ethos of their organisation, may feel it necessary to withdraw permission to use the facilities or to direct the manner in which they are being used. It is possible to envisage situations where this may give rise to actions under the legislation.

G. Should a same sex couple seek to be placed in a Catholic nursing home on a shared-room basis, or one party explicitly seeks to make a conjugal visit to their resident partner and this was forbidden by the management of the Catholic institution on the basis of the doctrinal position it is foreseeable (as in F above) that litigation could similarly result.

H. In relation to Catholic bookshops, it is possible to envisage a situation in which a Catholic bookshop manager is asked to sell some books, videos and other resources which are incompatible with the doctrinal position set out above and in refusing to do so becomes subject to an action under the Regulations on the basis either of the refusal to do so or as a result of the doctrinal explanation offered for such results. Similarly in the same bookshop persons could bring proceedings under the Regulations founded on an asserted affront to dignity arising from the contents of the morality or family life sections of the bookshop.'...

36. ... Article 2.3 [of Council Directive 2000/78/EC] provided that –

'Harassment shall be deemed to be a form of discrimination within the meaning of paragraph 1, when unwanted conduct related to any of the grounds referred to in Article 1 takes place with the purpose or effect of violating the dignity of a person and of creating an intimidating, hostile, degrading, humiliating or offensive environment. In this context the concept of harassment may be defined in accordance with the national laws and practice of the Member States.'

37. Harassment is defined in reg 3(3) and (4) [of the Regulations] as follows:

'(3) A person ("A") subjects another person ("B") to harassment in any circumstances relevant for the purposes of any provision referred to in these Regulations where, on the ground of sexual orientation, A engages in unwanted conduct which has the purpose or effect of—

(a) violating B's dignity; or

(b) creating an intimidating, hostile, degrading, humiliating or offensive environment for B.

(4) Conduct shall be regarded as having the effect specified in sub-paragraphs (a) and (b) (of para. (3)) only if, having regard to all the circumstances, including, in particular, the perception of B, it should reasonably be considered as having that effect.'

38. The applicants note that the European definition uses the conjunctive 'and' after the reference to violating the dignity of a person whereas the Regulations use the disjunctive 'or'. Further the applicants note the words of reg. 3(4) which are not found in the European version. In addition the applicants note that particular regard is to be had to the perception of the victim.

39. The version of harassment found in the Regulations entered Northern Ireland legislation in 2003 by amendment of the existing equality legislation. Accordingly the same wording as to harassment is to be found in relation to employment in Article 6A of the Sex Discrimination (Northern Ireland) Order 1976, Article 3A of the Fair Employment and Treatment (Northern Ireland) Order 1998 and the Employment Equality (Sexual Orientation) Regulations 2003. In addition the harassment provision was introduced as Article 4A of the Race Relations (Northern Ireland) Order 1997 in relation to the provision of goods, facilities and services, this being the statutory model for the Regulations.

40. The applicants' concern about the harassment provisions is shared by the House of Lords and House of Commons Joint Committee on Human Rights in their sixth report of Session

2006–07 on Legislative Scrutiny: Sexual Orientation Regulations, which was ordered to be printed on 26 February 2007. At paragraph 57 the Joint Committee expresses the concern that the harassment provision is drawn too widely and defined too vaguely. In paragraph 58 it is stated:

> 'The width and vagueness of the definition of harassment in the Northern Ireland Regulations give rise to a risk of incompatibility with both freedom of speech in Article 10 ECHR and freedom of thought, conscience and religion in Article 9. The potential interference with freedom of speech arises because people may feel inhibited from saying something if they fear that a person may perceive it is a violation of their dignity or is creating an offensive environment. The potential interference with freedom of religion and belief arises because explanations of sincerely held doctrinal beliefs might be perceived as violating a person's dignity or creating an offensive environment. The exemption for religious organisations in reg. 16 of the Northern Ireland Regulations does not provide an exemption for harassment so a person who invokes the exemption in that regulation risks being caught by the harassment provision if they explain their reasons for acting. As was explained in the debates on the Northern Ireland Regulations, where a person carrying out an exempt activity seeks to explain why a person has been excluded from that activity, there is a risk that the person being told will regard the explanation as violating their dignity or as offensive and therefore claim that they have been harassed.'

41. The Joint Committee recommended that the new Regulations for Great Britain contain a more precise and narrower definition of harassment so as to reduce the risk of incompatibility with the right to freedom of speech and freedom of religion and belief.

42. The experience of the 2003 amendments to the equality legislation has not demonstrated any excessive reach of the harassment provisions in relation to gender, race, religious belief or political opinion or sexual orientation in employment. The outlawing of harassment in relation to race, religion and gender involves interference with freedom of speech and a fair balance of rights has been sought to be achieved by permitting interference with such freedom of speech on the ground of the rights of others not to be subject to harassment on the basis of gender or race or religious belief. However in outlawing harassment on the ground of sexual orientation the competing right may not only be the right to freedom of speech but may in addition be the right to manifest a religious belief. Where the exercise of the right to freedom of speech also involves the manifestation of a religious belief there will be an added basis on which to seek to justify the action. This provides an added consideration in the case of sexual orientation that may not apply in relation to harassment on the grounds of gender, race or religious belief. This was a difference accepted by the respondent. It is not clear that any consideration was given to this difference when deciding to introduce the harassment provisions into the Regulations.

43. I have found an absence of proper consultation on the harassment provisions. By reason of that finding and of the extended reach of the harassment provisions beyond that of discrimination and statutory harassment, the wider definition of harassment than that appearing in the European Directive, the concerns of the Joint Committee and the added consideration required when the offending matter is grounded in religious belief, the harassment provisions in the Regulations will be quashed …

52. … The applicants contend that the Regulations are necessarily inconsistent with and in violation of the applicants' rights to manifest their religious beliefs. Any such interference would require to be justified by the respondent. In general the applicants contend that the Regulations have the effect that the protection afforded to sexual orientation in accordance with the right to respect for private life under Article 8 and Article 14 of the Convention outweighs the protection afforded to the manifestation of religious belief under Article 9 and 14 of the European Convention so that there is a lack of fair balance between the respective rights …

> 92. Further, the applicants make general complaints about the Regulations reflecting a lack of balance between competing rights, a preference for the Article 8 rights of those sought to be protected by the Regulations over the Article 9 rights of the applicants and the introduction of more limited exemptions for religious belief than applied in other legislation. There are inevitably different views about the proper balance between the respective interests and about the balance achieved by the Regulations. This balance is essentially a matter for the legislative decision-makers, subject to compatibility with other legal obligations. For the reasons appearing above I do not accept any generalised complaints about the Regulations.

The High Court's decision had the effect of nullifying the concerns expressed at paragraphs A and C of Archbishop Brady's evidence, as well as the latter part of paragraph H. But many of the other examples of sexual orientation discrimination he sought to defend have been found to, or would likely be regarded as, breaching both the Northern Irish Regulations and the SO Regs 2007. The prohibition by a college such as St Mary's University College (see para B) which, although linked with the Catholic Church, receives state funding, of an invitation to an LGB lobby group would amount to unlawful indirect discrimination against LGB students and the imposition of prohibitions on public displays of affection by LGB students or youth group members would amount to unlawful direct discrimination unless the organised religion exception applied (see p 646 below) or the same rule was applied to their heterosexual peers (paras B and F). We saw in Chapter 9 (as regards para D) that the religious beliefs of a counsellor will not generally justify discrimination because of sexual orientation though, again, exceptions apply in the case of activities carried out for the purposes of an organised religion. We shall see below, as regards para E, that the SO Regs 2007 have resulted in the closure of religious adoption and fostering agencies which do not fall within the narrow 'organised religion' exception, though others may be saved by s193 EqA (see further pp 640–644 below). A similar approach is likely to apply to Catholic nursing homes (para G) but, as we shall see in the discussion of *Lee v Ashers Bakers* at pp 637–638 below, the concerns expressed about bookshops are unlikely to materialise.

The Protected Characteristic

Section 12 EqA, Sexual Orientation

(1) Sexual orientation means a person's sexual orientation towards—
  (a) persons of the same sex,
  (b) persons of the opposite sex, or
  (c) persons of either sex.

(2) In relation to the protected characteristic of sexual orientation—
  (a) a reference to a person who has a particular protected characteristic is a reference to a person who is of a particular sexual orientation;
  (b) a reference to persons who share a protected characteristic is a reference to persons who are of the same sexual orientation.

The definition of 'sexual orientation' in the EqA is materially similar to that in the predecessor Regulations.[13] By contrast, the concept is not defined by the Employment Equality

[13] The SO Regs provided (reg 2(1)) that 'sexual orientation means a sexual orientation towards – (a) persons of the same sex; (b) persons of the opposite sex; or (c) persons of the same sex and of the opposite sex'. The EqA 2006, under which the SO Regs 2007 were made, defined sexual orientation as (s35) 'an individual's sexual orientation towards (a) persons of the same sex as him or her, (b) persons of the opposite sex, or (c) both'.

Directive or by most other instruments which prohibit discrimination on this ground. The rationale for defining 'sexual orientation' in the SO Regs was explained by the Government as follows:

Department of Trade and Industry, *Towards Equality and Diversity*, para 12.6

A concern voiced by some during negotiations on the text of the Directive last year was that – in addition to outlawing discrimination against people on the basis of their heterosexual, homosexual or bisexual orientation – it could also be used to protect those who have unlawful sex, in particular paedophiles. We do not believe that this is the intention of the Directive. Moreover, Article 2(5) allows member states to 'take measures … which, in a democratic society, are necessary for public security, for the maintenance of public order and the prevention of criminal offences, for the protection of health and for the protection of the rights and freedoms of others.'

The *Towards Equality* consultation paper, which predated the draft SO Regs, proposed outlawing orientation discrimination on grounds of 'heterosexual, homosexual or bisexual orientation.' This approach did not escape criticism:

Hazel Oliver, 'Sexual Orientation Discrimination: Perceptions, Definitions and Genuine Occupational Requirements' (2004) 33 *Industrial Law Journal* 1, 18–19, footnotes omitted

The concept of sexual orientation is in fact a very fluid one. Sexual orientation will often change over time, as people try out different sexual experiences. Although many individuals will clearly define themselves as heterosexual or homosexual, many others may not, and still more will have had experiences in the past that depart from their present sexual identity … the idea of requiring individuals to 'label' their own sexuality in this way can be criticised. The 1980s saw the development of a movement which challenged the importance of sexual orientation to an individual's identity and showed the limits of the categories of gay, lesbian and straight in defining sexual identity. This unwillingness to fit sexuality into rigid categories continues today, in particular within the gay, lesbian, bisexual and trans-gendered communities. Queer theory explores further this problem of defining sexual orientation and identity. Queer theory is difficult to define in itself, and different writers have different conceptions of its meaning, but at a basic level it can be summarised as an approach which deconstructs categories of identity as applied to human sexuality and gender. It should be noted that queer theory is not solely relevant to sexual orientation, and it is beyond the scope of this article to explore the applications of the theory in any detail. However, a queer theory analysis can be used to challenge the binary opposition of the categories heterosexual and homosexual, such that 'sexual identities might be conceived as multiplicitous, shifting, fluid and fragmented'. If a queer theory approach is applied to a GOR, it appears to become impossible to state with any certainty whether a person is of a 'particular' sexual orientation, as is required by the Regulations.

In this respect, sexual orientation is somewhat different from other types of discrimination, where it is generally clear what category the individual belongs to.

As with the other protected characteristics, a person may be discriminated against 'because of' sexual orientation for the purposes of s13 EqA (direct discrimination) irrespective of his or her own sexual orientation, thus protecting people from discrimination because of their association with others (see generally pp 38–42). The EHRC's *Technical Guidance for Schools* provides an example at §5.11 of a pupil refused a place at a Catholic school because his parents are a lesbian couple.[14]

[14] Available at https://www.equalityhumanrights.com/en/publication-download/technical-guidance-schools-england. The EHRC's Services, public functions and associations Statutory Code of Practice provides a similar example at §4.19 concerning access to a football club. The Code is available at https://www.equalityhumanrights.com/en/publication-download/services-public-functions-and-associations-statutory-code-practice.

Direct and Indirect Discrimination under the EqA

Section 23 EqA provides, so far as relevant, that:

> **Section 23 EqA, Sexual Orientation**
>
> (3) If the protected characteristic is sexual orientation, the fact that one person (whether or not the person referred to as B) is a civil partner while another is married is not a material difference between the circumstances relating to each case.

The EHRC's Employment Code of Practice provides the following example at §3.31:

> **EHRC, 'Employment', Statutory Code of Practice**[15]
>
> Example:
>
> A worker who is gay and in a civil partnership complains that he was refused promotion because of his sexual orientation. His married colleague is promoted instead. The fact that the worker is in a civil partnership and the colleague is married will not be a material difference in their circumstances, so he would be able to refer to his married colleague as a comparator in this case.[16]

The distinction between direct and indirect discrimination has been considered in Chapter 2. It is also discussed here because much of the recent case law on the distinction between direct and indirect discrimination have related to sexual orientation. In *Bull v Hall* the Court of Appeal (CA) appeared to extend the bounds of direct discrimination in ruling that discrimination between same-sex partners and married couples amounted to direct discrimination because of sexual orientation because, at the time, same-sex couples were unable to get married. There is, of course, no exact correspondence between unmarried couples and same-sex couples, though the CA thought that the case was directly analogous with *James v Eastleigh* [1990] 2 AC 751, discussed in Chapter 2. (The references below are to the SO Regs but the case is equally applicable to the EqA.)

***Bull v Hall* [2012] EWCA Civ 83, [2012] 1 WLR 2514**

The claimants, a civilly partnered same-sex couple, had booked a double room at a small hotel run by a married couple who believed that sex was acceptable only between married men and women. This had not been conveyed to the claimants, who were refused a double room on arrival. The judge at first instance ruled that the had been directly discriminated against because of their sexual orientation and that the 2007 Regulations were not incompatible with the defendants' Article 9 rights. The CA rejected the defendants' appeal.

Rafferty LJ, with whom Hooper LJ and Sir Andrew Morritt C agreed:[17]

> 3. The appellants contend that they have been attempting to live and act in accordance with their religious beliefs, including the relevant religious belief that monogamous heterosexual marriage is the form of partnership uniquely intended for full sexual relations and that both homosexual sexual relations and heterosexual sexual relations outside marriage are sinful.

[15] https://www.equalityhumanrights.com/en/publication-download/employment-statutory-code-practice.

[16] The EHRC's Services, public functions and associations Statutory Code of Practice, n 14 above, provides a similar example at §4.31 concerning differential treatment of married and civilly partnered couples as regards upgrades on anniversary holidays.

[17] Hooper LJ also agreeing with a separate judgment delivered by Sir Andrew Morritt.

> They argue that were they obliged to offer double beds to other than married couples they could no longer run their business and the inevitability of such closure founds their argument that the judge failed to balance their rights with those of the respondents. They contend that their religious beliefs engage both heterosexual and homosexual sexual practices. Whether those beliefs be considered outdated, uneconomic for those operating an hotel, or both, nevertheless they submit that in the particular circumstances of this case they must be entitled to manifest them …
>
> 12. The appellants … argue that the judge was wrong to hold … that there was direct discrimination … contending that their religious objection to a particular sexual conduct, that is, sexual relations outside marriage, was the basis for the restriction. That there was no direct discrimination was, they argue, underlined by many unmarried heterosexual couples being affected by the restriction …
>
> 40. … in my view notwithstanding lengthy submissions on various topics, the answer to this appeal lies in a consideration of *James*'s case. It is fatal to the appellants' case. An homosexual couple cannot comply with the restriction because each party is of the same sex and therefore cannot marry. In *James*'s case the male plaintiff could never have a pension aged 61. The restriction therefore discriminates against the respondents because of their sexual orientation just as the criterion at the swimming baths discriminated against Mr James because of his sex. For this reason alone it is directly discriminatory. Put another way, the criterion at the heart of the restriction, that the couple should be married, is necessarily linked to the characteristic of an heterosexual orientation. There has in my view been direct discrimination … on grounds of sexual orientation.

Rafferty LJ then turned to consider whether the defendants' Convention rights required a different approach to be taken and concluded that thy did not. Having considered the decision of the ECtHR in *Ladele v London Borough of Islington* [2009] EWCA Civ 1357, [2010] ICR 532, discussed in Chapter 9, she continued.

> 48. The arguments there set out are to my mind compelling. Their application to these facts is even clearer if, in para [56] [in which the Court of Appeal referred to the conclusion of the ECtHR in *Pichon v France* App No 49853/99 (2 October 2001, unreported) that Article 9 ECHR did not protect pharmacists who claimed that their 'religious beliefs justified their refusal to sell contraceptive pills'], for 'pharmacists' one substituted reference to the appellants, when it might have read:
>
> > 'Accordingly, the article did not protect hoteliers who claimed that their "religious beliefs justified their refusal to provide double beds to homosexual couples" as "the provision of hotel rooms is legal and occurs nowhere other than in a hotel", and the hoteliers could "manifest [their] beliefs in many ways outside the commercial sphere".'
>
> 49. I am fortified in my conclusion by a study of the judgment in *McFarlane v Relate Avon Ltd* [2010] EWCA Civ 880, [2010] IRLR 872. Laws LJ considered both jurisprudence and founding philosophy when he said:
>
> > '[22] In a free constitution such as ours there is an important distinction to be drawn between the law's protection of the right to hold and express a belief and the law's protection of that belief's substance or content. The common law and ECHR Article 9 offer vigorous protection of the Christian's right (and every other person's right) to hold and express his or her beliefs. And so they should. By contrast they do not, and should not, offer any protection whatever of the substance or content of those beliefs on the ground only that they are based on religious precepts. These are twin conditions of a free society.
> >
> > [23] The first of these conditions is largely uncontentious. I should say a little more, however, about the second. The general law may of course protect a particular social or moral position

which is espoused by Christianity, not because of its religious imprimatur, but on the footing that in reason its merits commend themselves. So it is with core provisions of the criminal law: the prohibition of violence and dishonesty. The Judaeo-Christian tradition, stretching over many centuries, has no doubt exerted a profound influence upon the judgment of lawmakers as to the objective merits of this or that social policy. And the liturgy and practice of the established Church are to some extent prescribed by law. But the conferment of any legal protection or preference upon a particular substantive moral position on the ground only that it is espoused by the adherents of a particular faith, however long its tradition, however rich its culture, is deeply unprincipled. It imposes compulsory law, not to advance the general good on objective grounds, but to give effect to the force of subjective opinion. This must be so, since in the eye of everyone save the believer religious faith is necessarily subjective, being incommunicable by any kind of proof or evidence. It may of course be *true*; but the ascertainment of such a truth lies beyond the means by which laws are made in a reasonable society. Therefore it lies only in the heart of the believer, who is alone bound by it. No one else is or can be so bound, unless by his own free choice he accepts its claims …

[25] So it is that the law must firmly safeguard the right to hold and express religious belief; equally firmly, it must eschew any protection of such a belief's content in the name only of its religious credentials. Both principles are necessary conditions of a free and rational regime.'[18]

50. The appellants rely on *Brockie*'s case [2002] 22 DLR (4th) 174. In that case a Christian printer was required to offer services to an homosexual group, but not required to print leaflets which actively promoted an homosexual lifestyle and which was dismissive of Christian beliefs. However, though in that case the printer was required positively to do something, here the appellants were not. They were not put in a position which would have asked them so to behave as to suggest, wrongly, to an interested public that the views which apparently lay in their mouth were those they genuinely held. Far from it. All that happened here was the desire of the respondents to rent a double-bedded room in a public hotel. I have no difficulty concluding that the discrimination here differs little from that in *Ladele*'s case. The appellants are able, as I have transposed the comments in *Pichon*'s case, 'to manifest [their] beliefs in many ways outside the professional [commercial] sphere'.

51. I conclude that, to the extent to which under the Regulations the restriction imposed by the appellants upon the respondents constitutes direct discrimination, and to the extent to which the Regulations limit the manifestation of the appellants' religious beliefs, the limitations are necessary in a democratic society for the protection of the rights and freedoms of others. The appellants simply seek a further exception from the requirements in the Regulations, which already provide exceptions, in the case, for example, of certain landlords and of those who permit others to share their homes[19]. The Secretary of State has drawn what she considers the appropriate balance between the competing claims of hoteliers and (amongst others) homosexuals. Her decision has been approved by affirmative resolution. This court would be loath to interfere with her conclusions.

A similar approach was taken by the CA in *Black v Wilkinson* [2013] EWCA Civ 820, [2013] 1 WLR 2490, in which a woman who ran a 'bed and breakfast' business at her family home sought to challenge a finding that she had directly discriminated against the claimants (a same-sex couple) by refusing to honour their booking for a double room because

[18] The *MacFarlane* case was one of the three (also including *Ladele*) decided by the ECHR in *Eweida v UK* (2013) 57 EHRR 8, discussed in Ch 9.

[19] See now Sch 5 para 4(b).

she did not allow same-sex couples to share a double room and did not knowingly allow unmarried heterosexual couples to do so either. Lord Dyson MR, with whom Arden and McCombe LJJ agreed, stated at §21 that had 'some difficulty in agreeing with the view that the decision in *James*'s case compels the conclusion that there was direct discrimination in *Bull v Hall*' and that '[t]he point in *James*'s case was that the Council's policy discriminated against men on the ground of their sex because it *explicitly* provided that the concession was not available to any men until they reached the age of 65' (original emphasis). Lord Dyson pointed out that the policy in *Bull v Hall* discriminated against all unmarried couples and did not regard it as material that same-sex couples could not marry. In his Lordship's view, '*Bull v Hall* was not a case of *direct* discrimination against a homosexual couple on the ground of their sexual orientation, since there were other unmarried couples who would also be denied accommodation on the ground that they too were unmarried. It was, however, a case of *indirect* discrimination because the defendants' policy in that case put homosexual couples at a disadvantage compared with heterosexual couples on the ground of their sexual orientation'.

Notwithstanding his direct disagreement with the decision of the CA in *Bull v Hall*, Lord Dyson regarded himself as obliged to follow it, remarking at §58 that the discrimination (even if properly characterised as indirect) was unjustified. Two of the three justices of the Supreme Court (SC) who characterised the discrimination as direct, however, did so on the express basis that it distinguished between (same-sex) civil partners and (heterosexual) married couples. This appeared to reinstate the orthodox position (that is, that direct discrimination will result from less favourable treatment of a criterion other than a protected characteristic only where there is an exact fit between that criterion and the protected characteristic for which it is a proxy).

***Bull v Hall* [2013] UKSC 73, [2013] 1 WLR 3741**

Lady Hale with whom Lord Toulson agreed and Lord Kerr concurred on direct discrimination:[20]

16. The distinction between direct discrimination … and indirect discrimination … is crucial: not because direct discrimination can never be justified, as Mr Robin Allen QC reminds us, but because the justifications are expressed in the legislation. There is no general defence of justification [for direct discrimination]. Yet the distinction is by no means easy to draw, as this case illustrates all too clearly.

17. Put simply, Mr and Mrs Bull state that they did not discriminate against Mr Preddy and Mr Hall on the ground of their sexual orientation but on the ground that they were not married to one another. They have applied exactly the same policy to unmarried opposite sex couples. While discrimination against a person on the ground that she is married was outlawed in the sphere of work by the Sex Discrimination Act 1975, it has never been unlawful to discriminate against the unmarried in any of the other areas covered by the Sex Discrimination Act 1975 and now the [EqA]. They accept that it was indirect discrimination, as opposite sex couples are

[20] Lady Hale having noted at §1 that it would have been 'unthinkable less than two decades ago' to question whether it was 'lawful for a Christian hotel keeper, who sincerely believes that sexual relations outside marriage are sinful, to refuse a double-bedded room to a same sex couple?' and whether it made 'any difference that the couple have entered into a civil partnership? … That they can now be asked is a measure of how far we have come in the recognition of same sex relationships since the repeal of s 28 of the Local Government Act 1988, in Scotland in 2000 and in England and Wales in 2003 …'.

able to marry while same sex couples currently cannot do so, and so the policy puts the latter at a particular disadvantage.

18. The Court of Appeal … based their finding of direct discrimination on the well-known, if controversial, case of *James v Eastleigh BC* …

19. Had it been available to them, their Lordships might well have cited the words of Advocate General Sharpston 20 years' later, in *Bressol v Gouvernement de la Communauteì Française, Chaverot v Gouvernement de la Communauteì Française* Case C-73/08 [2010] 3 CMLR 559 at [56]:

> 'I take there to be direct discrimination when the category of those receiving a certain advantage and the category of those suffering a correlative disadvantage coincide exactly with the respective categories of persons distinguished only by applying a prohibited classification.'

In this she was building on the opinion of Advocate General Jacobs in *Schnorbus v Land Hessen* Case C-79/99 [2000] ECR I-10997 at [33]:

> 'The discrimination is direct where the difference in treatment is based on a criterion which is either explicitly that of sex or necessarily linked to a characteristic indissociable from sex. It is indirect where some other criterion is applied but a substantially higher proportion of one sex than of the other is in fact affected.'

20. Applying Advocate General Jacobs's test, it can be argued that a marriage criterion is 'indissociable from sexual orientation', in that at present persons of heterosexual orientation can marry and persons of homosexual orientation cannot. I leave aside Mr O'Neill's argument [for the defendants] that persons of homosexual orientation are free to marry persons of the opposite sex: examples abound in history of people who have done so (I would instance the long, happy and fruitful marriage of Victoria Sackville-West and Harold Nicholson). They are not free to marry a person who shares their own orientation.

21. But applying the test as stated by Advocate General Sharpston, there is not an exact correspondence between those suffering the disadvantage of being denied a double bed, and those enjoying the correlative advantage of being allowed one, with the protected characteristic. While all same sex couples were denied, so too were some opposite sex couples. Furthermore, I note that in *Schnorbus* the criterion (of having served in the army) was one which men could meet but woman could not and in *Bressol* the criterion (of having the right to reside in Belgium) was one which all Belgian nationals could meet, but only some foreigner nationals; yet in both cases the Court of Justice held that the discrimination was indirect rather than direct.

22. We do not have to construe these regulations in accordance with the jurisprudence of the Court of Justice, because they are not implementing a right which is (as yet) recognised in EU law. But as the same concepts and principles are applied in the Equality Act 2010 both to rights which are and rights which are not recognised in EU law, it is highly desirable that they should receive interpretations which are both internally consistent and consistent with EU law.

23. *Schnorbus* and *Bressol* (which were applied by this court in *Patmalniece v Secretary of State for Work and Pensions* [2011] UKSC 11, [2011] 1 WLR 783) demonstrate that this case is not on all fours with *James*. There is not an exact correspondence between the disadvantage and the protected characteristic. In *Black v Wilkinson* [2013] EWCA Civ 820, [2013] 1 WLR 2490 at [21] Lord Dyson MR confessed to 'some difficulty in agreeing with the view that the decision in *James's* case compels the conclusion that there was direct discrimination in *Preddy v Bull*'. In his view, this was not a case of direct discrimination against a homosexual couple on the ground of their sexual orientation, since there were other unmarried couples who would also be denied accommodation on the ground that they too were unmarried.

24. Were this case solely about discrimination against the unmarried, I would agree with him. He found support in the decision of the Judicial Committee of the Privy Council in *Rodriguez v Minister of Housing of the Government* [2009] UKPC 52. This too was a complaint by a same

sex couple against a criterion which restricted the right to succeed to a government tenancy to couples who were married or had children together. It was a human rights case under the Constitution of Gibraltar, where the distinction between direct and indirect discrimination is not as crucial as it is in our domestic anti-discrimination law. Nevertheless, in the opinion of the Board, this was not direct discrimination on grounds of sexual orientation, because other unmarried couples suffered the same disadvantage. But it was more severe than most cases of indirect discrimination, because the criterion was one which the couple would never be able to meet: 'Thus it is a form of indirect discrimination which comes as close as it can to direct discrimination' (at [19]).

25. … The concept of marriage being applied by Mr and Mrs Bull was the Christian concept of the union of one man and one woman. That is clear from the reference to 'heterosexual married couples' in the statement of policy which was current at the time; it is even clearer from the amended policy, which read 'out of a deep regard for marriage (being the union of one man to one woman for life to the exclusion of all others)'; and was made clear to the couple by what Mr Quinn said when Mr Preddy told him that they were civil partners.

26. Civil partnership is not called marriage but in almost every other respect it is indistinguishable from the status of marriage in United Kingdom law. It was introduced so that same sex couples could voluntarily assume towards one another the same legal responsibilities, and enjoy the same legal rights, as married couples assume and enjoy. It is more than a contract. Like marriage, it is a status, in which some of the terms are prescribed by law, and which has consequences for people other than the couple themselves and for the state. Its equivalence to marriage is emphasised by the provision in reg 3(4) [now s23(3) EqA] that being married and being a civil partner is not to be treated as a material difference for the purpose of a finding of either direct or indirect discrimination …

27. Regulation 3(4) is by no means easy to construe. It does not state in so many words that it is unlawful to discriminate between married couples and civil partners. It expressly applies equally to direct discrimination under reg 3(1) and to indirect discrimination under reg 3(3). For that reason, it is difficult to regard it as turning what would otherwise be indirect discrimination into direct. It is ostensibly about a different aspect of the discrimination inquiry, which is whether the circumstances of the people being compared are the same or not materially different from one another. In other words, it provides that people who are married and people who are civil partners are to be regarded as similarly situated.

28. In *Maruko v Versorgungsanstalt der deutschen Bühnen* Case C-267/06, [2008] ECR I-1757 at [73] the Grand Chamber of the European Court of Justice held that it was for the national court to decide whether a surviving same sex 'life partner' was in a comparable situation to a surviving spouse. That decision is made for us by reg 3(4). But the Grand Chamber went on to hold that, if they were in a comparable situation, then to treat a surviving life partner less favourably than a surviving spouse, by denying him a survivor's pension, was direct discrimination within the meaning of the Equal Treatment Directive (2000/78) (at [72]). Interestingly, they so held despite the fact that the survivor and the Commission had argued that this was indirect discrimination (at [63]).

29. As this case is not within the scope of EU law, we are not bound to follow *Maruko*, but for the sake of consistency and coherence it is highly desirable that we follow the same approach. With or without reg 3(4) I have the greatest difficulty in seeing how discriminating between a married and a civilly partnered person can be anything other than direct discrimination on grounds of sexual orientation. At present marriage is only available between a man and a woman and civil partnership is only available between two people of the same sex. We can, I think, leave aside that some people of homosexual orientation can and do get married, while it may well be that some people of heterosexual orientation can and do enter civil partnerships. Sexual relations are not a precondition of the validity of either. The principal purpose

of each institution is to provide a legal framework within which loving, stable and committed adult relationships can flourish. I would therefore regard the criterion of marriage or civil partnership as indissociable from the sexual orientation of those who qualify to enter it. More importantly, there is an exact correspondence between the advantage conferred and the disadvantage imposed in allowing a double bed to the one and denying it to the other.

30. … The important question, as Lord Phillips emphasised in *R (on the application of E) v Governing Body of JFS* [2009] UKSC 15, [2010] 2 AC 728, is what criterion was being employed by the service provider when granting a service to one and denying it to another. The reason for adopting that criterion is irrelevant. When it came to denying a double bed to Mr Preddy and Mr Hall, which they would have given to a heterosexual married couple, Mr and Mrs Bull were not only applying the criterion that they were unmarried. They were applying a criterion that their legal relationship was not that of one man and one woman, in other words a criterion indistinguishable from sexual orientation. They would undoubtedly (as their revised policy makes clear) have denied a double bed to a same sex couple who were married under some foreign law which allows it (and would do once same sex marriage becomes law in the United Kingdom).

31. The matter can be tested by imagining a different additional criterion. What if hoteliers limited their double-bedded rooms to married couples over the age of 30? They would not only be discriminating against all unmarried people, which is permitted unless it is indirectly discriminatory against a person with some protected characteristic. They would also be discriminating against a married person who is under the age of 30. That would in my view clearly be direct discrimination on grounds of age. There would be an exact correspondence between the protected characteristic of age and the criterion used for the difference in treatment.

32. Furthermore, although this is a small point, if this is not direct discrimination, it is much harder to bring it within the definition of indirect discrimination in the 2007 regulations than is a marriage criterion alone. The criterion is not simply that 'you are unmarried' but also 'you are in a civil partnership'. Most people would not regard that as a criterion which would be applied to people irrespective of their sexual orientation: it is specific to those of homosexual orientation …

Does the Human Rights Act 1998 make a difference?

41. Under art 9 of the European Convention on Human Rights Mr and Mrs Bull have the right not only to hold the religious beliefs which they hold, but also to manifest them in 'worship, teaching, practice and observance'. The courts below held that their policy was a manifestation of their religious beliefs and that has not been challenged in this appeal …

45. The question, therefore, is whether it is 'necessary in a democratic society', in other words whether there is a 'reasonable relationship of proportionality between the means employed and the aim sought to be achieved' (see, for example, *Sessa v Italy* [[2015] 60 EHRR 32] at [38]). Mr O'Neill [for the defendants] makes an eloquent plea for 'reasonable accommodation' between the two competing interests …

46. In *Sessa v Italy* a Jewish lawyer complained that the refusal to adjourn his case to a date which did not coincide with the Jewish holidays of Yom Kippur and Sukkot was an interference with his right to manifest his religion. His complaint was dismissed by a majority of four to three. A powerful minority pointed out that, for a measure to be proportionate, the authority must choose the means which is least restrictive of rights and freedoms. Thus, seeking a reasonable accommodation may, in some circumstances, constitute a less restrictive means of achieving the aim pursued. Mr Sessa had given the Italian court ample notice of the problem and reorganising the lists to accommodate him would cause minimal disruption to the administration of justice – 'a small price to be paid in order to ensure respect for freedom of religion in a multi-cultural society' (at [13]).

> 47. I am more than ready to accept that the scope for reasonable accommodation is part of the proportionality assessment, at least in some cases. This is reinforced by the decision in *Eweida v UK* (2013) 57 EHRR 213, where the Strasbourg court abandoned its previous stance that there was no interference with an employee's right to manifest her religion if it could be avoided by changing jobs. Rather, that possibility was to be taken into account in the overall proportionality assessment, which must therefore consider the extent to which it is reasonable to expect the employer to accommodate the employee's right …
>
> 52. Sexual orientation is a core component of a person's identity which requires fulfilment through relationships with others of the same orientation. As Sachs J of the South African Constitutional Court movingly put it in *National Coalition for Gay and Lesbian Equality v Minister of Justice* [1998] 3 LRC 648 at [117]:
>
> > 'While recognising the unique worth of each person, the Constitution does not presuppose that a holder of rights is as an isolated, lonely and abstract figure possessing a disembodied and socially disconnected self. It acknowledges that people live in their bodies, their communities, their cultures, their places and their times. The expression of sexuality requires a partner, real or imagined.'
>
> 53. Heterosexuals have known this about themselves and been able to fulfil themselves in this way throughout history. Homosexuals have also known this about themselves but were long denied the possibility of fulfilling themselves through relationships with others. This was an affront to their dignity as human beings which our law has now (some would say belatedly) recognised. Homosexuals can enjoy the same freedom and the same relationships as any others. But we should not underestimate the continuing legacy of those centuries of discrimination, persecution even, which is still going on in many parts of the world. It is no doubt for that reason that Strasbourg requires 'very weighty reasons' to justify discrimination on grounds of sexual orientation. It is for that reason that we should be slow to accept that prohibiting hotel keepers from discriminating against homosexuals is a disproportionate limitation on their right to manifest their religion.
>
> 54. There is no question of (as Rafferty LJ put it) replacing 'legal oppression of one community (homosexual couples) with legal oppression of another (those sharing the defendants' beliefs)'. If Mr Preddy and Mr Hall ran a hotel which denied a double room to Mr and Mrs Bull, whether on the ground of their Christian beliefs or on the ground of their sexual orientation, they would find themselves in the same situation that Mr and Mrs Bull find themselves today.

Lord Kerr concurred on the basis that the claimants had clearly been treated less favourably than a married (heterosexual) couple from whose circumstances theirs could not be distinguished, and that this was because of their sexual orientation. Whether or not their sexual orientation operated on the defendants' minds was immaterial (citing *R (E) v Governing Body of JFS* [2009] UKSC 15, [2010] 2 AC 728, discussed in Chapter 7). Lord Toulson's speech was to the same effect as Lady Hale's while Lord Neuberger and Lord Hughes would have characterised the events as unjustified indirect discrimination. Whatever their individual reasoning the justices were unanimous in the view that the claimants had been subject to unlawful discrimination because of their sexual orientation.[21]

[21] See also *R (Cornerstone (North East) Fostering & Adoption Services v Ofsted)* [2021] EWCA Civ 1390, [2022] 2 All ER 516, discussed below and in Chs 9 and 10, in which the CA considered whether a policy of requiring that potential foster carers be married and act in compliance with Christian teaching on sexuality amounted to direct discrimination because of sexual orientation.

The SC was once again asked to consider the parameters of direct sexual orientation discrimination in *Lee v Ashers Baking Company Ltd*, an appeal from Northern Ireland's CA.

***Lee v Ashers Baking Company Ltd* [2018] UKSC 49, [2020] AC 413**

The claimant was a gay man who volunteered for QueerSpace, an organisation which campaigned for same-sex marriage in Northern Ireland. Ashers bakery was run by a Christian couple who believed that only heterosexual marriage was consistent with the Bible and acceptable to God. It refused the claimant's request to provide him with a cake iced with the slogan 'support gay marriage'.

The county court had accepted that the refusal of service amounted to direct discrimination on grounds of sexual orientation and belief and Northern Ireland's CA that it amounted to direct associative discrimination on grounds of sexual orientation (that aspect of the decision is considered in Chapter 2). The SC allowed Ashers' appeal. The bakers had not refused to provide Mr Lee with a service because he was gay, and would have refused to provide the cake he ordered to any customer irrespective of their sexual orientation. The county court had erred in concluding that support for same-sex marriage was indissociable from sexual orientation such that it stood as a proxy for the protected characteristic.[22]

Lady Hale (with whom Lords Mance, Kerr and Hodge and Lady Black agreed):

22. The District Judge did *not* find that the bakery refused to fulfil the order because of Mr Lee's actual or perceived sexual orientation. She found that they 'cancelled this order because they oppose same sex marriage for the reason that they regard it as sinful and contrary to their genuinely held religious beliefs. As the Court of Appeal pointed out, she did not take issue with the submission that the bakery would have supplied Mr Lee with a cake without the message 'support gay marriage' and that they would also have refused to supply a cake with the message requested to a heterosexual customer. The objection was to the message, not the messenger.

23. Not surprisingly, therefore, Mr Scoffield QC, who appears for the appellants, argues that it was not open to the judge to find that there was direct discrimination on grounds of sexual orientation. The reason for treating Mr Lee less favourably than other would-be customers was not his sexual orientation but the message he wanted to be iced on the cake. Anyone who wanted that message would have been treated in the same way …

24. Mr Scoffield also criticises the comparator chosen by the District Judge. She compared the treatment of Mr Lee, not with a person of different sexual orientation who wanted the same cake, but with a person of different sexual orientation who wanted a different message: 'support hetero-sexual marriage'. This, he argues, is inconsistent with [the definition of direct discrimination], which requires a comparison with the treatment of other 'persons' not messages; and with [the equivalent of s23(1) EqA] which requires that the relevant circumstances in each case must be the same, or not materially different.

25. The District Judge also considered at length the question of whether the criterion used by the bakery was 'indissociable' from the protected characteristic and held that support for same sex marriage was indissociable from sexual orientation (para [42]). This is, however, to misunderstand the role that 'indissociability' plays in direct discrimination. It comes into play when the express or overt criterion used as the reason for less favourable treatment is not

[22] It also erred in finding discrimination on grounds of religion where the religion was that of the respondent rather than the claimant. On this aspect of the case see further Ch 9.

> the protected characteristic itself but some proxy for it. Thus, in the classic case of *James v Eastleigh Borough Council* [1990] 2 AC 751, the criterion used for allowing free entry to the council's swimming pool was not sex but statutory retirement age. There was, however, an exact correspondence between the criterion of statutory retirement age and sex, because the retirement age for women was 60 and the retirement age for men was 65. Hence any woman aged 60 to 64 could enter free but no man aged 60 to 64 could do so. Again, in *Bull v Hall* [2013] UKSC 73, [2013] 1 WLR 3741, letting double-bedded rooms to married couples but not to civil partners was directly discriminatory because marriage was (at that time) indissociable from heterosexual orientation. There is no need to consider that question in this case, as the criterion was quite clear. But even if there was, there is no such identity between the criterion and sexual orientation of the customer. People of all sexual orientations, gay, straight or bi-sexual, can and do support gay marriage. Support for gay marriage is not a proxy for any particular sexual orientation …
>
> 35. In reaching the conclusion that there was no discrimination on grounds of sexual orientation in this case, I do not seek to minimise or disparage the very real problem of discrimination against gay people. Nor do I ignore the very full and careful consideration which was given to the development of the law in this area, to which Mr Allen QC [for the claimant] drew our attention at considerable length. Everyone, as art 1 of the Universal Declaration of Human Rights put it 70 years ago is 'born free and equal in dignity and rights'. Experience has shown that the providers of employment, education, accommodation, goods, facilities and services do not always treat people with equal dignity and respect, especially if they have certain personal characteristics which are now protected by the law. It is deeply humiliating, and an affront to human dignity, to deny someone a service because of that person's race, gender, disability, sexual orientation or any of the other protected personal characteristics. But that is not what happened in this case and it does the project of equal treatment no favours to seek to extend it beyond its proper scope.[23]

The SC rejected the claim of associative discrimination in *Lee v Ashers* on the facts found by the judge, but there is no doubt that discrimination by A against B because of C's sexual orientation will breach the EqA.

Harassment

We saw in Chapter 2 that sexual orientation harassment may occur, as in *English v Thomas Sanderson Blinds Ltd* [2008] EWCA Civ 1421, [2009] ICR 543, where a person is subject to unwanted treatment related to sexual orientation which violates their dignity or creates an intimidating, hostile, degrading, humiliating or offensive environment for them, irrespective of whether the person is straight or gay, and also irrespective of whether the harassers know or think that the person is gay. The same applies to all the protected characteristics.

It should be noted that harassment related to sexual orientation (like that related to religion or belief) is not regulated under Part 3 (services), Part 5 (premises), Part 6 (education)

[23] The claimant's application to the ECtHR was declared inadmissible because he had not expressly invoked Arts 8, 9 10 or 14 in the domestic and so had failed to exhaust domestic remedies: *Lee v UK*, App No 18860/19, [2022] IRLR 371.

or Part 7 (associations) EqA. By way of example, s29 EqA, which regulates discrimination and harassment in relation to goods, services and public functions, provides that:

Section 29 EqA, Provision of services, etc

(3) A service-provider must not, in relation to the provision of the service, harass—

(a) a person requiring the service, or
(b) a person to whom the service-provider provides the service …

(6) A person must not, in the exercise of a public function that is not the provision of a service to the public or a section of the public, do anything that constitutes discrimination, harassment or victimisation …

(8) In the application of section 26 [harassment] for the purposes of subsection (3), and subsection (6) as it relates to harassment, neither of the following is a relevant protected characteristic—

(a) religion or belief;
(b) sexual orientation.[24]

Some instances of harassment may amount to discrimination, if they involve less favourable treatment of an individual because of his or her sexual orientation which amounts to the subjection to a detriment of that individual to a detriment.[25] The EHRC's *Technical Guidance for Schools* provides an example at §3.29 of a teacher at a Church of England school who 'tells pupils that homosexuality is "wrong", and that gay and lesbian people will "burn in hell" unless they are "cured of the disease"', suggesting that this may amount to direct discrimination on the grounds of sexual orientation against a gay pupil in the class who is 'is deeply offended and intimidated'. The *Technical Guidance* further suggests at §3.7 that schools must ensure that their policies are non-discriminatory and that 'there should be no differentiation between the seriousness with which a school deals with bullying for reasons arising from a protected characteristic and the bullying for reasons not connected with a protected characteristic'.

EHRC's Technical Guidance for Schools[26]

Examples:

A school has a policy covering racial bullying and any pupil who participates in racial bullying is excluded for at least one day. However, the school does not have a policy dealing with homophobic bullying and pupils who participate in such bullying are usually given only a detention. This could lead to direct sexual orientation discrimination unless the bullying of homosexual pupils was not related to their sexual orientation …

Exceptions

We saw in Chapter 9 that religious organisations are provided with significant scope under the EqA to discriminate on grounds of *religion or belief*. This chapter is concerned with the situations in which religious organisations and others are permitted to discriminate on grounds of *sexual orientation*. It will become apparent, if it is not already, that it may be

[24] Sections 33(6), s85(1) and 103(2) EqA respectively (s85(10) also excluding harassment related to gender reassignment from Part 6 protection).

[25] Section 29(2)(c) EqA (this where the alleged discrimination concerns the provision of services. Subjection to a detriment is also regulated as an instance of discrimination by Part 6 (education: s85(2)(f)) and Part 7 (associations: s101(2)(d)), while Part 4 (premises) regulates discriminatory treatment of a person 'with respect to things done in relation to persons seeking premises' (s33(1)(c)).

[26] n 14 above.

difficult to disentangle discrimination because of religion or belief (generally the discriminator's) from discrimination because of sexual orientation (generally the person alleging discrimination). The general position is that the religion or belief of the discriminator is likely to go to the motivation, rather than the reason, for the discrimination (see discussion of *James v Eastleigh* and related case law in Chapter 2). But there are other cases where a person's sexual orientation or behaviour will have the effect of offending religious doctrine and making them religiously unfit in the eyes of a religious community to hold office, or perhaps to remain, within that community. Carrying such a judgment into effect is likely to amount to or involve discrimination *both* because of sexual orientation *and* religion or belief (or perhaps a lack thereof). Certainly, the fact that treatment complained of amounts to or involves discrimination because of religion or belief does not defend it from challenge as discrimination because of sexual orientation. This can be important because, as illustrated in the *Cornerstone* case extracted below, narrower defences are applicable to sexual orientation than to religion or belief discrimination.

Section 193 EqA

Section 193 EqA is set out in Chapter 4 at p 190. Like its various predecessor provisions, it provides an exception from the prohibition on discrimination (other than discrimination based on colour, or related to work) where benefits are restricted to 'persons who share a protected characteristic' pursuant to a charitable instrument, and the provision of the benefits is 'a proportionate means of achieving a legitimate aim', or 'for the purpose of preventing or compensating for a disadvantage linked to the protected characteristic'. Much of the litigation concerning s193 EqA has involved religious organisations seeking to discriminate on grounds of sexual orientation (though they have tended to characterise this discrimination as concerning religion or belief (adherence to orthodox religious norms).

One of the main areas of controversy about the SO Regs 2007, which prohibited sexual orientation discrimination in the provision of services for the first time in Great Britain, concerned their application to adoption and fostering organisations associated with churches (in particular the Roman Catholic Church) which generally accepted as adoptive parents only those who married (and therefore in heterosexual relationships) and which sometimes also imposed faith-related requirements the effect of which would be to exclude many LGB people. Faith-based adoption agencies were given a period of grace to comply with the SO Regs 2007, but this expired at the end of 2008 by which stage adoption agencies were no longer permitted to discriminate against LGB people or couples in placing children. According to a 2010 Christian Institute publication, the effect of the SO Regs 2007 was that two of the 13 Catholic adoption agencies in Great Britain had ceased to provide adoption services by that date while the remainder began to accept same-sex couples as adopters, generally after having severed ties with the Church.[27] The Scottish Catholic agency had 'successfully changed its charitable objects to allow it to continue to operate as an adoption agency in full accordance with its Roman Catholic ethos' by taking advantage of s193 EqA, while another agency, Catholic Care in Leeds, was challenging the Charity Commission's refusal to allow it to change its charitable objectives.[28] According to the Christian Institute, 'Cornerstone (North East) Adoption and Fostering Service ... continues to require prospective adopters to adhere to the Evangelical Christian faith'.

[27] https://www.christian.org.uk/resource/adoption-agencies-shut-under-equality-laws.

[28] The Charity Commission was and is responsible for deciding whether a charity's proposed objects meet the requirements of charity law, which involves an assessment of public benefit.

***Catholic Care (Diocese of Leeds) v Charity Commission for England and Wales* [2010] EWHC 520 (Ch), [2010] 4 All ER 1041**

The Catholic Care challenge referred to immediately above resulted in the decision of the High Court in this case, discussed at some length in Chapter 4. In short, the charity sought to change its Memorandum of Association to state that it would 'only provide adoption services to heterosexuals and such services to heterosexuals [would] only be provided in accordance with the tenets of the [Roman Catholic] Church' so that it could rely on to rely on the then equivalent of s193 EqA. The Charity Commission denied permission to make this change because the Commission interpreted the word 'benefits' as meaning only benefits of a charitable nature provided to the charity's beneficiaries (the adoptive children), and so concluded that there would be no benefit to the proposed change. The High Court allowed the charity's appeal and remitted the matter to the Charity Commission, which again refused permission to the charity to amend its objects. Catholic Care's appeal against this decision failed. In rejecting the charity's appeal Sales J (as he then was) accepted that the interest of children in being placed for adoption could justify discrimination on grounds of sexual orientation but accepted on the evidence that this had not been demonstrated on the evidence. The charity closed in 2013.

Cornerstone (North East) Adoption and Fostering Service, the evangelical Christian agency referred to in the Christian Institute report, also became involved in litigation. The decision well illustrates the tangled relationship between discrimination based on religion or belief and that based on sexual orientation.

***R (Cornerstone (North East) Fostering & Adoption Services v Ofsted)* [2021] EWCA Civ 1390, [2022] 2 All ER 516**

Cornerstone's Memorandum and Articles of Association provided that its objects were 'to provide a high quality adoption and fostering child care service according to Christian principles to alleviate the needs of children and young people who are, or may be, temporarily or permanently separate from their families and to promote the relief and care of children without families or parents able to care for them by the provision of substitute families able to meet their needs with the aim of improving the conditions of life and future of such children and young people.' The charity had contractual relationships with a number of local authorities on whose behalf it placed children. Cornerstone required all employees and potential adopters and foster carers to sign a Statement of Beliefs and a Code of Practice which required that they 'conduct themselves in a manner that will give proper expression to faith in Jesus Christ as Lord'; including through prayer, Bible reading and church attendance; honesty and sobriety; and 'abstain[ing] from all sexual sins including immodesty, the viewing of pornography, fornication, adultery, cohabitation, homosexual behaviour and wilful violation of your birth sex'. It also required that potential adopters and foster carers be married.

In 2011 the Charity Commission had accepted Cornerstone's assertion that it did not discriminate because of sexual *orientation* but on the basis of standards of sexual *behaviour*. Ofsted, which regulates adoption and fostering agencies as well as schools and other educational institutions, concluded that Cornerstone's policy breached the EqA and Articles 8 and 14 ECHR (and, accordingly, the Human Rights Act 1998 (HRA)) and ordered Cornerstone to change its policy. Cornerstone challenged this finding and instruction which it claimed involved a misinterpretation of the EqA and of Articles 8 and 14 ECHR, and claimed that Ofsted had discriminated against it on grounds of religion.

The High Court accepted that Ofsted had erred in deciding that Cornerstone had discriminated against potential foster carers on grounds of religion in view of the defences provided by the EqA, and because the discrimination was justifiable under Article 14 (see Chapter 9 for discussion of this aspect of the case), but otherwise rejected Cornerstone's claim. In particular, the judge found that Cornerstone's discrimination was not saved by s193 EqA because it was disproportionate to the articulated aims of increasing the pool of evangelical Christian foster carers; affording critical support to carers; allowing those within the evangelical Christian community to serve by promoting stable and durable placements; manifesting the beliefs of evangelical Christianity in the practice of Christian charity and the support of Christian family life to the benefit of the carers, the children cared for, Cornerstone and society as a whole; and increasing the number of foster placements available against what was alleged to be an overall national shortage of foster carers for the number of placements required for children. There was, the judge concluded, no evidence that there was any shortage of evangelical Christian carers or that recruiting such carers would respond to any difficulties in matching children and he 'fail[ed] to see how excluding a category of evangelical Christians (gay men and lesbians) from being foster carers achieves the aim which Cornerstone says it has of increasing the number of evangelical Christian carers'. The judge also 'fail[ed] to see how a discriminatory policy positively impacts on Cornerstone's aim of affording critical support to carers' or 'aids or assists in allowing those within the evangelical Christian community to serve by promoting stable and durable placements, unless it be said that gay and lesbian evangelical Christians cannot provide such placements, a position which, as I have said, I flatly reject'. He 'fully accept[ed] that Cornerstone is founded upon what it perceives to be evangelical Christian beliefs' but 'its policy on "homosexual behaviour" is driven, first and foremost, by its belief such conduct is simply not compatible with Christianity, and that it is sinful ... Cornerstone has failed to show by convincing evidence that its policy benefits children and young people in a way it would not if the policy did not discriminate. But conduct which is discriminatory on the grounds of sexual orientation that is pursued because of religious belief is not thereby justified'.

The High Court also ruled that Cornerstone was a hybrid public authority because it exercised functions on behalf of public authorities and ruled that that its policy breached Articles 8 and 14 ECHR so far as it discriminated on grounds of sexual orientation.

The CA rejected Cornerstone's appeal. It confirmed that Cornerstone's policy amounted to direct discrimination because of sexual orientation. It agreed with the assessment of proportionality by the judge below which, it was common ground, was equally applicable to the question of proportionality under s193 EqA and the alleged breaches of Convention rights by Cornerstone and Ofsted.[29] The Court stressed that particularly

[29] Also to indirect discrimination had this been in issue, which the CA did not accept (see Ch 2).

weighty reasons were required to justify differential treatment on the grounds of sexual orientation and agreed that Cornerstone's policy was disproportionate, though it would have accorded more weight than the High Court to some of those aims.

Jackson LJ (with whom Asplin and Davies LJJ agreed):

> 126. In *R (on the application of SC) v Secretary of State for Work and Pensions* [2021] UKSC 26, [2022] AC 223 … Lord Reed considered … sexual orientation discrimination, noting that the ECtHR had stated that differences in treatment require 'particularly serious reasons' by way of justification, while at [109]–[111] he described a similar approach to religious discrimination. However, he also noted that the court has taken a less strict approach in some cases of religious discrimination where other factors were relevant. He summarised at [115]–[116] the court's approach to justification generally and noted that it is a matter of some complexity. He identified a number of general factors that may be relevant in the circumstances of a particular case and concluded that, unless one factor is of overriding significance, it is necessary for the court to make a balanced overall assessment.
>
> 127. Here, 'other factors' are relevant to the overall assessment. It is of particular significance that Parliament has, in relation to religious organisations that offer a service to the public, given a clear indication that discrimination on the basis of sexual orientation is impermissible. The Judge described this feature as 'determinative' at [287] and 'conclusive' at [305]. I would prefer to regard it as a significant indicator of what Parliament intended when the question of proportionality is considered in the contexts of indirect discrimination generally under s 19, charities under s 193, and Convention rights under the HRA 1998. I would not treat it as conclusive because it is possible to envisage circumstances in which … different treatment on grounds of sexual orientation could be justified on the facts of a particular case, for example where there was good evidence that a significant number of children would not be fostered at all but for a discriminatory policy[30] …
>
> 129. Cornerstone draws attention to general statements from the ECtHR, such as those in *Manoussakis v Greece* (1996) 23 EHRR 387, where Jehovah's Witnesses had been convicted of establishing and operating a place of worship without prior authorisation. At [44] it was said that the restrictions imposed on the freedom to manifest religion called for very strict scrutiny. So, Mr O'Neill QC [for Cornerstone] argues, there is an equivalence: 'Your "very weighty reasons" are my "very strict scrutiny."' This is not the effect of the case law, either at European or domestic level. Enhanced protection on the ground of sexual orientation exists to counteract historic injustice towards homosexuals, the causes of which include religious beliefs.
>
> 135. The fact that the Charity Commission approached this case differently to *Catholic Care* does not in my view assist Cornerstone. Consistently with the outcome on Ground 1, the Commission's stance one way or another cannot determine whether the recruitment policy is a proportionate means of pursuing a legitimate aim.
>
> 136. Similarly, the ontological argument about the existence or non-existence of gay evangelical Christians is in my view a false trail. The Judge found at [203] that, as in any other community, there will be members of that faith community who will be homosexual … The Judge further

[30] Citing the judgment of Alito J in *Fulton v City of Philadelphia* (2021) 593 US 2021 in which the US SC struck down a ban imposed on a Catholic fostering agency because it would not place children with unmarried couples or with same-sex married couples in which the justice emphasised the fact that it had left children at risk of being left homeless. Jackson LJ further pointed out that in that case the US Constitutional protection of the free exercise of religion was also in issue.

inferred that a section of gay and lesbian evangelical Christians would want to foster through an agency founded on an evangelical Christian ethos and which would support them in all of the ways Cornerstone describes. That inference was in my view reasonable. The Judge was not obliged to adopt Cornerstone's doctrinal definition of evangelical Christians so as to find that gay and lesbian evangelical Christians are not merely unidentified but non-existent. That would be to substitute the precepts of the faith for the reality. If gay evangelical Christians wishing to foster are few and far between, it is no doubt to some extent because of those precepts, and not because people like that do not exist. Like the Judge, I therefore reject the proposition that there are no victims of this policy.

137. Furthermore, an important purpose of the EA 2010 is to support progress on equality and it must be recognised that religious doctrine does not stand still: see, for example the remarks of Lord Walker in *R (Williamson) v Secretary of State for Education and Employment* [2005] UKHL 15, [2005] 2 AC 246 at [57]. The law is entitled to have regard to the rights of those who might wish to be free of a discriminatory practice currently endorsed by their faith. Ms Hannett QC [for Ofsted] encapsulated these ideas in the submission that there is such a thing as 'regulatory virtue' in securing compliance with the EA 2010, though she did not rest her case on that alone. At first, that seemed to me to be a chilly submission, but on further thought I would accept that it is only by protecting those who are discriminated against in small numbers that equality can be progressed for wider communities. For completeness on the issue of victims, the *Northern Ireland Human Rights Commission* case was a decision about the statutory remit of that body and does not assist Cornerstone[31] …

142. Drawing matters together, I therefore accept that some of Cornerstone's arguments deserved to be placed in the balance in its favour on the question of justification. In consequence, I would hold that the real issue arose at stage four of *Bank Mellat* [[32]]: whether, balancing the severity of the measure's effects on the rights of the persons to whom it applies against the importance of the objective, the former outweighs the latter. As to that, I have reached the clear conclusion that the Judge was right to find that the different treatment arising under Cornerstone's recruitment policy was not justified, either through the lens of the EA 2010 or of the HRA 1998 …

The Court's reasonings on justification are further considered in Chapter 2 and the proportionality assessment to be conducted under s193 EqA is also considered in *R (Z) v Hackney LBC* [2020] UKSC 40 [2021] 1 WLR 4327, discussed in Chapter 3. The purpose of considering the *Cornerstone* case here is to demonstrate some of the practical implications of regulating sexual orientation discrimination.

Religious Organisations

Marriage

Schedule 3 paras 25A–25AA EqA are concerned with discrimination because of the religion or belief of the discriminator in the context of marriage and civil partnerships. Schedule 3 para 25A provides that it is not unlawful for a person to refuse to permit or take part in a marriage according to religious rites of a same-sex couple and para 25AA provides that

[31] *In re Northern Ireland Human Rights Commission* [2002] UKHL 25, [2002] HRLR 35, see discussion at p 268.
[32] *Bank Mellat v HM Treasury (No 2)* [2013] UKSC 38–39, [2014] AC 700, see p 60 above.

religious organisations and persons acting on their behalf may refuse to allow religious premises to be used in connection with the registration of civil partnerships, or to provide, arrange, attend, facilitate or participate in civil partnerships 'for the reason that the person does not wish to do things of that sort in relation to civil partnerships generally, or those between two people of the same sex, or those between two people of the opposite sex'. This provisions were added by the Marriage (Same Sex Couples) Act 2013, whose explanatory notes provide as follows:

Marriage (Same Sex Couples) Act 2013, Explanatory Notes[33]

Examples

- The governing body of a religious organisation meets to consider whether to opt in to conducting marriage of same sex couples according to its rites. It decides not to. This would be lawful and no member of the governing body, nor the organisation itself, could be forced, by legal action or otherwise, to change its decision.
- A religious organisation opts in to conducting marriage of same sex couples. However, one of the organisation's ministers does not approve of such marriage and does not wish to solemnize such a marriage. This would be lawful. The religious organisation arranges for an alternative minister to conduct the marriage ceremony for the same sex couple.
- A person who acts as an authorised person at marriages in her local church does not wish to do so in relation to same sex marriage ceremonies, even though the church has opted in to marriage of same sex couples. It would be lawful for her to refuse. A marriage registrar is asked to step in to cover that role, but does not wish to do so because he does not approve of marriage of same sex couples. It would be unlawful discrimination for him to refuse.
- An organist who usually plays at wedding services at a church does not wish to play at a wedding service of a same sex couple. This would be lawful because he is involved in the religious act of worship i.e. the religious ritual of the wedding service. This is the case whether he is a volunteer or employed by the church.
- A commercial photographer is asked to photograph a wedding of a same sex couple. It would be unlawful sexual orientation discrimination for her to refuse because she does not approve of marriage of same sex couples. This is because her role is not part of the religious marriage service.
- A volunteer flower arranger who usually decorates the place of worship for wedding services refuses to do so for a wedding of a same sex couple because she does not approve of such marriages. Her role is not part of the religious marriage service, but her refusal would nonetheless be lawful because the service she offers is to the church rather than to the public or a section of the public, so it is not covered by the Equality Act 2010. If a commercial flower arranger asked by a same sex couple to decorate their wedding venue refused to do so because he does not approve of marriage of same sex couples, this would be unlawful sexual orientation discrimination. This is because his role is not part of the religious marriage service and the service he provides is to the public and so is covered by the Equality Act 2010.
- A chaplain employed by a university is asked to solemnize the marriage of an employee of the university with a person of the same sex. Although his religious organisation has opted in to marriage of same sex couples, he refuses because he does not wish to marry a same sex couple. This is lawful. The university makes alternative arrangements by finding an alternative chaplain to conduct the ceremony.

[33] https://www.legislation.gov.uk/ukpga/2013/30/notes.

Work

The standard GOR defence provided by Schedule 9 para 1 EqA is discussed in Chapter 4 and referred to below. Here we are concerned only with Schedule 9 para 2, also discussed in Chapter 6, which provides that:

Schedule 9 para 2 EqA, Religious requirements relating to sex, marriage etc, sexual orientation

(1) A person (A) does not contravene a provision mentioned in sub-paragraph (2) by applying in relation to employment a requirement to which sub-paragraph (4) applies if A shows that—

(a) the employment is for the purposes of an organised religion,
(b) the application of the requirement engages the compliance or non-conflict principle, and
(c) the person to whom A applies the requirement does not meet it (or A has reasonable grounds for not being satisfied that the person meets it).

The provisions in para 2(2) are section 39(1)(a) and (c) and (2)(b)–(c) EqA (which regulate access to jobs, promotion, transfer or training and any other work-related benefits, facilities or services, and dismissal), and the equivalent provisions applicable to public and private offices. Schedule 9 para 2(3) makes similar provision as regards qualifications for posts to which para 2(1) applies. Schedule 9 para 2(4) then provides that the requirements referred to in para 2(1) include:

- not to be married or a civil partner of a person of the same sex;
- not to be the civil partner of a person of the opposite sex;
- requirements related to sexual orientation.

Schedule 9 paras 2(5) and 2(6) provide that the application of a requirement engages the compliance principle if it is applied so as to comply with the doctrines of the religion, and the non-conflict principle if, 'because of the nature or context of the employment, the requirement is applied so as to avoid conflicting with the strongly held religious convictions of a significant number of the religion's followers'.

Paragraph 2 applies in a narrower range of circumstances than Schedule 9 para 1 (because it applies only to employment for the purposes of an organised religion), but the defence it provides is significantly broader in that it does not contain any requirement that the discrimination be a proportionate means of achieving a legitimate aim. The provision and its predecessor has been relied on primarily in relation to discrimination on grounds of sexual orientation.

Schedule 9 para 2 is based on Article 4(1) of Council Directive 2000/78/EC which provides as follows:

Article 4(2), Council Directive 2000/78/EC

2. Member States may maintain national legislation in force at the date of adoption of this Directive or provide for future legislation incorporating national practices existing at the date of adoption of this Directive pursuant to which, in the case of occupational activities within churches and other public or private organisations the ethos of which is based on religion or belief, a difference of treatment based on a person's religion or belief shall not constitute discrimination where, by reason of the nature of these activities or of the context in which they are carried out, a person's religion or belief constitute a genuine, legitimate and justified occupational requirement, having regard to the organisation's ethos. This difference of treatment shall be implemented taking account of Member States' constitutional provisions and principles, as well as the general principles of Community law, and should not justify discrimination on another ground.

Provided that its provisions are otherwise complied with, this Directive shall thus not prejudice the right of churches and other public or private organisations, the ethos of which is based on religion or belief, acting in conformity with national constitutions and laws, to require individuals working for them to act in good faith and with loyalty to the organisation's ethos.

Article 4(2) expressly applies only to discrimination on grounds of religion. The SO Regs nevertheless included Reg 7(3) which was similar in effect to para 2 though it applied only to 'a requirement related to sexual orientation' whereas para 3 applies also to requirements concerning marriage/ civil partnership (see above). Much of the concern expressed in relation to Reg 7(3), and indeed to Article 4(2), involved the scope it might permit for religious organisations to discriminate against, for example, gay men and lesbian women on the grounds that active homosexuality is inconsistent with 'good faith and ... loyalty to [their] ethos.' The extract below gives a flavour.

Changing Attitude,[34] 'UK Secular News' (2003)

Following representations from the Archbishop's Council and other church groups, the government agreed to include a clause in the [SO Regulations] granting religious organisations the legal right to exclude gay and lesbian people from employment for the first time ... The decision was criticised by MPs from all parties as well as liberal sections of the church and gay rights groups. The legislation will enshrine in British law for the first time the right to discriminate against gays and lesbians in employment. It will allow any religious organisation to sack or refuse to employ a person on the grounds of 'sexual orientation.'

In a four-page submission to government, the Archbishops' Council argued the European directive would mean that 'actions taken by the church to enforce its own doctrines and beliefs in relation to sexual conduct could be found unlawful. For example a bishop who denied ordination to someone in a gay or lesbian relationship might be found to be discriminating unlawfully on grounds of sexual orientation.'... The Department of Trade and Industry conceded that the new clause would affect not only clergy but also teachers in church schools and employees of religious charities or hospitals. Sources close to the DTI claim Downing Street forced it to accept the clauses.

The Lesbian and Gay Christian Movement said the move would institutionalise homophobia in a way that 'makes section 28 look like a tea party.' LGCM's general secretary, the Revd Richard Kirker, said it would give Churches protection and privilege if they chose not to employ lesbian or gay people and added that government ministers had allowed themselves to become 'apologists for the most intolerant religious bigots'. LGCM accused the Government of capitulating to right-wing fundamentalists: the concessions won now allowed them to discriminate against lesbian and gay people.

In the *Amicus* case the High Court had considered a challenge to the inclusion of Reg 7(3) within the SO Regs.

***R (Amicus) v Secretary of State for Trade & Industry* [2004] EWHC 860 (Admin), [2007] ICR 1176**

Richards J:

89. The Secretary of State has made clear that [Reg 7(3)] is intended to form part of the implementation of article 4(1) of the Directive (the general derogation for occupational requirements) rather than of article 4(2) (the derogation in respect of differences of treatment based on a person's religion or belief where religion or belief constitutes an occupational requirement) ...

94. In his submissions for the Amicus applicants, Mr Singh contends that regulation 7(3) is unduly broad. It is additional to regulation 7(2), which applies to employment whether or not for the purposes of an organised religion, and it would be unnecessary unless it were capable

[34] An Anglican lesbian, gay, bisexual, transgender and heterosexual network.

of applying to a wider range of circumstances than regulation 7(2). A requirement related to sexual orientation can be applied, under regulation 7(3)(b), either (i) so as to comply with the doctrines of an organised religion or (ii) so as to avoid conflicting with the strongly held religious convictions of a significant number of the religion's followers. It thereby permits discrimination on grounds of sexual orientation in circumstances where the requirement does not pursue a legitimate objective or is not proportionate. The very absence of a specific requirement of proportionality, to be applied by the courts by reference to the facts of individual cases, is a particular ground of complaint. In addition, issue is taken with the authorising of discrimination on grounds of *perceived* sexual orientation, by regulation 7(3)(c)(ii), ie the same point as that already considered in relation to regulation 7(2)(c)(ii). All these matters, it is submitted, mean that the exception fails to meet the strict requirements of the derogation in article 4(1) of the Directive.

95. To illustrate those concerns, Mr Singh submits that regulation 7(3) appears to authorise discrimination in the following cases, among many others: (a) a church is unwilling to engage a homosexual man as a cleaner in a building in which he is liable to handle religious artefacts, to avoid offending the strongly-held religious convictions of a significant number of adherents; (b) a school for girls managed by a Catholic Order dismisses a science teacher on learning that she has been in a lesbian relationship, reasoning that such a relationship is contrary to the doctrines of the Order; (c) a shop selling scriptural books and tracts on behalf of an organisation formed for the purpose of upholding and promoting a fundamentalist interpretation of the Bible is unwilling to employ a lesbian as a sales assistant since her sexual orientation conflicts with the strongly held religious convictions of a significant number of Christians and/or of that particular organisation; (d) an Islamic institute open to the general public but frequented in particular by Muslims is unwilling to employ as a librarian a man appearing to the employer to be homosexual, reasoning that his sexual orientation will conflict with the strongly held religious convictions of a significant number of Muslims. In each of those cases, it is submitted, it is doubtful whether the characteristic of sexual orientation could be said to be a genuine and determining occupational requirement and in accordance with the principle of proportionality; and if those conditions *were* satisfied, the case would fall within regulation 7(2) and it would not be necessary to rely on regulation 7(3) …

103. The case for the Secretary of State is in summary that the concerns expressed about the width of regulation 7(3) are misplaced. The exception has a very narrow scope. The criteria are tightly drawn and are to be construed strictly (since this is a derogation from the principle of equal treatment). The exception represents a proportionate striking of the balance between the competing interests involved. Without prejudice to the decisions that might be reached by employment tribunals in individual cases, Miss Carss-Frisk suggests [for the Secretary of State] that it is unlikely that any of the examples put forward by Mr Singh would meet the conditions in regulation 7(3) …

115. The main question, as it seems to me, concerns the scope of the exception. If it had as wide a scope as was submitted by Mr Singh and Mr O'Neill [who appeared for the NUT], then it would be open to serious objection on the grounds that they put forward. But if it is as narrow in scope as contended for by Miss Carss-Frisk, the objection advanced loses much of its force. I think it clear from the Parliamentary material that the exception was intended to be very narrow; and in my view it is, on its proper construction, very narrow. It has to be construed strictly since it is a derogation from the principle of equal treatment; and it has to be construed purposively so as to ensure, so far as possible, compatibility with the Directive. When its terms are considered in the light of those interpretative principles, they can be seen to afford an exception only in very limited circumstances.

116. The fact that the exception applies, by regulation 7(3)(a), only to employment 'for purposes of an organised religion' is an important initial limitation. I accept Miss Carss-Frisk's

> submission that that is a narrower expression than 'for purposes of a religious organisation,' or the expression 'where an employer has an ethos based on religion or belief,' as used in the corresponding regulations relating to discrimination on grounds of religion or belief. I also accept the example she gave, that employment as a teacher in a faith school is likely to be 'for purposes of a religious organisation' but not 'for purposes of an organised religion.'
>
> 117. The conditions in regulation 7(3)(b) impose very real additional limitations. In my view the condition in regulation 7(3)(b)(i), that the employer must apply the requirement 'so as to comply with the doctrines of the religion,' is to be read not as a subjective test concerning the motivation of the employer, but as an objective test whereby it must be shown that employment of a person not meeting the requirement would be incompatible with the doctrines of the religion. That is very narrow in scope. Admittedly the alternative in regulation 7(3)(b)(ii) is wider; but even that is hemmed about by restrictive language. The condition must be applied 'because of the nature of the employment and the context in which it is carried out' – which requires careful examination of the precise nature of the employment 'so as to avoid conflicting with the strongly held religious convictions of a significant number of the religion's followers.' Again this is in my view an objective, not subjective, test. Further, the conflict to be avoided is with *religious convictions*, which must be *strongly held*; and they must be the convictions of a *significant number* of the religion's followers. This is going to be a very far from easy test to satisfy in practice …
>
> 119. One further point I should deal with in connection with regulation 7(3)(b) concerns its opening words, which refer to an employer applying 'a requirement related to sexual orientation.' Those words may in one way make the provision wider in scope than the regulation 7(2), where the relevant occupational requirement is expressed in terms of 'being of a particular sexual orientation.' I note that the choice of wording in regulation 7(3) was deliberate, so as to accommodate the concerns of some Churches about certain forms of sexual *behaviour* rather than sexuality as such. In my view the wording is apt to cover the point, and it may have been prudent to use such wording in order to avoid argument about the scope of the expression 'being of a particular sexual orientation.' I do not consider, however, that the point has a material effect on the present analysis. The protection against discrimination on grounds of sexual orientation relates as much to the manifestation of that orientation in the form of sexual behaviour as it does to sexuality as such. I have already mentioned this when looking generally at the fundamental rights in issue in this case. The wording of the derogation in article 4(1) of the Directive, which refers to a difference of treatment 'which is based on a characteristic related to' sexual orientation, is wide enough to embrace a difference of treatment based on sexual behaviour related to sexual orientation …

The approach taken by Richards J to Reg 7(3) SO Regs robbed the provision of much of its sting and this aspect of the decision was not appealed.

'A good loss: *R (Amicus–MSF section) v Secretary of State for Trade and Industry*' 130 *Equal Opportunities Review*

> The main challenge to reg 7(2), which applies where sexual orientation is a genuine and determining occupational requirement, and it is proportionate to apply the requirement, is that the GOR covers not only where a person does not in fact meet the requirement as to sexual orientation, but also where it is 'reasonable' for the employer 'not to be satisfied' that the person meets it. It was argued that allowing discrimination to be based on perceived sexual orientation could lead to employers stereotyping, such as acting on the basis of appearance. Mr Justice Richards

helpfully holds that if a decision is based on mere assumptions or social stereotyping, then it will not meet the requirement of reasonableness …

The scope of [Reg 7(3)] was a major concern of the trade unions bringing the judicial review application, and they succeeded in securing a ruling that will protect the overwhelming majority of their gay and lesbian members … The result of the ruling in this case is that there will be very few jobs in which it will be permissible to discriminate on grounds of sexual orientation. Neither of the GOR exceptions are likely to be applicable outside a religious or counselling environment, and even in such a context, following the High Court's ruling, it will be difficult for the employer to establish that discrimination on grounds of sexual orientation falls within the scope of the exception …

There is a further bonus in the High Court's judgment, the importance of which may transcend all the other points decided … the government has tried to draw between a person's 'orientation', which is protected, and manifestations of their orientation ….

The point arose in the judicial review application in the context of the meaning of a requirement 'related to' sexual orientation in reg 7(3)(b). Mr Justice Richards rules that 'the protection against discrimination on grounds of sexual orientation relates as much to the manifestation of that orientation in the form of sexual behaviour as it does to sexuality as such.' He adds that 'sexual orientation and its manifestation in sexual behaviour are both inextricably connected with a person's private life and identity.'

The application of para 2 was squarely in issue in the case immediately below, which is also discussed in Chapters 2 and 4.

***Reverend Canon Pemberton v Right Reverend Inwood* [2018] EWCA Civ 564, [2018] ICR 1291**

The claimant, a Church of England priest, married his male partner. As a result, the Bishop revoked his Permission to Officiate (PTO) at services, with the effect that he could not conduct services within the diocese. The Bishop also refused to grant the claimant an Extra Parochial Ministry Licence (EPM) which would have permitted him to be appointed chaplaincy and bereavement manager in a faith centre at a hospital, and so the discrimination complained of fell within Part 5 EqA (see Chapter 4). It ruled, however, that the discrimination was permitted by Schedule 9 para 2 EqA.

The CA accepted that EPML was a 'relevant qualification' though PTO was not, and that the Bishop had acted as a qualifications body in refusing EPML, though not in revoking the PTO, though it found that the Bishop had been entitled to discriminate against the claimant in pursuit of a GOR:

Asplin LJ:

48. Her Honour Judge Eady QC dealt with [para 3] in the following way:

'112. The question then arises as to whether the ET erred in concluding that the respondent had applied a requirement that engaged the compliance principle for the purpose of para. 2(5) Schedule 9? Here, I agree with the respondent, the 'doctrines' of the religion must refer to the teachings or beliefs of that religion, not to what might more narrowly be understood by 'doctrine' within a specific religious community such as the Church of England. Whilst a court will not simply accept an assertion as to the doctrines of a religion, it equally cannot be expected to enter into theological debate to determine those doctrines for itself. The ET was entitled to find that the doctrines – the teachings and beliefs – of the Church of England were as stated by Canon B30 and, with specific regard to same sex marriages permitted by the Act, as evidenced by the Pilling report and the Pastoral Guidance … That being so, it was equally entitled to accept that those doctrines were clear: marriage for the purposes of the Church of England was 'between one man and one woman'.

113. The ET had then to determine, however, whether the requirement applied by the respondent (that the claimant not be in a same sex marriage) was applied so as to comply with the doctrines thus identified. On this question, it is fair to say that the reasoning is hard to follow in places; the ET's conclusions … draw upon both the apparent incompatibility of the claimant's marriage with the doctrines of the Church and the conflict that thus arose with the claimant's 'canonical duty of doctrinal obedience'. That duty arose from the claimant's oath of canonical obedience and was owed to the respondent, as Bishop of the Diocese, to obey him in matters of canon law … The respondent's predecessor as bishop had written to the claimant on 17 March 2014, making clear his understanding of the Church's position in respect of same sex marriage and asking that the claimant follow the House of Bishops' Pastoral Guidance. The claimant had declined to do so. It was that combination of circumstances that the ET permissibly concluded led the respondent to apply the requirement that the claimant not be in a same sex marriage …'

49. Paragraph [202] of the ET decision is as follows:

'We then get the letter he wrote to Ms Toor on 5 July … [the 7 July letter]. So that is clear, is it not? The reason for not granting the licence is a) the Respondent's duty to uphold the Church's doctrine: marriage between a man and a woman only within the Church; and b) the Claimant having "clearly and consciously acted in a way which was fundamentally inconsistent" with therefore the reiteration of the doctrine via the Pastoral Guidance and the clear stricture in relation to the consequences for priest [sic] such as the Claimant if he did not. That to us interposes issues of incompatibility by way of the marriage doctrine and also breach of the doctrine, because that is what it is, of canonical obedience.'…

62. In relation to the second question, it seems to me that Her Honour Judge Eady QC was correct to conclude that 'doctrines' for the purposes of para 2(5) of Sch 9 must be read more widely than what is considered strictly by a particular church or religious organisation to be 'doctrine' by that organisation. As Mr Linden points out [for the defendant] para 2(5) uses the term 'doctrines' and not 'doctrine' and is intended to apply in relation to all religions. It seems to me that if one reads the sub-paragraph as a whole, in the context of the exception in para 2 as a whole, it should be construed to mean the teachings and beliefs of the particular religious organisation which may be wider than what it itself labels 'doctrine.' Even if that were not the case, in this case, Canon A5 itself refers to the 'doctrine of the Church of England' in wide terms and states merely that such doctrine is to be found 'in particular' in the specific documents referred to. Accordingly, it seems to me that Her Honour Judge Eady QC was correct to conclude that the ET was entitled to find that the doctrines, as in teachings and beliefs of the Church of England, were as stated in Canon B30 with specific regard in relation to same sex marriages to the statement of Pastoral Guidance from the House of Bishops. She was quite right to note that the Court cannot be expected to enter into a theological debate in order to determine the doctrines itself: see [112]. Indeed, the Court ought not to do so. She was also right to find that the ET was entitled to find that the doctrines in relation to marriage were clear.

63. It was not necessary, as Mr Jones suggested [for the claimant], that there should be an express provision prohibiting a priest from entering into a same sex marriage and spelling out the consequences if he did. The teaching and in fact, the doctrine of the Church of England (in the sense in which the Church uses the term) is quite clearly spelt out in Canon B30. Paragraph 1 of that Canon makes clear that the Church of England considers marriage to be between one man and one woman. By its very terms it delimits the concept of marriage in accordance with the teachings and doctrine of the Church in a way which excludes same sex marriage.

Furthermore, it is made clear in para 3 that a priest is expected to uphold what is described expressly as 'the Church's doctrine of marriage.' As Mr Linden pointed out, Canon B30 does not state expressly that the Church of England's doctrine of marriage does not include polygamy but it is quite clear that it does so.

64. Although the Marriage (Same Sex Couples) Act 2013 has extended the meaning of marriage, the position of the Church of England is carefully preserved in ss 1(3), (4) and 11. Mr Jones conceded that the Church of England does not accept same sex marriage as 'marriage' for its purposes at all. As the statement of Pastoral Guidance from the House of Bishops made clear at para 9, since the 2013 Act, there has been a divergence between the general understanding and definition of marriage in law and the 'doctrine of marriage held by the Church of England and reflected in the Canons and the Book of Common Prayer'. A clear statement on marriage and same sex marriage is contained at paras 9, 11, 12, 26, 27 and 28 of that document, including the need to obey the Church on these issues. Paragraph 26 states expressly that marrying someone of the same sex would be at variance with the teachings of the Church of England. Paragraphs 27 and 28 leave little to the imagination in relation to the effect upon a clergyman's 'good standing' of entering into a same sex marriage. This is all the more so when coupled with the form of the Preface to the Declaration of Assent and the Declaration itself contained at C15 of the Canons and the requirement to exemplify the teachings of the Church contained at C26, to which reference is also made in paras 23 and 26 of the statement of Pastoral Guidance.

65. In my view, the facts that the Bishop of Lincoln, in different circumstances, imposed a different sanction upon the Canon and that the Reverend Mr Cain (who was an incumbent at the time) was dealt with in another way are neither here nor there. Furthermore, although I do not consider that it has any particular weight at all, it seems to me that the Registrar's report to the Bishop of London in relation to Mr Cain points not only to 'doctrines' but also to 'doctrine' as including all the teachings of the Church of England. In addition, I consider the question of whether the oath of obedience is enforceable to be irrelevant. As Her Honour Judge Eady QC pointed out, the ET was entitled to take into account all of the matters she referred to at [113].

66. It follows that I also consider that Her Honour Judge Eady QC did not err in law in deciding at [113] of the EAT Determination that the ET was entitled to find that the requirement had been applied so as to comply (emphasis added) with the doctrines as found. Accordingly, I would dismiss the appeal in relation to Sch 9 para 2.

Services

Schedule 23 para 2, also discussed in Chapter 9, provides that an organisation which falls within para 2(1)[35] 'does not contravene Part 3, 4 or 7, so far as relating to religion or belief or sexual orientation, only by restricting:

Schedule 23, para 2(3) EqA, Organisations relating to religion or beliefi

(a) membership of the organisation;
(b) participation in activities undertaken by the organisation or on its behalf or under its auspices;
(c) the provision of goods, facilities or services in the course of activities undertaken by the organisation or on its behalf or under its auspices;
(d) the use or disposal of premises owned or controlled by the organisation'.[36]

[35] See Ch 9.

[36] Para 2(4) provides similarly that 'A person does not contravene Part 3, 4 or 7, so far as relating to religion or belief or sexual orientation, only by doing anything mentioned in sub-paragraph (3) on behalf of or under the auspices of the organisation'.

Organisations which fall within para 2(1) are those whose sole or main purpose is not commercial, and whose purpose is:

(a) to practise a religion or belief,
(b) to advance a religion or belief,
(c) to teach the practice or principles of a religion or belief,
(d) to enable persons of a religion or belief to receive any benefit, or to engage in any activity, within the framework of that religion or belief, or
(e) to foster or maintain good relations between persons of different religions or beliefs.

In addition, where sexual orientation discrimination is concerned, para 2(7) provides that the exception applies only where it is necessary to comply with the doctrine of the organisation, or to avoid conflict with strongly held religious convictions of a significant number of the religion's followers.[37] Schedule 23 para 2(10) provides that:

Schedule 23, para 2(10) EqA, Organisations relating to religion or belief

This paragraph does not permit anything which is prohibited by section 29, so far as relating to sexual orientation, if it is done—

(a) on behalf of a public authority, and
(b) under the terms of a contract between the organisation and the public authority.

Paragraph 2(11) also provides that 'In the application of this paragraph in relation to sexual orientation, sub-paragraph (1)(e) [which allows discrimination by organisations whose purpose is to (e) to foster or maintain good relations between persons of different religions or beliefs] must be ignored'.

The claimant in *Cornerstone* sought to rely on schedule 23 para 2. As we saw in Chapter 9, this succeeded in relation to discrimination on grounds of religion or belief. But para 2(10) precluded reliance on para 2(1) because of Cornerstone's links with public authorities. The High Court rejected Cornerstone's argument that (1) it did not provide services or perform a public function for the purposes of s29 EqA and (2) that, if it did, 'the conduct which is allegedly prohibited under section 29 is not made under the terms of a contract between it and a public authority', concluding that the phrase 'on behalf of' did not require a relationship of agency but covered a situation in which Cornerstone undertook a task that the local authority would otherwise have been required to undertake. The Court of Appel agreed.

Schedule 23, para 2(5) EqA, Organisations relating to religion or belief

'A minister does not contravene Part 3, 4 or 7, so far as relating to religion or belief or sexual orientation, only by restricting—

(a) participation in activities carried on in the performance of the minister's functions in connection with or in respect of the organisation;
(b) the provision of goods, facilities or services in the course of activities carried on in the performance of the minister's functions in connection with or in respect of the organisation.

As discussed in Chapter 9, para 2(5) permits ministers to restrict participation in 'activities carried on in the performance of the minister's functions in connection with or in respect of [a religious] organisation' and the provision of goods, facilities or services in the course of such activities, where (in the case of sexual orientation discrimination) the restriction is necessary to comply with the doctrine of the organisation, or to avoid conflict with strongly

[37] Or in a belief-based organisation, relevant beliefs.

held religious convictions of a significant number of the religion's followers.[38] As we saw in Chapter 9, the definition of 'minister' is narrow and it would not be possible for a religious organisation to rely on the exception in para 2(5) in relation to the kinds of activities referred to in para D of the examples provided by Archbishop Brady in the *Christian Institute* case (pp 623–627 above) unless the counselling was being provided by a priest. Schedule 23 para 2(1) might apply, however, to such counselling as long as it was delivered by an agency whose sole or main purpose was not commercial, and whose purpose was very closely connected with the Catholic religion. It might also apply to paras B insofar as a Catholic youth club was not delivering services on behalf of and under the terms of a contract between the club and a public authority. The example provided by Archbishop Brady in para F would appear to fall squarely within Schedule 23 para 2 because it would involve the imposition of restrictions on the use or disposal of premises owned or controlled by church/diocese, which is manifestly a non-commercial organisation falling within para 2(3).

The example referred to by the Archbishop in para G is more difficult. It is clear from the *Bull v Hall* case discussed at pp 623–624 that a hotel or bed and breakfast provider may not discriminate as regards sleeping accommodation on grounds of sexual orientation. To the extent that a church-run care home was contracted to local authorities for the provision of care services it would also be excluded from reliance on para 2(1) by para 2(1). Where this was not the case, however, it is possible that such a care home might fall within the para 2(1) exception if, for example, it was run by a Diocese or an order of nuns.

Work-Related Exceptions

The discussion of Schedule 9 para 2 relates to work but only in the context of employment for the purposes of organised religions. The normal GOR defence provided by Schedule 9 para 1 EqA is discussed in Chapter 4. That there are few circumstances in which sexual orientation discrimination is likely to be permitted by para 1 was recognised by the explanatory notes issued by the then Department for Trade and Industry in connection with the SO Regs and (RB Regs).

DTI, 'Explanatory Notes for the Employment Equality (Sexual Orientation) Regulations and the Employment Equality (Religion and Belief) Regulations', paras 75, 77–81[39]

It is very rare indeed that being of a particular sexual orientation is a genuine occupational requirement for a job ... In the vast majority of jobs, a person's sexual orientation has no bearing on whether or not they can carry out the job in question. However, a GOR may be justified in a small number of cases.

- For example, it may be possible to establish a GOR to be gay or lesbian, having regard to the context of the work, for persons in a position of leadership in, or representing the public face of, an organisation concerned with advising gay men and lesbians about their rights, or promoting those rights. In those circumstances there may be an issue of credibility which makes it a GOR for the person to be gay or lesbian in order to perform the functions of the post. On the other hand, for posts in the organisation which simply involve advising gays and lesbians about their legal rights, no GOR would apply because it is not essential to be gay or lesbian in order to offer good legal advice to gays and lesbians. The mere fact that the people receiving the advice might prefer to deal with a gay or lesbian adviser does not make it a GOR for the job.

[38] Or in a belief-based organisation, relevant beliefs.

[39] https://webarchive.nationalarchives.gov.uk/ukgwa/20070603164510/http://www.dti.gov.uk/er/equality/so_rb_longexplan.pdf.

In practice, if an employer already employs a person who does not have the required sexual orientation/religion or belief in a particular post, this will provide a very strong indication that having that sexual orientation/religion or belief is not a GOR for the post. Also, in many jobs, it will be sufficient that employees have some understanding of, and respect for, the religion or belief in question, or persons of the particular sexual orientation, as the case may be. If that is the case, then being of that particular sexual orientation/religion or belief would not be a genuine occupational requirement for the job.

Proportionate application

... Proportionality will depend on the facts of each case. But generally, an appropriate means is one which is suitable to achieve the aim in question, and which actually does so. A necessary means is one without which the aim could not be achieved; it is not simply a convenient means. This will include consideration of whether the aim could be achieved by other means which have lesser discriminatory effects.

- For example, it would not be proportionate for an employer to rely on a GOR to exclude persons of a particular sexual orientation ... when filling a vacancy if he already has other employees of that sexual orientation ... who could reasonably carry out those duties. (If it caused the employer excessive difficulties to make such arrangements, it would be justified not to do so). In this way an employer could recruit a new employee to a post with duties to which no GOR applied ...

The other work-related exception of general application to the prohibition on sexual orientation discrimination is found in Schedule 9 para 18, which provides as follows:

Schedule 9 para 18 EqA, Benefits dependent on marital status, etc

(1) A person does not contravene this Part of this Act, so far as relating to sexual orientation, by doing anything which prevents or restricts a person who is not married within sub-paragraph (1A) from having access to a benefit, facility or service—

  (a) the right to which accrued before 5 December 2005 (the day on which section 1 of the Civil Partnership Act 2004 came into force), or
  (b) which is payable in respect of periods of service before that date.

(1A) A person is within this sub-paragraph if the person is—

  (a) a man who is married to a woman, or
  (b) a woman who is married to a man, or
  (c) married to a person of the same sex in a relevant gender change case.

(1B) The reference in sub-paragraph (1A)(c) to a relevant gender change case is a reference to a case where—

  (a) the married couple were of the opposite sex at the time of their marriage, and
  (b) a full gender recognition certificate has been issued to one of the couple under the Gender Recognition Act 2004.

(2) A person does not contravene this Part of this Act, so far as relating to sexual orientation, by providing married persons and civil partners (to the exclusion of all other persons) with access to a benefit, facility or service.

The effect of this paragraph is to provide that people who are part of same-sex couples (other than couples which are same-sex because one has been legally recognised as changing gender in accordance with the Gender Recognition Act 2004) are not entitled to the same treatment as people who are in heterosexual marriages in respect of benefits which are associated with periods of service prior to December 2005 (this being the date in which Britain first formally recognised same-sex relationships). The significance of this is felt predominantly in relation to pension entitlement which is typically accrued on a gradual basis over years of employment. Someone who started work at 21, made pension contributions consistently over his or her working life and retired at age 65 in December 2021, for example, would be entitled to equal treatment as regards pension entitlements for a same-sex spouse only in respect of 17/45 years of service (just over one-third of the total) with the effect that the spouses's pension payment would likely be only about two-thirds that of a spouse of the opposite sex. This would be the case irrespective of the fact that the worker made the same contributions as a worker who was married to an individual of the other sex. Unsurprisingly, this state of affairs was subject to legal challenge in the following case which resulted in the effective nullification of para 18, though it remains on the statute book.

***Walker v Innospec Ltd* [2017] UKSC 47, [2017] ICR 1077**

The claimant was a gay man who had been in receipt of pension since 2003. He had entered into a civil partnership with his partner, with whom he had since 1993, shortly after the coming into force of the Civil Partnership Act 2004 in 2005, and had subsequently married him. He sought an assurance that, in the event of his death, this employer would pay the spouse's pension for which his pension scheme provided to his civil partner. The employer refused because the claimant's service predated 5 December 2005.

The claimant brought proceedings in the employment tribunal which ruled that para 18(1) must be read so as to be compliant with Council Directive 2000/78/EC. The EAT overturned this decision on the basis that the Directive did not have retrospective effect, the CA agreeing that the Directive required equal treatment only in respect of service and/or contributions paid after 2 December 2003, the deadline for its transposition. The SC allowed the claimant's further appeal. A majority ruled that the claimant's husband (assuming he survived the claimant to whom he and remained married) was entitled to the same treatment as a wife in respect of each of the claimant's years of service.

Lord Kerr (with whom Lady Hale Kerr and Lord Reed agreed[40]):

Some general considerations

18. ... The recognition of same-sex partnerships, which is not required by EU law, was motivated by an appreciation that formal equality for same-sex couples will always be deficient if they are unable to avail themselves of the legal benefits attendant on marriage. In her foreword to the consultation paper preceding the introduction of the Civil Partnership Act 2004, Jacqui Smith, the Minister of State for Industry and the Regions and Deputy Minister for Women and Equality, noted:

> 'Many [same-sex couples] have been refused a hospital visit to see their seriously ill partner, or have been refused their rightful place at their partner's funeral. Others find themselves unable to access employment benefits reserved only for married partners. Couples who have supported each other financially throughout their working lives often have no way of gaining pension rights. Grieving partners can find themselves unable to stay in their shared home or to inherit the possessions they have shared for years when one partner dies suddenly without leaving a will. In so many areas, as far as the law is concerned, same-sex relationships simply do not exist. That is not acceptable.'

[40] Lords Carnwath and Hughes ruling that the appeal should be allowed on more limited grounds.

19. Although EU law does not impose any requirement on member states to recognise same-sex partnerships, the European Court of Justice has held that if a status equivalent to marriage is available under national law, it is directly discriminatory contrary to the Framework Directive for an employer to treat a same-sex partner who is in such a partnership less favourably than an opposite-sex spouse (*Maruko v Versorgungsanstalt der deutschen Bühnen* (Case C-267/06) EU:C:2008:179, [2008] ECR I-1757). Thus in the UK it is unlawful as a matter of both EU and domestic law for an employer to deny a same-sex civil partner or spouse of an employee a benefit that would be provided to a spouse of the opposite sex.

20. That is not an end of the matter, however. When it introduced civil partnerships, Parliament also decided to include an exception to the prohibition on discrimination in the context of employment. That is now contained in para 18 of Sch 9 of the Equality Act 2010 …

22. The general rule, applicable in most modern legal systems, is that legislative changes apply prospectively. Under English law, for example, unless a contrary intention appears, an enactment is presumed not to be intended to have retrospective effect …

23. EU law is no different in this respect. As the Court of Appeal observed, the Court of Justice of the European Union (CJEU) has developed two principles to establish the temporal application of EU legislation – the 'no retroactivity' principle and the 'future effects' principle. These were described by the CJEU in *Land Nordrhein-Westfalen v Pokrzeptowicz-Meyer* (Case C-162/00) EU:C:2002:57, [2002] ECR I-1049, (paras 49–50) as follows:

> 'According to settled case law, in order to ensure observance of the principles of legal certainty and the protection of legitimate expectations, the substantive rules of Community law must be interpreted as applying to situations existing before their entry into force only in so far as it clearly follows from their terms, their objectives or their general scheme that such effect must be given to them …'

It also follows from settled case law that new rules apply immediately to the future effects of a situation which arose under the old rules …

26. The application of these principles presents a challenge when one is dealing with entitlement to an occupational retirement pension. Conventionally, the right to a pension accumulates over decades. During the time that the right is accruing, actuarial assumptions are made based on existing legal conditions, notwithstanding that the pension is payable in the future. Those assumptions are upset when, because of changes in social values, a new equal treatment provision is introduced. It is not immediately easy to identify the point at which entitlement to a pension becomes 'permanently fixed' – whether for example at the date of retirement or when the pension is paid …

The appellant's arguments

28. For the appellant, Mr Martin Chamberlain QC submits that the Court of Appeal has fundamentally misconstrued the nature of the issues involved in the jurisprudence of the CJEU. Mr Chamberlain argues that the line of cases on which the Court of Appeal relied[41] are all concerned with temporal limitations imposed on claims for equal pay for men and women, not for claims for equal treatment in relation to pension entitlement for heterosexual and gay men and women. Moreover, that limitation was, he says, introduced as an exceptional

[41] Case 43/75, *Defrenne v Sabena* EU:C:1976:56, [1976] ECR 455, [1976] ICR 547; Case C-170/84, *Bilka-Kaufhaus GmbH v Weber von Hartz* EU:C:1986:204, [1986] ECR 1607, [1987] ICR 110; Case C-262/88, *Barber v Guardian Royal Exchange Assurance Group* EU:C:1990:209, [1990] ECR I-1889, [1991] 1 QB 344; Case C-109/91, *Ten Oever v Stichting Bedrijfspensioenfonds voor het Glazenwassers-en Schoonmaakbedrijf* EU:C:1993:833, [1993] ECR I-4879, [1995] ICR 74; Case C-57/93, *Vroege v NCIV Instituut voor Volkshuisvesting BV* EU:C:1994:352, [1994] ECR I-4541, [1995] ICR 635 discussed by Lord Kerr at §§29–43.

measure to deal with the consequence of the abrupt, financially catastrophic impact that retrospective entitlement to equality of pay would have had on the economies of many member states of the EU …

43. The Court of Appeal in the present case understood the decision in *Ten Oever* [*v Stichting Bedrijfspensioenfonds voor het Glazenwassers-en Schoonmaakbedrijf* Case C-57/93, EU:C:1993:833, [1995] ICR 74] to establish a general principle of EU law, to the effect that entitlement to a survivor's pension is 'permanently fixed' as it is earned. It concluded that the same principle could be applied where the law is changed not by a judgment, but by legislation. It was influenced to this view by the opinion that the same policy considerations lay behind the no retroactivity principle and the CJEU's power to limit the retrospective application of its judgments. To an extent, the same policy considerations are in play. In both scenarios one can acknowledge the need to ensure legal certainty and to protect the legitimate expectations of those who rely on the law as it was thought to be.

44. But it is vital to keep the two concepts distinct. 'No retroactivity' and 'future effects' are principles of law which apply to all EU legislation, unless a contrary intention can be found. The *Barber* exception [the decision of the ECJ in *Barber v Guardian Royal Exchange Assurance Group* EU:C:1990:209, [1991] 1 QB 344; Case C-109/91 that its recognition that men should be entitled to benefit from occupational pensions at the same age as women should apply only in respect of benefits earned after the date of the judgment] is an example of a technique used by the CJEU to limit the generally retroactive application of its *judgments*, which it will only exercise in the most exceptional circumstances and where the impact would be truly 'catastrophic'. The court limits the temporal application of its judgments in cases where reliance has been placed on a different understanding of the law and legitimate expectations may be upset, but only in the most special circumstances. Therefore, how the court exceptionally applies a temporal limitation to one of its rulings has no inevitable bearing on the temporal application of legislation as a matter of principle …

46. I agree with Mr Chamberlain's analysis of the relevant jurisprudence and I turn now to consider his principal argument that two recent decisions of the Grand Chamber of the CJEU (which troubled the Court of Appeal because of their perceived incongruence with what that court considered to be the fundamental principles governing retroactivity) put success for Mr Walker's claim beyond doubt. Those decisions are *Maruko v Versorgungsanstalt der deutschen Bühnen* (Case C-267/06) EU:C:2008:179, [2008] ECR I-1757 (*Maruko*) and *Römer v Freie und Hansestadt Hamburg* (Case C-147/08) EU:C:2010:425 (opinion), EU:C:2011:286 (judgment), [2011] ECR I-3591 (*Römer*) …

55. From this it is clear that, unless evidence establishes that there would be unacceptable economic or social consequences of giving effect to Mr Walker's entitlement to a survivor's pension for his husband, at the time that this pension would fall due, there is no reason that he should be subjected to unequal treatment as to the payment of that pension …

56. … The point of unequal treatment occurs at the time that the pension falls to be paid. If Mr Walker married a woman long after his retirement, she would be entitled to a spouse's pension, notwithstanding the fact that they were not married during the time that he was paying contributions to his pension fund. Whether benefits referable to those contributions are to be regarded as 'deferred pay' is neither here nor there, so far as entitlement to pension is concerned. Mr Walker was entitled to have for his married partner a spouse's pension at the time he contracted a legal marriage. The period during which he acquired that entitlement had nothing whatever to do with its fulfilment …

58. … the financing of Innospec's retirement scheme should have been planned taking into account a possible change in Mr Walker's marital status. He could not have been denied

entitlement to a spouse's pension if, perfectly legally, he married a woman after he retired. His marriage to his current partner is just as legal as would be a heterosexual marriage. His entitlement to a spouse's pension is equally well founded ...[42]

Must effect be given to paragraph 18 or should it be disapplied – the second issue?

73. The appellant claims that, applying the principles established by *Kücükdeveci v Swedex GmbH & Co KG* (Case C-555/07) EU:C:2010:21, [2010] ECR I-365, para 18 must be disapplied. As Lord Mance explained in *R (Chester) v Secretary of State for Justice* [[2013] UKSC 63, [2014] AC 271 §§61-61] ... for the general principle of non-discrimination to apply, the context must fall within EU law. Both the EAT and the Court of Appeal considered that non-discrimination did not become a fundamental principle of EU law until the transposition deadline of the Framework Directive ...

74. Mr Chamberlain submits that this is incorrect, arguing that the CJEU did not say that non-discrimination only became a general principle of EU law in 2003. Its relevant finding was that Mr Römer's claim for equal pension benefits only came within the material scope of EU law from that time. Whether that is right or not need not be decided finally in this case because Mr Chamberlain's second argument disposes of the issue. That is that non-discrimination on grounds of sexual orientation is now a principle of EU law. It follows that any contemporary denial to his husband of a spouse's pension, calculated on all the years of Mr Walker's service, would be incompatible with the Framework Directive. In so far as para 18 authorises that, it must be disapplied on the basis of the principles articulated in *Kücükdeveci* and *Chester*...

Sexual Orientation and the ECHR/HRA

The protection afforded by the ECHR (in particular, Articles 8 and 14 ECHR) is evident from the discussion above, in particular in the decisions of the CA and SC in *Bull v Hall* at pp 632–636 above. The ECtHR had been active in challenging sexual orientation discrimination well before the CJEU or the domestic courts. Notwithstanding the parasitic nature of Article 14 ECHR (which prohibits discrimination) the European Court of Human Rights (ECtHR) developed a right not to be discriminated against because of sexual orientation from the Article 8 right to privacy read alone or in conjunction with Article 14. In *Dudgeon v UK* (1983) 5 EHRR 573 the ECtHR ruled that the criminalisation of same-sex sexual contact between adult males in private breached Article 8, a ruling it reiterated in *Norris v Ireland* (1991) 13 EHRR 186. In *Smith & Grady v UK* (2000) 29 EHRR 493 the Court considered the investigation and discharge from military service of the applicants pursuant to the then ban on LGB service personnel. The challenge in the domestic courts had failed, the CA ruling in *R v MOD ex p Smith* [1996] QB 517 that the policy could not be categorised as irrational. The ECtHR ruled that the intrusive investigations into the applicants' private lives and their subsequent discharge breached their Article 8 rights to a private life.[43] The decisions in *Smith & Grady* and the associated *Lustig-Prean & Beckett* cases resulted in the removal of the ban on gays in the military in 2001. The equalisation of the age of consent that year pre-dated the ECtHR's decision in *L & V v Austria* (2003) 36 EHRR 55 that unequal ages of consent

[42] At §§68–71 Lord Kerr considered and distinguished the CJEU's decision in Case C-443/15, *Parris v Trinity College Dublin* EU:C:2016:897, [2017] ICR 313 in which that Court rejected a claim for survivors' pension the denial of which was based on the applicant's status at age 60 by which point Ireland had not yet recognised civil partnerships for same-sex couples.

[43] See similarly *Lustig Prean & Beckett v UK* (2000) 29 EHRR 548.

for male same-sex sexual contact and for female same-sex and heterosexual sexual contact breached Article 14 read with Article 8. But the decision of the Labour Government to legislate in order to equalise the age of consent resulted from a successful challenge brought by Euan Sutherland and Christopher Morris to the unequal ages of consent in England and Wales.[44] The equalisation of adoption rights in 2002 also preceded the ECtHR's case law (*EB v France* (2008) 47 EHRR 21) as did the introduction of same-sex partnerships.

In the same year as it decided the *Smith* and *Lustig-Prean* cases the ECtHR decided in *Mouta v Portugal* (2001) 31 EHRR 47 that sexual orientation discrimination breached Article 14 read with Article 8. The ECHR jurisprudence was imported into the UK in October 2000 with the implementation of the HRA, but in *MacDonald v Ministry of Defence, Pearce v Governing Body of Mayfield School* [2003] ICR 937 the HL declined the invitation to interpret the SDA (as it then was) to regulate sexual orientation discrimination. The CJEU had proved similarly unwilling in Case C-249/96 *Grant v South-West Trains Ltd*, [1998] ECR I-3739 to apply the same expansive approach to the definition of sex discrimination as it had in Case C-13/94 *P v S & Cornwall* [1996] ECR I-2143, which concerned gender reassignment. In both cases legislation (Council Directive 2000/78 and the SO Regs) was imminent but provided cold comfort to the individual claimants.

Shortly after its decision in the *MacDonald* and *Pearce* cases the HL demonstrated a much more enthusiastic response both to the LGB equality and to the potential of s3 HRA (the interpretive obligation, discussed in Chapter 1) in *Mendoza v Ghaidan*. The case, in which the claimant challenged the rules regulating inheritance of statutory tenancies, stands as a high-water mark of the judicial approach to s3 HRA.

***Mendoza v Ghaidan* [2004] UKHL 30, [2004] 2 AC 557**

The claimant, a gay man, had lived since 1972 with his partner, who was the protected tenant of a flat in which they lived. After his partner died the landlord sought to evict the claimant on the basis that the tenancy had come to an end. The relevant statutory provisions would have allowed him to succeed to the tenancy had they been married, and to less (but some) protection had he been a member of the tenant's family. (At this time same-sex partners could neither marry nor form civil partnerships.) A county court judge ruled that the claimant was entitled to an assured tenancy as a member of the original tenant's family. On the defendant's appeal the CA ruled that it was required by s3 HRA to read the definition of 'spouse' to include a person living with the original tenant 'as his or her wife *or husband*' in order to avoid a breach of the claimant's rights under Article 8 and 14. The HL agreed.

Lord Nicholls (with whom Lords Steyn and Rodger and Lady Hale agreed):

> 29. … It is now generally accepted that the application of section 3 does not depend upon the presence of ambiguity in the legislation being interpreted. Even if, construed according to the ordinary principles of interpretation, the meaning of the legislation admits of no doubt, section 3 may nonetheless require the legislation to be given a different meaning [citing *R v A (No 2)* [2002] 1 AC 45] …
>
> 30. From this it follows that the interpretative obligation decreed by section 3 is of an unusual and far-reaching character. Section 3 may require a court to depart from the unambiguous meaning the legislation would otherwise bear. In the ordinary course the interpretation of

[44] (1996) 22 EHRR CD182, (1997) 24 EHRR CD22. The *Sutherland* case was suspended following the agreement to legislate and struck out by agreement in 2001 when the legislation came into effect.

legislation involves seeking the intention reasonably to be attributed to Parliament in using the language in question. Section 3 may require the court to depart from this legislative intention, that is, depart from the intention of the Parliament which enacted the legislation. The question of difficulty is how far, and in what circumstances, section 3 requires a court to depart from the intention of the enacting Parliament. The answer to this question depends upon the intention reasonably to be attributed to Parliament in enacting section 3.

31. On this the first point to be considered is how far, when enacting section 3, Parliament intended that the actual language of a statute, as distinct from the concept expressed in that language, should be determinative. Since section 3 relates to the 'interpretation' of legislation, it is natural to focus attention initially on the language used in the legislative provision being considered. But once it is accepted that section 3 may require legislation to bear a meaning which departs from the unambiguous meaning the legislation would otherwise bear, it becomes impossible to suppose Parliament intended that the operation of section 3 should depend critically upon the particular form of words adopted by the parliamentary draftsman in the statutory provision under consideration. That would make the application of section 3 something of a semantic lottery. If the draftsman chose to express the concept being enacted in one form of words, section 3 would be available to achieve Convention-compliance. If he chose a different form of words, section 3 would be impotent.

32. From this the conclusion which seems inescapable is that the mere fact the language under consideration is inconsistent with a Convention-compliant meaning does not of itself make a Convention-compliant interpretation under section 3 impossible. Section 3 enables language to be interpreted restrictively or expansively. But section 3 goes further than this. It is also apt to require a court to read in words which change the meaning of the enacted legislation, so as to make it Convention-compliant. In other words, the intention of Parliament in enacting section 3 was that, to an extent bounded only by what is 'possible,' a court can modify the meaning, and hence the effect, of primary and secondary legislation.

33. Parliament, however, cannot have intended that in the discharge of this extended interpretative function the courts should adopt a meaning inconsistent with a fundamental feature of legislation. That would be to cross the constitutional boundary section 3 seeks to demarcate and preserve. Parliament has retained the right to enact legislation in terms which are not Convention-compliant. The meaning imported by application of section 3 must be compatible with the underlying thrust of the legislation being construed. Words implied must, in the phrase of my noble and learned friend Lord Rodger of Earlsferry, 'go with the grain of the legislation.' Nor can Parliament have intended that section 3 should require courts to make decisions for which they are not equipped. There may be several ways of making a provision Convention-compliant, and the choice may involve issues calling for legislative deliberation …

35. In some cases difficult problems may arise. No difficulty arises in the present case. Paragraph 2 of Schedule 1 to the Rent Act 1977 is unambiguous. But the social policy underlying the 1988 extension of security of tenure under paragraph 2 to the survivor of couples living together as husband and wife is equally applicable to the survivor of homosexual couples living together in a close and stable relationship. In this circumstance I see no reason to doubt that application of section 3 to paragraph 2 has the effect that paragraph 2 should be read and given effect to as though the survivor of such a homosexual couple were the surviving spouse of the original tenant. Reading paragraph 2 in this way would have the result that cohabiting heterosexual couples and cohabiting heterosexual couples would be treated alike for the purposes of succession as a statutory tenant. This would eliminate the discriminatory effect of paragraph 2 and would do so consistently with the social policy underlying paragraph 2. The precise form of words read in for this purpose is of no significance. It is their substantive effect which matters …

Lord Steyn (who agreed with Lord Nicholls and with whom Lord Rodger and Lady Hale agreed), suggested that the courts had to date been too ready to issue declarations of incompatibility which should, in his words, be 'a measure of last resort'.

At the time of writing the future of the HRA is unclear, as discussed in Chapter 1. It is worth mentioning here some of the ECHR case law on sexual orientation which is likely to remain relevant to domestic protection in this area irrespective of any short-term domestic legislative changes:

- *Kozak v Poland* (2010) 51 EHRR 16: the denial to the applicant of any right to succeed to a tenancy because he was in a same-sex relationship with the tenant breached Article 8 and 14;
- *Oliari & Others v Italy* (2017) 65 EHRR 26: the failure to provide legal recognition of stable same-sex relationships breached Article 8;
- *Pajić v Croatia* (2018) 67 EHRR 12: the failure to treat same-sex and heterosexual couples the same as regards residence permits breached Article 14 read with Article 8;
- *Taddeucci and McCall v Italy* (App No 51362/09) 30 June 2016: the failure to treat same-sex couples who were unable to regularise their relationships differently, in relation to residence rights, than unmarried heterosexual couples, who could regularise their relationships breached Article 14 read with Article 8;
- *Oliari v Italy* (2017) 65 EHRR 26: the failure to provide legal recognition of a stable relationship, for residence purposes, of a same-sex couple married abroad breached article 8;[45]
- *Bayev v Russia* (2018) 66 EHRR 10: a legislative ban on the promotion of non-traditional sexual relations among minors violated Article 14 read with Article 10;[46]
- *Zhdanov v Russia* (App Nos 12200/08 & 2 others) 16 July 2019: the refusal to register the applicant organisations on the ground that they promoted LGBT rights breached Article 14 read with Article 11;[47]
- *Beizaras & Levickas v Lithuania* (2020) 71 EHRR 28: the failure to take appropriate steps to protect the applicants from threatened violence and harassment after they posted a picture of themselves kissing online breached Article 14 read with Article 8;[48]
- *B & C v Switzerland* (2021) 72 EHRR 16: returning the applicant to a non-European state (Gambia) where he would be at risk of ill-treatment as a gay man violated Article 3 ECHR.

[45] The state was not however required to recognise such marriages as marriages.

[46] See similarly *Alekseyev v Russia* (2019) 69 EHRR 16 (ban on a gay march).

[47] See similarly *Bączkowski v Poland* (2009) 48 EHRR 19.

[48] See similarly *Association ACCEPT v Romania* (App No 19237/16) 1 June 2021, unreported; *Genderdoc-M & MD v Republic of Moldova* (App No 23914/15) 14 December 2021, unreported.

11

Age

Age, Disadvantage and Discrimination

Introduction

Age discrimination was first regulated in the UK in 2006 by the Employment Equality (Age Discrimination) Regulations of that year ('Age Regs'), whose purpose was to implement the provisions of Council Directive 2000/78 in so far as they related to age. The Directive's prohibitions on discrimination related to religion and belief, sexual orientation and disability had been implemented some three years before by the Employment Equality (Religion and Belief) Regulations and Employment Equality (Sexual Orientation) Regulations ('RB Regs' and 'SO Regs'), and by amendments to the Disability Discrimination Act 1995 (DDA). The lag in the implementation of age discrimination provisions was permitted by the Directive.

The regulation of age discrimination (now by the Equality Act 2010, EqA) differs in several material respects from that related to the other protected characteristics considered in this book. The Age Regs, as they were initially implemented, expressly permitted compulsory retirement. By contrast with most of the other protected characteristics considered in this book, the prohibition on age discrimination did not extend beyond the sphere of employment until the implementation of the EqA. Even then, it remained lawful for employers to impose mandatory retirement ages until October 2012.[1] Age discrimination, uniquely, is capable of justification regardless of whether it is direct or indirect. Those aged under 18 are not protected from discrimination within Part 3 EqA (services, etc) and the prohibitions on discrimination by schools and in relation to premises does not apply as regards age.

In this chapter we will consider the legal approach to age discrimination under the EqA, under Council Directive 2000/78 and under Article 14 ECHR. First, however, it is important to understand the relationship between age and disadvantage.

Most of the characteristics protected by the EqA are associated with relative disadvantage across a number of spheres. Women and those belonging to most racially minoritised communities are disadvantaged materially and in terms of political power. LGBT people, whatever

[1] Employment Equality (Repeal of Retirement Age Provisions) Regulations 2011 (SI 2011/1069).

their material situation, have been subject to criminalisation and, at least until very recently, have been marginalised from society. Most disabled people experience material disadvantage and societal exclusion, and many people from minoritised religious communities' views are hampered by societal norms which are at odds with their own, or with those attributed to them.

The relationship between age and disadvantage is more complex. It is, of course, the case that the experience of disadvantage is not uniform across groups defined by reference to protected characteristics such as race, sex or religion. Further, in many cases, relative disadvantage is associated with, and or exacerbated by, the intersection of protected characteristics (including age). We shall see below, for example, that, among the elderly, women and people from racially minoritised groups are more likely to be poor. But age is more complex again in that, not only is disadvantage unevenly spread across those within particular age groups, as it is among women, Muslims, people with disabilities, etc, but individuals may be simultaneously advantaged and disadvantaged by age to a much greater extent than is the case with other protected characteristics. By way of example, *HM Land Registry v Benson* [2012] ICR 627 involved age discrimination challenges by individuals who would have been entitled, if made redundant, to very significant age-related payments, to decisions not to select them for redundancy because of the cost of so doing. *Woodcock v Cumbria PCT* [2012] EWCA Civ 330, [2012] ICR 1126 involved an age discrimination challenge to the provision of notice timed to avoid generating the claimant's age-related entitlement to a hugely enhanced redundancy package. And *Air Products plc v Cockram* [2018] EWCA Civ 346, [2018] IRLR 755 involved a challenge by a claimant who benefitted from being able to retire at 50 on a defined benefit pension to an attempt to level the playing field, as regards entitlement to incentive payments, between him and his younger colleagues who were not entitled to retire before 55 (this as a result of legislative changes) and who were entitled only to less valuable defined contribution pensions. All three cases are discussed below.

Another distinguishing feature of age is that, whereas other protected characteristics are relatively, though not completely, fixed, this is not the case with age. As Baroness Hale recognised in *Seldon v Clarkson Wright and Jakes* [2012] UKSC 16, [2012] ICR 716, further considered below:

> 4. … age is … a continuum which changes over time … 'Every human being starts life as a tiny infant, and none of us can do anything to stop the passage of the years. This means that younger people will eventually benefit from a provision which favours older employees, such as an incremental pay scale; but older employees will already have benefitted from a provision which favours younger people, such as a mandatory retirement age.[2]

The implications of this are not only that the distribution of costs and benefits by reference to age is likely to be more defensible than a distribution based on criteria such as sex or race, but also that changing the rules governing such distributions may deliver windfalls to older people at the expense of younger generations.

Many pensioners live in poverty and there is evidence that women begin to be subject to age discrimination at work from the age of 40 (men by 45).[3] But older people occupy many positions of power, both economic and political, and tend to be richer than those who both earn less (being younger) and have had less opportunity to accumulate material wealth. The average age of an MP elected in 2015 was 50.[4] The average age of chairs in the FTSE 100 was just under 65 in 2014, that of executive directors 53.06 and that of non-executive

[2] Citing Lord Walker in *R (Carson) v SSWP* [2005] UKHL 37, [2006] 1 AC 173.
[3] L Gratton and A Scott, *The 100 Year Life: Living and Work in an Age of Longevity*.
[4] https://www.parliament.uk/about/faqs/house-of-commons-faqs/members-faq-page2.

directors 59.89.[5] The youngest chairman was 45, the next youngest 50, 52 and 54 (one, one and four individuals respectively) while 48 were over 65, nine over 70 and one over 80. In 2019 the average age for FTSE 100 chairs, executives and non-executive directors was 58.5, 53 and 60 respectively.[6] And in 2013–14 the largest group of professors in UK universities was aged between 51 and 55 (4,040 in total) followed by those aged 46–50 (3,795), 56–60 (3,700), 61–65 (3,075), 41–45 (2,355) and 66+ (1,725).[7]

Older people have benefitted more as a class from increasing house prices in the UK and many have also been the beneficiaries of free third-level education while younger people increasingly find themselves juggling student loan repayments, exorbitant housing costs and insecure work.

Wealth

According to the Office for National Statistics, the distribution of wealth across British households between April 2016 and March 2018 is shown in Figure 11.1 below, which is taken from the ONS *Total wealth in Great Britain: April 2018 to March 2020*:[8]

Figure 11.1 Distribution of wealth by household age

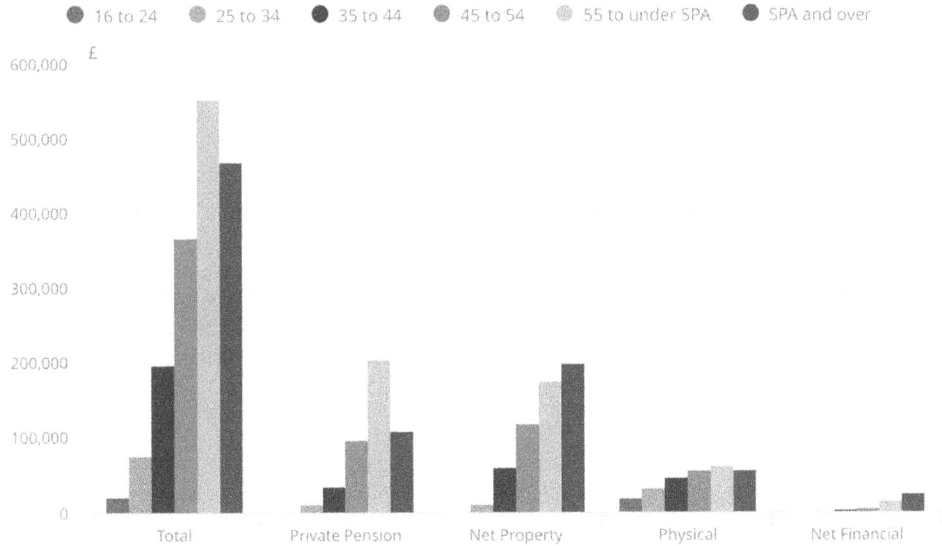

[5] https://www.theqca.com/article_assets/articledir_190/95112/NBBoardReview2014_Web.pdf. The figures for the FTSE 250 were similar.

[6] *A View at the Top: Boardroom Trends in Britain's Top 100 Companies*, available at https://www.icsa.org.uk/assets/files/free-guidance-notes/a-view-at-the-top-report.pdf.

[7] https://www.hesa.ac.uk/news/26-02-2015/age-and-gender-of-staff.

[8] Reproduced from fig 4, 'Median total household wealth by age of household reference person, GB, April 2018 to March 2020', available at https://www.ons.gov.uk/peoplepopulationandcommunity/personalandhouseholdfinances/incomeandwealth/bulletins/totalwealthingreatbritain/april2018tomarch2020. The 'household reference person' is the 'person that is the sole or joint householder or is responsible for household affairs' or, where there are joint householders, the person with the highest income or (where this is evenly shared) the older person'. 'SPA' refers to state pension age.

The relative wealth of older people in the UK, and the proportion of welfare payments directed towards them, has given rise to debates in the UK and elsewhere about 'intergenerational fairness'. The Resolution Foundation's Intergenerational Commission, which was convened to consider these questions, adopted the following categorisation: Silent Generation (born 1926–45), Baby Boomers (1946–65), Generation X (1966–80), Millennials (1981–2000) and the Latest Generation (2000+).

Intergeneration Commission final report, 'A New Inter-Generational Contract' (2018)[9]

Executive Summary

… Adults in Britain are positive about young people's access to information and entertainment, travel opportunities and the quality of their education. While there is still much to do, opportunities for women, ethnic minorities and lesbian, gay and transgender people are much better than for their predecessors …

… in their late 20s millennials (the generation born 1981–2000) have so far experienced unemployment rates that are around 25 per cent lower than those experienced by baby boomers (born 1946–65) at the same age … Employment rates for baby boomer women have been 5–7 percentage points higher at each age than for the pre-war silent generation (born 1926–45), and women in generation X … and the millennial generation have experienced big gains on top of those, in the child-rearing years in particular.

… While in the past every successive cohort had higher real earnings at each age, the millennial cohorts born 1986–90 (at age 26) and 1981–85 (in their early 30s) had similar earnings to the cohorts born 15 years before them when they were that age … Another trend that preceded the crisis and has endured even as employment has reached record highs is a shift towards lower-paying and less secure jobs among young people. Increases in self-employment since the early 2000s have been driven by younger workers without degrees; millennials have been more likely to work part time than generation X at the same age; and the fastest-growing occupations for those in their late 20s have been the lowest-paying ones – elementary, caring and leisure roles …

… So far millennial families are only half as likely to own their home by age 30 as baby boomers were by the same age. An even bigger reduction in access to social housing means that four-in-ten millennial families at age 30 live in the private rented sector, four times the rate for baby boomers when they were the same age … Millennials are spending an average of almost a quarter of their income on housing, up from an average of just 8 per cent among the silent generation at the same age [original emphasis throughout].

The report points out that younger generations benefit much less than older generations from generous defined benefit pension schemes and that, although a greater proportion of younger adults will be members of pension schemes, these are generally defined contribution schemes whose performance is heavily dependent on investment returns: 'A 1 percentage point decline in investment returns in each remaining year of working life would reduce retirement incomes for millennial men born 1984–86 by 8 per cent, well below the outcomes enjoyed by recent retirees'.[10] Overall, whereas older Baby Boomers 'have maintained significant income improvements on the silent generation, continuing the pattern of generational progress that

[9] https://www.resolutionfoundation.org/app/uploads/2018/05/A-New-Generational-Contract-Full-PDF.pdf.
[10] The impact of the COVID-19 pandemic is unlikely to be helpful in this regard.

was the norm across the age range in the second half of the 20th Century', the disposal income of Millennials at age 30 is no higher than it was for Generation X. And, whereas 'in 2001, 25–34-year-olds were consuming the same as 55–64-year-olds; they are now spending 15 per cent less'.

Select Committee on Intergenerational Fairness and Provision, 'Tackling intergenerational unfairness', Report of Session 2017–19, HL Paper 329 (2019), footnotes omitted

The rising cost of housing

60. One major pressure that younger generations are facing is increased housing costs. As Figure 1 shows, the two youngest generations are devoting a greater proportion of their overall income to housing than previous generations. People born between 1981 and 2000 appear to be spending over one and a half times more, as a proportion of their income, on housing at the age of 25 than the generation born immediately after the Second World War spent at that age. For previous generations, housing costs as a proportion of income have declined as individuals enter their 30s, but it is unclear whether this latest generation will experience a similar decline.

61. This increase in housing costs as a proportion of income does not appear to be caused by younger generations choosing to spend more to prioritise living space. The amount of floor space per person for those under 45 has fallen over the last 20 years whilst the amount for those over 45 has risen. Nor is it the case that younger generations are paying more to live closer to work. For the cohorts for which there are data, each cohort has had longer commutes than the generation before them had at their age …

Figure 1 Proportion of income spent on housing costs by generation: GB

Source: Intergenerational Commission, *Home Affront: Housing across the generations* (September 2017) p 31: https://www.intergencommission.org/wp-content/uploads/2017/09/Home-Affront.pdf.

Figure 2 Generational home ownership rates by age: UK

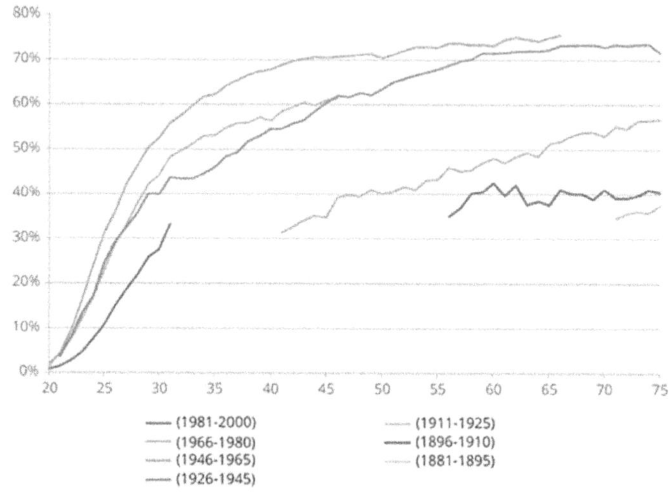

Source: Intergenerational Commission, *Home Affront: Housing across the generations* (September 2017) p 13: https://www.intergencommission.org/wp-content/uploads/2017/09/Home-Affront.pdf.

63. There have been many social and economic changes between generations that could delay buying a house. Younger generations are entering the labour market later, are less likely to live with a partner and are having children later, all of which could delay the decision to buy; conversely, they could themselves be delayed by housing costs. Adjusting for these demographic differences does account for some of the home ownership differences between generations, but there remains a large difference between home ownership rates.

Concern about the disproportionate political influence of older people has been widely expressed.

Joe Chrisp and Nick Pearce, 'Grey power: towards a political economy of older voters in the UK' (2019) *Political Quarterly*, footnotes omitted

Introduction

… in many advanced capitalist economies, including the UK, age-related inequalities in wealth have been growing, while levels of welfare state support for retired people and the working-age population have diverged. In the UK, the basic state pension and allowances for older people have been protected in the era of austerity, whereas there have been significant cuts to the benefits for the working age population. These trends have led to interest in the power of the 'grey vote' and even claims of 'gerontocracy'. Some commentators have speculated that age may become 'the new class' in British politics …

45 In common with other developed countries, the population of the UK is ageing as a result of increased life expectancy and the demographic bulge caused by the so-called 'baby boomer' generation. The ageing of the parliamentary electorate has also been accompanied by an increase in the proportion of older voters in the eligible voter population because of inward migration to the UK in recent decades from the EU and elsewhere of young people who are not entitled to vote in general elections …

The growing relative weight of older people in the voting-age population is coupled with considerable inequalities in voter turnout by age. A large age difference in turnout first opened up in the early 1990s and it has persisted in recent general elections … If we assume that both turnout and the proportion of those not entitled to vote due to their nationality remain constant, demographic change will mean that over 55s constitute over half of the voting public by 2020 …

> Evidence from the Bank of England, as well as research institutes such as the Institute for Fiscal Studies and the Resolution Foundation, has found that older people have benefited disproportionately from both monetary and fiscal policy in the post-financial crisis era. Older homeowners have seen their housing and pension wealth increase as a result of Quantitative Easing, while the austerity enacted by the Coalition and Conservative governments has given relative protection to the social security entitlements enjoyed by older people at the expense of those of the working age population …

Helen Lewis, 'Boomers Are Not Okay: Older voters warp their countries' policies because of political power. One British politician has a plan to end that dominance', *The Atlantic*, 27 November 2019

> … In Britain, age is now a better predictor of voting intention than social class. Overall, the Boomers voted for Brexit in 2016 and the Conservatives in 2017; their Millennial children voted Remain and Labour. The single biggest error that Theresa May, the prime minister in the lead-up to the 2017 election, made during that process was to float the idea that older people might have to contribute more to the spiraling costs of their own retirement care. The 'dementia tax' prompted an immediate, ferocious response, and May backed down.
>
> That is not an isolated example. A guiding principle of politics in Britain, and elsewhere in the West, is: What Boomers want, Boomers get. Working-age benefits, for example, have been frozen since the 2015 budget, but the state pension has consistently risen …
>
> Some Boomers argue that the word itself has become a cover for ageism; Millennials roll their eyes and reply with the phrase that has come to encapsulate their weariness: 'Okay Boomer'. Boomers have bent the gravity of politics toward themselves and their needs. They buy newspapers. They vote. They wield their spending power effectively. Their voice is loud. To build a fair and just society, the question then must be: On everything from elderly care to housing, how do you persuade them to vote against their own interests?

Lewis refers to David Willetts, former Conservative minister, who in 2010 wrote *The Pinch* in which he argued that British 'baby boomers' (born 1945–65) 'took their children's futures' by buying cheap houses, the value of which increased hugely and who enjoyed rising standards of living and good state and (often) private pension provision.

> Their Millennial children, by contrast, were having a tougher time – struggling to buy a house, watching their salaries stagnate, and looking ahead to a much less comfortable retirement. It was, Willetts wrote, selfish of the Boomers not to recognize, and mitigate, this situation. The trouble was the sheer number of Boomers. As a big generation, the Boomers had achieved political and cultural dominance. They were no more self-interested than any other group, but they warped government priorities …
>
> Arguments about Boomers versus Millennials crop up in other countries – hence the popularity of the 'Okay, Boomer' meme in the U.S. – but the problem is particularly acute in Britain, because of the country's steep fall in home ownership in recent decades. The British rental sector is much more 'mom and pop' – literally. 'Something like 20 percent of Boomers have a second property that they rent out,' Willetts said. That means there is a direct transfer of wealth from younger renters to older asset-owners …

The difficulties facing younger people have been exacerbated by the COVID-19 pandemic, which has impacted very significantly on the access of children and young people to education, as well as to society more generally, and has contributed to extraordinary economic circumstances, the brunt of which will be borne disproportionately by those children and young people.

Notwithstanding the relative wealth of older households, pension poverty remains a significant problem despite improvements over time. In August 2019 *The Observer* reported that elderly people in the UK suffered the highest rates of poverty in Western Europe and that the rise in the proportion of elderly people living in severe poverty (having an income of 40 per cent or less of the median) in the UK from 0.9 per cent to five per cent was 'the largest increase among western European countries'.[11] *The Observer* attributed this position to the UK's model of low state pension payments (16 per cent of average earnings) with means-tested additional payments. It reported that around 20 per cent of those aged 65+ in the UK had an income of 60 per cent or more of the median and that 'overall, those European countries that had made private pensions an important source of income for the elderly had seen a rise in financial inequality', quoting the author of the report who stated that 'The comparison shows that the shift toward increasing privatisation amplifies the already existing level of social inequality'. And Age UK reported in 2021 that, while levels of poverty among pensioners in the UK were lower than 20 years ago, '2.1 million (18 per cent) of pensioners in the UK live in poverty. Rates have risen since 2013–14 when 1.6 million (14 per cent) lived in poverty'.[12]

The risk of poverty was higher for Asian, Asian British, Black and Black British pensioners (at 30–33 per cent) than for white pensioners (16 per cent). The same organisation had reported in 2018, at a time when 1.9m pensioners were living in poverty, that 1.1m had incomes less than half of that of a typical household.[13]

The Centre for Ageing Better reported in 2017 that there was 'powerful evidence of gender inequalities in financial security in later life, with older women more financially insecure than older men. Female part-time workers or women with low-grade employment are at greater risk of financial insecurity.' Further, there was 'evidence that migrants and some people from minority ethnic communities are less likely to have adequate pension savings, resulting in financial insecurity in later life. Women from minority ethnic backgrounds are particularly at risk'.

Thomas Scharf and Caroline Shaw, *Inequalities in Later Life* (Centre for Aging Better, 2017).

Looking across the evidence, the review highlights a number of key messages around inequalities in financial security in later life:

- There is powerful evidence of gender inequalities in financial security in older age, with older women generally more vulnerable to financial difficulties than older men.
- Several studies suggest that marital status has more influence on the financial security of women than men in later life. This is especially the case for previously partnered women who go on to live alone.
- Employment history and socioeconomic background can compound the challenges faced by women when seeking financial security in later life. Women in part-time work or low-grade employment are particularly at risk of financial insecurity.
- Women who have spent most of their working lives in part-time employment are not financially better off in retirement than women who have been employed part-time for short periods or who have never worked.

[11] 'UK elderly suffer worst poverty rate in western Europe', *The Observer*, 18 August 2019, discussing B. Ebbinghaus, 'Pension Reforms and Old Age Inequalities in Europe', available at https://www.researchgate.net/publication/335228524_Pension_reforms_and_old_age_inequalities_in_Europe_From_old_to_new_social_risks.

[12] Age UK, 'Poverty in later life' (2021), available at https://www.ageuk.org.uk/globalassets/age-uk/documents/policy-positions/money-matters/poverty_in_later_life_briefing_june_2021.pdf.

[13] Age UK, *Poverty and financial disadvantage* (2018), available at https://www.ageuk.org.uk/globalassets/age-uk/documents/policy-positions/money-matters/poverty-and-financial-disadvantage-policy-position-nov-2018-clean.pdf; and see the 2021 report of the same name at https://www.ageuk.org.uk/globalassets/age-uk/documents/policy-positions/money-matters/poverty-and-financial-disadvantage-dec-2021.pdf.

- A gendered pension system ultimately means that women, who are more likely to be in part-time work or to take breaks from employment to care for family members, are restricted in their ability to accumulate personal and pension wealth.
- Much of the research finds there is an inter-sectional dynamic which can further diminish the prospect of women achieving financial security in old age, with racially minoritised women from ethnic minority backgrounds particularly at risk.
- Among groups of men who are disadvantaged under the current pension system, migrants and those from minority ethnic communities are identified as being less likely to achieve adequate pension savings, resulting in financial insecurity in later life.
- Migration incurs a penalty in terms of access to private pensions, regardless of the timing of migration and the length of time spent working in England.

Work

It is often suggested that older workers suffer from disadvantage in the workplace.

'Three-quarters of Brits say age discrimination is common in their workplace', ***Small Business*****, 12 December 2017**

A staggering 70.8 per cent of UK workers reveal discrimination around age is common in their workplace, rising to 85.3 per cent amongst those aged 55–64 … one third (30 per cent) of professionals have been turned down for a job because of their age, rising to 52.5 per cent amongst those aged 55–64 and 65.1 per cent amongst under 18s … More than half (57.1 per cent) of under 18s feel they're not taken seriously at work, because of their age, with a further 76 per cent of 25–34 year olds stating that they have been discriminated against at work because they were considered 'too young'. Eighty-nine per cent of 45–54 year olds said they have been discriminated against at work for being 'too old'…

Of those that said they were considered to be 'too young' for a job, nearly half (46.7%) said they were told they didn't have enough experience. In addition to this, 35.8% said the employer felt no-one would take them seriously. Conversely, for those considered to be 'too old', one in five (20.2%) were told that they would be too stuck in their own ways …

- 'I have been told that I was too old to retrain for a career change in my company.' …
- 'I was told by a career advisor that I should remove the number "70" from my email address because people might think I was born in 1970 and would consequently not consider me.' …
- 'I interviewed really well for a position but was told that because I was a middle-aged woman I was too set in my ways and may find it difficult to learn new things.'…
- 'I look much younger than I actually am and I feel my employer doesn't take me seriously at times.' …
- 'Senior management don't seem to take on board suggestions from myself or my younger colleagues but will listen and implement them once someone older has suggested the same thing.' …

It is clear from the foregoing that younger as well as older workers perceive themselves to be subject to work-related age discrimination, though much public attention is focussed on the position of older workers.

House of Commons Women and Equalities Committee, ***Older people and employment*****, Fourth Report of Session 2017–19, HC 359, footnotes omitted**

2. In 2014 Business in the Community estimated that up to 1.4 million people aged 50 to 69 had involuntarily left the labour market in the previous eight years. There were over one million people aged 50 or over out of work who would have been willing to work if the right opportunity arose, and 26 per cent of people aged 50 to 64 were jobless but would have liked to work.

The Government's *Fuller Working Lives* strategy itself acknowledges that 'There are almost one million individuals aged 50–64 who are not in employment but state they are willing to or would like to work.'

3. Women face particular difficulties in accessing work in later life. Women still do the majority of caring for children and other family members, and are more likely to be in part-time work. While the employment rate for women aged 50 to 64 has been rising for many years, it remains significantly below that of men at 67.5 per cent compared to 76.2 per cent for men. The gender pay gap, which our 2016 report showed to be particularly pronounced for women over 40, means that even when in work older women generally earn less and look forward to smaller pensions ...

14 .... Many witnesses pointed to the impact of wider ageism within society on employers, citing the greetings card industry as an example of 'casual ageism' which reflected the attitude that it is still acceptable to make jokes about people's age. Such attitudes among the public, it was argued, translated into the workplace, influencing the attitudes of employers as members of the public themselves.

15. These views were strongly corroborated by the individuals we heard from. A group of older job seekers told us in no uncertain terms that age discrimination was a regular occurrence. One individual 'over the usual retirement age' who wrote to us described his experience of seeking to access a Job Club at his local Jobcentre Plus. On arrival he was asked his age and, when he told them, he was 'summarily and brusquely thrown out – 'we don't deal with people like you'.' ...

The article extracted below discusses a number of tribunals and EAT decisions in age discrimination claims and explores some of the stereotypes associated with older workers.

Elaine Dewhurst, 'Are Older Workers Past Their Sell-by-Date? A View from UK Age Discrimination Law' (2015) 78 *Modern Law Review* 189, most references omitted

There is a common perception among many employers that productivity at work decreases with age ... Older workers are perceived to be 'stuck in their ways, and ... not interested in further training or promotion', inflexible, unadaptable, tired, sick, reluctant, bureaucratic, expensive, stagnant, lacking in technological competence and unable to learn or adapt to new technology. Perceptions abound that older workers do not have the potential to learn and develop and have no inclination to adapt to the times ...

Some general misconceptions revolve around the fact that employers consider older workers to be old-fashioned, difficult to train and unlikely to change or develop ...

Another perception is that those nearing retirement are lacking in potential and the cost of investment in such a worker and employment of such a worker is too high. In ... *Liladhar* v *Barnardo's Limited*[14] a 60 year old male internal auditor was selected for redundancy because he did not have an accountancy qualification, even though Mr Liladhar had requested the relevant training. The ET recognised that the employer had assumed that there was little point in investing in Mr Liladhar 'having regard to the likely duration of the claimant's future employment with the respondent. On the other hand, a younger person in whom such an investment was made would have ample opportunity to achieve a relevant qualification and make use of it in a productive context in the continued employment of the respondent'. The ET was of the view that a younger employee 'would almost certainly have been encouraged to achieve a relevant accountancy qualification' which was denied to the claimant in this case. In *Jessemey* v *Rowstock Ltd*[15] the cost of insuring an employee was raised by the employer as a reason for not extending his contract beyond the age of 65 years.

[14] (2010) ET No 3201718/2010.
[15] (2011) ET No 2700838/2011 and 27001156/2011.

Employers frequently use inappropriate age-related comments or actions in dealing with older employees which undermine the relationship between the employer and the individual worker. In *Nolan* v *CD Bramall Dealership Ltd*[16] the employer introduced a 64-year-old male senior service advisor as the '104 year old Service Team Leader', had referred to him as 'Yoda', and the employee had the letters on his number plate of his car changed from 'OAB' to 'OAP'. Similarly, in *Kerr v O'Hara Brothers Surfacing Ltd*[17] a 67-year-old male driver was frequently subjected to comments that he was too old for the job, was not scheduled for work on certain days when younger workers were and the employer indicated that they had treated the employee in this way for health and safety reasons. The ET held that there was no medical or other evidence that the claimant could not carry out his duties effectively. More particularly, the employer had not stated at what age they considered an employee unable to do certain tasks or provide any evidence why any particular age would mean that an employee could not carry out certain tasks.

Dewhurst suggests that there is limited evidence for a relationship between age and productivity, that the decline in work ability which she accepts may occur 'can be compensated for through other factors such as experience and interpersonal skills which older workers may have in abundance', and that 'the individual differences between older workers are so great that it is futile to generalise'. The premise of the article is that the stereotyping of older workers is commonplace. That some such stereotyping occurs is evident from the materials discussed in this chapter, but the broader evidence does not indicate a clear general relationship between age and workplace disadvantage.

Figure 11.2 shows that, taken in the round, UK workers' wages increase to reach a peak in the 40–49 age group before decreasing thereafter.

Figure 11.2 Pay for older and younger workers[18]

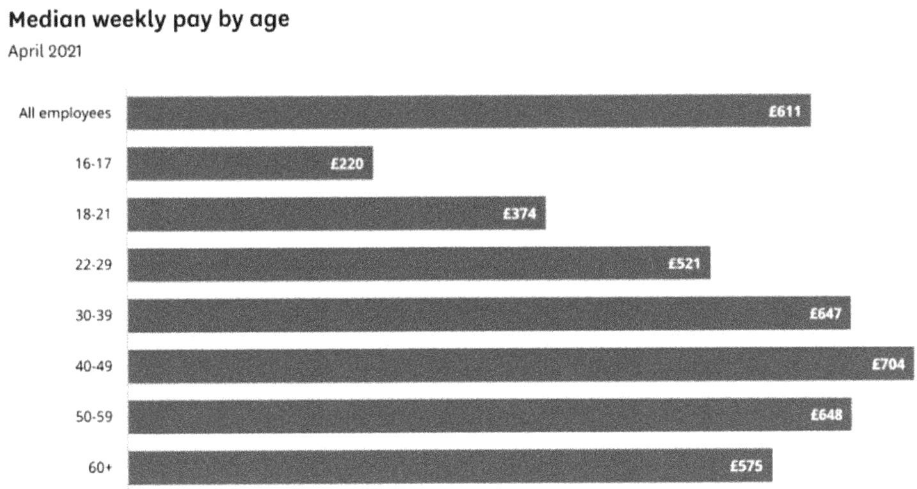

[16] (2012) ET No 2601000/2012.
[17] (2010) ET No 3302349/2012.
[18] Taken from House of Commons Library, 'Average earnings by age and region', 1 November 2021, available at https://commonslibrary.parliament.uk/research-briefings/cbp-8456.

It is the case that workers aged 50–59 earn less than those aged 40–49. It is worth noting, however, that they earn much the same as workers aged 30–39 and very significantly more than every other age group. The apparent decline in wages between 40–49 and 50–59 is also influenced by the varying proportions of individuals in different age groups between occupational categories.

Figures 11.3–11.5 below, which are based on ONS statistics for 2021,[19] show hourly pay (excluding overtime) within the various occupational classifications by sex and age. Male and female workers are considered separately to prevent distortion arising from the gender pay gap if the proportion of women within different age groups varies between occupational groups, as well as to show differences between men and women in the relationship between ages and wages. Women full-time and part-time workers have been considered separately because part-time workers account for 40 per cent of women, but only about 13 per cent of men workers.

Figure 11.3 Hourly pay of full-time male workers by age and occupation

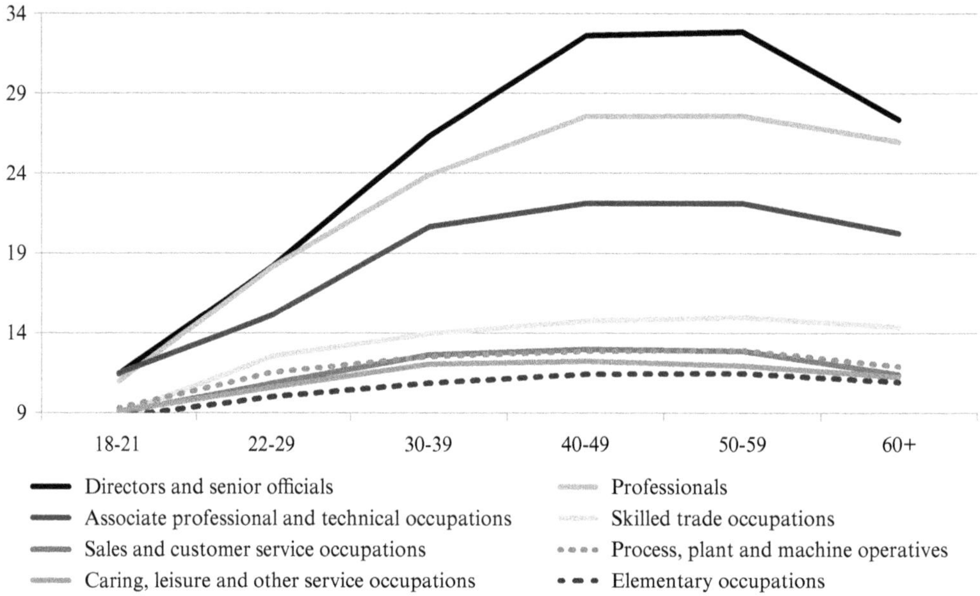

It is evident that male pay generally rises to peak between 40 and 59, thereafter declining fairly steeply for the highest paid (directors and senior officials), more gently for others. The pattern for women is different.

[19] https://www.ons.gov.uk/employmentandlabourmarket/peopleinwork/earningsandworkinghours/datasets/agegroupbyoccupation2digitsocashetable20.

Figure 11.4 Hourly pay of full-time female workers by age and occupation

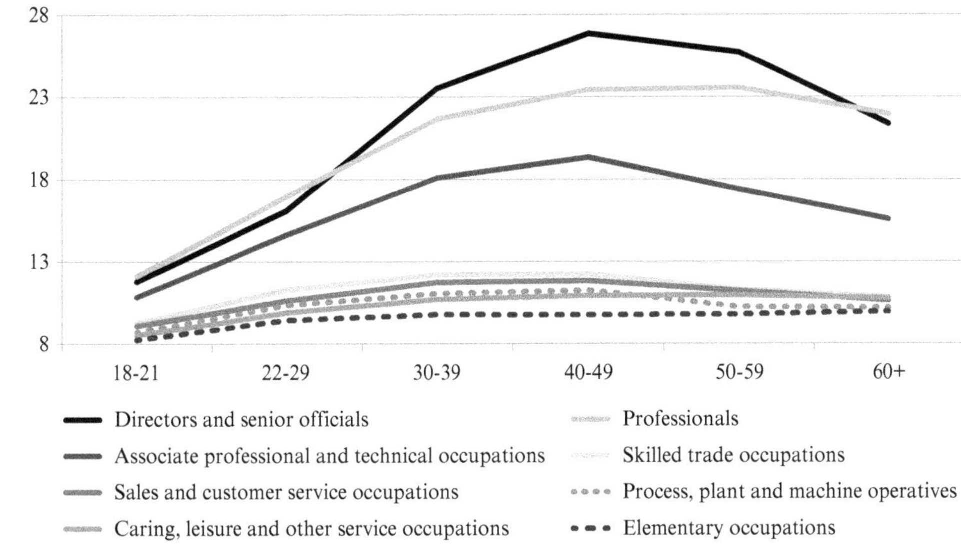

For full-time women workers, pay tends to peak at between 40 and 49 before declining relatively steeply for directors and senior officials, as well as for those in associate professional and technical roles. Women professionals have a trajectory more similar to that for men, though they earn less than their male peers. As is the case for full-time male workers, the variation is much more marked for better-paid workers than for those in relatively low paid occupations.

Figure 11.5 Hourly pay of part-time female workers by age and occupation

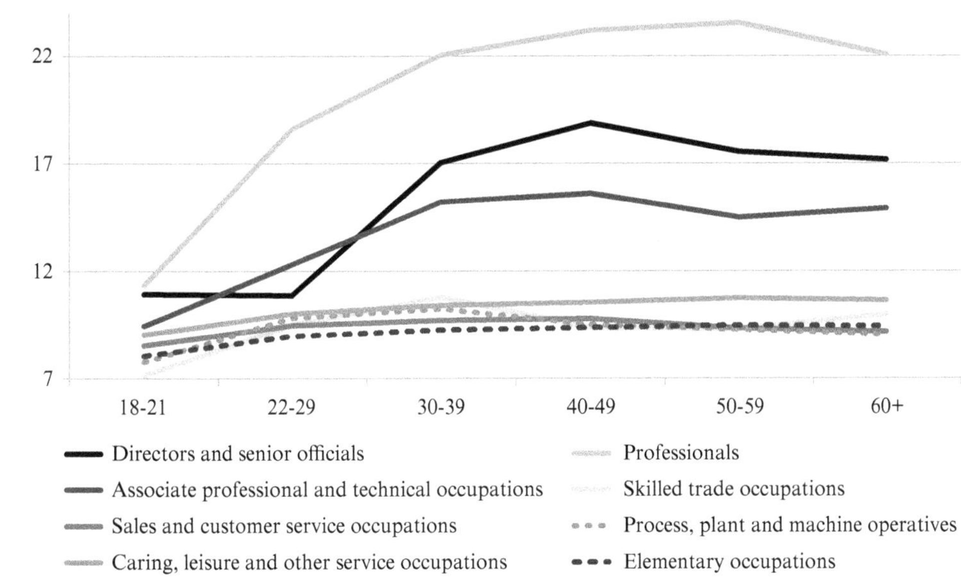

Women professionals working part-time have a similar wage to both male and female full-time professionals, though they earn somewhat less again than women professionals working full-time. The pattern of earnings for women working part-time in the lower paying professions is more varied than that for other workers, women in skilled trade occupations seeing peaks at 30–39 and 65+ while the wages of process, plant and machine operatives peak at 30–39 and the wages of women in caring, leisure and other service occupations and in elementary occupations remain relatively stable (presumably because underpinned by the NMW/National Living Wage).

The relatively low wages of younger workers is evident in all the figures above. This is not the only respect in which young workers are routinely disadvantaged. As Alysia Blackham, extracted below, points out, workers aged 16–24 experience much higher unemployment rates than others (16.2 per cent by comparison with 5.7 per cent in the last quarter of 2014; the figures in 2022 are 9.1 per cent and 2.9 per cent respectively) and are more likely to be employed in zero-hours, low-waged and precarious work.

Alysia Blackham, 'Young Workers and Age Discrimination: Tensions and Conflicts' (2019) 48 *Industrial Law Journal* 1, most footnotes omitted

> … While [established] practices [such as the use of lower youth wages for those under the age of 25; linking employment benefits to length of service or experience; and preferential treatment of older workers in cases of redundancy or termination] may be able to be justified … they likely undermine young people's labour market terms and conditions.
>
> … Those aged under 30 report experiencing higher levels of age discrimination than other age groups, making discrimination against young people at least as widespread as against older workers …. Despite the prevalence of young age discrimination, there has been minimal consideration of age discrimination against young workers in academic research, resulting in an 'ageist ageism literature'.[20] Studies of younger workers in employment have rarely extended to considering age discrimination in the workplace, and studies of age discrimination have rarely extended to discrimination against younger workers …

The other factor which needs to be considered in the case of younger workers is the prevalence of unpaid internships, which have become an increasing feature of young people's entry to sought-after jobs. In 2017 the Taylor Review into modern working practices condemned unpaid internships as 'an abuse of power by employers and extremely damaging to social mobility' and called on the government to eliminate them.[21] The Government responded that it would 'introduce new guidance and increase targeted enforcement activity to help stamp out illegal and exploitative unpaid internships', but little was done and in 2018 the Sutton Trust recommended a change in the law to require payment of any internship lasting longer than four months.

Carl Cullinane and Rebecca Montacute, *Pay as you go? Internship pay, quality and access in the graduate job market* (Sutton Trust, 2018)[22]

> Internships are an increasingly integral part of the graduate job market, yet are characterised by many features that are socially exclusive and afford advantages to those from better off backgrounds, serving as a drag on social mobility. This study uses survey data from young graduates and employers to paint a detailed picture of graduate internships for the first time.

[20] Citing K Rodham, 'Ageism, Young Academics and the Buffalo Stance' in I Glover and M Branine (eds), *Ageism in Work and Employment* (Aldershot, Ashgate, 2001) 176–77.

[21] *Good work: the Taylor review of modern working practices*, available at https://www.gov.uk/government/publications/good-work-the-taylor-review-of-modern-working-practices.

[22] https://www.suttontrust.com/wp-content/uploads/2019/12/Pay-As-You-Go-1.pdf.

How common are internships?

- 39% of graduates in their twenties have done an internship, including almost half (46%) of young graduates under 24. The average intern completes almost 2 internships each (1.8). Interns are more likely to be middle-class, and live in London or other urban areas.
- Graduate internships appear to be rising, with 46% of 21–23 year olds having completed one, compared to 37% of 27–29 year olds. They are also more likely to have taken on more each.
- Almost half (46%) of employers report offering internships, with large employers twice as likely to offer them as small businesses. While one in five employers (19%) report growing use of internships, this figure is 29% for large employers …
- Of the employers who offer internships, almost half report offering unpaid placements (48%). 27% offer expenses only internships and 12% no pay or expenses whatsoever.
- 70% of internships are unpaid, and over a quarter of graduates (27%) have completed at least one unpaid internship. Over half of unpaid placements were over 4 weeks in length (53%). 11% of unpaid internships undertaken were over six months.
- While internship numbers appear to be rising, there seems to be greater consciousness among employers of issues around pay. 56% of internships taken in the past two years were unpaid, compared to 69% of those taken five years ago or more. Younger interns are less likely to complete an unpaid opportunity than older interns.
- 5% of graduates have undertaken three or more unpaid internships. Completing more unpaid opportunities did not seem to lead to a greater likelihood of a paid opportunity, with many interns getting 'stuck' in a cycle of unpaid opportunities. While 62% of those doing their first and only internship were unpaid, this rises to 72% of those doing their fourth or more.
- Pay rates differed substantially across sectors. 89% of internships in retail, 86% of internships in the arts (TV, theatre, film, fashion), and 83% in media were unpaid. While just 26% of IT & telecoms and 32% of manufacturing internships were unpaid …

In December 2017 *The Independent* reported that work-related age discrimination was more commonly reported by those aged 25–34 than by 55+ workers.

'Majority of UK workers say age discrimination is common at work', *The Independent*, 11 December 2017

Almost three-quarters of UK workers feel age discrimination is common in the workplace, with both the youngest and oldest feeling most aggrieved, a new study reveals.

According to job-listings site CV-Library, a third of workers say that they have been rejected for a job because of their age, and over half of workers aged over 55 say they have been discriminated unfavourably because of their age.

The survey of 1,400 workers also found that over half of under 18s feel they're not taken seriously at work, and three-quarters of 25 to 34-year-olds consider themselves having been discriminated for being 'too young'.

Of those, under half said they were told by businesses that they didn't have enough experience.

Of those who say they were discriminated against for being too old, one in five said that they were told they would be too stuck in their own ways …

The Women and Equalities Committee stated in its 2017 report on older people and employment that over one million people aged 50 or over were out of work in 2014 'who would have been willing to work if the right opportunity arose, and 26 per cent of people aged 50 to 64 were jobless but would have liked to work'.[23] In December 2019 to February 2020,

[23] Fourth Report of Session 2017–19, HC359, https://publications.parliament.uk/pa/cm201719/cmselect/cmwomeq/359/35902.htm.

according to the Labour Force Survey (seasonally adjusted figures), the rates of employment, unemployment and economic inactivity for men and women by age were as follows.

Table 11.1 Employment, unemployment and economic inactivity for men and women by age

	Men			Women		
	Employment	**Unemployment**	**Economic activity**	**Employment**	**Unemployment**	**Economic activity**
16–17	20.4	29.4	29.0	27.5	18.7	33.9
18–24	64.3	11.8	72.9	63.2	9	69.5
25–34	90.4	3.2	93.4	80.1	3.2	82.8
35–49	91.2	2.3	93.4	80.5	2.6	82.7
50–64	76.8	3.3	79.4	68.6	2.6	70.4
65+	13.8	2.9	14.2	9.5	10	9.6

It can be seen that there is a significant fall-off in economic activity, though not a significant rise in unemployment, for both men and women between 35–49 and 50–64, with very low rates of economic activity thereafter and a high rate of unemployment for women. The high rate of unemployment for younger people is also worthy of note. The overall picture as regards the relationship between age, work and disadvantage is perhaps best described as mixed, with younger and older workers all reporting age-related discrimination and experiencing relatively lower wages than workers aged 30–49, while the upper echelons of business and the professions are dominated by workers aged 50+.

Health

Concerns are often expressed about discrimination against older people in access to health care.

Joan Costa-Font, 'The Covid-19 crisis reveals how much we value old age', references omitted[24]

The Covid-19 pandemic has hit the older population more than other age cohorts, as their weaker immune system makes it harder to fight diseases and infection. Although all age groups are at risk of contracting the virus, older people face significant risk of developing a severe illness. Of all coronavirus-related deaths so far, 95% occurred in those older than 60 years. More than 50% of all fatalities involved people aged 80 years or older.

Yet, not only older people are more exposed to the risk of contagion and death, but policy reactions have unveiled (i) the different social value older people have in different countries, (ii) the consequences of limited investment in quality long-term care across countries (in a context where nursing homes in many countries have become 'death homes'), and (iii) the lower priority that older people have in congested health care systems …

The lower social value of the elderly costs lives

Covid-19 brings about key trade-offs: shutting down economic activity and restricting people's freedoms, in exchange for improvements in wellbeing that encompass reduced fatalities, mainly among the older population. However, the social value or status of older individuals vis-à-vis other age groups in society is often overlooked in many policy responses …

[24] https://blogs.lse.ac.uk/usappblog/2020/04/25/the-covid-19-crisis-reveals-how-much-we-value-old-age.

Although with the ageing of the population older individuals certainly exert more political influence, their social value (or 'social standing' compared to other age groups) is very different across societies. Whilst many Asian countries report more positive perceptions towards older people, in many Western societies we observe a certain level of 'age aversion', where individuals praise youth stereotypes, and older people pretend to be younger to avoid the effects of ageism (or age discrimination) ... both in social media and in the press, we have seen an increase in discriminatory attitudes towards the elderly in these past few months (e.g., 'They're on their way out anyway') ...

The precarious state of long-term care services costs lives

... The Covid-19 pandemic has revealed how precarious is the funding and organisation of long-term care in a number of European countries ... Quarantines affect more severely older people, who are more likely to live alone and in need of care. Quarantine measures have had a large impact on caregiving. In many countries, caregivers have been forced to reside with older people in need to reduce the chance of contagion. But when older people are less disabled they are more likely to be left on their own, with unmet needs, or with the support of professional caregivers when available. However, many of these professionals were not regarded as key workers and in many cases could not provide their daily support.

Just like other long-term care services, nursing homes have experienced more than proportional fatalities .... This is in part the result of limited investment in quality of care, in many cases resulting from tight budgets and recent austerity reforms that have left institutions short-staffed ...

Lower priority for older people when health systems are congested costs lives

Another sign that older individuals exhibit a lower social valuation is the lower priority they receive when health care is congested amidst a pandemic, which means elderly people with health problems other than coronavirus are less likely to be treated when A&Es are at full capacity ... This applies to congested surgery theatres, when A&E and cancer surgeries are cancelled due to Covid-19, all of which overwhelmingly affect older people.

The lower priority of older patients when rationing health care has been a controversial issue in the literature. Since the 1970s, many medical ethicists and economists have adopted the view that when resources are limited, as they would in a pandemic such as Covid-19, one must consider the age of an individual. The basis for this is that there is a lifespan that we consider reasonable for an individual to live (a 'fair inning'), and the health system, and more generally the government, should focus on ensuring that everyone is given an equal chance to attain a reasonable age – which might be country specific (say, 80 in the UK). Hence, individuals older than such a cut-off age would not be prioritised by intensive care units, and more generally whenever health care was rationed.

Certainty, such a criterion has significant detractors, as medical technology changes the age cut-off one can regard as 'fair', and because social values are not necessarily consistent with a 'fair inning' criteria. However, survey evidence suggests that in many European countries a significant share of the population supports prioritising younger individuals, which affects how the health system's decision makers decide ... although in most countries people think 'age should make no difference', over 40% of the population in the UK, France and Japan think that someone who is 30 years old should be prioritised by the health system.

In the context of the pandemic, British doctors are asked to consider patients' age in critical care decisions. That is, they follow the Clinical Frailty Scale' recommended by the National Institute for Health and Care Excellence (NICE), which takes the patient's age into account. Similarly, the Italian health system prioritises younger patients following utilitarian premises that doctors should give priority to 'saving a life', and other European countries follow similar criteria. That implies a higher valuation for younger patients, who exhibit a higher capacity to benefit from critical care intervention. However, the nature of these choices is acknowledged by the latest ethics note of the British Medical Association, which states that 'some patients may be denied intensive forms of treatment that they would have received outside a pandemic ...'

The extract above makes reference to the Clinical Frailty Scale, which rates people from 1 ('Very fit … robust, active, energetic and motivated. These people commonly exercise regularly. They are among the fittest for their age') to 9 ('Terminally ill … with a life expectancy of <6 months'), interim scores including 4 ('Vulnerable … not dependent on others for daily help [but] often [with] symptoms [which] limit activities') and 7 ('Severely frail – Completely dependent for personal care' though 'not at high risk of dying (within ~6 months)').

The National Institute for Health and Care Excellence (NICE) is responsible for providing national guidance and advice to improve health and social care. NICE's COVID-19 Guidance was updated on 29 April 2020 to take account of concerns expressed, following NICE advice that the Clinical Frailty Scale should be applied to all adults on admission to hospital, that 'applying the score to people with learning disabilities, autism and other stable long-term disabilities, would put them at a disadvantage when decisions were made about admission to critical care in this time of intense pressure'. The reissued advice makes it clear that the 'tool should not be used in younger people, people with stable long-term disabilities (for example, cerebral palsy), learning disabilities or autism'.[25]

Figure 11.6 National Institute for Health and Care Excellence, March 2020 Covid-19 guideline

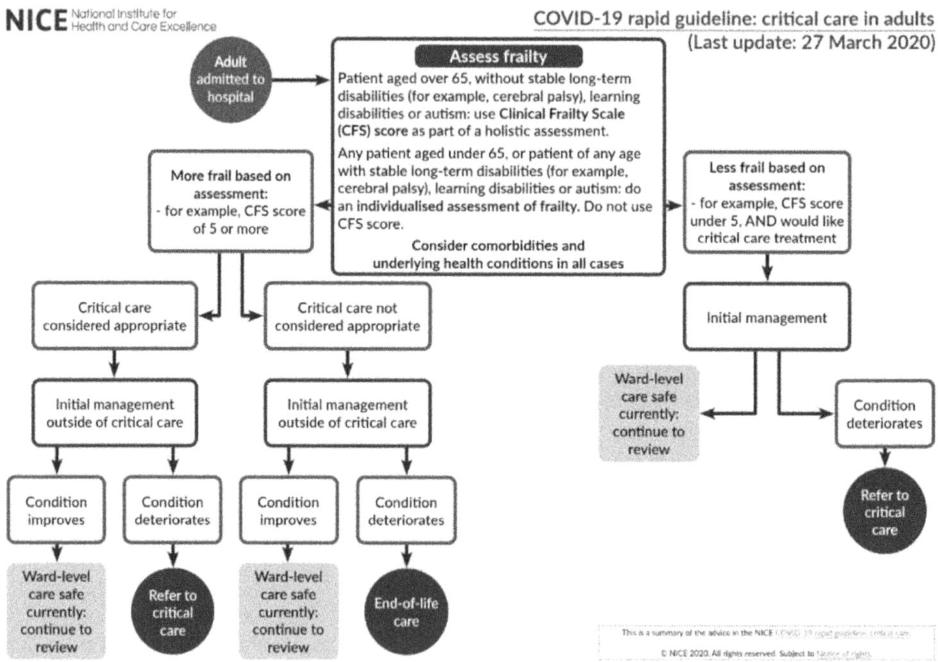

The Costa-Font blog post also refers to the BMA's ethical guidance on COVID 19 which, updated on 30 April 2020, states as follows:

> **BMA, 'Statement/briefing about the use of age and/or disability in our guidance'**[26]
>
> … neither age nor disability are in themselves relevant criteria for making decisions about treatment …

[25] https://www.nice.org.uk/news/article/nice-updates-rapid-covid-19-guideline-on-critical-care.
[26] https://www.bma.org.uk/media/2358/bma-statement-about-ethics-guidance-and-disability-april-2020.pdf.

> It is possible that, at some point, demand may outstrip the supply of available resources; in that case, incredibly difficult decisions will need to be made about who should have access to the limited intensive care resources available. These are decisions that nobody wants to make, but if we reach a point where there are simply not enough specialised intensive care beds and equipment for everyone, such decisions will become unavoidable. Doctors will be on the front line of making and implementing these agonising decisions and we cannot leave them to make these decisions alone; they need support and clear guidance in advance to make sure these decisions are being made in a fair and consistent way.
>
> All patients will continue to receive compassionate treatment and care, including symptomatic relief, but if decisions to choose between patients become unavoidable, our guidance is clear that they must be made consistently and solely on the basis of clinically relevant factors and the ability of patients to benefit.
>
> Under our guidance, the fact that someone is above a particular age, or that they have an existing medical condition is not, in itself, a factor that should be used to determine access to intensive treatment … A decision to exclude from treatment everyone above a particular age, or with a disability, would be both unacceptable and illegal …
>
> Treatment in an intensive care unit provides no guarantee of a positive outcome. The treatment is invasive and highly burdensome. Before commencing treatment for any patient, doctors must be reasonably confident that the patient has the physiological capacity to benefit from the treatment. Where, for example, the consequences of age or a pre-existing disability or medical condition mean that the patient is significantly less likely to survive this complex and demanding treatment, then it becomes a relevant factor …
>
> There is no easy way to make these decisions and we believe it is important that we, as a society, begin to discuss these issues now, in case they become necessary in the future. We are listening to the feedback we receive from individuals and organisations and speaking to specialist clinical, legal and ethical experts, as well as disabled people and others who may be affected our guidance. Our guidance will be kept under regular review.

NICE uses QALYS (Quality-adjusted life years) to determine the cost-effectiveness of medication and treatment. A QALY is, according to NICE:

> a measure of the state of health of a person or group in which the benefits, in terms of length of life, are adjusted to reflect the quality of life. One QALY is equal to 1 year of life in perfect health. QALYs are calculated by estimating the years of life remaining for a patient following a particular treatment or intervention and weighting each year with a quality-of-life score (on a 0 to 1 scale). It is often measured in terms of the person's ability to carry out the activities of daily life, and freedom from pain and mental disturbance.

NICE generally regards treatments that cost more than £30,000 per QALY as not being cost-effective,[27] and does not recommend them for adoption by the NHS. This does not apply to treatments for very rare conditions where the threshold is £100,000 per QALY.

The introduction of QALYs as a measure of healthcare interventions generated concerns about age discrimination, as the following extract shows.

John Harris, 'QALYfying the value of life' (1987) 13 *Journal of Medical Ethics* 117, footnotes omitted

> IV. THE ETHICS OF QALYS
>
> … The idea, which is at the root of both democratic theory and of most conceptions of justice, that each person is as morally important as any other and hence, that the life and interests of each

[27] £50,000 per QALY for end-of-life care.

is to be given equal weight … plays no part at all in the theory of QALYS. That which is to be given equal weight is not persons and their interests and preferences, but quality adjusted life-years. And giving priority to the manufacture of QALYS can mean them all going to a few at the expense of the interests and wishes of the many. It will also mean that all available resources will tend to be deployed to assist those who will thereby gain the maximum QALYS – the young …

VI. QALYS ARE AGEIST

Maximising QALYS involves an implicit and comprehensive ageist bias. For saving the lives of younger people is, other things being equal, always likely to be productive of more QALYS than saving older people. Thus on the QALY arithmetic we always have a reason to prefer, for example, neonatal or paediatric care to all 'later' branches of medicine. This is because any calculation of the life-years generated for a particular patient by a particular therapy, must be based on the life expectancy of that patient. The older a patient is when treated, the fewer the life-years that can be achieved by the therapy. It is true that QALYS dictate that we prefer people, not simply who have more life expectancy, but rather people who have more life expectancy to be gained from treatment. But wherever treatment saves a life, and this will be frequently, for quite simple treatments, like a timely antibiotic, can be life-saving, it will, other things being equal, be the case that younger people have more life expectancy to gain from the treatment than do older people …

DISCRIMINATION

The only way to deal between individuals in a way which treats them as equals when resources are scarce, is to allocate those resources in a way which exhibits no preference. To discriminate between people on the grounds of quality of life, or QALY, or life-expectancy, is as unwarranted as it would be to discriminate on the grounds of race or gender. So, the problem of choosing how to allocate scarce resources is simple. And by that of course I mean 'theoretically simple', not that the decisions will be easy to make or that it will be anything but agonisingly difficult actually to determine, however justly, who should live and who should die. Life-saving resources should simply be allocated in ways which do not violate the individual's entitlement to be treated as the equal of any other individual in the society: and that means the individual's entitlement to have his interests and desires weighed at the same value as those of anyone else. The QALY and the other bases of preference we have considered are irrelevant. If health professionals are forced by the scarcity of resources, to choose, they should avoid unjust discrimination. But how are they to do this?

Just distribution

If there were a satisfactory principle or theory of just distribution now would be the time to recommend its use. Unfortunately there is not a satisfactory principle available. The task is to allocate resources between competing claimants in a way that does not violate the individual's entitlement to be treated as the equal of any other individual – and that means her entitlement to have her fundamental interests and desires weighed at the same value as those of anyone else. The QALY and other quality-of-life criteria are, as we have seen, both dangerous and irrelevant as are considerations based on life-expectancy or on 'life-years' generated by the proposed treatment. If health professionals are forced by the scarcity of resources to choose, not whether to treat but who to treat, they must avoid any method that amounts to unjust discrimination …

… QALYs are not the answer …

PRIORITY IN LIFE-SAVING

… since each person's life is valuable, and since we are committed to treating each person with the same concern and respect that we show to any, we must preserve the lives of as many individuals as we can. To fail to do so would be to value at zero the lives and fundamental interests of those extra people we could, but do not, save. Where we cannot save all, we should select those who are not to be saved in a way that shows no unjust preference …

We should be very clear that the obligation to save as many lives as possible is *not the obligation to save as many lives as we can cheaply or economically save.* Among the sorts of disasters that force us to choose between lives, is not the disaster of overspending a limited health care budget!

There are multifarious examples of what I have in mind here and just a couple must suffice to illustrate the point. Suppose, as is often the case, providing health care in one region of a country is more expensive than doing so in another, or where saving the lives of people with particular conditions, is radically more expensive than other life-saving procedures, and a given health care budget won't run to the saving of all. Then any formula employed to choose priorities should do just that. Instead of attempting to measure the value of people's lives and select which are worth saving, any rubric for resource allocation should examine the national budget afresh to see whether there are any headings of expenditure that are more important to the community than rescuing citizens in mortal danger. For only if all other claims on funding are plausibly more important than that, is it true that resources for life-saving are limited …

A recent BBC television programme calculated that if a health authority had £200,000 to spend it would get 10 QALYS from dialysis of kidney patients, 266 QALYS from hip-replacement operations or 1197 QALYS from anti-smoking propaganda. While this information is undoubtedly useful and while advice to stop smoking is an important part of health care, we should be wary of a formula which seems to dictate that such a health authority would use its resources most efficiently if it abandoned hip replacements and dialysis in favour of advice to stop smoking.

Harris's suggestion that more money should be spent on 'rescuing citizens in mortal danger' looks like a reasonable one, but it is far from clear that available funds should be directed at immediate need rather than long-term preventative measures. Further, and whatever resources are committed to treatment rather than to preventative health measures, some element of selection will at times be unavoidable. It is the case that NICE's use of QALYs would have the effect that treatment which, for the same absolute cost, offer a 50 per cent chance of curing a childhood leukaemia will be regarded as more cost-effective than one which carries the same chance of curing advanced prostate cancer (typically found among older men). But Harris's charge of age discrimination is contested in the following blog, written by another academic philosopher in response to her article.

Richard Yetter Chappell, 'Are QALYs Discriminatory?'[28]

… There's something strange about insisting that each person's life has 'equal moral value', without bothering to assess how much each person stands to gain from continued life. One does not show equal concern towards two people by being indifferent to whether one receives a papercut or the other is beheaded … it is no kind of favouritism to prefer that a greater benefit be bestowed upon whoever is able to receive it. Egalitarians are simply confused to suggest otherwise …

Harris' central confusion is revealed in the following claim (p.121):

> If for example some people were given life-saving treatment in preference to others because they had a better quality of life than those others … this would amount to regarding such people as more valuable than others on that account.

This simply isn't true. Again, we do not ordinarily think that equal moral concern for persons entails being indifferent between a smaller benefit for one or a larger benefit for another. Rather, we may regard *people* with equal concern (i.e. treat them as being equally 'valuable' in themselves) by treating their welfare interests as mattering equally. And treating their interests equally should lead us to prefer that treatment go to whoever would benefit most from it.

Simply put: to say that someone would gain more from continued life is not to say that the *person* is more valuable than another. It is just to say that *what the person gains* is more valuable *to that person* than the alternative outcome is to the other person …

[28] https://www.philosophyetc.net/2009/11/are-qalys-discriminatory.html.

P.S. In principle, we need to assess possible harms and benefits in context: it's not as though a healthy year of life has constant value to all persons at all times … the next forty years of healthy life are worth much more to me than a subsequent forty (even if they're equally healthy, etc.), in light of what I want to achieve during my lifetime. So the real problem with QALYs is that they are *insufficiently* discriminating! But of course practical policies cannot be so perfectly fine-tuned, so QALYs may be the best *practicable* guide to efficient resource allocation …

In 2016, according to the ONS, there were 11.8m people in the UK aged 65+ (up from 9.1m in 1991), comprising 18 per cent of the total population (up from 15.8 per cent).[29] This group accounts about 55 per cent of welfare spending[30] and more than 40 per cent of NHS spending; according to a report in *The Guardian* in 2016: 'an 85-year-old man costs the NHS about seven times more on average than a man in his late 30s' and 'Health spending per person steeply increases after the age of 50'.[31] And the Department of Health estimated in 2010 that 70 per cent of total health and social care spending in England is on long-term health conditions which become more prevalent with age.[32]

Notwithstanding these figures, concerns are regularly expressed about the extent to which healthcare is rationed by factors related to age. This is evident from the materials extracted above. The Royal College of Psychiatrists reported in 2018 that older people were less well served by mental health services than younger people. The report referred to Department of Health estimates that 40 per cent of older people in GP clinics, 50 per cent of older people in hospitals and 60 per cent of those in care homes had a mental health problem, and stated that 'On an average day in a 500-bed hospital' 330 beds would be occupied by older people of whom 220 would have a mental health disorder: 100 depression, 100 dementia and 66 delirium. It went on to suggest that older people with mental health conditions are likely to be misdiagnosed as having dementia or a physical illness and less likely than younger people to be treated:

Royal College of Psychiatrists, *Suffering in silence: age inequality in older people's mental health care* (2018)

Two leading figures in old age psychiatry quote similarly alarming statistics … Common preconceptions among GPs appear to include notions such as that depression is an inevitable consequence of ageing, that diverting resources to younger people is more cost-effective, that older people are unsuited to IAPT and its processes, and that addressing physical and social issues among older people should take priority over psychological therapies. Meanwhile, studies have shown that patients aged 50–70 with pre-existing mental health conditions are particularly at risk if their continuing care is downplayed …

Among older people on acute hospital wards more than 60% have a serious mental disorder which often goes unrecognised and delays rehabilitation and discharge …

Discrepancies in funding

Reported total overall cash investment in older people's mental health services fell by 1% between 2010/11 and 2011/12, from £2.859 billion to £2.830 billion, according to the most recent audit. Taking inflation into account, the overall real-terms investment in these services fell by 3.1%. At the same time, older people's services were already underfunded by as much as £2.3 billion compared with services for younger adults. Achieving parity in service provision for adults aged 55–74 with those aged 35–54 was thought in 2008 to require a 24% increase in NHS mental health

[29] https://www.ons.gov.uk/peoplepopulationandcommunity/birthsdeathsandmarriages/ageing/articles/livinglongerhowourpopulationischangingandwhyitmatters/2018-08-13#how-is-the-uk-population-changing.

[30] House of Commons Library, 'Challenges of an ageing population' (2015), available at https://www.parliament.uk/business/publications/research/key-issues-parliament-2015/social-change/ageing-population.

[31] 'Ageing Britain: two-fifths of NHS budget is spent on over-65s', *The Guardian*, 1 February 2016.

[32] 'Challenges of an ageing population', n 30 above.

spending. There is no reason to think that the situation has improved since these figures were compiled … Since mental health problems affecting older people are often more complex, proportionally more investment is justified. Yet the tide of events seems to be moving the other way …

In 2013, the government said it wanted to achieve parity of esteem between physical and mental health. That commitment was followed by a promise of £1.25 billion for child and adolescent mental health, a national strategy for adult mental health and an investment of £1 billion to support its delivery. But the *Five Year Forward View for Mental Health* made no mention of a funding pledge for older people's services. The *Forward View* pays little attention to mental health care in the community, which is where most secondary mental health care is provided, including for older adults. Moreover, the services advocated do not distinguish between working-age and older adults, which has the unintended consequence of funnelling resources into services (such as crisis resolution teams) that work, with a few exceptions, only with the working-age population.

The implication in the 2018 report that young people fare better as regards mental health services than older people is open to question, much concern having been expressed over recent years about the chronic underfunding of mental health services for children and adolescents. Young Minds reported in 2018 on a 'crisis in mental health support for children and young people.' With about 75 per cent of those who sought treatment becoming more unwell while waiting for help from Child and Adolescent Mental Health Services (CAMHS), and frequently not being signposted to other forms of support.

Young Minds, *A new era for young people's mental health* (2018)[33]

… while waiting for help, young people may start to self-harm, become suicidal, or drop out of school, which can have a huge impact, not only on their education but on their families too. We also know that young people with emerging mental health problems, who do not meet the threshold for clinical services, are often left with no help at all. This cannot be right.

The government's recent plans to roll out Mental Health Support Teams in schools are a step in the right direction, but will cover less than a quarter of areas by 2022-3. And, after years of cuts, there is also a black hole in youth and community services …

Young people looking for mental health support can face barriers at every stage. This can be because of problems getting help at school, cuts to youth services, difficulties getting an initial referral to [CAMHS], high thresholds for treatment, delays between referral and assessment and delays between assessment and treatment. Even when young people are assessed as needing support from CAMHS, it does not guarantee timely treatment. Recent research by Health Service Journal showed that, in 2017/18, more than 500 young people had waited more than a year between assessment and the start of treatment. Around half of young people had waited more than 18 weeks.

These delays often mean that problems escalate. We have carried out a survey with more than 2,000 parents of children who have looked for mental health support. This showed that:

- Three-quarters (76%) of parents said that their children's mental health had deteriorated while waiting for support from [CAMHS].
- The longer children were left to wait, the more likely it was that their mental health worsened. 85% of parents whose children had waited more than six months said that their children's mental health had deteriorated, including 64% who said that their children's mental health had deteriorated a lot.
- Two-thirds (69%) of parents said that neither they nor their children had been signposted to any other form of support during the time they were waiting for support from CAMHS …

Less than 1% of the total NHS budget is spent on CAMHS.

Around 8% of the total mental health budget is spent on CAMHS.

[33] https://youngminds.org.uk/media/2620/a-new-era-for-young-peoples-mental-health.pdf.

Serious pressures on NHS budgets, themselves in significant part the product of an aging population, have resulted in increased tensions about the cost of healthcare for older people and the equivalence of treatment for older and younger people. Older people absorb a disproportionate amount of the NHS budget but are regularly in a position in which ailments which would be regarded as medical in the case of younger people may fall in the case of older people to be dealt with under social care arrangements, which is not generally free at the point of delivery. The chronic underfunding of social care by the state has itself contributed to the increasing pressure on the NHS, including by virtue of chronic shortages of suitable care home places to which vulnerable elderly people could be discharged from hospital. But efforts to address this problem, which has itself been caused in part by the exponential increases in demand resulting from an aging population, have been stymied by the disproportionate political power of (relatively affluent) older voters who are resistant to the adoption of measures which would threaten their ability (and/or that of their elderly parents) to pass accumulated wealth on through inheritance, rather than seeing it depleted for the purposes of funding social care.

Age Discrimination and the Law

The Human Rights Act 1998

Below we deal with the regulation of age discrimination by the EqA. Before this, it is useful to consider the potential impact of the Human Rights Act 1998 (HRA), which gives partial effect in domestic law to Article 14 (the prohibition on discrimination). We have seen in previous chapters that the HRA may provide an additional route to challenge discrimination which does not fall within the EqA. We have also seen that it can impact on the interpretation of the EqA. The potential for either of these routes is limited in the case of age discrimination because age attracts less protection than other characteristics under Article 14. This is made clear in the following case in which the Court of Appeal (CA) rejected an Article 14 challenge to a policy which discriminated between students aged up to 16 and 19+, on the one hand, and those aged 16–18, on the other, as regards school transport.

***R (Drexler) v Leicestershire CC* [2020] EWCA Civ 502, [2020] ELR 399**

The Council provided free transport to students with special educational needs up to age 16 if the schools which the authority designated as suitable to their needs were more than a set distance from their homes. Students aged 19 were also provided with free transport if the local authority regarded transport to be necessary to facilitate their attendance at the relevant institution. The local authority did not guarantee assistance to students aged 16–18, and adopted a policy by which such assistance, where it was provided, would generally be by way of a payment rather than the provision of transport. The policy's age-related distinctions echoed those of primary legislation which required local authorities to provide transport to those aged 5–16 and 19+ in the circumstances referred to in the local authority's policy, but did not impose this requirement in relation to students aged 16–18. The claim failed, the High Court having instructed itself in line with the decision of the SC (SC) in *R (DA) v Secretary of State for Work and Pensions* [2019] UKSC 21, [2019] 1 WLR 3289 that the test for justification in an Article 14 claim related to welfare benefits was 'whether it is manifestly without reasonable foundation', and found that the provision of transport in line with the statutory obligations imposed on the authority was justified.[34] The claimant's appeal to the CA failed.

Singh LJ (with whom Bean and Newey LJ agreed):

> 52 .... Even if the standard of review is different from the manifestly without reasonable foundation test, and is the conventional proportionality test, it is clear from authorities decided by the House of Lords and Supreme Court that a suitable margin of judgement must be afforded to the decision-maker in a context such as the present.
>
> 55. ... not all grounds of discrimination are treated in the same way under Article 14. It is recognised in the jurisprudence both of the European Court of Human Rights and in domestic courts under the HRA that certain grounds of discrimination are 'suspect', in particular race, sex, nationality and sexual orientation. These will therefore call for more stringent scrutiny than other grounds of discrimination. In the terminology used by the European Court of Human Rights, 'very weighty reasons' will usually be required to justify what would otherwise be discrimination on such grounds: see e.g. *R (Carson) v Secretary of State for Work and Pensions* [2005] UKHL 37; [2006] 1 AC 173, [paras 15-17 and 55-60] ... Lord Walker in particular drew on the terminology of 'suspect' grounds which is to be derived from American jurisprudence on the Fourteenth Amendment to the US Constitution (the 'equal protection' clause).
>
> 56. ... the courts recognise that they are not well placed to question the judgement made by either the executive or the legislature in relation to matters of public expenditure. This is both on the ground of relative institutional competence and on the ground of democratic legitimacy. The allocation of scarce or finite public resources is inherently a matter which calls for political judgement. This does not mean that the courts have no role to play but it does mean that they must tread with caution, affording appropriate weight and respect to the judgement formed by the executive or the legislature ...
>
> 76. ... in my view, the crucial point is not so much whether the 'manifestly without reasonable foundation' test is the applicable test; it is rather how the conventional proportionality test, even if that is the applicable test, should be applied given that the context is one in which a public authority is required to allocate finite resources and to choose priorities when it comes to setting its budget; and is also a context in which the ground of discrimination is not one of the 'suspect' grounds. In this context, it seems to me that there is no material difference between application of the conventional proportionality test, giving appropriate weight and respect to the judgement of the executive or legislature, and the 'manifestly without reasonable foundation' test.
>
> 77. Even if the correct test to be applied is not the one of manifestly without reasonable foundation, I have reached the clear conclusion that the Respondent was entitled to adopt the policy which it did and that it did not act unlawfully in breach of Article 14. In particular, I am convinced that the policy fell within the margin of judgement which is afforded to it even applying the conventional proportionality test. I bear in mind the following particular features of this case.
>
> 78. First, age is not a 'suspect' ground of discrimination, such as race or sex.

[34] Note that this test has been superseded (see discussion of *R (SC) v SSWP* [2021] UKSC 26, [2022] AC 223 in Ch 2), though this would be unlikely to have changed the outcome in *Drexler* had the SC decision preceded that case.

> 79. Secondly, this is an area in which the Respondent had to make difficult choices, in straitened financial circumstances, as to its priorities for public expenditure. It is better placed than the Court can ever be to know the needs of its local area and its residents. If cuts cannot be made to the budget in one context, they are likely to be necessary in some other context and will affect other people, who are not before the Court. Even if no cuts had to be made elsewhere, the gap in public finances would have to be filled in some other way, typically by raising taxes or borrowing, even assuming that those options are available. These methods all have consequences for other people. Sometimes this is called a 'polycentric' issue … This point goes to the relative institutional competence of the Respondent as compared with the Court. Furthermore, the Respondent has a democratic legitimacy which the Court does not …
>
> 80. Thirdly, the Respondent was seeking to 'track' the distinction which is made in primary legislation itself by Parliament as to the crucial importance of age once a person is above 16. That was not an end of the matter … There can be circumstances in which an apparent discretion in effect becomes a duty because to exercise the discretion the other way would contravene obligations in the HRA.
>
> 81. Nevertheless, in my view, the Respondent was entitled to take into account the difference in the statutory regime which applies to children under the age of 16, who are of 'compulsory school age', and those above 16 …
>
> 82. Fourthly, it is important to recall that the Respondent's policy admits of the possibility of exceptions to be made in case of real need. We were informed, and there is evidence before this Court, that some seven exceptions have indeed been made to the policy, even though its implementation was deferred by one year.
>
> 83. Finally, the policy envisages a system of appeals.
>
> 84. All of these factors, in my view, lead to the conclusion that the policy cannot be regarded as being unlawful under Article 14 It did have a legitimate aim (the saving of public money) – see *R (TP) v Secretary of State for Work and Pensions* [2020] EWCA Civ 37, at paras. 170-173 in the judgment of the Court, summarising the authorities on the relevance of cost when seeking to justify alleged discrimination – and the means chosen to achieve that aim complied with the principle of proportionality. This is not a case, such as might be envisaged hypothetically, where (for example) a cash-strapped local authority decided to adopt a policy under which school transport would continue to be provided for some people based on a wholly irrelevant ground such as sending boys by taxi to school but not girls.

This is not to say that age discrimination will never breach Article 14. In *Carvalho Pinto de Sousa Morais v Portugal* (2018) 66 EHRR 25 the ECtHR ruled that the applicant's Article 14 rights had been breached when the measure of damages ordered to be paid to her by reason of the loss of ability to have sexual intercourse as a result of botched gynaecological surgery was reduced because, the applicant having been 50 years old at the time of surgery and mother to two children, sex would have been less important to her than it would have been when she was younger. The ECtHR ruled that the assumption that sexuality was not as important for a 50-year-old woman with two children as it would be for someone younger age reflected a traditional notion of female sexuality being linked to child-bearing purposes, and ignored its physical and psychological relevance for the self-fulfilment of women as people. In earlier decisions the Portuguese Supreme Court had recognised that men's inability to have normal sex relations had affected their self-esteem and resulted in 'severe mental trauma' without taking account of their age. The Court found that the applicant had been the victim of discrimination on the basis of her age and sex. In *Khamtokhu v Russia* (2017) 43 BHRC 79, by contrast, the Court rejected challenges to sentencing guidelines which exempted women and those under 18 and over 65 from life imprisonment or serious offences. The Court ruled that there was no reason to question the difference in treatment between juvenile and adult offenders, the exemption of the former from life imprisonment applying across Council of Europe states in the interests of the rehabilitation of juvenile delinquents. The more favourable treatment of those aged 65+ was a measure designed to make the possibility of release for older prisoners a real possibility as it was for younger prisoners even in the event of a life sentence, and was within the margin of appreciation available to the state.

The Equality Act 2010

The EqA prohibits age discrimination in broadly similar terms to the prohibitions on discrimination because of other characteristics. The significant difference between age and the other protected characteristics is that direct age discrimination is, uniquely, subject to a general justification defence. Section 13 EqA having provided that '(1) A person (A) discriminates against another (B) if, because of a protected characteristic, A treats B less favourably than A treats or would treat others' goes on to state that

> **Section 13(2) EqA, direct discrimination**
>
> (2) If the protected characteristic is age, A does not discriminate against B if A can show A's treatment of B to be a proportionate means of achieving a legitimate aim'.

The justification of direct age discrimination is considered below and in Chapter 2 (the test for justification of direct age discrimination overlapping significantly with that for indirect discrimination generally). Also important in terms of core legal provisions is s5 EqA:

> **Section 5 EqA, direct discrimination**
>
> (1) In relation to the protected characteristic of age—
>
> (a) a reference to a person who has a particular protected characteristic is a reference to a person of a particular age group;
>
> (b) a reference to persons who share a protected characteristic is a reference to persons of the same age group.
>
> (2) A reference to an age group is a reference to a group of persons defined by reference to age, whether by reference to a particular age or to a range of ages.

The Explanatory Notes to the EqA state that an 'age group' would include, for example, 'over-50s' or '21-year-olds' while the EHRC's Statutory Code of Practice on Employment states that an age group could consist of persons 'older than' a claimant.[35]

The prohibition on age discrimination, harassment and victimisation applies across Parts 3 and 5-7 EqA (goods, services, facilities and public functions; education; work and associations) save that those aged under 18 are not protected by Part 3 or by the prohibition on discrimination by providers of further or higher education in access to recreational and training facilities, and Part 6 Chapter 1 (schools) and Part 4 (premises) do not apply to age.[36]

[35] Respectively, https://www.legislation.gov.uk/ukpga/2010/15/notes §37, and https://www.equalityhumanrights.com/en/publication-download/employment-statutory-code-practice, §2.4.

[36] Sections 28(1)(a), 93(9), 84(a) EqA.

Direct Age Discrimination

The question of comparators is considered in Chapter 2. The identification of the comparator may pose particular challenges in direct age discrimination claims. The EHRC's Employment Code of Practice remarks at §2.7 that the EqA 'does not specify the age group with which comparison should be made. It could be everyone outside the person's age group, but in many cases the choice of comparator age group will be more specific; this will often be led by the context and circumstances'.[37] It suggests that 'A female worker aged 25 could be viewed as sharing the protected characteristic of age with a number of different age groups. These might include '"25 year olds"; "the under 30s"; "the over 20s"; and "younger workers", and that such a worker 'might compare herself to the "over 25s", or "over 35s", or "older workers". She could also compare herself to "under 25s" or "18 year olds".' The appropriate comparator group will, of course, depend on the nature of the claim.

By contrast with the binary comparisons generally drawn in relation to other protected characteristics (male and female, white and Asian, straight and gay), a claimant's comparator may have a very similar age to the claimant depending on the specific discrimination complained of. In *Palmer v RBS plc* [2014] ICR 1288, for example, the 49-year-old claimant complained that she was discriminated against as regards redundancy/retirement by comparison with employees aged 50–55.

The domestic courts have, on occasion, been prepared to dismiss discrimination challenges on the basis that the very protected characteristic upon which the claim of discrimination rests (or something very closely related to it) has the effect of making the claimant and his or her comparator materially different in a way which blocks comparison between them. (Section 23(1) EqA, to which each of the predecessor legislation had equivalents, provides that 'On a comparison of cases for the purposes of [determining direct or indirect discrimination] there must be no material difference between the circumstances relating to each case.') This has, since the decision of the House of Lords in *Shamoon v Chief Constable of the RUC* [2003] UKHL 11, [2003] ICR 337, become less of a concern. But in *Lockwood v Department of Work and Pensions* a tribunal rejected an age discrimination challenge from a woman who had been awarded a lower payment on voluntary redundancy aged 26 (after eight years' service) than she would have been entitled to had she been over 35 on the basis that, *because of her age*, her circumstances were materially different from those of a comparator aged over 35. The CA ruled that the tribunal had erred in its approach.

***Lockwood v Department of Work and Pensions* [2013] EWCA Civ 1195, [2014] ICR 941**

The employment tribunal reasoned that younger employees had lesser financial and family obligations, could generally be expected to react more easily and rapidly to the loss of their jobs, that greater flexibility could be expected of them and that they were more likely to move into employment than older people. It also concluded that, had direct discrimination been established, it would have been objectively justified because the aim of the scheme was to produce a proportionate financial cushion until alternative employment was found or as a bridge to retirement and the receipt of a pension, and the use of banding by age was reasonably necessary to the scheme's administrative workability. The CA ruled that the tribunal had erred in its approach to comparators, though it

[37] n 35 above.

refused the claimant's appeal because it concluded that the discrimination was justifiable. (The legislative provision under discussion was reg 3(2) of the Age Regs, which provided that 'A comparison of [the claimant's] case with that of another person … must be such that the relevant circumstances in the one case are the same, or not materially different, in the other'.)

Rimer LJ (with whom Leweson and Treacy LJJ agreed):

> 34 …. The whole purpose of the comparison is as an aid to seeing whether or not the way in which the comparator was, or would have been, treated in the relevant circumstances supports the claimant's allegation that he was subjected to less favourable treatment on the ground of the protected characteristic.
>
> 35. … There was no difficulty [in this case] in identifying a comparator, namely someone over 35 who was, or would have been, otherwise in all material respects as regards his or her employment in the DWP in the same position as Ms Lockwood. For the employment tribunal then, however, to have held that the respective circumstances of the, say, 36-year-old comparator and the 26-year-old Ms Lockwood were materially different, so that Ms Lockwood failed to show less favourable treatment as compared with her comparator, was wrong.
>
> 36. First, Ms Lockwood's age of 26 did not make the relevant circumstances of her case materially different from that of the comparator. Her case was that it was because of her age that she was being discriminated against. Just as a comparison between a black claimant and a white comparator is not invalidated because of their difference in race, so the comparison between the 26-year-old Ms Lockwood and the 36-year-old comparator was not invalidated either. On the contrary, the comparison was relevant, valid and essential for the purposes of answering the question whether or not Ms Lockwood had suffered less favourable treatment on the ground of her age.
>
> 37. Second, once the comparison was made, there was only one answer to the question whether she had suffered such less favourable treatment, namely yes. That is because, on leaving her employment, she was paid substantially less money than was or would be paid to someone whose circumstances, age apart, were identical. The employment tribunal, however, rejected this straightforward conclusion. It instead approached the case by bringing into account in its assessment of the relevant circumstances the fact that, because Ms Lockwood was younger than the comparator and belonged to a generation whose members could adjust more easily and rapidly to the loss of jobs than their colleagues in their late thirties, her circumstances were materially different from those of the comparator.
>
> 38. Those considerations were, however, nothing more than features of being 26 rather than 36. The employment tribunal's reasoning appears to have been that, because a 26-year-old leaver can be assumed not to need as much money as a 36-year-old leaver, there was no less favourable treatment in giving the former a lower severance payment than the latter. Even if the premise was correct, the conclusion was self-evidently wrong. The premise, if right, may have provided grounds for justifying the disparity of the treatment between the different age groups. But that was a different question. There was, however, no question that Ms Lockwood suffered less favourable treatment than her comparator. The employment tribunal ought so to have found, and the appeal tribunal was wrong in failing to correct its error.

The discrimination in *Lockwood* was found to be justified. Section 13(2) EqA, which permits the justification of direct age discrimination, is extracted above. The provision is based on Recital 25 and Article 6 of Council Directive 2000/78.

Recital 2, Council Directive 2000/78

The prohibition of age discrimination is an essential part of meeting the aims set out in the Employment Guidelines and encouraging diversity in the workforce. However, differences in treatment in connection with age may be justified under certain circumstances and therefore require specific provisions which may vary in accordance with the situation in Member States. It is therefore essential to distinguish between differences in treatment which are justified, in particular by legitimate employment policy, labour market and vocational training objectives, and discrimination which must be prohibited.

Article 6(1), Council Directive 2000/78

… Member States may provide that differences of treatment on grounds of age shall not constitute discrimination, if, within the context of national law, they are objectively and reasonably justified by a legitimate aim, including legitimate employment policy, labour market and vocational training objectives, and if the means of achieving that aim are appropriate and necessary.

Such differences of treatment may include, among others:

(a) the setting of special conditions on access to employment and vocational training, employment and occupation, including dismissal and remuneration conditions, for young people, older workers and persons with caring responsibilities in order to promote their vocational integration or ensure their protection;
(b) the fixing of minimum conditions of age, professional experience or seniority in service for access to employment or to certain advantages linked to employment;
(c) the fixing of a maximum age for recruitment which is based on the training requirements of the post in question or the need for a reasonable period of employment before retirement.

An early challenge to the broad justification defence in the Age Regs failed in the High Court in *R (Age UK) v SSBIS* [2009] EWHC 2336 (Admin), [2010] ICR 260. The Court had referred to the CJEU a number of questions concerning whether the Directive regulated retirement ages (it did); whether Article 6 required the state to specify the kinds of differences in treatment on grounds of age which might be justified; and whether there was any significant difference between the test in Article 2(2) and the test in Article 6(1) (for the justification of indirect and direct discrimination respectively). The CJEU ruled that it was for the national court to ascertain whether the aims contemplated by the Age Regs fell within the social policy objective permitted by Article 6(1) of the Directive, and whether the justification defence was 'appropriate and necessary', stressing the heavy burden of proof imposed on the Member States as regards the legitimacy of the aim relied on to justify age discrimination.[38] On its return, the High Court accepted that the Government had established that its decision to allow direct discrimination to be justified was based on social policy concerns of protecting the confidence and integrity of the labour market despite the failure of the legislation to define the broad social policy reasons relied upon. It went on to state that, whereas the Government was entitled to a broad margin of appreciation as regards its social policy objectives, individual employers would not be so entitled in cases in which they sought to justify a particular case of discriminatory treatment.

The CJEU ruled in a number of early cases that the prohibition on age discrimination did not preclude compulsory retirement whether by reason of national legislation or, as is common in many continental European countries, by reason of a legally binding collective agreement.[39] In Case C-341/08, *Petersen v Berufungsausschuss für Zahnärzte für den*

[38] Case C-388/7, *R (Incorporated Trustees of the National Council on Ageing v SS Business, Enterprise and Regulatory Reform* EU:C:2009:128, [2009] ECR I-1569, [2009] ICR 1080.

[39] Case C-411/05, *Palacios De La Villa v Cortefiel Servicios* SA, EU:C:2007:604, [2007] ECR I-8531, [2009] ICR 1111; Case C-45/09, *Rosenbladt v Oellerking Gebäudereinigungsges mbH*, EU:C:2010:601, [2010] ECR I-9391;

Bezirk Westfalen-Lippe EU:C:2010:4, [2010] ECR I-47, the Court ruled that Article 6(1) of Council Directive 2000/78 did not preclude the imposition of a maximum age limit of 68 (subject to exceptions) on dentists providing services under the statutory health insurance scheme, which did not apply to dentists practising outside the scheme, if its aim was to distribute employment opportunities across the generations and if, taking into account the situation in the labour market concerned, the measure was appropriate and necessary for achieving that aim. (The Court went on to rule in *Petersen* that the national court was required to disapply any provision of national law which could not be interpreted consistent with the Directive, even if national law made no provision for so doing.)

While being relatively generous in the application of Article 6 to compulsory retirement, the CJEU from the start applied more rigorous scrutiny to arguments made under Article 2(5), which provides as follows.

> **Article 2(5), Council Directive 2000/78**
>
> This Directive shall be without prejudice to measures laid down by national law which, in a democratic society, are necessary for public security, for the maintenance of public order and the prevention of criminal offences, for the protection of health and for the protection of the rights and freedoms of others.

In *Petersen* (above) the CJEU ruled that Article 2(5) could not be relied upon to permit the imposition of the age limit under the statutory health insurance scheme unless the purpose of the legislation was to maintain the financial balance of the healthcare system, as distinct from the health of patients. And in Case C-447/09 *Prigge v Deutsche Lufthansa Ag* EU:C:2011:573, [2011] ECR I-08003, [2011] IRLR 1052 the Court ruled that the termination of commercial pilots' contracts when they reached 60, on grounds of public security and protection of health, breached Council Directive 2000/78 in circumstances in which national and international legislation fixed the age for compulsory termination at 65. This being the case, the measure did not fall within Article 2(5) of the Directive and Article 6(1) had to be interpreted to the effect that air traffic safety did not constitute a legitimate aim.

The CJEU has also been slower to accept the justifiability of age discrimination in relation to pay than it has been to permit compulsory retirement. In Case C-88/08, *Hütter v Technische Universität Graz* EU:C:2009:381, [2009] ECR I-5325, for example, it ruled that Council Directive 2000/78 precluded an employer from distinguishing in terms of pay between employees whose periods of service had been acquired before or after the age of 18. In Case C-499/08, *Ingeniorforeningen i Danmark v Region Syddanmark* EU:C:2010:600, [2010] ECR I-9343, the Court ruled that Council Directive 2000/78 did not permit the exclusion of workers from entitlement to severance pay intended to assist workers in finding new employment on the sole ground that they were entitled to a pension from their employer. The claimant, aged 63, had decided not to retire on being dismissed after 18 years' service and was seeking employment. The CJEU accepted that the purpose of the severance scheme was to protect long-serving employees and help them to find new employment, so as to fall within the category of legitimate employment policy and labour market objectives in Article 6. It ruled, however, that the scheme was disproportionate in that it excluded all those entitled to, rather than only those in receipt of, pensions.[40]

Cases C-159/10 and 160/10, *Fuchs v Land Hessen, Köhler v Land Hessen*, EU:C:2011:508, [2011] ECR I-6919, [2012] ICR 93; and Case C-250/09, *Georgiev v Tehnicheski universitet – Sofia, filial Plovdiv*, EU:C:2010:699, [2010] ECR I-11869.

[40] See, similarly, Case C-441/14 *Dansk Industri (DI), acting on behalf of Ajos A/S v Estate of Rasmussen* ECLI EU:C:2016:278, [2016] IRLR 552.

In Cases C-297/10 and C-298/10, *Hennigs v Eisenbahn-Bundesamt, Land Berlin v Mai* EU:C:2011:560, [2011] ECR I-7965, the CJEU ruled that the determination of pay by reference to age breached Council Directive 2000/78. The discrimination in issue arose from collective agreements, in one case under transitional arrangements following a movement away from age-related pay. The CJEU ruled that the discrimination was not objectively justified by a general relationship between age and experience, although the reward of experience was legitimate. Finally, in Case C-555/07, *Kücükdeveci v Swedex GmbH & Co KG* EU:C:2010:21, [2010] ECR I-00365, the Court ruled that the exclusion of service prior to an employee having reached the age of 25 from the calculation of continuous service for the purposes of statutory notice entitlement was not 'appropriate and necessary' to the achievement of the legitimate aims of facilitating the recruitment of younger workers by increasing the flexibility of personnel management, and recognising that young workers can generally react more easily and rapidly to the loss of their jobs and that greater flexibility can be demanded of them. The Court ruled in *Kücükdevec*, as it had in Case C-144/04, *Mangold v Helm* EU:C:2005:709, [2005] ECR I-9981, [2006] IRLR 143, that the prohibition on age discrimination in the Directive reflected the general principle of equal treatment in EU law.

The decisions of the CJEU considered above are significant to the approach to be taken by the domestic courts. The starting point for considering the justifiability of age discrimination in domestic law is the decision of the SC in *Seldon v Clarkson Wright and Jakes* in which Baroness Hale, for the SC, drew a number of principles from the case law of the CJEU.

***Seldon v Clarkson Wright and Jakes* [2012] UKSC 16, [2012] ICR 716**

The claimant was an equity partner in a firm of solicitors who was required to retire at the end of the year following his 65th birthday in compliance with the partnership deed. At the time the Age Regs permitted mandatory retirement of employees, but this did not apply to the claimant as a partner. His claim of direct age discrimination was rejected by a tribunal which ruled that the discrimination was justified by reference to the legitimate aims of (1) ensuring that associates were given the opportunity of partnership after a reasonable period, thereby ensuring that they did not leave the firm; (2) facilitating workforce planning by enabling realistic long-term expectations as to when vacancies would arise; and (3) limiting the need to expel partners by way of performance management, thus contributing to a congenial and supportive culture in the firm. The EAT accepted that the first two aims could have been met by any fixed retirement age, but ruled that there was no evidential basis for the assumption that performance would drop off at around the age of 65, and thus for choosing that age in order to achieve the third aim. It remitted the case to the tribunal to consider whether it was satisfied that the age discrimination was justified by reference to the first two aims ([2009] IRLR 267). The claimant's appeal was dismissed by the CA and the SC.

The claimant argued before the SC that the Age Regs failed to implement the test for justification of direct discrimination in Council Directive 2000/78 by applying the same test for direct as for indirect age discrimination: that the measure was a 'proportionate means of achieving a legitimate aim'. He also submitted that a discriminatory measure had to be justified in its application to a particular individual as well as generally.

Lady Hale (with whom Lords Brown, Mance and Kerr agreed, Lord Hope delivering a judgment in similar terms):

2. Age is a relative newcomer to the list of characteristics protected against discrimination. Laws against discrimination are designed to secure equal treatment for people who are seen by society to be in essentially the same situation …

3. The reasons why age may be relevant in more circumstances than the other characteristics may seem obvious, at least where this has to do with the comparative capabilities of people of different ages. A younger person may not have the same training and experience as an older person. An older person may have lost the mental or physical strength which once she had. But it will be seen from recital 25 above that the European legislators considered that age discrimination might be justified by factors which had nothing to do with the characteristics of the individual but had to do with broader social and economic policy. These factors would not justify direct discrimination on the ground of any of the other protected characteristics, so why should age be different?

4. The answer must be that age is different. As Ms Rose put it on behalf of the Secretary of State, age is not 'binary' in nature (man or woman, black or white, gay or straight) but a continuum which changes over time. As Lord Walker pointed out in *R (Carson and Reynolds) v Secretary of State for Work and Pensions* [2006] 1 AC 173, at [60], 'Every human being starts life as a tiny infant, and none of us can do anything to stop the passage of the years'. This means that younger people will eventually benefit from a provision which favours older employees, such as an incremental pay scale; but older employees will already have benefitted from a provision which favours younger people, such as a mandatory retirement age …

15. Both Mr Seldon and Age UK invite the Court to … [have] it firmly in mind that the purpose of all anti-discrimination legislation is to 'address the mismatch between reality and past assumptions or stereotypes. In the context of age discrimination these assumptions have usually concerned age as a proxy for continuing competence or capability or financial security or intentions about work'. These assumptions no longer hold good (if they ever did) in times of increasing longevity, where there are benefits both to individuals and to the wider society if people continue to work for as long as they can. Put simply, the younger generations need the older ones to continue to be self-supporting for as long as possible. So we should put such stereotypical assumptions out of our minds …

30. The Secretary of State accepts that only certain kinds of aim are capable of justifying direct age discrimination and that the apparently broad terms of reg. 3 [which applied the same justification test for direct and indirect age discrimination] must be read down accordingly. The distinction drawn in the evolving case law of the [CJEU] is between aims relating to 'employment policy, the labour market or vocational training', which are legitimate, and 'purely individual reasons particular to the employer's situation, such as cost reduction or improving competitiveness', which in general are not …

[Lady Hale discussed decisions of the CJEU including those discussed above, and in Case C-229/08 *Wolf v Stadt Frankfurt am Main* EU:C:2010:3, [2010] ECR I-1, discussed below, and suggested that the messages which could be taken from the European case law were as follows]:

50. (1) All the references to the European Court discussed above have concerned national laws or provisions in collective agreements authorised by national laws. They have not concerned provisions in individual contracts of employment or partnership, as this case does. However, the *Bartsch* case[41] … did concern the rules of a particular employer's pension fund; and

[41] Case C-427/06, *Bartsch v Bosch und Siemens Hausgeräte (BSH) Altersfürsorge GmbH*, EU:C:2008:517, [2008] ECR I-7245, concerning sex discrimination.

the *Prigge* case[42] … concerned a collective agreement governing the employees of a single employer, Deutsche Lufthansa.

(2) If it is sought to justify direct age discrimination under Article 6(1), the aims of the measure must be social policy objectives, such as those related to employment policy, the labour market or vocational training. These are of a public interest nature, which is 'distinguishable from purely individual reasons particular to the employer's situation, such as cost reduction or improving competitiveness' (*Age Concern*, *Fuchs*[43]).

(3) It would appear from that, as Advocate General Bot pointed out in *Kücükdeveci*,[44] that flexibility for employers is not in itself a legitimate aim; but a certain degree of flexibility may be permitted to employers in the pursuit of legitimate social policy objectives.

(4) A number of legitimate aims, some of which overlap, have been recognised in the context of direct age discrimination claims:

(i) promoting access to employment for younger people (*Palacios de la Villa*, *Hütter*,[45] *Kücükdeveci*);
(ii) the efficient planning of the departure and recruitment of staff (*Fuchs*);
(iii) sharing out employment opportunities fairly between the generations (*Petersen*, *Rosenbladt*,[46] *Fuchs*);
(iv) ensuring a mix of generations of staff so as to promote the exchange of experience and new ideas (*Georgiev*, *Fuchs*);
(v) rewarding experience (*Hütter*, *Hennigs*[47]);
(vi) cushioning the blow for long serving employees who may find it hard to find new employment if dismissed (*Ingeniørforeningen i Danmark*[48]);
(vii) facilitating the participation of older workers in the workforce (*Fuchs*, see also *Mangold v Helm*[49] …
(viii) avoiding the need to dismiss employees on the ground that they are no longer capable of doing the job which may be humiliating for the employee concerned (*Rosenbladt*); or
(ix) avoiding disputes about the employee's fitness for work over a certain age (*Fuchs*).

(5) However, the measure in question must be both appropriate to achieve its legitimate aim or aims and necessary in order to do so. Measures based on age may not be appropriate to the aims of rewarding experience or protecting long service (*Hütter*, *Kücükdeveci*, *Ingeniørforeningen i Danmark*).

(6) The gravity of the effect upon the employees discriminated against has to be weighed against the importance of the legitimate aims in assessing the necessity of the particular measure chosen (*Fuchs*).

(7) The scope of the tests for justifying indirect discrimination under Article 2(2)(b) and for justifying any age discrimination under Article 6(1) is not identical. It is for the Member States, rather than the individual employer, to establish the legitimacy of the aim pursued (*Age Concern*) …

55. It seems … that the United Kingdom has chosen to give employers and partnerships the flexibility to choose which objectives to pursue, provided always that (i) these objectives can

[42] Case C-447/09, *Prigge v Deutsche Lufthansa Ag* EU:C:2011:321, [2011] ECR I-08003, [2011] IRLR 1052, discussed above.

[43] Respectively *R (Incorporated Trustees of the National Council on Ageing*, n 38 above and *Fuchs*, n 39 above.

[44] Case 555/07, *Kücükdeveci v Swedex GmbH & Co KG* EU:C:2010:21, [2010] ECR I-00365, discussed above.

[45] Respectively *Palacios De La Villa*, n 39 above; Case C-88/08, *Hütter v Technische Universität Graz* EU:C:2009:381, [2009] ECR I-53258.

[46] Respectively Case C-341/08, *Petersen v Berufungsausschuss für Zahnärzte für den Bezirk Westfalen-Lippe* EU:C:2010:4, [2010] ECR I-47; *Rosenbladt*, n 39 above.

[47] Cases C-297/10 and C-298/10, *Hennigs v Eisenbahn-Bundesamt, Land Berlin v Mai* EU:C:2011:560, [2011] ECR I-7965.

[48] Case C-499/08, *Ingeniorforeningen i Danmark v Region Syddanmark* EU:C:2010:600, [2010] ECR I-9343.

[49] Case C-144/04, *Mangold v Helm* EU:C:2005:709, [2005] ECR I-9981, [2006] IRLR 143.

count as legitimate objectives of a public interest nature within the meaning of the Directive and (ii) are consistent with the social policy aims of the state and (iii) the means used are proportionate, that is both appropriate to the aim and (reasonably) necessary to achieve it.

56. Two different kinds of legitimate objective have been identified by the Luxembourg court. The first kind may be summed up as *inter-generational fairness*. This is comparatively uncontroversial. It can mean a variety of things, depending upon the particular circumstances of the employment concerned: for example, it can mean facilitating access to employment by young people; it can mean enabling older people to remain in the workforce; it can mean sharing limited opportunities to work in a particular profession fairly between the generations; it can mean promoting diversity and the interchange of ideas between younger and older workers.

57. The second kind may be summed up as *dignity*. This has been variously put as avoiding the need to dismiss older workers on the grounds of incapacity or underperformance, thus preserving their dignity and avoiding humiliation, and as avoiding the need for costly and divisive disputes about capacity or underperformance. Either way, it is much more controversial. As Age UK argue, the philosophy underlying all the anti-discrimination laws is the dignity of each individual, the right to be treated equally irrespective of either irrational prejudice or stereotypical assumptions which may be true of some but not of others. The assumptions underlying these objectives look suspiciously like stereotyping. Concerns about capacity, it is argued, are better dealt with, as they were in *Wolf* and *Prigge* under Article 4(1), which enables them to be related to the particular requirements of the job in question.

58. I confess to some sympathy with the position taken by Age UK. The fact that most women are less physically strong than most men does not justify refusing a job requiring strength to a woman candidate just because she is a woman. The fact that this particular woman is not strong enough for the job would justify refusing it to her. It would be consistent with this principle to hold that the fact that most people over a certain age have slower reactions than most people under that age does not justify sacking everyone who reaches that age irrespective of whether or not they still do have the necessary speed of reaction. But we know that the Luxembourg court has held that the avoidance of unseemly debates about capacity is capable of being a legitimate aim. The focus must therefore turn to whether this is a legitimate aim in the particular circumstances of the case.

59. The fact that a particular aim is capable of being a legitimate aim under the Directive (and therefore the domestic legislation) is only the beginning of the story. It is still necessary to inquire whether it is in fact the aim being pursued …

60. There is in fact no hint in the Luxembourg cases that the objective pursued has to be that which was in the minds of those who adopted the measure in the first place … while it has to be the actual objective, this may be an *ex post facto* rationalisation.

61. Once an aim has been identified, it has still to be asked whether it is legitimate in the particular circumstances of the employment concerned. For example, improving the recruitment of young people, in order to achieve a balanced and diverse workforce, is in principle a legitimate aim. But if there is in fact no problem in recruiting the young and the problem is in retaining the older and more experienced workers then it may not be a legitimate aim for the business concerned. Avoiding the need for performance management may be a legitimate aim, but if in fact the business already has sophisticated performance management measures in place, it may not be legitimate to avoid them for only one section of the workforce.

62. Finally, of course, the means chosen have to be both appropriate and necessary. It is one thing to say that the aim is to achieve a balanced and diverse workforce. It is another thing to say that a mandatory retirement age of 65 is both appropriate and necessary to achieving this end. It is one thing to say that the aim is to avoid the need for performance management procedures. It is another to say that a mandatory retirement age of 65 is appropriate and necessary to achieving this end. The means have to be carefully scrutinised in the context of the particular business concerned in order to see whether they do meet the objective and there are not other, less discriminatory, measures which would do so.

It is worth emphasising that the limitation of legitimate objectives in cases of direct age discrimination to those set out in Article 6 of Council Directive 2000/78 has no application to cases arising outside work (Part 5 EqA). Not only would the objectives set out in Article 6 mismatch those which might be pursued by discrimination in a non-work setting, but EU law does not regulate age discrimination (or discrimination because of sexual orientation, religion or belief or disability) outside work and so has no application in that context.

Lady Hale rejected the argument put for the claimant that in cases of direct discrimination the application of the general rule to the individual, as well as the general rule itself, required to be justified, remarking at §66 that this 'in many cases would negate the purpose of having a rule', though she did require that the rule had to be justified 'in the particular circumstances of the business'. As regards the fairness of the rule she made reference at §65 to the fact that 'In the particular context of inter-generational fairness, it must be relevant that at an earlier stage in his life, a partner or employee may well have benefited from a rule which obliged his seniors to retire at a particular age. Nor can it be entirely irrelevant that the rule in question [in *Seldon*] was re-negotiated comparatively recently between the partners'. While she took the view that the courts below had erred in applying the same approach to indirect and direct age discrimination she concluded that the aims of staff retention and workforce planning were 'directly related to the legitimate social policy aim of sharing out professional employment opportunities fairly between the generations (and were recognised as legitimate in *Fuchs*)' while that of limiting the need to expel partners by way of performance management was 'directly related to the 'dignity' aims accepted in *Rosenbladt* and *Fuchs*' (§67). She also regarded it as 'clear that the aims can be related to the particular circumstances of the type of business concerned' and concluded accordingly that the identified aims were legitimate:

> 68. As to whether the means chosen were proportionate, in the Article 6(1) sense of being both appropriate and (reasonably) necessary to achieving those aims, the case is already to go back to the ET on the basis that it had not been shown that the choice of 65 was an appropriate means of achieving the third aim. The question, therefore, was whether the ET would have regarded the first two aims as sufficient by themselves. In answering that question, I would not rule out their considering whether the choice of a mandatory age of 65 was a proportionate means of achieving the first two aims. There is a difference between justifying *a* retirement age and justifying *this* retirement age. Taken to extremes, their first two aims might be thought to justify almost any retirement age. The ET did not unpick the question of the age chosen and discuss it in relation to each of the objectives. It would be unduly constraining to deny them the opportunity of doing so now. I would emphasise, however, that they are considering the circumstances as they were in 2006, when there was a designated retirement age of 65 for employees, and not as they are now.

The tribunal ruled, on the case's remission, that there was no alternative to achieve the legitimate aims of 'retention' and 'workforce planning', other than mandatory retirement (the other justification argued before the SC having been abandoned). The remaining question was whether this justified the selection of 65 as the mandatory retirement age. The tribunal ruled that there was no single age of retirement which would have permitted the firm to balance its interests in retaining associates with the interests of partners in enjoying the benefits of their earlier loyalty and that the firm could have chosen 64 or 66 as readily as 65, but that partners had agreed the default retirement age of 65 which matched the state pension age and was the age at which the legislation then in place permitted mandatory retirement of employees. The CJEU had also upheld a retirement age of 65 in a number of cases. Mr Seldon appealed the tribunal's finding that the selection of 65 as the age of mandatory retirement had been justified, arguing that the tribunal should have selected 68 as the permissible age. The EAT ([2014] ICR 1275) ruled that tribunal had been entitled to conclude that the aims of retention and workforce planning had objectively justified the particular retirement age of 65.

Much of the CJEU case law upon which the SC relied in *Seldon* is criticised by Beryl ter Haar, who argues that in the 48 age discrimination cases decided by the CJEU that Court has been 'more lenient in justifying measures that are disadvantageous to older workers compared with measures negatively affecting younger workers'. Ter Haar critiques what she identifies as the 'two dominant theories': 'the complete life view and the fair innings argument' on the grounds that they 'are based on a form of distributive inequality over the course of time' while age discrimination 'may harm the dignity of a human being or a person's autonomy', particularly when it is 'based on stereotypes'. The 'complete life view approach' can favour older or younger workers equally but the 'fair innings argument' tends to favour younger workers. Ter Haar concludes that in 12 of 16 cases concerning discrimination against older workers the CJEU has not found discrimination:

Beryl ter Haar, 'Is the CJEU Discriminating in Age Discrimination Cases?' (2020) 13 *Erasmus Law Review*, footnotes omitted

> The contrast becomes even stronger when we realise that the three cases in the age category 'young' that reflect a complete life view approach either did not constitute age discrimination because something else was found (more) distinctive …[50] or fall under the exception of Article 6(2) FED[51]. In absolute numbers it means that older persons have had to accept disadvantageous treatment more often than younger persons.
>
> When evaluating the cases that seem to reflect the fair innings argument the CJEU seems to favour the position of young workers over that of older workers. This is the situation in cases affecting young people, as well as middle-aged and old people.[52]
>
> What we get is … a toxic combination: under the complete life view more measures have been accepted that negatively affect old people rather than young people; and under the fair innings argument more measures have been accepted that positively affect young people to the detriment of middle-aged and old people. The overall image of this combination is that the CJEU is more lenient in accepting disadvantageous measures for older people and more strict in protecting young people. Thus, while the relative numbers of measures that the CJEU found to be precluded by the FED do not indicate a significant difference in treatment between young and old, the reflective evaluation of the CJEU's rulings based on the theoretical approaches, especially the complete life view and fair innings argument, does indicate a significant difference. Maybe the CJEU is not aware of its bias, but by not having made a clear choice on how to evaluate age discrimination cases, a practice of unequal treatment has grown. The conclusion is, therefore, that the CJEU indeed discriminates in age discrimination cases.

In *McCloud v Lord Chancellor* a tribunal rejected the Government's attempt to justify direct age discrimination in relation to judicial salaries on the basis that it bore no rational relationship to the aims pursued by the measure. The CA upheld the tribunal's decision that transitional arrangements made under a new pension scheme for the judiciary discriminated directly and unlawfully on grounds of age. The scheme was less generous than the previous pension scheme, and the transitional provisions gave protection to those approaching pension age from all or part of the disadvantage they would otherwise have suffered in moving from the old to the new scheme. The challengers were younger judges who fell to be significantly disadvantaged as regards pensions by comparison with their older colleagues.

[50] Citing Case 49/18, *Escribano Vindel v Ministerio de Justicia* EU:C:2019:106, [2019] 2 CMLR 22; Case 154/18, *Horgan and Keegan v Minister for Education & Skills* EU:C:2019:113, [2019] IRLR 597.

[51] Citing Case 159/15, *Lesar v Beim Vorstand der Telekom Austria AG eingerichtetes Personalamt* EU:C:2016:451.

[52] Citing *Hütter*, n 45 above; *Kücükdeveci*, n 44 above; *Georgiev*, n 39 above; and *Fuchs*, n 39 above; Case C-229/08, *Wolf v Stadt Frankfurt am Main* [2010] ECR I-1; and Case C-258/15 *Salaberria Sorondo v Academia Vasca de Policía y Emergencias*, EU:C: 2016:873 [2017] ICR 302.

***McCloud v Lord Chancellor* [2018] EWCA Civ 2844, [2019] ICR 1489**

The Court:

35. The claims … are that the claimants were treated less favourably than those falling within the protected and/or taper groups on the grounds of age and that the less favourable treatment was not justified pursuant to s13(2) [EqA] …

41. The appellants have not been entirely clear in their assertion of their aims. The pleaded aim was 'to protect those closest to retirement from the financial effects of pension reform'. The claimants assert that this suffered from the defect that it said no more than that older members of the judiciary should be treated more beneficially than younger members and can, therefore, be said to be merely a re-statement of the discriminatory treatment. To the extent that it could be said to imply that the pension reforms would affect those closer to retirement most adversely, it was wrong on the facts since the effect of the transitional provisions was to give protection to the older members and not to the younger members.

42. There was a suggestion before the judge that a possible explanation was that older Judges would be more likely to have made fixed or concrete plans for retirement which would be difficult to change. But the judge dismissed that as no more than speculation without any hard evidence and at any rate of only minor consequence to older judges …

43. It was also suggested that the evidence supported a wish by government in the proposed pension reforms that all public sector persons should be treated consistently. Ten-year protection was given to older pensioners when the state pension was reformed; the large public sector unions had been given 10-year protection and the judges should therefore be in the same position.

44. Before the Employment Appeal Tribunal and this Court it was also suggested that the explanation for treating older judges more advantageously than younger judges was a 'moral and political aim' of being fair to those closest to retirement. Mr John Cavanagh QC for the appellants described this underlying reason as a 'moral one but affected by political aims' and submitted that any reliance on the appellants' lack of evidence was therefore misplaced.

45. The main ground of the appellants' appeal to the [EAT] was that in his consideration of both aims and means Judge Williams had erred in law by failing to accord to the appellants' aims and means the wide margin of discretion mandated by both domestic and European law. They also attacked his decision for focusing on the absence of evidence to conclude that the policy of protecting Judges was irrational when the aims were informed by moral or political or social value judgments. Likewise, in respect of aims, it was said that the judge applied his own judgment or standards of scrutiny rather than giving the government a wide margin of discretion. It was also said that the judge's decision on means was infected by his wrong conclusion about aims and that he also erred in considering process rather than outcome and that his reasoning on alternative means was directed towards different aims …

Margin of discretion/level of judicial scrutiny

69. It is … necessary for this court to come to a conclusion on the width of any appropriate margin of discretion in relation to both aims and means and indeed to decide whether there are two distinct lines of authority which needed to be (and were) reconciled in *Seldon*.

84. … we see no difference between the domestic authorities and the European authorities, let alone any attempt by the Supreme Court in *Seldon* to reconcile them. Nor do we consider the Equality Act 2010 imposes any greater burden on an employer in relation to age discrimination than does the Equality Directive. The terms of the statute derive straightforwardly from the Directive and they should be construed in the same way.

85. In that context it is axiomatic that the state or the government (if it is employer) must be accorded some margin of discretion in relation to both aims and means …

86. But, as Lady Hale said in para 59 of *Seldon*, establishing that an aim is capable of being a legitimate aim is only the beginning of the story. It is for the tribunal then, according an appropriate margin of discretion, to decide whether it is legitimate in the circumstances of the case. For this purpose, an aim must at least be rational and, if it is not, the employment tribunal is entitled to say so. Margin of discretion cannot rescue an aim that is irrational.

87. We would therefore hold that, where government has a legitimate interest in any issue which arises in a discrimination claim, it is to be afforded a margin of discretion but it is for the fact-finding tribunal to assess both whether the government has such a legitimate interest and the amount of discretion it should be afforded and then the tribunal should decide the case itself in accordance with ordinary principles.

92 …. In our view Judge Williams was entitled to say that an aim which protected older judges rather than younger judges when the older judges needed it least was irrational and that … it did not help to expand that by saying that older judges would have less time to prepare for pension reform. It does not seem to us that it adds anything either to say that it was somehow fairer to older judges to give them protection which they needed less than younger judges. Judge Williams' references to lack of evidence have to be seen in this light. The point is that there was just no evidence that older judges did need that protection more than younger judges …

93. As far as the wish for consistency is concerned while it is true that the judge did hold that the contention was based on generalisation rather than hard evidence, his real point was that, while consistency requires like cases to be treated alike, the judges' position was so different from those of other public servants that true comparisons could not be made.

94. Finally and importantly these matters are essentially for the employment tribunal judge to assess and this court (and indeed the Employment Appeal Tribunal) should, in our judgment, be slow to substitute our own judgment about the mass of evidence which there was before the tribunal for that of the employment judge. Moreover, as Lady Hale observed in *Essop v Home Office (UK Border Agency); Naeem v Secretary of State for Justice* [2017] UKSC 27, [2017] ICR 640 (at para 47), we must be able to detect an error of law. The quotations we have, at some length, made from the judgment of the employment tribunal in the previous paragraphs are a testament to his approach and the evidence; they speak for themselves as to the care and diligence with which he approached his task. We can detect no error of law.

The aims pursued by the discriminatory measures in *McCloud* were legitimate but there was a mismatch between end and means. In *RMT v Lloyd* the EAT reached similar conclusions in relation to two aims pursued by a discriminatory rule while finding another aim to be illegitimate because it was at odds with government policy.

***RMT v Lloyd* [2019] UKEAT 0281_18_1503, [2019] IRLR 897**

The claimant challenged the union's refusal to allow him to stand for election to its National Executive Council (NEC) on the basis that he would have reached the normal retirement age before the end of his three-year term of office, and was thus precluded from standing by the union's rules. The union sought to rely on (1) intergenerational fairness', arguing that the rule was intended to avoid the NEC from becoming increasingly old; (2) 'efficient planning as to the composition of the NEC', in particular the need to avoid the significant cost of additional elections if NEC members were to hold office for less than the three year term'; and (3) to achieve consistency with its policy to campaign for a younger retirement age.

A tribunal accepted that intergenerational fairness could be a legitimate aim but found that 87.5 per cent of the members of the NEC were between 41 and 60 and so the effect of the rule was 'if anything … to ensure that the composition of the NEC is steadfastly middle aged' and that it did 'nothing to ensure a mix of generations so as to promote the exchange of experience and new ideas'. As to the second aim relied upon by the union, it ruled that the union was not faced with many prospective NEC members who would be unable by reason of retirement to complete their three-year terms. Further, it did not require that paid officials who stood for re-election demonstrate that they would fulfil the full term before retirement. Finally, as to (3), the tribunal ruled that this policy clashed with that of central government, which was to raise the state retirement age, and could not therefore be considered a legitimate aim. The EAT refused the union's appeal, ruling as regards aim (3) that the decision of the Supreme Court in *Seldon* made it clear that no aim would be legitimate unless it was consistent with the social policy aims of the state. It might be argued that, while this would clearly be a defensible approach where the aims pursued were contrary to public policy, it is not obviously so where the difference is one between politically respectable views. While the EAT's approach may be defensible in the context of direct age discrimination, the requirement for consistency with the view of the government of the day has no place in the justification of indirect discrimination more generally.

We noted above the relative difficulty of challenging compulsory retirement ages before the CJEU. That Court has also been sympathetic to measures designed to facilitate the entry of young people into the labour market. In Case C-548/15, *de Lange v Staatssecretaris van Finaciën* EU:C:2016:850, [2017] IRLR 278, for example, the Court ruled that Council Directive 2000/78 permitted a provision of Dutch law which allowed people aged under 30 to deduct vocational training costs in full from their taxable income over a period of four years whereas those aged over 30 were limited to deducting no more than €15,000 pa. The Court accepted that the provision was designed to improve access to training for young people, and that this could be regarded as legitimate under Article 6(1). The scheme was capable of improving the position of young people on the labour market while older people benefitted from the allowance of €15,000 pa over an unlimited period, which covered the average cost of training. In view of the fact that older people had generally had the opportunity to undertake prior training and to work, and could therefore generally bear part of the cost of further training, the Court did not take the view that the Netherlands had exceeded the wide margin of discretion available to it under Article 6(1), though this was for the national court to determine.

Another example of this approach is the decision in Case C-432/14 *O v Bio Philippe Auguste Sarl* EU:C:2015:643, [2015] IRLR 1017, that neither Council Directive 2000/78 nor Article 21 of the EU Charter of Fundamental Rights precluded a provision of French law by which a payment (of 10 per cent total gross remuneration) generally made at the end of a fixed term contract by way of compensation 'for the insecurity' of the employee's situation was not applicable to contracts entered into with 'a young person [aged under 28] or a period falling within the school holidays or university vacations'. The applicant had sought the severance payment on completion of a four day fixed term contract during his university vacation. The CJEU concluded that the French legislature was entitled to consider that workers such as the applicant were not in the same situation as regards job insecurity as other workers, since work carried out on a fixed-term contract during school or university holidays was both temporary and ancillary.

It is not entirely clear that a 29-year-old university student would be in a different position from a 27-year-old, or that the position of the latter differs materially from that of a freelancer who chooses to take work only sporadically on fixed-term contracts. More questionable still was the decision of the CJEU in Case C-143/16 *Abercrombie & Fitch Italia Srl v Bordonaro* EU:C:2017:566, [2017] IRLR 1018 that the dismissal of the applicant from an 'on call' job when he reached the age of 25 was permitted by Council Directive 2000/78 and by Article 21. The CJEU ruled that the Italian legislation pursued a legitimate aim of employment and labour market policy (facilitating the entry of young people to the labour market) and used appropriate and necessary means, taking the unusual step of determining this rather than remitting the case to the national courts for a decision on the facts. The case is particularly worth of remark given the company's policy, publicly abandoned only in 2015, of hiring staff on the basis of physical attractiveness.[53] *Glamour* magazine reported in April 2015 that the move was 'a huge step for the brand whose image is based upon recruiting genetically gifted, often shirtless, models to work in its international chain of stores'.

The cases considered above have concerned direct discrimination. The SC has also considered indirect age discrimination in *Homer v Chief Constable of West Yorkshire Police* [2012] UKSC 15, [2012] ICR 704, considered in Chapter 2, in which other indirect age discrimination claims are also discussed.

Fairness, Cost and Justification

A number of age discrimination cases have involved challenges by claimants to distinctions drawn on the basis of age the purpose of which is to limit the benefits which would otherwise accrue to those claimants for reasons related, directly or indirectly, to their age. A particular complication which may arise in such cases is that the CJEU and the domestic courts do not permit costs savings alone to amount to a legitimate aim.[54] This difficulty surfaced in *Woodcock v Cumbria Primary Care Trust* in which the CA rejected an age discrimination claim by the chief executive of the North Cumbria Primary Care Trusts, who had been dismissed for redundancy. The claim arose because, his post having been made redundant and his application for redeployment having been unsuccessful, the precise timing of the claimant's dismissal was designed to minimise costs to the employer.

Woodcock v Cumbria Primary Care Trust [2012] EWCA Civ 330 [2012] ICR 1126

The claimant was entitled to 12 months' notice of dismissal. He was informed in August 2006 that that he was being formally placed at risk of redundancy and had spent some months in informal discussions before being invited in March 2007 to a meeting which was intended to be a redundancy consultation meeting prior to a decision whether to give him notice of dismissal. The claimant had been unable to attend that meeting and the meeting was not rearranged until 6 June 2007 by which stage the employer had realised that the claimant would reach his 49th birthday on 17 June 2007 and would, if provided with notice of dismissal after that date, have been in employment on his

[53] 'Abercrombie scraps hiring only attractive employee', *Glamour*, 25 April 2015.
[54] *Cross v British Airways* [2006] ICR 1239.

50th birthday at which point he would have been entitled to take early retirement on enhanced terms, which would have increased the cost of his redundancy by at least £500,000. The claimant was given 12 months' notice of dismissal on 23 May (prior to the consultation meeting), subject to the possibility of alternative employment being secured, and brought a claim for age discrimination when he was dismissed at the end of his notice period with a redundancy payment of £220,000.

A tribunal rejected the claim on the basis that, while the act of giving the claimant early notice of dismissal was discriminatory, it was justified by the legitimate aim of bringing about his dismissal for redundancy without incurring the additional costs to the trust of his turning 50 before the expiry of his notice. The claimant appealed, arguing on the basis of *Cross v British Airways* [2006] ICR 1239, that cost alone could not be a legitimate aim for the justification of discrimination. The EAT ([2011] IRLR 119) ruled that the tribunal had not relied upon cost alone but had applied the permissible 'cost plus' approach, the 'plus' being the factor of redundancy, also expressing the view that the requirement for 'costs plus', which it accepted was binding upon it, involved tribunals in an artificial approach.[55] The CA also rejected the claimant's appeal.

Rimer LJ (with whom Ryder and Arden LJJ agreed):

56 .... The case of *Cross* was the reserved judgment of the Employment Appeal Tribunal delivered by Burton J (the then President) and discussed a number of issues, including whether a provision, criterion or practice indirectly discriminatory on the grounds of sex was justifiable …

65. It is apparent from article 6(1) of the Directive and from its domestic implementation in regulation 3(1) that it is possible for an employer to justify treatment that, absent justification, would amount to direct age discrimination. It can do so, in the language of the latter, if the treatment is 'a proportionate means of achieving a legitimate aim'. Mr Gilroy's submission [for the claimant] is that the saving or avoidance of costs alone cannot be a legitimate aim. It can only be so if it is linked to a non-cost factor. Thus a consideration that, by itself, is inadmissible as justification becomes admissible if so linked; and, in such a case, it can play a part in the proportionality assessment.

66. There is, it seems to me, some degree of artificiality about such an approach to the question of justification. As Elias J observed in *Redcar and Cleveland Borough Council v Bainbridge* [2008] ICR 249, para 91: 'Almost every decision taken by an employer is going to have regard to costs.' Regulation 3(1), however, says nothing of the extent to which considerations of cost may feature in the justification exercise. It provides merely that what would otherwise be discriminatory treatment may be justified if it was 'a proportionate means of achieving a legitimate aim'. The relevant question must therefore be whether the treatment complained of was such a means. Accepting, as I make clear I do, that the guidance of the Court of Justice is that an employer cannot justify discriminatory treatment 'solely' because the elimination of such treatment would involve increased costs, that guidance cannot mean more than that the saving or avoidance of costs will not, without more, amount to the achieving of a 'legitimate aim'. That is entirely unsurprising. To adopt a simple example given by Mr Short, [for the employer] it is hardly open to an employer to claim to be entitled to justify the discriminatory payment to A of less than B simply because it would cost more to pay A the same as B. Such treatment of A could not, without more, be a 'legitimate aim'.

[55] See also the comments of Underhill LJ, as he was by this time, in *R (UNISON) v Lord Chancellor* [2015] EWCA Civ 915, [2016] ICR 1 in which he referred to his concerns, expressed in the EAT in *Woodcock*, about the 'crude dichotomy' between 'cost' and 'cost plus'.

67. If the trust's treatment of the claimant is correctly characterised as no more than treatment aimed at saving or avoiding costs, I would accept that it was not a means of achieving a 'legitimate aim' and that it was therefore incapable of justification. It would fall foul of the limitations upon justification explained in cases such as *Hill v Revenue Comrs* [1999] ICR 48. On the unusual facts of this case, I would not, however, regard that as a correct characterisation. The dismissal notice of 23 May 2007 was not served with the aim, pure and simple, of dismissing the claimant before his 49th birthday in order to save the trust the expense it would incur if was still in its employ at 50. It was served, and genuinely served, with the aim of giving effect to the trust's genuine decision to terminate his employment on the grounds of his redundancy. The appeal tribunal had no doubt that the dismissal of an employee on such grounds is a legitimate aim: 'It is an entirely legitimate aim for an employer to dismiss an employee who has become redundant.' I agree; and it cannot in my view cease to be a 'legitimate aim' simply because, if there is no dismissal, the employer will continue to incur costs that such dismissal is directed at saving.

68. I also agree with both the employment tribunal and the appeal tribunal that it was a legitimate part of that aim for the trust to ensure that, in giving effect to it, the dismissal also saved the trust the additional element of costs that, had it not timed the dismissal as it did, it would be likely to have incurred. In considering the timing of the steps it needed to take towards dismissing the claimant for redundancy it was obviously legitimate for the trust to have that consideration in mind, as it clearly did as early as March 2007. It would, in my view, have been irresponsible of the trust not to have done so. The claimant had, by 2007, no right, entitlement or expectation to the enjoyment of the enhanced benefits that he would have enjoyed had he remained in the trust's employment until he was 50. Had he in fact so remained so as to enjoy them, he would have been the beneficiary of a pure windfall. He could and would not have had any reasonable hope or chance of doing so if (a) he had been given notice to expire at the end of (or shortly after) June 2007, as ought to have happened … (b) he had been able to attend the meeting on 10 April 2007, as the trust had originally intended, and he had been given notice at or after that meeting; (c) it had been possible to arrange a subsequent meeting before June 2007, and he had been given notice after it; or (d) he had been given notice on or shortly after the meeting that was eventually fixed for 6 June 2007. If any of these things had happened, he could have had no possible grounds for complaint on age discrimination grounds.

69. The only difficulty generated by the case is that, on the employment tribunal's findings, the dismissal was tainted with discriminatory treatment on the grounds of age. That was because the difficulties in arranging an earlier consultation meeting with the claimant resulted in the trust taking the view in May 2007 that, because his 49th birthday was fast approaching, it needed to cut a procedural consultation corner in order to ensure that the notice expired before his 50th birthday. (In fact it was wrong about this: it could have given its dismissal notice immediately after the meeting of 6 June 2007; had it done so, it is difficult to see what complaint the claimant could have had.)

70. In my view that consideration goes, however, only to the proportionality of the treatment adopted by the trust. That required the striking of an objective balance between the discriminatory effect of the treatment of the claimant and the needs of the trust. The employment tribunal found that, in the circumstances, the treatment was proportionate …

71. Mr Gilroy submitted that the trust's action in removing the claimant's right of consultation so as to save costs was so patently a disproportionate action that the trust cannot get home on the proportionality element of the exercise. I am not persuaded by that. Both the employment tribunal and appeal tribunal explained why, in the very particular circumstances to which Underhill J referred, the trust's treatment was proportionate to the effect upon the claimant. The issue for us is whether, in making the proportionality assessment that it did, the employment tribunal erred in law. I agree with the appeal tribunal that it did not. On the contrary,

> I regard its decision as a well judged one. Ultimately, the essence of the case is (a) that the trust was fully entitled, and had effectively resolved, to terminate the claimant's employment prior to his 50th birthday; (b) the implementation of that intention was delayed through no fault of its own but through a chapter of accidents; and (c) whilst the consultation 'corner cutting' in theory deprived the claimant of an opportunity, in fact it deprived him of nothing of value, because, as the employment tribunal found, consultation would have achieved nothing ...

As we saw in Chapter 2, the CJEU and SC confirmed in *O'Brien v Ministry of Justice* that 'budgetary considerations cannot justify discrimination',[56] stating at §60 that the 'cost plus' argument was 'a subtle point which [which was] not without difficulty' but declining at §70 to express a view as to whether *Woodcock* had been properly decided.

Shortly prior to the decision in *Woodcock* the EAT had ruled in the case below that a tribunal had erred in finding that the claimant had been subject to age discrimination in being denied early retirement on cost grounds.

***HM Land Registry v Benson* [2011] UKEAT 0197_11_1002, [2012] ICR 627**

The employer, which needed to make cost savings, had authority from the Treasury to spend £50m from its reserves on three schemes to encourage staff to leave by voluntary redundancy or early retirement. Of this, £12m, plus an additional £1.9m from a separate pot, was available to spend on a scheme to offer early retirement to registration executives aged over 50 being offered early retirement, with those under 50 being offered the opportunity to volunteer for redundancy under the terms of the Civil Service Compensation Scheme. More applicants having applied for the scheme than the employer could accept, it decided to select employees so as to make the maximum number of staff cuts (and therefore future savings) with the monies available while retaining essential specialist expertise and a balance of grades of staff. The result of this was that the applications of the claimants, who were aged between 50 and 54, were rejected on the grounds of expense. The employer accepted that the cheapness criteria placed applicants in this age group at a particular disadvantage because they would have been especially expensive to terminate, but argued that the indirect age discrimination was justified. A tribunal ruled that the discrimination was not justified despite its finding that no other satisfactory method of selection had been shown to be possible. The tribunal took the view, however, that the employer had not established a 'real need' to limit its spending on the scheme, in the sense that additional funds could not be made available without insolvency.

Underhill P:

> 37. The essence of the tribunal's reasoning was that the appellant had not demonstrated a 'real need' to limit its spending on the scheme to £12m – or, to put it another way, to limit its spending on all three schemes to £50m. It held that it had not done so because it had not shown that payment of the additional £19.7m was 'unaffordable'. By that it evidently meant that the appellant had not shown that the funds were absolutely unavailable, in the sense that they could not be paid without insolvency: it pointed out that the appellant's reserves far exceeded that

[56] Respectively C-393/10, EU:C:2018:879, [2012] ICR 955; [2013] UKSC 6, [2013] ICR 499.

> amount (albeit that Treasury approval was needed to spend them) and that later in the same year, in the ATP, it contemplated spending a far greater figure. In our view, to apply a test of unaffordability in that sense is to fall into the error of treating the language of 'real need', or 'reasonable needs', as Balcombe LJ put it in *Hampson*, as connoting a requirement of absolute necessity. It is well established that that is not the case [citing the decisions of the Court of Appeal in *Barry* [1998] IRLR 138 and in *Cadman v Health and Safety Executive* [2005] ICR 1546, and of Elias P in the EAT in *CC West Midlands Police v Blackburn* [2008] ICR 505 … The effect of that principle, applied to a case like the present, seems to us to be that an employer's decision about how to allocate his resources, and specifically his financial resources, should constitute a 'real need' – or, to revert to the language of aim and means, a 'legitimate aim' – even if it is shown that he could have afforded to make a different allocation with a lesser impact on the class of employee in question. To say that an employer can only establish justification if he shows that he could not make the payment in question without insolvency is to adopt a test of absolute necessity. The task of the employment tribunal is to accept the employer's legitimate decision as to the allocation of his resources as representing a genuine 'need' but to balance it against the impact complained of …
>
> 38. We have not in reaching this conclusion lost sight of the fact that the cheapness criterion was indeed disproportionately unfavourable to employees in the claimants' age group, and we can well understand their disappointment at their non-selection. But it is fundamental that not all measures with a discriminatory impact are unlawful. Sometimes they have to be put up with. And we are bound to say, though this is not central to our reasoning, that in the present case the impact is not as severe as in many cases. Those affected did not lose their jobs or lose any other benefit which they had a positive expectation of receiving: rather, they lost out on the chance to take advantage of a benefit – admittedly a very substantial benefit – on which they had no right to count and which could indeed be described as a windfall. It is also important to emphasise that a central element in our conclusion is the tribunal's finding that the appellant had no real alternative, if it was to select at all, to using the cheapness criterion. We are not sure that that was an inevitable conclusion, and in other similar cases the evidence might well produce a different result. It does not, accordingly, follow from this decision that the use of a similarly discriminatory criterion will necessarily be justified in other cases.

The focus of the extract is on the question of necessity in the context of indirect discrimination. It is worth making the point, however, that the case is one in which cost was a determining factor, as it will frequently be, in the approach to selection for redundancy. The fact that this had a disparate impact on the claimants was the result of their own relatively privileged position (itself by reason of their age) did not render it unlawful. As *Harvey on Industrial Relations*, the leading practitioner text, suggests, 'While then it is clear that cost considerations alone cannot serve as a legitimate aim (as Lady Hale in *O'Brien* confirmed that a discriminatory rule or practice could only be justified by reference to a legitimate aim other than the simple saving of cost), this seems to draw a distinction between "cost" and "fair distribution of limited resources".'[57]

Harvey goes on to point out that *Benson* was expressly approved by the CA in the *Harrod* case.

[57] Division L [347.03].

***CC West Midlands Police v Harrod* [2017] EWCA Civ 191, [2017] ICR 869**

The challenge concerned the justifiability of a decision by a number of chief constables to rely on A19 of the Police Pensions Regulations 1987 compulsorily to retire officers who would be entitled to receive a pension of two thirds average pensionable pay ('⅔ APP'). These officers, who had at least 30 years' service, were all aged at least 48. The decision was made because of a need to reduce officer numbers in the face of significant budget cuts, A19 permitting compulsory retirement for the 'general interests of efficiency' of the force. The tribunal found in favour of a number of officers who challenged the decision as unlawful indirect discrimination, criticising the chief constables for failing to take into account the fact that most officers with 30 years' service retired voluntarily and that the additional savings to be made under A19 were therefore limited. It suggested that the chief constables should instead have sought to make the savings by (1) asking officers whether they intended to retire at ⅔ APP so as to determine whether it was necessary to make compulsory retirements; and (2) making use of part time working and (3) career breaks before, if necessary, (4) selecting any officers for compulsory retirement by reference to factors such as skills. The EAT allowed the chief constables' appeal ([2015] ICR 1311) and the CA rejected the claimants' appeals, ruling that the chief constables had been entitled to make the decision they did in order to achieve certainty of costs reduction and that it had not been for the tribunal to devise an alternative scheme involving the loss of fewer posts. The tribunal was entitled to require the chief constables to justify the selection but not the decision as to the numbers of officers who would have to go, and since the chief constables had been entitled to make compulsory retirements only from those with 30 years' service there was no other lawful method of selection available to them. In these circumstances the only possible conclusion was that their actions were justified and the age discrimination claims must fail.

***Heskett v Secretary of State for Justice* [2020] EWCA Civ 1487, [2021] ICR 110**

The claimant, a probation officer, complained of indirect age discrimination by reason of a pay freeze imposed in 2010 which disproportionately impacted himself and other younger staff members who were less likely than older colleagues to have reached the tip of the pay scale prior to the implementation of the freeze.[58] His claim was dismissed by a tribunal and by the EAT, and his further appeal dismissed by the CA. The main plank of the appeal had been a challenge to the EAT's acceptance that the absence of means was a legitimate aim for the purposes of justifying age discrimination, the previous authorities (*Woodcock v Cumbria PCT* and *Cross v British Airways plc*) having indicated that costs alone could not amount to a legitimate aim.

The claimant argued on appeal that the justification relied upon by the employer came down to cost was, accordingly, was impermissible. The EAT disagreed, distinguishing between reliance on cost alone, which was not a legitimate aim, and on an absence of means, and ruling that an organisation was entitled to seek to break even and to make decisions about how to allocate its resources. The tribunal had found that the employer had sought to spread the impact of externally imposed cost constraints fairly and was taking steps to address the recognised discriminatory effect of the pay policy, and it had been entitled to find that the employer's actions were justified.

[58] The impact of the freeze was that, whereas people had previously been able to progress annually by up to three points on the scale, this was reduced to one.

The discrimination in *Benson*, *Harrod* and *Heskett* was indirect. Another example of direct age discrimination which was justified by considerations of fairness arose in *Air Products plc v Cockram*, also considered in Chapter 4.

***Air Products plc v Cockram* [2018] EWCA Civ 346, [2018] IRLR 755**

The CA rejected a challenge by the claimant to the operation of a Long-Term Incentive Plan. Under the plan, all unvested awards were forfeited on termination of employment except in the case of employees who left employment on or after the relevant customary retirement age. In 2010, after UK pension law imposed a minimum pensionable age of 55 on most people, the company interpreted the customary retirement age as being 55. The claimant resigned at 50, by which stage he was entitled to a defined benefit (DB) pension, and sought the benefit of the exception to the forfeiture rule. The company defended the minimum age of 55 on the basis that it wished to achieve fairness between the generations and to treat employees consistently, and it believed that allowing employees who had a protected pension age of 50 (who were already advantaged by being able to retire earlier than younger employees, who had defined contribution (DC) pensions) to benefit from the retirement exception from that age would be unfair to those younger employees. The EAT allowed an appeal against a tribunal's decision that that the discrimination was objectively justified, stating that the tribunal had not given sufficient reasoning for accepting that the aim included intergenerational fairness. The company appealed. Much of the judgment concerned whether the tribunal had been entitled to reach the conclusions it did on the evidence before it. Of more interest here is the Court's approach to justification.

Bean LJ, with whom Leggatt LJ agreed:

16. The tribunal summarised the parties' positions on 'legitimate aim' at [90]–[91] of its decision:

'[90] The Respondent relies on three aims which it asserts are legitimate aims – (i) Intergenerational fairness and consistency; (ii) rewarding experience and loyalty; and (iii) ensuring a mix of generations of staff so as to promote the exchange of experience and new ideas …

17. On the question of intergenerational fairness and consistency as a legitimate aim, the tribunal made the following findings …

[99] We note that intergenerational fairness is in principle a legitimate aim. It is a broad objective, which may be manifest in different ways, depending on the circumstances. During submissions we discussed with Counsel whether the concept necessarily involves the division of resources between different age groups. For example, where there are limited opportunities for promotion, a provision designed to reduce opportunities for older employees in order to create more opportunities for younger employees might have the legitimate aim of intergenerational fairness. One generation's loss will be the other's gain. In the present case that factor appear[s] to be absent. If members of the defined benefit scheme take their LTIP benefits at below age 55, this does not affect the resource or financial benefit available to the members of the defined contribution scheme. As Mr Tatton-Brown put it [for the claimant], this is not a zero sum game.

[100] However, we are persuaded by Mr Stilitz [for the employer] that this is not a necessary aspect of intergenerational fairness. The categories of intergenerational fairness are not closed – 'It can mean a variety of things' (see *Seldon* above). We accept that limiting the advantage enjoyed by one age group over another is a legitimate social policy aspect of intergenerational fairness. Our conclusion is that the Respondent's aim is a legitimate aim.

18. As for the aim of rewarding loyalty, the tribunal made the following findings …

> [104] Mr Tatton Brown submitted that in the light of *Seldon* rewarding loyalty [could] no longer be regarded as a legitimate aim. We are not persuaded that this is so. In our view *Seldon* does not outlaw rewarding loyalty as a legitimate aim …

20. The tribunal went on to consider the question of proportionality at [109]–[120]:

> [109] … We are satisfied that the legitimate aims meet a real need, and that the discriminatory provision is appropriate to achieving the aims. The provision means that all employees are treated in the same way with regard to the LTIP awards, whichever pension scheme they are in. We accept this achieves intergenerational fairness.
>
> [110] The provision gives an incentive to remain in the Respondent's employment until at least age 55. Thereafter there is no disincentive to retirement. We accept this strikes a balance between rewarding experience and loyalty and encouraging retention …
>
> [114] Mr Stilitz submitted that 55 was the only age which would achieve the legitimate aims. The minimum pension age for employees in the defined contribution scheme is 55. It cannot be reduced. Therefore the only way of achieving consistency between the members of the two schemes is to treat 55 as the customary retirement age for all employees.
>
> [115] The aims would be undermined by permitting the retention of LTIP awards by any employee who left at a minimum age of 50. Ms Patterson made the valid point in evidence that in today's world 50 is a young age for retirement. Indeed, save for those with a protected pension age it is now not possible in the UK to draw a pension below the age of 55. Furthermore, adopting the age of 50 might be seen as unfair to employees who left at a younger age. It would appear arbitrary to decide on 50. Why not 52, or 48?
>
> [116] There was a rational basis for choosing 55. It ties in with the pension age. It is the lowest customary retirement age for any country where the Respondent operates. Viewed in that context it cannot be unfair to employees in the UK, who enjoy the lowest customary retirement age in the world. Indeed, reducing the age might be perceived to be unfair by employees in other countries who have a higher customary retirement age …
>
> [118] In weighing up the Respondent's needs against the discriminatory effect on the claimant, we had regard to the fact that the effect is not imposed by any action of the Respondent. It is triggered by the employee's decision to leave. In our view that is an important consideration …
>
> [119] Mr Stilitz accepted that the financial loss to an employee who leaves below age 55, including the claimant, can be significant, but he reminded us that some LTIP benefits are retained. Only unvested awards are forfeit.
>
> [120] Weighing up those factors, we are persuaded that the provision is a proportionate means of achieving the legitimate aims. Our unanimous judgment is that the complaint of age discrimination fails, and is dismissed ….

23. The employer sought permission to appeal to this court on these grounds: (1) The EAT erred in holding that the tribunal's decision was insufficiently reasoned; (2) the EAT substituted its own view for that of the tribunal; (3) the EAT acted perversely in remitting the matter to a different tribunal …

26. The employment tribunal had before them evidence from the employer's witness Ms Reese that the aim of the policy was to strike a balance between encouraging retention up to the age of 55 and then providing some incentive to retire in order to create opportunities for younger employees. The tribunal accepted this evidence, as they were plainly entitled to do …

32. … Mr Laddie [who appeared for the claimant on appeal] argued that the true aim of the minimum age of 55 to qualify for the retirement exception was to achieve consistency between

> the DB and DC schemes. This, he submitted, was not a social policy objective but an individual reason 'particular to this employer's situation' without any social policy component …
>
> 33. As the judgment in *Seldon* of Lord Hope of Craighead JSC at [75] makes clear, steps taken in the employer's best interests may nevertheless be directly related to what is regarded as a legitimate social policy. The crucial finding of the employment tribunal in the present case at para [100] is that 'limiting the advantage enjoyed by one age group over another is a legitimate social policy aspect of intergenerational fairness'. The claimant and a small number of colleagues were members of the DB scheme which had been closed to new entrants in 2005. Although not all DB scheme members were older than all DC scheme members, they were clearly older on average. Quite apart from the LTIP element, the DB scheme members had access to more generous pensions than their DC scheme colleagues and had the right to draw them at an earlier age. Removing the additional right of this group to have the benefit of unvested LTIP options which would be denied to their mainly younger colleagues outside the privileged group was in my view a legitimate social policy aspect of intergenerational fairness. At any rate, the employment tribunal as judges of fact were entitled so to find and I do not consider that anything in the judgments in *Seldon* prohibited them from doing so.
>
> 34. The tribunal found at paras [109]–[111] that the legitimate aims met a real need and that the discriminatory provision setting the minimum age to qualify for the retirement exception at 55 was appropriate to achieving those aims on the basis both of intergenerational fairness and of striking a balance between rewarding experience and loyalty and encouraging retention on the one hand and ensuring a mix of generations of staff on the other hand. Again, these are conclusions which the employment tribunal were entitled to reach, at least in relation to intergenerational fairness and the retention issue. Pointing (as Mr Laddie did) to the discrepancy between an employee of 54 who loses the unvested LTIPs on retirement and a 55-year-old who does not is not a convincing argument. Bright line rules are a common feature of benefits payable on retirement. And as Baroness Hale JSC observed in *Seldon*, 'where it is justified to have a general rule then the existence of that rule will usually justify the treatment which results from it.'

This line of cases illustrates the difficulties which may result from the adoption of a single legislative framework to regulate discrimination on multiple grounds. There should be no objection in principle to allowing a cost-based justification where, as here, the additional cost associated with an individual arises from an age-related advantage. Age-related advantages such as those at issue in *Woodcock* or *Benson* are different from other factors which are related to protected characteristics and which might make workers more expensive, such as pregnancy, because the additional costs associated with pregnancy are not experienced as a direct benefit to the pregnant woman. Nor do they rest on generalisations or assumptions, such as would be the case if an employer sought to shed staff who were thought more likely to become pregnant or to be subject to competing family-related demands (because they were women), or to take time off work for health-related reasons (because they were disabled, or relatively old). But because the EqA for the most part treats age the same as the other protected characteristics the courts have been required to develop the rather unconvincing 'cost plus' approach to justification which has the potential to open up discussions about cost (albeit with a theoretical 'plus') as a justification for other forms of discrimination.[59]

[59] Note that costs which actually result from disability are dealt with by the duty to make reasonable adjustments.

Exceptions

As is clear from this chapter, all age discrimination, direct as well as indirect, is capable of justification. In addition, the general exceptions discussed in Chapter 4 apply to age discrimination (these include acts done under statutory authority and the GOR defence applicable to work-related discrimination).

Section 195(7) EqA provides that sporting competitions may adopt age bands if necessary to secure 'fair competition or the safety of competitors, to comply with the rules of a national or international competition, or to increase participation in that activity', 'age-banded activity' being defined as 'a sport, game or other activity of a competitive nature in circumstances in which the physical or mental strength, agility, stamina, physique, mobility, maturity or manual dexterity of average persons of a particular age group would put them at a disadvantage compared to average persons of another age group as competitors in events involving the activity. This applies irrespective of the Part of the Act in relation to which discrimination is claimed. The other exceptions discussed below are specific to the Part of the Act in relation to which they are discussed.

Part 3 EqA: Services

Most significantly, though not formally cast as an exception to the prohibition on age discrimination, s28(1) EqA provides Part 3 'does not apply to the protected characteristic of … age, so far as relating to persons who have not attained the age of 18'. Schedule 3 para 6 further disapplies the prohibition on age discrimination to the exercise of local authority's functions concerning the provision of schools, and para 9 disapplies s29 EqA from 'anything done in connection with' school curricula, admission, transport or 'the establishment, alteration or closure of schools'. Schedule 18 para 1 provides that the Public Sector Equality Duty (PSED, discussed in Chapter 3) does not apply as regards the protected characteristic of age to the exercise of functions relating to the education of children or to the provision of benefits, facilities or services to pupils in schools or children in care.

Schedule 3 para 20A(1) provides that age-related discrimination 'in connection with the provision of a financial service' (which includes any service of a banking, credit, insurance, personal pension, investment or payment nature) does not breach s29 EqA, para 20A(2) providing that this exemption may only be relied on in cases in which the discriminator 'conducts an assessment of risk' which takes into account age where the assessment 'is carried out by reference to information which is relevant to the assessment of risk and from a source on which it is reasonable to rely'. The EHRC explains that 'a high street bank [may] offer[] a 'silver saver' account for customers over 60, with higher interest rates', but 'if … using age to assess risk, for example only providing car insurance up to age 75 or charging more for insurance as a customer gets older … would need up to date evidence from a reliable source, which shows that people over a certain age are a greater risk when driving'.[60] By contrast with the equivalent exception relating to disability (para 21), there is no requirement that it have been reasonable for the discriminator to discriminate.

Schedule 3 paras 30A–B and 30D EqA permit concessions to be granted on the basis of age, 'age related holidays' and the operation of minimum age limits for residential mobile home parks.[61] And Schedule 3 para 30C provides that, where a statutory age is imposed in

[60] https://www.equalityhumanrights.com/en/advice-and-guidance/age-discrimination.

[61] Introduced, with ss15A (immigration), 20A, 30A–D, 195(7) and Sch 16 para 1A EqA, pursuant to the Equality Act 2010 (Age Exceptions) Order 2012, which was made under s197 EqA, which allows a minister of the Crown to make additional exceptions to the prohibition on age discrimination.

relation to access to services, a service provider who displays a notice to that effect will not breach s29 EqA by refusing the service to a person who appears to them to be below the required age, and cannot establish otherwise. The explanatory notes to the Equality Act 2010 (Age Exceptions) Order 2012, which introduced this provision into the EqA, state that para 30C is intended to apply to 'schemes operated by those selling or providing goods or services that are subject to age limits created by or under legislation, such as alcohol, tobacco or entry to a cinema in respect of particular films'.[62] It is not clear why this provision is necessary in view of the fact that the prohibition on age discrimination in access to services etc does not apply to those aged under 18 (s28(1)(a)).

Part 5 EqA: Work

There have been no reported domestic cases on the GOR in the context of age discrimination but a number of the CJEU's decisions on age discrimination have concerned maximum ages for recruitment, which have invariably been considered under Article 4(1) (GOR) rather than Article 6 (justifiable direct age discrimination).

Case C-229/08 *Wolf v Stadt Frankfurt am Main*, EU:C:2010:3, [2010] ECRI-1, [2010] IRLR 244

The CJEU ruled that the GOR was capable of permitting a statutory maximum age limit of 30 for 'intermediate career' fire-fighters whose role was to engage in 'on the ground' fire-fighting which involved tasks which the medical evidence suggested could not be performed by those aged over 45–50. The maximum recruitment age was intended to ensure that these fire-fighters could perform the most physically demanding elements of the role for a comparatively longer period of their career than would otherwise be the case. The German Courts had ruled that the GOR did not apply because the applicant had been precluded from undertaking the physical tests designed to assess physical fitness, and referred to the CJEU the question whether Article 6 of the Directive permitted the discrimination in issue. The Court ruled that the possession of especially high physical capacities could amount to a GOR in this case given the nature of the activities carried out by fire-fighters, and that these capacities were age-related. It accepted that ensuring the efficient functioning of the fire service might be considered to require that the majority of fire officers be able to perform physically demanding tasks, and therefore to be younger than 45 or 50. This being the case, the imposition of a maximum age of 30 for recruitment to intermediate posts in the fire service was appropriate and necessary to the objective of ensuring the operational capacity and proper functioning of the professional fire service, and was justified under Article 4(1) of the Directive.

Case C-416/13 *Vital Pérez v Ayuntamiento De Oviedo*, EU:C:2014:2371, [2015] IRLR 15

The CJEU was asked to rule on the compliance with EU law of an age limit of 30 for recruitment to a local police force. The Spanish Government sought to rely on *Wolf*, arguing that age was a GOR in view of the need to safeguard the operational capacity and proper functioning of the service by ensuring that newly recruited officers could

[62] https://www.legislation.gov.uk/ukdsi/2012/9780111525692.

perform physically demanding tasks for a relatively long period. The CJEU emphasised that it was not the ground on which a difference of treatment was based, but a *characteristic related to that ground*, which constituted a GOR. It went on to rule that the characteristic in this case consisted of the possession of particular physical capacities, but that the age limit of 30 was disproportionate in view of the fact that other police local services had higher maximum ages for recruitment, or none at all, and that the national police service had abolished its maximum recruitment age of 30. The Court distinguished the decision in *Wolf* on the standard of physical fitness required of police officers was not as high as that of fire-fighters, further ruling that the process for recruiting police officers involved stringent physical tests which permitted the recruiters to determine whether police officers had the necessary physical capabilities without fixing a maximum age limit. Finally, the Court ruled that there was no evidence that the objective of safeguarding the operational capacity and proper functioning of the local police service required the maintenance of an age structure which required the imposition of a maximum age of recruitment at 30. The Court ruled that the same conclusion applied under Article 6(1) upon which the government had sought to rely.

Case C-258/15 *Salaberria Sorondo v Academia Vasca de Policía y Emergencias*, EU:C:2016:873 [2017] ICR 302

The CJEU accepted that a maximum age of 35 could be justified in recruitment of police officers for the Autonomous Community of the Basque Country, referring the case back to the national court to determine whether the age limit was appropriate and necessary to the objective of ensuring the operational capacity and proper functioning of the police service.

There are a significant number of additional exceptions to the prohibition on age discrimination in work. Schedule 9 para 4 provides that Part 5 EqA (work) does not apply in connection with age or disability to service in the armed forces and para 10 permits discrimination as regards benefits, facilities or services by reference to length of service on condition (in a case where the shorter-serving employee has accrued more than five years' service) that the discriminator 'reasonably believes' that the discrimination 'fulfils a business need'. Schedule 9 paras 11 and 12 permit wages to reflect the age differentials in the national minimum wage (NMW) and para 13 allows the calculation of enhanced redundancy payments by reference to age. Schedule 9 para 14 allows employers to discriminate between employees who have and have not reached state pensionable age or 65 (if the latter is greater) as regards access to insurance or a related financial service provided to employees 'in pursuance of an arrangement between the employer and another person, or where the employer's business includes the provision of insurance or financial services of the description in question, by the employer', and para 15 allows employers to provide assistance with childcare by reference to the age of children. Regulations made under Schedule 9 para 16 allow employers to make different payments to pension schemes according to employees' age.[63]

[63] Equality Act (Age Exceptions for Pension Schemes) Order 2010.

The exceptions permitting residential mobile home parks and the providers of cruise holidays have not provoked critical commentary, and the Club 18–30 holiday brand expired in 2018. More controversial are the provisions permitting discrimination, irrespective of justification, against younger workers. In the extract below, Alysia Blackham responds to the suggestion that holding down the minimum wage level for younger workers increases their prospects of finding work:

Alysia Blackham, 'Young Workers and Age Discrimination: Tensions and Conflicts' (2019) 48 *Industrial Law Journal* 1, most footnotes omitted

There is increasing recognition that lower minimum wages for young workers do not affect youth employment[64] … Reduced youth wages undermine young people's financial independence and contribute to family poverty. Indeed, young people in the UK are disproportionately at risk of poverty and social exclusion: in 2013, 32.5% of those aged 16–24 were at risk, compared with 22.4% of those aged 25–49. Lowering young people's employment entitlements contributes to this risk of poverty and supports the growth of low-pay work: in 2010, 40.6% of workers aged under 30 were employed in low-wage jobs, compared with 14.7% of those aged 30–49 …

Lower youth wages … are often explained on the basis that younger workers are less skilled and productive than their older colleagues … A disproportionate number of younger workers are employed in unskilled and service roles, where the productivity gains from experience are minimal … If younger workers are employed in low-skill sectors, then there is less of an argument that skill or experience matters in securing organisational productivity and efficiency. Lower wages for young people may therefore merely perpetuate less favourable treatment on the grounds of age and do not reflect differences in productivity. This, then, questions a key rationale for youth wages and challenges the use of length of service to determine pay rates in some roles and sectors …

Part 6 EqA: Education

Schedule 12 para 7 provides that the prohibition on age discrimination against students in higher and further education does not apply as regards the provision, arrangement or facilitation of care for children of a particular age group.

Part 7 EqA: Associations

Schedule 16 para 1A permits associations to provide concessions to people of particular age groups or who have been members for more than a specified number of years.

The main significance of the exceptions discussed above is that age discrimination which falls within them will be lawful without any requirement for justification, such as is otherwise required in the case of both direct and indirect discrimination.

[64] Citing S Sehkaran and R Lucas, *The National Minimum Wage and Young Workers: A Comparison between Urban and Rural Areas* (Manchester, Centre for Hospitality Employment Research, 2001); G Belchamber, 'Minimum Award Wages for Young Workers Must Be Reformed' (1999) 32 *Australian Economic Review* 390.

Index

www.ingramcontent.com/pod-product-compliance
Ingram Content Group UK Ltd.
Pitfield, Milton Keynes, MK11 3LW, UK
UKHW050649200926
475560UK00005BA/351

9 781509 966592